D1484124

BIRDS of AMERICA

BIRDS of AMERICA

EDITOR-IN-CHIEF
T. GILBERT PEARSON
President of the National Association of Audubon Societies

CONSULTING EDITOR
JOHN BURROUGHS

CONTRIBUTING EDITORS

EDWARD H. FORBUSH
State Ornithologist, Massachusetts

HERBERT K. JOB
Economic Ornithologist

WILLIAM L. FINLEY
Naturalist, Author, and Lecturer

L. NELSON NICHOLS
Member Linnæan Society

MANAGING EDITOR
GEORGE GLADDEN

ASSOCIATE EDITOR
J. ELLIS BURDICK
Associate Member of American Ornithologists' Union

ARTISTS
R. I. BRASHER
R. BRUCE HORSFALL
HENRY THURSTON

With 106 Plates in Full Color by
LOUIS AGASSIZ FUERTES

DOUBLEDAY & COMPANY, INC.
Garden City, New York

ISBN: 0-385-00024-3

COPYRIGHT, 1917, BY
THE UNIVERSITY SOCIETY, INC.

COPYRIGHT, 1936, BY
DOUBLEDAY & COMPANY, INC.

9 8 7

The original paintings by Louis Agassiz Fuertes, from which the color plates in this volume were made, are in the New York State Museum at Albany. The board of regents, in granting permission for their use in this volume, reserves the right to grant requests from other applicants for permission to reproduce such plates.

MANUFACTURED IN THE U. S. A.

ADVISORY BOARD

Arthur A. Allen. Ph.D.,
Assistant Professor of Ornithology, Cornell University.

Glover Morrill Allen, Ph.D.,
Secretary, Boston Society of Natural History

Morton John Elrod, Ph.D.,
Professor of Biology, University of Montana

Walter Kendrick Fisher, Ph.D.,
Associate Professor of Zoology, Leland Stanford University

G. Clyde Fisher, Ph.D.,
American Museum of Natural History

Harry S. Hathaway,
Naturalist, Rhode Island

Lynds Jones, Ph.D.,
Associate Professor of Animal Ecology, Oberlin College

Orin Grant Libby, Ph.D.,
Secretary, State Historical Society, North Dakota

Silas A. Lottridge, Ph.M.,
Naturalist, Author, and Lecturer

J. Walker McSpadden,
Author and Lecturer

Howard Taylor Middleton,
Wild Life Photographer

George Henry Perkins, Ph.D.,
State Geologist, Vermont

Albert Porter,
Editor and Lexicographer

S. F. Rathbun,
Naturalist, Washington

Paul M. Rea, A.M.,
Director, Cleveland, Ohio, Museum of Natural History

R. W. Shufeldt, M.D.,
Author and Wild Life Photographer

Harriet B. Thornber,
Secretary, Arizona Audubon Society

W. Clyde Todd,
Carnegie Museum, Pittsburgh

R. W. Williams,
United States Department of Agriculture

CONTENTS

PART I

CONTENTS

PART II

CONTENTS
PART III

PREFACE

HE actual and urgent need for this book is apparent to the large and steadily increasing number of persons who are intelligently interested in American ornithology. This need is due to the fact that in all the literature of that subject there is no single work which presents a complete review of what is known to-day about American birds.

The task of preparing a comprehensive account of the bird life of a continent is far too great to be accomplished in a natural lifetime by any individual working alone; and until recently there has been no systematic coöperation between students of our native birds. It is inevitable, therefore, that continued study of the subject, aided by such coöperation, should have revealed many errors of commission and omission in the labors of Wilson, Audubon, Bonaparte, and the other earlier students of this difficult and complex science. Nevertheless, it is clear that the work of these men laid the foundation of American ornithology; for their labors not only furnished much material of scientific value, but encouraged interest in and sympathy for birds, and thereby inspired further study of these beautiful and useful forms of animate life.

The ornithological pioneers mentioned recorded not only technical descriptions of birds, but were at much pains to present observations calculated to give the reader ideas about bird personality. Later writers have confined themselves generally to one or the other of these aspects of bird life — or to regional ornithology. Doubtless the development of these two schools has been due to the realization of the enormousness of the task of presenting both technical descriptions, and accurate as well as readable characterizations of the hundreds of species which occur on this continent. In the case of the technical student, however, it discloses also the fact that one who is intent upon gathering purely "scientific" data about birds — that is, statistics and details concerning their size, color, distribution, nidification, and so on — is likely to overlook, or at least to pay little heed to habits or characteristics which have no classificatory value.

Yet it is these very characteristics, rather than the purely scientific data, which make the strongest appeal to the imagination and the sympathies of the great majority of persons who are interested in birds. Indeed, it may be doubted whether any account of a bird, however accurate and detailed it is in its presentation of merely physical facts, is actually complete if it omits or curtails reference to traits which reveal the human and æsthetic significance of that bird's natural life. Surely, the cleverness and the fine courage which a mother bird displays in concealing and protecting her eggs, are as significant as are their mere number and color.

It is the purpose of this work to present accurately and sympathetically both of these phases of bird life, that is, the physical and the moral. The utmost pains have been taken to present a precise description of the external physical appearance of each bird selected for separate treatment. The size of the bird may be considered the basic fact in its identification, and this is restricted (except in a few instances) to the average length, because that is the dimension most clearly discernible in the living bird.

The color of the bird is even more important than its size, as a means of identification, and especial care has been taken in this particular. The most accurate and detailed descriptions of the coloration of American birds are those which are included in Robert Ridgway's monumental work, *The Birds of North and Middle America*, of which seven parts have been issued by the United States National Museum. These descriptions, however, are expressed in terminology much of which is comprehensible only to the trained and essentially scientific ornithologist. Therefore, in order to employ this material in the present work, it became necessary to substitute common words for the technical terms; but in doing this great care was taken to reproduce the exact meaning of the original text. By this expedient there has been presented in plain language a vast amount of scientifically accurate descriptive material which, in its original form, would be comprehensible for the lay reader only by the constant use of an unabridged dictionary. Similar changes have been made, when they were necessary, in using Ridgway's text for the paragraphs on the distribution of species, and in the sections which characterize the generic groups. The descriptions of birds not included in Parts I to VII of *The Birds of North and Middle America*, have been written by R. I. Brasher. Special identification or "field" marks have been italicised.

Although this precise and fairly complete physical description is essential for the purposes of scientific ornithology, and often is needed by the layman to supplement or corroborate his own observation, what Mr. Burroughs calls "the human significance of our feathered neighbors" is undoubtedly that which chiefly interests the very large and increasing army of bird lovers. This human significance is reflected in natural or acquired traits which, singly or combined, often give a bird a very definite personality. To the observer who learns to detect and understand these traits, the study of birds becomes far more than a mere science devoted to the collection and classification of physical facts. For once he has adopted this point of view, he begins to see something very like distinct character and personality in the bird world; and observing the manifestations of such traces of individuality becomes to him infinitely more interesting and significant than the mere noting of the size, contour, and plumage peculiarities of a bird, or its occurrence here, there, or elsewhere at this or that time of the year.

The characterizations, or life histories, of the species which receive separate treatment in the following pages, were prepared with especial regard for portraying their interesting and distinctive traits. In most instances this treatment reveals characteristics which serve to differentiate the species with much definiteness. It is, of course, true that individual differences may occur even within the species. For example, an individual bird may display what clearly seems to be unusual confidence in man, or uncommon cleverness in concealing its nest or protecting its young. And it is frequently remarked that a certain bird may be a much more accomplished singer than are the others of his species in the same vicinity. Nevertheless there is a general similarity between the habits and temperament of birds of the same species, and therefore a description of these habits will be found to apply to the average individual bird of the species concerned.

To the technical descriptive matter of especial interest to the systematic ornithologist, and the popular characterizations intended particularly for the non-scientific student of birds, has been added — wherever it is called for — much very important and interesting matter concerning the actual usefulness of birds. This subject of economic ornithology has been carefully investigated by the United States Bureau of Biological Survey, whose experts have gathered and compiled a great mass of statistics and other data concerning the food habits of birds, the object being to convey precise information as to which are the useful and which are the harmful species. It would be difficult to overstate the value of this work if its results were generally understood, for these researches demonstrate beyond peradventure the enormous usefulness of the birds in destroying insect pests which, but for this check of their natural rate of increase, would ruin every year many millions of dollars worth of crops, and threaten with defoliation and death many kinds of trees.

The Bureau of Biological Survey endeavors to disseminate this information as widely as possible, and in order to assist in this good work the data gathered by its experts have been freely used in the following pages. This has been done not only because of the obvious value and interest of the information thus conveyed, but because the reports and bulletins in which it is contained are likely within a few years to become unavailable through the exhaustion of the comparatively small supply printed. This, indeed, has already happened in the case of many of the most valuable bulletins, which are now unobtainable except in the larger public libraries and other repositories for such documents, and therefore have only very restricted circulation. Possessors of *Birds of America* will therefore have permanent access to the best of this very valuable material.

Finally, some explanation of the general form in which this work is presented may not come amiss in this connection. In their arrangement most ornithologies follow the evolutionary plan of proceeding from the lowest to the highest forms which, in the case of the birds, means from the Diving Birds which are considered by the scientists the lowest forms, to the Thrushes which are ranked as the highest. This is the order in which the birds are arranged in the Check-List of the American Ornithologists' Union, and the one which has been followed in these pages.

The Check-List of the American Ornithologists' Union includes the names of about twelve hundred birds to which systematic ornithologists accord full specific or "sub-specific" rank. This sub-specific distinction is often based upon very inconsiderable plumage differences of little or no interest or significance to the lay student of birds, while the character of the bird remains unchanged. In other words, a Robin is a Robin, whether he has white tips to the outer tail-feathers, as in the common Robin, or whether he lacks these spots, as in the Western Robin. *Birds of America* discusses about one thousand birds. It practically covers every species and subspecies with which a student of birds is likely to come in contact in North America.

The publishers wish to thank Mr. T. Gilbert Pearson, who, in addition to his services as Editor-in-chief, has given freely of the photographs and material assembled by the National Association of Audubon Societies; Mr. Herbert K. Job, for his photographs and helpful suggestions; Mr. Edward H. Forbush, for his advice, and, through him, the Massachusetts Board of Agriculture for ornithological literature printed by them; Mr. William L. Finley and Mr. H. T. Bohlman for pictures supplied; Dr. Jonathan Dwight, Jr., for valuable suggestions and criticisms, and permission to quote from *The Auk*; Dr. R. W. Shufeldt for critical suggestions; Mr. C. Walter Short for his interest and practical advice on manufacturing details; Mr. H. J. Vredenburgh for his careful supervision of the photo-engraving; Dr. Frank M. Chapman for permission to quote from his books; Mrs. Florence Merriam Bailey for permission to quote from her book, *Handbook of Western Birds of the United States*; Mrs. Mabel Osgood Wright, for permission to quote from her book *Birdcraft*; Mr. John Burroughs for permission to quote from his *Works*; Mr. C. William Beebe for photographs; Elizabeth Torrey and John W. Seabury for permission to quote from the *Works* of Bradford Torrey; Mr. Winthrop Parkhurst for permission to quote from the *Works* of H. E. Parkhurst; Mr. William Leon Dawson for permission to quote from *Birds of Ohio*, *Birds of Washington*, and *Birds of California*; Mrs. Olive Thorne Miller for permission to quote from *The Children's Book of Birds* and *A Bird Lover in the West*; Mr. F. Schuyler Mathews for quotations from his *Field Book of Wild Birds and their Music*; Mr. Ralph Hoffman for quotations from his *Guide to the Birds of New England and Eastern New York*; Mr. Walter H. Rich for permission to quote from his *Feathered Game of the Northeast*; Mr. H. T. Middleton, Mr. Silas A. Lottridge, Mr. A. A. Allen, and all others who have so generously contributed of their best in photographic studies; the United Fruit Company for the use of paintings for reproduction on the title pages; and the Hercules Powder Co., for quotations from *Game Farming for Profit and Pleasure*.

The following publishers have courteously granted these permissions: D. Appleton & Co. for quotations from the *Works* of Frank M. Chapman; Houghton Mifflin Co. for "To an Oriole" by Edgar A. Fawcett, quotations from *The Children's Book of Birds* and *A Bird Lover in the West* by Olive Thorne Miller, quotations from *Handbook of Birds of the Western*

United States by Florence Merriam Bailey, quotations from the *Works* of John Burroughs, quotations from the *Works* of Bradford Torrey, and quotations from *Guide to the Birds of New England and Eastern New York* by Ralph Hoffman; The John Lane Co. for quotations from *Birds by Sea and Land* by John Maclair Boarston; the Macmillan Co. for quotations from the *Works* of Mabel Osgood Wright; Elizabeth C. T. Miller for quotations from *Birds of Ohio* by William Leon Dawson; G. P. Putnam's Sons for quotations from *Field Book of Wild Birds and their Music* by F. Schuyler Mathews; T. Y. Crowell Co., for quotation from *Feathered Game of the Northeast* by Walter H. Rich; and Charles Scribner's Sons for quotations from the *Works* of H. E. Parkhurst.

To the United States Department of Agriculture and the members of the Biological Survey, to the New York State Museum and its director Dr. John M. Clarke, and to the American Museum of Natural History and its director Dr. Frederic A. Lucas and the members of its scientific staff are due special thanks for the material and pictures supplied by them.

Courtesy of H. T. Middleton

WILD-LIFE PHOTOGRAPHER SNAPPING A PIED-BILLED GREBE IN A POND

INTRODUCTION

By T. Gilbert Pearson, B. S.

THERE is to-day in the United States a very wide interest in the conservation of wild birds. This is manifested in the great interest which the public shows in proposed legislative enactments for bird-protection, in the propagation of various game-birds on private and public properties, in the building and erection of innumerable boxes for the convenience of nesting birds, and in the constantly increasing financial support given to the National Association of Audubon Societies, and its many affiliated state and local bird protection clubs throughout the country.

A lively curiosity has spread among all classes of thinking people as to the names of the birds they see, what they feed on, and something of their coming and going, with the result that the demand for bird books has become very great. No publisher of general literature would to-day deem his list of books adequate without one or more standard works on some phase of ornithology. Literary magazines constantly are publishing articles on the habits of birds, the migration of birds, the economic value of birds, the æsthetic interest in bird life.

There have been recorded in North America eight hundred distinct species of wild birds, and four hundred additional subspecies, or climatic varieties. This refers to the territory lying north of the Rio Grande — and not to Middle America, which includes Mexico and Central America. Naturally the individuals of some of these species are far more numerous than are others. For example, during historic times there probably never were more than a few thousand specimens of the California Vulture, while such common species as the Robin and the Mourning Dove run into the millions.

Some birds are extremely rare, for example only one specimen of the Scaled Petrel has ever been taken in North America, and that was in Livingston county, New York, although the natural habitat of all Petrels is on the open seas.

No one state contains all these various forms of bird-life. From the latest available information the following list shows the number of birds that have been recorded in the various states of the Union:

Alabama, 275; Arizona, 371; Arkansas, 255; California, 541; Colorado, 403; Connecticut, 334; Delaware, 229; District of Columbia, 293; Florida, 362; Idaho, 210; Illinois, 390; Indiana, 321; Iowa, 356; Kansas, 379; Kentucky, 228; Louisiana, 323; Maine, 327; Maryland, 290; Massachusetts, 369; Michigan, 326; Minnesota, 304; Missouri, 383; Nebraska, 418; Nevada, 250; New Hampshire, 283; New Jersey, 358; New Mexico, 314; New York, 412; North Carolina, 331; North Dakota, 338; Ohio, 330; Oregon, 328; Pennsylvania, 300; Rhode Island, 293; South Carolina, 337; Tennessee, 223; Texas, 546; Utah, 214; Vermont, 255; Virginia, 302; Washington, 372; West Virginia, 246; Wisconsin, 357; Wyoming, 288. For the remaining five states no list of birds has been published.

Among the twelve hundred species and subspecies there are a considerable number that are exotic and are never seen in this country save on rare occasions when blown far by storms they wander to our shores. Among this class may be mentioned such species as the Scarlet Ibis from South America, the Mew Gull from northern Europe, the Giant Fulmar of the southern oceans, and the Lapwing, Rook, and Wheatear from the old world.

Birds vary greatly in the extent of their natural range and here again comparison may be made between the California Vulture and the Robin; the one ranging in suitable localities from southern Florida to Alaska, the other being restricted to the California mountains. The bird of greatest range in the world is the Arctic Tern, which in the northern summer haunts the North American coastline from Maine to the Arctic seas, and during our winter feeds along the shores of the Antarctic continent. Most birds have a much more restricted range and but few are found in every state. Some species occur only along the Pacific coast, others only in the northeastern States and Canada, and still others are confined to the south Atlantic and Gulf States.

The earlier legislative enactments for bird-protection in the United States dealt almost entirely with game-birds. So persistently was this class of birds shot, trapped, and netted after the coming of the Europeans, that it soon became apparent that restrictive measures must be taken if some of the more popular game-birds were to be preserved for posterity. These laws at first were quite amateurish, but as a result of experience they later were established along certain definite lines, viz., first, those setting aside certain seasons of the year when the birds could be killed, the idea of this being to afford them protection during the period of incubation and caring for the young; second, forbidding certain methods of capture as for example "fire lighting" at night, netting, and shooting into flocks with large swivel guns; and, third, limiting the number that might be taken in a day or season.

It was found that the ordinary civil officers could not, or would not, enforce the game laws satisfactorily, hence there soon developed a plan of employing special state officers known as game wardens whose specific duty it was to see that the laws protecting birds and game were observed. In order to raise funds for the employing of these officers and also to increase the restrictions on gunners the custom arose of requiring hunters' license fees of all who desired to kill these State assets. These fees run from one dollar to three dollars for a resident of the State and from five to seventy-five dollars for a non-resident of the State. This hunting license fund in some of the larger States at times amounts to $200,000 or more annually.

It was not until about the middle eighties that public attention was drawn strongly to the desirability of preserving that group of birds usually referred to as "non-game birds." By a campaign of education the Audubon Society, first formed at that time, began to educate the public sentiment on the subject with the result that the law usually known as the Audubon Law and which has for its purpose the protection of this large group of birds, has been enacted in the Legislatures of all the States with the exception of six. By the enactment of the Federal Migratory Bird Law on March 4, 1913, a provision protecting these birds was created which covers the United States. On December 10, 1916, a treaty between this country and Great Britain was ratified, which extends protection to non-game birds in the Dominion of Canada.

The best place to study wild birds is on a Bird Reservation for here the birds have greatly lost their fear of man, and primitive conditions, so far as the birds are concerned, have thus largely been restored. In one of the protected sea-bird colonies of North Carolina I have photographed Royal Terns standing unafraid on the sands not twelve feet distant. They had become so accustomed to the warden in charge that they had regained their confidence in man. At Lake Worth I saw a man feed Scaup Ducks that swam to within two yards of his boat. In thousands of door-yards throughout the country wild birds, won by kind treatment, now take their food or drink within a few feet of their human protectors. This is because the door-yards have been made little bird reservations. I have a number of friends who regularly feed Chickadees in winter as the birds perch on their outstretched hands. It is astonishing how quickly wild creatures respond to a little reasonable treatment, as may readily be learned by any householder who will try the experiment. With a little patience any teacher may instruct her pupils in the simple art of making the birds feel at home in the vicinity of the school-house.

There are some kinds of birds that, as far as we know their history, have always built their nests in the holes of trees. Woodpeckers have strong chisel-shaped bills and are able to excavate nesting cavities, but there are others that do not possess such powers. These must depend on finding the abandoned hole of some Woodpecker, or the natural hollow of some tree. It not infrequently happens that such birds are obliged to search far and wide for a hole in which they can make their abode. It is the custom of those who take care of lawns and city parks to chop away and remove all dead limbs or trees that may die. As there are very few Woodpeckers that ever attempt to dig a nesting hole in living trees, such work of the axeman means that when the season comes for the rearing of young, all mated Woodpeckers must move on to where more natural conditions await them. This results in an abnormal reduction of the number of holes for the use of the weaker billed hole-nesting species which must now seek for the few available hollows and knot-holes. But even these places are often taken away from them for along comes the tree doctor, who on the pretext of aiding to preserve the trees, fills up the natural openings with cement and the birds are literally left out in the cold. It is plain to see, therefore, that one reason why many birds do not remain in our towns through the spring months, is due to the absence of places where they may lay their eggs and rear their young.

Photo by A. A. Allen

HOUSE WREN

Building its nest in a nesting box on a porch

To overcome this difficulty the Audubon Society several years ago began to advocate the building and erection of suitable nesting boxes, and to-day the practice is gaining wide usage. More people every year are putting such boxes upon poles or nailing them to trees about their homes, and city authorities in some instances now include bird-boxes among the annual expenditures in the care of their parks. Some of the boxes that may be purchased are very ornate and make beautiful additions even to the most carefully kept estates. One may buy these boxes at prices varying from thirty-five cents to thirty-five dollars each. It is not necessary, however, to buy the boxes to be put up for birds. Equally useful ones may readily be made in the Manual Training Department of the school, or in the basement or wood-shed at home. If one does not know how to begin one may buy a bird-box, or write to the Audubon Society for a free circular of directions, and construct similar ones for himself. People sometimes make the mistake of thinking it is absolutely necessary that such boxes should conform strictly to certain set dimensions. Remember, however, that the cavities in trees and stumps which the birds naturally use, show a wide variety of size, shape and location. A large, commodious, many-roomed, and well painted Martin house, makes a pleasing appearance on the landscape, but it may not be attractive to the Martins. As a boy I built up a colony of more than fifteen pairs of these birds by the simple device of rudely partitioning a couple of soap boxes. The openings of the different rooms were neither uniform in size or shape, but were such as an untrained boy would cut out with a hatchet. A dozen gourds each with a large hole in the side completed the tenements for this well contented Martin community.

There are a few simple rules on the making and placing of bird-boxes that should be observed.

1. In the case of all nest-boxes, except those designed for Martins, the opening should be several inches above the floor, thus conforming to the general plan of the Woodpecker's hole, or the natural cavity in a tree.

2. As a rule nest-boxes should be erected on poles from ten to thirty feet from the ground, or fastened to the sides of trees where limbs do not interfere with the outlook. The main exception to this rule is in the case of Wrens, where the boxes or gourds intended for their use may be nailed or wired in fruit trees or about out-buildings.

3. Martin houses should be erected on poles at least twenty feet high and placed well out in the open, not less than one hundred feet from buildings or large trees.

4. All boxes should be taken down after the nesting season and the old nesting material removed.

Much may be done to bring the birds about the home by placing food where they may readily get it. The majority of land-birds that pass the winter in Canada or the colder parts of the United States, feed mainly on seeds. Cracked corn, wheat, rice, sunflower seed, and bird-seed which may be purchased readily in any town, are therefore exceedingly attractive articles of diet. Bread crumbs are enjoyed by many species. Food should not be thrown out on the snow unless there is a crust or the snow has been well trampled down. Usually it should be placed on boards. Various feeding devices have been made of such character as to prevent the food being covered or washed away by snow or rain. Suet tied to the limbs of trees on the lawn will give comfort and nourishment to many a Chickadee, Nuthatch, and Downy Woodpecker. To make a bird sanctuary, therefore, nesting sites and food are among the first requirements. There appears to be no reason why town and city parks everywhere should not be made into places of great attraction for the wild birds.

At Meriden, New Hampshire, there is a tract of land containing thirty-two acres of field and woods, which is dedicated to the comfort and happiness of wild birds. It is owned by the Meriden Bird Club. The entire community takes an interest in its maintenance, and here birds are fed and nesting places provided. It is in the widest sense a "community sanctuary." There are now a number of these coöperative bird-havens established and cared for in much the same manner. One is in Cincinnati, another in Ithaca, New York, and still another at Greenwich, Connecticut.

The best equipped of this class of community bird-refuges, as distinguished from private estates, or Audubon Society, State, or Federal bird-reservations, is Birdcraft Sanctuary, located in Fairfield, Connecticut. This tract of ten acres was presented to the Connecticut Audubon Society in June, 1914. A cat-proof fence surrounds the entire place. That it may not look aggressive, it is set well inside the picturesque old wall. Stone gate-posts and a rustic gate greet the visitor at the entrance on the highway. There is a bungalow for the caretaker and a tool and workshop of corresponding style. Several rustic shelters and many seats are about. The various springs on the place were assembled into a pond. Trails were cut through the brush and the turf grass, and a charming bit of old orchard on the hill-top, was restored for the benefit of worm-pulling Robins. Stone basins were constructed for bird-baths, houses are put up for all sorts of birds, from Wren boxes, von Berlepsch model, Flicker boxes and Owl boxes, to a Martin hotel; and lastly, the natural growth has been supplemented by planting pines, spruce, and hemlocks for windbreakers, and mountain ash, mulberries, sweet cherries, flowering shrubs, and vines for berries. Not only were all these things done, but there has been built and equipped a small museum of Natural History, which for good taste and usefulness one would need to travel far to find its equal.

The interest in this subject is growing every day, in fact, America is to-day planning new homes for her birds — homes where they may live with unrestricted freedom, where food and lodging in abundance, and of the best, will be supplied, where bathing-pools will be at their service, where blossoming trees will welcome them in the spring, and fields of grain in the fall, quiet places where these privileges will bring to the birds much joy and contentment. Throughout this country there should be a concerted effort to convert the cemeteries, city parks, and estates into sanctuaries for the bird-life of this land.

With a little trouble, seasoned with good judgment, one may soon have birds feeding on a tray within a few yards of the window or even on the window sill. Abundant opportunity is thus given for photographing birds under the best possible conditions for successful results. With every possible convenience at hand one may get better pictures of birds on a feeding tray than one could ever hope to do in a state of wild Nature.

Photographing birds then is an excellent occupation, for the merest novice may hope for success. It is a good thing to do this too from the standpoint of the bird's well being. I have never known a bird photographer who was not a bird lover; for to know the birds is to protect them.

Photograph by W. L. Finley

H. T. BOHLMAN PHOTOGRAPHING A COLONY OF WHITE PELICANS AND CORMORANTS IN TULE LAKE, NORTHERN CALIFORNIA

Present operations in the United States, in the line of bird-reservations, grew out of the distinct need of preserving certain classes of birds from becoming extinct. The birds that we may distinctly call farm-land birds, such as the native Sparrows, the Warblers, Wrens, Orioles, and many other common insectivorous birds, have increased in America since the advent of white man.

It is chiefly the birds that could be commercialized, either for their flesh, or their feathers that have suffered great diminution in numbers in North America as a result of man's activities. An important effort to preserve this class of birds is now being carried on in the United States by the establishment of bird-reservations. Reservation work began in 1902, under the National Association of Audubon Societies. This is the best organized and most liberally financed bird protective organization in the world, and has been in active operation for many years.

One of the States that early adopted the Audubon Law was Florida. On the Atlantic coast of that state, in Indian River, there is an island of about four acres, where two thousand

Brown Pelicans have been coming, from the time whereof the memory of man runneth not to the contrary, to lay their eggs and rear their young. About the time this law was enacted long quills became very popular in the millinery trade. Some of us found that the millinery stores in large cities were selling feathers taken from the Bush Turkey, the Albatross, the Brown Pelican, and also from the old Turkey Buzzard of the South. Certain people tried to secure the repeal of the Florida law, so that the Pelicans might be killed for their feathers.

This caused the question to rise: Would it be possible to get the government of the United States to take hold of that island in some way? A man who kills a bird would rather be haled before a local magistrate where the jury probably would be composed of friends and neighbors, who themselves had killed birds. In such a case it was a simple matter

Photo by H. L. Dillaway Courtesy of Nat. Asso. Aud. Soc.

PARK RANGER AND CAMP ROBBER (GRAY JAY)

Mount Ranier in background

to leave the plough for a day and stand trial. But in a Federal court it is a different proposition. Here a man may have to travel half way across the state to attend court, and must appear before a jury composed of strangers — a situation to be dreaded.

There did not seem to be any way whereby this Federal control could be secured until the matter was finally taken up with President Roosevelt, who said, " If the land office will recommend that this land is not good for agricultural purposes we will make it a bird-reserve under the care of the Department of Agriculture, provided the Audubon Society will agree to hire a man to act as guardian on the island." In a very short time the matter was arranged, and the President declared the island a bird-sanctuary in perpetuity — a breeding place for wild birds for all time. He took a short cut in doing this for there was no specific law giving the executive such authority. Along the coast of Florida were found nine other small islands suitable for this purpose, and Mr. Roosevelt made them all Federal bird-reservations.

Later inquiry was made about places suitable for sanctuaries for other birds, for, bear in mind, many large birds over extended areas were threatened with extirpation to supply the demand for the market. Sea Gulls along the coast, Terns, Grebes, Ducks, Geese, and others in the West were in imminent danger from this cause. So the National Association of Audubon Societies began to look for breeding places of Ducks and other birds in the West. Examination was made in various parts of the country and many more bird reservations were the result. When President Roosevelt went out of office, we had thirty-eight bird reserves. President Taft took an interest in the subject and also segregated quite a number. One of the largest of these bird-sanctuaries is the delta of the Yukon, which is as large as the State of Connecticut.

One bird reserve was created in the western group of the Hawaiian Islands, including the Laysan Island. This, by the way, was raided in the summer of 1915 by Japanese feather hunters. The Pribilof Islands were also made a reserve, as well as the Aleutian Chain. There are to-day seventy United States bird-reserves in all. At first the Government made no appropriation to protect and guard these birds. Therefore, it became the duty of the Audubon Society to ask for aid from its members and friends who were willing to give money for an idea — people willing to provide funds to protect Egrets in Florida or Cormorants and Gulls on the Three-Arch Rocks in Oregon, whether or not they could ever hope to see personally the sanctuaries. After the lapse of six years, the Government made a small grant for the purpose, although, to-day, the Audubon Society owns and operates the patrol launches on the Government reserves, and still helps to pay the salaries of some of the wardens. The Government is appropriating more money each year to this work, and the gentlemen of the Biological Survey who have the work in charge are exercising every means at their command to successfully protect the birds.

T. GILBERT PEARSON PHOTOGRAPHING YOUNG HERONS

In the marshes of Klamath Lake, Oregon

President Wilson made the Panama Canal Zone a bird-reserve in 1913. There are many bird-reserves which the Audubon Society is protecting that are not on Government territory. These are cared for by the Society's paid agents. The islands along the coast of Maine are great breeding places for sea-fowl of various kinds. There are forty-two islands where they nest, and there are sixteen Audubon wardens in service there in summer. The Society also has wardens guarding islands along the coasts of Connecticut, New York, New Jersey, and North Carolina. There are still others in Florida and Louisiana. About sixty important colonies of water-birds are protected by the Audubon Society in the southern states. It has been able to buy some and to lease others. In some cases merely the consent of the owners is obtained. The result is that certain water-birds on the Atlantic coast, such as Herring Gulls and several species of Terns, have come back in great numbers.

The Audubon Society is trying to guard the Egrets in the South and we know of about twenty thousand of these birds left in the United States. Two of the Society's agents, while on guard, have been shot and killed by plume-hunters, and the colonies have been raided and the plumes sent to New York.

In North America the great nursery for wild Ducks and Geese is the region between the Great Lakes and Hudson Bay on the east and the Rocky Mountains on the west. There are three great flights of Ducks and Geese in autumn from that section of the country. Those heading for the Atlantic Seaboard chiefly cross the States diagonally, reaching the Atlantic Coast about Maryland. In a reactionary migratory movement, many of them go back along the coast at least to Long Island and swing back and forth, according to weather conditions. The other end of this movement goes down the coast. There is also a great flight down the Mississippi Valley. Under the migratory bird laws, the Mississippi, between Memphis and St. Paul, is a reservation. In the sunken ground of Arkansas there are two large bird-reserves, and on one of these many Ducks find a refuge. This was a famous place for market hunters in days gone by. More than 300,000 Ducks were taken there in one year. Another larger series of bird-reservations is situated in the State of Louisiana. These include 234,000 acres of marsh-land, where numbers of Ducks and Geese now find a safe refuge. These reservations were made by the private purchase of Charles Willis Ward, E. A. McIlhenny, Mrs. Russell Sage, and the Rockefeller Foundation.

This widespread interest in birds both on the part of the Government and private individuals has had happy results. Not only are our birds protected, but unusual opportunity has been given to study them. The advance in field work, coupled with the constant improvement of photography, has obtained results little short of astounding.

When the present work on *Birds of America* was projected, some months ago, we of the editorial board began as a first move, to take stock of the situation. We felt that the time was at last ripe for a new book on the subject that should be a final repository of all this vast treasure of scattered information. Patient field ornithologists, on the one hand, and laboratory naturalists, on the other, had given us wonderfully rich material which only awaited assembling. The task even ten years ago would have proved far more difficult. What was clearly needed, was to make a thorough canvass of the field and produce a work at once popular and scientific, and at the same time comprehensive—a record of our wild birds prepared in such form as to meet the needs of both the laymen and the trained naturalist. Ornithologists all over the country heartily endorsed the project; indeed we have seldom seen a work which aroused more enthusiasm in the doing than *Birds of America*. The official check list of the American Ornithologists' Union has been followed for classification, and we have included not only our common living birds as found to-day, but also many rarer forms and some recently extinct, such as the Passenger Pigeon. We have tried, in a word, to present a complete picture and story of our feathered wild bird life.

OUT-DOOR BIRD STUDY

BY EDWARD HOWE FORBUSH

State Ornithologist of Massachusetts

NATURALLY those who begin to study birds desire, first, to know their names and to be able to recognize them at sight. This is the A B C of bird study — the mere beginning — but nevertheless important. To learn to identify birds readily, the student needs good eyes and ears, a good opera-glass or field-glass, a notebook and pencil, a good book with colored illustrations, and some training in careful observation. It will be a great advantage if there is a museum accessible, where he can see mounted specimens. A small, light-weight opera-glass is all that is necessary for viewing the smaller birds; for water-fowl or sea birds a marine glass is most useful.

To learn the proper use of the opera-glass, select some bird, if possible, that is sitting still. Have your back to the sun. Focus the glass on the tree, and then the bird by noting the position of the branch and sighting the glass as you would a gun.

Note the size of the bird. It will be difficult at first to judge the size in inches, but you may compare it with certain common and well-known birds. You may have a scale of sizes, beginning with the Yellow Warbler or Chipping Sparrow, and reading like this: Chipping Sparrow, Song Sparrow, Bluebird, Catbird, Robin, Dove, Crow. Observe these birds well; note the size of each. Turn to your book, and get it in inches. Write it down; commit it to memory; have it always in mind. By making good use of such a scale, you may become expert in judging size by comparison.

Next, the shape of the bird is important. Note whether the bird as a whole is slim or stout. Some allowance may be made as to how the feathers are carried at the time. All birds can raise or lower the feathers of the body at will. If you can see the shape of the beak, you may be able to refer the bird at once to the family in which it belongs. If it is not much larger or smaller than a Song Sparrow, and has a short, conical bill, probably it is a Sparrow. If it is a little smaller than a Song Sparrow or about the size of a Chippy, and has a short but slender bill, a trifle curved, probably it is a Warbler, or belongs to some other insect-eating family.

The length and shape of the tail are important. Try to see whether the tail is long or short, rounded, square, or forked. If the bird is large, with a hooked beak and long tail, probably it is a Hawk. If the beak is long and straight, or nearly so, the tail short and the legs long, it must be a Heron, or some other wader.

The color of the bird is very important; indeed, it is about the only feature ordinarily observed. First, note the color of the upper part, *i. e.*, the top and sides of head, back and sides of neck, back, wings, and tail; next, that of the under parts — throat, front of neck, breast, and belly. Remember that the breast and belly often will seem darker than they really are, on account of being in shade; thus a pure white will seem gray. Be careful to note just where each color actually is; then note any conspicuous mark, for such a mark alone, taken with the size of the bird, often is enough to establish its identity.

Many birds have some prominent mark or color by which they may be identified in the field. In this work the notebook and pencil are indispensable. Note down — on the spot — size, shape, color, and markings, also shape and appearance of beak and tail (when you can get them), for future reference. This will help you to identify the bird, and to fix its identification in your memory.

The expert can determine many birds at a distance by their characteristic flight; and the beginner, by making good use of his opportunities, will soon learn to recognize a Buzzard by its wheeling flight, or a flying Green Heron by the downward bend of its wing-tips. All Woodpeckers have a bounding flight, as they travel by rising for a few wing beats and then sliding downward with the wings partly closed. The Goldfinch also has an up-and-down flight. The Pipit, the Yellow Palm Warbler and the Water-Thrushes all wag the tail up and down while moving about — something not habitual with most other birds. The gait of the bird on the ground may determine the species or at least the family. Crows, Grackles, Blackbirds, Oven-birds, and some others walk, while most birds progress by hopping, although now and then a hopping bird may surprise you by walking a few steps on clear, open ground.

The notes of birds serve as an excellent means of identification, although there are a few that imitate well the notes of others. Among these are the Crow, Blue Jay, Catbird, Brown Thrasher, and the famous Mockingbird.

As the novice will see colors in the wrong places or fail to see colors in the right places, so he will hear birds wrongly or fail to hear them at all. An ornithologist, if stricken blind, might still get an approximate idea of the number of birds of most species resident in a locality for most birds are vociferous.

Many people, however, have great difficulty in recognizing or remembering bird notes. Others are unable to differentiate between tones and calls of an entirely different quality. In studying bird songs, the notebook is indispensable. Write down in syllables what the bird seems to say as you hear it at the time. Accent it as the bird accents it, and if you are musical you may even get it by note. These notes may refresh your memory, and help fix the call or song in mind.

Birds do not really articulate, or, if they do, the sounds are mostly vowels; yet we imagine that they enunciate words. In learning the songs of birds you may take the notes of some common loud singer, like the Robin, as a standard, and by comparison determine how those of other species differ from it. This is good training for the ear. Some people cannot see any difference at first between the songs of the Robin and the Wood Thrush, but to the initiated they have nothing in common. In quality of tone, beginners usually see little difference between the songs of the Baltimore Oriole, the Robin, the Scarlet Tanager, and the Rose-breasted Grosbeak; nevertheless, the Oriole's lay is almost a pure whistle, the tune varying much with different individuals; the Robin's song is a bold warble, a little strident in places; the Tanager sings a weaker, finer note, like an undeveloped, hoarse Robin; and the Grosbeak has a beautiful warble, rather loud at times, but perfectly pure and mellow.

Unfortunately for the novice, a bird may have two or more distinct songs. Some commonly have many, while no two individual birds of certain species ever sing precisely the same tune; but this disparity only makes the study of their vocal powers more interesting. Occasionally a very gifted individual will eclipse the performance of all rivals. The caw of the common Crow is well known, but its love notes and its conversational abilities when ministering to its young are seldom recognized.

As one advances in the study, the manner in which birds feed, the character of the locality in which they are found, the location and construction of the nests, the size and color of eggs, all will tend toward fixing the identity of birds. In time, one learns to know many birds at a glance, until, almost unconsciously, he comes to the day when most of the birds he sees or hears are old friends.

Birds require food, shelter, nesting places, and protection from their enemies. In localities furnishing all these essentials birds always may be found in their seasons. A broad river valley, with fresh-water meadows, containing small, marshy ponds, if dotted with trees and bordered by farming lands, orchards, and wooded hills, should be an ideal place for birds.

When migrating, they appear to stop by preference only where there is an abundance of suitable food with which they may replenish the waste of tissues worn by long flights.

At such times birds that have found food attract by their calls others flying by or overhead; these also are heard or seen by others still; and so they gather from far and near.

Beginners in bird study usually choose the spring as the best time for making the acquaintance of the birds, but it is well to begin early in the year, when birds are few, and learn to recognize each species as it comes. It is also well to remember that the old males usually come first, and the females and young birds later.

Early mornings and late afternoons are usually the best times for observation, partly because most birds are then active and singing, and partly because there often is little wind movement then. The least motion is quickly noticed when the branches are still; but when the wind blows, birds are more likely to be overlooked. Also they are more shy and retiring on windy days, when they can spread their wings and be borne away with little effort.

Photograph by H. T. Bohlman

WILLIAM L. FINLEY MAKING PHOTOGRAPHIC STUDIES OF PELICANS

Cool days, with strong northwest winds, are unfavorable for bird study. Birds, excepting water-fowl and shore birds, usually seek shelter during heavy rains, but are active during light, warm showers.

People, whose study of birds must be confined mainly to the city, can best observe the common birds in large parks or cemeteries, where birds, being protected and seeing people continually, are unsuspicious and may be readily approached. Water birds may be found usually in spring and fall in ponds of large park systems.

July is one of the most interesting months in the bird calendar, for then there are many young birds about, and some of the birds that have reared their young begin to slip away toward the south and shore birds begin to come from the north.

The bird seeker must learn to notice every sound and movement in the woods and fields. He must try to follow every strange note to its source. The expert usually hears a bird before he sees it. Some birds are ventriloquists — when the bird is hidden by the leaves, the song seems to come first from one tree, then from another. For this reason the Scarlet Tanager can sometimes be found in summer by going around the place from which the sound of its voice seems to come, or by passing it, and then returning to it.

Many birds have the power of singing so softly that they seem to be far away when really just at hand. The Catbird does this quite commonly, and several other species occasionally sing their full songs in the fall as in the spring, except that they are audible only a few yards away. To find birds one must cultivate the senses of sight and hearing to the utmost.

The bird student soon finds that some localities are better supplied with bird-life than others. Many species, while migrating, follow or visit such coasts or broad river valleys as lie along or across their natural lines of migration.

Even the novice need not be taught how to approach the more common and familiar birds, which seem to court, rather than, to shun human companionship; but there are times when it becomes necessary to get close enough to a rare bird to examine it carefully or to observe its habits, while a near approach to a shy bird may tax the powers of the most skilful observer.

Courtesy of H. T. Middleton

WILD LIFE PHOTOGRAPHER MAKING A PORTRAIT STUDY OF GREAT HORNED OWL

To be successful in this, the beginner must imitate, in some respects the behavior of the fox or lynx, animals which are able occasionally to get near enough to wild birds to capture some that the human animal finds difficult to get within range of his field-glass. How are the wild animals enabled to do this? (1) They are inconspicuously or protectively colored. (2) Their feet are softly padded and their movements noiseless. (3) They go on all fours, crawling close to the ground, and, taking advantage of the cover, keep concealed as much as possible. (4) Their movements are so slow, at need, as to be imperceptible. In all these things we may imitate them.

Bird students often are dressed conspicuously, and shod with hard leather. Their tread, as it jars on the delicate senses of the lower animals, seems to shake the ground. The dead wood is broken under foot. They talk, laugh, and even shout with a loud voice. Standing erect, they are exposed to the view of birds for a mile or more around. Some of them wear large headgear, adorned with long feathers, and turn their heads about quickly.

They swing their arms, and move about, pointing, gesticulating and assuming attitudes, all of which no doubt seem menacing and fearsome to the shyer birds.

Even such students will see birds, for many of our feathered friends have become accustomed to strange sounds and antics. But the expert who sees all the birds has taken lessons from the fox — he hunts alone.

When one is in the company of others, nature never completely enthralls him. His attention is more or less distracted by his companions; he fails to see and hear all. The bird student should attend entirely to the birds, and then they will requite his singleness of purpose. When alone, he has no one to talk to, and no interruptions. The human voice warns all creatures from afar of the approach of their arch enemy, man; let it be stilled, and nature is at peace.

We many muffle the tread by wearing rubbers, or, better, shoes with rubber soles. Those having merely an outer lift and tap of rubber on heel and toe are best. The rubber will prevent the feet from slipping on rocks and pine-clad hillsides. The light canvas tennis shoes commonly used are not sufficient protection to the feet on rough, stony ground. Leather footgear should not be stiff or squeaky. We may avoid the rustling of dry leaves by choosing for our tramps the early morning, when the dew is on, or the hour succeeding a light shower. Care should be used not to tread on dry sticks so as to break them, as sharp sounds alarm all wild creatures.

In dress, avoid black, white, and all striking colors and contrasts. A dull, dead leaf color, like that of the shooting coats ordinarily sold to sportsmen, is good at any time. In spring and summer a dull green is very good. Certain grays and browns harmonize with natural objects.

The vision of most birds is far superior to our own or that of mammals; it is nearly, if not absolutely, perfect. Therefore it is necessary, in approaching shy birds, such as water-fowl or Hawks, to use, as cover, trees, shrubs, or grasses. Often one can advance only on hands and knees, or crawl prone like the serpent.

Frequently I have approached wild fowl by crawling in the paths made by raccoons, hares, opossums, and other animals under grasses and low shrubbery. At other times I have been obliged to creep or wriggle through short grass, in mud and water, to reach some desired point of observation. In such cases, when within sight of the birds a screen of vegetation must be kept always before the face, or the birds will take alarm and be off at once. Birds so wild that they will not allow a man on foot to come within a half a mile may be approached noiselessly in this way within twenty or thirty yards, but the labor and discomfort are great.

When nearing shy birds in this manner, keep under cover and do not raise the head. If it becomes necessary to take an observation, the head must be raised but little, and both raised and lowered so slowly that the motion will be imperceptible. Always approach against the wind, if possible, for the birds are then less likely to hear you. Do not allow the sun to strike on any metallic or glass object, for the reflection or flash will give the alarm. Many people will not take such pains in approaching birds. Others cannot, but must either decoy the birds within reach, watch them with long range glasses from wooded shores, or get up to them in less difficult and more conventional ways. Such people may see shy birds sometimes at rather close quarters by driving slowly along the country roads with a horse and carriage. The extra elevation given the observer by the vehicle increases his visual possibilities, and the birds have learned not to be suspicious of such an equipage on the road.

Birds sometimes may be approached on horseback better than on foot. Gunners sometimes employ grazing cattle as moving shields, behind which they near the game unnoticed.

When approaching shy birds on foot in the open, a zigzag, circular, or sidelong course may bring you much nearer than will a direct forward movement. It is well to avoid the

MR. FINLEY (ahead) AND MR. BOHLMAN CALL ON THE MURRES

appearance of stealth, and seem not to notice your bird. Make no quick movements, and do not hurry. Most birds meet violent deaths, and they must be constantly on the watch for their enemies. They are accustomed to flee for their lives from quick-moving creatures.

Shy water birds and marsh birds sometimes may be approached by the skilful use of a canoe. Let the canoe drift slowly along the marshy margin of a river, and watch the reeds and rushes closely. In this way Rails, Coots, Gallinules, and even Sandpipers are seen at close range. I have gotten very near resting flocks of shore birds by sitting or lying motionless in an Indian canoe, and drifting down upon them. The canoe may be used to advantage on a river not only in watching Bitterns, Rails, and other marsh birds, but also in going close to the smaller land birds in trees and bushes on the bank. For this purpose the canoe is much superior to the rowboat. It is noiseless, and the paddler is always facing ahead. Many birds may be seen at close range by working a sail-boat up or down a river before a light, fair breeze. A small boat covered with bushes, and sculled or allowed to drift down on birds sometimes is useful. A fast-sailing boat is one of the best devices for approaching swimming birds on a windy day. Such a boat, manoeuvred skilfully, will be upon the birds before they are aware of its nearness. During a squall I once drove a sloop so near a Merganser that the bird rose on the next sea as we swept past. There is an advantage in sailing down wind, as the bird must rise against the wind, and may come quite near, giving a good view, first of the breast and then of the back, as it turns away, The noisy naphtha launch is the abomination of the bird student. It has driven most of the water-fowl from our eastern rivers.

When birds have young in the nest they usually are less shy than at other times, forgetting their regard for their own safety in their solicitude for the welfare of their offspring. For this reason, if for no other, the bird student should strive to find the nesting sites. A word of caution is necessary here, however. Those who have found and watched bird's nests often complain that something usually happens to the eggs or the young birds. There are creatures always on the watch for an opportunity to rob birds' nests. The fox sometimes follows a man-track. Perhaps he has learned that the path of a man in the woods often leads to food. Too often the man-trail leads to wounded or dead birds and animals; the remains of a lunch may reward the fox. Sometimes fish heads and other offal are thrown around the camping place. So Reynard cunningly follows. Those who closely examine the nests of birds in trees or shrubbery are likely to be watched unawares by the astute and cautious Crow, the thieving Jay, the mischievous squirrel, or the bloodthirsty weasel. I have learned by sad experience that a close or frequent examination of a bird's nest in the woods only serves to call the attention of the bird's enemies. I have seen both Jay and squirrel following a man through the woods, keeping well hidden from his sight. If you approach a nest containing young, the cries of the parent bird may apprise all the wood folk of its location. Therefore, watch the birds with a glass, and do not go to the nest. Those who carelessly approach the nests of Herons or water-birds that breed in colonies are likely to drive the old birds away, and thus expose the eggs and young to the attacks of Crows, for Crows are quick to seize such opportunities.

When watching a nest, approach it with caution, and observe it from such a distance that neither young nor old will be much disturbed by your presence. Many interesting habits may be seen in this way, if a good glass is used.

He who, unable to go far afield, waits and watches for birds in some secluded spot, or imitates their notes and so calls them to him, may learn more of their ways than will the most active pedestrian. The country dweller may entice birds to the homestead by planting fruit-bearing trees, shrubs, vines, and other plants that will supply them with food. Even the urbanite possibly may attract a few Chickadees or Nuthatches in winter by putting out suet on trees; but other means are required to bring birds about the student in the field. You may facilitate your winter bird study by scattering millet seed in suitable spots along your walks, or by hanging bones and suet in favorably situated trees, which you can visit now and then. In spring or fall small grain will attract Thrashers, Blackbirds, Bob-whites, and Crows. Chestnuts and corn scattered about in the fall or early winter will gather all the Blue Jays in the countryside. In summer, if the person is carefully concealed, some of the shyest birds may be brought near by mimicking their notes. Many bird notes may be imitated by the voice.

It is difficult for most birds to understand the meaning of a silent human figure lying prone and half concealed. While so reclining I have been closely approached by Eagles and Vultures. Birds that recognize at once the upright figure of a man, and flee from it at sight, sometimes will manifest no fear of the same man stretched on the ground, and may even be curious enough to approach him. A concealed hunter sometimes will attract wild-fowl toward the shore by waving a rag on the end of a stick, or by using a small dog trained to gambol in the grass. There are easier and pleasanter ways, however, of attracting the shy birds of the woods.

Photo by Irene Finley

WILLIAM L. FINLEY MAKING FRIENDS WITH A DESERT SPARROW IN ARIZONA

All wood birds, both shy and rare, may be out-generaled by the quiet sitter. They seem to wonder what manner of thing this is that looks so like a man, but neither smokes nor swears, talks, laughs, nor tramps about. Slowly they draw near and peer at the curiosity, and finally they apparently conclude it to be harmless, and go about their usual avocations.

There is one great drawback, however, to this method. In summer our woods are infested with mosquitoes, as well as gnats and flies. A pair of light leather gloves, a net or veil, of a mesh smaller than ordinary mosquito netting, to wear over the hat and head, and a light blanket or wrap which can be carried in a shawl-strap, will enable one to keep quiet and yet defy the trouble-some insects. A light camp-stool also is useful.

One who desires to camp in the summer will need a different outfit. For more than twenty years I have used a small A tent, made of brown duck, with a flap to tuck under the blankets. It is seven feet long, four feet wide, and three feet high. A small line is sewed along the top, which may be tied at each end to a tree or stake, to support the tent. Eight loops of heavy twine are staked down with forked sticks, to hold out the sides. The ends are made of coarse cheese cloth, or fine netting, and the lower edges are provided with flaps to tuck under the blankets. A rubber blanket and a single light woolen one, with a cotton bag, to be filled nightly with moss or grass for a pillow complete the outfit, which may all be rolled up and carried by a strap handle or packed above a knapsack. The birds soon become accustomed to this tent, and even will alight upon it. For several evenings it was the favorite perch of a Screech Owl. From it I have watched the shore birds and seals on barren islands. In it I narrowly escaped being run over by two deer. The panther has circled around it, and once a wildcat actually walked on it, standing on my breast until I awoke. From such a tent, or from a screen of netting, you may watch the Ruffed Grouse or Partridge and her callow brood. You may camp in a heronry, and see the old birds come and go and feed their

Photograph by W. L.Finley

H. T. BOHLMAN TAKING A DIFFICULT SHOT AT A PIGEON GUILLEMOT'S NEST

On the rocks off the Oregon coast

young. I have camped on a small, dry mud bank in a great swamp, with no other dry land above water for miles around, being entertained by the nightly concerts of mosquitoes, Ducks, Herons, frogs, and alligators, without the least discomfort or inconvenience.

There are shelters in which one may remain concealed, varying in construction from the log camp of the sportsman to the bough camp of the Indian, or the " hide " or " blind " of the gunner. The umbrella blind used by bird photographers is an excellent device for watching birds, if set up in the shade. In full sunlight it is about as comfortable as a Turkish bath. If the birds to be watched are very wary it is best to set up the blind and leave it for several hours, that they may become accustomed to it. Then the observer should be accompanied by one or more persons when he goes to conceal himself within it. When his companions leave it will allay the birds' suspicions and curiosity may impel them to close approach. Wooden decoys used in connection with " blinds ", and bird-calls will enable a bird student

HERBERT K. JOB AT BLIND ON THE LOUISIANA RESERVATION

Here he secured wonderful films and pictures of Blue Geese within a few feet

to lure most shore birds as near to him as they will come to the gunner. A skilfully constructed blind placed on or near a long sand bar or point of the shore, and a few lumps of mud or turf judiciously distributed on the point, may enable one to get a good view of several species of wild-fowl. Apparently the flying birds at a distance mistake the clods for some of their number, and come on intending to alight. If wooden decoys were put out, the Ducks might discover their mistake and become suspicious; but on finding the objects to be mere clods, they sometimes will alight. The best decoys are live birds anchored so that they can swim about. Sometimes a single Grebe or Duck in a small pond will attract a flock of several species. Many game birds and water-fowl can be readily baited; but this is a method for those owning estates where birds can be protected, and should not be attempted by any bird student who would assemble the birds thus only to leave them to the tender mercies of the pot-hunter.

Those who wish to lure the sea birds may have some success with Gulls by putting out fish or offal upon some beach or bar, near a blind; but Gulls may be seen anywhere about the harbors of cities where they are not molested. To attract the birds of the ocean, however, one must go several miles to sea, where by throwing overboard cod livers, or some similar food, several species may be lured near the boat.

BIRD MIGRATION

By Wells W. Cooke

HE mystery of bird migration has proved a fascinating subject for speculation and study from earliest times. Long ago it was noticed that birds disappeared in fall and reappeared in spring, but, not knowing where they spent the intervening period, many fanciful theories were advanced to account for their disappearance, as hibernation in hollow trees or in the mud of streams or ponds. With later years, however, has come a fuller knowledge of migration, especially of the particular region in which each species passes the cold season, and more definite information in regard to the routes followed in the spring and fall journeys. But fuller knowledge has served to increase rather than to lessen interest in the subject. More persons to-day are watching birds and noting their times of arrival and departure than ever before.

A knowledge of the times of migration of birds is essential as a basis for intelligent study of their economic relations and is equally necessary in formulating proper legislation for bird protection — two subjects which form important parts of the work of the United States Biological Survey.

For more than 2,000 years the phenomena of bird migration have been noted; but while the extent and course of the routes traversed have of late become better known, no conclusive answer has been found to the question, Why do North American birds migrate? Two different and indeed diametrically opposite theories have been advanced to account for the beginnings of these migrations.

According to the more commonly accepted theory, ages ago the United States and Canada swarmed with non-migratory bird life, long before the Arctic ice fields advancing south during the glacial era rendered uninhabitable the northern half of the continent. The birds' love of home influenced them to remain near the nesting site until the approaching ice began for the first time to produce a winter — that is, a period of inclement weather which so reduced the food supply as to compel the birds to move or to starve. As the ice approached very gradually, now and then receding, these enforced retreats and absences — at first only a short distance and for a brief time — increased both in distance and in duration until migration became an integral part of the very being of the bird. In other words, the formation of the habit of migration took place at the same time that changing seasons in the year replaced the continuous semi-tropical conditions of the preglacial eras.

As the ice advanced southward the swing to the north in the spring migration was continually shortened and the fall retreat to a suitable winter home correspondingly lengthened, until during the height of the glacial period birds were for the most part confined to Middle and South America. But the habit of migration had been formed, and when the ice receded toward its present position the birds followed it northward and in time established their present long and diversified migration routes.

Those who thus argue that love of birthplace is the actuating impulse to spring migration call attention to the seeming impatience of the earliest migrants. Ducks and Geese push northward with the beginnings of open water so early, so far, and so fast that many are caught by late storms and wander disconsolately over frozen ponds and rivers, preferring to risk starvation rather than to retreat. The Purple Martins often arrive at their nesting boxes so prematurely that the cozy home becomes a tomb if a sleet storm sweeps their winged food from the air. The Bluebird's cheery warble we welcome as a harbinger of spring, often only to find later a lifeless body in some shed or outbuilding where the bird sought shelter rather than return to the sunny land so recently left.

As a matter of fact, however, only a small percentage of birds exhibit these pre-seasonal migration propensities. The great majority remain in the security of their winter homes until spring is so far advanced that the journey can be made easily and with comparatively slight danger; and they reach the nesting spot when a food supply is assured and all the conditions of weather and vegetation are favorable for beginning immediately the rearing of a family of young.

If, however, a longing for home is considered the main incentive to their northward flight, there arises the question as to why birds desert that home so promptly after the nesting season is over. Indeed, most birds start south as soon as the fledglings are able to shift for themselves. The Orchard Oriole, the Redstart, and the Yellow Warbler of central United States and the Nonpareil of the south all begin their southward journey early in July, long before the fall storms sound a warning of approaching winter and when their insect menu is particularly varied and abundant.

According to the opposite migration theory, the birds' real home is the Southland; all bird life tends by over-production to over-crowding; and, at the end of the glacial era, the birds, seeking in all directions for suitable breeding grounds with less keen competition than in their tropical winter home, gradually worked northward as the retreat of the ice made habitable vast reaches of virgin country. But the winter abiding place was still the home, and to this they returned as soon as the breeding season was over. Thus, in the case of the Orchard Oriole mentioned above, many individuals that arrive in southern Pennsylvania the first week in May leave by the middle of July, spending only 2½ months out of the 12 at the nesting site.

Whichever theory is accepted, the beginnings of migration ages ago undoubtedly were intimately connected with periodic changes in the food supply. While North America possesses enormous summer supplies of bird food, the birds must return south for the winter or perish. The over-crowding which would necessarily ensue should they remain in the equatorial regions is prevented by the spring exodus northward. No such movement occurs toward the corresponding southern latitudes. South America has almost no migratory land birds, for bleak Patagonia and Tierra del Fuego offer no inducements to these dwellers of the limitless forests of the Amazon.

The conclusion is inevitable that the advantages of the United States and Canada as a summer home and the superb conditions of climate and food for the successful rearing of a nestful of voracious young far over-balance the hazards and disasters of the journey thither. For these periodical trips did not just happen in their present form; each migration route, however long and complex, is but the present stage in development of a flight that at first was short, easily accomplished, and comparatively free from danger. Each lengthening of the course was adopted permanently only after experience through many generations had proved its advantages.

It may safely be stated that the weather in the winter home has nothing to do with starting birds on the spring migration, except in the case of a few, like some of the Ducks and Geese, which press northward as fast as open water appears. There is no appreciable change in temperature to warn the hundred or more species of our birds which visit South America in winter that it is time to migrate. It must be a force from within, a physiological change warning them of the approach of the breeding season, that impels them to spread their wings for the long flight.

The habit of migration has been evolved through countless generations, and during this time the physical structure and habits of birds have been undergoing a process of evolution in adaptation to the climate of the summer home. In spring and early summer climatic conditions are decidedly variable, and yet there must be some period that has on the average the best weather for the birds' arrival. In the course of ages there have been developed habits of migration, under the influence of which the bird so performs its migratory movements that on the average it arrives at the nesting site at the proper time.

The word " average " needs to be emphasized. It is the average weather at a given locality that determines the average time of the bird's arrival. In obedience to physiologic promptings the bird migrates at the usual average time and proceeds northward at the usual average speed unless prevented by adverse weather. Weather conditions are not the cause of the migration of birds; but the weather, by affecting the food supply, is the chief factor which determines the average date of arrival at the breeding grounds. After the bird, in response to physiological changes, has started to migrate, the weather it encounters en route influences that migration in a subordinate way, retarding or accelerating the advance by only a few days, and having usually only slight effect upon the date of arrival at the nesting site.

Local weather conditions on the day of arrival at any stated locality are minor factors in determining the appearance of a given species at that place and time. The major factors in the problem are the weather conditions far to the southward, where the night's flight began, and the relation which that place and time bear to the average position of the bird under normal weather conditions. Many, if not most, instances of arrivals of birds under adverse weather conditions are probably explainable by the supposition that the flight was begun under favorable auspices and that later the weather changed. Migration in spring usually occurs with a rising temperature and in autumn with a falling temperature. In each case the changing temperature seems to be a more potent factor than the absolute degree of cold.

The direction and force of the winds, except as they are occasionally intimately connected with sudden and extreme variations in temperature, seem to have only a slight influence on migration.

Some birds migrate by day, but most of them seek the cover of darkness. Day migrants include Ducks and Geese (which also migrate by night), Hawks, Swallows, the Nighthawk, and the Chimney Swift. The last two, combining business and pleasure, catch their morning or evening meal during a zigzag flight that tends in the desired direction. The daily advance of such migrants covers only a few miles, and when a large body of water is encountered they pass around rather than across it. The night migrants include all the great family of Warblers, the Thrushes, Flycatchers, Vireos, Orioles, Tanagers, shore birds, and most of the Sparrows. They usually begin their flight soon after dark and end it before dawn, and go farther before than after midnight.

Night migration probably results in more casualties from natural causes than would occur if the birds made the same journey by day; but, on the other hand, there is a decided gain in the matter of food supply. For instance, a bird feeds all day on the north shore of the Gulf of Mexico; if, then, it waited until the next morning to make its flight across the Gulf in the daytime it would arrive on the Mexican coast at nightfall and would have to wait until the following morning to appease its hunger. Thus there would be 36 consecutive hours without food, whereas by night migration the same journey can be performed with only a 12 hours' fast.

Migrating birds do not fly at their fastest. Their migration speed is usually from 30 to 40 miles an hour and rarely exceeds 50. Flights of a few hours at night, alternating with rests of one or more days, make the spring advance very slow, averaging for all species not more than 23 miles a day, but with great variations of daily rate among the different species. The exact number of miles which a particular bird makes during one day's journey has not yet been determined, and cannot be ascertained until the tagging or banding of birds by means of metal rings is carried out on a far more extensive scale than has yet been possible.

If migration were a steady movement northward with the same individuals always in the van, numerous careful observations might make it possible to approximate the truth; but instead of this, most migrations are performed somewhat after the manner of a game of leap-frog. The van in spring migration is composed chiefly of old birds, and as they reach their nesting places of the previous year they remain to breed. Thus the vanguard is constantly dropping out and the forward movement must depend upon the arrival of the next corps, which may be near at hand or far in the rear. Moreover, in our present state of knowledge we can not say whether a given group of birds after a night's migration keeps in the van on succeeding nights or rests and feeds for several days and allows other groups previously in the rear to assume the lead. It is known that birds do not as a rule move rapidly when migrating in the daytime, but from the meagre data available it may be inferred that the speed at night is considerably greater. During day migration the smaller land birds rarely fly faster than 20 miles an hour, though the larger birds, as Cranes, Geese, and Ducks move somewhat more rapidly. The result of timing Nighthawks on several occasions gave a rate of 10 to 14 miles an hour, the former being the more usual speed. This slow rate results from the irregularity of the flight, caused by the birds' capturing their evening and morning meals en route. In the evening the flight lasted about an hour and a half and in the morning about an hour. Thus a distance of approximately 30 miles would be traveled by each individual during the morning and evening flights.

Night migrants probably average longer distances in most of their flights, and this is known to be the case with some species. The Purple Martin, during the spring of 1884, performed almost its entire migration from New Orleans to Lake Winnipeg during only 12 nights — an average of 120 miles for each night of movement — and some late migrants like the Gray-cheeked Thrush, must make still greater distances at a single flight. That most of them can fly several hundred miles without stopping is proved by the fact that they make flights of 500 to 700 miles across the Gulf of Mexico.

The length of the migration journey varies enormously. A few birds, like the Grouse, Quail, Cardinal, and Carolina Wren, are non-migratory. Many a Bobwhite rounds out its full period of existence without ever going 10 miles from the nest where it was hatched. Some other species migrate so short a distance that the movement is scarcely noticeable. Thus, Meadowlarks are found near New York City all the year, but probably the individuals nesting in that region pass a little farther south for the winter and their places are taken by migrants from farther north. Or part of a species may migrate and the rest remain stationary, as in the case of the Pine Warbler and the Black-headed Grosbeak, which do not venture in winter south of the breeding range. With them fall migration is only a withdrawal from the northern and a concentration in the southern part of the summer home — the Warbler in about a fourth and the Grosbeak in less than an eighth of the summer area. In the case of the Maryland Yellow-throat, the breeding birds of Florida are strictly non-migratory, while in spring and fall other Yellow-throats pass through Florida in their journeys between their winter home in Cuba and their summer home in New England.

Another variation is illustrated by the Robin, which occurs in the middle districts of the United States throughout the year, in Canada only in summer, and along the Gulf of Mexico only in winter. Probably no individual Robin is a continuous resident in any section; but the Robin that nests, let us say, in southern Missouri, spends the winter near the Gulf, while his hardy Canada-bred cousin is the winter tenant of the abandoned summer home of the southern bird.

Most migratory birds desert the entire region occupied in summer for some other district adopted as a winter home. These two homes are separated by very variable distances. Many species from Canada winter in the United States, as the Tree Sparrow, Junco, and Snow Bunting; others nesting in northern United States winter in the Gulf States, as the Chipping, Field, Savannah, and Vesper Sparrows, while more than a hundred species leave the United States for the winter and spend that season in Central or even in South America.

Nor are they content with journeying to northern South America, but many cross the Equator and pass on to the pampas of Argentina and a few even to Patagonia. Among these long-distance migrants are some of our commonest birds; the Scarlet Tanager migrates from Canada to Peru; the Bobolinks that nest in New England probably winter in Brazil, as do Purple Martins, Cliff Sparrows, Barn Sparrows, Nighthawks, and some Thrushes, which are their companions both summer and winter. The Black-poll Warblers that nest in Alaska winter in northern South America, at least 5,000 miles from the summer home. The land bird with the longest migration route is probably the Nighthawk, which occurs north to Yukon and south 7,000 miles away, to Argentina.

But even these distances are surpassed by some of the water birds, and notably by some of the shorebirds, which as a group have the longest migration routes of any birds. Nineteen species of shorebirds breed north of the Arctic Circle, every one of which visits South America in winter, six of them penetrating to Patagonia, a migration route more than 8,000 miles in length. The world's migration champion, however, is the Arctic Tern.

The shape of the land areas in the northern half of the Western Hemisphere and the nature of the surface has tended to great variations in migratory movements. If the whole area from Brazil to Canada were a plain with the general characteristics of the middle section of the Mississippi Valley, the study of bird migration would lose much of its fascination. There would be a simple rhythmical swinging of the migration pendulum back and forth, spring and fall. But much of the earth's surface between Brazil and Canada is occupied by the Gulf of Mexico, the Caribbean Sea, and parts of the Atlantic Ocean, all devoid of

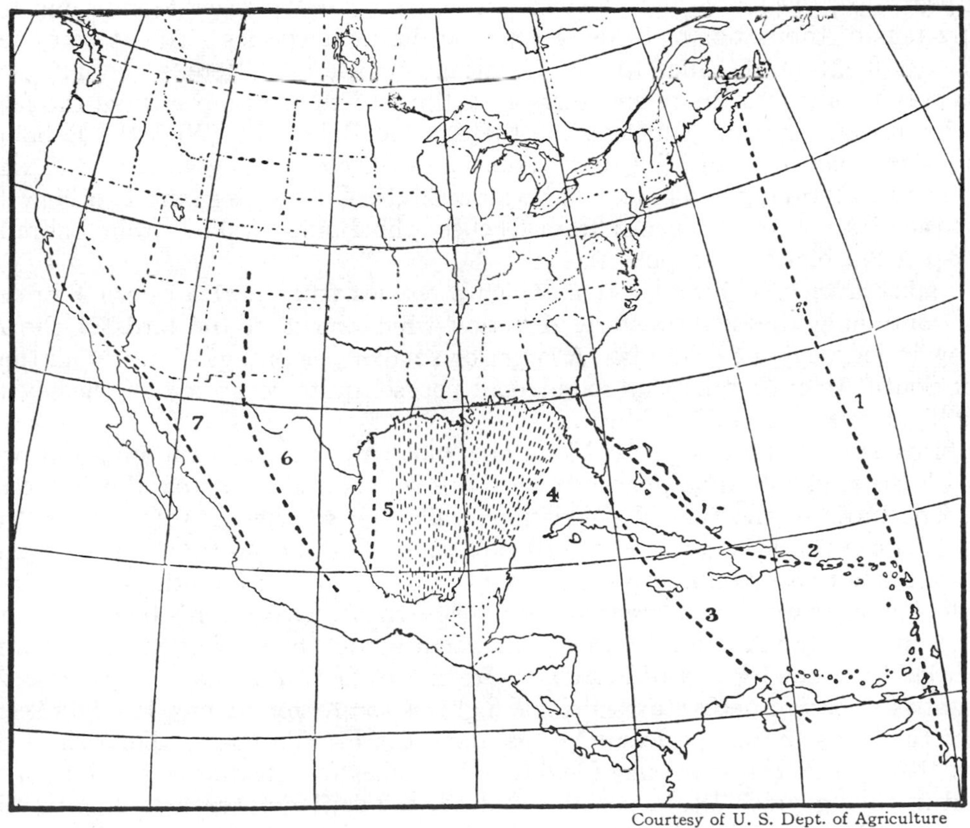

Courtesy of U. S. Dept. of Agriculture

PRINCIPAL MIGRATION ROUTES OF NORTH AMERICA

Most migrants use route No. 4, though this necessitates a flight of 500 to 700 miles across the Gulf of Mexico. A few traverse the more direct route No. 3, and still fewer, route No. 2. Only water birds make the 2,400-mile flight along route No. 1, from Nova Scotia to South America.

sustenance for land birds. The two areas of abundant food supply are North America and northern South America, separated by the comparatively small areas of Mexico and Central America, the islands of the West Indies, and the great waste stretches of water.

The different courses taken by the birds to get around or over this intervening inhospitable region are almost as numerous as the bird families that traverse them, and only some of the more important routes will be mentioned here.

Birds often seem eccentric in choice of route, and many do not take the shortest line. The 50 species from New England that winter in South America, instead of making the direct trip over the Atlantic involving a flight of 2,000 miles, take a somewhat longer route that follows the coast to Florida and passes thence by island or mainland to South America. What would at first sight seem to be a natural and convenient migratory highway extends from Florida through the Bahamas or Cuba to Haiti, Porto Rico, and the Lesser Antilles and thence to South America. Birds that travel by this route need never be out of sight of land; resting places are afforded at convenient intervals and the distance is but little longer than the water route. Yet beyond Cuba this highway is little used. About 25 species continue as far as Porto Rico and remain there through the winter. Only adventurers of some six species gain the South American mainland by completing the island chain. The reason is not far to seek — scarcity of food. The total area of all the West Indies east of Porto Rico is a little less than that of Rhode Island. Should a small proportion only of the feathered inhabitants of the eastern States select this route, not even the luxuriant fauna and flora of the tropics could supply their needs.

A still more direct route, but one requiring longer single flights, stretches from Florida to South America, via Cuba and Jamaica. The 150 miles between Florida and Cuba are crossed by tens of thousands of birds of some 60 different species. About half the species take the next flight of 90 miles to the Jamaican mountains. Here a 500-mile stretch of islandless ocean confronts them, and scarcely a third of their number leave the forest-clad hills for the unseen beyond. Chief among these is the Bobolink. With the Bobolink is an incongruous company of traveling companions — a Vireo, a Kingbird, and a Nighthawk that summer in Florida; the Chuck-will's-widow of the Gulf States; the two New England Cuckoos; the Gray-cheeked Thrush from Quebec; the Bank Swallow from Labrador; and the Black-poll Warbler from far-off Alaska.

The main-traveled highway is that which stretches from northwestern Florida across the Gulf, continuing the southwesterly direction which most of the birds of the Atlantic coast follow in journeying to Florida. A larger or smaller percentage of nearly all the species bound for South America take this roundabout course, quite regardless of the several-hundred-mile flight over the Gulf of Mexico.

The birds east of the Allegheny Mountains move southwest in the fall, approximately parallel with the seacoast, and apparently keep this same direction across the Gulf to eastern Mexico. The birds of the central Mississippi Valley go southward to and over the Gulf. The birds between the Missouri and the edge of the plains and those of Canada east of the Rocky Mountains move southeastward and south until they join the others in their passage of the Gulf. In other words, the great majority of North American birds bound for a winter's sojourn in Central or South America elect a short cut across the Gulf of Mexico in preference to a longer land journey by way of Florida or Texas. In fact, millions of birds cross the Gulf at its widest part, which necessitates a single flight of 500 to 700 miles. It might seem more natural for the birds to make a leisurely trip along the Florida coast, take a short flight to Cuba, and thence a still shorter one of less than 100 miles to Yucatan — a route only a little longer and involving much less exposure. Indeed, the earlier naturalists, finding the same species both in Florida and in Yucatan, took this probable route for granted, and for years it has been noted in ornithological literature as one of the principal migration highways of North American birds. As a fact, it is almost deserted except for a few Swallows, some shore birds, and an occasional land bird storm driven from its accustomed course, while over the

Gulf route night after night for nearly eight months in the year myriads of hardy migrants wing their way through the darkness toward an unseen destination.

To the westward a short route stretches a few hundred miles from the coast of Texas to northern Vera Cruz. It is adopted by some Warblers, as the Kentucky, the Worm-eating, and the Golden-winged, and a few other species, which seek in this way to avoid a region scantily supplied with moist woodlands.

Still farther west are two routes which represent the land journeys of those birds from western United States that winter in Mexico and Central America. Their trips are comparatively short; most of the birds are content to stop when they reach the middle districts of Mexico and only a few pass east of the southern part of that country.

Still another route is one which extends in an approximately north and south line from Nova Scotia to the Lesser Antilles and the northern coast of South America. Though more than a thousand miles shorter than the main migration route, it is not employed by any land bird. But it is a favorite fall route for thousands of water birds, notable among which is the Golden Plover.

All Black-poll Warblers winter in South America. Those that are to nest in Alaska strike straight across the Caribbean Sea to Florida and northwestward to the Mississippi River. Then the direction changes and a course is laid almost due north to northern Minnesota in order to avoid the treeless plains of North Dakota. But when the forests of the Saskatchewan are reached the northwestward course is resumed and, with a slight verging toward the west, is held until the nesting region in the Alaskan spruces is attained.

Cliff Swallows in South America are winter neighbors of the Black-poll Warblers. But when in early spring nature prompts the Swallows which are to nest in Nova Scotia to seek that far-off land, situated exactly north of their winter abode, they begin their journey by a westward flight of several hundred miles to Panama. Thence they move leisurely along the western shore of the Caribbean Sea to Mexico, and, still avoiding any long trip over water, go completely around the western end of the Gulf. Hence as they cross Louisiana their course is directly opposite to that in which they started. A northeasterly flight from Louisiana to Maine and an easterly one to Nova Scotia completes their spring migration. This circuitous route has increased their flight more than 2,000 miles.

Why should the Swallow select a route so much more roundabout than that taken by the Warbler? The explanation is simple. The Warbler is a night migrant. Launching into the air soon after nightfall, it wings its way through the darkness toward some favorite lunch station, usually one to several hundred miles distant, and here it rests and feeds for several days before undertaking the next stage of its journey. Its migration consists of a series of long flights from one feeding place to the next, and naturally it takes the most direct course between stations, not avoiding any body of water that can be compassed in a single flight.

The Swallow, on the other hand, is a day migrant. It begins its spring migration several weeks earlier than the Warbler and catches each day's rations of flying insects during a few hours of slow evolutions, which at the same time accomplish the work of migration. Keeping along the insect-teeming shores, the 2,000 extra miles thereby added to the migration route are but a tithe of the distance the bird covers in pursuit of its daily food.

The normal migration route for the birds of eastern North America is a northeast and southwest course approximately parallel with the trend of the Atlantic coast; the birds breeding in the interior take a line of flight parallel in general with the course of the three great river valleys — those of the Mississippi, the Red, and the Mackenzie — that form a highway rich in food supplies between their winter and summer homes. Many birds, however, follow migration routes widely differing from the normal. One of the most extreme exceptions is that of the Marbled Godwit. Formerly a common breeder in North Dakota and Saskatchewan, some individuals on starting for their winter home in Central America took a course almost due east to the Maritime Provinces of Canada and thence followed the Atlantic coast to Florida and continued southward; others went in the opposite direction, traveling westward to southern Alaska and southward along the Pacific coast to Guatemala. Thus birds which were neighbors in summer became separated nearly 3,000 miles during migration, to settle finally in close proximity for the winter.

The Connecticut Warbler, choosing another eccentric course, adopts different routes for its southward and northward journeys. All the individuals of this species winter in South America, and so far as known all go and come by the same direct route between Florida and South America across the West Indies; but north of Florida the spring and fall routes diverge. The spring route leads the birds up the Mississippi Valley to their summer home in southern Canada; but fall migration begins with a 1,000-mile trip almost due east to New England, whence the coast is followed southwest to Florida. The Connecticut Warbler is considered rare, but the multitudes that have struck Long Island lighthouses during October storms show that the species is at least more common than would be judged from spring observations, and also show how closely it follows the coast line during fall migration. The breeding of the Connecticut Warbler offers a fruitful field of investigation for some bird lover during a summer vacation, for there undoubtedly is a large and as yet undiscovered breeding area in Ontario north of Lakes Huron and Superior. Incidentally this route of the Connecticut Warbler is a conclusive argument against the theory that migration routes always indicate the original pioneer path by which the birds invaded the region of their present summer homes.

Another species having an elliptical migration route is the White-winged Scoter. This Duck breeds near fresh water in the interior of Canada and winters entirely on the ocean along the Atlantic and Pacific coasts of the United States. From its summer home west of Hudson Bay individuals that are to winter on the Atlantic travel 1,500 miles almost due east to the coast of the most eastern part of Labrador; thence they cross the Gulf of St. Lawrence and follow the New England coast to their winter home, which extends from southwestern Maine to Chesapeake Bay, with the center of abundance off Long Island and Massachusetts. In spring the birds return to their breeding grounds by an inland route traversing the valleys of the Connecticut, Hudson, and Ottawa rivers. Individuals that winter along the Pacific coast from Washington to southern California are known to pass by thousands up and down the coast as far north as that coast has a generally north and south trend; but as soon as the coast line turns westward near the northwestern part of British Columbia the birds disappear and are not known anywhere in the 500-mile strip between the Pacific coast and the Mackenzie Valley. Apparently this region is crossed at a single flight from the salt water of the coast to the fresh-water summer home on the great lakes of the Mackenzie Valley.

A migration route entirely different from any thus far mentioned is that of the Western Tanager, or Louisiana Tanager, as it was formerly called. From its winter home in Guatemala it enters the United States about April 20; another 10 days and the van is in central New Mexico, Arizona, and southern California, marking an approximately east and west line. The next 10 days the easternmost birds advance only to southern Colorado, while the western have reached northern Washington. May 10 finds the line of the van extending in a great curve from Vancouver Island northeast to central Alberta and thence southeast to northern Colorado. It is evident that the Alberta birds have not reached their breeding grounds by way of the eastern slope of the Rocky Mountains, a route which would naturally be taken for granted by anyone examining a map of the winter and summer homes. On the contrary, these Alberta breeders must have come by way of the Pacific coast to southern British Columbia and then crossed over the main range of the Rocky Mountains, which at this season (May 20) are still cold and partly covered with snow.

The shape of North America tends to a converging of the lines of migration toward the Gulf of Mexico, and consequently the east and west breadth of the migration route just south of the United States is usually less than the corresponding breadth of the breeding

William L. Finley and H. T. Bohlman photographing nest of Western Tanagers in top of fir tree, eighty feet from the ground

territory. The extent to which migration routes contract varies greatly with different species. The Redstart represents one extreme where the lines of migration are carried far eastward to include the Bahamas and the Antilles, while they also extend southward into Mexico. Thus the migrating hosts present a broad front with an east and west extension of 2,500 miles from Mexico to the Lesser Antilles.

The opposite extreme, a narrow migration route, appears in the case of the Rose-breasted Grosbeak. The breeding range extends from Nova Scotia to central Alberta, 2,500 miles, and the migration lines converge until the Grosbeaks leave the United States along 800 miles of the Gulf coast from western Florida to central Texas.

The case of the Bobolink is typical of many species nesting in North America and wintering entirely in South America. The summer home extends from Cape Breton Island to Saskatchewan, 2,300 miles, and the migration lines converge toward southeastern United States and then strike directly across the West Indies for South America. In this part of their journey the migration path contracts to an east and west breadth of about 800 miles and a very large percentage of the birds restrict themselves to the eastern half of it. In South America the region occupied during the winter has about one-fifth the breadth and one-third the area of the breeding range.

The route of the Scarlet Tanager is an extreme example of narrowness of the path traveled twice a year between winter and summer homes. The breeding range extends 1,900 miles from New Brunswick to Saskatchewan. The migration range is contracted to 800 miles from Florida to Texas as the birds leave the United States. The migration lines continue to converge until in southern Central America the limits are not more than 100 miles apart.

The Black and White Warbler presents some interesting phases of migration. It winters in Central America, Mexico, the West Indies, and the peninsula of Florida. Ordinarily it would not be possible to distinguish the spring migrants in Florida from the wintering birds, and the advance of migration could not be noted until the migrants had passed north of the winter range, but records of Black and White Warblers striking lighthouses of southern Florida indicate the beginning of the birds' northward migration flight from Cuba. This occurs on the average on March 4, and the birds do not appear in southern Georgia beyond their winter range on the average until March 24. Thus a period of 20 days is taken for the van of migration to move 400 miles across Florida, an average rate of 20 miles per day. This rate is about the slowest of all North American birds and is only slightly increased throughout the whole spring migration up the Atlantic coast to Nova Scotia, where the birds arrive about May 20, having averaged less than 25 miles a day for the whole 77 days after leaving Cuba.

Migration along the western border of the range is fully as slow as along the Atlantic coast; on the average, the first arrive at Kerrville, Tex., March 9 and in northern North Dakota May 10, having traveled 1,300 miles in 60 days, or 22 miles a day. Thence the speed is more than doubled to the northwestern limit of the range in the Mackenzie Valley.

Incidentally it may be remarked that the Black and White Warbler is one of the very few migrants which arrive in Texas and Florida before they appear at the mouth of the Mississippi. The van of most species reaches southern Louisiana earlier than southern Texas.

The Cliff Swallow is another species with a slow migration schedule. It must start northward very early, since by March 10 it is already 2,500 miles from the winter home and yet averages only 25 miles a day for the next 20 days while rounding the western end of the Gulf of Mexico. It more than doubles this rate while passing up the Mississippi and Ohio River valleys. The crossing of the Allegheny Mountains comes next, and there are only 200 miles of progress to show for the 10 days' flight. By this time spring has really come east of the Alleghenies, and the Swallow travels 60 miles a day to its summer home in Nova Scotia. It is to be noted that the Swallow works up to high rates of speed only when it is traveling on the diagonal, and that except during the ten days spent in crossing the mountains each 10 days' travel covers approximately 5 degrees of latitude.

One of the best examples of rapid migration is that of the Gray-cheeked Thrush. This bird remains in its South American winter home so long that it does not appear in southern United States until late April — April 25 near the mouth of the Mississippi and April 30 in northern Florida. The last week in May finds the bird in extreme northwestern Alaska, the 4,000 mile trip from Louisiana to Alaska having been performed in about 30 days, or about 130 miles a day.

Generally the later in the season a bird migrates the greater is its average speed, but not necessarily the distance covered in a single night. The early migrants encounter much bad weather, and after one night's migration usually delay several days before making the next flight. The later migrant finds few nights too unfavorable for advancing, so that short flights taken on successive nights greatly raise the average migration speed.

How do migrating birds find their way? They do not journey haphazard, for the familiar inhabitants of our dooryard Marten boxes will return next year to these same boxes, though meanwhile thay have visited Brazil. If the entire distance were made overland, it might be supposed that sight and memory were the only faculties exercised. But for those birds that cross the Gulf of Mexico, something more than sight is necessary. Among day migrants sight probably is the principal guide, but it is noticeable that these seldom make the long single flights so common with night migrants.

Sight undoubtedly does play a part in guiding the night journeys also. On clear nights, especially when the moon shines brightly, migrating birds fly high and the ear can scarcely distinguish their faint twitterings; if clouds overspread the heavens, the flocks pass nearer the earth and their notes are much more audible, and on very dark nights the flutter of vibrant wings may be heard but a few feet overhead. Nevertheless, something besides sight guides these travelers in the upper air. In Alaska a few years ago members of the Biological Survey on the Harriman expedition went by steamer from the island of Unalaska to Bogoslof Island, a distance of about 60 miles. A dense fog shut out every object beyond a hundred yards. When the steamer was halfway across, flocks of Murres, returning to Bogoslof after long quests for food, began to break through the fog-wall astern, fly parallel with the vessel, and disappear in the mists ahead. By chart and compass the ship was heading straight for the island, but its course was no more exact than that taken by the birds. The power which carried them unerringly home over the ocean wastes, whatever its nature, may be called a sense of direction. We recognize in ourselves the possession of some such sense, though imperfect and frequently at fault. Doubtless a similar but vastly more acute sense enables the Murres, flying from home and circling wide over the water, to keep in mind the direction of their nests and return to them without the aid of sight.

But even the birds' sense of direction is not infallible. Reports from lighthouses in southern Florida show that birds leave Cuba on cloudy nights, when they can not possibly see the Florida shores, and safely reach their destination, provided no change occurs in the weather. But at fickle equinoctial time many flocks starting out under auspicious skies find themselves suddenly caught by a tempest. Buffeted by the wind and their sense of direction lost, these birds fall easy victims to the lure of the lighthouse. Many are killed by the impact, but many more settle on the framework or foundation until the storm ceases or the coming of daylight allows them to recover their bearings.

A favorite theory of many American ornithologists is that coast lines, mountain chains, and especially the courses of the larger rivers and their tributaries form well-marked highways along which birds return to previous nesting sites. According to this theory, a bird breeding in northern Indiana would in its fall migration pass down the nearest little rivulet or creek to the Wabash River, thence to the Ohio, and reaching the Mississippi would follow its course to the Gulf of Mexico, and would use the same route reversed for the return trip in the spring. The fact is that each county in the Central States contains nesting birds which at the beginning of the fall migration scatter toward half the points of the compass; indeed, it would be safe to say all the points of the compass, as some young

Herons preface their regular journey south with a little pleasure trip to the unexplored north. In fall most of the migrant land birds breeding in New England move southwest in a line approximately parallel with the Allegheny Mountains, but we can not argue from this fact that the route is selected so that mountains will serve as a guide, because at this very time thousands of birds reared in Indiana, Illinois, and to the northwestward are crossing these mountains at right angles to visit South Carolina and Georgia. This is shown specifically in the case of the Palm Warblers. They winter in the Gulf States from Louisiana eastward and throughout the greater Antilles to Porto Rico; they nest in Canada from the Mackenzie Valley to Newfoundland. To migrate according to the " lay of the land," the Louisiana Palm Warblers should follow up the broad open highway of the Mississippi River to its source and go thence to their breeding grounds, while the Warblers of the Antilles should use the Allegheny Mountains as a guide. As a matter of fact, the Louisiana birds nest in Labrador and those from the Antilles cut diagonally across the United States to summer in central Canada. These two routes of Palm Warblers cross each other in Georgia at approximately right angles. It is possible to trace the routes of the Palm Warblers because those nesting to the east of Hudson Bay differ enough in color from those nesting farther west to be readily distinguished even in their winter dress. It must always be remembered, however, that from a common ancestry these two groups of Palm Warblers came to differ in appearance because they gradually evolved differences in breeding grounds and in migration routes and not that they chose different routes because they were subspecifically different.

The truth seems to be that birds pay little attention to natural physical highways except when large bodies of water force them to deviate from the desired course. Food is the principal factor in determining migration routes, and in general the course between summer and winter homes is as straight as the birds can find and still have an abundance of food at each stopping place.

It is interesting to note the relation between migration and molting. Most birds care for their young until old enough to look out for themselves, then molt, and when the new feathers are grown start on their southward journey in their new suits of clothes. But the birds that nest beyond the Arctic Circle have too short a summer to permit such leisurely movements. They begin their migration as soon as possible after the young are out of the nest and molt en route. Indeed, these Arctic breeders are so pressed for time that many of them do their courting during the period of spring migration and arrive at the breeding grounds already paired and ready for nest building, while many a Robin and Bluebird in the middle Mississippi Valley has been in the neighborhood of the nesting site a full month before it carries the first straw of construction.

Migration is a season full of peril for myriads of winged travelers, especially for those that cross large bodies of water. Some of the water birds making long voyages can rest on the waves if overtaken by storms, but for the luckless Warbler or Sparrow whose feathers become water-soaked an ocean grave is inevitable. Nor are such accidents infrequent. A few years ago on Lake Michigan a storm during spring migration forced to the waves numerous victims, as evidenced by many subsequently drifting ashore. If such mortality could occur on a lake less than 100 miles wide, how much more likely even a greater disaster attending a flight across the Gulf of Mexico. Such a catastrophe was once witnessed from the deck of a vessel 30 miles off the mouth of the Mississippi River. Large numbers of migrating birds, mostly Warblers, had accomplished nine-tenths of their long flight and were nearing land, when caught by a " norther," with which most of them were unable to contend, and falling into the Gulf they were drowned by hundreds.

During migration birds are peculiarly liable to destruction by striking high objects. The Washington Monument, at the National Capital, has witnessed the death of many little migrants; on a single morning in the spring of 1902 nearly 150 lifeless bodies were strewn around its base.

Every spring the lights of the lighthouses along the coast lure to destruction myriads of birds en route from their winter homes in the south to their summer nesting places in the north. Every fall a still greater death toll is exacted when the return journey is made. Lighthouses are scattered every few miles along the more than 3,000 miles of coast line, but two lighthouses, Fowey Rocks and Sombrero Key, cause far more bird tragedies than any others. The reason is twofold — their geographic position and the character of their lights. Both lights are situated at the southern end of Florida, where countless thousands of birds pass each year to and from Cuba; and both are lights of the first magnitude on towers 100–140 feet high. Fowey Rocks has a fixed white light, the deadliest of all. A flashing light frightens birds away and a red light is avoided by them as would be a danger signal, but a steady white light looming out of the mist or darkness seems like a magnet drawing the wanderers to destruction. Coming from any direction they veer around to the leeward side and then flying against the wind strike the glass, or more often exhaust themselves like moths fluttering in and out of the bewildering rays.

During the spring migration of 1903 two experienced ornithologists spent the entire season on the coast of northwestern Florida, visiting every sort of bird haunt. They were eminently successful in the long list of species identified, but their enumeration is still more remarkable for what it does not contain. About 25 species of the smaller land birds of the Eastern States were not seen, including a dozen common species. Among these latter were the Chat, the Redstart, and the Indigo Bunting, three species abundant throughout the whole region to the northward. The explanation of their absence from the list seems to be that these birds, on crossing the Gulf of Mexico, flew far inland before alighting and thus passed over the observers. This would seem to disprove the popular belief that birds under ordinary circumstances find the ocean flight excessively wearisome, and that after laboring with tired pinions across the seemingly endless wastes they sink exhausted on reaching terra firma. The truth seems to be that, endowed by nature with wonderful powers of aërial locomotion, many birds under normal conditions not only cross the Gulf of Mexico at its widest point but even pass without pause over the low swampy coastal plain to the higher territory beyond.

So little averse are birds to an ocean flight that many fly from eastern Texas to the Gulf coast of southern Mexico, though this 400 miles of water journey hardly shortens the distance of travel by an hour's flight. Thus birds avoid the hot, treeless plains and scant provender of southern Texas by a direct flight from the moist insect-teeming forests of northern Texas to a similar country in southern Mexico.

It may be well to consider the actual amount of energy expended by birds in their migratory flights. Both the soaring and the sailing of birds show that they are proficient in the use of several factors in the art of flying that have not yet been mastered either in principle or practice by the most skillful of modern aviators. A Vulture or a Crane, after a few preliminary wing beats, sets its wings and mounts in wide sweeping circles to a great height, overcoming gravity with no exertion apparent to human vision even when assisted by the most powerful telescopes. The Carolina Rail, or Sora, has small, short wings apparently ill adapted to protracted flight, and ordinarily when forced to fly does so reluctantly and alights as soon as possible. It flies with such awkwardness and apparently becomes so quickly exhausted that at least one writer has been led to infer that most of its migration must be made on foot; the facts are, however, that the Carolina Rail has one of the longest migration routes of the whole Rail family and easily crosses the wide reaches of the Caribbean Sea. The Hummingbird, smallest of all birds, crosses the Gulf of Mexico, flying over 500 miles in a single night. As already noted, the Golden Plover flies from Nova Scotia to South America, and in fair weather makes the whole distance of 2,400 miles without a stop, probably requiring nearly if not quite 48 hours for the trip.

Here is an aërial machine that is far more economical of fuel — *i. e.*, of energy — than the best aëroplane yet invented. The to-and-fro motion of the bird's wing appears to be an uneconomical way of applying power, since all the force required to bring the wing forward for the beginning of the stroke is not only wasted, but more than wasted, as it largely increases the air friction and retards the speed. On the other hand, the screw propeller of the aëroplane has no lost motion. Yet less than 2 ounces of fuel in the shape of body fat suffice to force the bird at a high rate of speed over that 2,400-mile course. A thousand-pound aëroplane, if as economical of fuel, would consume in a 20-mile flight not the gallon of gasoline required by the best machines but only a single pint.

The Canada Goose is typical of what may be called regular migration. This bird fulfills the popular notion of bird migration, *i. e.*, it moves northward in spring as soon as

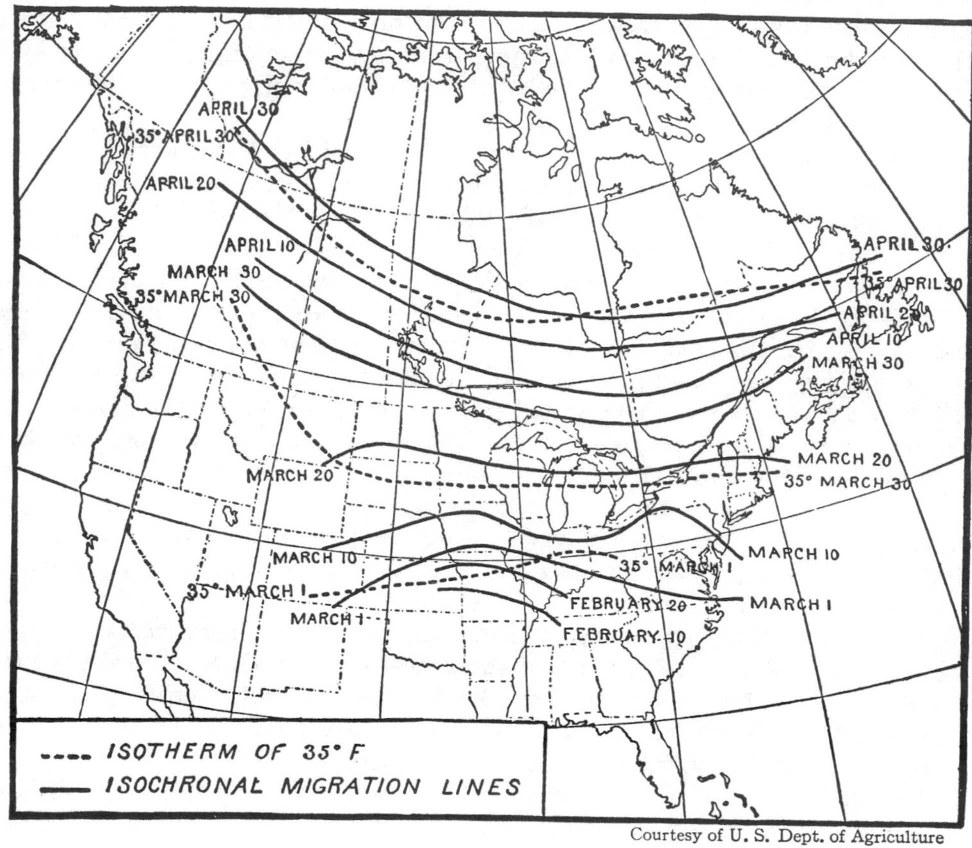

Courtesy of U. S. Dept. of Agriculture

MIGRATION OF THE CANADA GOOSE

An example of migration keeping pace with the advance of spring

the loosening of winter's fetters offers open water and a possibility of food. It continues its progress at the same rate as spring, appearing at its most northern breeding grounds at the earliest possible moment. The isotherm of 35° F. seems to be the governing factor in the rate of spring migration of the Canada Goose and the isotherm and the vanguard of the Geese are close traveling companions throughout the entire route. Moreover, the isochronal lines representing the position of the van at various times are approximately east-and-west lines during the whole migration period. But this so-called regular migration is performed by a very small percentage of species, the great majority choosing exactly the opposite course — to remain in their winter homes until spring is far advanced and then reach their breeding grounds by a migration much more rapid than the northward advance of the season.

Much has been learned about bird migration in these latter days, but much yet remains to be learned.

ORDER OF DIVING BIRDS

Order *Pygopodes*

MOST aquatic of all our birds are the Diving Birds. Not only are their bodies made so that they can propel themselves on land only with difficulty, but their food consists entirely of fish and other aquatic animals. Their flesh is coarse and unpalatable. They are the lowest form of bird life and are the most closely allied to the reptiles, from which birds are supposed to have originated. Birds of this order spend nearly their entire time in the water. They nest on the ground or on rocks. The young are covered with down when hatched, and as soon as this natal down is dry they are able to take to the water.

The scientific name given to this order, *Pygopodes*, is from two Greek words meaning " rump " and "foot," and refers to the position of the legs in relation to the rest of the body — a characteristic peculiar to this order. The tibia or drumstick is buried beneath the skin and feathers, bringing the heel joint close to the tail. The birds, therefore, sit or stand in an almost perpendicular position, and walk with great difficulty and awkwardness. The toes are either webbed or broadly lobed. Both body and neck are elongated, giving a boat-shaped appearance to the bird. The bill is horny and pointed and has no pouch; it can be opened very wide. The wings are very short, scarcely reaching the base of the tail. The latter is never long, and sometimes it is so rudimentary as to make the bird appear tailless. The plumage is dense, and there is no sexual variation in color. The body is almost entirely encased in a layer of fat.

According to the development of the tail, the Diving Birds are divided into two suborders: the first is the *Colymbi*, and contains the one family of Grebes; and the second is the *Cepphi*, and contains two families, the Loons and the Auks, Murres, and Puffins.

GREBES

Order *Pygopodes;* suborder *Colymbi;* family *Colymbidæ*

THE Grebes are much less pronounced, and consequently less interesting bird characters, than are the Loons, though both families have some of the same physical characteristics, notably skill in the water and clumsiness on land. They are smaller than the Loons and are more likely to be found in inland bodies of fresh water, though their migrations take them to the sea where they are by no means entirely out of their element. Like the Loons, when pursued the Grebes try to escape by diving and swimming under water, where they propel themselves by their feet; and generally they show decided disinclination to take to their wings, though they are swift and strong flyers. Grebes undoubtedly dive with remarkable quickness, but, as in the case of the Loons (and for the same reasons), their cleverness in this operation has been much exaggerated, as at any reasonable distance they are quite unable to dodge a rifle bullet, especially if it be propelled by smokeless powder.

Grebes have feet which are lobate, that is, each toe has one or more separate membranes which are joined only at the base. The toes are flattened and the nails short and round. The shanks are so flattened as to be nearly blade-like. The bill, which is cone-shaped, is about the length of the head. The head is generally ruffed or crested, at least in the breeding season, and the neck long. The wings are short and the tail is invisible. The plumage is compact, smooth, and rather hair-like; when well dressed by the bird it is absolutely waterproof, and, therefore, Grebes, though water birds, are never wet. The extreme posterior position of the legs causes the birds to sit up like Penguins. On land they sometimes progress on their bellies after the manner of seals. In flight the feet are extended backward and serve as a rudder, as the tail would in another bird.

A dense, matted, raft-like structure, made of rushes and the like, and often floating, but usually anchored to some aquatic plant, forms the nest of these strange birds. On this platform are laid from two to nine eggs of dull white or greenish-white. The nest is always damp and the eggs sometimes are hatched when they actually are partly covered with water. "When out of the shell," says one observer, "the young has not far to walk; he looks for a few moments over the edge of his water-drenched cradle and down he goes with the expertness of an old diver." Grebes usually are gregarious. When incubation of the full number of eggs has actually begun, the sitting bird upon leaving the nest (unless she is frightened away) completely conceals the eggs with moss and rushes.

Few birds have suffered more from the millinery trade than have the Grebes, whose dense and beautiful breast plumage has been much used for decorating hats. Legislation of various kinds curbs this barbaric practice in many parts of the country.

Photo by W. L. Finley and H. T. Bohlman

WESTERN GREBE

The most remarkable point about the food habits of Grebes is that the stomachs almost invariably contain a considerable mass of feathers. Feathers are fed to the young, and there is no question that they play some essential though unknown part in the digestive economy. As they are finely ground in the gizzards it is probable that finally they are digested and the available nutriment assimilated. Feathers constituted practically 66 per cent. of the contents of the 57 Horned Grebe's stomachs examined. However, it is not likely that they furnish a very large percentage of the nourishment needed by the birds. As the nutritive value of the feathers is unknown, this part of the stomach contents is ignored. The other items of food are assigned 100 per cent., and the percentages are given on that basis. Various beetles, chiefly aquatic, compose 23.3 per cent. of the food; other insects (including aquatic bugs, caddis and chironomid larvæ, dragon-fly nymphs, etc.), nearly 12 per cent.; fishes, 27.8 per cent.; crawfish 20.7 per cent.; and other crustacea 13.8 per cent. A little other animal matter is taken, including snails and spiders, and a small quantity of vegetable food was found in two stomachs.

It has been claimed that Grebes live exclusively on fish and do mischief in fish hatcheries. The results obtained by stomach examination show that they do not depend wholly or even chiefly upon fish. On the contrary, they eat a large number of crawfishes, which often severely damage crops, and consume numbers of aquatic insects which devour small fishes and the food of such fishes.

WESTERN GREBE

A. O. U. Number 1

Æchmophorus occidentalis (*Lawrence*)

Other Names.— Western Dabchick; Swan Grebe.

General Description.— Length, 24 to 29 inches. Color above, brownish-black; below, satiny-white. Head with short crest on top but none on sides; bill, slender; neck nearly the length of the body.

Color.— Adults: Forehead, dark ash; crest and narrow line down back of neck, sooty-blackish shading on upper parts into brownish-black; the feathers of back with grayish margins; primaries, dusky-brown, white at base; secondaries, white, some dark on outer webs; sides of head, chin, throat, and entire under parts, pure satiny-white; bill, yellowish-olive; feet, dull olive, yellowish on webs; outer edge and soles of feet, blackish; iris, orange, pink, or carmine with a white ring; a narrow bare space from bill to eye, lavender.

Nest and Eggs.— Nest: A matted structure of tule stems, grass, and water-plants, with a slight depression in the center; afloat on the water; usually lightly fastened to the living reeds so that it will move up and down but not be carried away from its position. Eggs: Sometimes 3 but usually 4 or 5, pale bluish-green but stained a light brown from contact with the decomposed vegetable matter of the nest.

Distribution.— Western North America; breeds from British Columbia, southern Saskatchewan, southern Alberta, and southern Manitoba south to northern California, Utah, and northern North Dakota; winters from southern British Columbia and California southward to central Mexico; casual east to Nebraska, Kansas, Wisconsin, Minnesota, and Quebec.

For years, the lake region of southern Oregon was the most profitable field in the West for the plume hunter. The Western Grebe was the greatest sufferer. This diver of glistening-white breast and silvery-gray back was sought not without reason. The Grebe hunters call the skin of this bird fur rather than feathers, because it is so tough it can be scraped and handled like a hide, and because the thick warm plumage seems more like the fur of a mammal than the skin of a bird. These skins, when prepared and placed on the market in the form of coats and capes, brought the prices of the most expensive furs.

Formerly there were immense colonies of Western Grebes living along the north shore of Tule, or Rhett, Lake, Lower Klamath Lake, and Malheur Lake. Plume hunters, however, sought out these big colonies and shot great numbers of the birds during the nesting season, leaving the eggs to spoil and the young to starve to death. This decreased the numbers so rapidly that within a few seasons the birds were exterminated in places.

Malheur Lake is a large body of shallow water surrounded on all sides by great stretches of tules. The whole border is a veritable jungle, an almost endless area of floating tule islands between which is a network of channels. Here is the typical home of the Western Grebe. In the edge of the tules, the Grebe gathers tule stems and other vegetation, making a floating raft

Photo by F. M. Chapman Courtesy of Nat. Asso. Aud. Soc.

TWO WESTERN GREBES JUST HATCHED

which is anchored. Around the edges of one of these islands, which was two acres in extent, we found between forty and fifty nests. The usual number of eggs was four or five.

On several occasions, we watched a Grebe chick cut his way out of the shell and liberate himself. After he gets his bill through in one place, he goes at the task like clockwork. He turns himself a little and begins hammering in a new place and keeps this up until he has made a complete revolution in his shell. The end or cap of the egg, cut clear around, drops off, and the youngster kicks himself out into the sunshine. It doesn't take his coat long to dry.

The Grebe parents have an interesting way of taking their young with them. The chicks ride on the back of the mother or father just under the wing-coverts with the head sticking out. Sometimes one may see an old Grebe carrying two or three young on his back. At the slightest alarm, the old bird raises the feathers and covers the chicks completely. One can readily tell when a Grebe has chicks on his back, even if not visible, because he appears to swim higher in the water. Normally, the body is almost submerged. An old Grebe not only swims, but dives readily, keeping the young in place on his back.

William L. Finley.

HOLBŒLL'S GREBE

Colymbus holbœlli (*Reinhardt*)

A. O. U. Number 2 See Color Plate 1

Other Names.—American Red-necked Grebe; Red-necked Grebe; Holbœll's Diver.

General Description.—Length, 19 inches. In Summer: Glossy greenish-black above, and silvery-white below. In Winter: Grayish-brown above, and grayish-white below. Neck shorter than body; bill, nearly as long as head; crest lacking or inconspicuous. Largest of the Grebes.

Color.—Adults in Summer: *Crown, back of neck, and upper parts, glossy greenish-black,* darker on head, more brownish on back where the feathers are edged with grayish; wing-coverts and primaries, dusky-brown; *secondaries, white* with brown tips and black shafts; *a broad area including chin, throat, and sides of head, silvery-gray,* lightening along juncture with black of crown; rest of neck and upper part of breast, deep brownish-rufous; under parts, silvery-white shaded along sides with pale ash, each feather with a dark shaft line and terminal spot, producing a dappled effect; bill, dusky, yellow below and at base; iris, carmine with a white ring. Adults in Winter, and Young: Crown, neck all around, and upper parts, grayish-brown, the feathers of back with lighter edges; sides of head and throat, whitish; under parts, grayish-white, the mottling of summer plumage obsolete; bill, obscured but showing some pale yellow below; iris, as in summer.

Nest and Eggs.—Nest: Attached to live rushes; constructed of reeds, decayed vegetable matter, grass, and mud. Eggs: 3 to 5, dull white, usually soiled with brownish.

Distribution.—North America at large, eastern Siberia, and southwest to Japan; breeds from northwestern Alaska across British America to northern Ungava, south to northern Washington, Montana, and southwestern Minnesota; common throughout the United States in winter; south to southern California, southern Colorado, the Ohio valley and North Carolina; casual in Georgia and Greenland.

Some Grebes colonize in breeding, as do the Western and Eared Grebes. In Holbœll's Grebe, however, we have the one large species of North America which is distinctly a lover of personal solitude. Its breeding grounds, or perhaps more properly waters, are the sloughs and marshes of the northwest States and Canadian provinces. Here, in the deep bogs, it places its soggy semi-floating pile of decaying vegetation amid the areas of reeds or canes growing from the water. One can seldom see the brooding bird on the nest. On being approached she hastily pulls débris over the three or four dirty-white eggs, completely covering them, then slips into the water and dives, showing herself no more until the intruder has surely vanished.

During the breeding season these Grebes are very noisy. The male (probably it is he) swims into the open water of the lakes, if such there be, and emits the most astonishing succession of yells and wailings, which probably are the happy expression of the torrent of his tender emotions, though to our ears they may rather resemble cries of distress. Later in the season he gets bravely over such manifestations of weakness, and is silent enough for anyone. Then he is usually seen "by his lonesome," out on some body of water, frequently on the ocean, well off the beach, where he can exercise to fine advantage his really great powers of diving.

Holbœll's Grebes are hardy birds, and often winter as far to the north as they can find open water, and are frequent in winter along our North Atlantic coast. They have a fatal tendency to linger too late in the northern lakes, and thus they get caught in the ice, or, driven to fly south, cannot find open water, and fall exhausted on the land or into snow banks. This is notably the case in the month of March, when they migrate north earlier than is safe. Since they cannot rise on wing except from water, as their wings are small, many of them perish out of their element. It is a common occurrence for farmers and others to pick them up in fields or roads, helplessly waddling about on legs set too far "aft" to make them handy ashore. But in the water there is no bird more swift and facile, better able to take care of itself, more able in the pursuit of the small fry which constitute its normal prey. HERBERT K. JOB.

Photo by H. K. Job

NEST OF HOLBŒLL'S GREBE

HORNED GREBE

Colymbus auritus *Linnæus*

A. O. U. Number 3 See Color Plate 1

Other Names.— Hell-diver; Water-witch; Devil-diver; Pink-eyed Diver; Dipper.

General Description.— Length, 14 inches. Color above, grayish-brown or dusky-gray; below, white. In summer, adults have crests or ruffs on cheeks and sides of head.

Color.— ADULTS IN SUMMER: Crown, chin, throat, and crest, *glossy greenish-black;* a stripe from bill through eye and above it, widening behind to nape, *brownish-yellow;* upper parts, grayish-brown; feathers, paler-edged; primaries, dusky-brown; *secondaries, white;* neck all around (except for dusky stripe behind), sides, and flanks, rich brownish-rufous; rest of under parts, silky-white; bill, dusky tipped with yellow; iris, carmine with white ring; feet, dusky outside, yellow inside. ADULTS IN WINTER, AND YOUNG: Ruff, obsolete; forehead, crown to level of eyes, a narrow strip down back of neck and upper parts, dusky-gray; feathers of back with lighter edges; wings, as in summer; chin, throat, and sides of head, pure silky-white; front of neck and lower abdomen, washed with gray; bill, dusky, yellowish or bluish-white below.

Nest and Eggs.— NEST: A buoyant platform of dead reeds, grass, and vegetation. EGGS: 3 to 7, white.

Distribution.— Northern part of northern hemisphere; breeds from the lower Yukon across British America to southern Ungava and the Magdalen Islands, south to southern British Columbia, across United States on about the parallel 45° to Maine; winters from southern British Columbia, southern Ontario, and Maine south to the Gulf coast and Florida; casual in Greenland.

Horned Grebes are commonly known as "Hell-divers" or "Water-witches," because of their facility in disappearing and the mystery as to where they go. This species often mystifies the hunter by sinking slowly backward until nearly out of sight or by diving and disappearing altogether, until the novice is ready to make oath that the bird has committed suicide for fear of his deadly marksmanship; but the Grebe merely submerges and swims beneath the surface until among the water plants, where it remains secure with its beak just protruding unnoticed above the water, or hidden by some overhanging leaf. When wounded it sometimes dives and swims along under water to the cover of overhanging vegetation on the bank, when it creeps ashore unseen and hides amid the verdant cover.

Photo by H. K. Job Courtesy of Outing Pub. Co.
HORNED GREBE (Spring Plumage)

This Grebe is one of the quickest of divers, often escaping a charge of shot by its activity in going under. When alarmed it lies very low in the water, and, if it can get its head and neck beneath the surface before the shot reaches the spot, its vital parts are likely to escape unharmed. It frequents small ponds and little streams with grassy banks, but where much persecuted by gunners seeks the larger lakes or the sea for greater safety. Ordinarily in swimming under water it does not appear to use its wings, but probably all diving birds utilize their wing power when in pursuit of elusive prey. Mr. C. W. Vibert of South Windsor, Connecticut, kept a bird of this species that was seen to raise its wings slightly when swimming beneath the surface.

When storms prevail at sea in fall and winter flocks of Grebes often are driven into the ponds of the interior. At such times they may be seen asleep on the water in the daytime with the head drawn down on the back and the bill thrust into the feathers of the shoulder or breast, keeping their place head to the wind by a sort of automatic paddling. Sometimes a sleepy bird uses only one foot and so swings about in a circle.

EDWARD HOWE FORBUSH.

EARED GREBE

Colymbus nigricollis californicus (*Heermann*)

A. O. U. Number 4

Other Names.— American Eared Grebe; Eared Diver.

General Description.— Length, 12 to 14 inches. Color above, dusky; below, white. In summer adults have *long, fan-shaped ear-tufts of fine feathers.*

Color.— ADULTS IN SUMMER: *Ear-tufts, golden-brown; crown, chin, throat, and neck all around, black;* upper parts, dusky; primaries, dusky; secondaries, white, dusky at base; sides, deep purplish-brown with a wash of the same color across breast and on under tail-coverts; under parts, silky white; abdomen, tinged with gray; bill, black; feet, olive, dusky outside and on soles; iris, red; eyelids, orange. ADULTS IN WINTER: No ear tufts; crown and narrow band on back of neck and upper parts, grayish-dusky; chin, throat, and sides of head, white; under parts, silvery-white; sides and flanks, tinged with gray.

Nest and Eggs.— NEST: A floating platform of reeds and vegetation, on shallow lagoons, ponds, or lakes. EGGS: 4 to 6, soiled white.

Distribution.— Western North America; breeds from Central British Columbia, Great Slave Lake, Saskatchewan, and Manitoba south to southern California, northern Arizona, northern Nebraska, and northern Iowa; winters from central California southward to Cape San Lucas and Guatemala; east to Kansas in migration; casual in Missouri, Indiana, and Ontario.

Out on the main part of Malheur Lake in southeastern Oregon, we came upon a colony of Eared Grebes. These birds were nesting well out in the open water. I counted one hundred and sixty-five nests scattered over an area of two or three acres. Some homes were but a few feet apart. The nest itself was a very interesting structure. It was built entirely of water weeds, commonly called milfoil, which grew in the shallow water. The nest consisted of the long slender runners pulled together from a distance of several feet around. It looked to me as if these weeds when piled together, would sink. On the contrary, I found the nest quite buoyant. Long red stems, kept alive by the water, often extended to the bottom. In a few cases, I found the birds had collected pieces of dry tule stems as a sort of lining to their platform nests. From a distance, the nest colony presented a line of blood-red against a background of green tules.

When we approached the Eared Grebe colony, paid no attention to this. I watched one bird as she pulled up the stems out of the water and from the lining of the nest covering her eggs completely, so when we came near, there was not an egg in sight. I do not know whether this habit develops more from the idea of protecting the eggs from enemies, or from the idea of keeping them warm when the mother is away. The

Photo by W. L. Finley and H. T. Bohlman

EARED GREBE (Spring Plumage)

Though a water-bird, it is never wet

everything was bustle and hurry. The birds were trying to cover their eggs before leaving. It seemed to be a habit in this colony to cover the eggs, while the Western Grebe on the same lake eggs often lie partly in the water. The sun, I think, helps a good deal in hatching the eggs during the day, the bird keeping a more careful vigil at night. WILLIAM L. FINLEY.

PIED-BILLED GREBE

Podilymbus podiceps (*Linnæus*)

A. O. U. Number 6 See Color Plate 1

Other Names.— Hell-diver; Devil-diver; Water-witch; Dabchick; American Dabchick; Pied-billed Dabchick; Dipper; Diedapper; Didapper: Divedapper; Carolina Grebe; Thick-billed Grebe.

General Description.— Length, 13 inches. Color above, brownish-black; below, lighter brown and white. Bill, short and thick; no crests.

Color.— ADULTS: Crown, back of head, and neck, grayish-black streaked with lighter; upper parts, brownish-black; sides of head and neck, brownish-gray; chin and throat, black; primaries and *secondaries, chocolate-brown; below, pale brownish-ash,* thickly mottled with dusky on sides; lower abdomen, mostly dusky; *bill, whitish, dusky on ridge and tip with a black encircling* *band* a little forward of the center; feet, greenish-dusky outside, leaden-gray inside; iris, brown; eyelids, whitish. ADULTS IN WINTER: General coloration on head and upper parts more brownish than in summer; the feathers of back with paler edges; neck, breast, and sides, light brown mottled with dusky; under parts, pure silky white; lower abdomen, grayish.

Nest and Eggs.— NEST: A floating structure of dead grass, reeds, mud, and vegetable matter, unattached or fastened to living rushes. EGGS: 6 to 9, white, sometimes tinged with greenish.

Distribution.— North and South America; breeds from British Columbia, southern Mackenzie, southern Keewatin, Quebec, and New Brunswick southward to Chile and Argentina; winters from Washington, Texas, Mississippi, and the Potomac valley southward.

The Pied-billed Grebe is the most widely distributed of the American Grebes and in the United States is the only one that breeds over most of the region east of the Mississippi. It is at home in the water to an astonishing degree, in fact "Water-witch" is one of the favorite local names by which it is known. It is a more accomplished swimmer than any Duck of which I have knowledge, for it possesses the wonderful faculty of lowering its body in the water to any desired stage of submersion, and this it can do either while swimming or while remaining stationary, as may suit its fancy. At times only the bill and eyes will appear above the surface, and in this attitude it can remain apparently without distress until the bewildered hunter or the disappointed Hawk has gone his way. As a diver it has few equals in the bird world. Many times, especially in the days when muzzle-loading shotguns were still in vogue, I have seen it dive at the flash of discharge and be safely beneath the surface before the death-seeking shot came over the water. "Hell-diver," by the way, is another name applied to Grebes as well as to Loons.

Drawing by R. I. Brasher

PIED-BILLED GREBE (½ nat. size)

A more accomplished swimmer than any Duck

The remarkable nest made by this species is quite in keeping with its other unusual and secretive characteristics. It is made of decaying vegetation brought up from the bottom of the shallow pond where it breeds. This unattractive mass is usually piled on a platform of green stems of water plants, which, because of their fresh condition, will readily float and are of sufficient buoyancy to bear the weight of the nest, the eggs, and the brooding bird. In Florida, where I have examined perhaps fifty of their nests, I never found more than six eggs in any one of them, but observers farther north speak of finding as many as eight and nine. In color they are dull white, unspotted, but sometimes tinged with greenish, and always soiled or stained.

When leaving its nest the Grebe pulls the water-soaked material well over the eggs, so that usually they are completely hidden from view. While in this condition anyone not acquainted with the nesting habits of the bird would surely pass it by unnoticed, never dreaming that in that little mass of floating, rotting water-plants the cherished treasures of a wild bird lay concealed.

Audubon said that the food of the Pied-billed Grebe "consists of small fry, plant-seeds, aquatic insects, and snails; along with this they swallow gravel." Wayne writes: "During the breeding season, the food consists mainly of leeches." They should never be shot, for they are worse than useless for food. They certainly do no harm, and an ever-increasing class of bird-students take much pleasure in spying upon their interesting movements.

They have many enemies, among which may be mentioned minks, fish, frogs, snakes, and musk-rats. Birds of prey undoubtedly take their share. One day with much labor I climbed an enormous pine tree to a nest of the Bald Eagle around which the old birds were circling. Upon reaching it after a prolonged and heart-breaking effort I found it to contain only one object — a Pied-billed Grebe, with its feathers still damp and the blood spots on its head but half dried.

T. Gilbert Pearson.

Photograph by A. A. Allen

PIED-BILLED GREBE

Swimming up to its newly hatched young that has struggled from the nest

LOONS

Order *Pygopodes;* suborder *Cepphi;* family *Gaviidæ*

AS a family the Loons of the present seem to be very much the same kind of birds as were those of which we have fossil remains in strata representing what the geologists call the Miocene Epoch of the Tertiary Period. They are birds of considerable size, and are famous especially for their skill and swiftness in swimming and diving and for their weird and unearthly cries. Their quickness in diving to escape danger is truly astonishing, and has, naturally enough, furnished occasion for frequent exaggeration, also excuses for much bad shooting by gunners who assert that they held true, but the Loon "dodged the shot." They have a peculiar faculty of sinking gradually in the water without apparent effort and with little or no rippling of the surface of the water.

Summer Winter

Drawing by R. I. Brasher

LOON (⅛ nat. size)

A clumsy, awkward traveler upon land, but almost unexcelled as a diver

Loons take wing with considerable difficulty, but once in the air their flight is swift and usually in a straight line. At all times the sexes present the same general appearance. Their prevailing colors are blackish or grayish above, with the under parts whitish; in summer the darker parts become speckled with white. These markings do not appear in the young nor in the winter plumage of the adults; the very young are covered with a sooty grayish down, changing to white on the lower abdomen. The head is never crested, but both head and neck are velvety. The plumage of the body is hard and compact. The wings are pointed, short, and rather narrow. The eighteen or twenty tail feathers are short and stiff. The hind toe is small and the front toes are fully webbed. The bill is stout, straight, narrow, sharp-pointed, and sharp-edged; it is so constructed that it serves as a spear for catching and holding the slippery fish which are the bird's chief diet.

Though related to the Auks, which show a highly developed gregarious instinct, the Loons are essentially solitary birds, and commonly are found singly or in pairs. The formation of ice in their natural habitats, however, at times forces a considerable number of individuals to occupy the same comparatively small stretches of open water.

The distribution of the Loons is circumpolar, and the single genus includes five species. In the breeding period they occur generally in the cooler regions of the northern hemisphere, and frequently some distance north of the Arctic Circle; in winter they scatter southward

Photograph of habitat group

Courtesy of American Museum of Natural History

LOONS

They are among the most aquatic of birds

into the temperate regions, especially along the seacoasts. The nests are rude structures, composed of moss and grass sometimes plastered with a little mud, and are built on the ground usually along the shore of a lake and frequently on top of the abandoned lodge of a muskrat. The birds seem to make no attempt to hide their nests, but the two eggs, by reason of their olive or brownish shades, which are broken by blackish or brownish spots, are decidedly inconspicuous.

The cry of the Loon has been variously described as mournful, mirthful, sinister, defiant, uncanny, demoniacal, and so on. At any rate, it is undeniably distinctive and characteristic, and is almost certain to challenge the dullest ear and the most inert imagination, while in those who know instinctively the voices of Nature, especially when she is frankly and unrestrainedly natural, it produces a thrill and elicits a response which only the elect understand.

LOON

Gavia immer (*Brünnich*)

A. O. U. Number 7 See Color Plate 2

Other Names.— Common Loon; Big Loon; Great Northern Diver; Imber Diver; Hell-diver; Ember-Goose; Walloon; Ring-necked Loon; Black-billed Loon; Guinea Duck; Greenhead.

General Description.— Length, 28 to 36 inches. In Summer: Upper parts, glossy black with white spots; under parts, white. In Winter: Upper parts, grayish-brown without spots.

Color.— Adults in Summer: Head and neck all around, glossy purplish-black with greenish reflections; a patch of sharp white streaks on lower throat; another of the same kind on each side of neck, separated in front, but sometimes meeting behind; *entire upper parts, wing-coverts, and inner secondaries, glossy black, thickly marked with white spots*— those of shoulders, inner secondaries, and back, large, square, and regularly arranged traversely, those of other parts oval, smallest on rump and wing-coverts; upper tail-coverts, greenish-black; primaries, dusky; *lower parts from neck, white;* sides of breast, streaked with black; bill and feet, black; iris, red. Adults in Winter, and Young: Crown, neck and upper parts, in general, grayish-brown, *the feathers of back with lighter edges;* primaries, black; tail, gray-tipped; sides of breast, mottled; chin, throat, and neck in front (narrowly), and under parts, white with some dark feathers on sides and under tail-coverts, thus no black or white spots; bill, dusky, bluish-white at base and below; feet, lighter than in summer; iris, brown.

Nest and Eggs.— Nest: Usually a hollow in the sand, without nesting material; in some localities a rough nest is constructed of sticks and reeds; occasionally the top of an old muskrat house is utilized. Eggs: 2, dark olive-gray, stained with brown and spotted with black.

Distribution.— Northern part of northern hemisphere; in North America breeds from Alaska across Arctic North America to Greenland, south to northern California, across the United States at about the parallel 42° to Nova Scotia; winters from southern British Columbia, the Great Lakes, and southern New England to Lower California, the Gulf coast, and Florida.

Of all the wild creatures which still persist in the land, despite settlement and civilization, the Loon seems best to typify the untamed savagery of the wilderness. Its wolf-like cry is the wildest sound now heard in Massachusetts, where nature has long been subdued by the rifle, ax, and plow. Sometimes at sea, when I have heard the call of the Loon from afar, and seen its white breast flash from the crest of a distant wave, I have imagined it the signal and call for help of some strong swimmer, battling with the waves.

It is generally believed that in migration at least the Loon passes the night upon the sea or the bosom of some lake or river. The Gulls, Auks, Puffins, and Cormorants, which live upon the sea, usually alight upon the high shores of some rocky island or on some lonely sand bar at night, but the Loon is often seen at sea when night falls, and its cries are heard by the sailors during the hours of darkness. Notwithstanding the general belief that it normally sleeps on the water, I believe that it prefers to rest on shore at night, when it can safely do so. Audubon satisfied himself that on its breeding grounds it was accustomed to spend the night on shore. On an island off the coast of British Columbia, where there was no one to trouble the birds, I once saw, just at nightfall, a pair of Loons resting flat on their breasts at the end of a long sandy point. Cripples instinctively seek the shore when sorely wounded, but on our coast a Loon must keep well off shore to insure its safety, and probably few but cripples ever land on shores frequented by man.

The Loon's nest is usually a mere hollow in the bog or shore near the water's edge on some island in a lake or pond. Sometimes the nest is lined with grasses and bits of turf; more rarely it is a mere depression on the top of a muskrat's house, and more rarely still it is placed on the shore of the lake or in some debouching stream. Where the birds are not much disturbed, and where food is plentiful, two or three pairs sometimes nest on the same island. No doubt there was a time when nearly every northern pond of more than a few acres contained its pair of Loons, in the breeding season, and this is true to-day of ponds in parts of some Canadian Provinces. The nest is usually so near the margin that the bird can spring directly into the water, but sometimes in summer the water recedes until the nest is left some distance inland.

The Loon is a clumsy, awkward traveler upon land, where, when hurried, it flounders forward, using both wings and feet. Audubon, however, says that his son, J. W. Audubon, winged a Loon which ran about one hundred yards and reached the water before it was overtaken. Its usual method of taking to the water from its nest is by plunging forward and sliding on its breast. It cannot rise from the land, hence the necessity of having the nest at the water's edge.

When the young are hatched the mother carries them about on her back a few days, after which they remain afloat much of the time until they are fully grown. If food becomes scarce in their native pond they sometimes leave it and travel overland to another. Dr. James P. Hatch of Springfield, Mass., says that early in the morning the parents and the well-grown young run races on the lake, using their broad paddles for propulsion and their half-extended wings for partial support. Starting all together they race down the lake, and then, turning, rush back to their starting point. Such exercises no doubt strengthen the young birds for the long flights to come.

The Loon finds some difficulty in rising from the water, and is obliged to run along the surface, flapping its short wings, until it gets impetus enough to rise. It is said that it cannot rise at all unless there is wind to assist it. Its great weight (from eight to nearly twelve pounds) and its short wings make flight laborious, but its rapid wing-beats carry it through the air at great speed. When it alights it often shoots spirally down from a great height, and plunges into the water like an arrow from a bow. It lands with a splash, and shoots along the surface until its impetus is arrested by the resistance of the water.

The Loon is almost unexcelled as a diver. It is supposed to be able to disappear so suddenly at the flash of a rifle as to dodge the bullet, unless the shooter is at point-blank range, but when two or three crack shots surround a small pond in which a Loon is resting it can usually be secured by good strategy. I once saw a Loon killed on the water with a shotgun, but the bird was taken at a disadvantage. It was on the Banana River, Fla., in January, 1900, and it had followed the fish (which were then very numerous) into the shallow water near the shore. Shoals extended out from the shore fully three hundred yards, so that the bird, in diving and swimming under water, could not use its wings to advantage. It was much impeded by the shoals and the vegetation on the bottom, and in swimming was so near the surface that its course could be followed readily by the ripple that it made. Two strong rowers were thus enabled to follow and overtake it. It escaped the first charge of shot, but its pursuers came so close the second time that the shot went home. In deep water, where the bird can use its wings and fly under water like a bolt from a crossbow, it can easily elude a boat. In old times the gunner used to "toll" the Loon within gunshot by concealing himself and waving a brightly colored handkerchief, while imitating the bird's call. But this will rarely succeed to-day in luring one within reach of a shotgun.

Loons are rather solitary in the autumn migration. They leave their northern homes and some begin to move southward in September, but many remain in the northern lakes until the ice comes. They move south along the larger rivers of the interior, but most of those near the Atlantic take the sea as their highway.

The Loon feeds very largely on fish. As it rests lightly on the surface it frequently thrusts its head into the water and looks about in search of its prey. When pursuing swift fish under water it often uses its wings, by means of which it can overtake the swiftest. This has been repeatedly observed. It can travel much faster under water in this manner than it can on the surface by use of the feet alone.

Edward Howe Forbush, in *Game Birds, Wild-Fowl and Shore Birds.*

The Yellow-billed Loon, (*Gavia adamsi*) White-billed Loon, or Adams's Loon, as it is variously called, is of the same general coloration as the Common Loon. The throat and neck patches, however, are smaller and the bill, which is larger and differently shaped, is pale yellowish white. It is subject to corresponding seasonal changes.

It breeds in northern Siberia, on the islands north of Europe, and in North America from northwestern Alaska, northern Mackensie, and Boothia Peninsula south to the mouth of the Yukon and to Great Slave Lake. Its nests and eggs, as far as known, are similar to those of the more familar Loon. In migration the Yellow-billed is found a little south of its breeding range, and specimens have been reported from Colorado and Greenland.

BLACK-THROATED LOON

Gavia arctica (*Linnæus*)

A. O. U. Number 9 See Color Plate 2

Other Names.— Arctic Loon; Arctic Diver; Black-throated Diver.

General Description.— Length, 27 to 30 inches. In Summer: Upper parts, glossy greenish-black with white spots; lower parts white. In Winter: Upper parts, grayish-brown without spots.

Color.— Adults in Summer: *Chin, throat, and front of neck, purplish-black,* shading gradually into *clear soft warm gray of crown, back of head, and hindneck,* deepest on forehead and face, lightest behind, and separated from black of front of neck by white streaks; a short crescent of white streaks across upper throat; sides of breast and neck striped with pure white and glossy black, the black diminishing behind into pure white of under parts; upper parts, glossy greenish-black, each feather on shoulders and back with two white square spots near end forming traverse rows; wing-coverts thickly specked with small oval white spots; a narrow dusky band across lower belly; under tail-coverts, with dusky spots; bill, black; feet, dusky; iris, red. Adults in Winter, and Young: Upper parts of head and neck, dark grayish-brown; sides of head, grayish-white finely streaked with brown; *upper parts, brownish-black, feathers with broad gray margins, giving a scaly appearance;* rump, brownish-gray; primaries and their coverts, brownish-black; secondaries and tail-feathers, dusky margined with gray; forepart of neck, grayish-white faintly dotted with brown, its sides streaked with same; lower parts, pure white; sides of body and lower tail-coverts, dusky edged with bluish-gray; bill, light bluish-gray, dusky on ridge; feet, dusky; iris, brown.

Nest and Eggs.— Nest: A depression in the tundra or constructed roughly of decayed vegetation. Eggs: 2, deep amber to pale greenish-gray.

Distribution.— Northern part of northern hemisphere; breeds from Kotzebue Sound, Alaska, west along northern coast of Siberia, on islands north of Europe, and from Cumberland Sound south to Ungava; winters in the southern Canadian provinces; rarely south to Colorado, Nebraska, Iowa, northern Ohio, and Long Island, N. Y.

The general appearance of the Black-throated Loon is like that of its relative, the Common Loon, but it is somewhat smaller and not nearly so well known in America since it is seldom seen south of the northern States. There seems to be no reliable record of its appearance south of Long Island. Throughout the interior of Norway and Sweden and far up into Lapland, it breeds quite commonly. It is considered to be of rare occurrence in most parts of the British Isles, but on the little islands in the fresh-water lochs from central Scotland northward, and on the Orkney and Shetland islands, may be found its nests.

Its habits also are like those of the larger member of its species. Its progress under water has been estimated at not less than eight miles an hour.

The Pacific Loon or Pacific Diver (*Gavia pacifica*) is confined to the West. It breeds from Point Barrow, Banks Land, northern Mackenzie, and Melville Peninsula, south to the base of the Alaskan Peninsula, Great Slave Lake, and central Keewatin and winters along the Pacific coast from southern British Columbia to Lower California, and Guadalupe Island. In coloration it is similar to the Black-throated Loon, but the gray of the head averages lighter and the light spots of the back larger and fewer in number.

RED-THROATED LOON

Gavia stellata (*Pontoppidan*)

A. O. U. Number 11 See Color Plate 2

Other Names.— Sprat Loon, Red-throated Diver; Little Loon; Cape Race; Cape Racer; Scape-grace.

General Description.— Length, 25 inches. Color above, brownish-black with white spots; below, white.

Color.—Adults in Summer: Crown and broad stripe down back of neck, streaked in about equal amounts with glossy greenish-black and white; *throat, sides of head, and sides of neck, clear warm gray* with a triangular *chestnut patch on lower throat;* upper parts, brownish-black with a green gloss, thickly spotted with dull whitish; primaries, dusky; tail, dusky, narrowly tipped with white; under parts, pure white, shaded along sides and on under tail-coverts with dusky brown; bill, dusky lead color; feet, black; iris, hazel. Adults in Winter, and Young: Crown and hindneck, bluish-gray; sides of neck, mottled with brownish and white; upper parts, brownish-black, *everywhere thickly marked with small oval and linear spots of whitish;* chin, throat, sides of head, white; no colored throat patch; under parts, as in summer; amount of spotting variable; in young birds spots usually lengthened into oblique lines, producing a regular diamond-shaped reticulation.

Nest and Eggs.— Nest: On banks of small ponds; a mere hollow in the ground. Eggs: 2, from deep reddish-brown to grayish-green, thinly spotted with brownish-black.

Distribution.— Northern part of northern hemisphere; breeds from Alaska across Arctic America to Greenland, south to Commander Islands, western Aleutian Islands, Glacier Bay, across British America to New Brunswick and Newfoundland; winters from southern British Columbia to southern California, and from the Great Lakes and Maine to Florida; rare in the interior; breeds also in Arctic Europe and Asia, and winters south to the Mediterranean and southern China.

The Red-throated Loon is mainly a salt-water bird while it sojourns in Massachusetts, although occasionally it is seen on some lake or river. Probably, like many other birds, it was oftener seen on fresh water in early times than now. It is still not uncommon on the Great Lakes, and David Bruce of Brockport, N. Y., stated that he had found it on Lake Ontario during every month of the year. In severe weather, when the lakes freeze, this bird, like the Common Loon, is sometimes taken on the ice, from which it is unable to rise, and is easily captured. In autumn it may be seen in small parties or flocks floating and feeding near our coasts. Like Grebes and some other water-fowl, it often lies on its side or back while afloat, exposing its white under parts while engaged in dressing or preening the plumage. This species migrates mainly along the coast in autumn, but as it is not so commonly seen there in spring, some portion of the flight may go north through the interior.

Its habits are similar to those of the Common Loon. It is perhaps equally difficult to shoot on the water. When surprised on land it seeks to escape by a series of hops or leaps, using both wings and feet.

Edward Howe Forbush, in *Game Birds, Wild-Fowl and Shore Birds.*

Photo by H. T. Middleton

BIRD-STUDYING

AUKS, MURRES, AND PUFFINS

Order *Pygopodes;* suborder *Cepphi;* family *Alcidæ*

IT is a curious and interesting fact that at opposite ends of the earth there should be forms of bird-life which, though entirely unrelated and differing from each other even in the signal respect that one is equipped with wings and uses them, while the other is flightless, nevertheless present similar and somewhat grotesque physical peculiarities, and much similarity in their habits. These birds are the Auks of the Arctic and the Penguins of the Antarctic regions, and their external similarity lies in the fact that in both the legs are set so far back on the body that the birds assume a man-like posture, and are clumsy and uncouth in their appearance on shore. In the water both are expert swimmers and divers, though here again they differ in that the Auks use their feet in swimming, whereas the Penguins swim entirely with their wings, and use their feet only in steering their course.

The Auks, Murres, and Puffins include diving Arctic sea-birds grouped under the scientific name *Alcidæ*, and embracing about a dozen genera and some thirty species. All members of the family are essentially birds of the Arctic regions, and are especially numerous on the Alaskan and Siberian coasts. Though the Auks resemble the Penguins superficially and in their habits, anatomically their nearest relatives are the Loons and Grebes. From the Loons, however, they differ in lacking a hind toe, and from the Grebes in the possession of a well-developed tail.

Photo by W. L. Finley and H. T. Bohlman

TUFTED PUFFIN ON NEST

Burrow unearthed

The wings are short, but they are used with great efficiency when the birds swim under water. In their sitting posture on land the birds' feet extend horizontally in front, and they appear to be resting on their rumps. On the sea they are in their element, and here they get all of their food, which includes fish, taken chiefly by pursuit under water, and other animal forms. Because of this life their plumage is remarkably thick and dense, and is much used by the Eskimos in making clothing.

In distribution the Auks are very unequally divided between the two northern oceans, the Atlantic having few forms in comparison with the Pacific. The largest number of species and the most diversified forms are found on the northern coasts of the Pacific, though the aggregate of individuals of any species found there does not, according to Dr. Coues, exceed that of several Atlantic Ocean species. The same authority says that a " more or less complete migration takes place with most species, which stray southward, sometimes to a considerable distance, in the autumn and return again to breed in the spring. A few species appear nearly stationary." Many of the migrating Auks pass the winter on the open sea or on drifting ice.

At the approach of spring weather, the birds return to their northern breeding grounds where they gather in immense numbers on rocky cliffs along the coast. No nest is built, but the single egg, which is laid in niches or on ledges, is covered constantly by one or the other of the parents. The color of the egg varies greatly with the different species. The young are helpless when they are hatched, and it is not known with certainty what methods are employed by the parents to get them to the water. It seems not unlikely that the chicks are sometimes carried to the sea by the adults, though doubtless many of them reach the water by scrambling and falling down the cliffs. These Auk colonies are frequently raided by foxes, weasels, and other predacious animals and birds, not to mention the Indians and Eskimos who depend largely upon the birds and their eggs for winter food.

TUFTED PUFFIN

Lunda cirrhata (*Pallas*)

A. O. U. Number 12

Other Name.— Sea Parrot.

General Description.— Length, 15 inches. Color above, black; below, brown; *bill, high, much compressed,* ridged on sides; a fold of naked skin at corner of mouth.

Description.— Adults in Summer: A tuft of straw-yellow feathers on each side of head about 4 inches long, completely surrounding eyes and continuous with white of face, forehead, and chin (narrowly); crown between the crests and entire *upper parts,* except a line on wing along fore-arm (which is white), *glossy blue-black;* entire under parts from chin, including most of sides of head, sooty-brownish, more grayish on abdomen; under tail-coverts, wings, and tail, black; *bill, feet, and eye-ring, vermilion;* base of bill, pale oily-green; rosette of mouth, yellow; iris, white. Adults in Winter: No crests or white on face; bill, mostly dusky with some touches of reddish; feet, pale salmon; iris, pale blue; otherwise like summer birds.

Nest and Eggs.— The single egg is laid on the bare ground at the end of a burrow or in natural cavities among rocks, sometimes within sight, sometimes as much as five feet from the entrance; it is dead-white, showing obscure shell markings of pale lavender or brownish.

Distribution.— Coasts and islands of the Arctic Ocean, Bering Sea, and North Pacific, from Cape Lisburne, Alaska, south to Santa Barbara Islands, California, and from Bering Sea to Japan; accidental in Maine and Greenland.

The islands of the north Pacific, scattered along the shores of British Columbia, form, with their surrounding waters and the verdant coast line, a veritable summer wonderland. Here the mirage makes birds sitting upon the water appear like fleets of ships. Sound is magnified until the explosion of a gun and its echoes roar along the shores, a carnival of sound. Swift tides boil through narrow, rocky passes, while the shimmering heat of summer gives a touch of wavering unreality to all the scene. In this enchanted realm thousands of queer birds move to and fro, and none is queerer than the Tufted Puffin.

Each looks like a masked caricature of a bird as it comes on, pushing its great red beak straight ahead, its red, splay feet spread widely, its long, cream-colored side plumes flying in the wind, and its little wings "working for two." In spring both male and female acquire a white face, which gives them a masked appearance, and the great, gaudily colored beak reminds one of Mr. Punch and his big red nose. The beak, a remarkable appendage, is much larger and showier in the breeding season than at any other time. There are eighteen horny plates, ingeniously formed and arranged, sixteen of which fall off after the breeding season, much reducing the dimensions of the basal part. The underlying plates are then brown in color. At the same time the white of the face with its plumes disappears, the entire head becomes blackish, and the bird remains merely a commonplace Puffin until the next breeding season.

On the Farallons, off the California coast, where these Puffins nest on barren rocks, they deposit their eggs in holes or cavities among the rocks, but on the northern coast, where each rocky islet has a cap of some four feet of earth, they burrow into this at the top of the precipice overlooking the sea. Some of their tunnels extend but a few inches. These are believed to be made by the young birds. Others delve deeply, and in an old colony a bank will be honeycombed in every direction. If one wishes to examine into their housekeeping, under these circumstances he must fasten a rope to rock or tree, rig a "bo'sun's chair," and let himself over the cliff, excavating with his hands like a dog digging out a woodchuck, the stream of dirt passing down the cliff until it reaches the sea far below. Even then he may not easily succeed in finding the eggs or young in the interminable labyrinth of passages penetrating the earth. Where the tops of islands are hilly, the Puffins dig into the turf, where the land slopes at an angle of about 45°, and often they go in to a depth of three or four feet.

The single egg, which appears white, is in reality spotted inside the shell structure, as may be seen by holding it up to a very strong light. The young one is a real Puffin, as it is covered with down like a powder puff, but as it sits at the mouth of the burrow it looks, at a distance, like a little rat peeping out of its hole.

There has been much speculation regarding the utility of the bill of the Puffin, and it has been suggested that it is used to crush mollusks, but this does not seem to be the case, at least during the breeding season, as small fish appear to form its principal food. Apparently it does not use its bill, but rather its feet, in digging, though this may be an error, and possibly both are used; but certainly the beak is an excellent weapon of defense as all who have attempted to dig out Puffins will testify. Nature has put the most powerful weapon of the mother bird where it will have most effect. As she sits facing the entrance to her burrow she can deliver the more effective blows in defense of her nest and young because of the great size and crushing strength of her weapon, backed as it is by her hard head and sturdy neck.

Puffins breed on islands occupied also by Gulls, Guillemots, Murres, Cormorants, and other birds. After the breeding season they go to sea where they remain all winter. Their habits and roosting places at this season are practically unknown.

The natives of the coasts and islands of the north Pacific catch Puffins in nets, using their bodies for food and their skins for clothing. The skins are tough and are sewn together with the feathered side in, to make coats or "parkas," as they are called. Thus the Puffins contribute to the comfort and welfare of these simple, primitive people. EDWARD HOWE FORBUSH

PUFFIN

Fratercula arctica arctica (*Linnæus*)

A. O. U. Number 13 See Color Plate 3

Other Names.— Common Puffin; Puffin Auk; Labrador Auk; Sea Parrot; Pope; Bottle-nose; Tammy Norie; Coulterner; Tinker.

General Description.— Length, 13 inches. Color above, black; below, white; *bill very deep* and ridged.

Description.— ADULTS IN SUMMER: Crown, grayish-black, separated by a narrow ashy collar from dark color of upper parts; sides of head with chin and throat, ashy; nearly white between eyes and bill, with a dark dusky patch on side of throat; upper parts,

Courtesy of the New York State Museum

HOLBOELL GREBE
Colymbus holboelli (Reinhardt)
WINTER
SUMMER

PIED-BILLED GREBE SUMMER
Podilymbus podiceps (Linnaeus)

HORNED GREBE
Colymbus auritus (Linnaeus)
WINTER
SUMMER

All ⅖ nat. size

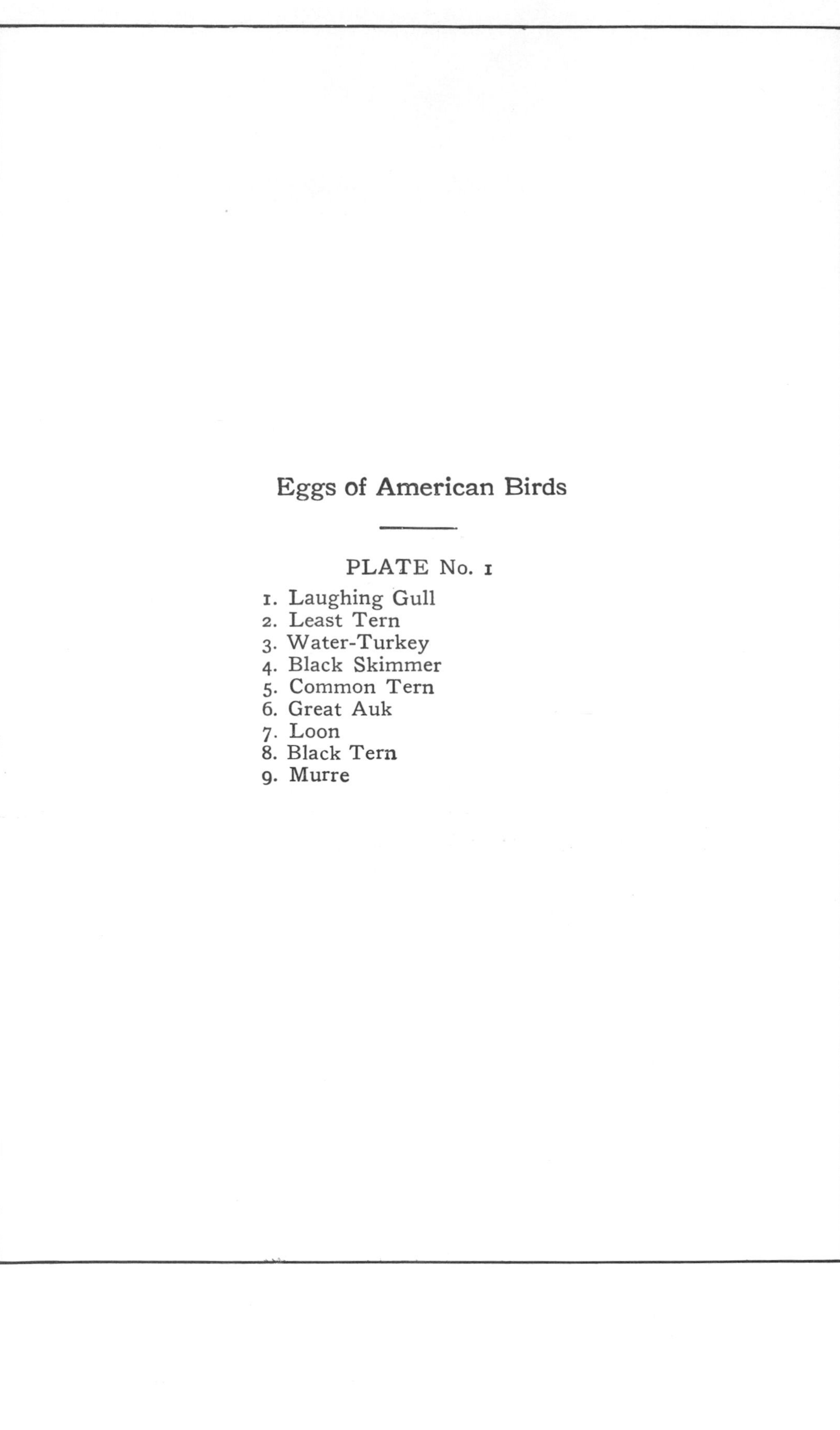

Eggs of American Birds

PLATE No. 1

1. Laughing Gull
2. Least Tern
3. Water-Turkey
4. Black Skimmer
5. Common Tern
6. Great Auk
7. Loon
8. Black Tern
9. Murre

EGGS OF AMERICAN BIRDS
(Plate Number One)

Eggs of American Birds

PLATE No. 2

1. Whip-poor-will
2. Nighthawk
3. Yellow-billed Cuckoo
4. Belted Kingfisher
5. Least Bittern
6. Sora
7. Bob-white
8. Red Phalarope
9. Wilson's Phalarope
10. Spotted Sandpiper
11. Wilson's Plover
12. California Quail
13. Semipalmated Sandpiper
14. Killdeer
15. Florida Gallinule
16. Sparrow Hawk
17. Ruffed Grouse
18. Wilson's Snipe
19. Woodcock
20. Sharp-shinned Hawk
21. White Ibis
22. Little Blue Heron
23. Clapper Rail
24. White-faced Glossy Ibis

Copyright, 1917, by The University Society, Inc.

EGGS OF AMERICAN BIRDS
(Plate Number Two)

Eggs of American Birds

PLATE No. 3

1. Crossbill
2. Purple Finch
3. Ruby-throated Hummingbird
4. Goldfinch
5. English Sparrow
6. Vesper Sparrow
7. Grasshopper Sparrow
8. Chipping Sparrow
9. Junco
10. Towhee
11. Crested Flycatcher
12. Phœbe
13. Indigo Bunting
14. Scarlet Tanager
15. Skylark
16. Kingbird
17. Gray Kingbird
18. Wood Pewee
19. Orchard Oriole
20. Baltimore Oriole
21. Blue Jay
22. Meadowlark
23. Bobolink
24. Cowbird
25. Red-winged Blackbird

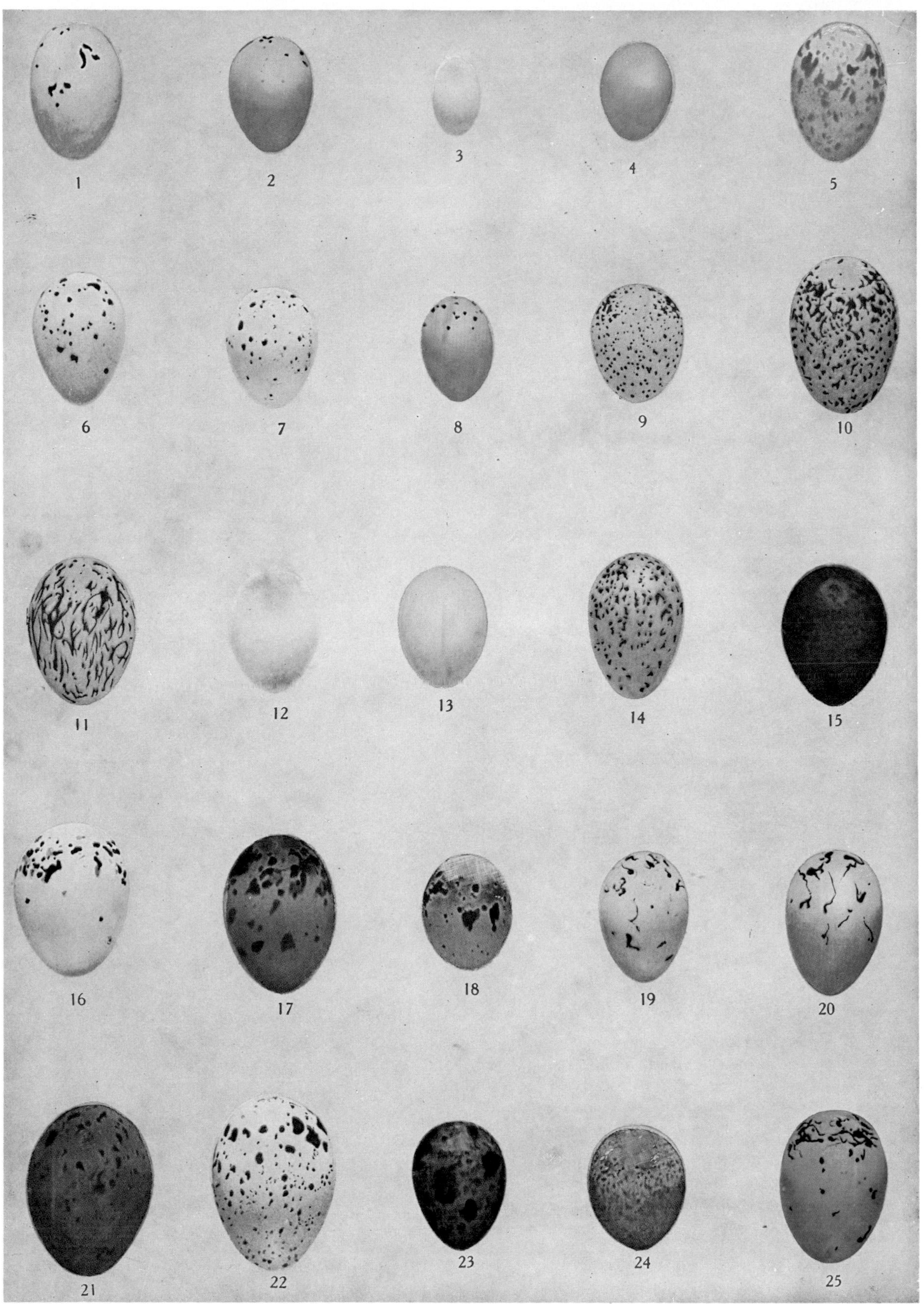

Copyright, 1917, by The University Society, Inc.

EGGS OF AMERICAN BIRDS
(Plate Number Three)

Eggs of American Birds

PLATE No. 4

1. Cedar Waxwing
2. Red-eyed Vireo
3. White-eyed Vireo
4. Warbling Vireo
5. Phainopepla
6. Blue-headed Vireo
7. Bell's Vireo
8. Black and White Warbler
9. Prothonotary Warbler
10. Worm-eating Warbler
11. Blue-winged Warbler
12. Oranged-crowned Warbler
13. Parula Warbler
14. Magnolia Warbler
15. Yellow Warbler
16. Water-Thrush
17. Yellow-throated Warbler
18. Prairie Warbler
19. Maryland Yellow-throat
20. Oven-bird
21. Yellow-breasted Chat
22. Chestnut-sided Warbler
23. Hooded Warbler
24. Redstart
25. Pipit

Copyright, 1917, by The University Society, Inc.

EGGS OF AMERICAN BIRDS
(Plate Number Four)

Eggs of American Birds

PLATE No. 5

1. Long-billed Marsh Wren
2. Chickadee
3. Bush-Tit
4. Brown-headed Nuthatch
5. House Wren
6. Sharp-tailed Sparrow
7. Bank Swallow
8. Golden-crowned Kinglet
9. Barn Swallow
10. Song Sparrow
11. Rose-breasted Grosbeak
12. Bluebird
13. Blue-gray Gnatcatcher
14. White-breasted Nuthatch
15. Wood Thrush
16. Abert's Towhee
17. Bendire's Thrasher
18. Olive-backed Thrush
19. Blue Grosbeak
20. Cardinal
21. Mockingbird
22. Catbird
23. Brown Thrasher
24. Robin
25. California Thrasher

Copyright, 1917, by The University Society, Inc.

EGGS OF AMERICAN BIRDS
(Plate Number Five)

Courtesy of the New York State Museum

RED-THROATED LOON
Gavia stellata (Pontoppidan)
SUMMER WINTER

COMMON LOON
Gavia immer (Brünnich)
SUMMER WINTER
All ⅙ nat. size

BLACK-THROATED LOON
Gavia arctica (Linnaeus)
SUMMER

BLACK GUILLEMOT
Cepphus grylle (Linnaeus)
WINTER SUMMER

BRÜNNICH MURRE
Uria lomvia (Linnaeus)
SUMMER WINTER
EGG

RAZOR-BILLED AUK
Alca torda Linnaeus
SUMMER

PUFFIN
Fratercula arctica (Linnaeus)
SUMMER

DOVEKIE
Alle alle (Linnaeus)
SUMMER WINTER

All ¼ nat. size

Courtesy of the New York State Museum

POMARINE JAEGER *Stercorarius pomarinus* (Temminck)
LONG-TAILED JAEGER *Stercorarius longicaudus* Vieillot
. ADULT
IMMATURE *S. parasiticus*

PARASITIC JAEGER *Stercorarius parasiticus* (Linnaeus)
DARK PHASE
INTERMEDIATE
LIGHT PHASE
SKUA *Megalestris skua* (Brünnich)

All ⅛ nat. size

Courtesy of the New York State Museum

RING-BILLED GULL
Larus delawarensis Ord
ADULT IN SUMMER IMMATURE

GREAT BLACK-BACKED GULL
Larus marinus Linnaeus
IMMATURE ADULT IN SUMMER

HERRING GULL
Larus argentatus Pontoppidan
IMMATURE ADULT IN SUMMER

GLAUCOUS GULL
Larus hyperboreus Gunnerus
END OF SECOND YEAR ADULT IN SUMMER
IMMATURE

All ½ nat. size

SABINE GULL ADULT IN SUMMER
Xema sabini (Sabine)
LAUGHING GULL ADULT IN SUMMER
Larus atricilla Linnaeus
KITTIWAKE
Rissa tridactyla (Linnaeus)
ADULT IN SUMMER
IMMATURE

BONAPARTE GULL
Larus philadelphia (Ord)
ADULT IN SUMMER
IMMATURE

IVORY GULL
Pagophila alba Gunnerus
IMMATURE ADULT IN SUMMER

All ⅙ nat. size

glossy blue-black continuous with a broad collar around neck in front, not reaching bill; under parts from neck, pure white; sides, dusky; *base of bill and first ridge, dull yellowish, next space, grayish-blue; rest of bill, vermilion, yellow below;* rosette of mouth, orange; feet, vermilion; iris, pale bluish-white; conical shaped projections above and behind eye, grayish-blue; eyelids, vermilion. ADULTS IN WINTER: Face, dusky; no eye-ring or appendages on eyelid; rosette of mouth, shrunken; feet, orange; most of horny appendages on bill have been shed, leaving it small and pale.

Nest and Eggs.— NEST: A burrow in the ground 1 to 4 feet in length. EGGS: 1, white or brownish-white, plain or marked with faint spots, dots, or scratches of lavender; laid at the end of burrow on a thin lining of grass.

Distribution.— Coasts and islands of north Atlantic; breeds in North America from Ungava south to the Bay of Fundy and Maine; winters south to Massachusetts; rarely to Long Island, and Delaware Bay.

Drawing by R. I. Brasher

PUFFIN (½ nat. size)

The Sea Parrot of the north Atlantic

" Whether at rest or on the wing, the Puffin is a curious looking creature," says John Maclair Boraston, the English ornithologist. "At rest they stand rank above rank on the topmost rocky ledges facing the sea, their black backs, collars, and crowns, white faces and underparts, combining with their erect attitude and disposition, incline to give them something of military uniformity and regularity. But when one noted the great tri-colored beak, the apparently spectacled eyes, and remarked the mild surprise with which the birds regarded our intrusion, one could not resist the idea that there was something ludicrously artificial in the make-up of the Puffin; for surely there never was a bird less bird-like in its appearance than the Puffin at rest. They were tame enough to allow us to approach almost within striking distance, had we been disposed to strike anything so mild-mannered as a Puffin. When the bird is on the wing, the flight is rapid, but labored, the wings beating violently, and as the bird flies, especially if returning to its burrow with fish, it utters a peculiar sound — a deep-throated, mirthless laughter, as it were, which may be imitated by laughing in the throat with the lips closed.

" It is a matter of speculation how the Puffin, which catches fish by diving, contrives to retain the first fish in its bill while it captures a second or a third. Possibly the tongue is used to hold it to the roof of the mouth, while the under mandible is lowered to make the later captures." (*Birds by Land and Sea.*)

Much of the grotesqueness of this bird's appearance is due to its uncouth beak, which is very large, flattened laterally, banded with red, blue, and yellow, and embossed with horny excrescences. These growths appear only in the mating season, and are sloughed off when that period is at an end, which means, as one observer puts it, that "the Puffin displays his wedding garments on his beak." Puffins are not likely to be seen near land after the breeding season is over. They are skillful swimmers and expert divers; in their diving they often descend to a great depth, and they are exceedingly quick and sure in their motions under the surface. At their breeding places the birds are likely to appear with remarkable punctuality, and they disappear with their young with corresponding regularity. In fact this departure is methodical to the extent that young birds which have not got the full use of their wings are left behind when the time for migrating arrives. It seems probable that the birds remain mated for life.

On land the bird places the whole length of the foot and heel on the ground and proceeds with a waddling stride. Robbing a Puffin's nest is dangerous business when either of the birds is at home, for they fight desperately and can inflict ugly wounds with their powerful mandibles and sharp inner nails.

The birds show strong affection for one another. If one is shot and falls in the water, others are likely to alight near it, swim around it, push it with their bills, and display in many ways their distress.

From old records we learn that in various parts of the Puffin's European range it was the custom to salt down large quantities of the young birds, to be eaten especially in Lent. To be sure the bird wasn't actually fish, but it tasted enough like fish to satisfy adaptable consciences among the devout.

CASSIN'S AUKLET

Ptychoramphus aleuticus (*Pallas*)

A. O. U. Number 16

Other Name.— Sea Quail.

General Description.— Length, 9½ inches. Color above, blackish; below, whitish; bill, shorter than head, wider than broad at base, its upper outline nearly straight.

Color.— *Upper parts, blackish-plumbeous;* head, wings and tail, nearly black; a grayish shade extending around head, neck, fore-breast, and along sides of body, fading to white on abdomen; bill, black, yellowish at base; feet, bluish in front, blackish behind and on webs; iris, white; a touch of white on lower eyelid.

Nest and Eggs.— The single egg, chalky-white or faintly tinged with green or blue, unmarked, is deposited in a burrow in the ground or in a crevice in rocks on an island or coast adjacent to the sea.

Distribution.— Pacific coast of North America from Aleutian Islands to latitude 27° in Lower California; breeds locally throughout its range.

While the Cassin Auklet has been found living on some of the rocky islands from the Aleutians to Lower California, yet I have never found one of the birds nesting on the rocks off the Oregon coast.

During the summer of 1903, Mr. Herman T. Bohlman and I camped for five days and nights on Three Arch Rocks which contain the greatest colonies of sea birds off the Oregon coast. Again in 1914, we lived for four days and nights on these rocks and climbed from top to bottom studying the various birds that live there. We have yet to see our first Auklet about Three Arch Rocks. This has led me to believe that it is rather uncertain as to just where the bird may be found. Mr. L. M. Loomis found the birds nesting on the Farallons and Mr. William L. Dawson found them nesting on some of the rocks off the Washington coast.

Because of its plump shape and size, it has been called a "Sea Quail." In his study of Cassin's Auklet on one of the islands off the Washington coast, Mr. William L. Dawson speaks of spending the night on the slope of the island where the Auklets had their nests. The birds burrow in under the soil, like the Petrels and Puffins, and are largely nocturnal in their nesting habits. The old birds come in at night to change places in the burrows. The Auklet chorus of birds in the burrows, he says, reminds one of a frog pond in full cry. Although the Auklets are quiet in daytime, yet the tumult increases as the night progresses.

William L. Finley.

CRESTED AUKLET

Æthia cristatella (*Pallas*)

A. O. U. Number 18

Other Names.— Snub-nosed Auklet, or Auk; Dusky Auklet; Crested Stariki; Sea Quail; Kanooska.

General Description.— Length, 9 inches. Color above, brownish-black; below, brownish-gray. Bill, shorter than head, with knob at base; a beautiful crest of from 12 to 20 slender black plumes springing from forehead, recurved gracefully over bill, about two inches long; a slender series of white filaments behind each eye, drooping downward and backward.

Color.— ADULTS: Brownish-black above, brownish-gray below; no white anywhere; bill, coral or orange, horn color at tip; feet, bluish-black; iris, white. YOUNG: Lacking bill plates, crests, and white filaments on side of head; a white spot below eye; iris, brown; otherwise as in adults.

Distribution.— Coasts and islands of Bering Sea and north Pacific, from Bering Strait south to Kodiak Island and Japan.

This is essentially a sea-bird of the far North, its normal habitat being the north Pacific Ocean and the islands of Bering Sea. In Yukon Harbor they have been seen in myriads. Their appearance there is thus described by Dr. Charles Townsend in a leaflet prepared for the National Association of Audubon Societies:

"The surface of the water was covered with them, and the air was filled with them. Large, compact flocks launched themselves into the air from the lofty cliffs, and careened toward the vessel with great speed and whirring of wings. Twilight did not come until after 9 o'clock, and during the long evening the birds were amazingly active. Flocks of them continued to come in rapid succession from the cliffs, many passing close to the ship at high speed and swinging about the harbor. After the anchor was dropped near the cliffs, a loud blast of the whistle made the Auklets still more abundant.

"These birds appeared to be nesting chiefly in crevices in the cliffs, although they could be heard under the boulders near the beaches. To discover the nesting localities is easy. One has but to walk along the great ridges of volcanic stones thrown up by the sea. The stones are rounded and sea-worn like pebbles, but they are gigantic pebbles and cannot readily be moved. The Auklets go far down among them, perhaps three or four feet, and can be heard chattering there during any part of the nesting-season. We found that a considerable part of the food of this and other kinds of Auklets consisted of amphipod crustaceans, or beach-fleas, as they are called, when found under bits of seaweed along the shore. The native Aleuts eat Auklets, just as they do most other kinds of sea-birds and capture them with nets that are like a large dip-net with a long handle.

Drawing by R. I Brasher

CRESTED AUKLET ($\frac{2}{3}$ nat. size)

A strangely ornamented bird

"We need not concern ourselves, I think, about the preservation of the Auklets. They dwell among the high cliffs and the boulder-strewn beaches of a thousand uninhabited islands, and know how to stow away their eggs so safely that neither natives nor blue foxes can get them easily."

LEAST AUKLET

Æthia pusilla (*Pallas*)

A. O. U. Number 20

Other Names.— Minute Auklet; Knob-nosed Auklet; Knob-billed Auklet; Choochkie.

General Description.— Length, 6½ inches. Color above, black; below, white; bill, shorter than head, with knob at base; no crest.

Description.— Adults in Summer: Front, top, and sides of head, sprinkled with white delicate feathers; a series of exceedingly fine hair-like feathers from back of eye down back of head and nape; some white on shoulders and on tips of some secondaries; otherwise entire upper parts, glossy-black; throat and under parts, white clouded with dusky, usually more thickly across breast; bill, red, darker above at base; legs, dusky; iris, white. Adults in Winter: Bristles of head, fewer and less developed; white of under parts, more extensive, reaching almost around neck; bill, brownish.

Nest and Eggs.— The single egg, chalky-white or faintly tinged with greenish or bluish, unmarked, is deposited in a burrow in the ground or in a crevice among rocks on an island or on a coast adjacent to the sea.

Distribution.— Coast and islands of the north Pacific; breeds from Bering Strait south to Aleutian Islands; winters from Aleutian and Commander islands south to Washington on the American side and to Japan on the Asiatic.

The Least Auklet is one of the commonest of the water fowl in Bering Sea. It congregates in countless thousands on the rocks in Bering Strait, making them look like great beehives. In the spring they are very playful, especially while they are in the water, where they chase each other in great apparent good nature, meanwhile keeping up an incessant but subdued chattering. Like the other Auklets, they build no nest, but lay a single egg deep in the crevice of a cliff, or among the rocks well below the surface, or in a burrow in the ground.

"A walk over their breeding grounds at this season," wrote Doctor Baird, "is exceedingly interesting and amusing, as the noise of hundreds of these little birds directly under foot gives rise to an endless variation of sound as it comes up from the stony holes and caverns below, while the birds come and go, in and out, with bewildering rapidity, comically blinking and fluttering. The male birds, and many of the females, regularly leave the breeding grounds in the morning, and go off to sea, where they feed on small water shrimps and sea fleas, returning to their nests and sitting partners in the evening." (*North American Birds.*)

ANCIENT MURRELET

Synthliboramphus antiquus (*Gmelin*)

A. O. U. Number 21

Other Names.— Gray-headed Murrelet; Black-throated Murrelet; Black-throated Guillemot; Old Man.

General Description.— Length, 10½ inches. Color above, dark slate; below, white; bill, small and short, *with no horny growth at base.*

Color.— Adults in Summer: Head, black, sooty on chin and throat; a conspicuous white stripe over each eye to nape, spreading on sides and back of neck into a series of sharp white streaks; a trace of white on each eyelid; upper parts, dark slate, blackening on tail; under parts, white; sides of body, velvety-black, the black feathers lengthening behind and overlaying the white flanks, extending upward in front of wings, meeting that of nape and there mixing with the white streaks; bill, yellowish-white, black on ridge and base; feet, yellowish, webs, black; iris, dark brown. Adults in Winter: Upper parts, darker, the slate obscured by dusky, especially on wing, tail-coverts, and rump; forehead, crown, and nape, sooty-black without white streaks; eyelids, sometimes largely white; no black on throat, but dusky mottling at base of bill; white of under parts extending nearly to eyes and far around on sides of nape.

Nest and Eggs.— The single egg, buff with markings of grayish-lavender and light brown, is deposited in holes or burrows in banks on the coast or on a sea island.

Distribution.— Coasts and islands of the North Pacific; breeds from Aleutian Islands to Near Islands and from Kamchatka to Commander Islands; winters from the Aleutians south to San Diego, California, and to Japan; accidental in Wisconsin.

The Ancient Murrelet is another of the diving birds which fairly swarm on many of islands along the southern coast of Alaska. It ranges as far south as California in summer, and then is common on the Commander Islands in the Bering Sea, where the natives call it the "Old Man," because of the curious feather arrangement on the sides and back of the head. These feathers are dropped as winter comes on, so that the significance of the popular name may not be apparent when the bird visits its southern feeding grounds.

The Ancient Murrelet is an expert diver, and swims very rapidly under water, where it pursues fish with such energy as sometimes actually to drive them to the surface.

BLACK GUILLEMOT

Cepphus grylle (*Linnæus*)

A. O. U. Number 27 See Color Plate 3

Other Names.— White-winged Guillemot; Sea Pigeon; Tysty; Geylle; Spotted Greenland Dove; White Guillemot; Scapular Guillemot.

General Description.— Length, 13 inches. Prevailing color, in summer, sooty-black; in winter, black and white; bill, slender and straight, *with no horny growth at base.*

Color.— Sooty-black; wings and tail, pure black; *wings with a large white mirror on both surfaces;* bill, black; mouth and feet, carmine, vermilion, or coral-red; iris, brown. This perfect dress is worn only two months. In August, wings and tail become gray, the white mirror is mixed with brown, head, neck all around, rump, and under parts, marbled with black and white, the bird looking as if dusted over with flour; back, black, the feathers white-edged; completion of the molt gives the following winter plumage: head and neck all around, rump, and under parts, pure white; back, hindneck, and head varied with black and white; wings and tail, black, the white mirror perfect.

Nest and Eggs.— Eggs: Deposited on the bare surface of the rock, in nooks and crannies of rocky islands on coast; 2 or 3, white or greenish-white, irregularly spotted and blotched with dusky and lavender shell markings.

Distribution.— Coasts of eastern North America and northwestern Europe, breeding from southern Greenland and Ungava to Maine; winters from Cumberland Sound south to Cape Cod; rarely to Long Island, N. Y., and New Jersey.

Drawing by R. I. Brasher

BLACK GUILLEMOT (½ nat. size)

Their black bodies, white-lined wings, and red legs make a color scheme well worth seeing

Along the coast of Maine the numerous rocky islands extending in an irregular line out to sea afford favorite nesting places for numerous sea-fowl, among which the Black Guillemot, or "Sea Pigeon," is by no means rare. Farther north they are more numerous and breed in numbers on Grand Manan Island, New Brunswick, at various places in the Gulf of St. Lawrence, and along the Labrador coast. In approaching their nesting islands one will observe what appear to be short, black Ducks swimming ahead of the boat, usually several together. One by one they will suddenly disappear, as with surprising swiftness they dive beneath the surface. Under water they are much at home, and by the use of wings, as well as legs, they take their submarine flight to a considerable distance before reappearing. Usually one does not see them again until they rise to the surface well beyond gunshot range. On taking wing they rise readily from the water. Their progress is swift, strong, and usually directed in a straight line. In flight they rarely rise more than a few feet above the water.

The Black Guillemot's nest is placed in the cleft of rocks well above the reach of high tides. While clambering over the great jumble of giant bowlders, that reach from the water to the higher ground on some of the Maine islands, I have often come upon these birds brooding their eggs or young. The first knowledge of their presence would be when one would spring out from among the bowlders and go dashing away to the sea. Their black bodies and white-lined wings, combined with the red of the dangling, wide-spraddled legs, made a color scheme well worth seeing. Hidden generally well from view is the nest, and often it would take a steam derrick to reach it. Not the slightest effort at nest building is attempted. The two handsomely spotted eggs are deposited on the bare rocky floor of the little cave. The young are covered with down, literally as black as the "ace of spades." The birds feed on various crustaceans and shell-fish which are secured by diving.

Many sea-birds of the North journey to southern waters to spend the winter, but the Sea Pigeon apparently sees no need for exerting itself to such an extent. In fact it can hardly be said to migrate at all, for it is rarely found south of Cape Cod, scarcely two hundred miles beyond its southernmost nesting grounds. At all times they are coast-wise birds, seldom being seen out of sight of land, and never under any circumstances going inland. T. GILBERT PEARSON.

PIGEON GUILLEMOT

Cepphus columba *Pallas*

A. O. U. Number 29

Other Name.— Sea Pigeon.

General Description.— Length, 13 inches. Prevailing color, in summer, sooty-black; in winter, black and white; bill, slender and straight, *with no horny growth at base.*

Plumage.— *White mirror of upper surface split by an oblique dark line* caused by extension of dark bases of greater coverts increasing from within outward until the outside ones are scarcely tipped with white; plumage and changes otherwise as in Black Guillemot.

Nest and Eggs.— Similar to those of the Black Guillemot.

Distribution.— Coasts and islands of the Arctic Ocean, Bering Sea and Cape Lisburne, and both coasts of the north Pacific from Bering Strait south to Santa Catalina Island, California, and to northern Japan.

Mr. Dawson says that the Pigeon Guillemot is "unquestionably the most characteristic water-bird of the Puget Sound region," and explains its sharing the popular name "Sea Pigeon" with the Bonaparte Gull as follows: "The Gulls are dove-like in posture (at least a-wing), and in their manner of flocking; while the Guillemot owes its name both to its plumpness and to its very unsophisticated, not to say stupid, appearance." (*Birds of Washington.*)

E. W. Nelson found this bird "the most abundant of the small Guillemots throughout the North, from Aleutian Islands to those of Wrangel and Herald, where we found it breeding abundantly during our visit there on the *Corwin.*" He notes that the birds are very conspicuous by reason of their white wing patches and bright red legs. When perched on the rocks they squat like Ducks, and when swimming they often paddle along with their heads below the surface.

For breeding operations a few pairs may take

possession of a group of small rocks, or a colony of several hundred may share cliffs with Cormorants, Tufted Puffins, and Glaucous Gulls. Mr. Finley observes (MS.) that off the Oregon coast these Guillemots nest in isolated places and not in colonies. "They like a crevice or a hole in the face of a cliff for a nest site." On land they have an awkward shambling gait, but in the water they are entirely at ease, and are swift swimmers and expert divers.

MURRE

Uria troille troille (*Linnæus*)

A. O. U. Number 30

Other Names.— Foolish Guillemot; Guillem, or Gwilym; Tinker; Tinkershire; Kiddaw; Skiddaw; Marrock; Willock; Scuttock; Scout; Strany; Lavy; Frowl.

General Description.— Length, 17 inches. Color above, brown; below, white. Bill, narrow and slender.

Color.— ADULTS IN SUMMER: *Head and neck all around, rich maroon-brown* shading on upper parts into dark slaty-brown; some feathers of back and rump with grayish-brown edges; secondaries, narrowly tipped with white; under parts, pure white; sides and flanks with dusky markings; bill, black, feet, dusky; iris, brown. ADULTS IN WINTER: White of under parts, reaching bill, on sides of head to level of gape, extending further around on sides of neck, leaving only a narrow line of dark color; the two colors shading without sharp line of demarcation.

Nest and Eggs.— A single egg, remarkably variable in coloration, is laid on the rock of cliffs, without any attempt at nest building; it varies from white to dark green, spotted, blotched, and scratched with black, brown, and lilac over the entire surface.

Distribution.— Coasts and islands of North Atlantic; breeds in North America from southern Greenland and southern Ungava south to Newfoundland and Magdalen Islands; winters south to Maine.

The common Murre's natural habitat is the northern Atlantic Ocean, and various islands therein, but in winter it wanders southward as far as New England, and possibly to New York, though the records of its appearances there seem not to be entirely reliable. On the water this bird looks much like a Duck, though its neck is shorter and its bill more pointed than is charac-

MURRE (½ nat. size)

Drawing by R. I. Brasher

teristic in that family. In their nesting places on ledges of rocky islets they sometimes gather in such numbers as to present a seemingly almost solid mass of birds, while the eggs are found lying so close together that it is actually difficult to walk without treading upon them.

All the Murres are oceanic birds, only visiting the rocks during the breeding season, and found inland only when driven there by storms. Their food consists of fish and various crustaceans; this particular species is especially partial to the fry of herrings and pilchards, which are captured at night in the open sea.

Doctor Chapman remarks that "long-continued studies of Murres on the coast of Yorkshire warrant the belief that, although the eggs of no two Murres (or Guillemot as it is termed in England) are alike, those of the same individual more or less closely agree, and that the same bird lays year after year on the same ledge. Murres perch on the entire foot or tarsus, and when undisturbed usually turn their backs to the sea and hold their eggs between their legs with its point outward. When alarmed they face about, bob and bow and utter their low-voiced *murre*."

CALIFORNIA MURRE

Uria troille californica (*H. Bryant*)

A. O. U. Number 30a

Other Names.— California Guillemot; California Egg-bird; Farallon Bird.

General Description.— Similar to the common Murre, but averaging about an inch longer.

Nest and Eggs.— Like those of common Murre.

Distribution.— Coasts and islands of the north Pacific; breeds from Norton Sound and Pribilof Islands south to the Farallons, California; winters from the Aleutian Islands south to Santa Monica, California.

The California Murre is the most abundant sea-bird on the off-shore rocks of the Pacific from Alaska to the Farallons. It is readily recognized by its snow-white breast and sooty-brown back. Its legs are placed clear at the end of its body, so it does a good deal of its sitting standing up. Its attempt to walk is a very awkward performance resembling a boy in a sack race. But in water the bird is very expert. It uses its feet as propellers and its wings as oars, flashing under water with such swiftness that it can overtake and capture a fish.

Photo by W. L. Finley Courtesy of Nat. Asso. Aud. Soc.

AN INCUBATING CALIFORNIA MURRE

During incubation the single egg is held between the legs with its point outward. Photo taken on island off the coast of Oregon

The Murre is a creature of the crowd. To see this bird in great colonies and to watch its home life, one gets the idea that a Murre would die of lonesomeness if isolated. They huddle together in such great numbers on the narrow sea ledges that they occupy every available standing place. There is not the least sign of a nest. The female lays a single egg on the bare rock. One egg is all that can be attended to under the circumstances. One might wonder why the birds persist in crowding so close together. Neighbors always seem to be quarreling and sparring with their sharp bills. They rarely hit each other, because they are experts at dodging. The babble is continuous; everyone talks at the same time.

The peculiar top-shape of the Murre's egg prevents it from rolling. The practical value of this may be seen every day on the sloping ledges. We tried several experiments and the eggs were of such taper that not one rolled over the edge. When an egg starts down grade, it does not roll straight, but swings around like a top and comes to a standstill. The shells are also very tough and not easily broken.

One day we lay stretched out on a ledge just

above a big colony where we could watch the ordinary run of life and not disturb the birds in any way. When a Murre arrived from the fishing grounds, he alighted on the outer edge of the shelf. Then, like a man in a Fourth of July crowd, he looked for an opening in the dense front ranks. Seeing none, he boldly squeezed in, pushing and shoving to right and left. The neighbors resented such behavior and squawked and pecked at the new arrival. But he pressed on amid much opposition and complaint until he reached his mate. They changed places and he took up his vigil on the egg. The mate, upon leaving the colony, instead of taking flight from where she stood, went through the former proceeding, often knocking over several neighbors who protested vigorously, jabbing at the parting sister. Arriving at the edge of the ledge, she dropped off into space. The continuous going and coming made an interesting performance for the onlooker.

WILLIAM L. FINLEY.

Photo by W. L. Finley and H. T. Bohlman

CALIFORNIA MURRES

Off Oregon coast on Three Arch Rocks Reservation

BRÜNNICH'S MURRE

Uria lomvia lomvia (*Linnæus*)

A. O. U. Number 31 See Color Plate 3

Other Names.— Franks' Guillemot; Thick-billed Guillemot; Thick-billed Murre; Brünnich's Guillemot; Polar Guillemot; Egg-bird.

General Description.— Length, 18 inches. Similar to common Murre in plumages and changes, but crown darker in contrast with throat and sides of neck; *bill, shorter and stouter* with cutting edge of upper jaw flesh-colored.

Nest and Eggs.— Indistinguishable from those of the Murre.

Distribution.— Coasts and islands of north Atlantic; breeds from southern Ellesmere Land, and northern Greenland to Hudson Bay and Gulf of St. Lawrence; resident in Greenland and Hudson Bay; south rarely in winter from Maine to South Carolina, and in interior to northern Ohio, central Indiana and central Iowa.

Brünnich's Murre comes as near being like the Antarctic Penguins as any other North American species. It is built primarily for swimming and diving, and is a poor walker, waddling awkwardly in an upright position.

Except as it may climb out of the cold water on a cake of ice, its only chance to exercise these poor gifts is during the short summer in the Far North on its breeding grounds. There the Murres, mingled with the other species, resort

Photo by H. K. Job   Courtesy of Houghton Mifflin Co.

BRÜNNICH'S MURRE

Presently it will lift its egg onto its feet and hold it there for incubation

to precipitous shores or rocky islands, from the Gulf of St. Lawrence away up to northern Greenland. I have visited the colony on Great Bird Rock, Magdalen Islands. Here, in June, I found them standing in rows on the narrow ledges of the cliff, usually with back to the sea, each bird holding between its legs one large pear-shaped egg. These eggs have very hard shells, and are so shaped that they roll in a circle, which helps to prevent their falling off the cliff. They are colored a great variety of tints of green, blue, buff, whitish, and are so variously marked that it is impossible to find any two alike. Usually the Murres crowd upon these ledges as thickly as they can find room to stand or squat.

From these ledges they throw themselves with confident abandon, and, with exceedingly rapid wing beats, circle out over the sea and back again to the rock. Otherwise they alight on the water with rather a heavy splash, and are apt to dive forthwith. They can be seen here and there swimming about, distinguishable from Ducks by the fact that their posterior part floats rather high — reminding one of the ancient ships as described by Vergil, with "lofty sterns."

Their hoarse baritone voice is almost human, and they are supposed to say *murre*. When I first heard them on the rocky ledges close at hand, I was involuntarily startled, so much did it sound to me like someone calling my boyhood nickname, "Herb, Herb!"

Unless one can visit a breeding colony, about the only way to cultivate their acquaintance is to get offshore in winter, on the bleak, wind-swept ocean, not much further south than Nantucket shoals, or, better, the coast of Maine. Miles off Cape Cod in mid-winter, from fishing vessels I have seen them by hundreds. Flocks of them dotted the ocean in all directions, or moved in lines swiftly through the air, to plunge into the water and disappear like stones, presently to bob up many rods further off. Occasionally at the entrance of harbors, in bitter cold weather, I have seen them perched on some slanting pole or beacon, from which they would plunge directly into the water.

Though oceanic in habit, this particular species seems to have a peculiar faculty, as has the Dovekie, for getting into trouble by wandering from its real element. After winter storms they are liable to be found far inland, sometimes stranded in a snow bank out in some field, or on the ice of a pond or stream, vainly seeking to find water. In such cases they are emaciated and must perish, as they are unable to rise on wing from any surface except water. When word comes of a queer unknown bird which stands upright on the ice or in the snow, it is a likely guess to call it a Brünnich's Murre.

HERBERT K. JOB.

RAZOR-BILLED AUK

Alca torda *Linnæus*

A. O. U. Number 32 See Color Plate 3

Other Names.— Razor-bill; Tinker.

General Description.— Length, 18 inches. Color above, black; below, white. Bill, flatly compressed; tail, pointed.

Color.— Adults in Summer: Head and neck all around, and upper parts, black, more brownish on former, a slight greenish-gloss on latter; tips of secondaries and entire under parts from neck, white; a sunken line of white from eye alongside of forehead to bill; bill, black, crossed by a white line; feet, dusky; iris, brown. Adults in Winter: White extending to bill, invading sides of head to level of eyes and neck; no white line from bill to eye; color of upper parts, duller.

Nest and Eggs.— Usually one egg, sometimes two, is laid on the bare rock of cliffs or islands along the coast, very variable in shape and size of markings; white or bluish, spotted and blotched with sepia or black, these spots sometimes wreathed in a circle around the large end; in others diffused over entire surface.

Distribution.— Coasts and islands of the north Atlantic; breeds on American side from southern Greenland to Newfoundland and New Brunswick; winters from New Brunswick and Ontario to Long Island and rarely to North Carolina.

The Razor-billed Auk presents a striking and interesting appearance in the water, which it rides as buoyantly as a cork. Like all of its kind, it is exceedingly quick and clever at diving, a method of escape which it always adopts in preference to flight, when it can. It slips under the surface with hardly any perceptible or audible splash, and it is quite impossible to tell where it will reappear. When fairly submerged the bird swims — using both wings and feet — with astonishing speed and often descends to a considerable depth. It feeds largely upon fish and various small marine creatures, and takes virtually all of its food from the sea. When it chooses to take to its wings, it can fly with much rapidity. In summer it is decidedly gregarious and the flocks often are seen far from land. If then overtaken by heavy gales, large numbers of the birds are drowned.

As the breeding season approaches, the birds abandon temporarily their nomad sea life and gather in large flocks at established breeding places, preferably on cliffs overlooking the ocean, and containing an abundance of niches and recesses, where the single egg is laid, no nest being made The incubating bird is very loath to leave the egg, and often when so engaged may be taken in the hand. There are many evidences that the birds mate for life.

Drawing by R. I. Brasher

RAZOR-BILLED AUK (⅓ nat. size)

It rides the ocean as buoyantly as a cork

GREAT AUK

Plautus impennis (*Linnæus*)

A. O. U. Number 33

Other Names.— Garefowl; Penguin; Wobble.

General Description.— Length, 30 inches. Color above, black; below, white.

Color.— Adults: Hood and entire upper parts including wings, black; ends of secondaries, white forming a traverse band; under parts, white extending to a point on throat; a white oval spot between bill and eye; bill, black with lighter grooves; feet, black; iris, brown.

Nest and Eggs.— Nest: Site probably similar to that of the Razor-billed Auk. Egg: 1, white or bluish-white, spotted and blotched with shades of umber-brown and sepia.

Distribution.— Formerly inhabited coasts and islands of the north Atlantic from near the Arctic Circle south to Massachusetts and Ireland, and probably south casually to South Carolina and Florida and the Bay of Biscay; now extinct.

The Great Auk was the most powerful and swiftest diving and swimming bird in North America. It had to be, as it could not fly. In order to survive it must be fast enough not only to pursue and overtake the swift-swimming fish in their native element, but also active enough to escape sharks and other predatory fish that otherwise might have exterminated it. Also it was obliged to follow the smaller migratory fish southward in winter and northward in spring.

It has been pictured often among the icebergs, but it was not a bird of the Arctic regions and was not found within the Arctic Circle. It is believed to have inhabited southern Greenland, but that was centuries ago when the climate of Greenland probably was warmer than it is now. In primitive times, when man was a savage, the Auk was safe upon its island home in the raging sea, which men in their frail canoes visited rarely and in small numbers; but civilized man, coming in large companies in ships that sailed the seven seas, armed with firearms, brought extermination to all flightless birds which came under his notice, and so the Great Auk was one of the first of the North American birds to become extinct in the nineteenth century, the century that will always be noted for its great destruction of birds and mammals at the hand of man.

The Great Auk had been known in Europe for centuries when it was first discovered in North America. This was in 1497 or 1498, when adventurous French fishermen began fishing on the banks of Newfoundland. The birds were taken there in such enormous numbers that it was unnecessary to provision the vessels, as the fleet could secure all the fresh meat and eggs needed by visiting the bird islands. Jacques Cartier, on his first voyage to Newfoundland in 1534, visited an "Island of Birds" which, from the course and distance sailed from Buena Vista, must have been what is now known as Funk Island, the last breeding place of the Great Auk in America, where the crews filled two boats with the birds in "less than half an hour" and every ship salted down five or six barrelfuls. He also found the Great Auk on the Magdalen Islands in the Gulf of St. Lawrence. The bird became known among the French fishermen as the *Pingouin* (Penguin). There were at least three Penguin islands about Newfoundland and another near the tip of the peninsula of Nova Scotia, while numerous birds apparently summered at the head of Buzzards Bay and about Cape Cod.

The Auk migrated from Labrador to Florida. It was common at Nahant, Mass., and about the islands in Massachusetts Bay in the early years of the nineteenth century and was taken now and then near Plymouth, but had disappeared at that time from the upper end of Buzzards Bay. When Audubon visited Labrador in 1832, he was told that fishermen still took great numbers from an island off the coast of Newfoundland, but, from all accounts, it seems probable that the bird was extirpated on the coasts of North America before 1840. Apparently the Great Auk was destroyed in America before it was extirpated in Europe, where the last recorded specimen was taken, off Iceland, in 1844.

Its destruction was accomplished first by the demand for the eggs and flesh for victualing fishermen and settlers, next by the demand for the feathers, and last by unrestricted shooting. When the supply of eider-down and feathers for feather beds and coverlets gave out, about 1760, because of the destruction of the breeding fowl along the coast of Labrador, some of the feather hunters turned to the Penguin islands off the coast of Newfoundland. Cartwright said (1775) that several crews of men lived all summer on Funk Island, killing the birds for their feathers; that the destruction was incredible; and that this was the only island that was left for them to breed upon. Nevertheless the species continued more or less numerous about the shores of Newfoundland until about 1823 and then gradually disappeared before continuous persecution. Dr. F. A. Lucas, who visited Funk Island in 1878, found such enormous numbers of the bones of this species that he concluded that "millions" must have died there. Today there are about eighty mounted specimens in existence and not many over 70 eggs preserved in museums and collections.

This Auk was readily alarmed by a noise, as its hearing was very keen, but it was not wary if approached silently. When on land it stood upright or rested on its breast, and its locomotion was slow and difficult, so that it might be easily overtaken and killed with a club. In the water, however, it was so swift that a boat propelled by six oars could not overtake one. It is believed to have fed mainly upon fish, but its habits never were studied and described, and, therefore, they are unknown. EDWARD HOWE FORBUSH.

DOVEKIE

Alle alle (*Linnæus*)

A. O. U. Number 34 See Color Plate 3

Other Names.— Little Auk; Sea Dove; Alle; Rotch; Ice-bird.

General Description.— Length 8½ inches. Color above, black; below, white; head and bill, formed like those of a Quail.

Color.— Adults in Summer: Head, neck all around, and upper parts, glossy blue-black; sides of head, neck, and throat, shaded with sooty-brown; three or four white streaks on shoulders; secondaries, tipped with white; under parts, pure white; bill, black; feet, flesh-color in front, black behind and on webs; iris, brown. Adults in Winter: White of under parts extending to bill, invading sides of head and neck and nearly meeting on nape; otherwise as in summer.

Nest and Eggs.— A single greenish-blue egg laid in crevices of rocky cliffs on islands or coasts near the sea.

Distribution.— Coasts and islands of north Atlantic; breeds from Kane Basin and Baffin Bay east to Franz Josef Land; winters from southern Greenland south to Long Island (N. Y.), and rarely to Delaware Bay and North Carolina; accidental near Melville Island, and in Wisconsin, Michigan, Ontario, and Bermuda.

The little Dovekies or "Sea Doves" breed along the coasts of Greenland and other sea islands of the Atlantic, north of latitude 69°, and in winter come down the coast where less ice abounds and where, consequently, food is more easily secured. New Jersey is about the usual limit of this species' southern journey. They stay in small flocks in the open sea and feed by diving. Apparently at this season they come on land but rarely.

Cape Hatteras, ornithologically, is a very interesting place. Here the warm waters of the Gulf Stream meet and neutralize the last remaining vestige of the cold bearing currents from the north. As the distribution of animal life is largely determined by climatic conditions, the North Carolina coast affected by these currents becomes the meeting place of many northward moving species that naturally inhabit warmer regions, and southward moving species from the cold countries to the north. The extreme southern migration of the Dovekie illustrates this interesting fact. A few miles north of Cape Hatteras I found, one December some years ago, one of these little wanderers. It was sitting on the beach in a tired-out condition and made but feeble attempts to escape when I took it in my hands. Then I discovered the cause of its emaciated condition: one foot was missing. Doubtless it had been bitten off by some fish. With its power of diving in the ocean thus reduced at least one-half, its chances for securing a livelihood were all but gone, and in the end the tide had cast it upon the shore. Within a few hours it died, despite the most energetic efforts to induce it to eat such food as was available.

The Eskimos kill many Sea Doves and use their feathered skins for making the bird-skin shirts with which they help ward off the biting frost of their country. The birds are taken in nets which the natives wield over the face of the cliff where the birds crowd together to breed.

"I have often thought," wrote Audubon, "how easy it would be to catch these tiny wanderers

Drawing by R. I. Brasher

DOVEKIE (⅓ nat. size)

These small Sea Doves manifest very little apprehension of danger from the proximity of man

of the ocean with nets thrown expertly from the bow of a boat, for they manifest very little apprehension of danger from the proximity of one, insomuch that I have seen several killed with the oars. Those which were caught alive and placed on the deck, would at first rest a few minutes with their bodies flat, then rise upright and run about briskly, or attempt to fly off, which they sometimes accomplished, when they happened to go in a straight course the whole length of the ship so as to rise easily over the bulwarks. On effecting their escape they would alight on the water and immediately disappear."

T. Gilbert Pearson.

ORDER OF LONG-WINGED SWIMMERS

Order *Longipennes*

BIRDS of the order of Long-winged Swimmers are cosmopolitan in distribution and are generally seen on the wing over or near water. In the order are three families: Skuas and Jaegers, Gulls and Terns, and Skimmers. They resemble most nearly the Tube-nosed Swimmers of all the water birds, but the character of the nostrils plainly distinguishes them without reference to internal anatomy. These birds have the nostrils lateral and open. The wings are long and pointed. Usually the tail is long. The legs are comparatively free and project from near the center of the body; the thighs are bare for a short distance; the tarsi are covered with horny shields of varying sizes. The toes are four in number, but the hind one, which is elevated, is very small (sometimes rudimentary); the front toes are webbed. Their bills are strong and thick; the Skuas, Jaegers, and Gulls have hooked, hawklike bills; the Terns have sharply pointed ones; and those of the Skimmers are bladelike.

Although there is no sexual variation in coloration in the species included in this order, there are seasonal and age differences. Their voices are shrill or harsh. Fish is the main item of their diet.

The eggs are few, usually numbering but three. The young are covered with down when hatched, but are helpless and the parents care for them in and out of the nest for some time.

SKUAS AND JAEGERS

Order *Longipennes;* family *Stercorariidæ*

THE Skuas and Jaegers are closely related to the Gulls and Terns; in fact they are Gulls with habits and structure modified sufficiently to justify their inclusion in a distinct family, the *Stercorariidæ*, while still remaining in the same order, the Long-winged Swimmers. Not the least striking of these modifications is a well-developed thieving propensity, with the result that they are often and variously called "Robber Gulls," "Sea Hawks," "Teasers," and "Boatswains." Generally they are aggressive and daring birds, graceful, skillful and powerful in flight, by reason of which they are able to overtake their weaker and more timid relatives and force them to disgorge their food, which the pursuer catches in its fall. Because of these practices they are often spoken of as parasites, but the practice itself is essentially predatory rather than parasitic. The birds' bad habits are not confined to this aërial robbery, however, for certain species are known actually to eat young birds and eggs, and even small mammals.

The Skuas and Jaegers have wings of only moderate length for this group, the primaries are unusually wide and are rounded at the ends. The tail is relatively very short, but is broad and nearly even, the middle pair of feathers being larger than the others in adults. The body is stocky and heavy and powerfully muscled. The claws are strong, sharp, and curved.

There is general tendency toward a sooty blackish coloration of the upper parts in the older birds with a gilding of the head and hindneck and a whitening of the shafts of the white feathers toward their bases. The young are smaller than the adults and are profusely streaked with rufous; several years are required to reach the color and dimensions of the adults.

SKUA

Megalestris skua (*Brünnich*)

A. O. U. Number 35 See Color Plate 4

Other Names.— Sea Hawk; Sea Hen; Bonxie; Skua Gull.

General Description.— Length, 22 inches. Color, blackish-brown.

Plumage.— ADULTS: *Blackish-brown, varied above with chestnut and whitish* (each feather dark-colored with a spot of chestnut toward end, shading into whitish along shaft); on nape and across throat, reddish-yellow with narrow white streak on each feather; crown and sides of head, with little whitish; wings and tail, dusky, white for some distance from base — concealed on tail by long coverts, but showing on primaries as a conspicuous spot; bill, black with gray cere; feet, black; iris, brown. Another plumage, not known to be characteristic of age or season, is uniform sooty-blackish *with the white wing spots very conspicuous.*

Nest and Eggs.— NEST: A depression in the grass; lined with grass and moss. EGGS: 2 or 3, olive or drab, irregularly marked and blotched with dark olive-brown and sepia.

Distribution.— Coast and islands of the North Atlantic; breeds on Lady Franklin Island (Hudson Strait), in Iceland, and on the Faroe and Shetland islands; winters on fishing banks off Newfoundland and Nova Scotia; rarely south to Long Island, N. Y.; in Europe south to Gibraltar.

The Skua is one of the largest and strongest members of its rapacious genus, and is much given to robbing the smaller sea birds, in the manner of its relatives. It occasionally strays along the North American coasts as far south as the northern boundary of the United States. There are records of its having been taken at least three times off the coast of Massachusetts. A single individual was shot on the Niagara River in 1886, and another was killed in 1896 by colliding with the lighthouse at Montauk Point, Long Island, N. Y.

Little seems to have been set down concerning the habits of the bird, which, however, probably do not differ essentially from those of the Jaegers. It does not assemble in flocks. Seldom are even two pairs seen together. It is famed for its courage and daring in attacking and teasing Gulls and forcing them to give up the fish they have caught. Indeed, its scientific name is an apt characterization — *megalestris* is from two Greek words which, translated, are "large pirate craft." In flight it has a striking appearance.

POMARINE JAEGER

Stercorarius pomarinus (*Temminck*)

A. O. U. Number 36 See Color Plate 4

Other Names.— Gull Hunter; Sea Robber; Gull Chaser; Jaeger Gull.

General Description.— Length, 24 inches. Color above, brownish-black; below, white.

Description.—ADULTS IN BREEDING PLUMAGE: Crown brownish-black extending below eyes and on sides of lower bill; back, wings, tail, upper and under tail-coverts, deep brownish-black; under parts from chin and neck all around, pure white — the sharp feathers of back and neck, light yellow; bill, horn color shading to black; feet, black; iris, brown. NEARLY ADULT: A row of brown spots across breast; sides barred with white and brown. INTERMEDIATE STAGE: Entire breast, brown mottled with white; upper tail-coverts and some wing-coverts, barred with white; feet, blotched with chrome yellow. In breeding and nearly adult plumage the *two central tail-feathers project about four inches and are twisted at right angles to the shafts;* in the intermediate plumage the central tail-feathers project only one inch and are *not* twisted; these central feathers are *rounded at the tip.* YOUNG OF THE YEAR: Whole body traversely barred with dull rufous; on head, neck, and under parts this color prevails, the bands very numerous, about same width as the dark color; on flanks and under tail-coverts the bars are wider, paler and almost white; on back and wing-coverts, brownish-black, nearly uniform, predominates; primaries and tail-feathers, dusky, darker at tips; head and neck, mostly pale rufous with a dusky spot in front of eye; feet, bright yellow. These plumages are evidently progressive with age and are independent of sex and season, and different from the following: DARK PHASE:

Plumage, blackish-brown all over, shading into black on crown, lightening on abdomen; primaries, whitish at base; feet, blotched with yellow and dusky; middle tail-feathers projecting but half an inch.

Nest and Eggs.— Nest: On the ground in northern marshes, of grass and moss. Eggs: 2 or 3, olive, pale greenish, or brownish, spotted with dark brown.

Distribution.— Northern part of northern hemisphere; breeds from Melville Island and central Greenland south to northern Alaska, northern Mackenzie, and Baffin Land, and also on Arctic islands of eastern hemisphere; winters off Atlantic coast south to New Jersey; in fall migration common along the California coast; winters south to the Galapagos, Peru, Africa, and Australia; accidental in Nebraska; occurs irregularly on the Great Lakes.

My first experience with that bold maritime robber, the Pomarine Jaeger, was on a day late in August, many years ago, when I crossed some Cape Cod sand-dunes and came in sight of the sea. Flocks of Terns and small Gulls were hovering over the water in all directions. Over them were big dark-colored birds with long tails coursing about with strong, swift flight. Now and then one of these would select for its victim a Tern which had just caught a fish, and give chase. No matter how the unfortunate one might dart and dodge, the Jaeger followed every move, and by savage attacks finally compelled it to drop the fish. Then by a spectacular swoop the robber would seize the booty in mid-air. When no victims are available for a hold-up, the Jaeger turns scavenger and picks up dead marine life like a true Gull, but its preference is for depredation.

Young—Dark Phase

Drawing by R. I. Brasher

POMARINE JAEGER (½ nat. size)

A bold maritime robber

On the fishing-banks out at sea, wherever the Shearwaters and Petrels gather, from August on through the autumn, I have usually found this Jaeger in attendance. With them are apt to be about as many Parasitic Jaegers and an occasional one of the Long-tailed species. The Jaegers are seen flying about, not close to the water like the others, but higher up, say fifty to seventy-five feet, as though to get a better view, to detect any weaker bird which makes a lucky strike. Though somewhat shyer than the rest, they are bold enough upon occasion, especially when eatables are being passed around. Sometimes I have brought them up quite close by making believe to throw something overboard. I have baited up numbers of them by throwing out fish livers, and made the most of the opportunity in securing photographs. At close range it was fascinating to study the different individuals as they appeared, owing to their great variations in plumage, all the way from the sooty phase to that of the adult with white under parts.

Jaegers are Arctic-breeding birds, not nesting in colonies, like the Gulls and Terns, but in scattered pairs. Such destructive birds would hardly make good colonizers. They are said to be great nest-robbers, and woe to the bird which leaves eggs or young exposed to these savages.

HERBERT K. JOB.

Photograph by H. K. Job Courtesy of Houghton Mifflin Co.

POMARINE JAEGER

In quest of a victim

PARASITIC JAEGER

Stercorarius parasiticus (*Linnæus*)

A. O. U. Number 37 See Color Plate 4

Other Names.— Skait-bird; Boatswain; Marlinespike; Teaser; Dung Hunter; Man-o'-war; Richardson's Jaeger; Black-toed Gull; Arctic Hawk Gull.

General Description.— Length, 20 inches. Color above, brownish-black; below, white. *Two middle tail-feathers, narrow and pointed, as well as elongated.*

Color.— ADULTS IN BREEDING PLUMAGE: Crown and back of head, crested, the feathers sharp and stiff; crown and whole upper parts, slaty brownish-black, shading into black on wings and tail; chin, throat, sides of head, neck all around, and under parts, pure white, the sharp feathers on back of neck, light yellow; under tail-coverts, dusky; bill, horn color, darker at end; feet, black; iris, brown. NEARLY ADULT: Under parts, white but mottled everywhere with dusky patches, heaviest across breast, on sides, and under tail-coverts; center line of throat and abdomen, nearly pure white; feet, with small yellow blotches or not; otherwise as in breeding plumage. DARK PHASE: Entire plumage, dusky, darker and more slate-colored above, lighter and browner below; crown, black; back of head and neck, yellow; wings and tail, black; feet, black. YOUNG OF THE YEAR: Entire plumage, barred with rufous and brownish-black; yellowish-rufous prevails on head and neck with dark shaft line on each feather; these shaft lines enlarge until between shoulders they occupy the whole of each feather except a narrow rufous border; on breast rufous becomes almost white, with traverse bars of brown, this pattern continuing over the entire under parts; primaries, dusky, narrowly tipped with rufous.

Nest and Eggs.— NEST: A depression in the ground near water, sparsely lined with grass and dead leaves. EGGS: 2 or 3, olive, greenish, gray, or brown, marked and blotched with shades of brown and pale lavender over entire surface.

Distribution.— Northern part of northern hemisphere; breeds from northwestern Alaska, Melville Island, and northern Greenland south to Aleutian Islands, central Mackenzie, central Keewatin, and on Arctic islands of Siberia and of northern Europe south to Scotland; winters from Aleutian Islands south to California, from New England coast southward to Brazil, in Australia, and from the coast of Europe south to the Cape of Good Hope; casual in interior to the Great Lakes, Missouri, Kansas, and Colorado.

As its name implies, the Parasitic Jaeger is a robber and lives largely on what it can take by force from its smaller brethren. It is large, and very strong and swift in flight, and the Eskimos call it "the cannibal" because, they say, once upon a time it killed and devoured men. It is much swifter and quicker than the Pomarine species, which it attacks and drives away, but it is less graceful on the wing. According to Edward W. Nelson, these birds bully and rob the Gulls and Terns, forcing them to disgorge fish which they have caught, and swooping below them snatch the food as it falls, very much in the manner of the Bald Eagle robbing the Fish Hawk.

These Jaegers often hunt in pairs and will then attack and rob even the Glaucous-winged Gull, which could make short work of its tormentors if it could only get at them. "But the parasites are too adroit, too elusive, and too desperately persistent," says Mr. Dawson. "The Gull hates to do it, but also he hates to be buffeted and hustled away from the fishing-grounds. 'Here, take it, you scum, and be off with you!'"

LONG-TAILED JAEGER

Stercorarius longicaudus *Vieillot*

A. O. U. Number 38 See Color Plate 4

Other Names.— Arctic Jaeger; Gull-teaser.

General Description.— Length, 23 inches. Color above, deep purplish-slate; below, white deepening into slate. During breeding season, crowns have slight crests. This is a smaller bird than the Parasitic Jaeger, the greater length being due *to the extremely long tail-feathers.*

Color.— Adults in Breeding Plumage: Lores and side of head above eye to nape, brownish-black; neck all around light straw-yellow; above with wing and tail-coverts, deep purplish-slate, deepening on primaries, secondaries, outside tail-feathers, and ends of central pair into lustrous *brownish-black;* chin, throat, and upper breast, white gradually shading into the dark slate of abdomen and under tail-coverts; bill, dusky with black tip; feet, grayish-blue; toes, webs, and claws, black; iris, brown. Immature: Changes of plumage identical with those of previous species. Dark Phase: Very rare.

Nest and Eggs.— Nest: Depression in the ground, scantily lined with dry grass and leaves. Eggs: 2 or 3, dark greenish, thickly spotted and blotched with brown.

Distribution.— Northern part of northern hemisphere; breeds on Arctic islands of Europe and Asia, and coasts of Kotzebue and Norton sounds, northern Mackenzie and northern Hudson Bay to northern Greenland; winters south to Gibraltar and Japan; in migration not rare off New England coast; casual on the Pacific coast south to California; accidental in Manitoba, Iowa, Illinois, and Florida.

Nelson describes the Long-tailed Jaeger as "the most elegant of the Jaegers in its general make-up, and especially when on the wing. At this time, the bird shows all the grace and ease of movement which characterize such birds as the Swallow-tailed Kite, and other species with very long wings and slender bodies. It appears to delight in exhibiting its agility, and two or more frequently perform strange gyrations and evolutions during their flight as they pass back and forth over the low, flat country which they frequent. It is, like the Parasitic Jaeger, found more plentifully along the low portions of the coast than at sea, and is very numerous along the coast of Norton Sound."

Like the other members of the genus, this Jaeger is a persistent and merciless robber of the smaller Gulls, swooping down on them and forcing them to disgorge fish or mollusks they have taken, and capturing the food as it falls. Flocks of Kittiwakes are likely to be accompanied by one or more of these Jaegers industriously engaged in this brigandism.

The species may be readily identified by the marked elongation of the central tail-feathers.

George Gladden.

Kittiwake (summer)

Photograph of habitat group

Courtesy of American Museum of Natural History

A SMALL CORNER OF BIRD ROCK

Brünnich's Murre Kittiwake (summer) Razor-billed Auk Kittiwake (winter)

GULLS

Order *Longipennes;* family *Laridæ;* subfamily *Larinæ*

THE Gulls comprise the subfamily *Larinæ* of the Gull and Tern family (*Laridæ*) which is part of the order of long-winged swimmers (*Longipennes*). There are about fifty species of Gulls, some of which are often found far inland, but most of which show an especial fondness for the seacoasts and their immediate vicinity. As a rule they are larger than their allies, the Terns, from whom they differ also in generally having almost square tails, though there are exceptions to this rule in the form of Terns with nearly square tails and of Gulls with tails which are more or less forked. An invariable difference, however, is in the structure of the upper bill, which is ridged and hooked at the end in Gulls and virtually straight in Terns. When hunting food, Gulls usually fly with their bill nearly on a line with the body, while Terns carry theirs pointed downward. Again, the Gulls alight freely on the water to feed, whereas the Terns hover and plunge for their food.

The Gulls show considerable variation in color, and some seasonal changes in plumage which have caused confusion in identifying species. "The predominating color of the adult birds," says Stejneger, "is white with a gray mantle, varying in shade from the most delicate pearl-gray to dark blackish-slate or nearly black, and the head is often more or less marked with black in summer. The seasonal change is not great, and affects chiefly the color of the head, which, in species with black heads, turns white in winter, while the White-headed Gulls usually get that part streaked with dark during the same season."

All of the species are web-footed and swim readily; they show little skill in diving, however, and the living fish they prey upon are chiefly the kind which come near the surface of the water, like the herring. On the wing they show perfect ease, and remarkable quickness and cleverness in their maneuvering, especially in the wind. It is certain, too, that they are capable of very long flights.

Gulls are markedly gregarious, and this instinct is especially in evidence during the breeding season, when several species may congregate on favorite nesting ledges to the number of thousands, if not millions. Their nests are composed usually of seaweeds and moss, and the eggs, usually no more than two or three, range in color from bluish-white to brownish, with blotches and spots of black, brown, or purplish.

Flocks of Gulls resting lightly on the waters of our harbors or following the wake of water craft are a familiar sight, but not every observer of the graceful motions of the birds is aware of the fact that Gulls are the original "white-wings." As sea scavengers they welcome as food dead fish, garbage, and offal of various sorts, and their services in cleaning up such material are not to be regarded lightly. It will surprise many to learn that certain Gulls render important inland service, especially to agriculture. At least one species, the California Gull, is extremely fond of field mice, and during an outbreak of that pest in Nevada in 1907–8 hundreds of Gulls assembled in and near the devastated alfalfa fields and fed entirely on mice, thus lending the farmers material aid in their warfare against the pestiferous little rodents. Several species of Gulls render valuable service to agriculture by destroying insects also, and in spring hundreds of Franklin's Gulls in Wisconsin and the Dakotas follow the plowman to pick up the insect larvæ uncovered by the share.

That at least one community has not been unmindful of the substantial debt it owes the Gull is attested in Salt Lake City, where stands a monument surmounted by bronze figures of two Gulls, erected by the people of that city "in grateful remembrance" of the signal service rendered by these birds at a critical time in the history of the community. For three consecutive years — 1848 to 1850 — black crickets by millions threatened to ruin the crops upon which depended the very lives of the settlers. Large flocks of California Gulls came to the rescue and devoured vast numbers of the destructive insects, until the fields were entirely freed from them. It is no wonder that the sentiment of the people of Utah, as reflected through their laws, affords Gulls the fullest protection. It would be well if such sentiment prevailed elsewhere throughout the United States. However, within the last few years much progress has been made in protecting these most beautiful dwellers of coasts and marshes.

IVORY GULL

Pagophila alba (*Gunnerus*)

A. O. U. Number 39 See Color Plate 6

Other Name.— Snow-white Gull.

General Description.— Length, 18 inches. White.

Color.—ADULTS: Entire plumage, *pure white;* shaft of primaries straw yellow; bill, dull greenish, yellow at tip and along cutting edges; feet, black; iris, brown; eyelids, red. YOUNG: Front and sides of head, dusky-gray; neck all around with irregular spotting of brownish-gray; shoulders and wing-coverts with brownish-black spots, thicker on lesser coverts; tips of primaries and tail-feathers with dusky spots.

Nest and Eggs.— NEST: In niches of cliffs; constructed of grass and seaweed, and lined with moss and a few feathers. EGGS: 2 to 4, olive-buff, spotted with different shades of brown and gray.

Distribution.— Arctic seas; breeds from Melville Island and northern Baffin Land to northern Greenland and Arctic islands of eastern hemisphere; winters in the extreme north, rarely south to British Columbia, Lake Ontario, and Long Island, N. Y.; in Europe south to France.

The first word of the scientific name of the Ivory Gull expresses its chief characteristic, just as the second word—*alba,* the Latin for " white " — is descriptive of its plumage. *Pagophila* is from two Greek words meaning " ice " and " loving." Hence this beautiful snow-white Gull is a rare visitant to the temperate zone of this continent from its home in the Arctic seas. The only verified record of the appearance of the bird in New York seems to be that furnished by William Dutcher of one shot in Great South Bay, L. I., near Sayville, in January, 1893. Another observer reports having seen a single member of the species near Mt. Sinai Harbor, in Suffolk County, N. Y. In summer it occurs frequently on the Arctic islands of the eastern hemisphere, and in winter it ranges southward to France. The greenish-yellow beak and the black legs are in striking contrast to its beautiful snow-white plumage. It differs from other Gulls in the comparative shortness of its beak, and slightly tapering tail.

The Ivory Gull is a glutton whenever it can obtain the flesh of seals or the blubber of whales. It will watch a seal-hole in the ice, waiting for the seal, whose excrement it devours.

KITTIWAKE

Rissa tridactyla tridactyla (*Linnæus*)

A. O. U. Number 40 See Color Plate 6

Other Names.— Common Kittiwake; Kittiwake Gull; Pick-me-up; Coddy-Moddy; Tarrock.

General Description.— Length, 18 inches. Color, white with pale grayish-blue mantle. *Hind toe, absent or rudimentary;* tail, slightly notched.

Color.— ADULTS IN SUMMER: Head and neck all around, under parts, and tail, pure white; mantle, pale grayish-blue; wing-coverts and secondaries similar, latter white on tips; *primaries, blackish-blue* with white oblong spaces on inner webs, the second, third and fourth with white tips; *feet, blackish; bill, light yellow* tinged with olive; iris, brown; eyelids, red. ADULTS IN WINTER: Back of head, nape, and sides of breast, shaded with color of back; a dusky patch behind eye and a small black crescent in front of eye: bill, dusky-olive; otherwise as in summer. YOUNG: Eye-crescent and spot behind eye as in winter adult plumage; a broad bar across back of neck, lesser and middle wing-coverts, inner secondaries, and a terminal bar on tail, black; first four primaries with outer webs, outer half of inner webs and ends for some distance, black; the rest, pearly-white.

Nest and Eggs.— NEST: On rocky ledges overlooking the water; made of grass and seaweed. EGGS: 2 or 3, sometimes 5, buff, brownish-gray, or greenish-gray, irregularly spotted with shades of brown and lavender.

Distribution.— Arctic regions; breeds from Wellington Channel and northern Greenland south to Gulf of St. Lawrence, and from Arctic islands of Europe and western Siberia to southern France; winters from Gulf of St. Lawrence south to New Jersey, and casually to Virginia, Bermuda, and the Great Lakes; accidental in Missouri, Colorado, and Wyoming.

The graceful and industrious little Kittiwake has several interesting and characteristic traits. It pursues its prey after the manner of the Terns, hovering over the water and plunging head foremost into the sea, with all of the dash and vigor of a Kingfisher. These Gulls are often seen following right whales apparently to get the fragments of fish rejected or dropped by those monsters. Observers who have watched the birds doing this say that they act as if they knew when the whales must rise to breathe.

The Kittiwake feeds mainly on fish, but will take almost any animal or vegetable refuse it can find. For drinking it prefers salt water to fresh, and it is often seen sleeping peacefully, floating on the great rollers, with its head tucked under its wing — literally "rocked in the cradle of the deep." It is a great wanderer, and decidedly democratic in its disposition, for it is often found in the company of other Gulls Terns, and various other sea-birds.

It takes its vernacular name from a fancied resemblance between its cry and the syllables "kit-ti-wake." In its scientific name, *Rissa* is its Icelandic name, and *tridactyla* is from the Greek, meaning "three-toed," and refers to an anatomical peculiarity of the species.

The Pacific Kittiwake (*Rissa tridactyla pollicaris*) is a geographical variation of the Common Kittiwake. The two differ but very little. The former occurs off the coasts of the north Pacific, Bering Sea, and the adjacent Arctic Ocean, breeding from Cape Lisburne and Herald Island south to the Aleutian and Commander Islands, and wintering from the Aleutian Islands south to northern Lower California.

Photograph by H. K. Job — Courtesy of Outing Publishing Co.

KITTIWAKE

In its nest on a cliff

GLAUCOUS GULL

Larus hyperboreus *Gunnerus*

A. O. U. Number 42 See Color Plate 5

Other Names.— Burgomaster; Burgomaster Gull; Ice Gull; Harbor Gull; Blue Gull.

Length.— 30 inches.

Color.— Adults in Summer: *Mantle, pale blue-gray; rest of plumage, entirely white;* bill, chrome yellow, more waxy on end with a bright vermilion spot at angle; legs, pale flesh color; iris, light yellow. Adults in Winter: Similar to summer plumage, but head and hindneck tinged with pale brownish-gray. Young: Upper parts, *whitish mottled with raw umber, pale reddish-brown, and dusky,* this coloration heaviest on back; under parts, nearly uniform pale brown; wings and tail, barred with same; bill and legs, pale flesh color, the former black-tipped; iris, brown.

Nest and Eggs.— Nest: In tussocks of grass; constructed of seaweed and dry grass. Eggs: 2 or 3, white to dark grayish-brown, blotched with brown and brownish-black.

Distribution.—Arctic regions; breeds from northwestern Alaska, Melville Island, and northern Greenland, south to Aleutian Islands, northern Mackenzie, and central Ungava, and on Arctic islands of eastern hemisphere; winters from the Aleutians and Greenland south to Monterey, California, the Great Lakes, and Long Island, N. Y., and casually to Bermuda, North Carolina, and Texas; in Europe and Asia south to the Mediterranean, Black, and Caspian seas, and Japan.

Under one of its popular names, the "Burgomaster Gull," the Glaucous Gull was made famous, or rather infamous, by Celia Thaxter's poem, which described its rapacious habits. This poem found its way into many school reading books of a generation ago. It gives a vivid and substantially accurate picture of the appearance and activities of a group of sea birds, and portrays one of the characteristics of the Burgomaster. Indeed, according to other observers, the bird not only robs smaller Gulls and other sea birds of the fish they catch, but eats their eggs and young and sometimes the adult birds themselves. It is recorded that a member of Ross's expedition to the Arctic regions shot one of these Gulls which, upon being struck, disgorged a Little Auk it had just devoured, and when dissected was found to have another member of the same species in its stomach.

Fishing fleets are likely to have the company of one or more of these Gulls, on the watch for any offal that may be thrown overboard. Under such conditions it has often been caught with a hook and line with a fish as bait. Though naturally timid and suspicious, its fondness for offal is likely to overcome its caution, and cause it to enter bays and even inland waters. Several specimens have been taken in the lower Hudson River and in New York Bay, and individuals have been seen in the Great Lakes.

A curious trait of this Gull is its apparent disinclination to alight in the water. In its natural habitat it alights generally on the highest point of an ice hummock. It displays none of the affection for its kindred which is characteristic of most of the Terns and Gulls, and will promptly desert either young or mate when they are in danger.

GREAT BLACK-BACKED GULL

Larus marinus *Linnæus*

A. O. U. Number 47 See Color Plate 5

Other Names.— Black-backed Gull; Saddleback; Coffin-carrier; Cobb; Wagell.

General Description.— Length, 30 inches. Color, white with a deep slate mantle.

Color.—Adults in Summer: *Mantle, deep dark slate with a purplish tinge;* secondaries, broadly tipped with white; primaries, black, white-tipped; rest of plumage, pure white; bill, chrome yellow, tip wax yellow with a large spot of bright vermilion on angle; legs, pale flesh color; iris, lemon-yellow; eyelids, vermilion. Adults in Winter: Similar to summer plumage, but head and neck streaked with dusky. Young: Above, dull whitish, mottled with brown and pale chestnut; wing-coverts and secondaries, dull brown with light edges; primaries, plain dusky, tipped with white; tail, brownish-black, fading to white at base, imperfectly barred with brown; forehead, crown, and under parts in general, dull whitish, mottled on abdomen with brown and dusky; throat, usually immaculate but sometimes like breast with faint brownish streaks.

Nest and Eggs.— Nest: Usually on small island; large and bulky; constructed of dry grasses and well-cupped. Eggs: 2 or 3, pale olive-gray, blotched with dark brown and black, with some purplish spots.

Distribution.— Coasts of North Atlantic; breeds from North Devon Island and central Greenland south to Nova Scotia, and to latitude 50° on European coasts; winters from southern Greenland south to the Great Lakes and Delaware Bay (casually to Florida), and the Canaries; accidental in Bermuda.

John Maclair Boraston, an English ornithologist, included the following characterization of the Great Black-backed Gull in his book *Birds by Land and Sea:*

"A staider and more deliberate flight marks the movements of the Great Black-backed and as he passes slowly before you, his eye on a level with your own, the brow seems to beetle in a set frown, and the glass catches the expression of the deeply set eye It seems an old eye, wise, authoritative. And, in fact, the bird may have been old when you were a child, for it requires four years for a Great Black-back to acquire all the marks of maturity, and its lifetime may well be a century. It will take offence at your presence more readily than the other Gulls, and as it passes, utters a low *Ha-ha-ha-ha!* and sails on solemnly leaving you admonished. If his displeasure is aroused, he will return again and again to swoop at you with menacing cry. 'The sea is mine,' he seems to say; 'and the smitten rocks. Get back to your brick-and-mortar cages with their glass peep-holes.' A century of the sea may well give a sense of prescriptive right."

This beautiful and dignified bird is frequently seen as a winter visitant off the shores of Long Island (between September and March) and on the Great Lakes. Its breeding places are confined to the Atlantic coast. It is very shy but exceedingly noisy. William Brewster says that he identified four distinct cries: "a braying *ha-ha-ha,* a deep *keow, keow,* a short barking note and a long drawn groan, very loud and decidedly impressive." The *keow* cry suggests the note of the Green Heron.

Drawing by R. I. Brasher

GREAT BLACK-BACKED GULL (⅜ nat. size)

Four years are required for this Gull to attain maturity

HERRING GULL

Larus argentatus *Pontoppidan*

A. O. U. Number 51 See Color Plate 5

Other Names.— Common Gull; Harbor Gull; Sea Gull; Lake Gull; Winter Gull.

General Description.— Length, 24 inches. Color, pure white with grayish-blue mantle.

Color.—Adults in Summer: Head, neck, tail, and under parts, pure white; *mantle, grayish-blue;* outer primaries, dusky with white spots and tips; center ones, color of mantle with ***black subterminal bar and***

narrow white tips; rest of primaries and secondaries, with white tips; bill, chrome yellow with red spot at angle; feet, brownish flesh color; iris, yellow. ADULTS IN WINTER: Similar to summer plumage, but head and neck streaked with dusky, and yellow of bill duller. YOUNG: Dull whitish, varied everywhere with shades of brown and dusky; tail, plain brown; primaries and secondaries, brown with white tips; bill, pale flesh color, dusky at end; legs, flesh color; iris, brown. There is much variation in the amount of dusky color in individuals; young of the year are sometimes almost entirely sooty-brown; this changes with the gradual acquisition of lighter tips and edges of the feathers, finally reaching the perfect adult plumage in three years.

Nest and Eggs.— NEST: Sometimes on the ground, occasionally in trees; ground nests usually mere depressions with scant nesting material; tree nests bulky and well constructed of strongly interwoven grass and moss. EGGS: 3, light bluish or greenish-white to dark olive-brown, irregularly blotched, spotted, and scrawled with dark brown and black.

Distribution.— Northern hemisphere; in America breeds from south-central Alaska, across British America to Cumberland Sound, south to British Columbia, across the United States on about the parallel 43° to Maine, and in Europe south to northern France and east to White Sea; winters from northern border of United States southward to Lower California and western Mexico, and from Gulf of St. Lawrence and the Great Lakes south to the Bahamas, Cuba, Yucatan, and coast of Texas, and in Europe to Mediterranean and Caspian seas.

The most abundant Gull along the Atlantic coast of the United States is the familiar Herring Gull. It is the species we find following the coast-wise ships looking eagerly for any scraps of food that are thrown overboard from the cook's galley. At low tide we may find them, often by hundreds, standing on the exposed bars and mud flats. They come into the harbors and fly about the piers. They wander far up the rivers and are continually met with even on the smaller lakes of the interior. Their food consists largely of fish, and the fact that some denizen of the deep may have been dead many days before the waves cast it upon the beach makes no difference with them. They are as fond of carrion as is a Vulture. One peculiar habit they have is the breaking of clam shells in a most unusual manner. When the water is low they sail over the mud flat until a clam is discovered. Dropping down they grasp it in their feet and fly away to a portion of the beach where the sand is packed hard and here from a height of forty or fifty feet they let it fall. I have seen one repeat this performance fourteen times before the shell broke and allowed it to enjoy the feast it so much craved.

Young

Adult

Drawing by R. I. Brasher

HERRING GULL
(½ nat. size)

The most abundant Gull along the Atlantic coast of the United States

Alighting at nest

A pair of adults

Nest and eggs

Young gull

HERRING GULLS

Photos by H. K. Job

Courtesy of Outing Publishing Co.

Herring Gulls breed on the rocky islands off the coast of Maine and thence northward. Frequently they assemble in very large numbers at this season. Probably 10,000 nest annually on Great Duck Island and the colony on the island of No-Man's-Land, Maine, has of recent years been even larger. The nests are made of grass and are often hidden in clumps of grass, by the side of logs or among piles of bowlders. Within a few days after hatching the young are able to run about and when a visitor walks through a breeding colony at this time the young birds go scuttling away in every direction like so many dirty little sheep. Although hard to catch they at once become docile when picked up. I have sometimes amused myself by laying them on their backs where they will often remain perfectly still until a row of half a dozen have thus been assembled.

Apparently these Gulls are their own worst enemies, as hundreds of young are annually killed by the old birds, who peck them on the head. Unfortunately the young appear to be unable to distinguish between parent and neighbors, and when an old one alights nearby they come up trustingly in quest of food; frequently swift death is their reward.

Formerly hundreds of thousands of this species were killed in summer for the millinery trade; but the Audubon Law now makes this a misdemeanor in every State where they are found, and wardens employed by the National Association of Audubon Societies to-day guard all the important breeding colonies in the United States.

There are nesting communities of them at various places in the interior as, for example, Lake Champlain, Moosehead Lake, and the Great Lakes. A very similar subspecies known as the Western Gull (*Larus occidentalis*) inhabits the Pacific coast of North America.

T. Gilbert Pearson.

CALIFORNIA GULL

Larus californicus *Lawrence*

A. O. U. Number 53

General Description.— Length, 23 inches. Color, pure white with pearly-blue mantle.

Color.—Adults in Summer: Mantle, pearly-blue; outer primaries, black with white spots and tips, the black grading to a narrow bar on sixth primary; secondaries, white-tipped; rest of plumage, pure white; bill, chrome yellow, a vermilion spot at angle below with a small black spot above; feet, dusky *bluish-green;*

Photo by W. L. Finley and H. T. Bohlman

CALIFORNIA GULLS

They generally nest in colonies on the inland lakes of western United States

webs, *yellow;* iris, brown; eyelids, red. Adults in Winter: Similar to summer plumage, but head and neck streaked with dusky and bill much duller. Young: Dull whitish, mottled with dusky on head, neck, rump, wing-coverts, and secondaries; back, grayish-blue, feathers with lighter edges; bill, dull flesh color; terminal half, dusky.

Nest and Eggs.— Nest: On the ground; constructed of small sticks and grass. Eggs: Usually 3 or 4, sometimes 5, pale bluish-white to brownish-clay color, blotched with dark brown and black zigzag markings.

Distribution.— Western North America; breeds from east-central British Columbia and Great Slave Lake south to northeastern California, northern Utah, and northern North Dakota; winters from its breeding range southward to Lower California and western Mexico; accidental in Kansas, Texas, Colorado, Alberta, and Hawaii.

RING-BILLED GULL

Larus delawarensis *Ord*

A. O. U. Number 54 See Color Plate 5

Other Names.— Common Gull; Lake Gull.

General Description.— Length, 20 inches. Color, pure white with pale bluish-gray mantle. Easily confused with the Herring Gull.

Color.—Adults in Summer: Mantle, pale bluish-gray; first primary, black, white spot near end; second, plain black; third, black with gray space on inner web; next three, black-tipped; rest of primaries and secondaries, color of mantle; rest of plumage, pure white; bill, greenish-yellow with a *broad band of black encircling it at angle;* feet, greenish-yellow; iris, pale yellow; eyelids, red. Adults in Winter: Similar to summer plumage, but head and neck behind *spotted* with dusky. Young: Above, mottled with brown and grayish-blue; wing-coverts, mostly dusky margined with lighter; secondaries and primaries, with a subterminal brownish area shading forward into gray; tail, with a broad subterminal band of dusky and indistinctly barred with brown; below, faintly mottled with brownish; bill, flesh color, dusky on terminal half; legs, dull greenish-yellow; iris, brown.

Nest and Eggs.— Nest: In the grass in marshes; built of dead reeds. Eggs: 2 to 3, bluish-white to dark brown, spotted and blotched with different shades of brown and lavender.

Distribution.— North America at large; breeds from southern British Columbia across British America to southern Ungava, south to Oregon, Colorado, North Dakota, central Wisconsin, central Ontario, northern New York (casually), and northern Quebec; winters from northern United States southward to Bermuda, the Gulf coast, Cuba, and southern Mexico.

Photo by H. K. Job Courtesy of Houghton Mifflin Co.

RING-BILLED GULLS RETURNING TO NEST

The versatility of the Gull shows his degree of intelligence. He is equipped for life on the water. His webbed feet are for swimming, but he doesn't seem to care whether nature equips him for the sea or not. His taste often runs to angle-worms instead of sardines. As the notion takes him, he will take up quarters about a pig-pen or a garbage pile, follow the plow as a Blackbird does, picking up angle-worms, or he will sail along in the wake of a vessel for days at a time to satisfy his taste for scraps.

The California and Ring-billed Gulls generally nest together in big colonies on the inland lakes through the western part of the United States. In many places, these birds are of great economic importance. I have seen them spread out over the fields and through the sagebrush and get their living by catching grasshoppers. In Utah, the Gull lives about the beet fields and alfalfa lands and follows the irrigating ditches. When the fields are irrigated and the water rushes along, seeping into holes and driving mice from their burrows, the Gulls flock about and gorge themselves on these rodents.

After the nesting season, large flocks of California and Ring-billed Gulls often collect along the southern coasts to spend the winter. While at Santa Monica, California, during the winter of 1905 and 1906, I often watched the flocks of Gulls returning every evening from far inland where they had been skirmishing during the day. I often saw them about the gardens and in the fields. A few miles from the ocean is the Soldiers' Home at Sawtelle The garbage is hauled two or three times a day over to the pig-pens. When the dump wagon reaches the pens, the driver not only always finds himself besieged by a lot of hungry porkers, but a flock of Gulls

Courtesy of Nat. Asso. Aud. Soc.

NEST AND EGGS OF CALIFORNIA GULL

is always at hand to welcome his arrival. They sit around on the ground or fences waiting patiently. The Gulls and pigs eat together. The Gull doesn't care if his coat gets soiled, for he returns to the shore each evening and takes a good bath before bedtime.

William L. Finley.

HEERMANN'S GULL

Larus heermanni *Cassin*

A. O. U. Number 57

Other Name.— White-headed Gull.

General Description.— Length, 20 inches. Head, white; body, bluish-gray.

Color.—Adults: Head all around, pure white, shading on neck into bluish-ash of under parts and into the *dark bluish-slate of upper parts;* rump and upper tail-coverts, clear ash; primaries, black with narrow white tips; tail, black narrowly tipped with white; *bill, bright red, black on terminal third;* feet, dusky-red; iris, brown; eyelids, red. Young: Head and throat, mottled with dusky and dull white; upper tail-coverts, gray; tail, broadly white-tipped; otherwise similar to adult plumage.

Nest and Eggs.— Nest: Probably similar to others of the genus. Eggs: Dull yellowish-drab, scatteringly marked with spots of brown and lilac.

Distribution.— Pacific coast of North America; breeds in Lower California and western Mexico; migrates north to southern British Columbia; winters from northern California southward to Guatemala.

As Mr. Dawson says, " Heermann's Gull is an inveterate loafer and sycophant. Of southern blood (we have just learned that he is bred on the islands off the coast of Mexico) he comes north in June only to float and loaf and dream throughout the remainder of the season. Visit the 'Bird Rocks' of Rosario Straits early in July and you will find a colony of Glaucous-wings distraught with family cares and wheeling to and fro in wild concern at your presence, while upon a rocky knob at one side, a white-washed club room, sit half a thousand Heermanns, impassive, haughty, silent. If you press inquiry they suddenly take to wing and fill the air with low-pitched mellow cries of strange quality and sweetness. And go where you will at that season, the Heermann's Gull is guiltless of local attachments — in the North." (*Birds of Washington.*)

Another observer notes that these Gulls display considerable intelligence in their pursuit of herring, when the fish are traveling in schools. The birds approach these schools from the rear and take the fish near the surface by diving for them. As the herring discover their pursuers they sink some distance, but the school continues to travel in the same direction. The Gulls seem to know this, for after having reached the head of the school, they circle to the rear, and follow along in the direction the herring are swimming until the fish come to the surface, when the birds renew their diving captures.

The systematic robbery of the Pelicans, an amusingly impudent performance, is also described by Mr. Dawson. "Often a long train of Pelicans is seen, as the tide is rising, slowly wandering around the bay, each one attended by one or more of these Gulls which are usually some distance behind. Whenever a Pelican awkwardly plunges into the water and emerges with its enormous scoop net full of fish, its parasites are sure to be ready and fearlessly seize the fish from its very jaws, the stupid bird never resenting the insult, or appearing to take the least notice of the little pilferers which it could easily rid itself of by one blow, or even swallow alive."

Photo by W. L. Finley and H. T. Bohlman

HEERMANN'S GULLS

They are inveterate loafers, and, while other Gulls are engaged with family cares, they stand on one side, impassive, haughty, silent

---

LAUGHING GULL

Larus atricilla *Linnæus*

A. O. U. Number 58 See Color Plate 6

Other Name.— Black-headed Gull.

General Description.— Length, 16 inches. Color, white with dark slate-gray mantle and almost black hood.

Color.—Adults in Summer: *Hood, dark slaty-black* extending further on throat than on back of head; a white spot above and below eye; neck all around, rump, tail, tips of secondaries and primaries, and entire under

Photograph by H. K. Job

Courtesy of Outing Publishing Co.

LAUGHING GULLS

On beach, Louisiana. Everywhere they add life, beauty, and interest to the scene

parts, white, the latter with a rosy tinge; *mantle, dark slate-gray; outer six primaries, black;* bill, deep carmine; feet, black; iris and edge of eyelids, carmine. Adults in Winter: Under parts, without rosy tint; head, white, mottled with dusky; bill and feet, dull. Young: Mantle, variegated with light grayish-brown; primaries, brownish-black, lighter on tips; secondaries, dusky on outer webs; tail, with a broad terminal band of dusky with narrow white tips; upper tail-coverts, white; bill and feet, brownish-black tinged with red.

Nest and Eggs.— Nest: On the ground in marshes; constructed of seaweed, sedges, and eelgrass. Eggs: 2 to 5, from dull grayish to dark olive, heavily marked with spots and splashes of brown, black, chestnut, and lavender.

Distribution.— Tropical and temperate coasts of North America; breeds from Maine (rarely) and Massachusetts (abundantly but local) south on the Atlantic and Gulf coasts to Texas, the Lesser Antilles, and Venezuela; winters from Georgia and Gulf coast south to western Mexico, Chile, and Brazil; casual in Colorado, Nebraska, Wisconsin, Ontario, and Iowa.

The Laughing Gull is well named, for seemingly it laughs. No great stretch of the imagination is required to assume that its loud cries are those of real mirth. It is a handsome creature in the breeding season, with its dark mantle, black head, and white breast faintly tinged with the color of the rose.

It breeds normally along most of the Atlantic coast of the United States. Until recent years it has been almost extirpated by constant persecution on the New England coast but now, under protection, its numbers are increasing. It nests on sandy islands, usually in tall thick grasses or shrubbery; in the north it builds a substantial warm nest of grasses and weeds, but in the south a mere hollow in the sand often suffices. In pleasant warm weather the birds are seen to leave their nests, trusting apparently to the heat of the sun, but in cool or stormy weather the female incubates closely. The young leave the nest soon after they are hatched and run about on the sandy soil, squatting and hiding in the thickest cover at the first alarm. Meanwhile the parents wheel high overhead, uttering their notes of apprehension. These birds are very gregarious and breed, as well as feed, in flocks.

Their food is largely composed of marine objects picked up on bars, beaches, flats, in the beds of estuaries and even at times in the salt marshes but ever near the sea. Audubon tells how the Laughing Gull robs the Brown Pelican in Florida. Waiting until the Pelican dives and comes to the surface the Gull alights upon its head and snatches the small fish from its enormous bill. Sometimes this Gull follows schools of porpoises for the small fish that they drive to the surface. Everywhere it adds life, beauty, and interest to the scene.

Photo by Herbert Mills Courtesy of Nat. Asso. Aud. Soc.

NEST AND EGGS OF LAUGHING GULL

Passage Key, Florida

Edward Howe Forbush.

FRANKLIN'S GULL

Larus franklini *Richardson*

A. O. U. Number 59

Other Names.— Prairie Pigeon; Franklin's Rosy Gull.

General Description.— Length, 14 inches. Color, white with dark bluish-slate mantle and dark slate hood.

Color.—Adults in Summer: *Hood, dark slate* extending around upper part of neck as well as on head; *eyelids, white;* mantle, dark bluish-slate; outer primaries, with dusky bars near tip, this color graduating from about 2 inches in width on first to a small bar on sixth; primaries and secondaries, white-tipped; tail, pale grayish-blue, the three outside pairs of feathers, white; neck all around, rump, and whole under parts, white, the latter with rosy tint; *bill, carmine crossed with black near end;* legs, dusky-red. ADULTS IN WINTER: Similar to summer plumage, but without hood; a few slaty feathers around eyes and on sides of head; no rosy tint below; bill and feet, dull. YOUNG: Traces of hood; outer 5 or 6 primaries, wholly black; mantle, gray or brown, varied with bluish-gray, according to age; tail, ashy-white with a broad black subterminal bar; under parts, white; bill, dusky, paler at base below; feet, flesh color; iris, dark brown.

Nest and Eggs.— NEST: On the ground among standing rushes and grass of marshes bordering lakes or rivers; constructed of dead rushes. EGGS: 3, varying from dull white to olive-drab, marked with bold blotches and zigzag lines of umber-brown and sepia.

Distribution.— North and South America; breeds from southwestern Saskatchewan and southwestern Keewatin to South Dakota, Iowa, and southern Minnesota; winters from the Gulf coast of Louisiana and Texas southward to Peru and Chile; very rare on the Atlantic coast; accidental in Utah, Ontario, Ohio, Virginia, and the Lesser Antilles.

A typical scene of the interior prairie region, say in the Dakotas or Manitoba, is the farmer plowing up the rich black soil, on a cold windy day in early spring, followed almost at his heels by a troup of dainty white birds which are picking up the worms and grubs exposed to view. He calls them "Prairie Pigeons," a pretty and appropriate title, though in reality they are Franklin's Gulls. Sometimes they have been called the Rosy Gull, because when the feathers of the under parts are opened up there is seen to be a faint rosy flush, as delicate as that of the tea-rose.

Photograph by H. K. Job — Courtesy of Outing Publishing Co.

FRANKLIN'S GULLS

On nesting ground

This Gull is as typical of the prairie as is the Western Meadowlark or the Prairie Horned Lark, though in a different way. I should characterize it as the "courser" of the prairies. Bands of them are usually seen flying steadily along in a line or some regular formation, uttering flute-like cries, perpetually on the move. To a degree they strike one as birds of mystery, especially if one be curious to know whither they are roaming. Obviously, however, they are flying either to or from their nesting-ground.

In their breeding habits they are about as distinct and spectacular as any other North American species. Selecting some marshy lake, where reeds or rushes grow from water, thousands of them will come together and build semi-floating nests of dead stems, partly buoyed by the vegetation and filled in from the bottom. If a person wade or push a boat to the edge of the colony, the air is full of indignant and screaming birds, always graceful and beautiful, no matter how excited they become. The nests are only a few feet apart, each containing two or three typical gull-like eggs by the last week of May. If the intruder keeps quite still, one or both of the owners may finally alight and stand on the nest, but neither will incubate as long as anyone is in sight. The downy young swim from the nests soon after they are hatched, and in a colony in

Photo by H. K. Job Courtesy of Outing Pub. Co.

FRANKLIN'S GULL

Dropping down among the reeds to its nest

late June and July the equatic vegetation seems alive with paddling puff-balls.

In their feeding habits during the warmer part of the year they are largely insectivorous. Out in the marshy lakes they feed a great deal upon nymphs of the dragon-fly, and on any insects or larvæ locally available. On the plowed fields they find many injurious grubs and cutworms. Later they are active in pursuit of grasshoppers.

Their flocking is very spectacular, both when they are preparing to leave in the fall, and when they arrive in spring. In selected places, especially near the nesting-grounds, the prairie is sometimes fairly white with them.

Gulls are supposed to be chiefly maritime birds, but this species is a seeming exception. In fact the Rosy Gulls are rarely seen either on the Atlantic or the Pacific coast of the United States, though in winter some of them at least come out along the Gulf coast, and follow it down into South America. But it would seem hard to one who has known it in the sloughs and on the prairies to picture it flying over the ocean, where it could easily be mistaken for the Laughing Gull. HERBERT K. JOB.

BONAPARTE'S GULL

Larus philadelphia (*Ord*)

A. O. U. Number 60 See Color Plate 6

Other Names.— Bonaparte's Rosy Gull; Black-headed Gull; Sea Pigeon.

General Description.— Length, 14 inches. Color, white with pale bluish-gray mantle and dark slate colored head.

Color.—ADULTS IN SUMMER: *Head, dark slate* reaching further in front than behind; *a white patch above and another below eye;* mantle, pale grayish-blue; most of *primaries with black tips;* neck all around, tail, and under parts, pure white, latter rose-tinted; *bill, black;* gape and eyelids carmine; feet, coral-red; webs, vermilion. ADULTS IN WINTER: *No hood;* crown and back of head, mottled with dusky; back of neck with tint of color of mantle; *a crescent before eye and patch on side of head, deep slate;* bill, light-colored at base below; feet, flesh color. YOUNG: No mottling on crown; a patch of dusky on side of head; wing-coverts and shoulders, dusky-brown with lighter edges; primaries and secondaries, dusky tipped; tail white with a subterminal dusky bar; bill, dull flesh color; feet, light flesh color; iris, brown.

Nest and Eggs.— NEST: On the ground in marshes, usually on elevated hummocks; constructed of small sticks and dead grasses. EGGS: 3, olive-gray with a wreath of dark and light brown spots around large end and some scattered markings of the same color over whole surface.

Distribution.— North America in general; breeds from northwestern Alaska and northern Mackenzie south to British Columbia and Keewatin; winters from Maine to Florida: on the Pacific coast from southern British Columbia to Lower California and western Mexico, and on the Gulf coast to Texas and Yucatan; in migration west to Kotzebue Sound and east to Ungava; casual in the Bahamas and Bermuda; accidental in Europe.

Bonaparte's Gull is one of the smaller American Gulls, and unlike most of that family is sometimes found in flocks which often resort to plowed fields and swamps where the birds feed on insects and earth-worms. Its favorite haunts, however, are coasts, rivers, and lakes, where it feeds much after the manner of the Herring Gull. Along the seacoast the Bonapartes are decidedly gregarious and often associate with Terns and other Gulls. Unlike their relatives, however, they are not given to following ferryboats and other craft from which offal and garbage are thrown overboard. In these surroundings their diet is chiefly marine worms and crustaceans which they find on tide flats, in channels, and on kelp-beds.

A peculiarity of this bird's flight, which is graceful and fairly swift, is that each stroke of the wings swings the body slightly upward. Its maneuvers on the wing are often very skillful, especially a trick it has of suddenly stopping its progress and sweeping backward and downward to inspect an object seen on the surface of the water. In general its flight is more like that of the Terns than the Gulls.

BONAPARTE'S GULL (½ nat. size)
Although a shore bird, it is often found in plowed fields feeding on earthworms
Drawing by R. I. Brasher

SABINE'S GULL

Xema sabini (*J. Sabine*)

A. O. U. Number 62 See Color Plate 6

Other Names.— Hawk-tailed Gull; Fork-tailed Gull.

General Description.— Length, 14 inches. Color, white with bluish-gray mantle and dark slate hood. *Tail, forked with the feathers rounded,* not pointed, at the ends.

Color.—Adults in Summer: Heads with hoods of dark slate *bounded behind by a narrow border of black;* mantle, bluish-gray; edge of wing, black; *five outer primaries and their coverts, black* with small white tips; *rest of primaries, white;* outer secondaries, white; the gray of mantle extending diagonally across to end of inner secondaries; neck, tail, and entire under parts, white, the last with rosy hue; bill, black to angle, yellow, chrome, or orange from angle to tip; gape, vermilion; feet, black; iris, reddish; edges of eyelids, orange. Adults in Winter: Entire head, white with some dark feathers on crown and sides; bill, duller; no rosy hue; otherwise as in summer plumage. Young: Head, back of neck, and upper parts in general, transversely barred with slate-gray and dull whitish; under parts, white; tail, white with a bar of black one inch wide on middle feathers, this color narrowing outward; bill, dusky flesh color; legs, flesh color.

Nest and Eggs.— Nest: A depression in moss or sand, lined with fine dry grass. Eggs: 2 or 3, deep olive-brown obscurely spotted and blotched with darker shades of the same.

Distribution.— Arctic regions to South America; breeds on the coast of Alaska from Kuskokwim River to Norton Sound, and in northern Mackenzie, northern Keewatin, and northern Greenland, and on Taimyr Peninsula in northwestern Siberia; in migration on both coasts of United States and casual in interior; winters along the coast of Peru.

Sabine's Gull is essentially an Arctic species, though it occasionally wanders as far south as the North Atlantic States and has been taken as a straggler on Long Island, on the Great Lakes, and on Great Salt Lake, Utah. In any of its plumages it may readily be recognized by its forked tail — whence one of its names. The normal diet of this Gull appears to be composed partly of marine insects, most of which probably are obtained on beaches where they are left by receding waves. The species seems first to have been described by Sabine, from specimens taken by his brother, a member of the Northwest Expedition of 1818, on one of a group of rocky islands off the coast of Greenland.

GEORGE GLADDEN.

TERNS

Order *Longipennes;* family *Laridæ;* subfamily *Sterninæ*

DISTRIBUTED throughout the world are over fifty species of Terns, ten occurring regularly in North America. These birds belong to the family *Laridæ* which includes the Gulls, and is part of the order of Long-winged Swimmers. All of the species are exceedingly graceful and expert on the wing, and some show extraordinary endurance in flight. This is true especially of the Arctic Tern, whose journey from the Arctic to the Antarctic and back each year, is one of the most astonishing known feats in the bird world.

The Terns are often called "Sea Swallows," and for obvious reasons, as several of the species are not unlike large Swallows both in appearance and in flight. They are generally smaller than the Gulls, and their bodies are more elongated, but in coloration they more or less resemble their larger relatives, whom they also resemble in their food and feeding habits, with the exception of their diving practices. The Terns hover and plunge for their food, while the Gulls alight on the water to feed. Because of this characteristic, Terns have often been called "Strikers."

Again like the Gulls, the Terns are decidedly gregarious and often breed in colonies of thousands on ledges; some of the species occasionally place their nests on the limbs of large forest trees. Generally the nests on the grounds are little more than mere depressions, and often they are placed so close together that in walking through a nesting place, it is difficult to avoid treading upon either the eggs or the young. When hatched, the young are covered with down of a mottled pattern, and, although sometimes they will enter the water of their own accord and swim about, they are dependent upon their parents until they acquire the power of flight.

GULL-BILLED TERN

Gelochelidon nilotica (*Linnæus*)

A. O. U. Number 63 See Color Plate 7

Other Names.— Marsh Tern; Egyptian Tern; Nuttall's Tern; Anglican Tern; Nile Tern.

General Description.— Length, 13 to 15 inches. Color, white with light bluish-gray mantle. Bill, *stout and short, and curved over at tip.*

Color.—ADULTS IN SUMMER: *Crown and crest, glossy greenish-black*, extending to level of eyes, leaving only a narrow white line on upper side of bill; mantle, light grayish-blue; primaries, grayish-black but heavily silvered, appearing much lighter; tail, color of mantle fading to pure white at base; chin, throat, neck all around, and under parts, pure white; *bill, black*, usually with narrow yellow tip; legs, greenish-black; iris, brown. ADULTS IN WINTER: The forehead and forepart of crown, white; black restricted to hind head and nape; side of head and a spot in front of eye, gray; otherwise similar to summer plumage.

Nest and Eggs.— NEST: A mere depression among the reeds of marshes; sometimes on sandy shores. EGGS: 3, olive-buff irregularly marked with umber-brown, blackish, and lavender.

Distribution.— Nearly cosmopolitan; breeds in North America, on coasts of Texas, Louisiana, North Carolina, Virginia (formerly to New Jersey), and in the Bahamas; wanders casually to Maine and Ohio; winters in southern Mexico, Central America, and all of South America; breeds also in Europe, Asia, and Australia, wintering to northern Africa.

It seems clear that the Gull-billed Tern is decreasing rapidly in numbers. Once common — or at least not actually rare — along the Atlantic coast, it now, according to Dr. Chapman, seldom, if ever, breeds north of Cobb's Island, Va., where it was found nesting in great numbers by Dr. Ridgway and Dr. Henshaw in 1879. Here Dr. Ridgway noted especially its cry, which he described as a chattering laugh, wherefore he thought it might well be named the Laughing Tern — its scientific name literally means "laughing swallow of the Nile." The same observer noted that the bird showed much more courage in defending its nest than do other Terns; it swooped downward and straight at the intruder, often nearly striking him with its bill, and in its attempt to change its course the rush of the air through its wings made a booming sound not unlike that produced by the Nighthawk when it checks its downward plunge.

This bird differs superficially from its kind in having a shorter and comparatively heavy bill, and a shorter and less distinctly forked tail. It is also less excitable than the Common Tern.

CASPIAN TERN

Sterna caspia *Pallas*

A. O. U. Number 64 See Color Plate 8

Other Names.— Imperial Tern; Caspian Sea Tern.

General Description.— Length, 20 to 23 inches. Color, white with grayish-blue mantle. Tail, *slightly* forked with outer feathers pointed; wings, long and slender.

Color.— Adults in Summer: Crown, glossy greenish-black; a white spot on lower eyelid; mantle, grayish-blue, but so heavily silvered when new as to appear light gray; rest of plumage, pure white; *bill, bright vermilion;* feet, black; iris, brown. Adults in Winter: The crown is broken by white and some dusky feathers show on wing-coverts.

Nest and Eggs.— Nest: A mere hollow scooped in dry sand. Eggs: 2 or 3, pale olive-buff, rather evenly marked with spots of dark brown and lavender.

Distribution.— Nearly cosmopolitan; breeds in North America at Great Slave Lake, Klamath Lake, Oregon, on islands of northern Lake Michigan, on coast of southern Labrador, and on coasts of Texas, Louisiana, Mississippi, South Carolina and (formerly) Virginia; winters from coast of central California to Lower California and western Mexico, and on the South Atlantic and Gulf coasts; casual in migration north to Alaska, James Bay, and Newfoundland.

Photo by W. L. Finley and H. T. Bohlman

COLONY OF CASPIAN TERNS

FORSTER'S TERN

Sterna forsteri *Nuttall*

A. O. U. Number 69 See Color Plate 7

Other Names.— Havell's Tern (immature); Sea Swallow.

General Description.— Length, 15 inches. Color, white with pale grayish-blue mantle. *Tail, forked for half its length.* Not distinguishable from either the Common Tern or the Arctic Tern except with specimens in hand.

Color.— Adults in Summer: Crown, glossy black not extending below eye; mantle, pale grayish-blue; primaries strongly silvered; entire under parts and rump, white; *the two long outside tail-feathers, white on outer web, dusky gray on inner; bill, orange-yellow,* terminal half, black with the extreme tip yellow; feet, bright orange; iris, brown. Adults in Winter: Crown variegated with white; nape, dusky; a distinct black bar on sides of head embracing eyes; outside tail-feathers, shorter than in summer; bill, dusky except at base below; feet, dusky yellowish.

Nest and Eggs.— Nest: In marshes; constructed of dead reeds and stems of water plants and lined with finer reeds. Eggs: 2 or 3, varying from pure white or pale green to warm brownish-drab irregularly spotted with brown, umber, and lilac.

Distribution.— North America at large; breeds in California, Oregon, Nevada, southwestern Saskatchewan, and Manitoba south to northern Colorado, northern Nebraska, northeastern Illinois and southern Ontario, and on the coasts of Texas, Louisiana, and Virginia; winters from southern California, Gulf of Mexico, and South Carolina southward to Guatemala; rare as far north as Massachusetts; casual in Brazil.

The Caspian Terns nest in colonies through the lake region of southern Oregon. They gather on one of the tule islands. We found two of the largest colonies on Lower Klamath and Malheur lakes, where these birds were living near a colony of California and Ring-billed Gulls. When we first visited Lower Klamath Lake, in 1905, we found these Gulls and Terns together with White Pelicans, Farallon Cormorants, Western Grebes, and Great Blue Herons, gathered in what might have been called one immense colony in the tules on the northwest side of the lake. Since that time, however, owing to disturbance, the birds have scattered; the Gulls, Terns, and Grebes have moved their colonies to other parts of the lake.

As one cruises about these lakes, he sees the graceful little Black and Forster's Terns flitting along over the surface, dropping here and there to pick up a bit to eat. The Caspian Tern is much larger than these two and is sometimes mistaken for a Gull. However, the exceedingly long wings, jet-black cap, and deep-red beak are

Photo by W. L. Finley and H. T. Bohlman

FORSTER'S TERN

On nest built on a muskrat house

the distinguishing features of this bird. We soon learned to recognize their harsh call note, for each morning they came flying over the camp, crying *Crack-a-day-o! Crack-a-day-o!*

Forster's Tern is readily recognized by its deeply forked tail; the outer feathers are very long and narrow. As it flits along over the water, its sharp bill is ever pointing downward and its eyes are watching the surface of the water. Because of its beautiful velvety plumage, the long pointed tail- and wing-feathers of this bird were formerly a much-sought adornment for women's hats.

While the Black Tern resembles Forster's Tern somewhat in size, yet Nature has made a striking difference in its dress. It can never be mistaken when once seen, for its fore parts are pure black and the wings and tail slaty-gray. This bird and the Forster Tern differ in their nesting habits from the Caspian, because they do not crowd together in a colony. They are sociable, however, and like company. The nests of both these birds are often a little floating mass of vegetation on the surface of the water, or oftentimes the nest is placed on a muskrat house. Where one nest is found, a few others are likely to be somewhere around in the same locality. I have at times found nests that contained eggs of both Forster's and Caspian Terns.

A peculiar habit of these swallow-like birds tended greatly toward their destruction at the hands of plume hunters. When a hunter shot one of them and it fell wounded to the surface, all the other Terns nearby would be attracted to the bird on the water and they hovered about and served as easy marks for the plumer.

By building a blind in which to hide nearby a colony of Caspian Terns on Malheur Lake, we had a splendid chance to study the home life of these birds. There were several hundred nesting close together, yet housekeeping was in no sense a communal matter. Each bird had its own particular nest spot and the invasion of that place by any other Terns meant a challenge for fight. When the Terns had young, their greatest anxiety seemed to be to keep them crouching low in the nest, so that they would not run away and get lost in the crowd. If a young bird did start to run out of the nest, he was immediately pounced upon by his own parents and pecked and beaten until he dropped flat to the ground or hid in the leaves. If a young bird ran to a neighboring nest or old bird for protection, he received a fusillade of blows that knocked him over. A young bird, therefore, that wandered from his own nest spot was likely to be pecked and beaten to death.

WILLIAM L. FINLEY.

ROYAL TERN

Sterna maxima *Boddaert*

A. O. U. Number 65 See Color Plate 8

Other Name.— Cayenne Tern.

General Description.— Length, 20 inches. Color, white with very pale bluish-gray mantle. A prominent glossy greenish-black crest on back of head.

Description.— ADULTS IN SUMMER: Crown, glossy greenish-black *not extending below eyes;* mantle, very pale bluish-gray, shading to white on rump and ends of inner secondaries; first five primaries with grayish-black spaces toward tips; rest of primaries and most of secondaries, pale pearl-blue; sides of head, chin, throat, rump, tail, and under parts, white; tail, forked for half its length; *bill, orange-red;* feet, blackish; iris, brown. ADULTS IN WINTER: Forehead, white; most of crown, variegated with black and white, the black extending forward on side of head as far as eye; tail, tinged with color of mantle and darkening toward tip into a deeper gray; less forked than in summer.

Nest and Eggs.— NEST: A hollow in the sand. EGGS: 2 or 3, whitish to yellowish-drab, blotched with dark umber, sepia, and lavender.

Distribution.— Tropical coasts north to United States; breeds in West Indies and on south Atlantic and Gulf coasts from Virginia to Texas; wanders casually to Massachusetts; not rare in summer from San Francisco Bay southward to western Mexico; winters from southern California and Gulf of Mexico south to Peru and Brazil, and on west coast of Africa from Gibraltar to Angola.

Because of its large size and conspicuous reddish bill the Royal Tern is one of the most striking birds to be seen along our southern coast. They may easily be distinguished from the smaller Gulls by the manner in which they hold their heads while in flight. A Gull's bill points forward on a plane with its body, while a Tern carries its bill pointed directly downward

Photograph by H. K. Job

Courtesy of Outing Publishing Co.

ROYAL AND CABOT'S TERNS

Air full of them — Battledore Island, Louisiana

like a mosquito. Their food consists chiefly of small fish which they gather by plunging directly into the water, usually from a height of several yards. So much force is put into the blow that the bird often disappears beneath the surface. In Florida these Terns often rob the slow-moving Brown Pelican of his hard-earned prey. They are distinctively birds of the salt water and rarely come inland. They seldom appear in small harbors, and we never find them flying about wharves and fish factories as we do the Gulls.

Like most sea-birds the Royal Terns assemble in colonies to rear their young. Their eggs are laid on the bare sandy islands with no attempt at concealment. No other birds in North America make their nests so near together; in fact, when they are incubating it is often difficult, at a little distance, to see the ground between them, so closely do they sit.

A few years ago I visited a colony nesting on Royal Shoal Island in Pamlico Sound, North Carolina, where probably there were some four thousand eggs scattered about on the sand among the shells. A high tide sometime before had washed at least a thousand of these from their resting places and left them in a great windrow along the beach. The bereaved birds had then moved over to higher ground on the other side of the egg area and scratched out new nesting places. In doing this they took possession of a plot of ground already occupied by a colony of Black Skimmers. They simply kicked the Skimmer's eggs away or covered them with sand and at once took up the duties of incubation serenely indifferent to the mild protestations of the discomfited Skimmers. Usually other species of Terns, and frequently Skimmers and Oyster-catchers, breed on the islands occupied by the Royal Terns but never, so far as I have observed, within the actual boundaries of their colony. The one exception to this is the rare Cabot's Tern which their big neighbors seem to have taken under their special protection. The two species fly together, feed together, nest together, and — perhaps — die together.

The Royal Terns were largely exterminated in many sections of their range by the gunners of the millinery trade some years ago, but under the protection of the wardens of the Audubon Society they are again increasing in numbers. Their chief breeding places today are on the islands off the coast of Virginia, North Carolina, South Carolina, and Louisiana.

T. Gilbert Pearson.

CABOT'S TERN

Sterna sandvicensis acuflavida *Cabot*

A. O. U. Number 67

Other Names.— Sandwich Tern; Kentish Tern; Boys' Tern; Ducal Tern.

General Description.— Length, 16 inches. Color, white with light bluish-gray mantle and tail.

Color.— Adults in Summer: Crown and crest, glossy greenish-black extending below eyes but leaving a space alongside of bill white to the end of the feathers; mantle, light bluish-gray shading on rump and upper tail-coverts into pure white; first four outer primaries with black space near ends; tail, color of mantle; *bill, black, the tip* for about one-half inch *bright yellow;* feet, blackish; iris, brown. Adults in Winter: Crown, white varied with black shaft lines; crest, brownish-black; outside tail-feathers, shorter than in summer; yellow tip of bill less in extent and duller; otherwise as in summer. Young: Forehead, crown, and nape, brownish-black variegated with white, upper parts, marked everywhere with irregular spots and transverse bars of dusky; primaries, as in adult; tail-feathers, tipped with dusky; bill, smaller and weaker, brownish-black, the extreme point only, and sometimes not that much, yellow.

Nest and Eggs.— Nest: On sandy shores, in colonies. Eggs: 2 or 3, creamy or buffy, irregularly spotted and scrawled with dark brown, chestnut, black, and lavender.

Distribution.— North and South America; breeds from North Carolina to Florida and Texas; winters from the Bahamas, Florida, and Louisiana south to Central America, Greater Antilles, Colombia, and Brazil; accidental in Ontario, Massachusetts, New Jersey and Lesser Antilles.

The Cabot's Tern in flight at a distance resembles its more famous relative the Arctic; however, it is a more stoutly built bird; also its tail is relatively shorter, while its head-feathers form a crest, which the bird can make quite conspicuous when it is angry or excited. In diving for its prey it often disappears entirely beneath the surface, and apparently descends to a much greater depth than do other Terns. When breeding in colonies, the Cabot's Terns often place their nests so close together that it is difficult to avoid stepping on them while one is exploring the premises.

Some ornithologists attribute the remarkable variation in the coloration of this Tern's eggs to the fact that they are incubated alternately by the male and the female, one bird being ready to cover the eggs the instant the other leaves them. Under these conditions the law of natural selection cannot operate in such a way as to eliminate an egg of conspicuous coloration, which is true of many Terns' eggs.

There is apparently reliable evidence that these Terns mate for life, and return year after year to the same nesting region, though not necessarily always to the same spot. English observers have noted that the birds change their actual breeding ground from time to time, though apparently the same general colony is likely to return to the same island.

Photo by H. K. Job

CABOT'S TERNS AND EGGS

Breton Island Reservation

COMMON TERN

Sterna hirundo *Linnæus*

A. O. U. Number 70 See Color Plate 7

Other Names.— Sea Swallow; Wilson's Tern; Summer Gull; Mackerel Gull; Lake Erie Gull; Bass-gull; Red-shank.

General Description.— Length, 15 inches. Color, white with mantle of pale pearl-blue.

Color.— Adults in Summer: Crown, lustrous greenish-black extending to lower level of eyes; mantle, pale pearl-blue deepening on back, ending abruptly on rump which, together with upper tail-coverts, is pure white; throat, chin, and sides of head, pure white shading insensibly to a much paler tone of color of mantle on entire under parts; outer primaries, grayish-black strongly silvered; secondaries, pure white shading to grayish-blue on end; *outer pair of tail-feathers, grayish-*

blue on inner webs, grayish-black on outer; rest of tail-feathers with inner webs, pure white, outer webs, pearl-gray; *bill, vermilion on basal half; rest, black with yellow on extreme tip;* feet, coral-red; iris, deep brown. ADULTS IN WINTER: Forehead and most of crown, white; under parts, nearly pure white; bill and feet, duller; otherwise as in summer. IMMATURE: Similar to winter adults, but back mottled or washed with light brownish and bill brownish.

Nest and Eggs.— NEST: Sometimes none, but generally a hollow in the sand lined with grass and dry seaweed. EGGS: 3, greenish-white to deep brown, spotted and blotched with brown, black, and lavender.

Distribution.— Northern hemisphere, northern South America, and Africa; breeds from Great Slave Lake, central Keewatin, and southern Ungava south to southwestern Saskatchewan, northern North Dakota, southern Wisconsin, northern Ohio and North Carolina; winters from Florida southward to Brazil; casual in migration on Pacific coast from British Columbia to Lower California. In eastern hemisphere, breeds in Europe and Asia and winters in India and Africa.

The level rays of the rising sun, coming up from the other side of the world, stream over the heaving sea, lighting up an islet where the surf beats unceasingly upon shifting sands. This islet of recent origin has risen from the sea, thrown up by the surging tempestuous waters of the Atlantic and is destitute of all vegetable life. As our boat lands through the plunging surf a cloud of white birds rises and storms about us with harsh resounding cries. *Tee'-arr, tee'-arr* they call with many variant sounds until all blend in one great monotone of angry entreaty. As we leave the beach a troop of downy young rises and moves toward the farther shore, augmented as it goes by others lying hidden behind every stone or shell or bunch of sea-drift until it seems like a feathered army marching in one continuous front across the isle. As they reach the farther shore they do not hesitate, but throw themselves into the surf, only to be tossed back again drenched and soggy upon the streaming sands. Stand back now, lie quietly down, and watch them swimming, tumbling in the surf, returning to the island, solicitously guarded by their watchful parents. We have found a colony of Common Terns! Now we see that there are many eggs laid on the bare sand or in slight hollows where a few stones or bits of seaweed have been collected by the parent birds.

Where nesting material is plentiful this Tern

Drawing by R. I. Brasher

COMMON TERN (⅓ nat. size)

It is useful to the fisherman, guiding him to schools of edible fish

sometimes builds a substantial nest of sticks, seaweed, and grasses, placing it just above high-water mark along the beach. At times it nests in thick grass on high islands, and on the Magdalen Islands Maynard found it breeding on the tops of grass-topped rocks 200 feet above the sea. The eggs are commonly laid in May or June but many are deposited as late as July. In New England, however, most of the young are able to fly early in August; and then the families join in flocks, leave their breeding places and forage over the country. At this season and in September some of them frequently go up the rivers and sometimes to inland ponds, where they probably find small fry in the warm waters.

In fishing they usually fly with the bill pointing downward, and, when they observe their prey, dive like a flash to the surface, often immersing the head but seldom going entirely under water. Several naturalists have followed the lead of Giraud in asserting that this bird, though web-footed, never dives and rarely swims, appearing to avoid the water, except as it is obliged to descend to the surface to procure food. It is true that it does not, like Gulls, rest often on the surface but in hot weather near its breeding grounds small parties may be seen floating on the waves bathing and throwing the spray about with the abandon and enjoyment of the true waterfowl — and they swim exceedingly well.

These birds are useful to the fishermen as they serve to mark the presence of schools of edible fish. These fish drive the small fry to the surface, the telescopic eyes of the Terns mark the disturbance from afar and when the fishermen see the gathering, plunging flocks they put off

Photo by O. E. Baynard Courtesy of Nat. Asso. Aud. Soc.

EGGS OF COMMON TERN

A hollow in the sand, a few bits of grass and dry seaweed, and the nest is ready for the three eggs

in their boats, well knowing that their work lies there.

This Tern feeds largely on small fry, shrimps and other small crustacea but also at times on grasshoppers and many flying insects.

EDWARD HOWE FORBUSH.

ARCTIC TERN

Sterna paradisæa *Brünnich*

A. O. U. Number 71 See Color Plate 7

Other Names.— Common Tern; Sea Swallow; Paradise Tern; Crimson-billed Tern; Long-tailed Tern; Short-footed Tern; Portland Tern; Pike's Tern.

General Description.— Length, 14 to 17 inches. Color, pale bluish-gray, lighter below.

Color.— ADULTS IN SUMMER: Crown, lustrous greenish-black encroaching on lores so as to leave only a slender white line of feathers on upper side of bill; mantle, pale bluish-gray; under parts, a little lighter shade of color of back, fading into white on chin, throat, and edges of black cap, *ending abruptly at under tail-coverts which are pure white;* outer primaries, silvery-gray; inner webs, mostly white; inner primaries, color of back, broadly tipped with white; tail, very long, pure white, with outer web of outside feather grayish-black; *bill, carmine;* feet, coral-red; iris, brown. ADULTS IN WINTER: Forehead, white; crown, white with narrow black shaft lines, widening behind and merging into solid black on nape; a dark stripe on side of head; under parts, nearly white; otherwise as in summer. IMMATURE: Like winter adult, but tip of bill black

Nest and Eggs.— Not distinguishable from those of the Common Tern.

Distribution.— Nearly cosmopolitan; breeds from Massachusetts north to northern Greenland, across Arctic regions to northern Alaska, and in entire Arctic regions of Europe and Asia; winters in Antarctic Ocean, south to latitude 74°; in migration, Pacific coast south to southern California, and Atlantic coast south to Long Island; accidental in Colorado.

Photograph by H. K. Job

ARCTIC TERNS

Feeding near breeding colony, Matinicue Rock, Maine

The world's migration champion is the Arctic Tern. It deserves its title of "Arctic," for it nests as far north as land has been discovered; that is, as far north as the bird can find anything stable on which to construct its nest. Indeed, so arctic are the conditions under which it breeds that the first nest found by man in this region, only 7½° from the pole, contained a downy chick surrounded by a wall of newly fallen snow that had to be scooped out of the nest by the parent. When the young are full-grown the entire family leaves the Arctic and several months later they are found skirting the edge of the Antarctic continent.

What their track is over that 11,000 miles of intervening space no one knows. A few scattered individuals have been noted along the United States coast south to Long Island, but the great flocks of thousands and thousands of these Terns which range from pole to pole have never been noted by an ornithologist competent to indicate their preferred route and their time schedule. The Arctic Terns arrive in the Far North about June 15, and leave about August 25, thus staying fourteen weeks at the nesting site. They probably spend a few weeks longer in the winter than in the summer home, and this would leave them scarcely twenty weeks for the round trip of 22,000 miles. Not less than 150 miles in a straight line must be their daily task, and this is undoubtedly multiplied several times by their zigzag twistings and turnings in pursuit of food.

The Arctic Tern has more hours of daylight and sunshine than any other animal on the globe. At the most northern nesting site the midnight sun has already appeared before the birds' arrival, and it never sets during their entire stay at the breeding grounds. During two months of their sojourn in the Antarctic the birds do not see a sunset, and for the rest of the time the sun dips only a little way below the horizon and broad daylight is continuous. The birds therefore have twenty-four hours of daylight for at least eight months in the year, and during the other four months have considerably more daylight than darkness.

WELLS W. COOKE, in *Bird Migration.*

ROSEATE TERN

Sterna dougalli *Montagu*

A. O. U. Number 72 See Color Plate 7

Other Names.— Graceful Tern; McDougall's Tern.

General Description.— Length, 15 inches. Color above, pearly-gray; below, delicate rose-pink.

Color— ADULTS IN SUMMER: Crown, glossy black reaching to lower border of eyes; mantle, delicate pale pearly-gray; neck all around and *entire under parts, a delicate rose pink;* primaries, grayish-black strongly silvered; *long tail-feathers, white on both webs;* bill, black, extreme tip, yellow, reddish at base; feet, vermilion; iris, brown. ADULTS IN WINTER: Forehead and cheeks, white; crown, hind head, nape, and sides of head, dusky mottled with white above; below, pure white without rosy tinge; lesser wing-coverts, brownish; tail, less forked, pearly-gray like back; bill, dull black with yellow tip and brown base. IMMATURE: Similar to winter adult.

Nest and Eggs.— Nesting similar and eggs indistinguishable from those of the Common Tern except by comparison.

Distribution.— Temperate and tropical regions; breeds locally from Sable Island to Long Island, N. Y., and from the Bahamas to the Lesser Antilles and Venezuela; formerly from Maine to Florida; rare migrant in Central America; winters from the Bahamas to Brazil; accidental in Ohio; occurs on the coasts of a large part of the eastern hemisphere.

The Roseate Tern is the embodiment of symmetry and grace — its flight the poetry of motion. Its elegant form tapers and swells in lines of beauty. Its lustrous plumage reflects the yellow rays of the sun and the pale refracted light of sea and sands in evanescent pink and rosy tints. These are seen in perfection only in the living bird and fade when the light of life fades from its eyes. The stuffed and distorted specimen on the museum shelf has lost the grace, beauty, and color of the living thing and remains but a sorry travesty of the life that is gone. It seems a bird of ethereal origin, fitted only for the balmy airs of tropic isles but it follows north the coast of both hemispheres and is found in Maine on one side of the Atlantic and in Scotland on the other.

Years ago, when fashion called for its plumage and there was none to save, this bird was almost exterminated on the Atlantic coast. The adults were shot on their breeding grounds and the young left to starve in the nests, but now, under protection, they are beginning to increase and may be found breeding with the Common Terns on isolated islands off the New England coasts. This Tern keeps mostly to the sea and its bays, sounds, and estuaries. Its nest is built often among low vegetation and the young can hardly be distinguished from the downy chicks of the Common Tern. The adult birds, however, are quite different from that species, a little slower and more graceful in flight. They may be readily identified by the black bill, the long graceful white tail, the rosy appearance of the breast and other under parts, and their incisive notes. When excited, they call *hoyit, hoyit,* ending with a prolonged cry, but the alarm note commonly heard is *cac, cac.* In the latitude of New England, about the first of August, the young are well able to fly, and they join the wandering flocks which visit the shores, far and near, before the southern migration begins.

EDWARD HOWE FORBUSH.

LEAST TERN

Sterna antillarum (*Lesson*)

A. O. U. Number 74 See Color Plate 7

Other Names.— Silver Ternlet; Sea Swallow; Little Striker; Little Tern; Minute Tern.

General Description.— Length, 9 inches. Color above, pale grayish-blue; below, satiny-white.

Color.—ADULTS IN SUMMER: Crown, glossy greenish-black with *a narrow white crescent with horns reaching above eyes and extending to bill,* but separated from white of cheeks by a dusky line through eye to bill; entire upper parts, including tail, *pale grayish-blue reaching to the black cap* and fading on sides of head and neck into satiny-white of all under parts; two outer primaries, black with white space on inner webs; rest of primaries, a darker shade of color of back; *bill, yellow tipped with black; feet, orange yellow;* iris, brown. ADULTS IN WINTER: Forehead, lores, and crown, white, the latter with black shaft lines; back of head and nape, dusky, connecting with a narrow streak through eye; hindneck, white; mantle, darker than in summer; edge of wing and a band along forearm, grayish-black; most of primaries, plain dusky.

Nest and Eggs.— NEST: In pebbly depression or on the dry sand of beaches. EGGS: 1 to 4, from pale greenish to dull drab, spotted over entire surface with splashes and dots of different shades of clear brown and some lavender.

Distribution.— Tropical and temperate America; breeds on coast of southern California and on Gulf coast from Texas eastward; also northward to Missouri (formerly Iowa) and northwestern Nebraska; has occurred in Wisconsin and South Dakota; breeds also from the coasts of Massachusetts, Virginia, North Carolina, and Florida south to the Bahamas, West Indies, British Honduras, and Venezuela; now rare everywhere; in migration occurs on the coasts of Lower California and western Mexico; winters from Gulf coast to Venezuela and Peru.

Unquestionably the most dainty of all the American sea-birds is the Least Tern. This petite little creature is adorned with a pair of silvery-gray wings that carry it on long voyages up and down the coast. From its winter home in the tropics it comes north in spring to California and Massachusetts and in both States it finds a summer home. A few pass up the Mississippi valley and it has been recorded as far north as South Dakota. Thirty years ago they swarmed literally by thousands in our Atlantic waters near the shore-line but the feather-hunters made sad work of them. There is a record of ten thousand having been shot for their feathers on Cobb Island, Virginia, in a single season. This was of course done in the summer and the orphaned young were left to perish on the beaches.

At one time large colonies existed in the sounds of North Carolina; but their numbers became so reduced that when the Audubon Society wardens were first established in that territory, in the spring of 1903, only sixteen eggs were laid in the bird colonies that year. They have responded splendidly to protection and although many years must elapse before we can hope to have them as abundant as formerly they are nevertheless increasing in a most encouraging way.

Like the other members of this family they prey mainly upon small fish which they capture by a swift plunge from the air. They do not confine themselves entirely to this diet, however, and often catch such insects as are found flying over the marshes.

Least Terns are usually seen in small scattered

flocks. They are very sympathetic and solicitous about the welfare of their fellows that chance to get into trouble. Any old Tern hunter will tell you that, if one be shot down, its friends will at once come and fly anxiously about emitting their little squeaky cries of anxiety. It was thus often possible to bag almost the entire company. When a flock was seen and the gunners found difficulty in obtaining the first bird to serve as a decoy, they were induced often to approach the boat by the simple expedient of tying a handkerchief to a stick and throwing it into the air. The sight of this object, which at a distance somewhat resembles a falling Tern, usually brought the birds on the run.

Like many other Terns the nest of this species is merely a slight depression hollowed out in the sand. The eggs are usually two in number, although as many as four are found at times. If not disturbed these Terns sometimes become quite tame and on more than one occasion I have been privileged to walk within fifteen feet of a resting bird before it took flight. Mated birds are very attentive to each other, and one of the most charming sights of a visit to a Least Tern colony is to see one of these little, gentle creatures feed his mate as she sits brooding her eggs on the shimmering sandy shore.

T. Gilbert Pearson.

Drawing by R. I. Brasher

LEAST TERN (⅗ nat. size)

The most dainty of all the American sea-birds

BLACK TERN

Hydrochelidon nigra surinamensis (*Gmelin*)

A. O. U. Number 77 See Color Plate 8

Other Names.—American Black Tern; Short-tailed Tern; Semipalmated Tern; Surinam Tern.

General Description.— Length, 9 inches. Upper parts, leaden-gray; head and under parts, black. Bill, very sharp and slender, shorter than head; wings, long and pointed with no distinct markings; tail, short and but slightly forked; feet, webbed only to middle of toes.

Color.— Adults in Summer: *Head and neck and entire under parts as far as the tail-coverts, jet black;* under tail-coverts, pure white; on back of neck and between shoulders the black shades into leaden-gray, which color extends over entire upper parts to the ends of tail-feathers; primaries, grayish-black; outer secondaries similar, inner secondaries like back; shoulder of wing, narrowly white-bordered; *bill, black;* gape, carmine; feet, dark red-brown; iris, brown. Adults in Winter: Forehead, sides of head, neck all around and entire under parts, pure white; crown, mixed gray and white, darker on nape with a dusky stripe above and another behind eye; upper parts, pale lead-gray; many feathers with white edges.

Nest and Eggs.— Nest: On dead reeds in marshes; a careless structure of a few dead sedges and grass. Eggs: 2 to 4, pale brownish-olive heavily marked with blotches and spots of light brown and sepia.

Distribution.— North and South America; breeds from southwestern British Columbia, Great Slave Lake, southern Keewatin, and western Ontario south to inland lakes of California, Nevada, Colorado, northern Missouri, and northern Ohio; rare on east coast of United States in autumn; winters from Mexico to Panama, Peru, and Chile; accidental in Alaska, Nova Scotia, and New Brunswick; casual in West Indies and the Bahamas.

The Black Tern is a species of really unique personality, and might be characterized as the " aquatic swallow " of the sloughs of the northwest. It may be recognized as the dark gray bird with black under parts, in general form and motions not unlike a Purple Martin, which may be seen flitting about over the prairies, especially in the vicinity of wet grounds or sloughs, pursuing insects like any Swallow. In late summer and early autumn these birds gather into large loose flocks, and are very much in evidence. Where the Franklin's Gull is found, the Black Tern hardly can fail to be present, though, as the Tern is much more widely distributed, the converse is not true.

Drawing by R. I. Brasher

BLACK TERN (½ nat. size)

A Tern with many Swallow habits

Here, in these sloughs and marshes, it breeds in abundance, and is one of the last of all to deposit its eggs — about the middle of June. The nest is the merest apology for such, being a slight depression, lined with a few wet stems, on some little hummock of mud or débris which may happen to project from the water. Sometimes the nests are partly floating, but heavy rains must work havoc with them. Two or three eggs are laid.

The parents are very solicitous when their home is approached. They dart about screaming and make angry swoops at the head of the intruder, in fact often striking hard with their bills. More than once I have suffered from their persistent attacks. On one occasion they hit me so hard on the top of the head that, even though I wore a cloth cap, their blows gave me a severe headache. After hatching, the young do not remain long in the frail nests, but quickly take to the water, and swim about through the aquatic vegetation, watched over by their parents, and brooded from time to time wherever they may crawl out upon any convenient spot.

As far as is definitely known, these Terns breed only in the western interior of the United States and Canada. On one occasion, however, when I landed on a low sandy island on the Atlantic coast, near Cape Charles, Virginia, I was surprised to find a considerable number of them, all in full adult plumage, with black breasts. They were with other species of Terns, and acted exactly as on their western breeding-grounds, hovering over me screaming, and dashing furiously at my head. Unfortunately there had been a high storm tide, which had destroyed every nest on this barren sand bar, including those of Forster's Terns and those of Black Skimmers. Both of these latter had constructed new nests and were resentful of intrusion. Where the Black Terns hovered there were little hollows in the sand, lined with grass, smaller than those of the other Terns, just the size that the species constructs in the West. It was unfortunate that I could not return to the island later, as I am positive they must have been breeding there, and this is the only case thus far known of any evidence of their breeding on the Atlantic coast.

Photo by H. K. Job Courtesy of Doubleday, Page & Co.

NEST OF BLACK TERN

The merest apology for a nest, being a slight depression, lined with a few wet stems, on some little hummock which may happen to project from the water

On another occasion also I witnessed a peculiar happening with the species. It is well known that they do not breed until two years old and in full plumage. In their second summer they are in an immature, white-breasted phase. In winter all migrate down into Central and South America, and only a comparative few of the immature plumaged birds of a year old are observed in our borders. In June, 1915, while cruising along the western coast of Louisiana, I saw great clouds of rather small birds, resembling in the distance flights of Golden Plovers such as I had seen many years ago, performing evolutions high in the air, and then settling down on the shores of a sandy inlet back of the outer beach. We managed to land and cross to it, and were amazed to find there swarms of Black Terns, nearly all in the one-year-old plumage, with a very few adults intermingled, fairly covering the flats for probably a couple of miles. There must have been tens of thousands of them, and their identity was proved by collecting a few. This would indicate that the young remain well to the south, not migrating north to any considerable extent until fully mature.

HERBERT K. JOB.

NODDY

Anoüs stolidus (*Linnæus*)

A. O. U. Number 79

General Description.— Length, 16 inches. Color of head and neck, gray; of body, brown. Tail, rounded, the *central* feathers longest.

Color.— Forehead, white; crown, leaden-gray; sides of head and neck all around, bluish-slate with a dark spot in front of eye; rest of plumage, deep brown blackening on wings and tail; bill, black; feet, dark reddish-brown; iris, brown.

Nest and Eggs.— NEST: In low bushes; constructed of sticks, leaves, and grass. EGGS: 1, warm buff, spotted and blotched with reddish-brown and lavender, chiefly around large end.

Distribution.— Tropical coasts. Breeds on Florida Keys, the coast of Louisiana, and in the Bahamas and West Indies; winters south to Brazil and Tristan da Cunha Island.

SOOTY TERN

Sterna fuscata *Linnæus*

A. O. U. Number 75 See Color Plate 7

Other Names.— Egg Bird; Wide-awake.

General Description.— Length, 15 to 17 inches. Color above, black; below, white.

Color.—ADULTS: Entire upper parts, black with a slight greenish-gloss; a white crescent on forehead extending above eyes, separated from white cheeks by a black band from eye obliquely downward and forward to bill; sides of head to eyes, half way around neck, and entire under parts, white; primaries and secondaries, black, lighter on inner webs of former, white on inner webs of latter; long outside tail-feathers, white; bill and feet, black; iris, red. YOUNG: Entire plumage, smoky-brown, grayish on abdomen; upper wing-coverts and shoulders, tipped with white giving a spotty appearance; feathers of back, rump, and upper tail-coverts, margined with dull rufous; primaries and tail, black, the latter but little forked; bill, black above, dull reddish below; eyes and feet, dusky-red.

Nest and Eggs.— On sandy beaches 1 to 3 eggs are dropped with slight attempt at a nest; the eggs are creamy or buff, sparsely spotted and splashed with light brown, Vandyke brown, and lavender.

Distribution.— Tropical and subtropical coasts, except Pacific coast of South America; breeds from Florida, Louisiana, and Texas throughout the Bahamas, West Indies, and tropical islands of the Atlantic; rarely north to Maine; winters from the Gulf coast to Brazil and the Falkland Islands.

As there is more or less similarity in the appearance, habits, and habitat of the Noddy and Sooty Terns it becomes proper as well as convenient to treat the two species together. For most of the following facts, we are indebted to John B. Watson's carefully prepared monograph, "The Behavior of Noddy and Sooty Terns," this being one of the *Papers from the Tortugas Laboratory of the Carnegie Institution of Washington.* Mr. Watson remarks that "extended statements of the instincts and habits of these birds are not extant." The habit of the birds of assembling on islands has been noted by various naturalists and travelers, but nearly all information concerning them has to do with their traits during the nesting season, and little is known of the remainder of their lives. What Mr. Watson records concerning their domestic conduct should, however, receive the careful attention of all who are interested in these comparatively little known birds.

Drawing by R. I. Brasher

NODDY (½ nat. size)

It greets a stranger bird with a nod of the head

Certain of the dictionaries inform the readers that the word "Noddy" means simpleton or fool, and that it is applied to the Tern in question because of the bird's tameness or stupidity, especially when on the nest. How much justification there is for this explanation will appear from Mr. Watson's description of the Noddy's conduct during the nidification period. As he shows, the name undoubtedly has reference to the bird's curious nodding habit, of which he gives the following description:

"This nodding reaction is one of the most interesting and ludicrous acts of the Noddy Tern. It is quite elaborate. Two birds will face each other, one will then bow the head almost to the ground, raise it quickly almost to a vertical position, and then quickly lower it. He will repeat this over and over again with great rapidity. The other bird goes through a similar pantomime. If a stranger bird alights near a group, he salutes those nearest, and is in turn saluted by them. During the pantomime a sound is rarely heard."

Mr. Watson observed these singular birds on Bird Key, a very small coral island about sixty-five miles west of Key West. The Terns arrived for the nesting season during the last week of April. It was observed that their food consisted of small fish of various kinds; that they never swam or dived, and that they never touched the water except when drinking, bathing, or fishing. They drank sea water, which they took on the wing by dipping the opened beak into the sea. They bathed by dipping the breast and head, and did not immerse the whole body. Frequently they followed schools of minnows which were driven to the surface by larger fish, and which they caught with their bills. This fishing was done by groups of Noddies and Sooties to the number of from fifty to one hundred.

Photograph by H. K. Job — Courtesy of Outing Publishing Co.

SOOTY TERN ON NEST

Mr. Watson noted that the Noddies left the island at about daybreak, fished for about two hours, and then returned to relieve their mates, who thereupon flew out to sea for their turn at fishing. Before the single egg is laid the male Noddy does all of the fishing and feeds the female. After the egg is laid the birds relieve each other at intervals of about two hours. During the laying and brooding season the male Sooty probably stays out over the water all day, but during the laying season he returns at night to feed the female, while in the brooding season he relieves the female. It seems probable that the birds feed within fifteen knots of the shore.

The courtship of the Noddy is a curious performance. It is begun by the male, who nods vigorously to the female. She responds by thrusting her bill down his throat while he regurgitates the fish he has caught. Then the male flies away to return presently with a stick, and the nest-building operation is begun without further ceremony. The nest is made of dead branches, or seaweed, or a combination of both, and it may be lined with shells, upon which the eggs are laid. The building may be done jointly by both sexes or, apparently, by either working chiefly unassisted. It is far from true that the brooding bird displays indifference when an intruder approaches, says Mr. Watson. On the contrary, though they may permit a very close approach, even to within handling distance, they strike savagely with their sharp beaks, and Mr. Watson says he has been attacked by the flying birds with such spirit that his hat was knocked off and his scalp cut by their bills. Incubation requires from thirty-two to thirty-five days, and the parents share the labor of feeding the young. The Noddies made use of nests of the previous season, by adding new material; and that this operation, apparently, was repeated several times seemed probable to Mr. Watson, as some of the nests were very large and bulky. But he found no proof that the same pair actually returned to the same nest. Often the birds built in low bushes, but in no instance was the nest placed directly on the ground, for it was noticed that even nests which seemed to be so placed were in reality resting on a worn-down turf of grass.

The nest of the Sooty Tern, on the other hand, was at the most no more than a shallow oval depression, hollowed out of the sand by the bird's claws. Sometimes this nest was fashioned under bayberry bushes, and occasionally a rim of leaves was gathered about the edge, but these leaves were only such as the bird could reach while she was covering the eggs. These birds have very definite ideas about their property rights, according to Mr. Watson. That is, they evidently consider a plot of ground from fourteen inches to two feet square within which their nest is placed as their private premises, and they will leave their eggs or even their young to drive away any other bird that comes within their domains. This jealousy causes almost constant commotion and uproar in the colony; for, if a bird upon returning to its mate does not alight literally within its own yard, and attempts to walk to its own nest, it will be set upon by every other bird through whose premises it passes. Against human intruders, however, it defends its home somewhat less vigorously than does the Noddy. The birds share incubation, and sometimes one will brood the eggs for two days in succession before being relieved. They never rest or swim on the water and, apparently, get so little sleep that they are called the "Wide-awake Terns."

Photo by Herbert Mills Courtesy of Nat. Asso. Aud. Soc.

A NODDY NESTING UPON THE BARE GROUND

Only a few sticks have been gathered around the rim of the nest

---

SKIMMERS

Order *Longipennes;* family *Rynchopidæ*

THE Skimmers constitute a single family, *Rynchopidæ*, which includes five species. Like the Loons and Grebes, they evidently are very old forms, as their fossil remains have been found in Patagonia in the strata of the Tertiary Period. In several respects they strongly resemble the Terns, but they differ from them and from all other birds in the curious structure of the bill, which is long, and much compressed laterally, the lower mandible, which is much longer than the upper, being as thin as a knife-blade. The upper mandible is peculiar in that it is movable. These differences are plainly modifications which fit the bird for its method of capturing its food (shrimps, small fish, and other animal forms) by skimming the surface of the water with the lower mandible, the upper being kept slightly raised meanwhile. This manner of feeding is suggestive of that of the whales. They hunt their food in companies and are partially nocturnal in their habits.

The birds generally are pure white below, and black, with some white tipping of the feathers on the upper parts. Their bodies are from sixteen to about twenty inches long, their wings slender and long, the tail short and slightly forked; the feet are small with the webs between the middle and the inner toes deeply notched.

Skimmers build no nest, but lay three or four eggs in a slight hollow in the sand. The Black Skimmer is the only member of the family which occurs in America.

Photograph of habitat group

Courtesy of American Museum of Natural History

BLACK SKIMMER, EGGS, AND YOUNG

BLACK SKIMMER

Rynchops nigra *Linnæus*

A. O. U. Number 80 See Color Plate 7

Other Names.— Cutwater; Scissorbill; Shearwater; Storm Gull.

General Description.— Length, 16 to 20 inches. Color above, black; below, white.

Color.— Crown, sides of head to below eyes, back of neck, and entire *upper parts, glossy black*; forehead, sides of head below eyes, sides of neck, and whole under parts, pure white with a rosy tint in spring; tips of inner four primaries and secondaries, white; tail, white, the central feathers black; basal half of bill, carmine, rest black; feet, carmine; iris, brown. Downy Young: Sand-colored.

Nest and Eggs.— Eggs: Deposited on the bare sand; 4, white to pale buff, spotted and blotched with dark browns and black and some lavender.

Distribution.— Tropical and temperate America; strictly maritime; breeds from Virginia (formerly New Jersey) to the Gulf coast and Texas; rarely north to the Bay of Fundy; winters from the Gulf coast to Colima, Mexico, and Costa Rica; casual in West Indies.

Five species of the Skimmer family inhabit the warmer portions of the earth. One of these, the Black Skimmer, reaches the shores of the United States and is distributed along the Gulf of Mexico from Texas to Key West, and northward along the Atlantic coast to Virginia. It is a large, long-winged bird, black above and white beneath. The bill of this bird is most unique, both mandibles being thin and flat like a knife-blade, and come together edgewise, and not like a duck's bill. The under one is an inch or more longer than the upper, and this is pushed forward under the surface of the water as the Skimmer with open mouth flies along the sea looking for the small marine animal-life upon which it feeds. In search of food they often follow along the narrow creeks through the marshes and at times enter the outer bays and river-mouths. They never go inland, nor do they travel very far to sea. When Skimmers first appear in spring along our southern beaches they come in flocks of hundreds or even thousands. At this season they are very restless and the flocks are continually taking flight from one beach or bar to another, and their shouts fairly drown the roar of the surf.

They are more or less gregarious throughout the summer, and assemble in colonies to rear their

Photograph by H. K. Job

Courtesy of Outing Publishing Co.

BLACK SKIMMERS

On Battledore Island, Louisiana

young. Their nesting places are situated on sand spits running out from shore or on small isolated islands of sand and sea-shells. The nest is a simple, unlined hollow in the sand which the bird makes by turning its body around many times. The eggs vary from three to five in number and are variously spotted and blotched, no two being exactly alike. If the nests are robbed, a second nest is soon made and another clutch of eggs is laid. Very often groups of breeding Skimmers assemble on the same sandy shore where Terns are nesting, but use a territory more or less separated from that occupied by the Terns. They are poor fighters and are little disposed to defend aggressively their rights. For this reason, and also because they begin to lay well after their neighbors have taken up their household duties, they are forced to take such accommodations as the Terns may deign to leave them. If you approach one of their nesting places the Skimmers will leap into the air and bear down upon you with hoarse cries, but I have never had one come near enough actually to strike me.

One of the local names for these birds is "Shearwaters." Along the Virginia coast they are known as "Storm Gulls." They are never shot for food, but their eggs are regularly taken by fishermen unless the colonies are carefully guarded. T. Gilbert Pearson.

T. GILBERT PEARSON HUNTING YOUNG HERRING GULLS HIDING IN THE WEEDS

Little Duck Island, Maine

ORDER OF TUBE-NOSED SWIMMERS

Order *Tubinares*

NOSTRILS opening through tubes are the distinguishing characteristic of this group of birds. Not only is the order cosmopolitan in distribution, but many of the species are found throughout the world. Two families—the Albatrosses and the Fulmars, Shearwaters, and Petrels—represent the order in North America. In the first of these families the tubes enclosing the nostrils are separated and placed one on either side of the bill; in the other the tubes are connected and are on top of the bill.

An unusual range in size is exhibited by the Tube-nosed Swimmers: the Storm Petrel is the smallest of the natatorial birds, while the Giant Albatross is unsurpassed in wing expanse in the entire bird kingdom. They are unequaled in the power of flight. As a rule they keep far off shore, only visiting land for the purpose of reproduction. They live practically in the air, flying low over the water and snatching their food of marine life and oily matter from the surface of the sea. So far as is known, but one egg is laid each season; some species nest in a burrow, but others lay the egg on the ground. The young are covered with down when hatched, generally of a sooty or gray color, but are helpless and in need of the parents' care for some time.

Birds of this order have no bright markings in their plumage and are usually gray, or black, and white. There are no sexual variations in coloration and the seasonal differences, if any, are undetermined. The plumage is very compact and oily. The wings are long, narrow, and pointed, and the tail rather short. The bill is hooked and enlarged at the tip, the upper mandible being longer than the lower and curved downward. The covering of the bill is in several horny plates, showing seams between. The three front toes are webbed and the hind toe, when present, is small and elevated.

ALBATROSSES

Order *Tubinares;* family *Diomedeidæ*

FEW birds make a stronger appeal to the imagination than do the Albatrosses, with their complete mastery of an art which has been a profound mystery to man until very recent years, and in which he can never hope to be more than a clumsy tyro in comparison with these great conquerors of the air. Much mystery has been made of the evident ease with which these great birds follow a rapidly moving ship for hours or even days at a time, with seldom or never an apparent movement of their wings. But an Albatross is not a supernatural creature and therefore cannot defy the laws of physics. Hence it is obvious that the bird must move as the result of the action of some motive force—either the pressure of the wind on its wings or the movement of the wings themselves. On this interesting subject we have a pretty definitely expressed opinion from a trained naturalist, the late Henry N. Moseley, one of the party of scientists who circumnavigated the globe in the *Challenger* expedition of 1872–1876.

"I believe," wrote Moseley, "that Albatrosses move their wings much oftener than is suspected. They often have the appearance of soaring for long periods after a ship without flapping their wings at all, but if they be very closely watched, very short but extremely

Photograph by J. J. Williams

Courtesy of Massachusetts Board of Agriculture

ALBATROSSES ON LAYSAN ISLAND, H. I.

quick motions of the wings may be detected. The appearance is rather as if the body of the bird dropped a very short distance and rose again. The movements cannot be seen at all unless the bird is exactly on a level with the eye. A very quick stroke, carried even through a very short arc can, of course, supply a large store of fresh momentum. In perfectly calm weather, Albatrosses flap heavily." (*Notes by a Naturalist.*)

Professor Hutton's description (in the *Ibis*) of the flight of the Albatross is probably as accurate as any:— "With outstretched, motionless wings he sails over the surface of the sea, now rising high in air, now with a bold sweep, and wings inclined at an angle with the horizon, descending until the tip of the lower one all but touches the crests of the waves as he skims over them. Suddenly he sees something floating on the water and prepares to alight; but how changed he now is from the noble bird, but a moment before all grace and symmetry. He raises his wings, his head goes back and his back goes in; down drop two enormous webbed feet straddled out to their full extent, and with a hoarse croak, between the cry of a Raven and that of a sheep, he falls 'souse' into the water. Here he is at home again, breasting the waves like a cork. Presently he stretches out his neck, and with a great exertion of his wings runs along the top of the water for seventy or eighty yards, until, at last, having got sufficient impetus, he tucks up his legs, and is once more fairly launched in the air."

Moseley's statement that Albatrosses flap heavily in calm weather should set at rest the oft-reported assertion that they never move their wings in flight, while the observation that there is actually some occasional movement even when the wings seem to be motionless must, of course, be accepted as entirely accurate, even though that acceptance necessarily destroys the cherished notion that the bird has and exercises supernatural powers. But even after it has been explained in perfectly cold-blooded scientific language, there should be enough of the truly remarkable left in the flight of the Albatross to create a profound impression upon any mind which does not insist upon seeing the supernatural where it does not exist. These notions of the supernatural are, of course, especially prevalent among sailors, who are famous for the variety and picturesqueness of their superstitions. And we are indebted to their Albatross superstition for having inspired Samuel Taylor Coleridge to write "The Rime of the Ancient Mariner," which, so Swinburne says, "for melody and splendor it were hardly rash to call the first poem in the language."

About sixteen species of the Albatross are known, and all are essentially birds of the subtropical or southern tropical seas, although the Black-footed and Laysan species sometimes wander as far north as Alaska, and either is occasionally seen off the Pacific coast of the United States. Though their wings when extended may measure twelve feet, or even more, their bodies rarely weigh more than eighteen pounds. The food of these great birds consists of fish, cuttlefish, jellyfish, offal, and refuse thrown overboard from the ships they follow. Such matter they seize eagerly, a habit which is taken advantage of by brutal or thoughtless persons who catch the bird by trolling with a long line and a hook baited with meat or fish.

BLACK-FOOTED ALBATROSS

Diomedea nigripes *Audubon*

A. O. U. Number 81

Other Name.— Goony.

General Description.— Length, 30 to 36 inches. Color above, dark chocolate-brown; below, gray. Tail, short; wings, very long and when folded reaching to or beyond tip of tail.

Color.— ADULTS: Top of head and upper parts, dark chocolate-brown; leaden-gray below whitening on front of head and at base of tail; a spot in front of eye and streak above it, black; feathers of upper parts with paler edges; bill, dusky; *feet, black*. YOUNG: Similar to adult, but less white on face, and upper tail-coverts dusky.

Nest and Eggs.— NEST: On the ground, usually on isolated islands of the ocean; there is little attempt at nest building, the single egg being surrounded merely by seaweed.

Distribution.— North Pacific; breeds on islands northwest of Hawaii and on Marshall Islands; occurs off the coast from southern Alaska to California and western Mexico, and off coasts of China and Japan.

I have a distinct picture in mind, when out on the Pacific, of a big dark long-winged bird coasting down the troughs of the waves and aëroplaning over the mountainous crests. I scarcely ever saw the bird light and feed on the water, yet of course, it follows the ship for scraps. The bird is more a part of the sea than the Gull. It curves in great circles over the maddened sea purely for the love of flying. I asked its name of one of the sailors and he called it a "Goony." I told him it was a Black-footed Albatross.

The Albatross will always be known in English literature through Coleridge's poem, "The Ancient Mariner." What a lesson against the wanton killing of a friendly bird!

WILLIAM L. FINLEY.

LAYSAN ALBATROSS

Diomedea immutabilis *Rothschild*

A. O. U. Number 82.1

General Description.— Length, 3 feet. Color above, smoky-brown; color below, white. Tail, short; wings, very long and when folded reaching to or beyond tip of tail.

Color.— Head, neck, lower rump, and under parts, white; back and shoulders, smoky-brown; wings and their coverts, blackish-brown; tail, black shading to white at base; bill, gray, blackish at tip, yellow at base below; feet, fleshy-pink; iris, brown.

Nest and Eggs.— The single egg is deposited on the ground on Laysan and adjacent islands of the North Pacific.

Distribution.— Laysan and Midway islands to San Geronimo and Guadalupe islands, Lower California.

The Laysan is the Albatross whose ruthless slaughter and narrow escape from complete extinction constitute an episode revealing the most heartless and hideous brutality ever perpetrated by man upon the bird-world, which is saying much. The island of Laysan, which gives its name to this beautiful and interesting species of one of the most wonderful of all the birds, lies in the Pacific Ocean about 700 miles west by north of Honolulu. It is barren, except for a scanty growth of shrubs, and therefore has never been inhabited by man, but for a great many years had been the home and breeding place of the Laysan Albatross, the Black-footed Albatross, the Sooty, White, Noddy, and Hawaiian Terns, the Bonin Petrel, two species of Shearwater, the Red-tailed Tropic-bird, two species of Booby, and the Man-o'-war-bird. A photograph of the island, taken in 1909, shows a great plain, about a mile in area, not only covered, but actually crowded, chiefly with Laysan Albatrosses.

For several years guano had been shipped from this island, and the Albatrosses were robbed more or less persistently of their eggs, but were not otherwise seriously molested. Then came the episode referred to above, which is described by Dr. William T. Hornaday in his book *Our Vanishing Wild Life:*

"At last, however, a tentacle of the feather trade octopus reached out to Laysan. In an evil moment in the spring of 1909, a predatory individual of Honolulu and elsewhere, named Max Schlemmer, decided that the wings of those Albatrosses, Gulls, and Terns should be torn off and sent to Japan, whence they would undoubtedly be shipped to Paris, the special market for the wings of sea-birds slaughtered in the Pacific. Schlemmer the Slaughterer bought a cheap vessel, hired twenty-three phlegmatic and cold-blooded Japanese laborers, and organized a raid on Laysan. With the utmost secrecy he sailed from Honolulu, landed his bird-killers upon the sea-bird wonderland, and turned them loose upon the birds. For several months they slaughtered diligently and without mercy. Apparently it was the ambition of Schlemmer to kill every bird on the island.

"By the time the bird butchers had accumulated between three and four carloads of wings, and the carnage was half finished, William A. Bryan, professor of zoölogy in the College of Honolulu, heard of it and promptly wired the United States Government. Without the loss of a moment the Secretary of the Navy dispatched the revenue cutter *Thetis* to the shambles of Laysan. When Captain Jacobs arrived he found that in round numbers about three hundred thousand birds had been destroyed, and all that remained of them were several acres of bones and dead bodies, and about three carloads of wings, feathers and skins. The twenty-three Japanese poachers were arrested and taken to Honolulu for trial, and the *Thetis* also brought away all of the stolen wings and plumage, with the exception of a shedful of wings that had to be left behind on account of lack of carrying space."

In 1911, the Iowa State University sent to Laysan a scientific expedition under charge of Professor Homer R. Dill. His report on the conditions he found is a terrible indictment, from which the following may be quoted: "An old cistern back of one of the buildings tells a story of cruelty that surpasses anything else done by these heartless, sanguinary pirates, not excepting the practice of cutting wings from living birds and leaving them to die of hemorrhage. In this dry cistern the living birds were kept by hundreds to slowly starve to death. In this way the fatty tissue lying next to the skin was used up, and the skin was left quite free from grease so that it required little or no cleaning during preparation. Many other revolting sights, such as the remains of young birds that had been left to starve, and birds with broken wings and deformed beaks were to be seen. Killing clubs, nets, and other implements used by these marauders were lying all about.

"This wholesale killing has had an appalling effect upon the colony. It is conservative to say that fully one-half the number of birds of both species of Albatross that were so abundant in 1903 have been killed. The colonies that remain are in a sadly decimated condition."

The prompt and effective interference of the Government was due to the fact that in February, 1909, President Roosevelt issued an executive order creating the Hawaiian Island Reservation for Birds, which includes Laysan Island and several other islands and reefs. But for that interference, the Laysan Albatross might have been reduced to a point which would have seriously threatened it with extermination.

Scientifically the Albatross is best known through Mr. Walter K. Fisher's photographs and descriptions. In May, 1902, he visited the Island of Laysan, where he found the Black-footed and Laysan Albatrosses breeding in great numbers. His account of their nesting habits, courting antics, and peculiar dances is well worth reading.

In the *Auk* for January, 1904, he writes: "The Albatross lays one egg on the ground, usually in a slightly raised mound with a shallow basin in the top. . . . The egg is laid about the middle of November. . . . The young are not hatched until February, and then begin the six months of hard work to feed the hungry babies. They grow slowly, for birds, and it is not till the last of July that the most venturesome follow their parents on short flights to the sea. A few weeks later all are on the wing, and with the old birds they scatter far and wide over the Pacific."

Speaking of the peculiar dance of the Albatrosses, Mr. Fisher says, "The old birds have an innate objection to idleness, and so for their diversion they spend much time in a curious dance, or perhaps more appropriately a 'cake-walk.' . . . At first two birds approach one another, bowing profoundly and stepping heavily. They swagger about each other, courtesying solemnly, then suddenly begin to fence a little, crossing bills and whetting them together, sometimes with a whistling sound, meanwhile pecking and dropping stiff little bows. All at once one lifts its closed wing and nibbles at the feathers beneath, or rarely, if in a hurry, quickly turns its head. The partner during this short performance assumes a statuesque pose, and either looks mechanically from side to side, or snaps its bill loudly a few times. Then, the first bird bows once, and pointing its head and beak straight upward, rises on its toes, puffs out its breast, and utters a prolonged nasal *Ah-h-h-h*, with a rapidly rising inflection and bovine quality. . . . Often both birds raise their heads in air and favor the appreciative audience with that ridiculous and indescribable bovine groan. . . . Occasionally while 'cake-walking' one will lightly pick up a straw or twig, and present it to the other, who does not accept the gift, however, but thereupon returns the compliment, when straws are promptly dropped, and all hands begin bowing and walking about as if their very lives depended upon it." GEORGE GLADDEN.

FULMARS, SHEARWATERS, AND PETRELS

Order *Tubinares;* family *Procellariidæ*

THE Fulmars, Shearwaters, and Petrels are the family *Procellariidæ* and with the Albatrosses form the order of Tube-nosed Swimmers. As the name of the order indicates, its chief point of difference from all other orders is the tubular form of the nostrils. Other characteristics are: the bill, hooked and enlarged at the tip and with the upper section longer than the lower and with the covering in several horny sections; the tail, rather short with twelve or fourteen feathers; the wings, usually long and pointed; and the hind toe, either small or lacking, and, if present, elevated. The plumage is compact and oily and shows a tendency toward uniformity in coloration. Often the bodies of the birds in this family are so fat that they can be used for illumination.

Over the oceans of the world are distributed nearly one hundred members of this family. About thirty-five are of regular or accidental occurrence in North America. Not a member is ever found inland unless driven there by a storm. Neither do any of them frequent the shores except for the purpose of reproduction. They spend practically all their time on the wing, and gather their food of marine animals and oily matter from the surface of the water.

So far as is known, the members of this group lay only a single egg. The Fulmars nest in colonies, like the Gulls, on the small islands near the shores of the North Pacific and North Atlantic. Of the nesting habits of the Shearwaters, very little is known; some breed on the islands of the North Atlantic, and it is probable that others breed on the islands of the southern hemisphere, coming north as the southern winter sets in. Some of the Petrels breed in the northern hemisphere and others in the southern. The species in this group concerning whose nesting habits we do know something usually deposit the lone egg in a burrow or a cavity. The young when hatched are covered with down, usually of a grayish color, and are cared for in the nest. At first they are fed by regurgitation on an oily fluid.

FULMAR

Fulmarus glacialis glacialis (*Linnæus*)

A. O. U. Number 86

Other Names.— Fulmar Petrel; Molly Hawk; John Down; Sea Horse; Mollimoke; Mallemuck; Noddy.

Length.— 18 to 20 inches.

Color.— Light Phase: Mantle, pale bluish-gray restricted to back and wings or extending also on head and tail; primaries and secondaries, dark ashy-brown; a dark spot in front of eye; rest of plumage, pure white; bill, yellow, tinged with green above and below; feet, pale gray; iris, brown. Dark Phase: Entire plumage, smoky-gray, paler below; feathers of upper parts, with darker margins; primaries, ashy-brown; bill, dull yellow; feet, dusky-gray; iris, brown.

Nest and Eggs.— The single white egg is deposited in a crevice of the rock.

Distribution.— North Atlantic; breeds from northern Greenland to Cumberland Sound, and east at least to Franz Josef Land; ranges north to latitude 85° and west to Melville Island; winters south to fishing banks off Newfoundland and to Georges Bank off Massachusetts, rarely to New Jersey.

The Fulmar is a circumpolar bird of the northern hemisphere. It breeds in countless numbers in Greenland, Franz Josef Land, Baffin Bay, Iceland, Spitzbergen, St. Kilda, and other regions throughout the northland. It is one of the largest of its family in the northern hemisphere, and an untrained or careless observer might mistake it for a Gull, but its peculiarly constructed bill separates it distinctly from that family, and puts it among the so-called "Tube-nosed Swimmers." Moreover, its flight is much more like that of the Albatross and differs sharply from that of the Shearwaters and Petrels. As Percy R. Lowe says (in *Our Common Sea-birds*): "With outspread wings, stretched stiff as a board, it will remain poised and balanced against a strong half-gale, or glide through the air with wonderful grace by the minutes together, now skimming over the crests of the waves or following down into their deep troughs, now stopping to alight, feet first, on the surface, in order to pick up some scrap food or some mollusk which it has espied. In coloration, too, the Fulmar approaches more nearly to the Albatross than to the rest of its family," while in nesting habits it "seems intermediate between the Albatross, which nests on the flat oceanic islands in the open, and the true Petrels, which nest in holes or burrows in the ground or loose rocks."

Another peculiarity of this bird is that it is almost voiceless. Even when its nesting places are invaded and hundreds or even thousands of the Fulmars take to their wings, they sail about in utter silence, like so many ghosts of birds. They are strictly pelagic in their habits except during the breeding season. On the ocean they are much given to following whaling ships for the blubber and oily scraps thrown overboard. This food they seem never to eat while on the wing, but invariably to devour it while floating on the surface of the water, after the practice of the Albatross. To the crews of the whalers and sealers the bird is well known, and to them it owes the names of "Mollimoke" and "Noddy."

GREATER SHEARWATER

Puffinus gravis (*O'Reilly*)

A. O. U. Number 89

Other Names.— Hagdon; Hag; Haglet; Wandering Shearwater; Common Atlantic Shearwater; Cinereous Puffin.

General Description.— Length, 18 to 20 inches; spread of wings, 36 to 45 inches. Color above, dark brown; below, white.

Color.— Upper parts, dark brown, shading on head to grayish-brown; usually lighter on hindneck, darkest on inner secondaries and rump, the feathers of back, rump, and wing-coverts edged with pale brownish-ash; crown, uniform brown extending on sides of head to level of gape, with line of demarcation from white

Drawing by R. I. Brasher

GREATER SHEARWATER (½ nat. size)

One of the "stiff-winged" flyers of the ocean

of throat distinct; upper tail-coverts, white with dusky bars or centers; primaries, brownish-black, lightening toward base; entire under parts, white with large dark brown patches on sides and flanks; *under tail-coverts, dark grayish-brown* with white tips; tail, brownish-black; bill, dusky horn color; feet, yellowish flesh color; iris, brown.

Nest and Eggs.— Little is known concerning its nesting: it is supposed to breed in a burrow on islands of the north Atlantic, laying a single white or yellowish-white egg.

Distribution.—Atlantic Ocean, from Arctic circle south to Cape Horn and Cape of Good Hope; occurs off the eastern coast of North America from June to November; occasionally visits the British Isles during the autumn months.

From the firm deck of a great ship out under the vast circle of the sky, surrounded by the heaving, racing ocean swells, the heart sickens at the thought of being left there alone. But to the Shearwater this is home. It needs no companionship and seeks none. On long slender wings, extending some three feet, it goes on, almost ever on, upon its lonely course. A series of rapid beats give it momentum for a prolonged glide upon stiffly extended pinions, even into the very teeth of the gale. Tipping to one side, the better to trim sail, it skims along never to reach a destination, for it seems always going, never arriving.

Photo by H. K. Job Courtesy of Outing Pub. Co.

GREATER SHEARWATER

Off the coast of Massachusetts

Such is the rather large gray sea-bird with white breast which we may meet from late spring to advanced autumn well off our Atlantic shores, hardly nearer than where land appears only as a distant haze. Though this is the most common of our Shearwaters, few of our human kind are privileged to enter its select social circle. Deep-water fishermen know the birds well, calling them "Hags" or "Haglets." Floating offal or grease thrown from the vessel, especially when anchored on the fishing-grounds, sometimes draws quite a concourse. At such times they can be enticed very close, and can even be caught with hook and line and be drawn squealing and fighting upon deck, from the hard surface of which they are unable to take wing.

In calm weather they can be seen resting on the water, and it is one of the few occasions when they seem really social, sitting around and chattering to one another. At such times they take to wing with some difficulty, for want of wind, and I have almost run them down by steering straight for them.

Their food, besides floating animal or vegetable matter, consists of various marine organisms, particularly small fish. The appearance of a school of the latter will quickly, as though by magic, draw a crowd, even though few or none may have been previously noticed. They plunge headlong into the water and flap about as though mad, or else remain on wing and patter with their feet over the surface. The frightened fish submerge, and immediately each bird is off on its lonely wanderings.

No one has yet discovered the breeding haunts of this singular creature, but they are undoubtedly on some desolate Antarctic island where, in a burrow or a hole in the rocks, the female deposits one large white egg, after the usual Shearwater manner. The southern summer, when they nest, is our northern winter. When nesting time is over, and the only bond but death strong enough to keep them quiet is relaxed, they renew their roaming. Oceans are hardly wide enough to circumscribe their energy, and thus, driven by the returning wanderlust, they visit us during our warmer months.

The best places to find Shearwaters, as well as the other " ocean wanderers," apparently are the fishing " banks," where fishing vessels congregate. I have found them in considerable numbers five to ten miles or more southeastward off Chatham, Mass., and off Cape Sable, Nova Scotia. Fishermen report them abundant on Georges, Grand, and other banks. Though seen from May or June to November, the period of July to September seems to represent the height of their season with us. HERBERT K. JOB.

SOOTY SHEARWATER

Puffinus griseus (*Gmelin*)

A. O. U. Number 95

Other Names.—Black Hag; Black Hagdon; Dark-bodied Shearwater.

General Description.—Length, 16 to 18 inches; spread of wings, 40 inches. Plumage, dark sooty-brown above and below.

Color.—*Uniform dark sooty-brown, blackening on wings and tail;* more sooty-gray below with paler throat; bill, dusky-bluish horn, the tube, ridge, and bill blackish; inside of leg and upper side of feet, flesh color; outside of outer toe and under side of feet, blackish.

Nest and Eggs.—Nest: Probably a burrow in the ground on sea islands of the South Atlantic, a single white egg being deposited at the end of the burrow.

Distribution.—Oceans of southern hemisphere; occurs in summer on the Pacific coast from southern Alaska to Lower California, and on the Atlantic coast from Gulf of St. Lawrence to South Carolina.

Photograph by H. K. Job Courtesy of Doubleday, Page & Co.

SOOTY SHEARWATER (foreground) AND GREATER SHEARWATER

CORY'S SHEARWATER

Puffinus borealis *Cory*

A. O. U. Number 88

General Description.— Length, 20 inches; spread of wings, 40 to 45 inches. Color above, brownish-ash; below, white.

Color.— Upper parts, brownish-ash; feathers of back, with pale tips; those on nape and sides of neck narrowly tipped with white; the ash on sides of head and neck and white of under parts gradually mingle; *tips of upper tail-coverts, white;* under eyelid, white in contrast with ashy-gray of head; wings and tail, brownish-gray; sides and flanks, tinged with ash; under tail-coverts, white, the longest tinged near ends with ash which extends nearly to tips of the longest tail-feathers; bill, greenish-black, yellow at base and on tip; feet, greenish-black; iris, brown.

Nest and Eggs.— Unknown but probably similar to others of the genus.

Distribution.— Coasts of Massachusetts, Rhode Island, and Long Island (August to November).

Somewhat smaller than the Greater Shearwater, the Sooty Shearwater very closely resembles it in habits and flight, but differs from it markedly in plumage, which at a distance looks as black as that of a Crow. It would seem decidedly strange that this bird escaped entirely the notice of Wilson, Nuttall, and Audubon, but for the fact that even now its nesting habits are unknown, nor have its nest and eggs been discovered.

Cory's Shearwater is even more a stranger; it has been seen only off the Atlantic coast between Massachusetts and Long Island, from August to November.

WILSON'S PETREL

Oceanites oceanicus (*Kuhl*)

A. O. U. Number 109

Other Names.— Common Stormy Petrel; Mother Carey's Chicken; Long-legged Storm Petrel.

General Description.— Length, 7 inches. Color, dark sooty-brown. *Legs, long and stilt-like; tail, square.*

Color.— Body, dark sooty-brown; wings and tail, black; wing-coverts, pale gray; upper and under tail-coverts, sides of rump, and base of tail, white; bill and feet, black, *latter with a large yellow spot on webs;* iris, brown.

Nest and Eggs.— Nest: In burrows or in crevices on Antarctic islands in February. Eggs: 1, white.

Distribution.— South polar regions north to Labrador and British Isles; common off the north Atlantic coast of America from May to September; accidental in Ontario.

Nearly everyone who crosses the Atlantic or makes a coasting voyage must have noticed those tiny dark-colored birds about the size of Swallows, with a conspicuous patch of white on the rump. On rapidly fluttering wing they circle about the vessel, or wander irregularly over the waves. At times they hover at some particular spot, pattering their feet in the unstable element while a-wing. These are Petrels, often called "Mother Carey's Chickens." They are so distinct from all other birds that no one who gets a fair look could possibly mistake them. The first ones are sighted several miles off shore, and they are quite inclined to follow vessels far out on the open ocean. They are birds whose home is on the ocean waves. Some of their scientific Latin names appropriately describe them as "runners on the sea."

Two species represent their kind on our Atlantic coast. One is slightly the larger with a forked tail, and is known as Leach's Petrel. The other, which has the tail square or slightly rounded at the end, is Wilson's Petrel. It is the species mostly seen off shore during our summer season. Like their relatives the Shearwaters, they breed on the far southern islands of the

Drawing by R. I. Brasher

WILSON'S PETREL (½ nat. size)

Its home is on the ocean's waves

Antarctic, nesting in February and laying a single white egg in a burrow. For a winter tour they wander thousands of miles and enjoy our northern summer, from about June to October.

Being summer tourists with us, they are better known than though they came with Boreas, and for the same reason it is this species which is generally observed in summer south of the latitude of Maine, as the other species is a northern breeder. Excursionists from New York City to the lower bay often see these birds in considerable numbers. One year, on July 13, a roasting hot day ashore, I was refreshed and delighted with the constant sight of these Petrels from the steamer flying between the heated wilderness of bricks and the New Jersey shore resorts. Sometimes I have almost lived with them while fishing offshore from Chatham, Mass. It was more fun than fishing to throw out fish liver, which floats, and draw the Petrels by scores around the stern. Especially on calm days they would come up so close that I have seen them caught by hand. It afforded splendid opportunity to watch them at close range as they emulated the Apostle Peter, from whom they are named because of their curious propensity to " walk " on the water. When caught they proved very unapostolic, and vomited up liver or ejected thus or from their nostrils some dark yellow, strongly scented oil. As they flew and fed so close at hand, their pretty little twittering was very noticeable.

The marvel of these birds is their well-nigh ceaseless activity. On a very few occasions, when the weather was calm and lowery, especially before storm, I have seen flocks of them huddled together upon the ocean " floor." At other times, one sees only that eternally restless

Photo by H. K. Job Courtesy of Houghton Mifflin Co.

WILSON'S PETRELS

" Walking " on the water

wandering, quartering over the ocean to pick up oily refuse or small marine life. When waves rage and break, they evidently must remain on the wing day and night. This is a life only for those to whom weariness is foreign.

HERBERT K. JOB.

LEACH'S PETREL

Oceanodroma leucorhoa (*Vieillot*)

A. O. U. Number 106

Other Names.— Common Fork-tailed Petrel; Leach's Fork-tailed Petrel; White-rumped Petrel.

General Description.— Length, 8 inches. Color, brownish-black. *Legs, short; tail, forked,* outer feathers more than ½ inch longer than middle pair.

Color.— Brownish-black, grayer on wing-coverts and below; primaries, black; upper tail-coverts, pure white; bill and feet, black; iris, brown.

Nest and Eggs.— NEST: In burrows on the ground. EGGS: Single, white, unmarked, or wreathed with fine light red spots around the larger end.

Distribution.— Both coasts of North America; breeds from the Aleutian and Copper islands, Bering Sea, south to Sitka, and from southern Greenland south to Maine and the Hebrides; casual in migration south to Virginia.

Leach's Petrel and Wilson's Petrel are supplementary each of the other. The former breeds north, the other south, but the latter meets its relative in the summer near its breeding grounds. The fact that I have never been able — perhaps partly from lack of abundance of opportunity — to meet any Petrels off our Atlantic coast in winter makes me wonder whether some day Leach's may not be found to return the compliment and visit its relative in its remote southern home.

All the Petrels I have identified off southern New England shores in summer have been Wilson's, which is natural enough, since Leach's is not known to breed south of Maine. There and northward I have found it nesting. Hundreds of them resort to the same barren islands. In the turf each pair digs a little burrow the size of a rat-hole, and about the middle of June each hole contains a single fragile white egg. As we land there is not a sign of a bird. But sometimes we can smell the peculiar odor like that of the oil they eject, characteristic and persistent and which lasts in mounted specimens for years.

Photo by H. K. Job

LEACH'S PETREL

Young and egg removed from burrow

Presently we notice the little holes, which run almost horizontally, just below the roots of the grass. A hand inserted up to the elbow lands in a little chamber where the brooding bird is now imprisoned. At the beginning of the breeding season I have found both male and female in the burrow; later, only one, which may be of either sex, as both sexes incubate. The other partner is supposed to be out at sea, but it is a curious fact that in daytime no Petrels are seen in the vicinity of the islands where they breed. Nor have they been proved to remain in other burrows or hide in holes of the rocks. After dusk the Petrels emerge from their burrows, and there are lively times. Dark forms dart around like bats, twittering, and also uttering a singular little plaintive " song," as it may well be called.

Where animals, such as dogs or cats, are kept by fishermen or lighthouse keepers on islands, I have found that they make a regular practice of digging out and eating Petrels, until the colonies are depleted or exterminated. Such practices should be prevented.

Later in the summer, investigation of the holes reveals the presence of soft, fuzzy young, covered with thick coats of gray down, lighter in color than the parents. I have found them as late as September without a single feather — perhaps the result of robbery of the nests. Such occurrences might have given rise to an old superstition that Petrels hibernate. Winter apparently drives them at least further south than our bleak north Atlantic coast.

Once I tried to make a captured Petrel of this species sit for its picture. Its ceaseless activity was something astonishing. No wonder it can outlast gales and billows in many a test of endurance.

Herbert K. Job.

FORKED-TAILED PETREL

Oceanodroma furcata (*Gmelin*)

A. O. U. Number 105

Description.— Length, 9 inches. General color, *light bluish-gray,* fading to white on chin, throat, and under tail-coverts; bend of wing and space around eye, dusky; bill and feet, black. Tail, slightly forked; bill, small and weak.

Nest and Eggs.— Nest: A hole in a bank; thinly lined with dry grass and fine roots. Eggs: Single, dull white with minute dark specks evenly dusted over the large end.

Distribution.— North Pacific and adjacent Arctic Ocean; breeds from Commander and Aleutian islands south to islands off Oregon; in migration occurs on both shores of Bering Sea north to Kotzebue Sound; wanders south to San Pedro, California.

KAEDING'S PETREL

Oceanodroma kaedingi *Anthony*

A. O. U. Number 105.2

Description.—Length, 8 inches. General color, *sooty-black;* upper tail-coverts and side of under coverts, white; wing-coverts, brownish; bill and feet, black. Tail, slightly forked; bill, small and weak. Similar to the Forked-tailed Petrel, but smaller in size and darker in color.

Nest and Eggs.— Nest: A burrow in a bank or under a pile of stones; lined with grass, pieces of bark, or chips of wood. Eggs: Single, white.

Distribution.— Pacific coast of North America; breeds on islands off Washington, Oregon, and California from Cape Flattery south to the Farallons; in migration south to Guadalope, Socorro, and Clarion islands.

On Three Arch Rocks off the Oregon coast, we found both the Forked-tailed and the Kaeding Petrels nesting. The latter birds, however, were far more abundant than the former. One might remain about these rocks for a month, climbing over them every day, and not know that a Petrel is there, for they are never seen flying about the rocks in daytime.

We climbed to the grassy slope on the north side of the outer rock. My first acquaintance with these two birds was when I dropped on my knees and dug out a single white egg. Then, as I dug a little farther, I saw a Kaeding's Petrel that had crawled back in the extreme corner to hide.

The Petrel nestling is a fluffy ball of down. One parent stays in the burrow with the nestling during the day, while the other is far out on the ocean. The parent feeds the young by thrusting the beak down his mouth and injecting into it a yellowish fluid. Both old birds are experts at this. If you take one out of the burrow, he will immediately " play Jonah " in your direction with surprising power of projection. A dose of rancid fish oil shot up your sleeve is not pleasing to your nerves or your nostrils.

I shall never forget the evening we made a dangerous trip to the top of the rock and hid on the north slope. As it grew dark, the Petrels began coming in to the island like a swarm of bats. Those in the burrows came chittering out to meet them. The ground beneath seemed full of squeakings and the air full of soft twittering and whistlings until it felt uncanny. We frequently felt the breath of swift wings, but it was like a fantasy, for not a bird could be seen, nor even a shadow. How one of these Petrels could find his own home and his mate in an acre of nesting holes hidden all about in the grass and in the darkness of night is one of those mysterious things that we cannot solve.

WILLIAM L. FINLEY.

STORM PETREL

Thalassidroma pelagica (*Linnæus*)

A. O. U. Number 104

Other Name.— Mother Carey's Chicken.

General Description.— Length, 5½ inches. Color, brownish-black. *Legs, short; tail, square.*

Color.— Glossy brownish-black, browner below; *upper tail-coverts, white with black tips;* under tail-coverts, streaked with white; bill and feet, black; iris, brown.

Nest and Eggs.— NEST: Holes excavated by the bird under rocks. EGGS: One, white.

Distribution.— Easterly parts of the Atlantic Ocean south to the Mediterranean and west coast of Africa; occasionally found on the Newfoundland Banks and off the coast of Nova Scotia; breeds on islands off Great Britain.

LEAST PETREL

Halocyptena microsoma *Coues*

A. O. U. Number 103

Other Name.— Wedged-tailed Petrel.

General Description.— Length, 6 inches. Color, brownish-black. *Tail, rounded.*

Color.— Lustrous brownish-black, without any white, darker on upper parts, blackening on wings and tail, slightly grayer on greater wing-coverts; bill and feet, black; iris, brown.

Nest and Eggs.— The single egg, white with a ring of black specks at end, is laid in a crevice of rocks, not in a burrow.

Distribution.— Eastern Pacific Ocean; breeds on islands off Lower California; south in migration to western Mexico, Panama, and Ecuador; occasionally found north of breeding range.

What the Wilson's and Leach's Petrels are to the western waters of the Atlantic, the Storm Petrel is to the eastern, and there is strong resemblance between the appearance and habits of the three birds. The Storm Petrel appears only occasionally off or near the American coast, and then doubtless in most cases accidentally.

Similar in its relation to the western coast is the Least Petrel, a Pacific Ocean form, seen occasionally off the coast of California, but essentially a bird of the islands far from either shore of that vast sea. This bird's habits are also distinctly Petrel-like and need no separate description.

ORDER OF TOTIPALMATE SWIMMERS

Order *Steganopodes*

SIX families are gathered in this order. All the members are large birds, two feet or more in length, but they differ greatly in appearance and habits. However, they agree in having all four toes joined with webs — hence the name "Totipalmate" has been applied to this group. Their bills are horny and are usually hooked and hard at the tip. Their mouths can be opened very wide; their tongues are small and knoblike. Each bird is equipped with a gular or throat pouch. The nostrils are very small or rudimentary.

Nests are built on the ground, on rocky ledges, or in brushy trees near the water. The eggs are single or few, usually plain-colored, but covered with a chalky incrustation. The young are hatched helpless and naked, but are soon covered with down. All of the Totipalmate Swimmers are carnivorous in diet, their food consisting almost entirely of fish.

TROPIC-BIRDS

Order *Steganopodes;* family *Phaëthontidæ*

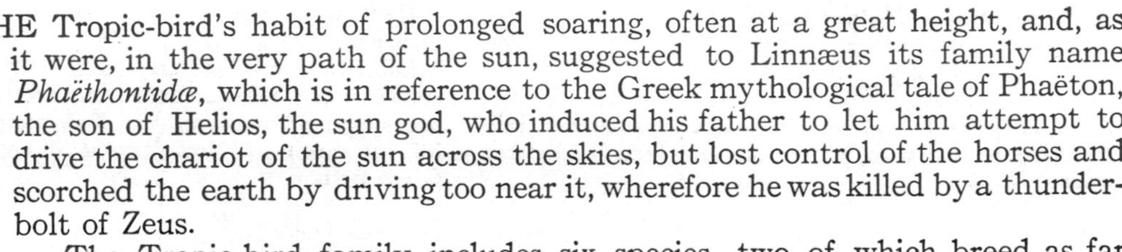

THE Tropic-bird's habit of prolonged soaring, often at a great height, and, as it were, in the very path of the sun, suggested to Linnæus its family name *Phaëthontidæ*, which is in reference to the Greek mythological tale of Phaëton, the son of Helios, the sun god, who induced his father to let him attempt to drive the chariot of the sun across the skies, but lost control of the horses and scorched the earth by driving too near it, wherefore he was killed by a thunderbolt of Zeus.

The Tropic-bird family includes six species, two of which breed as far north as the tropic of Cancer, and are often found about the West Indies, while individuals occasionally wander along the eastern coast of North America even as far north as Newfoundland. All have white plumage of satiny appearance, often with a pinkish tinge, and a black patch or bar in the eye region. The bill may be red, yellow, or orange in color, is pointed and somewhat curved, and the edges are toothed. The wings are long and rather slim; the tail is composed of from twelve to sixteen feathers, of which the central pair are much elongated and are slenderer than the others. Excepting the last-named peculiarity, the Tropic-birds resemble in their contour large Terns. They differ from the Man-o'-war-birds in general color, and in the shape of the bill, as well as in the absence of the throat sac, and the naked area about the eyes, and by the long central tail-feathers. The plumage of the sexes in the adults is alike, but the immature birds lack the long tail-feathers and show more irregularity in their marking.

The flight of the Tropic-bird differs from that of the Albatross in that it is accomplished by uniform, rather rapid, and entirely apparent wing-strokes, whereas the movement of the Albatross's wings usually is so slight as to be almost imperceptible. Nevertheless the Tropic-bird's flight performances are often very spectacular, and include frequent and thrilling dives from great heights into the ocean. Moreover, its power of sustained flight for enormous distances is fully established, though it frequently shows signs of exhaustion by dropping into the rigging of a ship in mid-ocean, an evidence of weariness which is seldom, if ever displayed by the great bird of the Ancient Mariner. It often follows ships for long distances, and is called by seamen the "Boatswain" or "Boatswain-bird," terms which sailors apply also to the Jaegers. Like many birds of great flight power, the Tropic-bird has a clumsy, shuffling gait on shore.

The food of the Tropic-bird consists chiefly of fish, squids, and the like, which are taken by diving from the wing. Its only note is a harsh croak or chatter. It breeds in colonies, and no nest is built. The single reddish-brown or buffy egg, more or less speckled with brown, purple, or gray, is laid in a hole or a crevice, or sometimes in a tree cavity, and incubation is shared by the pair. The bird engaged in this operation is not easily dislodged, but resists the intruder by pecking, snapping, and screaming. This spirit is taken advantage of by plumage collectors, who seize the sitting bird and pull out its tail-feathers to be used in "decorating" women's hats.

YELLOW-BILLED TROPIC-BIRD

Phaëthon americanus *Grant*

A. O. U. Number 112

Other Names.— Boatswain; Boatswain-bird; Bosen-bird; Longtail.

General Description.—Length, 32 inches. Prevailing color, white.

Color.— ADULT: General plumage, pure *white;* in breeding season tinged with rosy on under parts and long tail-feathers; lores, a stripe over and behind eye, and on side of head, black; a band on wing from inner coverts to inner secondaries, outer primaries, and shafts of tail-feathers, black; bill and feet, yellow; toes, black; iris, dark brown. YOUNG: Plumage, similar, but extensively marked with black bars or crescents on most of upper parts and with spots on tail.

Nest and Eggs.— The single egg, chalky-white heavily spotted with brown, is laid in crevices or crannies of rocks on isolated sea islands.

Distribution.— Florida and Bermuda south to the West Indies and the Atlantic coast of Central America; accidental in western New York, Nova Scotia, and Arizona.

Imagine to yourself a beautiful Dove with two central tail-feathers sweeping out behind to a distance of a foot and a half, and you will have a fairly correct mental picture of the Tropic-bird. As I have watched this creature from the deck of a steamer in the Caribbean Sea, or in the Pacific Ocean, and observed its exquisite form and grace, I have more than once vowed to myself that here indeed is the most appealing, if not the most graceful, of all birds on the sea. The plumage is silky white, with just enough black on the wings and head to emphasize the dazzling glory of the whole effect. They fly rapidly, and while feeding wing their way along over the water at an altitude of forty or fifty feet. "Longtails" is one of the names by which sailors know them.

The Yellow-billed Tropic-bird is an inhabitant of the coasts of tropical America and the nearby islands. The northernmost breeding grounds appear to be the rocky cliffs of the Bermuda Islands. Here up to a few years ago they came in spring by thousands to rear their young and would remain in the neighboring waters until the approach of cold weather would drive them again to the southward. They are not particularly popular with fishermen here, who complain that they eat many squids which should be left for men who want to use such bait when they desire to go angling. The nest is placed in holes and cracks of the rocky faces of the islands and sometimes among the low scrubby trees and bushes higher on shore.

As only a single egg appears to be laid in a season it will easily be seen that no great amount of persistent killing of the birds is necessary to reduce their numbers. Unless a sentiment is rapidly developed for their protection on these islands, the "Bosen-birds," as they are often called, will probably cease to grace these waters and one of the islands' natural beauties will be gone forever.

Writing in *Bird-Lore* in 1913, Karl Plath tells of the movements of the Tropic-birds on land as he watched them in the Bermuda Islands:

"One of the noticeable features of the Tropic-bird is its inability to walk upright or to stand on its legs; a fact which is not generally understood by taxidermists, who usually mount the bird standing on its feet like a Gull. The usual gait is an awkward waddle, or it proceeds in a series of hops. I have also seen them push themselves along by means of their feet. Before launching in the air, they creep awkwardly, with much flapping of wings, to a suitable height, and then drop, sometimes in the water before regaining their equilibrium, when they are among the most graceful of sea-birds." T. GILBERT PEARSON.

GANNETS

Order *Steganopodes;* family *Sulidæ*

THE Gannets constitute the family *Sulidæ*, and comprise the birds of that name (also called "Solan" Geese, "solan" being apparently from a Scandinavian term meaning "sea") and the Boobies. "Gannet" is thought to be derived from the Old English *gan*, meaning "gander" or "goose-like." There are eleven species in the family, and of these one is essentially a northern bird and migratory, while the others range along the tropical and subtropical coasts of the world. All are strictly sea birds, but they prefer the coastal waters and are not found at any considerable distance from land except when they are migrating. On the wing they move rapidly, alternating vigorous wing work with periods of sailing. They feed almost exclusively on fish, which they capture by diving from the wing, often from a height of forty feet or more, and with such force that they disappear entirely beneath the surface, their impact being sufficient sometimes to send the spray ten feet into the air. This constitutes one of the most picturesque and vigorous feats performed by any sea bird. Fish of considerable size are swallowed practically whole (which is made possible by a throat which can be greatly distended), and are disgorged for the young. All members of the family are highly gregarious, and nest in large colonies on uninhabited coasts or isolated islands. The bird builds a rude nest composed of seaweeds and grass and lays one or two eggs, chalky-white or dull white in hue.

The Gannets are comparatively large birds, their length being from about two to three feet. Their wings are relatively long, and acutely pointed, while the tail is wedge-shaped and consists of from twelve to eighteen feathers. Their legs are short and stout and placed nearly at the center of the body. The feet are completely webbed. The neck is rather long, and the head large. The bill is strong, cylindrical, and tapers to a point where it is slightly curved, though never actually bent into hook form. The plumage is compact and its characteristic coloration is white on the body with black or dusky wings and tail, though some species are sooty-brown or dusky.

BOOBY

Sula leucogastra (*Boddaert*)

A. O. U. Number 115

Other Names.— Brown Booby; Yellow-footed Booby; Catesby's Booby; Booby Gannet.

General Description.— Length, 30 inches. Color above, dark brown; below, white.

Color.— ADULTS: Plumage, dark brown, *abruptly white from neck on under parts;* bill and bare parts of head, variably colored, mostly dull greenish or yellowish; feet, similar; iris, white. YOUNG: Plumage, grayish-brown, paler below variegated with white on under parts from neck; bill and feet, obscured.

Nest and Eggs.— NEST: On low bushes of tropical keys; constructed of sticks and weeds; in some localities eggs deposited on bare sand or rocks, without any attempt at nest building. EGGS: 1 or 2, dull chalky white.

Distribution.— Atlantic coasts of tropical America and Pacific and Indian oceans; rare on south Atlantic and Gulf coasts of the United States from South Carolina to Louisiana; accidental on Long Island, N. Y., and in Massachusetts.

The Booby is a common bird in the West Indies and on the coasts of tropical lands to the south. While on ship-board in the Pacific Ocean off the coast of Panama and Nicaragua I observed these birds in sight at all hours of the day. Their flight is strong and easy, and the flapping is alternated with brief intervals of sailing. At times they would wheel on set wings and plunge headlong into the sea. Their food consists of marine animal life, fish evidently constituting the bulk of their menu, as the birds were usually more numerous in the neighborhood of schools of porpoises. On three occasions I saw Boobies standing on the backs of basking sea-turtles, one of which seemed not at all disturbed by the weight of two birds that were taking a rest on his broad carapace.

Boobies collect in numbers to nest on lonely isles. In *Camps and Cruises of an Ornithologist,* Doctor Chapman has written of the habits of a colony of fifteen hundred pairs of Boobies which he visited and studied in the spring of 1907. The place was a small island known as Cay Verde, lying on the outer fringe of the Bahama Islands. The nests were simple affairs placed on the ground. Two eggs are laid about a week apart, but for some reason rarely more than one young bird is reared. Of their domestic habits he writes:

"In spite of the apparent sociability expressed by their communal habits, the Boobies immediately resented the trespass on their home site by one of their own kind. Where the nature of the ground permitted, their nests were placed with more or less regularity six or eight feet from one another. As long as a bird remained within its own domain having a diameter of approximately six or eight feet, it was not molested, but let it or its young advance beyond these limits and they were promptly attacked.

" So closely, however, are the birds confined to their own little areas that difficulties of this kind are rare and under normal conditions peace reigns in the rookery. But when we walked through the rookery, the birds in escaping from the larger evil forgot the lesser one and inadvertently backed on to a neighbor's territory, the unusual cause of the trespass was not accepted as an excuse and they found the 'frying pan' was worse than the 'fire,' as the enraged owner, with bustling feathers, furiously assailed them with open bill, sometimes taking hold. At these times, and whenever the birds were alarmed, they gave utterance to hoarse, rancorous screams or screeches, though, as a rule, they were comparatively silent."

In summer Boobies occasionally range up the Atlantic coast as far as Georgia, but such visits are rare, for they are distinctly birds of tropical and subtropical seas. Unlike the Albatross and Petrel, they are seldom seen far from land.

T. Gilbert Pearson.

GANNET

Sula bassana (*Linnæus*)

A. O. U. Number 117 See Color Plate 9

Other Names.—Common Gannet; White Gannet; Soland Goose; Solan Goose; Solon Goose; Jan van Gent; Grand Fou.

General Description.—Length, 3 feet. Prevailing color, white. *Goose-shaped.*

Color.—Adults: Plumage, *white;* primaries and their coverts, black; head with a pale wash of amber-yellow; bill, grayish tinged with greenish or bluish; lores and throat sac, black; feet, black with greenish or bluish scales; iris, white or pale yellow. Young: Plumage, dark brown with a tinge of olive, spotted or streaked everywhere with white; on head and neck the spots tending to form streaks, on back and wing-coverts, triangular, usually one on end of each feather; primaries and tail, dusky. Intermediates between these two plumages are common, as it requires three years to reach perfect plumage.

Nest and Eggs.—Nest: On precipitous cliffs overlooking the sea; constructed principally of seaweed. Eggs: Single, pale greenish-blue, flaked with chalky-white.

Distribution.—Coasts of North Atlantic; breeds on Bird Rock and Bonaventure Island in the Gulf of St. Lawrence and on islands off British Isles; winters from North Carolina coast south to Gulf of Mexico, and on coasts of north Africa, Madeira, and the Canaries; occurs off eastern United States in migration; casual north to Greenland; accidental in Indiana and Ontario.

The Gannet is the largest bird of our north Atlantic coast. It is about three feet from tip of bill to end of tail. It is four feet and more between the tips of its outstretched wings, and its heavy body and muscular neck would make it a formidable antagonist, if it were pugilistic in its disposition. It is a white bird with black-tipped wings and its color renders it a conspicuous object as it flies about over the dark waters of the winter sea. The Gannet likes the association of others of its kind, hence if you find one you are pretty sure to see others in the immediate neighborhood. They range all down the Atlantic coast to Florida, and it is not an uncommon sight to see small flocks almost anywhere off the shores of the eastern United States, disporting themselves in the water just outside the breakers, or wheeling about in quest of fish.

They fly usually at a height of from sixty to a hundred feet above the water. Dr. F. A. Lucas says: "The height at which the Gannet flies above the water is proportionate to the depth at which the fish are swimming beneath, and Captain Collins tells me that when fish are swimming near the surface the Gannet flies very low and darts obliquely instead of vertically upon its prey. Should any finny game be seen within range, down goes the Gannet headlong, the nearly closed wings being used to guide the living arrow in its downward flight. Just above the surface the wings are firmly closed, and a small splash or spray shows where the winged fisher cleaves the water to transfix its prey. Disappearing for a few seconds, the bird reappears, rests for a moment on the water, long enough to swallow his catch, and then rises in pursuit of other game."

Drawing by R. I. Brasher

GANNET (¼ nat. size)

Like an animated spear it plunges into the ocean after its prey of fish

Gannets breed north of the United States. Bird Rock in the Gulf of St. Lawrence and Bass Rock at the Firth of Forth contain well-known breeding colonies of enormous numbers. The nests are usually built on ledges overlooking the sea. Where these are broad, the entire area is covered with nests, just enough space being left between them for the birds to come and go with comfort. Where the ledges are narrow and there is room only for a single row of nests, one will find nearly every brooding bird sitting with its tail pointed outward and its head in close proximity to the rocks. One egg is laid. It is covered with a calcareous deposit that can readily be scratched off. The young are hatched naked. The down, which appears in a few days, is of a yellowish hue. Immature birds have a peculiarly spotted appearance, as the brown feathers with which they are covered are each centered with a wedge-shaped dot of white.

It is extremely rare that the Gannet is found inland, the ones which have been occasionally reported doubtless being individuals that had lost their way, or had been driven by storms from the ocean, on whose bosom they are so much at home. T. Gilbert Pearson.

DARTERS

Order *Steganopodes;* family *Anhingidæ*

HE Darters (also called Anhingas and Snake-birds) comprise the family *Anhingidæ*, include four species, and are generally distributed throughout the tropic and semi-tropic regions of both hemispheres. They have an elongated body, covered with small feathers and soft down; a very long, slender, and snake-like neck; small, compressed head; and a slender, nearly straight, and very acutely pointed bill, nearly twice as long as the head, and like that of the Herons. In these respects (excepting the greater length and sinuosity of the neck, and the fact that the bill is not hooked, though it is somewhat serrated) they bear a general external resemblance to their nearest relatives, the Cormorants. The structure of the neck, however, is peculiar in that it is bent at the eighth or ninth vertebra, and is equipped with a singular muscular mechanism by means of which the bird may throw its bill forward with a rapier-like thrust, and impale its prey.

Darters' wings are long and pointed, while the tail is somewhat long, and is rigid, broad and fan-shaped; it is composed of twelve feathers which widen toward the ends; the outer pair are ribbed in a singular manner. The feet are short, and the legs are placed rather far back on the bodies, but the birds perch readily and with apparent ease. They are not marine in their habits, and are not likely to be found near the seacoasts, their favorite habitats being dense swamps. Their flight is swift, and they dive with astonishing ease and quickness. By nature they are timid and watchful; when frightened they drop from their perch into the water, and vanish not only noiselessly, but without causing more than very slight ripples. Once under water they swim very swiftly. When they are alarmed while swimming on the surface, they disappear by sinking gently backward, after the manner of the Grebes. Frequently they swim with the body submerged but with the head and neck protruding in a manner which strongly suggests a water snake.

These singular birds feed chiefly on fish, which they capture, not by diving, but mainly by a pursuit which is like that of the Loons and Grebes. They are gregarious and build, in brush near the water, rough nests in which they lay usually three or four eggs, of a pale bluish color and having a white chalk-like incrustation.

WATER-TURKEY

Anhinga anhinga (*Linnæus*)

A. O. U. Number 118

Other Names.— Anhinga; Darter; American Darter; Black Darter; Black-bellied Darter; White-bellied Darter (young); Snake-bird.

General Description.— Length, 3 feet. Color, black.

Color.— Adult Male: *Head, neck, and body, glossy greenish-black;* wings and tail, plain black, latter tipped with white; wings with a broad silvery gray band formed by greater and middle coverts; lesser wing-coverts, spotted, and shoulders, striped with silvery-gray; in breeding plumage, back of neck with a mane of long black feathers and a lateral series of hair-like brownish-white plumes; bill, yellow, dusky-green on ridge and tip; bare space around eye, livid-green; sac, orange; feet, dusky-olive and yellow; webs, yellow; iris, from carmine to pink. Adult Female: Throat and breast, light brown bordered behind with rich chestnut; feathers of back with brown edges and white centers; *head and neck, glazed brown* varied with rufous, buff, and whitish.

Nest and Eggs.— Nest: In swamps or bayous, on small trees or bushes over water; constructed of sticks, leaves, dry grass, roots, and moss. Eggs: 2 to 5, bluish or dark greenish-white overlaid with white chalky incrustation.

Distribution.— Tropical America north to western Mexico, Texas, Florida, southern Illinois and North Carolina; casual in Kansas; accidental in New Mexico and Arizona.

The Water-Turkey is no more a "Turkey" than the Nighthawk is a "Hawk," yet this is the name by which the American Darter is almost universally known to the people of the southern States where it is found. Of late years ornithologists have adopted the name, dropping the word "Anhinga," which was formerly used. This species haunts the shores of tree-fringed lakes and rivers, as well as the wider stretches of lakes and sloughs, if bushes or trees are here convenient upon which it can perch. It is a long-necked, long-tailed, and short-legged bird about three feet in length. The general color of the male is a glossy black. The female has the entire head, neck, and breast grayish-brown. They are silent birds and live mainly in the silent places of the wilderness. Their whole life seems to be pervaded with a haunting mystery. It is undoubtedly the bird to which the rural preacher referred when he said, "Where the Whangdoodle mourneth for its first-born."

Drawing by R. I. Brasher

WATER-TURKEY (⅛ nat. size)

A bird of haunting mystery

When you come upon one sitting on some limb deep in the swamp it will at times fly swiftly out of sight, only to return again and again, each time higher in the air until, having attained an altitude of several hundred feet, it will circle about apparently on motionless wings like a Hawk. Again, and especially if it does not suspect itself seen, it will drop from the perch into the water beneath with only the faintest splash, and after swimming to a safe distance will cautiously peer out with only its slender head and beak exposed. Often it swims with body out of sight and with its long neck protruding in a most eerie and snake-like fashion.

Photo by T. H. Jackson Courtesy of Nat. Asso. Aud. Soc.

NEST OF WATER-TURKEY

Orange Lake rookery, Florida

The Water-Turkey's food consists mainly of fish which it captures as it swims beneath the surface. When emerging from the water it often ascends some sloping log or bush with low hanging limbs. The toes of its stout webbed feet terminate in sharp claws which enable it to climb with ease. Here, with wings spread, it will remain for a time drying its feathers in the sunshine.

Courtesy of Nat. Asso. Aud. Soc.

FEMALE WATER-TURKEY

At Orange Lake rookery, Florida

They assemble in numbers, sometimes several dozen pairs together, for the business of nest building. Often they breed in colonies with Herons and Ibises, but not always; for I have found as many as twenty-five nests at a time, all clustered about in a dozen trees, and no other water birds near. The nest is a bulky affair of sticks and often some of the long gray Spanish moss is used. All the nests I have ever examined also contained freshly plucked leaves, which appeared to have been placed as a finishing touch just before the eggs were laid.

They inhabit the low countries, breeding in the coastal regions as far north as North Carolina and up the Mississippi valley to southern Illinois. They are fresh-water birds and rarely appear where the sea-water runs.

T. Gilbert Pearson.

CORMORANTS

Order *Steganopodes;* family *Phalacrocoracidæ*

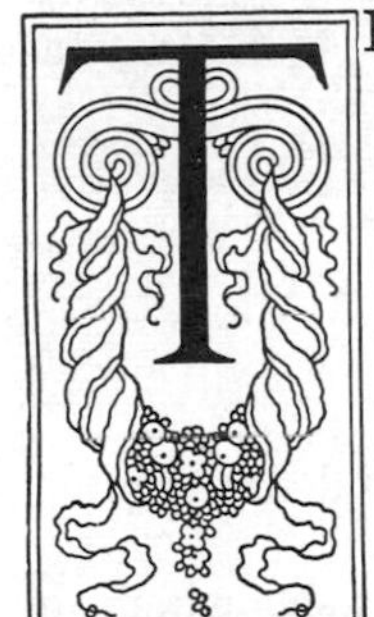

THE Cormorants comprise two genera, the *Phalacrocorax*, embracing the true Cormorants, or "Shags" as they are frequently called, and including about thirty species, and the monotypic *Nannopterum*, with Harris's Cormorant, the flightless and rare bird of the Galapagos Islands, as its single representative. This bird is very large and uses its wings only as fins in swimming.

Of the true Cormorants, about ten species occur in North America. They are chiefly maritime in their habitats, though some species are often found in fresh water far inland. They are disposed to be decidedly gregarious at all seasons, and during the breeding period they assemble in large colonies on ledges or rocky islands along the seacoast. When migrating they fly at a considerable altitude, but ordinarily they do not rise far above the water. They dive readily in pursuit of fish, but always from the surface or a low perch, and not from the air.

The superficial physical peculiarities of the Cormorants include a bare, expansible membrane under the lower mandible; a compressed bill of which the upper half is strongly hooked; nostrils which apparently in the adult do not admit air, the birds breathing through the mouth; and the claw of the middle toe armed with a comb-like process used in preening the plumage. The stiff and rounded tail of twelve to fourteen feathers is employed to assist the bird in walking and climbing. The birds are usually from two to three feet long, and the body is elongated and powerfully muscled. The neck is rather long and the legs are short and stout, and set far back. The wings are comparatively short, extending but slightly beyond the base of the tail. The plumage is very dense, and is generally dark in color, with greenish and bluish sheens. Frequently the head is crested, and during the breeding season may be further ornamented by plumes of slight feathers of hair-like structure.

That Cormorants can dive to a great depth is indicated by the record of one caught off the coast of England in a crab-pot 120 feet below the surface. They feed entirely on fishes, which they pursue and capture under water where they use both their feet and wings in swimming. If the fish captured has been seized in a position which makes swallowing it inconvenient, it is tossed into the air and caught again in a way which simplifies the swallowing operation. This diet gives the Cormorants' flesh a strongly fishy flavor, though this is less pronounced in the young birds and these are sometimes eaten.

Cormorants build rough nests, composed mostly of seaweeds, and placed usually on the ground, though sometimes in low bushes. The eggs are from three to five, of a greenish blue tinge, and covered with a crust of lime-like matter. The young are hatched naked but are soon covered with a black down. They feed by thrusting their heads down the throats of the parents and extracting the partly digested fish therefrom.

CORMORANT

Phalacrocorax carbo (*Linnæus*)

A. O. U. Number 119 See Color Plate 9

Other Names.— Common Cormorant; Shag.

General Description.— Length, 3 feet. Prevailing color, black. Throat sac, heart-shaped behind.

Color.— Adults in Breeding Plumage: General color, *glossy olive-black;* feathers of back and wing-coverts, bronze-gray, sharply edged with black; primaries, secondaries, and tail, more grayish-black; a conspicuous white patch on flank; numerous long white plumes on head and neck; a black crown crest about 1 inch long; bill, dusky; bare skin around eyes, livid greenish; throat sac, yellow, bordered behind by a band of white feathers; feet, black; iris, green. Adults in Winter: No crest or white feathers on head and rump. Young: Top of head and hindneck, brownish-black; back and wing-coverts, grayish-brown, the feathers with dark margins, some edged with white; throat, brownish-white; *under parts, whitish,* dusky on sides and across lower abdomen; bill, grayish-brown, black on ridge and tip; bare skin of face and sac, yellow.

Nest and Eggs.— Nest: On the ground, among rocks; constructed of sticks, moss, seaweed, and kelp. Eggs: 3 to 4, bluish-green coated with a white chalky substance.

Distribution.— Northern hemisphere; breeds from central Greenland south to Nova Scotia, and east through Europe and Asia to Kamchatka; winters from southern Greenland to Long Island, N. Y., rarely to Lake Ontario and South Carolina, and from the Mediterranean south to southern Africa, Australia, and Malay Peninsula.

Courtesy Nat. Asso. Aud. Soc.

NEST AND EGGS OF CORMORANT

The Cormorant is found generally throughout almost all of the northern hemisphere. From its breeding grounds in Labrador and Greenland it strays southward in summer, and occurs on the Atlantic coast in winter. It is seen occasionally on inland waters, but such visits probably are purely accidental, as its normal habitats are the seacoast and the mouths of large rivers.

Drawing by R. I. Brasher

CORMORANT (1/12 nat. size)

A bird of strange appearance and interesting habits

It lives almost entirely upon fish, which it captures under water by swimming with both wings and feet, sometimes at a considerable depth. In these operations it is very skillful and swift, while its powerful hooked bill forms an effective weapon for seizing and devouring its prey. The young are fed by regurgitation, during which the infant thrusts its bill far down the throat of the parent.

Courtesy of Nat. Asso. Aud. Soc.

YOUNG CORMORANTS

They are naked when hatched, and do not leave the nest for about a month

DOUBLE-CRESTED CORMORANT

Phalacrocorax auritus auritus (*Lesson*)

A. O. U. Number 120 See Color Plate 9

Other Names.— Crow Duck; Shag; Water-Turkey; Lawyer; Nigger Goose.

General Description.— Length, 33 inches. Prevailing color, greenish-black. *Throat sac, convex behind.*

Color.— Adults in Summer: Glossy greenish-black; feathers of back and wings, coppery-gray with narrow distinct black edges and black-shafted; two curly black crests on head; *no white flank patches or white feathers behind throat sac;* throat sac and lores, orange; bill, dusky; feet, black; iris, green; eyelids, blue. Adults in Winter: No crests; eyelids, not blue; bill, yellow, dusky on ridge; gular sac, red in front, yellow ocher behind. Young: Plain dark brown; grayish or whitish below.

Nest and Eggs.— Nest: On the ground; constructed of twigs and weeds; sometimes on ledges of sea islands where built of fresh seaweed and kelp. Eggs: 2 to 4, bluish-green with white chalky incrustation.

Distribution.— Eastern North America; breeds from central Saskatchewan, southern Keewatin, northeastern Quebec and Newfoundland south to northern Utah, South Dakota, southern Minnesota, and Penobscot Bay, Maine. Winters from North Carolina (casually Massachusetts) south to the Gulf coast; casual in Bermuda.

Cormorants are found in suitable places all over North America. They are wonderful divers and secure their prey while on their submarine excursions. They are very common on the coast and may easily be seen at many places, as, for example, on the Seal Rocks near the Cliff House at San Francisco, on Black Horse Island off the coast of Maine, and on almost every buoy and channel-stake about the harbors of Florida. On rocky coasts their nests are built on cliffs overlooking the sea, as on the Farallon Islands, California, and the Three Arch Rock Islands of Oregon. In the interior the nests are often built on the ground or on the rushes in the islands of lakes. In the swamps of the South, cypress trees are used, and along the Gulf coast of Florida large numbers breed on the low mangrove trees that cover the Keys.

Some years ago I visited a typical colony of these birds in Big Lake, in eastern North Carolina. Low-spreading cypress trees, their tops reaching, as a rule, not more than fifteen feet above the water, were the sites chosen for the nests. Eighteen trees scattered along the swampy shore for a mile and a half were thus occupied. A few trees contained but a single nest. Some were occupied by two, while in others six, eight, ten, and even twelve nests were noted. One tree contained thirty-eight, all of which contained either eggs or young. The number of occupants of a nest was in all cases either two or three. One hundred and fifty inhabited nests were counted in the community.

The eggs were pale bluish-white overlaid with a chalky coating and were about two and one-half inches long. When first hatched the young are naked and look like little, animated, greasy rubber bags. In a few days they assume a thick growth of black down.

The food of these birds must have consisted largely of eels, for in nearly every nest signs of eels were found, and the young upon becoming excited disgorged fragments of eels which showered down upon us as we attempted to climb the trees.

The Cormorants have many local names, such as "Shag," "Lawyer," and "Nigger Goose."

There are several subspecies of the Double-crested Cormorant. These are: the Florida Cormorant (*Phalacrocorax auritus floridanus*) of North Carolina, Florida, and the Gulf coast; the White-crested Cormorant (*Phalacrocorax auritus cincinatus*) of Alaska; and the Farallon Cormorant (*Phalacrocorax auritus albociliatus*) of the coast and inland lakes of the Pacific slope.

Market fishermen everywhere complain of the inroads these birds make on the food fishes of the sea, but a recent investigation carried out by the Canadian Government proved beyond doubt that the destruction wrought by Cormorants in the Gulf of St. Lawrence has been overrated greatly.

T. Gilbert Pearson.

Photograph by H. K. Job

YOUNG DOUBLE-CRESTED CORMORANTS
In rookery, Waterhen Island, Manitoba

BRANDT'S CORMORANT

Phalacrocorax penicillatus (*Brandt*)

A. O. U. Number 122

Other Names.— Penciled Cormorant; Tufted Cormorant; Townsend's Cormorant; Shag; Brown Cormorant.

General Description.— Length, 33 inches. Prevailing color, blackish. *Throat sac, heart-shaped behind; head, not crested;* bill, slender and nearly straight; tail, short.

Color.— ADULTS IN BREEDING PLUMAGE: General color, deep glossy greenish-black with violet or steel-blue reflections on neck and head; feathers of middle of back, plain, those of shoulders and wing-coverts with narrow black edgings; a series of yellow straight filamentous plumes two inches or more in length along each side of neck; many others longer and somewhat webbed on shoulders; *throat sac, dark blue;* a border of mouse-brown feathers behind gular sac; bill, dusky; feet, black; iris, green. ADULTS IN WINTER: Plumes, absent. YOUNG: Plain blackish-brown, more rusty below; abdomen grayish; shoulders and wing-coverts, paler-edged.

Nest and Eggs.— NEST: On ledges of rock islands; a compact structure of eel grass or seaweed, cemented with guano. EGGS: 3 to 5, light greenish-blue, with the usual chalky deposit.

Distribution.— Pacific coast, from Vancouver Island to Cape San Lucas.

Brandt's Cormorant is abundant on the Pacific coast. Its general demeanor, as it perches on rocks or snags, suggests that it is a rather dull and sluggish bird, but in reality it is very suspicious and wary, and this state of mind is shown plainly by its manner when it is in the water. Then its long neck is stretched to its fullest length, and its head is constantly turning from side to side, as if it feared the approach of an enemy from any direction.

The Cormorant dives readily and skillfully, and uses both its wings and its feet in making headway under water. In fact it seems quite as much at home in the water as a Duck, and yet, for some altogether mysterious reason, it has the very unducklike habit of perching in the sunshine, with wings spread, and evidently waiting for its plumage to dry. The Northern Raven and the Western Gull seem to have a special weakness for the eggs of the Cormorant, of which fact apparently it is very well aware; for, when the Ravens or Gulls are about, the Cormorant that is incubating will not leave the eggs until its mate is at hand to take its place immediately.

Photo by W. L. Finley and H. T. Bohlman

BRANDT'S CORMORANT AT NEST

Photograph of habitat group — Courtesy of American Museum of Natural History

BRANDT'S CORMORANTS AT MONTEREY, CALIFORNIA

PELICANS

Order *Steganopodes;* family *Pelecanidæ*

TWELVE species of these singularly grotesque but interesting birds are recognized, and they occur generally throughout the temperate and tropical regions of both hemispheres, three of them being North American. They are birds of considerable size, their bodies varying in length from fifty to seventy inches, while some have a wing expanse of nearly ten feet.

The distinctive feature of the Pelican is the great pouch which depends from its lower bill. As the bird's bill may be eighteen inches long, it will be realized that the capacity of this pouch, six inches or more in depth, is very considerable. Some of the species use this pouch very much as a scoop net is employed, and all of them store in it fish which they take to their young. Most of the bird's prey is captured in this manner, though some is taken by diving. Another physical peculiarity is the excrescence which develops at about the middle of the upper mandible during the breeding season. What, if any, purpose it serves is not known. It is shed coincidently with the fall molt.

The Pelican on land is very ungainly, its uncouth appearance being due in part to the awkward kink in its neck, which produces the impression of great discomfort. In point of fact, however, this position is due to the singular articulation of the eighth or ninth vertebra with the one on either side, so that it is really impossible for the bird to straighten its neck. The Pelican's flight is a combination of flapping and sailing, and though not rapid is steady and confident. A long line of these birds, flapping and sailing alternately, and often in nearly perfect unison, is an interesting spectacle.

These birds are decidedly gregarious and often breed in very large colonies. They build on the ground large nests composed of sticks. The eggs are from two to five in number and are bluish-white in color.

WHITE PELICAN

Pelecanus erythrorhynchos *Gmelin*

A. O. U. Number 125

Other Names.— American White Pelican; Common Pelican (of the North).

General Description.— Length, 5 feet; spread of wings, 9 feet. General color, white. Bill with pouch hanging from under side.

Color.— ADULTS: *Plumage, white with black primaries;* lengthened feathers of back of head, breast, and some of the lesser wing-coverts, pale straw-yellow; bill and feet, yellow tinged with reddish; lower part of bill, brighter than upper, which has the ridge whitish; pouch shading from whitish in front through yellow and orange to red at base; bare skin around eye, orange; eyelids, red; iris, pearly-white. YOUNG: Lesser wing-coverts and some feathers on head, grayish; bill and feet, dull yellowish; otherwise as in adults.

Nest and Eggs.— NEST: On the ground; constructed by the bird scraping the sandy soil into a heap about half a foot high and erecting a shallow platform of sticks and weeds on this base. EGGS: 2, dull chalky-white with a chalky incrustation.

Distribution.— Temperate North America; breeds from southern British Columbia, Great Slave Lake, and southwestern Keewatin to Manitoba, North Dakota (formerly southern Minnesota and South Dakota), Utah, and southern California; winters from southern California to Gulf States, Florida, and Cuba south to western Mexico and Costa Rica; casual in migration east to Atlantic coast, north to New Brunswick.

The American White Pelican was formerly found in the East as well as in the West, but the range of the bird has contracted until it is rarely seen on the Atlantic coast. The bird formerly nested in Minnesota, but the most eastern nesting site to-day within the United States is in North Dakota. A bird so conspicuous in size and color, and one that nests on the ground, can never rear its young free from the disturbances of predacious animals and man unless it can find a remote island upon which to breed. The natural home of the bird is on some sandy or tule island, where a large number of them nest together. This showy bird would soon have been extinct had it not been for the efforts of the National Association of Audubon Societies in seeking out the ancestral breeding places and having them set aside as Federal wild-bird reservations. The largest colonies of White Pelicans in the United States are found on Malheur Lake, Klamath Lake, and Clear Lake reservations in southern Oregon and northern California.

Through the western part of the United States, the Pelican season begins in April after the snow and ice have melted and lasts till August or September, when the young are able to care for themselves. Sometimes one will find eggs just hatching from May up to July. The Pelican generally lays two or three eggs and incubates about four weeks before they hatch.

The Pelican has a large skinny bag that hangs from the lower part of his bill. This, when distended, holds several quarts of water. When not in use, this sack is contracted so it occupies very little space. The White Pelican uses this as a dip-net by swimming along and scooping up the young fry. It was formerly thought that this pouch served to convey live fish swimming in water to the little Pelicans at home, but, as Audubon remarked long ago, it is doubtful whether a Pelican could fly at all with his burden so out of trim.

The first time I ever saw a motley crowd of half-grown Pelicans, I thought Nature had surely done her best to make something ugly and ridiculous. It was a warm day and the birds stood around with their mouths open, panting like a lot of dogs after a chase, their pouches shaking at every breath. When I went near, the youngsters went tottering off on their big webbed feet with wings dragging on this side and that, like poorly handled crutches. The youngsters huddled together by hundreds in a small place. Those on the outside pushed and climbed to get near the center, till it looked worse than any football scrimmage I ever saw.

One might wonder how such a huge-billed bird as a Pelican could feed helpless chicks just out of the egg. It was done with apparent ease. The old bird regurgitated a fishy soup into the front end of his pouch and the baby Pelican pitched right in and helped himself out of this family dish.

As the young bird grew older and larger, at each meal he kept reaching farther into the big pouch of his parent until finally, when he was half-grown, it was a most remarkable sight. The mother opened her mouth and the whole head and neck of her nestling disappeared down the capacious maw, while he hunted for his dinner in the internal regions.

William L. Finley.

Photo by W. L. Stevens Courtesy of *Field and Stream*

YOUNG PELICANS

Photograph of habitat group

Courtesy of American Museum of Natural History

WHITE PELICANS

Well might one wonder how such a huge-billed bird could feed helpless chicks just out of the shell

BROWN PELICAN

Pelecanus occidentalis *Linnæus*

A. O. U. Number 126

Other Name.— Common Pelican (of Florida).

General Description.— Length, 4½ feet; spread of wings, 6½ feet. General color, brown, darker above. Bill with pouch hanging from under side.

Color.— Adults: Head, white tinged with yellow on crown, the white extending down neck in a narrow border on side of pouch; rest of neck, dark chestnut; *upper parts, dusky brown,* each feather whitish-centered; wing-coverts, pale gray with white streaks; primaries, black; secondaries, dark brown with pale edges; tail-feathers, gray; under parts, grayish-brown striped with white on sides and flanks; lower fore-neck, variegated with ocher, chestnut, and black; bill, mottled with light gray and dusky, tinged in spots with carmine; bare space around eyes, blue; iris, white; eyelids, red; pouch, blackish; feet, black. In winter most of the neck is white. Young: Neck, plain brownish; other plumage similar but less intense than in adults.

Nest and Eggs.— Nest: In rookeries, on shores or marshy islands, usually on the ground or sometimes in low mangrove bushes; constructed of sticks, coarse grass, and weed stalks and lined with finer grasses. Eggs: 2 or 3, chalky-white.

Distribution.— Gulf coast of United States and Atlantic coast of Central and South America; breeds from Florida and Louisiana south to Brazil; rare in North Carolina; accidental in Wyoming, Nebraska, Iowa, Illinois, Indiana, Massachusetts, and Nova Scotia.

The Brown Pelican is an interesting southern and tropical bird, great of bulk, powerful in flight, and withal a mightly fisher. It is numerous on our Atlantic coast from South Carolina to Texas, where it breeds on various isolated islands. Fishermen dislike it because the pouch-net which it carries under its great beak is large, and its appetite for fish in proportion. But, considering that man's nets are so much vaster, and that two or three men kill more fish in one day than can thousands of Pelicans, surely there are fish enough in the ocean that we should not begrudge the lives of these interesting and spectacular birds. It is not Pelicans that will ever exterminate any species of fish, but only avaricious man, who all too often petrifies his soul and artistic sense through inordinate greed of hoarding. The poor Pelican never hoards, but only satisfies the stern behest of hunger.

The sight of the advancing wedge or line of

Photograph by H. K. Job — Courtesy of National Association of Audubon Societies

BROWN PELICANS

On East Timbalier Reservation, Louisiana

Photograph of habitat group

Courtesy of American Museum of Natural History

BROWN PELICANS

Interesting birds, great of bulk, powerful in flight, and mighty fishers

great Pelicans, with their heavy flappings and intervals of soaring, is impressive, as is the amazing headlong plunge into the sea after fish. Mirth-provoking is the sequel sometimes witnessed. The smaller Laughing Gull follows the great Pelican and hovers above the spot where it plunges. The Pelican soon emerges, holding the fish, which it has seized, in its bill. The fish, perchance, must be turned, and the mouthful of sea-water ejected. While the Pelican is arranging matters, the Gull alights on the great beak, leaning over to watch. No sooner is the bill opened than the sly Gull reaches in, seizes the fish, and flies away, we may well imagine laughing. The solemn old Pelican sits there blinking, too much astonished at first to move. Finally the dread truth seems to dawn on the dull mind. With a few disgusted flaps, away it goes in pursuit of another fish.

On some islands the Brown Pelican breeds on the mangrove trees, constructing quite a bulky nest of sticks. On others, which often are mere low sand-bars, the nest is a mere hollow in the sand, only slightly lined. Two or three large coarse-shelled white eggs are laid. On the trees they are comparatively safe, but on the ground storms and floods often wash them away and break up the nesting. The birds do not attempt to rescue eggs, when these are drifted together in windrows at high-water marks, but sit off on the water and solemnly ponder. Usually, in time, they will lay again.

Pelican Island, in Indian River, Fla., is the best-known breeding colony, the first such to be made a government reservation. Formerly there were mangrove trees, but these have died off, and the thousands of Pelicans nest on the ground. Now and then a storm floods the island and destroys all eggs and young. It is remarkable that in this protected colony the birds each year have nested earlier and earlier, until now laying is begun in November, though on the west coast of Florida the eggs are not laid until April and May.

On June 21, 1915, I visited a great colony of ten or twelve thousand breeding on East Timbalier Island, on the west coast of Louisiana, this also being a government reservation. Though it was so late in the season, the Pelicans had just laid their eggs; not one had yet hatched. The nests were all on the sand of the low island. Their lateness may have been due to robbery or disaster elsewhere earlier in the season. At any rate, it made them too late to mature the young before a terrible tropical hurricane visited the coast in August, and every one of the thousands of young birds on the islands perished.

Surely the birds have enough to contend with without having man as an enemy!

HERBERT K. JOB.

MAN-O'-WAR-BIRDS

Order *Steganopodes;* family *Fregatidæ*

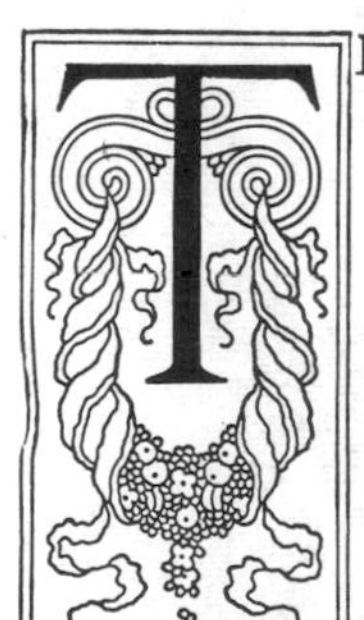

THE Man-o'-war-birds, or Frigate Birds, as they are often called, include two species constituting the family *Fregatidæ*. The larger (*Fregata aquila*) occurs in subtropical and tropical seas of both hemispheres, mainly north of the equator, and visits more or less regularly the coasts of California, Texas, and Florida, wandering northward occasionally as far as Nova Scotia. The other forms appear in the central Pacific and Indian oceans, and further south.

In general the Man-o'-war-birds' plumage is uniformly blackish in the adult males, while the females have the upper parts blackish and the sides and lower parts white. Other characteristic physical peculiarities are the unusually long and stoutly hooked bill, the very short shank, the serrated claw of the middle toe, the narrow web between the toes, and the pneumatic structure of the bones of the skeleton, which makes the body lighter than that of any other bird in proportion to the length of the wings, which are greatly elongated. The tail also is long and deeply forked like that of the Barn Swallow.

Their most curious physical feature, however, is the pouch or air sac of the male, which lies along the throat and, when fully distended, extends forward as far as the end of the bill, and downward so as to obscure the breast. When completely inflated (which is accomplished by means of tubes connected with the bronchi) it presents the appearance of a large, scarlet balloon. Doubtless this is a sexual manifestation, and plays a part in the courtship demonstration analogous to the Peacock's display of his upper tail-coverts, the strutting of the Grouse, and so on. When the pouch is deflated it is invisible beneath the plumage of the neck.

Like the Skuas and Jaegers, the Man-o'-war-birds are predatory in their habits, and get a large part of their food by robbing the Gulls and Terns, pursuing them and forcing them to drop or disgorge their food, which the pursuer catches as it falls. In their flight they are probably the most graceful and dashing of all birds. They soar for hours at a time with no apparent effort, and frequently make astonishing aërial dives from very great heights. They build their nests, sometimes on the ground and sometimes in stunted bushes, of small, dead twigs, and lay usually one, sometimes two, white eggs about the size of those of a domestic hen. In their breeding habits they are decidedly gregarious, and groups of nests are often placed very close to one another, even when there is no necessity for such proximity.

MAN-O'-WAR-BIRD

Fregata aquila (*Linnæus*)

A. O. U. Number 128

Other Names.— Hurricane Bird; Frigate Bird; Rabihorcado.

General Description.— Length, about 40 inches. Plumage, brownish-black.

Color.— Adult Male: *Plumage, brownish-black* with green or purplish reflections on head and shoulders, where the feathers are long and lance-shaped; below, plain; bill, various shades of whitish, flesh color, bluish, or blackish; bare space around eye, livid; sac, carmine to orange; iris, brown; feet, dusky. Adult Female: Less iridescent than male; feathers of back, less elongated; back of neck, brown; wing-coverts, mostly brown with darker centers and paler edges; *foreneck, breast, and sides, pure white.*

Nest and Eggs.— Nest: Usually on low trees or bushes, sometimes on rocks; extraordinarily small for the size of the bird, and flimsily constructed of a few dry twigs. Eggs: 1 to 3, plain white.

Distribution.— Tropical and subtropical coasts; in America north to southern California, Texas, Louisiana, and Florida; accidental in Kansas, Wisconsin, Iowa, Ohio, and Nova Scotia.

The Man-o'-war-bird is a genuine feathered aëroplane, if any bird is deserving of that distinction. Without moving its wings, seemingly for hours at a time, it calmly floats high in air, ascending in spirals, or drifting lazily along, directing its easy flight by changes of the angle of its "planes" so slight that any such effort is not apparent. In this respect, and perhaps in certain others, there is a resemblance to the Buzzards, which, in flight and lack of industry, manifest the soporific influences of the tropics. It is distinctly a tropical bird, seldom being seen further north than along the coasts of Florida, the Gulf States, and southern California.

Breeding is conducted mostly on tropical or subtropical islands, where crude nests of sticks are built on mangroves or low trees or bushes, in each of which one plain-white egg is laid. In the Bahamas large colonies of the birds nest, and eggs are usually seen in February. By late spring the period of nesting is over, and they forthwith appear in large numbers on our Florida and Gulf coasts. They are not definitely known to breed in the United States, though I think it probable that they do so occasionally, as there are reports of this on islands off the coast of Louisiana, and on an island near this group in June a member of our party picked up an egg, dropped on the sand, which clearly belonged to this species.

This bird is very impressive by reason of its size and the enormous stretch of its long, narrow wings, measuring some seven and one-half feet across. When a great flock of thousands soar on motionless pinions, they appear like an aërial army of invasion. Yet after all they are sluggish, lazy creatures. I have watched them go to roost at sundown in bushes or mangrove trees by the shore, and seen them sleeping, with head under wings, when the sun was some hours aclimb. Of course, they eat, but somehow I have seldom seen them actually securing food. Occasionally I have watched one snatch a fish or other marine creature from the surface of the ocean, but usually they are seen lazily floating in space, or else on their roosts or flocking on the beach.

On Bird Key, Dry Tortugas, off Florida, some hundreds of them stay in the Tern colony during the nesting season. While I was there they committed no depredations, but the warden says they attack the Terns as these are bringing fish for their young, compel them, through vicious swoops, to disgorge, and deftly catch the delicacy, usually before it reaches the water. Thousands of them, likewise, stay on Indian Key Reservation, Fla., near St. Petersburg, and wonderful soaring flights may be seen poised over the island. At close range their great hooked bills give them a rather fierce appearance, though of talons they have little to boast, their feet being weak and clumsy, fit only for perching. But their wings might well be the envy and despair of many another bird. HERBERT K. JOB.

Drawing by R. I. Brasher

MAN-O'-WAR-BIRD (⅛ nat. size)

A genuine feathered aëroplane

ORDER OF LAMELLIROSTRAL SWIMMERS

Order *Anseres*

BUT one family is included in this order; this, however, is divided into five subfamilies: Mergansers, River Ducks, Sea Ducks, Geese, and Swans. The general appearance and habits of this group are well known through their familiar representatives in barnyards and parks. There are about two hundred species scattered throughout all parts of the world; about fifty occur in North America. Economically they are among the most important of all birds.

The name given to the order is descriptive of the bill which is characteristic of all the members of the order except the Mergansers. This subfamily have round bills with saw-toothed edges, but the Ducks, Geese, and Swans have the bill flat and lamellate, or fitted along the edges with a series of flutings, with a membranous covering, and with a nail, or hard spot at the tip. Other characteristics of the Lamellirostral Swimmers are: tail generally short; wings moderately long; legs short and placed far apart, not so near the center of the body as in the Gulls and not so far back as in the Grebes; the knee joint buried in the general body covering and the thighs feathered nearly to the heel joint; toes four in number, hind toe free and elevated, front toes webbed; a peculiar waddling gait; neck usually long; plumage soft and dense, especially on the breast, with a copious covering of down.

The nest is placed on the ground, or among rocks, or in the hollow of a tree or stump. The eggs are usually numerous, of an oval shape, and plain in color. The young are covered with down when hatched, and as soon as this natal down is dry they are able to leave the nest and follow the mother.

There is a great variety of coloration among the birds of this order. With some species the female is the brighter, in others her dress is as plain as that of any Sparrow while the male is gaudily clad, and in other species there is no difference in coloration between the sexes. In some species the postnuptial molt of the male is not complete — an unusual proceeding in the bird world. This incomplete change is called the "eclipse plumage"; at this period these birds also lose their power of flight, because all the flight-feathers are shed at one and the same time. The eclipse plumage is worn only until the wing-feathers are regained, when it is shed and the distinctive male plumage again acquired.

MERGANSERS

Order *Anseres;* family *Anatidæ;* subfamily *Merginæ*

THE Mergansers constitute a small group (*Merginæ*) of fish-eating Ducks often called Fishing Ducks, Sheldrakes, or Sawbills. They are characterized by comparatively long, narrow, cylindrical bills, whose saw-toothed edges enable the birds to seize and devour fish of considerable size. This diet imparts a rank favor to the flesh of the various species, except that of the Hooded Merganser which evidently takes food enough of other kinds to counteract the effect of the fish eaten. This species and the common Merganser are also peculiar in that they nest in hollow trees or on a ledge of a cliff. All of the species have more or less striking and beautiful plumage and both sexes are usually crested. There are nine recognized species of Mergansers, three of which range throughout North America and as far south as Cuba.

MERGANSER

Mergus americanus *Cassin*

A. O. U. Number 129 See Color Plate 10

Other Names.— American Goosander; American Sheldrake; American Merganser; Greater Merganser; Pond Sheldrake; Big Sheldrake; Fresh-water Sheldrake; Winter Sheldrake; Buff-breasted Sheldrake; Buff-breasted Merganser; Fishing Duck; Fish Duck; Saw-bill; Big Saw-bill; Break Horn; Dun Diver (female); Morocco-head (female).

General Description.— Length, 25 inches. Adult males have the head and upper parts greenish-black, while the females and immature have the head red and the upper parts gray; all have the under parts white. Bill, cylindrical.

Color.— Adult Male: Head and upper part of neck, dark lustrous green; upper parts, glossy black shading to ashy-gray on rump and tail, this color running up back of neck acutely *but not reaching the green of head;* outer edge of shoulder and most of wing, pure white, crossed by one black bar formed by bases of greater coverts; primaries and outer secondaries, black, the latter shading to white and black inwardly; under parts, pure white, shaded along sides with pale pinkish where marbled with dusky; bill and feet, vermilion; hook of bill, black with some of the same color on ridge; iris, red. Adult Female: Head and neck, reddish-brown; the slight crest more brownish; chin, throat, and under parts, white; upper parts, ashy-gray, the feathers slightly darker centrally; white of wing restricted to a patch formed by secondaries and greater coverts; primaries, dusky; bill, reddish, paler at base with dusky ridge; feet, orange with dusky webs; iris, yellowish-red. Immature: Similar to adult female.

Nest and Eggs.— Nest: In hollow tree, on ground, or in crevices of rocks; constructed of moss, leaves, and grass, and warmly lined with down. Eggs: 6 to 10, pale buffy.

Distribution.— North America; breeds from southern Alaska across British America to southern Ungava and Newfoundland, south to Oregon, South Dakota, Minnesota, Michigan, Vermont, New Hampshire, Maine, and northern New York, and in mountains south to northern California, central Arizona, northern New Mexico, and Pennsylvania (formerly); winters throughout the greater part of its range south to northern Lower California, northern Mexico, Texas, Louisiana, Florida, and Bermuda.

In the dead of winter when the "white death" covers the land and even the ice-bound waters, we may find here and there in the courses of the larger New England rivers an open stretch where the floods foam over the rocks of a broken rapid. Here we may see a pair of large wild Ducks breasting the torrent, swimming and diving as composedly in the turmoil of waters as if they

Drawing by R. I. Brasher

MERGANSER (½ nat. size)

A fresh-water bird, rarely seen on salt water.

were taking their exercise in a placid lake. Their marking, the dark green glossy head of the male, its glistening light under parts, and the crested head of the female at once identify them as Mergansers, for this is the only American Duck the female of which is crested while the adult male is not. The feathers on the head of the male are elongated somewhat but he has no such crest as that of the female. The young of both sexes are more or less crested.

The birds are silent and if undisturbed they diligently dive and chase their finny prey beneath the surface. If disturbed they rise and fly to some other rapid, for only in such places can they find food in winter. Sometimes when suddenly alarmed they croak solemnly but this is rare. Ordinarily they fly at a speed of perhaps forty miles an hour but if startled they can distance a railroad train going at that speed.

This is a fresh-water bird, rarely seen on salt water except when driven there by very severe freezing weather. As soon as the ice breaks up in spring numbers of these sheldrakes may be seen in the ponds and rivers of the North following retreating winter to his lair.

The Merganser nests normally in hollow trees and is said to carry the young to the water in its bill. It feeds mainly on fish that are not much valued by man, such as minnows, chubs, and suckers, and in the salt water it devours also crustaceans and mollusks.

Its flesh as ordinarily cooked is so rank and strong that its flavor is not much superior to that of an old kerosene lamp-wick but some of the hardy gunners of the Atlantic coast know how to prepare it for the table in a way to make it quite palatable.

EDWARD HOWE FORBUSH.

RED-BREASTED MERGANSER

Mergus serrator *Linnæus*

A. O. U. Number 130 See Color Plate 10

Other Names.— Shelduck; Shell-bird; Long Island Sheldrake; Spring Sheldrake; Salt-water Sheldrake; Saw-bill; Common Saw-bill; Fishing Duck; Fish Duck; Red-breasted Sheldrake; Red-breasted Goosander; Sea Robin.

General Description.— Length, 24 inches. Adult males have the head and upper parts greenish-black, while the females and immature have the head red and the upper parts ashy-gray; all have the under parts white, but the males have a band of brownish-red on the breast. Both sexes have *a long crest of thin pointed feathers.*

Color.— ADULT MALE: Head and upper neck all around, dark mallard green; under parts, white, usually with pale pinkish shading; *fore-breast, brownish-red streaked with dusky; sides, finely waved with the same color;* fore-back, shoulders, and long inner secondaries, black; middle and lower back, gray waved with whitish and dusky; rump and tail, grayish; *a narrow black line extending up back of neck, reaching color of head;* wings, mostly white; inner secondaries, edged on outer web with black; lesser coverts, encircled by black; two black bars across wing behind greater coverts; primaries, dusky; bill, carmine, dusky on top and tip; feet, bright red; eyes, carmine. ADULT FEMALE: Crest, double; head, chestnut, more brown on crown and crest; throat, paler but not white; beneath, white, shaded on sides with ashy-gray; above, plain ashy-gray, the feathers dark centrally; white of wing restricted to a patch formed by ends of greater coverts and outer secondaries; the base and ends of greater coverts, dusky; primaries, plain dusky; bill, red, paler at base, with dusky ridge and tip; feet, dull reddish, webs darker; iris, red.

Nest and Eggs.— NEST: On the ground, in brush or crevices of rocks, near water; made of leaves, grass, and mosses, and lined with feathers and down from the parents. EGGS: 6 to 12, usually 9 or 10, olive buff.

Distribution.— Northern part of northern hemisphere; breeds in North America from Alaska along Arctic coast to Greenland (latitude 73°) south to British Columbia, Alberta, Minnesota, Wisconsin, northern New York, Maine, and Sable Island; winters throughout most of its range south to Lower California, Louisiana, and Florida; occurs casually in the Bermudas, Cuba, and Hawaii.

The Red-breasted Merganser is a swift and rather silent flyer, and an exceedingly expert diver. While swimming on the surface it sometimes raises and lowers its crest. This is more of a marine species than the American Merganser, but is nevertheless not uncommon in the interior of the country, particularly in the lake regions, during migration.

In the winter, most of the birds of this species which are seen in Massachusetts appear to be full-plumaged males, while in summer the few which remain with us appear to be females. Some of them, however, may be males in the "eclipse" plumage. I have noticed that practically all the birds seen in winter in Florida are females or young. This, together with the fact that most of those seen in Massachusetts in winter are males, seems to indicate that the hardy males do not go so far south in winter as do the females and young.

The Red-breasted Mergansers feed largely on fish, diving and charging through the schools of small fish, which they seize and hold fast with their saw-toothed bills. Thoreau notes that he saw Sheldrakes (presumably of this species) chasing fish by both swimming and flying along the surface. A few shell-fish are eaten at times.

EDWARD HOWE FORBUSH, in *Game Birds, Wild-Fowl and Shore Birds.*

Courtesy of S. A. Lottridge

RED-BREASTED MERGANSER

A swift and rather silent flyer, and an exceedingly expert diver

---

HOODED MERGANSER

Lophodytes cucullatus (*Linnæus*)

A. O. U. Number 131 See Color Plate 11

Other Names.— Hooded Sheldrake; Little, Wood, Swamp, Pond, Mud, Pickax, or Summer, Sheldrake; Little Fishing, or Fish, Duck; Little Saw-bill Duck; Saw-bill Diver; Round-crested Duck; Fan-crested Duck; Tree Duck; Wood Duck; Spike-bill; Hairy-crown; Hairy-head; Moss-head; Tow-head; Tadpole; Water Pheasant.

General Description.— Length, 17½ inches. Males are black above and white below; females are grayish-brown above and whitish below. Bill, narrow and thin. The adult male has a thin semi-circular crest capable of being opened or shut like a fan.

Color.— ADULT MALE: Head, neck, and upper parts, black shading to brown on lower back; *crest, mostly white with narrow black border behind and wider black space in front;* the white extending a little below level of eyes; breast and under parts, white, invading the black area just in front of wings by two broad streaks; a white speculum with two black bars formed by the outer webs of secondaries and greater coverts; inner secondaries, black with white center stripes; sides below, regularly and finely waved with rufous and black; under tail-coverts, waved with dusky; bill, black; feet, yellowish; iris, yellow. ADULT FEMALE: Crest bushy; head and neck, grayish-chestnut, browner on crown; back and sides, dusky-brown, the feathers with paler edges not waved; speculum of wing, smaller and crossed by only *one* dark bar; throat and under parts in general, whitish; bill, dusky, orange at base below; feet, brownish.

Nest and Eggs.— Nest: In hollow trees, lined with grass, leaves, feathers, and down. Eggs: 6 to 10, ivory white.

Distribution.— North America at large; breeds from central British Columbia, Great Slave Lake, across British America to Newfoundland south to southern Oregon, northern New Mexico, southern Louisiana, and central Florida; winters in southern British Columbia, across the United States on about latitude 41° south to Lower California, Mexico, the Gulf States, and Cuba; rare in northeastern part of range; recorded from Alaska, and from Europe and Bermuda.

The Hooded Merganser is a distinctively American bird and is the most beautiful of its family. Vivacious, active, elegant in form, graceful in carriage, its presence adds a peculiar charm to the little ponds and streams on which it delights to disport. It frequents clear streams and muddy pools alike, and its white and black plumage strongly contrasted against the shining water and the surrounding foliage makes a picture not soon forgotten. One who has seen a small flock of this species playing on the dark waters of a tiny shaded pool with two or three beautiful males darting about among the others, opening and closing their fan-like crests and throwing the sparkling drops in showers over their glistening plumage, will rarely find anywhere a finer and more animated picture of bird life.

It is well known that this bird nests in hollow trees and that the young are either carried to the water by the mother soon after they are hatched, or are pushed out of the nest and, falling unhurt to the ground, are led to the water by the parent. She seems to be rather a silent bird, but has a hoarse croak at times and probably has vocal means of communication with her little ones. This Duck is exceedingly swift on the wing, a proficient diver, and a fast swimmer both on and under the surface. Its toothed bill places it with the fish-eating Ducks, but it feeds on vegetable matter also, and Col. John E. Thayer says that "it readily eats corn." No doubt it could be domesticated, and if so it would make a great addition to the ornamental waterfowl on parks and large estates. Notwithstanding its unpalatable fishy flavor it is shot by gunners at every opportunity and has decreased greatly in numbers where formerly it was common.

Edward Howe Forbush.

DUCKS

Order *Anseres;* family *Anatidæ;* subfamilies *Anatinæ* and *Fuligulinæ*

UNDER the general term "Duck" are included a very large variety of forms, some of which do not measure up to the popular notion of what a real Duck is. From the scientific point of view, the Ducks include a large group of birds constituting the subfamilies River Ducks and Sea Ducks of the order *Anseres* or Waterfowl. Most of them have the body longer than the neck, and a broad, flattened bill, while the front of the tarsus is fitted with overlapping scales. The sexes are unlike in color. The characteristic "waddle" of the Duck on land is due to the fact that its legs are placed far back on its body, an arrangement which, however, increases its skill in swimming and diving. The wings are rigid, strong, and usually pointed, and capable of driving the bird's body at great speed; the plumage is exceptionally dense and soft.

Wild Ducks fall naturally into the two groups known as River or Pond Ducks and Sea or Bay or Diving Ducks. The Sea Ducks (which are found virtually all over the world) differ from the River Ducks in having the hind toe broadly lobed or webbed, and include species mainly of large size. The terms "Sea" and "River" should not be taken too literally, for certain species of each group may be found on the ocean, on rivers, or on bodies of fresh water well inland. The Sea Ducks, of which about seventy species are recognized, feed mainly on mollusks, shellfish, and the roots and seeds of aquatic plants, which they get by diving, often to a considerable depth, as is proved by the fact that in Lake Erie Old-squaw Ducks have been caught in fishermen's nets at depths of from eighty to one hundred feet

Most of their feeding is done in daytime, and at evening they go out to sea where they pass the night often several miles from shore.

The River Ducks, of which there are about seventy species, get most of their food by searching the bottom in water so shallow that diving is not necessary. With a few exceptions — notably the Canvas-back — their flesh is more palatable than is that of the Sea Ducks. Again, the Sea Ducks often go in enormous flocks, while the River Duck flocks are comparatively small, rarely exceeding forty or fifty individuals. The range of the River Ducks, like that of the Sea Ducks, is very wide, representatives of the group occurring in both hemispheres. The plumage of both groups displays a very great variety of colors, from the plain hues of the Black Duck to the remarkably gaudy and variegated Wood Duck. Usually the secondary quills of the wings show patches of varied or iridescent color and this patch is called the speculum.

Excepting the Wood Duck, all of the American River Ducks build their nests, which are composed of grasses, leaves, moss, and the like, on the ground, sometimes on dry land at a distance from water, but more frequently in swampy land, where the grass is high enough for concealment. Their eggs usually show shades of green, buff, or cream colors. The Sea Ducks also build ground nests of leaves, grasses, twigs, seaweed, and the like, which are lined with down from the breast of the sitting bird. The eggs number from four or five to a dozen or more, and are buffy, greenish, bluish, or cream in color.

MALLARD

Anas platyrhynchos *Linnæus*

A. O. U. Number 132 See Color Plate 12

Other Names.— Common Wild Duck; Stock Duck; English Duck; French Duck; Green-head (male); Gray Duck (female); Gray Mallard (female).

General Description.— Length, 22 to 24 inches. Color of male: head, green; back, grayish-brown; under parts, gray with purplish-chestnut breast. Color of female: dusky-brown and tawny, variegated and lighter below than above.

Description.— Adult Male in Winter and Breeding Plumage: Frequently several of the upper tail-coverts curl upward. *Head and upper neck, glossy green,* with shadings of purple and deep Prussian blue; *around neck, a white ring;* back, grayish-brown, more brown in center and on shoulders; lower back, rump, and tail-coverts, glossy black; tail, mostly whitish with center feathers long and recurved; *speculum, violet, purplish, and greenish, framed in black and white tips of greater coverts and secondaries,* forming all together two black and two white bars; lesser wing coverts, plain grayish; breast, rich purplish-chestnut; rest of under parts, silvery-gray finely zigzagged with dusky; bill, olive; feet, orange-red; iris, brown. Adult Male in Summer: Similar to female. Adult Female: Entire body, variegated with dusky-brown and tawny, with yellowish-brown edges to most of feathers, lighter in color below than on back; head and neck, quite buffy with streaks of brownish; *wing as in male;* feet, dull yellow; bill, dusky spotted with orange; iris, brown. Immature: Similar to adult female.

Nest and Eggs.— Nest: On the ground in a tussock of grass or weeds; built of fine reeds, grass, or leaves; well lined with down. Eggs: 6 to 10, pale olive or buffy-green.

Distribution.— Northern hemisphere; in North America breeds from Pribilof Islands and northwestern Alaska across British America to Greenland, south to Lower California and across the United States on about the parallel of 37°; winters from Aleutian Islands, Montana, Wyoming, Nebraska, southern Wisconsin, Ohio, Maryland, and Nova Scotia (rarely) south to Mexico, the Lesser Antilles, and Panama; casual in Bermuda and Hawaii.

Asked to name the one duck most important to the human race, the economist would reply at once — "The Mallard." Other ducks are numerous in certain lands but the Mallard occupies most of the northern hemisphere and is abundant wherever it has not been destroyed or reduced in numbers by man. Wild Mallards have furnished mankind with countless tons of food from time immemorial and domesticated Mallards have provided our race with vast

Courtesy of the New York State Museum

Louis Agassiz Fuertes.

ARCTIC TERN ADULT IN SUMMER
Sterna paradisaea Brünnich
GULL-BILLED TERN ADULT IN SUMMER
Gelochelidon nilotica (Linnaeus)
LEAST TERN
Sterna antillarum (Lesson)
IMMATURE ADULT IN SUMMER

SOOTY TERN ADULT IN SUMMER
Sterna fuscata Linnaeus

BLACK SKIMMER
Rynchops nigra Linnaeus
ROSEATE TERN ADULT IN SUMMER
Sterna dougalli Montagu
All ⅛ nat. size

FORSTER'S TERN
Sterna forsteri Nuttall
ADULT IN SUMMER IMMATURE

COMMON TERN
Sterna hirundo Linnaeus
ADULT IN SUMMER IMMATURE

Courtesy of the New York State Museum

Plate 8

CASPIAN TERN
Sterna caspia Pallas
IMMATURE ADULT IN SPRING

ROYAL TERN
Sterna maxima Boddaert
ADULT IN WINTER ADULT IN SPRING

BLACK TERN
Hydrochelidon nigra surinamensis (Gmelin)
ADULT CHANGING TO WINTER PLUMAGE
ADULT IN SPRING IMMATURE

All ⅙ nat. size

COMMON CORMORANT *Phalacrocorax carbo* (Linnaeus)
ADULT IN BREEDING PLUMAGE IMMATURE
DOUBLE-CRESTED CORMORANT *Phalacrocorax auritus auritus* (Lesson)
ADULT IN BREEDING PLUMAGE IMMATURE
GANNET *Sula bassana* (Linnaeus)
ADULT IMMATURE
All ⅙ nat. size

Courtesy of the New York State Museum

Plate 10

Louis Agassiz Fuertes

RED-BREASTED MERGANSER *Mergus serrator* Linnaeus
FEMALE MALE

AMERICAN MERGANSER *Mergus americanus* (Cassin)
FEMALE MALE

RUDDY DUCK *Erismatura jamaicensis* (Gmelin)
FEMALE MALE

BUFFLE-HEAD *Charitonetta albeola* (Linnaeus)
MALE FEMALE

All ⅛ nat. size

Courtesy of the New York State Museum

HOODED MERGANSER *Lophodytes cucullatus* (Linnaeus)
MALE FEMALE
¼ nat. size

Courtesy of the New York State Museum

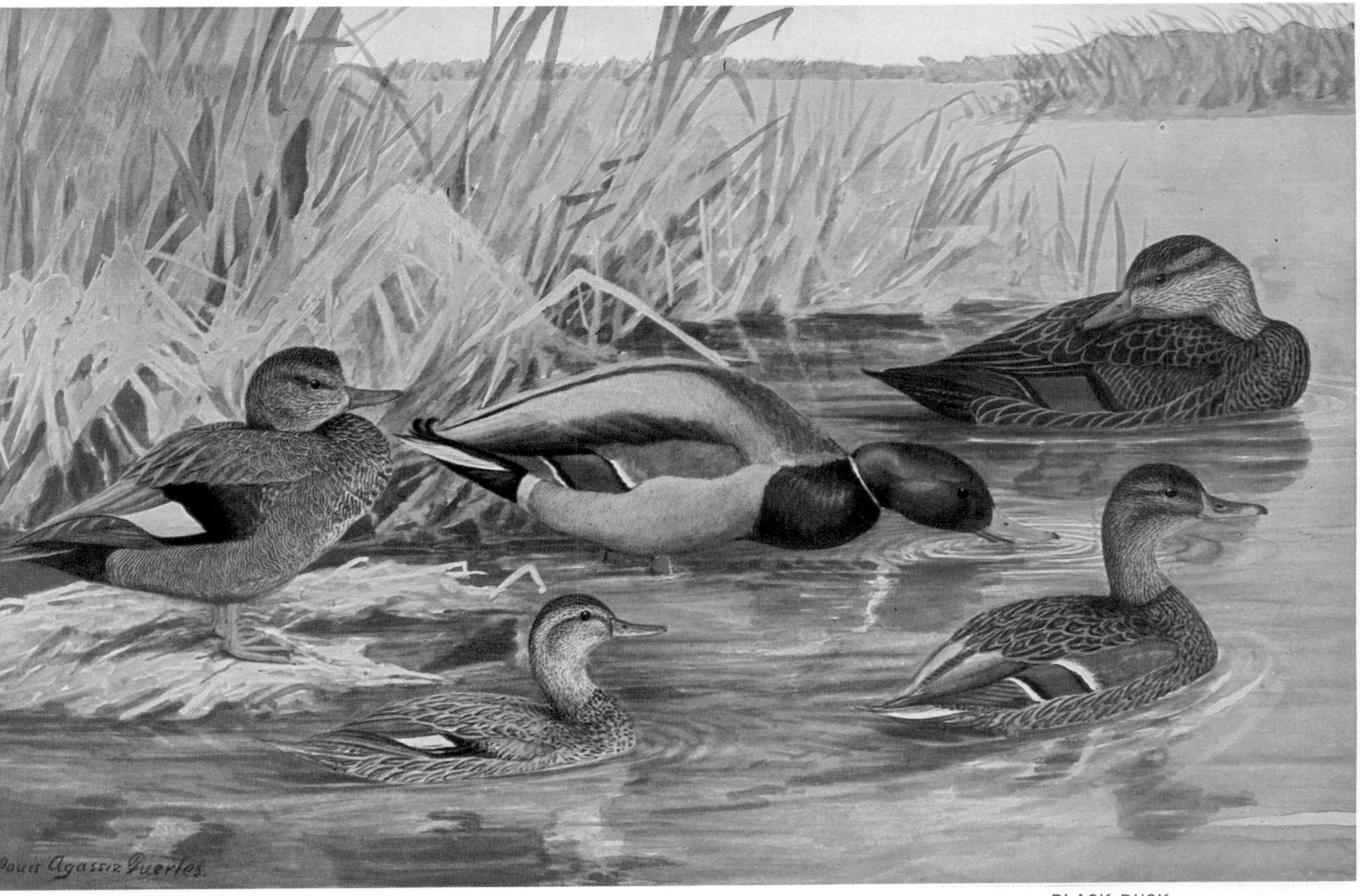

GADWALL
Chaulelasmus streperus (Linnaeus)
MALE FEMALE

MALLARD
Anas platyrhynchos Linnaeus
MALE FEMALE

BLACK DUCK
Anas rubripes Brewster
MALE

All ⅙ nat. size

Courtesy of the New York State Museum

Plate 13

BALDPATE
Mareca americana (Gmelin)
MALE FEMALE

EUROPEAN WIDGEON
Mareca penelope (Linnaeus)
MALE FEMALE

GREEN-WINGED TEAL
Nettion carolinense (Gmelin)
MALE FEMALE

All ⅙ nat. size

Courtesy of the New York State Museum

Louis Agassiz Fuertes.

SHOVELLER
Spatula clypeata (Linnaeus)
FEMALE MALE

WOOD DUCK
Aix sponsa (Linnaeus)
FEMALE MALE

BLUE-WINGED TEAL
Querquedula discors (Linnaeus)
MALE FEMALE

All ¼ nat. size

PINTAIL *Dafila acuta* (Linnaeus)

MALE FEMALE

⅙ nat. size

REDHEAD
Marila americana (Eyton)
MALES

CANVASBACK
Marila valisineria (Wilson)
FEMALE MALES
All ¼ nat. size

Courtesy of the New York State Museum

RING-NECKED DUCK
Marila collaris (Donovan)
MALE FEMALE

LESSER SCAUP DUCK
Marila affinis (Eyton)
MALE FEMALE

SCAUP DUCK
Marila marila (Linnaeus)
MALE FEMALE

All ¼ nat. size

AMERICAN GOLDEN-EYE *Clangula clangula americana* (Bonaparte)
MALE FEMALE
⅓ nat. size

KING EIDER *Somateria spectabilis* (Linnaeus)
FEMALE MALE
AMERICAN EIDER *Somateria dresseri* Sharpe
FEMALE MALE
HARLEQUIN DUCK *Histrionicus histrionicus* (Linnaeus)
MALE FEMALE

All ⅙ nat. size

Courtesy of the New York State Museum

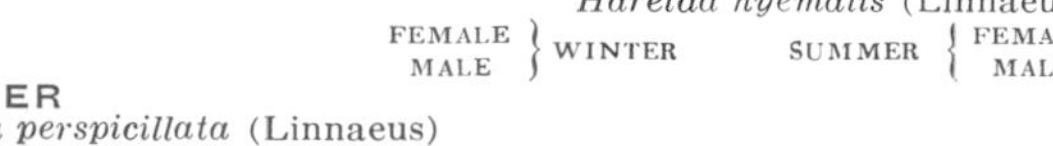

OLDSQUAW
Harelda hyemalis (Linnaeus)
FEMALE } WINTER SUMMER { FEMALE
MALE } { MALE

AMERICAN SCOTER
Oidemia americana Swainson
MALE FEMALE

SURF SCOTER
Oidemia perspicillata (Linnaeus)
FEMALE MALE

WHITE-WINGED SCOTER
Oidemia deglandi Bonaparte
MALE FEMALE

All ⅛ nat. size

Courtesy of the New York State Museum

Plate 21

BLUE GOOSE
Chen caerulescens (Linnaeus)
ADULT IMMATURE

SNOW GOOSE
Chen hyperborea nivalis (Forster)
IMMATURE ADULT

AMERICAN WHITE-FRONTED GOOSE
Anser albifrons gambeli (Hartlaub)
ADULT IMMATURE

All ⅛ nat. size

Courtesy of the New York State Museum

Plate 22

Rouis Agassiz Fuertes.

WHISTLING SWAN
Olor columbianus (Ord)

CANADA GOOSE
Branta canadensis canadensis (Linnaeus)

BRANT
Branta bernicla glaucogastra (Brehm)

BLACK BRANT
Branta nigricans (Lawrence)

All $\frac{1}{2}$ nat. size

quantities of eggs, flesh, and feathers for thousands of years. The Mallard, bred while in domestication, forms an important part of the food supply of China, the most populous country on the globe, and now the Pekin Duck is the staple stock of many a huge poultry plant in America. The Mallard is the chief waterfowl of most game preserves, on some of which 10,000 birds are reared annually. It has gained its ascendancy among the waterfowl of the world by taking advantage of every opportunity to increase and multiply. It never overlooks a chance. One spring day Dr. William T. Hornaday, director of the New York Zoological Park, found in Montana a little water hole hardly ten feet across; all about in every direction for miles and miles stretched a desert of sage-brush shimmering in the sun. As he dismounted to drink, a female Mallard sprang from her nest in the sage-brush by the side of the little pool. One can understand from this episode how the Mallard has been able to spread over the northern hemisphere.

The Mallard is wary, wise, handsome, and strong. When in security it is one of the noisiest of all Ducks and its loud quack has become typical of the Duck the world around, but when in danger it can steal away as silently as the shades of night. It is a hardy bird, remaining in the North even in winter wherever open fresh water and food may be found. The female nests very early in the season, lines the nest and covers the eggs with down, and rarely leaves them until the young are hatched. Then she leads them to water, watches over them, driving away their weaker enemies and decoying away the stronger, while the little ones skulk, dive, or hide among the water plants. Inherited experience has taught them the way of life; but many are seized by great fish, frogs and turtles, and no doubt the Hawks capture some. The brood is large, however, and the survivors are many.

When advancing winter seals the waters of their northern home and warns them to be gone, then there is a great flight from northwest to southeast, for few Mallards breed in the East, but many winter there. They reach the Atlantic from Maine to the Carolinas and, moving south, spend the winter largely in the southern States.

EDWARD HOWE FORBUSH.

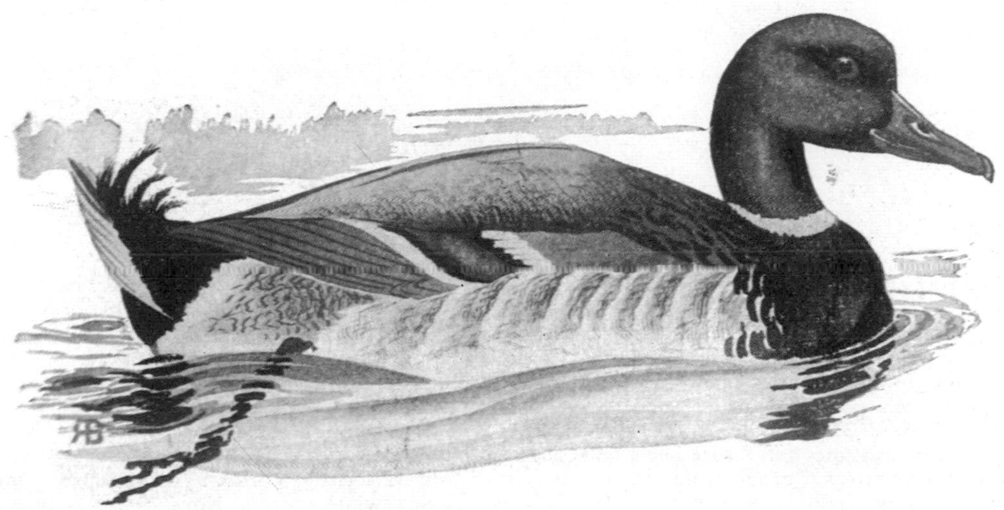

Drawing by R. I. Brasher

MALLARD (½ nat. size)

The chief waterfowl of most game preserves

"The Mallard is quite omnivorous in regard to its food. The animal food consists of small frogs, tadpoles, toads, lizards, newts, small fish, fish fry, snails, mussels, leeches, earthworms, mice, and similar small game that it finds about the pond and in the edges of the woods. Its vegetable food includes grass, many species of seeds and aquatic plants, grain, nuts, acorns, fruits, etc. It is particularly fond of wild rice. In the South the Mallard is one of the friends of the rice farmer, as it destroys the scattered rice or volunteer rice of the field, which, if left to grow, would greatly reduce the value of the crop. It is serviceable to the southern people in another way, as it feeds very largely upon crayfish, which burrow into and undermine the levees and dikes.

Examinations of one hundred and twenty-six stomachs of Mallards, made at the Biological Survey, revealed 17 per cent. animal food and 83 per cent. vegetable. The most important items of the animal food were dragon-fly nymphs, fly larvæ, grasshoppers, beetles, and bugs. Mollusks, earthworms, and crustaceans were found. The principal elements of the vegetable food, as found by the experts of the Biological Survey, were the seeds of the smartweeds, seeds and tubers of pondweed and of sedges. Other items of importance were the seeds of wild rice and other grasses, of burr reed, hornwort, water shield and widgeon grass. A great many vegetable substances of less importance were included in the Mallard's diet, of which the following are worthy of note; wild celery, algæ, roots of arrowhead; fruits, such as grapes, dogwood, sour gum, and bayberries; and the seeds of such small aquatic plants as millweed, horned pondweed, and mermaid weed." (Forbush, in *Game Birds, Wild-Fowl and Shore Birds.*)

Photo by Edward Fleischer

FEMALE MALLARD

BLACK DUCK

Anas rubripes *Brewster*

A. O. U. Number 133 See Color Plate 12

Other Names.— Dusky Duck; Black Mallard; Dusky Mallard; Red-legged Duck; Summer Black Duck; Spring Black Duck.

General Description.— Length, 22 to 24 inches. Color, dusky-brown. Darker than female Mallard and not so much white in the wing.

Color.— *General plumage, dusky-brown,* paler below; crown, darker than sides and throat, being quite blackish with pale brown streaks; ground color of neck, grayish-brown with dark streaking; wing-coverts, dusky-gray, the lesser ones varied with light edges; greater coverts, tipped with black and edging *purplish-blue speculum;* below, the lighter edgings of feathers in excess of darker centers; above, the reverse; bill, olive; feet, orange-red with dusky webs; iris, brown.

Nest and Eggs.— Nest: On the ground; a rather large well-made structure of weeds and grass with a deep cup; lined with down and feathers. Eggs: 6 to 12, very pale buff or pale greenish-buff.

Distribution.— Eastern North America; breeds from central Keewatin and northern Ungava south to northern Wisconsin, northern Indiana and southern Maryland; winters from Nova Scotia south to southern Louisiana and Colorado; in migration west to Nebraska and central Kansas; casual in Bermuda; accidental in Jamaica.

The Black Duck and the Mallard are in certain ways supplementary each of the other. The former is the common Wild Duck of the eastern half of North America; the latter, of the western half, though they overlap considerably. They are enough alike in form, size, and habits to be called popularly "Black" Mallard and "Gray" Mallard. There is, nevertheless, a decided difference in temperament. Though the wild Mallard is a very shy bird, it soon loses this fear in captivity, as is seen in the fact that it is the progenitor of the domesticated Mallard. The Black Duck, under restraint, remains the same shy, timid skulker it always was. In fact I know of no Duck more implacably wild.

In the eastern half of the United States it breeds, in suitable localities, in the Middle States and as far north as well up into Labrador. The locations chosen for its nesting are thick, bushy swamps, reedy bogs, the higher edges of meadows, tracts of weeds or low brush on small islands, and the like. As with all Wild Ducks, the nest is hard to discover, except by accidentally flushing the female from the eggs. My first experience was in plodding through the thick of an alder swamp, when a big bird suddenly shot from the ground almost into my face, revealing a dozen large yellowish-white eggs under the vegetation.

Nesting is quite early in Connecticut, sometimes

as soon as the first days of April, but more generally from about April 20 to the first week in May. The broods keep very close in the thick swamps, and seldom show themselves on open water, unless it be close to thick aquatic reeds or grass. During August they take to wing, and the number of them reared in the vicinity can be judged somewhat by their evening flights. They are crepuscular and considerably nocturnal, flying and feeding during the night and at dawn and dusk.

The planting of wild-duck foods has become a real art. Captured birds are induced to breed in marshy enclosures. The eggs are given to domestic poultry, which raise the young somewhat tamer. These hand-reared birds breed much more readily than the wild parents. Many of the young are allowed to go wild, and these, through "the homing instinct," return in spring to breed in the locality. HERBERT K. JOB.

"In the interior the food of this species is largely vegetable, particularly in the fall. In the spring more animal food is taken. The vegetable food includes grass roots taken from meadows, roots, and shoots of aquatic plants, wild rice, grains, weed seeds, hazel nuts, acorns and berries. The animal food includes small frogs and toads, tadpoles, small minnows, newts, earthworms, leeches, and small shell-fish. The food of the Black Duck has the same practical interest for the game preserver as has that of the Mallard, for the Black Duck is closely related to the Mallard, thrives almost equally well on grain, and when grain fed, becomes a very excellent bird for the table." (Forbush, in *Game Birds, Wild-Fowl and Shore Birds.*)

Photograph by H. K. Job

BLACK DUCKS

Just after alighting

The Black Duck is notably hardy, and can endure almost anything in the line of cold, so long as it can find open water in warm springs or small streams, where its food of aquatic animals or plants is accessible. I have seen it in wooded swamps in mid-winter, where there was open the merest little channel of a small stream. At times, in regions along the sea-coast, it flies out on the bays, or the open sea in daytime, to take refuge from disturbance.

Important practical projects have been carried out by private enterprise to establish the breeding of this and other species of Wild Ducks in large tracts of swampy land, where there are ponds.

FLORIDA DUCK

Anas fulvigula fulvigula *Ridgway*

A. O. U. Number 134

Length.— 22 inches.

Color.— Lighter colored than the Black Duck, the buff markings in excess of the dark ones, giving a lighter general tone; cheeks, chin, and throat, *plain* pale buffy; bill, olive; nail, black and dark spot at base; feet, orange-red; iris, brown.

Nest and Eggs.— Similar to the Black Duck.

Distribution.— Northwestern to southern Florida.

The Florida Duck is one of our little-known species of water-fowl because its range is very limited and nowhere does it seem to be abundant. It closely resembles the common Black Duck of the northern States, practically the only difference being the absence of streaks on the neck and also the fact that it is of smaller size. So far as known at the present time it is confined to Florida and the coast country of Louisiana. On the palmetto prairies of Hillsboro County, Florida, I discovered some one summer swimming about with their young in the small sloughs and grassy ponds of the region. When pursued the female would flutter away with a great splashing and giving every evidence of a highly nervous state of mind. The young meantime scampered for cover, with bodies raised high out of the water, propelling themselves forward at a most astonishing rate. The male bird was in no case seen in company with his family. Another time I came upon several of them at Lake Flint and again at Lake Hicpochee in the Okechobee country. Here they were feeding in the shallow water in company with numerous Coots which abound in the region. They are great birds to dabble and seem thoroughly to enjoy the sensation of muddying the waters. Frequently they quacked to each other, but their notes seemed to me to be indistinguishable from the call of the Black Duck.

Along the Louisiana coast there exist extensive salt and brackish water marshes through which wide creeks or bayous wind their serpentine way to the open sea. This is a haven for the myriads of Ducks and Geese that repair here to spend the winter. Upon the approach of spring, however, they depart for their northern breeding grounds and the deserted marshes are left to the mosquitoes, the snakes, and the alligators. And yet a few scattered birds tarry and brave the discomforts of the sweltering summer days. Should you at this season quietly paddle a pirogue along the smaller bayous, there would be a chance of coming upon the rare, elusive Florida Duck and her brood, and you might get a glimpse, or even a quick photograph, of them before they hurry into the marsh and disappear.

T. Gilbert Pearson.

The Mottled Duck (*Anas fulvigula maculosa*) is a geographical variation of the Florida Duck and is resident in southern Texas and southern Louisiana. The two forms differ but little.

GADWALL

Chaulelasmus streperus (*Linnæus*)

A. O. U. Number 135 See Color Plate 12

Other Names.— Gray Duck; Gray Widgeon; Creek Duck; Bleating Duck; Speckle-belly; Blarting Duck; Red-wing.

General Description.— Length, 22 inches. Males are brownish-gray above and gray below; females are like female Mallards, but smaller and wing-patch is like that of the male. The only River Duck with a pure white, black-bordered wing-patch. Wings, long and pointed; tail with 16 feathers.

Description.— Adult Male: Wide low crest on top of head. Head and neck, grayish-brown, darker on crown and nape; sides of head, throat, and neck, speckled with dusky; lower neck, breast, sides of body, and foreback, dusky with crescentic bars of whitish on breast and waved with lighter along sides; lower back, dusky shading into black on rump and upper tail-coverts; shoulders, tinged with brown; lesser wing-coverts, gray; *middle coverts, chestnut; speculum, white,* formed by outer webs of secondaries, framed in velvet-black of greater coverts and bordered behind with black and ash; abdomen, white minutely zig-zagged with gray; under tail-coverts, velvet-black. Adult Female: No crest. Above, variegated with dusky and tawny-brown, very similar to female Mallard, without any crescentic or wavy marks of male; breast and abdomen, white with dusky spotting; wing as in male, without chestnut coverts.

Nest and Eggs.— Nest: A slight hollow in a bunch of grass or reeds, usually near water; constructed of dry grass; lined with down and feathers. Eggs: 8 to 12, creamy or buffy-white.

Distribution.— Nearly cosmopolitan; in North America breeds from southern British Columbia, central Alberta and central Keewatin south to southern California, southern Colorado, northern Nebraska and southern Wisconsin; winters from southern British Columbia, Arizona, Arkansas, southern Illinois, and North Carolina south to Lower California, central Mexico, and Florida; accidental in Bermuda, Cuba, and Jamaica; rare in migration on the Atlantic coast of the Middle and New England States north to Newfoundland.

In North America this almost cosmopolitan species, the Gadwall, breeds mainly, if not entirely, in the western provinces. There is reason to believe that the Gadwall was once not uncommon in New England; but within the last half century not many specimens are known to have been taken. Wilson believed it to be rare in the "northern parts of the United States," and it was probably always less common in the New England States than in the West and South; but I am convinced, by the statements of the older ornithologists and by descriptions given me by some of the older gunners, that the Gadwall was more often seen in the early part of the last century than it now is, and that some of the so-called Gray Ducks which were then killed here were of this species.

Photo by H. K. Job Courtesy of Outing Pub. Co.
GADWALL DUCKLINGS

The Gadwall is a swift flier, resembling the Baldpate or Widgeon when in the air. It is quite distinctly a fresh-water fowl, and gets much of its living along the shores of lakes and rivers, concealed by the reeds, grasses, and bushes that grow near the shore or overhang it. It is a good diver at need, and is seen usually in pairs or small "bunches," often in company with other Ducks.

When approached from the land they usually make no attempt at concealment, but swim toward open water and take wing, making a whistling sound with their wings, that is not so loud as that made by the Baldpate. This is an excellent bird for the table, which accounts largely for its present rarity. It is fond of grain and is easily domesticated. It breeds naturally in the latitude of Massachusetts, and it might prove a great acquisition to the game preserve or to the farm-yard if it could be propagated in sufficient numbers. It seems a promising species with which to experiment with this end in view.

The food of this bird consists of the tender shoots of grasses, blades and roots of aquatic plants, seeds, nuts, acorns, insects, mollusks and other small forms of aquatic life, including small fish.

Photo by H. K. Job Courtesy of Outing Pub. Co.
NEST OF GADWALL

Edward Howe Forbush, in *Game Birds, Wild Fowl and Shore Birds.*

EUROPEAN WIDGEON

Mareca penelope (*Linnæus*)

A. O. U. Number 136 See Color Plate 13

Other Names.— Widgeon; Whistler; Whewer; Whew; Whim.

Length.— 18 to 21 inches.

Color.— Adult Male: Differs from the Baldpate in having head and neck uniform cinnamon-red; top of head, creamy or white; rest of plumage similar. Adult Female: Differs in having entire plumage more suffused with yellowish-brown.

Nest and Eggs.— Similar to those of the Baldpate.

Distribution.— Northern part of the eastern hemisphere; occurs in winter and in migrations rarely in Wisconsin, Michigan, New York, Nova Scotia, Newfoundland, and Greenland south to Nebraska, Missouri, Indiana, Ohio, North Carolina and Florida, and in Alaska, British Columbia, and California.

The European Widgeon is an Old World species which occasionally appears in the western hemisphere. Normally it breeds among the grassy swamps and lakes of Norway and Sweden and is accounted the most abundant of the Ducks in Lapland. Sometimes it breeds on the lakes of northern Scotland but it is always an abundant winter visitor to southern Scotland and throughout England. In size and general character it closely resembles the Baldpate.

BALDPATE

Mareca americana (*Gmelin*)

A. O. U. Number 137 See Color Plate 13

Other Names.— American Widgeon; Bald Widgeon; Green-headed Widgeon; Southern Widgeon; California Widgeon; White-belly; Bald-head; Bald-crown; Ball-face; Smoking Duck; Wheat Duck; Poacher.

General Description.— Length, 18 to 21 inches. Males are brownish-gray above, and brownish-red and white below. Females are yellowish-brown above, and brownish and white below. Bill, small, widest near the base; tail with 14 feathers.

Description.— Adult Male: Head with short crest.

Drawn by R. I. Brasher

BALDPATE (½ nat. size)

A shy, wary, and garrulous Duck

Forehead, crown and back of head, white; a broad patch of glossy green on side of head extending around and down back of neck where it meets its fellow; cheeks and rest of neck, whitish with dusky spots; throat, dusky; back, shoulders, and rump, pale brownish-gray finely waved with dusky; breast, light brownish-red with pale gray edgings on feathers; sides of body, the same color waved with dusky; rest of lower parts, pure white except under tail-coverts which are black; lesser wing-coverts, plain gray; middle and greater coverts, pure white forming a large area, edged behind by black tips of the greater coverts; *speculum, glossy green bordered behind by black;* long inner secondaries, black with sharp white edges; rump and upper tail-coverts, white; the outside feathers of latter, dusky; primaries and their coverts, and tail, pale brownish-gray; this perfect plumage seen only in old drakes; bill, grayish-blue, black at tip and base below; feet, the same with dusky webs; iris, brown; usually the whole head and neck are pale brownish-yellow speckled with greenish and dusky. Adult Female: Head and neck all around, pale grayish; crown and back of neck, more brown with dusky spots; upper parts, yellowish-brown barred on back with dusky; shoulders spotted with the same; rump and upper tail-coverts, mixed brownish and white; tail, grayish-brown, the feathers white edged; wing, as in male but white area mottled with grayish; breast, brownish; rest of under parts, white; bill, feet, and eye, as in male.

Nest and Eggs.— Nest: On the ground in marshes; a neat well-built structure (for a Duck) of grass and weeds; lined with feathers and down from the breast of the bird. Eggs: 8 to 18, pale buffy.

Distribution.— North America in general; breeds from northwestern Alaska, northern Mackenzie, and central Keewatin south to Oregon, Nevada, Utah, Colorado, Kansas, southern Wisconsin, and northern Indiana; winters from southern British Columbia, southern Illinois, Maryland, and Delaware (casually Massachusetts and Rhode Island) south to southern Lower California, the West Indies, and Costa Rica; rare in migration to northern Ontario, northern Quebec, and Newfoundland; accidental in Hawaii, Bermuda, and Europe.

In the East the Baldpate or American Widgeon is a shy and wary bird and a great tell-tale. Quick to take the alarm itself, it is not slow to communicate it to others; and whenever a few Baldpates mix with a flock of other Ducks the sportsman must "mind his eye," or all his stratagems, disguises, and concealments will fail. In the Far West it is less wary.

Wild isolated lakes and rivers not much frequented by other Ducks often are chosen by the Baldpate as favorite nesting spots. Here they nest, usually among bushes or trees amid the dead leaves, often on high ground and not always near the water, but the eggs are well concealed and covered with their blanket of down. While the females are incubating, the males gather and, like the males of other River Ducks, go into the "eclipse" plumage, which closely resembles that of the female and leaves them inconspicuous in color during the summer while they molt and grow new wing quills.

As the season of migration approaches the Baldpates begin to move southward and many are shot in the northwestern States while flying from pond to pond; but they soon become shy, flying high over marshes and keeping well out of range of suspicious points, and by the last of October when they appear on the Atlantic coast they are difficult to kill.

The usual note of this bird is a soft whistle which is repeated often when the flock is on the wing. The flight is either in a line nearly abreast or in a group much like a flock of pigeons. Whenever anything alarms one of the flock a louder whistle warns all the others to shy off or climb the air.

The species is very fond of wild celery, but is a poor diver and depends somewhat upon the flocks of Redheads, Canvas-backs, Scaups, and Coot to dive for its food which it steals from their bills the moment they appear above water. The male may be recognized by the conspicuous white of the forehead and wing-coverts.

Courtesy of Nat. Asso. Aud. Soc.

NEST AND EGGS OF BALDPATE

The largest families are found among Ducks, Grouse, and Quails, the young of which are able to leave the nest as soon as the natal covering is dry

Edward Howe Forbush.

GREEN-WINGED TEAL

Nettion carolinense (*Gmelin*)

A. O. U. Number 139 See Color Plate 13

Other Names.— Green-wing; Red-headed Teal; Winter Teal; Mud Teal.

General Description.— Length, 14 inches. Males are gray and red above, and whitish and red below; females are brown above, and whitish below.

Description.— Adult Male: Head, slightly crested. *Head and upper neck, rich chestnut with a glossy green patch behind eye,* blackening on lower border and on back where it meets its fellow, bordered below by a whitish streak; upper parts, grayish, very finely waved with dusky; *speculum, velvet-black on outer half, rich glossy green on inner;* primaries and wing-coverts, grayish; greater coverts with chestnut tips margining the speculum in front; breast, warm brownish; rest of lower parts, whitish speckled with round dusky spots on breast; sides, grayish, finely waved with dusky; a white crescent in front of wing; bill, dusky lead color, darker below; feet, bluish-gray; iris, brown. Adult Female: Head (no crest) and neck, light warm brown, whitening on throat and darkening on crown, spotted with dark brown; upper parts, dark brown, each feather with distinct tawny edgings; sides of body, the same; rest of lower parts, whitish; wing as in male but speculum duller. Young of the Year: Resemble adult female.

Nest and Eggs.— Nest: On the ground, usually in a thick growth of grass or among willows; constructed of dry grass; lined with feathers and down. Eggs: 8 to 11, sometimes 12, pale buff.

Distribution.— North America at large; breeds from the Aleutian Islands across British America to Newfoundland, south to central California, northern New Mexico, northern Nebraska, northern Illinois, southern Ontario, Quebec, and New Brunswick; winters from Aleutian Islands, British Columbia, Nevada, southern Nebraska, northern Indiana, western New York, and Rhode Island (casually Nova Scotia) south to southern Lower California, the West Indies, and Honduras; accidental in Hawaii, Bermuda, Greenland, and Great Britain.

Teals might be called the bantams of the duck tribe, as regards size. Their swiftness of flight is in inverse ratio to mere bigness, and probably there is nothing more rapid that flies. The celerity with which a Teal can vault into the air when alarmed is astonishing. In all its movements it evinces a real grace, a peculiar charm. From the culinary standpoint, surely there is nothing more luscious in the realm of waterfowl, no, not even the vaunted Canvas-back.

Photo by H. K. Job Courtesy of Outing Pub. Co.

NEST OF GREEN-WINGED TEAL

The Green-wing and the Blue-wing are the two Teals of North America which are well known and widely distributed. Of the two the Green-wing is the hardier, lingering in the northern States late in the fall and even at times well into the winter, as long as there is any open water at all to be found in the ponds or at warm spring-holes. It is also, on the whole, the more northerly of the two, both in its winter range and in its breeding.

Of late years both species have been growing regrettably scarce in the eastern districts of the country. When found at all it is usually only a single bird or a pair. But in parts of the central and western districts there are still good flocks to be seen.

The nesting of the Green-wing is mostly in the Northwest, not so commonly on the sloughs of the open prairies of the Dakotas and southern Manitoba as in the more brush-grown regions further west and north. It grows more numerous as one penetrates into northern Manitoba and western Saskatchewan. In the latter it likes the alkaline ponds, and in the former the poplar forest lakes. The nest has seemed to me one of the most difficult of Ducks' nests to discover, in that it is usually located well back from water, sometimes near the edge of meadow and forest. These Teals frequent the open marshy pools, but my search for their nests in the grass nearby was usually in vain. They were generally discovered by accident. One was found near the cabin of an Indian half-breed by the edge of a cattle-pasture, amid grass, weeds, and low brush.

Others were under low bushes at the drier edges of meadows, back from the lake almost to the forest.

On a large island of a big alkaline lake in Saskatchewan it was my good fortune to discover my first nest of this species, which made the twentieth kind of Duck whose nesting I had discovered. The island was high and dry, open, overgrown with prairie grass and tracts of low brush. Many kinds of Ducks were nesting here and they kept flushing from their eggs close in front of me as I tramped about — Pintails, Gadwalls, Shovellers, Mallards, both Scaups, Blue-winged Teals, and others. Suddenly up fluttered a small duck with green on the wings. In the thick of the grass was a nest lined with soft down, containing a complement of eggs.

I have hatched and reared the young and find them hardy and easy to manage.

Herbert K. Job.

"The Green-winged Teal is fond of wild oats and rice, and takes seeds of various grasses and weeds, also chestnuts, acorns, wild grapes, berries, insects, crustaceans, worms, and small snails. Audubon states that he never found water lizards, fish, or even tadpoles in stomachs of this Teal. He regarded it, when fed upon soaked rice or wild oats, as far superior to the Canvas-back, and considered it the most luscious food of any American Duck. Possibly it might be domesticated to advantage, as it has been bred in captivity in a small way." (Forbush, in *Game Birds, Wild-Fowl and Shore Birds.*)

BLUE-WINGED TEAL

Querquedula discors (*Linnæus*)

A. O. U. Number 140 See Color Plate 14

Other Names.— Blue-wing; White-faced Teal; Summer Teal.

General Description.— Length, 16 inches. Males are variegated dark and light brown above, and purplish-gray and yellowish-gray below with spots of black. Females are dark brown above, variegated with lighter, and whitish below, mottled with brown.

Color.— Adult Male: Crown, grayish-black; *a large white black-edged crescent in front of eye;* rest of head, purplish-gray; lower hind-neck and fore-back,

Photo by H. K. Job Courtesy of Nat. Asso. Aud. Soc.

FLIGHT OF BLUE-WINGED TEALS

Louisiana

variegated with brownish-black and yellowish-brown; lower back and rump, dark brown with a greenish tinge; *wing-coverts and outer webs of some of the shoulder feathers, dull cobalt blue; speculum, rich mallard green* enclosed by white tips of greater coverts and secondaries; some inner secondaries, greenish-black on outer web, greenish-brown on inner, striped lengthwise with reddish-buff; breast, very pale purplish-gray; rest of under parts, yellowish-gray with innumerable round black spots on breast, sides, and below, changing to bars on flanks behind; under tail-coverts, black; a patch on each side of rump, pure white; bill, ashy, darkening on ridge and tip; feet, yellow, webs duller; iris, brown. Adult Female: Head and neck, dull buff; crown, brownish-dusky streaked with brownish-black; cheeks and chin, whitish, markings small or obsolete; upper parts, dark brown with pale yellowish-brown edgings to all feathers; below, grayish-white, slightly more brown on breast, mottled on breast with dusky spotting and on sides and flanks with V-shaped brownish marks; wings as in male but speculum duller; bill, greenish-dusky; feet, paler yellow. Young of the Year: Resemble adult female.

Nest and Eggs.— Nest: In marshes or on dry ground; constructed of grass and weed stems and lined with feathers and down. Eggs: 8 to 12, pale buffy.

Distribution.— Western hemisphere; breeds from central British Columbia, across British America to Newfoundland, south to Oregon, Nevada, New Mexico, Missouri, Indiana, northern Ohio, western New York (occasionally Rhode Island), and Maine; winters from about the parallel 36° south to the West Indies and South America as far as Brazil and Chile; accidental in Bermuda and Europe.

The Blue-winged Teal is quite similar to the Green-winged in many of its ways. One difference is that it is less able to endure cold. Before the heavy frosts of late autumn arrive, it is well to the southward. I have been told by hunters in Louisiana that in late October and November large columns of them pour along the Gulf coast and pass on into Texas and Mexico. However, a good many remain in Louisiana on the great reservations for the winter. In the winter of 1915–16 I saw there considerable numbers of this species, associating with the Green-wing, sometimes in flocks of several hundreds. Both kinds became quite gentle under protection, and would swim up within a few feet of blinds and of our cabin window and feast on rice which was scattered for them.

Drawing by R. I. Brasher

BLUE-WINGED TEAL (½ nat. size)

It becomes quite gentle and tame under protection

Quite a number of the Blue-wings remain each summer to breed in Louisiana. The general impression seemed to be that this is a rather new thing, and that they are breeding further south than usual because of protection. For the same reason, since the abolition of spring shooting, they are said to be nesting more and more in the central-western States. The Green-wing, however, still elects to go well to the north.

Photo by H. K. Job Courtesy of Outing Pub. Co.

BLUE-WINGED TEALS

About one month old

The Blue-wing is the common summer Teal of the open prairie regions of the northwest. In selecting its nesting-site it does not retire as far from the water as the Green-wing, but generally chooses the thick growth of prairie grass of the preceding year's growth, only a few rods back from the shallow marshy sloughs. Sometimes, however, it is placed on the dry prairie, half a mile from water.

The mother Blue-wing always approaches her nest with great caution, not flying directly to it, but, alighting at a distance, she sneaks through the grass and weeds. In leaving the nest she pulls over it the blanket of gray down which she has plucked from her breast as a lining, entirely concealing the eggs, and making the nest practically invisible. After returning she sits very close, allowing herself almost to be stepped on before she will leave. Confident of her powers of concealment, she seems more apt than most other Ducks, except perhaps the other Teals, the Pintail, and the Shoveller, to nest carelessly near the haunts of man, in the prairie regions of her choice. The nests of these confiding Duck mothers may be placed beside a path or road, in a cattle-yard, or near a house. One summer I was at a hunter's camp just back from Lake Manitoba, and many times a day we followed a little path to the water. One day a boy walked a little off the trail, and came tearing back to camp to report having flushed a Duck from her eggs. It was a nest of this species, only a dozen feet from the path, in the prairie grass.

The Blue-wing prefers little shallow marshy pools, or meadows and bogs, to the larger open waters. Its food in the ponds includes much vegetable matter, seeds, grasses, pondweeds, etc. It also at times devours snails, tadpoles, and many insects.

Photo by H. K. Job Courtesy of Outing Pub. Co.

NEST OF BLUE-WINGED TEAL

Formerly in North Dakota I used to see it, often with the Shoveller or the Pintail, almost wherever there was the merest puddle by the roadside, in spring and early summer. Let us hope that it may continue abundant and intimate on the western farm. HERBERT K. JOB.

CINNAMON TEAL

Querquedula cyanoptera (*Vieillot*)

A. O. U. Number 141.

Other Names.— South American Teal; Red-breasted Teal.

General Description.— Length, 17 inches. Males have the head and under parts chestnut, and the upper parts brown. Females are dark brown above, variegated with lighter, and whitish below, mottled with brown.

Color.— ADULT MALE: *Head, neck, and entire under parts, rich purplish chestnut,* browner on crown and chin, blackening on center of abdomen; under tail-coverts, dark brown; fore-back, a lighter shade of same color crossed by brown curved bars; lower back and rump, greenish-brown, the feathers edged with paler; wing-coverts, cobalt-blue; some of the shoulder feathers, blue on outer web with a yellow center stripe; others, dark green, also with center stripe; *speculum, bright green* framed between white tips of greater coverts and white ends of secondaries; bill, dusky; feet, orange, webs, darker; iris, brown. ADULT FEMALE: Quite similar to female Blue-winged Teal, but larger with longer bill and under parts with some tinges of the chestnut color of the male; bill, dusky, paler below and along edges; feet dull yellowish; iris, brown.

Nest and Eggs.— NEST: In tall grass, usually near water; very well constructed of woven grass and lined with feathers and down. EGGS: 9 to 13, creamy-white.

Distribution.— North and South America; breeds in North America from southern British Columbia, southwestern Alberta, Wyoming, and Western Kansas south to northern Lower California, southern New Mexico and southwestern Texas; winters from southern California, central New Mexico and southern Texas south to southern Lower California and central Mexico; rare east of the 100th meridan; occurs in South America from Peru and Brazil south to the Falkland Islands.

There are several curious facts concerning the Cinnamon Teal. It seems to have been first described from a specimen taken in the faraway Straits of Magellan early in the 19th century. Its first recorded appearance in the United States apparently was in Louisiana near the town of Opelousas in 1849, but strangely enough it is now seldom seen in that State. At about that time, indeed, it appeared frequently in the lower valley of the Mississippi, but its normal range now appears to be much further to the west and south, for reasons which are not apparent. It is now essentially a bird of the West.

A flock of Cinnamon Teals in the water are likely to present an enlivening spectacle, as the males often engage in some sort of play not unlike the boy's game of leap-frog.

"The Cinnamon Teal nests very commonly in the lake region of southern Oregon. I have seen it nesting all through this section from Klamath Lake to Malheur Lake. In some places in southern Oregon it is more abundant than the Mallard or the Pintail. I think sportsmen often mistake the female for the Blue-winged Teal, because of the blue wing-markings." (W. L. Finley, MS.)

SHOVELLER

Spatula clypeata (*Linnæus*)

A. O. U. Number 142 See Color Plate 14

Other Names.— Spoonbill; Spoonbill Duck; Spoonbill Teal; Broady; Blue-winged Shoveller; Red-breasted Shoveller; Shovel-bill; Swaddle-bill; Butter Duck; Cow-frog.

General Description.— Length, 17 to 21 inches. Males have the colors green, white, blue, black, grayish-brown, and red in patches, while the females are pale brownish-yellow with spots and streaks of dusky. Both sexes have the bill long and clumsy and broadened at the tip.

Color.— Adult Male: Head and neck, dark glossy green; lower neck and *fore-breast, pure white,* extending almost around body; a narrow line from green of head down back of neck and back, dark grayish-brown shading into black on rump and upper tail-coverts; shoulders, broadly white; *wing-coverts and some outer feathers of shoulders, dull cobalt;* speculum, rich green set between white tips of greater coverts and black and white tips of secondaries; the long inner secondaries, greenish-black with white stripe; *lower breast, abdomen, and sides, purplish-chestnut,* lightening behind, followed by a white space; center tail-feathers, dusky; outer ones, white; under tail-coverts, black; bill, purplish dusky; feet, vermilion or orange; iris, orange or yellow. Adult Female: Ground color all over, pale brownish-yellow closely and narrowly streaked on crown, finely spotted on sides of head and neck all around with dusky; feathers of back and sides, broadly brownish-black, leaving only narrow edges of the lighter color; wing as in male but coloration duller; bill, yellowish shading to dull greenish at tip with some orange below and at base; iris, yellow; feet, dull orange.

Nest and Eggs.— Nest: Located in the marshes or in dry grass or under bushes; constructed of grass and leaves, and lined with feathers and down. Eggs: 8 to 14, olive-greenish or buffy.

Distribution.— Northern hemisphere; in North America breeds from Alaska, Mackenzie and southern Keewatin south to southern California, central New Mexico, northern Texas, northern Missouri and northern Indiana; winters from southern British Columbia across the United States on about the parallel 35° south to the West Indies, Colombia, and Hawaii; in migration occasional in Bermuda, and north to Nova Scotia and Newfoundland.

Drawing by R. Bruce Horsfall

SHOVELLER (½ nat. size)

A quaint Duck, always carrying with it a prodigious spoon

Though it is the wise practice to try to establish only one vernacular name for each species, I think that this Duck is better known as " Spoonbill " by the average hunter and out-door person. Nor is this name absurd, as is sometimes the case with popular names. The bird certainly carries quite a prodigious spoon with it upon all occasions, and is never at a loss to use it deftly in its natural haunts. A popular name for it might well have been " mud-sucker." The great bill is edged with a long fringe of bristles, and the quaint little Duck, almost top-heavy in appearance, paddles through the slough, constantly dabbling in water and ooze, which it takes into its bill, and, ejecting the refuse through its " sieve," retains whatever nutritious matter there may be.

This is another fresh-water Duck which is scarce in eastern districts but common in the West. There it frequents the shallow sloughs and bogs. It seems to be more strictly insectivorous than some of the other Ducks. Though they were abundant in Louisiana in winter, and were associated with the many Pintails and Teals which ate the rice put out for them, the Shovellers seldom touched it, not that they were particularly shy, but apparently because they preferred the natural fare of bugs and aquatic growths.

I have watched the Shovellers a good deal, as they nested in the prairie sloughs of the Northwest. In spring the male is a very gaudy creature, far outshining his plain little wife as they swim in the slough. They are then quite tame and easy to observe, and I have seen them in roadside pools, and even in swampy barnyards, where it seemed that they must be domesticated Ducks, until suddenly they flew away.

Nesting is usually in rather thick grass, frequently only a short distance back from the edge of the slough, or even in a tussock on quite moist ground. Yet, on the other hand, it is often far back on the dry prairie, quite a distance from water. Really there is no accounting for the tastes of individual Ducks.

Speaking of taste, in another sense, many people have the idea that the Shoveller is a lean, scrawny sort of bird, always thin and poor eating. My experience has been that, on its winter grounds in the South, it is fat and luscious, quite as good as one of those delicious little morsels, the Teals.

It is a rather delicate bird, and does not stand the cold as well as many other Ducks. Hence it migrates fairly early and goes well to the South. If kept in captivity over winter in the North, both it and Teals should have some shelter from the worst of the winter weather. I have known them, in very bitter cold, to have their bills accumulate balls of ice as the water trickled down the bristles and froze. Probably no better plan could be employed for wintering these delicate Ducks than the model aquatic house which we have adopted for this purpose at the experiment station of the National Audubon Society at Amston, Conn. It is a small house built out in the water on posts, the inside being a swimming-pool and a float, with large frame windows to the south and west, to utilize all possible sunshine. There the Ducks thrive in comfort all winter, without having the water freeze, even when 15 degrees below zero outside, and in spring they are not reduced in vitality, and are in fine condition to breed. HERBERT K. JOB.

Photo by H. K. Job Courtesy of Outing Pub. Co.

YOUNG SHOVELLERS

"Audubon states that repeated inspections of stomachs of these species disclosed leeches, small fish, earthworms, and snails. It feeds also on aquatic plants, grasses, grass seeds, and bulbs, which it procures along the shores of small ponds which it frequents. It often feeds by wading and dabbling in the mud, straining mud and water through its peculiarly constructed bill. Dr. James P. Hatch states that it feeds on aquatic insects, larvæ, tadpoles, worms, etc., which it finds in shallow, muddy waters; also crustaceans, small mollusks and snails." (Forbush, in *Game Birds, Wild Fowl and Shore Birds.*)

PINTAIL

Dafila acuta (*Linnæus*)

A. O. U. Number 143 See Color Plate 15

Other Names.— Male: Sprig-tail; Split-tail; Spike-tail; Picket-tail; Peak-tail; Sharp-tail; Sprit-tail; Spring-tail; Spindle-tail; Kite-tail; Pigeon-tail; Pheasant-dock; Sea-pheasant. Female: Gray Duck; Pied Gray Duck; Pied Widgeon. Either Sex: Winter Duck; Lady-bird; Long-necked Cracker; Harlan; Smee.

General Description.— Length, 24 to 30 inches. Males are gray above and whitish below; females are brown, varied on body with ocher and dusky. Both sexes have the head small and not crested, the neck long, and the tail long and pointed with 16 feathers; in the male *the two central tail-feathers are from 5 to 9 inches in length.*

Color.— Adult Male: Head and neck above, dark brown glossed with green and purple; back of neck with a stripe shading into the gray color of back; back, finely waved with dusky and white; shoulder-feathers and long inner secondaries, striped lengthwise with velvety-black and silvery-gray; lesser wing-coverts, plain gray; *greater coverts, tipped with rufous or cinnamon,* edging front of speculum; speculum, greenish in front, bronzy with violet reflections behind where edged with the white tips of secondaries; *two long central tail-feathers, black;* the remaining fourteen tail-feathers, gray; throat, white running up behind back of head in a narrow stripe; breast, abdomen and sides, whitish, finely waved with black on sides; under tail-coverts, black; bill and feet, grayish-blue; iris, brown. Adult Female: Head and neck all around, warm yellowish-brown with indistinct streaking; rest of plumage, varied with ocher, plain brown, and dusky; tail without long central feathers; wing, as in male but much smaller; bill, dusky bluish; feet, dull grayish-blue; iris, brown.

Nest and Eggs.— Nest: On the ground, usually in tall bunches of prairie grass, near water; made of dry grass, snugly and warmly lined with down. Eggs: 7 to 10, pale greenish to olive-buff.

Distribution.— Northern hemisphere; in North America breeds on Arctic coast from Alaska to Keewatin and south to southern California, southern Colorado, northern Nebraska, northern Iowa, and northern Illinois; winters from southern British Columbia, Nevada, Arizona, southern Missouri; southern Wisconsin, southern Ohio, Pennsylvania (rarely), and Delaware south to Porto Rico and Panama, and in Hawaii; in migration occasional on the Atlantic coast to northern Ungava, Greenland, and Newfoundland, and in Bermuda.

In other writings I have characterized the Pintail as the greyhound among waterfowl. It is an interesting, agile, swift-flying, hardy species, the male being wonderfully garbed in a most effective blending of gray, white, and brown, surpassing many other birds of more gaudy hues. Though shy enough ordinarily, it becomes readily accustomed to man. The young are easy to rear and grow up very tame. I predict that the time is not far distant when the domesticated Pintails will be almost as familiar as tame Mallards, and will be raised on preserves and estates

Photograph by H. K. Job Courtesy of Outing Publishing Co.

PINTAILS

Flying past blind and decoys, Little Vermilion Bay, Louisiana for sporting purposes, for food, or for ornament.

Though Pintails breed in the northerly parts of the continent, they also do so in our northwestern States. They are hardy and early, arriving in spring often before all the ice is out of the lakes. In northern Manitoba I have seen young on June 25 that were fully fledged except that the primaries were not quite long enough for flight. The eggs must have been laid in late March or April when conditions there are decidedly wintry. The nest is usually in dry grass or in a clump of weeds. Small dry islands are favorite locations. Otherwise it seems to be placed quite regardless of proximity to water. Frequently I have found it far back on the dry prairie, probably a mile from the nearest slough. It is perhaps more flimsily built than with most other Ducks, and often has rather less down than the average. The number of eggs in a clutch has seemed to me, in my experience, to run slightly less than with other species, seven or eight being most common, and seldom over nine or ten.

In migration it is not at all common in eastern waters, but in the Mississippi valley and west it is probably next to the Mallard in abundance. It prefers shallow ponds and marshy areas where grass and sedge grow from the water. In the sloughs where it breeds, the mated pairs swimming about make a beautiful sight. Even in autumn when the male has lost for the time his distinctive plumage, the birds are quite distinct, owing to their slender forms and long necks, and their movements always have the air of grace and good breeding. In fact the Pintail is one of my special favorites. Though I prefer it alive, I must admit that it is very fine on the table, and that I had just as soon eat it as any other Duck. On one of my winter jaunts in Louisiana, the hunters of the party provided many a Pintail, and it was considered that one Duck at a meal for each man was just the right amount.

By November the Pintails are abundant on the marshes of Louisiana where, in some localities, they winter by thousands. In the winter of 1915 I found it the general testimony that this species had increased wonderfully in abundance during the last few seasons, which result was attributed directly to the stopping of spring shooting — that outrage against reason and conservation, now made an offense by Federal Law and by our International Treaty. They were fond of grain, and, on putting this out, various Ducks, but chiefly Pintails, would assemble in large numbers to feast upon it, becoming so bold that I was able to film and to photograph large numbers of them from blinds, and even from the windows of our cabin on the marsh.

HERBERT K. JOB.

WOOD DUCK

Aix sponsa (*Linnæus*)

A. O. U. Number 144 See Color Plate 14

Other Names.— Summer Duck; The Bride; Bridal Duck; Wood Widgeon; Acorn Duck; Tree Duck.

General Description.— Length, 20 inches. Males are green, blue, and purple above with white streaks, and red, yellow, and white below. Females are brown above, and yellowish-brown and whitish below. Both sexes have long, full crests; the bill narrow, higher at base than wide; the tail long with soft, broad feathers.

Color.— ADULT MALE: Head, including crest, iridescent green and purple; a narrow white line from bill over eye to rear of crest; another commencing behind eye and running to nape; a broad white patch on throat forking behind, one streak curving upward behind eye, the other curving on side of neck; above, lustrous violet and bronzy green; shoulders and long inner secondaries, velvet-black glossed with purple and green; a greenish-blue speculum bounded by white tips of secondaries behind; primaries, white-edged and frosted on webs near end; upper tail-coverts and tail, deep dusky black; *sides and front of lower neck and breast, rich purplish-chestnut evenly marked with small V-shaped white spots;* a large black crescent in front of wing preceded by a white one; sides, yellowish-gray waved with fine black bars; rest of *under parts, white;* lengthened flank feathers falling in a tuft of rich purplish-red below wing; bill, white in center, black on ridge, tip, and below, with a square patch at base of lake-red; feet, yellowish-orange; iris and lids crimson. ADULT FEMALE: Crest small; head and neck, grayish-brown, darker on crown; feathers at base of bill narrowly all around, chin, upper throat, and *a broad circle around eye running into a streak behind, pure white;* upper parts, brown with some gloss; fore-neck and sides of body, yellowish-brown streaked with darker; breast spotted indistinctly with brown; abdomen, white; bill, grayish with a white spot in center, reddish at base; feet, dusky yellow; iris, brownish red.

Nest and Eggs.— NEST: In a hollow tree from 20 to 40 feet from ground, lined with feathers and down. EGGS: 8 to 14, creamy-white.

Distribution.— Temperate North America; breeds from southern British Columbia eastward on about the parallel 46° to New Brunswick and Nova Scotia, south to central California, Texas and Florida; winters chiefly in United States from about 37° southward; accidental in Bermuda, Mexico, Jamaica, and Europe.

The Wood Duck is one of the most richly and beautifully colored birds of the United States, and, for a migratory bird, is peculiarly ours, in that it breeds nearly all over our national domain, from north to south, and in winter it mostly remains within our borders. More than any other Duck it is a woodland bird. It frequents ponds and streams which are bordered by woods, and makes excursions, a-wing or a-foot, or both, back from water into the real woods, where it devours nuts, as well as whatever insect or other small life it encounters. I have examined specimens, taken in the fall, which had their crops completely filled with whole acorns. Such a meal, surely, should "stand by" for a long time!

Photo by H. K. Job

MALE WOOD DUCK

The regular natural nesting site is in a hollow tree, preferably in the woods, and it is often quite a distance back from water. Owing to the increasing scarcity of large hollow trees, these Ducks seem at times hard pressed to find suitable locations. On a farm in Connecticut back from a pond, an old apple tree growing in a pig-pen by the barn was cut down, and, in chopping open a hollow branch, eleven eggs of the Wood Duck were discovered, though never had a Duck been seen about the premises. About a mile from this place another farmer showed me a nest with ten eggs at the top of the hay in his barn, up near the roof. The mother Duck came through a broken clapboard up near the peak of the roof, dug a hollow in the hay, and lined it with down from her breast. Still another nest, on this same farm, was in an apple tree of the orchard. A couple of miles away another was in a large maple beside the highway, so low down than one could just peer in from the ground. It is surprising through what a small hole a Duck can pass to enter and leave a nest. In one case which I witnessed, a Golden-eye, emerging from quite a narrow slit, had fairly to wriggle from side to side to force its way out.

After the nesting season the Wood Ducks are seen in small flocks, probably family parties. They frequent the wooded swamps, and fly out to the more open ponds and streams about dusk. Where dead trees or branches have fallen into water, a typical sight, to be witnessed by creeping very silently through the bushes, is a row of these beautiful Ducks standing on the fallen timber enjoying the sunshine, some asleep, with bills under the wing-coverts, others preening their feathers, but all appearing very well contented with their lot in life.

This bird was classed by the Government as one of our vanishing species. This aroused widespread concern, and caused a number of States to prohibit shooting for terms of years; the same action was adopted also by Federal regulations. There seems now to be a marked change for the better, in which result artificial

Courtesy of S. A. Lottridge

NEST AND EGGS OF WOOD DUCK

The regular nesting site is in a hollow tree, preferably in the woods, and is often a distance from water

propagation is playing an important part. It had been found that this Duck, through somewhat peculiar but perfectly practicable methods, can be bred and reared in captivity, birds thus raised bringing high prices. Quite an industry arose in breeding American Wood Ducks in Holland and selling them in America. Now we have learned the process ourselves, and anyone who desires can breed these beautiful birds in almost any small fenced pool or pond. To those who desire it, the National Association of Audubon Societies, through its Department of Applied Ornithology, imparts detailed information and furnishes literature. HERBERT K. JOB.

REDHEAD

Marila americana (*Eyton*)

A. O. U. Number 146 See Color Plate 16

Other Names.— American Pochard or Poachard; Red-headed Broadbill; Raft Duck; Red-headed Raft Duck.

General Description.— Length, 23 inches. Males have the head red, the neck and fore part of the body blackish, and the remainder of the body silver-gray above and on the sides with a center line below of white; females have the head duller and paler and the back browner. Both sexes have the *bill short, the skull rounded and high-arched, the feathers on the head presenting a puffy appearance,* and the hind toe with a web or lobe.

Color.— ADULT MALE: The entire head and the *neck all around, rich pure chestnut* with bronzy reflections; back, white crossed with fine black wavy lines, the colors about *equal* in amount, producing a distinct silvery-gray shade; sides of body, the same; lower neck and fore-parts of body with rump and tail-coverts above and below, blackish; wing-coverts, gray finely dotted with white; speculum, ash, bordered inside with black; center line of body below, whitish; bill, dull blue with a black band on end; feet, grayish-blue with dusky webs; *iris, yellowish-orange.* ADULT FEMALE: Head and upper neck, dull brownish-red, fading to whiter on cheeks, chin, and a space behind eye; upper parts, brownish, the feathers with paler edges; breast and sides, brownish, remainder of lower parts, white; bill, dull grayish-blue with brown belt near end; feet and iris, as in male.

Nest and Eggs.— NEST: On ground near water or in a clump of dead reeds over the water; bulky but well-constructed and lined with down. EGGS: 7 to 10, pale olive or light buff.

Distribution.— North America; breeds from southern British Columbia, central Alberta, central Saskatchewan, and southwestern Keewatin south to southern California, Utah, southern South Dakota, southern Minnesota, and southern Wisconsin; winters from southern British Columbia, Utah, New Mexico, Kansas, Illinois, Maryland, Delaware, and Massachusetts south to Lower California, central Mexico, and Florida; accidental in Jamaica; in migration casual in Alaska and regularly on the Atlantic coast north to southern Labrador.

In the Redhead we have the counterpart of the Canvas-back. The young of either can hardly be distinguished save by the shape of the bill, especially in the downy stage. Later they grow more apart, yet they retain many resemblances. Many a person who thinks he has eaten Canvas-back has very likely dined instead on Redhead.

It is usual to find the Redhead the more numerous of the two, though along the Gulf coast of Louisiana, where Audubon found Redheads in plenty, I have found them now to be rare, even in sections where the Canvas-back is abundant. Like the latter, it is found mostly on the sea-coast or on the larger bodies of water inland. It feeds much by diving, catching small fish and other aquatic life. Also it is partial to roots and shoots of aquatic plants. I have

Photo by H. K. Job Courtesy of Outing Pub. Co.

YOUNG REDHEADS

Eighteen days of age

watched both species together diving, and both exhibit the same skill and celerity in this pursuit, with no noticeable difference.

This species, like the others, breeds in the sloughs and marshes of the Northwest, in about the same localities, but is generally the more common. Wherever I have found the Canvas-back breeding, the Redhead has been there too, whereas the converse is not true; there are many sloughs in which Redheads breed where there are no Canvas-backs. If there is any distinction in the choice of nesting-sites, I should say that the Redhead is even more apt than the other to build out in reeds or canes growing in quite deep water. In northern Manitoba, on Lake Winnipegosis, in places where the Canvas-back was nesting in meadows in the sedge, with water not knee-deep, I found Redhead nests among the outer reeds on the margins of boggy ponds, where one needed a canoe to reach them.

Perhaps the Redhead is not more prolific than any other Duck, but I have found larger numbers of eggs in some of their nests than is at all usual with others, the maximum number being twenty-two, the most I ever found in a wild Duck's nest, and all fertiie and advanced in incubation. The eggs are quite different from those of the Canvas-back, being yellowish-white in color, and with a very smooth glossy surface, almost like billiard balls, and easy to recognize.

Photo by H. K. Job Courtesy of Outing Pub. Co.

NEST OF REDHEAD

Built over water on edge of channel in a clump of flags and rushes

In the Northwest where wild Ducks nest in abundance, it is not uncommon for individual Ducks to lay in each other's nests. The Redhead and the Ruddy Duck seemed to me to be especially addicted to the practice. They laid rather freely in each other's nests, and frequently palmed off their offspring thus on the unsuspecting Canvas-back.

Photo by H. K. Job Courtesy of Outing Pub. Co.

HARDY AND DOCILE

Some more young Redheads

Both kinds have been kept and studied in captivity. I have reared both from the egg to maturity, and under my direction have had both kinds breed. Though the young of both were quite easily reared, the Redhead presents fewer difficulties than the Canvas-back. It breeds more readily under favorable conditions, and the young are especially hardy and docile, though the young Canvas-backs, too, are quite manageable. Most experimenters, in time past, have had much less difficulty in keeping Redheads than Canvas-backs under artificial conditions.

As a result of this line of experimental research, I am confident that in the not distant future both kinds will regularly be propagated on estates where there are suitable ponds.

HERBERT K. JOB.

CANVAS-BACK

Marila valisineria (*Wilson*)

A. O. U. Number 147 See Color Plate 16

Other Names.— White-back; Bull-neck; Can.

General Description.— Length, 24 inches. Males have the head red, the lower part of the neck and the fore part of the body blackish, and the remainder of the body grayish-white above with a center line below of white; females have the head and neck yellowish-brown and the body grayish-brown. Both sexes have *the profile long and sloping* (*lines of head and bill nearly one*), bill three times as long as wide, and hind toe with web or lobe.

Color.— ADULT MALE: Feathers of entire head and upper neck (all around) dark reddish-brown, obscured on the crown and in front of eye and throat by dusky; upper parts, white very finely waved with narrow black zigzag bars, the general effect much lighter than in the Redhead; rest of plumage substantially as in that bird but upper tail-coverts and rear parts in general, grayer; *bill, plain dusky bluish, not banded;* feet, grayish-blue; *iris, red.* ADULT FEMALE: Very similar to the female Redhead; head and neck, more brownish without rufous shade but easily distinguished from that bird *by the much longer and differently shaped bill;* iris, reddish-brown; bill and feet, as in the male Canvas-back.

Nest and Eggs.— NEST: Usually in tall rushes or reeds near water; bulky; constructed of dry grass and reeds; lined with down. EGGS: 6 to 10, pale olive green.

Distribution.— Whole of North America, breeding from Oregon, Nevada, Nebraska and southern Minnesota northward to southwestern Keewatin, Great Slave Lake, Fort Yukon, and central British Columbia; winters from southern British Columbia, Nevada, Colorado, Illinois, Pennsylvania, and western New York south to central Mexico and Gulf coast; in winter formerly abundant in Maryland, Virginia, and North Carolina, now rare; occasional south to Florida, and casual in the West Indies, Bermuda, and Guatemala; in migration north rarely to New Brunswick and Nova Scotia.

CANVAS-BACK (½ nat. size)

The king of waterfowl, famous for the flavor of its flesh

Drawing by R. I. Brasher

Though the Canvas-back has acquired a great reputation for the flavor of its flesh, it is probable that this characteristic taste depends upon

Photo by H. K. Job Courtesy of Doubleday, Page & Co.

TYPICAL NEST OF CANVAS-BACK

the local food supply. Various water-plants besides the spicy wild celery please His Majesty, the assumed king of waterfowl, so he is not always spiced up. At various times when I have eaten Canvas-back, I really could not distinguish it from other good-meated wild Ducks. In northern Manitoba the local hunters, I was told, when shooting, usually single out Mallards first, finding them meatier and fully as tasty.

None the less is the Canvas-back a most fascinating waterfowl. Swifter than the proverbial arrow, the flocks fairly sing like bullets, as they pass down wind. Wonderfully agile and graceful are their movements in the water, especially when they leap headlong for the dive, leaving one to guess where they may reappear. I once watched two Indians in the Northwest, each in a canoe, out on a large lake, try to catch a large young Canvas-back not yet quite able to fly. It took them about an hour of the liveliest sort of work before the bird rose, winded, to the surface and let one of them pick it up.

Its breeding-grounds are the marshes and sloughs of the interior Northwest — North Dakota, Manitoba, Saskatchewan, and on up into the trackless wilds. There I have often found its nest, a semi-floating pile of dead stems, usually amid a clump of reeds or rushes, or else in long sedge, but always in vegetation growing from water usually at least knee deep. The nest is a sort of deep wicker-basket, lined with dark gray down, in contrast with the white down of the Redhead. The eggs usually number eight to eleven, and are of a peculiar lead-bluish color, with some olive tinge, differing from that of any other Duck. The ducklings are of a decided yellow-olive color. From the first they may be distinguished from others by the straight profile of the upper mandible, always characteristic of the Canvas-back.

A most hardy species, it is driven southward only by the actual freezing of the lakes. Numbers of them stay in Lake Cayuga, New York, and other similar bodies of water, till they sometimes freeze in and perish. One of their principal lines of migration is southeast across country from the breeding-grounds of the Northwest out to the Atlantic coast at Chesapeake Bay — a noted winter resort of the species.

Photo by H. K. Job Courtesy of Outing Pub. Co.

CANVAS-BACK

About six weeks old

Despite incessant persecution, I think that the Canvas-back is on the increase, owing to the stopping of the suicidal practice of spring shooting. Recently, I was studying waterfowl in the Mississippi Delta country, and was anchored off the exit of Pass, in a dense fog. This suddenly lifted, and we saw, stretched out before us, a solid "bed" of Ducks, surely half a mile long and one hundred yards wide. The guide and I estimated that there were thirty-five thousand, over one-half of which were Canvas-backs. And this was but one of many such hordes along that coast. Cheer up, friends of wild birds, the "King" still lives!

Herbert K. Job.

SCAUP DUCK

Marila marila (*Linnæus*)

A. O. U. Number 148 See Color Plate 17

Other Names.— Mussel Duck; Green-head; Black-neck; Gray-back; Blue-bill; Greater Blue-bill; Blue-billed Widgeon; Broad-bill; Raft Duck; Flock Duck; Shuffler; Black-head; Big Black-head; Floating Fowl; American Scaup Duck; Greater Scaup Duck; Troop-fowl.

General Description.— Length, 20 inches. Males have the fore parts black, and the rest of the body white marked with black; females are dusky-brownish above and yellowish-brown below. Both sexes have the bill short and wide, and the hind toe with web or lobe.

Color.— Adult Male: *Entire head, neck, and fore parts of body, black with green and bluish reflections;* middle of back, shoulders, and most of under parts, white, everywhere except on flanks and abdomen marked with fine transverse zigzag lines of black; wing-coverts similar but more obscurely waved; greater coverts, tipped with black; *speculum, white framed in black* of greater coverts and ends of secondaries; primaries, brownish-black; *bill, dull bluish-gray* with black nail; feet, bluish-gray; webs, dusky; iris, yellow. Adult Female: *A belt of pure white around face at base of bill;* black parts of male replaced by dusky-brown; upper parts in general, dusky-brownish without black marking; wing, as in male; below yellowish-brown, duskier on breast and along sides; center line of body, whitish; bill, legs, and eyes as in male.

Nest and Eggs.— Nest: In marshy ground, made of weeds, grass and lined with down. Eggs: 9 to 12, pale buffy-olive or olive-gray.

Distribution.— Northern part of northern hemisphere; in North America breeds from about the parallel 48° northward, rarely on Magdalen Islands, in Ontario, and Michigan; winters from Maine to Florida and the Bahamas, and from Alaska, Nevada, Colorado and Lake Ontario south to southern California, southern New Mexico, and southern Texas; in migration rare in central Ungava, Newfoundland, and Nova Scotia.

Photograph by A. A. Allen

SCAUP DUCKS

Flying over Cayuga Lake

Scaup is the European name of this bird but it will hardly be recognized under that title by American gunners. Here it is known as the Broad-bill, Blue-bill, Blue-billed Widgeon, Widgeon, etc. It seems more inclined to migrate to salt water than does the Lesser Scaup, but this may be because its winter habitat is more northern and it is more likely to be driven to the open sea by the freezing of the fresh water. It is common in winter in the unfrozen marshes and lakes of central New York, but if these freeze it must go to the sea or starve. Therefore, the species is often more numerous in the late winter and early spring on the coastal waters than it is in the autumn and early winter while the lakes remain open.

These birds breed mainly in the Northwest in marshes and about numerous small ponds. Those that migrate to the Atlantic coast winter chiefly from Massachusetts to Chesapeake Bay, while farther south their place is taken mainly by the Lesser Scaup. They are swift flyers, showing a stripe of white on the wing as they pass in a characteristic waving line. The male may be distinguished from the male Lesser Scaup, which he closely resembles, by the color of the head which has a greenish luster in contrast with the purplish cast common on that of the lesser bird. At a distance both appear black; therefore, they are called Black-heads, indiscriminately. The white faces of the females of both species are very conspicuous.

The Scaup is an excellent diver and when it has been feeding in the interior on the roots of the wild celery (*vallisneria*) and other water plants, its flesh is fit for the epicure, and even when it feeds on the eel grass and other vegetation on salt marshes and flats it is fairly well flavored, but after it has fed for a time in salt water on crustaceans and mollusks it grows fishy and is not highly prized for the table.

EDWARD HOWE FORBUSH.

LESSER SCAUP DUCK

Marila affinis (*Eyton*)

A. O. U. Number 149 See Color Plate 17

Other Names.— Black Jack; River Broad-bill; Creek Broad-bill; and names of the Scaup Duck with or without qualifying terms.

Length.— 17 inches.

Description.— ADULT MALE: Varies principally from the Scaup Duck in size; *iridescence of head chiefly purple;* flank feathers finely marked with black in a zigzag pattern; otherwise similar. ADULT FEMALE: Very similar to the female Scaup Duck but smaller and with breast and sides more inclined to rufous-brown.

Nest and Eggs.— Similar to Scaup, eggs averaging smaller.

Distribution.— North America at large; breeds from the northern borders of the United States northward; more rarely to southern Montana, Colorado, northern Iowa, northern Indiana, and western Lake Erie; winters from southern British Columbia, Nevada, Colorado, Lake Erie, and New Jersey south to the Bahamas, Lesser Antilles, and Panama; rare in migration in Newfoundland, New Brunswick, and Nova Scotia.

The species of marine Duck which is probably under more general observation than any other is the Lesser Scaup. These are the Ducks which are seen in great "rafts" or "beds" just offshore in harbors or bays in winter and early spring nearly all along the Atlantic coast, from Long Island Sound to Florida. They feed, by diving, largely on mollusks or other sluggish marine life.

A flock settles on the water over some mussel-bed or clam-flat, and the members are soon diving actively. Another passing flock sees and joins it, and so on, until there may be several thousands. These usually stretch out into a long column, and keep swimming to windward, after satisfying their hunger, the white-penciled backs of the males glistening brilliantly in the sunshine.

In some localities, where they are not persecuted, these flocks become quite tame. At Tampa, Florida, they swim up right among the vessels lying at the wharves. The greatest sight is at Palm Beach, Florida, in Lake Worth. There flocks of them swim close up to the boat-landings back of the hotels. Guests throw out bread and are wonderfully amused to see wild Ducks fight for food within six to ten feet of their benefactors. Sometimes they even take food from the outstretched hand. The strangest part of this is that when they fly outside the protected area they become as shy as ever.

Hardy, like all the marine Ducks, they are especially late in arriving in autumn along the Atlantic coast of the United States. Little is seen of them till November. At first they seem inclined to keep out on the open sea, and the gunners get little chance at them before severe cold drives them in.

One reason for this tardiness is that, next to the White-winged Scoter, the Scaup is ordinarily the last Duck to breed. They nest in the same prairie marshes of the Northwest as do the Canvas-back and Redhead. There I have found that their layings are not complete until about the middle of June. The first young broods are generally seen in the sloughs toward the middle of July. As it is ten or eleven weeks before they can fly, the young are not a-wing before late September or early October.

The nests are not usually built out over the water like those of the Canvas-back and Redhead, but either in weeds or grass on a dry shore, a little back from the water's edge, or else in a firm tussock of meadow grass, right at the margin of a boggy slough, where the female can slip into the water from the nest.

I have raised the young by hand, and find them especially interesting. At first they are rather wild, great on jumping, but soon they become very docile. Their soft downy suits are of rich dark olive-brown color, and they erect their crown-feathers somewhat under excitement, which gives them quite a striking appearance.

HERBERT K. JOB.

Photograph by H. K. Job — Courtesy of Houghton Mifflin Co.

LESSER SCAUP DUCKS

At Palm Beach, Florida, in March

RING-NECKED DUCK

Marila collaris (*Donovan*)

A. O. U. Number 150 — See Color Plate 17

Other Names.— Ring-bill; Moon-bill; Marsh Blue-bill; Black Jack; Bunty; Ring-billed Blackhead; Bastard Broad-bill; Ring-necked Scaup Duck; Ring-necked Scaup; Ring-neck; Ring-billed Duck.

General Description.— Length, 18 inches. Males have head, upper parts, and breast black, and remaining lower parts white; females have upper parts brown, and lower parts yellowish-brown and white.

Color.— ADULT MALE: Head and neck all around lustrous black with purple reflections; extreme chin, white; *chestnut ring around lower neck;* fore-breast and upper parts, black; speculum, bluish-gray; under parts from breast, white; lower abdomen and sides, finely marked with black; tail and under tail-coverts, black; wings, dark brown; *bill, black with bluish-gray base and a band of same color near tip;* feet, grayish blue with dusky webs; iris, yellow. ADULT FEMALE: Forehead, narrowly, sides of face more broadly, pure white; rest of head, umber-brown, lightening on cheek and throat; *a white eye-ring;* upper parts, dusky-brown; breast, sides of body, brown, variegated with lighter; abdomen, white; wing as in male; speculum, duller, bill, legs, similar to male; iris, brownish-yellow.

Nest and Eggs.— NEST: On the ground in marshes; made of dry grass and leaves and lined with down. EGGS: 6 to 12, usually 9 or 10, rarely 15, grayish-white to buff.

Distribution.— North America in general; breeds from northern California, North Dakota, northern Iowa and southern Wisconsin northward; winters from southern British Columbia, New Mexico, northern Texas, southern Illinois and New Jersey south to Porto Rico and Guatemala; occurs in migration north to Newfoundland, Nova Scotia, and Quebec.

Distinctive peculiarities about the Ring-necked Duck are that it is almost never seen in large flocks, and seldom in open water. It swims buoyantly, and is much given to raising its head with a swan-like movement of its neck, and to erecting the feathers on the back of its head. It rises readily, from water or land, its wings whistling faintly; its flight is swift and direct. It is expert at diving and in that way captures many minnows, crawfish, snails, tadpoles, and frogs, though a considerable portion of its food consists of the roots of aquatic plants and seeds.

Nowhere is this Duck recorded as very common. It resembles the Lesser Scaup in appearance, size, and habits, and the two species mingle together.

GOLDEN-EYE

Clangula clangula americana *Bonaparte*

A. O. U. Number 151 See Color Plate 18

Other Names.—Golden-eyed Duck; American Golden-eye; Garrot; Whistler; Whistle-Duck; Whistle-wing; Brass-eyed Whistler; Whiffler; Jingler; Merry-wing; Great-head; Bull-head; Iron-head; Cub-head; Copper-head; Cur; Spirit Duck.

General Description.— Length, 20 inches. Males have the head greenish-black, the fore part and sides of the body white, and the back and tail black; females have the head and back brown and the under parts grayish. Both sexes have fluffy crests, and bills that are short, high at the base, and narrowed near the tip.

Color.— ADULT MALE: *Head and neck, glossy greenish-black; a large oval spot in front and below eye, white;* lower neck, under parts, middle and greater wing-coverts, most secondaries, and some shoulder-feathers, white; long inner secondaries, edge of wing, primary coverts, primaries and back, black; tail, ashy; some flank feathers with narrow dusky streaks on top edge; bill, dusky with *yellow tip;* feet, orange, dusky webs; *iris, yellow.* ADULT FEMALE: Chin, upper throat and head all around, brown; neck and entire lower parts, dull whitish, shaded on breast and sides with ashy; upper parts, brownish; some feathers of upper back with lighter edges; upper tail-coverts, tipped with pale brown; bill, feet, and eye as in male; white wing spaces much more restricted.

Nest and Eggs.— NEST: In hollow tree, made of grass, leaves, and moss and lined with down. EGGS: 9 to 12, light greenish.

Distribution.— North America; breeds from central Alaska, across British America to Newfoundland, south to southern British Columbia, southern Montana, northern North Dakota, northern Michigan, northern New York, and northern New England; winters from about the parallel 43° south to southern California, central Mexico and Florida.

The Golden-eye is commonly known as the Whistler because of the peculiar penetrating whistle made by its wings in flight. There are times when these cutting strokes can be heard even before the bird itself can be clearly made out. The Whistler breeds from just above the latitude of Massachusetts northward to the limit of trees, making its nest in a hollow tree near some fresh-water pond or river. It breeds in the interior of Alaska, but is very rarely seen on the coast. It is found almost throughout the interior of North America, and is distinctively a fresh-water bird until the frosts of winter begin to close the ponds and rivers, when most of the Whistlers in New England go to the salt water. Some, however, still remain in the unfrozen fresh waters of the North, South, and West.

The Whistler is a remarkably active bird,

dives like a flash, and rarely comes well to decoys. It has learned to be extremely wary and cautious, but in stormy weather it often keeps close to shore, which gives the shore gunner his chance. It does not always dive for its food, but sometimes dabbles in the mud along the shore with Blue-bills or other Ducks. Offshore it feeds largely on mussels, which it dislodges and brings up from the bottom. Audubon found it feeding on crawfish on the Ohio River. Wayne says that in South Carolina a small mussel of salt or brackish water is its favorite food. Knight has observed it feeding on these and also on some vegetable substances. He states that it eats small fish and fry also, and along the coast it feeds on mussels and other mollusks; but Elliot believes that in the interior the Whistler feeds on vegetable matter, such as grasses and roots.

When feeding there and when it first comes to the salt water, in autumn, the young are fairly tender and well-flavored, being about on a par with the Blue-bill as a table delicacy. Some of the residents of Cape Cod consider it superior to the Scoters. Nuttall says that it eats fresh-water vegetation, such as the roots of Equisetums and the seeds of some species of Polygonums.

EDWARD HOWE FORBUSH, in *Game Birds, Wild-Fowl and Shore Birds.*

BARROW'S GOLDEN-EYE

Clangula islandica (*Gmelin*)

A. O. U. Number 152

Other Names.— Rocky Mountain Garrot; Rocky Mountain Golden-eye.

Description.—ADULT MALE: Coloration exactly as in Golden-eye except that the *white spot in front of eye is triangle-shaped* and white of wing is divided by a dark bar formed by bases of greater coverts; averages larger than the Golden-eye; bill, differently shaped, being shorter and deeper at base. ADULT FEMALE: Indistinguishable from the female Golden-eye in color but separable by shape of bill.

Nest and Eggs.— NEST: In hollow trees; made of grass, leaves, and weed stems and lined with feathers and down. EGGS: 6 to 10, dull greenish.

Distribution.— Northern North America; breeds from south-central Alaska and northwestern Mackenzie to southern Oregon and southern Colorado, and from northern Ungava to central Quebec; winters from southeastern Alaska, central Montana, the Great Lakes, and Gulf of St. Lawrence south to central California, southern Colorado, Nebraska, and New England; accidental in Europe; breeds commonly in Iceland, and is a rare visitor to Greenland.

Drawing by R. I. Brasher

BARROW'S GOLDEN-EYE (¼ nat. size)

An active bird, diving like a flash, and rarely coming well to a decoy

Barrow's Golden-eye closely resembles the American Golden-eye. It is not easy to distinguish between the males at a distance and it is impossible to tell with certainty to which species the females and young belong. Their habits are also similar but the Barrow's breeds farther south and winters farther north. Its note is a low croaking sound.

BUFFLE-HEAD

Charitonetta albeola (*Linnæus*)

A. O. U. Number 153 See Color Plate 10

Other Names.— Buffle-headed Duck; Buffalo-headed Duck; Bumblebee Duck; Butter Duck; Butter-ball; Butter-box; Butter-back; Spirit Duck; Wool-head; Hell-diver; Conjuring Duck; Marionette; Dipper; Dipper Duck; Dapper; Dopper; Robin Dipper; Little Black and White Duck (male); Little Brown Duck (female).

General Description.— Length, 15 inches. Males are black above, and white below; females are grayish-brown above, and whitish below.

Color.—ADULT MALE: Head, puffy and crested, and iridescent, purple, and green; *a large white patch on each side behind eye, running some distance below eye and joining its fellow over top of head;* neck all around, under parts, shoulders, nearly all wing-coverts, and most secondaries, pure white; some shoulder feathers edged with black, forming a narrow lengthwise line; back and upper parts, black; tail, grayish; bill, dull bluish-gray with black tip and base; feet, pale flesh color; iris, brown. ADULT FEMALE: Head, thinly crested, dusky-gray with a *lighter patch on side;* upper parts, grayish-brown; *wings* the same *with small white areas;* below, whitish shaded on sides of neck and body with ashy; bill, feet, and iris, as in male.

Nest and Eggs.— NEST: In hollow trees or stumps near water; lined with down and feathers. EGGS: 9 to 14; from creamy-white to buff or dull olive.

Distribution.— North America; breeds from Maine, Ontario, Iowa, northern Montana, and British Columbia north to Alaska; winters from British Columbia, Aleutian Islands, Idaho, Colorado, Missouri, southern Michigan, western New York, and New Brunswick south to northern Lower California, central Mexico, Louisiana, and Florida.

This little Duck is widely known on fresh waters, for it is by nature a fresh-water bird, which in autumn and winter frequents the seashore. It was named Buffle-head (or Buffalo-head) because of its large fluffy head, which looks particularly big when its feathers are erected. The Buffle-head was not much sought by gunners until within recent years. Its great weakness is a fondness for decoys.

The male is a handsome bird; its bright contrasting tints are highly ornamental, but, as is usual among Ducks, the female is dull and inconspicuous in color and much smaller. My youthful experience with the Dipper Duck convinced me at the time that it could dive quickly enough to dodge a charge of shot; but its immunity from danger probably was due more to my inexperience and to the inferior quality of the gun and ammunition used than to the quickness of the bird. However, it dives like a flash, and is very likely to escape unless the gunner, warned by experience, uses a close shooting gun, judges well his distance and holds exactly right. When a few are together one usually keeps watch when the others are under water and warns them of danger by its short quack.

In flight it hurls itself through the air with tremendous speed, its rapidly moving wings almost forming a haze about its glancing form, which buzzes straight away as if bound for the other end of the world. It alights on the water with a tumultuous splash, sliding along for a little distance over the surface. When it has once alighted it seems to prefer the water to the air, and will often dive, rather than fly, to escape danger. It is sometimes so fat that in the Middle States it is known as the Butter-box or Butter-ball, but the flesh is not usually of a very good quality. As with all Ducks the quality of its flesh depends largely on the character of the food it has recently eaten, and this species, like others, is much more palatable when killed in the interior than when taken on the sea-coast.

In February the males begin their mating antics, when they have a habit of stretching forth the neck and erecting the glossy feathers of the head as it is moved back and forth, so as to display their beauties to the best advantage in the sunlight. They are quite quarrelsome in the mating season and fight furiously for the possession of favored females.

Nuttall says that the Buffle-head feeds principally upon fresh-water and submerged vegetation, and that it sometimes visits the salt marshes "in quest of the laver (*Ulva lactuca*)," as well as crustacea and small shell-fish. Audubon states that it feeds on shrimps, small fry, and bivalves in salt water, and on crawfish, leeches, snails, and grasses in fresh water. It also takes locusts, grasshoppers and many other insects.

When it is considered that the minnows on which the Buffle-head feeds to a considerable extent eat eggs of trout and other food fishes, it seems probable that it is a useful bird, and certainly it is a very interesting one. Its diminution on the Atlantic sea-board has been deplorably rapid. In 1870 Samuels regarded it as a "very common and well known bird" in New England and abundant in migration. At its present rate of decrease, another century will see its extinction as surely as the last century saw that of the Great Auk and the Labrador Duck. Its rate of decrease should be watched, and, if necessary, a close season should be declared for several years in every State and province where it breeds or which it visits in its annual migrations. It is unsafe to procrastinate in matters of this kind.

EDWARD HOWE FORBUSH, in *Game Birds, Wild-Fowl and Shore Birds.*

OLD-SQUAW

Harelda hyemalis (*Linnæus*)

A. O. U. Number 154 See Color Plate 20

Other Names.— Long-tailed Duck; Long-tail; Swallow-tailed Duck; South-southerly; Old Wife; Old Injin; Old Granny; Old Molly; Old Billy; John Connolly; Uncle Huldy; Coween or Cowheen; Calloo; Cockawee; Scoldenore; Scolder; Quandy; Squeaking Duck; Winter Duck; Hound.

General Description.— Length, male 23 inches; female 16 inches. In summer the males are black and brown above, and white below; in winter they show more white and less dark; females are grayish-brown above, and whitish shaded with dark below. Both sexes are without crests, have comparatively short necks, and short bills; males have long slender tails, the two central feathers of which are elongated.

Color.—ADULT MALE IN SUMMER PLUMAGE: Lores *broadly, space above eye, sides of head and cheeks, silvery gray; forehead, crown, and back of head, blackish-brown;* rest of neck all around, upper back, and breast, dark chocolate-brown; upper parts and long tail-feathers, blackish; shoulders, yellowish-brown striped with darker; shorter tail-feathers, whitish; wing, dusky; under parts, white; bill, flesh color with black tip and base; feet, bluish-gray with dusky web; iris, yellow, orange, or red. ADULT MALE IN WINTER: *Head, neck, fore-back, and upper breast, white; a gray patch commencing in front of eye, including cheeks and side of head, extending down side of neck* in a point, changing to rufous; upper parts, including long tail-feathers, black; shoulders, broadly white; lower breast with a large patch of deep brown rounded behind, running up and meeting black of back; rest of under parts, pure white. ADULT FEMALE IN SUMMER: Head, neck, and upper parts, dark grayish-brown, paler on throat, with a grayish-white patch around eye and another below on side of neck; under parts, white shaded across breast and on sides with ashy-brown; bill, mostly dusky with a light space in center. ADULT FEMALE IN WINTER: Crown, back of head, and back of neck, mottled grayish and brown; rest of head and neck, white with a dusky patch back of eye; upper parts, dusky-brown; shoulders, mixed with lighter brown and gray; breast shaded with grayish; rest of under parts, white; bill, dusky.

Nest and Eggs.— NEST: Placed under bushes or grass near water; constructed of grasses and dry weed stems and lined with feathers and down. EGGS: 5 to 9, from dull pea-green to light olive-buff.

Distribution.— Northern hemisphere; in North America breeds from Alaska across British America to Labrador, principally beyond the tree limit; winters from the Aleutian Islands to Washington and from the Gulf of St. Lawrence south to the Great Lakes and North Carolina and rarely to Colorado, Texas, Louisiana, and Florida.

Drawing by R. I. Brasher

OLD-SQUAW (¼ nat. size)

It has earned this name from its propensity to ceaseless chattering

We class the Old-squaws among the Sea Ducks and seemingly they do prefer to live about sea-water. They occur inland, however, on many of the larger rivers and lakes. On the Pacific side of the continent, California is their southern limit, and on the Atlantic coast they go down to North Carolina and sometimes to Florida. The summer home is in the high northern latitudes. Their food consists mainly of shellfish and crustaceans. Wayne reports finding them in company with Surf Ducks feeding on mussels along the South Carolina coast.

As they are not regarded as good for the table, market-hunters seldom kill them, and only the less experienced sportsmen shoot them if other Ducks are within reach. Their habits, including their manner of flying, feeding, and diving, are very similar to those of the Scoters, with which birds they much associate.

Along the North Carolina coast the Old-squaws assemble in large flocks, especially in the spring. At this time they are often very noisy; in fact no wild Duck in North America has so much to say to his fellows as this handsome species. This propensity for ceaseless chattering is given as the reason for naming the bird "Old-squaw." Many hunters call it "Old South-southerly," through some fancied resemblance between those words and the notes of the bird. Another local name is "Long-tail," the extended tail-feathers of the male, especially in the spring plumage, giving point to this name.

Old-squaws are said to indulge in a variety of interesting aërial evolutions during the mating season. At great speed they chase one another through the air and often dart down to the water and disappear, as they carry on the chase for a brief time beneath the surface.

T. Gilbert Pearson.

HARLEQUIN DUCK

Histrionicus histrionicus (*Linnæus*)

A. O. U. Number 155 See Color Plate 19

Other Names.— Painted Duck; Mountain Duck; Rock Duck; Lord-and-Lady; Squealer; Sea Mouse.

General Description.— Length, 17 inches. Males are deep bluish-slate; females are brown above, and grayish-brown below. Both sexes have small crests, short bills, and long, sharp tails.

Color.—Adult Male in Full Plumage: General color deep bluish-slate with a purplish tinge blackening on top of head, lower back, rump, and tail, a darker shade on head and neck than on breast and back; a white patch between bill and eye curving upward and backward, changing to chestnut along nape; a round white spot on side of head, a long white streak on side of upper neck, a white collar around neck, complete or not — all these marks with black borders; a white crescentic bar in front of wings; two white streaks on back; outer webs of inner secondaries and a bar across end of greater coverts and some of the secondaries, also white; speculum, dull purplish; sides and flanks, broadly chestnut with a small white spot at root of tail; bill, dull olive, lightening on sides; feet, grayish-blue with dusky webs; iris, brown. Three years required to reach this perfect plumage; male usually seen intermediate between this and plumage of female. Adult Female: Head, neck, and upper parts, dull dark brown, deepest on head and rump; lower parts grayish-brown whitening on abdomen; a lighter spot in front of eye, another larger one below it and still another one further back on side of head, all obscure whitish; bill, dusky; feet, dull leaden-gray; iris, brown. Young: Similar to adult female in summer.

Nest and Eggs.— Nest: In hollow tree or stump, under driftwood or in crevices of rock, usually near swiftly running streams; constructed of weeds, grass, and leaves and lined with down and feathers. Eggs: 6 to 8, pale cream or buffy.

Distribution.— Northern North America and eastern Asia; breeds from Alaska, on the Arctic coast, to Greenland, south to British Columbia, central Mackenzie, northern Ungava, and Newfoundland and in the mountains to central California and southwestern Colorado, northeastern Asia, and Iceland; winters on the Pacific coast from Aleutian Islands to California, in the interior to Colorado, Missouri, Lake Michigan, and western New York, and on the Atlantic Coast from Gulf of St. Lawrence regularly to Maine, rarely to New Jersey, and accidentally to Florida; accidental in Europe and not rare in Asia south to Japan.

Harlequin, well named! fantastically decorated, but still a thing of beauty. Delightful in color, elegant in form, graceful in carriage, rightly are its little companies called the "Lords and Ladies" of the waters. This is the loveliest of the Sea Ducks, but its beauty is reserved mainly for the cold and inhospitable North, and the wave-lashed rocks of isolated ledges in the wintry sea. It breeds principally in the Far North along the coasts of the Arctic Ocean. Yet, strange as it may seem, some individuals prefer the glacial streams in the mountains, and follow the higher ranges as far south as California, where they rear their young amid snow-clad peaks and disport themselves in the foaming mountain torrents until the rigors of approaching winter drive them to the sea.

Nests have been found on the ground, in holes in rocks and banks, and in hollow trees. The downy young take to the water as soon as they become strong and then they tumble about among the rocks and rushing waters perfectly at home as are their parents on the sea. In the breeding season the Harlequin is quite a solitary bird but there appear to be many unmated or infertile ones or possibly those that have finished breeding, which may be found on the sea in May and the summer months. Such little flocks, often led by a full-plumaged male, enjoy themselves on the waters of Puget Sound among the outer islands, diving, playing about on the surface and dressing their plumage, apparently without a care in the world. On the Atlantic coast they are scarcer now in Maine and rarer still to the southward but in some severe winters flocks are seen south of Nantucket and Marthas Vineyard off the coast of Massachusetts. They are fond of swift waters, mad currents, tide rips and flowing seas; are tremendously tough and hardy, and feed largely on mussels, which they get by diving, often to considerable depths. When nesting along mountain streams they eat many insects.

Edward Howe Forbush.

LABRADOR DUCK

Camptorhynchus labradorius (*Gmelin*)

A. O. U. Number 156

Other Names.— Pied Duck; Skunk Duck.

General Description.— Length, 29 inches. Males were black with white heads and markings; females were grayish-brown above, and grayish-white below.

Color.—Adult Male: Head and upper neck, white with a longitudinal black stripe on crown and nape; lower neck, ringed with black continuous with that of upper parts; below this a white half-collar continuous with that of shoulders; rest of under parts, black; wing-coverts and secondaries, white, some of the latter margined with black; some long shoulder-feathers, pearly-gray; primaries, their coverts, and tail-feathers, brownish-black; bill, black with orange base and edges; feet, grayish-blue with dusky webs; iris, chestnut. Adult Female: Above, grayish-brown; several secondaries white, forming a speculum, but no white on wing-coverts or shoulders; below, grayish-white barred with dull brown; a spot on side of head and another in front of eye, white; bill, feet, and iris, as in male.

Nest and Eggs.— Unknown.

Distribution.— Formerly along the northern Atlantic Coasts; supposed to have bred in Labrador and to have wintered from Nova Scotia south to New Jersey; now extinct.

The most remarkable fact about the Labrador Duck, which seems to have been common on the Atlantic coast one hundred years ago, is that it is now extinct and no one knows why. If it is a fact that it bred only on rocky islands about the Gulf of St. Lawrence and the coast of Labrador, the feather hunting of the eighteenth century and the egging and shooting of the nineteenth probably resulted in its extinction, but no one, now living, knows to a certainty that it bred in Labrador. John W. Audubon was shown nests at Blanc Sablon that were said to be those of this species. Newton writes that it was common in summer on the coast of Labrador until about 1842. Major King writes (1886) that it was common on the northern shore of the Gulf of St. Lawrence and bred there, but gives no dates. I have seen no other evidence of its breeding in Labrador. There are no definite records of its nesting, and not one of its eggs is in existence. It may have bred much farther north but so far the records show that no one has ever seen it to the northward. We must be satisfied, then, with the probable explanation that, like the Great Auk, the species bred more or less locally and was exterminated in much the same way. Probably the exact facts never will be known.

The history of the bird is brief. It was first made known to science by Gmelin in 1788, nearly thirty years after the New England feather hunters had ceased to raid the islands where it was believed to breed, the birds having become so reduced in numbers that feather hunting was no longer profitable. Audubon never saw it alive, but asserted that it remained off the coasts of Maine and Massachusetts all winter and was unknown south of Chesapeake Bay. Dekay (1844) averred that the bird was well known to gunners on the New York coasts, but Giraud, writing about the same time, regarded it as rare there. Elliot says that between 1860 and 1870 he saw a considerable number of the species in the New York markets, but that a full-plumaged male was exceedingly rare although no one imagined that the species was on the verge of extinction. The last Labrador Duck on record died by the hand of man near Long Island, New York, in 1875. According to Dutcher's summary, there are only forty-two recorded specimens in existence in the museums and scientific collections of the world.

Little is known about the habits of this Duck. It frequented sandy shoals off the New England coast and was so tame and confiding that it was not difficult to shoot.

It was said to feed largely on shellfish, and Audubon relates that a bird stuffer at Camden, New Jersey, had many fine specimens taken with hooks baited with mussels. It was a strong flyer and a good diver and, as is the case with most Sea Ducks, its flesh was rank and fishy. It was hardy and in every way well fitted for the battle of life but was not able to cope with civilized man. It is significant that its extinction occurred in the nineteenth century when marked improvements in firearms were accompanied by the extermination of far more species of birds than in any other century since the dawn of history.

Edward Howe Fobrush.

LABRADOR DUCKS

A group of mounted specimens in the American Museum of Natural History, New York City

SPECTACLED EIDER

Arctonetta fischeri (*Brandt*)

A. O. U. Number 158

Other Name.—Fischer's Eider.

General Description.—Length, 22 inches. Males are white above and grayish-black below; females are yellowish-brown, streaked and barred with darker. Both sexes have dense patches of velvety feathers around the eyes, outlined with black, suggesting spectacles; very fine, stiffened frontal feathers; and crown feathers lengthened into a short hanging hood in the male, slightly indicated, or not, in the female.

Color.—Adult Male: Most of head, neck all around, most of back, lesser and middle wing-coverts, long inner secondaries and a patch on side of rump, white; frontal feathers on head, nape, and cheeks strongly tinged with pale sea-green; spectacle area pure silvery-white framed as aforesaid, with black; rest of plumage, including wings, grayish-black; bill, orange; feet, yellowish; iris, white surrounded with a light blue ring. Adult Female: Varies as do all Eiders; general coloration, yellowish-brown, streaked on head and neck, and barred on body, except abdomen, with black and brown.

Nest and Eggs.— NEST: On the ground among rocks; made almost entirely of feathers and down from the bird's breast. EGGS: 5 to 8, light olive.

Distribution.— Very locally distributed on coast of Bering Sea and adjacent Arctic Ocean; breeds in Alaska from Point Barrow to mouth of the Kuskokwim and on the northern coast of Siberia west to mouth of Lena River; winters in Aleutian Islands.

The Spectacled Eider is essentially an Alaskan Duck, as far as its habitat on this continent is concerned, and is most commonly seen in and near Norton Sound, where it breeds. Its principal winter home seems to be on the islands of the Aleutian Archipelago. Like the Emperor Goose, this Duck is likely to fly near the surface of the water or the land; its normal progress on the wing is very swift and steady. During July and August the birds undergo a severe molt which deprives them even of the use of their wing-feathers. When they are thus helpless the Eskimos kill them wholesale with sticks and clubs. The natives also make caps of the heavily feathered skins of this Eider, and use the bright green plumage for headdresses of various kinds.

Drawing by R. I. Brasher

SPECTACLED EIDER (½ nat. size)

The Eskimos make caps of its skin

NORTHERN EIDER

Somateria mollissima borealis (*Brehm*)

A. O. U. Number 159

General Description.— Length, 24 inches. Males are white above, and black below; females are pale rufous-brown, variegated with darker.

Color.—ADULT MALE: Crown, glossy blue-black, including eyes, and separating behind to receive white of hind neck; *head, neck all around, fore-breast, most of back, most of wing-coverts, long inner secondaries, and sides of rump, white* tinged with creamy-pink on breast; sides of head washed with pale sea-green; middle of rump, upper tail-coverts, tail, lower back, and under parts from breast, deep sepia black; bill, yellowish, brownish in center with white tip; legs, yellowish; iris, brown. ADULT FEMALE: Ground color of entire plumage, pale rufous-brown, darker on crown, streaked on side of head and neck and variegated elsewhere with transverse bars of black and chestnut-brown; abdomen, plain grayish-brown.

Nest and Eggs.— NEST: Between stones, on rocks

or banks, or any suitable hollow; made of seaweed and lined with down plucked from the breast of the bird; additional down is added as incubation proceeds, and the quantity is often so great as to conceal the eggs entirely. EGGS: 6 to 10, greenish-drab.

Distribution.— Northeastern North America; breeds from Ellesmere Land and Greenland south to northwestern Hudson Bay and southern Ungava; winters in southern Greenland, south rarely to Maine and Massachusetts.

The Northern Eider is a North American race of the common Eider of Europe and is almost identical with it. It nests on islands off the northern coast of Labrador.

This bird furnishes much of the eider-down that is gathered by the Greenlanders, and it is not improbable that it was one of the species sought by the feather hunters on the coast of Labrador in the eighteenth century.

EDWARD HOWE FORBUSH, in *Game Birds, Wild-Fowl and Shore Birds.*

EIDER

Somateria dresseri *Sharpe*

A. O. U. Number 160 See Color Plate 19

Other Names.—American Eider; Common Eider; Eider Duck; Dresser's Eider; Drake (male); Sea Duck (female); Black and White Coot (male); Isle of Shoals Duck; Squam Duck; Wamp; Canvas-back.

Description.— Length, 24 inches. This Eider differs from the Northern Eider in shape of bill; in latter base of bill extends along each side of forehead between the narrow pointed extension of crown feathers, this lateral extension being very narrow and ending in a point, whereas in the Eider the processes are more than twice as broad with obtuse rounded ends; the sides of head are more extensively greenish but otherwise the coloration is similar.

Nest and Eggs.— NEST: On the ground, in grass, in crevices between rocks, or in any sheltered locality; made of moss, seaweed, and lichens and lined with gray down from breast of the bird, the lining being added gradually during the month of incubation. EGGS: 6 to 10, usually 6, plain dull greenish-drab.

Distribution.— Northeastern North America; breeds from southern Ungava and Newfoundland, on the southern half of Hudson Bay to southeastern Maine; winters from Newfoundland and Gulf of St. Lawrence south on Atlantic Coast to Massachusetts, rarely to Virginia, and in interior rarely to Colorado, Iowa, Wisconsin, Ohio, and western New York.

Eiders are native to both Europe and America but the European and Northern Eiders differ from the American in the shape of the processes of the bill, which extend upward and backward toward the eyes. These maxillæ are less attenuated and more rounded at the ends in the American species than in the European and the Northern. This is one of the famous species that are responsible for the greater part of the eider-down of commerce. The female plucks from her own breast the down to line her nest and, as is the case with other species, she felts this down into a blanket or mantle which not only lines the nest but extends up so that she can cover the eggs with a flap or coverlet of the same warm substance. In Iceland, Norway, and some other parts of Europe the down is considered so valuable that the birds are conserved, tended, and protected, so that they become almost as tame as domesticated fowls. Nesting places are made for them in the turf or among the stones, and some of them even nest on the sod roofs of the houses, where sods are removed or arranged for their accommodation. In some places the nests are so numerous that it is impossible to step among them without endangering the sitting birds. Some birds become so tame while on the nest as to allow the inhabitants to stroke their feathers. When the first downy lining and the eggs are removed from the nest by the down gatherers, the female plucks her breast again, renews the lining, and lays more eggs. If her treasures are removed a second time, it is said that the male denudes his breast for a third lining. The down and eggs taken are not sufficient to interfere with the breeding of the birds, and both the birds and the inhabitants prosper in the partnership.

We do it differently in America. The coast of Labrador formerly was a great breeding ground of the Eider Duck. Before the year 1750, vessels were fitted out in New England for the Labrador coast for the express purpose of collecting feathers and eider-down. The crews landed on the coasts and islands when the young birds were still unfledged and while the parents were molting their flight quills and unable to fly. They surrounded the birds, drove them together and killed them with clubs, thus destroying "millions" for their feathers alone, as there was no market for their flesh. This was continued until not long after 1760, when the birds had become so reduced in numbers that feather hunting became unprofitable and was given up. In the meantime, and ever since, eggers, fishermen, and settlers have destroyed both birds and eggs, until the vast Eider nurseries of the Labrador coast are little more than a memory, and now we import eider-down gathered by the wiser and more humane people of the Old World.

However, the Eider is by no means extinct in this country. It still breeds in the more inaccessible regions of northern Ungava and about Hudson Bay and a few are preserved in Maine under the protecting care of the National Association of Audubon Societies. The nests are hidden away carefully under thick shrubbery on rocky islands where the waves of the Atlantic break ceaselessly on jagged rocks and the birds when not on their nests keep at sea.

The only note I have ever heard from one of these birds was a hoarse croak when the female was suddenly startled from her nest, but the male is said to have a soft note in the breeding season.

In migration they seem to be rather silent birds, flying in long undulating lines and alternately flapping and sailing. The Massachusetts gunners call them Sea Ducks for they seem to prefer the outer ledges jutting into the sea. Numbers frequent the islands south of Cape Cod in winter where they feed largely on mussels for which they dive sometimes in at least ten fathoms of water. They are hardy and handsome. Their flesh is fishy and unattractive. If protected on their breeding grounds they might become in time a great source of revenue to the people of the northern coasts.

Photo by T. G. Pearson Courtesy of Nat. Asso. Aud. Soc.

NEST OF EIDER

At Way Ledge, near Isle au Haut, Maine

EDWARD HOWE FORBUSH.

KING EIDER

Somateria spectabilis (*Linnæus*)

A. O. U. Number 162 See Color Plate 19

General Description.— Length, 22 inches. Males are white above and brownish-black below; females are light brown, streaked and barred with darker. Males have the bill with immense square frontal processes bulging high above rest of bill; bills of females are less developed but retain the same general outlines.

Color.—ADULT MALE: Fore parts, most of wing-coverts, and a spot on each side of rump, white, tinged on side of head with pale sea-green, and on breast with creamy-brown; *top of head and back of neck, pearl-gray; eyelids and spot below eye, black;* rest of plumage, deep brownish-black, including the long inner secondaries; a black V-shaped mark on chin; bill, reddish-orange, the enlarged part surrounded in front, on top, and rear with a black border; tip, white; feet, yellowish-orange with dusky webs; iris, brown. ADULT FEMALE: Hardly separable from other female Eiders in coloration, but easily distinguished by the shape of bill; the bill, yellowish, dusky at end, with white tip.

Nest and Eggs.— NEST: In depressions of ground or among rocks; composed entirely of down. EGGS: Usually 6, but sometimes more, light olive-gray to grayish-green.

Distribution.— Northern part of northern hemisphere; breeds along the whole coast of northern Siberia, Bering Sea, and Arctic coast of America from Icy Cape east to Melville Island, Wellington Channel, northern Greenland, northwestern Hudson Bay, and northern Ungava; winters on Pacific coast from Aleutian Islands to Kodiak Island, in the interior rarely to the Great Lakes, and from southern Greenland and Gulf of St. Lawrence south regularly to Long Island, rarely to Georgia; accidental in California and Iowa.

The King Eider is an arctic species and its habits resemble those of the common Eider. It is a deep-water Duck, feeding mostly on mussels. The female lines her nest with down, as do the other species, and it forms part of the eider-down of commerce, which is gathered by the natives in Greenland.

The raised frontal processes at the base of the bill, which adorn the head, develop immensely in the breeding season, bulging high above the rest of the bill. These processes are soft, and are supported upon a mass of fatty substance. They shrink and become more depressed in winter, when the general formation of the beak is not much different from that of other Eiders. The female, however, does not resemble the male, and is not easily distinguished in the field from that of the American Eider. When in hand, the general resemblance of the bill and the head feathering to that of the male may be noted.

EDWARD HOWE FORBUSH, in *Game Birds, Wild-Fowl and Shore Birds.*

SCOTER

Oidemia americana *Swainson*

A. O. U. Number 163 See Color Plate 20

Other Names.— MALES: Black Scoter; Sea Coot; Black Coot; Black Sea Coot; Fizzy; Broad-billed Coot; Hollow-billed Coot; Pumpkin-blossom Coot; Booby; Butter-bill; Black Butter-bill; Butter-billed Coot; Butter-nose; Copper-bill; Copper-nose; Yellow-bill. FEMALES: Brown Coot; Gray Coot; Smutty Coot.

Description.— Length, male 21 inches; female 17 inches. ADULT MALE: *Entirely black,* less glossy below; bill, black, with a yellow protuberance at base; feet, dusky; iris, brown. ADULT FEMALE: Sooty-brown, paler below, lightening on abdomen, with dusky speckling; sides and flanks waved with dusky; throat and sides of head, distinctly whitish; bill, dusky and not peculiar; feet, dull olive with black webs; iris, brown.

Nest and Eggs.— NEST: On ground near water; made of coarse grass, feathers, and down. EGGS: 6 to 10, pale buff.

Distribution.— Northern North America and eastern Asia; breeds in northeastern Asia and from Kotzebue Sound to Aleutian Islands, including Near Islands; also on west shore of Hudson Bay, Ungava, and Newfoundland; winters on Asiatic coast to Japan and from islands of Bering Sea south rarely to Santa Catalina Island, California; in the interior not rare on the Great Lakes, and casual or accidental in Missouri, Louisiana, Nebraska, Colorado, and Wyoming; on the Atlantic coast abundant during migration from Newfoundland and Maine south, but rarely as far as Florida.

We have no means of knowing the early history of any one of the Scoters as they all were generally grouped together as "Coots" or "Black Ducks" by the early historians. The Scoters or "Coots," as they are called by the gunners and fishermen, are typical diving Ducks. They are very muscular and powerful in build. The bony framework is strong, the skin tough, and the feathers strong, coarse, and very firmly attached to the skin. The whole structure seems to be formed to resist the tremendous water pressure that they encounter while diving at great depths. Fishermen, both along the Massachusetts coast and in the lake region of Wisconsin, have told me that they have taken these diving Ducks in nets set from 50 to 100 feet below the surface. This may be an exaggeration. Under water they use both legs and wings for propulsion, and are even more at home there than in the air. If threatened with danger they are as likely to dive as to fly, and sometimes, when in full flight, they have been seen to dive. The Scoters are universally known as Coots along the New England coast, a name derived probably from the French fishermen who first established the fishing industry on the banks of Newfoundland. The true Coot, however, is a lobe-footed fresh-water bird.

As food, Ducks of this genus are regarded as nourishing but not very appetizing. Some writers have gone so far as to stigmatize them as abominable; but the people of Cape Cod are able, by parboiling, etc., to make a dish of even the old birds, which, though it may "taste a little like crow" to the uninitiated, serves as an agreeable variant to a diet of salt fish.

A cultured Boston lady assures me that when she attempted to cook a Coot it drove everybody out of the house, and that she had to throw away the kettle that it was cooked in. Nevertheless, I have found the young palatable if properly prepared, though hardly equal to the celery-fed Canvas-back. Many Scoters are shot for food and sold in the markets, but large numbers are killed merely for sport, and either left to lie where they fall or to drift away on the tide.

The American Scoter, Black Coot, or Little Gray Coot, as it is commonly called, while a common bird, is the least numerous of the three Scoters. While at times it keeps by itself it is quite as likely to mix with flocks of the other Scoters. The flight of the Scoters is swift. I have heard it estimated at 200 miles an hour with a strong wind, but this is probably exaggerated. They may possibly fly at the rate of over 100 miles an hour under favorable conditions, but this is a high rate of speed for any bird. This bird usually flies in lines at some distance from the shore, and the flocks are often led by an old experienced male, who will lead his following high in air while passing over the boats where gunners lie in wait.

In migration this bird is often seen in flocks of 100 or more, and in smaller groups at other times, but it associates with the other two species. Little is known about its early abundance, but it is probable that on the Atlantic it has decreased more in proportion to its former numbers than the other two common species. It is far more numerous now on the Pacific coast than on the Atlantic. So little is known of its breeding grounds in northeastern North America that Professor Cooke is obliged to reason, by exclusion, that as we have no record of its breeding west of Hudson Bay until we reach the Yukon valley, nor in Labrador south of about latitude 52 degrees, the multitudes seen in winter on the Atlantic coast must breed east of Hudson Bay, in northern Ungava. As this is one of the least explored regions of the world, it is quite possible that vast numbers of Scoters and Mergansers breed there. It breeds mainly in fresh-water marshes and ponds in the north and also upon islands in the sea. It is a very expert diver, and

Drawing by R. I. Brasher

SCOTER (¼ nat. size)

As food, this Duck is nourishing, but not very appetizing

is often able to get so nearly under water at the flash of a gun that the shot injures it very little if at all.

Its food consists largely of mussels, and when feeding on fresh water it prefers the fresh-water clams to most other foods. Thirteen Massachusetts specimens were found to have eaten nearly 95 per cent. of mussels; the remaining 5 per cent. of the stomach contents was composed of starfish and periwinkles. It is a common belief that all Scoters feed entirely upon animal food, but this is not a fact. Along the Atlantic coast they appear to subsist mostly on marine animals, but, in the interior, vegetable food also is taken.

Edward Howe Forbush, in *Game Birds, Wild-Fowl and Shore Birds.*

WHITE-WINGED SCOTER

Oidemia deglandi *Bonaparte*

A. O. U. Number 165 See Color Plate 20

Other Names.— Velvet Scoter; Velvet Duck; Lake Huron Scoter; White-winged Surf Duck, or Sea Coot or Scoter; Black White-wing; Black Surf Duck; Pied-winged Coot; Uncle Sam Coot; Bell-tongue Coot; Bull Coot; Brant Coot; Sea Brant; May White-wing; Eastern White-wing; Assemblyman.

General Description.— Length, male 23 inches; female 20 inches. General color of male, black; female, brown above and gray below. Bill swollen at base over nostrils and on sides; feathers of lores come close to nostrils.

Color.—Adult Male: *Black,* paler below, more brownish on sides; a small white spot under and behind eye; *speculum white,* formed by tips of greater coverts and most of secondaries; bill, black at base and on knob, a white space in front of knob; sides of bill reddish shading to orange on tip; feet, orange or red with black webs and joints; Iris, pale yellow. Adult Female: Sooty-brown above; pale grayish below; a large space in front of and below eye, and another back of it on side of head, whitish; closely resembles the other two female Scoters but can always be distinguished by the *white speculum;* bill smaller than in male and grayish-dusky; feet, dull flesh color with black webs; iris, dark-brown.

Nest and Eggs.— Nest: Usually concealed under overhanging bushes, small spruces, or willows; sometimes near salt water, at other times 2 or 3 miles from the sea; a depression in the ground, lined with a little grass and, after the clutch is complete, with a little down. Eggs: 5 to 14, usually 7 or 8, pale salmon-buff or flesh color.

Distribution.— North America; breeds from the coast of northeastern Siberia, northern Alaska, northern Mackenzie, and northern Ungava south to central British Columbia, Alberta, northern North Dakota, and southern Quebec; winters on the Asiatic coast to Bering Island, Japan, and China, and in North America from Unalaska Island to San Quintin Bay, Lower California, the Great Lakes (casually to Colorado, Nebraska, and Louisiana), and the Atlantic coast from the Gulf of St. Lawrence south (rarely) to Florida; non-breeding birds occur in summer as far south as Rhode Island and Monterey, California.

The White-winged Scoter, the largest of the three dark-colored marine Ducks commonly called " Sea Coots " along the Atlantic coast and readily distinguished from the other two by its white wing-bars, is very familiar to gunners. Toward the end of August flocks of adult males, flying southward, begin to be noticed along the New England coast. The lighter-colored females and young are not due till about the middle of October and later. Then there is a great procession of them past the headlands, flying swiftly and low over the water. They stream by in single files, in wedge-shaped formation, or in irregular columns, the three kinds being often intermingled.

The " coot shooters," starting out at the first glimmer of dawn, or before, anchor their boats in a line straight out from some headland, about a gunshot apart, and lie low, after anchoring out wooden decoys in front. The Scoters, coming swiftly on, may swing around the boats further out to sea, or rise higher in the air. Often, however, trusting to their swiftness, they dash through the line. Then the guns speak. On some mornings when there is a big flight it sounds like a regular battle. Scoters are thickly armored, however, with feathers, down, fat, and a tough hide, and many a time I have heard the impact of the shot on their bodies when there was not the least visible effect. They fly more especially early in the morning, but on lowery, windy days, particularly when a storm is brewing, I have watched them pass by thousands all day long.

Such big thick-set birds, floating rather high on the water, make themselves quite conspicuous, and are easily recognized. They like to gather over submerged beds of mussels and other bivalves, and feed upon them by diving. Being very hardy birds, they do not go as far south in winter as many of the Ducks. Large numbers of them remain in the winter about Nantucket and Long Island. Few get as far as the southern States.

This Scoter is the most southerly of the three in its breeding range. I have found quite a number of their nests in North Dakota and Manitoba. Though so hardy, they are the last of the water-birds to breed. Usually they finish laying from June 20 to July 1. When beginning to lay, the female swims ashore, preferably on an island, and creeps into the thickest weeds or brush she can find near by. There she scratches a hollow, lays a very big creamy-white egg, and rakes the soil over it. Next day she digs it out, adds another, and buries both. When the set is nearing completion she plucks down from her breast and lines the nest. Examining a nest of eggs before incubation begins is like digging potatoes.

She sits very close, and when almost stepped on tries to scurry through the weeds to the water. Once I caught a Scoter leaving her nest. She did not act frightened, but gazed quietly at her captor. Suddenly she gave a violent flap, slipped to the ground, and managed to get to the water first. The young are large for ducklings, clad in black and white suits of down, and walk almost erect, reminding one of little men. HERBERT K. JOB.

The stomachs of nine White-winged Scoters from Massachusetts waters, examined by Mr. W. L. McAtee, of the Biological Survey, contained

Photo by H. K. Job Courtesy of Doubleday, Page & Co.

NEST OF WHITE-WINGED SCOTER

of mussels, about 44 per cent.; quohogs, 22 per cent.; periwinkles, 19 per cent.; hermit crabs, 9 per cent.; the remainder was caddis larvæ and algæ and other vegetable matter. Three birds from Nantucket had eaten only the common mussel.

SURF SCOTER

Oidemia perspicillata (*Linnæus*)

A. O. U. Number 166 See Color Plate 20

Other Names.— Surf Duck; Surf Coot; Surfer; Sea Coot; Bay Coot; Gray Coot; Brown Coot; Box Coot; Spectacle Coot; Butterboat-billed Coot; Hollow-billed Coot; Speckle-billed Coot; Blossom-billed Coot; Horsehead; Horse-head Coot; Patch-head; Patch-head Coot; Patch-polled Coot; White-head; White Scop; Baldpate; Skunk-head; Skunk-head Coot; Skunk-top; Pictured-bill; Plaster-bill; Morocco-jaw; Goggle-nose; Snuff-taker.

General Description.— Length, 21 inches. Predominating color of male, black; female, sooty-brown above, gray below.

Color.—ADULT MALE: *Black, glossy above, duller below; a triangular white patch on forehead pointing forward; another one on nape pointing downward; no white on wings;* basal half of bill, white with a large round spot of black, this bordered above and behind by red and yellow in a very narrow line; front half, yellowish-orange crossed by a white band; upper half, crimson and orange; feet, orange-red with dusky webs and joints; *iris, white.* ADULT FEMALE: Above, sooty-brown; below, gray; two whitish patches on side of head, thus scarcely different from females of other two species. Distinguished from female Scoter by larger bill, and from female White-winged Scoter by absence of white speculum.

Nest and Eggs.— NEST: On the ground in a bunch of marsh grass; more rarely in the low branches of dwarf spruces; constructed of grass and plant stems, and lined with down. EGGS: 5 to 8, cream color.

Distribution.— North America; breeds on the Pacific coast from Kotzebue Sound to Sitka, and from northwestern Mackenzie and Hudson Strait to Great Slave Lake, central Keewatin, and northern Quebec; non-breeding birds occur in summer in northeastern Siberia and south on the Pacific coast to Lower California, and in Greenland and south on the Atlantic coast to Long Island; winters on the Pacific coast from the Aleutian Islands south to San Quintin Bay, Lower California, on the Great Lakes, and south casually to Colorado, Kansas, Iowa, Illinois, and Louisiana, and on the Atlantic coast from Nova Scotia to North Carolina, rarely to Florida; casual in the Bermudas; frequent in Europe.

The Sea Coots are birds of the ocean and the larger lakes of the interior during the period of their sojourn in the United States. Now and then a few may be seen on some of the more important rivers, but one need not look for them on small ponds and in marshes where many other wild Ducks love to dwell.

From the studies which economic ornithologists have made of their feeding habits we learn that about 80 per cent. of the food of coastwise specimens consists of mussels which they procure by diving. They also eat periwinkles, algæ, and eel-grass. The flesh of few, if any, birds whose diet consists largely of fish or shell-fish is really palatable; and it would seem that this fact alone would protect the Scoter from gunners. Nevertheless they are extensively shot, particularly where the supply of other Ducks is not very great. This is partially true along the New England coast.

Here they are hunted in a communal fashion. The gunners of a locality agree on a day when they will go Coot shooting. At least fifteen or twenty boats must go, if success is to be attained. The boats are anchored in line offshore from some headland that separates two bays where the birds are accustomed to feed, and are stationed at a distance of about one hundred yards from each other. All this is done very early in the morning for by sunrise the companies of Coots will begin to pass. They fly swiftly and the man who secures many must be a good shot.

Speaking of the Scoter as an article of food, Walter H. Rich in *Feathered Game of the Northeast says:*

"They are unusually tough customers either in life or at the table. Most of our cooks believe it impossible to so prepare this bird as to make it decent food for any but a starving man. The best recipe I have seen runs somewhat as follows: First, skin your fowl and let it parboil in saleratus water at least one day, or until it can be dented with a fairly sharp ax. If your courage holds out, the game is now ready to stuff and bake as you would any other Duck, except that you must put enough onions into its inside to take away all Coot flavor. Arriving at this stage of proceeding there are two lines of retreat yet open to you; either throw your delicate morsel away or give it to someone against whom you hold an ancient grudge — on no account should you try to eat it."

The summer home of the Surf Scoter is in the Far North; none is known to rear its young in the United States. Those occasionally found within our borders in summer are either cripples, as the result of winter shooting, or are non-breeding individuals. Audubon describing a nest he found in Labrador writes that it was hidden among tall grasses and raised about four inches above the ground. It was made of weeds and lined with down of the bird in a manner similar to the nest of the Eider Duck.

T. Gilbert Pearson.

RUDDY DUCK

Erismatura jamaicensis (*Gmelin*)

A. O. U. Number 167 See Color Plate 10

Other Names.— Dumpling Duck; Daub Duck; Deaf Duck; Fool Duck; Sleepy Duck; Butter Duck; Brown Diving Teal; Widgeon Coot; Creek Coot; Sleepy Coot; Booby Coot; Ruddy Diver; Dun Diver; Sleepy Brother; Butter-ball; Batter-scoot; Blatherskite; Bumblebee Coot; Quill-tailed Coot; Heavy-tailed Coot; Stiff-tail; Pin-tail; Bristle-tail; Sprig-tail; Stick-tail; Spine-tail; Dip-tail; Diver; Dun-bird; Dumb-bird; Mud-dipper; Spoon-billed Butter-ball; Spoonbill; Broad-billed Dipper; Dipper; Dapper; Dopper; Broad-bill; Blue-bill; Sleepy-head; Tough-head; Hickory-head; Steel-head; Hard-headed Broad-bill; Bull-neck; Leather-back; Paddy-whack; Stub-and-twist; Light-wood-knot; Shot-pouch; Water-partridge; Dinky; Dickey; Paddy; Noddy; Booby; Rook; Roody; Gray Teal; Salt-water Teal; Stiff-tailed Widgeon.

General Description.— Length, 16 inches. Males are red above and white below; females are brownish-gray above and grayish below. Both sexes have the forehead rather low; the neck thick; the bill long and broad and curving upward, but tip overhanging and curved downward; and the tail composed of 18 stiff feathers, often spiny-pointed.

Color.—Adult Male in Spring: Forehead, crown, sides of head to below eye and nape, dusky-black; face, lores, chin, and sides of head, pure white; neck all around, upper parts, and sides, rich glossy chestnut; lower parts, silvery-white, "watered" with dusky; wing-coverts, primaries, and tail, blackish-brown; under wing-coverts, white; bill and feet, rather bright bluish-gray, latter with dusky webs; iris, brown; eyelids, bluish. Male in Fall, and Adult Female: Upper parts, brownish-gray, spotted and traversed with dusky; below, pale gray and whitish, with darker transverse marks on sides; crown and nape, dusky-brown, with two indistinct dusky streaks alongside of head; under tail-coverts, white; bill, feet, and eyes, as in spring male but much duller.

Nest and Eggs.— NEST: In the abandoned homes of Coots or on the shores of lakes, ponds, or streams; a bulky structure of dry reeds, rushes, and grass, so large and buoyant that it will float. EGGS: 9 to 14, creamy or light buff.

Distribution.— North America; breeds from central British Columbia, Great Slave Lake, southern Keewatin, and northern Ungava south to northern Lower California, central Arizona, northern New Mexico, northwestern Nebraska, southern Minnesota, southern Michigan, southern Ontario, and Maine, and rarely and locally in southern Lower California, Kansas, Massachusetts, Valley of Mexico, Lake Dueñas, Guatemala, and in Cuba, Porto Rico, and Carriacou; winters from southern British Columbia, Arizona, New Mexico, southern Illinois, Maine, Pennsylvania, and south to the Lesser Antilles and Costa Rica; rare in migration to Newfoundland and Bermuda.

Drawing by R. I. Brasher

RUDDY DUCK (⅓ nat. size)

A sprightly, comical little Duck, whose flesh is a passable substitute for that of the Canvas-back

The sprightly, comical little Ruddy Duck is a distinctly North American species and is distributed widely over the continent. It is perfectly at home on or under water and dislikes to leave it, often preferring to attempt escape by diving rather than by flying. This makes it easy game for the gunner, as a flock will sometimes remain in a salt pond so small that any part of it may be reached from the shore with a shotgun, diving at every shot until those left alive essay to fly and most of them pay the penalty of their simplicity with their lives. They can dive so quickly that they often escape unharmed. Like the Grebes they possess the power of sinking slowly down backward out of sight, but like them also they rise from the water with some labor and difficulty. They are extremely tough, hardy little birds and gunners know them by such names as Tough-head, Hard-head, Steel-head, etc. Other local names, such as Booby, Noddy, and Fool Duck, indicate a lack of respect for the birds' perspicacity.

When the famous Canvas-back first showed signs of scarcity on the Atlantic coast, a price

Photo by H. K. Job

A PAIR OF RUDDY DUCKS ON BREEDING-GROUND

was put upon the head of the Ruddy Duck to meet the market demand. Unfortunately for its safety it feeds upon delicate grasses and other vegetable aliment in preference to sea-food. Therefore, its flesh is a passable substitute for that of the Canvas-back. So the market gunners have pursued it until its numbers are no longer legion and its chances for extinction are good.

The male is a handsome bird in the breeding season but presents rather a ridiculous appearance in mating time, as he swims pompously about with his head lifted proudly and drawn away back toward the spread tail, which is raised and thrown forward as if to meet it.

This Duck nests in prairie sloughs, where the broods remain until after all the other breeding Ducks have departed. Old and young are regular gourmands and, according to Gurdon Trumbull, gunners near the mouth of the Maumee River told of finding them floundering helplessly fat, on the water and in some seasons floating about dead or dying in numbers. But this was before the days of the market demand for their flesh. They do not have so much time to get fat now.

EDWARD HOWE FORBUSH.

GEESE

Order *Anseres;* family *Anatidæ;* subfamily *Anserinæ*

THE Geese in scientific terminology constitute the subfamily *Anserinæ*, of the family *Anatidæ* (Goose-like swimmers), included in the order *Anseres*-(Water fowl). They comprise nine or ten genera and about forty species, of which ten or twelve occur in the United States. Of these, however, only two or three species are actual residents of this country, and the remainder are no more than migratory visitants south of the Canadian boundary.

The group are closely related to the Swans, from which they differ in having the neck shorter than the body, and the lores feathered; they are also closely allied to the Ducks, from most of which they differ in having the tarsus enclosed in small, hexagonal scales, and in the similarity in color of the sexes. They also lack the cere, or soft swollen surface at the base of the upper bill, which is characteristic of the Ducks. Still another marked difference is shown in the feeding habits of the Geese, which often take them into fields far away from water. This habit is due to the fact that Geese walk much more readily than do Ducks, because of their legs being set further forward on their bodies. Their food is almost wholly vegetable. In the water they take seeds and roots of aquatic plants, which they get by searching the vegetation below the surface, an operation which they accomplish by completely immersing the head and long neck, tipping the body meanwhile so that the tail points straight upward. On land they feed in the spring on sprouting grain, and in the fall on corn, oats, wheat, and barley, taken from the stubble fields.

Geese nest invariably on the ground and usually line their nests with their own down to which sometimes soft grasses are added. The eggs, from four to six or eight in number, are white. The coloration of several species of Geese varies greatly according to their habitat and the seasons.

Owing to their great powers of flight the Geese cover immense distances in their annual migrations, many species nesting well within the Arctic Circle, and ranging far to the south in winter.

SNOW GOOSE

Chen hyperboreus hyperboreus (*Pallas*)

A. O. U. Number 169

Other Names.— Wavey; Common Wavey; Little Wavey; White Brant; Lesser Snow Goose; Common Snow Goose; White Goose; Mexican Goose.

Length.— 25 inches.

Description.— Bill, short and high at base. ADULTS: *Pure white,* the head washed with rusty brown; *primaries, gray at base, black at ends;* bill, pale carmine-red with white tip and black cutting edge; feet, pinkish-red; eyes, dark brown. YOUNG: Entire plumage, gray, lightening below; streaked on head and neck very faintly with darker; more or less waved on back with same; secondaries and primaries, dusky, the former with lighter edges; bill and feet, much darker than in adult.

Nest and Eggs.— Unknown.

Distribution.— North America; breeds from mouth of the Mackenzie east probably to Coronation Gulf and Melville Island; occurs on the Arctic coast of northeastern Asia, but not known to breed there; winters from southern British Columbia, southern Colorado, and southern Illinois south to northern Lower California, central Mexico (Jalisco), Texas, and Louisiana, and on the Asiatic coast south to Japan; generally rare in eastern United States.

Drawing by R. I. Brasher

SNOW GOOSE (½ nat. size)

Flocks, at rest, appear like banks of snow

The Snow Goose is a western bird, closely resembling the Greater Snow Goose, which is confined mainly to eastern North America. In the old days, about which the ancient hunter loves to tell, great flocks of White Geese, resting upon the western prairies, appeared like banks of snow. The enormous numbers of the past are gone, but the white birds are more or less abundant still in migration in the Far West and they are numerous in winter along the Pacific coast of the United States.

This bird breeds beyond the Arctic circle and reappears in the United States in September. The flocks like to rest on some lake at night and to feed by day in the open fields. Farms where they can pick up waste grain are favorites, and they are destructive to young grain just sprouting from the soil. As the migrating flocks come in at night they present a beautiful and impressive sight. They fly in a wide rank presenting a curved front not so angular as the V-shaped flock of the Canada Goose. Winging steadily along, high and serene, their extended pinions barely moving, their snowy forms borrowing rosy tints from the sunset sky, they seek a harbor of security; but as they seem about to pass on, and leave the placid lake far behind, the flock lengthens, turns upward at an angle of fifty or sixty degrees, and then, hanging on down-bent rigid wings, floats softly down and down, drifting and still falling a thousand feet or more and at the end, with a few quick flaps, dropping to the water, and so they come to rest. Sometimes when near their goal they zigzag down more like a falling Canvas-back. The young are easily distinguished from the adult birds by their grayish plumage.

The Snow Goose is difficult to approach and is not highly regarded by the epicure. Were it not for its taste for sprouting grain it might maintain its numbers for many years.

EDWARD HOWE FORBUSH.

The Greater Snow Goose (*Chen hyperboreus nivalis,* color plate 21) is similar in color to the Snow Goose, but larger in size. It breeds on Whale Island, in Ellesmere Land, and in North Greenland, but its full breeding range is unknown. In the winters it is found from southern Illinois, Chesapeake Bay, and Massachusetts (rarely) south to Louisiana, Florida, and the West Indies. Sometimes during migration it is seen west to Colorado and east to New England and Newfoundland.

Audubon said he found this Goose in fall and winter in every part of the United States that he visited and other early writers record great flocks on the Atlantic coast. Its numbers have been greatly reduced; this is probably due not only to its conspicuousness, but also to the superior flavor of its flesh.

BLUE GOOSE

Chen cærulescens (*Linnæus*)

A. O. U. Number 169.1 See Color Plate 21

Other Names.— Blue-winged Goose; Blue Wavey; Blue Brant; Blue Snow Goose; White-headed Goose; Bald-headed Brant; White-headed Bald Brant; Brant.

General Description.— Length, 28 inches. Head, white; body, gray. Bill, short and high at base.

Color.—ADULTS: *Head and upper neck, white;* face stained with rusty; neck below, back, and breast, dusky-gray fading into whitish below, into fine *bluish-gray on wings,* and into whitish on rump and upper tail-coverts, broadly-barred across the back and on sides with dusky-gray; wing-coverts, pale grayish-brown; most of secondaries, dusky edged with gray; primaries, black; bill and feet, pinkish-red; cutting edges of bill, black and tip white; iris, dark brown. YOUNG: General color, brownish, streaked on side of neck and barred on back with pale gray; under tail-coverts whitish; wing as in adults; bill and feet, dusky flesh color; iris, brown.

Nest and Eggs.— Unknown.

Distribution.— Eastern North America; breeding range unknown, but probably interior of northern Ungava; winters from Nebraska and southern Illinois south to coasts of Texas and Louisiana; rare or casual in migration in California, and from New Hampshire to Florida, Cuba, and the Bahamas.

Until within a very few years the Blue Goose was generally considered a rare species. In a winter trip to the delta of the Mississippi River, in 1909–10, I was astonished to find that the immense concourses of Geese, by scores of thousands, which were said to be " Brants " were in reality, nine-tenths of them, Blue Geese. The Canada Geese did not consort with them, and there were only a few White-fronted and Snow Geese in their company.

At daybreak they could always be found out on the flats off from the exits of certain "passes" into the Gulf. They kept up a tremendous clamor which could be heard a couple of miles away. Being exceedingly shy, they would rise and disappear up or down the coast if anyone approached within half a mile of them; consequently even the market gunners get very few. Farther westward, on the Wild Life Refuges, they make rendezvous for the night in certain localities on the marshes. At Cheniers au Tigres the cattle men complained that these great hordes of Geese, spending the nights, and sometimes days, on the marshes used for pasturing cattle, pulled up every root of the grass from many acres, creating depressions which filled with water and became ponds. The cattle men actually had youths employed to ride about on horseback and shoot at the Geese to drive them off.

They breed very far north, perhaps on the Arctic islands north of the American continent. Very little is known about its breeding habits. It is a remarkable fact that in winter nearly the whole of the species in a body seems to resort to the Gulf coast of Louisiana, or not further than Texas, hundreds of thousands being concentrated within a comparatively short coast-line.

In January, 1916, I had a remarkable experience with Blue Geese. On a certain point on the shore of Vermilion Bay, La., there is a rather small gravel-spit, known as "the goose-bank," to which from time immemorial, great numbers of Geese have always resorted during the winter to eat gravel for digesting their food. Wishing to secure photographs and motion pictures of Blue Geese, we built a blind at one end of this spit, scattered corn, and returned some four weeks later. The weather was bad and the Geese did not show up. After five days of dreary waiting amid fog and hosts of mosquitoes, patience had its reward.

Photo by H. K. Job — Courtesy of Nat. Asso. Aud. Soc.

BLUE GEESE

The photographer waited five days to get this picture

Hardly was I hidden in the blind that morning before the Geese began to come. After considerable circling they alighted on the shore and came up to get the gravel. The "seance" lasted four hours, and during that time I had upwards of a thousand Blue Geese, and a few Snow Geese, within as near as six feet. They ate, drank, bathed, and dozed, without any suspicion of my presence. Noisy fellows, they talked so much that they seemed not to hear the clattering of the picture machine, even when only a dozen feet away. It was one of the most thrilling experiences of a lifetime.

HERBERT K. JOB.

WHITE-FRONTED GOOSE

Anser albifrons gambeli *Hartlaub*

A. O. U. Number 171a See Color Plate 21

Other Names.— American White-fronted Goose; Laughing Goose; Harlequin Brant; Gray Brant; Pied Brant; Prairie Brant; Spectacled Brant; Speckled Brant; Yellow-legged Goose; Speckle-belly.

General Description.— Length, 30 inches. Plumage, grayish-brown with dark patch on lower breast. Bill, comparatively low at base.

Color.— *Lores, forehead, and fore-crown, white,* bordered behind by blackish; head, neck, breast, and upper parts in general, dark grayish-brown, feathers of back with lighter edges, forming regular and distinct transverse bars; upper tail-coverts, white; secondaries and ends of primaries, dusky, ashy at base; greater coverts and secondaries bordered with whitish; sides of body below, grayish-brown; a large patch more or less broken of deep blackish-brown on lower breast and abdomen; bill, pink with white tip (the bill is yellow in breeding season); feet, chrome-yellow; iris, dark brown. YOUNG: General tone of color browner, no black below; no white on head; tip of bill, black or dusky; otherwise similar.

Nest and Eggs.— NEST: A shallow depression in the ground, lined with grass, feathers, and down; usually near fresh-water lakes. EGGS: 5 to 7, creamy-white.

Distribution.— Central and western North America; breeds on and near the Arctic coast from northeastern Siberia east to northeastern Mackenzie and south to lower Yukon valley; winters commonly from southern British Columbia to southern Lower California and Jalisco, and rarely from southern Illinois, southern Ohio, and New Jersey south to northeastern Mexico, southern Texas, and Cuba, and on the Asiatic coast to China and Japan; rare in migration on the Atlantic coast north to Ungava.

The White-fronted Goose was formerly an uncommon spring and autumn migrant on our coast (Howe and Allen). Dr. J. A. Allen (1879) terms it a rare migrant, spring and fall, and says that Dr. Brewer states that it was more common thirty or forty years ago, as was the case with many of our other Ducks and Geese. It is now regarded as a mere straggler on the entire Atlantic coast.

It is known as a Brant in some of our western States, where it is abundant in migration. Formerly it was common as far east as the Ohio River.

The flight of the White-fronted Goose is similar to that of the Canada Goose. There is the same V-shape formation, and at a distance it might be readily mistaken for that of the Canada Goose. Audubon states that in Kentucky this Goose feeds on beechnuts, acorns, grain, young blades of grass, and snails.

EDWARD HOWE FORBUSH, in *Game Birds, Wild-Fowl and Shore Birds.*

CANADA GOOSE

Branta canadensis canadensis (*Linnæus*)

A. O. U. Number 172 See Color Plate 22

Other Names.—Wild Goose; Common Wild Goose; Cravat Goose; Big Gray Goose; Bay Goose; Reef Goose; Black-headed Goose; Canada Brant; Honker; Long-necked Goose.

General Description.— Length, 35 to 43 inches. Head, black; body, brownish-gray. Neck, long and slender.

Color.— Head and neck, black; *a broad circular patch extending from upper side of head around throat to an equal distance on other side,* not reaching lower bill, leaving chin black; rest of plumage, brownish-gray, more ashy below; all feathers with paler edges; *upper and under tail-coverts, white;* bill and feet, black; iris, brown.

Nest and Eggs.— NEST: Usually on a mound in marshes; constructed of grass, reeds, and leaves and lined with down; rarely old nests of Hawks or Eagles are appropriated. EGGS: 6 to 7, dull white.

Distribution.— North America; breeds from limit of trees in valley of the lower Yukon, northwestern Mackenzie, and central Keewatin south to southern Oregon, northern Colorado, Nebraska, and Indiana; formerly bred casually south to New Mexico, Kansas, Tennessee, and Massachusetts; winters from southern British Columbia, southern Colorado, southern Wisconsin, southern Illinois, and New Jersey (rarely southern Ontario and Newfoundland) south to southern California, Texas, and Florida; accidental in Bermuda and Jamaica.

Photograph of habitat group

Courtesy of American Museum of Natural History

WILD GEESE ON CRANE LAKE, SASKATCHEWAN

The young birds are about two weeks old

The Canada Goose is the best known member of the subfamily *Anserinæ* in eastern and central North America. Nearly everyone is familiar with the sight of the V-shaped bands of these splendid birds as they migrate southward in autumn, or in spring when they again turn their wing-beats toward the frozen pole. The great breeding grounds of this Goose are in the British provinces, few, if any, of the eastern flight pausing in spring south of the Canadian border. In the western States, however, they breed commonly in many localities. Thus, I have found their eggs on islands in lakes of North Dakota, and come upon the young attended by the parents in Oregon and northern California. It is a rather curious fact that shortly after the young have hatched, the parents begin a molt of feathers which is frequently so extensive that the birds lose the power of flight. At this season they must of course depend entirely upon their wonderful ability to swim, when in search of food, or endeavoring to escape their enemies.

Photo by T. G. Pearson Courtesy of Nat. Asso. Aud. Soc.

NEST AND EGGS OF CANADA GOOSE

Stump Lake, North Dakota

Canada Geese are not flesh eaters, the grain-fields of the great Northwest being their special delight. During the fall migration they often come here in great numbers and feed on the grain scattered among the stubble at harvest time. Along the lower Mississippi River they may often be seen in the fields of Tennessee and Arkansas. Like most Geese, while feeding, they have one or more sentinels constantly on the lookout for danger. Furthermore the members of a feeding flock are continually rising up and looking about, so that there are always a number of heads in the air.

These birds assemble in enormous numbers on favorite feeding grounds in Chesapeake Bay and in the sounds of North Carolina. In Currituck Sound I have seen one flight that was two hours in passing a given point. They came in one long wavy rank after another, from twenty to thirty of these extended lines of Geese being in sight at a time. The Canada Goose is highly esteemed as an article of food, and when one stops to think of the incessant gun-fire to which they have long been subjected, it is hard to understand why their numbers have not materially decreased. T. Gilbert Pearson.

The Canada Geese "feed largely on vegetable matter, the roots of rushes, weeds, grasses, etc., grass, and many seeds and berries, and swallow quantities of sand as an aid to digestion. Geese either feed on shore, when they pluck up grass and other vegetation, or they bring up food from the bottom in shoal water by thrusting their heads and necks down as they float on the surface. Like the Brant, they feed on eel-grass, which grows on the flats in salt or brackish water, in tidal streams, and marshy ponds. Sometimes they are destructive to young grass and grain." (Forbush.)

Hutchins's Goose (*Branta canadensis hutchinsi*) is precisely like the Canada Goose in everything except size; its length is but 25 to 34 inches, and its weight is generally three or four pounds, rarely exceeding six pounds. It breeds in the Arctic region of North America and migrates south in winter chiefly through western United States and the Mississippi valley. Sometimes it visits northeastern Asia. Throughout its range it is variously known also as Goose-brant,

Photo by H. K. Job

NEST AND EGGS OF CANADA GOOSE

Saskatchewan

Little Canada Goose, Little Wild Goose, Small Gray Goose, Little Gray Goose, Short-necked Goose, or Mud Goose.

The White-cheeked Goose (*Branta canadensis occidentalis*) and the Cackling Goose (*Branta canadensis minima*) are other geographical varieties of the Canada Goose. The former is found in the Pacific coast district of North America, breeding from Prince William Sound and Mitkof Island south to northeastern California, and wintering from Washington to south California. It is like the Canada, but the under parts are darker and the white cheek patches are usually separated by a black throat patch. The Cackling Goose is like the White-cheeked but smaller in size. It breeds in the western Aleutians and Norton Sound south to the northern coast of the Alaskan peninsula. In the winter it may be found from British Columbia south to San Diego county, California; it has sometimes been reported from Colorado, Iowa, Wisconsin, and Illinois.

BRANT

Branta bernicla glaucogastra (*Brehm*)

A. O. U. Number 173a — See Color Plate 22

Other Names.— Common Brant; Eastern Brant; White-bellied Brant; Light-bellied Brant; Brant Goose; Clatter Goose; Crocker; Quink; Black Brant; Brent Goose; Burnt Goose.

General Description.— Length, 24 inches. Color above, brownish-gray; below, ashy-gray and white. Neck, long and slender.

Color.—Adults (sexes alike): *Head, neck, throat, and breast, black; on each side of neck a series of 5 or 6 white streaks;* upper parts, brownish-gray, the feathers lighter edged; rump, darker; upper tail-coverts, white; primaries and secondaries, dusky; lower breast, pale ashy-gray fading on abdomen and lower wing-coverts to white; bill and feet, black; iris, brown. Immature: Similar, but not so much white on sides of neck and wing-coverts, and the secondaries tipped with white.

Nest and Eggs.— Nest: A depression in the ground on marshy ground or sandy beaches; made of grass, moss, and feathers and lined with down. Eggs: 4 to 6, grayish-white.

Distribution.— Northern hemisphere; breeds on Arctic islands north of latitude 74° and west to about longitude 100°, and on the whole west coast of Greenland; winters on the Atlantic coast from Massachusetts, south to North Carolina, rarely to Florida; has been recorded in the interior from Manitoba, Ontario, Colorado, Nebraska, Wisconsin, Michigan, Indiana, and Louisiana; accidental in British Columbia and the Barbados.

BLACK BRANT

Branta nigricans (*Lawrence*)

A. O. U. Number 174 — See Color Plate 22

Description.— Like the Brant, but black of head and breast extending over most of under parts, fading on abdomen and under tail-coverts into lighter; white neck patches usually larger and meeting in front.

Nest and Eggs.— Nesting similar to and eggs indistinguishable from the Brant's.

Distribution.— Western North America; breeds on the Arctic coast and islands from Point Barrow east to near mouth of Anderson River, north probably to Melville Island; common on Siberian coast, Chukchi Peninsula, and west to New Siberian Islands; winters on the Pacific coast from British Columbia south to San Quintin Bay, Lower California, in the interior of Oregon and Nevada, and on the Asiatic coast south to Japan; recorded as a straggler to Massachusetts, New York, and New Jersey.

The Brant is the smallest of our wild Geese and is known to the United States only as a winter visitor. Its summer home is beneath the very shadow of the frozen pole, for its nest is built well within the Arctic circle. When the first breath of autumn sweeps over our southland the wild water-fowl begin to appear, and every successive gale from the North brings its teeming thousands. Not among the first arrivals but soon to follow comes the Brant. It does not visit the rivers and lakes of the interior like most of its kin, but follows down the coast to feed principally in the salt and brackish waters of the bays and sounds of Virginia and North Carolina. Here it may be found in thousands and tens of thousands. I recall once sailing through Pamlico Sound from Ocracoke to Cape Hatteras, a distance of thirty miles, and there was not a minute during the entire trip but what newly startled flocks were in the air before us.

When the weather is fair Brants gather in very large companies to feed on the eel-grass growing in the shallow water of the shoals, or at high tide to drift a chattering host upon the bosom of the slow-heaving sound. When strong winds blow these large "rafts" are broken up and small companies of from two to a dozen fly about seeking companionship. It is then that the gunners get in their deadly work. In a small blind erected on four posts standing on a shoal, often three or four miles from land, the hunters take their stand. Anchored in the water about them are from fifty to one hundred wooden decoys representing Ducks and Brant. It is to these dummy sirens that the small flocks of Brant come; they "draw to the idols," the local gunners say. They are awkward, slow-flying birds and poor indeed is the marksman who cannot make a good score with a shotgun under such conditions.

Another popular way of hunting them is by means of a battery. This may be described as a coffin with canvas wings. It is anchored on the Brant's feeding grounds and when the gunner lies down in it he is effectively concealed unless to a bird almost directly overhead. This is probably the most deceptive device used by man to outwit the wary wild fowl. I have known bags of one hundred Brant to be made from a single battery in a day. In viewing such sights one is led to wonder that any of these game-birds have been able to escape the terrific slaughter to which they have long been subject by the hand of man.

Drawing by R. I. Brasher

BRANT (½ nat. size)

The smallest of the wild Geese

On the Pacific coast of North America the Black Brant is found. It is very similar to the eastern species, but has more black on the underparts and the front of the neck as well as the sides has white markings.

T. Gilbert Pearson.

EMPEROR GOOSE

Philacte canagica (*Sevastianoff*)

A. O. U. Number 176

Other Names.— Painted Goose; Beach Goose.

General Description.— Length, 28 inches. Head and tail, white; body, bluish-gray. Bill, small and but little elevated at base.

Color.— ADULTS: Head, sides and back of neck, and tail, white, the first two tinged with amber-yellow; throat, blackish; rest of plumage, bluish-gray; feathers above and below with black subterminal crescents white-tipped, producing a scaly appearance; bill, flesh color with white tip; feet, orange-yellow; iris, brown. YOUNG: Head, dusky speckled with white on top; otherwise similar to adult.

Nest and Eggs.— NEST: A depression on marshy islands bordering the sea, at first without semblance of nesting material, but as the number of eggs to be laid nears completion, the depression is lined with grass, leaves, and down. EGGS: 5 to 8, dull whitish.

Distribution.— Coasts of Alaska; breeds from Kotzebue Sound south to mouth of Kuskokwim, on St. Lawrence Island, and also on Chukchi Peninsula, Siberia, near East Cape; winters from the Commander and Near islands east through the Aleutians to Bristol Bay and Sitka; casual in British Columbia and California; accidental in Hawaii.

Edward W. Nelson, who made a special study of the Emperor Goose in Alaska, and prepared for the National Association of Audubon Societies a leaflet in which he records some of his interesting observations, says that this is the "least known and the most beautiful" of all the wild geese which make their summer home in the Far North, in both the Old and the New worlds. For these reasons it seems proper to give here some account of the bird, even though its visits to the United States proper are confined to occasional appearances in northern California.

The main wintering place of the Emperor Goose, according to Mr. Nelson, appears to be on the southern side of the Peninsula of Alaska and the Aleutian Islands, where the Aleuts know it as the "Beach Goose." The Eskimos of the Yukon delta Mr. Nelson found wearing "parkies" or outer garments made of the skins of Emperor Geese, sewed together. Their native name for the bird is "nachau-thluk." As to his observations of the bird's habits in the Yukon region Mr. Nelson writes:

"At first the Emperor Geese were difficult to approach, but as their numbers increased they became less shy. When on the wing, they were easily distinguished from the other Geese, even at considerable distances, by their proportionately shorter necks and heavier bodies, as well as by their short, rapid wing-strokes, resembling those of the Black Brant. Like the latter, they usually flew near the ground, rarely more than thirty yards high, and commonly so close to the ground that their wing-tips almost touched the surface on the down stroke. While flying from place to place, they give at short intervals a harsh, strident call of two syllables, like *kla-ha, kla-ha, kla-ha,* entirely different from the note of any other Goose I have ever heard. They are much less noisy than either the White-fronted or Cackling Geese, which often make the tundra resound with their excited cries.

"Almost at once after their arrival on the islands, the Emperor Geese appeared to be mated, the males walking around the females, swinging their heads and uttering low love notes; and incoming flocks quickly disintegrated into pairs which moved about together, though often congregating with many others on flats and sandbars. The male was extremely jealous and pugnacious, however, and immediately resented the slightest approach of another toward his choice; and this spirit was shown equally when an individual of another species chanced to come near. When a pair was feeding, the male moved restlessly about, constantly on the alert, and at the first alarm the pair drew near one another, and just before taking wing uttered a deep, ringing *u-lugh, u-lugh;* these, like the flight-notes, having a peculiar deep tone impossible to describe. At low tide, as soon as the shore ice disappeared, the broad mud-flats along shore were thronged with them in pairs and in groups. They were industriously dabbling in the mud for food until satisfied, and then congregated on bars, where they sat dozing in the sun or lazily arranging their feathers.

"Early in June, they began depositing eggs on the flat, marshy islands bordering the sea. The nests were most numerous a short distance back from the muddy feeding-grounds, but stray pairs were found nesting here and there farther inland. One must have lain with neck outstretched on the ground, as I afterward found was their custom when approached, for the Eskimo and I passed within a few feet on each side of her; but, in scanning the ground for nesting birds, the general similarity in tint of the bird and the obvious stick of driftwood beside her had completely misled our sweeping glances.

"The same ruse misled us several times; but on each occasion the parent betrayed her presence by a startled outcry and hasty departure soon after we had passed her and our backs were presented. They usually flew to a considerable distance, and showed little anxiety over our visit to the nests. When first laid the five to eight eggs are pure white, but they soon become soiled. When the complement of eggs to be laid approaches completion, the parent lines the depression in the ground with a soft, warm bed of fine grass, leaves, and feathers from her own breast. The males were rarely seen near the nests, but usually gathered about the feeding-grounds with others of their kind, where they were joined now and then by their mates.

"The young are hatched the last of June or early in July, and are led about the tundras by both parents until August, when the old birds molt their quill-feathers and with the still unfledged young become extremely helpless. At this time, myriads of other Geese are in the same condition, and the Eskimos made a practice of setting up long lines of strong fish-nets on the tundras to form pound-traps, or enclosures with wide wings leading to them, into which thousands were driven and killed for food. The slaughter in this way was very great, for the young were killed at the same time. Fortunately, in 1909, President Roosevelt made a bird-reservation covering the delta of the Yukon and the tundra to the southward, which includes the main breed-ground of the Emperor Goose, and thus took a long step toward perpetuating this fine bird."

SWANS

Order *Anseres;* family *Anatidæ;* subfamily *Cygninæ*

THE Swans constitute a subfamily (*Cygninæ*) of the family *Anatidæ*, and may be considered as comprising two genera, which include about eight species. The "true" Swans English ornithologists group in a single genus, *Cygnus*, while by American scientists they are called *Olor* from the Latin, meaning Swan. They are large, and almost exclusively aquatic birds and are characterized by the length of the neck, which may be even longer than the body, the number of vertebræ ranging from twenty-three to twenty-five, while the Geese have less than twenty. The Swans are famous for their stately appearance in the water, due largely to the constantly changing but always graceful arching of their necks. The plumage is generally pure white, though the head is sometimes marked with rusty hues.

Like the Geese, the distribution of the Swans is very wide, their range including much of the Arctic regions, where they build their rude nests, composed chiefly of reeds, in which are deposited about six eggs of a greenish hue. Their food consists mainly of the seeds and roots of water plants, though they are accused of destroying great quantities of fish-spawn.

WHISTLING SWAN

Olor columbianus (*Ord*)

A. O. U. Number 180 See Color Plate 22

Other Names.— Swan; Common Swan; Wild Swan; American Whistling Swan.

Length.— 4½ feet.

Description.— *Nostrils nearer the tip of the bill than the eyes.* ADULTS: Entire plumage, pure white; bill, black with *a yellow spot at base in front of eye;* feet, black; iris, brown. YOUNG: Plumage, ashy-gray, darker on neck where washed with pale rufous; bill, partly flesh color; feet, yellowish flesh color.

Nest and Eggs.— NEST: On the ground in or on the borders of marshes; a large structure of grass, moss, weed stalks, and herbage of different kinds. EGGS: 3 to 6, dull white.

Distribution.— North America; breeds from north-

Photograph of habitat group

Courtesy of American Museum of Natural History

WHISTLING SWAN

Incubating on its nest of moss, etc., on Southampton Island, Hudson Bay

ern Alaska south to Becharof Lake, Alaska Peninsula, and on Arctic islands from about latitude 74° south to northern Mackenzie and northwestern Hudson Bay; in migration occurs west to Bering Island; winters on the Pacific coast from southern British Columbia, rarely south to southern California, and in the interior from Lake Erie and southern Illinois to coast of Louisiana and Texas, and on Atlantic coast from Delaware and Maryland to South Carolina, rarely north to Massachusetts and south to Florida; casual in northern Mexico; accidental in the British Isles and in the Bermudas.

On the coasts and islands of the Arctic Sea, in far-off archipelagoes of the great frozen North, the Whistling Swan builds its huge nest. When the mother leaves it she covers the eggs carefully with the mossy nest lining to insure warmth and safety. The eggs are hatched by the last of June and the cygnets are led to the water where they feed and grow under the midnight sun. Soon the parents molt out all their flight-feathers and, as the whole family is then unable to fly, they often fall victims to the natives who hunt them remorselessly at this season, but native tribes are few; the country is a wide wilderness and many of the birds escape the dangers of the north. Late in September or in October they are on their way southward where they are to face greater perils.

Courtesy of National Association of Audubon Societies and of Mr. John Heywood

SWANS IN WINTER ON HEYWOOD ESTATE, GARDNER, MASSACHUSETTS

Showing how waterfowl keep open a hole in the ice

It is hard to see just why this bird is called the Whistling Swan. Its calls have great variety; some high-keyed notes may come from the younger birds but the old males sound the bass horn. As the flock passes over, high in air, the leader utters a high note like that of a flageolet which Elliot describes as sounding like *whŏ-whŏ-whŏ* and this, repeated by flock after flock, may have given the bird its name.

The flight seems to divide into three sections; one following the Atlantic coast; another the Mississippi valley, and a third the Pacific coast. The flocks pass mainly overland in an unwavering line at great heights. In fair weather they seem to avoid civilization, flying so high as to be unnoticed by human eyes and making but few stops, therefore they are considered scarce in most of the northern States of the Union. Very rarely, when caught in storms and over-weighted with sleet and snow, they are forced to come to the ground.

Such a catastrophe occurred to the flocks in northwestern Pennsylvania on March 22, 1879. Swans came down in many places in four counties, in ponds, streams, fields, or villages. Large numbers were killed by men and boys with guns, rifles, and clubs. Twenty-five were captured alive in one village, as they were worn out and helpless after their battle with the storm. Most of those that alighted within sight of human habitations were slaughtered wantonly. (George B. Sennett, in *Bull. Nuttall Orn. Club,* 1880.) In some cases the Great Lakes are their refuge, if they can reach those waters, and often they are saved by alighting under the lee of some point or island, but now and then a flock comes down in the Niagara River and is carried over the falls. Whenever this happens and the wearied and often injured birds are cast up against the ice bridge or along the shores, people come in crowds and kill with guns or clubs the birds that have passed alive through the fury of the elements.

There is no safety for a Swan in this country except it be high in air or far out on open water. Such refuge is found on the broad waters of the South. The great flocks that once frequented the coast in winter from Massachusetts to South Carolina are gone, but the species still winters in large numbers on the Carolina coasts.

The song of the dying Swan has been regarded as a pleasing myth for many years, but Elliot asserts that he heard it once at Currituck Sound, when a Swan, mortally wounded in the air, set its wings and, sailing slowly down, began its death-song, continuing it until it reached the water " nearly half a mile away." The song was unlike any other Swan note that he had ever heard. It was plaintive and musical and sounded at times like the soft running of an octave. Inquiry among local gunners revealed the fact that some had heard similar sounds from Swans that had been fatally hurt. Need we wonder that the Swan was a favorite bird of mythology? EDWARD HOWE FORBUSH.

TRUMPETER SWAN

Olor buccinator (*Richardson*)

A. O. U. Number 181

Description.— *Larger than Whistling Swan;* nostrils midway between tip of bill and eyes. ADULTS: Plumage, pure white or with wash of rusty on head; *bill, lores* and feet, *black;* iris, brown. YOUNG: Bill and feet, not perfectly black; plumage, grayish; head and upper neck, rusty. Length, 5 feet.

Nest and Eggs.— NEST: On an elevated knoll near water; constructed of grass, stalks, feathers, and down. EGGS: 5 to 7, dull white.

Distribution.— Interior and western North America; breeds from the Rocky Mountains to western shore of Hudson Bay and from the Arctic Ocean to about latitude 60°; fromerly bred south to Indiana, Missouri, Nebraska, Montana, and Idaho, and casually west to Fort Yukon and British Columbia; winters from southern Indiana and southern Illinois south to Texas, and from southern British Columbia to southern California; casual in migration in the Rocky Mountain region of United States; accidental in New York and Delaware. Now of rare occurrence nearly everywhere.

The Trumpeter Swan, the largest of North American wild fowl, represents a vanishing race. In most parts of North America it is a bird of the past. Formerly it ranged over the greater portion of the continent. Today it is seen rather rarely in the wilder regions of the interior.

Great flights of Swans were observed by the early settlers on the Atlantic seaboard from Maine to Georgia. No one knows what proportion of these were Trumpeters, but, as the Trumpeter was recorded on the Atlantic coast as late as the last half of the nineteenth century, there is some reason for the belief that some of the early flocks were of this species. It was once the prevailing Swan of California and was abundant in Oregon and Washington, but it has now practically disappeared from the Pacific coast. It always was a bird of the fresh waters and did not, like the Whistling Swan, often frequent salt water bays and estuaries. When the country was first setted the Trumpeter bred in the northern United States, and from there northward to the fresh-water lakes and ponds in the vicinity of Hudson Bay, where it was very numerous, and even to the shores of the Arctic Ocean.

Little is known about the breeding habits of

this bird, but, like the Canada Goose, the male guards and defends the female, eggs, and young.

In autumn when the grip of the frost congealed the surface of its native lakes and streams the Trumpeter gathered in mighty flocks, circled high in air and moved southward in great flights using the V-shaped formation so characteristic of migrating Canada Geese. This is written in the past tense as there are no longer any great flights of the species. Then, as now, the Mississippi valley was a highway of bird migration and there, at times, in autumn, when the icy north wind blew, the sunset sky was overcast by clouds of waterfowl moving in dim strata near and far, in varying lines, crossing, converging, ascending, descending, but all trending southward toward waters as yet untouched by the frost. The rushing of their wings and their musical cries filled the air with a chorus of unrelated sounds, blending in rough harmonies. Above them all, in the full light of the setting sun great flocks of Cranes passed along the sky, and higher still in the glowing firmament rode the long "baseless triangles" of the Swans, sweeping across the upper air in exalted and unswerving flight, spanning a continent with the speed of the wind, their forms glistening like silver in the sunset glow. They presented the most impressive spectacle in bird life ever seen in North America. When at last they found their haven of rest they circled with many hoarse trumpetings in wide spirals from that giddy height reconnoitering the country as they swung lower and lower until, their apprehensions at rest, they sailed slowly down to drink, bathe, feed, and rest on quiet, peaceful waters.

Swans feed almost entirely by reaching down in shallow water and pulling up the vegetation from the bottom with the bill. Animal food such as shellfish is taken to some extent, mainly in the spring.

The reason for the rapid decrease of the Trumpeter is not far to seek. It is the largest and most conspicuous of waterfowl. Wherever, in settled regions, Swans were seen to alight, every kind of a firearm that could do duty was requisitioned and all men turned out to hunt the great white birds. They were not much safer in the almost uninhabited North, as the demands of civilization pursued them there. The records of the traffic in Swans' down tell the story of decrease in the territory of the Hudson Bay Company. Just previous to the middle of the nineteenth century about five hundred Swans' skins were traded annually at Isle à la Crosse and about three hundred were taken yearly at Fort Anderson. These were mainly skins of the Trumpeter Swan. The number sold annually by the Company slowly decreased from 1312 in 1854 to 122 in 1877. In 1853 Athabasca turned out 251, in 1889 only 33. In 1889 and 1890 Isle à la Crosse sent out but two skins for each outfit. (Preble, *North American Fauna.*) So the demands of fashion and the blood lust will follow the Trumpeter to the end.

EDWARD HOWE FORBUSH.

ORDER OF LAMELLIROSTRAL GRALLATORES

Order *Odontoglossæ;* family *Phœnicopteridæ*

UNTIL comparatively recent times the Flamingoes were associated by ornithologists — as they still are by many others — with the Storks and Herons. It is now known that they constitute an order which is the link between the order of Lamellirostral Swimmers and that of the Herons, Storks, and Ibises. The Persians recognized this relationship to the Geese when they gave to the Flamingo the name of *Kaj-i-surkh*, or Red Goose.

Of the seven species comprising the Flamingo family, five occur in this hemisphere, but only one comes within the borders of the United States. The family has several peculiar and interesting characteristics. In the first place, the plumage of all Flamingoes is very beautiful, the prevailing colors varying from rosy pink to bright scarlet. Again (and unlike the Herons, Cranes, and Ibises) the Flamingo's long neck is not due to multiplication of the vertebræ, of which there are but eighteen, but to the lengthening of the separate bones. Furthermore, the bird's bill is quite distinct in its structure: the lower mandible is a boxlike affair, broad and deep, into which the upper mandible, which moves freely, closes like a lid, and the sides are fitted with gill-like processes, which act as sieves, while the whole is bent sharply downward near the tip. This curious organ is thrust into the mud in an inverted position, the point being directed backward. In this manner the bird seeks its food, which consists of frogs, shellfish, mollusks, and aquatic herbage, strained from the mud by the sieve apparatus.

Any bird or beast of strange appearance and unusual habits is likely to be credited with almost any weird practice. The Flamingo furnishes an illustration of this in the accounts of its nesting habits which long passed current, and some of which are still believed by many. For probably the oldest and one of the most graphic of these accounts we are indebted to William Dampier, the seventeenth-century English freebooter and explorer, who thus described the nesting of the Flamingo (near Curaçao) in his famous book, *A New Voyage Around the World:*

" They build their Nests in shallow Ponds, where there is much Mud, which they scrape together, making little Hillocks, like small Islands, appearing out of the Water, a foot and a half high from the bottom. They make the foundations of these Hillocks broad, bringing them up tapering to the top, where they leave a small hollow pit to lay their Eggs in; and when they either lay their Eggs, or hatch them, they stand all the while, not on the Hillock, but close by it with their Legs on the ground and in the water, resting themselves against the Hillock, and covering the hollow nest upon it with their Rumps: For their Legs are very long; and building thus, as they do, upon the ground, they could neither draw their legs conveniently into their Nests, nor sit down upon them otherwise than by resting their whole bodies there, to the prejudice of their Eggs or their young, were it not for this admirable contrivance, which they have by natural instinct. They never lay more than two Eggs, and seldom fewer. The young ones cannot fly till they are almost full grown; but they will run prodigiously fast; yet we have taken many of them."

Of course, neither Dampier nor anybody else ever saw Flamingoes incubating their eggs in this manner; what he wrote was what had been told him, or what he conjectured would have to be done by a bird with such tremendously long legs; for we know, as a matter of fact, that Flamingoes cover their eggs very much as other birds do, that is to say, by sitting on them with their legs doubled up and the knees stretched out backward and coming about under the end of the tail. Yet undoubtedly by a great many ornithologies, or by detached articles still in circulation, this absurd invention is still perpetuated.

Photograph of habitat group

Courtesy of American Museum of Natural History

A FLAMINGO COLONY

The nests are made by scooping up mud with the bill and patting it into shape with bill and feet

FLAMINGO

Phœnicopterus ruber *Linnæus*

A. O. U. Number 182

Other Names.— Scarlet Flamingo; American Flamingo.

Description.—ADULTS: Plumage, scarlet; primaries and most secondaries, black legs, lake red; bill, black on end, orange in middle, base and bare skin of head, yellow. This perfect plumage rare; birds as usually seen are mostly dull pink with vermilion and scarlet only on wings. YOUNG: The young are hatched in white down with a straight bill, which gradually acquires the crook. First plumage, grayish-white with dusky wings; this passes through pink, rosy, and red to its full scarlet, several years being required to perfect the plumage. Length of adult, 4 feet.

Nest and Eggs.— NEST: A conical structure on remote inaccessible islands, of mud or marl scraped up by the bird's bill, about 18 inches in diameter at the base and about a foot across the top; from a few inches to more than a foot high. EGGS: 1 or 2, white.

Distribution.— Atlantic coast of subtropical and tropical America, from the Bahamas, Florida Keys, and Yucatan to Brazil, and in the Galapagos; accidental in South Carolina.

The great Scarlet Flamingo is a rare bird in the United States. Occasionally a few are seen at the extreme southern end of Florida and there was undoubtedly a time, many years ago, when they bred in that region. I saw a specimen at Palm Beach in 1908 that had been recently killed near there, but they probably never wander much north of this point. They frequent shallow lagoons or flooded mud flats, and are usually found in flocks.

In 1904 Dr. Frank M. Chapman found and studied a colony of perhaps two thousand pairs that were nesting on the island of Andros in the Bahama Islands. His intimate photographic studies made at this time were the greatest ornithological triumph in bird photography that had then been attained. It may be added that his published notes constitute practically all we know today of the nesting habits of this bird. The nests in this Flamingo city, he tells us, were pillars of dried mud, a foot or more in height, that had been scraped up by the birds from the immediate vicinity.

On each of these one white chalky egg was laid. While incubating, the old birds do not sit astride the nest as shown in many old illustrations, but double their legs under them. There was no cover in the way of trees or bushes for a long distance, but here on the semi-flooded, marl-covered plain the birds were fairly secure from human intrusion, as the region was isolated and particularly difficult to approach.

Upon first entering his photographic blind which he had erected near the field of Flamingoes' nests, Dr. Chapman had grave apprehensions as to whether the birds, all of which had flown to a distance, would return to their eggs. In *Camps and Cruises of an Ornithologist* he tells us something of their behavior, when, after his companion had departed from the neigborhood, he crouched in his blind and waited.

Drawing by Henry Thurston

FLAMINGOES ($\frac{1}{18}$ nat. size)

Rare birds in the United States

"Without further delay, the birds returned to their homes. They came on foot, a great red cohort marching steadily toward me. I felt like a spy in an enemy's camp. Might not at least one pair of the nearly four thousand eyes detect something unnatural in the newly grown bush almost within their city gates? No sign of alarm, however, was shown; without confusion, and as if trained to the evolution, the birds advanced with stately tread to their nests. There was a bowing of a forest of slender necks as each bird lightly touched its egg or nest with its bill; then, all talking loudly they stood up on their nests; the black wings were waved for a moment and bird after bird dropped forward on its egg. After a vigorous wriggling motion, designed evidently to bring the egg into close contact with the skin, the body was still, but the long neck and head were for a time in constant motion, preening, picking material at the base of the nest, dabbling in a nearby puddle, or perhaps drinking from it. Occasionally a bird sparred with one of the three or four neighbors which were within reach, when, bill grasping bill, there ensued a brief and harmless test of strength."

T. GILBERT PEARSON.

Photo by Leo E. Miller of the American Museum of Natural History

FLAMINGOES IN THE ZOOLOGICAL PARK, BUENOS AIRES

ORDER OF HERONS, STORKS, IBISES, ETC.

Order *Herodiones*

UNDER this order are grouped the long-legged wading birds generally found along shores or on muddy flats. Their necks are long, but are easily bent into a strongly curved S-shape. Their wings are rounded, long, and broad, and the tail short. The toes are four in number, all on the same level, long, slender, and without webs. The head is more or less naked with small, elevated nostrils, and the skull slopes gradually to the base of the bill. The bill is variable and divides the order into three suborders: the Spoonbills and Ibises (*Ibides*) have the bill grooved along the side from nostril to tip, a peculiarity not found in the other members of the order; the Storks and Wood Ibises (*Ciconiæ*) have the bill very thick at the base and curved near the tip which is rather blunt; the Herons, Egrets, Bitterns, etc. (*Herodii*) have the bill straight and sharp-pointed. The first of these suborders, as its name indicates, contains two families, and the others one each.

Their food is principally fish, reptiles, amphibians, mollusks, and other aquatic animals. The food is seized by a quick, straight thrust of the bill. Because of the structure of their feet, they are naturally good perchers and generally nest in trees. The nests are clumsy and crude, the eggs few. The young are naked, or nearly so, when hatched, and are fed and cared for in the nest by the parents.

SPOONBILLS, IBISES, AND STORKS

Order *Herodiones;* families *Plataleidæ*, *Ibididæ*, and *Ciconiidæ*

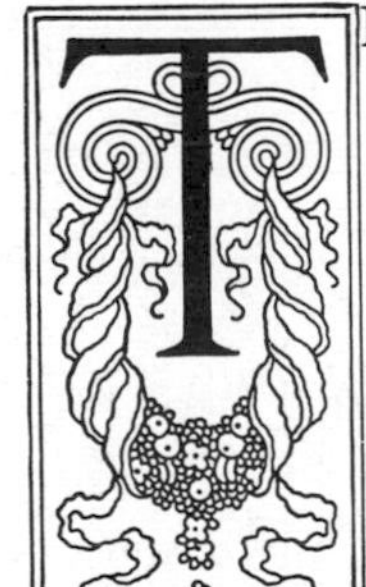

THE Spoonbills are distributed quite generally throughout the tropical and subtropical regions and are grouped in three genera including five or six species, of which the only American representative is the Roseate Spoonbill. As a family they are gregarious, especially during the breeding period, when they gather sometimes in very large colonies in marshes and bayous and build platform-like nests in low trees or bushes. The eggs number from three to five, and are white, spotted with varying shades of brown.

Structurally the Spoonbills are similar to the Ibises, except in their possession of the curious spoon-shaped bill which gives them their name. This is plainly a special adaptation, and is made use of by the bird in obtaining its food, which consists of frogs, aquatic insects, shellfish, mollusks, and small fish, and which the bird captures by submerging its bill and swinging it from side to side in a semicircular sweep imparted by a corresponding movement of the body. While thus feeding the birds stalk about with grave and dignified mien, seldom making long pauses, as do the Herons, to wait for their prey to approach. While resting, either in a tree or on land, they often stand for an hour or more on one leg, after the manner of many of their kind. Their flight is accomplished by an easy flapping operation, and is accompanied by some soaring, with head and legs outstretched meanwhile.

The plumage of the Spoonbills varies from almost pure white to the beautiful combination of white and rose or pinkish tints which characterize the species found in this country. During the breeding season the adults develop a fine crest, which depends from the nape of the neck. Spoonbills have no true vocal organs, though the windpipe is very long, and at the lower end coils approximately in the form of a figure eight, somewhat after the manner of that of the Cranes. The common call is a harsh *quack*, and the birds often make a clattering sound by snapping their mandibles together.

As the Spoonbills differ from the Ibises in the peculiar structure of their bill, so the Ibises are unlike the Storks, their close relatives, in the differentiation of the same organ, which is evenly curved, somewhat slender, more or less cylindrical, and comparatively soft, except at the tip, while that of the Storks is generally straight, rigid, and hard. Of the eighteen or more members of the Stork family scattered over the warmer parts of the earth, only one, the Wood Ibis, is regularly found in America north of the southern boundary of the United States.

Certain of the Ibis species are gregarious in the breeding season, while others are rather solitary. The nests may be placed in low bushes, on trees, or occasionally among reeds, or even in holes in ledges or cliffs. They are composed of plant-stems and sticks, and may or may not be lined with straw, roots, or herbage. The eggs are from two to four in number and may be greenish-blue, pale blue, olive-green, greenish-white, or sometimes brownish, while some of the lighter-colored forms may show brownish or reddish markings. The range of the Ibis is virtually cosmopolitan. About thirty species are known, and these are referable to about twenty genera. About one-third of the species are of New World occurrence.

Remarkable variation in both proportions and coloration are shown in this family; some species are graceful in their outlines and others are clumsy and uncouth, while plumage colors range from neutral or dull tints to gaudy and brilliant hues. Most of the species walk with marked grace and deliberation, while the flight is generally like though perhaps rather more rapid than that of the Spoonbills. The Ibises' diet includes aquatic insects, shellfish, mollusks, worms, small fish, frogs, grasshoppers, beetles, and lizards. In their search for their food, when it is in the water, the birds sweep the bill to and fro, though they also use it frequently for probing in mud or soft sand.

The Ibis was one of the most sacred birds of the ancient Egyptians, and as such was the subject of many myths and superstitions. Even to-day it is one of the characteristic birds of the Nile valley, and in lower Egypt it is called *Abou-mengel*, " Father of the Sickle," the reference being, of course, to its curved bill. Herodotus credited the bird with being a destroyer of snakes, and Cuvier recorded finding the remains of a reptile in the stomach of a mummied Ibis, but it seems clear that such creatures do not form part of the bird's normal diet.

ROSEATE SPOONBILL

Ajaia ajaja (*Linnæus*)

A. O. U. Number 183

Other Names.— Pink Curlew; Rosy Spoonbill.

General Description.— Length, 32 inches. Plumage, white with some pink or red. Adults have the head and throat bare.

Color.— Upper neck and back, white, sometimes tinged with pink; *wings and under parts, delicate rose-madder;* plumes of lower foreneck, lesser wing-coverts, upper and under tail-coverts, rich carmine; shafts of wing- and tail-feathers, carmine; tail, brownish-yellow with a patch of same color on sides of breast; the skin of the bald head varied with dull green, orange, and black; bill, with various shades of green, blue, yellow, and black; legs, lake red; iris, carmine. Young: Head, feathered; general plumage, white tinged with pink on wings, tail, and abdomen; edge of wing, dark brown. Three years are required to reach the perfect adult plumage.

Nest and Eggs.— Nest: A platform of sticks in dense tropical marshes, usually in cypress trees or mangrove bushes, from 8 to 20 feet above ground. Eggs: 3 or 4, white or buffy, blotched and spotted with various shades of brown.

Distribution.— North and South America, from Texas, Louisiana, Florida, and Georgia south to Patagonia and the Falkland Islands; formerly casual north to Pennsylvania and the lower Ohio valley (Indiana and Illinois); accidental in California, Colorado, Kansas, and Wisconsin.

There is no large wading bird of North America that bears such brilliant feathers as the Roseate Spoonbill. The general plumage is pink with the lesser wing-coverts of the adult a bright carmine color. This part of the plumage is known as the "drip." The bill is long and flatly spoon-shaped. The bird gets its food by wading, swinging its opened bill from side to side through the mud and water, as it advances. Formerly the Spoonbills, or "Pink Curlews," as the Florida hunters know them, were extensively shot and their feathers shipped to Jacksonville where they were made into fans to sell to winter tourists. Today the birds are extremely rare, thanks to the energy of the plume-hunter and the bird-shooting tourist. But for the wardens employed by the National Association of Audubon Societies they would probably now be extinct in Florida. A few are sometimes seen in Louisiana and possibly a thousand are left in Florida, but unless public sentiment in that State should receive a radical and sudden shift toward conservation, the bird will probably not long survive.

Spoonbills travel in flocks, sometimes in company with Ibises. They fly in long diagonal lines, each bird being behind and just to one side of the one in front. When seen among the dark green foliage of the mangrove trees, or while in flight, their wings reflect the sunlight and they show to advantage and make an unusual appeal to the bird-student. For the most part they are silent, although when feeding or when about their nests a low croaking note is constantly uttered, as though the birds were conversing among themselves.

Dr. Frank M. Chapman, speaking of the actions of the young in a nesting colony he visited in Mexico, says:

"When their parents returned they were all attention and on the alert for food. On such occasions they usually stood in a row on the edge of the nest facing the old birds, and in a most comical manner swung the head and neck up and down. I have seen balanced mechanical toys which would make almost exactly the same motion. The toys, however, were silent, while the little Spoonbills all joined in a chorus of tremulous, trilling whistles, which grew louder and more rapid as the parent approached.

Drawing by Henry Thurston

ROSEATE SPOONBILL ($\frac{1}{9}$ nat. size)

One of the rarest and most brilliant waders of the South

"What their parent brought them I could not see, nor for that matter, could they. But with a confidence born of experience, the bird that had first opportunity pushed its bill and head far down into its parent's mouth to get whatever was there. This singular operation sometimes lasted as long as ten seconds, and it was terminated only by the parent which, much against the will of its offspring, disengaged itself; then after a short rest a second youngster was fed and thus in due time the whole family was satisfied."

T. Gilbert Pearson.

WHITE IBIS

Guara alba (*Linnæus*)

A. O. U. Number 184

Other Names.— Spanish Curlew; Stone Curlew (young); White Curlew.

Length.— 26 inches.

Color.— Adults: *Plumage, pure white; tips of several outer primaries, glossy black*; bare face, bill, and legs, orange, red, or carmine, the bill tipped with dusky; iris, pale bluish-white. Young: Dull grayish-brown; rump, base of tail, and under parts, white; bare space on head, restricted and dull yellowish; bill, yellowish-orange; legs, bluish-gray; iris, brown.

Nest and Eggs.— NEST: Usually in mangrove thicket; constructed from twigs of those bushes. EGGS: 3 to 5, grayish-blue or whitish, blotched and spotted with dull yellow, rufous, and umber-brown.

Distribution.— North and South America, from Lower California, Texas, and South Carolina south to West Indies, Brazil, and Peru, and casually to Great Salt Lake, South Dakota, Illinois, Vermont, Connecticut, and Long Island; winters from Gulf of Mexico southward.

Some years ago the National Association of Audubon Societies purchased as a bird-reservation a portion of Orange Lake, Florida, that contains an island which has long been the breeding place of innumerable water-birds. Those years when the water is not too high to cover their food White Ibises to the number of about nine thousand pairs come here to breed, as do the Egrets, Herons, and Water Turkeys that are present every season. Their nests are built in the low alder trees that cover the island and are placed at all heights from one to fifteen feet. They are bulky and their weight added to that of the heavy birds plays sad havoc with the branches. The eggs are beautifully spotted; the young are crested with black down. At times the trees are so covered with White Ibises that at a distance they appear to be weighted down with snow.

Drawing by Henry Thurston

WHITE IBIS (⅓ nat. size)

A flock returning to their nests at evening is a pretty sight

The birds, of course, have their natural enemies. This island literally swarms with water moccasins in summer. They take many of the eggs and perhaps some of the newly hatched young. Vultures roost on the island and they devour many young. The most annoying of all the creatures that disturb the Ibises, however, are the Fish Crows. Numbers of them are on the island all day long and the quantities of eggs they consume is astonishing. When the nest is robbed these birds will lay again, and the Crows keep them producing eggs for many weeks. The warden in charge estimated that in the summer of 1913 every female Ibis laid an average of eleven eggs, although four is the normal number for a bird each season.

These birds fly in long ranks and make a very pretty sight when towards evening they begin coming in from their feeding grounds which are often many miles away. Low over the water to avoid the wind they come into view, rank after rank as far as the eye can see. With black-tipped wings sweeping up and down with never a pause the birds advance until near the island when they rise in unison and scatter about among the trees to spend the night.

In the United States the White Ibis breeds as far north as the swamp country of southern Illinois and the rice regions of South Carolina. I have seen them on the coast as far north as Beaufort, North Carolina, but only in the late summer, and only then the immature birds who exhibit the same wanderlust as the young of some

Photo by T. H. Jackson Courtesy of Nat. Asso. Aud. Soc.

NEST AND EGGS OF WHITE IBIS

At Orange Lake, Florida

species of Herons. The young birds before they assume the adult plumage are called " Stone Curlews " by the fishermen, and the old birds, which are popularly supposed to be of a different species, are usually referred to as " Spanish Curlews " or " White Curlews." The White Ibis is in no sense a Curlew, but its long, rounded, curved bill has doubtless suggested this name to many interested but unscientific observers.

T. GILBERT PEARSON.

GLOSSY IBIS

Plegadis autumnalis (*Linnæus*)

A. O. U. Number 186

Other Names.— Bay Ibis; Green Ibis; Ord's Ibis; Liver; Black Curlew.

Description.— Length, 24 inches. ADULTS: *Rich purplish-chestnut* shading on head, back, wings and tail, to glossy purplish-green; sides and under tail-coverts dusky-green; primaries, greenish-black; bare skin around eye slaty-blue; *no white feathers on face;* bill, dusky; legs, dark grayish; iris, brown. YOUNG: Head and neck, grayish-brown streaked with whitish; upper parts, dull dusky-green; below, grayish-brown.

Nest and Eggs.— NEST: In marshy ground or low bushes; constructed of dead reeds, plant stems, etc.; rather well built and well cupped. EGGS: 3, deep dull bluish-green.

Distribution.— Tropical and subtropical regions, mainly of eastern hemisphere; rare and local in southeastern United States from Louisiana to Florida, and in the West Indies; casual north to Missouri, Wisconsin, Michigan, Ontario, and Nova Scotia.

Photo by O. E. Baynard Courtesy of Nat. Asso. Aud. Soc.

GLOSSY IBIS

Two adult birds, one nest, and four young, Bird Island, Orange Lake, Florida

WHITE-FACED GLOSSY IBIS

Plegadis guarauna (*Linnæus*)

A. O. U. Number 187

General Description.— Length, 24 inches. Predominating color, rich purple.

Color.—ADULTS: Head, neck, and entire under parts, rich purplish-chestnut tinged with iridescent violet on head and nape; back and wing, iridescent violet-green and purple; shoulders, rich wine-red, less lustrous than wing; primaries, green with brassy luster; rump, upper tail-coverts, and tail, green with purplish reflections; lower tail-coverts, similar, contrasting with chestnut abdomen; *bare area on head, lake red; a margin of white feathers surrounding bare space on head,* including chin; bill, dusky, reddening on tip; legs and feet, dull reddish; iris, red. YOUNG: Plumage, entirely green; bill, dusky, blotched or banded with pinkish-white; legs, black; this coloration changing through brownish or grayish to the mature iridescent plumage.

Nest and Eggs.— NEST: On reed beds; constructed of dead reeds attached to upright stalks of living ones; very well and compactly built with a well-shaped cup. EGGS: 3 or 4, deep bluish-green.

Distribution.—Temperate and tropical America from southern Oregon, Arizona, Texas, and Florida south through Mexico to southern South America; casual north to British Columbia, Wyoming, and Nebraska.

The Glossy Ibis and the White-faced Glossy Ibis are identical in appearance, except that the former does not possess the small patch of white feathers in the region about the base of the bill. Both birds are inhabitants of tropical and subtropical America. They are extremely rare in eastern United States and appear to be confined largely to Florida. The only place they have been known to nest in that State in many years is on the Audubon Society's bird-island in Orange Lake. As many as seven pairs have built their nests here in a season.

In April, 1914, I hid in the top of a willow

Courtesy of Am. Mus. Nat. Hist.

WHITE-FACED GLOSSY IBIS (⅛ nat. size)

He is capable of a flight of ten or twenty miles in search of breakfast

tree on this island to watch the actions of the thousands of nesting Herons and White Ibises in the bushes below and about me. While thus concealed I had the good fortune to see six of these rare birds. At a distance they appear to be dull black, but upon coming closer the plumage was seen to possess a rich metallic luster that shone with various hues of green and purple as the birds turned in the sunlight. One that lit in a bush nearby had a white face which marked it as a White-faced Glossy. The nests were built in the bushes in a manner similar to that of the other Herons and Ibises. They were very substantial structures of sticks and twigs.

The Glossy Ibis is the species most generally supposed to be found in the West Indies and Florida, the White-faced Glossy on the other hand being regarded as a western bird. The latter breed in the extensive marshes of Malheur Lake in southeastern Oregon, making their nests in the interminable jungles of the tule reeds that here cover the marshes far and wide.

They are gregarious birds at all times and after the nesting season wander about from one feeding ground to another. The people of the Malheur country esteem them highly as food, and despite the law they are at times killed and eaten. In the coastal regions of Texas these Ibises are met with in various sections and here also they are shot. " Black Curlew " is the name by which gunners usually know them. They frequent the low, moist grounds about lakes, or over-flooded meadows. Often the feeding grounds are long distances from their nests, but the Glossy Ibis is a good flyer and quite capable of taking a flight of ten or twenty miles to get its breakfast. The food consists of crustaceans, especially crawfish, and water insects of various kinds. Frogs at times fall beneath the lightning stroke of the long curved bill. There should be a strong law in every State where this elegant wader is found, making the deed of killing one a misdemeanor punishable by heavy fine — and the law should be rigidly enforced. T. GILBERT PEARSON.

WOOD IBIS

Mycteria americana *Linnæus*

A. O. U. Number 188

Other Names.— American Wood Stork; Colorado Turkey; Goard, or Gourd, Head; Iron Head; Gannet.

Description.— Length, 4 feet. ADULTS: *White; wing-quills, primary coverts, and tail, glossy greenish-black;* the bald head and neck, grayish-blue, creamy, and yellowish; bill, dusky along ridge, dingy yellowish on sides and below; legs, bluish-gray; iris, dark brown. YOUNG: Dark gray with blackish wings and tail; head and neck, downy feathered, becoming bald after first molt.

Nest and Eggs.— NEST: A platform of sticks in trees, sometimes 100 feet up; the same sites are occupied every year and the nests sometimes become very bulky from the addition of material each season. EGGS: 2 or 3, white.

Distribution.—Temperate and tropical America from southern California, Arizona, Texas, Ohio valley, and South Carolina south to Argentina; casual north to Montana, Wisconsin, New York, and Vermont.

Of all the various species of Storks known to inhabit the earth, only two are found in North America. One of these, the Jabiru (*Jabiru mycteria*) of tropical America, occasionally wanders north to Texas, but the other species, the Wood Ibis, is with us in goodly numbers. They breed in the southern United States, chiefly in Florida. They are gregarious at all times, although now and then small bands wander away from the main flock. I once saw at least five thousand of these birds in a drove feeding on a grassy prairie of central Florida. When disturbed by the report of a gun they arose, a vast white and black mass, and the roar of their wings coming across the lake resembled nothing so much as the rumbling of distant thunder.

They breed in colonies numbering hundreds or thousand of pairs, and they always select the tallest trees for nesting sites. For several years the Audubon Society has been guarding a colony in "Big Cypress" swamp of south Florida. In the rookery nearly every tree has its nest and some of the cypresses with wide-spreading limbs hold six or eight of them. This colony occupies an area of from two hundred to five hundred yards wide and about five miles in length. Here, as in other rookeries, Fish Crows are a great scourge. All day a stream of Crows can be seen flying from the pine woods to the swamp, or returning with eggs stuck on the end of their bills.

I had the opportunity to witness the rather odd manner in which these birds sometimes get their prey. The water was low at this season and in the pine flats various ponds, which ordinarily cover many acres, were partially or entirely dried up. One of these, now reduced to a length of about one hundred feet and with a width perhaps half as great, contained many small fish crowded together. Thirty-seven Wood Ibises had taken possession of this pool and seemed to be scratching the bottom, evidently for the purpose of making the already thick water so muddy that the fish would be forced to the surface. The numerous downward strokes of the bare, bony heads fully demonstrated the effectiveness of their enterprise. "Goard Head," "Iron Head," and "Gannet" are the appellations given to these birds by many swamp-dwellers to whom the name Wood Ibis is unknown.

Photo by H. K. Job Courtesy of Doubleday, Page & Co.

YOUNG WOOD IBIS

After the breeding season these Storks wander north as far as Pennsylvania and Michigan. Often one may find them on the wide marshes, either salt- or fresh-water, standing perfectly still for an hour or more at a time, the long heavy bill pointed downward and resting on the skin of the thick, naked neck. On such occasions they seem to represent the personification of dejection.

T. Gilbert Pearson.

HERON FAMILY

Order *Herodiones;* suborder *Herodii;* family *Ardeidæ*

AS hungry as a Heron" is a simile which should mean much to a student of birds, for Herons as a class are gaunt and voracious creatures who always seem to be half famished, and actually are more or less emaciated, no matter how plentiful is their food supply. Structurally the family is characterized by the possession of four toes, with the hind one on the same plane as the three front ones, and the claw of the middle one equipped with a comb-like process on the inner side; a slender body, long neck, and a long and sharply pointed bill; comparatively long but noticeably rounded wings; and a bare space about the eyes and on the sides of the head. There is great variation in the plumage, which is free and pliable, and is likely to be extended on the back, as in the case of the beautiful nuptial plumes of the Egrets. On the abdomen, rump, and certain other parts are curious patches of down which are characteristic of the family.

Several of the American Herons are gregarious during the breeding period, when large colonies place their bulky nests near together in tree-tops; but in their feeding habits they usually are solitary. Some species capture their prey by standing motionless and waiting for it to come within reach; others pursue on foot frogs, crawfish, and the like in shallow water. Their flight is deliberate, but powerful and certain, and is accomplished by incessant flapping, and little or no sailing or soaring. Unlike the Cranes and Ibises, the Herons in flight carry the neck folded and the head drawn in near the shoulders. Their eggs number from three or four to six, are unspotted and are whitish or bluish-green in color. Of the true Herons there are about twelve species, which are from one foot to four feet and more in length. The family is represented in virtually all parts of the North American continent excepting the regions of continuous cold or drought.

Drawing by R. I. Brasher

BITTERN (½ nat. size)

It is an adept at concealment

BITTERN

Botaurus lentiginosus (*Montagu*)

A. O. U. Number 190 See Color Plate 23

Other Names.—American Bittern; Stake Driver; Thunder Pumper; Butterbump; Mire Drum; Bog Bull; Indian Hen; Marsh Hen; Poke.

General Description.— Length, 24 to 34 inches. Color above, brown, blackish, white, and tawny mixed; below, yellowish.

Color.— Crown, dull brown with buffy stripe over eye; rest of upper parts, streaked and minutely *freckled with brown, blackish, white, and tawny*; chin and upper throat, whitish; under parts, yellow and tawny-white, each feather with a brown darker-edged stripe; center of throat and neck, white with brown streaks; a brown mustache on side of throat; wing-quills, greenish-black with a glaucous shade and tipped with brown; tail, brown; bill, pale yellow with dusky ridge; *legs, dull greenish-yellow*; iris, yellow.

Nest and Eggs.— Nest: On the ground among reeds in a swamp; roughly and loosely constructed of dead rushes. Eggs: 3 to 5, brownish with a gray shade.

Distribution.— North America; breeds from central British Columbia, southern Mackenzie, central Keewatin, southern Ungava, and Newfoundland south to southern California, northern Arizona, Kansas, the Ohio valley, and North Carolina, and less frequently in southern United States; winters from California, Arizona, southern Texas, the Ohio valley, and Virginia south to Cuba and Guatemala, and casually to the Bahamas, Porto Rico, Jamaica, and Great Britain.

Thoreau says that the Bittern is the genius of the bog. It frequents the ooze, and delights in the quaking false bottom where the first unwary step may plunge the adventurer into slimy depths. Here it steals about, hidden among the rank marsh growth; here it makes its nest and woos its mate. But it is not confined to the marsh; it is common in large meadows and may even be seen hunting grasshoppers in nearby upland pastures. The Bittern is an adept at concealment. It has a habit of standing among the grass or reeds with its bill cocked up at such an angle that even when in full sight it remains unnoticed because of its close resemblance to a rail or a stake. Its penciled foreneck imitates the reeds and all its colors are inconspicuous. It has learned the art of moving almost as slowly as the minute hand of a clock so as to escape observation while changing position.

The most remarkable characteristic of the Bittern is its song, but the result of its efforts can hardly be called musical. While producing the sound the bird looks as if trying to rid itself of some distress of the stomach and the resulting melody sounds much like the sucking of an old-fashioned wooden pump when some one tries to raise the water. The bird suddenly lowers and raises its head and throws it far forward with a convulsive jerk, at the same time opening and shutting the bill with a click. This is accompanied by a sound which resembles a hiccough. This is repeated a few times, each time a little louder than before, while the bird seems to be swallowing air. This is succeeded by the pumping noises which are in sets of three syllables each resembling *plunk-a-lunk* or, as some people will have it, *plum pudd'n*. The lower neck seems to dilate with the air taken in and remains so until the performance is over, when the neck is deflated.

There is a peculiar acoustic property about the sound. Its distance and its exact location are very hard to gage. The volume seems no greater when near than when at a considerable distance, but as the distance increases the sound is no longer heard and in the place of each set of syllables there comes to the ear only a single note closely resembling the driving of a stake, which can be heard from afar. Hence the name "Stake Driver," often applied to this bird. These notes, although common in spring, particularly at morning and evening, are not noticeable and their resemblance to pumping and stake-driving is a protection to the bird.

Photo by H. K. Job Courtesy of Outing Pub. Co.

BITTERN ON NEST

Another remarkable characteristic consists of white nuptial plumes upon the sides of the neck or breast, which appear to be always concealed, except when the birds are performing their mating antics, when a plume is raised on each side high above the shoulder and becomes conspicuous against the darker plumage of the upper parts. The young — helpless, homely, and awkward — are exposed to many dangers in their lowly nest. Minks, muskrats and water snakes roam about them; keen-sighted Hawks, Eagles, and Owls sweep over the marsh; but the watchful mother is ever ready to defend them, and with her dagger-like bill and long neck she is no mean antagonist. When danger threatens she bristles to twice her usual size and with glaring eyes and ready, open beak becomes a dauntless defender.

EDWARD HOWE FORBUSH.

LEAST BITTERN

Ixobrychus exilis (*Gmelin*)

A. O. U. Number 191 See Color Plate 23

Other Names.— Dwarf Bittern; Little Bittern; Least Heron.

General Description.— Length, 11 to 14 inches. Color above, greenish-black; below, brownish-yellow.

Color.— ADULT MALE: Crown, back, and tail, glossy greenish-black; a streak down back of neck; most of wing-coverts, and outer edges of inner secondaries, pure chestnut; other wing-coverts, brownish-yellow; primaries, dusky, tipped with chestnut; front and sides of neck and under parts in general, brownish-yellow; white streaks along throat line; sides of breast with a broken brownish-black patch; a whitish streak on upper side of shoulder-feathers; bill, pale yellow with dusky ridge; skin of lores, light green; legs, dull greenish; iris and toes, yellow. ADULT FEMALE: Crown, brownish; back, brownish-chestnut with 2 white streaks along shoulders; wings, similar, but coverts more spotted with brown.

Photo by A. A. Allen

LEAST BITTERN

On its nest in the marsh

Nest and Eggs.— NEST: Usually in a bunch of cat-tails; a rough platform of dead reeds, raised above the water on a bed of decayed rushes. EGGS: 3 to 6, bluish-white.

Distribution.— Temperate North America and northern South America; breeds from southern Oregon, southern Saskatchewan, southern Manitoba, southern Quebec, and Nova Scotia south to the West Indies and Brazil; winters from Florida and Gulf of Mexico southward.

Reed-grown ponds, grassy margins of lakes, and expanses of fresh-water marshes form the abiding places of the Least Bittern. Only a little over a foot in length, it is the smallest of all our Herons. Because of its retiring habits and secretive disposition it is known to few besides the inquisitive ornithologist, whose enthusiasm for the subject leads him into the forbidden haunts of the Bittern. Even then it is rarely seen until suddenly it springs from its hiding, at times almost beneath your feet, and in an awkward and laborious manner flies away a few rods and drops again into the marsh. More rarely it may be seen clinging to the stem of some rush or reed much in the manner of a Wren. It has not been given to many to hear the soft cooing spring notes of the male, but most summer marsh-waders are familiar with the startled *qua* with which it begins its flight when disturbed.

Although the Least Bittern is found in summer as far north as Maine and Manitoba, it is much more abundant in the southern States. A few pass the winter in Florida, but the bulk of these birds migrate farther south. In spring they arrive in the Carolinas and Arkansas by middle April, and a few weeks later their summer disposition in the northern States is complete. A fairly compact platform of plant stems and grasses serves as a nest, on which from three to six elliptical pale bluish eggs are laid. It is usually situated in clusters of tall grass or reeds and at a distance varying from one to four feet from the water.

In many of the fresh-water ponds of Florida certain small areas, near the shore, are covered with a thick growth of buttonwood bushes. These are popular places for small colonies of the Boat-tailed Grackle, the big shiny Blackbird of the country. In the midst of these Blackbird villages one may often find a Least Bittern's nest. They do not assemble in colonies like most members of the family, the two or three nests sometimes found in the same neighborhood evidently having been placed close together more because the different pairs chanced to like the location, than from any desire for the companionship of their kind. Although I have always found these Bitterns partial to fresh water in the summer, Arthur T. Wayne states that in South Carolina they also breed regularly in salt marshes, and that during migration they constantly frequent such locations.

To find a nest full of young Least Bitterns is an event to remember. Standing at their full height with bills pointed skyward they remain as motionless as though cast in bronze. The alternate light and dark streaks on their breasts and throats blend perfectly with the coloring of the reeds about them. Evidently they know that so long as they are still they are perfectly hidden.

A rare and closely allied bird variously known as Cory's Least Bittern (*Ixobrychus neoxenus*), Cory's Bittern, or Cory's Dwarf Bittern, has been found in Florida, Ontario, Michigan, and perhaps elsewhere.

T. GILBERT PEARSON.

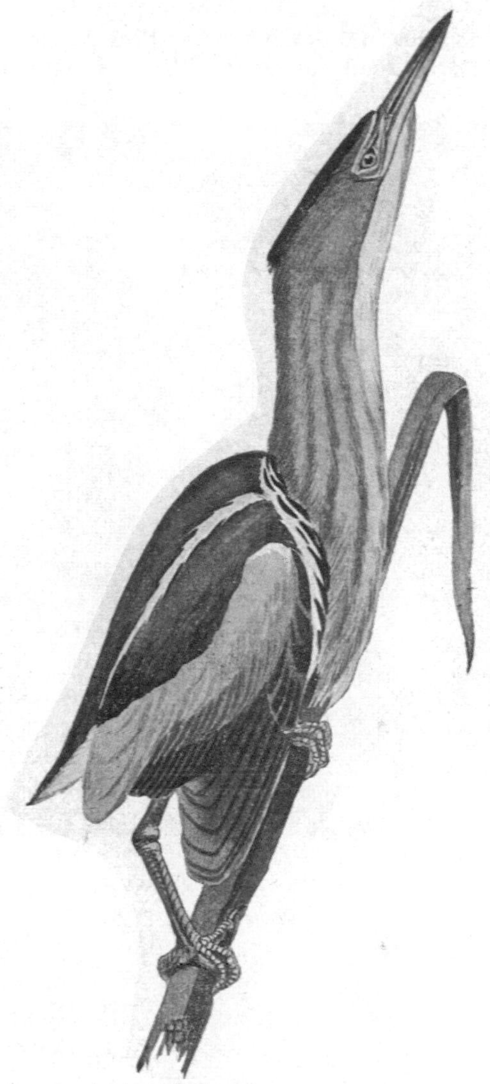

Drawing by R. I. Brasher

LEAST BITTERN (⅔ nat. size)

The smallest of the Herons in "the frozen position"

GREAT WHITE HERON

Ardea occidentalis *Audubon*

A. O. U. Number 192

Other Name.— Florida Heron.

General Description.— Length, 48 to 54 inches. Head not crested, but in breeding season with a few feathers long and flowing; plumage, *pure white;* bill, yellow, greenish at base; legs and feet, yellow; iris, chrome yellow; bare space around eye, bluish and green.

Nest and Eggs.— NEST: In low bushes or high trees; a simple platform of sticks. EGGS: 3 to 5, bluish-green.

Distribution.— Region bordering Gulf of Mexico from southern Florida south to Cuba, Jamaica, and Yucatan; casual north to Anclote River and Micco, Florida.

The Great White Heron is equal in size to the common and well-known Great Blue Heron. It is not the proud possessor of beautiful aigrette-plumes, such as adorn the Egrets, and consequently has not been so extensively shot. It occurs mainly on the islands of Jamaica and Cuba, but is not uncommonly found along the coast of Florida. In 1911 I discovered a colony of seven pairs breeding on the island in Tampa Bay, on the Gulf coast of Florida. This appears to be the northern limit at which they have thus far been found in the nesting period. The nests were about twelve feet above the water and rested among the stronger topmost limbs of mangrove trees. They were huge affairs, made of sticks, and those examined contained either three or four eggs. The little colony covered a territory about eighty feet in diameter. One hundred feet away a number of Florida Cormorants and Louisiana Herons were beginning to build their nests. Apparently the three species were dwelling together in harmony.

Photo by H. K. Job Courtesy of Houghton Mifflin Co.

YOUNG GREAT WHITE HERON

In nest, Florida Keys

Cruising among the Florida Keys and coral reefs near Cape Sable one may often see these giant Herons feeding in the shallow places which everywhere abound. They haunt such localities in south Florida, but one need not look for them inland. Their great size and white plumage render them conspicuous marks which may be seen for a long distance. I have always found the Great White Heron extremely shy and difficult to approach. Its judgment seems never at fault in determining what is the exact range of a hunter's rifle. T. Gilbert Pearson.

GREAT BLUE HERON

Ardea herodias herodias *Linnæus*

A. O. U. Number 194 See Color Plate 24

Other Names.— Red-shouldered Heron; Blue Crane; Crane; Common Blue Crane.

General Description.— Length, 42 to 50 inches. Color above, slaty-blue; below, black. Head, crested and with long plumes.

Color.— Adults: Forehead and top of head, white; *sides of crown and crest, black;* neck, pale gray, marked on throat with white, rusty and black streaks; chin and cheeks, white; *upper parts, slaty-blue*; shoulders, grayer; tail, slaty-blue; inner wing-quills, slaty-blue shading into black primaries; plumes of lower neck and breast, gray; abdomen, black with white and rufous streaking; under tail-coverts, white; bill, yellow with dusky ridge; legs and feet, dusky, soles yellow; bare space around eye, greenish and blue; iris, chrome yellow. Young: No crest or lengthened feathers on head; entire crown, blackish; general color above, brownish-slate, the feathers edged with rufous; lesser wing-coverts, reddish-brown; below, ashy.

Nest and Eggs.— Nest: Usually in tall trees along river banks; a large and bulky structure of limbs, twigs, and some dry grass. Eggs: 3 to 6, blue or greenish-blue.

Distribution.— Western hemisphere; breeds from southeastern British Columbia, central Alberta, central Manitoba, northern Ontario, and Prince Edward Island south to southern Lower California, northern Texas, and South Atlantic States (except Florida); winters from Oregon, the Ohio valley, and Middle States south to the West Indies, Panama, and Venezuela.

The Great Blue Heron is the largest of the truly American herons, and is known as a stately, dignified, and interesting bird by those who have observed it in other ways than over the sights of a shotgun or rifle. This pursuit is legalized in certain regions where the bird is believed to be even more destructive to the spawn and young of game fish than to its other prey of frogs, crawfish, small snakes, salamanders and various water creatures which are more harmful than useful, not to mention grasshoppers and meadow mice. Under these conditions it becomes difficult to approach one of these alert and far-sighted birds even to within field-glass range. A stalk of this kind is, however, well worth while if it brings the observer to within observation distance, for his reward will be an exhibition of stealthy and skillful fishing which is bound to command his admiration.

Much of this fishing the Heron does without stirring from the position he takes in shallow water among reeds or near the shore. Motionless as a statue he stands, his long neck doubled into a flattened S and his keen eyes searching the water nearby. As a frog or fish approaches he holds his rigid position until the creature comes within striking range, and the Heron knows what that is to a small fraction of an inch. Then suddenly the curved neck straightens out and simultaneously the long, rapier-like bill shoots

Photo by W. L. Finley and H. T. Bohlman

GREAT BLUE HERON

downward with a stroke which is quicker than the eye can follow and seldom misses its mark. In a second the fish or frog has disappeared, and the fisherman has resumed his statuesque pose. Again, the great bird may be seen stalking slowly through shallow water, lifting each foot above

Photo by H. K. Job Courtesy of Outing Pub. Co.

A COLONY OF GREAT BLUE HERONS

the surface, and sliding it into the water again so gently as to cause hardly a ripple; and woe to the crawfish or salamander that does not observe that approach.

Like most Herons, the Great Blue is a solitary bird in its habits except during the breeding season. Then the birds show a strongly marked gregarious instinct by forming colonies, generally in isolated swamps, where they build their huge nests and bring up their young, which are fed by regurgitation. These heronries are most interesting institutions for the bird-student. Occasionally several nests are placed in a single tree, and frequently colonies are found which include 150 or more nests. Unless the birds are seriously molested they are likely to return for many successive years to the same nesting-site.

It is well known that members of the Heron family feed to a great extent on fish and other forms of aquatic life, and consequently do not live far from water. The Great Blue Herons at times depart from this family trait and visit hillsides, cultivated fields, and drier meadows in search of pocket gophers, ground squirrels, and field mice, which they greedily devour. Pellets collected in an inland nesting colony of these Herons showed that a very large proportion of the food of the young is made up of these injurious rodents. The Herons, like other flesh-eating birds, digest their food rapidly and are disposed to gorge themselves when opportunity offers. It is fair to assume as a low average that a pair of Herons with four or five young will consume twelve to fifteen gophers per day.

George Gladden.

EGRET

Herodias egretta (*Gmelin*)

A. O. U. Number 196 See Color Plate 24

Other Names.—American Egret; White Heron; White Egret; Greater Egret; Great White Egret; Great White Heron; Long White.

Description.— Length, 41 inches. No crest, but a magnificent train of long plumes springing from back and extending a foot or so beyond tail in breeding season; *plumage, entirely white;* bill, yellow; legs and feet, black; lores and iris, yellow.

Nest and Eggs.— Nest: Merely a platform of sticks in mangroves or in trees. Eggs: 3 to 5, plain bluish-green.

Distribution.— Temperate and tropical America; breeds in Oregon and California, and from North Carolina, Florida, the Gulf coast, and Mexico south to Patagonia; formerly bred north to New Jersey and Wisconsin; winters from the Gulf of Mexico southward; casual in Manitoba, Quebec, New England, and Nova Scotia.

The treatment which man has accorded the Egret is not only an evidence of his power over weaker animals, but stands as a blot on this country's history. The long white plumes, which this bird bears on its back in the mating and nesting season, have long been sought as adornments for women's headwear. The only way to get these "aigrettes" is to shoot the bird, and shoot it at the time it is engaged in the care of its nestlings. At other seasons it is wild, and only with great difficulty can one approach to within shooting distance, before it takes wing.

The plumes are acquired early in the year but not until the birds have accumulated in colonies, and laid their eggs, can the hunter hope for success. Even then the wise millinery agents wait until the rookery is ripe. By "ripe" they mean when the eggs have hatched. If the shooting begins in a colony before this time, the birds will frequently desert their nests and eggs. Thus in order to get the most satisfactory results the plume-hunter must be content to wait until the young appear, and the instinct of parental care is so aroused that the old birds will return again and again despite the fact that they see their companions falling all about them before the guns of the inhuman hunters. This method of attack on any species if long continued means its doom. When old and young alike perish no chance remains to perpetuate the species.

In the far West a few Egrets still are found, but very rarely. They appear never to have reached the abundance there that they did in the Southern States. At one time the lake-shores of Florida teemed with tens of thousands of these elegant, long-legged white creatures. Several years ago I visited rookeries containing great numbers of them, but even then the work of destruction was going on. While visiting a plume-hunter's camp in 1886 I was told that the New York feather dealers paid ninety cents for the plumes of every bird. Since that time the price has gone up and up until recently tourists at Miami and Palm Beach have been paying $10 and more for the scalp of each bird brought in by the white hunters and Seminole Indians of the Everglade country.

For several years past the National Association of Audubon Societies has been employing guards to protect the few remaining breeding colonies as far as they are known. These nesting places are distributed from the coastal region of North Carolina southward to the Florida Keys, but it is debatable whether the species can be saved, although without the efforts of the Audubon Society the bird would probably have disappeared entirely by this time.

This member of the Heron family often associates in the nesting season with other Herons. The loose nests of twigs are placed in the top of bushes or on the limbs of cypress trees high above the waters of the sequestered swamps into which these birds have long since been driven.

T. Gilbert Pearson.

Photograph of habitat group — Courtesy of American Museum of Natural History

EGRETS

These birds have been brought to the verge of extinction by plume hunters

SNOWY EGRET

Egretta candidissima candidissima (*Gmelin*)

A. O. U. Number 197

Other Names.— Little Egret; Lesser Egret; Common Egret; Snowy Heron; Little Snowy; Little White Egret; Little White Heron; Bonnet Martyr.

Description.— Length, 24 inches. Plumage, pure white; bill and legs, black; toes, yellow; bare space around eye, greenish-yellow; iris, chrome yellow. A long crest on crown, another from back of about 50 feathers, the latter recurved, and another on lower neck.

Nest and Eggs.— Nest: Usually among mangroves or in swampy willow ponds; a simple platform of sticks. Eggs: 2 to 5, pale bluish-green.

Distribution.— Temperate and tropical America; formerly bred from Oregon, Nebraska, Indiana, Illinois, and New Jersey south to Chile and Argentina; now breeds locally in the United States from North Carolina to Louisiana; winters from Florida southward; casual in British Columbia, Ontario, Massachusetts, and Nova Scotia.

Much smaller than the Egret, the Snowy Egret is nevertheless adorned in the breeding season with "aigrettes," growing on the back between the wings, that are quite as valuable in the market as those produced by the larger bird. The plume-feathers are much shorter, more delicate, and are recurved at the end. They are the "cross aigrettes" of the millinery trade. To the plume-hunters the bird is known as the "Little Snowy," to distinguish it from the larger species called by them the "Long White."

Photo by H. K. Job Courtesy of Outing Pub. Co.

SNOWY EGRET ON NEST

Showing "aigrette" plumes

Snowy Egrets once bred as far north as New Jersey, but now their northern breeding limit is North Carolina. Although found inland in Florida, they are elsewhere in their range in the United States more distinctively inhabitants of the tide-water regions. Owing to protection afforded them from the millinery feather hunters of recent years by Audubon Society wardens, they appear to be increasing in a few sections, notably about Charleston, South Carolina. Apparently the largest gathering of breeding birds is in a splendid Heron colony that has developed under the special care of E. A. McIlhenny at Avery Island, Louisiana. The rookery is in the trees and bushes of a small artificial pond within 200 yards of Mr. McIlhenny's house, and among the many interesting entertainments he gives his guests is to take them out to the edge of the yard of a spring evening that they may watch the Herons and Snowy Egrets coming home to roost or to relieve their mates on guard at the nests.

Like that of other Herons the food of this bird consists of such small forms of life as inhabit the sloughs and marshes of their territory. The young are fed extensively on small fish that are regurgitated into their throats by the parent bird. The Snowy Egret has a plumage of spotless white. The legs are black and the feet are bright yellow. By observing the coloring of the feet and legs one need never mistake it for the immature Little Blue Heron, which, except for the absence of "aigrettes," it much resembles.

T. Gilbert Pearson.

LOUISIANA HERON

Hydranassa tricolor ruficollis (*Gosse*)

A. O. U. Number 199

Other Names.— Lady of the Waters; Demoiselle.

General Description.— Length, 27 inches. Color above, slaty-purple; below, white. The lengthened feathers of head and neck, sharp with well-defined edges; the back train-feathers, fringe-like.

Color.— ADULTS (SEXES ALIKE): Crown, sides of head, most of neck, back, and wings, slaty-purple; chin and throat, white, broken behind with color of head; the long feathers of crest, white; lower back and rump, white but concealed by feathers of train which extends beyond tail; *lower parts, mostly white;* bill, black — bluer toward base; legs, grayish; iris, red; bare space around eye, light lilac. YOUNG: No crest or plumes. Neck and back, brownish-red; rump, center of throat, and under parts, white; wings and tail, pale lavender-blue; legs, dusky green. Individuals show variations between this and adult plumage but *are never white.*

Nest and Eggs.— NEST: In mangrove or willow swamps; in communities or in company with other Herons; a frail platform of sticks. EGGS: 3 to 5, bluish-green.

Distribution.— Southern North America; breeds from North Carolina and the Gulf States to the West Indies, Mexico (both coasts), and Central America; winters from South Carolina southward; casual in Indiana, New Jersey, and Long Island.

Though characteristically a southern species, the Louisiana Heron ranks among the most abundant Herons in this country, since in the Southern States it is decidedly the most abundant of the numerous Herons. In every way it is a beautiful bird, distinct and distinguished in its royal purplish garments contrasted with sharply defined white under parts. It is graceful and gentle, not shy, and is quite well known, feeding along the edges of swamps and meadows, or on the borders of streams and ponds.

Of social disposition, its nesting is mainly in rookeries, sometimes of large size. In E. A. McIlhenny's celebrated Egret and Heron colony at Avery Island, La., this is the most abundant species, many thousands of them nesting in this forty-acre tract. Reasons for their abundance are primarily that the plumes which grow from their backs at the nuptial season, though quite pretty, fortunately have not been in demand for millinery purposes. Then, further, they are tamer in disposition than some others, and apparently are not so easily frightened from a locality by human intrusion.

The rookeries are usually in a wooded swamp, generally among low, rather thick trees, and par-

Courtesy of Am. Mus. Nat. Hist.

LOUISIANA HERON (¼ nat. size)

The most abundant Heron in North America

ticularly on small wooded or bushy islands, where such can be found. On the Louisiana Coast reservations, where the islands were treeless, these Herons were content to nest directly on the ground, or on the smallest of bushes, sometimes hardly a foot up. The nests are frail platforms of sticks, and are similar to those of most other Herons, as are their eggs, which are blue, rather small, and from three to five in number.

Photo by H. K. Job   Courtesy of Nat. Asso. Aud. Soc.

LOUISIANA HERON

On nest on ground

On various occasions I have pitched my little photographic tent among their nests, preferably at night, leaving it till morning, when I would enter it and have a companion withdraw. The birds had soon become accustomed to it as a part of the landscape, and, not being able to "count noses," would soon return and settle down to brood their eggs or small young, or would come to feed the latter. It was most interesting and exciting to sit there, as though a member of the tribe, and watch all the singular, remarkable ways and actions, selecting the quaintest of these for photographic records.

These rookeries are the more interesting in that it is usual for various species of Herons to congregate together. In such colonies I have found, besides representatives of this species, the Snowy and American Egrets, Black-crowned and Yellow-crowned Night Herons, Little Blue and Great Blue Herons — certainly a lively assortment. Since, however, the Louisiana Heron is the most abundant of all, there are plenty of rookeries, especially the smaller ones, where it is found alone. In such places there is the wildest of confusion when one enters. The larger young climb from the nests from branch to branch, using both bills and feet to aid them. The less said about cleanliness and odor the better. Yet despite their slovenly ways it is remarkable how clean and trim the Herons look! They spend hours preening their feathers, so that, after all, in their own peculiar way they are orderly.

Most of them retire beyond our borders in winter, but on the Gulf coast I have seen a few of them at that season, still wading in the shallows and striking swiftly with their sharp bills at the small fish and other aquatic forms which constitute their bill of fare. HERBERT K. JOB.

LITTLE BLUE HERON

Florida cærulea (*Linnæus*)

A. O. U. Number 200

Other Name.— Blue Egret.

Description.— Plumes on shoulders and throat. OLD ADULTS: General plumage, dark slaty-blue shading to purplish-red on neck and head; bill, black shading to bluish at base; legs and feet, black; iris, yellow. YOUNG ADULTS: In perfect plumage, pure white, but usually showing traces of blue, especially on end of primaries. Length, 24 inches.

Nest and Eggs.— NEST: In trees or bushes over or near swamps; constructed like those of the rest of the genus. EGGS: 2 to 4, bluish-green.

Distribution.— North and South America; formerly bred from Missouri, Indiana, Illinois, and New Jersey to western Mexico and south to Argentina and Peru; in the United States now breeds locally on the coast from North Carolina to Texas; wanders casually to Nebraska, Wisconsin, Ontario, New England, and Nova Scotia; winters from South Carolina southward.

In that portion of the United States that the Little Blue Heron inhabits it is one of the most common members of the Heron family. It is generally seen in flocks, inhabiting the shallow ponds and grassy lake-sides of the Southern States. With slow deliberation they wade carefully along, their bright yellow eyes scanning the shallows in quest of the fish, water-insects, or frogs upon which they subsist. Upon the approach of evening they take flight and with measured wing-strokes pass across the country, sometimes for several miles, to a favorite roosting place in the trees of a swamp, or on some island. In spring they assemble in colonies, often by hundreds, and build their nests in the small trees or bushes of some isolated and favorite pond. These "rookeries" are usually inhabited also by other species of Herons and sometimes by other varieties of water birds.

The young are first covered with white down which later is replaced by white feathers. Not until two years of age do they assume the blue plumage of the adult. During the second summer individuals may be seen representing all stages in this change of feathers. Some are white with only a few blue feathers showing, while others, further developed, are entirely blue except for scattering spots of white. The Little Blue Heron is one of the comparatively few birds that mates and rears young while yet clothed in the feathers of youth. I recall visiting a colony of perhaps forty pairs on one occasion, every bird of which was still in the white phase of plumage.

Because of their white appearance they are often mistaken for Egrets and many times these rarer birds are reported as being seen in a neighborhood, when a closer inspection by a competent observer would easily reveal the mistake.

After the nesting season the birds wander all over the country hunting for good feeding grounds. It is an odd fact worthy of mention, that the young take trips farther afield than do their parents; and thus it happens that in the late summer immature Little Blue Herons are constantly recorded far to the north of their breeding grounds, where the adult birds are seen only at very rare intervals, if at all. Old Herons possess a very pretty tuft of long plumes on their backs in summer, but these decorations never appear on the bird while in the white plumage.

Being fish eaters their flesh is not at all esteemed as a table delicacy, but in remote regions the colonies are often raided for their eggs for which some people profess a fondness. Their chief natural enemies appear to be water moccasins and alligators, with which most rookeries are infested. The former climb into the trees and swallow the eggs, the latter devour the young when they fall from the nest.

T. Gilbert Pearson.

Photo by H. K. Job Courtesy of Houghton Mifflin Co.

LITTLE BLUE HERON

GREEN HERON

Butorides virescens virescens (*Linnæus*)

A. O. U. Number 201 See Color Plate 23

Other Names.— Little Green Heron; Green Bittern; Fly-up-the-creek.

General Description.— Length, 18 inches. Color above, dark green; below, dark brown.

Color.— ADULTS: Crown (including a long soft crest), lengthened feathers of back and shoulders, *lustrous dark green*; the back plumes with a glaucous cast; *wing-coverts, green* with well-defined tawny edges; neck, rich dark purplish-chestnut; center of throat, white with dusky streaks; below, dark brownish; abdomen, streaked with white; primaries, secondaries, and tail, greenish-dusky; edge of wing, white; bill, dusky-greenish, yellow at base below; bare space around eye, bluish-green; legs, yellow; iris, yellow. YOUNG: No crest; top of head, brown; sides of neck and body, brownish streaked with lighter; throat and center line of neck, white with dusky streaks; back, plain greenish-brown; wing-coverts and secondaries, with white edgings and white tips; under tail-coverts, grayish-white; bill, greenish with dusky ridge; legs, pale greenish-gray; iris, yellow.

Nest and Eggs.— NEST: Frequently in the woods but usually near water; a frail platform of twigs in a tree or bush. EGGS: 3 to 6, pale greenish.

Distribution.— Eastern North America; breeds from southern South Dakota, northern Wisconsin, southern Ontario, southern Quebec, and Nova Scotia south to the West Indies; winters from the West Indies southward, and rarely in southeastern United States; casual in Colorado.

Though a comparatively small Heron, the Green Heron is perhaps the best known member of his family in this country, and probably most people who see him dismiss him as a gawky, awkward, and rather stupid bird with habits which are not exactly tidy. This is because he is usually seen when he utters his harsh alarm note and flops clumsily along to a nearby perch, where he stretches his neck, jerks his tail, and gazes around in a fuddle-headed manner.

Those who really know the bird, however, realize that when he is about his business of

Photograph by R. W. Shufeldt

GREEN HERON

Perhaps he is the best known member of his family in this country

Photograph by A. A. Allen

GREEN HERON

At its nest in the willows fringing a pond

catching fish, frogs, salamanders, and the like, he is very far from stupid or clumsy. Then he steps along in the shallow water or through the weeds with true Heron stealth, and the thrust of his long bill, as he seizes his prey, is as accurate as and a great deal quicker than that of an expert swordsman. When flushed to a perch, the bird has a curious habit, if it sees it is observed, of suddenly becoming absolutely rigid, or "freezing," to use the term commonly employed. This apparently is done for the purpose of escaping further observation. It is an interesting fact that young Herons, at a signal from the old bird, often employ the same ruse, and stand as motionless as statues, sometimes until the intruder has approached to within a few feet.

Unlike other members of its family, the Green Heron is not gregarious in its breeding habits. Occasionally a few birds place their nests near together, but this apparently is accidental, for there are no true rookeries of Green Herons, and the birds lead a distinctly lonely life.

Photo by S. A. Lottridge

YOUNG GREEN HERONS

Removed from the nest by the photographer

BLACK-CROWNED NIGHT HERON

Nycticorax nycticorax nævius (*Boddaert*)

A. O. U. Number 202 See Color Plate 24

Other Names.— Night Heron; American Night Heron; Qua-bird; Quawk; Squawk; Gardenian Heron.

General Description.— Length, 26 inches. Color above, black and ashy-gray; below, white. Head crested and, in breeding plumage, with a few long white cord-like plumes from back of crown.

Color.— Adults: *Crown, back, and shoulders, black;* rest of upper parts, wings, and tail, pale ashy-gray; forehead, sides of head, and throat, white shading into very pale lavender on neck; rest of under parts, white; bill, black; legs, yellow; iris, red; bare space around eye, yellowish-green. Young: Entire plumage, grayish-white, streaked on head, breast, and beneath with dark brown; streaked and spotted on back with rusty and whitish; wing-coverts, brown with conspicuous white triangular tips; primaries, dusky-brown; bill, dull yellowish; feet, pale greenish-yellow; iris, brown.

Nest and Eggs.— Nest: In trees, bushes, or on ground; a large but loosely constructed affair of branches and twigs. Eggs: 3 to 6, pale sea-green.

Distribution.— North and South America; breeds from northern Oregon, southern Wyoming, southern Manitoba, northern Quebec, and Nova Scotia south to Patagonia; winters from northern California and Gulf States southward; casual in winter north to Massachusetts and southern Illinois.

Though not strictly a nocturnal bird, as it moves about more or less in the daytime, the Black-crowned Night Heron feeds chiefly in the evening or after the night has fallen. As the twilight deepens it may be seen flying heavily toward its favorite feeding places, and now is most frequently heard the loud and raucous *quawk* from which is has received one of its popular names.

The bird's preferred hunting grounds are shallow tidal creeks, the edges of ponds, and swamps which include pools. Here it hunts, usually alone and often at a distance of several miles from its breeding place, so that the feeding of the young frequently involves long flights from the hunting ground to the nest.

Its hunting methods differ from those of its relative, the Great Blue Heron. Instead of

Photo by W. L. Finley and H. T. Bohlman

BLACK-CROWNED NIGHT HERON ON NEST

standing rigid, and knee-deep in water, as that big fisherman does, the Night Heron moves about briskly, holding its head lowered and its neck curved, all ready for the quick stroke which means death to the frog or fish at which it is aimed.

Photo by H. T. Middleton

YOUNG NIGHT HERONS

This Heron's most interesting characteristic is its gregariousness, which causes it to collect in large colonies during the nesting period. These heronries usually are situated in an isolated patch of woods, and their population may include several hundred pairs of birds, not to mention as many groups of four or five young birds. Indeed, as a pair will frequently raise two broods in a season, it is not uncommon to find the adult birds feeding at the same time two sets of youngsters, one composed of fledglings in the nest and the other of birds able to clamber about in the branches.

YELLOW-CROWNED NIGHT HERON

Nyctanassa violacea (*Linnæus*)

A. O. U. Number 203

General Description.— Length, 24 inches. Plumage, bluish-gray, lighter below. Head, crested and, in breeding plumage, with a few long white cord-like plumes from back of crown.

Color.— Adults: Top of head and patch under eye, creamy white; sides of head and chin, black; rest of plumage, bluish-gray, darker on back, the feathers with black centers and pale edges; lighter below; head and neck, and most of crest, white *tinged with very pale tawny*; wings and tail, dusky-slate; bill, black; feet, black and yellow; iris, orange; lores and space around eye, greenish. Young: Above, brownish-gray with a strong olive tinge, streaked and spotted with brownish-yellow; below, streaked with brown and white; sides of head and neck, yellowish-brown streaked with darker; top of head and neck variegated with white; bill, black with much greenish-yellow below; lores and legs, greenish-yellow; iris, yellow.

Nest and Eggs.— Nest: A platform of sticks in trees of swampy areas. Eggs: 4 to 6, dull bluish.

Distribution.— Warm temperate and tropical America; breeds from southern Lower California, Kansas, southern Illinois, southern Indiana, and South Carolina south to Brazil and Peru; casual north to Colorado, Ontario, Massachusetts, Maine, and Nova Scotia; winters from southern Lower California and southern Florida southward.

Although the name of Yellow-crowned Night Heron suggests that this bird is a "night" bird, in reality it is quite as diurnal in its habits as any of the more common Herons. Many times I have come upon it in the fresh-water marshes or on mud flats by the sea where it was evidently feeding and it would fly away with all the assurance of a bird whose sight was unimpaired by the sunlight. It is a solitary species and is little known to many bird-students. Rarely are more than two or three found at a time and generally they are seen singly. It is a southern species and probably never breeds north of Illinois and North Carolina. Wayne states that they "breed only in small colonies of two or three pairs." This refers to the South Carolina birds of which he writes, but in Florida I have found the facts to be otherwise. In that State I have examined several of their colonies and they numbered from twelve to twenty pairs in each instance. Ap-

Drawing by Henry Thurston

YELLOW-CROWNED NIGHT HERON (⅛ nat. size)

A solitary and little-known species

parently they do not associate in colonies with other Herons, but always form their own village.

In Hillsboro County, Florida, some years ago, I waded out in a large pond thickly grown with trees through the foliage of which the sun rarely pierced to the dark scum-water beneath. The object of my venture was to discover whether any Egrets were breeding among a company of Herons, whose squawks told me they were nesting in the trees surrounding an open place in the center of the pond. Submerged logs, fallen limbs and aquatic moss made the going difficult. The place was infested with water-moccasins and alligators, and the nervous strain soon began to tell. Upon reaching a point perhaps sixty yards from shore where the water and slime was breast deep, I was startled beyond all description by a sudden hoarse cry and heavy flapping directly overhead. Unknowingly I had waded into the midst of a colony of Yellow-crowned Night Herons.

Photo by H. M. Laing Courtesy of Outing Pub. Co.

NOT SINGING, BUT HUNGRY

Young Night Herons

While occupying the same pond with the other Herons, they were at least two hundred feet from the nearest nest of any other species. Before leaving I counted sixteen nests, all of which appeared to be occupied.

These birds are supposed to feed largely upon mussels and crawfish and along the coast many small crabs are consumed. They retire to the far south in the autumn and do not reappear in the northern part of their range until March. After the nesting season many of the young wander far inland and in North Carolina I have seen them during the month of August more than two hundred miles from the coast.

T. Gilbert Pearson.

Photo by S. N. Leek

NEST OF GREAT BLUE HERON

Showing the four bluish eggs

ORDER OF MARSH-DWELLERS

Order *Paludicolæ*

BIRDS of this order vary greatly in size and appearance — the Little Black Rail is but five inches long, while the Cranes average about four feet. Structurally all are alike in having the hind toe elevated. Two habits are common to the entire order. The first of these is that of dwelling in marshy places, and the second is that of always flying with the neck extended. The young are hatched with a covering of down and are able to run about soon after leaving the shell, although requiring more or less attention from the parents.

The order is divided into two suborders: the Long-legged Marsh-dwellers (*Grues*), which includes two families, the Cranes and the Courlans; and the Henlike Marsh-dwellers (*Ralli*), which consists of the single family of Rails, Gallinules, and Coots.

CRANES AND COURLANS

Order *Paludicolæ;* suborder *Grues;* families *Gruidæ* and *Aramidæ*

THOUGH superficially similar to the Herons in some respects, the Cranes constitute a distinct group in a different order. They are the family *Gruidæ* of the Marsh-dwellers and are really more closely related to the Rails than to the Herons. When in flight they may be distinguished from the Herons by their habit of carrying the neck extended at full length. But they are similar to the Herons in having the head more or less bare, while they differ from them in that their plumage is dense and compact, rather than loose. The family includes about twenty species, of which only three occur on this continent. Their favorite habitats are marshes and plains, and their diet includes not only frogs, snakes, field mice, and lizards, but grain and considerable vegetable food. Most of the Cranes have singularly loud and resonant cries, this being especially true of the Sandhill Crane. This resonant quality of the Crane's cry is due probably to the curious peculiarity and great length of the bird's windpipe. Though this organ is about normal in the chick just hatched, it becomes elongated and coiled as the bird matures, and is accommodated in the keel of the breastbone. In the Whooping Crane, when this development is complete, nearly thirty inches of the trachea may be thus packed away, and the entire length of the organ, from the throat to the lungs, may be fully five feet.

Another distinguishing characteristic of the Cranes is the fact that the chicks are covered with down when they are hatched, and are able to run about a few hours after they leave the shell. The American species range over the entire continent as far south as Cuba and Mexico. They are migratory from the northern portions of their range, but less so or not at all in the south.

The Courlans comprise another family, the *Aramidæ*, of the Marsh-dwellers. But two species are known: one found in South America, and the other, the Limpkin, in Central America, Mexico, the West Indies, and Florida.

WHOOPING CRANE

Grus americana (*Linnæus*)

A. O. U. Number 204

Other Names.— White Crane; Great White Crane; Garoo.

General Description.— Length, 4½ feet; spread of wings, 7½ feet. Plumage, white. Head with bare spot on each side below eyes, *extending to a point on back of crown* and sparsely covered with short hairs.

Color.— Adults: *White; primaries and coverts, black;* bare part of head, carmine; bill, dusky-greenish; legs, black; iris, yellow. Young: Entire head, feathered. General plumage, whitish, variegated with rusty-brown.

Nest and Eggs.— Nest: On the ground; a well-built structure of marsh grass and reed stems, from one and a half to two feet in diameter and eighteen inches high. Eggs: 2, olive or buffy, blotched with large irregular spots of brown.

Distribution.— North America; bred formerly from northern Mackenzie south to Illinois and Iowa; now mainly restricted to southern Mackenzie and northern Saskatchewan; in migration formerly not rare on the Atlantic coast from New England to Florida and casual west to Colorado and Idaho; winters from the Gulf States to central Mexico.

The Whooping Crane was named and described by Linné in the eighteenth century. Previous to that time all three American species were lumped together as Cranes.

Many of the narratives of the early voyagers and settlers tell of Cranes migrating and nesting along the Atlantic coast. During the first century after the discovery of the country, Cranes evidently were more or less numerous all along this coast, from Florida to New England, but the word has been used so frequently to denote the larger Herons that one might be inclined to place little faith in the statements of sailors and colonists were it not for two facts: (1) In those days Cranes were well-known and conspicuous birds in England and other countries of which these voyagers were natives, or which they had visited, and undoubtedly they were familiar with these birds, and could distinguish them from Herons. (2) In the lists of birds given by these early adventurers, Herons, "Hearnes" and "Hernshaws," "Bitterns," and "Egrets" or "Egrepes" are also referred to, showing that they distinguished the Cranes from the Herons. The common European Heron was a large species (resembling the Great Blue Heron of America) which, at that time, was called the Hernshaw, Hearneshaw, or Heronshaw. It is often impossible to determine which species of Crane was referred to in these early narratives and lists of birds, as usually no description is given; but now and then we find a reference to a bird that must have been the Whooping Crane.

The Whooping Crane is the only bird of North America that can be described as "almost as tall as a man." The Whooping Crane stands about five feet high when stretched to its full height, but being white it appears taller, while the Sandhill Crane is not so conspicuous on account of its color and does not appear so large.

Probably there were few Cranes inhabiting Massachusetts when the Pilgrim Fathers landed at Plymouth, except along the coast, on the islands, and on the meadows and marshes of the river valleys, for most of the State was then covered with primeval forest; and while Cranes are sometimes found in open woods, they are shy and wary birds, and prefer the open country, where they can discern their enemies from afar.

The fact that they sometimes ate the corn proves that they were actually Cranes, not Herons, and also helps to explain their early disappearance from Massachusetts. They paid with the death penalty for eating the corn. Also, as these birds occupied the only natural open lands — those that were first sought by settlers — they were driven out within a few years after settlement began. Even had they not attacked the corn they must soon have succumbed because of their large size, their white color, and their general conspicuousness. In the early days the Indians used to steal upon the Cranes and shoot them with arrows. Now the few survivors of this species in the West will hardly come knowingly within a mile of the white man.

John Lawson, in his *History of Carolina,* says that Cranes are sometimes "bred up tame" and are excellent in the garden to destroy frogs and other vermin.

This bird is long-lived and grows wary as the years go by; it now frequents prairies, marshes, and barren grounds, over which it stalks, always alert and watchful. It flies low, its wings sometimes almost brushing the grass tops, but in migration it rises to such tremendous heights that it may pass over a large region unnoticed by man.

Photograph of habitat group

Courtesy of American Museum of Natural History

THE SANDHILL CRANE IN FLORIDA

When standing erect it is nearly the height of a man

It feeds on frogs, fish, small mammals, and insects, and is said to take corn and other cereals and the succulent roots of water-plants.

Nuttall, describing the flights of the Whooping Crane up the Mississippi valley in December, 1811, says, "that the bustle of their great migrations and the passage of their mighty armies fills the mind with wonder." It seemed, he says, as though the whole continent was giving up its quota of the species to swell this mighty host, and the clangor of their numerous legions, passing high in air, was almost deafening. His statement, that this great host of Cranes was passing nearly all night, will give some idea of the immensity of this great flight.

The Whooping Crane is doomed to extinction. It has disappeared from its former habitat in the East and is now found only in uninhabited places. It can hardly be said to be common anywhere except perhaps locally in the far North. Only its extreme watchfulness has saved thus far the remnant of its once great host.

EDWARD HOWE FORBUSH, in *Game Birds, Wild-Fowl and Shore Birds.*

SANDHILL CRANE

Grus mexicana (*Müller*)

A. O. U. Number 206 See Color Plate 24

Other Names.— Brown Crane; Upland Crane; Field Crane; Southern Sandhill Crane.

General Description.— Length, 4 feet; spread of wings, 6½ feet. Plumage, slaty-gray. *Head with bare spot forking behind,* not reaching on sides below eyes, and thinly sprinkled with hair.

Color.— ADULTS: Plumage, *slaty-gray;* primaries and their coverts, ashy-gray but little darker than general color; cheeks and throat, lighter inclined to whitish; bill and feet, black; iris, brown. YOUNG: Head, feathered. Plumage, variegated with rusty and brown.

Nest and Eggs.— NEST: On the ground, usually on a slight knoll of open grassy flats; generally a mere depression in the ground, lined with dry grass and weed stems. EGGS: 2, from pale olive to buffy-brown, marked over entire surface with spots of burnt-umber.

Distribution.— North America; resident in Louisiana and Florida; bred formerly from southern British Columbia, Saskatchewan, Manitoba, and western Ontario south to California, Colorado, Nebraska, Illinois, and Ohio; formerly in migration east to New England; now rare east of the Mississippi, except in Florida, and rare as a breeder in the southern half of its former breeding range; winters from California, Texas, and Louisiana south to Mexico.

The virtual extermination, or at best the extreme rarity, of the great Whooping Crane, leaves the much smaller Sandhill Crane by far the largest representative of that interesting family in America. For it should be remembered that the various Herons — notably the Great Blue Heron — which are commonly called "Cranes," not only are not Cranes at all, but differ radically from them in both disposition and habits.

If not in size, then in its conspicuous and striking characteristics, the Sandhill Crane is a fit successor to his towering relative, whose days seem to be numbered. Nor is the bird a weakling at that, for the height of the male when he stands erect is nearly that of a man of average stature, while the bird's great wings carry his compact and muscular body with perfect ease and at a high speed. The bird's wariness bespeaks intelligent caution rather than weakness or fear. Indeed, when the Sandhill Crane is crippled by a broken wing or otherwise, he may become an exceedingly ugly antagonist for the man who attempts to overpower him, because of the skill, strength, and quickness with which he will then employ his long and dagger-like bill in defending himself. Many a hunter's dog has been blinded or otherwise badly injured by the vicious thrusts of this very dangerous weapon, which the Crane does not hesitate to use when he is at bay and fighting for his life.

Unlike the Herons, this Crane spends much of its time, and gets the food which it seems to relish most, on dry land. Hence it is often found on the plains and prairies, sometimes in small flocks but oftener in pairs or singly. Its diet includes a large percentage of roots, bulbs, grains, and the like; and it is especially fond of corn which it takes from the shock. Insects, frogs, lizards, snakes, and mice are also included in its bill of fare, but not in sufficient numbers to make its flesh "strong" as is that of the Herons and other wading birds. In fact, this Crane's flesh is excellent for the table, and it has been persistently hunted for food.

On the fenceless prairies and the treeless marshes, where its keen eyes can detect afar off the approach of an enemy, the demeanor and habits of this fine, brave bird challenge the admiration of the man who appreciates alertness, courage, and strength in wild life. Not for an instant is the great bird off his guard. Moving in deliberate and dignified strides he pauses occasionally and lowers his head to thrust his long bill into the soft earth, or to seize a dozing frog or an unwatchful insect; but in a few seconds up again comes his head, and his eyes search the surrounding country. If the approach of his chief enemy, man, is discovered, the Crane surveys the intruder for a few minutes and then, with a few long, running strides takes to his wings, at the same time sounding his wild and defiant cry.

This cry of the Sandhill Crane is a veritable voice of Nature, untamed and unterrified. Its uncanny quality is like that of the Loon, but is more pronounced because of the much greater volume of the Crane's voice. Its resonance is remarkable and its carrying power is increased by a distinct tremolo effect. Often for several minutes after the birds have vanished, the unearthly sound drifts back to the listener, like a taunting trumpet from the under-world.

George Gladden.

The Little Brown Crane (*Grus canadensis*) is like the Sandhill Crane except for its smaller size. It breeds from northern Alaska, Melville Island, and Boothia Peninsula south to central Alaska, southern Mackenzie, and central Keewatin. During migration it occurs through the interior of the United States and winters south to Texas and Mexico.

LIMPKIN

Aramus vociferus (*Latham*)

A. O. U. Number 207

Other Names.—Courlan; Crying-bird; Clucking-hen; Carau.

Description.— Length, 28 inches. Color, olive-brown, paler on face, chin, and throat, streaked or spotted everywhere with white; bill, dusky; legs, greenish-dusky; iris, brown. The young are paler and duller than the adults.

Nest and Eggs.— Nest: On the ground near water, sometimes a short distance above ground in a maze of vines or thick bushes; constructed of grass, leaves, dead vines, moss, and other old vegetation. Eggs: 4 to 7, usually 5 or 6, varying from pure white to buffy, spotted and splashed with brown and gray.

Distribution.— Florida, Greater Antilles, and both coasts of Central America; casual north to South Carolina; accidental in Texas.

Of the Courlan family only two species are known, one of these being the Limpkin of Central America, Mexico, the West Indies, and Florida. It may be described as a very large Rail with many of the habits of an Ibis. In the Everglades of Florida it is a common bird and while crossing that vast waste in the month of May I found many flocks, some of which numbered as high as forty individuals. Their flight is peculiar. With dangling legs the bird springs from the glades and goes off on wings that have a jerky motion, strongly suggestive of the movements of the wings of a mechanical beetle. In alighting the wings are held high above the back and in this attitude the bird drops from sight. The food consists largely of the big fresh-water snail found in many parts of the State. These snails in places abound in the shallow waters and are easily procured by this long-legged wading bird. In the cypress swamps I have come upon piles of empty shells from which the snails had been extracted by these birds. In doing this the shell is rarely broken.

In the swamps along the Oklawaha River, lumbermen of recent years have cut much of the timber. Stumps, from four to ten feet in height, are everywhere left standing. The jungle hates a bare place and soon these stumps are covered with vines. Here, on the top of these vine-clad pillars, the Limpkins often build their nests. Farther south you may find them in tall bunches of saw-grass or isolated custard-apples bushes in the glades. The nests are made chiefly of such varieties of twigs and leaves as are obtainable in the neighborhood. From four to seven brown spotted eggs are laid.

Limpkins at times are very noisy creatures. Their usual call possesses a quality of unutterable sadness, as though the bird was oppressed beyond measure by the desolateness of its surroundings. For this reason the name "Crying-bird" is usually given them by the natives. In the spring and early summer they largely haunt the swampy shores of streams and lakes, but in the autumn they gather in great numbers in the more open savannas. Thousands thus pass the winter months on the pond-covered prairies about the headwaters of the Caloosahatchee River, west of Lake Okechobee. The Limpkin is highly esteemed for food, but owing to the difficulties of hunting them in their retreats there is strong likelihood of the species persisting in Florida for many years to come.

A few years ago many were to be found in the swampy country of northern Florida, within fifteen or twenty miles of the Georgia line, and two or three specimens have even been taken in South Carolina. T. GILBERT PEARSON.

Courtesy of Am. Mus. Nat. Hist.

LIMPKIN

A long-legged wading bird of Florida and tropical America

RAILS, GALLINULES, AND COOTS

Order *Paludicolæ;* suborder *Ralli;* family *Rallidæ*

ABOUT fifty genera, embracing one hundred and eighty species constitute this family, the *Rallidæ*, which includes the Rails (*Rallinæ*), Gallinules (*Gallinulinæ*), and Coots (*Fulicinæ*). The distribution of these birds is virtually cosmopolitan, and about fifteen species occur, regularly or casually, in North America. They are from small to fair-sized birds, with noticeably compressed bodies,— well adapted to rapid progress through thickly growing reeds and rushes,— long necks, small heads, short, rounded wings, short tails, and long, strong legs and feet. The bill is short and henlike in the Coots and Gallinules, but long and slightly curved toward the end in the Rails. The plumage is subdued and blended in color. A family peculiarity is that of running, rather than flying, to escape danger, a trait apparently responsible for the extermination of certain species which had lost the power of flight through disuse of the wings, and the steady diminution of others for the same reason.

"Rails and Gallinules are marsh birds, very secretive in habits, keeping well under cover of the dense rushes and grasses, except at night or in the twilight, when they venture out on the muddy shores. When silently floating along the marshy stream, one may often see them standing motionless near their favorite coverts, or walking deliberately along the margin flirting their upturned tails and bobbing their necks in henlike fashion. Their cries are also loud, and remind one of the different notes of our domestic fowl. Consequently all our species of the family, from the Virginia Rail to the Coot, have received the common name of Mud Hens. The flight of Rails and Gallinules is feeble and hesitating. They usually take wing as a last resort, and then proceed with dangling legs, in a direct course, low over the tops of the rushes, dropping abruptly in a few rods amidst the grass, as if exhausted by their unwonted exertion. They are perfectly at home on the ground, and dart among the dense weeds with marked freedom, the long toes keeping them from sinking in the mud or submerged vegetation, their thin bodies gliding easily between the reeds." (Eaton.)

All of the Rails, Gallinules, and Coots nest on the ground, and as a rule lay large sets of eggs. The young are covered with down when hatched, and are able to run about very soon after leaving the shell.

KING RAIL

Rallus elegans *Audubon*

A. O. U. Number 208 See Color Plate 25

Other Names.— Fresh-water Marsh Hen; Great Red-breasted Rail; Mud Hen.

General Description.— Length, 19 inches. Upper parts, tawny-olive streaked with darker; lower parts, chestnut. Forehead entirely feathered down to base of bill; bill long and slender.

Color.— Adults: Crown, sides of head, back of neck, and rest of *upper parts, tawny-olive* streaked from center of neck to tail with blackish-brown; an indistinct whitish line from bill over and behind eye; chin and upper throat, white; *neck and breast, rich chestnut;* rest of under parts, white traversed by broad bars of olive-brown; wing-coverts, olive-brown; secondaries, dusky-brown edged with lighter; primaries, plain dusky-brown; a narrow white semi-circle below eye; bill, yellowish, dusky on ridge and tip; legs, pale dusky-greenish; iris, reddish-brown. Downy Young: Glossy black.

Nest and Eggs.— Nest: On the ground in marsh grass; built of dead reeds and grass, well concealed from above by interlacing of surrounding grass. Eggs: 6 to 12, dull white to pale buff, thinly spotted with reddish-brown and lilac.

Distribution.— Eastern North America; breeds from Nebraska, southern Minnesota, Ontario, New York, and Connecticut south to Texas, Florida, and Cuba; winters mainly in the southern part of its breeding range; casual north to South Dakota and Maine.

This large and handsome Rail, the King Rail, closely resembles the Virginia Rail except in size. Its retiring habits probably account for our lack of knowledge regarding it. Little seems to be known of it except that it appears to prefer fresh marshes to salt marshes. I have never seen it alive.

Dr. Bachman, in South Carolina, seems to have had a better opportunity of observing its habits than any one else who has written about it. He states that he found twenty pairs breeding within a space having a diameter of thirty yards, and that the nests were placed on the ground, being raised up six or eight inches by means of withered weeds and grasses; but Wayne, who has also found numerous nests, finds them in rushes or buttonwood bushes, from eight to eighteen inches over water. He noted that the female laid an egg each day after 11 A. M. and on laying the twelfth began at once to incubate. This Rail frequents the swampy borders of rivers and fresh-water ponds overgrown with vegetation. The stomach of one specimen was filled with seeds of *Arundo tecta;* that of another contained a quantity of oats.

Edward Howe Forbush, in *Game Birds, Wild-Fowl and Shore Birds.*

Photo by H. T. Middleton

KING RAIL

CLAPPER RAIL

Rallus crepitans crepitans *Gmelin*

A. O. U. Number 211 See Color Plate 25

Other Names.— Common Clapper; Marsh Clapper; Mud Hen; Sedge Hen; Meadow Hen; Salt-water Marsh Hen.

General Description.— Length, 16 inches. Color above, brownish-gray; below, lighter. Forehead entirely feathered down to base of bill; bill, long and slender.

Color.— Adults: Forehead, dusky; crown, sides of head, neck, upper parts, and lower parts as far as abdomen, *pale olive-ash* streaked on back, shoulders, and rump with olive-brown; lores and throat, whitish; abdomen and under tail-coverts, pale brownish-white traversed with broad indefinite bars of brownish-gray; wing-quills and tail, plain dusky-brown; bill, yellow, dusky on ridge and tip; feet, pale greenish-dusky; iris, reddish-brown. There is much variation in the shades of plumage, fall and winter birds being much darker and with browner shades. Downy Young: Glossy black.

Nest and Eggs.— Nest: A platform of dead reeds and grasses on the ground in meadows. Eggs: 6 to 15, white to buff, dotted and blotched with chestnut and some lavender.

Distribution.— Salt marshes of the Atlantic coast; breeds from Connecticut to North Carolina; winters mainly south of New Jersey; casual north to Maine.

Grassy salt marshes are the haunts of the Clapper Rail. From Connecticut southward to the Florida Keys they are undoubtedly more numerous than any other species found in these marshes. One does not find them everywhere in their range but in the localities they like best the grass seems to swarm with them. It is ordinarily very difficult to flush them and one may wade or push a boat through the marsh for hours and never see one while all the time their tantalizing calls are heard near and far. Their facility in keeping out of sight is most remarkable. From Virginia southward they are much hunted during the months of September and October. They are shot from small boats when the tide is high and the flooded marshes afford no shelter wherein the birds may hide. While one man poles the boat a second stands in the bow and fires at the

Drawing by R. I. Brasher

CLAPPER RAIL (½ nat. size)

A noisy salt-water marsh bird

slow-flying game as it rises from the scant cover of the exposed tops of the grass.

During the breeding season one may find many nests within a small area. The following description of one of their favorite nesting colonies is quoted from my notes made at the time of my visit:

"'Jacks Grass' is a low island of perhaps twenty acres on the North Carolina coast near New Inlet. It has no trees, but is covered generally with grass eight or ten inches long. Small clumps of rushes growing rarely over three feet high are scattered over the island, and in nearly every one of these a Clapper Rail's nest was found. These were composed of marsh-grass blades and stalks, and were built from six to eight inches above the wet sod. The fragments of grass used varied from four to six inches in length, shorter pieces being employed for the top layers. The nests measured about eight inches across the top, and were of uniform width from the bottom. On May 13 two of the nests examined each held eight slightly incubated eggs, and one nest of ten eggs was seen. One was found with two freshly deposited eggs, and another had four incubated eggs. Egg-shells from which the young had but shortly departed were found in one instance. Usually the nests were not screened from view by any arching of the rushes above them. Along the banks of the tide creeks that traversed the island the marsh grass was often two or more feet in length. Here were many covered runways of the birds, some of which were several yards in length."

Three distinct subspecies, or climatic varieties, of this Clapper Rail have been recognized by naturalists. One is the Louisiana, or Henshaw's, Clapper Rail (*Rallus crepitans saturatus*), chiefly distinguished by having its feathers darker colored than the common variety; the Florida Clapper Rail (*Rallus crepitans scotti*), a form that is still darker; and Wayne's Clapper Rail (*Rallus crepitans waynei*), found from North Carolina southward. Two closely allied but distinct species occurring elsewhere in North America are the California Clapper Rail (*Rallus obsoletus*), of the salt marshes of the Pacific coast, and the Caribbean Clapper Rail (*Rallus longirostris caribæus*), found in Texas and the West Indies. The general habits of all are very similar to the more familiar eastern bird.

Photo by P. B. Philipp Courtesy of Nat. Asso. Aud. Soc.

NEST AND EGGS OF CLAPPER RAIL

Stone Harbor, New Jersey

T. Gilbert Pearson.

VIRGINIA RAIL

Rallus virginianus *Linnæus*

A. O. U. Number 212 See Color Plate 25

Other Names.— Little Red-breasted Rail; Small Mud Hen; Fresh-water Marsh Hen; Long-billed Rail.

General Description.— Length, 11 inches. Like the King Rail except for smaller size.

Color.— Adults: Crown, back of neck, and upper parts, pale olive-brown, streaked on back and rump with dark brownish-black; *sides of head and cheeks, ashy;* lores and a narrow semi-circle below eye white; chin and upper throat, white; *neck and breast, rich chestnut;* abdomen and under tail-coverts, dusky with narrow white traverse bars; wing-coverts, chestnut; secondaries, brownish-black edged with olive; primaries and tail, plain brownish-black; *bill, flesh color,* dusky on ridge and tip; legs, dark flesh color; iris, reddish-brown. IMMATURE: Darker above than adults; under parts, blackish. DOWNY YOUNG: Sooty black with yellowish bill.

Nest and Eggs.— NEST: In a tuft of grass or reeds in meadows; rather compactly constructed (for a Rail) of dry reeds. EGGS: 6 to 12, cream or buffy, thinly spotted with chestnut or lavender.

Distribution.— North America; breeds from British Columbia, southern Saskatchewan, southern Keewatin, Ontario, southern Quebec, and New Brunswick south to southern California, Utah, Kansas, Missouri, Illinois, New Jersey, and eastern North Carolina, and in Toluca valley, Mexico; winters from Oregon, Utah, and Colorado to Lower California and Guatemala, also in the lower Mississippi States, and from North Carolina (casually Massachusetts) to Florida; occurs casually north to northern Quebec and Newfoundland.

In general habits I have not noticed any very distinctive difference between the Virginia Rail and the Sora, unless it be that birds of the former species are more inclined to keep by themselves in solitude or in pairs, whereas a good many Soras may be found, even during breeding time, in the same bog. The nesting is entirely similar. With neither species, as a rule, can one flush the sitting bird directly from the nest, for it slips off upon hearing the approach. In a few cases, where I came up very silently, I have seen them slip off through the grass, especially when I approached with caution nests already located.

Courtesy of S. A. Lottridge

VIRGINIA RAIL

It hides away in marshes and is little known

On one occasion, by concealing my camera in a bower of rushes near a nest, I secured some photographs. Despite all my care I found it next to impossible to see the bird on the nest before pulling the thread attached to the shutter. So I laid my line of communication further off and pulled at a venture, after waiting a reasonable time. In each case except one I secured my subject.

The young, as with other kinds, are tiny black creatures, which have a most amazing way of disappearing in a bog. Seeing the sprite in the grass, we may do our best to make a grab, but the reward is likely to be only a handful of grass and black slime.

Though it is hard to see the nesting bird for identification, the eggs of both the Virginia Rail and the Sora are distinct and characteristic. Though of the same size, those of the former are lighter in ground color, being yellowish-white, whereas those of the Sora are a more decided buff in hue. The birds, too, are distinct, the Sora having a little short bill, while the subject of our sketch has quite a long bill and a redder shade of plumage.

This bird is one of the coterie, always to be associated together, which are found in the bogs and meadows — Virginia Rail, Sora, Red-winged Blackbird, both Marsh Wrens, Bittern and Least Bittern, sometimes Swamp Sparrow, and, in the West, the Coot and Yellow-headed Blackbird, as well as Redhead, Ruddy Duck, Canvas-back, and others. It is a most interesting fraternity, and the fascination of their company has made and keeps me a regular "bog-trotter."

HERBERT K. JOB.

Photo by H. K. Job Courtesy of Outing Pub. Co.

VIRGINIA RAIL ON NEST

SORA

Porzana carolina (*Linnæus*)

A. O. U. Number 214 See Color Plate 26

Other Names.— Carolina Rail; Common Rail; Soree; Meadow Chicken; Carolina Crake; Little American Water Hen; Chicken-billed Rail; Chicken-bill; Rail-bird; Ortolan; Mud Hen.

General Description.— Length, 9 inches. Color above, olive-brown; below, gray. *Bill short and stout;* forehead entirely feathered down to base of bill.

Color.—ADULTS: Forehead, lores, face, *chin, and throat* (narrowly), *black;* crown, neck, and upper parts, including tail, *olive-brown;* back with dark-brown traverse bars and streaked narrowly with white; line over eye, sides of head, and *under parts, pure gray,* more olive on sides of body where barred with white transversely; abdomen barred with white; tail-coverts, whitish, tinged with rufous; bill, yellow, with extreme tip black; feet, light yellowish-green; iris, carmine. IMMATURE: *No black on foreparts;* throat and abdomen, whitish; *neck and breast, washed with cinnamon.* DOWNY YOUNG: Glossy black, with a tuft of orange-colored bristly feathers on the breast.

Nest and Eggs.— NEST: On the ground in meadows; a carelessly constructed affair of grass and weeds. EGGS: 7 to 13, more rarely 16, pronounced drab, spotted with chestnut and lavender over entire surface.

Distribution.—North America; breeds from central British Columbia, southern Mackenzie, central Keewatin, and Gulf of St. Lawrence south to southern California, Utah, Colorado, Kansas, Illinois, and New Jersey; winters from northern California, Illinois, and South Carolina through the West Indies and Central America to Venezuela and Peru; accidental in Bermuda, Greenland, and England.

The Soras are curious birds, which remind one of very tiny dark-colored bantam hens. They spend their lives mainly in slipping through the tangles of the fresh-water bogs, in the universal search for something to eat. Success in their mission is demonstrated by the fact that, though slenderly built, supposedly "thin as a rail," by autumn they are quite generally loaded with fat. From their arrival in May until their final departure south in October they live in close retirement and are seldom seen. But throw a stone into one of these seemingly tenantless bogs, and it is surprising what a chorus of yells and cackling sounds may arise, as though its coverts sheltered a sizable poultry farm.

During my boyhood I had constant opportunity to study Soras and Virginia Rails in an almost bottomless "cat-tail" bog, in the suburbs of Boston, Mass., on the edge of the town of Brookline, now groomed up into a fine city park and lake. It was my delight to flounder through it with boy companions, and find many sorts of nests. I shall never forget how one day a boy tried a short cut to a nest, contrary to my advice, got in all over, and finally, in tears, floundered ashore, swimming through black ooze of the consistency of New Orleans molasses. His return home through the city was a constant ovation, as may be imagined.

Here I found many a Sora's nest, including one

which contained sixteen eggs, the largest number that I ever found in a Rail's domicile, eight to ten being usual, and thirteen not infrequent. The nests are little platforms of dry grass or rush leaves, quite well hollowed. Sometimes they are in a cluster of reeds or rushes, a little above the level of the water, or under a thick tussock of meadow grass. But, after much searching, I found that the more typical location, both for the Sora and the Virginia Rail, was just out of the bog, in open meadow, where, on comparatively firm ground, rather short meadow-grass grew from just a little water. There the Rails constructed a little pile or island of grass, raised slightly above the water. The stems of the rather sparse grass held it together, and the ends were twisted and tied by the birds to form over it a sort of rounded canopy. In walking over the meadow I learned to find nests by noting this arching of the grass, even at some distance. Rails are nocturnal, and toward dusk one may watch them at the edges of the bog trotting out to feed. Their migrations are quite mysterious. Some frosty morning the meadows suddenly are found to be alive with them. Then the gunners get their innings. In some localities, such as the meadows along the Connecticut River, near its mouth, Rail shooting becomes a regular industry. At high tide boatmen pole flat skiffs through the grass. The Rails flutter up with their characteristic flight, making easy marks.

Courtesy of Am. Mus. Nat. Hist.

SORA

Their peculiar flight makes them easy targets for gunners

In Louisiana I found this species common in winter on the marshes back from the Gulf coast, on the reservations. Toward evening I could watch them from the windows of our camp, as well as during cloudy days. They came out from the reeds and fed on the rice which we scattered, sometimes venturing even under the house.

HERBERT K. JOB.

Photo by H. K. Job

NEST AND EGGS OF SORA

YELLOW RAIL

Coturnicops noveboracensis (*Gmelin*)

A. O. U. Number 215 See Color Plate 26

Other Names.— Little Yellow Rail; Yellow Crake.

General Description.— Length, 7 inches. Prevailing color, brownish-yellow, paler below and streaked above with dark. Forehead entirely feathered to base of bill; bill short and stout.

Color.— ADULTS: Crown (narrowly), neck, and upper parts, broadly and regularly streaked with *yellowish brown and burnt umber,* this fusing on crown and shading on sides of neck and sides of breast into reddish-brown spots; the dark streaks of back and wings, crossed by narrow white semi-circles, *the wings, showing considerable white in flight;* sides of head and neck, chin, throat, breast, and abdomen, yellowish-brown; under tail-coverts, plain brownish; sides of body, with some traverse spots of brown and white; lores and a streak below eye extending on side of face, brown; bill, yellow; feet pale yellowish flesh color; iris, brownish-red. DOWNY YOUNG: Black.

Nest and Eggs.— NEST: On the ground in meadows; constructed of dry grass. EGGS: 6 to 10, creamy-buff, spotted with fine rusty-brown.

Distribution.—Chiefly eastern North America; breeds from southern Mackenzie, central Keewatin, and southern Ungava south to Minnesota and Maine; winters in the Gulf States, rarely in California, Illinois, and North Carolina; casual in Nevada, Utah, and Bermuda.

The Yellow Rail is seen rather rarely in Massachusetts. I have met with it alive only once. It probably is more common in migration than is believed generally, as it is very small and its habits are secretive. It is even more reluctant than the other Rails to take wing; hence it is seen rarely, but is sometimes caught by dogs and cats. When forced to take wing it flies in the same hesitating, fluttering manner as the other Rails, but rather swifter and sometimes to a considerable distance. It can swim and dive well in case of necessity.

Wayne states that in South Carolina he found it nearly impossible to flush these birds with a dog when their only cover was short dead grass. His dog caught nine and flushed but one. Fresh-water snails were found in their stomachs.

EDWARD HOWE FORBUSH, in *Game Birds, Wild-Fowl and Shore Birds.*

BLACK RAIL

Creciscus jamaicensis (*Gmelin*)

A. O. U. Number 216 See Color Plate 26

Other Names.— Little Black Rail; Black Crake.

General Description.— Length, 6 inches. Upper parts, black barred with white; head, throat, and chest, slate color. Forehead entirely feathered down to base of bill; bill short and stout.

Color.— ADULTS: Forehead and crown, dusky; hind-neck and fore-back, dark chestnut; rest of *upper parts, deep brownish-black,* finely barred with white; head, neck, and breast, dark slate; abdomen and under tail-coverts, deep blackish-brown, traversed with narrow

Drawing by R. I. Brasher

BLACK RAIL (½ nat. size)

The smallest of the American Rails

white bars; lores and a line through and back of eye, dusky; wing-quills and tail, dusky with some white spots. DOWNY YOUNG: Black.

Nest and Eggs.— NEST: A very well-made and deeply cupped structure of fine grasses and weed stems; well concealed in a depression of the ground. EGGS: 6 to 9, white, sparsely spotted with small chestnut dots.

Distribution.— Eastern North America; breeds from southern Ontario and Massachusetts south to Kansas, Illinois, and South Carolina; winters from Texas east through the Gulf States and south to Jamaica and Guatemala; casual in Bermuda.

The Black Rail, the smallest Rail in America, is believed to be a very rare bird in New England, where it has been recorded only from Maine, Connecticut, and Massachusetts, in which States it possibly breeds. So far as our present information goes, Massachusetts appears to be near the northern limit of its breeding range on the Atlantic coast, but it may go farther north.

Records are received with caution, as the black, downy young of larger Rails are mistaken for Black Rails. Wayne appears to be the first observer who has actually seen the female Black Rail on her nest in the United States, and recorded it. The nest was in an oat field, and the standing grain, where the nest was, had been cut. The bird is so secretive that, as related by Wayne, two men and a dog searched four hours for the male in the oat field before it could be secured, although it was calling incessantly. This bird may not be as rare as it is rated.

The Black Rail runs swiftly, like a mouse, through the herbage, and seldom flies, although in migration it has reached the Bermuda Islands. Gosse quotes a Mr. Robinson who says that in Jamaica it is so foolish as to hide its head and cock up its tail, thinking itself safe, when it is easily taken alive.

EDWARD HOWE FORBUSH, in *Game Birds, Wild-Fowl and Shore Birds.*

Courtesy of Am. Mus. Nat. Hist.

BLACK RAIL

PURPLE GALLINULE

Ionornis martinicus (*Linnæus*)

A. O. U. Number 218 See Color Plate 27

Other Name.— Sultana (Jamaica).

General Description.— Length, 14 inches. Head, neck, and under parts, purplish; upper parts, olive-green. Head with frontal shield extending from base of bill and covering forehead; toes slender and without lobes; bill shorter than head.

Color.— ADULTS: Head, neck, and under parts, *deep purplish-blue;* abdomen black; *under tail-coverts white;* back and upper parts in general, olive-green; wing-coverts, blue-edged; wing- and tail-feathers dusky with outer webs bluish-green; frontal shield, pale cobalt; basal half of bill, carmine, front half yellow; a narrow white streak on side of face at base of bill; legs, chrome-yellow; iris, red. IMMATURE: Upper parts, washed with brownish; under parts, mottled with white. DOWNY YOUNG: Glossy-black with numerous white hair-like feathers on head.

Nest and Eggs.— NEST: Placed in reeds over water; constructed of dead rushes. EGGS: 6 to 10, creamy, thinly spotted and dotted with brown and lavender.

Distribution.— Tropical and subtropical America; breeds from Texas, Tennessee, and South Carolina south through Mexico and the West Indies to Ecuador and Paraguay; winters from Texas, Louisiana, and Florida southward; irregularly north in summer to Arizona, Nebraska, Wisconsin, Ontario, Quebec, Nova Scotia, and New Brunswick; accidental in England and Bermuda.

The Purple Gallinule has been richly endowed with beautiful feathers. With the single exception of the male Wood Duck it must be regarded as possessing the most striking colors of any of our southern water-birds. On the rice plantations along the Ashley River above Charlestown, South Carolina, I found this species very abundant and often saw them run across the road ahead of our buggy. There was much water about and they seemed to pass frequently from one pond or ditch to another, their stout, fairly long legs sending them forward at a good speed when haste was desired.

Photo by T. H. Jackson Courtesy of Nat. Asso. Aud. Soc.

NEST AND EGGS OF PURPLE GALLINULE

Orange Lake, Florida

With much vividness do I recall one spring morning when, while I was fishing from a boat in Levy Lake, Florida, these birds were much in evidence. It was during the mating season and they were the personification of activity. There was here an abundant growth of water lilies, and the birds seemed to take the greatest pleasure in walking over the lily pads, their yellow legs twinkling in the sunlight. As they walked, their tails jerked in a most pert and amusing manner. When springing from pad to pad their wings would be held high above the head. One of them clucking and displaying his superb plumage to every possible advantage approached some bushes which grew near shore and climbing the limbs proceeded with many flutters and loud bursts of guttural notes to climb upward until it reached the branches of a dense magnolia tree. Here from a height of twenty feet its purple plumage shone with a most resplendent beauty under the full glare of the morning sun. The whole performance combined to make a picture not easily forgotten.

When making short flights, and especially when chasing each other, the legs hang down as if ready for immediate use in case of emergency. They swim well although they are not web-footed. The long slender toes must be very

Drawing by R. I. Brasher

PURPLE GALLINULE (½ nat. size)

A southern water bird of superb plumage

serviceable in aiding them to run over the insecure pathway paved only with the floating leaves of the water lilies or to climb among the tangles of grass and water-plants.

The Purple Gallinule appears in its summer home in April or May and after a perfectly proper period of courtship nest building is begun. This interesting receptacle for the eggs is usually built in reeds or rushes a few feet above the water. Not long ago I examined six nests in a pond in lower Louisiana. Without exception these were constructed of grass-stems and rushes, each being built in a separate bunch of thick rushes. The surrounding stalks were pulled down in such a manner as to hide each nest completely from view. They were located above the water at heights varying from two to five feet. In the Mississippi valley the Purple Gallinule does not breed much north of Missouri. In the East and South (except Florida) it is confined largely to the tide-water sections.

T. Gilbert Pearson.

FLORIDA GALLINULE

Gallinula galeata (*Lichtenstein*)

A. O. U. Number 219 See Color Plate 27

Other Names.— American Gallinule; Common Gallinule; Red-billed Mud Hen; Water Hen; Water Chicken.

General Description.— Length, 14 inches. Prevailing color, blackish. Forehead covered by naked shield at base of bill; toes slender and without lobes; bill slender, sharp, and nearly as long as head.

Color.— Adults: Head, neck all around, breast, and under parts, *dark slate*, duskier on head and neck, and whitening behind; upper parts, brownish-slate; wings and tail, dusky; sides of under tail-coverts, edge of wing, outer web of first primary, and stripes on flanks, white; *bill, frontal plate, and a ring around upper part of leg, red;* tip of bill, yellow; a narrow white stripe on face at base of bill; legs, greenish-yellow; iris, red. Young: Similar to adults, but duller, with whitish under parts, and brownish bill and forehead.

Nest and Eggs.— Nest: In the marshes; constructed of dry reeds; often placed on a buoyant platform of the same material, capable of rising and falling with the water; in some places it is built on dry parts of the meadow. Eggs: 6 to 12, buffy-white, rather sparsely spotted with brown.

Distribution.— Tropical and temperate America; breeds from central California, Arizona, Nebraska, Minnesota, Ontario, New York, and Vermont south through the West Indies and Mexico to Chile and Argentina, and in the Galapagos and Bermuda; winters from southern California, Arizona, Texas, and Georgia southward; casual in Colorado, Quebec, Nova Scotia, New Brunswick, and Maine.

Photograph by A. A. Allen

A FLORIDA GALLINULE TURNING ITS EGGS

So hen-like in many of its movements is the Florida Gallinule that one can readily understand why its near relative in Europe should be named the Moor Hen. In habits it much resembles both the King Rail and the Coots, and its home is in the same character of country occupied by both of these species. It is a bird of the ponds and marshes of our southern country, although it occasionally breeds as far north as Minnesota and Maine. Like the Rails it often has more or less favorite pathways through the thick marsh grass, and like the Coot is sometimes seen swimming about in shallow weed-grown waters. When thus occupied the head bobs back and forth with each stroke of the feet. They cannot rightly be said to assemble in flocks, although as many as a dozen are at times seen feeding near together. Often they come on shore for food or assemble in small companies to sun and rest at some favorite rendezvous. At a distance they somewhat resemble the Coot, but a nearer view will reveal the difference. The bright scarlet bill and head-shield is a field mark for identification quite distinct from the white bill of the Coot.

Drawing by R. I. Brasher

FLORIDA GALLINULE (⅜ nat. size)

The source of many of the henlike noises heard in fresh-water marshes

Florida Gallinules possess a wonderful repertoire in the matter of calls. They are all very harsh, but they suggest the entire range of passions. For example, there is the appealing *ticket, ticket* of the lovelorn male, the petulant *tuka, tuka* of despondency, and the questioning explosive *chuck* of inquiry. They are very noisy birds and their notes are among the most familiar and constantly heard calls of the rush-grown lakeside. When the incubation of the eggs begins, the volume of sounds decreases perceptively. Rarely have I heard one call at night, for this bird is not so nocturnal as the Rails and many of the Herons.

Like most birds, the Gallinule is very cleanly and bathing is one of its frequent diversions. In flight it is most ungainly and when flushed its passage through the air is attended with every indication of extreme weariness.

The Gallinule's nest is worth a wade in the pond to discover. It is made of flags or rushes, and is placed from just above the water to a height of a foot or two. It is wedged in among a clump of rushes or in a rush-hidden bush. Frequently it is a foot and a half in diameter and several inches thick. The central cavity is slightly sunken and is just large enough to hold the six to twelve spotted eggs that are laid. Incubation begins as soon as egg-laying commences, with the result that some young appear from a week to twelve days before the others. Among their enemies may be mentioned the cotton-mouth moccasin that swallows their eggs and the frogs and alligators that snap up the young when swimming.

T. GILBERT PEARSON.

COOT

Fulica americana *Gmelin*

A. O. U. Number 221 See Color Plate 27

Other Names.—American Coot; Mud Hen; Water Hen; Marsh Hen; Moor-head; Meadow Hen; Water Chicken; Pond Hen; Mud Coot; Ivory-billed Coot; White-bellied Mud Hen; White-bill; Hen-bill; Crow-bill; Sea Crow; Pond Crow; Crow Duck; Flusterer; Blue Peter; Splatter; Shuffler; Pelick; Pull-doo.

General Description.— Length, 16 inches. Prevailing color, slate, dark above and light below; forehead, covered by naked shield at base of bill; bill stout, nearly as long as head; *toes lobed along edges.*

Color.— Adults: Entire plumage, dark slate-gray, blackening on head and neck, tinged with olive on back; under tail-coverts, edge of wing, *tips of secondaries,* and ends of some primaries, *white; bill, white* with small spots of reddish near end and at base of frontal shield; frontal shield, brown; *feet, pale olive-greenish;* iris, red. Downy Young: Blackish above, whitish below, with numerous orange-colored hair-like feathers on throat and upper parts. Immature: Similar to adults, but lighter below, and bill flesh color.

Nest and Eggs.— Nest: Constructed of dead reeds, grasses, and bits of decayed vegetation; afloat on the water or in the reeds nearby. Eggs: 7 to 16, creamy, finely and regularly spotted over entire surface with specks of dark brown and black.

Distribution.— North America; breeds from central British Columbia, southern Mackenzie, Manitoba, Quebec, and New Brunswick south to northern Lower California, Texas, Tennessee, and New Jersey, and also in southern Mexico, southern West Indies, and Guatemala; winters from southern British Columbia, Nevada, Utah, the Ohio valley and Virginia south to Colombia; casual at Fort Yukon, Alaska, and in Greenland, Labrador, and Bermuda.

Many people think that the Coot is a Duck because it is usually seen swimming. As a matter of fact, however, it belongs to the Rail tribe. Its feet are not webbed straight across, but each toe has a sort of scallop of lobes, which answer just about as well in paddling. Another popular mistake is to apply the name Coot to those marine Ducks which are properly called Scoters, not "Sea Coots."

The real Coot, while having some limitations, is notably versatile with its feet. Not that it is exactly a feathered Pavlowa, but with marked ability it can run, walk, swim, and "skitter." In the "Mud Hen skitter," which might well be

Photo by W. L. Finley and H. T. Bohlman

COOTS

Their odd ways make one laugh

made a new dance for society, it can beat even the celebrated dancer, for it is practiced on a peculiar floor, the surface of the water — as the flock flutter away, pattering with their feet as they go.

The favorite haunts of the Coots are the shallow ponds or bogs, where reeds or rushes grow from the water. In such places they make their nests, which are platforms of dead stems woven together in a sort of wicker-basket fashion, piled up from the bottom of the water, and partly supported by the stems of the aquatic plants, being rather deeply hollowed. The eggs number from seven or eight to fourteen or sixteen, and are distinguishable by the small "pepper-spot" markings evenly sprinkled over them. One egg is laid each day and incubation begins with the first egg. Consequently they hatch one by one, each youngster promptly leaving the nest to swim off, probably to be tended by the other parent.

The young are singular creatures, covered with a sort of black down with orange-colored hairs projecting from the neck and head, the latter being bald on top, and the bill and adjacent parts bright red. I have hatched some in incubators and reared them to maturity. At first small and feeble, they become active and bold, rushing at me and shrieking for food with raucous screams. If there is a more amusing bird anywhere, I should like to see it!

Though the Coot is rather tame, it is difficult to see it on the nest, but it is easy to watch it swim away, bobbing its head after the approved fashion of the skittering fraternity. Numbers breed, scattered about, in the same slough. On migration they are seen mostly in small parties, or often singly. They breed from the northern States north, and in winter are abundant in swampy parts of the southern States where they gather in large flocks.

In Louisiana I found them in great numbers in winter on the fresh-water marshes. When I "baited a blind," to photograph wild Ducks, it was always the Coots which ventured up first to try the food. The Ducks used them as buffers for danger, and swam up after the Coots proved to them that it was safe. They often came up on the steps of the camp to get food, and were known to walk into the house, perhaps thinking they heard the dinner-bell.

They are easily kept in captivity, but in the breeding season are said at times to make a rather too free use of their sharp bills. However, their odd ways make one laugh, and I recommend the funny Coot as an antidote for "the blues."

HERBERT K. JOB.

Photograph by H. K. Job — Courtesy of National Association of Audubon Societies

COOTS AND TEALS

The Ducks used the Coots as buffers for danger

ORDER OF SHORE BIRDS

Order *Limicolæ*

SHORE birds include seven closely related families — so closely related that no suborder has been established within this order. The various species frequent open areas, usually along watercourses, ocean beaches, or marshes. They average small in size, the largest North American species being the Long-billed Curlew, and the smallest being the Least and Semipalmated Sandpipers, or Peeps, so abundant in the spring, summer, and fall everywhere in the maritime districts. In color they are generally brown or blackish above, mottled and streaked with buff or whitish. The wings are long and pointed, the primaries graduating rapidly from outer to inner, the secondaries reversing this order — this giving a V-shape to the open wing. Many species are capable of sustained flight, and perform almost incredible journeys during migration. The tail is short. The legs are long and thin with long, slender, usually unwebbed, toes.

The food of the Shore Birds is the mollusks, crustaceans, and insects, found in the mud or along the moist strand of their habitat. They nest on the ground, usually laying four eggs, which are so well spotted or blotched with dark colors that they are quite inconspicuous among the grass or pebbles. When hatched the young are covered with down of a gray or brown color marked with blackish. At the approach of an " enemy " these downy chicks lie flat on the ground in an endeavor to escape detection.

Shore Birds have mellow, piping or whistling, voices, which can be heard for some distance. They are greatly prized as game birds and have been hunted to such an extent that it is not uncommon to hear them spoken of as " our vanishing shore birds."

PHALAROPES

Order *Limicolæ;* family *Phalaropodidæ*

LITTLE swimming Sandpipers " the Phalaropes were aptly called by Dr. Coues. They are essentially birds of the northern hemisphere, and all of the three species occur in North America, though only one, Wilson's Phalarope, is actually a permanent resident of this continent. A peculiar and interesting characteristic of the family is that the usual differences between the sexes of most species are reversed in the case of the Phalaropes; which is to say, the females are not only the larger and have the more striking plumage, but they are the aggressors in the courtship performances and the males do the nest-building and incubate the eggs.

All of the Phalaropes are comparatively small birds — from seven to nine inches long — and have noticeably thick, duck-like plumage to protect their bodies from the freezing waters in which they are often found, and a bill in which the lateral groove is prolonged nearly to the hardened and pointed tip, while the bill itself is as long as or longer than the head. The toes are equipped with marginal webs. The legs are normally long and slender. The wings are long, flat, and pointed, with the outer primaries longest and the inner secondaries elongated, giving the wing in flight a V-shaped appearance. The tail is short, stiff, broad, and rounded.

Dr. Coues's popular name for the Phalaropes is in recognition of their pelagic, or at least aquatic, habits, which often take them many miles out to sea, even in the dead of winter. The nests are mere depressions in the ground and sometimes are thinly lined with grass. Three or four eggs are laid but only about two young are successfully hatched and raised.

The baby Phalaropes are covered with down at birth and within a short time after leaving the shell are able to run about.

The Northern and Wilson Phalaropes are known to be of great economic value, because they destroy immense numbers of more or less harmful insects. The investigations of W. L. McAtee, a Government biologist, showed that 53 per cent. of the food of twenty-eight Northern Phalaropes consisted of mosquito larvæ, the insects eaten including the famous mosquito of the marshland of New Jersey. Wilson's Phalarope is known to feed upon bill-bugs, which often do considerable damage to corn. Undoubtedly far more has been done by the Phalaropes and other shore birds toward the extermination of mosquitoes in New Jersey than has been accomplished by the State's expenditure of large sums of money. Mr. McAtee's investigations showed that the Phalaropes also feed freely upon the crane flies ("leather-jackets"), grasshoppers, the clover-root curculio, the wireworms and their adult forms, the click beetles, the diving beetles which are a nuisance in fish hatcheries, and various species of marine worms which prey upon oysters.

RED PHALAROPE

Phalaropus fulicarius (*Linnæus*)

A. O. U. Number 222 See Color Plate 28

Other Names.—Whale-bird; Red Coot-footed Tringa; Gray Phalarope; Flat-billed Phalarope; Sea Snipe; Bank-bird; Brown Bank-bird; Gulf-bird; Sea Goose.

General Description.— Length, 8 inches. In summer, upper parts mottled and striped with black and pale brown, under parts entirely red; in winter, gray above and white below; but always distinguishable from other Phalaropes by the short, stout, tapering bill (dagger-shaped). The front toes have lobed or scalloped webs.

Color.— Adult Male in Summer: *Forehead, lores, chin, lower side of head, throat, and entire under parts, dull cinnamon-brown;* crown, nape, back of neck, and upper parts, yellowish-brown; crown streaked with brownish-black; rest of feathers above, with broad dark centers; wing-coverts dusky, the greater coverts showing white for most of their exposed portions; primaries brownish-black; a white ring around eye and a whitish area above and behind eye; basal half of bill, yellow, end dusky; feet, yellowish; iris, brown. Adult Female in Summer: Forehead, crown, chin, nape (narrowly), back of neck, wings, and middle tail-feathers, sooty-brown; lores, cheeks, sides of head, over eye and larger part of greater wing-coverts, white; *throat, neck (broadly), breast, and entire under parts, rich wine-red;* back, shoulders, and long inner coverts ochery-white, each feather with a broad center streak of brownish-black; primaries and wing-coverts, dusky, the latter edged with dull white; bill, yellowish, tipped with black; feet, yellowish-brown; iris, deep brown. Adults in Winter: Forehead, most of crown, sides of head, throat, breast, and rest of *under parts, pure white;* back of head, a spot in front of, another below, and one behind eye, a narrow streak down back of neck, upper back and primaries, plain dusky-gray; lesser and middle wing-coverts, grayish-ash edged with white, center coverts showing white space as in summer; rest of upper parts, *nearly uniform pale grayish-ash,* some of the feathers with darker centers; bill, mostly dusky; feet, dull yellow; iris, brown.

Nest and Eggs.— Nest: A hollow in ground; sometimes thinly lined with moss and dry grass. Eggs: 3 to 4, dull greenish or yellowish-gray, spotted with various shades of brown.

Distribution.— Northern and southern hemispheres; in North America breeds from northern Alaska, Melville Island, and northern Ellesmere Land south to mouth of the Yukon, northern Mackenzie, central Keewatin, Hudson Strait, and southern Greenland; winter home unknown but probably on the oceans, at least as far south as Falkland and Juan Fernandez islands; migrates along both coasts of United States; casual in migration in interior south to Colorado, Kansas, Illinois, and Maryland.

It is unfortunate that the Red Phalarope breeds far in the north, for the chance of studying its habits would be unusually interesting. After depositing the eggs the female loses her interest in home-ties and the smaller, more protectively-colored male meekly performs the household duties of incubation and assumes all the care of starting the youngsters toward maturity, while his mate looks on or gads about the country seeking new feeding grounds.

"When migrating this is a bird of the open waters, usually the sea, where it feeds and rests in flocks, swimming as gracefully and safely as a duck, and found along the shore only when driven in by storms." (Barrows.)

Their food is worms, soft, small marine animalcula, insects, and crustacea, which live in their marshy habitat. In the North it feeds on the animal-life which forms the food of the right whale — hence its name of Whale-bird.

NORTHERN PHALAROPE

Lobipes lobatus (*Linnæus*)

A. O. U. Number 223 See Color Plate 29

Other Names.— Sea Goose; Mackerel Goose; Web-footed Peep; Bank-bird; White Bank-bird; Sea Snipe; Whale-bird; Hyperborean Phalarope; Red-necked Phalarope.

General Description.— Length, 7 inches. Color above, ashy-gray; bill very slender, cylindrical, and sharp (needle-like); front toes with lobed or scalloped webs.

Color.— Adult Male in Summer: Forehead, throat, breast, and *lower parts, pure white;* crown, sides of head, back of neck, upper back, ashy-gray; forehead and front part of crown, mottled with ashy; lores, dusky; *a broad area of rufous extending from nape downward across upper breast, interrupted on upper breast with dusky streaks*; sides of breast much mottled with ashy-gray and white; flanks and sides marked with arrowhead-shaped dusky spots; shoulders, rufous-brown, each feather with blackish center and white tipped; wing-coverts and primaries, dusky, the greater coverts with rear portion white; a white semi-circle above and another below eye; bill, black; iris, brown; feet, dusky gray. Adult Female in Summer: Head from chin, back of neck, shoulders, and back, plain grayish-ash; throat and lower side of head, white, bordered behind and below with a large patch of rich tawny, this color including upper breast; under parts, white, broken on side of breast, sides, and flanks, with ashy-gray; *a broad V-shaped stripe of yellowish-brown on back; two narrow ones of same color on shoulders;* wing-coverts and primaries, dusky, the greater coverts broadly white on ends, forming a conspicuous bar, a white semi-circle above and another below eye; bill, black; legs and feet, bluish-gray; soles of feet, greenish-yellow; iris, deep brown. Adults in Winter: *Forehead, broad line over eye running along side of head and meeting white of chin, breast, and lower parts, pure white;* a broad streak behind eye, crown, back of neck, and *upper parts, plain light ash,* varied with white edges of feathers, these lighter edges forming a V-shaped mark on back and more extensive on shoulders, becoming narrower on longer wing-coverts behind; sides of breast, mottled with ash; sides and flanks, with a faint tinge of gray, thinly spotted with darker; wing as in summer; a wash of pale rufous on sides of neck; a

Drawing by R. I. Brasher

NORTHERN PHALAROPE (female; ⅔ nat. size)

She leaves all the family duties to the less handsome, more modest male

dusky spot in front of eye; eye-ring, white interrupted before and behind; bill, bluish-black; feet, livid; iris, deep brown.

Nest and Eggs.— NEST: A hollow in ground lined with grass or leaves. EGGS: 4, greenish or buffy, thickly blotched with various shades of brown.

Distribution.— Northern and southern hemispheres; in North America breeds from northern Alaska, Melville Island, and central Greenland south to Aleutian Islands (including Near Islands), valley of the upper Yukon, northern Mackenzie, central Keewatin, southern James Bay, and northern Ungava; winter home unknown, but probably the oceans south of the equator; in migration occurs nearly throughout the United States and in Mexico, Central America, Bermuda, and Hawaii.

Like the Red Phalarope, the Northern Phalarope breeds in the extreme north. It has a curious habit of whirling around several times in succession on the surface of the water, creating miniature whirlpools, evidently with the intention of stirring up the tiny marine life on which it feeds. I have seen many flocks on the ocean, well off the shore of the New England coast, during August and September, floating like thistle-down but not going through the gyrations they perform on the shallow inland ponds, which would indicate that in the latter they find food absent in the former.

R. I. BRASHER.

Photo by W. L. Finley and H. T. Bohlman

NORTHERN PHALAROPE

Female in summer plumage

WILSON'S PHALAROPE

Steganopus tricolor *Vieillot*

A. O. U. Number 224 See Color Plate 30

Other Name.— Summer Phalarope.

General Description.— Length, 9 inches. Color above, gray; bill longer than head and very slender; front toes with marginal webs, but the membrane not scalloped.

Color.— Adult Male in Summer: Forehead, crown, and upper parts in general, including wings and tail, dull grayish, streaked on back, shoulders, and wing-coverts with darker gray; lores and a broad stripe over and behind eye, whitish; throat and a patch on nape, white; rest of under parts, dull white, washed on side with pale yellowish; a rusty area on side of neck, bordered above with dusky; dusky spot in front of eye and an indistinct one of the same color, behind; bill, dusky; feet, dull horn; iris, brown. Adult Female in Summer: Crown, pale ash changing to white on a narrow stripe on back of neck, this color changing again on back to *ash,* continuing down and becoming white on rump and upper tail-coverts; *a broad black area commencing behind eye, running halfway down neck where widening and changing into rich purplish-chestnut, extending along back in a narrower streak;* shoulders, the same color, bordered on each side with grayish; wings, pale grayish-brown; primaries, dusky; tail, mottled with gray and white; chin and throat, pure white; rest of *under parts, white;* sides of neck, breast, and flanks washed with pale rufous; a large white spot over eye, bordered in front with black streak; a smaller spot of white below eye; bill, dusky; feet, horn blackish; iris, brown; *no white patch on wing.* Adults in Winter: Crown, back of neck, and upper parts, ashy-gray, each feather usually edged with whiter; wing-coverts and secondaries, dusky-gray edged with pale yellowish-white; primaries, plain dusky; upper tail-coverts, line over eye, and under parts, white, shaded on sides of breast with grayish; a dusky spot in front of eye; an indistinct streak behind eye of light dusky; bill, dusky; legs, yellow; iris, brown. Young: Brownish-black above, this soon succeeded by coloring of winter adult.

Nest and Eggs.— Nest: A slight depression in the ground; lined with grass. Eggs: 3 or 4, creamy, buff, or drab, spotted, specked, and scratched with brown of different shades.

Distribution.— North and South America; breeds from central Washington, central Alberta, and Lake Winnipeg south to eastern California, southern Colorado, southern Kansas, northern Iowa, and northwestern Indiana; winters from central Chile and central Argentina south to Falkland Islands; casual in migration on Pacific coast from southern British Columbia to Lower California and on Atlantic coast from Maine to New Jersey.

Photo by W. L. Finley and H. T. Bohlman

MALE WILSON'S PHALAROPE RETURNING TO HIS TASK OF INCUBATING

Though I have met the other two kinds of Phalaropes out on the open Atlantic well off-shore, to find Wilson's Phalarope one has to journey to the northwest interior. There I have found these beautiful, gentle birds breeding beside the marshy sloughs of North Dakota, Manitoba, and Saskatchewan. The best-known, most widely advertised peculiarity of Phalaropes is their family relationship. The female is the larger and brighter-colored, and is said to do the courting; the demure little male — mere man — incubates the eggs and cares for the young, while the wives flock together in the sloughs as though they had organized women's clubs or other social coteries. Thus I have watched parties of these giddy little ladies sporting about, and then, tramping through the meadow grass on the prairie a few rods back from some other slough, have flushed the male from the nest so well hidden in the grass. The four eggs are decidedly pointed and are very boldly and thickly streaked with black.

To the credit of the female it must be said that she is not entirely without the heart of the mother. The cries of her husband, in times of seeming danger, soon bring her to the rescue, and she runs or flies about with him, scolding, though he usually leads in the performance of the various protestations.

On one occasion, during the spring migration, in early June, I met a considerable flock of Northern Phalaropes on a shallow alkaline slough in northern Manitoba, but at the most I have only seen Wilson's Phalarope in small parties. Like all the tribe these are graceful in every motion, notably in swimming, bobbing their heads and necks prettily forward as they progress.

Despite the above reversals of social usage, the female is far from being a virago. The birds are gentle in manner and inconspicuous, and the average person passing through their haunts probably would not notice them. Though small, they are, like other shore birds, swift and strong in flight, and in winter they journey as far south as Chile and Argentina.

Photo by H. K. Job Courtesy of Outing Pub. Co.

WILSON'S PHALAROPE

The male of this species attends to the work of raising the family

HERBERT K. JOB.

AVOCETS AND STILTS

Order *Limicolæ;* family *Recurvirostridæ*

THE Avocets and Stilts include eleven or twelve species which occur, usually in flocks, throughout the warmer regions of the world. As a family they are comparatively large birds, and have exceedingly long legs, long necks, and long, slender bills, curved more or less upward, in which the nostrils are set within the quarter nearest the base.

Of the Avocets, there are four species, one occurring in North America, another in South America, a third in Europe, and a fourth in Australia. Each of these has a rudimentary hind toe, and the front toes webbed, in which latter respect they differ from most wading birds. Their wings are rather short and their tails are short and square. Their plumage is thick and duck-like. They feed on aquatic insects, shellfish, and the like, which they capture chiefly in shallow water by sweeping the bill from side to side with a movement which suggests the swinging of a scythe. The Avocets swim easily, when they need to, and usually are comparatively tame. They are from fifteen to eighteen inches long and in coloration are generally black and white, with the legs of a bluish tinge. They build rude nests on the ground in swampy places; the eggs are three or four in number, of olive or buff color profusely marked with dark brown spots.

Of the true Stilts there are seven or eight species, only one of which occurs in America. The family differs from the Avocets in having no web between the middle and inner toes; in being considerably smaller, with an average length of about thirteen inches; and in having the wings long and pointed. The common American species occurs in both continents and is found most often in small flocks on muddy flats, where the bird walks with long, deliberate strides, probing the mud with its long bill or catching fish in the shallow waters. Physically and in their habits, there is considerable general similarity between the Stilts and the Avocets.

The young of both Avocets and Stilts are covered with down at birth and shortly after leaving the shell are able to run about. This natal down is soon replaced by the first or juvenal plumage.

AVOCET

Recurvirostra americana *Gmelin*

A. O. U. Number 225

Other Names.—American Avocet; Blue Stocking; Blue Shanks; Irish Snipe.

General Description.— Length, 18 inches. Color, white with some black areas; bill, flattened and upturned; three front toes webbed.

Color.— Adults in Summer: *White, changing imperceptibly to chestnut-brown of head and neck;* shoulders and wings, black; some secondaries and coverts, white; tail, pearl-gray; bill, black; legs, dull blue; iris, red or brown. Adults in Winter: Head and neck, pearl-gray; otherwise like summer plumage. Young: Head and neck, washed with chestnut, the black feathers edged with same color; bill, nearly straight.

Nest and Eggs.— Nest: In the marshes, hidden in the grass and constructed of grass and weed stems. Eggs: 3 or 4, pale olive or buffy, uniformly and thickly spotted with burnt umber and other shades of brown.

Distribution.— North America; breeds from eastern Oregon, central Alberta, and southern Manitoba (rarely north to Great Slave Lake) south to southern California, southern New Mexico, northwestern Texas, northern Iowa, and central Wisconsin; winters from southern California and southern Texas to southern Guatemala; casual from Ontario and New Brunswick to Florida and the West Indies, but rare east of Mississippi River.

Courtesy of American Museum of Natural History

AVOCET

The most showy of North American shore birds

The Avocet stands out among North American shore birds as the most showy of them all. Its white body and black and white-striped wings reveal its presence at a great distance. It is a large bird, being about a foot and a half long. This, added to the fact that it makes a most acceptable dish when served on the table, is responsible for the extended persecution to which it has been subjected by gunners. One of the names by which shooters know it is "Blue Shanks," the color of its long, bare legs being responsible for this. While searching for wild Ducks' nests on the marshes of the Klamath River in Oregon I first came upon these remarkable birds. Evidently a small group was nesting in the neighborhood, for upon our appearance three birds came into view and at once set up a great outcry. Our first view of them was when they came flying toward us giving vent to their alarm and resentment at our approach. They flew overhead and circled about much as is the custom of Willets under like circumstances. Their screaming soon brought others, who may have been their mates called from the nests by the general alarm. At times they alighted on the ground at a safe distance, or settled in the water of the slough. Here the maneuvers of head-bobbing and wing-waving were most amusing. Sometimes the body would be all but submerged and with head laid out along the water the bird would swim away just as a wounded wild Goose will often try to escape the fowler.

The Avocet's nest is a depression in the ground in the vicinity of water and is lined with grass. The young upon emerging from the spotted eggs are able to run almost at once.

Audubon has this to say in reference to their feeding habits:

"They search for food precisely in the manner of the Roseate Spoonbill, moving their heads to and fro sideways, while their bill is passing through the soft mud; and in many instances, when the water was deeper, they would immerse their whole head and a portion of the back, as the Spoonbill and Red-breasted Snipe are wont to do. When, on the contrary, they pursued aquatic insects, such as swim on the surface, they ran after them, and, on getting up to them, suddenly seized them by thrusting the lower mandible beneath them, while the other was raised a good way above the surface, much in the manner of the Black Shearwater [Black Skimmer], which, however, performs this act on wing. They were also expert at catching flying insects, after which they ran with partially expanded wings."

In the United States the Avocet is to-day confined almost entirely to the territory lying west of the Mississippi River. The Federal Migratory Bird Law extends protection to it at all times, and it is to be hoped this splendid game bird may be spared the melancholy fate of the Eskimo Curlew and the Whooper Swan.

Photo by H. T. Bohlman Courtesy of Nat. Asso. Aud. Soc.

NEST AND EGGS OF AVOCET

Like several other shore birds, the Avocet makes itself very useful by destroying diving beetles, which are predatory in their habits and do much damage to fish hatcheries by feeding upon insects which are the natural diet of fishes. It also feeds freely upon grasshoppers and upon bill-bugs, which injure the corn crops. Snails and marine worms also part of its diet.

T. Gilbert Pearson.

BLACK-NECKED STILT

Himantopus mexicanus (*Müller*)

A. O. U. Number 226

Other Names.— Stilt; Longshanks; Lawyer.

General Description.— Length, 13 inches. Color above, black, sharply contrasting with the white of under parts; legs very long.

Color.— Adults: *Back, shoulders, and wings, glossy black, continuing up back of neck,* on crown, enlarging on side of head, and including the eyes; a spot over and behind eye, one beneath eye, forehead, forepart of crown, lores, chin, sides of head below eye, sides of neck, entire under parts, rump, and upper tail-coverts, white; tail, ash; bill, black; iris, red; legs, flesh color. White of rump covered by the wings in life. In the female the black is often dingy. Young: Upper parts, brown, marked with whitish.

Nest and Eggs.— Nest: A depression in the sand or a frail structure of grass and small stems hidden in a bunch of weeds. Eggs: 3 or 4, buffy or olive-brown, thickly spotted and blotched with dark brown.

Distribution.— Temperate North America and northern South America; breeds from central Oregon, northern Utah, and southern Colorado to southern California, southern New Mexico, southern Texas, coast of Louisiana, and in Mexico, and from central Florida and Bahamas throughout the West Indies to northern Brazil and Peru; formerly bred north to New Jersey; winters from southern Lower California, southern Texas, southern Louisiana, and southern Florida south through Central America and the West Indies to northern Brazil, Peru, and the Galapagos; casual in migration to Nebraska, Wisconsin, and New Brunswick.

The Black-necked Stilt has been brought to verge of extermination along the Atlantic coast by the spring and summer shooting. It is not uncommon in the West and South, being particularly abundant about the alkaline lakes and pools of the Great Basin, where it is often seen in the company of the Avocet.

Courtesy of S. A. Lottridge

BLACK-NECKED STILT

The bird walks with long deliberate strides

" On the ground, whether walking or wading, the bird [the Black-necked Stilt] moves gracefully, with measured steps; the long legs are much bent at every step (only at the joint, however) and planted firmly, perfectly straight; except under certain circumstances, there is nothing vacillating, feeble, or unsteady, in either the attitudes or the movements of the birds. When feeding, the legs are bent backward with an acute angle at the heel joint to bring the body lower; the latter is tilted forward and downward over the center of equilibrium, where the feet rest, and the long neck and bill reach the rest of the distance to the ground." (Coues.)

When the birds light they raise their wings straight up above the body for a moment, then close them slowly over the back. Many water birds have this same habit; and it is undoubtedly a recognition mark to keep in touch with the rest of the flock as the pose is a very conspicuous one, enabling the bird to be seen from a long distance.

The Black-necked Stilt's diet is known to include in considerable quantities several species of the predacious diving beetles which, because they prey upon insects that are the natural food of fishes, are counted a nuisance in all fish hatcheries. In this respect its economic value is a matter of fact, not of theory. Grasshoppers are destroyed in large numbers by this bird, and also bill-bugs which feed upon corn.

R. I. Brasher.

SNIPES, SANDPIPERS, ETC.

Order *Limicolæ;* family *Scolopacidæ*

THE Snipes, Sandpipers, and the closely allied species which form the family *Scolopacidæ* of the order of Shore Birds, or Wading Birds, are represented in all the habitable parts of the world, but during the breeding season they are found with few exceptions only in the northern parts of the northern hemisphere. There are about one hundred species in the family, about half of which number occur regularly or occasionally in America.

The members of this family vary greatly in size, shape, and color, but in general they are of small or medium size and never reach the average size of Herons. Usually the bill is long and soft-skinned, generally straight, roundish, and slim, but sometimes curved either upward or downward and in one species, the Spoon-bill Sandpiper of eastern Asia, the end is spoon-shaped. The head is feathered to the bill. The legs are of moderate length. The wings are normally long, flat, and pointed. The tail is rather short, stiff, broad, and rounded.

As indicated by the name of the group in which this family has been placed, its members are seldom found far from the shores of bodies of water or from moist lands. They migrate and pass the winter in flocks, but during the breeding season are not gregarious. Like other shore birds, they all, with the exception of the European Green Sandpiper and the American Solitary Sandpiper, nest on the ground. The eggs usually number four, but seldom does a pair succeed in bringing more than two young birds to maturity during a season. The babies are clothed with down when hatched, and are precocial, that is, they are not cared for in the nest by their parents, but are able to run about within a very short time after leaving the shell.

Many of the species in this group are greatly prized as game birds, and to this fact is due to a large extent the decrease in their numbers. The development of land for agricultural purposes has restricted their breeding grounds, and this is an indirect, but nevertheless another, cause for their lessening numbers. Not only because of their food value are the birds entitled to protection, but also because of their usefulness. They search out and destroy many creatures that are detrimental to man's interests. Among the pests which they eat are grasshoppers, army worms, cutworms, cabbage worms, cotton worms, boll weevils, rice weevils, Texas fever ticks, horseflies, and mosquitoes.

WOODCOCK

Philohela minor (*Gmelin*)

A. O. U. Number 228 See Color Plate 31

Other Names.—American Woodcock; Woodhen; Big-headed Snipe; Big Mud Snipe; Blind Snipe; Whistling Snipe; Wood Snipe; Night Partridge; Night Peck; Timber Doodle; Hookum Pake; Labrador Twister; Bogsucker; Bog-bird; Pewee; Whistler; Big-eyes.

General Description.— Length, 11 inches; color above, brown; below, pale orange-brown; head, large; neck, short; *eyes, large* and set far back and high; *bill, very long* and compressed, the lower section shorter than the upper into which it fits at the tip, and the upper section capable of being flexed like a finger; wings, short and rounded; *three outer primaries, scythe-shaped; legs, short and stout with thighs feathered;* toes, without webs.

Color.— Above, finely blended and varied with black, warm browns, gray, and russet, the brown predominating, the gray tending to form streaks above and below shoulders; forehead, grayish; *three square patches of black extending from top of crown to nape and separated by narrow gray bars;* a black stripe from gape to eye; chin, whitish; rest of under parts, pale orange-brown with a few black spots on sides of chest; primaries, plain brownish; bill, brownish flesh color, dusky on ridge and tip; feet, flesh color; eye-ring, white; iris, dark brown.

Nest and Eggs.— Nest: On ground, on brushy bottoms or in open woods, usually not far from water; a depression in the leaves without lining. Eggs: 3 or 4, buffy to grayish-white, irregularly and thickly spotted with pale reddish-brown.

Distribution.— Eastern North America; breeds from northeastern North Dakota, southern Manitoba, northern Michigan, southern Quebec, and Nova Scotia south to southern Kansas, southern Louisiana, and northern Florida; winters from southern Missouri, the Ohio Valley, and New Jersey (rarely Massachusetts) south to Texas and southern Florida; ranges casually to Saskatchewan, Keewatin, Colorado, Newfoundland, and Bermuda.

During the day the Woodcock sits quietly in a shadowy retreat, usually in the swamps, but often in open upland woods. It may also be flushed in "slashings," where will be found the "form" of old leaves where it had nestled. The swampy coverts which "Mr. Big-eyes" prefers are clean, sweet localities, where alders and willows like to grow. The bird is by no means confined to such resorts for it may be found nesting well up in the hills, though even there a favorite resort is generally not far away, to which it travels in the evening and forages for its nocturnal supper. Often in the evening I have seen it against the fading west, bound for its own particular restaurant. Even after night had fallen its familiar *scape* could be heard.

Some of our birds are enveiled in mystery and the Woodcock is not the least strange of this coterie. It often lives where its presence is unsuspected. One of the best Woodcock covers I have known was within the limits of the city of Brooklyn. Fortunately this knowledge was not shared by others, so the birds were little hunted. Into this retreat the birds would come silently some April night, and from it they would disappear some October day as mysteriously.

The flight is swift though short, sometimes accompanied with a clattering sound, at others as silent as an owl's. I have frequently seen them collide with limbs when flushed. This may be due to the fact that the birds' eyes are placed far back in the head, or it may be because they are watching the intruder and cannot look forward and behind at the same time.

Drawing by R. I. Brasher

WOODCOCK (⅔ nat. size)

A game bird that is not disturbed by the advent of agriculture

The mother Woodcock has a curious and interesting habit of flying off, when disturbed, with a young chick grasped between her feet or between her thighs. If she has an opportunity, she will convey all her babies, one at a time, to a place of security.

At courting time, and all through the period of incubation, the male indulges in a curious aërial dance. Soon after sunset he whirls up in spirals, chirping and twittering, to a height of fifty or sixty feet, then circles horizontally and descends, giving voice to his ecstasy in a continuous "cheeping" until he reaches the ground where he struts like a tiny turkey-gobbler, with drooping wings and upright spread tail, changing his notes to a series of rather hard *paiks*. On moonlight nights, I have listened to this serenade until after 9 o'clock.

A dish of angleworms can hardly be considered appetizing; but, transmuted in the Woodcock's interior machinery (he is really one hundred per cent. angleworm), there seems to be no difference of opinion among epicures when the bird is brought to the table on toast.

The Woodcock's diet includes also in considerable quantities such harmful insects as the crane fly (" leather-jacket "), and various species

Photo by H. K. Job Courtesy of Outing Pub. Co.

WOODCOCK ON NEST

Its nest is a depression among fallen leaves

of more or less destructive grasshoppers. To this extent its feeding habits are of distinct benefit to man.

R. I. Brasher.

WILSON'S SNIPE

Gallinago delicata (*Ord*)

A. O. U. Number 230 See Color Plate 32

Other Names.— Common Snipe; English Snipe; American Snipe; Meadow Snipe; Marsh Snipe; Bog Snipe; Gutter Snipe; Jack Snipe; Shadbird; Alewife-bird; Shad Spirit.

General Description.— Length, 12 inches. Color above, mainly brownish-black; bill long and slender, upper section overlapping under. Seldom found away from fresh-water marshes.

Color.— Ground color of head, neck, throat, and *breast, pale brownish-white;* sides of head, neck, and *breast, spotted with pale and dark brown;* two dusky stripes from bill over crown to back of head; another from gape to eye and extending a little behind and a small patch on cheeks; back and shoulders, brownish-black mixed with chestnut and brown; shoulder-feathers, broadly edged with brownish-white, forming two longitudinal stripes on each side; wing-coverts, brownish, feathers edged with whitish, secondaries with brown spots coalescing along shaft; primaries and their coverts, dusky-brown, the outer one white-edged; upper tail-coverts, brown with narrow black bars; *tail-feathers, black at base, then bright rufous with a narrow subterminal black bar* and white-tipped; abdomen, white; *sides of body, shaded with brown, barred with numerous traverse streaks of dusky;* under tail-coverts, rufous with dusky bars; bill, brownish flesh-color, dusky on ridge and tip; feet, greenish-gray; iris, brown surrounded by white ring interrupted in front and behind.

Nest and Eggs.— Nest: A grass-lined depression in marshy ground. Eggs: 3 or 4, grayish-olive, spotted and streaked with chestnut, burnt umber, and black.

Distribution.— North America and northern South America; breeds from northwestern Alaska, northern Mackenzie, central Keewatin, and northern Ungava south to northern California, southern Colorado, northern Iowa, northern Illinois, Pennsylvania, and New Jersey; winters from northern California, New Mexico, Arkansas, and North Carolina through Central America and West Indies to Colombia and southern Brazil; remains in winter casually and locally north to Washington, Montana, Nebraska, Illinois, and Nova Scotia; accidental in Hawaiian Islands, Bermuda, and Great Britain.

As its scientific name implies, the Wilson's Snipe is truly a delicacy, and in many more ways than from the culinary standpoint. Every phase of its life assumes a peculiar interest, when one comes to know it well. Sportsmen, naturally, are fond of it, and refer to it familiarly as " Jack Snipe."

In the breeding season its ways are most singular and entertaining. It breeds on the northern borders of the United States and north to the Arctic Sea. On the Magdalen Islands I have watched it with both amusement and amazement. The background is of the mossy bogs and marshes, interspersed with shallow ponds and clumps of small spruce. There, in May and June, we may see and hear the male bird darting about in wide circlings up in the sky, like a sort of feathered meteor, producing with its wings a humming, murmuring sound, not unlike that accompanying the flight of the "Whistler" or Golden-eye. Then the mode of the performance changes. The singular, long-billed creature now flies low, emitting a vocal yelping or cackling, in general form not very different from that of the Yellow-legs, only continuous, lasting for several minutes at a spell. Presently it alights on a spruce tree or a stub and continues its vociferations.

Possibly the female may indulge also in the circling and winnowing performance, for I have seen two or more birds at a time executing this, and in one case we thus traced a bird to its nest. Watching where it alighted, after much flying around, a member of our party flushed it from a nest of four handsomely marked, pointed eggs, in the grass near a little bush. I embraced the opportunity to set the camera by the nest, with thread attached, and thus secured some interesting pictures.

Photo by H. K. Job Courtesy of Outing Pub. Co.

WILSON'S SNIPE ON NEST

The usual haunts of this Snipe are open meadows or fresh-water marshes, where the ground is wet and soft, and where there is grass enough to conceal it. It migrates down across the United States from mid-September to freezing-up time, and is much hunted. Flushing suddenly from the grass, it darts off with rapid, erratic flight, uttering reiterated squeaky notes, commonly represented as *scaip, scaip,* or *escape,* suiting the action to the word. It winters from the Southern States to as far south as Brazil.

On the Louisiana marshes, in the winter of 1915–16, I found it very abundant. Usually it is found in scattered parties on the meadows, but here I found it in large flocks, sometimes noting several hundred in flight in a compact mass. Smaller parties, or "wisps," say of twenty to

Drawing by R. I. Brasher

WILSON'S SNIPE (3/5 nat. size)

A favorite with sportsmen

forty, were frequently darting about, especially toward evening. Near the camp of Messrs. Ward and McIlhenny, where I stayed, there were a series of muddy flats, interspersed with bunches or patches of grass, which were fairly alive with Snipe. In the morning I could see one or more of them lying beneath many a tussock dozing. Unless flushed, they stayed there until sundown, or till it became overcast, whereupon they could be seen running about over the open mud and shallow water, busily probing for worms. By building a blind at the edge of one of these flats and carefully awaiting sudden intervals of sunshine late in the afternoon, I secured motion pictures and others of them thus engaged.

HERBERT K. JOB.

The food of Wilson's Snipe is known to include crane-flies ("leather-jackets"), locusts, grasshoppers, crawfishes, and the predacious diving beetles which cause trouble in fish hatcheries and destroy much of the natural insect food of fishes. To the extent that it preys upon these insect forms — and that is very considerable — it must be reckoned a useful bird.

DOWITCHER

Macrorhamphus griseus griseus (*Gmelin*)

A. O. U. Number 231 See Color Plate 33

Other Names.— Robin Snipe; Sea Pigeon; Driver; Red-breasted Snipe (summer); Brown Snipe (summer); Brown-back (summer); Gray Snipe (winter); Gray-back (winter).

General Description.— Length, 11 inches. Color above, in summer, brownish-cinnamon; in winter, slate-gray. Bill long and slender, upper section overlapping under. Found on sand bars and mud flats, and not in bogs.

Photograph by H. K. Job

DOWITCHERS

A flock on Breton Island Reservation

Color.— IN SUMMER: Ground color of neck, head, breast, and upper parts, brownish-cinnamon; head and neck, narrowly streaked with dusky-brown; feathers of back, with broad blackish-brown centers; *rump, upper coverts, and tail, white, barred with dusky;* wings, grayish-dusky, the coverts edged with lighter; secondaries, broadly edged and tipped with white; *under parts, rufous,* paler or whitish behind; breast and sides, thickly speckled with dusky; a series of dusky specks from gape through and behind eye; bill and feet, dull dusky-greenish; iris, brown. IN WINTER: Forehead, head, neck, back, shoulders, and long inner secondaries, dark gray, the feathers on back with dusky centers and paler edges; lower back, *rump, and tail, pure white,* with roundish spots of dusky; wing-coverts, like back; secondaries, white-edged and -tipped; primaries dusky-brown; *under parts, white;* throat, sides of breast, and sides, strongly shaded with gray; a dusky stripe from gape through and behind eye; the white stripe between this and crown, pronounced; cheeks and side of head, mottled with pale dusky; lower tail-coverts with roundish dusky spots; bill, dusky, greenish at base; legs, dully greenish-gray; iris, brown with white crescent below.

Nest and Eggs.— NEST: A depression in the ground

on borders of marshy lakes and ponds; a loose structure of grasses and leaves. EGGS: 4, greenish-olive to light clay-color, spotted with dark brown.

Distribution.— Eastern North and South America; breeding range unknown, but probably northern Ungava; winters from Florida and the West Indies south to northern Brazil; in migration regularly on the Atlantic coast, and occasionally in Illinois, Indiana, and Ontario; accidental in Greenland, Bermuda, Great Britain, and France.

The Dowitcher's regular food includes several species of destructive grasshoppers, diving beetles which do much damage in fish hatcheries besides destroying insects which are the natural food of fishes, and various marine worms which prey upon oysters. Its usefulness to man, therefore, is very considerable.

It is a bird of the open meadows, feeding along marshy shores and on sand bars bared by the receding tide, in flocks, and often in the company of other waders. This gregarious instinct, combined with its gentleness, is a fatal trait, and enables gunners to slaughter them unmercifully and sometimes to exterminate every individual in a "bunch." To turn a 12-gauge "cannon" loose among these unsuspicious birds, winnowing in over the decoys with friendly notes of greeting, is about as sportsmanslike as shooting into a bunch of chickens. To catch them with a camera requires skill and patience, and herein lies the hope for future existence of our disappearing wild life — substitution of the lens for the gun!

The call of the Dowitcher is a rather low-pitched series of whistles:— *pheu-pheu-pheu-pheu-pheu,* without the diminuendo of the Yellow-leg's notes.

The Long-billed Dowitcher (*Macrorhamphus griseus scolopaceus*) differs from the common Dowitcher in its larger size, richer coloration, and longer bill. But the two can only be unerringly separated by a close comparison with the specimens in the hand. The Long-billed Dowitcher is known locally as the Greater Long-beak, the Greater Gray-back, and the Red-bellied Snipe. It is found in western North America and South America; it is "supposed to be rare or casual on the Atlantic coast and declared to be the only representative of the genus in the west — which would be important if it were a fact. Nesting and habits same as stock form." (Coues.)

STILT SANDPIPER

Micropalama himantopus (*Bonaparte*)

A. O. U. Number 233 See Color Plates 33, 34

Other Names.— Long-legged Sandpiper; Frost Snipe; Mongrel; Bastard Yellow-legs.

General Description.— Length, 9 inches. Upper parts, in summer, mottled with blackish-brown, white, chestnut, and dusky; in winter, ashy-gray. Under parts, whitish barred with dark. Legs long and slender; toes webbed at base; bill long, slender, and *slightly curved.*

Color.— IN SUMMER: *Forehead, crown, a line from gape through eye broadening on side of head, rufous;* center of crown, dusky; a whitish streak from bill over and back of eye; upper parts, blackish-brown, each feather edged and tipped with white or chestnut; upper tail-coverts, barred with white and dusky; tail, mottled white and ash; wing-coverts, grayish, the feathers edged with lighter; primaries and secondaries, grayish-brown, latter edged with white; under parts from throat, whitish, sometimes with a pale rufous wash, spotted on breast, *barred everywhere below with brownish;* bill, dusky-greenish, darkening at tip; *legs, dusky yellowish-green;* iris, brown with a white crescent below. IN WINTER: Above, ashy-gray, crown narrowly streaked and feathers of back more broadly edged with lighter; wing-coverts, brownish-ash, the feathers lighter-edged; primaries and secondaries, dusky, the latter edged with whitish; a dusky streak from bill through and behind eye; under parts from chin, white, narrowly and thinly barred with dusky; bill, dusky; legs, dull brownish-yellow; iris, brown with a white crescent below.

Nest and Eggs.— NEST: A depression in the ground lined with a few leaves and grass. EGGS: 3 or 4, grayish-white or light drab, boldly marked with spots of chestnut, brown, and lavender, more numerous at the large end.

Distribution.— North and South America; breeds near the coast of Mackenzie and probably south to central Keewatin; winters in South America south to Uruguay and Chile; casual in winter in southern Texas and Mexico; in migration occurs in western Mississippi valley, West Indies, and Central America; less common on the Atlantic coast, and casual in British Columbia, Newfoundland, and Bermuda.

Although considered rare, the Stilt Sandpiper is more numerous along the Atlantic coast than is supposed, since it is frequently mistaken for the Yellow-legs by gunners or by those not trained to close observation. The similarity of the two species is acknowledged by the popular name, "Bastard Yellow-legs," which the sportsmen of Long Island have given to the Stilt Sandpiper. The different color of the long legs will always be a distinguishing mark, however, between these cousins.

It flies in flocks, or individuals may join forces with other species. A Stilt Sandpiper among a number of Semipalmated Sandpipers is instantly noted, his long legs raising his body conspicuously above his smaller companions. Its general habits of feeding are similar to those of the smaller Sandpiper.

KNOT

Tringa canutus *Linnæus*

A. O. U. Number 234 See Color Plates 33, 34

Other Names.— Red Sandpiper; Red-breasted Sandpiper; Red-breasted Plover; Freckled Sandpiper; Ash-colored Sandpiper; Canute's Sandpiper; Gray-back; Silver-back; Robin Snipe; White Robin Snipe; Robin-breast; Beach Robin; Red-breast; Buff-breast; Buff-breasted Plover; Horsefoot Snipe; White-bellied Snipe; May-bird; Blue Plover; Silver Plover.

General Description.— Length, 10 inches. In summer, color of upper parts grayish-brown and the breast rufous-brown; in winter, plain gray above and white below. Bill straight, longer than the head, and flattened and enlarged at tip; toes slender and not webbed at base.

Color.— Adults in Summer: Upper parts, grayish-brown narrowly streaked on crown and back of neck with dusky; feathers of back and shoulders, tipped and edged with grayish-white, those of shoulders, tinged with yellowish-brown; *rump and upper tail-coverts, white* with traverse bars of dusky-brown; tail, grayish edged with ashy-white; line over and back of eye, *sides of head, chin, throat, and under parts, plain rufous-brown* shading into lighter on flanks, into white on under tail-coverts; latter with arrowhead spots of dusky; wing-coverts and secondaries, grayish edged with lighter; primaries, plain dusky gray; bill and feet, greenish-black; iris, brown. Adults in Winter: *Above, plain grayish;* crown, streaked with darker gray, feathers of back, wing-coverts, and secondaries, edged, or not, with whiter; rump and upper tail-coverts, white with dusky spots and bars; primaries, dusky, lighter

Drawing by R. I. Brasher

KNOT (3/8 nat. size)

A bird that is known on the shores of every continent

tipped; *below, white;* sides of breast and sides, with dusky markings more distinct and wedge-shaped on sides; an indistinct dusky line from gape through and back of eye; legs and bill, dusky-greenish; iris, brown.

Nest and Eggs.— Nest: A depression in the ground, lined with grass. Eggs: 4, light pea-green, speckled with brown.

Distribution.— Northern and southern hemispheres; breeds from northern Ellesmere Land south to Melville Peninsula and Iceland, and also on Taimyr Peninsula, Siberia; winters south to southern Patagonia, and from the Mediterranean to South Africa, India, Australia, and New Zealand; casual in winter on the Atlantic coast of the United States; in migration occurs on the Atlantic coast of North America and over most of the eastern hemisphere; rare in the interior of North America and on the Pacific coast.

A flock of Knots tripping along the beach in their spring plumage with rufous breasts gives the observer the impression that some Robins have acquired nautical propensities and come down to the ocean for a change of food. While following the retreating surges gleaning minute crustacea left stranded by the recession of the waves they talk in soft low notes to one another and are so preoccupied that they often come within a few feet of a motionless watcher.

After nesting in the extreme North they return to the coast in the autumn with an entirely different dress, no longer with the robin's breast, but with a soft gray above and white below.

Like some other maritime birds, individuals often remain as far south as Long Island, New York, all summer, being apparently not interested in marital duties — wise bachelors or old maids who prefer a good table and comfortable climate to the long journey and inclemency of the Arctic Circle, where those with a proper sense of domestic responsibility settle down for a few weeks and raise a family.

When not harassed by gunners they are remarkably gentle and unsuspicious, and I have laid in a hollow scooped out of the sand while a flock fed all around me, one or two actually peeping over the edge of the pit, within three feet of my face!

The Knot is an industrious eater of grasshoppers which are injurious to crops, and of crawfishes which do much damage in rice and corn fields in the South and to levees by boring into and weakening them. It also feeds upon the marine worms which are destructive parasites of the oyster, and upon the diving beetles which prey upon the natural insect food of fish. For these services it is entitled at least to such protection as will guard against any decrease of the species. R. I. Brasher.

PURPLE SANDPIPER

Arquatella maritima maritima (*Brünnich*)

A. O. U. Number 235 See Color Plate 34

Other Names.— Rock Sandpiper; Rock Snipe; Rock Plover; Rock-bird; Rockweed Bird; Winter Rock-bird; Winter Snipe.

General Description.— Length, 9 inches. Principal colors, black and white. Legs short and strong. General build, short, thick, and squatty.

Color.— Adults in Summer: *Upper parts, black;* crown, streaked with yellowish or grayish-white; back and shoulders varied with chestnut, pale buff, or whitish, the reddish color on sides, the paler colors tipping the feathers; sides of head, with a rufous wash, separated from the crown by a whitish line; under parts, white shaded on throat and breast with tawny and here and there streaked with blackish; rest of lower parts with dusky-gray markings; rump and upper tail-coverts, plain dusky; wings, dusky; lesser wing-coverts, narrowly tipped with white; greater coverts, broadly tipped with the same; secondaries, mostly white increasing in size toward the inner feathers; inner tail-feathers, dusky; outer ones, gray. Adults in Winter: Entire upper parts, soft blackish-brown with purple reflections, each feather lighter bordered; greater and lesser wing-coverts, inner secondaries, and shoulders, edged and tipped with white; secondaries, broadly tipped with white; primaries, deep dusky; upper tail-coverts and middle tail-feathers, like color of back; outside tail-feathers, light ashy; throat and *breast, brownish-ash* shading into the white of rest of under parts; feathers of side, with wedge-shaped light dusky centers; lores, dusky; eye-ring, whitish; bill, yellow with dusky tip; feet, dull orange-red.

Nest and Eggs.— Nest: Slight depression in the ground, thinly lined with dry grass. Eggs: 4, grayish olive, boldly and distinctly marked with rich burnt umber over the entire surface.

Distribution.— Northern hemisphere; breeds from

Melville Island, Ellesmere Land, and northern Greenland south to Melville Peninsula, Cumberland Sound, and southern Greenland, and in Norway, Russia, Siberia, Iceland, and Faroe Islands; winters from southern Greenland and New Brunswick to Long Island; casual in migration to the Great Lakes, Georgia, Florida, and Bermuda, and in the Eastern Hemisphere south to Great Britain and the Mediterranean.

A member of the Snipe family feeding on the wintry beach seems almost as much out of place as a Hummingbird and the observer is likely to think the bird's journey has been interrupted by injury.

I have seen Purple Sandpipers on the rocky Maine coast in December, searching carefully in seaweed for their food and apparently indifferent to the cold. As nearly as I could make out they seemed to be feeding on small mussels and clams, which they swallowed shell and all.

Although nowhere common in America, since its principal line of migration follows through Norway into other parts of Europe, it can be found during the winter months as far south as Long Island, N. Y., where, like the Ipswich Sparrow, it is less rare than is generally supposed because few observers brave the open wind-swept dunes in winter.

Two varieties of the Purple Sandpiper occur in Alaska. These are the Aleutian Sandpiper (*Arquatella maritima couesi*) and the Pribilof or Black-breasted Sandpiper (*Arquatella maritima ptilocnemis*). When first described these two subspecies were supposed to be separate species from each other and from the Purple Sandpiper, although a close relationship between the three was acknowledged. Careful study has established their exact status. In their respective winter plumages the Aleutian and Purple Sandpipers are not distinguishable and in the other seasons there is very little real difference between them, but the Aleutian both breeds and winters within the boundaries of Alaska, occasionally straying over to Plover Bay, Siberia. The Pribilof Sandpiper breeds on the St. Lawrence, St. Matthew, and Pribilof islands and winters on the coast of southeastern Alaska.

R. I. Brasher.

PECTORAL SANDPIPER

Pisobia maculata (*Vieillot*)

A. O. U. Number 239 See Color Plate 35

Other Names.— Grass Snipe; Jack Snipe; Grass-bird; Meadow Snipe; Cow Snipe; Brownie; Brown-back; Triddler; Hay-bird; Fat-bird; Short-neck; Squat Snipe; Squatter; Krieker; Marsh Plover.

General Description.— Length, 9 inches. Color above, brownish-black; below, white marked with dusky on breast. *Tail double notched, the middle tail-feathers pointed and longer than all the others.*

Color.— Crown, streaked with blackish-brown and chestnut; sides of head, *neck, and breast, pale yellowish-brown, spotted with dusky brown; upper parts, brownish-black, each feather edged with ashy or chestnut,* shoulder feathers with lighter margins; outer upper tail-coverts, white with arrowhead spots of dusky; lesser coverts, brown with broad brownish-ash edges; secondaries and greater coverts, brownish, edged and tipped with white; primaries, dusky black; *central tail-feathers, brownish-black* with lighter edges; rest of tail-feathers, ashy, margined with white; throat, abdomen, and under tail-coverts, white; sides, yellowish-brown spotted with dusky; bill and legs, dusky-greenish; broad, indistinct stripe above, and a ring around, eye, whitish.

Nest and Eggs.— Nest: On the ground; a mere depression, sparsely lined with grass. Eggs: 4, greenish-drab, spotted and blotched with brown.

Distribution.— North and South America; breeds on the Arctic coast from northern Alaska to mouth of Yukon and northeastern Mackenzie; winters in South America from Peru and Bolivia to northern Chile, Argentina, and central Patagonia; in migration very rare on Pacific coast south of British Columbia, except in Lower California; common in fall migration in Mississippi valley and on the Atlantic coast, rare in spring; casual in northeastern Siberia, Unalaska, and Greenland; accidental in Hawaii and England.

"During the mating season the male Pectoral Sandpiper develops a great pouch, formed of the skin of the throat and breast, which he is able to inflate until it is nearly as large as the body. He now becomes a song bird, and flutters upward twenty or thirty yards in the air, as if emulating the famous Skylark, and, inflating his great pouch, glides down again to the ground; or he flies slowly along the ground, his head raised high and his tail hanging straight down, uttering a succession of booming notes. As he struts about the female his low notes swell and die away in musical cadences." (Forbush.)

Although migrating in flocks the "Kriekers" scatter when a good feeding meadow is reached, and are generally flushed from the grass singly. They prefer the bayside meadows, and are seldom seen along the margins of ponds or on the beaches. It is probable that they "fatten up" on some favorite food further north, for they are extremely fat when they arrive on the Long Island (N. Y.) marshes in September. They "lie" well, flushing within easy gunshot range with a flight similar to that of Wilson's Snipe but less rapid. The zigzags are shorter, the course rapidly straightens out, and if the "sportsman" waits a few seconds after they spring, it is not difficult to add them to the "bag." When the early morning mists of September hang low over the meadows Pectoral Sandpipers, magnified by the fog, appear nearly as large as Wilson's Snipe.

R. I. Brasher.

WHITE-RUMPED SANDPIPER

Pisobia fuscicollis (*Vieillot*)

A. O. U. Number 240 See Color Plate 35

Other Names.— Bonaparte's Sandpiper; Schintz's Sandpiper; Sand-bird; Bull Peep.

General Description.— Length, 7 inches. In summer, the upper parts pale brownish with dusky stripes and the lower parts white with brownish markings; in winter, brownish-ash above and whitish below. Middle tail-feathers pointed and longer than others.

Color.— Adults in Summer: Crown and upper parts, pale brownish, each feather with a large dusky center, forming stripes on back; crown, striped with dark brown; shoulders, more chestnut; *rump and upper tail-coverts, white;* central tail-feathers, brownish-black, the rest light grayish, broadly edged and tipped with white; sides of head, neck, and breast, washed with pale yellowish-brown, spotted with darker; an indistinct dark brown streak from bill through and behind eye; wing-coverts and secondaries, grayish-brown edged with lighter; primaries, dusky; chin and throat, white; abdomen and rest of under parts, white; bill and feet, dusky-greenish; iris, brown surrounded by a white ring. Adults in Winter: *Crown, back of neck, back, and shoulders, brownish-ash,* indistinctly streaked with darker; *rump and upper tail-coverts, white;* central tail-feathers, dusky; the rest, light ash; some feathers of shoulder and back, deep chestnut edged with white; wing, as in summer; a broad streak over eye, chin, throat, and under parts in general, whitish faintly spotted with pale brown; a streak from bill through and behind eye, dark brownish-ash; bill, dusky horn, lighter at base; feet, dusky-greenish; iris, brown surrounded by a white ring.

Nest and Eggs.— Nest: A depression in the ground lined with a few leaves. Eggs: 4, light olive or olive-brown, boldly spotted and marked with deep sepia, chiefly at large end.

Distribution.— North and South America; breeds along the Arctic coast from northwestern Mackenzie to Cumberland Island; has occurred in summer west to Point Barrow and east to Greenland; winters from Paraguay to southern Patagonia and the Falkland Islands; in migration most abundant in the Mississippi valley, less so on the Atlantic coast; casual in the Bermudas, Great Britain, the West Indies, and Central America.

The White-rumped Sandpiper is usually found among the Least and Semipalmated Sandpipers tripping over awash seaweed or running along the shore. They seldom associate with flocks of their own kind, but prefer the company of other species. In autumn plumage they can be easily confused with the smaller Sandpipers, but close scrutiny will reveal the white upper tail-coverts — a conspicuous identification mark. Their habits are similar to those of other members of the family and they are naturally unsuspicious unless repeatedly disturbed.

An important part of the diet of the White-rumped Sandpiper consists of grasshoppers of species known to be injurious to crops. This is a real service to man which should not be overlooked when measures for the adequate protection of the birds are considered.

BAIRD'S SANDPIPER

Pisobia bairdi (*Coues*)

A. O. U. Number 241 See Color Plate 35

Other Name.— Grass-bird.

General Description.— Length, 7 inches. Color above, brownish-black; below, white with pale brownish on breast. Resembles the Pectoral Sandpiper but smaller and breast less heavily streaked.

Color.— ADULTS: Entire upper parts, brownish-black, each feather bordered and tipped with light reddish-yellow, these tips broader and nearly pure white on shoulders; coverts and secondaries like back, latter lighter tipped; central tail-feathers, brownish-black; remainder, successively lighter, all narrowly bordered with white; *breast pale brownish with faint spots and streaks of dusky;* throat and under parts, white; bill and legs, dusky; iris, brown. YOUNG IN AUTUMN: Sides of head, throat, breast, and upper parts, including wings, nearly uniform pale yellowish-brown, each feather darker centrally; crown (strongly), sides of head, throat, and breast (more faintly), streaked or spotted with brown; rest of under parts, white; bill, dusky, lighter at base; legs, dull olive.

Nest and Eggs.— NEST: A depression in the ground under shelter of tuft of grass, lined with a few leaves and grasses. EGGS: 4, buffy, spotted with shades of chestnut-brown.

Distribution.— North and South America; breeds along the Arctic coast from Point Barrow to northern Keewatin; winters in Chile, Argentina, and Patagonia: occurs regularly in migration from the Rocky Mountains to the Mississippi River, and in Central America and northern South America, and irregularly in autumn on the Pacific coast from Alaska to Lower California and on the Atlantic coast from Nova Scotia to New Jersey; casual in summer in Guerrero, Mexico; accidental in England and South Africa.

Although it is slightly larger than the Least and Semipalmated Sandpipers it is not easy to distinguish the Baird's Sandpiper from those species. Its general color in the field is more yellowish-brown and it is found almost exclusively along the prairie sloughs and lagoons of the Middle West. Its habits are similar to other small Sandpipers; it runs along the shore in the same confiding way, and unless frightened will sometimes feed almost at the observer's feet.

LEAST SANDPIPER

Pisobia minutilla (*Vieillot*)

A. O. U. Number 242 See Color Plate 35

Other Names.— Peep; Wilson's Stint; Ox-eye; Mud-peep; Sand-peep; Little Sand-peep.

General Description.— Length, 6 inches; the smallest Sandpiper, and not heavier than an English Sparrow. Color above, grayish-brown; below, white with the breast darker. Much like the Semipalmated Sandpiper, but the feet with *no* webs.

Color.— ADULTS IN SUMMER: *Entire upper parts, dusky brown* striped on head and neck with chestnut, each feather on back and shoulders edged with chestnut and tipped with whitish; center tail-feathers, blackish edged with chestnut, others, gray edged with white; wing-coverts and secondaries, brownish edged with bay; secondaries, tipped with white; primaries, dusky; breast, washed with pale rusty and spotted with brown; a diffuse streak from bill through and back of eye, dusky; bill and *legs, dusky greenish;* iris, brown with white eye-ring; throat, abdomen, and rest of under parts, white. ADULTS IN WINTER: Entire upper parts, pale grayish-brown, each feather darker centrally; secondaries and primaries, white-tipped; breast, shaded with very pale brownish-gray, spotting obsolete; bill as in summer; *feet, yellowish-green.*

Nest and Eggs.— NEST: Near water; a mere depression in the ground, lined with leaves and grass. EGGS: 3 or 4, creamy-buff to light drab, heavily spotted with chestnut and lavender.

Distribution.— North and South America; breeds from northwestern Alaska, southern Arctic islands, and northern Ungava to Yakutat Bay, Alaska, valley of the Upper Yukon, northern Mackenzie, central Keewatin, southern Ungava, Nova Scotia, and Sable Island; winters from California, Texas, and North Carolina through the West Indies and Central America to Brazil, Chile, and the Galapagos; in migration occurs throughout the United States and west to northeastern Siberia and the Commander Islands, north to Greenland, and in Bermuda; accidental in Europe.

To the lover of unspoiled Nature our grand open sea beaches would not seem like the real thing were it not possible at times to see flocks of innocent little Sandpipers running gracefully along the margin, chased by the advancing waves. The tiniest atom of its tribe, the Least Sandpiper, accompanied by several other kinds, is still with us, and is perhaps increasing, thanks to the outlawry of shooting them under the Federal Law. It will be a sorry day when we need such tiny things for food, each one affording but a mere taste.

Drawing by R. I. Brasher

LEAST SANDPIPER ($\frac{2}{3}$ nat. size)

The baby among shore birds

This species and the Semipalmated Sandpiper consort together and resemble each other so closely that it is hard at a distance to tell them apart. There is a slight distinction in habit, in that the Least Sandpiper is more apt to be found on marshes, while the other prefers the beach, though there is no certain distinguishing of them in this way. As things go, they are comparatively common in May and again in August and the first part of September quite generally over the country, wherever there are any considerable bodies of water, particularly on both our seacoasts, also in the Mississippi valley, and on the shallow prairie sloughs of the Northwest.

Whereas most of the larger shore birds cross to the interior of the continent to breed, the Sandpipers as a class seem not to avoid the northern Atlantic coast in the spring flight and in the nesting season. This is true of the Least Sandpiper. Though it breeds in the far Northwest, it also does so on our eastern coasts, well to the north.

It was my good fortune to be able to study its nesting habits when I found it breeding on the Magdalen Islands, Gulf of St. Lawrence. Picture there, on these islands, broad expanses of meadowy country, carpeted with short grass and moss, interspersed with patches of low spruce and juniper, and dotted with small shallow ponds. Here, in early June, we may listen to a sweet, twittering little song, and spy the author, not a Warbler but our little Sandpiper, the male bird, circling about on quivering wings, singing to his little mate who loiters on the edge of a

Photo by H. K. Job Courtesy of Houghton Mifflin Co.

AN ANXIOUS MOTHER

Least Sandpiper watching the photographer near her babies

One day, a June 13, a tiny bird fluttered almost from beneath the feet of my companion, and there was our first nest of the Least Sandpiper, a little hollow in the northern moss, lined with dry bayberry leaves, and holding four eggs, large for the size of the bird, and wide across, though somewhat pointed. The tiny owners trailed around at our feet in abject despair. Finally we compromised by persuading the female to allow me to photograph her on the nest, after which we parted company.

On another occasion, beside the crude cart-road leading to the fisherman's house where we were staying, a pair of these birds appeared greatly worried over our passing. They ran about, alighted on the wire fence, and scolded plaintively. This set us to searching, but it was some time before I discovered the four tiny young, very recently hatched, huddled together on the ground among the sparse grass of the adjoining pasture, and a tell-tale egg-shell near by. Little buff-colored balls of down, ornamented with black spots, they were as pretty bird-babies as I have ever seen. Somehow, these episodes with breeding shore birds of Arctic proclivities, in this crisp northern clime, appealed to me with very special fascination.

HERBERT K. JOB.

RED-BACKED SANDPIPER

Pelidna alpina sakhalina (*Vieillot*)

A. O. U. Number 243a See Color Plates 33, 34

Other Names.— American Dunlin; Black-bellied Sandpiper; Brant-bird; Red-back; Red-backed Dunlin; Lead-back; Ox-bird; Fall Snipe; Crooked-billed Snipe; Crooked-bill; Little Blackbreast; Winter Snipe; Simpleton; Stib; Black-heart Plover (Ontario).

General Description.— Length, 9 inches. In summer, upper parts chestnut and the lower parts white with a black patch; in winter, upper parts dark ashy-gray, under parts pale ashy-white. Bill, rather long and terminal third bent slightly downward.

Color.—ADULTS IN SUMMER: *Crown, back, shoulders, rump, and upper tail-coverts, chestnut,* crown, streaked with dusky, rest of feathers of upper parts with dusky centers, many with whitish tips (especially behind); tail, wing-coverts, and secondaries, ashy-gray; *secondaries, broadly white-tipped,* coverts with darker centers; primaries dusky, some inner ones edged with white at base; sides of head, back of neck, chin, throat, and rest of under parts, white; *abdomen, with a broad velvety-black patch;* other whitish parts above, streaked with pale dusky; bill, dusky-yellow; legs, dark horn-color; iris, brown with a dusky spot in front. ADULTS IN WINTER: Entire upper parts, dark ashy-gray, lightening over eye and streaked with whitish on back of neck; feathers of back, faintly outlined with lighter; wing-coverts and secondaries, more brownish; feathers, darker centrally, secondaries narrowly white-tipped; primaries, deep dusky, the inner ones whitish at base forming a conspicuous *white spot;* chin, throat, and rest of under parts, pale ashy-white; black area of summer plumage entirely absent; under parts from throat, obsoletely streaked with dusky; bill and legs, dusky-greenish; iris, brown.

Nest and Eggs.— NEST: A hollow in the ground, in or near salt marshes or fresh-water lakes and ponds. EGGS: 4, pale greenish to brownish-buff, spotted with dull umber, chestnut, and sepia.

Distribution.— North America and eastern Asia; breeds on the northern coast of Siberia west to mouth of the Yenisei, and from Point Barrow to mouth of Yukon, and in Boothia and Melville peninsulas, and northern Ungava; winters on the Pacific coast from Washington to southern Lower California and from New Jersey (rarely Massachusetts) south to Louisiana and southern Texas, and in Asia from China and Japan to the Malay Archipelago; rare in migration in the interior of the United States except about the southern end of Lake Michigan.

Although the Red-backed Sandpiper is found often in the interior of North America, in New England it is confined mainly to the neighborhood of the sea and largely to the salt marshes, but also frequents sand bars and mud flats. It is an active little bird usually keeping in companies, which run about nimbly and fly very rapidly, performing varied evolutions in concert, as if drilled to act together. In the breeding season it has a rather musical flight song, which never is heard except in its northern home, so far as I know. When frightened or flying it has a hoarse, grating note.

There seem to be two well-defined migration routes of this species: one from Alaska and Siberia down the Pacific coast of North America, and one from Hudson Bay, Ungava, and the lands to the north down the Atlantic coast.

The Atlantic birds winter mainly in the United States, and the Pacific birds are common in winter only as far south as southern California. The future of this species, therefore, is in our hands. It can be protected or exterminated by the people of the United States and Canada. In spring the eastern migration passes more to the westward, and the species appears in numbers on the Great Lakes, becoming rare to the northeast of Massachusetts.

The Red-backed Sandpiper feeds largely on worms, crustaceans, and insects.

EDWARD HOWE FORBUSH, in *Game Birds, Wild-Fowl and Shore Birds.*

SEMIPALMATED SANDPIPER

Ereunetes pusillus (*Linnæus*)

A. O. U. Number 246 See Color Plate 35

Other Names.— Peep; Little Peep; Sand-peep; Black-legged Peep; Ox-eye; Sand Ox-eye.

General Description.— Length, 6½ inches. Principal color above, chestnut; below, white with spots on breast. *Toes, webbed at base;* bill, straight and enlarged at tip; tail, double-notched.

Color.— ADULTS IN SUMMER: Above, varied with black, pale chestnut, ashy, and white, each feather dusky centrally with a reddish edge and whitish tip; *rump and upper tail-coverts, dusky,* more whitish on sides; central tail-feathers, brown, others, ashy-gray; wing-coverts and secondaries, brownish and rufous, edged with lighter; primaries, plain dusky; a dusky line from gape through and behind eye and a white line above; lower parts, pure white tinged with pale rufous on breast, where spotted with pale dusky; bill, black; legs, dusky green; iris, brown. ADULTS IN WINTER: Above, plain ashy, the feathers lighter-tipped; light ends of secondaries, less conspicuous as is also the line through eye; under parts, pure white with dusky spotting very faint; bill, legs, and iris, as in summer.

Nest and Eggs.— NEST: A hollow in the ground, lined with dry grass. EGGS: 3 or 4, from grayish to olive, usually boldly spotted and splashed with brown or chestnut, but sometimes finely dotted over entire surface.

Distribution.— North and South America; breeds from the Arctic coast of North America south to mouth of Yukon and to southern Ungava; winters from Texas and South Carolina through West Indies and Central America to Patagonia; migrates mainly east of the Rocky Mountains; casual in British Columbia, Pribilof Islands, and northeastern Siberia; accidental in Europe.

Photograph by H. K. Job

TURNSTONES AND SEMIPALMATED SANDPIPERS

The Semipalmated Sandpiper is a sociable little bird usually found in company with other small Sandpipers, especially in that of the Least Sandpiper to which it is similar in general habits and appearance. It is partial to the open sand beaches — following the receding waves, seizing its minute crustacean food from the backwash, and cleverly eluding the returning surf. It is more of a sand bird and less of a mud bird than the Least Sandpiper. Positive identification in life is impossible unless a very close view is obtained, enabling the observer to see the semi-webbed feet.

It is constantly on the move, but, notwithstanding its great activity, it becomes very fat when food is abundant. On a windy day I have seen little groups of them settle down under the lee of a marsh tussock, preening their feathers and indulging in a siesta of repletion, keeping up a continuous peeping of contentment. These loafing spells become more frequent as the autumn days wane, and they are loath to leave a sunny nook under a bank sheltered from the strong northwest wind. I have sailed a sharpie within ten feet before they would take wing with querulous *tu-weets tu-weets* of resentment.

In its winter plumage the Western Sandpiper (*Ereunetes mauri*) can only be distinguished from the Semipalmated by its longer bill; in the summer the color of its upper parts is richer and more rusty with stronger markings. The curious and remarkable thing about this bird is that while it breeds in a narrow strip of territory along the northwestern coast of Alaska, it is a common winter resident in the south-eastern United States from North Carolina to Florida and Louisiana.

This long journey across the continent is not paralleled by any other shore bird; it is, however, comparable to that of several species of ducks. Just what route this migration follows is unknown as there are no records from the interior to show which way the birds passed. The Western Sandpiper also winters from Lower California to Venezuela. The individuals that pass the winter in eastern South America probably migrate over the seas from Florida.

R. I. Brasher.

SANDERLING

Calidris leucophæa (*Pallas*)

A. O. U. Number 248 See Color Plates 33, 34

Other Names.— Ruddy Plover; Beach-bird; Surf Snipe; White Snipe; Beach Plover; Whitey; Bull Peep.

General Description.— Length, 8 inches. In summer, principal color above, chestnut; in winter, pale bluish-ash. Under parts always white, but the breast finely spotted in summer. *Only three toes* (hind toe missing); front toes with narrow marginal webs.

Color.— Adults in Summer: Entire upper parts, varied with black, ash, and chestnut, on back and shoulders each feather black centrally, broadly margined with reddish and tipped with white; wing-coverts, secondaries, and primaries ashy, the feathers lighter on edges of coverts, *secondaries, white-tipped,* and *a white spot at base of primaries;* rump, upper tail-coverts, and central tail-feathers, dusky, tipped and edged with ashy white; rest of tail-feathers nearly white; under parts, white, finely spotted with dusky and chestnut on sides of throat and breast; bill and legs, dusky; iris, brown. Adults in Winter: Upper parts, pale bluish-ash, the crown narrowly streaked with darker and the feathers on back fading into white on edges; shoulders and inner secondaries, with darker centers; wing-coverts, like back; *secondaries, largely white;* primaries, dusky, whitening at base; an indistinct dusky line from bill through eye; line above eye, cheeks, and entire under parts, pure white; bill and legs, black; iris, brown.

Nest and Eggs.— Nest: A depression in the ground, lined with grass or leaves. Eggs: 4, light olive-brown, speckled and spotted with different shades of brown, chiefly at large end.

Distribution.— Northern and southern hemispheres; breeds from Melville Island, Ellesmere Land, and northern Greenland to Point Barrow, Alaska, northern Mackenzie, Iceland, and in northern Siberia; winters from central California, Texas, Virginia, and Bermuda to Patagonia, and casually to Massachusetts and Washington; also from the Mediterranean, Burma, and Japan to South Africa and various Pacific islands, including Hawaii.

In the sunny days of September, where the white-maned horses of the sea, urged onward by the winds, charge in long rows and thunder down upon the sands of Cape Cod, the Sanderling is in its element. Matching the very sand in color it is almost invisible while squatted on the upper beach at high tide, waiting for the recession of the waters; but as the ebb begins, the little flock scatters along the shore, retreating before each wave, following down the backwash, until sometimes forced to fly by the oncoming surge, intent upon the flotsam and jetsam of the sea washed up for their delectation, spread for a brief moment upon the sloping sands and then carried back into the deep. The Sanderling neglects no opportunity. It follows its prey at times until up to its breast in the wave but always nimbly avoids immersion. Because of this habit, the Sanderling is beter known to many as the Surf Snipe. If disturbed the little flock rises, flies out over the surf and turns, flying up or down the beach, now low in some great sea hollow, now just skimming the crest of a foaming breaker, but they soon swing in again and dropping upon the sands resume their absorbing occupation.

The Sanderling's common note is a sharp *chit.* The bird may be distinguished from the little "Sand-peeps," which it much resembles, by its larger size, and from other Sandpipers by its light color and whitish head. When in flight it shows a line of conspicuous white spots on the wing. When in hand it may be readily distinguished from all other Sandpipers by the lack of a hind toe — a characteristic of the Plovers. In the spring and autumn migrations the Sanderling is not uncommon on the Great Lakes and is recorded from various parts of the Mississippi valley, but the sea is its first love. Its flights are largely made over the ocean and it can rest on the water if necessary and swim with the ease of a duck.

EDWARD HOWE FORBUSH.

HUDSONIAN GODWIT

Limosa hæmastica (*Linnæus*)

A. O. U. Number 251 See Color Plate 38

Other Names.— Red-breasted Godwit; Ring-tailed Marlin; Spot-rump; Field Marlin; Goose-bird; Black-tailed Godwit; Black-tail; American Black-tailed Godwit; White-rump; Smaller Dough- or Doe-bird.

General Description.— Length, 16 inches. In summer, color of upper parts brownish-black mottled with lighter colors, under parts, chestnut; in winter, upper parts plain dull ashy, under parts lighter ash shaded with buffy; always a white spot just above the tail.

Color.— ADULTS IN SUMMER: Upper parts brownish-black with greenish gloss, variegated with rufous, yellowish, or white, lighter colors scalloping edges of feathers; *rump, blackish; upper tail-coverts, conspicuously white;* tail, black, white at base and white-tipped; head and neck, streaked with dusky; *under parts, rich chestnut crossed with numerous black bars,* these bars tending to spots on breast and neck; rear under parts, crossed also with white bars; bill, pale reddish, terminal third black; legs, bluish-gray; iris, brown. ADULTS IN WINTER: General plumage, plain dull ashy lightening on head, neck, and under parts where shaded with pale buffy; tail, as in summer; *upper tail-coverts, conspicuously white;* bill, flesh-colored with dusky tip; feet, bluish-gray. Plumages intermediate between the two are common.

Nest and Eggs.— NEST: A hollow scooped out of the ground, lined with a few leaves and grasses. EGGS: 4, dark olive-drab marked with still darker brownish shade of the ground color.

Distribution.— North and South America; breeds from the lower Anderson River southeast to central Keewatin; winters in Argentina, Patagonia, and the Falkland Islands; in migration occurs principally east of the Great Plains, most commonly on the Atlantic coast in autumn and in the Mississippi valley in spring; casual in Alaska.

The Godwits constitute a genus (*Limosa*) of the Snipe and Sandpiper family, and include about half a dozen species of which two are American birds. Two others, the Pacific Godwit (*Limosa lapponica baueri*) and the Black-tailed Godwit (*Limosa limosa*), are included in check-lists of North American avifauna — the first because a few individuals have strayed from Siberia to the islands off Alaska and there reproduced their kind, and the second because of its accidental occurrence in Greenland. The Godwits are characterized by a very long and slightly upward-curved bill, which is grooved nearly to the tip; the shanks are partly bare; the middle or outer toes are partly webbed; the wings are long and pointed; the tail in length equals or somewhat exceeds the wing. Their prevailing color is reddish or brownish, but there is considerable variation of color according to age, sex, and season.

Marked peculiarities of the genus are that the females are larger than the males, and that incubation is performed by the males. The birds are found in marshes, salt-water meadows, and along the shores of bays or lakes. They place their nests on the ground, but not invariably near water, and lay three or four eggs, of a generally drab hue, marked with dark brown. Their food, which consists of aquatic insects, shell-fish, worms and the like, they capture by probing the sand or mud with their long bills, or by following retreating waves and snatching up the small creatures thus left stranded.

Of the Hudsonian Godwit Mr. Forbush says: "During my boyhood I frequently heard old gunners about Boston tell their tales of the Goose-bird which was well and favorably known all along our coast. But it is impossible now to tell with certainty whether these tales referred to one or both of the Godwits. The Hudsonian Godwit is now less rare than the larger species, but few are seen or taken regularly on the Massachusetts coast. It is shy, like its larger relative, but a good bird caller finds no difficulty in luring it to his decoys.

"The breeding range and migration of this species are more or less shrouded in mystery. The eggs have been found once by MacFarlane in the Anderson River region, which proves that the birds breed near the coast of the Arctic Sea, and that is about all we know of its breeding range, except that it summers in Keewatin. We must assume that the species goes to South America by sea, like the Eskimo Curlew, and lands on Cape Cod and Long Island in numbers only when driven there by storms. It was considered rare by Wilson and Audubon, as it probably never was seen on the coast of the Middle and Southern States in any numbers unless driven in by a severe storm." (*Game Birds, Wild Fowl and Shore Birds.*)

The Hudsonian Godwit feeds to a considerable extent upon mosquitoes and horse-flies, as examination of its stomach has amply proved. It is therefore to be counted a useful bird, since the insects it destroys are known to be harmful.

MARBLED GODWIT

Limosa fedoa (*Linnæus*)

A. O. U. Number 249 See Color Plate 38

Other Names.— Great Marbled Godwit; Great Godwit; Red Curlew; Brant-bird; Marlin; Red Marlin; Brown Marlin; Spike-billed Curlew; Spike-bill; Badger-bird; Dough- or Doe-bird.

General Description.— Length, 21 inches; largest shore bird, except the Long-billed Curlew. Prevailing color, reddish, darker above; no white spot at base of tail. Bill curved slightly upward.

Color.— A light dull yellowish-rufous, browner and richer above but varying much in intensity with individuals; broad line over eye, sides of head, chin, and upper throat, more whitish; an indistinct dusky line from bill through and behind eye; crown, brownish; neck all around, spotted with dusky; upper parts with brownish-black center on each feather; rump, tail-coverts, and tail, barred with blackish and brown; primaries, rufous, outer webs and ends of a few outer ones dusky; *throat, breast, and sides, traversely barred with brown, the markings narrow;* bill, flesh-colored, dusky on ridge and terminal half; legs, bluish-ash; iris, brown.

Nest and Eggs.— Nest: On the ground in a dry field but not far from water; a depression, lined with grass. Eggs: 4, creamy-buff to light olive-drab, thickly spotted with various shades of umber brown.

Distribution.— North America; breeds from valley of the Saskatchewan south to North Dakota (formerly to Iowa and Wisconsin); winters from southern Lower California, Louisiana, Florida, and Georgia to Guatemala and Belize; casual in California in winter; in migration occurs on Pacific coast north to British Columbia, and on the Atlantic coast to the Maritime Provinces (formerly) and south to the Lesser Antilles; accidental in Alaska.

My first acquaintance with the Marbled Godwit was one beautiful June day in North Dakota, when I was wading in a large slough, deep not only in mud and water, but in the delights of inspecting nests of Canvas-back, Redhead, Ruddy Duck, and various other interesting water birds. All at once I began to hear loud outcries, and a flock of about twenty big brown birds with long straight bills swept past me and alighted in the grass just back from the shore. In great excitement I followed, and with my binoculars had a splendid view of them as they strode about on their stilt-like legs and caught insects.

Not until I visited Saskatchewan did I locate their breeding-grounds. There I found them nesting in scattered pairs, véry commonly over the dry prairies. Like the large Curlew, they are partial to an alkaline country. Though they are always in the general vicinity of some slough, their actual nesting is back on the dry prairie.

Photo by H. K. Job Courtesy of Outing Pub. Co.

GREAT MARBLED GODWIT

On Saskatchewan prairie

Amid the rather short dry prairie grass a slight hollow is selected, a frail nest of grass constructed, and four large handsome eggs are deposited the latter part of May or early in June. The nest is not especially concealed, except by the vastness of the surroundings and the blending coloration of the brooding bird, who sits quite close, so that the nest is found largely by accident. One day while driving our team and outfit over the trackless prairie, we were startled by an almost human scream, as a large brown bird fluttered from under the feet of the horses. Lucky it was that the nest was not trampled, so I was able to take photographs of it. My companion on the trip, A. C. Bent, afterwards found another nest on which the female sat so persistently that actually he lifted her from it by hand without having her make the slightest effort to escape.

When the young are hatched, the birds become almost as violent and noisy in their demonstrations as the Willet. They follow one around on the prairie, flying about, alighting nearby, and trotting off, ever shrieking that incessant din of *god-wit, god-wit,* from which I assume their name may have been derived. On one occasion a Godwit followed me nearly all day and kept up this screaming, until in the afternoon it got so hoarse that its voice would break into a sort of gasp or croak, as though it had a bad cold. Hence I nicknamed this absurd creature my "Catarrh-bird." Under these circumstances they were so tame that I was able to take with a reflecting camera all the photographs of them that I needed.

Formerly this species was quite abundant along the Atlantic coast on its migrations, whereas now it is only an accidental straggler. I have seen a few in winter in Louisiana, but most of them migrate beyond our borders to warmer climes. It is a handsome, interesting species which, like nearly all the larger shore birds, is in danger of extermination unless the radical measures already enacted are rigidly enforced.

HERBERT K. JOB.

The Marbled Godwit is of very real service to farmers by reason of the fact that it feeds freely upon various species of grasshoppers which are very injurious to crops. It should, therefore, receive adequate protection, especially during its breeding season.

GREATER YELLOW-LEGS

Totanus melanoleucus (*Gmelin*)

A. O. U. Number 254 See Color Plate 36

Other Names.— Big Tell-tale; Greater Tell-tale; Tell-tale Godwit; Yellow-shins; Winter Yellow-legs; Big Yellow-legs; Big Yellow-legged Plover; Greater Yellow-shanks; Cucu; Big Cucu; Long-legged Tattler; Stone-bird; Stone Snipe; Yelper.

General Description.— Length, 15 inches. Color above, blackish-brown; below, white with brown spots on breast and neck. Bill longer than head, slender, and either straight or with end half very slightly curved upward; *legs and toes long and slender.*

GREEN HERON *Butorides virescens virescens* (Linnaeus) IMMATURE ADULT

LEAST BITTERN *Ixobrychus exilis* (Gmelin) FEMALE MALE

AMERICAN BITTERN *Botaurus lentiginosus* (Montagu)

All ¼ nat. size

AMERICAN EGRET
Herodias egretta (Gmelin)
SANDHILL CRANE
Grus mexicana (Müller)

BLACK-CROWNED NIGHT HERON
Nycticorax nycticorax naevius (Boddaert)
ADULT IMMATURE
GREAT BLUE HERON
Ardea herodias herodias Linnaeus
ADULT IN SUMMER IMMATURE

All ½ nat. size

Courtesy of the New York State Museum

VIRGINIA RAIL *Rallus virginianus* Linnaeus
DOWNY YOUNG — ADULT

IMMATURE

KING RAIL *Rallus elegans* Audubon

CLAPPER RAIL *Rallus crepitans crepitans* Gmelin

All ½ nat. size

Courtesy of the New York State Museum

YELLOW RAIL
Coturnicops noveboracensis (Gmelin)
ADULT
DOWNY YOUNG of Little Black Rail

BLACK RAIL
Creciscus jamaicensis (Gmelin)
ADULT

SORA
Porzana carolina (Linnaeus)
ADULT
DOWNY YOUNG

All ¾ nat. size

Courtesy of the New York State Museum

PURPLE GALLINULE
Ionornis martinicus (Linnaeus)

FLORIDA GALLINULE
Gallinula galeata (Lichtenstein)

AMERICAN COOT
Fulica americana Gmelin
ADULT DOWNY YOUNG

All ⅖ nat. size

Courtesy of the New York State Museum

RED PHALAROPE *Phalaropus fulicarius* (Linnaeus)

FEMALE — MALE — AUTUMN AND WINTER PLUMAGE

All ¾ nat. size

Courtesy of the New York State Museum

FEMALE

NORTHERN PHALAROPE *Lobipes lobatus* (Linnaeus)
AUTUMN AND WINTER PLUMAGE

MALE

All ⅗ nat. size

Courtesy of the New York State Museum

WILSON'S PHALAROPE *Steganopus tricolor* Vieillot

AUTUMN AND WINTER PLUMAGE — FEMALE — MALE

All ⅔ nat. size

Courtesy of the New York State Museum

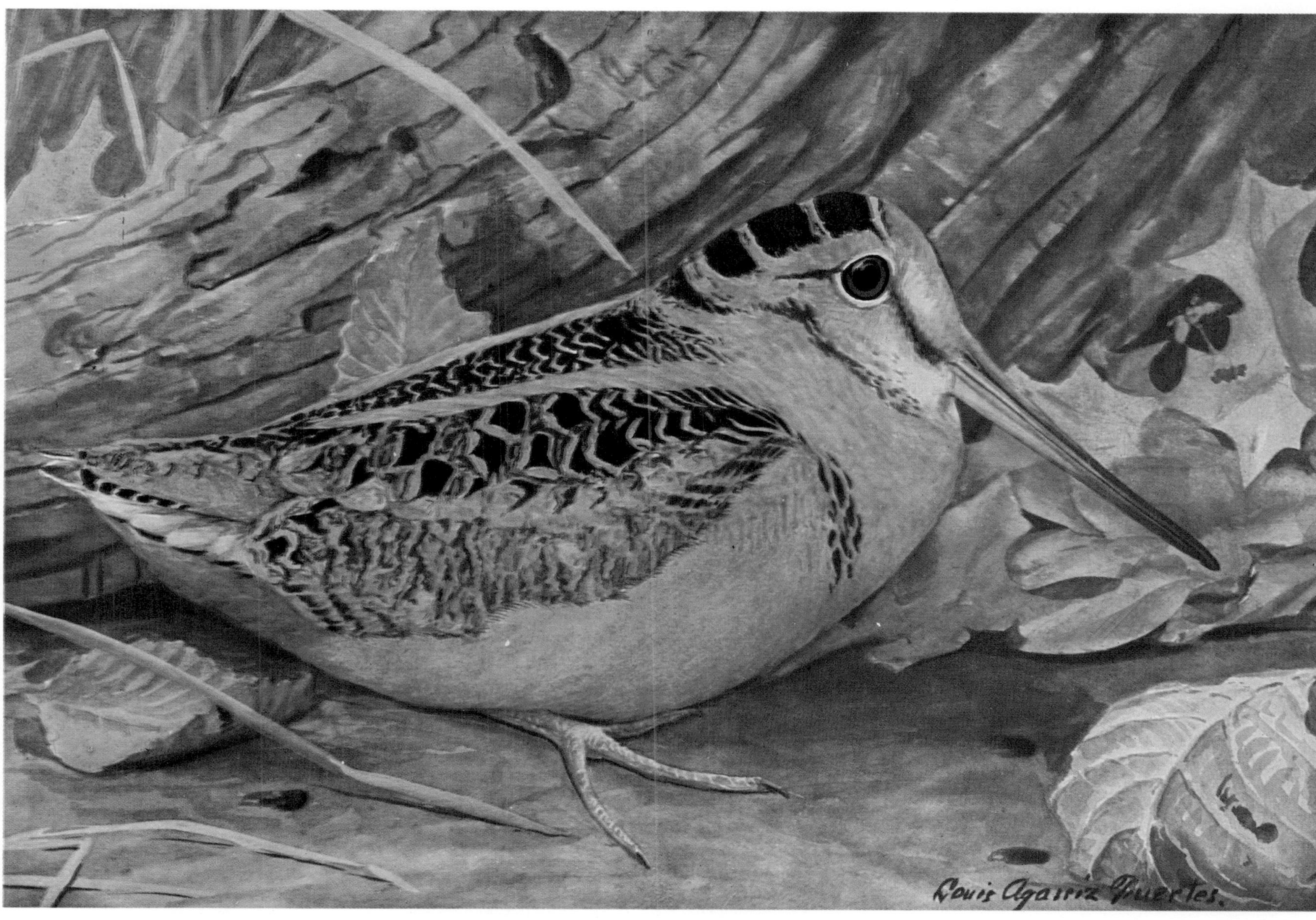

AMERICAN WOODCOCK *Philohela minor* (Gmelin)

⅞ nat. size

Courtesy of the New York State Museum

WILSON'S SNIPE *Gallinago delicata* (Ord)

⅞ nat. size

Courtesy of the New York State Museum

RUDDY TURNSTONE
Arenaria interpres morinella (Linnaeus)
SANDERLING
Calidris leucophaea (Pallas)

STILT SANDPIPER
Micropalama himantopus (Bonaparte)

RED-BACKED SANDPIPER
Peliana alpina sakhalina (Vieillot)

KNOT
Tringa canutus Linnaeus

DOWITCHER
Macrorhamphus griseus griseus (Gmelin)

BREEDING PLUMAGES
All ½ nat. size

Courtesy of the New York State Museum

PURPLE SANDPIPER
Arquatella maritima maritima (Brünnich)
SANDERLING
Calidris leucophaea (Pallas)

RED-BACKED SANDPIPER
Pelidna alpina sakhalina (Vieillot)
STILT SANDPIPER
Micropalama himantopus (Bonaparte)

DOWITCHER
Macrorhamphus griseus griseus (Gmelin)
KNOT
Tringa canutus Linnaeus

AUTUMN AND WINTER PLUMAGES
All ½ nat. size

Courtesy of the New York State Museum

PECTORAL SANDPIPER *Pisobia maculata* (Vieillot)

WHITE-RUMPED SANDPIPER *Pisobia fuscicollis* (Vieillot) SPRING AUTUMN

BAIRD'S SANDPIPER *Pisobia bairdi* (Coues)

LEAST SANDPIPER *Pisobia minutilla* (Vieillot) AUTUMN SPRING

SEMIPALMATED SANDPIPER *Ereunetes pusillus* (Linnaeus) SPRING AUTUMN

All ½ nat. size

SOLITARY SANDPIPER
Helodromas solitarius solitarius (Wilson)

GREATER YELLOW-LEGS
Totanus melanoleucus (Gmelin)

SPOTTED SANDPIPER
Actitis macularia (Linnaeus)
IMMATURE — ADULT

YELLOW-LEGS
Totanus flavipes (Gmelin)

SUMMER PLUMAGES
All ½ nat. size

Courtesy of the New York State Museum

WILLET
Catoptrophorus semipalmatus semipalmatus (Gmelin)
SPRING AUTUMN

UPLAND PLOVER
Bartramia longicauda (Bechstein)

BUFF-BREASTED SANDPIPER
Trynyites suoruficollis (Vieillot)

All ⅔ nat. size

LONG-BILLED CURLEW
Numenius americanus Bechstein
HUDSONIAN CURLEW
Numenius hudsonicus Latham

ESKIMO CURLEW
Numenius borealis (J. R. Forster)

All ⅔ nat. size

MARBLED GODWIT
Limosa fedoa (Linnaeus)
HUDSONIAN GODWIT SPRING
Limosa haemastica (Linnaeus)

Color.—ADULTS: Head, neck, breast, and lower parts, white streaked with dusky brown on forehead, crown, and back of neck, spotted with arrowhead marks on front of neck, breast, and sides; chin, throat, and sides of head, with small dusky markings; a conspicuous white eye-ring with a dusky spot in front; lores, whitish; *upper parts from neck, wing-coverts, and secondaries, blackish-brown,* each feather broadly edged and tipped with lighter, greater coverts and secondaries, barred; quills, plain dusky brown; *rump and tail, white,* the latter narrowly streaked with light brown; bill, greenish-dusky, lighter basally; *legs, light chrome yellow.* YOUNG: Similar to adults, but lighter above, the streaks below limited to the neck and upper breast, and the legs yellow.

Nest and Eggs.— NEST: A mere depression, usually unlined, in the ground. EGGS: 4, grayish or deep buff, spotted with rich dark brown and lavender over the entire surface but more thickly at large end.

Distribution.— North and South America; breeds from Lake Iliamna, Alaska, and southern Mackenzie to southern British Columbia, Ungava, Labrador, and Anticosti Island; winters from southern California, Texas, Louisiana, and Georgia (casually North Carolina) south to Patagonia; occurs in Bermuda in migration.

On Hatteras Island, North Carolina, about five miles north of its famous lighthouse, there is, in ordinary seasons, an extended series of shallow, grassy beach-ponds. During the month of May, these are inhabited by large numbers of shore birds of many kinds. I have seen here at least ten thousand on the wing at a time when disturbed from their feeding by the discharge of a gun.

Drawing by R. I. Brasher

GREATER YELLOW-LEGS (½ nat. size)

Easily attracted to decoys, hence a favorite with gunners

Among the feathered squadrons there are always many Yellow-legs. When Hudsonian Curlews are absent the Greater Yellow-legs is the largest bird among them. This gathering place at Cape Hatteras is similar to many others all up and down the coast. Yellow-legs are the sentinels of such assemblies, and keep a sharp lookout at all times. They watch and listen and are first to give the alarm. With shrill cries they leap upon the wing and go flying away, generally collecting into a company as they proceed. Sometimes they do not go far, but circle back and fly about in the offing, rarely ceasing to call. In motion their wing-beats are deliberate, and, when approaching others among which they are preparing to settle, they have a way of slowly sailing on extended wings that renders them an easy shot for the gunner.

Yellow-legs are extensively hunted, although as food their flesh does not rank so high as some others of the Sandpiper family, as for example Woodcock and Upland Plovers. They are shot chiefly over wooden models cut out and painted to represent the bird and stuck up in the mud near a shooting blind. To these decoys they often come with little hesitation, especially if to this deception the hunter adds an additional lure by imitating their call with a fair degree of accuracy.

There is a widespread idea that these birds appear later in the autumn than the Lesser Yellow-legs, so they are much called " Winter Yellow-legs." " Tattler " and " Tell-tale " are also popular names for this species. The breeding grounds are mainly north of the United States, to which territory they retire in May, but by July many individuals are back. In fact, the tide of the migration of the Yellow-legs that ebbs and flows along our coast and interior waterways, seems never to cease, for every month in the year they are found in many Southern States. One reason for this is the fact that not all are mated any one season and numbers of the unpaired birds do not go north at all. In the Gulf States many Greater Yellow-legs pass the winter, but the great bulk go farther afield and scatter throughout the lands to the south as far as Patagonia.

Their food consists of minnows and such insects and other small forms of life as are obtainable in and about the water. Where bars and mud flats are exposed at low tide, there the Yellow-legs are wont to come. Along the shores of ponds, lakes, and rivers of the interior they are found, and in fact, few, if any, shore birds have so extended a range.

T. GILBERT PEARSON.

YELLOW-LEGS

Totanus flavipes (*Gmelin*)

A. O. U. Number 255 See Color Plate 36

Other Names.— Common Yellow-legs; Lesser Yellow-legs; Little Tell-tale; Lesser Tell-tale; Lesser Yellow-shanks; Yellow-legged Plover; Summer Yellow-legs; Little Yelper; Small Cucu; Little Stone-bird; Little Stone Snipe; Lesser Long-legged Tattler.

General Description.— Length, 11 inches. An exact miniature of the Greater Yellow-legs, from which it differs only in size.

Nest and Eggs.— NEST: A depression in the ground under shelter of tuft of grass or bushes, or in the open. EGGS: 4, creamy, buffy or clay-color, usually boldly marked, splashed, or blotched with burnt umber, blackish, and lavender, but sometimes with small spots over entire surface.

Distribution.— North and South America; breeds from Kotzebue Sound, Alaska, northern Mackenzie, central Keewatin, and southern Ungava to the valley of the upper Yukon, southern Saskatchewan, and northern Quebec; winters in Argentina, Chile, and Patagonia, and casually in Mexico, Florida, and the Bahamas; in migration occurs mainly east of the Rocky Mountains (rare in spring on the Atlantic coast) and in the Pribilof Islands, Greenland, and Bermuda; accidental in Great Britain.

Photograph by H. K. Job

YELLOW-LEGS IN MANITOBA SLOUGH

The Lesser Yellow-legs formerly was one of the most numerous of all the shore birds of North America, and still holds its numbers better than many other species.

No longer ago than 1870 the flocks were quite numerous about some of the inland ponds and lakes in Massachusetts in August, particularly in dry seasons, when the ponds were low. I remember that they were always watchful, but they were readily attracted by a whistled imitation of their call, and if even one was shot out of the flock the others hovered about until many had paid the penalty of their sympathetic concern. Of late years at those same ponds, a single bird or a pair is seen occasionally, but the flocks are gone, perhaps never to return. Its habits are similar to those of the Greater Yellow-legs, and it feeds largely on insects, including ants.

EDWARD HOWE FORBUSH, in *Game Birds, Wild-Fowl and Shore Birds.*

SOLITARY SANDPIPER

Helodromas solitarius solitarius (*Wilson*)

A. O. U. Number 256 See Color Plate 36

Other Names.— Green Sandpiper; American Green Sandpiper; Wood Sandpiper; American Wood Sandpiper; Solitary Tattler.

General Description.— Length, 9 inches. Color above, dark olive-brown, speckled with white; below, white with dark spots on breast and neck; the barred tail-feathers are very conspicuous in flight. *Bill, slender, straight, and longer than head.* Seldom found elsewhere than near inland lakes and woodland streams.

Color.—*Above, dark glossy olive-brown* streaked with whitish on head and neck, elsewhere finely speckled with white; upper tail-coverts, whitish, heavily spotted with color of back; middle tail-feathers, brownish-olive, *remainder, white, barred with 3 or 4 bands of olive-dusky; below, white;* breast and sides of neck, shaded with brownish, streaked and spotted with dusky; sides, with some bars of dusky; bill, dusky-greenish; legs, dull greenish; iris, brown, rarely white.

Distribution.— North and South America; summers from central Keewatin, northern Ungava, and Newfoundland south to Nebraska, Illinois, Indiana, Ohio, and Pennsylvania; probably breeds regularly in the northern part of its range, locally and casually in the southern part; winters from the West Indies to Argentina; recorded from Greenland, Bermuda, and Great Britain.

That dark and dainty sprite, the Solitary Sandpiper, is almost the only Sandpiper of the wooded wilderness. It is a bird of mountain, forest, hill, and plain, but is rarely, if ever, seen on the sandy beaches of the sea, where other Sandpipers play. It is not so solitary as its name would imply but it frequents solitary places where other Sandpipers seldom or never appear. It is seen singly or in small scattered companies of a few individuals about mountain lakes or streams, near little ponds, ditches, or muddy, stagnant pools, almost anywhere throughout its range, and even occasionally on tidal streams and in salt marshes. At times it frequents the same feeding ground with Yellow-legs or Spotted Sandpipers, but may be distinguished from the former by its much smaller size and dark legs and from the latter by the great quantity of white on its spread tail and its darker upper parts. Its notes, *peet-weet, peet-weet,* are very similar to those of the Spotted Sandpiper and it has the same habit of nodding or bowing its head but its hinder parts are not quite as active and expressive as are those of its spotted congener.

There is some uncertainty about our knowledge of the breeding habits of this bird. It has been reported as nesting on high mountains, on the ground, in the nests of other birds, and in hollow trees, all of which may be true, but at the present time we have little reliable data regarding its home life. In the breeding season it is seen singly or more rarely in pairs and then it is known to alight upon the tree-tops and to emit a rather weak and ineffective flight song. It is graceful and elegant, moves lightly and easily and flies swiftly and often wildly, erratically, and high in the air like a Snipe. When the ponds and lakes are low during a long drought in August or September, the Solitary Sandpiper may be seen along the exposed mud flats and sandbars, often going into the water up to its belly. In the autumn it has a habit of wading in stagnant ditches and stirring up the bottom by advancing one foot and shaking it rapidly. This is done so delicately that it does not roil the water, but it starts from their hiding places the minute organisms that lie concealed there, and the bird, plunging in its bill and head, often clear to the eyes, catches them deftly as they flee from the disturbance. This bird seems to feed very largely on aquatic insects, small mollusks, etc., but it destroys grasshoppers, moths, and other destructive land insects, some of which it pursues and catches easily on the wing.

Edward Howe Forbush.

The Western, or Cinnamon, Solitary Sandpiper (*Helodromas solitarius cinnamomeus*) is not always distinguishable from the eastern Solitary Sandpiper. It averages larger and the spots on the upper parts are or approach a cinnamon brown. It occurs in western North and South America, breeding north of the United States.

WILLET

Catoptrophorus semipalmatus semipalmatus (*Gmelin*)

A. O. U. Number 258 See Color Plate 37

Other Names.— Semipalmated Snipe; Spanish Plover; Stone Curlew; Duck Snipe; Will-willet; Pill-will-willet; Bill-willy; Humility; Pied-wing Curlew.

General Description.— Length, 16 inches. Color, gray, light below and dark above, with dark markings; a good deal of white on wings, and the rump and upper tail-coverts white. Bill, slender, straight, and longer than head; *toes, webbed at base.*

Color.—Adults in Summer: General color, ashy, lighter below; crown and back of neck streaked with dusky; shoulders and back with spots and specks of the same color; *rump, upper tail-coverts, and tail, white,* the tail barred with narrow traverse streaks of brown; primaries, dusky-brown with a *large white space at base,* this color invading secondaries; primaries beneath, blackish, the white showing two conspicuous areas in flight; lores, whitish; a dusky streak from bill to eye; throat, narrowly streaked; breast and sides, thickly marked, with narrow traverse arrowhead bars; bill, bluish-horn, blackening toward tip; legs, pale lavender; iris, brown. Adults in Winter: Above, light ashy with a tinge of brown, with little or no darker marking; upper tail-coverts, white; wing, similar to summer plumage; below, pale ashy or white shaded with gray on breast and sides; sides of head, pale brown; bill, paler than in summer; a white eye-ring.

Nest and Eggs.— Nest: In a tussock of grass or weeds, close to the water, in fresh- or salt-water marshes; a carelessly built structure of small reeds and grass. Eggs: 4, greenish-white or dark brownish-olive, boldly marked with spots in various shades of brown and lavender.

Distribution.— North and South America; breeds from Virginia (formerly Nova Scotia) south to Florida and the Bahamas; winters from the Bahamas to Brazil and Peru; accidental in Bermuda and Europe.

Drawing by R. I. Brasher

WILLET (⅓ nat. size)

A noisy, self-assertive bird

Here is a noisy, self-assertive bird, if there ever was one. Willet life, literally, is a perfect " scream." And yet this forward creature has been nicknamed " Humility," because it probes for worms in the humble mud in the intervals between the periods when it lifts up the voice on high. Constitutionally, the bird seems unable to keep its mouth shut, as though it had blown off the safety valve and was compelled to keep going, from sheer inability to stop, with a compelling motor power behind. Its relatives, the two species of Yellow-legs, have somewhat the same inquisitive and assertive dispositions, though apparently in lesser degree. Gunners have frequently lodged complaint that the noisy Willet warns away their game.

The acme of its fantastic performance comes during the nesting season, particularly when the young are abroad. Then as long as one is minded to remain on the marsh, the birds, fairly beside themselves, fly about yelping and screaming. On Smith's Island, Va., I watched one, perched on the dead fork of a bush out on a broad marsh. With absolute mechanical precision, for a quarter of an hour at a stretch, with hardly an apparent pause to get breath, the bill would open and shut, like clock work, to the tune of *yip, yip, yip,* and so on, rapidly reiterated. When it took to wing it would start up its *pill-willet* cries.

Usually the nest is hard to find. I have watched the birds on the marshes of the southern coast and by the sloughs on western prairies, but never had the luck to locate a nest till about May 10, 1904, when I was on a cruise along the coast of South Carolina. We landed on an uninhabited island, mostly marsh, but with a beach in front, backed by a narrow ridge of sand between beach and marsh. Clumps of coarse beach grass grew all along this ridge, and from nearly every other clump, as we advanced, a Willet sprang from her four large dark mottled eggs, until on that one island we had examined over fifty nests. These were frail structures of dry grass, lining hollows scratched in the sand under the grass clumps.

It need not be assumed from this that the Willet is an abundant bird, for it is another of our rapidly " vanishing shore birds." Formerly it was common along our Atlantic coast, but now the sight of one is a rarity.

During the fall migration, it is seen casually in muddy sloughs or on the flats and marshes of the sea-coast more reserved than is its wont, as though sobered by the thought of exile from the fields of its vocal exploits. During winter it is absent on its annual junket to varied southern scenes as far remote as Brazil and Peru.

Photo by H. K. Job Courtesy of Houghton Mifflin Co.

WILLET ON NEST

HERBERT K. JOB.

The Western Willet (*Catoptrophorus semipalmatus inornatus*) differs from the eastern Willet in larger size and in shades of color, but its general appearance and habits are the same. This geographical variety breeds from central Oregon, southern Alberta, and southern Manitoba, south to northern California, central Colorado, southern South Dakota, and northern Iowa, and on the coasts of Texas and Louisiana; in winter it occurs from central California, Texas, Louisiana, and the Gulf coast of Florida to Mexico and Lower California. It is sometimes found in the Atlantic State during migration.

UPLAND PLOVER

Bartramia longicauda (*Bechstein*)

A. O. U. Number 261 See Color Plate 37

Other Names.— Bartramian Sandpiper; Bartram's Sandpiper; Bartram's Plover; Upland Sandpiper; Uplander; Hill-bird; Field Plover; Highland Plover; Pasture Plover; Grass Plover; Prairie Plover; Prairie Pigeon; Prairie Snipe; Papabotte; Quaily.

General Description.— Length, 12 inches. Color

above, blackish-brown; below, grayish-white. *Bill, shorter than head; gape, wide; neck, long; tail, long and graduated;* outer and middle toes webbed at base; inner toe free. Found mainly in pastures and old fields away from water, even at the sea-shore.

Color.—Above, blackish-brown, all feathers edged with tawny or whitish, the brown prevailing on crown and back, the lighter edgings of latter producing a streaked effect; on long inner secondaries, the dark color mere small bars; wing-coverts marked with whitish; primaries, dusky, *outer one barred with white;* rump and upper tail-coverts, plain brownish-black; middle tail-feathers, dark brown with rufous edges and irregularly barred; rest of tail-feathers, orange-brown with numerous broken bars or spots of black and a sub-terminal black bar; line over eye and under parts, grayish-white, tinged with yellowish-brown on breast and sides of head; breast and sides, with each feather marked by a brownish arrowhead-shaped spot; bill, yellowish-green, dusky at tip; legs, yellowish-olive; iris, brown.

Nest and Eggs.— Nest: A slight depression in open dry prairies, lined or not with grass. Eggs: 4, pale buffy or cream, spotted with dark brown and lavender.

Distribution.— North and South America; breeds from northwestern Alaska, southern Mackenzie, central Keewatin, central Wisconsin, southern Michigan, southern Ontario, and southern Maine to southern Oregon, northern Utah, central Oklahoma, southern Missouri, southern Indiana, and northern Virginia; winters on the pampas of South America to Argentina; in migration occurs north to Newfoundland and in Europe; accidental in Australia.

My early recollections of the Upland Plover, once a familiar game bird, are of open rolling grassy tracts on Cape Cod, Mass., interspersed with patches of bayberry bushes, in late July and August, and some very shy brown birds that, despite most of my attempts to stalk them, would rise wildly well out of gunshot and with shrill cries fly on to the next hillside, alighting and watching in an erect attitude, their heads projecting from the short sparse grass.

Upland Plover shooting is now becoming a thing of the past, under the protection of Federal Law. This is as it should be, for here we have another species which is in great danger of extermination. Little by little, both through excessive shooting and by the destruction of nests in cultivated areas, it has been growing more and more scarce. Once it was a common bird in the Eastern States, but now only an occasional lone pair is found there. The grassy prairies of the Northwest are now its principal breeding ground, but owing to their increased reclamation for agricultural purposes, it is being further pushed out. This is a lamentable declension from the days when in New England it was comparable in abundance to the Meadowlark, and pairs were nesting in nearly every field.

Classing it as a "shore bird," is only on the basis of structure and relationship, for otherwise there is no bird which is less fond of the vicinity of water. Its haunts are dry grassy fields, where it lives chiefly on insects injurious to the fields, such as cutworms and grasshoppers. Here is where it nests, the last of May and early June. The female sits closely, and on the prairies of North Dakota, Manitoba, and Saskatchewan I have found nests only by flushing the brooding bird, which allows one almost to step upon her before she will leave. The nest is in rather thick bunches of prairie grass, a simple affair of dry grass leaves. Four is the invariable number of eggs which I have found. The bird is almost exactly the color of dead grass, and even when the nest has been found and revisited, it is astonishing how hard it is to discern the brooding bird. In one case she allowed me to open by hand the grass which covered her, set up the camera and photograph her within two feet of the lens. Shy as the birds become under persecution, they are gentle in nesting time. On the western prairies they are much less shy than in the East.

As soon as the young are able to fly, in July, they all begin to migrate south, and most of them are gone before August is far advanced. This was the reason why the older laws allowed Upland Plover shooting in July. In the summer of 1912 I was in Manitoba. At the opening of this early hunting season, a gunner came out near our camp and shot nearly forty Upland Plovers, while his boy picked up little downy chicks and carried them in his pocket. I reported this to the head authorities, who are excellent conservationists, and the law was changed. It will need the best of care, by every State and Province, and the coöperation of public sentiment, to save from extinction this beautiful and valuable species. Herbert K. Job.

The investigations of the Government biologist show that the Upland Plover is naturally an industrious destroyer of many different species of noxious insects. There can be no doubt that the bird feeds upon the highly destructive locust, and also upon grasshoppers, the clover-root curculio, bill-bugs (which destroy much corn), crawfish, which are a pest in corn and rice fields and also weaken levees by their burrowing, and various grubs which damage garden truck, corn, and cotton crops.

BUFF-BREASTED SANDPIPER

Tryngites subruficollis (*Vieillot*)

A. O. U. Number 262 See Color Plate 37

Other Name.— Hill Grass-bird.

General Description.— Length, 8 inches. Color below, buff; above, dusky brown. Bill shorter than head, slender, hard at tip; gape wide; tail rounded, central feathers projecting; *toes not webbed.* Prefers dry upland fields and is rarely seen on the shore.

Color.—Adults in Summer: Above, dusky-brown, finely streaked on head with pale yellowish-buff, this streaking running down back of neck to feathers of back and shoulders which are edged and tipped with tawny; primaries, secondaries, and coverts, grayish-brown, the last two with lighter edges; *inner webs of primaries and both webs of secondaries, pearly white marbled with black;* lores, sides of head to above eye, throat, breast, and all under parts, plain buff unmarked except by a few brownish spots on side and chest; central tail-feathers, brown; others, rufous with a subterminal dusky bar; bill, dusky; legs, dusky-greenish; iris, brown. Adults in Winter: The broad edgings of feathers above, narrowed to whitish semi-circles; under parts, whiter; wing and tail, as in summer.

Nest and Eggs.— Nest: A depression in the ground, sparsely lined with grass and withered leaves. Eggs: 4, grayish or pale olive-buff, sharply spotted with rich burnt umber.

Distribution.— North and South America; breeds along the Arctic coast from northern Alaska to northern Keewatin; winters in Argentina and Uruguay; most abundant in migration in the Mississippi valley; occasional on the Atlantic coast in fall; casual on the Pacific coast north to St. Michael, Alaska, and to northeastern Siberia; straggles to Bermuda and Europe.

The Buff-breasted Sandpiper is rather a rare bird upon the Atlantic coast, and possibly always has been, as it breeds in northern Alaska and its main migration route does not touch the Atlantic coast.

Formerly it was very abundant in Texas, and still is common there, but decreasing. The reports of its decrease in the West are very impressive. Apparently it is on the way to extinction.

It is usually a very gentle and confiding bird and pays little attention to the hunter. It is valuable as an insect eater, particularly in the West, but in its pursuit this fact is overlooked and its food value only is considered. Doctor Hatch found it living upon crickets, grasshoppers, ants and their "eggs," and other insects, and on minute mollusks taken from the shores of shallow ponds in the warmest part of the day.

Edward Howe Forbush, in *Game Birds, Wild-Fowl and Shore Birds.*

SPOTTED SANDPIPER

Actitis macularia (*Linnæus*)

A. O. U. Number 263 See Color Plate 36

Other Names.— Peep; Peetweet; Teeter-peep; Teeter-tail; Teeterer; Tip-up; Tilt-up; Sand Lark; See-saw; Sand-peep; Sand Snipe; River Snipe.

General Description.— Length, 7 inches. Color above, ashy-olive; under parts pure white, unspotted in winter, but in summer with round black spots. Bill straight, slender, and about as long as head; outer and middle toes, webbed at base; inner toes, free; tail, rounded and half as long as wing. This is the only Sandpiper which has *large* and distinct spots on its under parts; it nearly always teeters when alarmed; and in flight shows a white line on the wings. Found most often near streams and ponds.

Color.—Adults in Summer: Crown and upper parts, including wings, soft ashy-olive, finely varied with dusky, in streaks on head and neck, elsewhere in wavy irregular crossbars; line from bill to eye and back of it, olive-dusky; a line over eye and entire under parts, pure white; *under parts, as far as under tail-coverts, with numerous sharp, circular black spots,* more crowded on the female; primaries and secondaries, brownish-black, largely *white* at base, not showing in folded wing; feet, grayish flesh color; bill, flesh color with black tip; iris, brown surrounded with a white ring. Adults in Winter, and Young: As in summer, but without marking above or below; breast, slightly grayish and wing-coverts more strongly outlined with lighter.

Nest and Eggs.— Nest: A depression in the ground in the vicinity of water; rather well constructed of grass, leaves, and weed stems. Eggs: 4, creamy, buffy, or grayish, blotched with blackish and purplish-gray.

Distribution.— North and South America; breeds from tree limit in northwestern Alaska, northern Mackenzie, central Keewatin, northern Ungava, and Newfoundland south to southern California, Arizona, southern Texas, southern Louisiana, and northern South Carolina; winters from California, Louisiana, and South Carolina to southern Brazil and central Peru; straggles to Great Britain and Helgoland.

Probably there is no shore bird more widely and intimately known all over the country than the Spotted Sandpiper, which is popularly nick-

Photo by S. A. Lottridge

NEST AND EGGS OF SPOTTED SANDPIPER

named " Teeter " or " Tip-up," from its nervous habit of constantly tilting its body, and " Peet-weet " from its notes. As typically seen, it runs along the shore of a pond or stream, stops and wags its head and body up and down several times, then runs again, and, if further approached, flies out over the water with a peculiar quivering flight, the wings being held straight out, with alternations of quivering downward beats and brief intervals of soaring. Usually it circles back and alights not far from the same place. It is not by any means, however, confined to the vicinity of open water, but is often seen in meadows, and even on dry uplands, particularly in cultivated fields where crops are growing.

Most shore birds breed far to the north, but here is one species which is remarkably impartial in its topography. Though it breeds in northern Alaska, it also does so nearly all over the United States, even down on the Gulf of Mexico, alike on seaboard and interior. In this praiseworthy originality it is entirely unique, surpassing even the Robin, which does not breed so far south.

In the northern States I have usually found fresh eggs during the last week of May, generally four in number. The nest may be found in many sorts of situations. Probably that most preferred is just up from the shore of a pond or stream, under a bunch of grass or a clump of weeds. Usually nests are quite well hidden, but I have seen them easily visible, under sparse weeds on open gravelly shore. However, they are often placed quite a distance from water, in pastures or among crops, quite often in fields of corn or potatoes.

Some shore birds " act up " to draw away intruders from their nests, when these are being approached. The Spotted Sandpiper makes no such attempt until after being flushed, when both birds appear and run about anxiously.

The female is a close sitter, and discloses her secret by fluttering out when closely approached. Owing to this habit, I have inspected dozens of nests, whereas, if the bird would discreetly withdraw, the well-hidden nest would seldom be found, except when placed in cultivated fields.

Photo by H. K. Job

SPOTTED SANDPIPER ON NEST

Some of these birds winter on our southern coasts, but the majority pass on further, penetrating into Brazil and Peru. HERBERT K. JOB.

LONG-BILLED CURLEW

Numenius americanus *Bechstein*

A. O. U. Number 264 See Color Plate 38

Other Names.— Big Curlew; Hen Curlew; Old Hen Curlew; Sickle-bill; Sickle-billed Curlew; Sabre-bill; Smoker.

General Description.— Length, 26 inches. Prevailing color red, darker above than below. Its appearance is similar to that of the Marbled Godwit, but it is easily distinguishable from the latter by its longer and *curved* bill, the upper section of which is longer than the lower and slightly knobbed at the tip. Toes, webbed at base.

Color.— Crown, rufous-brown with blackish streaks; back and shoulders, brownish-black varied with cinnamon-brown, each feather having several indentations of this color; wing-coverts, with more rufous and whitish; secondaries and tail-feathers, pale brownish barred with dusky; inner primaries, rufous-brown, changing to dusky on outer ones; entire under parts, varying from yellowish-brown to rufous, usually deepening to chestnut under wings and fading to whitish on throat and sides of head; breast, with dusky streaks tending to arrowheads; bill, dusky above, pale flesh-color below; legs, bluish-gray. Very constant in plumage irrespective of age, sex, or season.

Nest and Eggs.— Nest: A grass-lined depression in the ground on open prairies. Eggs: 3 or 4, pale buffy to grayish-buff, spotted with darker brown and lavender.

Distribution.— North America; breeds from central British Columbia, southern Saskatchewan, and Manitoba to northeastern California, northern New Mexico, and northwestern Texas; winters from central California and southern Arizona south to Guatemala, and on the Atlantic coast from South Carolina to Florida, Louisiana, and Texas; formerly a regular migrant north to Massachusetts and rarely to Newfoundland, now a straggler east of the Mississippi, north of Florida; casual in the West Indies.

From being an abundant species on the south Atlantic coast a century ago, this interesting, spectacular species, the Long-billed Curlew, is now almost unknown in the eastern United States. The only time I ever saw it in the East was about 1886, in August, over the marshes of Marshfield, Mass., when I saw a single wedge-shaped flock of these great birds with absurdly long down-curved bills. Audubon found them coming to roost at night by thousands, on November 10, 1831, on an island off the coast of South Carolina. Seeing that, in May, 1904, probably on the same island, I saw some ten thousand Hudsonian Curlews come to roost at dusk, I could not but wonder if he could have been mistaken in the species. At any rate, where it was once well known it is now unknown. The species is in real danger of extinction, and it is well that the Federal Law now places them under absolute protection.

My personal experience with this great Curlew has been chiefly in summer, in the nesting season, on the prairies of Saskatchewan. Evidently it is gradually disappearing, for during extended explorations in North Dakota, from May to October, I failed to see a single one. Various settlers told me that it had been common in "the eighties" and previously, but that it had since become rare. It seems to prefer those prairie regions where the soil has an alkaline tinge and the sloughs are surrounded by the typical bare alkaline flats. In such regions in Saskatchewan

Courtesy of S. A. Lottridge

LONG-BILLED CURLEW

This interesting species is now almost unknown in the eastern United States

I found them in scattered pairs. Conspicuous in size, they also make themselves so by their reiterated loud, high-pitched, trilling cries, especially when they have young or eggs in the vicinity. They are shyer than the Marbled Godwits which share with them these alkaline plains.

Photo by H. K. Job Courtesy of Outing Pub. Co.

YOUNG LONG-BILLED CURLEWS

The nest is a simple hollow in the prairie, amid rather sparse grass, lined with dry stems. Three or four very large eggs make the usual complement. It is hard to find, as the male bird gives the alarm when an intruder approaches, and the female joins him. Perhaps they become somewhat accustomed to the cowboys who ride around after the cattle, since all of the nests which I knew about were discovered by cowboys on horseback through flushing the bird from the nest. Though the anxious parents are in evidence, flying or trotting about at a distance and whistling, they give no definite clue as to the direction in which the chosen spot is located.

One evening at sundown after a forty mile drive over the plains, we were approaching a ranch, in rolling prairie country, when we noticed two birds squatting together in the short grass. They proved to be young of this species, quite large, yet still in the downy stage, very pretty and interesting. There was just enough light to take photographs of them by time-exposures. Meanwhile the parents were flying about, swooping angrily past us at close range, screaming most vociferously. Altogether it was a spectacle which I would not have missed for a good deal.

HERBERT K. JOB.

The Long-billed Curlew is evidently a persistent eater of the highly injurious locust, as is shown by the fact that ten stomachs of the bird were found by Government experts to contain forty-eight locusts each. This would be sufficient reason for giving it a place among the birds of great economic value to man. But the bird's usefulness does not stop here, for it is known to feed freely also upon various injurious grasshoppers, and it is more than likely that its diet includes other noxious insects, so that its usefulness is beyond question of a doubt.

HUDSONIAN CURLEW

Numenius hudsonicus *Latham*

A. O. U. Number 265 See Color Plate 38

Other Names.— Jack Curlew; Jack; Striped-head; Crooked-billed Marlin; American Whimbrel; Short-billed Curlew.

General Description.— Length, 18 inches. Can be distinguished from young Long-billed Curlews only at close range.

Color.— *Top of head, uniform blackish-brown with well-defined whitish central and side stripes;* a distinct streak of dusky from bill through and behind eye and a pronounced broad whitish streak above it; upper parts, blackish-brown variegated with white, ocher, or pale brown in the same pattern as the Long-billed Curlew but tone less rufous; primaries and their coverts, dusky, the former *broken-barred with paler;* tail, ashy-brown with a number of narrow blackish bars; beneath, very pale brownish-white; breast, with dusky streaks changing to arrowheads or broken bars on sides; bill, dusky, yellowish below for about one-third its length, darkest at tip; feet, grayish-blue; iris, dark brown.

Nest and Eggs.— NEST: Like that of Long-billed Curlew. EGGS: 4, creamy to pale olive-gray, boldly marked with shades of umber-brown.

Distribution.— North and South America; breeds on the coast of Alaska from mouth of Yukon to Kotzebue Sound, and on the coast of northern Mackenzie; winters from Lower California to southern Honduras, from Ecuador to southern Chile, and from British Guiana to mouth of the Amazon; migrates mainly along the Pacific and Atlantic coasts; rare in the interior; casual on the Pribilof Islands and in Greenland and Bermuda; accidental in Spain.

Why should the long, slender bills of the Curlew and the Ibis be bent downward? One might as well ask why the similar bills of the Godwit and the Avocet should be bent upward and those of the Woodcock and the Snipe remain almost straight. These questions never have been satisfactorily answered. They remain among the fascinating problems of ornithology yet to be solved.

The Hudsonian Curlew, or Jack Curlew, as it is commonly called by gunners, is an illustration of the Darwinian theory. It has survived, while other species have disappeared, because it was fitter — better able to avoid the hunter. No bird is more exposed to persecution, as it migrates the entire length of North and South America, from the Arctic Ocean to the Straits of Magellan, but it frequents places rather remote from the centers of civilization, breeds in the Far North, is extremely shy and difficult to stalk, and so perpetuates its race.

Drawing by R. I. Brasher

HUDSONIAN CURLEW (¼ nat. size)

It is extremely shy and difficult to stalk

The main lines of its migration are down the east and west shores of both continents but there is also a scattering flight through the interior. Little is known about the bird's breeding habits but as soon as the young are grown the slow migration begins. The main flight moves from the west coast of Hudson Bay to the shores of New England and southward. The birds appear on the islands of the St. Lawrence River early in August and reach their maximum numbers there late in the month.

When feeding they usually scatter about over the ground, moving slowly and sedately, except when in pursuit of some particularly lively prey. Berries they pick from the bushes with their bills. They feed in fields where grasshoppers abound and in blueberry patches. Along the coasts, where the species is most common, the flocks frequent flats, beaches and low grassy hills not far from the sea. When flying to or from their feeding grounds they usually pass about thirty yards high, except on windy days, when they fly close to the ground or water. In New England they feed at the edge of the water or wade in shallow pools picking up their food with the head apparently held sidewise. Fiddler crabs and the large gray sand spiders form an important part of their diet. These Curlews also consume June bugs and other beetles and some worms. They are sometimes seen singly, flying and circling high in air, and occasionally a small flock is noted migrating like a flock of Geese or Ducks. Formery they were numerous on Cape Cod and Nantucket, but now-a-days most of them pass out to sea, though many still visit the marshes of the Carolinas. In spring they have a soft, rather mournful call, *cur-lew,* and the alarm note is *pip-pip-pip-pip.*

EDWARD HOWE FORBUSH.

Courtesy of *Recreation*

HUDSONIAN CURLEW

ESKIMO CURLEW

Numenius borealis *(J. R. Forster)*

A. O. U. Number 266 See Color Plate 38

Other Names.— Fute; Dough- or Doe-bird; Little Curlew; Prairie Pigeon.

General Description.— Length, 15 inches. Color like that of the Hudsonian Curlew, but more reddish. Bill slender, curved, and about twice the length of head; toes, webbed at base.

Color.— Upper parts, brownish-black variegated with pale cinnamon-brown; *crown, without central light line;* streak over eye of whitish; under parts, tawny ocher to whitish, marked everywhere with dusky streaks, bars, or arrowhead spots, these markings very numerous except on chin; bill, black, paler at base below; feet, lead-gray; iris, brown.

Nest and Eggs.— Nest: Usually on the open plains; a mere depression in the ground, lined with a few dry leaves or grass. Eggs: 4, ground color variable, from pale green, gray, or brown to olive-drab, with numerous bold markings of sepia and umber-brown, more crowded around large end.

Distribution.— North and South America; breeds on the Barren Grounds of northern Mackenzie; winters in Argentina and Patagonia; now nearly extinct.

It is a great pity that we must speak of the Eskimo Curlew in the past tense. Its disappearance is but another tribute to the effectiveness of modern fire-arms and the short-sighted selfishness of the average American hunter. In the seventies and early eighties Eskimo Curlews in countless numbers came annually to the coast of Massachusetts and earlier writers mention them as being very plentiful in the Carolinas. Their summer home was in the Barren Grounds and other regions in the northern part of North America. In autumn they collected in Newfoundland in enormous flocks. One observer declares that they came in millions that darkened the sky. After following down the coast to Nova Scotia they launched out over the ocean for South America, and many of them never sighted land until they reached the West India Islands. Whether during this long journey they ever rested on the water, or whether they continued their voyage without pause, is not known. Autumn gales, however, diverted many of them from their course and they landed on the Bermuda Islands as well as along the coast of the northern States. Tens of thousands thus came to the islands and beaches of New England where, according to Forbush, they were mercilessly shot for food. Because at this season they were always extremely fat they were known generally as "Dough-birds."

After reaching South America the Curlews proceeded southward, spreading out over the continent as far as Patagonia. Here they passed the winter. In March and April the great flights would appear on the shores of those States bordering on the Gulf of Mexico. Passing a gantlet of gun-fire the survivors journeyed up the Mississippi valley to northern Canada, and so on to their breeding grounds. It will thus be seen that their migrations were among the most extensive of any undertaken by our North American birds.

Since 1900 perhaps a dozen specimens have come to the attention of ornithologists — all dead birds — and it is of course possible that a few may still exist. But the great flocks are gone and the species is doomed.

Like all the Curlews this bird was an inhabitant of regions where water abounds. Along the coast they fed in the beach-pools and marshes but not generally on the sandy beaches so commonly frequented by Sandpipers and some of the Plovers.

In the spring and summer their great joy was to wade in the ponds, sloughs, and shallow, grassy lakes of the interior. They were of no special economic value to the farming interests of the country, for they did not feed on insects injurious to crops, but they were of much value as a food product, and with proper laws enforced for their conservation the great flocks might have been spared indefinitely for the pleasure and benefit of mankind.

T. Gilbert Pearson.

PLOVERS

Order *Limicolæ;* family *Charadriidæ*

THE Plovers comprise the family *Charadriidæ* of the order of Shore Birds and include about seventy-five species of comparatively small birds, which, during the breeding season, have a cosmospolitan distribution. The birds generally are migratory and they are likely to cover great distances in their journeys between their summer and winter homes, this being particularly true of the Golden Plover. Eight species occur in North America. Externally the Plovers differ markedly from the Snipes in having a comparatively short and pigeon-like bill, which is hardened and somewhat swollen at the end, and is ill-adapted for probing in mud or soft sand, and they must, of necessity, feed from the surface. For this reason, also, Plovers are often found feeding in the dry uplands not frequented by the Snipe. Furthermore, in the Plovers the body is relatively shorter and plumper than in the Snipes, and the neck is much shorter and thicker. Plovers' wings are long and pointed, and, except in a few species, when folded extend to or beyond the end of the tail, which is comparatively short, generally rounded, and consists of twelve feathers. Their plumage varies greatly, and in some species shows considerable seasonal changes.

They nest on the ground and lay usually four eggs, which are marked or spotted with dark colors in a manner that makes them hard to detect among the pebbles by which they are likely to be surrounded. But one brood is raised in a season. The young when hatched are covered with soft buff or grayish down, spotted with blackish. Whether or not the chicks know that these colors are protective, it is certain that they lie very still among the pebbles and grass when an intruder approaches, and therefore may easily be overlooked.

Plovers' voices usually are mellow, piping whistles which have singular carrying power.

BLACK-BELLIED PLOVER

Squatarola squatarola (*Linnæus*)

A. O. U. Number 270 See Color Plate 39

Other Names.— Black-breast; Black-breasted Plover; Bull-head; Bull-head Plover; Beetle-head; Bottle-head; Chuckle-head; Hollow-head; Owl-head; Whistling Plover; Whistling Field Plover; Pilot; May Cock; Swiss Plover; Ox-eye; Four-toed Plover; Gump; Gray Plover (autumn); Mud Plover; Pale-belly (young).

General Description.— Length, 12 inches. In summer, upper parts black and white, lower parts black; in winter, whitish all over but tinged with brown above. *Four toes,* but hind toe very small; outer and middle toes webbed at base; bill rather short.

Color.—Adults in Summer: *Forehead, crown, sides of head to upper level of eye, back of neck, and sides of same, pure white* with a few dusky spots on nape and center of neck; rest of upper parts, including coverts, shoulders, and inner secondaries, white, each feather with a small exposed dusky area, these forming bars on the inner secondaries; tail and upper coverts, barred with dusky; *below, including lores, chin, throat, part of side of head, breast, and abdomen, pure blackish-brown;* under tail-coverts, white; primaries, dark brown blackening at ends *with large white areas* at base; bill and feet, dusky-gray; eye, remarkably large and lustrous, deep brown. Adults in Winter: Ground color all over, whitish; upper parts, tinged with pale brown; crown, yellowish streaked with dusky; sides of head, back of neck, throat, and breast, finely streaked with brownish; feathers of back, of wing-coverts, and of inner secondaries, with wedge-shaped dusky centers; rest of under parts, unmarked, thus showing none of the black area so conspicuous in summer; bill, feet, and eye as in summer; intermediates between these two plumages, showing an admixture of black and white below, are very common. Young: Upper parts, lighter with a golden shade on each feather; under parts, whitish; breast, streaked with grayish.

Nest and Eggs.— Nest: A mere depression in the ground, lined with grass and leaves. Eggs: 4, light buffy-olive to deep olive-buff, heavily spotted with sepia or black.

Distribution.— Nearly cosmopolitan; breeds on the Arctic coast from Point Barrow to Boothia and Melville peninsulas, and also on the Arctic coast of Russia and Siberia; winters from the Mediterranean to South Africa, in India and Australia, and from California, Louisiana, and North Carolina to Brazil and Peru; in migration occurs throughout the United States and in Greenland and the Bermudas; accidental in the Hawaiian Islands.

The largest of our Plovers, the Black-bellied or Black-breast, is also the shyest. I recall that once, in boyhood, I was trying to creep up on a flat to get a shot at a small flock — of course in vain. A fisherman said to me, as I returned: "Sonny, you might as well try to walk up to an old Black Duck in broad daylight as to them 'ere Plovers."

Drawing by R. I. Brasher

BLACK-BELLIED PLOVER (½ nat. size)

The largest and shyest of the Plovers

Thanks to their wariness, it is quite possible, even at the present, to see small parties or flocks of these stout birds standing well out on the flat, at the water's edge. At the first approach of danger, off they go, with their mellow call of *tee-u-ree-e*. Plump bodies and large heads, as well as the white rump, white on the extended wings, and the conspicuous black patch under the wings against light feathers, make them easy of distinction from the darker Golden Plovers. Unlike the latter, which resort to dry fields to secure grasshoppers and other insects, these "Beetle-heads," as they are sometimes called by fishermen and gunners, mostly confine themselves to flats and beaches and to pools in the marsh.

Solid though they are, comparatively, I made the discovery one day that they could go where I could not. A small flock were feeding well out at the water's edge, at low tide, on a muddy shore, in winter, on the coast of Louisiana. I managed to wade out with my heavy motion-picture camera near enough to show them up with the telephoto lens. When I started to return, I thought I should have to stay there. When I pulled the tripod legs out of that tenacious mud, I sank down so that I could not extricate myself without putting down the tripod again and leaning on it till it was as deep in mud as before. Theoretically this might have continued forever, but finally I managed to stagger to dry land without disaster.

As with the Golden Plover, there is decided difference between the plumages of adult and young, notably so in the case of this species. These "pale-bellies" are readily distinguished. They arrive on the New England coast early in September, whereas the adults begin to appear about July 25. The young linger late in the fall, sometimes being noted well through November.

Even back in the palmy days when the Golden Plover was sometimes abundant, it seemed to me that the Black-breast did not habitually fly about in such large flocks as its relative, nor did these smaller flocks fly as high or perform such sightly evolutions in the air. They were, however, accustomed, in some localities, to congregate in a very large mass on some favorite dry sand-bar or flat, to scatter again when they left the rendezvous.

Photo by H. K. Job Courtesy of Houghton Mifflin Co.

BLACK-BELLIED PLOVER ASLEEP

Also like the Golden Plover, they breed on the Arctic coast and penetrate on the southward migration as far as Peru. But their routes are quite different, and some of them winter on our Gulf and south Atlantic coasts.

Herbert K. Job.

GOLDEN PLOVER

Charadrius dominicus dominicus (*Müller*)

A. O. U. Number 272 See Color Plate 39

Other Names.—American Golden Plover; Green Plover; Three-toed Plover; Whistling Plover; Three-toes; Common Plover; Spotted Plover; Field Plover; Green-back; Golden-back; Brass-back; Greenhead; Pale-breast; Muddy-breast; Muddy-belly; Bull-head; Toad-head; Hawk's eye; Squealer; Field-bird; Pasture-bird; Frost-bird; Trout-bird; Prairie-bird; Prairie Pigeon; Pale-belly (young).

General Description.— Length, 11 inches. Upper parts conspicuously spotted with yellow, lower parts black. Bill small and slender; *no hind toe;* wings long. Bobs its head very frequently.

Plumage.—Adults in Summer: Forehead, broad stripe over and behind eye and continuing down side of neck and breast, pure white; *crown, back of neck, back, and shoulders, blackish-brown,* streaked on crown and back of neck, and each feather of rest of upper parts sharply indented all around with golden yellow; wing-coverts and secondaries, more brownish, but showing some golden-yellow spotting; primaries, plain dusky-gray darkening at tips and whitening at base, but no pronounced white areas as in the Black-breasted Plover; tail, white with brownish bars; lores, throat, side of head in front of white stripe, breast, and under parts, pure brownish-black; bill, dusky; feet, lead color; eye, large and lustrous brown. Adults in Winter: Above, somewhat as in summer but colors less intense; more greenish-yellow and paler brown; sides of head, neck, breast, and under parts in general, brownish or grayish-white, narrowly streaked on sides of head and throat, mottled on neck, breast, and abdomen, with dark grayish-brown; an obscure dusky stripe behind eye; bill, legs, and eye as in summer. Young: Above, dusky mottled with dull whitish spots, becoming yellow on the rump; below, ashy, deeper on lower neck and breast.

Nest and Eggs.— Nest: A slight depression in the moss or ground. Eggs: 4, creamy-white to buffy-brown, spotted boldly with blotches of brown and black.

Distribution.— North and South America; breeds from Kotzebue Sound along the Arctic coast to mouth of the Mackenzie, and from Melville Island, Wellington Channel, and Melville Peninsula south to northwestern Hudson Bay; winters on the pampas of Brazil and Argentina; migrates south across the Atlantic from Nova Scotia and New Brunswick; a few pass south through the Mississippi valley, and all migrate north by this route; in migration to California, Greenland, and Bermuda; formerly abundant, now becoming rare.

In the Golden Plover we have a noble and beautiful species which has woefully decreased in numbers and may even be in danger of extermination. Its wonderful migrations have been much written about. Breeding along the Arctic coasts of northwestern North America, the Golden Plovers in August proceed eastward to Labrador, and down the coast to the peninsula of Nova Scotia. Thence they launch forth over the open Atlantic, straight south, passing several hundred miles off the New England coast, unless driven ashore by easterly gales. Continuing, they

Courtesy of American Museum of Natural History

GOLDEN PLOVER

(Winter plumage)

A noble and beautiful species which has woefully decreased in numbers

pass the West Indies, cross the Gulf of Mexico and appear on the coast of Brazil. Being able to alight on the water and feed among masses of drift-weed makes such a long journey possible. Reaching land, they keep on down to the pampas of Argentina. Returning north to breed, they pass, in April and May, up through the interior United States, especially the Mississippi valley, neglecting the Atlantic coast, and thus again reach the breeding grounds.

The autumnal flight on the New England coast used to be a great event, watched for with eagerness by the local gunners. If a tropical hurricane came up the coast between about August 20 and the middle of September, with its violent onshore gales from the northeast, there would be a wonderful influx of Golden Plovers, driven off their course, accompanied by equally great flocks of the Eskimo Curlew, now, alas, probably extinct.

The last really great flight of both these species which I witnessed was in late August, 1883, at Chatham, Mass., at the southern end of the projection of Cape Cod. The wind was shrieking, and I hardly could stand against it on the exposed headlands, where I watched great compact masses of these wonderful birds, high in air, blowing in from the sea. They alighted, as was their wont, on the upland grassy pastures as well as on the marshes, where they eagerly levied toll on their favorite grasshopper diet, while the gunners also took toll of them. Thus early in the season all were in the changing adult plumage, the pale-bellied young not arriving till about mid-September.

In Nova Scotia, before they launched forth on their great voyage, I have watched large flocks of them perform wonderful aërial evolutions over the marshes, swinging high and low many times before alighting. They came quite readily to tin or wooden decoys before a well-placed blind. During the spring flight, in May, I have watched them on the North Dakota prairie, when they were in their exquisite breeding plumage. As they faced me, their coal-black breasts so blended with the black loam soil that it was hard at first to make them out. Apparently realizing their concealing coloration, they would stand perfectly still till I came within fifteen or twenty paces, whereupon they would dart off together in their swift flight, piping their melodious calls.

HERBERT K. JOB.

KILLDEER

Oxyechus vociferus (*Linnæus*)

A. O. U. Number 273 See Color Plate 39

Other Names.— Killdeer Plover; Noisy Plover; Chattering Plover; Killdee.

General Description.— Length, 10 inches. Color above, olive-brown; below, pure white. A front view of the bird shows *four black* bands, two on head and two on breast. Wings, long and, in flight, showing a white V; tail long and rounded; bill slender.

Color.— ADULTS: Forehead, white from eye to eye, prolonged below; above this, a black band; a brownish-black patch from gape along lower side of head; a white collar around neck continuous with white throat; a broad diffuse stripe of the brownish-black back of eye; crown, back, shoulders, wing-coverts, and secondaries, plain olive-brown; *rump and upper tail-coverts, orange-brown* deepening to chestnut behind; several inner pairs of tail-feathers, olive-brown shading into black, then lightening again and changing into rusty tips, others with the orange-brown at rump, black subterminal bars, and pure white tips, the outer pair, mostly white, with several broken black bars on inner webs; primaries, dusky with a white space on outer webs and a longer one on inner webs; secondaries, mostly white, but with black areas increasing from within outward; *a black breast-band encircling neck; below this a white space, and below this again another black breast-band not extending around neck;* rest of under parts, pure white; bill, dusky; legs, leaden gray; iris, brown; eyelids, orange or red. YOUNG: Black of adults replaced by gray; feathers of upper parts marked with rusty-brown.

Nest and Eggs.— EGGS: Deposited on the bare ground in fields, usually near water; 4, dull buffy, thickly spotted and blotched with brown and sepia.

Distribution.— North and South America; breeds from central British Columbia, southern Mackenzie, central Keewatin, and central Quebec south to the Gulf coast and central Mexico; winters from California, Arizona, Texas, Indiana, New Jersey, and Bermuda south to Venezuela and Peru; casual in Newfoundland, Paraguay, and Chile; accidental in Great Britain.

The Killdeer gets its name from its loud, strident, and frequently reiterated cry, which somewhat resembles the words "Kill deer" or the syllables "Kill-dee." It is a true Plover, and a member of the important shore-bird family which are usually to be found near the water or in moist places. But the Killdeer also occurs frequently on perfectly dry land, many miles from

Courtesy of American Museum of Natural History

KILLDEERS

Adults and young in first plumage

ponds, streams, or the ocean. It seems to be especially fond of freshly plowed fields, where it feeds voraciously upon worms, grubs, and bugs of various kinds. On the ground it runs about rapidly and in a somewhat nervous manner, frequently uttering its somewhat petulant cry, which, under these conditions, is sometimes abbreviated to the last syllable, *dee*.

The Killdeer is especially solicitous about its eggs or young. When the incubating bird is flushed from her nest, she resorts to all of the tactics of the ground-building birds, fluttering away with one or both wings dragging as if broken, sometimes almost rolling over, often stopping to gasp and pant as if totally exhausted, and keeping up meanwhile an incessant screaming. In the meantime the male bird circles around at a safe distance, adding his protests and denunciation, and the two continue the uproar until the intruder has withdrawn.

On the wing the bird is swift, graceful and somewhat erratic, for which reason it has been much pursued as "game" by amateur gunners and others who should have known better. This "sport" is forbidden by the Federal Migratory Bird Law, which prohibits the hunting of these birds until 1918. The bird should, indeed, be protected at all times, not only because the shooting of it is killing for the mere sake of killing, since its flesh is not edible, but because it makes itself exceedingly useful by destroying great quantities of noxious insects.

There can be no doubt as to the economic value of the Killdeer's feeding habits, for its regular diet is known to include mosquitoes, the fever tick, which spreads the dreaded Texas fever among cattle; crane flies ("leather-jackets"), which are destructive to wheat and grass; grasshoppers, the clover-root curculio, various weevils which attack cotton, grapes and sugar beets; bill-

Photo by H. T. Middleton

EGGS OF KILLDEER

Laid in a depression of the ground

bugs which often do much damage to corn; wireworms and their adult forms, the click beetles; the southern cornleaf beetle; horse flies; crawfishes; the diving beetles which are injurious in fish hatcheries; and the marine worms which prey upon oysters.

George Gladden.

SEMIPALMATED PLOVER

Ægialitis semipalmata (*Bonaparte*)

A. O. U. Number 274 See Color Plate 39

Other Names.— Semipalmated Ring Plover; Ring-necked Plover; Ring-neck; Ring Plover; Red-eye; Beach-bird.

General Description.— Length, 7 inches. Upper parts color of wet sand; lower parts white; *one* black ring around neck. Bill short; outer and middle toes webbed to the second joint; hind toe missing.

Color.—Adults: A narrow black bar extending from eye over top of bill to other eye with the white space above it, and this in turn bordered by another black stripe reaching from eye to eye across front of crown; below eye (narrowly) and behind it a dusky stripe; a white bar around back of neck continuous with white of chin and lower sides of head; below this, *a broader bar of dusky encircling neck and upper breast; crown and upper parts, dark brownish-gray;* tail, like back darkening toward end, white-tipped; primaries, dusky; narrow, white spaces at base; secondaries, largely white except long inner ones which are like the back; greater coverts, white tipped; entire under parts, white; bill, yellow, with black tip; feet, pale flesh color; eye-ring, bright orange; iris, hazel. Young: Black of adults replaced by brownish-gray; feathers of upper parts with buffy edgings.

Nest and Eggs.— Nest: A mere depression in the ground, lined with leaves or grass. Eggs: 4, buffy to olive-buff, spotted and blotched with dark brown and black.

Distribution.— North and South America; breeds from Melville Island, Wellington Channel, and Cumberland Sound to the valley of the upper Yukon, southern Mackenzie, southern Keewatin, and Gulf of St. Lawrence; winters from southern Lower California, Louisiana, and South Carolina to Patagonia, Chile, and the Galapagos; casual in Siberia, Greenland, and the Bermudas.

The Semipalmated Plover is the common Plover of the Atlantic seaboard, for during the migrations there are probably more of them to be seen than of all the other Plovers combined, but even at that they are far from being numerous as they once were. In my boyhood I have seen flocks of hundreds, while now it is a matter of dozens. Yet we are fortunate in having them still with us to illustrate the Plover type on our beaches and flats — birds with heads proportionately large, with robin-like actions in racing off for a few yards, then standing still to gaze and meditate, though with the body more horizontal than the Robin, then stooping to conquer the small marine life at their feet.

Drawing by R. I. Brasher

SEMIPALMATED PLOVER (¾ nat. size)

A graceful little Plover and skillful in the art of concealment

They frequent both beaches and flats, preferably the latter, and sometimes pools on the marsh. Here they scatter out in feeding but bunch together in flight. From the flats, before we discover them, comes that singularly attractive characteristic call which always makes my pulses bound in response. When they take to wing these notes are speeded up and reiterated as the flock circles out over the water and dashes past. They are with us in May, and again in August and September, being more numerous in the latter period, reinforced by the new generation. Through August we see the adults, with their distinct black breast-bands, but it is not till September, usually, that the grayer young begin to appear, illustrating one of the strange phases of bird habits, that in many cases the young make the long untried journey southward after most of the parents have gone on before. They are found in the interior, as well as on the coast, but mostly along the larger bodies of water, or on marshes where there are shallow sloughs and mud-flats.

The breeding-grounds are mostly in the Far North, even beyond the Arctic Circle. The southernmost point where they are known to breed is the Gulf of St. Lawrence. There I have studied them, on the Magdalen Islands, finding a scattered colony on a long sandflat, bordering a lagoon, that stretched for miles between two of the larger islands. The little creatures would run ahead of me, piping plaintively. Careful looking finally revealed a number of their nests, back from the lagoon, in the sand and broken shells above high-water mark, or further back in the tracts where sparse tufts of beach-grass grew from the sand. The nests were more than the mere scratched-out hollows of the Piping Plover, in having at least a few grass-stems or scraps of dried sea-weed surrounding the hollow, or even partly filling it. The eggs were usually four, sometimes only three, handsome, boldly marked, resembling, save for their pyriform shape, Terns' eggs more than those of Piping and Wilson's Plovers.

Breeding seemed to be at its height the tenth of June. By that time a very few young were just hatched. They are darker than the Piping Plover chicks, but have similar ways. I had quite an experience in catching and tethering one of them to a blade of grass. Sitting quietly on the sand near by, I watched the mother run about anxiously, and finally venture up to snuggle the baby, while I took snapshots of them with the reflecting camera. HERBERT K. JOB.

The Semipalmated Plover's diet includes several species of injurious grasshoppers, as well as mosquitoes which seriously molest cattle and certain species of which it is now well known

Photo by H. K. Job Courtesy of Houghton Mifflin Co.

SEMIPALMATED PLOVER

Brooding tethered chick

may be carriers of dangerous diseases. It is known also that the bird feeds upon locusts. The usefulness of this Plover is, therefore, beyond question.

RINGED PLOVER

Ægialitis hiaticula (*Linnæus*)

A. O. U. Number 275

Other Names.— Ringed Dotterel; Ring Plover.

General Description.— Length, 7½ inches. Coloration very similar to that of the Semipalmated Plover, but usually the white spots on the lower eyelids and a white patch behind the eye are better marked. No web between middle and inner toes; hind toe missing.

Nest and Eggs.— NEST: A slight depression in the sand amid broken shells. EGGS: 4, pale buff or cream color, spotted with dark reddish-brown approaching black.

Distribution.— Eastern Arctic America and Old World; breeds from central Europe and Turkestan to Siberia, Spitzbergen, Iceland, Greenland, and Cumberland Sound; winters on shores of the Mediterranean and throughout Africa; accidental in Barbados, Chile, India, and Australia.

The well-known Ring Plover of Europe was long supposed to be confined to that continent, but it is now known that the bird breeds freely in Greenland and there are definite records of its appearance in America, one specimen having been taken at Great Slave Lake. It resembles the Semipalmated Plover, though it is somewhat larger, the black band on the breast is wider and the white stripe on the forehead extends backward and downward over the eye, while it lacks the web between the middle and inner toes of the Semipalmated. Its general habits are ploverlike.

This Plover must be considered a very useful bird because it persistently destroys several species of grasshoppers which are known to be injurious to crops. It should, therefore, be protected against molestation which is at all likely to lessen materially its numbers, or to change its normal habits.

PIPING PLOVER

Ægialitis meloda (*Ord*)

A. O. U. Number 277

Other Names.— Ringneck; Pale Ringneck; White Ringneck; Belted Piping Plover; Western Piping Plover; Clam Bird; Mourning Bird; Beach Plover; Sand Plover.

General Description.— Length, 7 inches. Upper parts, color of dry sand; under parts, snowy white. *Toes, not webbed;* hind toe missing; bill short.

Color.— Forehead, white; a black band on front of crown from eye to eye; lores, streak behind eye, chin, throat, sides of head, a half collar around back of neck, and entire under parts, pure snowy white; crown and *upper parts, very pale ashy-brown;* a black band on upper breast tending to encircle neck but not meeting; an indistinct dusky streak behind eye; primaries, dusky with white spaces at base; secondaries and greater coverts, mostly white; long inner secondaries, similar to back; upper tail-coverts and base of tail, white, latter blackening toward end, and outer pair of feathers, entirely white; an orange-red ring around eye; basal half of bill, orange yellow, front half, black; feet, yellowish; iris, brown. Adult Female: The crown bar is usually dark brown and the breastband much reduced and brownish. Young: No trace of dark color on head, and little, if any, on sides of neck; feathers of upper parts with pale or rusty edgings; bill, mainly black.

Nest and Eggs.— Eggs: Generally laid among stones on the beach; 4, clay color or creamy-white, thinly and uniformly marked with sepia specks, sometimes mere points.

Distribution.— Eastern North America; breeds locally from southern Saskatchewan, southern Ontario, Magdalen Islands, and Nova Scotia south to central Nebraska, northwestern Indiana, Lake Erie, New Jersey (formerly), and Virginia; winters on the coast of the United States from Texas to Georgia, and in northern Mexico; casual in migration to Newfoundland, the Bahamas, Greater Antilles, and Bermuda.

Truly a bird of the beach-sand is the Piping Plover. With propriety it might have been named the "Sand Plover." It looks the part, for it lives on the sand and so closely resembles the sand in color that it is rendered almost invisible till it moves. Then whoever it is that approaches may notice a whitish streak projecting itself ahead over the intensely bright dry sand so rapidly that it might more readily seem to be something flying than running. Its piping calls are plaintive and pretty, harmonizing finely with the general spirit of the extended beach, the dazzling sand, and the flowing sea with its monotonous undertone.

Somehow the sea-beach hardly seems fully genuine without it. None the less many of our beaches have lost this little gem of a resident. With the advent of increasing throngs of summer visitors, the eggs are stepped on or picked up, and the birds are shot by vandals or are forced to move on. At some times it has seemed that these birds would be exterminated, but law and public sentiment have come to the rescue, and in some quarters they still cling tenaciously to their old haunts. They are found not only on the sea-coast, but on the sandy or pebbly shores of the larger inland lakes.

The eggs of this Plover generally number four and are laid in a rather deep, well-rounded cavity, in almost clear sand, when there is such, but otherwise on shingle or pebbly areas, at the top of beaches. They are laid in the latitude of southern New England during the latter part of May or in early June. I have even found fresh eggs in July, but such cases are more likely second layings, after the first set is destroyed, as shore birds as a class seem to rear but one brood each season. The eggs are distinct from those of other allied species in being finely speckled instead of coarsely marked.

Photo by H. K. Job Courtesy of Doubleday, Page & Co.

NEST OF PIPING PLOVER

The young look like little bunches of cotton-batting blowing over the sand. Though born out in the open glare of the sun on the hot sand, they cannot at first endure much heat, but are carefully brooded by their parents, or else hide under drift-weed or in the clumps of beach-grass.

The food of these little Plovers is the tiny

marine life cast up by the waves on the broad white beaches where they spend their innocent lives and beautify the impressive surroundings. The sight of a big man with a gun chasing the little things has always seemed to me an atrocity, happily now made a crime, both by State enactments and by the laws of the nation.

HERBERT K. JOB.

SNOWY PLOVER

Ægialitis nivosa *Cassin*

A. O. U. Number 278

Other Name.— Snowy Ring Plover.

General Description.— Length, 7 inches. Color above, ashy-gray; below, snowy-white; *no complete white ring around neck. Bill slender,* shorter than head; hind toe missing.

Color.—ADULT MALE IN SUMMER: Forehead, line over eye, sides of head and whole under parts, snowy white; broad black bar from eye to eye; crown, pale orange-brown; narrow black streak from back of eye tending to meet its fellow on nape; rest of upper parts, pale ashy-gray; several pairs of tail-feathers, like back, darkening toward ends; two or three outside pairs, entirely white; primaries, dusky with a brownish central space; greater coverts, ashy-gray, white-tipped; primary coverts, darker, also white-tipped; outer secondaries, dark brown, long inner ones, color of back; a broad black patch on each side of breast, not meeting on back of neck or front of breast; bill and feet, black; iris, brown. ADULT FEMALE IN SUMMER: Band over eye and stripe back of it, with breast patch, dusky-gray; otherwise similar to male. ADULTS IN WINTER: Black parts replaced by grayish brown; otherwise similar to summer plumage.

Nest and Eggs.—NEST: A depression in the sandy beach. EGGS: 3, pale buff or clay color with numerous scratchy markings of dark brown and black.

Distribution. — Western United States, to South America; breeds from central California, northern Utah, and southern Kansas south to northern Lower California and southern Texas; winters from southern California and Texas south along both coasts of Central America, and on the west coast to Chile; casual in Oregon, Wyoming, Ontario, Louisiana, Florida, Bahamas, Cuba, Venezuela, and Brazil.

Something like poetic license must be invoked as an excuse for calling this Plover "snowy," since in point of fact only about half, and that the lower half, of the bird is white, while the upper parts generally are buffy-gray. It is essentially a bird of the western United States. Its note is similar to that of the Piping Plover and so are its habits, especially that of searching for marine crustacea and worms along the seashore, following the receding waves and retreating before them as they come sliding in.

The male and female take turns at incubating the eggs and the bird who is on the nest is fed by the other. But for the tracks made by the birds in these visits, the eggs usually would be exceedingly hard to find, as their color often makes them blend perfectly with the sand and drift about them.

The breeding habits of the birds were closely observed at Santa Barbara, California, by Henry W. Henshaw, and the following graphic description of their conduct when their nest was discovered is included by Dr. Baird in *North American Birds:* "Great was the alarm of the colony as soon as his [Mr. Henshaw's] presence was known. They gathered into little knots, following him at a distance with sorrowful cries. When her nest was seen to be really discovered, the female would fly close by him and make use of all the arts which birds of this kind know so well how to employ on like occasions. With wings drooping and trailing on the sand, she would move in front till his attention was secured, and would then fall helplessly down, and, burying her breast in the sand, present the very picture of despair and woe, while the male bird and the other pairs expressed their sympathy by loud cries."

WILSON'S PLOVER

Ochthodromus wilsonius (*Ord*)

A. O. U. Number 280

General Description.— Length, 8 inches. Color above, ashy-gray; below, pure white. Head large; bill long and large; outer toes webbed halfway.

Color.—Adult Male in Summer: Forehead, white, extending backward above eye; narrow black band across fore crown, *not* reaching eyes; lores, dusky; a white collar continuous with throat, around neck; upper parts, pale ashy-gray tinged with brown or ocher on back of head and neck, feathers of back and wing-coverts, with lighter edges; primaries and central tail-feathers, dusky; the outer pair whitish; others, color of back, growing darker toward end, and white-tipped; a black half ring on fore-breast not completed around neck; rest of under parts, pure white; secondaries, except inner ones, mostly white on inner web, darker on outer; bill, black; legs, flesh color; iris, dark brown; *no colored ring around eye.* Adult Male in Winter: Black replaced by dusky-gray. Adult Female: Black on breast of male replaced by dark gray, with a rusty tinge; otherwise similar to summer male. Young: Differ only from the adult female in having no black on crown or lores.

Nest and Eggs.— Eggs: Laid among the loose pebbles of the open beaches; 3, pale olive or greenish-gray, spotted and splashed all over with blackish-brown.

Distribution.— Southern North America; breeds from Texas eastward along the Gulf coast, and from southeastern Virginia (formerly New Jersey), south to the northern Bahamas; winters from southern Lower California, Texas, and Florida south to southern Guatemala and probably to the West Indies; casual in Nova Scotia and New England, and at San Diego, California.

Wilson's Plover looks like a bleached and faded copy of the Semipalmated, or else a more robust and darker type of the Piping Plover. Its much larger and stouter bill, however, proclaims its identity, as does the fact that it is seen in summer on the southern coast, southward of the breeding range even of the Piping Plover, though these ranges may overlap occasionally on the coast of Virginia. Its favorite haunts are the more retired sand beaches and bars from that State southward and on the Gulf coast, preferably on the ocean front, though it feeds to some extent back on the flats or along inlets. Following the water-line, we meet it singly or in pairs, though there may be several pairs along a good stretch of beach. Later in the summer, from about July, when the young are on wing, there may be a semblance of flocking.

By keeping our eyes well "peeled," carefully watching the sand as we walk along, we may spy the spotted eggs lying in a slight cavity of the sand, usually among scattered shells or bunches of weeds or grass, in the dry flat area of white sand above high-water mark. The only nest-building, aside from the scratching out of the hollow, is to line it with a few chips of broken shell. It is hard to see what particular purpose this may serve, unless possibly to make the eggs a little less conspicuous. At the best they are not readily found, and the birds themselves give little clue to the whereabouts of their treasures. They are not very shy, and patter along the sand ahead, uttering flute-like notes. For a while they keep flying on ahead, and presently will circle out over the water to the rear.

Photo by H. K. Job Courtesy of Houghton Mifflin Co.

WILSON'S PLOVER

Its favorite haunts are the more retired sand beaches

I have found their eggs in southern Florida in late April, and on the shores of South Carolina toward the middle of May.

Herbert K. Job.

MOUNTAIN PLOVER

Podasocys montanus (*J. K. Townsend*)

A. O. U. Number 281

Other Name.— Prairie Plover.

General Description.— Length, 9 inches. Color above, grayish-brown; below, white; bill slender; tail short, less than half the length of wing; hind toe missing; no web between middle and inner toes.

Color.—Adults in Summer: Above, uniform grayish-brown, usually pure but in some cases the feathers edged with tawny or ocher; a sharp black line from bill to eye; a black bar across fore-crown varying in width from a mere line to a band nearly half the length of the crown in width; central tail-feathers, color of back, blackening toward end, outer ones, pale, all white-tipped; *below, pure white without belt or patches* but breast sometimes shaded with rusty or gray; primaries, blackish, some of the inner ones white toward base; bill, black; legs, lead color; iris, brown. Adults in Winter: Black crown bar and loral stripe, absent; plumage, more rusty; otherwise, as in summer. Young: No pure white or black markings, and even more buffy than winter adults.

Nest and Eggs.— Nest: On the open prairies; a depression in the ground, lined with leaves and grass. Eggs: 3 or 4, cream to light olive, finely and thickly dotted with sepia, black, and lavender.

Distribution.—Western North America; breeds from northern Montana and western Nebraska south to northern New Mexico and northwestern Texas; winters from northern California and southern Texas to southern Lower California and central Mexico; accidental in Florida.

On the central table-land of the Rocky Mountains, near Sweetwater, Wyoming, was captured the first specimen of the Mountain Plover to be described. From the altitude of this point, the bird received its name. In reality, however, its unofficial name of Prairie Plover is more appropriate. It frequents the barren prairies as well as the well-watered regions of the western United States but not the marshes and beaches.

It is a quiet bird, attending consistently and constantly to its business of chasing and capturing insects. It feeds freely upon locusts, as is shown by the fact that sixteen stomachs of the bird which were examined, contained an average of forty-five locusts each. Also included in its diet are various species of harmful grasshoppers and it deserves, therefore, to be considered a useful bird.

SURF-BIRDS AND TURNSTONES

Order *Limicolæ;* family *Aphrizidæ*

THE Surf-birds and Turnstones constitute the family *Aphrizidæ* of the order of Shore Birds. There are but three species, all of which occur in North America. The subfamily of Surf-birds seem to be more closely related to the Sandpipers than to the Plovers, and the only known species is the one which is found on the coasts and islands of the Pacific. The Turnstone subfamily includes two species. Structurally they are related to the Plovers and the Surf-birds. The bill is shorter than the head, and is curved slightly upward, a peculiarity which assists the bird in turning over stones in search of its food, and from which it derives its name. The legs are short and stout, the wings long and pointed, the tail short and slightly rounded, and the plumage parti-colored in summer and neutral in winter. The birds lay four eggs, usually on almost barren rocky coasts, and conceal them very cleverly by selecting a nesting site with which their varied colors harmonize very closely.

SURF-BIRD

Aphriza virgata (*Gmelin*)

A. O. U. Number 282

Other Name.— Plover-billed Turnstone.

General Description.— Length, 10 inches. Color above, dark ashy-brown streaked and varied; below, dull white with dark markings; bill stout with rounded tip; tail, slightly notched.

Color.— Adults in Summer: Above, dark ashy-brown streaked with whitish on head and neck and varied with chestnut and black on back and wing-coverts; *upper tail-coverts and basal half of tail, pure white; rest of tail, black tipped with white;* primaries, dusky, tipped with white; greater coverts, white-tipped; large space on secondaries, also white; under parts, dull white or ashy variegated with brownish-black marks; throat and fore-breast, narrowly streaked, these streaks changing on breast proper to crescentic bars; rest of under parts, sparsely spotted; bill, black; legs, greenish-yellow; iris, brown. Adults in Winter: Head, neck, breast, and upper parts generally, uniform dusky-brown with darker shaft lines; no white or reddish; wings and tail, as in summer; beneath, dull white faintly spotted. Young: Above, brownish-gray with white edgings to feathers; below, white streaked with dusky.

Nest and Eggs.— Unknown.

Distribution.— Pacific coast of North and South America; breeding range unknown, but probably in the interior of northwestern Alaska; winters in Chile to Straits of Magellan; occurs in migration from Kobuk River, Alaska, to southern South America.

Ornithologists have been divided as to whether the Surf-bird should be considered a Plover or a Turnstone, and after much argument have compromised by giving it distinct generic rank. Evidently the bird occurs frequently on the Hawaiian and other islands in the Pacific Ocean, and it is known also to visit the Pacific coast of the United States, but nowhere is it abundant. Its breeding grounds are unknown. The bird frequents the outer beaches of the sea-coasts, where it permits the spray from the heavy surf to dash over it; hence the name given to it.

RUDDY TURNSTONE

Arenaria interpres morinella (*Linnæus*)

A. O. U. Number 283a See Color Plate 33

Other Names.—Turnstone; Sea Dotterel; Sea Quail; Sand-runner; Stone-pecker; Horsefoot Snipe; Brant-bird; Bead-bird; Checkered Snipe; Red-legs; Red-legged Plover; Chicken; Chicken Plover; Chicken-bird; Calico-back; Calico-bird; Calico-jacket; Sparked-back; Streaked-back; Chuckatuck; Creddock; Jinny; Bishop Plover.

General Description.— Length, 9 inches. Upper parts chestnut, black, and white; lower parts black and white; bill with sharp tip inclined upward; tail slightly rounded.

Color.—Adult Male in Spring and Summer: Forehead, cheeks, sides of head, and back of neck, white with a bar of black from side of neck to below eye, continuing forward and meeting its mate over base of bill and enclosing a white loral patch; another black streak on side of neck; top of head, streaked with black and white; *lower hind neck, back and shoulders, variegated with black and chestnut; rump and upper tail-coverts, snowy-white,* the latter black in center; tail, white with a broad subterminal black band; center tail-feathers, white-tipped; wing-coverts and inner secondaries, mixed black and chestnut; greater coverts, mostly white; *middle secondaries, entirely white* becoming gradually more dusky outwardly, producing an oblique white wing bar; primaries, dusky, largely white at base; *under parts, snowy-white; breast and throat, jet-black, encircling a white patch;* bill, black; *feet, orange-red;* iris, deep brown. Adult Female in Spring and Summer: Less strongly colored; chestnut replaced by plain brown, especially on wing-coverts; darker parts restricted; black not glossy. Adults in Winter: Chestnut absent, the blacks mostly replaced by browns or grays, the patch on chest smaller and much broken.

Nest and Eggs.— Nest: A hollow scratched in the ground and lined with bits of grass or seaweed. Eggs: 4, greenish-gray spotted and blotched heavily with yellowish and umber-brown.

Distribution.— North and South America; breeds on Arctic shores from Mackenzie River east, probably to Melville Peninsula, and north to Melville Island; winters from central California, Texas, Louisiana, and South Carolina to southern Brazil and central Chile.

Shore birds as a class are foremost among the earth's greatest travelers. The typical species of this class breed on the Arctic tundra, and, when winter approaches, migrate nearly to the further end of the South American continent. Such a wanderer is the Turnstone, a beautiful species, richly colored, and possessed of great powers of flight. The month of May finds it rapidly passing across the United States, following both the Atlantic and Pacific coasts and also through the interior. In the latter it is found along the larger bodies of water, but also on the sloughs of the prairies, especially where alkaline conditions produce open muddy shores. Some flocks are seen as late as the first week of June. Returning bands begin to appear as soon as the last of July, and during August the main southbound tide is on.

Courtesy of Am. Mus. Nat. Hist.

TURNSTONE (⅔ nat. size)

His method was not unlike that of the proverbial bull in the china-shop

Their prevailing habit is to keep in compact flocks, more often about a dozen, when often they fly in lines, as well as bunched up. None the less they are also found scattering, two or three, or even a lone one. They fly very fast, usually with a sort of trilling, rapidly reiterated series of notes. They are well known to hunters, frequently by the names of Chicken Plover, Calico-bird, and others.

Their favorite haunts are stony beaches on the open coast and also inlets with gravelly or partly muddy shores. For feeding purposes they carry no knife, like the Oyster-catcher, but have an arrangement no less effective for their purpose — a wedge-shaped bill. How they use this I had one exceptional chance to watch. It was in late afternoon toward the middle of September, on a sandy shore, slightly muddy, where shells and débris had been washed up. The select company was "one little Turnstone and I," the latter armed with binoculars, the former too busy to notice intruders. He was a fine gentleman, dressed in the gaudiest "calico" possible for the fall fashions, yet not too proud to work for his supper. His method was not unlike that of the proverbial bull in the china shop, for he trotted about, "tossing" nearly everything that came in his way. Inserting the "wedge" under a pebble, a shell, or what not, he would give a real toss of his imperious head, and flop over it would go. Presently he tackled a shingle, and had a hard time to budge it. He tried it on all sides, and then again, until at last he lifted and threw it over. His efforts seemed to be well rewarded, for he fed there some little time, as though many slugs and worms had taken refuge beneath it. It is in search of such prey that the turner of stones operates, a cog in the wheel of the system of nature, which decrees that every possible corner and crevice of the great system shall have its guardian, even the tiny spot of ground beneath the pebble on the beach.

HERBERT K. JOB.

The Turnstone's diet is not confined to the animal food mentioned, but includes grasshoppers of species which often menace seriously various crops. Its service in keeping down these pests is undoubtedly very valuable, and for this reason alone the bird deserves careful protection at all times.

The Black, or Black-headed, Turnstone (*Arenaria melanocephala*) averages a trifle smaller than the Ruddy Turnstone. In its summer plumage the crown and upper back are black with a greenish-bronzy gloss; the rest of the head, neck, throat, and chest are black, the forehead and sides of the head spotted with white, and a white spot in front of the eye; the rest of the under part of the body is white. In the winter, the head, neck, and chest are sooty-black without spots. The nesting and other habits of this Turnstone duplicate those of the Ruddy Turnstone. It occurs on the Pacific coast of North America, breeding from Kotzebue Sound south to the valley of the lower Yukon, and wintering from British Columbia south to Lower California. Sometimes it wanders north to Point Barrow, Alaska, and over to northeastern Siberia.

OYSTER-CATCHERS

Order *Limicolæ;* family *Hæmatopodidæ*

THE Oyster-catchers (*Hæmatopodidæ*) include ten species, and are virtually cosmopolitan in their distribution. Three species occur in North America, and all are essentially maritime birds. They are found (excepting by accident) only along the ocean fronts, where they get the principal parts of their diet, oysters, clams, mussels, and various shell-fish, whose shells they force apart with their strong, wedge-shaped bills. They also feed on marine worms and insects.

These birds have very stout legs and strong feet from which the hind toe is lacking. The plumage is chiefly black on the upper parts and white underneath. The bill of the living bird is bright red. On the ground Oyster-catchers walk with a deliberate and dignified stride, or run with ease and considerable speed. Their flight also is swift and graceful, though when flushed when they are feeding they are not likely to fly far. They build no nest but lay in a slight depression in the sand usually three eggs, which are buffy white, blotched and speckled with dark brown. Various observers have declared that incubation is performed entirely by the female, but that she covers the eggs only at night or on cloudy days and at other times leaves her work to the sun and the hot sands.

OYSTER-CATCHER

Hæmatopus palliatus *Temminck*

A. O. U. Number 286

Other Names.—American Oyster-catcher; Mantled Oyster-catcher; Brown-backed Oyster-catcher; Sea Crow.

General Description.— Length, 21 inches. Head black, back brown, and under parts white.

Color.— *Entire head and neck all around, glossy bluish-black,* frequently with a glaucous shade; *back,* shoulders, rump, and upper tail-coverts, *dusky-brown,* the side and central coverts white; *tail, white at base,* then brownish shading to blackish at ends; inner secondaries, dusky-brown, outer ones, pure white; greater coverts, broadly tipped with white forming a conspicuous area in combination with the white of secondaries; primaries, dusky-blackish at ends; *entire under parts from the breast, pure white;* bill, vermilion or coral-red, yellowish at end; legs, pale purplish flesh color; iris and eye-ring, red or orange.

Nest and Eggs.— Nest: A slight depression on sandy beaches. Eggs: 2 or 3, white or cream, spotted and blotched with dark brown, black, or lavender.

Distribution.— Coasts of North and South America from Texas, Louisiana, and Virginia (formerly New Jersey), south on both coasts of Mexico to the West Indies, southern Brazil, and central Chile; casual north to New Brunswick; breeds probably throughout its range.

Should we seek out the loneliest of the barren beaches or bars of glistering sand which are so characteristic of the coasts of the southern States, here and there at considerable intervals we are likely to meet scattered pairs of a rather large shore bird, very conspicuous from its black and white plumage. With high-power binoculars we can see their large bright-red bills, though they are so very shy that we could hardly distinguish this last feature without such aid. They are Oyster-catchers, birds which literally carry about with them each its oyster-knife, in order to be able to feed upon the oysters, mussels, clams, or other shell-fish which they encounter. Locally they are sometimes called "Sea-Crows" by the fishermen, which is not an inapt descriptive title, though their notes, which are clarion flute-like calls, are certainly more melodious than crow-talk.

Though they are often seen upon the more retired beaches of the mainland, the real type location is the little "sea island," of very small and low degree, which at high tide is a mere little strip of white sand, with areas of shell cast up by the sea. This is where, the year around, we may find the curious birds and from April to June their nests. Really it seems almost like pleasantry to imply that they ever have a real nest. To provide such homes for its eggs, all the bird needs to do is to squat on the sand, turn around a few times, and there will be found as good a habitation as it ever cares to occupy. In more ways than one is this home insecure, for it requires but a sudden heavy squall or storm to raise the water level and drive the waves over the low bar. The water may be over it but a short time, yet the mischief is done. This and other birds of the sea never appear to claim their eggs or to make any effort to save them after they have once been floated off even for a short distance.

Drawing by R. B. Horsfall Courtesy of Nat. Asso. Aud. Soc.

OYSTER-CATCHERS AT HOME

Possibly the prodigal parents may not think the eggs worth saving, so small is their number. Two eggs is the clutch I have always found, though sometimes they are said to have three. Where

Drawing by R. I. Brasher

OYSTER-CATCHER (⅓ nat. size)

Each carries with him his own oyster-knife

the Oyster-catchers are seen flying on ahead as one advances, and then returning in a circuit, it is likely that there are eggs or young not far off. The eggs are hard to find, though they lie right out in the open, on the highest and driest part of the bar, often among shells and bunches of drifted sea-weed, with which they aptly blend. The young are even harder to discover, unless they are seen to run. I have searched a bar, as it were, with a fine-tooth comb before detecting the little creatures — exactly the color of the sand — lying outstretched by some weed or bit of débris.

Photo by H. K. Job Courtesy of Houghton Mifflin Co.

OYSTER-CATCHER

On nest, South Carolina

One very absorbing experience which I have had was in photographing an Oyster-catcher at her nest. The open sand-flat afforded no possible concealment. At night I placed a bunch of seaweed near the two eggs. In the morning I set the camera under this, and, attaching a spool of strong thread to the shutter, had my friends bury me in the sand, at the thread's end, all but head and arm. When the rest of the party left the island, the birds walked right past me, gazing without fear at the apparently disconnected head cast up by the waves. Soon the female was shielding her eggs from the blazing Carolina sun. Then excitedly I pulled the thread and the picture was mine! HERBERT K. JOB.

The Black, or Bachman's, Oyster-catcher (*Hæmatopus bachmani*) is peculiar to the Pacific coast of North America, breeding from Prince William Sound, Alaska, west through the Aleutian Islands and south to central Lower California, and wintering from southern British Columbia to Lower California. It averages about two inches shorter than its eastern congener. Its head and neck are dull bluish-black, and the rest of its plumage brownish-black. In habits it, also, is strictly a shore-bird.

Photo by Clyde Fisher Courtesv of Nat. Asso. Aud. Soc.

ON ORANGE LAKE

The Island, here shown, was purchased by the National Association of Audubon Societies for a bird reservation

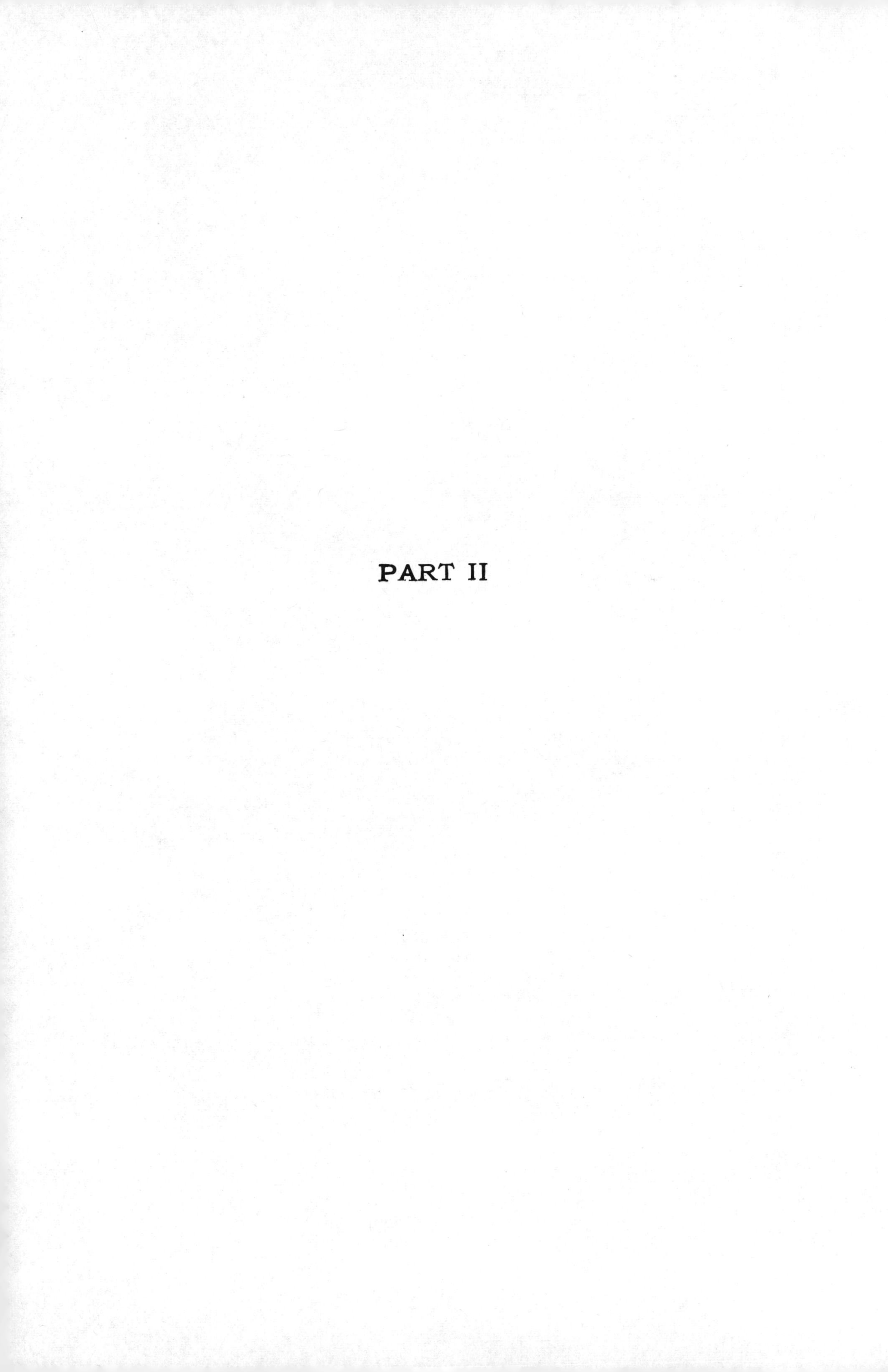

PART II

ORDER OF GALLINACIOUS BIRDS

Order *Gallinæ*

GROUND-DWELLING birds constitute this order. They are fowl-like in form and appearance: the bill is stout, convex, and short; the legs are stout and moderately long; the front toes webbed and the hind toe elevated; the wings are short, rounded, arched, and strong; the tail varies in length in the different species; the head is small; and the body heavy.

Birds of this order are polygamous. The eggs are numerous and large. The young are covered with down when hatched and are able to run about very soon after leaving the shell. Gallinaceous Birds obtain their food almost entirely from the ground, and in getting it they indulge in a great deal of scratching of the soil. The flesh of most species is edible and is generally light-colored.

Representatives of the order are found on every continent, but only the one suborder *Phasiani* has representatives (four families) of regular occurrence in the United States and Canada.

BOB-WHITES AND QUAILS

Order *Gallinæ;* suborder *Phasiani;* family *Odontophoridæ*

THE true Quails and Partridges are Old World birds and their American representatives are the Bob-whites and Quails. There are about seventy species in the western hemisphere, most of which are confined to the tropics and only seven of which are found north of the southern border of the United States.

These birds are rather small in size with heads completely feathered and sometimes crested; the nostrils covered with a naked scale; the legs stout and moderately long; the tarsi and toes naked; the front toes webbed at the base, the hind toe raised and rather small; the wings short, rounded, arched, and strong; the tail varying from less than one-half to about four-fifths the length of the wing; and the body heavy. A great variation in plumage is shown between the members of this family.

The eggs of the Partridges are numerous and large and the young when hatched are covered with down and are able to care for themselves.

The Quails of the United States, because of their interesting habits and marvelous diversity of form and color, are a notably attractive group. All are handsome birds, but the most striking and beautiful species live in the Southwest and on the Pacific coast. Only one occurs in the Eastern States. The others are widely distributed from Texas to California and Oregon. Their range was, and still is, continuous along the entire southern border of the country from the Atlantic to the Pacific; but there is an irregular belt along the northern border and a large area in the interior, comprising the Great Plains, the northern three-fourths of the Great Basin, and the Rocky Mountains, in which they appear to have been originally wanting.

With few exceptions our Quails welcome the extension of agriculture, and the added food supply in farmed areas results in an increase of their numbers. This is equally true of the Bob-white of the East and of some of the desert species of the West. So fully does the Bob-white appreciate the advantages of the farm that its range has increased with the extension of the cultivated area, especially west of the Mississippi.

Their cheerful disposition, their beauty, and their value as food usually win for the Quails a welcome to any farm. But, as the investigations of the Biological Survey show, these birds, with rare exceptions, not only are harmless, but usually are very useful to agriculture. This is particularly true of the Bob-white, which constantly feeds on injurious weed seeds and insects, and thus renders valuable service to the farmer. In return for this good service it is but fair that these birds should be treated with friendly care and interest.

BOB-WHITE

Colinus virginianus virginianus (*Linnæus*)

A. O. U. Number 289 See Color Plate 40

Other Names.— Quail; Bob-white Quail; Partridge; Virginia Partridge.

General Description.— Length, 10 inches. Plumage above, chestnut, black, ashy, and tawny, mixed; below, different shades of brown with black marks. Feathers of crown, somewhat erectile. Found in open field.

Color.— Adult Male: Forehead, lores, line over eye extending to back of head, chin, and throat, white; the line from gape, below eye, and side of head deep dusky; crown, back of head, neck all around, and upper parts of breast, reddish-brown; upper parts, a mixture of chestnut, black, ashy, and tawny, this last color edging feathers of shoulder and inner secondaries, forming a continuous line when wing is closed; under parts, white tinged with warm brown on chest, each feather with several narrow V-shaped spots of black, sides of body, flank, and wing-coverts, brownish-red, abdomen marked more or less with double crescentic black bars; upper part of breast outlining white throat, deep dusky brown; primaries, brown; tail, ash; bill, dusky horn almost black; iris, deep brown. Adult Female: Differs from male in having the throat buff instead of white, less black on breast and coloration less intense, the reddish tints of male being supplanted by a dull pinkish hue; black crescents of under parts, narrower; bill, horn color.

Nest and Eggs.— Nest: On the ground under old rail fences, sheltered by a thick growth of grass or small bushes, or at the foot of stumps; constructed of dry grasses, leaves, or weed stalks. Eggs: 12 to 18, pure white.

Distribution.— Eastern North America from South Dakota, southern Minnesota, southern Ontario, and southwestern Maine south to eastern and northern Texas, the Gulf coast, and northern Florida west to eastern Colorado; introduced in central Colorado, New Mexico, Utah, Idaho, California, Oregon, and Washington.

The call of Bob-white is one of the cheeriest sounds in nature. Nearby, it commands attention; distant, it harmonizes with other sounds of summer, yet never palls upon the ear. It names the bird. Northerners call him Quail; Southerners, Partridge; but he has named himself and ornithologists have decided that he is the prior authority. His cry is interrogatory. It is pleasing, heartening, delightful. Farmers translate it as *more wet,* saying that it foretells rain. And this prophecy is always welcome in the drouth of summer.

Photo by H. K. Job Courtesy of Outing Pub. Co.

BOB-WHITE

She was undisturbed by the camera

Everything about the bird is so attractive that men have always loved him — and hunted him. Perhaps there is no other wild bird to which the American people are more indebted. He delights in the farm; is the friend and companion of man; a destroyer of weeds and pernicious insects; a close-lying, swift-flying game bird; and, last as well as least, is the joy of the epicure. From the standpoint of the greatest good to the greatest number he is supreme; his wide range and easy accessibility make him always immediately available. He is the bird for field trials where staunch dogs show their training. Annually each autumn something like 400,000 sportsmen go out from the cities in this country to hunt Bob-white. In many cases the rental of the privilege of shooting more than pays the taxes on the farm. Thus Bob-white pays indirectly most of the taxes in many school districts and so settles for the education of the children on the farms.

After the spring rains, when the warm south winds give promise of coming summer, the birds are mating and the call of the "Quail" is heard on all sides. They are good-natured, affectionate birds, but now during the rivalries of the mating season the males become quarrelsome and sometimes fight fiercely. The mating over, the happy pairs settle down, each to its allotted place. Rarely two females use the same nest and there is some indication of polygamy in such cases. The male, however, is very attentive to his mate, is a good provider, and has been known to assume the entire charge of the brood upon the death of the female, brooding, feeding, and protecting them at all times like the fondest mother.

The young are hatched after about twenty-four days of incubation. They all pop out of the shell at about the same time and are ready to leave the nest as soon as their natal down is dry. A farmer in mowing one day overran a nest as the young were hatching. He was astonished to see the little ones, just from the shell, run away and hide in the grass. Thus nature provides for their safety. When surprised by a sudden intruder the mother tries to lead him away by many wiles, while the tiny chicks squat close to the ground and remain invisible until danger has passed. As the young grow they keep together, never going back to the nest but wandering about in the vicinity. They frequent weedy gardens, potato fields, grain and stubble fields, bushy pastures and stump lots as well as the edges of woods. The ordinary, more or less neglected farm is a paradise for them.

The birds of a bevy are very fond of each other and always keep together if possible. When scattered by the common enemy they soon commence their plaintive two-syllabled call and are never satisfied until they are reunited, when they converse together using a great variety of tender low notes. They sleep side by side in a circular group on the ground, heads out, ready to burst away like a "feathered bombshell" if surprised by the enemy. When hunted they often take refuge in almost impenetrable thickets and swamps. They have learned by necessity the art of concealment. A full-plumaged male will flatten himself and disappear on ground almost as open as a well kept lawn, and the full bevy needs only a few overhanging fern fronds or a leafy spray to render their concealment perfect. At need, Bob-white can disappear in the open before one's very eyes and reappear again from the same spot as if he had for the time being put on the cloak of invisibility. Sometimes he appears to give no scent and the dogs cannot find him.

There is some evidence of occasional southward migration for comparatively short distances. These occur at the approach of winter. Severe northern winters sometimes almost exterminate the bevies. Resting on the ground as they do at night, a heavy snowstorm may cover them. If, as sometimes occurs, rain follows the snow and is succeeded by freezing weather a crust is formed that imprisons the poor birds by thousands and starvation follows. Continued deep snows alone may decimate the species by covering deeply their food and the gravel so necessary to their digestion. Those who feed Bob-white in winter always should include coarse sand or grit with the grain.

Hard winters and an increasing number of gunners have reduced greatly the numbers of this bird in the northern parts of its range, but we are beginning to learn how to propagate it artificially. In the coming years it may be quite possible to breed the species in unlimited numbers. This gives hope for its future in all parts of its range. EDWARD HOWE FORBUSH.

The Bob-white Quail is fond of farming regions, especially where wheat and the other small grains are cultivated. It thrives in the South on cow-peas and many other foods which are plentiful. It is quite as important to see that the foods the birds require at different seasons

Photo by R. W. Shufeldt

TEXAS BOB-WHITE (½ nat. size)

Except for paler coloration and smaller size, it is like the common Bob-white

of the year are plentiful, and that they have proper covers and protection, as it is to see that their enemies are controlled. Good shooting depends on a proper attention being given to all of these matters. Briers, both berry and flower briers, the blackberry, the wild rose, and many others, make safe and attractive covers and they also furnish much food. The young Quails live largely on insects found in the fields and woods. Later they eat many berries and the seeds of plants, including weeds. In the fall they glean the stubbles for the grain lost at the harvest and in winter they often live on sumac, wild rose hips and other plants which are seen above the snow. At this season many birds will perish unless food be supplied. A little corn, served with grit at established feeding places will save hundreds of birds during a severe winter.

The Florida Bob-white (*Colinus virginianus floridanus*), a smaller and darker form of the better known common Bob-white, is found in the peninsula of Florida except in the extreme northern part.

The Texas, or Texan, Bob-white (*Colinus virginianus texanus*) is a paler variety and occurs from the southeastern corner of New Mexico to southern Texas and south into northern Mexico.

Photographs by H. K. Job

Courtesy of Outing Publishing Co.

BOB-WHITES

Nest and brood — Seven weeks old

MASKED BOB-WHITE

Colinus ridgwayi *Brewster*

A. O. U. Number 291

Other Names.— Arizona Bob-white; Hooded Quail; Ridgway's Colin; Ridgway's Quail.

General Description.— Length, 10 inches. Plumage above, reddish-brown, brown, black, and gray, mixed; below, orange-chestnut.

Color.— Adult Male: Forehead, sides of head and neck, black with or without a white line over eye; *crown, hind head, and nape, mixed black, white, and pale brown;* hindneck and shoulders, grayish-reddish-brown; back, rump, and upper tail-coverts, minutely spotted with blackish, brown, and grayish-white; wing-coverts, tawny, each feather barred with blackish, edged and tipped with dull white; primaries, dusky-brown, edged with white, inner web scalloped with the same color; secondaries, dusky barred and speckled with pale raw umber and cream; the inner secondaries and shoulder-feathers, broadly edged with yellowish white; tail, above bluish-ash finely speckled and waved with whitish, below gray lightly and irregularly barred and waved with grayish-white; under parts, orange chestnut usually immaculate except on flanks where feathers are usually tipped with an oval white spot behind a subterminal black bar; lower tail-coverts with a wedge-shaped black spot bordered with whitish; bill, black; feet, horn color; iris, brown. Adult Female: Forehead, lores, a broad stripe over and behind eye, chin, and throat, pale warm buffy; crown, sides of head (narrowly), neck, and upper parts in general, variegated with gray, brown, and tawny; beneath, dull pinkish buff lightly crossed with brown crescentic marks, these absent on flanks which are more brownish-buff.

Nest and Eggs.— Nest: A shallow excavation on the ground under the shelter of grass or bushes. Eggs: As far as known, 6, white, unmarked.

Distribution.— Middle part of southern border of Arizona south to central-northern Sonora.

The plumage of the Masked Bob-white is strikingly different from that of his eastern cousin. He is a handsome little chap in his bright chestnut-colored waistcoat, which looks red in the sunlight, and like most of his tribe he seems to be very well aware of the fact. Wherefore he announces himself with the same cheerful and confident tones which have given him and his relatives their common name. One observer notes that toward evening the short introductory note, which is usually subdued, is omitted altogether. When the covey is scattered, especially in the evening, they are assembled by means of a peculiarly soft and rather plaintive two-note call, resembling the syllables *hoo-we.*

From much of their normal range in the Southwest these attractive and interesting little birds have been driven by advancing agriculture and the accompanying man with a gun, intent upon destroying every living thing for food or for "sport."

In the vicinity of Tucson, Arizona, not so very many years ago, the birds were so plentiful, tame, and persistent in their habit of keeping closely bunched in coveys of fifteen or twenty, that it was no uncommon thing to kill five or six at a single shot — on the ground, of course. And yet many people wonder about the disappearance of wild life!

George Gladden.

MOUNTAIN QUAIL

Oreortyx picta picta (*Douglas*)

A. O. U. Number 292

Other Names.— Plumed Partridge; Mountain Partridge.

General Description.— Length, 12 inches. Plumage above, olive-brown; below, grayish-brown and chestnut. A crest of two straight feathers about two inches long.

Color.—Adults: The lores and the extreme chin, whitish; patch below eye and extending a short distance behind, and throat, orange-chestnut bordered on top by black and behind by whitish space; rest of front parts of body, grayish-brown more tinged with olive or pale rufous above; back, wings, and tail, plain olive-brown; the inner secondaries and shoulders bordered with buff or tawny forming a conspicuous lengthwise streak when wings are folded; primaries and tail, brownish, the latter finely flecked with the color of the back; abdomen, rich chestnut, the sides and flanks with broad bands of black and rufous; center of lower abdomen and thighs, whitish or pale chestnut; under tail-coverts, black streaked with chestnut; crest, black; bill, dusky with paler base; feet and iris, brown.

Nest and Eggs.— Nest: Placed on the ground under the shelter of tufts of weeds, grass, or small bushes. Eggs: 6 to 12, sometimes 18 or 20, creamy white, deposited on a bed of dead leaves or grass.

Distribution.— Humid districts of the Pacific coast from southwestern Washington south to Monterey County, California; introduced on Vancouver Island.

The mountain climber in California may now and then hear a high, clear, sweet, plaintive call *quit quit quit queeah* from the slope above him and may even catch a glimpse of a handsome bluish-plumed bird disappearing into the chapparal. A near view shows it to be the elegant Mountain Quail, the largest and in some ways the finest of its tribe. In California it seems to prefer the brush, chapparal, or timber to the open country, and the mountains to the valleys or plains, but in Oregon and Washington, where the climate is cooler, it seeks lower levels and is quite common in some of the coast valleys of southern Oregon, while in Washington it can exist even on the plains.

The systematists have divided it into three subspecies: the Mountain Quail of the humid coast region south to Monterey County, California, which has been introduced into western Washington and Vancouver Island; the Plumed Quail (*Oreortyx picta plumifera*) of the semi-arid regions from Oregon south to Inyo and Ventura counties, California, and east to the edge of Nevada; and the San Pedro Quail (*Oreortyx picta confinis*) of the San Bernardino and San Gabriel mountains in southern California and the San Pedro Martir Mountains in Lower California. The distinctions between these races relate mainly to coloration and the differences are not great. Their habits are much alike.

The male has a cheery call somewhat like the last note of the common call of Bob-white. Any boy can whistle it. Also he has a crowing note which has been compared to that of a young bantam cock. When the flock is startled its members emit a chuckling sound slightly similar to that which comes at such times from a bevy of eastern birds, but here the resemblance ceases.

The Mountain Quail rarely raises more than one brood in a season but its broods are large and occasionally eighteen or twenty eggs have been found in a nest. The tiny, downy chicks when first hatched are striped down the back with brown and yellow, streaked on each side of the head and speckled over the body with brown and black. After the first few days the little plumelets on the head begin to develop, forming a slight top-knot. The chicks are full of vitality, very active, and so easily frightened at the first alarm that they will scatter like a charge of shot and hide in an instant. When the young are small the female sometimes emits a scolding note somewhat similar to that of a guinea hen. As they grow toward maturity they frequent the chapparal, and are quite at home in the thickets. When scattered they are called together again by a note that Edwin Sandys likens to the cry of a young Wild Turkey.

This Partridge loves the high mountain glens and their foaming streams. It rarely gathers in large packs as does the Valley Quail but the members of a single brood, or perhaps two, associate together. In Oregon it thrives on bushy hillsides along the smaller streams. When pursued it is more likely to take to its legs than to its wings and to lead the hunter an arduous chase, by running until beyond gunshot and then flying fast and far. As winter comes on the flocks start on foot down the mountain trails and roads which lead into the valleys. In the spring they return to the highlands in the same way, but in mild winters there seems to be little,

Courtesy of American Museum of Natural History

CALIFORNIA VALLEY QUAIL

Beautiful, lively, and loquacious

if any, migration. This bird cannot adapt itself to civilization as well as the Valley Quail but disappears before the advance of settlement and should be assiduously protected because of its beauty and utility. EDWARD HOWE FORBUSH.

The food of the Mountain Quail of the arid regions has been studied in the laboratory of the United States Biological Survey. The stomachs examined, twenty-three in number, were collected in California. The food consisted of animal matter 3 per cent., and vegetable matter 97 per cent. The vegetable food consisted of grain, 18.20 per cent.; seeds, practically all of weeds or other worthless plants, 46.61 per cent.; fruit, 8.11 per cent.; and miscellaneous vegetable matter, 24.08 per cent. The grain included wheat, corn, barley, and oats. (Judd.)

SCALED QUAIL

Callipepla squamata squamata (*Vigors*)

A. O. U. Number 293

Other Names.— Blue Quail; Cotton Top.

Description.— Length, 9½ inches. Crest short, not entirely distinct from crown-feathers. General color, fine bluish-ash, more bluish on throat and neck, whiter on abdomen which is tinged with brown centrally; head and the full broad crest of soft blended brown feathers tipped with pure white; feathers of neck all around, upper breast, and upper back, sharply edged with crescentic lines of black; exposed surface of wing tinged with light ocher brown, the inner secondaries strongly edged with buff, forming a lengthwise stripe; side feathers, bluish-ash, each feather with a white stripe bordered on both sides with brown; rest of under parts, a blending of rusty or pale brown with elongated arrowhead or heart-shaped darker spots; bill, dusky; legs, brownish-horn; iris, dark brown.

Nest and Eggs.— NEST: A slight hollow scooped out of the sand under the protection of a clump of weeds or grass; lined with a few leaves or coarse grasses. EGGS: 8 to 16, creamy or pale buffy-white, minutely speckled with a darker shade of buff or shades of brown, distributed regularly over entire surface.

Distribution.— From central Arizona to western Texas, north to southern Colorado and over most of the Panhandle of Texas, east nearly to central Texas, and south to the valley of Mexico.

The Scaled Quail and the Chestnut-bellied Scaled Quail (*Callipepla squamata castanogastris*) are two excellent wild food birds, identical in appearance save that the last named has a chestnut patch on the belly. The birds are found in the Rio Grande valley, Texas, and northern Mexico; the first named form is found also in New Mexico, southern Arizona and the valley of Mexico. Like the other western birds, they are runners. An observer who once had a flock in his room for a time says: "The speed they made when they started on a course around the room against the wall was most remarkable. I would have backed them against the fastest Gambels or Valley Quails that ever ran on a desert or prairie." The country inhabited often is full of thorns which prevent the use of dogs and render the shooting comparatively uninteresting. Natural foods undoubtedly are sufficiently plentiful in most parts of their range, since the birds once were very plentiful. The control of their enemies would seem to be all that is necessary to perpetuate these birds.

Two or three broods are reared in a season, the

Photo by R. W. Shufeldt

SCALED QUAIL

Adult male in breeding plumage (from life)

cock assisting in the care of the young but not in incubation.

Although the Scaled Quail is a desert species, it comes into more or less direct relation with agriculture, sometimes feeding upon cultivated land and about farm buildings. Half of its food consists of the seeds of weeds. It is highly insectivorous, fully one-fourth of its food consisting of insects. The dryness of its food makes this Quail dependent on water, and the sight of a number of them is a sure indication of a nearby supply of water.

CALIFORNIA QUAIL

Lophortyx californica californica (*Shaw*)

A. O. U. Number 294

Other Names.— Valley Quail; Top-knot Quail; California Partridge; Helmet Quail.

General Description.— Length, 11 inches. Males are ashy-brown above, and slaty-blue and tawny below with chestnut patch; females are ashy-brown above and below. Both sexes have the head adorned with a glossy black crest, narrow at the base and gradually widening into gracefully recurving plumes.

Color.—Adult Male: General color of plumage of *upper parts, deep ashy brown* with a strong olive tinge, the feathers of nape and neck black-edged and centered with fine white dots between; front half of crown, brownish-yellow; rear portion and back of head, light brown; forehead, whitish with fine black lines; a white stripe from above eye along upper side of head to nape, bordered above by a narrow black stripe which extends across to front of crown; a black stripe from back of eye running toward neck and circling across upper breast; chin and throat, black bounded behind by another white stripe circling backward and around front of breast cutting off the black of throat; fore-breast, deep slaty-blue; rest of under parts, tawny with *a large area of rich chestnut on abdomen,* where marked with circular edgings of jet black except in center of chestnut patch; inner secondaries and shoulder-feathers, broadly marked with brownish-orange; sides and flanks, like color of back with broad sharp longitudinal white stripes; under tail-coverts, tawny, each feather with a wedge-shaped spot of blackish-brown; bill, dusky horn; legs, brownish-horn; iris, deep brown. Adult Female: Head and neck all around and breast, plain olive-gray without any markings on head; lower parts, without the chestnut and warm colors of the male but scaled like his, sides with white streaks; crest very much shorter.

Nest and Eggs.— Nest: A slight hollow lined with grass, under brush heaps, beside a rock, bushes, old fences, or other shelters, sometimes in gardens or even in "stolen" chicken nests. Eggs: 12 to 16, creamy, beautifully marked with spots and blotches of old gold, sometimes pale brown and chestnut over entire surface.

Distribution.— Humid districts of Pacific coast region from southwestern Oregon south to Monterey County, California; introduced into Vancouver Island, Washington, and Colorado.

The California Quail — elegant, graceful, and lovely — is one of the liveliest of all American game birds. During daylight it is in motion most of the time, and, even when settled quietly on stump or fence, its head or eyes are constantly moving that it may catch the first glimpse of any of its many enemies. Although it often seems tame and confiding during the close season or where not hunted, it leads the hunter a merry chase after the shooting season begins, and its habits of sprinting and long-distance running are likely to baffle any but well-trained dogs.

It is known commonly in California as the Valley Quail, to distinguish it from the Mountain Quail of the higher lands; but ornithologists now recognize two subspecies, the California Quail and the Valley Quail (*Lophortyx californica vallicola*) both entirely distinct from the Mountain Quail. The first is a bird of the humid coast region and has been introduced into Washington. The second, which differs only slightly from the first, is chiefly a bird of the drier or sub-arid regions of the interior, from the Klamath Lake region in Oregon south to Cape San Lucas and east to Nevada, but it is not an inhabitant of the more eastern desert region where its place is taken by Gambel's Quail. The species represented by the two subspecies lives in the valleys and on the foothills in California from near sea level to perhaps a mile above it.

Our little Quail is not only beautiful and lively, it is loquacious also. No bird perhaps has a more varied and pleasing language for if there is such a thing as bird-talk this bird surely is an accomplished conversationalist. The hunter soon learns to know the meaning of some of its notes. There is a common scolding call, resembling a little the crowing of a cock, something like *ka-ka-kao.* Some assert that the bird is merely swearing in Spanish, *Caraho!* Its calls vary. One has been rendered *kuk-kuk-ka* or *kuck-kuck-ke;* but *coo-coò-coo* with the accent strongly on the second syllable, which is pitched higher than the others, represents very well the call most commonly heard. Hunters translate its calls into various phrases, which it seems to imitate, such as "Cut it out," "Cut me too," "Oh go way," etc.; but these imaginative renditions hardly hint at the expressive powers of the Quail's language, which may be heard at its best when the young and old are in flocks together.

In spring, while the female sits on the nest, the male is attentive and watchful. His cry as he occupies some elevated perch nearby on stump, rock, or fence shows that he is on guard. The little chicks exhibit their inherited liveliness soon after they leave the egg, and have been seen to run away and hide from sudden danger with pieces of their natal shell still sticking to their backs. They are little striped, downy, bobby things with trifling top-knots. As they grow older the families gather until in early fall they assemble in "packs," usually not far from some spring or other water, where they can drink and bathe. It is believed that they post sentinels after the fashion of Crows, especially when the flock is feeding or dusting near a road or passing over rather open ground where cover is insufficient or scattered. One bird then takes an elevated position and remains on watch until relieved by another. The sentinel is frequently changed. In the flocking season a Quail perched in full view is a sign that the flock is near at hand. The little company is easily startled; a sudden motion, a falling leaf, the snapping of a twig or the rustling caused by a dog is enough to set them scurrying. When suddenly alarmed by the rush of man or beast coming rudely upon them they are likely to rise and fly in all directions, but perhaps more often they will skulk and run, fast and far. When the flock is alarmed, its members give the danger signal, a loud whispering sound such as may be produced by blowing the breath out suddenly between the teeth. Then begins a rapid extended scoot through the chapparal or underbrush.

This Quail has decreased much in numbers since the latter part of the last century. Where "packs" of thousands once lived, now only hundreds can be found. It has been destroyed in part for the market and in part by the farmers, for although it is a feeder on insect pests it eats grain and it long ago learned the virtues of grape juice and therefore earned the hostility of certain grape growers and paid dearly for its luxurious tastes.

Photo by W. L. Finley and H. T. Bohlman

CALIFORNIA QUAIL

EDWARD HOWE FORBUSH.

GAMBEL'S QUAIL

Lophortyx gambeli *Gambel*

A. O. U. Number 295

Other Names.— Arizona Quail; Gambel's Valley Quail.

General Description.— Length, 10 inches. Color above, bluish-ash; below, bluish-ash and white. Crest of soft recurved feathers.

Color.— ADULT MALE: Upper parts, plain bluish-gray with neck feathers with dark shaft lines; crest, black; crown, reddish-brown; forehead, black streaked with white; *a black stripe in front of chestnut crown patch; below this a streak of white;* a black stripe from back of eye running backward and circling across upper breast; chin and throat, black with a white stripe between it and the eye stripe; inner secondaries edged with white; forebreast, clear ash like color of back; rest of under parts, buffy whitish; *center of abdomen with a large pure black patch;* sides rich chestnut with broad sharp white stripes; under tail-coverts, white streaked with dusky; bill, black; iris, brown. Adult Female: Top of head, uniform grayish-brown from bill to neck; crest, brown, smaller and with a less number of feathers than in male; throat, dull whitish with some dark streaks; no head markings or black patch below where feathers are dull whitish with dusky longitudinal streaks; otherwise similar to adult male.

Nest and Eggs.— Nest: A hollow in the sand beneath a creosote bush, mesquite, cactus, yucca, or a tuft of grass; sparsely lined with grass or leaves. Eggs: 10 to 12, white or buffy-white, irregularly speckled, blotched, or clouded with shades of brown or lavender.

Distribution.— Desert region of southern California, southern Nevada, Arizona, and southwestern Utah, east to the southwestern corner of Colorado, and also in southwestern New Mexico to the Rio Grande valley and the El Paso region of extreme western Texas, and south into northeastern corner of Lower California and to Guaymas, Sonora.

One November evening as the sun went down I found myself in camp by a small group of water-holes far up in a desert cañon of the Santa Catalina Mountains of Arizona. I was alone, my guide having gone back several miles to look for the third member of the party whose absence had caused some uneasiness. I was sitting on a bowlder enjoying the wild, unusual surroundings when I was startled by a low *Chā-Chéā, Chā-Chéā,* which came from the little thicket behind me. This was followed at once by another call of a like nature, then another and another. I had no idea as to the nature of the language or from whom it emanated. Throwing over me the rotting remains of an old tent cover lying near I crouched among the bowlders and waited. The calls increased in number, the soap weed seemed filled with them and then suddenly out stepped a splendid Gambel's Quail, the first I had ever seen. Its long head-plume waved gradually as it advanced. Quickly others appeared and before long there before me, not twenty feet away, more than forty birds rimmed the edge of the water-hole. After a day spent in the desert they had come to the only place for miles around where water could be found in order to drink before going to roost. In a few minutes they began flying up into one of the few stunted, scrubby trees which grew in the cañon. So intent had I been watching them that I failed to note a second company nearly as large which had come to another water-hole perhaps twenty yards away. But this was not all. They continued to arrive until fully two hundred had taken up their quarters for the night in the scrubby trees around our camp. Now and then there was a flutter as some bird changed its perch. There was also much conversation after they had settled for the night, just as other folk are sometimes known to talk after going to bed.

Later I met them many times on the desert and watched them as with low words of caution they ran from the cover of one creosote bush or cactus plant to another. It was rare that I saw them take wing; even when the guide one day declared that he proposed to vary our diet of peccary and bacon that night with a mess of broiled Quail, and began to shoot them, the survivors preferred to trust their legs rather than their wings while in quest of safety.

The Gambel's Quail is a prolific bird. Ten or a dozen beautifully spotted and blotched eggs are laid and the long dry summers of the country it inhabits are very conducive to the health and happiness of little ground-running birds. There is plenty of food to be found, too, here in these glorious deserts, and should you spy a flock at eating time you might find a menu something like this: grasshoppers, ants, grain, berries and mesquite beans. Surely this feathered racer of the desert is thrice blessed with dainties.

T. Gilbert Pearson.

MEARNS'S QUAIL

Cyrtonyx montezumæ mearnsi *Nelson*

A. O. U. Number 296

Other Names.— Montezuma Quail; Messena Partridge; Fool Quail; Fool Hen; Black Quail.

General Description.— Length, 9 inches. Males are streaked above with black, reddish, and yellowish-brown, and below they are red and gray; females are barred above with black, brown, and lavender, and below they are pale lavender-brown. Both sexes have the bill very stout; the tail less than half the length of the wing; and an elongated square-cut crest of soft, blended, depressed feathers.

Color.—Adult Male: Plumage of upper parts streaked with black, reddish, and yellowish-brown;

forehead black with small streaks of white changing to brown crest; a black throat patch; a black streak on cheeks and one of the same color over eye continuous with another from gape along lower side of head, meeting that of the throat and enclosing a broad oval white space; remainder of head and broad space below throat patch, white; below the white area is another narrower streak of black extending from nape across front of chest; *wings, marked with round black spots,* the primaries, browner and spotted with white or buff; sides of neck, sides and flanks, ashy with large round white spots; middle line of breast and abdomen, rich dark chestnut; under tail-coverts, velvet-black; bill, blackish; feet, bluish-gray; iris, deep brown.

Adult Female: Head without stripes, mostly a warm grayish-cinnamon; upper parts variegated and finely barred with black, tawny, and dull lavender, the feathers with broad white shaft streaks; general color beneath, pale lavender-brown; chin whitish; neck, bluish-ash, freckled and bordered with black; breast and sides with blackish shaft streaks.

Nest and Eggs.— Nest: On ground; rather well made for a bird of this genus, entrance sometimes concealed and partially arched over. Eggs: 8 to 12, white.

Distribution.— Arid regions from central Arizona and central New Mexico east to central Texas, and south to the mountains of northern Coahuila, and Chihuahua, and eastern Sonora.

Mearns's Quail is an interesting bird. It is about the size of the Bob-white, but it is unmistakable on account of its peculiar markings. The head is black and brown, marked with white. The upper parts are brown barred with black, the sides of the breast and flanks are almost black and dotted with white, which causes the bird to look something like a dark little Guinea Hen. They are nowhere common, and, possibly, now are extinct in the United States, excepting the birds purchased and owned by breeders. Their flesh is excellent and no doubt they could be made an attractive addition to the game bag.

It is a confiding bird and like some of its relatives has earned the name of "Fool Hen" by making no attempt to protect itself and by allowing itself to be killed with a stick or stone.

The habits and food of this Quail vary considerably with the locality. It is easily tamed and is quite at home in cultivated fields. Away from civilization (according to Dr. Judd) it prefers districts covered with open forest, with alternate areas of grass and scattered bushy undergrowths, or hillsides covered with grass and bushes. Bendire records finding this species in rocky ravines.

Photograph by R. W. Shufeldt

MEARNS'S QUAIL

Mounted specimen in United States National Museum

GROUSE

Order *Gallinæ;* suborder *Phasiani;* family *Tetraonidæ*

HE Grouse include the larger forms of the rough-footed, fowl-like game birds. They are characterized by completely feathered legs (except in the case of the Ruffed Grouse and its subspecies, the Canada Ruffed Grouse), and by the fact that the nostrils and nasal grooves are concealed by feathers. The toes are naked, except in the Ptarmigans, and are equipped along the edges with comb-like growths, which are shed from time to time. The tail, which may be rounded, forked, or pointed, has from sixteen to twenty-two feathers. The region about the eye generally is more or less bare and some species have a naked spot on the side of the neck. The commonest colors in the Grouse's plumage (which is dense and soft) are various shades of brown, red, and gray, with dark greens and purples appearing in some species; but conspicuous colors and striking patterns do not occur. The male birds usually show more pronounced colors than the females, and there are some seasonal variations, especially in the Ptarmigans. Many species of Grouse prefer open plains and some even inhabit deserts. Generally, however, Grouse prefer the woods and spend most of their lives on the ground, where they get the greater part of their food and always build their nests; but some of the species when flushed will usually alight in trees nearby. Their nests are roughly fashioned of twigs and leaves. The eggs number from about six to twice as many, or more, of a brownish cast, more or less spotted or blotched, especially in the case of the Ptarmigans.

Grouse subsist upon seeds, buds, berries, snails, worms, insects and various other animal and vegetable forms. They are polygamous, excepting the Ptarmigans, and the courtship performances of the cocks include various kinds of strutting and dancing, and also the peculiar drumming demonstrations, especially of the Ruffed Grouse. Also the cocks frequently fight savagely for the possession of the hens. Generally Grouse seem intentionally to depend upon their colors for concealment, and often will lie crouched on the ground until they are almost trodden upon. When they do take to flight, it is usually at great speed and with a whir of the wings which is fairly startling. This is especially true of the Ruffed Grouse.

The flesh of all of the Grouse has a very fine flavor, excepting that of a few of the species which at times subsist largely upon spruce buds and other resinous growths. The family comprises about twenty-five species and numerous subspecies, distributed throughout the northern parts of the Old and New worlds, but is especially well represented in North America, where it reaches its highest development.

DUSKY GROUSE

Dendragapus obscurus obscurus (*Say*)

A. O. U. Number 297

Other Names.—Blue Grouse; Pine Grouse; Pine Hen; Gray Grouse; Fool Hen.

General Description.— Length, 22 inches. Color above, slaty-black; below, bluish-ash. No crest; tarsus, feathered; tail, fan-shaped with feathers (20) broad and obtuse; tail and wing about the same length.

Color.—Adult Male: Ground color of the plumage of head, neck, and upper parts in general, slaty black almost completely obscured by narrow traverse mottling of bluish-ash, these markings becoming pale brown on shoulders and secondaries; shoulder-feathers with white shaft streaks and terminal spot of white; lores and line back of eye, broken gray and white, producing an indistinct streak; tail, brownish-black marbled with gray tipped with a broad slate-gray bar; throat, broken slate and white; checks dusky-black; rest of under parts, dark bluish-ash in front, lighter behind; feathers of lower parts margined with white, broader on the flanks and under tail-coverts; bill, black; comb, over eye, and neck drum, yellow; iris, orange-brown. Adult Female: Above, dusky-black, the plumage varied by traverse bars of yellowish-brown, broader and more regular in front, broken and mottled with other shades of brown, behind; beneath, as in the male, bluish-ash, broken along the center line of the abdomen; the throat and sides with broken traverse bars of yellowish-brown; middle tail-feathers much mottled intruding on the ashy tip.

Nest and Eggs.— NEST: A slight depression in the ground under grass or bushes or alongside of a log; thinly lined with dry grass or pine needles. EGGS: 7 to 10, cream or pale buffy, spotted and speckled over the entire surface with sharply defined spots of reddish brown.

Distribution.— Rocky Mountains from northern Utah and northern Colorado to central-western New Mexico and central Arizona, and west to East Humboldt Mountains, Nevada.

The Dusky Grouse is a western bird, the largest and finest of American wood Grouse. It is next in size to the Sage Hen and weighs two and one-half to three and one-half pounds. There are four recognized races of this Grouse, namely: the Dusky Grouse (*Dendragapus obscurus obscurus*) of the American Rockies, the Sooty Grouse (*Dendragapus obscurus fuliginosus*) of the Pacific coast ranges, Richardson's Grouse (*Dendragrapus obscurus richardsoni*) of the Canadian Rockies and south to Montana and Wyoming and the Sierra Grouse (*Dendragapus obscurus sierræ*) of the mountains of southern Oregon, California and south to Mt. Pinos. The various races are known locally by several expressive and descriptive names, the most common of which are Blue Grouse, Gray Grouse, Pine Grouse, Pine Hen, and Fool Hen.

The Dusky Grouse is an inhabitant of coniferous forests from sea level to timber line whereever its favorite trees grow. It haunts great woods of fir, pine, and cedar, but seems to be most common on the edges of the timber and along the rare openings near the streams. Here in a quiet glade, where the stream glides under a natural bridge formed by a giant fallen tree, along the moss-grown trunk of which wild beasts have worn a narrow pathway, the Blue Grouse woos his mate. Mounted perhaps upon a fallen log, he struts about with tail erect and drooping wings. Now his neck puffs and swells, the feathers on its sides spreading and turning outward, their light inner surfaces exposed, forming white rosettes with a great red inflated air-sac showing in the center, and so he blossoms to the sight of his waiting mate, watching among the ferns. The comb-like fiery wattles above his eyes distend as he struts toward her, bows low, and deflates the air sacs, expelling the air with a deep *boom boom boom*. This, like similar sounds produced by other Grouse, is more or less ventriloquial, and seems almost as loud at a considerable distance as when close at hand. When it is uttered, as is sometimes the case, from a limb among the dense foliage the concealed bird is very difficult to discover.

The love season over, and the eggs laid, the female retires and becomes imperceptible, so closely does she resemble her surroundings, as she sits motionless on her crude ground nest, which is placed often in the open near the timber, sometimes beneath a log or bush. Here, secure in her invisibility, she sits until almost stepped upon; for the moment she leaves the nest the eggs become conspicuous, and she seems to lack the artifices that the Ruffed Grouse employs to lead the disturber away, though sometimes she does her best. Mrs. Irene G. Wheelock asserts that the male also attends and guards the young, but this is an exceptional habit among American Grouse. In autumn when the young birds are grown the individuals of each family remain together.

In the wilderness, where this Grouse seldom has been hunted, it barely moves out of the hunter's path, and, if flushed, merely hops or flutters into the lower branches, turning its head from side to side and regarding the disturber of its peace with innocent wonder, hence the name Fool Hen; but if hunted much it soon becomes "educated" and its habits then are more like those of the Ruffed Grouse under similar conditions although it is more likely to take to tall trees.

There is some mystery about where the Dusky Grouse spends the winter. After the snow is deep, however, it is believed that the birds stay day and night in coniferous trees where they find shelter and food among the heavy foliage which, resinous and unpalatable though it is, forms the principal part of their sustenance, while the rain and snow falling on the trees give them all the water they need. If this is the case, however, it would be interesting to know how they get gravel to assist in digesting their food or what they substitute for gravel when that is unobtainable. Keen-eyed Indians on snowshoes, in the dead of winter, have little trouble in finding and killing these birds on the trees. Now and then a Grouse flies down to the surface and writes his autograph on the snow and they are said to burrow into the drifts as the Ruffed Grouse does, and sleep there, but little is known about their winter habits. The Dusky Grouse is a bird that deserves a better acquaintance. It is well worth knowing.

EDWARD HOWE FORBUSH.

The Dusky Grouse are mountain as well as forest-loving birds, and they often wander from the spruce and fir forests above the timber line in their search for berries and other food. In winter they descend to the valleys. They are not migratory, such movements being made solely in search of food and to escape the severe weather of the higher altitudes. The food of the Dusky Grouse consists of insects, which form a large part of the food of the young birds, grasshoppers being the principal insect eaten, and fruits, seeds, and leaves.

Like the Spruce Grouse, the Dusky Grouse is a browser and is one of our chief foliage-eating birds. Dr. Judd says it spends most of its time in pine forests feeding on needles, buds, and flowers. In the summer many berries are eaten, among them the abundant wild gooseberries, currants, strawberries, huckleberries, and bear-berries. The flesh is white, tender, juicy, and delicious. Later in the season it is affected by the change in diet and it often has then a bitter and resinous taste which renders it highly undesirable.

HUDSONIAN SPRUCE PARTRIDGE

Canachites canadensis canadensis (*Linnæus*)

A. O. U. Number 298 See Color Plate 41

Other Names.— Canada Grouse; Black Grouse; Wood Grouse; Wood Partridge; Spotted Grouse; Cedar Partridge; Swamp Partridge.

General Description.— Length, 17 inches. Males are black and gray above, and black below, variegated with white; females are brown, tawny, and black above, and dull-whitish below, barred with black. Both sexes are without crests or ruffs; tarsus feathered to the toes; tail with 16 feathers.

Color.—Adult Male: Plumage of entire upper parts, wavy-barred with black and gray; some rufous markings on back and wings; white markings on shoulders and wing-coverts; lores, whitish; throat and sides of head below eye, black bordered with broken white; a bright yellow or reddish-colored comb over eye of naked skin; *tail, black broadly tipped with orange-brown;* under parts, deep glossy black much variegated with white; under tail-coverts tipped with white; sides and breast with white crescented bars. Adult Female: Entire upper parts, umber brown varied with tawny and ocher and traversely barred with black; lores and a short streak behind eye together with an obscure patch on side of throat, whitish; beneath, dull whitish much mixed with tawny particularly on breast; nearly everywhere wavy-barred with blackish; shorter in front, more heavily behind; flanks, streaked

Drawing by R. I. Brasher

HUDSONIAN SPRUCE PARTRIDGE (½ nat. size)

The champion fool among birds

with white; tail mottled with buff and tipped very narrowly with orange-brown.

Nest and Eggs.— NEST: On the ground, well-concealed under low conifer branches, brush heaps, or tamarack; constructed of dry twigs and leaves and lined with moss and grass. EGGS: 8 to 14, buffy or reddish-brown, blotched and spotted with different shades of darker brown.

Distribution.— From the eastern base of the Rocky Mountains west of Edmonton, Alberta, east to Labrador Peninsula; also a disconnected area in Alaska from Bristol Bay to Cook Inlet and Prince William Sound.

There is no such bird as the Spruce Partridge. It is the Spruce Grouse (*Canachites canadensis*); but it is called Spruce Partridge in common parlance to distinguish it from the Birch Partridge (Ruffed Grouse) and ornithologists have adopted the popular misnomer, well knowing it to be incorrect. In recent years this Grouse has been divided into three races or subspecies, differing slightly in plumage but hardly any in habits. The races are: (1) Hudsonian Spruce Partridge (*Canachites canadensis canadensis*), (2) Alaska Spruce Partridge (*Canachites canadensis osgoodi*), and (3) Canada Spruce Partridge (*Canachites canadensis canace*). These three races (each in its allotted place) inhabit most of the wooded regions of Canada and Alaska except southern British Columbia, Alaska, and central Alberta, where another species, Franklin's Grouse (*Canachites franklini*), takes their place.

The Spruce Partridge is a bird of the northern wilderness. Only one of the three races of *Canadensis* ever reaches the United States, and that one, the Canada Spruce Partridge, touches only a few of the northern States, in most of which it is now nearly or quite extinct. The Spruce Partridge is a dweller in dark spruce woods and tamarack swamps, north into boreal regions, probably as far as its favorite trees extend. The extermination of the southern race over much of its range in the United States is a blot on our history, as the bird always was harmless and interesting. It is hardy and fearless. It is too confiding, however, to exist in the neighborhood of civilized man — the most bloodthirsty and destructive of all animals. In the mating season the male struts about with bristling feathers, head, neck, and tail raised, tail expanded and body held level. The drumming is not done exactly like that of the Ruffed Grouse, but the bird performs by beating the air with its wings as it climbs up a leaning tree trunk, or else it flies from the ground, sometimes nearly to the tree tops, often only a few feet in air, and drums suspended with beating wings.

In its native wilds this bird exhibits the most charming confidence in mankind. The hunters know it as the champion fool among birds. The Indian boy shoots it with a blunt-headed arrow or even knocks it down with a stick as it walks by unconcernedly or sits on a limb regarding the intruder with happy curiosity. Full-grown birds have been caught in the hand or beheaded with a switch. The hunter meets a brood in the trail and they merely step aside and watch the passer with a sort of affectionate regard. As civilization approaches, the Spruce Partridge disappears, for man destroys every wild creature that confides in him. If any escape they learn by experience, but the Spruce Partridge is too slow to learn. There is little excuse for killing it as the flesh is dark and unpalatable, having a strong flavor of spruce and fir foliage which forms a great part of its food. In summer it feeds more or less on insects and berries and, as the flesh is improved in flavor by this diet, the bird is hunted most then and in early autumn when the young are at their best. Its only possible chance for salvation is its residence in the northern wilderness where white men are few and far between.

EDWARD HOWE FORBUSH.

Photo by H. E. Anthony

SPRUCE PARTRIDGE

A bird of the northern wilderness

FRANKLIN'S GROUSE

Canachites franklini (*Douglas*)

A. O. U. Number 299

Other Names.— Franklin's Spruce Grouse; Fool Hen; Mountain Grouse; Wood Grouse; Tyee Grouse.

Description.—Adult Male: Size, shape, and color of the Hudsonian Spruce Partridge; tail, longer and more even with broader feathers, but *without terminal orange bar;* its upper coverts broadly tipped with pure white. Adult Female: Differs from the female Spruce Partridge in having the tail-coverts white tipped and tail tipped with white instead of orange-brown; otherwise the birds are indistinguishable.

Nest and Eggs.— Nesting habits, and number and color of eggs are similar to those of the Spruce Partridge.

Distribution.— Southern Alaska, central British Columbia, central Alberta, south to Oregon, Idaho, and Montana.

The popular name "Fool Hen" is applied to the Franklin's Grouse and various other species of northern Grouse, and to other species of gallinaceous game birds, who fail to act promptly on the well-known fact that the average man will murder them on sight. This misplaced confidence by the Franklin's Grouse persists in a degree which is almost incredible. Often, a flock of them feeding on a trail will do no more than step aside as the destroyer approaches, or if they actually take to their wings they will perch in nearby trees, and regard their enemy with friendly curiosity, declining to move even when their confidence is rewarded by a volley of sticks and stones. George Bird Grinnell records an instance of one bird who sat quite still on a limb while a man shot at him several times with a rifle. The man was a bad shot but finally a bullet cut a foot off the Grouse, whereupon the bird simply shifted its weight to the other foot, and continued to sit still until the marksman was at last successful. Indeed it seems quite hopeless that this Grouse will ever become a real game-bird, which is to say, a bird who flies for his life at the distant approach of man.

Photo by T. H. Riggall Courtesy of *Field and Stream*

FRANKLIN'S GROUSE

Regarding its enemy with friendly curiosity

The strutting of this Grouse is an elaborate and rather amusing performance. It involves much prancing about, during which the bird distends his red eyebrows until they nearly meet over the crown of the head, meanwhile spreading his tail to its utmost width, then closing half of it on one side and half on the other, alternately, these movements being accompanied by a sound like the rustling of silk. The plumage of this species resembles that of the Hudsonian Spruce Partridge.

The Franklin's Grouse was first described by Lewis and Clarke in the report of their exploring expedition to the Pacific coast in 1804–1806. But, despite the fact that the bird has been known for over a century, comparatively little is known of its nesting habits. From the few records available, these habits do not differ from those of the Spruce Partridge.

RUFFED GROUSE

Bonasa umbellus umbellus (*Linnæus*)

A. O. U. Number 300 See Color Plate 41

Other Names.— Grouse; Shoulder-knot Grouse; Partridge; Drumming Grouse; Birch Partridge; Pheasant; Drumming Pheasant; Mountain Pheasant.

General Description.— Length, 18 inches. Color above, reddish-brown, spotted; below, yellowish, barred with dark. Both crested and ruffed; tail and wings of equal length; tail with 18 broad, blunt feathers, and somewhat double notched, so that it is nearly half-diamond shape when spread; tarsus partly feathered in front.

Color.—ADULTS: Lores, cream; crown, variegated black, brown, and yellow; nape more softly blended with gray and reddish-brown; back and shoulders, cinnamon-rufous, each feather with a broad yellowish-white center stripe, this stripe mottled on both sides with brownish-black; lower back, rump, and upper tail-feathers, tawny-brown mixed with gray, speckled with heart-shaped spots of yellowish-white; *tail, warm brown or grayish-ash,* crossed with six or seven narrow bands of blackish-brown, the subterminal one much wider, the feathers tipped with whitish; throat, dull ocher; rest of under parts, whitish tinged with pale brown or pale yellow; the breast, narrowly but boldly crossed with traverse bars of burnt umber or sepia, sides and abdomen with large traverse wedge-shaped spots of dusky and brown, under tail-coverts and thigh-feathers faintly marked or immaculate; ruff, purplish-black; wing-coverts, a warm brown or cinnamon with a narrow shaft streak of white; secondaries and primaries, dusky, the former edged and tipped with yellowish-white, the outside webs of latter with a number of elongated spots of yellowish white. YOUNG: Similar to adult.

Nest and Eggs.— NEST: On the ground, in thickets, dense underbrush, on the borders or in large woods, alongside of a log or at the base of a large tree; constructed of old leaves, a few feathers, weed stems, grass, and roots. EGGS: 6 to 15, usually 10 or 12, varying from whitish through cream to a pale brown, usually without spots but sometimes lightly speckled with shades of brown.

Distribution.— Eastern United States from Minnesota, Michigan, southern New York, and southern Vermont south to eastern Kansas, northern Arkansas, Tennessee, and Virginia, and in the Alleghenies to northern Georgia.

The bird called Partridge or Birch Partridge in the North and Pheasant in some of the middle and southern States is really a typical forest Grouse. It is a hardy dweller in rough, cold lands. Dark forests, rocky mountain sides, deep thickets, and sheltered swamps are its favorite hiding places in summer or winter. It likes the dim and silent woods, far from the haunts of man, but will tolerate his presence if only he leave intact the stately trees; it is no lover of open plains and where the woods are destroyed it soon disappears.

Most country boys in the northern United States well remember their first experience in the woods with this brave and hardy bird. No sound of the forest is more startling than the sudden thunderous roar of beating pinions with which it rises, sometimes almost from under foot, scattering the fallen leaves like a little whirlwind, tearing its way through rustling leaves and bending twigs, winning distance and concealment in one breathless instant. A stirring dash, a swirl of leaves and it is gone, leaving the slow, blundering human biped startled and staring with open mouth and fast-beating heart. It is not necessary for this Grouse to rise with such bluster for it can fly and alight as quietly as most birds, but the sudden whir speaks eloquently of fear and is the bird's method of escaping quickly, confounding its enemies, and sounding the alarm to its companions in danger. Often the swift bird escapes before the startled gunner has fairly caught sight of it.

The four recognized races of this Grouse — the Ruffed Grouse (*Bonasa umbellus umbellus*), the Canada Ruffed Grouse (*Bonasa umbellus togata*), the Gray Ruffed Grouse (*Bonasa umbellus umbelloides*), and the Oregon Ruffed Grouse (*Bonasa umbellus sabini*) — extend the range of the species over much of the wooded regions of the United States and Canada and it is known more widely than most other game birds, but its habits can hardly be said to be so well known, as wherever it is much hunted it becomes extremely shy and suspicious, and some of its ways are, even now, the subject of dispute. Probably no one man has lived long enough to learn all its wiles. Its wildness in settled regions is the more remarkable when we realize that when the first explorers came to this country this Grouse had so little fear of mankind that it would sit on a low limb gazing curiously at the intruder and could be killed with a stick. Only a few years ago in the great untrodden forests of British Columbia I found it similarly unsuspicious. The young when reared artificially from the egg are so tame that they are in danger of being trodden underfoot. Fortunately the bird has so capable a brain that a brief experience with the " man behind the gun " serves to " educate " it and if it survives its first few experiences with flying shot it becomes quite another bird.

It is only the solitary woodsman that is likely to observe the habits of the Ruffed Grouse. He who has learned the art of sitting quietly on a log or waiting patiently in the cover of the thickets may gradually come to know many of its ways. Its drumming is one of the commonest sounds of the woods. Under favorable circumstances the sound will carry a mile. Yet many have never been conscious of hearing it, few have ever actually seen the performance, and to this day those who have watched the birds drum in confinement are in dispute as to whether the sound is made by the wings striking the air or the feathers of the breast. The sound serves three purposes: first, as a call to the female, second, as a challenge to combat; and third, as an expression of the abounding vigor and vitality of the male. It serves the first purpose admirably, as probably all the females within hearing come to the sound if they hear no other drummer, for the Ruffed Grouse is a polygamist and has been observed to mate with two or more females within a few minutes. The second purpose is served when one drummer approaches another's station, for then a fight is likely to ensue until one or the other is whipped and driven away. The third purpose apparently is the only one served in the autumn, when the mating season is over and when the birds drum as a healthful exercise to expend their surplus energy.

Drawing by R. I. Brasher

RUFFED GROUSE ($\frac{1}{3}$ nat. size)

Its experience with man has taught it to be suspicious and shy

It seems, at first sight, very unfortunate that Grouse nest on the ground where their nests are easily accessible to the prowlers of the forest, but if they built in trees, which they almost never do, their large nests would be conspicuous and readily seen by their enemies. The sitting bird covers her eggs, and so closely does she resemble her surroundings that even the keen-eyed Hawk passes her unawares. Also she seems to leave no scent at nesting time, for trained pointer and setter dogs have been unable to find a mother bird on the nest so long as she remained motionless. Often the nest is sheltered under log, stump, or tree, sometimes near the den of the fox, often near that of the skunk; but these prowlers seem to find it only if they fall upon it by accident, thus starting the bird, or if they see her enter or leave it. When the fox blunders on her retreat she bristles up and flies directly at his head. This startles him but does not divert him and his mouth is soon full of scrambled eggs.

The little ones with their pipings and flutterings would not long be safe in their lowly nest and so they leave it as soon as the natal down is dry and thenceforth become wanderers on the face of the earth. They do not stray far from the neighborhood, but patter about day by day, and gather under the mother's wings wherever night overtakes them. She is ready to defend them with her life, if need be, or to entice away any enemy by crying and fluttering in the path like a wounded bird. This ruse often is successful with a boy or a dog, but does not deceive Reynard, who quietly retires, lies down to await the mother's return, and, when the chicks rise from their concealment at her call, springs among the frightened brood and marks one for his own.

In feeding, the little ones scatter through the woods, searching for insects on the forest floor or jumping and fluttering up to the overhanging foliage in search of their elusive prey, while the mother follows, watchful for any enemy that may be upon the trail. In about a week from the time they leave the egg the chicks can use their wings and within three weeks, though still no larger than very small chickens, they have learned to fly considerable distances and to rise quite high in air.

As their feathers grow they learn first to sleep on the ground in a circle about the mother and next to roost in shrubs and trees. As the summer wanes the growing birds make dusting places in dry spots along wood roads or southerly hillsides where they wallow and dust their feathers in the manner of a domestic fowl, to free themselves of parasites.

Photograph by H. K. Job — Courtesy of Outing Publishing Co.

RUFFED GROUSE ON NEST

When autumn comes they are nearly full-grown but their numbers have decreased about one-half as they have many enemies. Now they visit the wild apple trees and grape vines or search for beechnuts and acorns among the fallen leaves. About the middle of October they begin to wander about and often are found dead in queer places where they have flown against some obstacle such as a high wire fence or the side of a building. This is the unexplained "crazy season." They are now preparing for winter, laying in stores of fat, growing a long downy covering for body and legs and putting on their snowshoes, which consist of little horny comb-like appendages that grow from the sides of the toes to help support the weight of the body on the snow.

Now comes the hunting season, when the bird has need of all its wits. Its many wiles and stratagems are known more or less to the hunter. Commonly upon rising it goes behind a tree trunk or some thick foliage and keeps this between itself and its pursuer. Often it doubles upon its trail, circles, and lies close until the hunter has passed, rising behind him and getting safely away. Sometimes it flies rapidly out of sight but alights high in some tall, thick pine where it remains motionless until the coast is clear, and so, in one way or another, a few birds manage to survive the season and then they face the winter. As the inclement season comes on, they leave the heights and come down into the more sheltered valleys and swamps where they subsist on buds, foliage, twigs, and dried berries until vernal breezes blow and nature calls them again to the mating. EDWARD HOWE FORBUSH.

The Ruffed Grouse can be kept plentiful even in closely settled farming regions, provided small woods or thickets be left or are planted, and foods suitable for different seasons of the year are provided. Young birds are largely insectivorous. More than 95 per cent. of the diet of the young Grouse examined by Dr. Judd was insects. Newly hatched chicks eat the most; as they grow older they eat fruit, and later they feed on mast, grain, and buds. The study of the food habits of the young has not been as extensive as it should be, but it indicates that the chicks eat grasshoppers, cutworms, certain beetles, ants, parasitic wasps, buffalo tree-hoppers, spiders, grubs, and caterpillars. Undoubtedly many small insects and their eggs which are found in the woods and adjacent fields will be added to the list. The beetles seem to be preferred, but Dr. Judd says the Grouse he shot in September, in New Hampshire, were feeding largely on red-legged grasshoppers, which were abundant in the pastures where the birds foraged. The vegetable food consists largely of seeds, fruit, buds and leaves. Mast, including hazelnuts, beechnuts, chestnuts, and acorns, are staple foods, the acorns being the largest supply in many regions. Acorns of the scrub oak, scrub chestnut oak, white oak, and red oak are swallowed whole. The Ruffed Grouse undoubtedly eats grain and often procures it along woodland roads, where it resorts to dust and to feed on the abundant berries.

More than one-fourth of the yearly food of this bird is fruit. Its diet includes the hips of the wild rose, grapes, partridge berries, thorn apples, wild crab apples, cultivated apples, wintergreen berries, bayberries, blueberries, huckleberries, blackberries, raspberries, strawberries, cranberries, sarsaparilla berries, and others, wild and cultivated cherries, plums, haws, sumacs, including the poison sumac and poison ivy, which are taken with immunity.

Sportsmen are well aware of the fondness of this Grouse for wild grapes and apples, and they often find them in places where grapes are plentiful and in old fruit orchards, especially on abandoned farms. The wild rose-hips and sumac are excellent winter foods because they can be obtained above the snow. Wild and cultivated sunflowers furnish excellent food, and many other fruits and seeds of varying importance are on the Ruffed Grouse's bill of fare.

Birch, poplar, willow, laurel, and other buds are eaten by the Ruffed Grouse, and the budding, practiced for the most part during the winter, enables it to survive the severe winters of the northern States and Canada, when other foods are buried in deep snows. The several species of birch buds are a staple.

WILLOW PTARMIGAN

Lagopus lagopus lagopus (*Linnæus*)

A. O. U. Number 301

Other Names.— Ptarmigan; Common Ptarmigan; Willow Grouse; White Grouse; Snow Grouse.

General Description.— Length, 17 inches. In summer males are brownish-rufous above, barred with black, and white below; females are tawny-brown, above and below, barred and spotted with black. In winter both sexes are white. The feet are completely feathered, the tail has 14 feathers, and the tail-coverts reach to the end of the tail.

Color.—ADULT MALE IN SUMMER: Head, neck, and

breast, rich chestnut or cinnamon-rufous, top of head spotted with black, chest and neck with bars of the same color; entire upper parts except wings, more brownish-rufous, broadly and closely barred with black; most of the wings and rest of the under parts, white. ADULT FEMALE IN SUMMER: Entire plumage except wings, tawny-brown, heavily spotted and barred above, and uniformly barred below with black. ADULTS IN WINTER: Snowy white; *tail-feathers, black tipped with white;* middle pair with tail-coverts which extend to end of tail, white.

Nest and Eggs.— NEST: A mere depression in the ground, lined with leaves, grass, or feathers. EGGS: 7 to 12, varying from pale yellowish to dark chestnut-brown, heavily spotted with rich browns and black.

Distribution.— Arctic regions; in America breeds from northern Alaska, northern Banks Land, and central Greenland south to eastern Aleutian Islands, central Mackenzie (in the mountains to west-central Alberta), central Keewatin, James Bay, and southern Ungava; south in winter to northern British Columbia, Saskatchewan valley, Minnesota, Ontario, and Quebec; accidental in Wisconsin, Michigan, New York, Maine, and Massachusetts.

The extreme northern portion of the northern hemisphere is the summer home of the Willow Ptarmigan. Here, often well above the tree line on the boundless moss-covered tundra where the ground thaws only to a depth of a few feet, the student may seek for this bird. The rich chestnut-brown plumage in no way renders it conspicuous in summer and in winter when all the region about it is perpetually white, the Ptarmigan has a coat as white as the snowy wastes it inhabits. From seven to twelve spotted eggs are laid in the simple grass- or feather-lined nest on the ground. One observer states that all the coloring matter can so be washed from a freshly laid egg that only the pale creamy white of the shell is left.

The male of many of the Gallinaceous birds, not content with one mate, gathers unto himself several helpmates. The male Willow Ptarmigan, let us record, is not one of these polygamous individuals. He has only one mate and for her sweet sake he wages furious battles in spring with other covetous blades of the frozen wastes. For her he undergoes punishment and loses many feathers. So frequent and so furious are these battles that apparently few except the strong birds are able to win and be the proud head of a family. Such provision is doubtless wise in a country where the conditions of climate are certainly not ideal for bird-life. During the mating season the male is very noisy and his hoarse calls and hoots may be heard on all sides. The uproar reaches its greatest height between 10 P. M. and 2 A. M., this being the period of the twenty-four hours when there is less daylight, and doubtless takes the place of the dawn which birds farther south are fond of making resonant with their songs.

The Willow Ptarmigan is migratory and after the breeding season retires southward as far as Sitka in south Alaska, and the central British provinces. A few have even been known to wander to the northern edge of the United States.

The food of this bird in summer consists of various insects and herbs. In autumn it finds many berries and in winter it appears to subsist almost entirely on the buds and terminal twigs of the dwarf alder and willow that flourish in bush-grown gullies of the tundra.

Ptarmigans constitute a popular article of diet with the human inhabitants of the Far North. A method at times employed in hunting them is thus described by Mr. E. W. Nelson:

"At the Yukon mouth on the evening of May 24, these Ptarmigans were uttering their hoarse notes all about. As we were sitting by the tent my interpreter took my rifle and going off a short distance worked a hump of snow to about the size of one of these birds. Fixing a bunch of dark-brown moss at one end of the snow to represent the bird's head, he set his decoy upon a bare mossy knoll; then retiring a short distance behind the knoll he began imitating the call of the male until a bird came whirring along, and taking up the gauntlet lit close by its supposed rival and fell victim to the ruse."

T. GILBERT PEARSON.

Allen's Ptarmigan (*Lagopus lagopus alleni*) is similar to the Willow Ptarmigan, having the same seasonal variations, but in all plumages the primaries are usually mottled with fuscous or have some fuscous along the shaft. It occurs on the rocky barrens of Newfoundland and feeds on seeds and berries.

ROCK PTARMIGAN

Lagopus rupestris rupestris (*Gmelin*)

A. O. U. Number 302

Description.— Length, 15 inches. ADULTS IN SUMMER: Entire plumage with the exception of wings and tail, which are white, brownish-yellow barred with blackish-brown; the lower parts of the male, except breast and sides, white. ADULTS IN WINTER: Pure white, *the tail black and a black stripe from the bill to eye and behind it.* IMMATURE IN FIRST WINTER: Similar to adult female in winter.

Nest and Eggs.—Nest and location similar to the Willow Ptarmigan. EGGS: 6 to 10, indistinguishable from those of the Willow Ptarmigan.

Distribution.— Arctic America; breeds from Melville Island to Melville Peninsula and south on the Barren Grounds from Alaska to Ungava; also above the limit of trees south to central Yukon; south in winter to southern Mackenzie and southern Ungava.

The habits of the Rock Ptarmigans are much like those of their relative, the Willow Ptarmigan, though they are not such prolific breeders. During the nesting season their coloration so closely resembles that of their surroundings that they are unlikely to be discovered except by accident. Like other birds which build on the ground, they seem to be aware of this fact, and will let an intruder almost tread upon them without stirring.

The Rock Ptarmigan is common on the mainland of Alaska where it is to be found chiefly on high ground in the summer months, whence it is driven into the valleys by the fierce winter storms.

The scientists recognize six variations of this species; they are: Reinhardt's Ptarmigan (*Lagopus rupestris reinhardi*), Nelson's Ptarmigan (*Lagopus rupestris nelsoni*), Turner's Ptarmigan (*Lagopus rupestris atkhensis*), Townsend's Ptarmigan (*Lagopus rupestris townsendi*), the Adak, or Chamberlain's, Ptarmigan (*Lagopus rupestris chamberlaini*), and Dixon's Ptarmigan (*Lagopus rupestris dixoni*).

Photos by I. S. Howe — Courtesy of Nat. Asso. Aud. Soc.

ROCK PTARMIGANS

These pictures were taken Christmas Day on Turkey Creek, near Morrison, Colorado: they are a good illustration of the protective value of the dress of the Ptarmigans; the shadows on the snow can be seen at a greater distance than can the birds

WHITE-TAILED PTARMIGAN

Lagopus leucurus leucurus (*Swainson*)

A. O. U. Number 304

Other Names.— Mountain Quail; Snow Grouse; Rocky Mountain Snow Grouse; White Quail.

Description.— Length, 13 inches. Entire foot feathered; tail less than ⅔ length of wing; tail-coverts reaching to end of tail. ADULTS IN SUMMER: Tail, most of wing, and lower parts from breast, pure white; rest of plumage, finely marked with grayish-brown, white, and black, varying with almost every specimen. ADULTS IN WINTER: *Entirely snow white;* bill, black. YOUNG: Tail, gray.

Nest and Eggs.— NEST: On ground in open situations; sometimes a mere depression in the ground, at others, quite a well-built structure of grass, leaves, and weed stalks, lined with feathers. EGGS: 10 to 16, pale buffy or light rusty-brown spotted or marbled with small dots or burnt-sienna over entire surface.

Distribution.— Rocky Mountains from northern British Columbia and central Alberta south to Vancouver Island, Washington, northwestern Montana, Colorado, and northern New Mexico.

It was on Piegan Pass in Glacier National Park, Montana, that I first saw the White-tailed Ptarmigan. An hour before we had left the tree line behind and had since been climbing steadily. Snow fields were all about us and beds of heather were abundant, in fact it was clear that we were now in the heart of the Ptarmigan country. We had all but reached the summit when suddenly, within thirty feet of the trail and almost on a level with my eyes, as I sat on my horse, a Ptarmigan appeared with five young. Their color matched their surroundings so nearly that had they elected to sit still no eye in the party would have detected them. A low clucking call from the mother bird was the only sound we heard. She exhibited no uneasiness and made no move to leave. Twenty minutes later, when a halt was made and some of us walked back with our cameras, the little family was still in the same place, and readily allowed themselves to be photographed at a distance of twelve feet. Here on these Alpine heights the Ptarmigan lives, with the Rosy Finches and the Pipits for its neighbors.

In winter when all the world the Ptarmigan knows is covered deep in snow, we find that nature has also worked a miracle with the bird, for then its plumage is of snowy whiteness. In few birds is protective coloration exhibited to such an extent as in these Ptarmigans that live along " the top of the world."

T. GILBERT PEARSON.

Photo by Nelson W. Logue — Courtesy of Nat. Asso. Aud. Soc.

WHITE-TAILED PTARMIGANS IN SUMMER PLUMAGE

Male — **Female**

Taken July 14, 1905, at Willow Lake, Colorado, above the timber line, elevation 11,500 feet. All the white is snow

PRAIRIE CHICKEN

Tympanuchus americanus americanus (*Reichenbach*)

A. O. U. Number 305

Other Names.— Prairie Hen; Pinnated Grouse; Prairie Grouse.

General Description.— Length, 18 inches. Color above, yellowish-brown, spotted with black; below, white barred with dusky-brown. Tail, short, rounded, and with 18 feathers; tarsus, feathered to base of toes; toes, webbed at base; a tuft of narrow, stiff feathers about 3 inches long on each side of neck overlying an area of bare skin; head with a slight soft crest. Neck tufts of female much smaller and less conspicuously colored.

Color.—Adults: Plumage above, yellowish-brown much broken by broad traverse spots or irregular bars of deep black, this color in excess of lighter tints; forehead, crown, and sides of head, deep buff; crown, much mottled with black and brown spots; a stripe from gape, beneath the eye, to nape, plain brownish-black; primaries and tail, plain dusky, the former with round spots of pale ocher on outer webs; tail, narrowly tipped with white; throat, plain buff bounded by a streak of dusky above, thus two stripes on side of head; rest of lower parts, dull whitish, everywhere barred with numerous sharply defined bands of dusky-brown; neck-tuft, rusty and pale buff at the neck, shading into deep black at ends.

Nest and Eggs.— Nest: On the ground in open prairie country, sheltered by grass tufts or bushes, or exposed; a slight hollow in the soil, thinly lined with grass and a few feathers. Eggs: 8 to 12, light drab or dull buffy usually unmarked, sometimes lightly sprinkled with brown.

Distribution.—Southeastern Saskatchewan and southern Manitoba to eastern Colorado, northeastern Texas, Arkansas, western Kentucky, and Indiana; probably extinct east of Indiana but formerly reached southwestern Ontario, Michigan, and northwestern Ohio.

The Prairie Chicken or Grouse, including the somewhat smaller form, Attwater's Prairie Chicken (*Tympanuchus americanus attwateri*), which is found in Texas and Louisiana, still occurs, in sadly diminished numbers, from Manitoba, Michigan, and Indiana to Texas and westward to the Great Plains where, as in the Dakotas, it has extended its range with the advancement of civilization. The Prairie Grouse weighs about two pounds and its flesh is tender, juicy, and delicious. Some prefer it to the flesh of the Ruffed Grouse. It certainly is a magnificent wild food bird and well worth preserving.

Grouse cannot stand the ordinary destruction by natural enemies and the destruction by guns at the same time. Since the birds continued to vanish after shooting had been prohibited, it is evident that there are other causes for this besides shooting. The destruction of their foods and covers is sufficient to account for the loss. Cats, rats, and roving dogs in many places prevent any increase in their numbers. Prairie fires and floods often exterminate them on large areas. The same may be said of the Sharp-tailed Grouse, and of the Prairie Chicken of the northwestern States which once was plentiful as far west as California; this bird has suffered, also, from loss of its food and covers. The prairie grasses, the wild rose, the wild sunflower, and many other food plants often are absolutely destroyed on the big wheat farms where these birds formerly were abundant and where they are now extinct or nearly so. In addition to food the briers afford safe protection when a Hawk or other enemy approaches. If we give their natural enemies a good chance to eat them, by destroying the Prairie Chickens' nesting sites and covers, and if we destroy absolutely their winter foods on vast areas, we must not expect the birds to return to places from which they have been extirpated merely because we have enacted laws prohibiting shooting.

In explanation of the picture, "The Love-making of the Prairie Chicken," Dr. Frank M. Chapman writes: "On frosty spring mornings, as the sun rises over the prairies, one may at times hear a singular, resonant, booming note, *boom-ah-b-o-o-m, boom-ah-b-o-o-m*. It is the love-song of the Prairie Hen. He may be near at hand or possibly two miles away, so far does this sound, unobstructed by tree or hill, carry in the clear air. It is well worth following, however, for we may find the maker of it, with perhaps ten to fifty of his kind, engaged in a most remarkable performance. During the mating season, from March until early in May, the Prairie Hens of a certain district or area gather before daybreak to take part in these courtship demonstrations. The feather-tufts on either part of the neck are erected like horns, the tail raised and spread, the wings drooped, when the bird first rushes forward a few steps, pauses, inflates its orange-like air-sacs, and with a violent, jerking, muscular effort, produces the startling

Photograph of habitat group

Courtesy of American Museum of Natural History

THE LOVE-MAKING OF THE PRAIRIE CHICKEN

During the mating season, the males of a certain area gather in the early morning and indulge in queer antics before the females, which are suggestive of a dance

boom, which we may have heard when two miles distant. At other times, with a low cackle, he springs suddenly into the air, as though quite unable to control himself, and finally he comes within striking distance of a rival who has been giving a similar exhibition. Then, with much clashing of wings, a fight ensues which often strews the nearby grass with feathers. These tournaments of display and combat are doubtless designed to arouse the attention of the females, but they also occur when only males are present. Within an hour or two after sunrise, the time varying with the ardor of the birds, the competition is over for the day and the rivals feed peacefully together, until they enter the lists the following morning."

The food habits of the Prairie Grouse are well known. They eat many insects, especially grasshoppers, from May to October, and are valuable aids to the farmer for this reason. In the fall and winter the food of the Prairie Grouse is mainly vegetable—fruit, leaves, flowers, shoots, seeds, and grain. Dr. Judd says: "Like the Bob-white and the Ruffed Grouse, the Prairie Grouse is fond of rose-hips, and the abundant roses of the prairie yield 11.01 per cent. of its food." In Kansas and many other States the wild sunflowers, goldenrod, and other natural foods were tremendously abundant, but throughout most of the range of the Grouse these foods have been destroyed absolutely. It would pay to restore some prairie grass, wild roses, sunflowers, and other covers and food which are essential to the bird's existence. No farmer or sportsman can be expected to give the land, time, labor, and money needed to save the Grouse simply as a bait for trespassers. This Grouse is fond of the stubble as a feeding ground and it can be made profitably abundant on many farms, but it must have winter foods and covers, and it must be protected from its enemies if any shooting is to be done; otherwise it will become extinct.

The Lesser Prairie Chicken (*Tympanuchus pallidicinctus*) occurs on the Great Plains, from Kansas south to west-central Texas; its plumage is similar to that of the Prairie Chicken but paler.

HEATH HEN

Tympanuchus cupido (*Linnæus*)

A. O. U. Number 306

Other Name.— Eastern Pinnated Grouse.

General Description.— Length, 17 inches. Color above, rusty-brown; below, rusty-white. Tarsus, lightly feathered to the toes; a tuft of less than ten stiff, pointed feathers on each side of the neck, overlying a naked area which is capable of being inflated to the size of a small orange; tail, short with eighteen stiff feathers.

Plumage.—Adults: Ground color above, rusty-brown; shoulders with white tips to the feathers; everywhere barred with even broad markings of blackish-brown, much narrower on neck and tending to spots on crown; below, rusty white, traversely barred with numerous reddish-brown bars, these darker bars much in excess of lighter ones; neck-tufts black. Sexes generally alike, but the female is sometimes darker, with bars beneath dull black and tail dark brown with many fine irregular rusty bars.

Nest and Eggs.— Nest: On ground; a depression, lined with grass, weed stems, and leaves. Eggs: 6 to 12, creamy to yellowish-green, unspotted.

Distribution.— Island of Marthas Vineyard, Massachusetts; formerly in suitable portions of New England, New York, and the Middle States.

The Heath Hen possibly was once a smaller eastern race of the Prairie Chicken, but, all connecting links having been destroyed, it now stands as a distinct species, having been set apart by William Brewster (*Auk,* Jan., 1885). No one knows how much ground this bird formerly occupied, but now it is confined to the island of Marthas Vineyard, Massachusetts, where the State Commissioners of Fisheries and Game are trying to save it from extinction. It is believed to have occupied formerly all suitable country along the Atlantic seaboard from Massachusetts to Virginia, but no one has any data regarding its western limit. Audubon and Wilson believed it to be identical with the Grouse that inhabited the barrens of Kentucky in their day, but possibly it did not range west of the Appalachians. It is recorded in numbers in the Connecticut valley in Massachusetts, but no records of its existence farther west in that State have been found.

It was numerous once in suitable localities

over its range, being so abundant in Boston that laborers and servants are said to have stipulated with their masters not to have it upon the table more than a few times a week. (Chamberlain, *A Popular Handbook of the Ornithology of the United States and Canada.*) It remained more or less common locally until after the year 1800, but between that time and 1869 it appears to have been exterminated from the mainland and to have been preserved on Marthas Vineyard only by special protection. Its numbers there dwindled until 1906 when a destructive fire swept over the breeding range and the number was reduced to less than fifty. Since then, under stringent protection, the remnant has so increased that the colony has been estimated (1916) at from five hundred to one thousand birds.

The Heath Hen or Heth'en, as it is called on Marthas Vineyard, is a bird of dry, sandy, scrubby plains, or barrens. It long occupied such regions in Massachusetts, Long Island, New York, and New Jersey and still prefers them in its last retreat on Marthas Vineyard, where it keeps mainly to the dry sandy plains in the interior which have been swept by fires for centuries and which now support a growth composed of scattering low pitch pines, scrub oaks, and other still smaller shrubbery. From this cover the birds make forays to the open farm lands, which they frequent more or less, to the shore, and more rarely to the woods, but in some parts of the island which are wooded with a good growth of oak and pine, the Heath Hen is rarely seen. Also it seems to be rare or practically absent in the western end of the island, which is largely a region of hilly pastures.

The habits of this bird are much like those of the Prairie Chicken. The booming of the males is not so deep in tone, but the wooing antics are much the same. The mother and her young sleep on the ground, but the males, and possibly also the females, often alight on the tops of small trees, and flocks have been known to alight and remain for some time on the roof of a farm house. This bird is believed to drink only rain or dew that it finds on vegetation. The Heath Hen feeds in spring and summer on grasshoppers and other insects, tender foliage, and berries. In winter it has to subsist largely on dried leaves, buds, and acorns, but it is fond of corn and peas and sometimes is destructive in gardens.

If the Massachusetts authorities continue to handle their problem wisely there is hope that the Heath Hen may yet be introduced and propagated under protection in other parts of its former habitat.

EDWARD HOWE FORBUSH.

SHARP-TAILED GROUSE

Pediœcetes phasianellus phasianellus (*Linnæus*)

A. O. U. Number 308

Other Names.— Prairie Chicken of the Northwest; Northern Sharp-tailed Grouse; Spike-tail; Pin-tail; Pin-tailed Grouse; Sprig-tailed Grouse; White Grouse; White-belly; Black-foot; Sharp-tail.

General Description.— Length, 20 inches. Color above, yellowish-brown, sprinkled with black; below, whitish. *No tufts on side of neck,* but the patch of distensible skin is hidden; head, slightly crested; tarsus feathered to base of toes; toes with a fringe of horny processes in winter; tail, graduated and much shorter than wing with feathers square at tips and middle pair extending some distance beyond the others; middle tail-feathers of female shorter than those of male.

Color.— Head and neck, deep buffy; a dull whitish area on each side of neck and a whitish stripe behind eye; upper parts everywhere closely and evenly variegated with blackish-brown, dull chestnut, and grayish, these marks smallest on rump, reddish tones most pronounced on back, and the lighter colors everywhere sprinkled with blackish; wing-coverts, like back but each feather with a conspicuous rounded white spot; crown and back of neck also like back but smaller pattern, the bars mostly traverse; throat, light buff, unmarked; under parts, buffy-white toward throat, *clearer white below;* breast with numerous U- and V-shaped spots of dark brown; similar but smaller spots scattered over rest of under parts except on middle of abdomen; primaries, brownish; secondaries with square yellowish-white spots tipped with white, the inner ones varied with colors of back; four middle tail-feathers, also like back, others white on inner webs, mottled on outer; bill, dark horn-color, flesh-colored below; iris, light brown.

Nest and Eggs.— NEST: A hollow in the ground, lined with coarse grass and feathers. EGGS: 10 to 16, grayish-olive uniformly spotted with brown rarely larger than a pinhead.

Distribution.— Central Alaska and northwestern British Columbia east through central Keewatin to central-western Ungava, and south to Lake Superior and the Parry Sound district, Ontario; casual east to Saguenay River, Quebec.

The Sharp-tailed Grouse is commonly confused with the Prairie Chicken but most gunners recognize it at once by its acuminate tail and the absence of neck tufts. They designate it by such names as Sharp-tail, Pin-tail, Sprig-tail, Spike-tail, White-belly, etc.

The species formerly was known to naturalists as *Pediœcetes phasianellus,* the Sharp-tailed Grouse. It has been divided into three subspecies, differing chiefly in the shades of coloration. The Sharp-tailed Grouse is the more northern race which is confined to Canada and Alaska. This is a very dark bird with heavy, dark markings on the upper parts. The Columbian Sharp-tailed Grouse (*Pediœcetes phasianellus columbianus*) is much paler in tint, with the dark markings less conspicuous, and frequents the plains of the western region, from central British Columbia and central Alberta south to California, Utah, and Colorado, though now practically extinct in California. The Prairie Sharp-tailed Grouse (*Pediœcetes phasianellus campestris*) is native to the prairie regions of southern Canada and the northern United States. These races have similar habits except as they may be modified somewhat by differences of environment. Therefore a description of the habits of one race may be taken as typical of the species.

With the first promise of spring on the Great Plains the remarkable mating antics of the Sharp-tail begin. As a spectacle this erratic dance would furnish amusement to a Hottentot. The birds have a meeting place where they gather at the booming calls of the male at early dawn and again at sunset. At first they appear to be standing quietly, then one begins the dance by partly spreading its wings in a horizontal direction, lowering its head, raising and spreading its tail, distending the air-sacs and then, bristling up, runs across the floor of the meeting place, stamping its feet so hard and fast as to produce a drumming sound, uttering also what Ernest S. Thompson terms a sort of "bubbling crow," beating the air with its wings, and vibrating its tail with a low rustling sound. Immediately all join the dance. Some circle to the right, others to the left, passing each other stiffly, charging back and forth, bowing, squatting, and posturing. Faster and faster goes the dance; more and more madly swings the giddy whirl until the excited birds jump over the backs of

Drawing by R. I. Brasher

SHARP-TAILED GROUSE (½ nat. size)

This bird prefers thickets or the edges of timber

their companions, strut, swell, and even fight The performance resembles in some ways an Indian war dance and each bird seems to be anxious to make as much noise and show as possible. The dance goes on day after day until the mating season is over and often begins again in autumn.

The nest, usually placed in the open, shaded perhaps by grasses, weeds, or bushes, is not very carefully concealed except when the female is sitting. Then her colors and markings blend so perfectly with the surroundings that no eye can find her and she will sit on the nest until trodden upon, rather than expose her eggs to hostile eyes. She rarely leaves it until the young are hatched and gets her food, consisting of buds and grasshoppers, close by. The young birds leave the nest when hatched and live on the ground and they have only to squat to become imperceptible to the ordinary eye. When the brood has scattered the mother calls them together with a hoarse raucous croak.

About the middle of autumn they begin to alight in trees and to gather in large "packs." When startled and about to fly they utter a sharp cackling sound and this is repeated from time to time in the flight, which resembles that of the Prairie Chicken, as they alternately flap and sail. This bird seems to prefer shrubbery or the edges of the timber to the open plains, particularly in winter. EDWARD HOWE FORBUSH.

The food of the Sharp-tailed Grouse is similar to that of the Prairie Grouse. Many grasshoppers and other insects are eaten, the young being highly insectivorous like all the other Grouse, the Quails, and the Turkeys. The vegetable food comprises leaves, buds, and flowers, weed seeds, fruit, and grain. Since this is the more northern species, it naturally relies more on buds than the Prairie Grouse does, and in winter it eats birch buds, willow buds, and others. It is well worth preserving and could easily be restored and made plentiful and profitable on many of the big wheat farms of the northwestern and Pacific coast States. The Sharp-tail is very fond of wheat, but it cannot secure the grains beneath the snow during the long winters, and it perishes because the wild roses and other winter foods have been destroyed. A handsome border to a private road, fence, or path, containing wild roses and sunflowers and prairie grasses, could be made to yield a good crop of Grouse, many of which might be shot on the stubbles in the autumn without any danger of extermination. Some stock birds should be left, of course, and the Prairie Falcon, the coyote, the snake and other enemies should not be permitted to devour them.

SAGE HEN

Centrocercus urophasianus (*Bonaparte*)

A. O. U. Number 309

Other Names.— Cock of the Plains; Sage Cock; Sage Grouse.

General Description.— Length, male, 25 to 30 inches; female, 20 inches. Color above, black, brown, and yellowish-white, variegated; below, yellow-white. Tarsus, feathered to toes; tail, longer than wings, graduated, and with the 20 feathers pointed.

Color.— MALE: Above, varied with black, grayish-brown, and dull yellowish-white; the wing-coverts, streaked with whitish; tail with the marbling tending to form bars; on side of neck a patch of feathers with stiff shafts changing to hair-like filaments at ends about 3 inches long; in front of these feathers a naked patch of yellow skin capable of great distension; above them a tuft of white down feathers covered with long plumes of black; chin and throat, blackish usually with a definite white collar behind; rest of lower parts, yellow-white with a large black area on abdomen. ADULT FEMALE: Plumage similar to male, but lacking black throat and with no peculiar feathers on neck; tail, much shorter and with narrower feathers. YOUNG: Similar to adult female but brownish above.

Nest and Eggs.— NEST: Slight depression in the ground, scratched out by the bird, usually under sage bushes. EGGS: 7 to 9, dull yellowish-olive to greenish-brown, marked with round spots of dark brown.

Distribution.— Sagebrush plains from southern British Columbia, southern Saskatchewan, and northwestern North Dakota, south to middle-eastern California, northwestern New Mexico, and northwestern Nebraska.

The Sage Hen is unique. It is the largest of American gallinaceous birds, excepting only the Wild Turkey. It is one of the most remarkable fowls of the world. Nevertheless, the American people are fast exterminating it. It exceeds all other Grouse in size, with the possible exception of the great Black Grouse or Capercallie of Europe, and its peculiar nuptial performances go far to establish it as one of the wonders of animated nature which should be carefully preserved for all time. Ordinarily it does little injury to man's crops or chattels. Why then should it be exterminated?

Thus far the systematists have not been able to find a subspecies of the Sage Hen. Everywhere it has the same habits, frequenting the high, dry alkali plains, sometimes at an altitude of more than seven thousand feet, among the sagebrush (*Artemesia*). It stands or falls with the sagebrush and in these days it commonly falls. We are told now that it is disappearing in Oregon and Washington, gone from the Black Hills, and thinning rapidly in numbers elsewhere. Like all the game birds of the open it can hide or fly from its natural enemies, but cannot withstand the combination of man, dog, and gun, with shooting at all seasons of the year. The young are preferred for the table as they have less sage flavor than their parents, and when the callow young are destroyed the species cannot last, as the adults are not immortal. The old birds are "tougher than tripe," in more ways than one. Nevertheless, they may be eaten if properly prepared. Edwin Sandys says that he is willing to admit that "an aged sage hen doth possess that sageness that one might expect with advancing years," but carved with bowie knife or hatchet it will sustain human life. Its flavor is improved by drawing the bird as soon as it is dead.

Photo by W. L. Finley and H. T. Bohlman

PORTRAIT OF SAGE HEN

The Sage Cock has a sharp cackle, ***kek, kek, kek,*** which voices its alarm when flushed, but its mating notes are not what one would expect from a bird of its size. It begins its "drumming" or croaking very early in the season, sometimes even in fine winter weather. The mating grounds are in conspicuous places, such as a barren flat or moraine, and the birds may be readily watched from a distance with a powerful glass. From twenty-five to one hundred or more males congregate in these places. They are polygamous and the females come to them from all quarters at sunset or early in the morning. The males being in full dress and vigor late in February or in March in the United States, or later in higher latitudes, assemble at their chosen spots on fine mornings and, standing erect, hold their drooping wings well away from their sides, raise and spread the tail, which often works from side to side, while the loose skin of the neck is drawn in and out and the great pale sacs on the sides of the neck are distended until the white feathers surrounding them bristle out in all directions. The air sacs when inflated are not semi-globular in shape, as in the Prairie Chicken, but irregular, bulbous, and enormous, sometimes protruding an inch above the head and well out in front. The skin between the sacs is next drawn in with a sucking motion, bringing them nearly together and the air is expelled from the throat, producing peculiar guttural grunting or croaking sounds, some of which have been described by Bendire as resembling the purr of a cat, but louder. Bond says that it produces an "inconsequential chuckling noise," while Burnett describes it as resembling the sound of an old pump, thus, *punk de punk, punk*—the first note low and the last two higher in pitch. The cocks strut with tail widely spread and erect, the acuminate tail-feathers standing out separately like so many spikes, sometimes dragging the wings on the ground, and dance with the pomp of a Pouter Pigeon. Rival, jealous males frequently fight viciously, but the battling consists mostly in seizing one another by the head or neck and beating with the wings and is not sanguinary or long continued. One of their habits at this time is to lower the breast to the ground and push it along. In some localities this is done so frequently that the feathers on the lower neck become worn down to mere shafts, appearing like so many bristles. Sometimes in their enthusiasm they even roll in the dust. Bond says that the cock inflates its neck until the whole neck and breast present a balloon-like appearance and then, bending forward, throws the entire weight of its body on the distended portions, sliding along on the bare ground for some distance and concluding by expelling the air with a variety of cackling, chuckling, or rumbling sounds.

In May when the song of the Sage Thrush begins, the mating of the Sage Hens is about over. Then the females make their nests, often near some spring or stream. The mother bird on the nest is a difficult object to see. She seems to know it and sits very close. For this reason she is regarded as foolish and sometimes is known as "fool hen." The little ones are ready to run about fifteen minutes after they leave the shell, so Burnett informs us, are colored like little Turkeys, and "peep" similarly. Also they have a plaintive whistle, *ra-do-ra-do*. At night they nestle themselves under the mother's wings, only a row of little heads showing outside. As the summer wanes, the Sage Hens and their well-grown young often spend the days on flats, near streams or near water holes. By November the young are full-grown, but are lighter in color than their mother.

The Sage Grouse seldom is to be found far from the sagebrush. Where this grows high along the river bottoms the birds often lie closely and they match their environment in color, so that the hunter may walk into the midst of a brood without seeing them and they may rise on all sides. They labor into the air with noisy wings, but fly fast when well under way. Where they have been much hunted they are likely to rise beyond gunshot and start for the horizon.

Late in the season when they have become wary they assemble in "packs." In winter they are said to retire from some exposed localities to the valleys or to the shelter of the timber. Although they feed largely on the leaves of the sage, insects form a considerable part of the food of the young, and in some regions they attack grain, alfalfa, and garden plants. Their habits are such that they are exposed to the inclemency of the weather, which ordinarily seems to affect them little. Sometimes, however, they become drenched by severe rains so that they are unable to rise from the ground. Hailstorms sometimes kill the young and even the full-grown birds.

EDWARD HOWE FORBUSH.

TURKEYS

Order *Gallinæ;* suborder *Phasiani;* family *Meleagridæ*

HE Turkeys are distinctively American birds. Formerly ranked as a separate family, they are now regarded as the only native American representatives of the Pheasant family. They are confined to North America and to Central America, and the only species now recognized are the Common Turkey, of which the ornithologists describe five forms—Merriam's Turkey (*Meleagris gallopavo merriami*), the Florida Turkey (*Meleagris gallopavo osceola*), the Rio Grande Turkey (*Meleagris gallopavo intermedia*), the American Wild Turkey (*Meleagris gallopavo silvestris*) and the type species which is not found in the United States—and the Yucatan Ocellated Turkey, smaller but with even more brilliant plumage. Our Common Turkey is still found in a slightly different form in Mexico, whence it was introduced into Europe about 1530.

Elon H. Eaton remarks that "the scientific name of the family is a misnomer, being the original name of the Guinea Hen, and if the popular impression of the origin of the common name is correct, this is a misnomer also, but it is probable, as has been suggested, that the common name has reference to the call note of the bird, which resembles the syllables *turk, turk, turk.*"

Turkeys have the head and neck naked except for a few stiff bristles, and wrinkled and wattled, with an erectile process growing on the forehead. The tarsus is naked, covered with scales, and, in the male, spurred. The tail is broad and rounded with fourteen to eighteen blunt feathers. The male has a "beard" of coarse black bristles hanging from the center of upper breast.

WILD TURKEY

Meleagris gallopavo silvestris *Vieillot*

A. O. U. Number 310a

Other Names.— American Turkey; Eastern Turkey; Northern Turkey; Wood Turkey; American Wild Turkey.

General Description.— Length, male, 4 feet; female, 3 feet. Prevailing color, iridescent copper-bronze. Head and neck, naked.

Color.—Adult Male: The naked skin of the head and neck, different shades of red, the excrescences more purplish or blue; the feathers are broad with square ends, each one well defined, giving the bird the appearance of being covered with scales, their ground color coppery-bronze, abruptly margined with velvet-black, the bronze assuming a greenish or purplish shade where the two colors meet; lower back and rump, black with little or no gloss; upper and under tail-coverts, dark purplish-chestnut with a subterminal bar of black; tail, dark-brownish with numerous traverse bars of black and a broad subterminal bar of the same color from two inches wide on the outer feathers to about one inch on the central ones, spaces between the black bars speckled with dusky; bill, yellowish-white tinged with red; legs, red, the scales outlined with yellowish-white; claws, black; iris, deep brown. Adult Female: Head and neck, smooth, pinkish or pale reddish; rest of the plumage very much duller than in the male and with little or no metallic gloss.

Nest and Eggs.— Nest: Placed on the ground, in tall dense weeds or tangled thickets; very well concealed. Eggs: 9 to 18, usually 9 to 12, warm yellowish-white evenly dotted over the entire surface with reddish-brown.

Distribution.—Eastern United States from Nebraska, Kansas, western Oklahoma, and eastern Texas east to central Pennsylvania, and south to the Gulf coast; formerly north to South Dakota, southern Ontario, and southern Maine.

When, early in the sixteenth century, the Spanish conquerors invaded Mexico, they found the natives in possession of some large domesticated birds which were extremely toothsome. Some were transferred to Spain and it was found they would breed readily in captivity. In time these birds were introduced into France and England, and by and by emigrants brought them back to America. The Turkey in its native condition is distinctively a North American species. The wild birds in this country today chiefly inhabit deep woods and the borders of swamplands. In the southwest one may look for them among the chaparral in the neighborhood of streams, or in the oak and piñon groves.

At one time they were very abundant in many places, and early writers tell of their custom of gathering in flocks of hundreds and migrating on foot for long distances in quest of forest mast upon which they fed extensively. This habit of collecting in large flocks may still be noted in some regions, as for example on some of the islands off the coast of Georgia.

Wild Turkeys are polygamists, a strong gobbler having two or three hens under his observation. When the laying time approaches, the hens steal away and make their nests in the grass or bushes in some open place in the woods, or abandoned bush-grown fields. They hide their nests with great care, not only to avoid foxes and other predatory animals, but to prevent detection by the gobbler. It is unanimously believed that he will break the eggs if he comes upon a nest. After the nesting season, groups of from ten to forty birds may be found feeding together in the bottom lands or coming into the crop field at dawn.

They are usually hunted with dogs. A well-trained Turkey dog upon finding a group of birds rushes barking among them, thus causing the Turkeys to fly in all directions. The hunter goes to the spot, erects a small blind of logs or brush, calls in his dog, and sits down to wait for a time. In about an hour he begins to sound his call, imitating the get-together notes of the Turkey. If fortune smiles upon him he will in the end get two or three birds, for the Turkeys have the habit of reassembling at the place from which they scattered when disturbed.

T. Gilbert Pearson.

Photograph of habitat group — Courtesy of American Museum of Natural History

WILD TURKEYS IN THE WEST VIRGINIA MOUNTAINS

Close relatives of our domesticated Turkey

PHEASANTS

Order *Gallinæ;* suborder *Phasiani;* family *Phasianidæ*

WITHIN recent years a new industry, the rearing of Pheasants, has begun to engage attention in the United States, and propagating ventures, ranging from the single pen with one or two pairs of birds to the pheasantry of many acres and thousands of birds, are scattered throughout the country. Some of these experiments have been conducted by the States through their game officials; others, by associations and individuals. In a few cases large expense has been incurred and great care and attention have been bestowed on the experiments. Efforts have been made also to stock numerous public and private parks, preserves, and aviaries. To supply the demand, not only have pheasants been imported from the Old World, but many persons in this country have undertaken to rear them. In view of the widespread and rapidly increasing interest in the subject, the Department of Agriculture has made a special investigation of the methods of Pheasant raising. The results are here condensed in the form of practical suggestions for the benefit of those interested in the industry.

The true Pheasants are a strictly Old World genus and the species which have been introduced into this country are totally different and distinct from the Ruffed Grouse (called "Partridges" in most of the northern States), which is popularly but quite inaccurately called "Pheasant" in the southern, and also in some of the northern States, notably Ohio and Pennsylvania. This blunder originated in the early settler's habit of applying to American birds the names of more or less similar European species, though in this instance it must have required a considerable tax on the imagination to detect any resemblance between the strikingly colored and very long-tailed European Pheasants and the neutral hued, always short-tailed Grouse of the New World.

A few words as to different kinds of Pheasants are essential to a proper understanding of the subject of Pheasant propagation. The Ring-necked Pheasant usually imported from China, its natural home, has a broad white ring about the neck. It is variously called Ring-neck Pheasant, Chinese Pheasant, China Pheasant, China Torquatus Pheasant, Chinese Ringneck, Mongolian Pheasant, Denny Pheasant, and Oregon Pheasant.

The English Pheasant has no ring about the neck. It is imported from Europe, but in comparatively small numbers, and is known as the English Pheasant, Dark-necked Pheasant, and Hungarian Pheasant.

The English Ringneck Pheasant, a hybrid between the English and Ring-necked Pheasants, has been brought from Europe in large numbers. It is generally correctly named, but is sometimes designated as English Pheasant, Ringneck Pheasant, and even Mongolian Pheasant. It often has more or less of the blood of the Versicolor Pheasant, of Japan. In England both the English Pheasant and the English Ringneck are referred to as the Common Pheasant.

The Mongolian Pheasant which has a more or less complete white ring about the neck, but in other respects resembles the English Pheasant more than it does the Ringneck, is the rarest of the four kinds in American preserves and aviaries. It is a native of the region about Lake Balkash, Central Asia.

The Bohemian Pheasant and the White Pheasant are merely color phases, chiefly of the English Pheasant and the English Ringneck. The Reeves Pheasant, a large and striking bird with a tail sometimes five or six feet long, is usually met with in aviaries, though it has been placed in game coverts in Europe and, to a very limited extent, in the United States, and may still be found on certain Scotch estates, where it ranks very high as a game bird. It normally inhabits east-central Asia.

Two of the best known and most commonly imported Pheasants are the Golden and Lady Amherst, both of the genus *Chrysolophus*, originally from the mountains of eastern Tibet and western and southern China. Both are favorite aviary birds, and the Golden Pheasant has been liberated in various game covers in America and Europe, but with indifferent success. The Silver Pheasant is often seen in parks and aviaries, but the numerous other members of the genus, usually called Kaleeges (or Kalijes), are not often imported into this country. The home of the genus is the Indo-Chinese countries and the lower ranges of the Himalayas.

The Eared Pheasants, large, dull-colored birds of the higher ranges of central and eastern Asia, are known in American aviaries mainly through the Manchurian Pheasant, the most northerly member of the genus. These Pheasants lack the timidity so characteristic of most of the Pheasant family and would probably lend themselves readily to domestication. At present their high price is practically prohibitive of any extensive attempt to domesticate them, but, should they become more common, they would be excellent subjects for such experiments.

Photo by H. T. Middleton

WILD RING-NECKED PHEASANT (HEN)

The English Pheasant (*Phasianus colchicus*) derives its specific name from the ancient country of Colchis, on the eastern shore of the Black Sea. It was imported thence into Europe by the Greeks, probably under Alexander the Great, and was by them reared for food. Its propagation in confinement was continued in the days of the Roman Empire, under which it appears to have been carried on throughout much of Europe and as far west as Britain. It was introduced into Ireland and Scotland before the close of the sixteenth century. It is now acclimatized practically all over Europe, and has been introduced into the United States, Canada, Australia, and New Zealand.

Efforts to acclimatize Pheasants in the United States are of comparatively recent origin, though earlier than is popularly supposed. Richard Bache, an Englishman who married the only daughter of Benjamin Franklin, imported from England both Pheasants and Partridges, which he liberated on his estate in New Jersey, on the Delaware River near where the town of Beverly now stands. But, although he provided both shelter and food for them, the birds had all disappeared by the following spring.

A second attempt was made early in the nineteenth century by the owner of a New Jersey estate situated between the Hackensack meadows and the Passaic River, opposite Belleville. A park was fenced and stocked with deer and English Pheasants, but despite feeding and careful protection these birds likewise disappeared during the winter.

Robert Oliver of Harewood, near Baltimore, Md., for many years imported foreign game, including not less than one hundred English Pheasants. These increased rapidly and were in time turned out, some at Hampton, some at Brookland Wood, and a large number at Harewood. Those liberated at Hampton and Brookland Wood bred, and were occasionally seen afterwards, but those turned out at Harewood soon disappeared, the last being seen in 1827. In 1829–30, Mr. Oliver liberated at his estate at Oaklands, in Anne Arundel County, more than twenty Pheasants of his own raising. On Mr. Oliver's death his son Thomas continued the experiments, but they proved unsuccessful.

These initial importations were followed by similar attempts to stock private preserves, but met with like failure. In 1880, however, a successful effort was made to introduce the

Ringneck Pheasant into Oregon, and since then acclimatization experiments have followed broader lines and have assumed greater importance.

The failure of many efforts to add Pheasants to our fauna is largely due to insufficient knowledge of their habits and the character of their normal environment. It is useless to undertake to acclimatize a bird in a region differing widely in climatic and other physical conditions from those to which it has been accustomed.

It must be remembered, also, that introduced birds have to adapt themselves to a new flora and fauna, and that this is often a slow process and frequently fails. If liberated in the wilds, they must be provided with reserve food and shelter until able to care for themselves, which may take several years. In Oregon the Ringnecks put out came at first regularly to farm-yards to feed with the domestic fowls; and English Ringnecks liberated on Grand Island, Michigan, were driven back by severe weather to the pens from which they had been allowed to escape a few months before.

If Pheasants are imported for stocking preserves, suitable coverts should be prepared for them. In their native country Pheasants frequent the margins of woods, coming into open tracts in search of food, retreating into thick undergrowth when alarmed. An ideal Pheasant country is one containing small groves with underbrush and high grass between the trees, thorny hedges, berry-growing shrubs, water overgrown with reeds, and occasional pastures, meadows, and cultivated grain-fields. Bleak mountains, dry sandy wastes, and thick woods are not frequented by Pheasants normally; nor do they seek pines, except for protection. A small grove of mixed evergreen and deciduous trees on the southern slope of a hill furnishes favorable shelter. On the preserve additional shelter should be provided in winter.

Photo by W. T. Davis Courtesy of Nat. Asso. Aud. Soc.

PHEASANT'S NEST

Gardiners Island, New York

Henry Oldys, in *Pheasant Raising in the United States.*

ENGLISH PHEASANT

Phasianus colchicus *Linnæus*

Length.— Male, 36 inches or less according to development of the tail, tail up to 21 inches; female, about 24 inches, tail 12 inches. Slightly larger than the Ring-necked Pheasant.

Spread of Wings.— 32 inches.

Weight.— Male, about 3 pounds; female, about 2 pounds.

Description.— Male: Tail very long, coneate, tapering; head with ear tufts and finely mottled sides; head and neck peacock-blue, glossed with metallic reflections of green, bronze, and purple; sides of head, bare, scarlet; back, orange-brown, variegated with dark green, buff, and black; rump and upper tail-coverts, rufous, with black and reddish variegations; tail, olive-brown, edged with purplish-rufous, and barred with black; breast, glossy, coppery chestnut, edged with purplish; no rings about the neck. Female: Plain blended light brown and dusky.

RING-NECKED PHEASANT

Phasianus torquatus *Gmelin*

Length.— 34 inches when the tail is full-grown.

Spread of Wings.— 32 inches.

Weight.— 2¾ pounds or more.

Description.— Similar in general color to the English Pheasant, but male with a conspicuous white ring about the neck; top of head, more greenish-bronze and a whitish line on sides of crown; the sides, golden buff spotted with black; the upper wing-coverts, pale grayish-blue; the sides of the rump, grayish-blue; abdomen, greenish-black.

ORDER OF PIGEONS AND DOVES

Order *Columbæ;* family *Columbidæ*

THE names Pigeon and Dove, applied to birds of this group, are synonymous or interchangeable. The former is French (Italian, *piccione* or *pipione*, Latin *pipio*); the latter is akin to the Dutch *duif* (Danish *due*, Icelandic *dufa*). The name *Dove* is commonly applied to the smaller members of the group, though in England the largest species is called the Ring Dove; and, as Professor Alfred Newton remarked in his *Dictionary* of *Birds*, "no sharp distinction can be drawn between Pigeons and Doves, and in general literature the two words are used almost indifferently while no one species can be pointed out to which the word Dove, taken alone, seems to be absolutely proper."

Pigeons are monogamous, but nevertheless are to a degree fickle or inconstant in their affections, at least in the domesticated species, and are by no means the peaceful birds they are popularly supposed to be — fierce, bloody, and stubborn conflicts often occurring during the breeding season. The eggs number one or two and are usually immaculate white but sometimes are immaculate buff. The nest is a very simple affair, usually flat and frail, composed of twigs, straw, or similar materials, placed in a tree, upon stumps, rocks, or walls, clefts of cliffs, in buildings, or on the ground. Both sexes take equal part in nest building, incubation, and care of the young. The latter are hatched naked, except for scattered bits of filamentous down, and are fed first by a fluid secreted in the crop of the adult and later with moistened or partially digested seeds or grain from the parents' crop, the young one in both cases inserting its bill into the parent's mouth, the regurgitation of the food by the parent being accompanied by a violent or spasmodic jerking of the body and wings.

The food of Pigeons consists principally of grains, seeds, and fruits, and salt is seemingly a necessity to them. In drinking, the bill is immersed to the nostrils, and the water drawn in in a continuous draft, a method in which they are, so far as known, unique among birds. The voice of Pigeons is, usually, a soft *coo*, varied in strength and modulation according to species. It is sometimes extremely loud in proportion to the size of the bird, one of the smaller American species, the blue Ground Dove, producing a sound resembling that made by blowing one's breath into the mouth of a bottle, but nearly as loud as the bellowing of a bull. In others the voice is plaintive or even mournful.

The Pigeons have the head small; neck short; bill horny at the tip, compressed, and with a tumid swelling near the base about the nostril; wings pointed, flat, powerful, with rapid whistling flight; legs short, the tarsus scaled on the sides and back and sometimes in the front as well; front toes cleft to the base or with a slight membrane between the middle and outer toes; hind toe level with the front toes, thus making them arboreal as well as terrestrial in their habits because they can perch easily; body plump and full-breasted; and eye region usually more or less naked. The plumage is peculiarly dense, but is easily detached from the very tender skin.

Pigeons are found throughout the temperate and tropical portions of the world, but are most numerous in the eastern hemisphere, especially in the islands of the Indo-Malayan and Australian regions, where the most beautifully colored species occur, many of them being among the handsomest of birds. More than five hundred and fifty species and subspecies are known, of which only about one hundred species and subspecies occur in America, and only seventeen of these are of regular or even rare occurrence north of the southern boundary of the United States.

BAND-TAILED PIGEON

Columba fasciata fasciata *Say*

A. O. U. Number 312

Other Names.—White-collared Pigeon; Wild Pigeon.

General Description.— Length, 16 inches. Head and under parts, purplish-drab; upper parts, brownish-gray and bluish-gray.

Color.— ADULTS: Head, purplish-drab becoming paler and usually more grayish on cheeks and throat, which are sometimes distinctly more grayish in contrast with color of crown; *across nape or upper hindneck, a bar of white;* below this, the whole hindneck, metallic greenish-bronze, the feathers with sharp outlines, producing a somewhat scaled effect; back, shoulders, and front lesser wing-coverts, grayish-brown, very faintly glossed, in certain lights, with bronzy; rump and upper tail-coverts, neutral gray; *tail, brownish-gray with a band of darker gray* to dull black across the middle portion separating the darker and lighter gray areas; rear lesser wing-coverts, middle coverts, and greater coverts, brownish-gray, the greater coverts, narrowly edged with white; inner secondaries, similar but more brownish, without distinct whitish edgings, the outer ones much darker, distinctly though narrowly edged with whitish; primaries and coverts, dusky, the first narrowly edged with white; under parts, purple-drab usually somewhat clearer or more reddish on under parts of body and more grayish on throat, the abdomen (at least the lower portion), anal region, and under tail-coverts, white; under wing-coverts, pale neutral gray; bill, yellow, the tip black; iris, pale yellow next to pupil with outer ring of pink or lilac; eyelids, red; legs and feet, clear cadmium-yellow. YOUNG: Very different in coloration from adults, only the tail, wings, and primary coverts being similar; no white bar on nape nor metallic feathers on hindneck; crown, hindneck, sides of neck, and sides of head, brownish-gray, much paler on chin and upper throat; smaller wing-coverts, margined with paler, as are also feathers of chest; shoulders sometimes suffused with brown.

Nest and Eggs.— NEST: A slight, frail platform of small, narrow twigs in trees or bushes or in forests, near water; sometimes on ground with slight nesting material. EGGS: 1 or 2, porcelain-white.

Distribution.— Western United States north to southwestern British Columbia and Montana, from Pacific coast to Rocky Mountains; east to Montana, western North Dakota, Colorado, New Mexico, and western Texas; southward over nearly the whole of Mexico and through the highlands of Guatemala to northern Nicaragua.

Drawing by R. Bruce Horsfall

BAND-TAILED PIGEON (½ nat. size)

A fine bird, in danger of becoming extinct

The most striking example of the disappearance of a species in American natural history is that of the Passenger Pigeon. The Band-tailed Pigeon of the West might have followed in the path of the eastern bird within a few years, had our people not been aroused to its necessity for protection. The enactment in 1913 of the Federal law for the protection of migratory birds was the most important step ever taken in saving this as well as other species of American birds. Under the provisions of this act, the Band-tailed Pigeon has been removed entirely from the list of game birds that can be killed until September 1, 1918.

The Band-tailed Pigeon, often called Wild Pigeon, is sometimes mistaken for the Passenger Pigeon. It ranges up and down the Pacific coast with an occasional record as far east as Colorado and western Texas. The habit of the Pigeon collecting in large bands in certain seasons has made it possible in the past for hunters to kill enormous numbers. This, coupled with the fact that the bird does not reproduce itself rapidly, usually laying but a single egg, is sufficient reason why it can be exterminated readily.

Twenty-five or thirty years ago, men made a business of netting Band-tailed Pigeons in the Willamette valley, Oregon, for the market. Mr. O. G. Dalaba of Corvallis, Oregon, says that he caught a great many in the coast hills in the early nineties. He says he got twenty-five dozen birds at one spring of the net at Eddyville and many others got away. At that time, they were shipped to Portland and San Francisco by way of steamers from Yaquina Bay. He shipped as many as eighty dozen at a time. The birds were accustomed to collect around mineral springs or at watering places at certain seasons of the year.

During the winter of 1911 and 1912, Mr. W. Lee Chambers reported an immense flight of Band-tailed Pigeons from Paso Robles south to Nordhoff all through the coast mountains. Great numbers of the birds were killed and shipped to San Francisco and Los Angeles. One hunter shipped over two thousand birds. A great many hunters from all through southern California turned out daily to shoot Pigeons. This was a good example of a certain time and place where perhaps a large portion of the existing numbers of Pigeons collect together and stay about in one locality until they are practically destroyed. It would take very few occurrences like this to exterminate the species.

William L. Finley.

PASSENGER PIGEON

Ectopistes migratorius (*Linnæus*)

A. O. U. Number 315 See Color Plate 40

Other Names.—Wild Pigeon; Pigeon; Wood Pigeon; Red-breasted Pigeon; Blue-headed Pigeon.

General Description.— Length, 17 inches. Prevailing color above, grayish-blue; below, reddish-fawn. Tail, very long, graduated for more than half its length, the feathers (12 in number) narrowed terminally and obtusely pointed; wings, long and pointed.

Color.— Adult Male: Head, including nape, plain bluish-gray, paler on chin and upper throat; hindneck similar, but glossed with golden or coppery-bronze; the sides of neck, brilliant golden-bronze changing to metallic purple-bronze; back, slate-gray tinged with grayish-brown or olive-brown; shoulders and inner secondaries, grayish-brown, some of the former with a large oblong black spot (mostly concealed) on outer web, the rear shoulder-feathers also with inner web edged with black; inner wing-coverts, similar in color to shoulders but usually slightly (often distinctly) more grayish, passing on outer coverts into slate-gray; outer secondaries, dull brownish-black or dusky, usually narrowly edged terminally with paler; primary coverts and primaries, dark grayish-brown, the latter (except outermost) narrowly margined with dull whitish, the edgings on outer web growing much broader basally, and often orange-cinnamon, at least in part; lower back and upper rump, clear bluish-gray, passing into more brownish-gray on upper tail-coverts; middle pair of tail-feathers, darker brownish-gray passing into dusky terminally; next pair with outer web light gray, inner web white, the next three pairs similar but with white of inner web passing into pale gray basally, the outermost with outer web white — all (except middle pair) with a sub-basal roundish black spot on inner web, preceded by a spot of cinnamon-rufous; lower throat, foreneck, chest, breast, and sides, plain reddish-fawn color, passing into white on abdomen, anal region, and under tail-coverts; bill, black; iris, scarlet or scarlet-vermilion; bare eye space, livid flesh color; legs and feet, lake-red or pinkish-red. Adult Female: Distinctly duller in plumage than the adult male: the head, more brownish-gray; the back, shoulders, and secondaries, more decidedly brownish; the shoulders and wing-coverts, more heavily spotted with black; the reddish-fawn color of the foreneck and rest of under parts, replaced by light drab, passing into pale drab-gray on breast and sides and metallic gloss of hindneck and sides of neck less brilliant; iris, orange or orange-red; bare eye space, pale grayish-blue; legs and feet, paler lake-red than in adult male.

Nest and Eggs.— Nest: Before its extermination, nested in myriads; in the extensive forests sometimes fifty or more of their frail structures of twigs seen in a single tree. Eggs: 1 or 2, pure white.

Distribution.— Now extinct, the last living specimen having died in the Cincinnati Zoological Garden, September 1, 1914. Formerly perhaps the most numerous of all birds, inhabiting practically the whole forested area of eastern North America, breeding northward to middle western Keewatin, northern Ontario, Quebec, northern Maine, New Brunswick, and Nova Scotia, southward to Kansas, northern Mississippi, Kentucky, and Pennsylvania; migrating southward to the Gulf coast (Florida to Texas), casually to Cuba, eastern Mexico, and Guatemala; westward regularly, along the Missouri River to eastern Montana and to western Texas, accidentally to Nevada, Wyoming, eastern Oregon, western Washington, and British Columbia; accidental in British Isles, Europe, and the Bermudas.

More interest is evidenced in the history of the Passenger Pigeon and its fate than in that of any other North American bird. Its story reads like a romance. Once the most abundant species, in its flights and on its nesting grounds, ever known in any country, ranging over the greater part of the continent of North America in innumerable hordes, the race seems to have disappeared during the nineteenth century, leaving no trace.

The Passenger Pigeon was described by Linné in the latter part of the eighteenth century; but it was well known in America many years before. In July, 1605, on the coast of Maine, in latitude 43° 25′, Champlain saw on some islands an "infinite number of Pigeons," of which he took a great quantity. Many early historians, who write of the birds of the Atlantic coast region, mention the Pigeons. The Jesuit Fathers, in their first narratives of Acadia (1610–13), state that the birds were fully as abundant as the fish, and that in their seasons the Pigeons overloaded the trees. Passing from Nova Scotia to Florida, we find that Stork (1766) asserts that they were in such plenty there for three months of the year that an account of them would seem incredible. John Lawson (1709), in his *History of Carolina,* speaks of prodigious flocks of Pigeons in 1701–02, which broke down trees in the woods where they roosted, and cleared away all the food in the country before them, scarcely leaving one acorn on the ground. The early settlers in Virginia found the Pigeons in winter "beyond number or imagination." The Plymouth colony was threatened with famine in 1643, when great flocks of Pigeons swept down upon the ripened corn and beat down and ate "a very great quantity of all sorts of English grain." But Winthrop says that in 1648 they came again after the harvest was gathered, and proved a great blessing, "it being incredible what multitudes of them were killed daily."

These great flights of Pigeons in migration extended over vast tracts of country, and usually passed in their greatest numbers for about three days. This is the testimony of observers in many parts of the land. Afterwards, flocks often came along for a week or two longer. Even as late as the decade succeeding 1860 such flights continued, and were still observed throughout the eastern States and Canada, except perhaps along the Atlantic coast.

About 1850 indications of the disappearance of the Pigeons in the East began to attract some notice. They became rare in Newfoundland in the 60's, though formerly abundant there. They grew fewer in Ontario at that time; but, according to Fleming, some of the old roosts there were occupied until 1870.

Alexander Wilson, the father of American ornithology, tells of a breeding place of the Wild Pigeons in Shelbyville, Ky. (probably about 1806), which was several miles in breadth, and was said to be more than forty miles in extent. More than one hundred nests were found on a tree. The ground was strewn with broken limbs of trees; also eggs and dead squabs which had been precipitated from above, on which herds of hogs were fattening. He speaks of a flight of these birds from another nesting place some sixty miles away from the first, toward Green River, where they were said to be equally numerous. They were traveling with great steadiness and rapidity, at a height beyond gunshot, several strata deep, very close together, and "from right to left as far as the eye could reach, the breadth of this vast procession extended; seeming everywhere equally crowded." From half-past one to four o'clock in the afternoon, while he was traveling to Frankfort, the same living torrent rolled overhead, seemingly as extensive as ever. He estimated the flock that passed him to be two hundred and forty miles long and a mile wide — probably much wider — and to contain two billion, two hundred and thirty million, two hundred and seventy-two thousand pigeons. On the supposition that each bird consumed only half a pint of nuts and acorns daily, he reckoned that this column of birds would eat seventeen million, four hundred and twenty-four thousand bushels each day.

Audubon states that in the autumn of 1813 he left his house at Henderson, on the banks of the Ohio, a few miles from Hardensburgh, to go to Louisville, Ky. He saw that day what he thought to be the largest flight of Wild Pigeons he had ever seen. The air was literally filled with them; and the "light of noonday was obscured as by an eclipse." Before sunset he reached Louisville, fifty-five miles from Hardensburgh, and during all that time Pigeons were passing in undiminished numbers. This continued for three days in succession. The people were all armed, and the banks of the river were crowded with men and boys, incessantly shooting at the Pigeons, which flew lower as they passed the river. For a week or more the people fed on no other flesh than Pigeons. The atmosphere during that time was strongly impregnated with the odor of the birds. Audubon estimated the number of Pigeons passing overhead (in a flock one mile wide) for three hours, traveling at the rate of a mile a minute, allowing two Pigeons to the square yard, as one billion, one hundred and fifteen million, one hundred and thirty-six thousand. He estimated, also, that a flock of this size would require eight million, seven hundred and twelve thousand bushels of food a day, and this was only a small part of the three days' flight.

Great flights of Pigeons ranged from the Alleghenies to the Mississippi and from Hudson Bay to the Gulf of Mexico until after the middle of the nineteenth century. Even two decades later, enormous numbers of Pigeons nested in several States.

Their winter roosting places almost defy description. Audubon rode through one on the banks of the Green River in Kentucky for more than forty miles, crossing it in different directions, and found its average width to be rather more than three miles. He observed that the ejecta covered the whole extent of the roosting place, like snow; that many trees two feet in diameter were broken off not far from the ground, and that the branches of many of the largest and tallest had given way. The birds came in soon after sundown with a noise that sounded "like a gale passing through the rigging of a close-reefed vessel," causing a great current of air as they passed; and here and there as the flocks alighted, the limbs gave way with a crash, destroying hundreds of birds beneath. It was a scene of uproar and confusion. No one dared venture into the woods during the night, because of the falling branches.

The nesting places sometimes were equal in size to the roosting places, for the Pigeons congregated in enormous numbers to breed in the northern and eastern States. When food was plentiful in the forests, the birds concentrated in large numbers; when it was not, they scattered in smaller groups. The last great nesting place of which we have adequate record was in Michigan, in 1878. Prof. H. B. Roney states, in the *American Field,* that the nesting near Petoskey, that year, covered something like 100,000 acres, and included not less than 150,000 acres within its limits. It was estimated to be about forty miles in length and from three to ten miles in width. It is difficult to approximate the number of millions of Pigeons that occupied that great nesting place.

Audubon, who described the dreadful havoc made among these birds on their roosting grounds by man, says that people unacquainted with them might naturally conclude that such destruction would soon put an end to the species; but he had satisfied himself, by long observation, that nothing but the gradual diminution of the forests could accomplish the decrease of the birds, for he believed that they not infrequently quadrupled their numbers during the year, and always doubled them. The enormous multitudes of the Pigeons made such an impression upon the mind that the extinction of the species at that time, and for many years afterwards, seemed an absolute impossibility. Nevertheless, it has occurred. How can this apparent impossibility be explained? It cannot be accounted for by the destructiveness of their natural enemies, for during the years when the Pigeons were the most abundant their natural enemies were most numerous. The extinction of the Pigeons has been coincident with the disappearance of bears, panthers, wolves, lynxes, and some of the larger birds of prey from a large portion of their range.

The aborigines never could have reduced appreciably the numbers of the species. Wherever the great roosts were established, Indians always gathered in large numbers. This, according to their traditions, had been the custom among them from time immemorial. They always had slaughtered these birds, young and old, in great quantities; but there was no market among the Indians, and the only way in which they could preserve the meat for future use was by drying or smoking the breasts. They cured large numbers in this way. Also, they were accustomed to kill great quantities of the squabs in order to try out the fat, which was used as butter is used by the whites. Lawson writes (1709): "You may find several Indian towns of not above seventeen houses that have more than 100 gallons of pigeon's oil or fat."

But it was not until a market demand for the birds was created by the whites that the Indians ever seriously affected the increase of the Pigeons. Kalm states, in his monograph of the Pigeon, that the Indians of Canada would not molest the Pigeons in their breeding places until the young were able to fly. They did everything in their power to prevent the whites from disturbing them, even using threats, where pleading did not avail.

When the white man appeared on this continent, conditions rapidly changed. Practically all the early settlers were accustomed to the use of firearms; and wherever Pigeons appeared in great numbers, the inhabitants armed themselves with guns, clubs, stones, poles, and whatever could be used to destroy the birds. The most destructive implement was the net, to which the birds were attracted by bait, and under which vast numbers of them were trapped. Gunners baited the birds with grain. Dozens of birds sometimes were killed thus at a single shot. In one case seventy-one birds were killed by two shots. A single shot from the old flint-lock, single-barreled gun, fired into a tree, sometimes would procure a back load of Pigeons.

The Pigeons were reduced greatly in numbers on the whole Atlantic seaboard during the first two centuries after the settlement of the country, but in the West their numbers remained apparently the same until the nineteenth century. There was no appreciable decrease there during the first half of that century; but during the latter half, railroads were pushed across the plains to the Pacific, settlers increased rapidly to the Mississippi and beyond, and the diminution of the Pigeons in the West began. Already it had become noticeable in western Pennsylvania, western New York, along the Appalachian mountain chain and in Ohio. This was due in part to the destruction of the forests, particularly the beech woods, which once covered vast tracts, and which furnished the birds with a chief supply of food. Later, the primeval pine and hemlock forests of the northern States largely were cut away. This deprived the birds of another source of food — the seed of these trees. The destruction of the forests, however, was not complete; for, although great tracts of land were cleared, there remained and still remain vast regions more or less covered by coppice growth sufficient to furnish great armies of Pigeons with food, and the cultivation of the land and the raising of grain provided new sources of food supply. Therefore, while the reduction of the forest area in the East was a large factor in the diminution of the Pigeons, we cannot attribute their extermination to the destruction of the forest. Forest fires undoubtedly had something to do with reducing the numbers of these birds, for many were destroyed by these fires, and in some cases large areas of forest were ruined absolutely by fire, thus for many years depriving the birds of a portion of their food supply. Nevertheless, the fires were local and restricted, and had comparatively little effect on the vast numbers of the species.

The net, though used by fowlers almost everywhere in the East from the earliest settlement of the country, was not a great factor in the extermination of the Pigeons in the Mississippi valley States until the latter half of the nineteenth century. With the extension of railroads and telegraph lines through the States, the occupation of the netter became more stable than before, for he could follow the birds wherever they went. The number of men who made netting an occupation after the year 1860 is variously estimated at from 400 to 1000. Whenever a flight of Pigeons left one nesting place and made toward another, the netters learned their whereabouts by telegraph, packed up their belongings, and moved to the new location, sometimes following the birds a thousand miles at one move. Some of them not only made a living, but earned a competency, by netting Pigeons during part of the year and shooting wild-fowl and game birds during the remainder of the season. In addition to these there were the local netters, who plied the trade only when the Pigeons came their way.

Possibly the last great slaughter of Pigeons in New York, of which we have record, was some time in the 70's. A flock had nested in Missouri in April, where most of the squabs were killed by the pigeoners. This flock then went to Michigan, where they were followed by the same pigeoners, who again destroyed the squabs. The Pigeons then flew to New York State, and nested near the upper Beaverkill in the Catskills, in the lower part of Ulster County. It is said that tons of the birds were sent to the New York market from this nesting place, and that not less than fifteen tons of ice were used in packing the squabs.

During the 70's most of the Pigeons concentrated in the West. They often passed the winter in Texas, Arkansas, Missouri, the Indian Territory and contiguous regions, and the summer in Michigan and adjacent States and in the Canadian northwest. At this time some very large nets were used, grain beds were made, and the birds were allowed to come and feed there until from 200 to 250 dozen were taken sometimes at one haul.

Still, people read of the "mysterious" disappearance of the Passenger Pigeon, wonder what caused it, and say that it never has been satisfactorily explained. The New York market alone would take 100 barrels a day for weeks, without a break in price. Chicago, St. Louis, Boston and all the great and little cities of the North and East joined in the demand. Need we wonder why the Pigeons have vanished?

The birds that survived the slaughter at Petoskey in 1878 finally left the nesting place in large bodies and disappeared to the North, and from that time onward the diminution of the Pigeons was continuous. Some of the netters asserted that this great flight was swallowed up in Lake Michigan, and that the Pigeons then became practically extinct. This statement had no foundation in fact. It is probable that when they left Petoskey in 1878 they retired into inaccessible regions of Canada, beyond reach of the rail and telegraph, to breed again. In April, 1880, they again passed through Michigan.

There were many smaller nestings for years after the Petoskey nesting of 1878, but the records are meager, for apparently no naturalist visited them. The Petoskey nesting of 1878 was unusually large for that time, for the reason that the birds at three large breeding places in other States or regions were driven out by persecution, and joined the Petoskey group. After this the birds exhibited a tendency to scatter to regions where they were least molested. There seem to have been two great nestings in Michigan in 1881.

Our Canadian records of the species at this time are meager. Mr. Ernest Thompson Seton says that it bred in Manitoba in considerable numbers as late as 1887; but he also says that the last year in which the Pigeons came to Manitoba "in force" was in 1878; next year they were comparatively scarce, and each year since they have become more so.

A flock was seen in Illinois in 1895, from which two specimens were taken. At that time the netting of the birds had been practically given up, and most of the dealers had seen no Pigeons for two seasons. It finally ceased, on account of the virtual extinction of the birds.

A large correspondence and a careful search through some of the literature of the latter part of the century leads to the belief that the Pigeons were common and in some cases abundant in portions of the West from 1880 to 1890, though gradually decreasing. After 1893 the reports became more vague and less trustworthy, except in a few cases. Small flocks were seen and specimens taken in the last decade of the nineteenth century in Canada, and in Wisconsin, Nebraska, Illinois, Indiana and other western States and even in some of the Eastern States. Chief Pokagon reported a nesting of Pigeons near the headwaters of the Ausable River in Michigan in 1896. In 1898 a flock of about 200 birds was said to have been seen in Michigan; one was taken; and in 1900 about fifty birds were reported.

While the big nestings of 1878 and 1881 in Michigan were the last immense breeding places of Passenger Pigeons on record, the species did not become extinct in a day or a year; they were not wiped from the face of the earth by any great catastrophe; they gradually became fewer and fewer for twenty to twenty-five years after the date set by the pigeoners as that of the last great migration.

Efforts have been made to account for the supposed sudden disappearance of the Pigeons by tales of cyclonic sea disturbances or lake storms, which are supposed to have drowned practically all of them. Undoubtedly thousands of Pigeons were destroyed occasionally, during their flights, by storms or fogs at sea or on the Great Lakes. There are many rather unsatisfactory and hazy reports of such occurrences. The earliest of these is recorded by Kalm, who says, in his account of the Passenger Pigeon, that in March, 1740, about a week after the disappearance of a great multitude of Pigeons in Pennsylvania and New Jersey, a sea captain named Amies, who arrived at Philadelphia, stated that he had seen the sea covered with dead Pigeons, in some cases for three French miles. Other ship captains, arriving later, corroborated this tale. It was said that from that date no such great multitudes of Pigeons were seen in Pennsylvania. Kalm published this in 1759, but after that date the Pigeons again came to Pennsylvania in great numbers; which shows that the drowning of this multitude had no permanent effect on the numbers of the birds. This story in some form has cropped up at intervals ever since.

Schoolcraft (1821), while walking along some parts of the shore of Lake Michigan, saw a great number of the skeletons and half-consumed bodies of Pigeons, which he says are overtaken often by tempests in crossing the lake, and "drowned in entire flocks." Vast numbers of Eagles and Buzzards were seen feeding upon them.

Some of the Pigeons may have been driven by persecution to the Far North to breed, in the latter part of the nineteenth century, and they may have been destroyed by unseasonable storms, for many species are subject to periodical reduction by the elements; but the whole history of the last thirty years of the existence of the Passenger Pigeon goes to prove that the birds were so persistently molested that they finally lost their coherence, were scattered far and wide, and became extinct mainly through constant persecution by man. While they existed in large colonies, the orphaned young were taken care of by their neighbors. This communal habit of feeding preserved the species so long as the birds nested in large colonies; but when they became scattered the young starved when their parents were killed.

The Passenger Pigeon was not a suspicious bird, as birds go: it was easily taken. It reproduced slowly, laid but few eggs, and, when its innumerable multitudes were reduced and its flocks were dispersed, the end came rapidly.

It often is asked how it was possible for man to kill them all. It was not possible, nor was it requisite that he should do so, in order to exterminate them. All that was required to bring about this result was to destroy a large part of the young birds hatched each year. Nature cut off the rest. She always eliminates a large share of the young of all creatures. The greater part of the Pigeons taken in summer and fall were young birds. The squabs were sought because they brought a high price in the market. The young when out of the nest were less experienced than the adults, and therefore more easily taken. Sometimes the Pigeons were so harassed that all their nestings were broken up, and few young were raised that season; thus the natural increase was practically cut off, and constant diminution was assured. Extermination must have resulted under such conditions, even if no man ever killed an adult Passenger Pigeon. The Pigeons were not immortal. Even if undisturbed by man, they "gave up the ghost" in a few years; but they were not undisturbed. No adequate attempt to protect them was made until they practically had disappeared. Whenever a law looking toward the conservation of these birds was proposed in any State, its opponents argued before the legislative committees that the Pigeons "needed no protection"; that their numbers were so vast, and that they ranged over such a great extent of country, that they were amply able to take care of themselves. This argument defeated all measures that might have given adequate protection to this species. That is why extinction finally came quickly. We did our best to exterminate both old and young, and we succeeded. The explanation is so simple that all talk of "mystery" seems sadly out of place here.

Photo by R. W. Shufeldt

THE LAST PASSENGER PIGEON

She died in the Cincinnati Zoological Park in 1914

Ornithologists believe that the migrations of this Pigeon were made mainly in pursuit of food, and with little reference to the seasons of the year. Undoubtedly, however, the tendency was to migrate north in the spring and south in the fall, like other birds of passage. Some of the pigeoners say that the Pigeons nested in the southern States in winter; but of this there is no authentic record.

The accounts of the early settlers in Massachusetts show that there was a northward migration of Pigeons through New England in March, and they sometimes lingered about Hudson Bay until December, feeding on the berries of the juniper. The roosts of the Pigeons were so extensive and the birds frequenting them were so numerous that it was necessary for them to fly long distances daily in order to secure food enough for their wants. In migration their flight was very high and swift. Audubon estimates that they flew a mile a minute, and others have asserted that they sometimes traveled 100 miles an hour. This was probably an exaggeration.

In searching for food in a country where it was plentiful, the birds flew low, and, upon reaching good feeding ground, swung in large circles while examining the place. Some flocks were composed of young birds, others were mostly males, and still others almost entirely females.

Their roosting places were preferably in large and heavy timber, sometimes in swamps. In most of the larger roosts, the trees, undergrowth, and all vegetation on the ground were soon killed by a heavy deposit of guano. About sunset the Pigeons in all the country for many miles around began to move toward the roost, and soon after sundown they commenced to arrive in immense numbers, some from a distance of 100 miles or more. Birds poured in from all directions until after midnight, and left the roost again at sunrise.

Audubon says that a messenger whom he sent out from a Pigeon roost reported to him that the uproar of the birds arriving could be heard three miles away. A most remarkable attribute of the Pigeon was its disregard of the presence of human beings in its roosting and nesting places. Any one who entered quietly one of these spots when the birds were there would be surrounded by the unsuspicious creatures in a few minutes. The nests formerly were placed in trees of great height, in some locality near water, where food was plentiful; but after the primeval forests were cut off, the Pigeons nested sometimes in low trees. This contributed to their doom. The best description of the nesting of these birds that I have seen is given by Chief Pokagon, in the *Chautauquan*. He was a full-blooded Indian, and the last Pottawottomi chief of the Pokagon band. He says:

"About the middle of May, 1850, while in the fur trade, I was camping on the head waters of the Manistee River in Michigan. One morning on leaving my wigwam I was startled by hearing a gurgling, rumbling sound, as though an army of horses laden with sleigh bells was advancing through the deep forests toward me. As I listened more intently, I concluded that instead of the tramping of horses it was distant thunder; and yet the morning was clear, calm and beautiful. Nearer and nearer came the strange commingling sounds of sleigh bells, mixed with the rumbling of an approaching storm. While I gazed in wonder and astonishment, I beheld moving toward me in an unbroken front millions of pigeons, the first I had seen that season. They passed like a cloud through the branches of the high trees, through the underbrush and over the ground, apparently overturning every leaf. Statue-like I stood, half-concealed by cedar boughs. They fluttered all about me, lighting on my head and shoulders; gently I caught two in my hands and carefully concealed them under my blanket.

"I now began to realize they were mating, preparatory to nesting. It was an event which I had long hoped to witness; so I sat down and carefully watched their movements, amid the greatest tumult. I tried to understand their strange language, and why they all chatted in concert. In the course of the day the great on-moving mass passed by me, but the trees were still filled with them sitting in pairs in convenient crotches of the limbs, now and then gently fluttering their half-spread wings and uttering to their mates those strange, bell-like wooing notes which I had mistaken for the ringing of bells in the distance.

"On the third day after, this chattering ceased and all were busy carrying sticks with which they were building nests in the same crotches of the limbs they had occupied in pairs the day before. On the morning of the fourth day their nests were finished and eggs laid. The hen birds occupied the nests in the morning, while the male birds went out into the surrounding country to feed, returning about 10 o'clock, taking the nests, while the hens went out to feed, returning about 3 o'clock. Again changing nests, the male birds went out the second time to feed, returning at sundown. The same routine was pursued each day until the young ones were hatched and nearly half-grown, at which time all the parent birds left the brooding grounds about daylight. On the morning of the eleventh day after the eggs were laid, I found the nesting grounds strewn with egg shells, convincing me that the young were hatched. In thirteen days more the parent birds left their young to shift for themselves, flying to the east about sixty miles, when they again nested. The female lays but one egg during the same nesting.

"Both sexes secrete in their crops milk or curd with which they feed their young until they are ready to fly, when they stuff them with mast and such other raw material as they themselves eat until their crops exceed their bodies in size, giving to them an appearance of two birds with one head. Within two days after the stuffing they become a mass of fat — "a squab." At this period the parent bird drives them from the nests to take care of themselves, while they fly off within a day or two, sometimes hundreds of miles, and again nest.

"It has been well established that these birds look after and take care of all orphan squabs whose parents have been killed or are missing. These birds are long-lived, having been known to live twenty-five years caged. When food is abundant they nest each month in the year."

It seems improbable, however, that they bred

in winter. The nesting usually occupied four or five weeks. The female, when sitting, never left the nest until the flight of males returned, when she slipped away, just as her mate reached the nest. Thus the eggs were kept covered all the time. The adult birds never ate the nuts and acorns in the immediate vicinity of the nesting place, but went to a distance for their food, and left the mast in the neighborhood for the young to feed on when they came out of the nest. It is said that for miles around there were no caterpillars or inchworms in the oak woods for several years after a nesting, as the adults secured practically all of them for the young, thereby protecting the forests against their insect enemies. When the young were first pushed out of the nest by the parents, they went to the ground, and fed mainly in the lower parts of the woods until they became expert in flying. They passed over the ground, the lower ranks continually flying over those in front, scratching out all the edible material, those flying overhead striking off the nuts as they flew by. The young birds were able to reproduce their kind in about six months.

Chief Pokagon asserts that while the old birds were feeding they always had guards on duty, to give an alarm in case of danger. The watch bird as it took flight beat its wings together in quick succession, with a sound like the roll of a snare drum. Quick as thought each bird repeated the alarm with a thundering sound, as the flock struggled to rise, leading a novice to imagine that a cyclone was coming.

In feeding, the birds were very voracious. They scratched among the leaves and unearthed every nut or acorn, sometimes almost choking in their efforts to swallow an unusually large specimen. During the breeding season they were fond of salty mud and water, and the pigeoners, learning of this, were accustomed to attract the birds to their death by salting down " mud beds," to which the poor Pigeons flocked in multitudes, and over which, when they were assembled, the pigeoners threw their nets.

The food of the Pigeons consisted mainly of vegetable matter, except for the grasshoppers, caterpillars and other insects, worms, snails, etc., which they ate, and which they fed to their young. Acorns, beechnuts and chestnuts, with pine and hemlock seeds, were among their principal staples of supply. They also fed on the seeds of the elm, maple and other forest trees. Buckwheat, hempseed, Indian corn and other grains, cherries, mulberries, hollyberries, hackberries, wild strawberries, raspberries and huckleberries, and tender shoots of vegetation, all attracted them. They sometimes went to the Barren Grounds in the far North in vast numbers, to feed on blueberries. They often descended upon the fall-sown wheat and rye fields in such numbers that the farmers had to watch their fields, or lose their crops. Oats and peas were favorite foods. No doubt they also fed largely on the seeds of weeds, as the Mourning Doves, Bob-whites, and many other terrestrial feeders do; but I find no record of this. They were fond of currants, cranberries, and poke berries, and no doubt of many other kinds of berries, and rose hips. We know little of their food habits, for no scientific investigation of their food ever was made.

EDWARD HOWE FORBUSH, in *Game Birds, Wild-Fowl and Shore Birds.*

MOURNING DOVE

Zenaidura macroura carolinensis (*Linnæus*)

A. O. U. Number 316 See Color Plate 42

Other Names.— Carolina Dove; Wild Dove; Turtle Dove; Dove.

General Description.— Length, 12½ inches. Prevailing color above, grayish-blue; below, reddish-fawn. Tail, longer than wing, strongly graduated, consisting of 14 relatively narrow and tapering feathers.

Color.— ADULT MALE: Forehead and over eye, fawn color usually paler on front of forehead, passing into dull slate-gray on back of head; hindneck, brownish-gray, the lateral portions (sometimes also lower portion) highly glossed with metallic purplish-bronze; back, shoulders, upper tail-coverts, wing-coverts, and inner secondaries, grayish-brown; the rump similar but usually grayer, passing into slate-grayish laterally; these secondaries, usually also greater coverts, with a number of rather large square and roundish black spots; outer secondaries, primaries, primary coverts, neutral-gray, the primaries narrowly edged with white, these edgings broader on outermost quills; middle pair of tail-feathers similar in color to back, but usually rather grayer, sometimes darkening terminally; next pair, grayer with a dusky bar (usually oblique) across middle portion of inner web; third pair, similar but with the dusky (or black) bar more distinct, extending across part of outer web (the bar more or less V-shaped); fourth and fifth pairs, with the black bar broader, extending entirely across both webs, and with the gray of ends passing into grayish-white terminally; sixth pair, similar to fifth but ends mostly white; seventh (outermost) pair, similar but with outer web entirely white; general color of under parts reddish-fawn color, deeper (sometimes nearly fawn color) on foreneck and chest, becoming much paler on chin and upper throat, behind passing through light pinkish-cinnamon on abdomen and pinkish-buff on anal region to cartridge-buff on longer under tail-coverts; sides of head, similar in color to forehead but sometimes slightly paler, relieved by *a small spot of black, glossed with blue on side of head;* sides and flanks and under wing-coverts, clear bluish-gray; bill, black, the mouth lake-red, the tumid nasal valves somewhat glaucous; iris, dark brown; bare eye space, pale blue, tinged above eye with pale green; legs and feet, lake-red. ADULT FEMALE: Similar to the adult male but coloration duller; less reddish below, where passing into or tinged with light drab on foreneck and chest; black spots on secondaries and wing-coverts larger and more numerous, the shoulders sometimes with a few black spots or broad streaks; metallic gloss on sides of neck more restricted and less brilliant, and black head spot smaller and without blue gloss.

Nest and Eggs.— NEST: Placed in trees (usually low down), bushes, cactus, dense brier thickets, or on ground or on cliff; a frail structure of twigs, so flat that the fact that the eggs do not roll off oftener is remarkable. EGGS: 1 or 2, white; 2 and sometimes 3 broods in a season.

Distribution.—North America; breeds from British Columbia, Saskatchewan, Manitoba, Ontario, and southern Nova Scotia south throughout the United States and Mexico, and locally in Lower California, and Guatemala; winters from southern Oregon, southern Colorado, northern Ohio, and North Carolina to Panama; casual in winter in Middle States.

MOURNING DOVE
(3/8 nat. size)

It is frequently mistaken for the extinct Passenger Pigeon

Drawing by R. I. Brasher

The best-known characteristic of the Mourning Dove is its call — it can hardly be considered a song — which may suggest hopeless sorrow, or the tenderest love and devotion, according to the mood of the listener. Another peculiarity which attaches to the bird is the fact that it is frequently mistaken, by untrained observers, for the probably altogether extinct Passenger Pigeon. Indeed, probably all of the "Passenger Pigeons" reported during the past twenty years have been Mourning Doves; this, at least, has so often proved to be the case that ornithologists take little interest nowadays in announcements that a flock of the Pigeons has been seen.

The nest of this bird is an astonishingly poor makeshift, composed chiefly of a handful of twigs thrown together so loosely that the eggs are in danger of rolling out of it, or falling through the interstices. Neither the hopeless woe nor the love-sick hypothesis nor both seem to account for this slovenliness. Very likely if the birds employed some of the time and ardor they usually put into billing and cooing in trying to construct a safe and substantial home, the result would be a better nest; but after all their poor workmanship is probably due primarily to the fact that both their bills and their feet are ill-adapted to nest-building.

A peculiarity by means of which the Mourning Dove may certainly be identified, is the sharp whistling of its wings while it is in flight. Another distinctive habit of the bird, especially during the mating and nesting season, is that of the male in rising from its perch, with violent flapping of wings (which, like those of the domesticated pigeon, seem to strike over his back), and flying at a sharp angle to a height of a hundred feet or more, when the flight ceases and the bird returns to the same or another perch, by sailing on motionless wings which are usually held at a downward angle, like those of a gliding Snipe or Sandpiper. This performance seems to be purely a sexual manifestation intended to impress the female.

The breeding habits of this bird present several peculiarities. It is one of the earliest of spring arrivals, its appearance being about contemporaneous with the Robin, Bluebird, and Meadowlark. The breeding period — within the bird's normal northern habitat — extends virtually from May to September. Incubation occupies about two weeks and three or even four broods are reared in a season. An Ohio observer reports that he has found the birds incubating in that State during every month excepting December and January, and that he has found fresh eggs in a nest still occupied by birds not mature enough to fly. Another peculiarity is the parent bird's manner of feeding her young, which is done by regurgitation; that is, the young take their food, mixed with a light-colored fluid called "pigeon's milk," from the crop of the parent. The young are slow to develop their power of flight, and so it happens that the mother bird is often seen sitting crosswise on the nest with the heads and tails of her infants protruding on either side of her body.

Apparently because of the strong and swift flight of the Mourning Dove, it was for many years considered a "game" bird in several of the States, especially in the South. Under the Federal Migratory Bird Law of 1913, however, it was classed as a migratory bird, and in that character was given the protection to which it is entitled. GEORGE GLADDEN.

Photograph by A. A. Allen

A MOURNING DOVE BROODING ITS YOUNG

The Mourning Dove is one of the most useful of birds; it feeds extensively on weed seeds, frequently eating insects, especially grasshoppers, but on the whole preferring a vegetable diet. It has been accused of injuring ripening peas but this accusation has not been substantiated.

Photograph by C. M. Oswalt Courtesy of Outing Publishing Co.

NEST AND EGGS OF MOURNING DOVE

The nest is an astonishingly poor makeshift, composed chiefly of a handful of twigs loosely thrown together

---

WHITE-WINGED DOVE

Melopelia asiatica (*Linnæus*)

A. O. U. Number 319

Other Name.— Singing Dove.

General Description.— Length, 12 inches. Prevailing color above, gray; below, brown on breast and gray on abdomen. Tail shorter than wing, moderately rounded, consisting of 12 feathers, these broader terminally; wing rather large and pointed.

Color.— Head, fawn color, paler in front and passing into a much darker hue (sometimes approaching dark purple-drab) on crown and back of head; hindneck, similar in color to back of head but somewhat lighter; back, shoulders, and wing-coverts, plain deep buffy-brown, light sepia, or umber; the middle pair of tail-feathers (sometimes longer upper tail-coverts also) similar, sometimes more decidedly brown; *outer wing-coverts, mostly white forming a conspicuous elongated patch from bend of wing to extremity of greater coverts,* the latter with basal portion gray, as are also the coverts along inner margin of the white area; primaries, primary coverts, and outer secondaries, dull black, the outer webs of secondaries, broadly edged with white at the tips, the primaries very narrowly edged with white (except basally) and margined terminally with light or pale brownish-gray; rump, light slate-gray or dark gull-gray, usually tinged with buffy-brown; the upper tail-coverts, either wholly brown or mixed brown and gray; tail-feathers (except middle pair), slate-gray very broadly tipped with very pale gray to grayish-white, and crossed by a band of slate-black or blackish-slate between the paler and darker areas; a spot below the eye of blue-black or black glossed with steel-blue; sides of neck, glossed with metallic reddish-bronze to greenish-bronze; sides of head and neck, throat, foreneck, chest, and upper breast (sometimes whole breast), wood-brown, paler (sometimes dull whitish) on chin and upper throat, passing into pale gray on posterior under parts, including under tail-coverts; the anal region, white; sides and flanks and under wing-coverts, deeper gray; under surface of tail, slate-black broadly tipped with white or grayish-white; bill, black; iris, orange to orange-red or coral-red; bare eye-space, pale grayish-blue to campanula-blue; legs and feet, lake-red.

Nest and Eggs.— Nest: In bushes or low trees; a slight frail structure of sticks and weeds. Eggs: 2, creamy-white.

Distribution.— Eastern Cuba; southern Bahamas; Haiti; Jamaica; Old Providence Island; and lower Rio Grande valley in Texas; southward through Mexico, Central America, and Panama (?) Occasional in southern Florida, Louisiana, and south-central Texas.

The White-winged Dove has been credited with a trick of lying very close when it is on the ground, in fact till it is almost stepped on, and then taking flight with a whirring of wings; but Mr. W. L. Finley says that in the three months he once spent in the neighborhood of Tucson he did not notice this habit. (MS.)

The characteristic note is Owl-like rather than Dove-like, which is to say it is bold and emphatic rather than timid and melancholy or lovesick. In uttering it the Dove inflates its throat as does a Pouter Pigeon. "Mr. Herbert Brown said the peculiar note of the White-winged Dove always reminded him of the crowing of a young rooster just learning. He was deceived entirely the first time he heard it; he was satisfied he was near a farm house, but upon investigation, he found no one living in the locality, but he did discover a Dove that was doing the crowing." (W. L. Finley, MS.)

Its note, its numbers, and its whirring flight make the White-winged Dove perhaps the best known bird of the torrid cactus deserts and mesquite valleys of the southwest.

In its flight the white bands on the bird's wings and tail are plainly visible.

GROUND DOVE

Chæmepelia passerina terrestris (*Chapman*)

A. O. U. Number 320

Other Name.— Mourning Dove.

General Description.— Length, 6½ inches; smallest of American Doves. Color above, grayish-brown; below, grayish-reddish. Wing moderate with rounded tip; tail from ⅔ to ¾ length of wing, decidedly rounded, with 12 feathers, these relatively broad and with broadly rounded tips.

Color.— Forehead, front of crown, sides of head and neck, and under parts, light grayish-reddish, paler on chin and upper throat, deepening into pinkish light purple-drab on chest, and passing into brownish-gray behind, the under tail-coverts paler on margins; feathers on sides of head and neck and lower throat narrowly margined with darker, those of foreneck and chest more broadly or more distinctly margined, and with a central broadly wedged-shaped spot of dusky; rear of crown, back of head, and hindneck, bluish-gray, the feathers narrowly margined with dusky; back, shoulders, inner secondaries, front lesser wing-coverts, rump, and upper tail-coverts, plain grayish-brown; wing-coverts (except front lesser coverts), similar in color to chest, etc., passing into a more grayish hue on greater coverts, the inner coverts with spots (the rear ones wedge-shaped and oblique) of metallic blackish-purple; outer secondaries dull brownish-black, narrowly edged with paler; primary coverts, dull black with basal half chestnut; primaries, chestnut with terminal portion and outer webs (except basally) of longer quills, dull black, the shorter primaries tipped and edged with black; middle tail-feathers, brownish-gray; the rest, dull black, the outermost ones margined terminally (especially on outer web) with whitish; bill, coral-red or orange-red, dusky at tip; iris, orange-red; legs and feet, flesh-color or pink.

Nest and Eggs.— Nest: On the ground or from 2 to 20 feet above it in bushes, stumps, vines, or small trees; simply a few curved twigs with the addition sometimes of pine-needles. Eggs: 2, pure white or creamy white.

Distribution.— Florida, including Keys, South Carolina, and westward near the Gulf coast through Alabama to Louisiana into western Texas, southern Arizona and Lower California; occasional or casual northward to North Carolina, Virginia, District of Columbia, Maryland, Pennsylvania, New Jersey, New York City, and Tennessee.

The Ground Dove is the smallest of the North American Pigeons. It is a dainty, trusting little bird and often allows one to walk within a few yards of it before taking flight. The larger part of its life is spent on the ground, where it seems to obtain all its food. On short legs it walks sedately along in a rather rapid manner, prettily bobbing its head as it goes, and picking up seeds of grass and weeds by the way. It does not occur north of North Carolina and is rare in that State. It increases in numbers as one advances farther south, and reaches its greatest abundance in Florida, where it is found in most parts of the State. Elsewhere in the East it lives mainly near the coast. It is distributed along the Gulf coast in suitable localities as far west as Texas.

In the more open places in the woods as well as about lakes and on plantations you may come across it almost anywhere. In many towns it lives in numbers and in companies of twos or threes frequent the gardens and quiet streets. Throughout the spring and summer its soft cooing notes are repeatedly heard issuing from the orange trees or grape-vines. Its soft plaintive note has won for it the name of "Mourning Dove" by many people who in turn give the name "Turtle Dove" to the species to which this name rightfully belongs.

The breeding season of few birds extends over such an unusually long period. I have found nests with fresh eggs as early as February 28, and every month afterward until September 26. It is rather curious that an entirely different character of nesting site seems to be chosen at different times of year. The nests I have found in the early spring were always on the top of rotting stumps. Later nearly all nests discovered were on the ground in grain-fields or weed patches, the one exception being nests found on the fronds of cabbage palmetto trees. In the months of July, August, and September, of more than forty nests examined, all were either on the larger boughs of orange trees, or resting on the horizontal supports of scuppernong grape-vines. These notes were made over a period of six years' observation in Alachua County, Florida. The nest is always a simple affair of dried grasses with occasionally small twigs for support. Two white eggs are laid. The young are fed by the process of regurgitation.

We might expect this little Dove to be the personification of gentleness, but the contrary condition is often apparent. Frequently they wage battles among themselves, in which, however, nobody ever seems to get hurt. They will also attack, without hesitation, almost any other bird that they think is trying to deprive them of their food.

A very similar allied species, known as the Mexican Ground Dove (*Chæmepelia passerina pallescens*) is found in the desert regions of the southwest. Their simple nests are often built in the mesquite trees growing along the dry arroyos.

Ground Doves are seldom disturbed by the people of the country they inhabit; in fact, many superstitious negroes have solemnly assured me that it would bring the worst kind of bad luck to anybody who should be so unwise as to kill one.

T. GILBERT PEARSON.

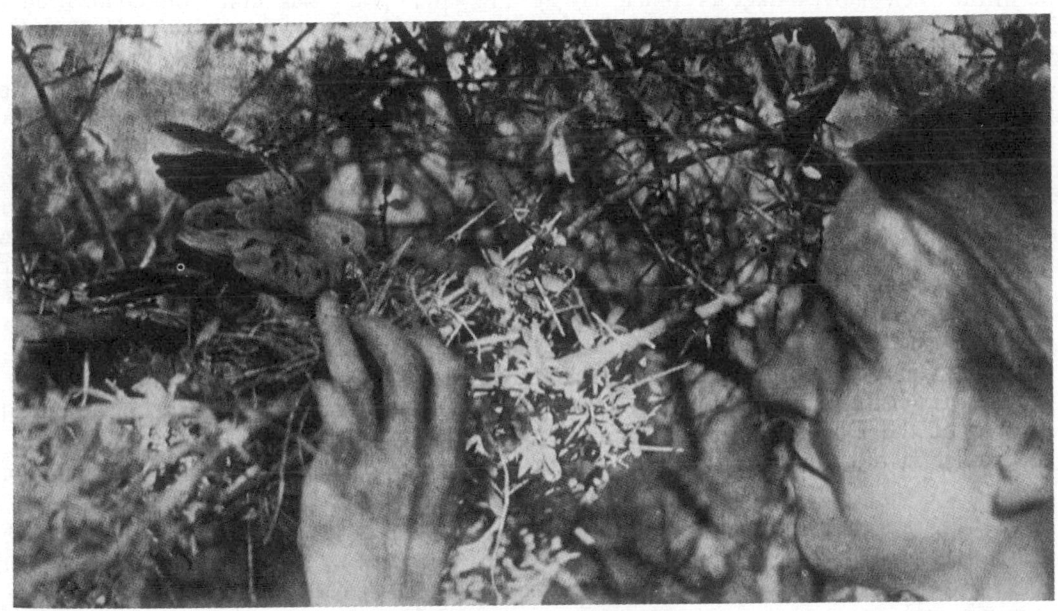

Photograph by W. L. Finley — Courtesy of Nat. Asso. Aud. Soc.

MEXICAN GROUND DOVE

She raised her wings and spread her tail in anger

INCA DOVE

Scardafella inca (*Lesson*)

A. O. U. Number 321

Other Name.— Scaled Dove.

General Description.— Length, 8 inches. Color above, grayish-brown; below, grayish-red and buff. Tail, as long or longer than wing, double rounded, with 12 feathers, all relatively narrow and tapering terminally; wing, rather short and much rounded.

Color.— General color of upper parts, grayish-brown passing into pale écru-drab on forehead, the wing-coverts, paler grayish-brown, sometimes dull grayish-white, especially on outer coverts; each feather of crown, back of head, hindneck, back, shoulders, wing-coverts, rump, and upper tail-coverts, rather broadly margined terminally with sooty-black, producing *a conspicuous barred or scaled effect;* primary coverts, chestnut broadly margined terminally with black; primaries, chestnut with terminal portion dark grayish-brown, this increasing in extent on outer webs of outermost quills; outer secondaries, chestnut broadly edged and tipped with dusky, the more inner ones mostly dusky, with pale edgings; middle pair of tail-feathers grayish-brown, usually tipped with dusky; second pair, similar but with tip more extensively dusky, the third with still more of dusky and, usually with white on terminal portion; remaining tail-feathers, dull black or dusky passing into grayish-brown basally and broadly tipped with white, the white increasing in extent toward the outermost, on which it occupies approximately the outer half of inner web and two-thirds, or more, of outer web; sides of head and neck, foreneck, and chest, pinkish pale écru-drab to dull pale grayish-red, passing into dull white on chin and upper throat and into very pale buff on rear under parts, the feathers (except on chin and throat, rarely foreneck also) margined terminally with sooty-black, the bar thus formed broadest on sides and flanks, narrowest (often very narrow, sometimes obsolete) on chest and foreneck; bill, blackish; iris, dull orange to bright red; legs and feet pale flesh color to carmine-pink.

Nest and Eggs.— Nest: In bushes, frequently close to houses, a rather (for the genus) well-built platform of twigs. Eggs: 2, white.

Distribution.— Southern Texas, southern Arizona, and Lower California and southward through Mexico, Guatemala, and Honduras to Nicaragua.

The little Inca Dove, like its much larger White-winged relative, often seems very tame or very stupid, for it is likely not to take wing (where it has not been molested) until it is almost trodden upon. In fact, where it comes much in contact with human beings, it becomes about half-domesticated. This is especially the case in farming country where the bird trots around in barnyards or along the roads, busily picking up grain or weed seeds, and uttering meanwhile a hard and quite undovelike note.

The following is from Mr. W. L. Finley's Arizona notes on the Inca Dove: "One cannot live in Tucson for a day without making the acquaintance of the little Inca Dove. This diminutive member of the Dove family was formerly a home dweller in the cactus and mesquite, but in later years has taken on civilization and is scarcely found outside the city limits. He likes a tree that borders a city lawn, and he likes to make love on a telephone wire, dropping down to the dooryard for his dinner and making himself at home with the chickens.

"We heard the Inca before we saw him. We did not have to listen; we could not help hearing him from dawn till dark. Of all wooing birds, this Dove is the most constant. A pair of lovers will sit on the telephone wire by the hour and keep up a mournful cooing, that to some people is positively disconcerting. But all the world should love a lover. The song is really more suggestive of a funeral procession than of a wedding journey." (MS.)

George Gladden.

ORDER OF BIRDS OF PREY

Order *Raptores*

BECAUSE of their rapacious habits, more than because of their physical characteristics, these birds have been grouped in one order. Each member of the order is equipped with a strongly hooked bill with a soft area or cere at the base. The only other birds that have similar bills are the Parrots, but these latter have their toes arranged differently, being "yoke-toed," or having two toes pointed forward and two backward, while the Birds of Prey either have three toes permanently pointed forward, as in the Eagles, or the outer toe may be turned at will to the front or to the back, as in the Owls.

Three suborders are recognized. The first is that of the American Vultures (*Sarcorhamphi*), or Carrion-feeders—thus separated from the others because, not having feet suitable for the slaughter of living prey, they feed upon dead or dying animals, and because they have the head and part of the neck without feathers. It includes but one family. Both the second and the third suborders have the head well feathered. In the suborder Diurnal Birds of Prey (*Falcones*) the eyes are placed at the sides of the head so that the two eyes never look in the same direction. The third suborder is the Owls (*Striges*), birds which have the eyes directed forward, so that both look in the same direction, and surrounded by disks of radiating feathers. The Owls are divided into two families, the Barn Owls and the Horned Owls. The Diurnal Birds of Prey include three families: the Eagles, Hawks, and Kites; the Falcons, Caracaras, etc.; and the Ospreys.

VULTURES

Order *Raptores;* suborder *Sarcorhamphi;* family *Cathartidæ*

THE Vultures comprise a New World family named *Cathartidæ* from a Greek word meaning "cleanser" or "scavenger." The nine species in this group live chiefly upon decaying flesh, and never attack living animals excepting—and this very rarely—creatures which are disabled or are dying of disease or injuries. They range from the tropics northward to temperate America—in the case of the common Turkey Vulture—and include the great Condor of the Andes, which is exceeded in wing extent only by the California Vulture—now almost extinct—and the Wandering Albatross.

The bill is stout, blunt, and hooked; the talons are dull and only slightly curved, and the feet are clumsily formed and not adapted to seizing and killing or holding prey, as are those of the Eagles, Hawks, and Owls. The wings are broad and have eleven primaries and from twelve to twenty-five secondaries. The tail is rounded or even with from twelve to fourteen quill feathers. The head and long neck of the adults usually are bare, though in the King Vulture a short down covers the neck and extends to the crown of the head. This bare skin is rough and is frequently brightly colored. The eyes usually are conspicuous. The plumage and size of the sexes are alike. The Vultures walk when on the ground instead of hopping. Their attitude gives the impression of listlessness.

The Vultures build no nests, but lay one, two, or three eggs in rock cavities, caves, hollow trees or stumps, or on the ground. The eggs, may be greenish, white, or buff and with or without markings of gray or reddish-brown. The young are naked when hatched, but very soon they are covered with a white or buff down. They are fed sometimes by regurgitation; and the adults have a habit, when frightened or angered, of vomiting exceedingly offensive smelling matter. Turkey Vultures and Black Vultures sometimes roost in company, but speaking generally the Vultures are not gregarious.

All Vultures are famous for their majestic flight and for their marvelously keen eyesight, which, rather than their sense of smell, enables them to discover their food. By making perfect use of the air currents one of these great birds will mount for thousands of feet, or soar for hours at a time, without once flapping its wings.

CALIFORNIA VULTURE

Gymnogyps californianus (*Shaw*)

A. O. U. Number 324

Other Names.— California Condor; Queleli.

Description.—Length, 4 to 4½ feet; spread of wings, 9 to 11 feet. Wings, long, folding beyond end of square tail; head and neck, bare; skin, smooth, yellow or yellowish-orange and red; plumage, sooty-blackish commencing over shoulders with a semi-ruff of linear feathers, those underneath of similar character but less clearly defined; the feathers of upper parts with browner tips; wings and tail, black; outer webs of greater wing-coverts and secondaries grayish; wing-coverts and outer secondaries edged with whitish; *under wing-coverts, pure white;* bill, dark brown changing gradually to dull reddish on cere; iris, deep red; feet, horn with a patch of red on knees.

Nest and Eggs.— Nest: A recess among rocks in most inaccessible mountains, more rarely in hollow of a stump or tree trunk. Eggs: 1 or 2, plain greenish-white, unmarked.

Distribution.— Coast ranges of California from Santa Clara County south to northern Lower California; casual north to southern Oregon and east to Arizona; formerly north to Columbia River.

The California Vulture is as large as the Condor of the Andes and when full-grown will measure nine to eleven feet from tip to tip of the wings when they are spread. It differs from its South American brother in dress. Its head and neck are bare and brilliantly colored in orange and red. Its coat is plain brown or blackish. It will weigh from twenty to twenty-five pounds. The Condor seldom, if ever, attacks living creatures; it always plays a waiting game. It never carries food in its talons, because its foot is not made like the Eagle's for gripping and carrying prey. No bird is gentler in disposition or more affectionate in his home life.

The range of the California Condor is more restricted than that of any other bird of prey. The few left in the wild state live almost entirely in the coastal mountainous regions of southern California and a part of Lower California. Unless careful protection is given these few Condors remaining in the these wild mountainous regions, this largest of flying birds will soon cease to be a part of the natural history of California.

If you were to start on a hunt for the California Condor, you might search for years, as we did, without success. In the whole world's collections, less than a dozen of these birds are to be seen alive. In the various museums of the world, one can find almost twice as many eggs of the Great Auk, a bird now extinct, as of this Condor.

The main cause which has been given for the decrease in Condors seems to be that when stock-raising became common in California years ago, the rangers were compelled, in order to secure pasture during the dry months, to drive their herds back into the more remote mountainous parts. Here they invaded the retreats of panthers, grizzlies, and coyotes. These preyed upon the calves and sheep and did considerable damage. The quickest and best device for getting rid of these animals was by baiting carcasses with poison. The Condors came to feed upon the poisoned animals and large numbers of the big birds were undoubtedly killed in this way.

William L. Finley.

Photo by W. L. Finley and H. T. Bohlman

A PAIR OF CALIFORNIA VULTURES

For years Mr. Finley and Mr. Bohlman searched for living birds of this species. They were rewarded by obtaining this remarkable picture

TURKEY VULTURE

Cathartes aura septentrionalis *Wied*

A. O. U. Number 325 See Color Plate 43

Other Names.— Carrion Crow; Turkey Buzzard.

Description.— Length, 2½ feet; spread of wings, 6 feet. Tail, long, and rounded; wings, when folded, reaching to or beyond the tip of tail; head and upper part of neck, entirely bare or with only a few bristles, and with skin deeply corrugated. ADULTS: Head and upper neck of a *reddish tinge* and some shades of blue and white; neck and upper parts, blackish glossed with green or purple; beneath, dull brownish-black; feathers above, broadly edged with dull-grayish brown; secondaries edged with gray; shafts of wing- and tail-feathers, pale brown or yellowish white; bill, dull whitish; iris, brown; feet, flesh-colored.

Nest and Eggs.— EGGS: Commonly 2, sometimes 1, and very rarely 3; laid, from February to June, in a cave, a cavity between rocks, in a hollow log, or on the ground; white or creamy, variously spotted with lavender or purplish brown blotches.

Distribution.— From southern Lower California and northern Mexico north to southern British Columbia, Saskatchewan, western Manitoba, northern Minnesota, southern Ontario, western and southern New York, and New Jersey; casual in Wisconsin, Michigan, northern Ontario, and New Brunswick; winters throughout most of its regular range in the East, but further west retires to California, Nebraska, and the Ohio valley.

The Turkey Vulture is ugly to the last degree, except in flight, but it is an invaluable health-protector in warm latitudes, where it exists on all forms of carrion, being guided to its food by a sense of sight — not smell. What it lacks in beauty and grace afoot it compensates for a-wing. Its circling form, on motionless, widely outstretched pinions, is seldom absent from the skyscape of its habitat as it soars in great circles, scanning the ground below. For hours at a time, in fair weather, it will remain on the wing.

There can be little question that its eyesight is

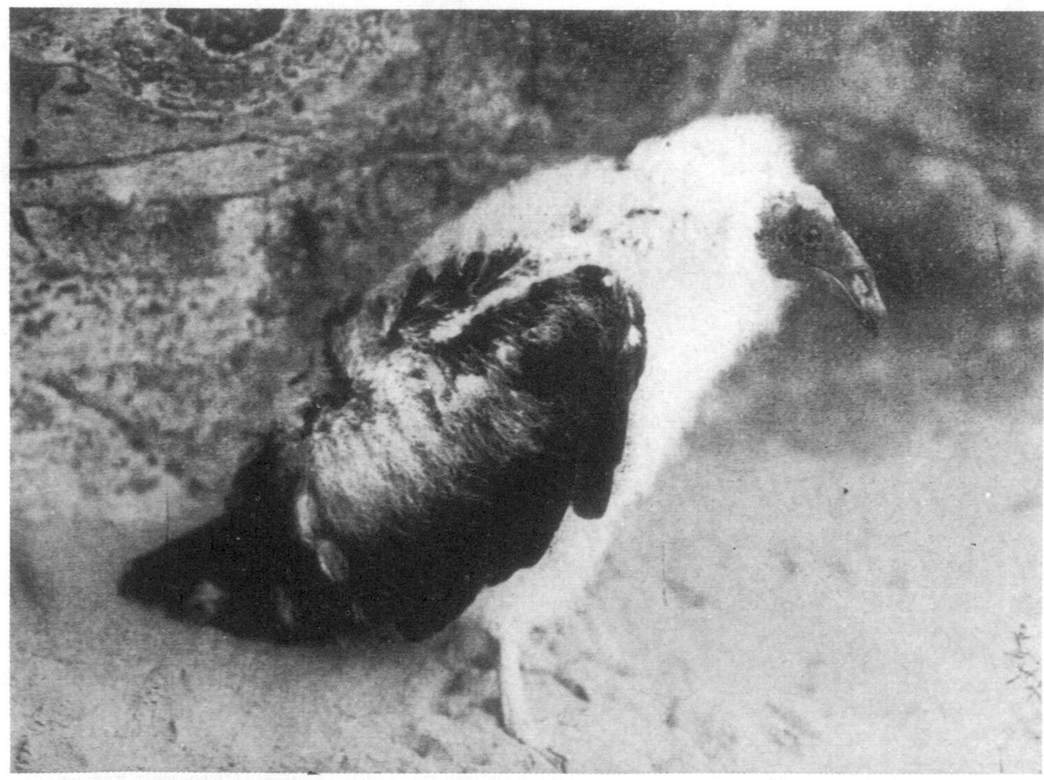

Photo by W. L. Finley and H. T. Bohlman

HALF-GROWN TURKEY VULTURE

He is ugly to the last degree except in flight

many times more powerful than human vision. Suddenly it will appear from nowhere in the sky above, coming directly downward to a dead animal no larger than a cat which it has seen, although it was out of sight itself. If one descends, others are discovered shooting in long slants toward the spot; these in turn are followed by others until all the Vultures which were in the air for many miles around have congregated at the feast.

"The food of the Turkey Buzzard is mainly carrion, but it also eats snakes, toads, and probably rats, mice, and occasionally young birds that chance to fall in its way. It does not, however, attack poultry or game birds, nor does it regularly search for and destroy the nests of other birds. On the whole it is a beneficial species and should be rigorously protected." (Barrows.)

At Cocoanut Grove, Florida, we amused ourselves by catching some of these ungainly birds with a lasso laid on the ground and encircling some bait. A number fought to escape; others simulated death, remaining in an apparently unconscious condition for ten minutes at a stretch. We decorated them with paper collars and cuffs and a few bits of ribbon, then released them and they flew aloft like aërial mountebanks.

R. I. Brasher.

BLACK VULTURE

Catharista urubu (*Vieillot*)

A. O. U. Number 326

Other Names.— Black Buzzard; Carrion Crow; Black Scavenger.

Description.— Length, 27 inches; spread of wings, 4½ feet. Head, naked; feathers of neck extended up back of head in a point; wings, when folded, do not reach to the tip of the tail; compared with the Turkey Vulture, its tail is *decidedly shorter*, wing-strokes more frequent, is built more stumpily and weighs

Photo by H. K. Job

BLACK VULTURES

On the street in Charleston, South Carolina

more. ADULTS (SEXES ALIKE): Head and a part of the neck, covered with a *black* wrinkly and lumpy skin; general color of entire plumage, blackish; *shafts of primaries, white fading to dull gray at base*; bill, blackish, the tip, dull yellowish-white; iris, brownish-hazel; legs, grayish-white with black claws.

Nest and Eggs.— EGGS: 1 to 3, laid on the ground under the protection of logs or bushes or in rock cavities; pale greenish or bluish-white marked irregularly round the larger end with various shades of brown or brownish-purple; deposited from March to May.

Distribution.— From western Texas, Kansas, Illinois, Indiana, and southeastern Virginia, south through the Southern States, Mexico, and Central America to southern South America; casual in Ohio, New York, Maine, Quebec, New Brunswick, and Nova Scotia.

To the visitor for the first time in the South the appearance of that dusky scavenger the Black Vulture, calmly walking around in the streets as domesticated and as unafraid as the English Sparrow of northern cities, strikes him as a little odd.

The careful disposal of dead animals, so necessary in the North, is not required within bounds of this bird's habitat. Anywhere that animals are slaughtered will be found numbers of these Vultures waiting patiently on fences roofs, or any convenient perch, for their share of offal. They are carefully protected, a heavy fine being imposed by law for their destruction. So universal is the recognition of their services that even without any lawful protection it is doubtful if any would be destroyed.

They are easy to distinguish, even at a distance and in the air, from the Turkey Vulture by the short squarish tail and more blocky outlines. Nearby the white under wing-coverts are distinctive.

EAGLES, HAWKS, AND KITES

Order *Raptores;* suborder *Falcones;* family *Buteonidæ*

THE Eagles, Hawks, and Kites comprise the family *Buteonidæ*. They are diurnal birds of prey. Like the Owls, the Falcons, and the Vultures, they have strongly hooked bills with a cere or waxlike membrane around the base. Their feet have three toes permanently pointed forward and one turned backward; the claws or talons are long, curved, extremely acute, and flexibly jointed to the toes. The tarsus is shorter than the tibia, scaled in front, and partly feathered. The leg is well feathered, usually below the knee joint, and the long feathers (the "flag") are well developed. The wings are ample and usually somewhat rounded in shape. The tail is variable as to relative length and shape but usually contains twelve feathers. In general appearance these birds are heavy. Their prey is killed by the sharp claws and torn to pieces with the bill.

The *Buteonidæ* are found both in the eastern and in the western hemisphere. In the United States and Canada are twenty species of regular or accidental occurrence.

Many of the species included in this family return to the same neighborhood and often to the same nest, year after year, and some are known to mate for life. They breed slowly, rearing but one brood a year, though, if the first set of eggs be destroyed, another will be laid. The period of incubation is about four weeks; the young when hatched are covered or partially covered with down, but before they leave the nest they are fully feathered.

The food habits and the economic value of these rapacious birds are thus summarized by Dr. A. K. Fisher: "The young grow slowly and need a relatively large amount of food. To satisfy their hunger requires constant foraging on the part of the parents, and the strain of rearing the family is probably twice that of any of the other land birds. Even the adults are large eaters, gorging to the utmost when the opportunity presents; and as digestion is very rapid and assimilation perfect, a great quantity of food in relation to the body weight is consumed every day. Hawks and Owls often swallow their smaller victims entire, and tear the larger ones into several pieces, swallowing each fragment as it is detached. After

Photograph by E. R. Sanborn

BALD EAGLE

A majestic bird, whether at rest or in flight

the nutritious portion of the food has been absorbed, the indigestible parts, such as hair, feathers, scales, bones, and other hard parts, are rolled into a solid ball by the action of the muscles of the stomach. These masses, known as 'pellets,' are regurgitated before fresh food is taken. The pellets contain everything necessary to identify the food. To the wholly beneficial class belong the large Rough-legged Hawk, its near relative, the Squirrel Hawk or Ferruginous Rough-leg, and the four Kites—the White-tailed Kite, Mississippi Kite, Swallow-tailed Kite, and Everglade Kite. The chiefly beneficial class contains a majority of our Hawks and Owls, and includes the following: Marsh Hawk, Harris's Hawk, Red-tailed Hawk, Red-shouldered Hawk, Short-tailed Hawk, Sennett's White-tailed Hawk, Swainson's Hawk, Short-wing Hawk, Broad-winged Hawk, Mexican Black Hawk, Mexican Goshawk, Sparrow Hawk, and Audubon's Caracara. The class in which the harmful and beneficial qualities balance includes the Golden Eagle, Bald Eagle, Pigeon Hawk, Richardson's Pigeon Hawk, Prairie Falcon, and Great Horned Owl. The harmful class comprises the Gyrfalcons, Duck Hawk, Sharp-shinned Hawk, Cooper's Hawk, and Goshawk."

SWALLOW-TAILED KITE

Elanoides forficatus (*Linnæus*)

A. O. U. Number 327

Other Names.—Swallow-tailed Hawk; Swallow-tail; Fork-tailed Kite; Snake Hawk.

General Description.— Length, 24 inches. Head and under parts, white; upper parts, black. Wings, long and reaching nearly to the tip of the deeply forked tail; feet, stout but very short, the tarsus feathered halfway in front; talons, short, well-curved, scooped out, and sharp-edged on the under surface. Outer tail-feathers about 8 inches longer than middle-pair.

Color.— ADULTS: *Crown, head, and neck all round, and entire under parts including under wing-coverts, pure snowy white;* back, wings, and tail, glossy-black with varying luster, principally violet and greenish-blue; shoulder feathers and lesser wing-coverts with a pronounced bronzy cast; bill, bluish black; cere, pale bluish; feet, pale bluish-green with light-colored claws. YOUNG: Similar to adults, but with head and neck narrowly streaked with blackish, and most of dark flight feathers edged and tipped with white.

Nest and Eggs.— NEST: Usually in the top of tall trees near water courses; composed of dry twigs, sticks, hay, and occasionally moss. EGGS: 2 or 3, sometimes 4, white or buffy, boldly blotched and speckled, chiefly around the larger end in handsome patterns, with rich chestnut-brown and cinnamon.

Distribution.— North and South America; breeds locally from southeastern Saskatchewan, northern Minnesota, southern Wisconsin, southern Indiana, and South Carolina south through eastern Mexico and Central America to Peru, Bolivia, and Paraguay; accidental west to New Mexico and Colorado and north to northern Wisconsin, Ontario, New York, Maine, Massachusetts, and in England; casual in the Greater Antilles; winters south of the United States.

In Florida Everglades where the Miami River rises, I had the pleasure and satisfaction of studying those remarkable birds the Swallow-tailed Kites. Gifted with extraordinary wing and tail surfaces they live almost entirely in the air, floating, soaring, and circling with all the buoyancy and dash of their minor prototypes, the Barn Swallows, to whom they bear a singular resemblance in shape, color, action, and superlative wing power — in fact in nearly everything but size.

The three birds I observed were feeding on small snakes, apparently water moccassins, which were neatly snatched from their lurking places in the reeds and devoured on the wing. This aërial feeding was gracefully performed by a forward thrust of the talons holding the food, a mouthful being taken by bending the head suddenly downward. One of the birds carried aloft a small alligator, perhaps a foot long, but the morsel proved too obdurate and was dropped. At times they made long downward sweeps like the drop of Nighthawks, apparently in a spirit of play.

No other North American bird approaches the Swallow-tail in the grace and beauty of its flight; the Duck Hawk alone equals it in speed. The former conveys the impression of lightness in the air; the latter, of power and impetuosity.

Incubation starts in March in the southern

parts of its range and it may be as late as June in the northern districts.

Before migrating these Kites assemble in small companies, circling slowly in ascending spirals until sometimes out of eye-range like the maneuvers of the Red-tailed Hawks before leaving us in the autumn. Their call note is a high-pitched shrill *ke wee wee,* the first note short, somewhat like the cry of the Broad-winged Hawk.

The Swallow-tail feeds upon snakes, grasshoppers, wasp grubs, caterpillars, lizards, frogs and other small reptiles and he is not known to attack birds or quadrupeds. R. I. BRASHER.

Drawing by R. I. Brasher

SWALLOW-TAILED KITE (½ nat. size)

The most graceful in flight of all North American birds

WHITE-TAILED KITE

Elanus leucurus (*Vieillot*)

A. O. U. Number 328

Other Name.— Black-shouldered Kite.

General Description.— Length, 17 inches. Upper parts, light bluish-ash; under parts and tail, white. Wings, pointed and about twice as long as tail and when closed reach nearly to end of tail; two outer wing-quills notched; feathers of wings broad and tips obtuse; feet, very small; tarsus, feathered half-way down in front; claws, small, little curved, and not grooved beneath.

Color.— Except top of head and tail, upper parts light bluish-ash; lower parts, *top of head, and tail,* with the exception of the two center feathers, *pure white;*

two center tail-feathers, a lighter ash than black; a *spot in front of eye* formed by bristly feathers and extending narrowly above the eye, and *a large patch on the shoulder* embracing lesser and middle wing-coverts, *deep black;* bill and claws, black; cere and feet, yellowish-orange; iris, deep carmine. Young: Crown, nape, and upper parts generally thickly marked with broad streaks of dusky brown tinged with rufous; shoulders, umber-brown tipped with rusty; all wing-feathers, narrowly tipped with white; tail-feathers with a bar of dark ashy, near the tip; below, tinged with rusty and pale yellow-brown with elongated wedge-shaped spots of umber and blackish.

Nest and Eggs.— Nest: In the tops of trees, preferably live oaks; made of small twigs and larger sticks and lined with grass. Eggs: 3 to 5, dull whitish, so heavily marked over entire surface with blotches of red and mahogany-brown as usually to obscure the ground color.

Distribution.— North and South America; breeds in California, Texas, Oklahoma, South Carolina, and Florida; casual in southern Illinois, Louisiana, Mississippi, and Alabama; winters in California and Florida and south rarely to Guatemala; resident in South America from Argentina and Chile to Venezuela; accidental in Michigan.

All the Kites are birds of marked individuality and their identification in life is not difficult. The white square tail and black shoulders of the White-tailed Kite are quite distinctive field marks. Its favorite haunts are along the borders of streams and marshes, where it frequently perches on some tree overlooking its hunting grounds.

Drawing by R. I. Brasher

WHITE-TAILED KITE (½ nat. size)

A fine flyer and a beautiful bird of the South and West

Its method of hunting is not unlike that of the Marsh Hawk — crossing over the fields or hovering almost stationary aloft like a Sparrow Hawk when it sees its game and dropping upon it like a plummet. Unlike the Swallow-tailed Kite, this species does not confine its food to insects and reptiles but preys sometimes on small birds and frequently on quadrupeds, especially field mice. Chipmunks, lizards, snakes, and grasshoppers are found on its menu.

These birds are less likely to desert disturbed nests than the Swallow-tailed Kites. They utter plaintive calls of anxiety while their home and its neighborhood are under investigation. The nest is placed on a tree, usually near the water. R. I. Brasher.

MISSISSIPPI KITE

Ictinia mississippiensis (*Wilson*)

A. O. U. Number 329

Other Name.— Blue Kite.

Description.— Length, 14 inches. Plumage, bluish-gray. Two outer primaries notched on inner web, next two with edge cut away but less abruptly; wings and tail, moderate in length; feet, short and stout; tarsus, scantily covered with feathers about half-way down in front; web partially connecting middle and outer toes; claws, stout and much curved; bill, small and sturdy; its upper cutting edge almost toothed.

Color.— Adults: Front of head, pure silvery white

shading into pale bluish-gray and this color grading imperceptibly into the *dark bluish-gray* of the entire upper and lower plumage; lores, eyelids and cere black; gape of mouth, orange; lesser wing-coverts, primaries, and upper tail-coverts, darker bluish-gray (almost black), the primaries tinged with chestnut rufous at base of inner and outer webs; tips of the secondaries, silvery white; *tail, nearly pure black;* bill, black; feet orange-yellow; iris, deep red. YOUNG: Head, neck, and lower parts, dull yellowish-white, each feather with a long oval spot of blackish-brown, more reddish-brown on lower portion; chin, throat, and a broad stripe over eye, white; upper parts, brownish-black, the feathers narrowly edged with yellowish-white; primary-coverts, secondaries, and primaries, sharply margined on ends with white; tail, black with three bands of more slaty tint, and corresponding rows of white spots on inner webs.

Nest and Eggs.— NEST: In high tree-top; usually an old nest of some other species remodeled with additional material and lined with Spanish moss or green leaves. EGGS: 2 or 3, pale bluish-green, usually unmarked but sometimes with faint spots or stains.

Distribution.— Southern Kansas, Iowa, Illinois, southern Indiana, and South Carolina south to Texas and Florida; winters in Florida and southern Texas and south rarely to Guatemala; accidental in Colorado, South Dakota, Wisconsin, and Pennsylvania.

Its uniform bluish-gray plumage, with darker wings and tail, easily distinguishes the Mississippi Kite in life.

This compact, well-built bird possesses much more courage and spirit than others of its kindred. Only the Swallow-tailed Kite surpasses it in flight power, but it is stronger and much more determined than that species. Its aërial performances are quite up to the Kite standard; it soars with motionless pinions in great circles, sweeps or dashes with vigor and grace, or hovers in the air watching for its humble quarry. It is a tireless flyer.

Although the almost toothed bill indicates an approach to falcon traits, it confines its captures to lizards, small snakes, frogs, grasshoppers, and particularly to a large species of beetle belonging to the cicada family. This latter it deftly picks from tree branches without ceasing its flight. Its food is eaten on the wing after the manner of the Swallow-tailed Kite.

R. I. BRASHER.

EVERGLADE KITE

Rostrhamus sociabilis (*Vieillot*)

A. O. U. Number 330

Other Name.— Snail Hawk.

General Description.— Length, 18 inches. Plumage, bluish-gray. Five outer primaries notched on inner webs; upper section of bill, lengthened and hooked.

Color.— ADULTS: Prevailing color, dark bluish-gray blackening on secondaries, primaries, and tail and with a tinge of brownish on wing-coverts and feathers of neck and head with a bluish-green shade; base of tail with upper and under-coverts, white increasing on tail in extent from the center to outside feathers; tail, tipped with a band of pale gray about an inch wide; bill and claws, black; base of bill, cere, and feet, bright orange; iris, red. YOUNG: Above, brownish-black with a chalky cast on back. Each feather rather broadly tipped with yellowish-rufous; crown and sides and back of head longitudinally streaked with the same; line over eye, sides of head and lower parts, dull ocher; throat and cheeks, streaked with dusky; other lower parts thickly marked with elongated spots of brownish-black; upper tail-coverts, white with black shaft lines; lower tail-coverts unmarked; tail with basal third white and a terminal band of brownish-ash.

Nest and Eggs.— NEST: In a bush, small tree, or clump of grass; a flat structure of sticks, grasses, old stalks, and leaves and lined with a few dried heads of saw-grass, the whole rather carelessly put together. EGGS: 2 or 3, dingy white, irregularly splashed, spotted, or blotched with yellow-brown, light olive-brown, and dark sepia.

Distribution.— Tropical Florida, Cuba, eastern Mexico, Central America, and eastern South America to Argentina; migratory in northern Florida.

The formation of the bill of the Everglade Kite enables it to extract from its shell the fresh-water snail (*Pomus depressus*) on which it feeds almost exclusively. This snail is very abundant in the shallow lagoons of the Everglades, and this Kite's distribution in the United States is confined to that region.

The birds usually resort to some eminence in

the "hammock" as a feeding station; to these spots the delicacies are carried, the snail dexterously removed from its armor, and the empty shell left with others. Amid the wastes of sawgrass, palmetto, and cypress, inhabited only by a remnant of the Seminole tribe of Indians, may be found heaped-up mounds of these empty shells.

On the corduroy road built by General Taylor during the Seminole war and which extends into the almost impassable area of the 'glades west of where the town of Palm Beach now stands, I found several of these curious shell mounds, but I saw only one pair of birds. They were very tame, permitting me to approach within thirty feet before they left their perch in a cypress and swept out over the "prairies." Their flight was like that of the Marsh Hawk and the similarity was accentuated by the white band at base of the tail.

R. I. Brasher.

MARSH HAWK

Circus hudsonius (*Linnæus*)

A. O. U. Number 331 See Color Plates 43, 48

Other Names.— Harrier; Marsh Harrier; Blue Hawk (adult); Mouse Hawk; Frog Hawk; Bog-trotter; White-rumped Hawk.

General Description.— Length, 19 inches; spread of wings, 45 to 52 inches. Males have the fore and upper parts light ashy, and abdomen white; females are dark umber-brown above, and brownish-white below. Both sexes have the face encircled with an imperfect ruff, somewhat as in the Owls.

Color.— Adult Male: In perfect feather, head, neck, breast and upper parts, pale light ashy; rest of under parts, pure white with a few drop-shaped rusty spots; in most specimens there is a dusky wash on back, shoulders, and secondaries; five outer primaries, blackish; all primaries and secondaries with large white areas at base of inner webs; tail, bluish-ash banded with 5 or 6 obscure dusky bars, the terminal one darkest, and mottled with white at base of feathers; *upper tail-coverts, pure white.* Adult Female: Upper parts, dark umber-brown; feathers of head and neck edged laterally with yellowish-rufous; lores, line over and line below eye, dull yellowish-white with a dusky stripe between them running back from the rear angle of the eye; lesser wing-coverts, indented with pale rufous; tail, deep umber crossed by 6 or 7 regular but obscure bands of blackish, the lateral feathers being lighter; sides of head, dull rufous faintly streaked with dark brown; the facial disk, pale cream color also streaked with dark brown; chin and throat, plain dull yellowish-white; beneath, variable shades of dull white to brownish-yellow, thickly streaked with broad longitudinal stripes of dark umber-brown more numerous laterally;

Photograph by A. A. Allen

A MALE MARSH HAWK AT ITS NEST IN THE MARSHES

upper tail coverts, white. YOUNG: Similar to adult female but darker everywhere and with but four dark bands on tail.

Nest and Eggs.— NEST: On the ground in a tangle of weeds or grassy hummocks; neatly constructed, for a Hawk, of fine dried marsh grass; rather bulky, a foot or more in diameter. EGGS: 2 to 9, but usually from 4 to 6, dull white, faintly tinged with a greenish or bluish shade; no characteristic spots but often blotched with a very pale brown and other neutral-colored tints.

Distribution.— North America; breeds from northeastern Siberia, northwestern Alaska, northwestern Mackenzie, central Keewatin, northern Quebec, and Prince Edward Island south to the southern border of the United States; winters from southern British Columbia, Colorado, Iowa, the Ohio Valley, and New York (occasionally Massachusetts) south to the Bahamas, Cuba, and Colombia.

The Marsh Hawk is a bird of very wide distribution in the United States, being found in nearly all open localities. Slowly and steadily with a gliding flight the Harrier quarters back and forth across the fields with the care and precision of a well-trained pointer dog. Not a square yard is overlooked. Suddenly the forward flight is checked with almost a back somersault and as abruptly as though he had run into a wall; a short interval of hovering, then a descent that as often misses as captures the quarry below. When caught the prey is devoured on the spot.

The courting maneuvers of the male above the female are interesting. Sweeping in great semi-circles, gradually lessening in diameter, he stops suddenly on the top of a swoop, closes his wings, drops, turns head over tail, drops again, turns over and swings upward from the last somersault, just clear of the ground, on another ecstatic performance. These wild movements are usually executed in a silence unbroken except for the sound of rushing wings. Both parents take part in rearing the young and are very courageous in defending the home from intruders, especially after the eggs are hatched.

In the spring, Marsh Hawks are seen always in pairs; but after the young are able to fly they generally hunt in family parties, and later in the season twenty to fifty individuals will flock together.

Photograph by H. K. Job — Courtesy of Outing Publishing Co.

NEST AND YOUNG OF MARSH HAWK

The food of the Marsh Hawk varies with the season and with local conditions. In some parts of the country it is principally birds, and in others it is exclusively small quadrupeds, and of these field mice are the favorites. An average pair rearing young would destroy in the neighborhood of 1000 field mice during the nesting period. If we place a value of two cents on each mouse, which is a very conservative estimate, they would be worth twenty dollars for that short period, to a farmer, and more if he owned an orchard of any size. Rabbits, tree squirrels, ground squirrels, lizards, snakes, and frogs are found on the menu of this bird.

SHARP-SHINNED HAWK

Accipiter velox (*Wilson*)

A. O. U. Number 332 See Color Plate 44

Other Names.— Pigeon Hawk; Sparrow Hawk; Bird Hawk; Chicken Hawk; Bullet Hawk; Little Blue Darter.

General Description.— Length; male, 11 inches; female, 12 to 14 inches. Spread of wings, 23 to 27 inches. Color above, dark bluish-slate; below, white. *Tail, square* or slightly notched at tip; *five* outer primaries notched on inner webs.

Color.— Adults: Head, nape, back, shoulders, wings, rump, and upper tail-coverts, *dark bluish-slate;* primaries and tail, more brownish; the tail barred by four well-defined bands of brownish-black, the last subterminal and broader than the rest, the first concealed by the upper coverts; feathers of back of head, snowy white beneath the surface but showing when the feathers are erected; side of head, pale rufous; lores, cheeks, chin, throat and lower parts, pure white; chin, throat, and cheeks, marked with fine blackish shaft streaks; chest, abdomen, sides, flanks, and elongated leg feathers with numerous traverse broad bars of reddish rufous, these bars centrally heart-shaped and rather narrower than the white ones; on the sides the rufous predominates, the bars broadly arrowhead-shaped, connected along shafts; lower tail-coverts, pure white; bill, dark horn color; iris, cere, and feet, yellow; claws, black. Young: Above, umber-brown; feathers of head, edged with dull light rufous; feathers of rest of upper parts bordered with the same color; the shoulders and rump showing roundish spots of white; tail as in adult but more brownish; below, dull white, tawny or yellowish, boldly striped lengthwise with dark umber or reddish-brown; feathers, generally black-shafted; sides of head and neck more narrowly streaked; broad, light stripe over eye.

Nest and Eggs.— Nest: Usually in a conifer, rarely on a ledge of rock; constructed of small sticks with or without a lining of leaves or bark; remarkably large for the size of the bird. Eggs: 4 or 5, dull bluish or greenish-white, boldly marked with large spots and blotches of different shades of brown, sometimes inclined to form a wreath around larger end, sometimes evenly distributed; occasionally reduced to small spots or so thickly placed as almost to obscure the ground tint.

Distribution.— North America; breeds nearly throughout the United States and Canada from northwestern Alaska, northwestern Mackenzie, southern Keewatin, central Quebec, and Newfoundland southward; winters from British Columbia, Colorado, Iowa, northern Ohio, and Massachusetts south to Panama.

Although the Sharp-shinned Hawk has a body but little larger than a Robin's, this relentless buccaneer, like his larger relative, the Cooper's Hawk, fully upholds the traditions of Hawks for destructiveness. Fortunately the persistent campaign of education, teaching the difference between "good" and "bad" birds of this family, is having its effect, and agriculturists are realizing that but few birds of prey are more harmful than beneficial. Opinion is gradually crystallizing into the conviction that but three Hawks deserve destruction — this species, the Cooper's Hawk and the Goshawk. There are individuals of other species who acquire a taste for poultry and it may become necessary to eliminate a particular individual, but the wholesale destruction of Hawks brings punishment on ignorance by an increase of quadruped and insect pests.

Photo by H. K. Job

A NESTFUL OF BABY SHARP-SHINNED HAWKS

This murderous little villain will destroy all small birds unfortunate enough to live within its hunting grounds. At times it seems to "see red," attacking with blind fury birds much larger than itself. I saw one tackle a Screech Owl and have no doubt he would have killed it had there been no interference, handicapped as the Owl was by daylight. Quick as he is, the Flicker often escapes his onslaught by dodging around a limb, but is caught if attempting flight. A family of six young Flickers were killed, one after the other, because experience had not taught them to hug the branch; the Hawk's swift plunges frightened them into flight, and the little demon nailed them before they had gone ten feet!

R. I. Brasher.

The Sharp-shinned Hawk, a miniature of Cooper's Hawk, is fully as destructive to bird life as its larger cousin. Although rarely attacking full-grown poultry, it is very partial to chickens and often almost exterminates early broods which are allowed to run at large. No birds, from the size of Doves, Robins, and Flickers to the smallest Warblers and Titmice, are safe from its attacks. In examinations of the stomachs of this Hawk the remains of nearly fifty species of birds were recognized, and the list is of so much interest that it is given here:

Arizona Quail, Mourning Dove, Downy Woodpecker, Red-shafted Flicker, Yellow-shafted Flicker, Chimney Swift, Cowbird, Orchard Oriole, Grackle, Housefinch, Goldfinch, Savannah Sparrow, Western Savannah Sparrow, White-throated Sparrow, Field Sparrow, Chipping Sparrow, Tree Sparrow, Junco, Song Sparrow, Fox Sparrow, English Sparrow, Abert Towhee, Red-eyed Vireo, Black and Yellow Warbler, Black-throated Green Warbler, Yellow-rumped Warbler, Bay-breasted Warbler, Black-poll Warbler, Pine-creeping Warbler, Oven-bird, Maryland Yellow-throat, Blackcap, Western Blackcap, Canada Warbler, Mockingbird, Catbird, Crissal Thrasher, Cactus Wren, Carolina Wren, Red-breasted Nuthatch, Chicadee, Ruby-crowned Kinglet, Gray-cheeked Thrush, Hermit Thrush, Robin, and Bluebird.

To show how universally this species feeds on small birds, it is only necessary to say that of 107 stomachs containing food 103, or 96¼ per cent., contained the remains of birds. Mammals and insects seem to be taken rarely, mice and grasshoppers being the ones most frequently chosen.

A. K. Fisher, in *The Food of Hawks and Owls.*

COOPER'S HAWK

Accipiter cooperi (*Bonaparte*)

A. O. U. Number 333 See Color Plates 43, 44, 46

Other Names.— Pigeon Hawk; Chicken Hawk; Quail Hawk; Big Blue Darter; Swift Hawk; Striker.

Description.— Length: male, 18 inches; female, 20 inches. Spread of wings, 30 to 36 inches. Same proportions as Sharp-shinned Hawk, but larger and with *tail round; five* outer primaries notched on inner webs. Adults: Plumage exactly the same as Sharp-shinned Hawk's excepting top of head usually darker shade than

ADULT MALE COOPER'S HAWK
(¼ nat. size)
The most destructive species of Hawk

Courtesy of Am. Mus. Nat. Hist.

color of upper parts, and in high plumage a clearer and more uniform bluish-slate. IMMATURE: Plumage also similar to the corresponding age of the Sharp-shinned.

Nest and Eggs.— NEST: Usually in tall trees from 10 to 50 feet from the ground in secluded woodlands; often an old Crow's or some other Hawk's nest is appropriated; being frequently occupied for a number of years in succession, and, additional material being added each spring, some of the nests become very large and bulky structures. EGGS: 3 to 6, pale bluish or greenish-white, sometimes plain but usually spotted with pale reddish-brown.

Distribution.— North America; breeds from southern British Columbia, southern Alberta, southern Keewatin, central Quebec, and Prince Edward Island south to southern border of the United States; winters from southern British Columbia, Colorado, Nebraska, Ohio, and Massachusetts south to Costa Rica, and occasionally farther north.

The resemblance between Cooper's Hawk and the Sharp-shinned is not confined to color, but extends to habits, the Cooper being, if anything,

Photo by H. K. Job Courtesy of Outing Pub. Co.

COOPER'S HAWKS

Too young to leave the nest, but old enough to be curious

because of its superior size, fiercer and more destructive. It will dash into the farmyard like a bolt, passing within a few feet of individuals and carrying off a young chicken with incredible swiftness. The attack is accomplished so suddenly that, unless the gun is in hand, the robber always escapes. There is no time to run even a few yards for a weapon — the thief is gone before it can be reached. If there is plenty of thick cover in the run, chickens will often escape, especially the more active breeds, like Leghorns. At my home in the Taconic Hills near Kent, Conn., I have repeatedly seen them strike, but as the foliage is dense and brushy they have invariably been unsuccessful in securing the quarry. In four years we have not lost a chicken by Hawks.

Cooper's Hawk is preëminently a "chicken Hawk," and is by far the most destructive species we have to contend with, not because it is individually worse than the Goshawk, but because it is so much more numerous that the aggregate damage done far exceeds that of all other birds of prey. Although not so large as the Goshawk, it is strong enough to carry away a good-sized chicken, Grouse, or cottontail rabbit. It is especially fond of domesticated Doves, and when it finds a cote easy of approach or near its nesting site, the inmates usually disappear at the rate of one or two a day until the owner takes a hand in the game. The arboreal and ground squirrels appear to be the mammals most frequently taken by Cooper's Hawk. Remains of chipmunks, red squirrels, and gray squirrels have been found in the stomachs. R. I. BRASHER.

GOSHAWK

Astur atricapillus atricapillus (*Wilson*)

A. O. U. Number 334 See Color Plate 45

Other Names.— American Goshawk; Blue Hen Hawk; Blue Darter; Partridge Hawk; Dove Hawk; Chicken Hawk.

General Description.— Length: male, 22 inches; female, 24 inches. Spread of wings, 43 to 47 inches. About the same proportions as the Sharp-shinned Hawk and Cooper's Hawk. Color above, bluish-slate; below, white.

Color.— ADULTS: Top and back of head, black, the white under surface of the feathers much exposed on back of head; *a broad conspicuous white stripe over eye extending to back of head,* finely streaked with black; rest of upper parts, uniform bluish-slate; tail, darker and barred by five broad faintly defined bands of blackish and tipped with whitish; primaries, dusky slate; lores and cheeks, dull grayish-white; lower parts, white, everywhere except on throat and lower tail-coverts traversed with numerous narrow bars of slaty color, more broken on the breast, more regular on flanks and thighs; chin, throat, and cheeks with very fine black shaft lines; these shaft lines also evident on rest of under parts; bill, dark-bluish horn color; iris, red; cere, legs, and feet, yellow; claws, black. YOUNG: Above, dark brown, the feathers margined with rusty, this color changing on neck and shoulders to whitish or dull buffy; wings and tail, barred with dusky and light brown; under parts, yellowish-white thickly marked with lance or drop-shaped dark brown streaks; tail more strongly barred than adult's; a broader white tip; cere and feet, duller yellow; iris, yellow; bill, more brownish.

Nest and Eggs.— NEST: Usually in a conifer at a great height and in the most inaccessible depths of evergreen woods; constructed of sticks, twigs, weed stalks, and leaves, and lined with strips of bark, grass, and hemlock twigs. EGGS: 2 to 5, pale bluish-white, sometimes faintly spotted with pale buffy-brown but normally immaculate.

Distribution.— North America; breeds from northwestern Alaska, northwestern Mackenzie, central Keewatin, and northern Ungava south to Michigan and New Hampshire, and in the mountains south to Pennsylvania and New Mexico; winters from Alaska and the southern Canadian Provinces south to northern Mexico, Texas, Oklahoma, Missouri, Indiana, and Virginia; accidental in England.

Drawing by R. I. Brasher

GOSHAWK (⅓ nat. size)

Savage, fearless, and the merciless foe of poultry and game birds

It is fortunate for the American hen that the Goshawk resides mostly north of the United States, migrating southward only in winter when its toll from the poultry yard is necessarily limited because the birds are confined to their houses. It is the most destructive of the Hawks to game birds, the Ruffed Grouse suffering particularly from its depredations.

Though swift in attack its flight is even and its death is often accomplished with a rifle in the hands of a fair shot. Like most *Raptores,* hunger deprives it of caution. It will follow the hunter and snatch a wounded bird almost from beneath his feet, although this performance means its own destruction. Unless the adult is hungry, young Goshawks are more audacious than their elders and because of their brownish plumage their deeds are frequently attributed to the harmless Red-tail. The Goshawk is the most symmetrical and clean-cut of all its family not excepting even the Peregrine Falcon, and often (with me at least) is allowed to escape because of its splendid form and spirit. Its destructiveness cannot obliterate the appreciation its prowess arouses.

The Western Goshawk (*Astur atricapillus striatulus*) differs in having the markings of the under parts much more numerous; the upper parts are darker and incline to blackish on the back. This form inhabits the Arctic parts of the Pacific coast and breeds from Alaska south to the Sierra Nevadas of California. In winter it may be found in southern California and east to Colorado.

R. I. BRASHER.

HARRIS'S HAWK

Parabuteo unicinctus harrisi (*Audubon*)

A. O. U. Number 335

Description.— Length: male, 20 inches; female, 23 inches. Lores, nearly naked with numerous bristles; inner web of five outer quills notched. ADULTS: General plumage, blackish varying from dark umber-brown to a distinct dusky-black shade; the wings and tail, generally darker; *lesser and a part of the middle wing-coverts and feathers of the leg, a deep rich chestnut; upper and lower tail-coverts and base of tail, broadly white;* end of tail, also white for one inch or more; sides of head with a few white streaks; bill, horn color; cere and legs, yellow; iris, brown. YOUNG: Plumage, more brownish, streaked on head and neck with yellowish-brown; back and shoulders varied with chestnut and rusty-brown; chestnut wing patch duller and much broken by darker feathers; white band at base of tail less sharply defined; terminal white band on tail narrower or missing; below, tawny-white broadly streaked with dark brown and dusky; thigh feathers *barred* with white.

Nest and Eggs.— NEST: In a tree or bush and varying greatly in size and finish; different species of cacti, Spanish bayonet or mesquites are most frequently selected as a site; a platform constructed of sticks, twigs, and weed stems and lined with grass, moss, and roots. EGGS: 2 to 4, dull white or greenish-white, plain, or lightly spotted with faint yellowish-brown or lavender.

Distribution.— Southeastern California, southern Arizona, southern New Mexico, abundant in some parts of southern Texas, rarely reaching east to Louisiana and Mississippi; south to Cape San Lucas and Panama; accidental in Iowa.

Harris's Hawk is tame and unsuspicious. Unless hunting it is rather slow in flight but it possesses plenty of dash and swiftness when pursuing prey. In the monotonous regions of mesquite and sagebrush thickets of the southwestern deserts, any form of life arouses interest, and the traveler follows with pleasure the free swings of Harris's Hawk coursing low over the brush, searching for the wood-rats or chipmunks which constitute its principal food. It is not averse to association with Caracaras and Vultures and often joins them in their meals of carrion.

RED-TAILED HAWK

Buteo borealis borealis (*Gmelin*)

A. O. U. Number 337 See Color Plates 43, 46, 47

Other Names.— Red Hawk; Hen Hawk; Chicken Hawk; Red-tail; Eastern Red-tail; Red-tailed Buzzard; Buzzard Hawk; White-breasted Chicken Hawk.

General Description.— Length: male, 22 inches; female, 24 inches. Spread of wings, 50 to 56 inches. Color above, dark brown; below, whitish. Four outer primaries notched on inner webs; long, broad wings; wide-spreading tail of medium length.

Color.— ADULTS: Plumage above, dark brown mixed or mottled with gray and whitish; under parts, white or whitish, usually washed with buff on sides of breast and with abdomen streaked with dark brown or blackish; *tail, bright rust-red* or rufous above, usually with a distinct black bar near the end, the tip, whitish; iris, brown; bill, dusky horn color; cere, legs, and feet, yellow. YOUNG: Dark streaks on abdomen so thick as to form a broad band of blackish; the tail, gray crossed by about eight narrow bars of blackish; iris and bill, yellow; feet, duller yellow; otherwise similar to adults.

Nest and Eggs.— NEST: A large and bulky structure generally placed well up in the forks of a large tree from 40 to 80 feet above ground; constructed of quite large sticks and lined with smaller twigs, bits of bark, and usually with the tips of hemlock branches, fern leaves, or moss; the same nest is occupied year after year and the annual addition of material adds to the bulk. EGGS: 2 to 4, dull whitish or bluish-white, and exhibiting a wide variation in form and markings; some plain, others heavily blotched with many shades of brown and red and still others with a few faint spots of pale lavender-gray which may form wreaths around either end or be fairly well distributed over entire surface.

Distribution.— Eastern North America, from Saskatchewan, Wisconsin, and Illinois east to central Keewatin and Newfoundland, and south to eastern Texas, northeastern Mexico, the Gulf coast, Florida, and the Greater Antilles.

The Red-tailed Hawk's shrill *kee-er-r-r* attracts our attention to its circling flight over the rocky hillsides of its favorite haunts. It is a slow-moving species. Frequently it is seen perched on a tree look-out where it watches for the small quadrupeds, especially mice, which form its principal food.

Although known throughout the country as

Photo by S. A. Lottridge

RED-TAILED HAWK

A useful species for keeping down the rodent population

"Hen Hawk," the Red-tailed very seldom raids the chicken-yard. Where mice, squirrels and their kind are plentiful, it never does so. A divergence from this fact by an individual who has acquired the poultry taste may warrant that particular bird's destruction, but personally I would rather let these Hawks have a chicken or two for their services in keeping down the mouse and rat population. In four years of chicken-farming this toll has not been required, although many pairs nest and live around my farm. One day an investigation of shrill squeals from a tall chestnut revealed three Red-tails quarreling over a young woodchuck, so fiercely that I walked directly beneath the fighting trio before they took alarm and fled, letting the object of the fracas drop to the ground.

Krider's Hawk (*Buteo borealis krideri*) is a light-colored race, nearly pure white below with but few markings on abdomen, the subterminal tail-bar very faint or wanting, the upper side of the tail light chestnut, and a mixture of much white in plumage of the upper parts. It is found on the Great Plains from Wyoming, North Dakota, and Minnesota south to Nebraska and Missouri, and in winter to Wisconsin, Illinois, Texas, Louisiana, and Mississippi.

The Western Red-tail (*Buteo borealis calurus*) is much darker than the stock form; normal specimens show heavier and darker bars and spots below; in extreme cases it is uniform deep brown with the tail rich red crossed by several black bars. This variation occurs in western North America from Alaska and Mackenzie southward to Cape San Lucas and Guatemala, east to western part of the Great Plains; it is found casually in Illinois and Ontario.

Harlan's Hawk (*Buteo borealis harlani*) is nearly uniform black; its tail is much mottled with grayish, rufous and white, and has a subterminal band of black. It is geographically distributed over the lower Mississippi valley and the Gulf States from Louisiana to Georgia and Florida; sometimes it occurs in Colorado, Texas, Kansas, Nebraska, Iowa, Illinois, and Pennsylvania.

The Alaska Red-tail (*Buteo borealis alascensis*) is a larger dark-colored subspecies, inhabiting southeastern Alaska from Yakutat Bay to the Sitka Islands. R. I. BRASHER.

Photograph by H. K. Job Courtesy of Outing Publishing Co.

HOME-LIFE OF RED-TAILED HAWK

From its abundance, wide distribution, and striking appearance the Red-tailed Hawk is probably the best known of all the larger Hawks. Since it is handicapped by the misleading name "Hen Hawk," its habits should be carefully examined. There is no denying that both it and the Red-shouldered Hawk, also known as "Hen Hawk," do occasionally eat poultry, but the quantity is so small in comparison with the vast numbers of destructive rodents consumed, that it is hardly worth mentioning. While fully 66 per cent. of the Red-tail's food consists of injurious mammals, not more than 7 per cent. consists of poultry, and it is probable that a large proportion of the poultry and game captured by it and the other buzzard Hawks is made up of old, diseased, or otherwise disabled fowls. It is well known to poulterers and owners of game preserves that killing off the diseased and enfeebled birds, and so preventing their interbreeding with the sound stock, keeps the yard and coveys in good condition and hinders the spread of fatal epidemics. It seems, therefore, that the birds of prey which catch aged, frost-bitten, and diseased poultry, together with wounded and crippled game, are serving both farmer and sportsman.

Abundant proof is at hand to show that the Red-tail greatly prefers the smaller mammals, reptiles, and batrachians, taking little else when these can be obtained in sufficient numbers. If hard pressed by hunger, however, it will eat any form of life, and will not reject even offal and carrion; dead Crows from about the roosts, poultry which has been thrown on the compost heap, and flesh from the carcasses of goats, sheep and the larger domesticated animals are eaten at such times. Immature Hawks are more apt to commit depredations than adults, the reason probably being that they lack skill to procure sufficient quantity of their staple food. A large proportion of the birds eaten consists of ground-dwelling species which probably are snatched up while half concealed in the grass or vegetation. Among the mammals most often eaten and most injurious to mankind are the arboreal and ground squirrels, rabbits, voles and other mice. The stomachs of the Red-tailed Hawks examined contained the Abert squirrel, red squirrel, three species of gray squirrels, two species of chipmunks, Say's ground squirrel, plateau ground squirrel, Franklin ground squirrel, striped ground squirrel, harvest mouse, common rat, house mouse, white-footed mouse, Sonoran white-footed mouse, wood rat, meadow mouse, pine mouse, Cooper lemming mouse, cotton rat, jumping mouse, porcupine, jack rabbit, three races of cottontails, pouched gopher, kangaroo rat, skunk, mole, and four kinds of shrews. The larger insects also, such as grasshoppers, crickets, and beetles, are sometimes extensively used as food.

A. K. Fisher, in *The Food of Hawks and Owls.*

Photograph by G. N. Leek

YOUNG RED-TAILED HAWK

RED-SHOULDERED HAWK

Buteo lineatus lineatus (*Gmelin*)

A. O. U. Number 339 See Color Plate 47

Other Names.— Red-shouldered Buzzard; Big Chicken Hawk; Hen Hawk; Winter Hawk.

General Description.— Length: male, 20 inches; female, 22 inches. Spread of wings, 44 to 50 inches. Color above, reddish-brown; below, lighter reddish-brown, barred and streaked. Four outer primaries notched on inner webs; outer webs spotted with white or buff.

Color.— Head, neck, and back, deep rufous, each feather with a blackish center stripe; chin, throat, and cheeks, dull white with a dusky indistinct mustache; *under parts, light rufous,* abdomen, sides, and middle of breast with transverse bars of buff; thigh feathers, pale ochraceous; lower tail-coverts, plain whitish; *lesser wing-coverts, rufous or chestnut* with black shaft streaks; shoulders and middle wing-coverts broadly edged with rufous; secondaries, dark brown tipped and crossed with two bands of whitish; primaries, dusky-black fading at tips into grayish-brown with square spots of white on outer webs; rump, uniform brownish-black; upper tail-coverts banded with the same color; **tail,** brownish-black barred with six sharply defined narrow bands of white, the last at the tip and the first two concealed by upper coverts; bill, bluish horn color; cere and legs, yellow; *iris, brown.* Young: Above, plain dark brown without orange-brown or rusty markings; *lesser wing-coverts, rusty* but not so pronounced as in the adult plumage; head, neck, and under parts, white or yellowish-white, rather heavily streaked with drop- or arrow-shaped marks of dark brown; tail, brown crossed by a number of lighter and darker bars; *iris, yellow.*

Photo by H. K. Job Courtesy of Outing Pub. Co.

NEST OF RED-SHOULDERED HAWK

This nest was later used by Barred Owls

Courtesy of Am. Mus. Nat. Hist.

RED-SHOULDERED HAWK (⅛ nat. size)

A species which is very valuable to the farmer

Nest and Eggs.— Nest: Usually placed in the fork of a lofty elm, birch, maple, or beech (seldom in a conifer); a large bulky structure made almost entirely of sticks. Eggs: 3 to 5, dull white or bluish-white, erratically spotted and blotched with umber and yellowish-brown.

Distribution.— Eastern North America; breeds from Manitoba, southern Keewatin, southern Quebec, Nova Scotia, Prince Edward Island, south nearly to the Gulf States, west to edge of the Great Plains; winters south to the Gulf coast.

Although quite as common in many localities as the Red-tail, the Red-shouldered Hawk is less often seen, since it keeps more within the shade of woods and especially so in swampy tree-covered areas. It is a lighter-built bird than the Red-tail and more impetuous in pursuit of its prey. Its call — a shrill *kee-yoo* — is sharper and with less " burr " on the last note. Any one familiar with both species can identify them in life almost as far as they can be seen. The young require more careful inspection, but the slenderer and less-feathered legs with more heavily streaked breast serve to identify them. Usually the Red-shouldered Buzzards are found in pairs; they evidently mate for the entire year and possibly for life. The young and parents often remain together throughout the autumn.

The Florida Red-shouldered Hawk (*Buteo lineatus alleni*) differs from the common Red-shouldered Hawk only in size, being much smaller; its range is restricted to the south Atlantic and Gulf States, from South Carolina through Texas into Mexico.

The entire under parts of the Red-bellied Hawk (*Buteo lineatus elegans*) are sometimes rich dark reddish, almost effacing the usual markings, but typical specimens have a ruddy-colored breast, this color fading into lighter on the abdomen; the wings and tail are barred with white as in the Red-shouldered. This form occurs from the Rocky Mountains to the Pacific and from British Columbia south to Lower California and Mexico.

The Red-shouldered Hawks are very valuable to the farmer. They are more nearly omnivorous than most of our birds of prey, and are known to feed on mice, birds, snakes, frogs, fish, grasshoppers, centipedes, spiders, crawfish, earthworms, and snails. About 90 per cent. of their food consists of injurious mammals and insects, and hardly 1½ per cent. of poultry and game. It is folly to destroy this valuable bird, and everywhere it should be fostered and protected.

ZONE-TAILED HAWK

Buteo abbreviatus *Cabanis*

A. O. U. Number 340

Description.— Length: male, 19 inches; female, 21 inches. Spread of wings, 47 to 53 inches.

Color.— Adults: Entire body, a uniform glossy coal-black; viewed from above the *tail is black, narrowly tipped with white and crossed with three bands* of slate color increasing in width and distinctness from front to rear, and narrowly tipped with white; viewed from below, three pure white zones appear, since the ashy is on outer webs only, with white on inner web; wings when folded quite black, but inner webs basally marked with light and dark bars and spotted with white; feet, yellowish; bill, dark blackish-horn. Young: Similar to adults but the snowy white bases of the feathers, especially on head and neck, more inclined to show through; tail banded with more numerous and less regular bars with the inner webs of the feathers mostly white.

Nest and Eggs.— Nest: From 15 to 50 feet from ground on the horizontal branches of tall cottonwoods, ash, sycamores, box elders, or cypress trees, along borders of streams; constructed of coarse sticks and twigs and lined with leaves or Spanish moss. Eggs: 2 to 4, dull white, spotted or blotched with warm chestnut or umber-brown, chiefly at large end.

Distribution.— Southern Arizona, southern New Mexico, and southwestern Texas, south through Mexico and Central America to Venezuela and British Guiana; casual in southern California.

Little is known of the life history of the Zone-tailed Hawk. Its favorite haunts are banks of streams, and it builds its nest and lives among the cottonwoods. In Texas and New Mexico, these wanderers from Mexico are said to frequent cañons and to dive down the perpendicular sides, like Clarke's Nutcracker, almost to the stream at the bottom. It is a lightly-built bird. Its food consists of small mammals, lizards, frogs, and beetles, grasshoppers, and other insects.

SWAINSON'S HAWK

Buteo swainsoni *Bonaparte*

A. O. U. Number 342

Other Names.— Brown Hawk; Black Hawk; Hen Hawk.

Description.— Length: male, 20 inches; female, 22 inches. Spread of wings, 50 to 56 inches. Three outer primaries notched on inner webs.

Color.— Every possible gradation of coloration between the normal and melanistic phases is exhibited by different individuals. Adult Male in Normal Plumage: Above, grayish-brown; tail tinged with hoary and with about 9 or 10 dusky bands; *forehead, chin, and throat, white; chest, broadly bright chestnut* with black shaft lines; rest of under parts, whitish usually barred and spotted with brown; iris, brown; feet and cere, yellow; bill and claws, bluish-black. Adult Female in Normal Plumage: Chest, grayish-brown; otherwise like male. Darker or Melanistic Phase (both sexes): Entire plumage sooty-brown. Young: Entire upper parts, dark brown, each feather tawny-edged; head, neck, and under parts, buff or buffy white; wings and tail, barred with darker brown.

Nest and Eggs.— Nest: Placed almost anywhere — on the ground, in bushes, or on ledges — but generally it is placed in the tallest trees toward the end of horizontal branches; constructed of small branches and twigs, and lined with a few leaves, moss, or feathers; sometimes old nests are rehabilitated. Eggs: 2 to 4, normally 2, white, greenish-white, or buffy-white, usually spotted or blotched with reddish-brown; sometimes unmarked.

Distribution.— North and South America; breeds from southern British Columbia, Fort Yukon, Alaska, northwestern Mackenzie, and Manitoba south to Chile; casual in Quebec, Ontario, Maine, and Massachusetts; winters from South Dakota southward.

Swainson's Hawk is a western bird which occurs eastward occasionally, specimens having been taken in many of the eastern States. In many cases where it has been reported, however, this identification was probably incorrect.

Photo by S. A. Lottridge

IMMATURE SWAINSON'S HAWK

On the sage plains of Washington, Oregon, and adjoining States the characteristic Hawk is Swainson's. There it is very abundant. It prefers the open prairies, coursing over these uninhabited wastes with slow circling flight until its quarry is sighted when it is transformed into the quick alert hunter intent on securing the prize.

"Compared with the majority of our Hawks it is gentle and unsuspicious in disposition, living in perfect harmony with its smaller neighbors. It is no unusual sight to find other birds nesting in the same tree; and the Arkansas Kingbird goes even farther than this, sometimes constructing its home under the nest of these Hawks or in the sides of it. The food of Swainson's Hawk consists almost entirely of the smaller rodents, principally striped gophers and mice, as well as grasshoppers and the large black cricket which is very common as well as destructive in certain seasons, and the bane of the farmers in eastern Oregon, and other localities in the Great Basin, destroying and eating up every green thing as they move along. I cannot recall a single instance where one of these birds visited a poultry yard. From an economic point of view I consider it by far the most useful and beneficial of all our Hawks." (Bendire.)

The adult in normal plumage is likely to be mistaken for the immature Red-tail or possibly for the Red-shouldered Hawk, but it lacks the rufous wing-coverts, and has a broad pectoral band of gray, brown, or cinnamon, separating the white throat from the nearly white under parts. The fact that this hawk has only three primaries notched on the inner webs will separate it from either the Red-tailed or the Red-shouldered Hawk.

BROAD-WINGED HAWK

Buteo platypterus (*Vieillot*)

A. O. U. Number 343 See Color Plate 48

Other Name.— Broad-winged Buzzard.

General Description.— Length: male, 14 inches; female, 18 inches. Spread of wings, 33 to 38 inches. Color above, dark brown; below, white, barred and streaked. *Three* outer primaries notched on inner webs; wing never more than 13½ inches long.

Color.— Crown, back of head, and nape, blackish-brown broken by dull rufous behind; back, shoulders, and upper parts, dark grayish-brown, the feathers with black shaft line and plain dark brown centers; primaries and secondaries, deep dusky on outer webs and at ends and barred with darker; tail, similar to color of back, crossed with three narrow grayish-white bars; line back of eye and sides of head, grayish-white finely streaked with dusky and brown; lores, whitish; a diffused but strongly marked mustache from gape to breast but throat white; breast, pale yellowish-brown shading into whitish under coverts, thickly traversed on breast with broad arrowhead bars of reddish-brown, these bars wider on sides and flanks, narrower on thigh feathers, and each with a central dark shaft line; greater coverts edged with rufous or raw umber; bill, dark horn color; cere and feet, yellow; claws, black; iris, deep brown. YOUNG: Above, blackish-brown variegated with raw umber, chestnut, or dull whitish edgings to all feathers; streaks above and behind eye and sides of head, pale yellowish-brown streaked with brownish; throat, white as in adult; under parts, yellowish-white with a tinge of tawny, boldly marked on sides and flanks with longitudinal drop- and arrowhead-shaped dark brown spots, center line of breast and abdomen with a few narrow streaks or plain; tail, dark brown crossed with 6 or 8 lighter bars on both webs of middle feathers, on outer webs of the others; all tail-feathers tipped with white.

Nest and Eggs.— NEST: Usually placed in the crotches of trees from 10 to 80 feet above ground; roughly and coarsely constructed of sticks and bits of bark and lined with small roots, bark strips, moss, or feathers and sometimes decorated with green sprigs. EGGS: 2 to 5, usually 2 or 3, very pale greenish or grayish-white heavily marked with brown spots.

Distribution.— Eastern North America; breeds from central Alberta, southeastern Saskatchewan, northern Ontario, New Brunswick, and Cape Breton Island south to the Gulf coast and central Texas, mainly east of the Mississippi; winters from the Ohio and Delaware valleys south to Venezuela and Peru.

The Broad-winged Hawk is a common though locally distributed Hawk, partial to deep woods. It will remain motionless for hours, apparently asleep but in reality wide awake, for the least movement in the brush below of a prospective victim will send him from his perch like an arrow. He is more silent and more fond of solitude than other Hawks. His call note is much weaker, closely resembling that of the Wood Pewee, but louder, higher pitched, and with the last note short and less plaintive than the notes of the Flycatcher, and having a certain ventriloquistical quality which makes it difficult to judge the distance of the author.

As far as my experience goes, it seems to be a beneficial and harmless species, confining its food to small animals, frogs, mice, etc., and seldom molesting the farmer's chickens. Agriculturists with whom I have talked do not always share this view but then it is difficult to eradicate an idea so firmly intrenched as the belief that all Hawks are demons.

Of the economic status of this species, Dr. A. K. Fisher, says: "The Broad-winged Hawk feeds largely on insects, small mammals, snakes, toads, and frogs, and occasionally on small birds. It is especially fond of the larvæ or caterpillars of the large moths which feed upon the leaves of fruit and shade trees. These insects are too large and formidable for the smaller insectivorous birds to attack; hence their principal enemies are Hawks, of which the one under consideration is the most important. It feeds extensively also upon grasshoppers, crickets, cicadæ, May beetles and other coleoptera. Like the other Buzzard Hawks, it is fond of meadow mice, and eats also considerable numbers of chipmunks, shrews, red squirrels, and occasionally rabbits and moles. Probably the greatest damage done by this Hawk is the destruction of toads and snakes, which are mainly insectivorous and hence beneficial to the farmer."

Drawing by R. I. Brasher

BROAD-WINGED HAWK (½ nat. size)

A beneficial and harmless species

R. I. BRASHER.

Photo by H. K. Job — Courtesy of Outing Pub. Co.

BROAD-WINGED HAWK

Approaching its nest with a piece of bark in its mouth

SENNETT'S WHITE-TAILED HAWK

Buteo albicaudatus sennetti *Allen*

A. O. U. Number 341

Other Name.— White-tail.

General Description.— Length: male, 22 inches; female, 24 inches. Spread of wings, 50 to 56 inches. Color above, ash; below, white, barred on sides. *Three* outer primaries notched on inner webs.

Color.— Adult Male: Upper parts, including crown, sides of head, and neck, clear ash, tinged on shoulders with reddish; *lesser wing-coverts, pure reddish-brown not extending to edge of wing; rump, upper coverts, and tail, pure white, with a broad black band near* the tip and numerous fine irregular blackish cross lines; entire *under parts, pure white* lightly crossed with fine dark bars on sides and usually on thigh feathers; the greater coverts and secondaries like back but slightly darker gradually deepening to dusky-black on primaries, the inner webs of which are more brownish and crossed with numerous darker bars, speckled basally with white increasing in firmness and extent on secondaries; bill, blackish-horn; feet and gape, yellow; claws, black; cere, dull greenish. Adult Female: Similar to adult male but colors generally darker and reddish-brown of wing-coverts more extensive. Young: Crown, sides of head and neck, throat, lower breast and upper abdomen, back, and wings, clear sepia-brown; region over eye and rear part of sides of head with a few very narrow white streaks; lores, a rather broad streak below eye, and edge of wing, white; throat streaked with whitish; lower abdomen, thighs, under tail-coverts, white with heart-shaped spots of sepia; tail, *grayish-ash* shading to darker brown at end where tipped with white, crossed or not with very faint darker bars; wing-coverts outlined with paler brown; bill, horn color; legs, yellow; claws black; cere, livid.

Nest and Eggs.— Nest: Placed in low trees or bushes within 10 feet of ground; a large rough bulky structure of sticks and grasses usually destitute of lining. Eggs: 2 or 3, dull white, faintly and lightly spotted with yellowish-brown.

Distribution.— From central Texas south to southern Mexico.

Sennett's White-tailed Hawk is an exceedingly handsome bird and a straggler over our border from Mexico. Its banded white tail and conspicuous chestnut wing patch give it a distinction shared by no other Hawk. Though its habits are not very well understood they are probably similar to those of others of the genus.

R. I. Brasher.

ROUGH-LEGGED HAWK

Archibuteo lagopus sancti-johannis (*Gmelin*)

A. O. U. Number 347a See Color Plates 43, 48

Other Names.— American Rough-legged Hawk; Rough-leg; Rough-legged Buzzard; Black Hawk; Mouse Hawk.

General Description.— Length: male, 20 inches; female, 22 inches. About the size of the Red-tailed Hawk, but much lighter built and with more slender feet and longer, more pointed wings; *four* outer primaries deeply notched on inner webs; *feathers of legs extending to the toes.*

Color.— Intermediate stages between normal and melanistic plumages are common. Adults (Normal Coloration): Upper parts, grayish-brown, margined with whitish and buffy; wings and tail barred with gray and whitish; inner webs of primaries and under surfaces of wing-feathers, white toward their bases; tips of wings and patch on middle under wing-coverts, black; under parts, white or buffy, spotted and streaked with blackish, forming a dark band across the abdomen. Young: End portion of tail, plain grayish-brown except for white tip; under parts more heavily marked with black, the band across abdomen, broad and unbroken; otherwise similar to adults. Dark or Melanistic Phase (common to all ages and to both sexes): Uniform sooty-black, except base of tail and a portion of the bases of the wing-feathers which are white.

Nest and Eggs.— Nest: Usually placed in large trees but sometimes on ledges; a large bulky structure of interlaced sticks, grasses, and weeds and lined with small twigs, finer grasses, and other fibrous vegetable material, well felted together. Eggs: 2 to 5, usually 2 or 3 varying from dingy to buffy-white and sprinkled with blotches of dark brown.

Distribution.— North America north of Mexico; breeds from the Aleutian Islands, northwestern Alaska, Arctic coast, and northern Ungava, south to central British Columbia, southern Mackenzie, southern Ungava, and Newfoundland; winters from Oregon, Colorado, Minnesota, and the northern boundary of eastern United States, south to central California, southern New Mexico, Texas, Louisiana, and North Carolina.

The Rough-legged Hawk breeds in Alaska and Canada and is but a winter migrant to the States. Its favorite haunts are in open meadows or in country covered with scrub and brush. It is the nearest to nocturnal of all our Hawks. Its plumage is soft and fluffy, its flight noiseless, and, when observed in the twilight sweeping quietly over the open spaces where field mice abound, it is easily mistaken for an Owl. When mice are abundant one or two Rough-legs will hunt for weeks in the vicinity, effectually controlling these pests and saving many fruit trees, especially the young ones, from destruction. While watching for rabbits on moonlit nights I have more than once been startled by the sudden appearance of a dark form swooping noiselessly down on a luckless mouse playing on the snow crust. A swift dash —a tiny squeak — then the quick disappearance of captor and victim into the shadows.

The Ferruginous Rough-leg (*Archibuteo ferrugineus*) is quite similar in its habits to the common Rough-leg. The adults have the top, back, and sides of head streaked equally with blackish and white; rest of the upper parts, blackish and chestnut in about equal amounts; the tail silvery ash tinged with rufous and with white tip and base; the under parts, pure white from bill to end of tail; and legs, chestnut barred with black. It breeds from southern Washington, southwestern Saskatchewan, and southern Manitoba to southern California, Utah, Colorado, and Kansas, and winters from Montana to Lower California and northern Mexico. The Ferruginous Rough-leg is rarely found east of the Mississippi.

Of the value to man of these two species, Dr. A. K. Fisher says: "The Rough-legged Hawk and the Ferruginous Rough-leg, or Squirrel Hawk, as it is sometimes called on account of its fondness for ground squirrels, so destructive in the West, are among our largest and most beneficial Hawks. The winter range of the Rough-leg is determined more by the fall of snow than by the intensity of cold, the main body advancing and retreating as the barrier of snow melts or accumulates.

"Meadow mice and lemmings form the staple food of this bird. In this country lemmings do not reach our territory except in Alaska, but in the north of Europe they occasionally form into vast, migrating devastating hordes which carry destruction to crops in the country invaded. The vole, or meadow mouse, is common in many parts of this country, and east of the Mississippi River without doubt is the most destructive mammal to agriculture. It destroys meadows by tunneling under them and eating the roots of grass. This mouse also destroys grain and various kinds of vegetables, especially tubers, but probably does even more damage by girdling young fruit trees. In 1892 considerable areas in southeastern Scotland were overrun by meadow mice and a large amount of property was destroyed during the 'vole plague.' Just such invasions are to be expected in any country where predacious mammals and birds are reduced to a minimum in the supposed interest of game preservation. This wholly upsets nature's balance, and the injurious rodents are left practically without an enemy to control their increase. Attempts have been made in some of our States to reduce the number of Hawks and Owls by offering bounties for their heads, but fortunately the work has not been carried far enough to do the harm that has resulted from the long-continued efforts of gamekeepers in Great Britain.

"The Ferruginous Rough-leg is as fully beneficial as its relative, though the character of its food differs somewhat. In many parts of the country inhabited by it, meadow mice, which play such an important part in the economy of the other bird, are scarce or wanting, but are replaced by nearly as destructive rodents, the ground squirrels. Upon these this large and handsome Hawk wages continuous warfare, and great is the service it performs in keeping their numbers in check. Rabbits, prairie dogs, and occasionally pouched gophers are eaten. It is humiliating to think how many of these two noble Hawks are ruthlessly murdered, and to reflect that legislators put bounties on their heads to satisfy the ignorant prejudices of their constituents." R. I. BRASHER.

BALD EAGLE

Haliæetus leucocephalus leucocephalus (*Linnæus*)

A. O. U. Number 352 See Color Plates 43, 49

Other Names.— White-headed Eagle; White-headed Sea Eagle; American Eagle; Black Eagle; Gray Eagle; Washington Eagle. The last three names refer to the immature Bald Eagle.

General Description.—Length: male, 30 to 35 inches; female, 34 to 43 inches. Spread of wings, 6½ to 7¾ feet. Plumage, dark brown. *Tarsus, bare for an inch or more above base of toes;* five outer primaries deeply notched on inner webs.

Color.— ADULTS: Entire head, neck, upper tail-coverts, and tail, white; rest of plumage, dark brown, many of body feathers with paler margins, and the wing-feathers nearly black; bill, cere, and feet, bright yellow; iris, pale yellow or yellowish-white. IMMATURE, FIRST YEAR: Plumage, mainly black; no white on head, only small freckles of white on inner webs of tail-feathers, but all body feathers, snowy white below the surface; bill, black; feet, yellow; iris, brown. IMMATURE, SECOND AND THIRD YEARS: Head and neck, mainly black, the long narrow feathers at the back of the neck, tipped with brown or gray; tail, black, the inner webs of most of the feathers, sprinkled or mottled with whitish; body feathers, above and below, mixed brown, black, and gray, sometimes streaked and margined with pure white; bill, dark horn color; cere and feet, yellow; iris, brown.

Nest and Eggs.— NEST: In large trees from 20 to 90 feet above ground, sometimes in niches of rocky cliffs; a large coarsely built affair of good-sized sticks, roots, twigs, seaweed, bits of turf, vine or plant stalks and lined with roots or grass. EGGS: 2, rarely 3, ivory white with a granular surface.

Distribution.— United States to southern Lower California and northern Mexico, breeding in suitable location throughout its range; rare and local in California and in arid interior.

In flight or at rest the Bald Eagle is majestic, its white head and tail lending dignity to its imposing form. The Eagle as a type has inspired many literary tributes. Tennyson's two stanzas refer presumably to the Gray Sea Eagle of Europe, which sometimes visits the western hemisphere, but they might well have been addressed to our Bald Eagle:

> He clasps the crags with crooked hands;
> Close to the sun in lonely lands,
> Ring'd with the azure world, he stands.
>
> The wrinkled sea beneath him crawls;
> He watches from his mountain walls,
> And like a thunder-bolt he falls.

In prose perhaps nothing finer has been written than Mr. Burroughs's expression:

"He draws great lines across the sky; he sees the forests like a carpet beneath him; he sees the hills and valleys as folds and wrinkles in a many colored tapestry; he sees the river as a silver belt connecting remote horizons. We climb mountain-peaks to get a glimpse of the spectacle that is hourly spread out beneath him. Dignity, elevation, repose, are his. I would have my thoughts take as wide a sweep. I would be as far removed from the petty cares and turmoils of this noisy and blustering world." (*Far and Near.*)

The Bald Eagle frequents the shores of lakes and rivers. His food consists very largely of fish and he very seldom or never nests at any great distance from where this food can be obtained in abundance. He is almost non-migratory, only deserting his home during the coldest weather when the waters are frozen over. Frequently he is seen soaring high in the air in search of something to eat. His power of sight is famous and often he will spy the object of his quest when at a distance of two or three miles and make a direct line for it. Most of his food is dead fish gathered from the surface of the water or from the shores of lakes and rivers but when he cannot find the dead fish he often robs the Osprey compelling it to drop the fish it has just captured. Sometimes the Eagle fishes for himself but he is not an expert fisherman. Occasionally he joins the Crows and Ravens when they are feeding upon carrion. In the winter time he often attacks waterfowl, but is rarely successful if the fowl be upon water, for just as the Eagle drops for his prey the latter dives beneath the surface of the water and escapes. He kills many rabbits, squirrels, mice, and snakes, but on the whole he confers no decided benefits on the agriculturist. On rare occasions an Eagle has been known to pick up a hen or to destroy a young lamb but these are not common offenses.

The male Bald Eagle has a high clear call which is represented by the syllables *cac-cac-cac*. The female's cry is more harsh and broken and Dr. Fisher compares it to the loud laugh of a maniac. They have a screaming note which much resembles the voice of a sea gull and has been likened to that of a small fox or of a dog.

The nest, a bulky and conspicuous affair, is placed high up in a large tree generally so situated that a wide view of the surrounding country can be obtained. Year after year the same pair of Eagles occupy the nest, making slight repairs to it each spring. Bald Eagles mate for life and apparently they are very fond of each other. Family cares are undertaken very early in the season; in Florida, eggs are laid in December or January; in the Middle States, in February or March; and in districts further north, a little later.

About thirty days are needed for incubation and only one brood is reared a season. When the baby Eagles are hatched they are covered with a whitish down but they acquire their first plumage before they are able to fly. Three years must pass before maturity is reached. During these years the young Eagles are noticeably different in color from the adults and during the first year after leaving the nest they are larger than either of the parents, the expanse of the wing being often a foot more. These large immature birds deceived Audubon who thought they were a distinct species and named them "Birds of Washington."

Courtesy of Nat. Asso. Aud. Soc.

BALD EAGLE'S NEST

Florida

In northwestern Alaska, northwestern Mackenzie, central Keewatin, and northern Ungava south to British Columbia and the Great Lakes occurs a larger but otherwise similar Eagle known as the Northern Bald Eagle (*Haliæetus leucocephalus alascanus*).

GOLDEN EAGLE

Aquila chrysaëtos (*Linnæus*)

A. O. U. Number 349 See Color Plate 49

Other Names.— Ring-tailed Eagle; Black Eagle; Mountain Eagle; Gray Eagle; Brown Eagle.

General Description.— Length, about 3 feet; spread of wings, 7 to 7½ feet. Plumage, dark brown. *Legs feathered to the toes.*

Color.— Adults: Dark brown with a faint purplish gloss becoming lighter on wing-coverts, tail- and thigh-feathers; feathers of back of head, nape, and sides of neck with separate, spear-head-shaped tips, of *a deep golden brown;* primaries, secondaries, and tail, more blackish; tail, white or grayish at base; bill, bluish horn; legs, cere, gape, and line over eye, yellow; claws, black; iris, brown. Young: Darker and larger than adults; tail, white at very base and with a broad black terminal bar; golden-brown of back of head, etc., less apparent and duller; otherwise as in adults.

Nest and Eggs.— Nest: Usually on inaccessible cliffs, sometimes in large trees — sycamores, pines, or oaks; constructed of good-sized sticks and lined with hay, twigs, or green grass. The birds return every year to the same site, adding material each season until the nest sometimes becomes 4 or 5 feet in diameter and nearly the same height. Eggs: 2, white, beautifully marked with bold spots, specks, and blotches of chestnut, sienna, and shades of purple, more heavily at large end.

Distribution.— Northern part of northern hemisphere; in the Old World south to north Africa and the Himalaya; in North America from northern Alaska, northwestern Mackenzie, central Keewatin, and northern Ungava south to middle Lower California, central Mexico, western Texas, South Dakota, Manitoba, southern Keewatin, central Ontario, New Hampshire, Maine and Nova Scotia and in the Alleghenies to southwestern North Carolina; less common east of the Mississippi.

The aerie was in the top of a storm-battered old pine on the east slope of the Cascades. It looked impossible to climb, yet the going up was not so hard. Excitement led me on. As I climbed, the task became more precarious. My heart beat wilder each time the pair of Bald Eagles circled near. I finally straddled the big limb below the nest and worked a hazardous way through five feet of dead limbs and debris.

I had read so many stories of fierce Eagles that I half persuaded myself I should be attacked, but I wasn't. After a careful study extending over several years, I have found that forty-eight such cases out of every fifty may be set down as false in the beginning. Investigation will show the forty-ninth is without truth, and there might possibly be a slight cause for the fiftieth. I have the records of over a hundred nests of the Bald and Golden Eagles that have been robbed and in not a single case did the birds put up a fight.

The pair of Eagles were winding slowly around the blue dome of the sky. I moved the youngsters over and climbed in beside them to visit. Here were the nestlings of noble birth. Of the millions of people who daily see our national emblem on the coins and arms of our country, few know anything of the Eagle as a bird. Few know of the home-life and habits. Fewer still have ever seen an Eagle wild and free.

In North America, we have two Eagles that are of general distribution: the Bald Eagle, found in the wilder places throughout the United States, and the Golden Eagle, now restricted almost entirely to the mountainous regions of the West. The term "bald" originated from the white head which is an unmistakable mark of identity of the full-grown bird and at a distance gives the impression of baldness.

The Bald Eagle is much the same general color as the Golden Eagle up to the time it is three years old. In the time of Audubon, these young Bald Eagles were considered a separate species. At the age of three years, the Bald Eagle attains maturity and the white feathers appear on the head and neck. To distinguish one species from the other, look at the lower joint of the leg. If this is covered with feathers down to the toes, it is a Golden Eagle; if the leg is naked, it is a Bald Eagle.

In some ways, the Golden Eagle is a nobler bird than his white-headed cousin. The Bald Eagle is a resident along the big rivers, on the shores of lakes and on the islands of the sea. Its favorite food is fish. It often catches these, or compels an Osprey to pay tribute. In some places, it lives almost entirely on the dead fish it finds along the shores. The Golden Eagle is more of a hunter. It has seldom been known to touch dead animals.

In the coast mountains of California, we finally found an aerie of a Golden Eagle that could be photographed. To the branch of a tall sycamore bending out toward the valley, the Eagles had carried a cartload of sticks and made a platform five feet across.

We made a close study of the castle in the

MR. FINLEY (right) AND MR. BOHLMAN (left) PREPARING TO MAKE PHOTOGRAPHIC STUDIES OF THE GOLDEN EAGLE'S HOME-LIFE

The nest was about 60 feet up in a sycamore tree, and contained two young Eagles. The camera was focused, a thread was attached to the shutter, and the pictures were taken from a distance by pulling the thread after the return of the parents

sycamore. These Eagles were successful hunters. We never saw the time when their larder was empty. The food of the young Eagles consisted almost entirely of ground squirrels. The first visit I made to the aerie after the Eaglets were hatched, I found the bodies of four ground squirrels lying on the rim of the nest. For miles along the lower hills, the ground was perforated with the burrows of these rodents. On rocky lookouts above, the Eagles had their regular watch-towers where they kept vigil.

The Golden Eagle cradled her eggs in the big sycamore the first week in March. The period of incubation lasted a month, for the eggs hatched on April 3d. At first the Eaglets were covered with soft, white down, rather poor garments for a hunter, but this coat lasted a full month. During this time, the youngsters grew from the egg till they weighed as much as a good-sized hen. Then black pinfeathers began to prick up through the down, first appearing on the wings and back. It was not till the first week in June that the Eaglets were fairly well clothed. The wings and feet were still very weak. The wing-feathers were slow in gaining the strength that was necessary to handle such heavy bodies. It required the continued efforts of both parents to hunt food for such ravenous children. It took many days of practicing on the nest edge by flapping their wings and much parental persuasion before the young Eagles sailed out from the castle in the sycamore. WILLIAM L. FINLEY.

The food of the Golden Eagle consists of fawns, rabbits, woodchucks, prairie dogs, and ground squirrels among mammals, and Turkeys, Grouse, and waterfowl among birds. At times it attacks also the young of domesticated animals, notably lambs, pigs, goats, and poultry. It has been known to attack calves and colts, but such instances must be exceptional and when the birds are hard pressed by hunger.

Over extensive areas of the West the Golden Eagle unites with other birds of prey to keep many species of noxious rodents in check, and must be considered beneficial. In the more thickly inhabited regions, however, where such food is scarce, they often do great damage by carrying off lambs, young pigs, kids, and poultry. As many as four hundred lambs are reported to have been taken from contiguous ranges in one season. It thus will be seen that in one region the bird should be protected and in another kept in check.

FALCONS

Order *Raptores;* suborder *Falcones;* family *Falconidæ;* subfamily *Falconinæ*

THE Falcons are in some respects the most remarkable, as they certainly are the most famous, of the birds of prey. Their savage and predacious disposition, swiftness of flight, and extraordinary keenness of vision suggested centuries ago their employment in the pursuit of other birds and small mammals, and thus arose the ancient sport of falconry, which is still followed to some extent in the Orient, though its obvious cruelty finally caused its abandonment in western Europe. In days when hawking was at its height in England, the rank of the individual could be told by the particular species of Falcon which he carried on his wrist: the Gyrfalcon was carried by royalty, the Peregrine Falcon was carried by an earl, the Goshawk by a yeoman, the Sparrow Hawk by a priest, and the Kestrel by a servant.

The true Falcons have the bill sharply hooked, toothed, and notched. The projecting bony eye-shield gives the bird a peculiarly stern and domineering expression. The legs are muscular; the talons curved, strong, and very sharp; the wings, long, strong, and pointed; the tail, rigid and comparatively short; the general build, powerful. The flight of all the species is remarkably swift, and the birds' movements on the wing are very quick and certain. Without apparent effort they overtake and kill in flight the swiftest flying Ducks, as well as Pigeons and Grouse. Their courage is great and they do not hesitate to attack birds much larger and stronger than themselves. Birds pursued by Falcons seem to realize that their only chance for escape is to keep above the enemy, and it often happens, therefore, that both birds may fly so high as to disappear entirely. Eventually, however, the relentless pursuer will rise above his victim, and then in a few moments will come the savage and certain downward plunge, and the clutch of the merciless talons which means death in midair.

Because of these qualities the Falcons, with a few exceptions, such as the American Sparrow Hawk, are highly destructive to other birds; yet their bravery, skill, fleetness, and determination challenge the admiration of man, and often enlist his protection, or at any rate stay his hand which would be raised against a destroyer less courageous and less picturesque.

The nests of the Falcons are less bulky than are those of the Hawks and some species lay their eggs on a bare rock or in a hollow tree. The number of eggs varies from two to five but is most often four.

WHITE GYRFALCON

Falco islandus *Brünnich*

A. O. U. Number 353 See Color Plate 50

Other Name.— Greenland Gyrfalcon.

General Description.— Length: male, 22 inches; female, 24 inches. Spread of wings, 50 to 55 inches. Plumage, white. Tarsus covered with feathers about ⅔ down on front and sides, the feathers meeting at the back.

Color.— Adults: *Entire plumage, white,* the feathers of back, shoulders, middle and lesser wing-coverts with pale ashy drop-shaped crescents or arrow-head spots, the number varying with the individual; bill, bluish-horn, darker at tip; cere, edges of eyelids, and feet, livid bluish; claws, blue-black; iris, brown. Young: Differing from adults only in being more heavily marked above and below, with dark brown in longitudinal streaks and spots.

Nest and Eggs.— Nest: In cavities of cliffs; composed of sticks, seaweed, and other materials which happen to be handy. Eggs: 2 to 4, whitish, so heavily spotted and suffused with different shades of reddish-brown as almost to appear uniformly of that color, with some spots of darker brown.

Distribution.— Arctic regions; resident in Greenland; in winter rarely south to Ontario, Nova Scotia, and Maine.

GRAY GYRFALCON

Falco rusticolus rusticolus *Linnæus*

A. O. U. Number 354

Description.— Differs from White Gyrfalcon only in color. Adults: General color, gray with darker markings; above about equally divided between the pale bluish-gray and the darker bars, crescents, or spots; *on head and neck, lighter shades prevailing;* under parts, whitish, *striped, streaked, or spotted with dusky*; bars of tail, well marked, the light and dark ones about equal in width; bill, bluish; cere, and feet, bluish-gray; iris, brown. Young: Upper parts, browner; head, more narrowly streaked with darker shades; under parts more heavily streaked.

Nest and Eggs.— Nest: On cliffs or in trees. Eggs: Not distinguishable from those of the White Gyrfalcon.

Distribution.— Arctic regions; breeds in Arctic America from Alaska east to southern Greenland; in winter casual south to British Columbia, Kansas, Wisconsin, Ontario, and Maine.

CYRFALCON

Falco rusticolus gyrfalco *Linnæus*

A. O. U. Number 354a See Color Plate 50

Other Name.— MacFarlane's Gyrfalcon.

General Description.— Length, 24 inches; spread of wings, 50 to 55 inches. Color above, grayish-brown; below, white, streaked. Tarsus feathered half-way down the front and sides.

Color.— Adults: Upper parts, brownish-gray or grayish-brown, slightly marked with buffy-white; *head, unstreaked; under parts, white heavily streaked with grayish-brown*; a pronounced black mustache; tail closely barred with light and dark of about equal widths; bill, bluish horn color; legs, bluish-gray; claws, black; iris, brown. Immature: Similar to adults, but head sometimes slightly streaked with lighter, and back almost uniform.

Nest and Eggs.— Nest: On ledges of cliffs; composed of sticks and small twigs and lined with feathers and other soft materials. Eggs: 2 to 4, commonly 3 or 4, varying from dull yellowish-red to a deep burnt-umber, finely and evenly speckled with reddish-brown.

Distribution.— Arctic regions; breeds in Ellesmere Land, northern Greenland, and east to Franz Josef Land; in winter casual south to Minnesota, New York, Rhode Island, Massachusetts, and Maine.

BLACK GYRFALCON

Falco rusticolus obsoletus *Gmelin*

A. O. U. Number 354b See Color Plate 50

Description.— A dark phase of the Gyrfalcon; uniformly dusky or brownish-slate, upper parts without bars, except broken ones on tail and under parts almost black with a few inconspicuous streaks or spots of buff.

Nest and Eggs.— Similar to those of the Gyrfalcon.

Distribution.— Breeds in Ungava; south in winter to Nova Scotia, Quebec, Ontario, and Maine; casually to New York, New Hampshire, Massachusetts, and Rhode Island.

The White Gyrfalcon, the Gray Gyrfalcon, the Gyrfalcon, and the Black Gyrfalcon form a subgenus of the *falco* genus in the Falcon family, known as *hierofalco,* a word signifying " sacred or noble Falcon." They are Arctic birds and never come very far south of the Arctic circle. All of these northern Falcons were formerly in great demand for the sport of hawking. Their flight is much swifter than that of the Peregrine or Duck Hawk, and they are very tenacious of grip when they have captured their prey, but they do not equal in dash and spirit the smaller Peregrine.

Drawing by R. I. Brasher

GYRFALCON (⅜ nat. size)

A visitor from " Greenland's icy mountains "

The White Gyrfalcon is seldom found even in mid-winter south of the 50th parallel. According to Holbœll they are the most abundant Falcon in Greenland, where they breed in January. They prey chiefly upon waterfowl and Ptarmigans; usually they build near bird rocks from which they obtain the young without much trouble. He mentions having seen one with a young Kittiwake in each foot, and two Sandpipers carried in the same manner. He did not regard its rapidity of flight as very great. He had for years kept Pigeons and lost only two young birds which were seized when at rest. Almost every day, especially in October and November, these Falcons would chase the old Pigeons unsuccessfully. They were not very shy and were occasionally decoyed and killed by throwing a dead bird toward them.

They go southerly along the coast of Greenland from September to November; at this time they are often seen fighting with the Ravens and will approach quite close to the houses of the Danes.

PRAIRIE FALCON

Falco mexicanus *Schlegel*

A. O. U. Number 355

Other Names.— American Lanner (female) or American Lanneret (male).

General Description.— Length: male, 18 inches; female, 20 inches. Color above, brownish-ash; below, white, spotted. Outer primary notched on inner web; back of tarsus, broadly bare.

Color.— Adults: Above, brownish-ash, each feather with a paler border, crown more uniform, back of head and *nape more streaked;* primaries, darker brown, sharply edged with paler; tail, pale brownish-gray with barring or indentations of whitish, tip, white; under parts, dull white marked everywhere except on throat with firm spots of dark brown, more drop-shaped on breast, more oval on abdomen, enlarging and tending to form bars on flanks, absent or very few on under tail-coverts; a broad dark-brown streak from gape forming a mustache; bill, dark bluish horn, yellow at base and below; feet, yellow; iris, brown. Young: Differ from adults in showing more light brown above and in being more heavily spotted below on a buff or ocher ground; feet, livid.

Nest and Eggs.— Nest: On cliffs or on the steep faces of cut banks of streams; constructed of sticks with a lining of grass. Eggs: 2 to 5, creamy-white, almost entirely obscured with spots and splashes of cinnamon and chestnut.

Distribution.— From eastern border of the Great Plains and from southern British Columbia and southeastern Saskatchewan to southern Lower California and southern Mexico; casual east to Minnesota and Illinois.

The Prairie Falcon is the American representative of the Lanners and Lannerets of the eastern hemisphere. With short quick wing beats, like the Duck Hawk's flight, it sweeps over the western prairies and sage brush deserts. It is a bird of the open, resorting to the perpendicular side of cañons or isolated buttes to rear its young. From these commanding eminences its keen vision ranges over the many square miles of territory from which it takes its toll of birds and small rodents, especially of ground squirrels. Though ordinarily shy these Falcons are bold, daring hunters, pursuing and capturing their food with an impetuosity which almost equals the Duck Hawk's.

Their cry of *Wert-wert-wert-wert-wert* is a more mellow call than that of other Hawks, resembling the notes of the Rough-leg at nesting time. They utter two other calls — a rattling *k-r-rr,* rising in pitch at end, and a whining "kruk" very similar to the "clap" of the Flicker.

DUCK HAWK

Falco peregrinus anatum *Bonaparte*

A. O. U. Number 356a See Color Plates 43, 51

Other Names.— Peregrine Falcon; American Peregrine; Great-footed Hawk; Wandering Falcon; Tercel (male).

General Description.— Length: male, 18 inches; female, 19 inches. Spread of wings, 40 to 46 inches. Color above, bluish-ash; below, yellowish, barred. Outer primary notched on inner web; tarsus broadly bare at the base, only slightly feathered in the front, and about the length of the middle toe with claw; upper section of bill with an additional point or tooth near the tip and a corresponding notch in the lower section.

Color.— Adults: Feathers of extreme forehead, whitish; crown, sides of head to level of eyes behind, space in front and below eyes, *dark slate color; rest of upper parts, a fine dark bluish-ash,* all the feathers with paler edges but these lighter markings more obsolete on rump and upper tail-feathers; tail crossed with 5 or 6 narrow bars of black, the one nearest the tip much broader, tail, tipped with white; greater wing-coverts and secondaries barred; primaries, dark dusky-black tipped with whitish; *a strong black streak from gape forming a mustache,* and almost cutting off the *light yellowish under parts,* a patch of similar color on the side of the head; *throat whitish,* usually unmarked, as is also the breast; rest of under parts, closely and regularly barred with blackish brown, more pronounced and larger on sides and under tail-coverts; thigh feathers finely and regularly barred transversely with the same color, these markings tending to broad arrow-head shapes; bill, bluish-black, more yellow at base; cere, gape, and feet, yellow; claws, blackish; iris, dark brown. Young: The extreme forehead, lores, throat, and patch on side of head, plain pale tawny-white; crown, streak behind eye, mustache, and entire upper parts, plain brownish-dusky; all the feathers, including coverts and secondaries, edged with lighter; primaries, darker dusky-brown tipped with lighter; tail, ashy, tipped with pale yellowish-white and crossed with 4 or 5 very narrow bars of light ash; beneath, pale tawny or yellowish-white marked lightly on breast, more heavily below, with wedge-shaped longitudinal spots of deep brown; bill, bluish-horn; cere and feet, dull yellow; claws, black; iris, brown.

Nest and Eggs.— NEST: Usually in crevices on inaccessible cliffs, more rarely in natural cavities of trees; no apparent attempt at any construction. EGGS: 3 or 4, dull white, usually so heavily colored with spots, blotches, and specks of reddish or dark brown as to obscure the ground color.

Distribution.— North and South America; breeds locally (except in northwest coast region) from Norton Sound, Alaska, northern Mackenzie, Boothia Peninsula, and western central Greenland south to central Lower California, Arizona, southwestern Texas, Kansas, Missouri, Indiana, Pennsylvania and Connecticut (in mountains to South Carolina); winters from southern British Columbia, Colorado, and New Jersey (occasionally further north) to the West Indies and Panama; occurs also in South America south to northern Chile.

The Peregrine Falcon (*Falco peregrinus peregrinus*) of the Old World is the noble Falcon of the days when hawking was the chief of sports. Casually it is found in Greenland but its best known American representative is the Duck Hawk. The only difference between the two birds is in the coloration of the throat and upper breast; in the Duck Hawk these are generally unmarked, but in the Peregrine they are marked with blackish-brown.

The quick wing beats resembling the flight of a Pigeon are quite different from the flight of the majority of other Hawks and readily identify the Duck Hawk in the field. Its strength and bearing appeal to our primitive sense of admiration for courage. While such traits are admirable, others less commendable cannot be ignored. The toll of life taken by the strong we accept as part of the scheme of things but wanton destruction revolts us and a Duck Hawk is sometimes so carried away by lust of slaughter that it will strike bird after bird from a flock of Sandpipers and leave the victims where they fall.

After the young are reared the parents proceed

DUCK HAWK (½ nat. size)

A fierce destroyer but a splendid success as a bird

Drawing by R. I. Brasher

to exemplify the fitness of the name given them by the scientists — *falco,* sickle, *peregrinus,* wandering, and *anatum,* of the Ducks. They seek maritime districts and change their diet from Partridges, Pigeons, Flickers and the like to shore birds and Ducks.

The usual method pursued in obtaining its prey is to rise in spirals until it is above the victim and then to drop directly upon it; seldom is it unsuccessful. Sometimes it captures its victims by direct chase or by a sudden assault. That they do not always look carefully before they strike was proved by one which passed over me while I was concealed in a duck-blind, struck one of the decoys, and knocked the head off. This is not an unusual incident, declare baymen who do a great deal of Duck shooting.

Considering the peculiar advantages the Duck Hawk possesses in the struggle for existence, it is remarkable how comparatively rare it is. Among birds it has no superior. The inaccessible location of its nest prevents animal depredations; even a wild-cat would think twice before attacking its home. The insatiable " egg-collector " is its worst enemy. R. I. Brasher.

Peale's Falcon (*Falco peregrinus pealei*) is a duskier slate above than the Duck Hawk, its crown is like its back, its breast is more heavily spotted with blackish, and there are broad bars of dusky on its under parts. This Black Hawk, as it is also called, inhabits the Pacific coast region from the Aleutian Islands to Oregon. It breeds throughout its range and is accused, in Alaska, of living largely on Auklets and Murrelets.

PIGEON HAWK

Falco columbarius columbarius *Linnæus*

A. O. U. Number 357 See Color Plate 52

Other Names.— Pigeon Falcon; American Merlin; Bullet Hawk; Little Blue Corporal.

General Description.— Length: male, 11 inches; female, 13 inches. Color above, dark brown; below, whitish. Two outer primaries notched on inner webs; tarsus but slightly feathered in front, broadly bare on back, and longer than middle toe without claw; not more than 4 blackish or 5 light bands crossing the tail.

Color.—Adults in Normal Plumage (as usually seen); Above, dark umber-brown, interrupted on neck by whitish streaks, most of feathers with paler edges and dark shaft lines; primaries, blackish with lighter tips and numerous oval transverse spots of cinnamon on inner webs; tail, umber-brown barred with about four narrow light ocher bands and tipped with white; beneath varying from dull white to a rich warm buff heavily streaked longitudinally with dark umber-brown except on throat which is distinctly whitish and marked only with fine shaft streaks; sides of head, buff finely penciled with dark streaks merging into a mustache extending from gape to bottom of throat; forehead and spot in front of eye, whitish; a dark line above and behind eye; bill, bluish horn; cere and feet, chrome yellow; claws, black; iris, deep brown. Adult Male in Full Plumage: Forehead, line over eye, lores, and throat, white; crown, back, shoulders, rump, coverts, and secondaries, fine purplish ash; crown, streaked with black; feathers of back, shoulders, and coverts with a strong distinct black shaft line; primary coverts barred with dusky; tail, grayish-ash banded with two exposed bars of blackish and a broad subterminal one of the same color tipped with white; primaries, deep dusky edged with whitish and with a number of transverse oval spots of whitish on inner web; the white line over eye continued to back of neck; sides of head, neck all around, breast, and under parts in general, a fine warm buffy, streaked narrowly on cheeks and sides of head, more strongly on neck and beneath, with blackish; the thigh feathers merely with black shaft streaks; a narrow but distinct dusky mustache; bill, bluish-horn; cere, skin around eye, and feet, chrome-yellow; claws, black; iris, deep brown. Young: Practically the same as normal plumage of adults, but birds of the year are usually lighter with more tawny and wider edges of feathers on upper parts.

Nest and Eggs.— Nest: On ledges, in branches of trees, or, occasionally, in a hollow tree; the tree nests constructed of sticks, weed stems, grass, or moss and lined with feathers and strips of soft inner bark; the ledge nests with very little material. Eggs: 4 or 5, white, thinly spotted, evenly or wreathed around either end, or so heavily splashed and blotched with rich chestnut-brown as to obscure the ground color.

Distribution.— North America to northern South America; breeds from northwestern Alaska and northwestern Mackenzie south in the mountains to California and southern Oregon, and from central Keewatin, northern Ungava, and Newfoundland south to northern Michigan, central Ontario, and Maine; winters from California and the Gulf States (casually further north) south through Mexico, Central America, and the West Indies to Ecuador and Venezuela.

The Pigeon Hawk is a stocky, well-built, impetuous miniature of the Duck Hawk, which it closely resembles in color and habits. It is widely distributed but nowhere common in the United States. This is fortunate, for its principal food is birds.

Many migrants from the New England States cross the Sound to Long Island, following the Great South Beach westward. I have found this Hawk most abundant there during October, pursuing the shore birds, especially Sanderlings and Ringed Plovers. Strong northwest winds are prevalent along this beach in the autumn and the Pigeon Hawks tack across the wind on their way westward and south. The short "board" is made directly into the wind's eye, then a long slant with the breeze on the quarter carries them well on their way to the westward. Sometimes a number of Hawks of different species can be seen as far as the eye can reach up and down the beach going through these maneuvers, crossing and recrossing each other on the different "tacks."

A darker colored form of the Pigeon Hawk is the Black Pigeon Hawk or Black Merlin (*Falco columbarius suckleyi*). The throat of the male is streaked with black, and the rest of the lower parts are brownish-black with chestnut and whitish markings; the lower parts of the female and the young male are heavily marked with dusky and the spotting of the wings is faint or absent. It inhabits the northwest coast region from northern California to Sitka, Alaska, and it is similar to the stock species in nesting and habits.

Richardson's Pigeon Hawk or Richardson's Merlin (*Falco columbarius richardsoni*) averages lighter in coloration than the Pigeon Hawk and its tail is crossed by five dark bands and six light ones. Otherwise, in color, in habits, and in nesting it is similar to the Pigeon Hawk. It is found in the interior of western North America; it breeds in the region of the Great Plains from southern Alberta and the middle of the Saskatchewan valley to northern Montana and North Dakota. It winters south to southern Lower California, northwestern Mexico, and southern Texas. It has also been seen in California, Missouri, and South Carolina.

R. I. Brasher.

SPARROW HAWK

Falco sparverius sparverius *Linnæus*

A. O. U. Number 360 See Color Plate 52

Other Names.—American Sparrow Hawk; American Kestrel; Rusty-crowned Falcon; Grasshopper Hawk; Mouse Hawk; Kitty Hawk; Windhover; Short-winged Hawk.

General Description.—Length, 11 inches. Color above, cinnamon-rufous; below, pale rusty and whitish. Two outer primaries notched on inner webs; tarsus but slightly feathered in the front, broadly bare on back, and decidedly longer than the middle toe.

Color.—Adult Male: Crown and back of head to about level of eyes, fine bluish-ash, enclosing a patch of chestnut; sides and back of neck, yellowish-white with a spot of dusky-ash on each side of neck; back and shoulders, cinnamon rufous, evenly barred with black; wing-coverts and secondaries, fine bluish-ash, the middle coverts and inner secondaries with subterminal wedge-shaped spots of black; primaries, pale dusky tipped with yellowish; tail, cinnamon rufous with a broad subterminal bar of black tipped with white; lores, throat, and sides of head, white with *a black streak below eye and another bordering the white area behind;* breast and upper abdomen, pale rusty; rest of under parts, whitish spotted on lower breast with small round blackish dots, on flanks with paler blackish wedge-shaped spots; under tail-coverts, pure white; outer tail-feathers, mostly white with black bars; bill, pale bluish-horn; cere, feet, and bare skin around eye, yellow; claws, black; iris, deep brown. Adult Female: Head and neck, as in adult male but usually with fine black shaft streaks on crown; back, shoulders, wing-coverts, secondaries, rump, and tail, cinnamon rufous; tail, banded with 5 or 6 imperfect black bars, the subterminal one broader, more distinct, feathers tipped with white; secondaries, dusky centrally, rufous showing as narrow edgings and tips, rest of upper parts including the coverts, barred with dusky; primaries, grayish dusky edged with yellowish-white; chest and lower parts in general pale yellowish-white with pale brownish longitudinal streaks; thigh feathers more whitish and unmarked; bill, feet, etc., as in adult male.

Nest and Eggs.—Eggs: Deposited in natural cavities of trees, deserted Woodpecker holes, in rock cavities, holes in banks, artificial nesting boxes, or in crannies of outbuildings, without nesting material; 4 or 5, ground color varying from creamy-white to reddish-buff, specked, spotted or clouded with shades of Indian red and brown, usually largest and more numerous or somrtimes wreathed at greater end; some eggs minutely dotted all over with dark brown, some so heavily splashed as to conceal the ground color.

Distribution.— North America east of the Rocky Mountains; breeds from the Upper Yukon, northwestern Mackenzie, southern Keewatin, and Newfoundland south to Texas and the eastern Gulf States (except Florida); winters from Kansas, Indiana, Ohio, and Massachusetts south through Mexico to Costa Rica.

The Sparrow Hawk is the smallest and the most sociable of our Hawks; it often nests in hollows of old orchard trees near farm houses or in dead trees alongside of roads.

"Windhover" is a very appropriate name, for they are much given to hovering over fields and pastures; they remain almost stationary for many minutes suspended in the air with quick-beating wings, and scan the ground below for grasshoppers and mice. Its familiar call of *killy-killy-killy-killy-killy-killy* attracts attention to its position.

Small birds are sometimes captured, but so rarely that I have not in many years' observations seen the deed performed, although I have found feathers of other birds in their nests.

Of all the Falcons, the Sparrow Hawk is the most beneficial. Of its food, Dr. A. K. Fisher says: "At times it attacks small birds and young chickens, but these irregularities are so infrequent that they are more than outweighed by its good services in destroying insects and mice. Grasshoppers, crickets, and other insects form its principal food during the warm months, while mice predominate during the rest of the year. Terrestrial caterpillars, beetles, and spiders also are eaten to a considerable extent. As might be expected, a large proportion of the birds captured are taken during the nesting season, the Hawks then having less time to procure their favorite food. It is at this time also that they commit depredations in poultry yards. During late fall and winter, meadow mice and house mice form a large part of their food, the former being taken in fields and meadows and the latter around corn stacks and about barns and outbuildings."

R. I. Brasher.

The Desert Sparrow Hawk (*Falco sparverius phalæna*) is larger than the stock form, with longer tail; its colors are paler, with more rufous and a larger crown patch. The female has the dark bars of upper parts narrower; those of tail more broken or incomplete. It inhabits western North America, breeds from British Columbia and southwestern Saskatchewan south to southern California, New Mexico, and western Texas east to Wyoming and western Nebraska, and winters from British Columbia and Colorado south to Guatemala.

Photo by S. A. Lottridge

SPARROW HAWK

The smallest and most sociable of our Hawks

The Little Sparrow Hawk (*Falco sparverius paulus*) has been honored with subspecific distinction because specimens smaller than the average have been captured in Florida, beyond the confines of which State it is requested not to roam!

CARACARAS

Order *Raptores;* suborder *Falcones;* family *Falconidæ;* subfamily *Polyborinæ*

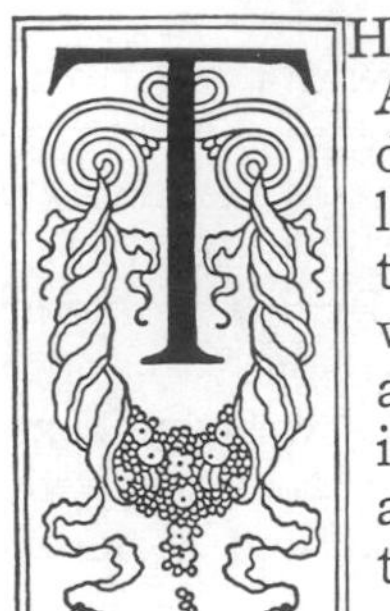

THE Caracaras are vulture-like Hawks found chiefly in Central and South America. They are diurnal birds of prey. The name is an attempt to reproduce in syllables the bird's raucous cry. All of the species have long, unfeathered legs and plumage in which black and white predominate. The feathers on the crown are elongated sufficiently to form a crest which can be raised at will, and there are well developed bristles on the cheeks. The Caracaras are essentially carrion feeders and for this reason they are valuable, especially in the cattle-raising regions in South America where they have become quite abundant. "Their flight is strong, rapid, and direct, and bears no resemblance to that of a Vulture." (Chapman).

The Caracaras are divided into three genera, *Polyborus*, *Milvago*, and *Ibycter*, of which the first-named comprises four species, including the Audubon Caracara. All of these birds build in trees, or on ledges, large nests composed of sticks and leaves, and lay two or three eggs thickly speckled and blotched.

AUDUBON'S CARACARA

Polyborus cheriway (*Jacquin*)

A. O. U. Number 362

General Description.— Length, 25 inches. Fore parts whitish, barred with black; rest of plumage black. Skin of face nearly bare, the chin and sides of head having blackish bristles; bill, long, compressed, and slightly hooked; tarsus, nearly twice as long as middle toe without claw.

Color.— Adults: Throat, neck all around, front part of back, and breast, dull whitish barred with black; upper and under tail-coverts, white; tail dull white with numerous bars of blackish, the terminal one being much broader than the others; crown and rest of plumage, blackish; bill, dull horn; cere, red or yellow; feet, yellow; claws, black; iris, brown. Young: Plumage more brown, darker markings of body, longitudinal streaks, not transverse bars; tail, as in adult.

Nest and Eggs.— Nest: Built in trees, bushes, sometimes in cliffs; large bulky structures composed of branches lined with small sticks, roots, and grasses, and with a slight depression. Eggs: 2 or 3, light chestnut to dark reddish or umber-brown, speckled, blotched, or clouded with yellowish or rufous-brown, burnt-umber, or purple madder, sometimes distributed over entire egg; in others more numerous at one end.

Distribution.— Northern Lower California, Arizona, Texas, and Florida south to Guiana and Ecuador; accidental in Ontario.

Photo by O. E. Baynard Courtesy of Nat. Asso. Aud. Soc.

AUDUBON'S CARACARA, ONE DAY OLD, AT EDGE OF NEST

Perched upright in the cactus or mesquite, with a strange grandfatherly appearance, or flying slowly with stiff outstretched neck, Audubon's Caracara strikes the observer with singular grotesqueness. An odd performance in which it indulges is to throw the head so far backward as to touch the shoulder feathers, emitting while in this position, its hoarse raucous call. Among themselves they are quarrelsome, stronger individuals attacking and sometimes severely injuring weaker ones. These fracases, though apparently starting in a spirit of play, often end in a general fight.

Though usually carrion feeders, in some maritime locations the Caracaras lay tribute on Pelicans as they come ashore, compelling them by attacks from above to disgorge the fish with which their pouches are filled.

Drawing by R. I. Brasher

AUDUBON'S CARACARA (½ nat. size)

Perched upright in a cactus, it has a strange grandfatherly appearance

OSPREYS

Order *Raptores;* suborder *Falcones;* family *Pandionidæ*

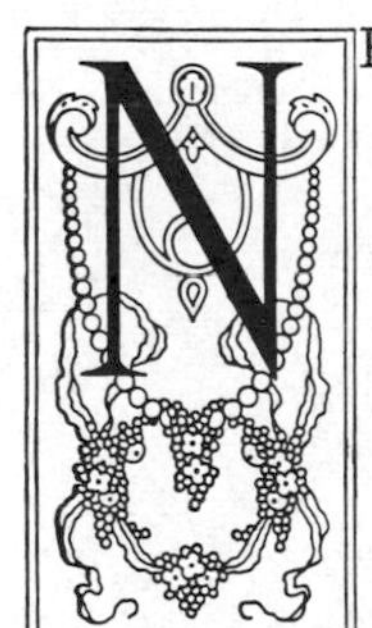

NEWTON, the English ornithologist, explained that "Ospray" or "Osprey" is "a word said to be corrupted from 'ossifrage,' in Latin *Ossifraga,* bone-breaker. The Ossifraga of Pliny and some other classical writers seems to have been the Lammergeier; but the name, not inapplicable in that case, has been transferred — through a not uncommon but inexplicable confusion — to another bird which is no breaker of bones, save incidentally those of the fish it devours."

Three or four species of Ospreys have been described, but most ornithologists are now agreed that there is but a single true species, the European Osprey (*Pandion haliaetus*), of which the American Osprey and the Australian Fishing Eagle are subspecies. In all of these forms the feet are large, very strong, equipped with scale-like processes, and with the claws long, sharp, and powerful; the outer toe is reversible, like that of the Owls; the legs are long and closely feathered. The bill has no tooth, but is much hooked. The plumage is oily and overlapping, the quills and tail-feathers pointed and rigid. The wings are long and pointed, the tail short.

The Ospreys, or Fish Hawks, as they are usually called in America, have a very wide distribution, being found everywhere except in New Zealand, Iceland, Australia, the southern part of South America and, of course, the extreme Arctic and Antarctic regions. Their food consists solely of fish taken alive. Because of this characteristic they are never found far from water in which fish may be had. Since the Ospreys cannot dive, as do the Ducks, the fish they catch are of the varieties found in shallow water or near the surface.

The Ospreys are not more sociable than other raptorial birds; but an abundant food supply together with freedom from interference will often result in a number of them nesting near one another, and sometimes quite a large colony will develop. They return year after year to the same site and even rehabilitate the old nests by the addition of more material.

OSPREY

Pandion haliaëtus carolinensis (*Gmelin*)

A. O. U. Number 364 See Color Plate 43

Other Names.— American Osprey; Fish Hawk; Fishing Eagle.

General Description.— Length, 2 feet; spread of wings, 4½ to 5½ feet. Upper parts, dark brown; head and under parts, white.

Color.— ADULTS: Head, neck, and *entire lower parts, pure white; a broad brownish-black stripe across upper side of head to nape;* head narrowly streaked with blackish coalescing toward center; nape, pale yellowish-white thinly streaked; breast with large heart-shaped spots of brown on each feather, the shaft black (these spots more numerous in female, fewer in male); rest of lower parts unmarked; *back, shoulders, wings, and tail, deep burnt-umber* with a faint purplish gloss; tail barred with seven even bands of dusky, inner webs and tip, white; the feathers of the upper parts are edged with paler; bill, bluish-black; cere and feet, grayish-blue; claws, black; iris, yellow or red. YOUNG: More marked with buffy and brownish on neck and under parts; upper parts, edged and notched with whitish; tail, more barred.

Nest and Eggs.— NEST: In a tree or on the ground; composed principally of coarse sticks, seaweed, and any old rubbish which is handy. EGGS: 2 to 4, usually 3, yellowish or dull white, spotted and blotched with Indian red and different shades of brown, sometimes so heavily at the large end as to obscure the ground color; some marked at small end, and others almost plain

Distribution.— North and South America; breeds from northwestern Alaska, northwestern Mackenzie, central Keewatin, southern Ungava, and Newfoundland south to Lower California, western Mexico, and the Gulf coast; winters from the southern United States through Lower California and Mexico to the West Indies and Central America; occurs also in South America south to Peru and Paraguay.

Drawing by R. I. Brasher

OSPREY (⅛ nat. size)

His feet are perfect fish traps

Photograph by G. W. Leek

OSPREY SETTLING ON ITS NEST

The Osprey's feet, with their rough, spiny projections, long and well-curved claws, are perfect fish traps: add powerful wings and tail, with plenty of muscular energy to operate them, and we have a combination which rarely misses its finny prey.

Its keenness of vision is of a very high order, and it is able to see a neutral colored fish from a height of many feet. Though most plunges begin within a hundred feet or so of the surface, dives of three hundred or more feet are not uncommon. Kingfishers seize their prey with their bill but the Osprey, like other raptorial birds, uses its feet only. The captive is always carried head forward. Some authorities suggest that this position makes wind resistance less, but it seems more reasonable to me to suppose that placing the talons one in front and one behind is done the better to control the spasmodic jerks of the expiring fish.

Occasionally the Osprey mistakes the size of its quarry, and I saw one on the St. Lucie River in Florida dragged under by a large intended victim. The Osprey finally succeeded in getting its claws free, but was so nearly drowned that it lay on the yacht's deck for ten minutes before recovering sufficiently to fly.

Where protected — and I am glad to say that is everywhere in the East — it often nests in colonies, one of the largest of which is on Gardiners Island, off the eastern end of Long Island. Its harmless character is so well understood by the Purple Grackles that frequently they build their own homes in the interstices of the large bulky nest which the Fish Hawk builds.

R. I. Brasher.

Photograph by H. T. Middleton

OSPREY

Courtesy of the New York State Museum

AMERICAN GOLDEN PLOVER *Charadrius dominicus* Müller
SPRING AUTUMN

BLACK-BELLIED PLOVER *Squatarola squatarola* (Linnaeus)
SPRING AUTUMN

KILLDEER PLOVER *Oxyechus vociferus* (Linnaeus)

SEMIPALMATED PLOVER *Aegialitis semipalmata* Bonaparte

All ⅖ nat. size

BOB-WHITE *Colinus virginianus virginianus* (Linnaeus)
MALE AND FEMALE
½ nat. size

Courtesy of the New York State Museum

CANADA SPRUCE PARTRIDGE *Canachites canadensis canace* (Linnaeus)

MALE AND FEMALE

⅔ nat. size

RUFFED GROUSE *Bonasa umbellus umbellus* (Linnaeus)

FEMALE MALE, STRUTTING

¼ nat. size

Courtesy of the New York State Museum

PASSENGER PIGEON *Ectopistes migratorius* (Linnaeus)

YOUNG MALE FEMALE

⅓ nat. size

MOURNING DOVE *Zenaidura maeroura carolinensis* (Linnaeus)

FEMALE YOUNG MALE

⅓ nat. size

APPEARANCE OF DIURNAL BIRDS OF PREY IN FLIGHT

TURKEY VULTURE
BALD EAGLE
RED-TAILED HAWK
DUCK HAWK
ROUGH-LEGGED HAWK
COOPER'S HAWK
OSPREY
MARSH HAWK—FEMALE

COOPER'S HAWK
Accipiter cooperi (Bonaparte)
IMMATURE FEMALE

All ⅓ nat. size

SHARP-SHINNED HAWK
Accipiter velox (Wilson)
ADULT MALE

GOSHAWK
Astur atricapillus atricapillus (Wilson)
IMMATURE ½ nat. size ADULT

RED-TAILED HAWK *Buteo borealis borealis* (Gmelin)
ADULT
COOPER'S HAWK *Accipiter cooperi* (Bonaparte)
ADULT FEMALE
¼ nat. size

Courtesy of the New York State Museum

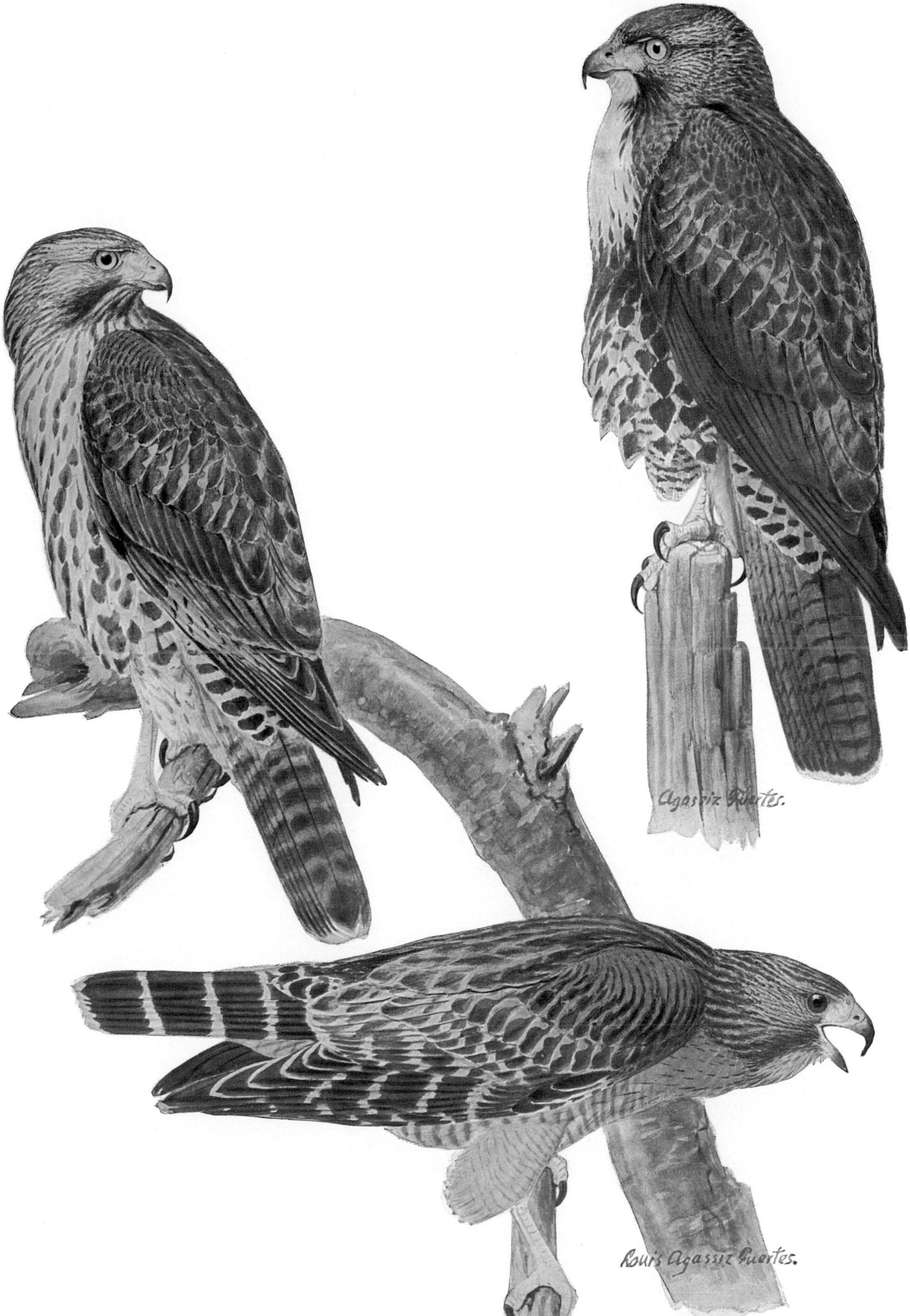
Agassiz Fuertes.
Louis Agassiz Fuertes.

RED-SHOULDERED HAWK
Buteo lineatus lineatus (Gmelin)
IMMATURE ADULT

RED-TAILED HAWK
Buteo borealis borealis (Gmelin)
IMMATURE

All ⅓ nat. size

BROAD-WINGED HAWK *Buteo platypterus* (Viellot)
ADULT IMMATURE

ROUGH-LEGGED HAWK
Archibuteo lagopus sancti-johannis (Gmelin)
Black phase

MARSH HAWK *Circus hudsonius* (Linnaeus)
MALE

All ¼ nat. size

GOLDEN EAGLE *Aquila chrysaëtos* (Linnaeus)
⅙ nat. size

BALD EAGLE *Haliaeetus leucocephalus leucocephalus* (Linnaeus)
IMMATURE
⅙ nat. size

GYRFALCON
Falco rusticolus gyrfalco Linnaeus

WHITE GYRFALCON
Falco islandus Brünnich

BLACK GYRFALCON. *Falco rusticolus obsoletus* Gmelin

All ¼ nat. size

DUCK HAWK *Falco peregrinus anatum* Bonaparte

FIRST YEAR MALE — ADULT FEMALE — CHICKS AND EGG

All ⅓ nat. size

MALE SPARROW HAWK *Falco sparverius sparverius* Linnaeus

FEMALE

ADULT PIGEON HAWK *Falco columbarius columbarius* Linnaeus IMMATURE

All ½ nat. size

BARN OWL
Aluco pratincola (Bonaparte)

LONG-EARED OWL
Asio wilsonianus (Lesson)

⅓ nat. size

Courtesy of the New York State Museum

GREAT GRAY OWL *Scotiaptex nebulosa nebulosa* (J. R. Forster)

SNOWY OWL *Nyctea nyctea* (Linnaeus)

BARRED OWL *Strix varia varia* Barton

All ⅓ nat. size

OWLS

Order *Raptores;* suborder *Striges;* families *Aluconidæ* and *Strigidæ*

OWLS are nocturnal birds of prey and in the field of usefulness are the complement of the Hawks—the Hawks working by day and the Owls by night. Like the other raptorial birds Owls capture their prey with their feet. If the victim is not too large, it is swallowed entire and the hair and bones disgorged afterward in the form of pellets. It is the examinations of these pellets which have proved beyond a doubt that the Owls should be classified among the beneficial birds.

The eyes of Owls are directed forward so that both look in the same direction and to look to the side they are obliged to turn the head; the eyes are surrounded by radiating systems of feathers called facial disks, which are bounded, except directly in front, by a line or rim of small, narrow, stiff, compactly webbed, differently formed, and somewhat recurved feathers. For scientific purposes the Owls are divided into two families, the *Aluconidæ*, or Barn Owls, and the *Strigidæ*, which includes the Horned or Eared Owls, the Barred Owls, the Screech Owls, and all the other Owls.

Speaking generally, the Barn Owls have the face heart-shaped, with the lower apex very prominent. The various species have a complete and conspicuous facial ruff, relatively small eyes, elongated bill, long legs with feathering on the posterior part reversed (pointed inward), inner toe as long as the middle toe, the head without ear-tufts. The eyes are very small (beadlike), surrounded by a very conspicuous line of differently formed feathers. The wing is very long; the tail less than half as long as the wing and more or less distinctly notched. The claws are very long and sharp. The plumage coloration is prevailing white, buff, or tawny, and is usually more or less freckled or otherwise variegated (at least on the upper parts) with brown or dusky. The range of the genus is nearly cosmopolitan, the colder regions excepted. Nearly 30 forms are recognized, of which about one-third are American, but only one of which is found in the United States.

Unlike the Barn Owls, the *Strigidæ* have the face more or less circular, or at least not pointed below, while the leg-feathers (if present) are not reversed or recurved, but are pointed downward. The head is frequently surmounted by a pair of more or less distinct, often very conspicuous, ear- or horn-like tufts of feathers, and the eyes are, as a rule, large and prominent; but there are numerous genera in which these features are not present.

As in the Barn Owls, the *Strigidæ* have the plumage remarkably full, soft, and downy, and in coloration more or less protective. The sexes are invariably colored essentially alike. Frequently the plumage is dichromatic, different individuals of the same species, wholly independent of sex or age, differing remarkably in coloration, the extreme phases being represented by birds of a gray or brownish gray color on the one hand and others of a more or less cinnamon-rufous or brick-red hue, individuals of intermediate coloration being usually much less numerous than those representing the extremes. These distinct phases are constant from first plumage to old age, and are frequently to be found in one brood of young.

The *Strigidæ* are more nearly cosmopolitan than the Barn Owls, being absent only from Polynesia, representatives of the family existing in Madagascar, New Zealand, the Hawaiian Islands and the Arctic districts. Thirty recent genera and nearly three hundred species and subspecies are recognized, of which eighteen genera and about one hundred species (including subspecies) are American.

Owls generally place their nests in holes in trees or banks, or they may use the deserted nest of a Hawk or a Crow. The eggs are from three to five in number and are invariably pure white. Young Owls are thickly covered with white down.

BARN OWL

Aluco pratincola (*Bonaparte*)

A. O. U. Number 365 See Color Plate 53

Other Names.— Monkey-faced Owl; Golden Owl; White Owl; Monkey Owl; American Barn Owl.

General Description.— Length, 18 inches; spread of wings, 44 inches. Plumage, whitish-tawny, speckled with black.

Color.— Average Plumage: Ground color of upper parts, bright *ochraceous-buff* but this overlaid with a delicate *mottling of dusky and grayish-white,* forming a mottled grayish effect, each feather, except of wings and tail, with a streak of black inclosing a small heart-shaped, roundish, or drop-shaped (rarely linear) subterminal spot of white; wings with the darker mottlings condensed into indistinct transverse bands, which are about 4 in number on secondaries and 5 on primaries; tail, varying from ochraceous-buff to white, mottled with dusky, and crossed by about five bands of mottled dusky; *face, white,* tinged with purplish-brown, and with an area of dark red-brown in front of and narrowly surrounding eye; facial circle or rim, soft ochraceous-buff above (down to ears), deeper ochraceous-buff below, where feathers of rear border are tipped with dark brown; *under parts, white,* but this suffused or overlaid by ochraceous-buff and with numerous small but distinct spots or dots of black; bill, dull yellowish; iris, dark brown. Dark Extreme: Under parts, wholly ochraceous-buff, speckled with black; upper parts as in average plumage or somewhat darker; face more strongly tinged with purplish-brown. Light Extreme: Face (except spot below eye) and entire under parts, pure white, the latter sometimes immaculate; facial rim, white with tips of feathers (in part, at least) orange-buff; wing and tail, sometimes uniformly mottled or the latter sometimes white with bands of mottled dusky.

Nest and Eggs.—Nest: Almost anywhere—in church towers, outbuildings, hollow trees, holes in steep banks, deserted nests, or even in ground burrows; constructed of a few sticks, hay, straw, bones, or other refuse. Eggs: 3 to 11, usually 5 to 7, dull white, unspotted.

Distribution.— Greater part of United States and Mexico; breeding north to Long Island, New Jersey, Pennsylvania, western New York, Ohio, northern Indiana, northern Illinois, southern Nebraska, Colorado, and upper Sacramento valley, northern California, and occurring, more or less irregularly, farther northward to Massachusetts, Vermont, Ontario, Michigan, Wisconsin, Minnesota, Oregon, and southern British Columbia; southward over whole of Mexico, whole of Lower California, and eastern Central America to eastern Nicaragua, at least in winter.

Courtesy of S. A. Lottridge

YOUNG BARN OWLS

Some years ago, I had a good opportunity to make an intimate study of a Barn Owl family. They had a nest in the gable end of my neighbor's barn and occupied it for a number of years. This year they had three young, and at three weeks old they were the funniest, fuzziest, "monkey-faced" little creatures I had ever seen. They blinked, snapped their bills, and hissed like a box full of snakes. They bobbed and screwed around in more funny attitudes than any contortionist you ever saw.

We crept out one night and hid in a brush heap by the barn. Before long the scratching and soft hissing of the young Owls told us that their breakfast time had come. The curtain of the night had fallen. The day creatures were at rest. Suddenly a shadow flared across the dim-lit sky. The young Owls in some way knew of the approach of food, for there was a sudden outburst in the nest box like the whistle of escaping steam. Again and again the shadow came and went. Then I crept into the barn, felt my way up and edged along the rafters to the old box. As soon as food was brought, I lit a match and saw one of the half-grown young tearing the head from the body of a young gopher.

Barn Owls are always hungry. They will eat their own weight in food every night, and more, if they can get it. To supply such ravenous children, their parents ransack the gardens, fields and orchards industriously night after night and catch as many mice, gophers, and other ground creatures as a dozen cats. For this reason, it would be difficult to find birds that are more useful about any farming community. Yet many times people kill these Owls through ignorance of their value or from idle curiosity.

A case is on record where a half-grown Barn Owl was given all the mice it could eat. It swallowed eight, one after another and the ninth followed all but the tail, which for a long time hung out of the bird's mouth. In three hours, this same bird was ready for a second meal and swallowed four more mice.

The Owl is not particular when he eats. He put his feet on his game to hold it, then tears it to pieces with his hooked beak, swallowing the entire animal, meat, bones, fur, and all. In the stomach, the nutritious portions are absorbed and the indigestible matter is formed into round pellets and disgorged. About the Owl's roost or near its home, one may often find these pellets in great numbers. A scientist, by examining these, can tell exactly what the bird has been eating. He can also get a careful estimate of the size and number of the Owl's meals.

The best known record we have concerning the food of the Barn Owl is that which was made from a pair that occupied one of the towers of the Smithsonian Institution at Washington, D. C. Dr. A. K. Fisher, who is our greatest authority on the food of Hawks and Owls, examined two hundred pellets from this pair of birds. These showed a total of 454 skulls. There were 225 meadow mice, 2 pine mice, 179 house mice, 20 rats, 6 jumping mice, 20 shrews, 1 star-nosed mole and 1 Vesper Sparrow.

Photo by S. A. Lottridge

BARN OWL

It is always hungry and will eat its own weight in food every night

WILLIAM L. FINLEY.

LONG-EARED OWL

Asio wilsonianus (*Lesson*)

A. O. U. Number 366 See Color Plate 53

Other Names.— American Long-eared Owl; Cat Owl; Lesser Horned Owl.

General Description.— Length, 16 inches; spread of wings, 40 inches. Color above, a mottling of blackish-brown and grayish-white; below, white and buff, barred and spotted with brown. Ear-tufts conspicuous.

Color.— Adults: Above, mottled with blackish-brown and grayish-white, the former predominating, especially on back; shoulders with a few irregular, indistinct spots of white on outer webs; primary coverts, dusky with transverse series of mottled grayish spots, these becoming more buffy basally; ground color of primaries, grayish, especially on inner quills, passing into buffy basally (extensively on outer quills), the grayish portion finely mottled, transversely, with dusky, and crossed by about seven transverse series of square blackish-brown spots, those in front about as wide as the buffy or mottled grayish interspaces; secondaries crossed by about nine or ten bands of dusky; general color of wing-coverts like back, but growing paler toward edge of wing, their tips also pale (sometimes nearly white); tail banded like secondaries; ear-tufts with center portion (broadly) plain black, the edges of the feathers (broadly) buff, passing into white (usually broken by blackish lines or mottling) terminally; forehead and behind ears minutely speckled with blackish and white; "eyebrows" and lores, grayish-white, the eyes surrounded by blackish, this widest in front, above, and below; face, plain dull ochraceous; facial disk, black becoming broken into a variegated collar across throat; chin and upper throat, plain white; general color of under parts, buff, the exposed surface of the feathers, however, white; breast with large longitudinal center blotches of clear sooty-brown; sides and flanks with center stripes of sooty-brown crossed by as broad, or broader, transverse bars of the same; abdomen, leg plumes, and legs, plain buff, passing into nearly white on lower leg and on toes, the thigh-plumes usually with a few arrowhead spots of brownish; under tail-coverts with center narrow stripes or streaks of dusky, these Y-shaped forward; under wing-coverts, plain ochraceous, the under primary coverts blackish-brown, forming a conspciuous spot; bill, dull black; iris, bright lemon-yellow. Young: Wing- and tail-feathers (if developed) as in adults; other portions broadly barred with blackish-brown and grayish-white, the latter predominating anteriorly; "eyebrows" and loral bristles, black; legs, white.

Photograph by H. T. Middleton

LONG-EARED OWL

With ear-tufts elevated

Photo by R. W. Shufeldt

LONG-EARED OWL

An industrious mouser, doing an enormous amount of good

Nest and Eggs.— Nest: Built in dense growth of coniferous trees, from 10 to 40 feet up, a carelessly made affair of sticks and lined with grass, old leaves, or feathers; frequently an old Crow's, Hawk's or squirrel's nest is appropriated and repaired; more rarely it is placed on the ground. Eggs: 3 to 7, usually 4 or 5, white.

Distribution.— Temperate North America; north to Newfoundland, southern Quebec, northwestern Ontario, southern Keewatin, southern Mackenzie, British Columbia, and coast of southern Alaska; breeding southward to Virginia, Arkansas, northern Texas, southern California, etc.; winters over greater part of its range and southward to central Mexico.

Most Owls whose habits are essentially nocturnal pass the daylight hours in hollow trees or in other cavities or recesses in which little or no light can enter. The Long-eared species, however, though it does all of its hunting at night usually spends the day perched in thick foliage of evergreen or other densely leaved trees. When discovered in such a hiding place its characteristic performance is to raise itself to its full height, compress its feathers close to its body and elevate its ear-tufts, in which protective and rather comical pose, it looks more like a stub, or "a piece of weatherbeaten bark than a bird."

Unlike that of the Great Horned Owl and other members of the Owl family, this bird's flight is rather wavering and uncertain, suggesting that of a Whip-poor-will; but like theirs it is entirely noiseless, and silence is, of course, more effective than mere speed with a great rushing of wings would be to a bird of its habits. It has several characteristic cries, one of which resembles the yapping of small dogs, and another the mewing of kittens, while at close quarters with an intruder it is likely to snap its beak and hiss with a great show of ferocity. This Owl is not infrequently seen in considerable flocks.

The Long-eared Owl is an industrious mouser, and molests comparatively few birds. Dr. Fisher examined 107 stomachs of this Owl, of which fifteen were empty. Of the ninety-two remaining, eighty-six, or over 93 per cent., contained remains of small mammals. As the bird

Photo by H. K. Job Courtesy of Outing Pub. Co.

YOUNG LONG-EARED OWLS

is common all over the United States, it does an enormous amount of good. Like the Sparrow Hawk, this Owl is easily destroyed, and so is one of the greatest sufferers when bounties are paid for the destruction of birds of prey.

SHORT-EARED OWL

Asio flammeus (*Pontoppidan*)

A. O. U. Number 367 See Color Plate 56

Other Names.— Marsh Owl; Swamp Owl; Prairie Owl.

General Description.— Length, 14 inches; spread of wings, 42 inches. Color, a variegation of yellowish-white and dark brown. Ear-tufts, rudimentary and inconspicuous.

Color.— Adults: General color of head, neck, back, shoulders, rump, and under parts, light ochraceous to buffy-white (the individual variation being very great), each feather, except on rump, with a center stripe of dark brown or blackish-brown, the stripes broadest on shoulders, back of head, hindneck, back, and chest with the ochraceous (or buffy) and brown about equal in extent, but on the under parts the brown stripes becoming gradually narrower behind, until on abdomen and sides they form narrow lines; flanks, legs, anal region, and under tail-coverts, immaculate, the last nearly (sometimes quite) pure white, the legs more deeply buffy or ochraceous; rump more reddish-buffy or ochraceous, with indistinct crescentic markings of brown; wing-coverts coarsely variegated with irregular markings of dusky-brown and ochraceous or buffy, the latter in form of indentations or confluent spots along edges of feathers, broadest on outer webs; secondaries, dusky-brown crossed by about five bands of ochraceous or buffy, the last one terminal; primaries, ochraceous or buff on inner two-thirds (more or less), the end portion dusky-brown, tipped (broadly) with buffy, this becoming indistinct or obsolete on longest quills, the dusky-brown continued in three to five irregularly transverse series of square spots on outer webs, leaving, however, a large basal area of plain ochraceous or buffy, which sometimes passes into white in front; primary coverts, plain blackish-brown, with one or two indistinct transverse series of ochraceous spots on middle portion; tail, ochraceous or buff passing into white, crossed by about five bands of blackish-brown, about equal in width to the ochraceous or buffy interspaces on middle feathers but becoming narrower on outer ones, the ochraceous or buffy interspace on the former enclosing central transverse spots of dusky, the terminal ochraceous or buffy band broadest on all the feathers; "eyebrows," lores, chin, and throat, dull white, the loral bristles with black shafts; face, dingy ochraceous-white or dull buffy-white, the eyes broadly encircled with black; facial rim minutely speckled with pale ochraceous or buffy and blackish, except immediately behind ear, where uniform blackish; under wing-coverts, immaculate pale buff to white, the terminal half of under primary coverts, plain blackish-brown (forming a conspicuous spot); under surface of primaries for greater part, immaculate buffy-white, but terminal portion, and preceding this, one or two very broad bands, dusky; bill, blackish; iris, bright lemon-yellow. YOUNG: Above, dark sooty-brown, the feathers broadly tipped with ochraecous-buff; face, uniform brownish-black; under parts, plain pale dull ochraceous or buffy, tinged forward with smoky-grayish.

Nest and Eggs.— NEST: Placed on the ground of marshy levels, beneath bushes, grass clumps, or in a slight depression; a carelessly constructed affair of a few sticks and grass, lined with finer grass and some feathers of the parent bird. EGGS: 4 to 7, white, unspotted.

Distribution.— The whole of continental North and South America, from coast of Arctic Ocean to Patagonia, also Tierra del Fuego, Falkland Islands, and Juan Fernandez and Mas-a-tierra islands, off Chile; breeding, locally, nearly throughout its range except in more southern portions of eastern United States, where not ascertained to breed south of Massachusetts, northern Ohio, northern Indiana, Missouri, Kansas, and Colorado; winters practically throughout United States and in Cuba; also found throughout Europe and northern Asia and other portions of the eastern hemisphere except Australia.

Marshes and bogs are the preferred habitat of this small and rather stupid Owl, the Short-eared, and the bird is seldom seen perched in a tree. It is also un-Owl-like in that in cloudy or foggy weather it may do considerable hunting during the day. Seen under such conditions, skimming along near the ground, the bird's long wings make it appear much larger than it is.

Another of this Owl's peculiarities is its gregarious instinct, as manifested in winter and during the migration period. Then it is likely to gather in colonies or flocks of a hundred or more individuals, some of which probably have come from the bird's northern range.

Though this Owl's ear-tufts are smaller than are those of the Long-eared species, the bird's

Photograph by H. K. Job

NEST OF SHORT-EARED OWL

Nine young, all sizes, and feathers and remains of prey

ear openings are much larger, in fact almost cavernous in their proportions. This remarkable development is due to the bird's dependence upon its sense of hearing. For in the long grass the movements of much of its prey cannot be seen, and must therefore be heard; and close observation of the Owl will show that much of its hunting is done with its ears rather than eyes.

Of the economic value of this Owl, Dr. A. K. Fisher reports: "Fully 75 per cent. of its food consists of mice; as many as six of these mammals have been found in one stomach. In the West it probably feeds also on the small ground squirrels. Among birds, the Sparrows inhabiting the meadows and prairies are most often taken. In an interesting article by Peter Adair, in the 'Annals' of Scottish Natural History for October, 1893, on the disappearance of the short-tailed vole that caused the vole plague in Scotland in 1890–1892, the statement is made that farmers and shepherds attribute its disappearance largely to its natural enemies, stress being laid on the services of the Owl, Kestrel, Rook, and Black-headed Gull among birds and the stoat and weasel among mammals. These men are also of the opinion that this vole plague resulted from the destruction of birds of prey. When the plague first began the Short-eared Owl was hardly known in the district, but, swarming thither, it bred till it was so numerous that it became an important factor in reducing the number of voles."

BARRED OWL

Strix varia varia *Barton*

A. O. U. Number 368 See Color Plate 54

Other Names.— Hoot Owl; Rain Owl; Wood Owl; Round-headed Owl; Swamp Owl.

General Description.— Length, 20 inches; spread of wings, 44 inches. Plumage, brown, barred with whitish. No ear-tufts or horns.

Color.— ADULTS: Fore and upper parts, *broadly and regularly barred with pale buff and deep brown,* the latter color always terminal, the brown bars rather broader than the paler ones on upper parts, but on the neck and chest rather narrower; breast also barred with brown and whitish, but the brown bars connected by a center streak, thus separating the whitish into pairs of spots on opposite webs; each feather of abdomen, sides, and flanks with a broad center longitudinal stripe of darker brown, the under tail-coverts with similar but rather narrower stripes; anal region immaculate buffy or buffy-white; legs with numerous but rather faint transverse spots or bars of brown; general color of wings and tail, brown; middle and greater coverts with roundish transverse spots of white on outer webs, the lesser coverts, plain deep brown; secondaries, crossed by about six bands of pale grayish-brown passing into paler on edges, the terminal band passing into whitish on margin; primary coverts with four bands of darker buffy-brown or ochraceous-brown; primaries with transverse series of square spots of pale brown on outer webs (growing deeper brown on inner quills), the last terminal (there are about eight spots on longest primary); tail, crossed by six or seven sharply defined bands of pale brown, the last terminal; face, grayish-white or pale brownish-gray, with concentric semicircular bars of brown; "eyebrows" and lores, dull grayish-white with black shafts; a narrow crescent of black against front angle of eye; facial circle a mixture of blackish-brown and buffy-white bars, the former predominating across foreneck where the brown forms disconnected transverse spots; *bill, dull buff-yellowish; iris, very dark brown or brownish-black,* the pupil appearing blue by contrast; naked portion of toes, dull yellowish or yellowish-gray, the large scales, more decidedly yellow, the soles, deep yellow; claws, dark horn color, becoming blackish terminally. YOUNG: Head, neck, and entire under parts broadly barred with rather light brown and pale buffy and whitish, the brown and pale bars about equal in width; back, scapulars, and wing-coverts similarly barred but the bars broader, the brown ones of a deeper shape, and each feather broadly tipped with white; wing- and tail-feathers (if developed) as in adults.

Nest and Eggs.— NEST: Almost always in a hollow tree, on the old chips, but sometimes in a deserted Crow's or Hawk's nest. EGGS: 2 to 4, usually 3, white, unspotted.

Distribution.—Middle eastern North America; breeds north to Newfoundland, southern Quebec, northern Ontario, southern Keewatin, Manitoba, and Saskatchewan; west to eastern Montana, eastern Wyoming, and eastern Colorado; south to Virginia, western North Carolina, northwestern South Carolina, northern Georgia, Tennessee, Kentucky, southern Illinois, Missouri, and northern Arkansas, and occasionally to Louisiana.

The Barred Owl is a bird of the deep solitudes. Where in the low grounds along the rivers or on lake-shores nature has built her densest growth of forest trees, or where, in forbidding swamps, trees and vines struggle for the mastery in one interminable jumble, there you will find the Barred Owl and his mate. If it be in the spring you may hear his big voice booming through the solitudes. For when night has fallen the big Swamp Owl must be up and doing. *Whoo, whoo, whoo, who, who, to-hoo-ha!* he shouts, emphasis and great stress being laid on the last two syllables as though he would question your presence, and challenge your right to invade his domain. The volume and variety of these *who, who* call notes is one of the wonders of the wilderness and when two or three males get to discussing affairs together the animation they inject into the melody is quite alarming to a timid person not accustomed to the sounds. Of all the Owls, these bar-breasted fellows are pre-eminently the most proficient hooters.

This owl-music is usually heard mainly in the fore part of the night. Long before midnight it dies down, only to spring up again before sunrise. During the day they seldom call except in rainy or cloudy weather. On moonlight nights their serenade is at times continuous. They seem to possess a certain amount of curiosity, and will often respond to a human imitation of their notes even though it be but rudely rendered. In Florida on one occasion five of these birds came close about my camp one night and from the trees overhead looked down at the fire while every one in his own language hooted and called with an energy worthy of a better subject.

Drawing by R. I. Brasher

BARRED OWL (½ nat. size)

The most proficient hooter among the Owls

Barred Owls begin nesting as early as March or April. They appear never to build a nest of their own and not infrequently select a deserted nest of a Crow or a Hawk. More often they seek the hollow of some tree and here well up from the ground lay their white eggs. These usually number two in Florida, although farther north four are frequently found.

Photo by H. K. Job Courtesy of Outing Pub. Co.

YOUNG BARRED OWL

Mr. Job found it in a hollow tree

"The egg of a Barred Owl in the nest of a Red-shouldered Hawk has twice been found by Dr. Louis Bennet Bishop; both times in the same piece of woodland, which had been reduced from an extensive tract by wood-choppers, thus leaving few suitable nesting-places for large birds. One contained three eggs of the Hawk and one of the Barred Owl, with the Owl on the nest; the other contained two eggs of the Hawk and one of the Barred Owl, with the Red-shouldered Hawk on the nest. As the Hawk's eggs were in both instances further advanced in incubation this species was probably the original owner of both nests." (Reported in *Birds of Connecticut.*)

The food consists of such animal matter as they find it most easy to obtain. Dr. A. K. Fisher, who has studied much about the food of Owls, states that of a large number of stomachs examined fully 50 per cent. of those that had recently received food contained mice. These birds also eat frogs, lizards, crawfish, spiders, and various insects. Now and then one catches a domestic fowl that has had the temerity to leave the shelter of the hen-house and go to roost in some tree. Small birds are also taken at times. This is probably the reason why all wild birds have such a dislike for an Owl, and one of the many interesting sights of the woodland is to watch a band of Blue Jays leading a mob of feathered friends in an attack on a sleepy sun-dazed, and altogether discomfited Barred Owl.

T. Gilbert Pearson.

The Florida, or Allen's, Barred Owl (*Strix varia alleni*) is limited to the coast strip of the South Atlantic and Gulf States from South Carolina to Florida and Texas. Its coloration is similar to the type species but its toes are wholly naked except a strip on the outer side of the middle toe.

The Texas Barred Owl (*Strix varia albogilva*) is very much more limited in its geographical distribution than the Florida; it is found only in the mesquite area of middle southern Texas. Like the Florida it has the toes without feathers, but its general color is much paler — the upper parts more conspicuously barred, the bars nearly pure white; the tail-bands, broader, whiter, and more sharply defined; stripes on under parts narrower and a lighter brown and the buff, decidedly paler; legs much paler buffy or buffy-white and much less distinctly mottled, sometimes immaculate; the bill and feet are much larger.

The Spotted Owl (*Strix occidentalis occidentalis*) and its variant the Northern Spotted Owl (*Strix occidentalis caurina*) are the western representatives of the Barred Owl — the Spotted Owl is often called the Western Barred Owl. They are smaller than the eastern Owl and have the bars of the upper parts and the stripes of the under parts replaced with spots. The colors of the Spotted Owl are much the same as those of the Barred Owl; but the Northern Spotted Owl is decidedly darker, the brown being darker in shade and more extended in area, and the amount of white being correspondingly reduced. The Spotted Owl occurs in the mountains of southern California, Arizona, New Mexico, and southern Colorado south to northern Lower California and northwestern Mexico. The Northern Spotted Owl is found in the Pacific coast district of British Columbia, Washington, Oregon, and northern California.

GREAT GRAY OWL

Scotiaptex nebulosa nebulosa (*J. R. Forster*)

A. O. U. Number 370 See Color Plate 54

Other Name.— Spectral Owl.

General Description.— Length, 30 inches; spread of wings, 60 inches. Plumage, grayish-brown, darker and waved above, lighter and streaked below.

Color.— Adults: General color of upper parts, dusky grayish-brown or sooty, broken by transverse mottlings (mostly on edges of feathers) of grayish-white, the uniformly sooty centers of the feathers producing an effect of irregular dusky stripes, most conspicuous on back and shoulders; the front parts with edges of feathers more regularly barred, the mottling more profuse on rump and upper tail-coverts, producing a more grayish appearance; outer webs of wing-coverts variegated by whitish mottlings; primary coverts with very indistinct bands of paler brown; secondaries crossed by about nine bands (one terminal, three concealed by greater coverts) of pale grayish-brown, fading into paler (sometimes whitish) on edges of outer webs; primaries crossed by nine transverse series of square spots of mottled pale brownish-gray, on outer webs, those nearer the tips indistinct, except the terminal crescentic bar; inner secondaries and middle tail-feathers with coarse mottling or marbling of dusky-brown or sooty and grayish-white, the markings usually with a tendency to form irregular, broken bars; rest of tail, dusky crossed by about nine paler bands, these merely marked off by a narrow line or edging of whitish or pale brownish-gray inclosing a grayish-brown, sometimes slightly mottled, space, though toward base of the tail-feathers the mottling is more confused and the bands confused or broken up; ground color of under parts, grayish-white, each feather of neck, chest, breast, and abdomen with a broad, irregularly saw-toothed center stripe of dusky-brown or sooty; sides, flanks, anal region, and under tail-coverts, narrowly banded or barred with sooty-brown and grayish-white, the legs with narrower, more irregular bars; "eyebrows," lores and chin, grayish-white, with a dusky space immediately in front of eye; face, grayish-white with distinct concentric semicircular bars of dusky-brown; facial circle, dark brown passing into white on foreneck, where interrupted by a spot of brownish-black on throat; *bill, light dull yellow*; *iris, lemon-yellow.* DOWNY YOUNG: Buffy-white, the down on the hindneck, back, shoulders, and wings, dark sooty-brown basally, the tips pale dull buff or pale brownish-buffy.

Nest and Eggs.— NEST: In conifers, usually at a good height; constructed of sticks, twigs, and moss and warmly lined with feathers. EGGS: 2 to 4, white and small for size of the bird.

Distribution.— Northern North America; breeding from tree limit in Alaska and northwestern Mackenzie southward to northern British Columbia, central Alberta, northwestern Idaho, northern Manitoba, and northern Ontario; in winter migrating southward to Rhode Island, Connecticut, New Jersey, Pennsylvania, northern Ohio, northern Illinois, Minnesota, North Dakota, Wyoming, Colorado, Oregon, and northern California.

The Great Gray Owl has received from the scientists a name with a very appropriate and poetical interpretation; *scotiaptex* is from two Greek words which mean "the Eagle-Owl of darkness"; *nebulosa* is Latin and means "cloudy" or "gray."

This big and powerful Owl is forced to do much of its hunting in daylight for the very good reason that in a large area of its natural range there is no true night. Occasionally it strays into the United States. Elon H. Eaton states that "in the Adirondacks [N. Y.] it is probably more common as a winter visitor than is supposed, but throughout the remainder of the State is only of rare and irregular occurrence." Its decided preference, however, is evidently for the thick forest of the northland, "in which," Dr. Fisher says, "it dwells doubtless to the very limit of the trees."

According to Dr. William Healey Dall it is a stupid bird and may sometimes be caught in the hands. Its diet consists chiefly of small mammals (hares, meadow mice, and squirrels) and Ptarmigan and smaller birds. Its cry resembles that of the Screech Owl.

The Great Gray Owl exceeds the Great Horned Owl in measurements, but its weight is seldom more than that of the Barred Owl. Its plumage is unusually thick and fluffy and makes the bird appear a great deal heavier than it really is.

The Lapp Owl (*Scotiaptex nebulosa lapponica*) is an Old World variant of the Great Gray Owl which occasionally strays into Alaska. It is lighter colored than the Great Gray. It is considered very rare even within its natural range in the upper portions of forest belt of the Arctic regions of Europe and Asia.

RICHARDSON'S OWL

Cryptoglaux funerea richardsoni (*Bonaparte*)

A. O. U. Number 371 See Color Plate 55

Other Names.— American Sparrow Owl; Sparrow Owl; Arctic Saw-whet Owl.

General Description.— Length, 11 inches; spread of wings, 24 inches. Color above, brown, spotted with white; below, white, spotted with dark.

Color.— ADULTS: General color of upper parts, deep brown; crown, thickly spotted with white, the spots of roundish form; hindneck with very large, partly concealed, irregularly heart-shaped or variously formed spots of white; shoulders with large, partly concealed spots of white, the exterior ones with outer webs mostly white, margined terminally with brown; wing-coverts near edge of wing and some of the greater coverts with large roundish spots of white; rear half of secondaries crossed by two rows of small white spots (on edge of outer web); outer webs of primaries with roundish white spots, these growing smaller on innermost quills; tail crossed by four or five transverse rows of white spots, these not touching shaft on either web; face, including "eyebrows," grayish-white, the portion immediately above upper eyelid and in front of eye, dark sooty-brown or blackish, the sides of head intermixed with dusky; area above and behind ears uniform dark brown, the latter dotted on rear portion with white; sides of neck, mostly white, some of the feathers tipped with brown; chin, cheeks, and space below ears, immaculate white; across middle of throat, a broken band of mixed brown and white, the former predominating; ground color of under parts, white, slightly tinged, in places, with pale buff, *the breast* (except in center) *with large spots of brown, the sides and flanks, broadly striped with the same, the under tail-coverts with narrower stripes; legs, buff, usually clouded with brown;* under wing-coverts, buffy white, spotted or streaked with brown; under surface of wings, grayish-brown spotted with white, the spots larger and more roundish on secondaries and inner primaries, narrower and oblique on longer and outermost primaries; bill, horn color; iris, lemon-yellow. YOUNG: Wing- and tail-feathers (only) as in adults; rest of upper parts plain deep sooty-brown, the ear-region and part of the region back of the eye, uniform sooty-black; "eyebrows," lores, and corners of the mouth, dull white, the feathers with black shafts; under parts, plain vandyke-brown, intermixed on rear portions with dull buffy.

Nest and Eggs.— NEST: In hollow trees, or among branches of trees, or in bushes. EGGS: 2 to 7, white, unspotted.

Distribution.—Northern North America; breeding from the limit of tree growth in Alaska, Yukon, and Mackenzie south to northern British Columbia, northern Alberta, northern Manitoba, Nova Scotia, and Magdalen Islands; south in winter (regularly or casually) to Massachusetts, Rhode Island, Pennsylvania, southern Ontario, northern Illinois, Wisconsin, Minnesota, Colorado, northwestern Idaho, southern British Columbia, Washington, and eastern Oregon.

Richardson's Owl is not only nocturnal in its habits, but apparently is made almost completely blind by the sunlight, for, according to Dr. Fisher, "many specimens have been captured alive by persons walking up and taking them in their hands. On this account the Eskimos in Alaska have given it the name of 'the blind one.'"

Dr. Merriam describes the call of this Owl as a "low liquid note that resembles the sound produced by water dropping from a height;" hence the Montagnais Indians call it *phillip-pile-tshch,* which means "water-dripping owl." This name, indeed, has more than mere physical significance for the Indians who use it. Their legend is that once upon a time the largest Owl in the world, who was very proud of his great voice, tried to imitate the voice of the waterfall and to drown out its roar. But the impertinence of this ambition so angered the Great Spirit that he humiliated the huge bird by transforming him to a pygmy and changing his voice to the feeble notes which resemble the slow dripping of water.

GEORGE GLADDEN.

SAW-WHET OWL

Cryptoglaux acadica acadica (*Gmelin*)

A. O. U. Number 372 See Color Plate 55

Other Names.— Acadian Owl; White-fronted Owl; Kirtland's Owl; Sparrow Owl.

General Description.— Length, 8 inches; spread of wings, 18 inches. Color above, brown, spotted with white; below, white, spotted with dark.

Color.— ADULTS: General color of upper parts, nearly vandyke brown; the crown, narrowly streaked with white, the streaks sometimes restricted to forehead and sides of crown; lower hindneck with large, mostly triangular, concealed spots of white; shoulders with outer webs mostly white, margined terminally with brown; outer larger wing-coverts with a few spots of white; outer webs of outer primaries, spotted along edge with white; tail, crossed by two or three interrupted narrow bands of white and margined at tip with the same, the transverse spots forming the bands not touching shaft on either web; lores, space above and around eye, and chin, dull white, the eye margined above and in front with dusky, this in front of eye sometimes spreading over greater portion of lores; sides of head, dull buffy white to cinnamon-buff, broadly streaked with brown; across middle of throat and thence, on each side, to the ear ruff, a band of brown or chestnut-brown spots or streaks, this sometimes advancing in front middle portion, forming a patch on upper throat; ear-ruff, streaked with brown and white, the former predominating; rest of under parts, white tinged or suffused with pale buff, broadly striped or longitudinally spotted with chestnut-brown; under tail-coverts, immaculate white or, more rarely, with small and indistinct spots or streaks of pale brown; *legs, pale buff* to cinnamon-buff, the toes, paler (dull white or buffy white); under wing-coverts, buffy white to light cinnamon-buff, becoming white along edge of wing; under primary coverts white, broadly and abruptly tipped with grayish brown; under surface of wings, grayish-brown, the inner webs of secondaries and primaries with large spots of white, the outer primaries sometimes with a few small, narrow, oblique white spots, sometimes immaculate; bill, black; iris, lemon-yellow; naked portion of toes, pale dull yellowish, YOUNG: Wing- and tail-feathers (only) as in adults; "eyebrows" and forward portion of forehead, white, in strong contrast with the uniformly blackish-brown or (more rarely) lighter brown of ear region; rest of crown, together with upper parts (except wing- and tail-feathers), plain, deep brown; chin and sides of throat, dull white; throat, chest, and breast, plain brown (lighter than upper parts); rest of under parts, plain tawny-buff or cinnamon-buff.

Nest and Eggs.— NEST: In a hollow tree or stump, or in deserted Woodpecker and squirrel holes. EGGS: 3 to 6, white.

Distribution.—Northern North America; breeding from Nova Scotia and New Brunswick westward through Quebec, Ontario, Manitoba, and Alberta to British Columbia, and extreme southern Alaska, southward to Massachusetts, Pennsylvania, mountains of Maryland, northern Indiana, northern Illinois, southern Nebraska, Colorado, New Mexico, central Arizona, higher Sierra Nevada of California, and Oregon; in winter migrating irregularly (according to severity of the season) southward to Virginia, southern Ohio, southern California, etc., casually to North Carolina, South Carolina, Georgia and Louisiana; casual or accidental in Mexico and Guatemala.

If sound sleeping be a sign of a clear conscience, the Saw-whet Owl must have very few sins on its mind, for so deep is its slumber, huddled up in a spruce thicket or some other dense foliage, that frequently even clumsy man captures it alive. A more tragic result is the capture of the sleeper by its arch-enemy, the Barred Owl, or by some other carnivorous prowler on noiseless wing or padded foot. Doubtless the number of these captures would become large enough in time to make the bird rare indeed, but for the fact that it often selects as a bedchamber an old Woodpecker's nest, or a hollow tree, where it is comparatively safe from most of its enemies during the daylight hours; at night its senses are so alert that it can generally elude them.

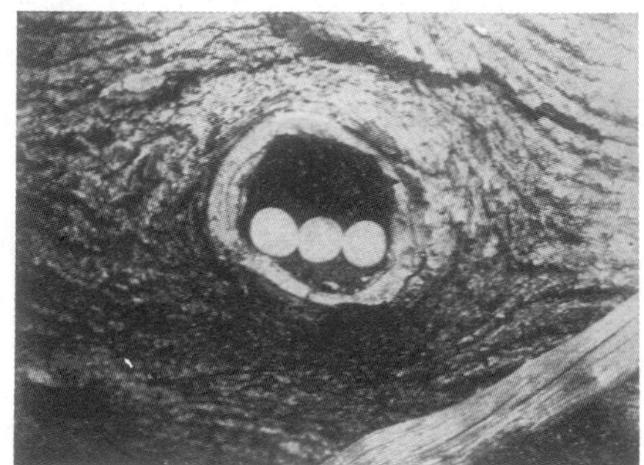

Courtesy of S. A. Lottridge

EGGS OF THE SAW-WHET OWL

Courtesy of S. A. Lottridge

SAW-WHET OWL

Photographed in a wood-house on the Orange Mountains, New Jersey

The Saw-whet is a non-migratory species, but is a good deal of a wanderer nevertheless, with the result that a locality which has known it well one year may see nothing whatever of it for several years thereafter. These wanderings are chiefly in search of food and occur especially during the fall and winter months. The bird's flight is singularly like that of the Woodcock; so much like it, in fact, that Dr. Fisher, who made a special and very careful study of American Owls, once shot a flying Saw-whet supposing it to be a Woodcock, and did not discover his mistake until his dog pointed the dead bird.

This Owl's cry, most frequently heard during March and April, has a peculiar scraping or rasping quality which suggests the sound made by filing a large-toothed saw; and hence its popular name.

A grayer variety of this owl, found on Queen Charlotte Island and in British Columbia south to the Puget Sound region, has been named the Northwestern Saw-whet Owl (*Cryptoglaux acadica scotæa*).

SCREECH OWL

Otus asio asio (*Linnæus*)

A. O. U. Number 373 See Color Plate 56

Other Names.— Little Horned Owl; Gray Owl; Red Owl; Little Dukelet; Mottled Owl; Shivering Owl.

General Description.— Length, 10 inches; spread of wings, 22 inches. Dichromatic; in gray phase, brownish-gray dappled; in red phase, pattern the same but color chestnut-red. Ear-tufts, large and conspicuous; four or five outer primaries notched or cut away on inner webs; toes scantily feathered toward their tips.

Color.— Gray Phase — Adults: Above, brownish-gray finely mottled and streaked with black or dusky, each feather with an irregular center streak, or chain of small spots connected along shaft, of the same; inner webs of ear tufts coarsely mottled with grayish-white, brownish-white, or pale buffy; shoulders, mostly dull white to light buff, tipped and narrowly margined with blackish; across upper nape an indication of a lighter colored band, in the form of irregular grayish-white or buffy spots, and across lower hindneck often another of buffy (mostly concealed) spots; secondaries, crossed by several narrow bands of paler buffy-grayish or pale dull buffy, each enclosing an irregular dusky bar or transverse spot of dusky, the general color, however, so broken by mottlings that the bands are sometimes indistinct; outer webs of outermost middle and greater coverts, with a large spot of white or pale buffy on or near the tip; outer webs of inner primaries, with square spots of lighter cinnamon, these becoming larger and paler on the three or four longest primaries; tail, crossed by seven or eight irregular, broken, narrow bands of lighter grayish-brown; face, dull grayish-white, with an area of deep, mottled or streaked, brown immediately above eye; "eyebrows," sides of head, and below eyes, narrowly barred with dusky, the feathers of lores with conspicuously black shafts and bristly tips; facial rim, mostly black, especially from behind ears to sides of throat; chin dull white; throat, dull white suffused with pale cinnamon-buff, narrowly barred and streaked with black; a small area of immaculate dull white in center of foreneck; center line of abdomen, together with anal region, immaculate buffy white; rest of under parts, white (sometimes faintly tinged with pale buff), broken by a rather dense narrow irregular barring of black and broad center streaks of the same, these connected or confluent with the bars, and on sides of breast enlarged into conspicuous spots, which are often edged with light rusty; frequently, on sides and flanks, pairs of the black bars enclose a space of pale brown; legs light cinnamon-buff, fading into dull whitish on lower and rear portions of tarsi, the thighs nearly immaculate but leg-plumes heavily barred with dark brown, at least on upper portion; longer under tail-coverts with rear portion barred or spotted with black and light brown; bill, pale dull greenish-blue; iris, bright lemon-yellow, the eyelids jet-black; toes and basal portion of claws, yellowish-gray, the terminal portion of claws, dusky. Young: Wings and tail as in adults; upper parts, deep grayish-brown indistinctly and rather broadly barred with dusky, many of the feathers tipped with dull white; under parts, dull white broadly barred with grayish dusky; no streaks on upper or under parts. Rufescent Phase — Adults: General pattern of coloration much as in the gray phase, but the gray or brown everywhere replaced by bright chestnut-rufous, the upper parts without the blackish; streaks narrower and linear; face, plain light cinnamon-rufous, the lores and over eye, whitish; under parts with pattern less intricate, the blackish or dusky bars of the gray phase replaced by transverse spots of cinnamon-rufous. Young: Similar to young of the gray phase, but the grayish or grayish-brown markings rufescent.

Nest and Eggs.— Nest: In a deserted Woodpecker hole, in natural hollow in a tree or stump, in outbuildings, or in boxes placed in trees for their use. Eggs: 4 or 5, white, laid on a few sticks, bits of grass, leaves, and feathers.

Distribution.— Eastern North America from Minnesota, Ontario, and New Brunswick south to northeastern Texas and Georgia, and west to about the 100th meridian; accidental in England.

One wonders how the man who named this bird the "Screech" Owl, would feel about a real screech, and how he would describe it. For the bird's characteristic cry is a singularly mournful and plaintive little wail, with never the slightest suggestion of a screech about it. Any term which would have denoted lament, apprehension, and incidentally a severe chill, would have been appropriate; in fact the name, "Shivering" Owl, by which the bird is commonly known in the South, has the advantage of being doubly significant, since the shivering note gives superstitious folk the "shivers" also.

From the naturalist's point of view, the most remarkable peculiarity of this Owl is what is technically called its "dichromatism," which means its tendency to develop two very distinct plumage phases, a red and a gray. There is no satisfactory explanation of this curious idiosyncrasy. As William Dutcher says, "a bird of one color may be mated with a bird of another color, and all of their young may be of one color, either red or gray, or the parents may be of one color and the young of mixed colors; hence this is often called the Mottled Owl. The only other Owl that might possibly be confounded with it is the Saw-whet [Acadian], which lacks ear-tufts, is brown, and does not have black wing-shafts." One instance is reported in which a captive gray Screech Owl was fed liver exclusively, and its plumage changed to red; but, as this was only a single experiment, it cannot be considered conclusive proof that the color change was due to the diet.

Courtesy of Am. Mus. Nat. Hist.

SCREECH OWL

In the South this bird is better known as the Shivering Owl

Another interesting peculiarity of the bird is that apparently the male and female mate for life, or at least retain that relationship for several years. This is one of the comparatively few instances of monogamy in the bird world. Polygamy is more common, but with the great majority of birds the association of the male and the female is purely a temporary affair, and in many instances the male deserts the female before the young are fully able to shift for themselves. A pair of Screech Owls may, however, continue their relationship until it is broken by the death of one or the other; and as the species is not migratory, it may even happen that the same pair will continue to use the same nest, in winter as well as summer, until they are driven away, in which event they are quite likely to resume housekeeping in the same neighborhood.

It remains to be said that the almost invariable rule of extreme cleanliness in the care of their nests or nesting places, characteristic of most American wild birds, is not generally observed by these Owls, whose habitations are often exceedingly filthy. GEORGE GLADDEN.

Scattered over North America are eight variants of the Screech Owl. The Florida Screech Owl (*Otus asio floridanus*) occurs in the coast districts of the South Atlantic and Gulf States from South Carolina to Florida and Texas; it is smaller and darker, with the under parts more densely or heavily penciled, in both phases, than the type species.

The Texas, or McCally's, Screech Owl (*Otus asio mccalli*) is limited to the lower Rio Grande valley, both in Texas and in Mexico; it is larger than the Florida Screech Owl but smaller than the common Screech Owl and paler than either; in the gray phase it is much more coarsely mottled above than in any other form of the species.

The California, or Bendire's, Screech Owl (*Otus asio bendirei*) is similar to the gray phase of the eastern Screech Owl, but the other parts are more tinged with grayish and the darker pencilings are finer and more generally distributed, nearly, if not quite, obliterating the immaculate white throat and abdominal area which are always present in the type species. There is no rufous phase in this form. Its distribution is limited to southwestern Oregon and California.

Photo by H. K. Job Courtesy of Outing Pub. Co.

YOUNG SCREECH OWL

In position of defense

The Rocky Mountain Screech Owl (*Otus asio Maxwelliæ*) was named in honor of Mrs. M. A. Maxwell of Boulder, Colorado, a noted taxidermist and hunter. It is found in the foothills and on the adjacent plains of the eastern Rocky Mountains from southeastern Montana to central Colorado. It is conspicuously lighter in color than any other form, with the white purer and more extended and the colored parts paler.

MacFarlane's Screech Owl (*Otus asio macfarlanei*) is larger and very much darker than the Rocky Mountain; in coloration it is similar to the California but is also larger than that form. It occurs from the interior of British Columbia south to eastern Washington, Oregon, and western Montana.

Photograph by A. A. Allen

SCREECH OWL

Brooding her young in the hole of a dead maple

Kennicott's Screech Owl (*Otus asio kennicotti*) is large, like MacFarlane's, but its coloration is much darker and browner, the general tone of the upper parts inclining to tawny-brown, with the lighter markings brownish buff or paler cinnamon, the under parts suffused with pale cinnamon, and the legs light tawny; the gray phase is relatively rare. This form is found in the northwest coast region from Oregon to Sitka.

Aiken's Screech Owl (*Otus asio aikeni*) is smaller and much darker than the Rocky Mountain; it is distributed over the foothills and plains of east-central Colorado, south to central New Mexico and northeastern Arizona, and east to central Texas.

The Mexican, or Arizona, Screech Owl (*Otus asio cineraceus*) is similar to the Aiken's Screech Owl, but it is more delicately penciled both above and below, the pencilings on the under parts averaging denser and more numerous; it is found in southeastern California, northern Lower California, Arizona, New Mexico, and northwestern Mexico.

A species closely allied to the Screech Owls is the Spotted Screech Owl (*Otus trichopsis*). It is somewhat like the Texas and Mexican Screech Owls, but smaller; the coloration is much darker, with coarser mottling on the upper parts; the lower hindneck is crossed by a collar of white spots. It occurs from southern Arizona south to Guatemala.

Another related species is the Flammulated Screech Owl (*Otus flammeolus flammeolus*) and its variant form, the Dwarf, or Idaho, Screech Owl (*Otus flammeolus idahoensis*). In these two Owls the toes are entirely naked, the ear-tufts, short (almost rudimentary), the upper parts, grayish (cinnamon-brown in red phase), finely mottled and marked with blackish, the facial circle, bright cinnamon to deep brown. The Flammulated Screech Owl is found in Arizona and northern Colorado south to central

Mexico and the highlands of Guatemala; the Dwarf Screech Owl occurs in southern British Columbia, eastern Washington, and Idaho south to San Bernardino Mountains, California.

"The little Screech Owl is well known throughout the greater part of the United States. With the exception of the Burrowing Owl, it feeds more extensively on insects than any of the other Owls. It is also a diligent mouser, and feeds more or less on crawfish, frogs, toads, scorpions, lizards, and fish. Of 254 stomachs examined, birds were found in about 15 per cent. Among insects, grasshoppers, crickets, beetles, and cutworms are most often eaten. As many as fifty grasshoppers have been found in one stomach, eighteen May beetles in another, and thirteen cutworms in a third. During the warmer parts of the year it is exceptional to find a stomach not well filled with insect remains. Meadow mice, white-footed mice, and house mice are the mammals most often taken, while chipmunks, wood rats, flying squirrels, and moles are less frequently found. The Screech Owl is fond of fish and catches many, especially in winter, when it watches near the breathing holes on the ice, and seizes the luckless fish which comes to the surface. Most of the birds destroyed by this Owl are killed either in severe winter weather or during the breeding season, when it has hard work to feed its young. As nearly three-fourths of the Owl's food consists of injurious mammals and insects, and only about one-seventh of birds (a large proportion of which are destructive English Sparrows), there is no question that this little Owl should be carefully protected." (Fisher.)

GREAT HORNED OWL

Bubo virginianus virginianus (*Gmelin*)

A. O. U. Number 375 See Color Plate 57

Other Names.— Big Hoot Owl; Cat Owl; Virginia Owl; Virginia Horned Owl.

General Description.— Length, 24 inches; spread of wings, 60 inches. Color above, sooty-brown or dusky, mottled with grayish-white; below, whitish, barred with dark. Ear-tufts very conspicuous, about 2 inches in length; toes fully feathered; 3 or 4 outer primaries notched or cut away on inner webs.

Color.— Adults: Plumage in general, tawny basally, this partially exposed on crown and hindneck, on shoulders, rump, and sides of breast, sometimes on other portions of the under parts; general color of upper parts, dark sooty-brown or dusky, much broken by coarse transverse mottling of grayish-white, the dusky greatly predominating on crown and hindneck, where forming broad ragged or coarsely and irregular saw-toothed longitudinal stripes which become blended on forehead; shoulders and some of the middle and greater wing-coverts with inconspicuous irregular spots or blotches of whitish; secondaries more minutely mottled (producing a more grayish effect), and crossed by about five to eight bands of mottled dusky; primary coverts, darker, crossed by three of four bands of blackish; primaries with ground color more ochraceous or buffy, finely mottled or penciled, and crossed by six to nine transverse series of square spots of dusky; ground color of tail, light tawny, transversely mottled with dusky, more whitish terminally, and crossed by six or seven bands of mottled dusky, these about equal in width to the paler interspaces and bands broken or sometimes even quite obliterated on middle tail-feathers where the darker markings have an oblique or, sometimes, even longitudinal tendency; ear-tufts with outer webs black, their inner webs mostly ochraceous; "eyebrows," dull whitish, the feathers with blackish shafts; face, dingy ochraceous or dull tawny, passing into dull whitish around eyes; a crescentic mark of black bordering upper eyelid and confluent with black of ear-tufts; facial circle, black, except across throat; a conspicuous, crescentic area of immaculate white across foreneck, the feathers white to extreme base; rest of under parts with white predominating, but tawny or ochraceous prevalent on sides of breast and showing as the base color wherever the feathers are disarranged; sides of chest, breast, and abdomen, sides, and flanks, with numerous sharply defined transverse bars of brownish black, these narrower and less sharply defined on front, the center of upper breast immaculate white; a series of large spots or blotches of black on chest, below the white collar; under tail-coverts with bars farther apart than on other under parts; legs and toes, dull tawny to pale buff, usually immaculate or nearly so, more rarely flecked or spotted with dusky; bill, dull slate-black or blackish-slate; iris, bright lemon-chrome yellow; bare portion of toes, light brownish-gray or ashy; claws, horn color, passing into black terminally. Young: Wings and tail as in adults; downy plumage of head, neck, and body, ochraceous or buff, relieved by detached, rather distant, bars of black.

Nest and Eggs.— Nest: Generally, in a deserted Hawk's, Crow's, Eagle's, Osprey's, or Caracara's nest or (in some parts of its range) in a cave, on a ledge, or in a hollow tree; constructed of twigs, weed stalks, roots, and feathers when in an old nest, or eggs deposited on the bare ground amidst a collection of old bones, skulls, fur, and feathers of quadrupeds and birds. Eggs: 2 or 3, white.

Distribution.— Eastern North America from Ontario, Quebec, New Brunswick, and Newfoundland south to the Gulf coast and Florida, west to Wisconsin, eastern Minnesota, Iowa, and eastern Texas.

"Tiger of the Air" is the term which has been applied to this great Owl, and fitly, too, it must be admitted, for the big bird undeniably is courageous, powerful, and bloodthirsty. That he is highly destructive must also be conceded, for it has been demonstrated beyond question of a doubt not only that he is bold, persistent, and generally successful in his raids upon domestic poultry of all kinds, but that he is highly skillful and deadly in his pursuit of game birds, song birds, rabbits, and squirrels.

The tiger comparison applies well to the Owl's manner of hunting, for the sweep of his great wings in the silent air is as noiseless as the tread of the big cat's padded feet upon the soft earth. Through the woods and over the meadows he glides as silently as a shadow, and to the unwatchful rabbit or the slumbering Partridge that shadow is the shadow of certain and sudden death. For such creatures the Owl's lightning-like swoop, and the murderous clutch of his great talons, are as pitiless and as inescapable as the spring of the tiger upon the helpless lamb.

To the poultry-farmer this Owl is a veritable terror; for, once the bird has acquired a preference for a diet of domesticated fowls, and has learned that they are easier to capture than are the wild creatures, nothing short of death is at all likely to deter him. For young Turkeys he is likely to develop an especially strong craving, and one instance is recorded of the loss by a farmer of fifty-nine young Guinea-fowl, taken in a single autumn by the same Owl. In such instances the bird is likely to become fastidious to the extent that he will devour only the brains of his prey, and leave the flesh untouched. Of the mammals he has been known to kill even the woodchuck, and he and other members of his family are apparently the only rapacious birds who frequently dine on the skunk, with the well-known results which, however, evidently do not in the least trouble the Owl.

The bird's breeding habits are peculiar. In the general latitude of Michigan the eggs are laid before the first of March, and many instances are recorded of their being laid as early as the first week in February, or even in the latter part of January, when the winter has been unusually mild. It is by no means uncommon to find an Owl stolidly incubating under a thick blanket of snow. Two eggs are the normal complement, and there is evidence that frequently they are laid with an interval of several days between them, for often a nest is found to contain a partly fledged bird and an unhatched egg. This peculiarity has prompted the dubious inference that the interval between the eggs is deliberately planned, so that the later one may be protected by the fledgling when the mother is away from the nest. It is much more probable that the interval represents natural operations which are imperfect, rather than designed.

Courtesy of Am. Mus. Nat. Hist.

GREAT HORNED OWL (¼ nat. size)

A bold, persistent, and powerful raider

"Dr. Louis Bennett Bishop and Mr. Herbert K. Job have both noted an unusual habit of the parent birds in apparently destroying the nest when the young become old enough to balance themselves in the fork of the tree, thus removing the conspicuous nest and leaving the bird well protected by the harmony of its colors with the bark of the tree." (Reported in *Birds of Connecticut.*)

The hooting cry of Owls is perhaps as famous as is the note of any bird. In fact, it is so famous that uninformed or careless listeners apply the term "hoot owl" to any bird who has a hooting call. As a result such persons often confuse two or more distinct species, especially the Great Horned Owl and the Barred Owl, though there is a marked difference between the hoots of these two birds, that of the Great Horned being much the stronger and more characteristic. This bird also has a series of yelps, not unlike those of a dog, and a catlike squall, to which may be due one of its popular names, "Cat Owl," though the appearance of the bird's head with its conspicuous ear-tufts is not unlike that of a cat.

Photo by H. K. Job Courtesy of Outing Pub. Co.

GREAT HORNED OWL

When huddled up on the nest attending to incubation duties its resemblance to a cat is very marked

The *"oot-too-hoo, hoo-hoo"* call, with the syllables variously divided and differently accented is, however, the characteristic utterance of this remarkable and interesting bird. Sometimes, when heard at a distance, the audible notes, two long ones followed by two short ones, strongly suggest the warning which a locomotive engineer sounds with his whistle when he approaches a crossing. Usually the cry, like that of most Owls and of the night-birds generally, has an uncanny and weird significance, in which are blended distinct suggestions of threat, defiance, and scorn, as befits the fearless and savage nature of this veritable "tiger of the air."

George Gladden.

The name of the genus to which the Great Horned Owl belongs is *Bubo,* which is Latin for Eagle-Owl. This genus has seven other representatives in North America. The Western, or Pallid, Horned Owl (*Bubo virginianus pallescens*) is similar to the Great Horned but smaller and lighter. It is found in western North America (exclusive of the high mountains) from eastern Oregon, Montana, and Minnesota south to southeastern California, Arizona, New Mexico, western Texas, and northeastern Mexico.

The Pacific, or California, Horned Owl (*Bubo virginianus pacificus*) is found in the interior of California, north to south-central Oregon, and east to San Francisco Mountain, western Arizona. It is slightly smaller than the Western Horned Owl, generally darker, the feet more heavily mottled with dusky, and the face usually with more decided tinge of tawny.

The Dwarf Horned Owl (*Bubo virginianus elachistus*) occurs in southern Lower California; it is similar in coloration to the Pacific Horned Owl but much smaller.

The Dusky Horned Owl (*Bubo virginianus saturatus*) is similar to the Pacific Horned Owl but much darker, especially the upper parts; it is found from the interior of Alaska south along the coast to south-central California, and in the Rocky Mountains to Arizona and New Mexico.

The Arctic Horned Owl (*Bubo virginianus subarcticus* or *Bubo virginianus wapacuthu*) is paler than the Western Horned Owl, the upper parts with much more of white and less of black, the under parts less heavily barred, and the feet paler, usually immaculate buff or buffy white.

It breeds from northwestern Mackenzie and central Keewatin to the southwestern Saskatchewan; in winter it travels southward to Ontario, Wisconsin, northeastern Illinois, North Dakota, Montana, Idaho, and Colorado.

The Labrador Horned Owl (*Bubo virginianus heterocnemis*) is similar to the Dusky Horned Owl; but its bill is larger, its rear under parts lighter, its feet paler and less heavily mottled, and its upper parts usually with less of a tawny admixture. It occurs on the coast of Labrador and Ungava; in winter it is found in Newfoundland, Ontario, and Toronto.

The Saint Michael Horned Owl (*Bubo virginianus algistus*) is larger than the Pacific Horned Owl and with the tawny parts intensified in color. It is found in the coast region of northern Alaska from Bristol Bay and the Yukon delta northward.

As a result of his investigations of the habits of this group of Owls, Dr. A. K. Fisher reports:

"The large and handsome Great Horned Owl is found throughout the United States where suitable timber exists for its habitation. It is a voracious bird, and its capacity for good or evil is very great. If the more thickly settled districts where poultry is extensively raised could be passed by, and the bird considered only as it appears in the great West, it would earn a secure place among the beneficial species, for it is an important ally of the ranchman in fighting the hordes of ground squirrels, gophers, prairie dogs, rabbits, and other rodents which infest his fields and ranges. Where mammals are plenty it does not seem to attack poultry or game birds to any considerable extent, but in regions where rabbits and squirrels are scarce, it frequently makes inroads on fowls, especially where they roost in trees. Undoubtedly rabbits are its favorite food, though in some places the common rat is killed in great numbers; we have a record of the remains of over one hundred rats that were found under one nest. The following is a list of the mammals taken from the stomachs examined: Three species of rabbits, cotton rat, two species of pouched gophers, two species of wood rats, chipmunk, two species of grasshopper mice, white-footed mouse, plateau ground squirrel, Harris ground squirrel, musk rat, fox squirrel, five species of meadow mice, one short-tailed shrew, the house mouse, common rat, black bat, red-backed mouse, flying squirrel, shrew, and kangaroo rat. Besides mammals and birds, insects (such as grasshoppers and beetles), scorpions, crawfish, and fish are also taken. The Great Horned Owl does a vast amount of good, and, if farmers would shut up their chickens at night instead of allowing them to roost in trees and other exposed places, the principal damage done by the bird would be prevented."

SNOWY OWL

Nyctea nyctea (*Linnæus*)

A. O. U. Number 376 See Color Plate 54

Other Names.— Great White Owl; Ermine Owl; Harfang; Wapacuthu; Arctic Owl.

General Description.— Length, 24 inches; spread of wings, 60 inches. Color, white with dark spots. Ear-tufts almost or quite lacking; 4 or 5 outer primaries notched or cut away on inner webs near tips; feet densely covered with hair-like feathers, hiding the black claws.

Color.— Adult Male: Entire plumage, pure white, sometimes nearly immaculate but usually broken with transverse spots or bars of clear slaty brown on crown, back, and shoulders, the wing- and tail-feathers with subterminal spots of dusky; under parts, usually marked on abdomen, sides, and flanks with narrow bars of clear slaty brown, but these sometimes wholly absent; bill, black; iris, lemon-yellow; claws, black. Adult Female: Much darker than the adult male, only the face, foreneck, center of breast, and the feet being immaculate, other portions being heavily barred with dark brownish-slate, the crown and hindneck spotted with the same; bill, etc., as in adult male. Young: Uniform dusky brown or deep sooty-grayish, paler on legs and feet.

Nest and Eggs.— Nest: A slight depression on a knoll, lined with some dried grass and a few feathers. Eggs: 3 to 10, generally 5 to 7, white or pale cream.

Distribution.— Northern parts of northern hemisphere; in North America breeding from far within the Arctic Circle southward to northern Ungava, central Keewatin, central Mackenzie, and northern British Columbia; in winter southward to more northern United States, irregularly (according to severity of the season), but sometimes numerously, to Virginia, Illinois, Kansas. Colorado, and mouth of Columbia River, casually or rarely to South Carolina, Louisiana, Texas, and California; accidental in the Bermudas.

The fine, strong, and picturesque Snowy Owl comes to us as a migrant from the northland where it breeds, and where the long days in summer make its habits chiefly diurnal. This fact has been discovered too late by many a Crow engaged with his brethren in the pleasing diversion of mobbing the big white specter sitting on a limb motionless, and presumably blind, because obviously an Owl. For, let one of the black tormentors come near enough and the ghost suddenly launches out on strong, silent wings, the great talons strike and close, and there is a Crow who would have been wiser but for the circumstance that he is very dead.

Drawing by R. I. Brasher

SNOWY OWL (⅛ nat. size)

A clever fisherman as well as hunter

In the regions far to the north, where this Owl breeds and therefore does its most persistent hunting, it preys upon small rodents, Ptarmigans, Ducks and other waterfowl, and, according to Captain Bendire, will kill and devour even the Arctic hare, an animal often twice as heavy as the Owl. It is very fond of fish and is said to be expert at catching them alive. It will also eat dead fish washed up on the shore, when other food is scarce.

So swift is its flight that it is able to overtake even Grouse in flight. Duck hunters are often startled by the sudden descent of the great bird upon their decoys. In its migrations it is believed to be more destructive to game and other useful birds than the Barred Owl, but less so than the Great Horned Owl.

For unknown reasons the winter migrations of the Snowy Owl sometimes amount to veritable invasions. In New York, for example, this phenomenon was observed in the winters of 1876–1877, 1882–1883, 1889–1890, and 1901–1902, when, according to Mr. Eaton, " dozens of specimens were collected in various parts of the State, notably on Long Island and near the shores of Lake Ontario."

Of its economic value Dr. A. K. Fisher says: " On account of its size and strength the Snowy Owl is capable of doing great good in destroying noxious mammals. The stomachs examined were collected between the last of October and March and the contents make a very good showing for the bird. Although a number of water birds were found, a large proportion consisted of mammal remains. One stomach contained fourteen white-footed mice and three meadow mice, and in others as many as five to eight of these little rodents were found. The common rat appeared in a number of stomachs and seems to be considerably sought after. It is a lamentable fact that this useful bird is slaughtered in great numbers whenever it appears within our limits." GEORGE GLADDEN.

AMERICAN HAWK OWL

Surnia ulula caparoch (*Müller*)

A. O. U. Number 377a See Color Plate 55

Other Names.— Day Owl; Canadian Owl; Hudsonian Owl.

General Description.— Length, 17 inches; spread of wings, 34 inches. Color above, dark brown, speckled with white; below, white, barred with brown. No ear-tufts; facial disk, poorly developed, making the face hawk-like; 3 or 4 outer primaries notched on inner webs; *tail, long and rounded;* feet, heavily feathered.

Color.— ADULTS: Plumage above, rich dark brown, darker in front, where passing into black or brownish-black on hindneck and crown, lighter and more grayish-brown behind, each feather of crown with a central small spot of white, those on forehead more circular, those on back of head more linear, as well as less numerous, the hindneck with larger V-shaped or wedge-shaped spots, streaks, or bars of white; a narrow streak of brownish-black from above middle of eye backward along upper edge of ears, where it bends abruptly downward across terminal portion of the latter; confluent with this at about the middle of its vertical portion is another but broader blackish stripe which passes down side of hindneck, and another passes from back of head down center line of hindneck; between these black stripes a whitish area; back, plain brown; a conspicuous elongated patch of white immediately above wing; rump with sparse, transverse, spots of white, the upper tail-coverts with broader and more regular bars of same, about equal to the brown ones in width; outermost middle and greater wing-coverts with an ovoid spot of white on outer webs; secondaries crossed by about three series of ovoid spots of white (on edges) and very narrowly tipped with white; outermost primary coverts with one or two series of white spots; primaries with about 7 series of white spots, all the primaries margined at tips with white; tail, crossed by seven or eight very narrow bands of white (the last one terminal), these bands becoming less distinct (sometimes obsolete) on lateral feathers; "eyebrow," lores, and face, grayish-white, the grayish appearance caused by black shafts to the feathers, the grayish-white of face continued across lower part of throat, separating a large space of dark brown from an indistinct brown collar across upper chest, this collar confluent with the lower end of the black bands on the head; ground color of under parts, white, everywhere barred with chestnut-brown or burnt-umber, the bars sharply defined, averaging rather more than half as wide as the white interspaces, except on upper chest, where the white is so much in excess as to form a broken patch, below which the brown bars are broader, and somewhat coalesced; on legs and toes the bars narrower, more sparse, and less regular; bill, yellowish; iris, lemon-yellow. YOUNG: Upper parts, dark sooty-brown or sepia, the feathers of crown and hindneck tipped with dull grayish-buff, which forms the predominating color; feathers of shoulders and of the space between indistinctly tipped with dull grayish-buff; lores and sides of head, plain brownish-black, the rest of face, dull whitish; under parts, dull whitish, deeply shaded across chest with dark sooty brownish, the other portions being broadly but rather indistinctly barred with brown, these markings narrower and more confused toward the front and on the legs.

Nest and Eggs.—NEST: In an abandoned Woodpecker hole, natural cavities, sometimes on rocks or stumps, or in old nests of other birds, relined with feathers and moss. EGGS: 3 to 7, white.

Distribution.—Northern North America; breeding northward to limit of trees in Alaska, Yukon, Mackenzie, Keewatin, and Ungava, southward to Labrador; Newfoundland (?), central Alberta, Montana (casually?), and southern British Columbia; winters, regularly, southward as far as Massachusetts, Rhode Island, eastern Pennsylvania, New Jersey, New York, southern Ontario, Ohio, southeastern Indiana, Michigan, southern Wisconsin, northern Illinois, Minnesota, Missouri, Nebraska, and Washington; accidental in Bermuda (?) and in British Isles.

Like the Snowy Owl, the Hawk Owl is a winter visitor to our Northern States from the Arctic regions, where, also like his big white cousin, he has learned to hunt effectively in broad daylight. He is likely to be seen in the latitude of the northern third of Michigan from about the last week of October until about the first of February, when he begins to move toward his northward range, several weeks ahead of the Snowy Owl.

The Hawk Owl is of much less frequent occurrence in its southern range than is the Snowy, but like the latter species it sometimes, and for no apparent reason, appears in unusual numbers. One of these visitations, for example, occurred in northern New England in October and November, 1884, when scores, if not hundreds, of these Owls were shot.

The bird is appropriately named "Hawk" Owl; not only is its appearance Hawk-like but its manner of hunting is similar, in some respects, to that of the Hawks, or at any rate very unlike that of most of the Owls. For, besides its daylight hunting, the bird has the habit of perching conspicuously on a dead stub, or in plain sight at the top of a tree, whence it watches for its prey with true Hawk-like alertness. When frightened from such a perch, it usually swoops downward to about the level of the undergrowth and then flies rapidly to another good observation point, which it reaches by an abrupt upward glide. Its flight, however, is entirely Owl-like in its noiselessness.

Its common note, a shrill cry, is uttered usually when the bird is thus in flight. Its prey includes chiefly mice, squirrels, and birds, hawked for in broad daylight.

The American Hawk Owl, as its name implies, is the American representative of the European Hawk Owl (*Surnia ulula ulula*). The latter is found in the northern parts of the Old World but casually it strays over to Alaska. It is much lighter than the American species, the black and brown areas being lighter and less extended and the white ones more extended. In habits, however, the two are alike.

BURROWING OWL

Speotyto cunicularia hypogæa (*Bonaparte*)

A. O. U. Number 378

Other Names.— Billy Owl; Ground Owl.

General Description.— Length, 9½ inches. Color above, brown spotted with light; below, whitish, barred with brown. Tail, square or slightly rounded, only about half as long as wing; head, relatively small; legs, long; 3 outer primaries with inner webs cut away.

Color.— Adults: Above, brown with pale brownish-buff to dull buffy-white spots, these largest on back, shoulders, and wing-coverts, where often roundish, and on hindneck, where mostly longitudinal, smaller on crown, where often intermixed with streaks of the same color; secondaries with the spots arranged in 4 or 5 transverse series, the outer webs of primaries with similar spots, which become larger on longer quills; tail, crossed by 5 or 6 narrow, interrupted bands of pale dull buffy, usually suffused with deeper buff and narrowly tipped with pale buff; *a stripe over eye of dull brownish-white,* the lores and around eye the same color but usually stained with pale brown, the former with shafts of the feathers, black; side of head, brown, indistinctly streaked with paler; chin, cheeks, and lower side of head, immaculate dull white or buffy white, this white area extending upward at rear end behind lower half, or more, of ear region; throat, buff, barred with dark brown, the bars usually most developed (sometimes coalesced) behind, forming a transverse band, which on each side is continued upward behind the whitish area; foreneck and upper center of chest, immaculate buffy white; rest of under parts, pale buff, deeper buff and immaculate on thigh plumes and thighs (the feathering of leg, the anal region, center of lower abdomen, and the under tail-coverts likewise immaculate), elsewhere broadly barred with brown, the brown predominating on chest or upper breast (especially laterally), where the buff is often in form of small, roundish, or sometimes even longitudinal spots; bill, dull light grayish or yellowish; iris, clear lemon-yellow; toes and naked part of leg, dull grayish or horn color. Young: Wings and tail (if developed) as in adults; crown, hindneck, and back, mostly plain light grayish-brown to buffy brown; under parts and upper tail-coverts immaculate buff, the sides of chest (sometimes whole of upper chest), shaded with brown; throat band, uniform brown.

Nest and Eggs.— Eggs: Deposited from 5 to 10 feet from entrance of abandoned prairie-dog, skunk, fox, or badger burrow, in an enlarged chamber, upon a collection of weed stalks, dried broken bits of horse or cow-dung, bits of skin, or any convenient material; 5 to 11, usually 5 to 7, white.

Distribution.— Unforested portions of western United States and southwestern Canada, from Pacific coast to western Minnesota, South Dakota, Nebraska, middle Kansas, Texas, and southeastern Louisiana; north to Washington (casual), southern British Columbia, southwestern Saskatchewan (breeding), and western Manitoba; southward through Lower California to Cape San Lucas and through Mexico to Guatemala; reappearing in western Panama; accidental in New York City and Newburyport, Massachusetts (escaped from captivity?).

Courtesy of S. A. Lottridge

FLORIDA BURROWING OWL

Contrary to the usual Owl custom the Burrowing Owl is diurnal in its habits, and evidently can see in the bright noonday glare quite as well as any of our familiar song birds. It is very active and exceedingly odd in many of its movements. Frequently on the western plains or deserts I have come across one of them standing at the mouth of its burrow or perched on a sagebush or fence-stake and have been greeted with a series of bows so profound and deferential as to be most disconcerting.

The nest is always made in a hole in the ground. A fox den, a badger burrow, or a prairie-dog hole, deserted by the original owners, make a suitable abode for the Burrowing Owl. Where these are not convenient and the soil is not too hard for its efforts, the Owl digs its own burrow. Sometimes one may come across a solitary pair far from any others of their kind, and again several pairs will be found inhabiting the same locality. Five to seven eggs are laid. These are pure white, as if Nature did not feel called upon to distribute her coloring matter on eggs that birds insist on hiding in the blackness of an underground chamber.

These Owls appear to eat almost anything they can lay their claws on. Ground squirrels, snakes, lizards, and grasshoppers all fall beneath their attacks. They are known to catch birds — even such large species as the Nighthawk succumb to their ferocity.

On the palmetto prairies of the south Florida mainland, as well as on some of the islands along the coast, is found the Florida Burrowing Owl (*Speotyto cunicularia floridana*) which is very closely related to the western bird of the same name. In *The Auk* for January, 1892, S. N. Rhoads tells of his experience of visiting a nesting colony that was three miles long and contained several hundred pairs of "Ground Owls," as they are locally called. Here in the loose sand it was easy for the birds to make their own nesting burrows. These ran along so close under the grass roots that grazing cattle often broke holes through from the top. The burrows were from four to seven feet in length with an enlarged oven-shaped pocket at the end. The nesting material consisted of pieces of dry cow-droppings and fragments of turf among which the eggs were mixed more or less indiscriminately.

The old birds it seemed were kept very busy gathering food for their offspring. Of the appetite of the young he writes: "The voracity of the young is phenomenal. I kept several, of different ages, in a tin box for several days. Besides eating everything, fresh or putrid, that was offered, they attacked and devoured each other. I was forced to kill the three remaining cannibals to preserve them."

T. Gilbert Pearson.

PYGMY OWL

Glaucidium gnoma gnoma *Wagler*

A. O. U. Number 379

Other Name.— Gnome Owl.

General Description.— Length, 6½ inches. Dichromatic; in grayish-brown phase, upper parts grayish-brown spotted with light and under parts white streaked with dark; in rufescent phase, upper parts much browner with the spots cinnamon. No ear-tufts; tips of outer primaries narrow.

Color.— Grayish-brown Phase: General color of upper parts, grayish brown, the crown and hindneck with numerous irregular but mostly roundish small spots of pale dull buff; across lower hindneck an interrupted collar of white and immediately below this another of black followed by large, mostly concealed, spots of pale tawny; back, shoulders, wing-coverts, rump, and upper tail-coverts with minute irregular (often V-shaped) spots or bars of pale buffy brownish, buffy, or whitish, these markings mostly concealed; outer shoulder-feathers with large spots of buffy or buffy-white on both webs, the spots largest, however, on outer webs; outermost middle and greater wing-coverts with larger spots of white; primary coverts, plain dark brown, darker terminally, their inner webs, however, spotted with white; wings, dusky grayish brown, their outer webs with transverse spots or broad bars of paler grayish-brown, these becoming white or partly white on outer secondaries and ends of longer primaries; tail, dark to dusky grayish-brown, crossed by 6 or 7 interrupted bars of white, these much broader on inner webs, and on both webs falling far short of the shaft; "eyebrows" and lores, dull white, the latter with conspicuous black bristly shafts; chin and cheeks, immaculate white; a band of brown across throat; foreneck and middle line of breast and abdomen, immaculate white; sides of chest, brown tinged with tawny, transversely spotted with pale cinnamon-buff, the sides more grayish, irregularly spotted with white; rest of under parts, white broadly streaked with dark brown, the streaks becoming black or brownish black on flanks and next to the immaculate white center area; legs, soiled dull white mottled with grayish-brown; bill, pale grayish-yellow, darker basally; iris, lemon yellow; toes, light yellowish-brown. Rufescent Phase: Similar in pattern of coloration to the grayish-brown phase, but general color of upper parts much browner with the spotting (especially that on crown and hindneck) cinnamon or cinnamon-buff, and with throat-band and sides of breast cinnamon-brown.

Nest and Eggs.— Nest: In hollow stumps, or trees from 8 to 75 feet from the ground, usually in deserted Woodpecker holes, generally in coniferous forests, but the nest in deciduous trees. Eggs: 3 or 4, white or very pale cream.

Distribution.— Western North America from Caribou district, interior of British Columbia, south in mountains to Guatemala and east to eastern Montana, Colorado, and New Mexico.

Dr. Coues gave the Pygmy Owl an excellent character, saying that "it is a very straightforward, ingenuous, unsuspicious little bird, meddling with no affairs but its own, and innocent enough to expect like treatment from others, expectations, however, not often realized"— either in birdland or elsewhere, he might have added.

A physical peculiarity wherein the bird is strangely un-Owl-like is that when it is in flight its wings make a distinct whistling sound, whereas the flight of the remainder of its tribe in this country is as silent as the passing of a shadow. Moreover, like a few other members of its family, it is quite able to do, and does, much of its hunting in broad daylight, even in the bright sunshine, though probably it is most active in the dim light of the evening and early morning. Dr. Fisher corroborates Dr. Coues' statement about the unsuspicious nature of the bird by noting that it responds promptly to an imitation of its call (which resembles the syllables *klook, klook*), and in this way may be decoyed from a considerable distance; and he adds that "it hides in the pines or other thick foliage, where it sits upright near the trunk and is practically invisible to the observer."

Besides not being noiseless this Owl's flight is rather jerky and uneven, suggesting that of the Sparrow Hawk, this being true especially when the bird is hunting insects, which it often catches by pouncing upon them on the ground from low branches or stumps. These dives are executed after the manner of the Shrike, that is, with closed wings, followed by a fluttering upward flight. It is a very courageous bird, and kills and eats other birds as large as the Robin and squirrels or other rodents twice its own size. The Indians are very superstitious about this bird, and believe that killing one will bring terrible misfortunes upon the slayer.

The California Pygmy Owl (*Glaucidium gnoma californicum*) is a browner variety of the Pygmy and is limited to the Pacific coast region from southwestern British Columbia south to Monterey, California. Speaking of this subspecies, Mr. W. L. Finley says (MS.): "We have had one or two cases in which the California Pygmy Owl has killed canaries in cages. One of our wardens killed one of these birds as it was eating a Meadowlark which it had caught; it had evidently caught the bird in broad daylight."

ELF OWL

Micropallas whitneyi (*J. G. Cooper*)

A. O. U. Number 381

Other Name.— Whitney's Owl.

General Description.— Length, 6 inches. Dichromatic; in gray phase, upper parts brownish-gray spotted with yellowish and under parts a mixture of white, gray, and light brown; in brown phase, upper parts nearly snuff-brown. No ear-tufts; tail, square or slightly rounded, less than half as long as wing; tarsus, scantily haired or bristled, not feathered; 4 outer primaries notched on inner webs.

Color.— Gray Phase — Adults: Above, brownish-gray to grayish-brown, the crown, hindneck, back, shoulders, rump, upper tail-coverts, and lesser wing-coverts with small irregular spots of buff or pale tawny, these larger and deeper pale tawny or cinnamon-buff on forehead; an interrupted narrow collar of white across lower hindneck; outer webs of feathers on shoulders, mostly white, margined terminally with blackish; middle and greater wing-coverts with a large, semi-ovoid spot of white on terminal or subterminal portion of outer web; secondaries crossed by about five series of semi-circular spots of pale cinnamon-buff, these passing into white on outer edge; primary coverts with three series of dull cinnamon-buff spots; outer webs of primaries with about 6 conspicuous spots of cinnamon-buff, these not touching shafts; tail crossed by about 4 or 5 narrow, interrupted bands of pale brownish buffy or buffy and white, these not reaching shaft on either web; "eyebrows," white, the feathers narrowly tipped with black; "face," cinnamon to cinnamon-buff, the last sometimes partly dull rusty whitish; a white cheek spot, margined behind by a blackish bar; throat cinnamon to cinnamon-buff, this extended laterally to behind the black cheek bar, where sometimes barred with blackish; rest of under parts, a confused mixture of white, grayish, and dull light cinnamon or light buffy brown, the white predominating behind, the grayish and cinnamon prevailing forward, the colored areas narrowly and irregularly barred with dusky; under tail-coverts, white, with subterminal irregular spots of pale buffy brown or narrow center streaks of dusky; under wing-coverts, white, suffused with pale buffy brown and irregularly spotted with deep grayish brown, the edge of wing, however, immaculate white; bill, pale horn color with yellowish edges; iris, lemon yellow. Young: Similar to adults but crown nearly immaculate deep brownish-gray, and without any cinnamon-buff on face or throat, or buffy brown on under parts, the latter irregularly marbled or clouded with white and light brownish-gray narrowly barred with darker. Brown Phase: Much browner than the grayish (usual) phase, the general color of the upper parts nearly snuff-brown; otherwise not different, the pattern of the coloration being identical.

Nest and Eggs.— Nest: In the giant cactus, an abandoned Woodpecker's hole being almost always utilized, but sometimes in a hollow tree. Eggs: 2 to 5, pure white.

Distribution.— Southern and Lower California, east to southern Texas, south over the tableland of Mexico to Puebla.

Arizona is a land of extremes. We may expect to find gray and brown birds to match the colors of the desert; we also find birds of most brilliant hue. There are also extremes in size. Here in the desert lives the dwarf of all Owls. When we made his acquaintance, we found he was no bigger than an English Sparrow. What a tiny baby in comparison to the Great Horned Owl!

When the late Mr. Herbert Brown, who was a splendid naturalist and outdoor man, asked us to go Owl hunting, we accepted. The next morning, he came early with a team and light wagon. In the back of the wagon, he had three short ladders, which I discovered later had been built especially so they fitted together and made a ladder long enough to reach up near the top of the tallest cactus. No matter how expert one is at climbing, he would have some difficulty without a ladder in getting up where the Elf Owls nest, for they prefer the highest Woodpecker's hole in the top of the giant cactus.

In the semi-desert country around Tucson, the Woodpeckers find very few trees, not nearly enough for nesting places. As a substitute, they take the giant cactus. When they drill a cavity into the green cactus trunk, the sap oozes out and hardens, making a hard-shelled house that is very permanent. Oftentimes when the cactus falls to decay, one may pick up these gourd-shaped homes made by the Woodpeckers. In many places, one may see the candelabra-like branches of the giant cactus riddled with Woodpecker holes. These furnish secure homes for the little Elf Owl and we had no difficulty in finding plenty of these tiny Owls by using the long ladder.

The Elf Owl is abundant about Tucson. Mr. Brown said, "Their food consists largely of ants, beetles, and grasshoppers." The bird is almost entirely nocturnal in habits and is seldom seen moving about in the daytime. It is a constant night hunter, flitting about over the desert for insects, very seldom preying on other birds or animals.

WILLIAM L. FINLEY.

Photo by W. L. Finley and H. T. Bohlman

ELF OWL

No bigger than an English Sparrow, but still an Owl

ORDER OF PARROT-LIKE BIRDS

Order *Psittaci;* family *Psittacidæ*

THE order of Parrot-like birds (*Psittaci*) is characterized by a relatively short, hooked bill; feet with four toes, two forward and two backward, and perfectly adapted for grasping and climbing as well as for holding food when eating; tongue short, usually thick and fleshy, sometimes with the tip brush-like or fringed; tail-feathers usually numbering twelve; secondaries acutely conical; and by various other anatomical peculiarities. They are noisy in the wild state, their voices harsh and unmusical. Many of the species, but not all, learn to speak in captivity.

The typical Parrots occur throughout the tropical and most of the subtropical portions of both hemispheres. They are the only Parrot-like birds found in America or Africa. The species of typical Parrots are very numerous, more than five hundred and fifty being known, of which number, however, only one, the Carolina Paroquet, is a resident of the United States, and but one other, the Thick-billed Parrot, casually crosses the international boundary at the south.

Parrots, it is believed, mate for life. Their eggs are immaculate white and are usually deposited in the trunks of trees; the young when hatched are either partly or entirely covered with down and are cared for in the nest.

The Parrot family are not good walkers, but they can climb, and they fly exceedingly well, often going long distances in search of their food of fruit and seeds. Bright colors predominate in the plumage and there is but slight, and in many species no, sexual variation in coloration.

CAROLINA PAROQUET

Conuropsis carolinensis (*Linnæus*)

A. O. U. Number 382

Other Names.— Kelinky; Carolina Parrakeet.

General Description.— Length, 13 inches. Color, green with yellow head.

Color.— Forehead, front of crown, lores, space below eyes, and upper part of cheeks, orange; rest of head and neck (all round), clear lemon yellow; back and shoulders, clear yellowish-green, the rump, brighter and less yellowish-green; lesser and middle wing-coverts, deep Paris green margined with paler and brighter green; greater coverts and inner secondaries more yellowish-green, paler and more yellowish-green terminally and along margin of outer webs; secondaries (except innermost ones) and primary coverts, dark green, the primaries similar but becoming darker and duller terminally (especially on inner webs, where passing into dusky on margin), the longer primaries (except outermost) broadly edged with pale greenish-yellow basally; upper tail-coverts and tail, clear light parrot green with black shafts, the shafts of middle feathers, whitish basally; under parts of body, including foreneck and under tail-coverts, clear light apple green, the under wing-coverts, similar but more yellowish-green, sometimes intermixed with yellow; bend of wing, orange intermixed with yellow; anal region and lower portion of thighs, yellow, sometimes tinged with orange; under primary coverts and under surface of primaries. brownish-gray, tinged with yellowish-olive, the under surface of tail similar but more strongly tinged with yellowish-olive; bill, light cream-buff or cream-white; iris, dark brown; bare eye space, pale flesh color or pinkish white; legs and feet, pale flesh color or pinkish white.

Nest and Eggs.—Nest: In hollow tree. Eggs: 3 to 5, white.

Distribution.— Formerly inhabiting the Atlantic coastal plain of the United States, from Florida to Virginia (occasionally to eastern New York), and west to Texas, Oklahoma, Colorado, and north to Iowa and Wisconsin, but now totally extirpated over much the greater part of its former range and so nearly extinct that only a few small colonies may yet exist in remote and uninhabited parts of southern Florida.

The Carolina Paroquet is to-day nearly, if not quite, extinct, no record of its appearance having been made for several years. Once common in the Southern States from Maryland and Colorado, they have passed away before the guns of the white man. Observers tell us that they traveled about the country in flocks and their inroads on fruit orchards won for them a dislike that in the end meant their inevitable destruction. When a flock was shot into, the survivors after flying a short distance would return again and again to their fallen companions until sometimes an entire company would be wiped out.

Many of the early writers and explorers give accounts of their appearance and habits. Thus John Lawson, Gentleman, in his *History of Carolina,* published in London in 1714, writes: "The Parrokeetes are of a green colour, and orange-coloured half way up their heads. Of these and the Allegators there is none found to the northward of this Province. They visit us first when mulberries are ripe, which fruit they love exceedingly. They peck the apples to eat the kernels, so that the fruit rots and perishes. They are Mischievous to Orchards. They are often taken alive and will become familiar and tame in two days. They have their nests in hollow trees in low swamp ground. They devour the Birch Buds in April, and lie hidden when the weather is frosty and hard."

Many years have now passed since the Carolina Paroquet was seen in the Carolinas. Florida is, or was, its last stand. Dr. Frank M. Chapman found fifty or more individuals in the southern part of that State in 1889. Writing of his experiences he says: "Late in the afternoon of our arrival we started a flock of seven Paroquets from a productive patch of thistles which proved to be their favorite food. Evidently their meal was finished and they were ready to retire, for they darted like startled Doves through the pines, twisting and turning in every direction, and flying with such rapidity, they were soon lost to view; the ring of their sharp, rolling call alone furnished proof it was not all a vision."

Two days later he again came upon a flock of which he writes: "Several were skillfully dissecting the thistles they held in their feet, biting out the milky seed while the released fluffy down floated away beneath them. There was a sound of suppressed conversation; half-articulate calls. We were only partially concealed behind a neighboring tree, still they showed no great alarm at our presence; curiosity was apparently the dominant feeling."

Photo by R. W. Shufeldt

CAROLINA PAROQUET

This is a picture of a live bird, although the species is almost extinct

Following Dr. Chapman's discovery other observers occasionally reported finding them, but these reports became less frequent as time passed and of late years have altogether ceased.

T. Gilbert Pearson.

THICK-BILLED PARROT

Rhynchopsitta pachyrhyncha (*Swainson*)

A. O. U. Number 382.1

General Description.— Length, 16 inches. Color, green with red on head, bend of wing, and thigh.

Color.— Forehead, front of crown, space over eye, and front lesser wing-coverts, deep poppy red or dull carmine; lower portion of thighs, light poppy red; a spot of dark reddish-brown or blackish-brown immediately in front of bare eye space, this dark color extending, narrowly, along the upper margin of the naked eye space; under primary coverts, clear chrome-yellow, forming a conspicuous patch on under side of wing; under surface of wing-feathers and tail-feathers, plain brownish-slate color, tinged with olive in certain lights; rest of plumage, yellowish parrot green or bright oil green, brighter on sides of head, slightly lighter (sometimes duller) on under parts, bend of wing sometimes (in older individuals?) partly red; bill, dull black; iris, brownish-red; legs and feet, dull black.

Nest and Eggs.— Nesting unknown, but probably similar to the rest of the genus — nest in a hollow tree, and eggs white.

Distribution.—Mountains bordering the Mexican tableland, northward casually to the Chiricahua Mountains, Arizona.

The Thick-billed Parrot appears to be either very stupid or very curious — excessive curiosity is likely to convey the impression of stupidity — for it has an exasperating habit of following travelers in flocks which keep up such an uproar that every other bird and beast is likely to become alarmed and either make off or conceal itself. This is nowise pleasing to the traveler who happens to be a naturalist or an ornithologist, and therefore intent upon observing the wild-life forms, many of which would remain in sight long enough to be looked at but for the racket made by the Parrots.

The birds are most likely to be encountered in the piñon pine forests, where they feed freely upon the seeds which they extract with their beaks from the tough cones. In the United States they are found chiefly in the cañons of the Chiricahua Mountains, in Arizona.

George Gladden.

Photo by C. William Beebe (copyrighted)

THICK-BILLED PARROT

The only species of its order which finds it way across the Rio Grande

ORDER OF CUCKOOS, ETC.

Order *Coccyges*

SEVERAL groups of birds with little outward resemblance to one another have been grouped in this order. There are three suborders, each with one family. The first suborder, *Cuculi*, and family, *Cuculidæ*, contains the Cuckoos, Anis, and Road-runners. The second, or *Trogones*, includes the Trogons, but one species of which enters the United States. The third suborder is that of the Kingfishers (*Alcyones*).

CUCKOO FAMILY

Order *Coccyges;* suborder *Cuculi;* family *Cuculidæ*

BIRDS of the Cuckoo family are long-tailed, mostly arboreal, but sometimes terrestrial and ground-scratching. The toes are arranged in pairs, two pointing forward and two backward. There are eight to ten feathers in the tail. The nostrils are exposed, and the bristles at the corners of the mouth are either inconspicuous or missing. The bill is extremely variable as to size and shape, but is always compressed and more or less decurved at the tip.

The young are hatched naked and are cared for in the nest. The nest (if any) is of very rude construction. The eggs are extremely variable as to coloration and number and are usually deposited at intervals so that eggs and young are often found in the same nest at the same time. Many foreign species are parasitic in their reproduction, laying their eggs in the nests of other birds, and allowing their young to be reared by the foster parents, often at the sacrifice of the latter's progeny, who are frequently unceremoniously crowded or thrown from the nest by the interloper.

The Cuckoo family is a very extensive group of nearly world-wide distribution, only the colder regions, where their insect food is wanting, being without any representatives of it. The group is much more numerously represented in the eastern than in the western hemisphere, only eleven of the forty-six genera and forty-three of the two hundred and two species enumerated in Sharpe's *Hand-list of the Genera and Species of Birds* being American. All the American forms are peculiar, however, none of the genera being represented elsewhere and none being parasitic as is the common European bird. This family includes: the group which bear the family name, Cuckoo, five species and subspecies of which are found in the United States; the Road-runners or Ground Cuckoos; and the Anis.

As a rule the Cuckoos are birds of dull plumage, a more or less plain grayish, brown, or partly rufous coloration prevailing; but there are exceptions in some of the Old World genera. No American species of the group is remarkable for showy coloration.

GROOVE-BILLED ANI

Crotophaga sulcirostris *Swainson*

A. O. U. Number 384

Other Names.— Tick Bird; Black Witch; Jew Bird.

General Description.— Length, 12 to 14 inches. Plumage, black. Upper bill with several distinct curved grooves and ridges, parallel with curve of ridge.

Color.— Dull black, faintly glossed with violet on wing-coverts, wings, and middle tail-feathers, still more faintly glossed with greenish on primaries and under parts; feathers of head and neck rather broadly edged with dull purplish-bronze, the shoulders and back and smaller wing-coverts with a broad U-shaped submarginal mark of dull greenish-bronze, the terminal margin of each feather and a narrow border to the bronzy submarginal mark, black; feathers of chest with similar but narrower and less distinct markings; bill, black or brownish-black, often partly grayish-brown or horn color; naked skin of loral and eye regions, dull black; iris, dark brown; legs and feet, black.

Nest and Eggs.— Nest: In tree, frequently orange or lemon, or thorny bush; bulky, flat; constructed of thorny twigs, sticks, lined with fibrous roots or green leaves. Eggs: 3 to 5, milky blue.

Distribution.— The whole of Mexico and Central America, southward to Peru, Venezuela, and British Guiana; north regularly (breeding) to Rio Grande valley in Texas and Lower California, casually to Louisiana, Florida, Kansas, and southern Arizona.

The Groove-billed Ani is another of the border birds which barely earns the right to be considered one of Uncle Sam's feathered wards, by establishing a residence only in southern Texas. According to Captain Bendire its habitat is chiefly the lowlands, and the birds are seldom seen at an altitude of more than 700 feet above the sea. Their apparent fondness for the company of cattle is due not only to the fact that they feed upon insects started up by the movements of the animals (which the disreputable Cowbird also does), but to their feeding upon parasites which they find on the animals' skins, thereby doing the steers a service similar to that performed by the famous Rhinoceros Bird for its burly companion.

This work the Anis do mainly at night when the animals are lying down, though they have been seen in daylight perched on the animals' backs, and one observer asserts that they will cling to a cow's tail and clear it of insects to its extremity. In flight, the Anis give the impression of being very loose-jointed creatures, their wings flopping clumsily and their tails blowing about in the breezes as if insecurely attached.

Judging from the living birds only, no one would suspect that the Anis were related to the Cuckoos; their appearance and habits are very different. The Anis are gregarious and live in open districts. Even in their nesting they are social birds, several females laying their eggs in the same nest.

ROAD-RUNNER

Geococcyx californianus (*Lesson*)

A. O. U. Number 385

Other Names.— Ground Cuckoo; Chaparral Cock; Snake Killer; Lizard Bird; Churca; Paisano; Correcamio; Cock of the Desert.

General Description.— Length, 20 to 24 inches. Color above, olive streaked with tawny-brown and buffy-whitish; below, whitish streaked on chest. Tail, long and graduated; feathers of head bristle-tipped; entire plumage, coarse and harsh.

Color.—Feathers of forehead and anterior part of crown, blue-black centrally, each with a broad lateral spot of russet often edged with buffy-grayish, the rest of crown (including bushy crest on the back of the head), blue-black, broken by edgings of tawny-brown; hindneck and upper back, blue-black, the feathers broadly edged with light tawny-brown passing into dull buffy-whitish on edges, producing a conspicuously streaked effect; feathers of lower back, shoulders, and wing-coverts, similarly marked, but the central area of each feather, olive glossed with bronze-greenish, and edged with black, the paler markings on wing-coverts larger and paler, in form of longitudinal spots; greater coverts, olive glossed with bronze, and with a large terminal spot of white on each web; inner secondaries olivaceous, glossed with bronze-greenish edged narrowly with black, and broadly margined (on both webs) by dull whitish; primary coverts, olive-dusky broadly margined at ends with dull white; primaries, blackish, faintly glossed with greenish, margined terminally with dull white and crossed, near middle portion, by a broad band of the same, composed of marginal spots on outer webs only; rump, plain grayish-brown; upper tail-coverts and middle pair of tail-feathers, bronzy-olive glossed with purplish and margined with dull white; remaining feathers, glossy blue-black on outer webs, more greenish on inner webs, tipped, and narrowly margined (on outer web) with white, decreasing in extent to the second pair; lores, dull whitish, the feathers with projecting black bristle-like shafts; cheeks and space below eyes, mixed dull whitish and pale tawny-brownish, barred and spotted with black; sides of head, streaked with black and dull whitish; chin and throat, mostly dull white; foreneck, sides of neck and chest light ochraceous-buff passing into whitish on edges of feathers, each feather with a center streak of black, these streaks narrow in front, much broader on sides of neck and chest; rest of under parts, plain grayish buffy-white; inner webs of lateral tail-feathers, pale gray on under surface in front of the white tip; bill, dusky horn color; iris, golden yellow to orange; bare eye space around blue in front passing into bluish-white beneath and behind eye, the rear portion orange-red; legs and feet, pale bluish, the large scales of leg pale yellowish or cream color margined with pale bluish.

Nest and Eggs.— NEST: Usually in cacti, mesquite, sage brush, or thorny bushes; a large coarse structure of sticks, lined with grass, feathers, strips of bark, snake skin, or rootlets, with slight depression. EGGS: 4 to 6 usually, but sometimes 2 or 12, chalky white or pale yellowish.

Distribution.— California, Colorado, Kansas, and western and middle Texas, south through Lower California and the table-land of Mexico to Puebla.

The Road-runner is one of the most striking characters of the cactus belt of the Southwest. When we first went to Tucson, Arizona, we were anxious to find a Road-runner. Day after day, we searched through the cactus and kept our eyes open. We found several old nests and occasionally we would catch a glimpse of a slim, long-tailed bird running through the cactus. One day when we least expected it, a Road-runner slid across the road, hopped up into a cholla cactus and was instantly lost to sight in the thorny mass. We drove around the bush slowly, once, twice, closer and closer till we could see through the tangle. But no Road-runner! She had disappeared, and yet she could hardly have escaped without our seeing her. A slight movement in the cactus — there she was, sitting bolt upright holding a lizard in her bill. Until she moved, she was as completely hidden as if she had not been there.

In this nest were one fresh egg, one egg just ready to hatch, two featherless black-skinned young birds, and two young ones about grown and ready to leave home. This certainly verified the statement of Elliott Coues: "Perfectly fresh eggs and newly hatched young may be found together, and by the time the last young are breaking the shell, the others may be graded up to half the size of the adult."

I have occasionally seen an old Road-runner that takes a delight in out-distancing a team of horses, but sometimes a Road-runner is not accustomed to our modern method of traveling. One day a friend was spinning down the Oracle Road in his automobile when, at the turn, a Road-runner dropped into line ahead and set the pace down the smooth stretch. The driver turned on a little more gasoline. The Road-runner looked over his tail at the horseless carriage. It was gaining on him! As the machine bore down on the astonished bird, the feathered racer was scared. He cocked his tail suddenly to put on the brake, made a sharp turn to the left, dodged through the cactus and creosote and away he went at top speed as far as he could be seen.

Photo by W. L. Finley and H. T. Bohlman

ROAD-RUNNER

While some people accuse the Road-runner of killing other birds, especially young Quail, our experience showed that he lived almost entirely on lizards. The young birds in the nest were fed on lizards almost from the time they were out of the egg. The reptile was always killed and then thrust head down into the mouth of the youngster. The tail for a time would hang out of his mouth, but as the head end was digested, the young bird gulped a little now and then, until finally the end of the tail disappeared.

William L. Finley.

YELLOW-BILLED CUCKOO

Coccyzus americanus americanus (*Linnæus*)

A. O. U. Number 387. See Color Plates 58

Other Names.— Rain Crow; Rain Dove; Storm Crow; Chow-Chow; Kow-Kow.

General Description.— Length, 11 or 12 inches. Color above, grayish-brown; below, white.

Color.— Above, plain grayish-brown, faintly glossed with bronzy, usually becoming more grayish on forehead, the outer webs of *primaries, suffused with rufescent brown,* sometimes nearly uniform dull cinnamon-rufous; middle pair of tail-feathers, usually becoming more dusky terminally, the remaining tail-feathers, black, faintly glossed with bluish or greenish, passing into grayish-brown basally, each *tail-feather, very broadly tipped with white,* this decreasing in extent from the outermost, on which the white extends much farther on the outer web than on the inner; sides of head, grayish-brown, sometimes concolor with crown and hindneck, sometimes much darker; below eye, lower portion of sides of head, and entire under parts, dull white, faintly shaded with pale bluish-gray, except on under parts of body and under tail-coverts, which are sometimes very faintly tinged with pale buffy; bill, slate-black above, yellow on more than basal half below, and on cutting edge above; iris, dark brown; naked eyelids, grayish; legs and feet, pale bluish-gray.

Nest and Eggs.—Nest: Generally in fork of a tree as high as 25 feet up; a frail structure of twigs, grass, leaves, and catkins, so shallow that it is remarkable the eggs do not roll out oftener. Eggs: 2 to 6, pale dull, greenish-blue.

Drawing by R. I. Brasher

YELLOW-BILLED CUCKOO (½ nat. size)

Mysterious and secretive in habits, but highly useful

Distribution.— Parts of North and South America; breeds from North Dakota, Minnesota, southern Ontario, Quebec, and New Brunswick south to Louisiana and northern Florida, and west to South Dakota, Nebraska, and Oklahoma; migrates through the West Indies and Central America; winters in South America south to Ecuador, Bolivia, and Argentina.

BLACK-BILLED CUCKOO

Coccyzus erythrophthalmus (*Wilson*)

A. O. U. Number 388. See Color Plate 58

Other Names.— Rain Crow; Kow-Kow.

General Description.— Length, 11 or 12 inches. Color above, olive-brown; below, white.

Color.— Above, plain olivaceous hair-brown, glossed with bronze, passing into a more grayish hue on forehead, the inner primaries and outer secondaries sometimes slightly more rufescent basally; *tail-feathers* (except middle pair) *narrowly but conspicuously tipped with dull white* and crossed by a broad subterminal bar of dusky; loral region, brownish-gray, like forehead; sides of head, grayish-brown, like hindneck, etc.; cheeks, space below eyes, chin, throat, and upper chest, pale buffy-grayish; rest of under parts, plain dull white, the under tail-coverts more buffy or brownish-white; upper bill, black; lower bill, pale grayish-blue dusky terminally; iris, deep brown; naked eyelids, bright red; legs and feet, pale bluish-gray.

Nest and Eggs.— NEST: A more carefully constructed nest than the Yellow-billed Cuckoo's; placed in small trees or bushes, usually within 8 feet of the ground; made of twigs, strips of bark, rootlets, and weed stems, lined often with small catkins, and very shallow. EGGS: 2 to 5, plain dull bluish-green.

Distribution.— North and South America; breeds from southeastern Alberta, southern Manitoba, southern Quebec, and Prince Edward Island, south to Kansas, Arkansas, North Carolina, and mountains of Georgia; winters in South America from Colombia to Peru.

Few birds are more widely known that the Cuckoo. He has his place in the Bible, and was honored by the consideration of Aristotle and Pliny. In mythology the bird figures more than once, and especially when Jupiter appeared to Juno in its form. Wordsworth's lines

> O Cuckoo! shall I call thee bird?
> Or but a wandering voice,

though of course addressed to the European species, apply as well to ours.

The frequency with which the English Cuckoo has been put into verse by the poets of its country, its parasitic habit of laying its eggs in the nests of other birds, and the ubiquity of the so-called "cuckoo clock," have conspired to make the name of the bird very well known in this country. In point of fact, the American Cuckoo is a totally different bird from the English one — different in size, different in color, and very different in habits and disposition. In the first place, the American Cuckoo does not make a practice of laying its eggs in other birds' nests; indeed, it nearly always builds a nest of its own, such as it is, and brings up its family as every other self-respecting bird does. As to the

Photo by H. K. Job — Courtesy of Outing Pub. Co.

BLACK-BILLED CUCKOO ON NEST

cuckoo-clock, its performance does not even remotely suggest the American Cuckoo's song which, in fact, is simply a series of guttural *chucks* and *clucks,* most unbird-like and wholly unmusical. Finally, the English bird has a decidedly Hawk-like appearance, while the American species looks a little like an attenuated pigeon, with a disproportionately long neck and tail.

The comparatively slight difference between the appearance and habits of the two species, the Yellow-billed and the Black-billed, makes it proper to consider them jointly. Sometimes Mrs. Yellow-billed Cuckoo employs Mrs. Black-billed to bring up her children, and at other times the Black-billed offspring are deposited in the Yellow-billed home. Both species are known as the

Courtesy of Nat. Asso. Aud. Soc.

YOUNG YELLOW-BILLED CUCKOO

" Rain Crow " because of the belief — especially among farmers — that their guttural cry predicts rain. But why " Crow," a bird which is uniformly and famously black all over, while the Cuckoo varies from white to brown, but is essentially a light-colored bird? This is one of the queerest freaks of popular terminology, and suggests that we have to thank for it somebody who couldn't tell black from white.

Both of these Cuckoos are essentially birds of mystery. Not only in their rather unearthly call, but in their specter-like comings and goings, and general behavior, they are not like unto other birds. So one is not surprised to learn that the Black-billed, at any rate, is a nest-robber, and is generally recognized as such in the bird-world. Mr. Burroughs mentions three instances in which Robins have actually killed Cuckoos; in one case the Robins caught the robber in the very act, and so pecked and mauled him that he died of his injuries. Audubon gave the same bad character to the Yellow-billed, which, he said, " robs smaller birds of their eggs which it sucks upon all occasions, and is cowardly without being vigilant. On this account it falls prey to several species of Hawks, of which the Pigeon Hawk may be considered its most dangerous enemy." But the Pigeon Hawk is the enemy of all birds that it can overtake and kill, and these include many species larger than itself.

In his manner the Cuckoo gives the impression of being deeply preoccupied and quite absent-minded. He slips in and out of trees like a ghost. Upon first alighting, he looks about him as if he were dazed, but almost immediately recovers himself and proceeds to search for his preferred fare of " tent " caterpillars of which he destroys great numbers, thereby placing himself in the category of highly useful birds. In flight, the Yellow-billed species is readily identifiable by the white markings on its long tail. These markings are different from those shown in the tail of the Mourning Dove, which otherwise — though after all very faintly — resembles the Cuckoo.

George Gladden.

The California, or Western, Cuckoo (*Coccyzus americanus occidentalis*) is the western replica of the Yellow-billed Cuckoo from which it differs only in size.

The Mangrove Cuckoo (*Coccyzus minor minor*) and the Bahama Mangrove, or Maynard's, Cuckoo (*Coccyzus minor maynardi*) are found in the Florida Keys and the West Indies south through Mexico to Central America and northern South America. They are plain grayish-brown above, faintly glossed with bronzy; the tail-feathers are tipped with white, the middle pair more narrowly than the others; upper parts of sides of head dull black; the underparts are dull ochraceous-buff or cinnamon-buff; their bills are black above and yellow underneath. Maynard's Cuckoo is smaller than the Mangrove Cuckoo.

Probably no group of insects contains a greater number of orchard pests than the order Lepidoptera, which comprises butterflies and moths, with their larvæ, or caterpillars. Tent caterpillars, cankerworms, fall webworms, tussock moths, and a host of others are among the worst enemies of the fruit grower. It is, therefore, fortunate that there are in the United States two birds that subsist, to a great extent, upon caterpillars, apparently preferring them to any other food. These are the Cuckoos, the Yellow-billed and the Black-billed.

For years it has been a matter of common observation that these birds feed largely on caterpillars, but, until a number of stomachs had been examined, it was not known how great a proportion of their food is made up of these harmful insects. The examinations indicated that caterpillars of various species, including some of the most destructive, constitute more than 48 per cent. of their food. One stomach contained at least 250 tent caterpillars, probably a whole colony, in the young stage. In another 217 heads of the fall webworm were counted, and this probably fell far short of the real number, as these larvæ are very small, and in many instances nothing but jaws remained undigested.

Many caterpillars are protected from the attacks of birds and parasitic insects by a covering of hair, and hairy caterpillars are only rarely eaten by most birds. Cuckoos, however, seem to prefer them to the smooth kind, and apparently eat them whenever they can be found. Caterpillar hairs are often stiff, bristly, and sharp at the end, like minute thorns, and it frequently happens that when a Cuckoo's stomach is opened and emptied it is found to be completely furred on the inside by hairs which have pierced the inner lining and become fast. Cuckoos eat many noxious insects besides caterpillars, such as beetles, bugs, and grasshoppers. Unfortunately, they are naturally rather shy birds, preferring the edges of the woodland and groves to the more open cultivated grounds and orchards. If, however, they are unmolested, they soon gain confidence, and in many cases frequent shade trees about houses and lawns, or even in the very heart of the city.

TROGONS

Order *Coccyges;* suborder *Trogones;* family *Trogonidæ*

THE Trogons are forest birds, and therefore arboreal, passing their entire life among the trees, where they nest in natural cavities or in those abandoned by Parrots or the larger Woodpeckers. They feed chiefly on fruits and insects, both of which they take while flying. As a group the Trogons are celebrated for their beauty of plumage, some of the species being among the most beautiful of birds, the magnificent Quetzál (*Pharomachrus mocinno*), of Guatemala, excelling even the far-famed Birds of Paradise in the gorgeous beauty of its plumage and exquisite grace of form.

The Trogons are found in the tropics of both hemispheres; but they are most numerous in America, where eight genera and about thirty-two species occur. One species only is found north of Mexico, the Coppery-tailed Trogon, and it is rare.

The special characteristics of the Trogon family are: bill short (much shorter than the head), broad at the base, and the edges toothed; the gape or corners of the mouth well covered with bristle-tipped feathers; feet weak, the lower section of the leg shorter than the longest front toe, and front toes united for about half their length; wing short, rounded, and very concave underneath; tail longer than the wing and composed of twelve feathers; plumage dense and soft and easily detached; colors bright, brilliantly metallic in adult males, and the under parts of the body pure red, orange, or yellow; young usually spotted and without bright colors.

COPPERY-TAILED TROGON

Trogon ambiguus (*Gould*)

A. O. U. Number 389.

General Description.— Length, 11¾ inches. Males are metallic bronze-green above, and geranium-red below; females are brown above, and pale geranium-red below.

Color.—Adult Male: Forehead (sometimes part, occasionally whole of crown, also), black; back of head (usually part of crown), hindneck, back, shoulders, and forward portion of lesser wing-covert region, bright metallic-green, bronze-green, or golden-bronze, passing into metallic pure green or bronze-green, on rump and upper tail-coverts; middle pair of tail-feathers bright bronze or copper-bronze, changing to a greenish hue in some lights (the color sometimes more greenish basally), broadly and abruptly tipped with black or bluish-black, the next pair of feathers similarly colored on outer web, but inner web darker and more purplish-bronze passing into blackish basally, the terminal black area broader and less sharply defined; remaining tail-feathers very broadly tipped with white (this white terminal area margined basally by a narrow and usually interrupted bar of black); wing-coverts, delicately marked with fine wavy lines of black and white; primaries, slate-black, the outer webs mostly pale gray or grayish-white; lores, cheeks, ear region, chin, and throat, uniform black or slate-black; chest, bright metallic bronze-green, bronze, or copper-bronze, succeeded by a crescentic band of pure white; the remaining under parts, pure geranium-red; thighs, slate-black or blackish-slate, the longer feathers broadly tipped with pink or pinkish-white; bill, yellow; naked eyelids, red or orange; iris, dark brown; feet, brownish. ADULT FEMALE: Forehead, and at least forward portion of crown, slate color or brownish-slate, passing into plain brown on back of head, hindneck, back, and shoulders; the rump and upper tail-coverts similar but (especially the latter) paler; wing-coverts, similar in color to rump and upper tail-coverts; middle pair of tail-feathers, vandyke-brown to chocolate-brown, broadly and abruptly tipped with black; next pair, blackish-brown or brownish-black, the outer web edged (except terminally) with lighter brown; remaining feathers, extensively tipped with white; lores and under eye region, dark-slaty or blackish; ear region crossed obliquely by a broad bar of pale brownish-buff or brownish-white and tipped by an oblique bar of black; a broad brownish-white eye-ring, interrupted on upper and lower eyelids; cheeks, chin, and throat, brownish-slate to grayish-brown, passing into brown (like color of back) on chest; and crossed immediately behind brown jugular area by a crescentic band of brownish-white or pale brownish-buff; lower abdomen, flanks, anal region, and under tail-coverts, light geranium-red; thighs, slate color, the longer feathers broadly tipped with whitish; bill, yellow (duller than in adult male); iris and feet as in adult male. YOUNG: Head, neck, and breast, dull brownish-gray or grayish-brown; an eye-ring and an oblique bar across ear region of white; tail similar to adult female; remainder of upper parts, brown; under parts in general, grayish-white; wing-coverts with buffy spots margined with black.

Nest and Eggs.— NEST: A hole in a bank, about 18 inches deep. EGGS: 3, dull white.

Distribution.— From southern Arizona and extreme southern Texas south over greater part of Mexico.

The Coppery-tailed Trogon utters its call in the manner of the Peacock, sitting bolt upright on a limb, its long tail hanging straight down, and its bill pointed at the zenith. This call is a series of soft and rather musical notes not unlike those of a contented hen. Those who examine mounted specimens should remember that the geranium-red color of the breast plumage is likely to fade considerably after the skin is removed from the bird's body.

KINGFISHERS

Order *Coccyges;* suborder *Alcyones;* family *Alcedinidæ*

THE Kingfisher family is nearly cosmopolitan and is very numerously represented in the eastern hemisphere, especially in the Malay Archipelago and thence to New Guinea, where a great variety of types are found, many of them among the most beautiful of birds. There are about 200 species in all. The group is poorly represented in America, where occur only two genera with about 11 species and subspecies. Only one genus is found north of the Rio Grande.

The American Kingfishers are a well-marked group of birds. Their heads are large, completely feathered, and more or less crested, though sometimes only the feathers at the back of the head and on the nape are slightly elongated. Their bills are long, strong, straight, and much deeper than wide at the base. Their wings are moderate to rather short with the longest primaries always longer than the longest secondaries; the tip of the wing is rather pointed. Tail feathers number twelve, and the tail is from one-half to two-thirds as long as the wing and is slightly rounded. The feet are relatively very small; the first toe is much shorter than the inner toe and connected with the second so as to form with it and the others a broad flattened sole, the surface of which is conspicuously granulated.

In coloration none of the American Kingfishers have the bright hues of the spectrum though some have the upper parts of a rather dull metallic bronze-green. In all of the American forms the sexes are more or less different in coloration.

As their name implies, they feed chiefly on small fishes, though some of the Old World species are forest birds and subsist on reptiles and other forms of animal life. Although small fishes are the principal portion of the diet of Kingfishers, they destroy also a few aquatic insects which do injury to the young of fish and frogs.

Some of the forest-inhabiting species of the eastern hemisphere nest in cavities of trees, but the true Kingfishers nest in holes which they dig in banks. The five to eight eggs are invariably pure white. The young are hatched naked and are cared for in the nest after the manner of perching birds.

BELTED KINGFISHER

Ceryle alcyon (*Linnæus*)

A. O. U. Number 390 See Color Plate 58

Other Names.— Kingfisher; the Halcyon.

General Description.— Length, 12 inches. Color of upper parts and of belt, bluish-gray; under parts, white; females with a reddish band across abdomen. Head, crested.

Color.— Adult Male: Above, including sides of head, clear bluish-gray interrupted by a white collar across hindneck; feathers of crown (especially those of crest) with a center streak of black, those of back, wings, etc., with very slender black shaft-streaks, wing-coverts and secondaries usually with a few minute irregular white markings, the latter with portion of outer web next to shaft and most of inner web, black; primary coverts and primaries, slate-black, the first minutely tipped with white, the primaries with basal half spotted with white, the inner ones, together with the outer secondaries, rather narrowly tipped with white; middle pair of tail-feathers, bluish-gray with a center streak of black (this sometimes confined to shaft), the latter usually margined on each side by small white spots; remaining tail-feathers, slate-black, the outer web (except of lateral pair) broadly edged with bluish-gray, the inner black portion spotted with white, the inner webs barred with white; outermost similar but without distinct, if any, bluish-gray edging, the white spots reaching to outer margin; a conspicuous spot of white in front of eye and another but smaller white spot immediately beneath eye; rear of cheeks, sides of neck, chin, throat, and foreneck, immaculate white, the front of cheeks deep bluish-gray or broadly streaked with the same; *a broad band of bluish-gray across chest;* rest of under parts, white, the sides and flanks mostly bluish-gray (usually intermixed or flecked with white); under wing-coverts, and greater part of basal half of inner webs of primaries, immaculate white; bill, black; iris, dark brown; legs and feet, livid slate color. Adult Female: Similar to the adult male *but with a band* (sometimes incomplete or interrupted) *across lower breast, together with sides and flanks, cinnamon-rufous,* the innermost under wing-coverts sometimes tinged or suffused with the same.

Nest and Eggs.— Nest: At extreme end of a burrow in the bank, from 4 to 15 feet long. Eggs: 5 to 8, laid on the bare floor of the enlarged extremity of the tunnel.

Distribution.— North America and northern South America; breeds from northwestern Alaska, northwestern Mackenzie, central Keewatin, northern Quebec, and Newfoundland south to the southern border of the United States; winters from British Columbia, Nebraska, Illinois, Indiana, Ohio, and Virginia south to the West Indies, Colombia, and Guiana, and irregularly as far north as Massachusetts, New Hampshire, and Ontario.

Drawing by R. I. Brasher

BELTED KINGFISHER (male; ⅓ nat. size)

A feathered Ike Walton who is a stickler for his fishing rights

This is one of the pronounced and picturesque personalities of the feathered world — a handsome, sturdy and self-reliant bird who makes his living by the persistent, skillful, and largely harmless practice of an ancient and respected art.

It seems worth while to emphasize at once

Photo by H. K. Job Courtesy of Outing Pub. Co.

YOUNG KINGFISHER

Emerging from its nest-burrow

the character and purpose of the Kingfisher's activities. Too many of his human imitators fear, or even believe, that he is destructive to game fish, especially brook trout. But it seems that this charge cannot be substantiated, and that the bird catches chiefly minnows, chubs, and related shallow-water fish which are pests to the fisherman. And it is known that a very considerable part of his diet is composed of crawfish, frogs, and even injurious beetles and locusts, which he takes when the fishing is bad, because of rough water, or for other reasons. Consequently, most discerning and well-informed disciples of the immortal Izaak are disposed to take their hats off to this brother fisherman-in-feathers who is always good company on a trout brook and is never without his click-reel.

What wonderful eyesight he must have — little, if any, less keen than that of the Eagles and the Hawks. Many of his dives after his prey he makes from a fluttering halt in his flight, ten or fifteen feet above the surface of the water; but not infrequently he makes his plunge, like a blue meteor, from a perch fifty feet or more from the water, striking it with an impact which, one would think, would completely knock the wind out of him. It is as graceful and daring a "high dive" as is to be seen anywhere. But think of the vision which must be required to see, at that distance, a fish, often no more than two or three inches long, and generally several inches below the surface!

Angling has been called the "contemplative sport," and it is true that the typical trout fisherman likes to fish alone, though at other times he may not be a noticeably unsocial person. Nor, if he is a true sportsman, will he be secretive with his friends as to his favorite fishing grounds. With the Kingfisher it is different. Very likely he enjoys fishing; at any rate, he acts as if he does; but after all, for him fishing is a serious business, not a diversion. Consequently, he is not a gregarious bird, and furthermore he is likely to have pretty definite ideas about his "fishing rights." That is, after he has established himself in a certain locality, he resents the appearance therein of any other Kingfisher and he will attack and drive away any intruders if he can. It is hardly fair to consider this sheer selfishness. For him, fishing is pretty hard work, demanding both patience and skill; and besides, the supply of fish he can catch is never actually bountiful. So he cannot be blamed for keeping a sharp lookout for trespassers on his preserve.

Though the Kingfisher may sometimes actually spear fish with his long bill, he generally seizes them with it, and usually flies immediately to a nearby perch where he beats his prey to death and then swallows it, head foremost, an operation which sometimes is not accomplished without much squirming and writhing. Or, if he has young to feed, he flies straight to his burrow in a nearby bank.

"Among the many legends connected with the

Photo by H. H. Cleaves Courtesy of Nat. Asso. Aud. Soc.

KINGFISHER

Flying from nest in bank, Princess Bay, Staten Island, New York

European Kingfisher," says William Dutcher, "one relates that originally it was somberly clothed; but that a Kingfisher was liberated from Noah's ark and flew toward the setting sun, whereupon the sky was reflected from its back, while its breast was scorched by the rays of the sun, and ever afterwards its plumage showed the colors of the evening sky. Another beautiful old fable is that Alcyone, daughter of Æolus, grieved so deeply for her husband, who had been shipwrecked, that she threw herself into the sea, and was immediately changed into a Kingfisher, called 'Halcyon' by the ancient Latin-speaking people.

"Pliny says: 'Halcyons lay and sit about midwinter when daies be shortest; and the time whiles they are broodie is called the halcyon daies; for during that season the sea is calm and navigable.' [The popular belief was that the seven days preceding the shortest day of the year were used in building the nest, and the seven days following were devoted to hatching the eggs. These fourteen days were called 'halcyon days.'] Even now the adjective 'halcyon' represents calm and peaceful days devoted to pleasant outings in woods or fields or along ocean-beaches, or to paddling up some quiet river, all the while learning to know the trees and wild flowers, and the songs and forms of birds."

GEORGE GLADDEN.

TEXAS KINGFISHER

Ceryle americana septentrionalis *Sharpe*

A. O. U. Number 391.

Other Name.— Texan Green Kingfisher.

General Description.— Length, 8 inches. Color above, green; below, white; males with a patch of chestnut-rufous on the chest. No crest.

Color.—ADULT MALE: Above, including sides of head (except cheeks), dark metallic bronze-green, darker and duller on crown, especially the forehead, interrupted by a white collar across hindneck; forehead freckled with whitish; wing-coverts, usually immaculate, but sometimes with a few minute spots or streaks of white; secondaries with a sub-basal narrow band of white, continuous across both webs, this white increasing in extent on inner secondaries where it involves the whole basal half; about midway between this band and tip of secondaries is another band, composed of small white spots confined to outer portion of outer web, this followed by another one of much smaller white spots, while usually each secondary has a minute white terminal spot or edging; inner primaries, usually with a single small white spot on outer web; middle pair of tail-feathers, mostly blackish, glossed with bluish or bluish-green, usually spotted on inner web with white, sometimes wholly blackish; next pair, blackish, the inner web with roundish white spots; four outer feathers (on each side), immaculate white for basal half or more, the terminal portion, blackish broken by white spots or bars on inner web; front of cheeks, greenish-black, the remainder white (sometimes spotted with greenish-black in front or along lower portion), forming a conspicuous stripe which involves the side of neck; chin, throat, and center of upper foreneck, immaculate white; sides of upper foreneck, chest, and side portion of upper breast, deep chestnut-rufous; rest of under parts, white, the sides and flanks heavily spotted with greenish-black, this heavy spotting extending across lower breast; under tail-coverts with spots of greenish-black; under wing-coverts, white, with a large V-shaped area of dusky; inner web of wings with large spots of white; bill, black; iris, dark brown; legs and feet, dusky. ADULT FEMALE: Similar to the adult male but without any chestnut-rufous, the upper chest, immaculate buffy-white or pale buff (like foreneck,

Photograph by A. A. Allen

BELTED KINGFISHER WITH SMALL SUCKER

throat, and chin), the lower chest crossed by a broad band heavily spotted with greenish-black, the lower breast, also with a similar, but usually less distinct, band; white of under parts tinged with buff, especially the chin, throat, and upper chest, which are sometimes wholly light buff.

Nest and Eggs.— NEST: A burrow in a bank. EGGS: 5 or 6, pure porcelain white, thin-shelled, deposited in the hollowed-out end of the cavity on the bare floor.

Distribution.— Southern Texas and Mexico, south to Panama.

The Texas Kingfisher, since it occurs only in the southern parts of Texas, is essentially a Mexican, if not a Central American, bird. The rattle of this small fisherman is like that of the lusty northern Kingfisher, but absurdly weaker. Like its big relative, however, it has very strong convictions as to its fishing rights, and fiercely attacks any member of its species which ventures on its preserve. It usually watches for fish from a rock in the stream, or even from a sand bar. On land it waddles awkwardly, jerking its tail as it proceeds.

Drawing by R. I. Brasher

TEXAS KINGFISHER (½ nat. size)

Like the northern species, this Kingfisher nests in a hole which it digs in a bank, and the work of excavation is shared by the male and the female, who take turns. Floods due to cloudbursts destroy many of these nests in the bird's Texan range.

Photo by C. William Beebe (Copyrighted) Courtesy of Houghton Mifflin Co.

TEXAS KINGFISHER

ORDER OF WOODPECKERS

Order *Pici;* family *Picidæ*

AS implied by the vernacular name of the group the Woodpeckers are preeminently distinguished for their habit of pecking the bark and decayed wood of trees in their search for grubs and other insects, and for excavating deep cavities in the trunks and branches of trees in which to deposit their eggs. While by no means peculiar to the group, these habits are nevertheless more highly developed and more universal in the Woodpeckers than in any other birds.

The Woodpeckers are essentially arboreal in their habits and obtain the larger part of their food from trees. Their physical conformation especially adapts them to this mode of life. Their legs are rather short and stout and the toes are furnished with strong sharp claws. With the exception of the genus *Picoides*, or Three-toed Woodpeckers, all North American Woodpeckers have four toes, two of which point forward and two backward. As a further aid in maintaining their hold on the trunks of trees their tails are composed of stiff feathers terminating in sharp spines which can be pressed against the bark and so serve as a prop to hold the bird in an upright position while it is at work. Thus Woodpeckers are enabled to cling easily to the trunks and branches and to strike hard and effective blows with their beaks upon the bark or wood.

Since much of the food of this family is obtained from solid wood, a wise Creator has provided most of them with a stout beak having a chisel-shaped point which forms an exceedingly effective wood-cutting instrument. The most interesting and peculiar point in the anatomy of these birds, however, is the tongue. This is cylindrical in form and very long. At the front end it generally terminates in a hard point with barbs upon the sides. On the inside end the typical Woodpecker tongue is extended in two long slender filaments of the hyoid bone which curls up around the back of the skull; in most species these extensions stop between the eyes, but in other members of the family they pass around the eye and in some others enter the right nasal opening and extend to the end of the beak. In this last case the tongue is practically twice the length of the head. The rear end of the tongue is enclosed in a muscular sheath by means of which it can be pushed out from the mouth to a considerable length and used as a most effective instrument for dislodging grubs or ants from their burrows in wood or bark.

While most birds must of necessity content themselves with such insects as they can find on the surface or in open crevices or flying in the air, the Woodpeckers are enabled by their physical construction to devote their energy to those larvæ or grubs which are beneath the bark. They locate their hidden prey with great accuracy and often cut small holes directly to the burrows of the grubs.

Woodpeckers are found in all wooded portions of the world except on the island of Madagascar and in the entire Australian region. The group is nearly equally represented in the two hemispheres, the western claiming about 22 families and 225 species and subspecies, the eastern 27 families and a little more than 200 species and subspecies. In the United States, exclusive of outlying possessions, there are now 45 species and subspecies of this family, most of which are of decided economic importance. As a family they are much less migratory than most other birds, and the majority of the species occupy the same range throughout the year, and this adds materially to their value to farmers. Their food consists so largely of wood-boring grubs, hibernating insects, and insects' eggs and pupæ that their supplies do not fail even in the coldest weather.

With the possible exception of the Crow no birds have been subject to so much criticism as the Woodpeckers. When they are seen scrambling over fruit trees and their holes are found in the bark it is concluded that they must be doing harm. The Woodpeckers, except a few species, rarely disfigure a healthy tree. But when they find a tree infested by wood-boring larvæ, they locate the insects accurately, draw them out, and devour them. If, in the years that follow, the borings formerly occupied by these insects are used by a colony of ants, they in their turn are dug out and destroyed.

Usually the Woodpeckers nest in excavations in trees which they chisel out themselves. The Flicker's bill is less powerful than those of other members of his family and he takes advantage of natural cavities more frequently than the others. These nests vary in size from the large ones in lofty trees belonging to the powerful Ivory-billed and Pileated Woodpeckers to the tiny home of our familiar Downy. The Gila Woodpecker nearly always selects the giant cactus, the Ivory-billed usually a cypress, but the remainder of the family have no particular preference for the kind of tree. In very thinly wooded or treeless countries the few species of Woodpeckers which occur there are from necessity more or less terrestrial, making their excavations in banks of earth or even depositing their eggs in cavities already existing, such as the brain cavity of the skull of a large mammal. The eggs of Woodpeckers are invariably glossy, immaculate white. They number 4 to 8 and are deposited on small chips at the bottom of the excavation, no attempt being made to construct anything like a true nest.

Most of the Woodpeckers have a wavy, galloping flight. much like that of the Goldfinches.

IVORY-BILLED WOODPECKER

Campephilus principalis (*Linnæus*)

A. O. U. Number 392

Other Names.— Woodcock; Logcock; Woodchuck; Ivory-bill.

General Description.— Length, 21 inches. Plumage, blue-black.

Color.— Adult Male: General color, glossy blue-black, the primaries and tail duller black, or with bluish gloss less distinct; nasal plumes, front of lores, stripe on sides of head and neck (*commencing usually beneath middle of eye* and much narrower on this portion) white, these stripes continued behind along each edge of shoulders; secondaries (except basal portion), terminal portion of primaries (extensively), except five or six outermost, and under wing-coverts, white; sometimes a few feathers on flanks and anal region tipped with white; crest, bright red; bill, ivory-white; iris, clear lemon-yellow; legs and feet light gray, the larger scales paler and somewhat yellowish-gray, the claws pale horn color. Adult Female: Similar in coloration to the adult male, *but crest wholly glossy blue-black.*

Nest and Eggs.— Nest: Usually high up in a cypress; entrance oval. Eggs: 3 to 5, white.

Distribution.— Southeastern United States, north to coast district of North Carolina and in the Mississippi Valley to southern Indiana, southern Illinois, Missouri, Oklahoma, western Kentucky, Arkansas, west to Texas (Brazos and Trinity rivers), south to the Gulf coast, and in Florida to the Big Cypress district south to Caloosahatchie River; now extirpated over much of the greater portion of its former range and existing only in scattered or isolated localities in the lower Mississippi valley and the Gulf States, chiefly in Florida and Alabama.

This magnificent bird is the largest of all the North American Woodpeckers. It is just about the size of a Crow, in fact it is fully four inches longer than the Fish Crow so common along our rivers and coast-line. The most striking feature of its appearance is its head. This is adorned with a bill that resembles a glossy ivory dagger, nearly three inches in length, and the flaming red crest at the back of the head of the male is one of the most animated feathered objects in nature. The Ivory-billed Woodpecker is a bird of astonishing strength and vigor. Often beneath a diseased tree which it has attacked, in quest of boring beetles or insect larvæ, huge piles of bark and slabs of wood are found which give convincing evidence of its power as a feathered axman.

This is a bird of the deep forest solitudes. It is a great traveler and during the course of a day wanders over a vast expanse of territory. Unfortunately for us it has been unable to withstand the advances of civilization even to the extent to which the big Pileated Woodpecker has survived, and to-day it must be numbered among those species of which we are accustomed to speak as being "nearly extinct." Probably it has entirely disappeared from our southern Atlantic coast, as well as from the Mississippi River country, with the exception of some of the Louisiana swamps. A few still persist in the almost limitless swamps of Florida, but so far as the vision of the average man is concerned, the bird has already gone to join the Dodo and the Great Auk.

Alexander Wilson, writing in the early part of the last century when the Ivory-billed was still found as far north as North Carolina, speaks of a "vulger prejudice" existing in the minds of the people against it. Yet there appears to be little evidence that gunners ever paid any special attention to the bird. Its almost total disappearance, therefore, is not easily explained.

The nesting holes of this species are dug from dead or living trees located far in the most inaccessible regions of the deep cypress swamps. There, too, are the haunts where the bird seeks its food. They are very noisy, and in the nesting season as they chase each other about, or later when the young have left the nest, their loud cries may be heard piercing the swampy gloom for hundreds of yards.

Wilson, writing of one he wounded and confined in his room in a hotel in Wilmington, North Carolina, says: "In less than an hour I returned, and, on opening the door he set up a distressing shout, which appeared to proceed from grief that he had been discovered in his attempts to escape. He had mounted along the side of the window, nearly as high as the ceiling, a little below which he began to break through. The bed was covered with large pieces of plaster, the lath was exposed for at least fifteen inches square, and a hole large enough to admit the fist, opened to the weather-boards; so that, in less than another hour he would certainly have succeeded in making his way through."

The analysis of the food of the Ivory-billed Woodpecker indicates that this species, were it not for its small numbers, might be of considerable economic value. The insects which form the animal portion of its food are mostly of an injurious character. These powerful birds are able to reach the wood-boring grubs in places where smaller species fail and their large bodies require a great quantity of such food. The vegetable portion of their food shows no indication that this Woodpecker is likely to take any products of agriculture. Its shy, retiring habits strengthen this inference.

In his *Food of the Woodpeckers of the United States,* F. E. L. Beal says of the Ivory-bill: "When we see how much good this Woodpecker is capable of doing as a guardian of the forest, it seems deplorable that it should be allowed to be exterminated. Wise legislation, backed by

Drawing by R. I. Brasher

IVORY-BILLED WOODPECKER (¼ nat. size)

The boss carpenter of the bird world — the biggest, handsomest, and rarest of American Woodpeckers

intelligent public opinion, may retard, if not absolutely prevent, the present destruction and allow the bird to regain something of its former abundance. There is room for this splendid species and much need for its services in the great southern forests."

T. Gilbert Pearson.

HAIRY WOODPECKER

Dryobates villosus villosus (*Linnæus*)

A. O. U. Number 393 See Color Plate 59

Other Names.— Guinea Woodpecker; Sapsucker or Big Sapsucker (incorrect); Harry.

General Description.— Length, 9½ inches. Upper parts, black and white; under parts, white.

Color.— Adult Male: Crown, uniform glossy blue-black; a band of scarlet on hindhead usually interrupted in middle portion by an extension of the black of crown; rest of upper parts, black, the center of back (broadly) white, the wings (including middle coverts) spotted with white, the spots on greater coverts and wing feathers arranged in regular transverse series; *two outside tail-feathers on each side, entirely white,* the third white except basal portion of inner web, the fourth with greater part of outer web and rear portion of inner web, white; nasal tufts dull white to dull brownish-yellow, the bristly shafts blackish; a broad white stripe above sides of head narrower in front where extending over eye (sometimes confluent with whitish of nasal tufts); a broad white stripe below and back of eye confluent in front with nasal tufts, behind extending to sides of neck; between these two white stripes a broad black stripe involving whole of sides of head and part of region around eye, behind confluent with black of hindneck; a black cheek stripe (usually broken in front by admixture of white), continued and gradually widening behind where confluent with a lateral extension of the black of hindneck, and also sending off a short branch along side of chest; underparts, immaculate white; bill, deep grayish horn color; iris, reddish-brown. Adult Female: Similar to the adult male but *without any red on head.*

Nest and Eggs.— Nest: Generally in a dead tree. Eggs: 4 to 6, white.

Distribution.— Northeastern United States from Nebraska, eastern Colorado, and Oklahoma east to middle and northern parts of Eastern States.

One is tempted to think of the Hairy Woodpecker as but an overgrown Downy, or his big brother. Two and a half inches longer than Downy is our big Hairy of the Trees, and his voice is a big rollicking variation of Downy's, deeper and stronger but with the same happy ring. If one's observation of him is imperfect he might easily be mistaken for Downy, for his manners and coloration pattern are very much like his smaller relative. Not nearly so common as the Downies, the Hairies nevertheless are to be found scattered over about the same area and in the same kind of natural conditions. They are just rare enough so that an enthusiastic bird student hearing the strong call of Hairy will quicken his step and add more alertness to his observation for the pleasure of meeting big Harry again.

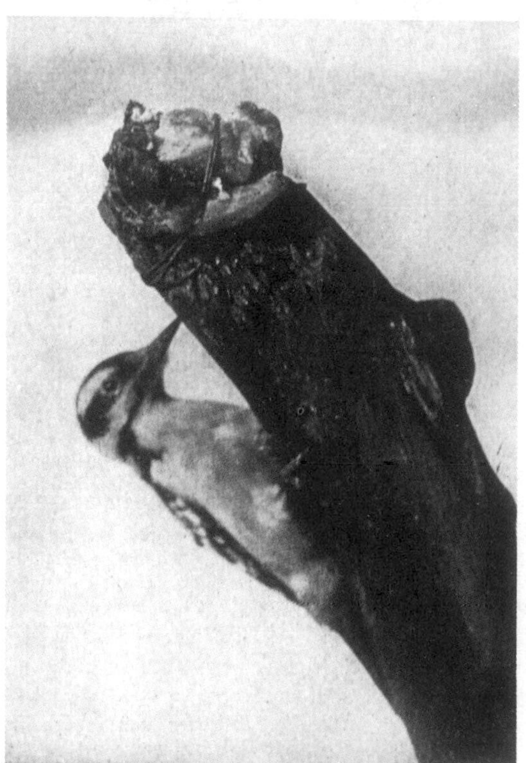

Photo by G. C. Job Courtesy of Outing Pub. Co.

HAIRY WOODPECKER

Indulging his craving for meat by investigating a piece of suet tied to a dead branch

In Canada and the northern border of the United States Hairy is over three inches longer than Downy. Here he is called the Northern Hairy (*Dryobates villosus leucomelas*). He seems astonishingly large to the bird-student who finds him far up in the northern forests. Correspondingly small is the Hairy of the Southern States, there called the Southern, or Audubon's, Hairy (*Dryobates villosus auduboni*).

Newfoundland has a Hairy Woodpecker (*Dryobates villosus terrænovæ*) which is intermediate in size between the familiar Hairy and the Northern Hairy; he also has less white on his back and wings.

Western America has four slightly variant forms. The Rocky Mountain Hairy Woodpecker (*Dryobates villosus monticola*) is similar in size to the Northern Hairy but the white spots on the wing coverts are either reduced in size or absent altogether. Harris's Woodpecker (*Dryobates villosus harrisi*) is found along the Pacific coast from Alaska to northern California. Cabanis's Woodpecker (*Dryobates villosus hyloscopus*) lives in the interior districts from northern California, southern Utah, northwestern and central New Mexico, extreme southwestern Texas, south to the mountains of western Mexico. The range of the Queen Charlotte Woodpecker (*Dryobates villosus picoideus*) is limited to the Queen Charlotte Islands, British Columbia. These last three varieties are about an inch smaller than the Northern and Rocky Mountain Hairies, and their differences from one another are comparative.

L. Nelson Nichols.

The Hairy Woodpecker is a bird from which the orchardist and forester have nothing to fear and much to gain. The number of useful insects which he eats is insignificant while the number of destructive larvæ which he devours must have a very great effect in reducing the number of these pests. More than three-fourths of the food of this Woodpecker consists of animal matter and less than a fourth of the remainder is fruit and this is mostly wild fruit. The ratio between the animal food and the vegetable matter does not vary greatly during the year; the wood-boring larvæ upon which this bird so largely feeds can be obtained at all times of the year and the same is true of most of its vegetable food.

Photo by S. A. Lottridge

NEST AND EGGS OF HAIRY WOODPECKER

Section of stub removed

DOWNY WOODPECKER

Dryobates pubescens medianus (*Swainson*)

A. O. U. Number 394c See Color Plate 59

Other Names.— Little Guinea Woodpecker; Little Sapsucker (incorrect); Tommy Woodpecker; Black and White Driller.

General Description.— Length, 6½ inches. Upper parts, black and white; under parts, white

Color.— Adult Male: Crown, sides of head, center of hindneck, sides of back, shoulders, and upper tail-coverts, black faintly glossed with bluish; four middle tail-feathers, black, without gloss; wings, dull black, passing into dark brownish slaty on primary coverts and terminal portion of primaries, the middle coverts with a rather large roundish spot of white near end and a sub-basal roundish or transverse spot of the same; greater coverts with a roundish sub-terminal spot of white on outer web and a sub-basal roundish spot (concealed) of same on both webs; secondaries crossed by four transverse series of roundish white spots, the first concealed by greater coverts, the last smaller and terminal; outer webs of primaries with similar but more elongate and square spots, about four in number on longest quills besides a smaller terminal spot or margin; a broad center stripe of white on back, this sometimes slightly streaked with black; *two lateral tail-feathers on each side, white, with two broad black bars across rear portion,* the upper one usually broken or interrupted; third feather with rear half of outer web, white, the terminal portion of inner web with one or more broad white bars or spots; nasal tufts, dull white, the bristle-like shafts black terminally; a white stripe over side of head, continued, narrowly, above eye, its rear end in contact with a bright red nape band; a broad stripe of white, extending in front beneath eye, to lores, where confluent with the duller white of nasal tufts, its rear end involving sides of neck; cheeks, grayish intermixed with black in front, continued behind as a gradually widening "solid" black stripe which curves upward behind the white area and connects with the black of back; under parts, plain dull grayish-white, more whitish on chin and throat, the under tail-coverts usually barred or flecked with black; under wing-coverts, mostly immaculate dull white, but with a black patch; inner webs of wings, dull slaty with large spots of white, except on rear portion of longer primaries; bill, dark horn-grayish; iris, brown or reddish-brown. ADULT FEMALE: Similar to the adult male, but without any red on head, the band replaced by a white one and this usually divided by a center black area.

Nest and Eggs.— NEST: Generally in a dead tree. EGGS: 4 to 6, white.

Distribution.— Northern and central parts of eastern North America from southeastern Alberta, Manitoba, and southern Ungava south to eastern Nebraska, Kansas, and the Potomac valley, and in mountains to North Carolina.

The little black and white Woodpecker of eastern North America has been named the Downy. It is a convenient, homely, and short name for a genial, friendly little bird. Maybe

Photo by H. K. Job Courtesy of Outing Pub. Co.

DOWNY WOODPECKER AT WORK

Tommy Woodpecker would be better, for his boyish, buoyant disposition makes friends for him wherever he goes. He is best known in the open woodland rather than in the dense forest. He seems to be pretty well scattered over the entire area of northeastern America, but never to be very common anywhere. Yet hardly a maple-shaded village, or city park, or farmer's wood lot or thinly timbered swamp but hears the bright, clear, quick, rattling call of little Downy. Watch carefully where the call came from, and he may be seen — or sometimes heard and not seen — tapping into a limb of a tree. Or he may swing down, looping across an open space to another tree that promises another grub or tree parasite. If he is not too busy he will rattle out his joyous call again to whatever ear may hear.

The casual observer who does not handle the birds should not expect to find anything downy about the Downy Woodpecker, or hairy about the Hairy Woodpecker. They are both plain black and white Woodpeckers with ordinary looking feathers when viewed from a short distance. Both the Downy and the Hairy Woodpeckers excavate holes during the fall, in which they pass the winter nights.

There are five other varieties of the Downy scattered over temperate North America: Southern Downy Woodpecker (*Dryobates pubescens pubescens*) in the South Atlantic and Gulf States from North Carolina to eastern Texas; Gairdner's Woodpecker (*Dryobates pubescens gairdneri*) along the Pacific coast from southern British Columbia to northern California;

Photo by S. A. Lottridge

EGGS OF DOWNY WOODPECKER

A section of the stub was removed

Batchelder's Woodpecker (*Dryobates pubescens homorus*) in the mountains from southern British Columbia to New Mexico and Arizona; the Northern, or Nelson's, Downy Woodpecker (*Dryobates pubescens nelsoni*) in northwestern Alaska and southwestern Mackenzie to central Alberta; and the Willow Woodpecker (*Dryobates pubescens turati*) along the coasts and in the valleys of California except on the northwest coast and the desert ranges. The differences between these forms and between them and the common Downy are slight variations in coloration and size. L. NELSON NICHOLS.

The Downy Woodpecker is one of the fruit-grower's friends. Besides picking up various pests he locates burrows of the flat-headed apple-tree borer and extracts the insects in considerable numbers. He is also an enemy of the codling moth. Caterpillars appear to be a very acceptable food for Downy, as they constitute 16½ per cent. of his yearly diet. A large proportion of them are of the wood-boring species which he digs out of the wood; others are surface feeders which he takes from the leaves and bark.

The proportion between the animal and vegetable parts of the food of the Downy Woodpecker is practically the same as in the case of the Hairy Woodpecker. Less than 6 per cent. of the entire food is fruit and very little of this is cultivated. Grain of all kinds aggregates less than 2 per cent.

The one charge that can be brought against this Woodpecker is that of disseminating the seeds of the poison ivy. These seeds are a favorite winter food for many birds. Unfortunately they germinate freely after they have been voided. Since the insect food eaten by Downy is almost all of harmful species it should be considered fortunate that he can live on this food when it is difficult for him to procure anything else, and his one sin should be forgiven him.

RED-COCKADED WOODPECKER

Dryobates borealis (*Vieillot*)

A. O. U. Number 395

General Description.— Length, 8 inches. Upper parts, black and white, barred; under parts, white.

Color.— ADULT MALE: Crown, hindneck, lores, and broad cheek stripe, extending behind to sides of neck, where wider than in front, glossy blue-black; nasal tufts, dull whitish; around eye and sides of head white, forming a large patch which extends behind onto sides of neck and in front sends a narrow branch to above middle of eye; *streak of scarlet-vermilion, along side of head* immediately above the white ear area; extreme upper back, sooty black, usually with concealed spots or streaks of whitish; rest of back, together with shoulders, broadly barred with sooty black and white, the two colors equal in extent; upper rump also barred with black and white but less regularly or distinctly; lower rump, upper tail-coverts, and four middle tail-feathers, black; two outer tail feathers white (usually stained), with basal portion of inner web, black, the white portion of inner web with three broad bars or transverse spots of dull black; third tail-feathers with whole, or nearly all, of inner web black, also the basal half of outer web; wings, sooty black, the middle and rear lesser coverts variously spotted with white, the greater coverts with two transverse rows of white spots, the secondaries crossed by four (exposed) narrow bands or broad bars of white; outer webs of primaries (except two outermost) with spots of white; inner webs of wings (except terminal half of longer primaries) with large spots of white; under parts, white, the sides of chest longitudinally spotted or broadly streaked with deep black, the sides, flanks, and under tail-coverts with smaller spots and streaks of dusky; bill, blackish; iris, brown. ADULT FEMALE: Similar to the adult male, but without any red streak on sides of head.

Nest and Eggs.— NEST: In a living pine and usually high up. EGGS: 2 to 5, usually 3 or 4, glossy white.

Distribution.— Pine forests of eastern United States, from Florida to eastern Texas; north to central Virginia, eastern Tennessee, western Kentucky, and southeastern Missouri; casually to New Jersey and eastern Pennsylvania.

This is distinctly a bird of the southern United States, not being found north of Virginia or farther west than Oklahoma. It is an inhabitant of the open pine-woods which cover so much of our southern territory, and rarely, if ever, is it met with where the terrain is heavily wooded. In small bands they go trooping through the trees, searching the limbs, twigs, and cones for the insect diet upon which they largely subsist. Rarely will one see them except in the tree-tops, as they seem to prefer to feed there rather than lower down along the trunks. In general appearance they much resemble the common and familiar Downy, and by many people are often mistaken for this bird. Unlike it, however, they keep well away from human habitations and generally avoid entirely such places as fruit orchards and shade-trees. An easy field mark for distinguishing the two is to be found in the coloring on the head of the males. On the Downy a scarlet band stretches across the nape, while the Red-cockaded rejoices in a small scarlet streak on either side of the back of the head.

The student who goes afield for the first time to study the nesting habits of this bird will find certain surprises awaiting him. To begin with, the nesting cavity is always dug in a living pine tree. Wise lumbermen do not cut a tree that has a nest of this bird in it, for if they do they will have their labor for nothing. The tree has a dead heart. How the little Woodpecker knows this in advance has not yet been revealed. The small entrance-hole goes directly in, usually slanting slightly upward, until the softer dead wood is encountered, then it is dug straight down for about a foot. Here on a bed of fine chips, picked from the side of the hole, the three or four glossy white eggs are laid.

These birds have a strong attachment for their nesting-tree and not only return to it year after year, but will rear their young in the same nest for several consecutive seasons, if the condition of the tree continues to be satisfactory. Sometimes they are not permitted to do this, for along comes that bully of the woods, the Red-bellied Woodpecker, who after enlarging the entrance-hole takes it for his own.

And now comes the most curious habit of this interesting bird. Before a single egg is laid each spring the birds peck hundreds of small holes through the bark about the nest from which the turpentine at once begins to flow. This soon makes a shining, sticky surface all around the tree for two or three feet above the nest and for several feet below it. Why this is done we can only conjecture, although the birds doubtless have a very good reason. It is certainly true that none of the ants that sometimes attack young birds could crawl across this no-man's-land, and it is equally true that the nest will not be troubled by the flying squirrels that are everywhere abundant in the pine-forests of the South.

Of the total food of the Red-cockaded Woodpecker over four-fifths is insects and the remainder is vegetable matter, mostly seeds of conifers. About one-half of 1 per cent. of its whole food is made up of useful beetles. Other items on its meat diet are wood-boring weevils, leaf-eating beetles, ants, bark lice, soldier bugs, caterpillars, crickets, eggs of cockroaches, grasshoppers and spiders. In addition to the conifer seeds it eats seeds of the bayberry, poison ivy, and magnolia and some wild fruits. It does little, if any, damage to the products of husbandry.

T. Gilbert Pearson.

TEXAS WOODPECKER

Dryobates scalaris bairdi (*Malherbe*)

A. O. U. Number 396

Other Names.— Speckle-cheek; Texan Downy.

General Description.— Length, 7½ inches. Upper parts, black and white, barred; under parts, grayish-white.

Color.— Adult Male: Crown, bright red, the feathers dark grayish sooty basally, and with a white spot in middle portion, the red tips gradually increasing in length toward the nape, so that the white spots are concealed behind but exposed on the crown, where also the basal dusky shows; forehead with very little, if any, red, passing into brownish in front; *hindneck, back, shoulders, and rump broadly, sharply, and regularly barred with black and white,* the black bars narrower than the white, and less distinct on rump; shorter upper tail-coverts, black, usually with a white spot or bar; longer upper tail-coverts and four middle tail-feathers, uniform black; lateral pair, brownish-white, crossed by about six broad bars of black, those on basal portion of outer web usually reduced to spots next to shaft; next pair similar, but with about basal half of inner web, uniform black; fourth pair, black with broad white spots, or broadly and irregularly edged with white, on about terminal half of outer web, the inner web sometimes with one to three white spots on terminal portion; wings, black, the middle coverts with a central, usually heart-shaped, spot of white, the lesser coverts (at least the posterior ones) with a smaller and more rounded white central spot, the greater coverts crossed by two transverse series, or bands, of white spots, the secondaries with six similar white bands, the first concealed by greater coverts, the primaries similarly marked; nasal tufts, dull brownish-white to pale brown; broad stripes of brownish-white above and below side of head, extending beneath eye to base of nasal tufts, the two sometimes confluent on side of neck, behind the black ear stripe; cheeks, dull whitish anteriorly, barred with dusky in front with black behind, where the black is continued backward as a narrow stripe, which usually sends a lateral branch upward to meet the rear end of the black ear stripe; under parts, dull grayish-white, paler on chin and upper throat, flanks, and under tail-coverts, the sides of chest and breast marked with streaks or, usually, drop-shaped spots of black, the sides spotted, the flanks transversely spotted or barred, the under tail-coverts with transverse bars or spots of the same, usually of V-shaped form; under wing-coverts, dull brownish-white, sparsely (sometimes indistinctly) spotted or streaked with black or dusky; inner web of wings dull slate or dusky, with large, roundish spots of white, arranged in transverse series, on inner half of web; bill, horn color; iris, brown. ADULT FEMALE: Similar to the adult male, but without any red, the crown uniform black, passing into sooty brown on front of forehead.

Nest and Eggs.— NEST: In trees, when they are convenient, or in gate-posts or in telegraph or telephone poles. EGGS: 4 or 5, white.

Distribution.— Southeastern California, southern Nevada, Utah, Colorado south to central Texas and northern Mexico.

This is a sort of Downy Woodpecker of the southwestern border. It is perhaps commoner than any other Woodpecker in western Texas, where it is frequently seen in both the hard-wood and the soft-wood timber of the Guadalupe and other mountains. In the hot and arid valleys it is to be found chiefly in the willow, cottonwood, mesquite and yucca growths.

In its appearance it is similar to Nuttall's Woodpecker, though it has no bars on its black middle tail-feathers. In the mountainous country it often associates with the Ant-eating Woodpecker and the Red-shafted Flicker. Its note, though thin and rather weak, is often persistent enough to betray its presence, while its curiosity prompts it to do much peering around tree-trunks at the stranger. Though it nests in trees where suitable ones are available, it frequently sets up housekeeping in telegraph poles or gate posts.

The Texas Woodpecker shows the ruling characteristic of its family in its choice of food, for the largest item is wood-boring beetle larvæ. Next in importance are the caterpillars and these include a number of cotton worms. Ants make up the remainder of its food.

The San Lucas Woodpecker (*Dryobates scalaris lucasanus*) is similar to the Texas Woodpecker except that the outer tail-feathers are barred only on the terminal half. It is found in southern California south to southern Lower California.

NUTTALL'S WOODPECKER

Dryobates nuttalli (*Gambel*)

A. O. U. Number 397

General Description.— Length, 7½ inches. Upper parts, black and white, barred; under parts, white.

Color.— ADULT MALE: Forehead and greater part of *crown, black* conspicuously streaked (except sometimes on forehead) with white, the streaks narrowly wedge-shaped; extreme rear of crown, back of head, nape, and upper hindneck, scarlet-vermilion, this color separated, on each feather, from a dusky basal area by a small V-shaped or drop-shaped spot of whitish; lower hindneck, upper back, lesser wing-coverts, upper tail-coverts, and four middle tail-feathers, uniform black; rest of back, together with shoulders and rump, broadly barred with black and white, the bars of the two colors equal in width; middle and greater wing-coverts, black, the former with a single subterminal roundish spot of white, the latter with two roundish white spots on outer web; wing feathers, black, broadly barred with white, their inner webs with larger roundish spots of the same; outermost feathers, white, with one complete subterminal bar of black and a second incomplete or interrupted bar, the basal portion of inner web usually with some black; next one similar but with more black at base and with second subterminal interrupted bar reduced to a pair of small, widely separated spots, or absent; third with more than basal half black and without second (sometimes without any) subterminal black spot or bar; nasal tufts and front of loral region, dull whitish or light yellowish dusky behind; rear of lores, narrow mouth stripe (extending back beneath eye), a broader stripe on side of head, continued more broadly along sides of neck, together with under parts white, the under parts of body usually tinged with pale brownish buffy; sides of head and broad cheek stripe (the latter continued posteriorly over lower sides of neck, where much expanded), black; sides and flanks, spotted with black, the markings more longitudinal on sides of breast, more transverse on flanks; under tail-coverts, barred or spotted with black; bill, horn color; iris, brown. ADULT FEMALE: Similar to the male, but crown and hindneck uniform black or else (in earlier spring), with very small or scattered white streaks.

Nest and Eggs.— NEST: In dead limbs or old tree-stubs; not far from the ground. EGGS: 4 to 6, white.

Distribution.— California (west of Sierra Nevada), southwestern Oregon and northern Lower California.

All of the climbing birds are, of course, pretty good at climbing, that being their business; but this little Woodpecker has a trick of flying up and lighting on the under side of a limb, and while thus upside down turning around a few times, like an inverted weather-cock, which makes one gasp, and wonder if he has any nerves at all.

Another peculiarity of the bird is his manifest preference for oaks and other deciduous trees, which he frequents virtually to the exclusion of the conifers. The first word of his scientific name *"Dryobates"* is a combination of two Greek words meaning "oak" and "treader"; so literally he and his relatives, the Hairy, Downy, Red-cockaded, and Texas Woodpecker families, are "treaders of oaks."

Of his temperament, Mrs. Bailey gives the following interesting glimpses: "He has the full strength of his convictions and will drive a big Flicker from a sycamore and then stretch up on a branch and call out triumphantly. Two Nuttalls trying to decide whether to fight are an amusing sight. They shake their feathers and scold and dance about as if they were aching to fly at each other, but could not quite make up their minds to so grave a matter."

The bird evidently prefers to attend strictly to business, and is likely to become so absorbed in hammering away at bark or wood where his prey lurks, that often one may approach to within a very short distance without disturbing him. The black crown, the black and white bars on the back (suggesting the American Three-toed Woodpecker), and the white feathers on the sides of the tail are marks by which the bird may easily be identified.

In the mountains of southwestern New Mexico and southern Arizona and south into northwestern Mexico lives another member of the "oak-treader" family. He is known by the name of Arizona Woodpecker (*Dryobates arizonæ*). His upper parts are plain brown except for the red nape. He is a little longer than the Texas Woodpecker.

The animal food of Nuttall's Woodpecker is composed chiefly of insects which are either pests or of no positive benefit. The bird eats some fruit, but this is largely and probably entirely wild varieties. Nothing worse can be said of this bird than that it possibly helps in the distribution of the seeds of poison oak.

Photo by W. L. Finley and H. T. Bohlman

NUTTALL'S WOODPECKER

Practically all the insects which it eats are either pests or of no positive benefit

WHITE-HEADED WOODPECKER

Xenopicus albolarvatus (*Cassin*)

A. O. U. Number 399

General Description.— Length, 8½ inches. Body, black; head, white.

Color.—Adult Male: *Head, all round* (except rear of crown, upper nape, and a streak behind eye) *together with foreneck, plain white,* the nasal tufts tinged with brownish; rear of crown and nape with a band of bright poppy red; rest of plumage, uniform slightly glossy, black, duller black on wings, the primaries extensively white on basal half of both webs, this white extending much farther on outer than on inner web; bill, slate-blackish; iris, brownish-red or dull carmine. Adult Female: Similar to the adult male, but without any red on head or nape.

Nest and Eggs.— Nest: In stub of pine or fir tree, usually from 4 to 15 feet from ground. Eggs: 3 to 7, white.

Distribution.— Cascade and Sierra Nevada Mountains, from southern British Columbia southward through Washington and Oregon to southern California: east to western Idaho and western Nevada.

The White-headed Woodpecker is a typical bird of the yellow pine timber, ranging from the mountains of southern British Columbia through Oregon and Idaho and especially along the eastern slopes of the Cascades and Sierra Nevadas. The bird gets its food from insects in the bark of the pine, not so much by boring into the tree as by prying off the scales or layers of the bark. It is a quiet worker and eats a great number of larvæ that tunnel into the bark and the other insects that crawl under the scales of the bark for shelter in winter.

Drawing by R. I. Brasher

WHITE-HEADED WOODPECKER (⅔ nat. size)

A quiet worker among the yellow pine timber

Dr. James C. Merrill says: " One would think that the peculiar coloration of the White-headed Woodpecker would make it very conspicuous and its detection an easy matter, but this is by no means the case, at least about Fort Klamath. On most of the pines in this vicinity there are many short stubs of small broken branches projecting an inch or two from the main trunk. When the sun is shining, these projections are lighted up in such a manner as to appear quite white at a little distance, and they often cast a shadow resembling the black body of the bird. In winter when a little snow has lodged on these stubs, the resemblance is even greater, and almost daily I was misled by this deceptive appearance, either mistaking a stub for a bird or the reverse."

Mrs. Florence Merriam Bailey records much the same experience with this bird. " Impossible as it would seem at first sight, I have found that the snow-white head often serves the bird as a disguise. It is the disguise of color pattern, for the black body seen against a tree trunk becomes one of the black streaks or shadows of the bark, and the white head is cut off as a detached white spot without bird-like suggestions. On the other hand, when the bird is exploring the light-barked young Shasta firs or gray barkless tracts of old trees, the white of the head tones in with the gray and is lost, the headless back becoming only a shadow or scar. But the most surprising thing of all is to see the sun streaming full on the white head and find that the bird form is lost. The white in this case is so glaring that it fills the eye and carries it over to the light streaks on the bark, making the black sink away as insignificant. All this applies, however, only when the bird is quiet; in motion he is strikingly conspicuous, and in flight his white wing streak makes another good recognition mark."

William L. Finley.

The most pronounced characteristic of the White-headed Woodpecker is its fondness for the seeds of pines. These constitute more than half of its food. The remainder of its food is insects and half of these are ants.

ARCTIC THREE-TOED WOODPECKER

Picoides arcticus (*Swainson*)

A. O. U. Number 400 See Color Plate 60

Other Name.— Black-backed Three-toed Woodpecker.

General Description.— Length, 9½ inches. Upper parts, black and white, the black predominating; under parts, white.

Color.— Adult Male: Crown, bright yellow to orange; rest of head except (usually) extreme front of forehead, hindneck, and sides of neck, uniform glossy blue-black; rest of *upper parts, black,* or sooty-black, the shoulders and back broadly margined with glossy blue-black, the lesser wing-coverts narrowly margined with the same, the middle wing-coverts and upper tail-coverts margined with deeper black than central portion; outer webs of wings, except inner secondaries, spotted with white; four middle tail feathers, black, the next pair mostly black, extremities brownish-white, usually tipped with black, the three lateral pairs mostly white, tinged terminally with brownish; nasal tufts dusky, sometimes finely streaked with paler; extreme front of forehead, usually white, grayish white, or pale grayish, a broad white stripe extending thence across lores and beneath eyes to side of neck; cheeks, black or blue-black, forming a stripe which extends behind across sides of neck, where usually confluent with the black neck area; under parts, white, the sides and flanks broadly barred with black, the bars less regular and sometimes broken into spots or streaks on front of sides; bill, slate color; iris, reddish-brown or chestnut. Adult Female: Similar to the adult male, but without any yellow on crown, the entire crown being uniform glossy blue-black.

Nest and Eggs.— Nest: In a tree, usually an evergreen, not over 15 feet up. Eggs: 4 to 6, white.

Distribution.— North America; north to central Alaska, Yukon, southern Mackenzie, central Keewatin, and northern Ungava; breeding southward to Maine, New Hampshire, Vermont, northern New York, northern Ontario, northern Michigan, northern Minnesota, Montana, Wyoming, Oregon, and northeastern California; in winter, irregularly southward to Massachusetts, Connecticut, Pennsylvania, southern Ontario, northern Ohio, northeastern Illinois, Wisconsin, eastern Nebraska, and in Sierra Nevada to latitude 39° or farther.

Drawing by R. I. Brasher

ARCTIC THREE-TOED WOODPECKER (½ nat. size)

Too much interested in his own affairs to pay attention to you

The Arctic, or Black-backed, Three-toed Woodpecker is a bird of the northern forests. Observations of this bird are made very rarely except in the belts of spruce and balsam. Even there one is more sure of finding them in the burned areas where the dead stubs rise thirty and more feet high. The bird is never common anywhere. Manly Hardy wrote from Maine to Captain Bendire that this bird "is rarely, if ever, found in any numbers far from burnt tracts; if in green growth, usually singly, or at most in pairs; but on newly burnt lands specimens may be found by the score, and their sharp, shrill *chirk, chirk* can be heard in all directions."

The very rarity of this bird makes the finding of one an event in bird observations. The three toes will not be observed as the bird clings to a tall dead stub or a thick branched spruce, but the plain black back and the yellow front of the head of the male are distinctive.

To some the Arctic Woodpecker is a stupid bird, but its lack of fear of hunters and its interest in its own affairs of hunting for worms has made it an easily studied bird in the field. This habit may have tempted many a man with a gun to blaze away at it.

THREE-TOED WOODPECKER

Picoides americanus americanus *Brehm*

A. O. U. Number 401 See Color Plate 61

Other Names.—American Three-toed Woodpecker; White-backed Three-toed Woodpecker; Ladder-back Woodpecker.

General Description.— Length, 8½ inches. Upper parts, black and white — a white line down the back, interrupted with black; under parts, white.

Color.—Adult Male: *Crown, yellow;* forehead, black, spotted with dull white, especially toward the back (next to yellow of crown); rest of crown, lores, around eyes, sides of head, and hindneck, uniform glossy blue-black, sometimes with a narrow streak of white behind the eye, often with whitish spots or streaks on back of head (next to yellow of crown); rest of upper parts, dull black (sometimes forming a rather distinct but broken collar), *back and upper rump barred* or transversely spotted, along center with white, the outer webs of wings also spotted with white, except inner secondaries, the innermost of which have white spots along edge of inner web; two lateral tail-feathers on each side, with terminal half or more white, the third, extensively white terminally, this white stained with brownish, especially on ends; nasal tufts, light grayish-brown, finely streaked with black; a streak or narrow stripe of white around the mouth and passing beneath eyes; beneath this a cheek stripe of glossy blue-black, usually broken by white tips to the feathers; under parts, white, the sides and flanks, broadly barred with black, sides of breast with bars more irregular, sometimes broken into spots and streaks; bill, grayish horn color. Adult Female: Similar to the adult male, but without any yellow on head, the entire crown glossy blue-black, usually streaked or spotted with grayish-white on forehead and crown, but sometimes immaculate.

Nest and Eggs.— Nest: In a tree, usually an evergreen, and not over 12 feet up. Eggs: Usually 4, white.

Distribution.— Northern North America, from central Ungava to northern Minnesota, southern Ontario, northern New York, Maine, and New Hampshire; casual in winter to Massachusetts.

The Ladder-back Woodpeckers are divisible into three regional varieties, the American, the Alaska (*Picoides americanus fasciatus*), and the Alpine (*Picoides americanus dorsalis*). The American Three-toed Woodpecker is a rarer bird in the United States than the Arctic Woodpecker. Far into the Canadian north beyond the Great Slave Lake it becomes the commonest of Woodpeckers. The Alaska Three-toed Woodpecker is not at all common even in Alaska, but it is also rarely found as far south as northwestern Washington. The variety called the Alpine Three-toed Woodpecker is a Rocky Mountain bird from Arizona to Canada, and appears to prefer the pine belts rather than the upper spruce belts.

There have been so few observations of the Ladder-back and so much taken for granted of their calls and customs, that the accounts of their habits are quite confusing. In the Adirondacks Dr. Merriam and Mr. Bagg have made extensive observations. The birds there have nesting holes in any kind of evergreen. The most remarkable characteristic of this bird is that it is non-migratory. Only the Hudsonian Chickadee, Canada Jay and Spruce Grouse are as perfectly non-migratory as the Three-toed Woodpecker.

Quiet as is the Arctic Three-toed, the American Three-toed is even more silent. It might easily be passed by unnoticed by the bird student, anxious though he might be to see a real rarity.

The great bulk of the food of the Three-toed Woodpeckers, both the Arctic Three-toed and the Ladder-backed Three-toed, consists of the larvæ of wood-boring beetles or moths. These are eaten with great regularity throughout the year but more of them in the colder months than in summer. In the dead of winter when all insect life seems to be at a standstill these birds still obtain their daily food. Snugly tucked away in crevices in the bark of trees are the beetles waiting for the return of summer; the larvæ repose in their burrows of solid wood and would seem to be safe from all disturbance; but the Three-toed Woodpeckers are not afraid of cold weather or of hard work and they tear open the hiding places in the bark or chisel into the solid wood and thus get their breakfasts, dinners, and suppers.

YELLOW-BELLIED SAPSUCKER

Sphyrapicus varius varius (*Linnæus*)

A. O. U. Number 402 See Color Plate 62

Other Names.— The Sapsucker; Yellow-bellied Woodpecker; Red-throated Sapsucker.

General Description.— Length, 8½ inches. Upper parts, black barred with brownish-white; lower parts, red, black, and yellow.

Color.—Adult Male: Forehead and *crown, bright poppy-red* or crimson, bordered behind by a crescent of glossy blue-black, extending laterally to above middle of eye; nape (at least laterally) white or brownish-white, rarely tinged with red; back and shoulders, black faintly glossed with greenish blue, broken by heavy spotting of white or brownish white, the white prevailing on sides of back, the black in center; rump and upper tail-coverts, mostly black laterally, mostly white (usually immaculate) centrally; tail, black, the inner web of middle pair of feathers, white with several larger or smaller oblique spots or bars of black, the lateral feathers margined terminally with white (except in abraded plumage); wings, black, the exposed portion of middle coverts and outer web of greater coverts (except inner one), white, *forming a conspicuous longitudinal patch,* the outer webs of primaries and ends of secondaries with large elongated spots of white, the inner secondaries with much white on ends; a broad and sharply defined band of white originating at nasal tufts and extending between eye and cheek regions to sides of neck; a narrower stripe of white behind eye extending to nape; a cheek stripe of black, becoming narrower behind where confluent with a *large crescent-shaped throat patch of uniform glossy blue-black; chin and throat, bright poppy-red,* center under parts, pale yellow; sides and flanks, dull white or brownish white broken by V-shaped markings of blackish; under tail-coverts, white, sometimes with a few shaft-streaks or other markings of blackish; bill, brownish-black; iris, brown. Adult Female: Similar to the adult male, *but chin and throat white instead of red,* and frequently with red of crown reduced in extent, often altogether wanting, the whole forehead, crown, and back of head sometimes uniform glossy black, sometimes with small whitish streaks or arrow-head spots.

Nest and Eggs.— Nest: In dead or decaying tree, 15 to 60, usually 40, feet from ground. Eggs: 4 to 7, white.

Distribution.— Eastern North America, breeding from northern Missouri, northern Indiana, northern Ohio, Massachusetts, etc., north to Mackenzie, central Keewatin, central Quebec, and Cape Breton Island, west to Alberta and southward on Allegheny Mountains to North Carolina; wintering from Pennsylvania, Ohio valley, etc., southward (occasionally farther northward); migrating southward over greater part of Mexico and Central America; also in winter to the Bahamas, Cuba, Jamaica, and the Bermudas; accidental in Greenland and casual in eastern Wyoming and eastern Colorado.

The Yellow-bellied Sapsucker and its western variant, the Red-naped Sapsucker (*Sphyrapicus varius nuchalis*), are the most migratory of all the Woodpeckers. During migration the male birds precede the females. At this period the Sapsucker apparently cares little for insects and he shows that trait of his character which has given him his name by boring numerous rows of holes through the bark of sap trees. Sometimes these holes are merely single punctures but more often a number of punctures are made close together so that squarish spaces are formed nearly half an inch in diameter. Frequently these are placed so near together that their area is greater than that of the remaining bark. Trees thus attacked often die. At this time too, is often heard the bird's snarling and squealing note as he chases his rivals away from the tree which he has selected.

The Downy Woodpecker is often charged with the wrong-doing of the Yellow-bellied Sapsucker; but the truth of the matter is that Downy never makes holes deep enough to draw out the sap, and he doesn't in any way injure the tree.

In the breeding range of the Sapsucker it is an ordinary occurrence for campers to be awakened at break of day by the noise he makes drumming on some dry branch or on some hard dry strip of bark which has a hollow space underneath it. To produce this sound of drumming he braces himself with tail and feet, and stretching backward as far as he can, lets fly his head and neck with all the force of the contracted muscle; this is done so rapidly that his head is practically invisible. This drumming often serves the purpose of a love-song in the mating season.

The mature female Sapsuckers have scarlet crowns, but the young females have black ones and apparently they do not receive their scarlet feathers until after the second summer.

The tongue of the Sapsucker differs from those of the majority of Woodpeckers; it cannot be pushed out as far and the end is brush-like, lacking the sharp points, and is used to sweep in the sap.

Dr. Merriam calls the Sapsuckers "noisy, rollicking fellows"; he was speaking of them in the spring of the year when it is more than probable that they had become over stimulated from the sap which the heat of the sun had fermented. In the fall they are quiet and reserved.

The Yellow-bellied Sapsucker is one of the few Woodpeckers that have more vegetable matter than animal matter in their diet; the vegetable matter is about 51 per cent. of the total food. The examination of a number of stomachs showed that ants amounted to over 34 per cent. of the whole food. They are evidently a favorite food for they are eaten regularly throughout the year. Bark lice, stink-bugs, spiders, May-flies, sun-flies, grasshoppers, crickets, tree-hoppers, caterpillars and moths constitute the remainder of the animal food. Fruit amounted to 28 per cent. of the total food, but it was probably the wild fruit or berries which had been left on the bushes. Conifer seeds and poison ivy seeds with some rubbish, such as the outer bark of trees, make up about 6 per cent.

While the animal food of this bird should be reckoned in its favor, it must be remembered that the damage it inflicts on trees in eating the sap and the cambium is very serious and is often so extensive that it cannot be balanced by the good that the bird does in other directions. Investigation by the Biological Survey show that the damage to timber, especially in the Southern States, is extensive and serious.

Drawing by R. I. Brasher

YELLOW-BELLIED SAPSUCKER (½ nat. size)

A noisy, rollicking fellow

RED-BREASTED SAPSUCKER

Sphyrapicus ruber ruber (*Gmelin*)

A. O. U. Number 403

General Description.— Length, 8½ inches. Head, red; upper parts, black spotted with white; under parts, yellow.

Color.— *Head, neck, and chest, bright red;* nasal tufts, front and lower portion of lores, dull yellowish-white; lores next to eye, black, this sometimes continued, narrowly, along edge of forehead; red below eyes lighter than that of cheeks, the latter blackish at front end; rest of under parts, very pale straw-yellow, the breast washed with bright red, the sides, flanks, and under tail-coverts less yellowish-white, broken by mostly V-shaped markings of dusky grayish; general color of upper parts (except head and neck), black, broken by a double series (converging behind) of white spots down middle of back, *a longitudinal white patch on wing-coverts* (involving most of middle coverts and outer webs of greater coverts) and white spots on outer web of primaries and at tip of inner secondaries, the inner web and tip of upper tail-coverts also white, and inner web of middle pair of feathers with oblique, square spots of white; bill, brownish-black; iris, brown.

Nest and Eggs.— Nest: In an aspen, maple, or willow, 15 to 25 feet from the ground. Eggs: 5 or 6, white.

Distribution.— California; from northern California to mountains of southern California, east to western slope of Sierra Nevada; south in winter to southern Lower California.

Although the Red-breasted Sapsucker nests throughout our Oregon woods, I do not find his home very often. I see more of him through the winter season when he skirmishes about the orchard for food. Last winter I saw one about our place several times. I tried to approach him, but he shied around to the opposite side of the tree and kept peeking around at me in a very coy manner. Whenever I approached within fifteen or twenty feet, he flitted to the next tree, generally keeping the tree between us.

This Sapsucker sometimes arouses the wrath of the farmer in girdling his trees for sap. There would be less complaint if this red-headed resident stayed more in the woods, but he insists on an occasional tasting of the apple trees. He likes the soft maples, willows, and aspens. These are also his nesting sites. The chips on the ground at the foot of the tree are the surest indication of a nest. The doorway to his home seems very small for the size of the bird. It is from one and one-fourth to one and one-half inches in diameter and at times it is such a close fit that Mrs. Sapsucker can just squeeze in.

Mrs. Florence Merriam Bailey relates a very interesting experience with a mother Sapsucker and her young. "The last week in July at Donner Lake, we found a family of dull colored young going about with their mother, a handsome old bird with dark red head and breast. They flew around in a poplar grove for a while, and then gathered in a clump of willows, where four young clung to the branches and devoted themselves to eating sap. The old bird flew about among them and seemingly cut and scraped off the bark for them, at the same time apparently trying to teach them to eat the sap for themselves; for though she would feed them at other times she refused to feed them there, and apparently watched carefully to see if they knew enough to drink the sap. When the meal was finally over and the birds had flown, we examined the branch and found that lengthwise strips of bark had been cut off, leaving narrow strips like fiddle-strings between. At the freshly cut places the sap exuded as sweet as sugar, ready for the birds to suck." WILLIAM L. FINLEY.

These Woodpeckers do not "suck" the sap, as the quotation from Mrs. Bailey would seem to imply, but sweep it in with their brush-like tongues.

The habits of the Red-breasted Sapsucker vary with the locality. In some places it doesn't seem to indulge in the Yellow-bellied Sapsucker's habit of girdling trees for the sap and the cambium or soft inner bark. Reports from other places say that it does more serious mischief than its relative, fruit trees, especially prune and apricot, and evergreens being frequently killed by reason of its punctures. Ants constitute the largest item of animal food, amounting to 42½ per cent. They are eaten every month in the year except possibly February. Beetles of all kinds amount to 4 per cent. and none of them are useful species. Caterpillars and locusts' eggs are also eaten. Altogether the animal matter amounts to 69 per cent. of the total food.

The Northern Red-breasted Sapsucker (*Sphyrapicus ruber notkensis*) is slightly larger, and its coloration is darker and brighter; the red of the head, neck, and chest averages brighter and the whitish spots on the back are usually smaller — sometimes obsolete. It is found in the coast and forest districts from Alaska to northern California and in winter to southern California.

WILLIAMSON'S SAPSUCKER

Sphyrapicus thyroideus (*Cassin*)

A. O. U. Number 404

Other Names.— Williamson's Woodpecker; Brown-headed Woodpecker (female).

General Description.— Length, 9 inches. MALE: upper parts, black with three white patches; under parts, black and yellow. FEMALE: head brownish-gray; upper parts, black and brownish-gray with white spot; under parts, black, brownish-buffy, and yellow.

Color.— ADULT MALE: *Greater part of head and neck, back, shoulders, chest, and sides of breast uniform, glossy greenish blue-black;* a white stripe behind eye and over the ear, extending to sides of nape, where considerably expanded; a white stripe below eye and under ear originating on and involving nasal tufts and extending to beneath end of ear region; a *center stripe of bright poppy-red on lower chin and upper throat;* abdomen and center of breast, bright sulphur (sometimes nearly lemon) yellow; sides, flanks, and under tail-coverts, white, broadly striped and spotted with black, the markings V-shaped on flanks and under tail-coverts; lower rump and upper tail-coverts, white, the lateral portions of the former and outer webs of latter largely black; tail, black; wings, black, the middle coverts and outer webs of greater coverts (except inner ones), white, *forming a very conspicuous large longitudinal patch on wing,* the second, or third, to fifth primaries (counting from outermost) usually with a

number of small white spots on outer web; bill, black in summer, purplish slaty brown in winter; iris, deep reddish-brown. ADULT FEMALE: Very different from male; crown and hindneck, deep drab, the back of head and nape streaked (sometimes also narrowly barred) with black; back and shoulders, broadly barred with black and pale drab or (in worn summer plumage) dull brownish white, the paler bars usually narrower than the black ones; wings (including coverts) black, barred with pale drab or dull brownish white; rump and upper tail-coverts, white, spotted or barred with black on sides; tail black, the middle feathers crossed with oblique bars of white (at least on inner web), the lateral ones barred with white on ends; sides of head, drab, paler (sometimes whitish) around eyes, the cheeks usually streaked or flecked with black; chin and throat, plain light drab, rarely with a center streak of red; chest, usually barred with black and pale buffy-brown, with a tendency to a black patch, frequently with a large and well-defined patch of unbroken glossy greenish-black, sometimes covering whole throat and foreneck; sides and flanks, regularly barred with black and pale brownish-buffy; abdomen and center portion of breast, immaculate yellow (primrose to nearly lemon-yellow); under tail-coverts, white, with V- or U-shaped bars of black; bill, etc., as in adult male.

Nest and Eggs.— NEST: In an old tree or stump, usually 5 to 60 feet from the ground. EGGS: 3 to 7, white.

Distribution.— Mountain forests of western North America; breeds from southern British Columbia south to southern California, southern Arizona, and central New Mexico; winters in southern California east to western Texas and south into Mexico.

There are two curious and interesting facts about this handsome bird. The first is that the male is the only one of the four-toed American Woodpeckers who has no red feathers on the top of his head — or his nape. All of the others, from the big Ivory-bill to the little Downy, are more or less red-headed.

The second peculiarity is that for twenty years after their discovery (in 1853), the male and female Williamson's Sapsuckers were duly recorded and gravely described by ornithologists as distinct species, the female under the name of "Brown-headed Woodpecker." It was in 1873 that Henry Henshaw, later chief of the United States Biological Survey, noticed the singular circumstance that the Williamson's Sapsucker and the so-called "Brown-headed Woodpecker" had a way of occupying the same apartments. Now it appears that instead of immediately entertaining visions of complicated hybridization, and conjuring up consequent opportunities to discover "new species," Mr. Henshaw reflected that, as a matter of fact, radical differences between the plumage of the male and the female birds of the same species were so common as to have become commonplace. Wherefore he very reasonably conjectured, and thereafter definitely demonstrated, that the "Brown-headed Woodpecker" was none other than Mrs. Williamson, ornithologically as well as "cohabitologically," and was evidently quite willing so to be and remain. Result: exit one superfluous species; also the shadow of a scandal in birdland.

William L. Sclater says it "appears to be uncertain" whether this bird is actually a "sapsucker," that is, whether it bores holes in the bark of trees for the purpose of getting their sap, as does its eastern namesake, and adds the interesting observations that if it excavates a hole for a nest, it usually selects for that purpose an old pine or spruce tree or a rotten stump; also that apparently it returns for several successive years to this site though a new excavation is made each year. It would be interesting to know

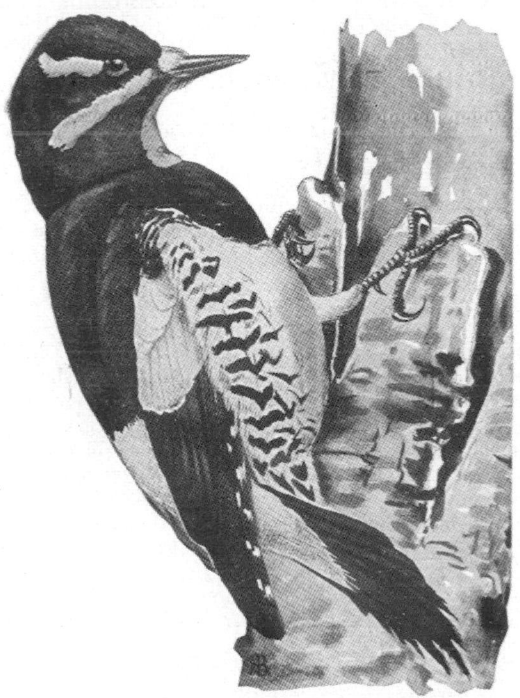

Drawing by R. I. Brasher

WILLIAMSON'S SAPSUCKER (½ nat. size)

Nature gave the male of this species no red feathers for his head

how Mr. Sclater satisfied himself about the return of the same bird to the same tree, though this does not seem inherently improbable since it has been established that other species of birds do return, year after year, to the same nesting site. And in the case of this Sapsucker definite identification might be possible through some individual peculiarity if, as Mr. Sclater says, the male does most of the work both of excavation and of incubation. Mr. Sclater also says, " When the female is on the nest, he [the male] sits on a branch nearby and warns her of danger by a special tapping."

The bird's characteristic cry resembles the syllables *huit, huit,* according to one transliteration of them. Generally speaking, the species is rather silent and shy, and is likely to work and stay near the tops of tall trees. Its hammering is less vigorous than that of other Woodpeckers, and is described by Mr. Torrey as " curiously slow, distinctive drum-taps."

The Williamson's Sapsucker eats ants and cambium, the former being the chief item in its animal diet and the latter taking the same place among its vegetable foods. It is of little economic interest except in connection with forests.

PILEATED WOODPECKER

Phlœotomus pileatus pileatus (*Linnæus*)

A. O. U. Number 405 See Color Plate 63

Other Names.— Logcock; Great Black Woodpecker; Cock of the Woods; Wood Hen; Wood Cock; Great God Woodpecker; Good God Woodpecker; Lord God Woodpecker; Wood Kate.

General Description.— Length, 15 to 19 inches. Plumage, slate-black with white and red markings. Head with conspicuous crest; bill, longer than head with wedge-like tip; outer hind toe shorter than outer front toe.

Color.— Adult Male: Crown, including *conspicuous crest, bright poppy-red,* approaching crimson on forehead; a rather narrow stripe of yellowish-white behind eye and beneath this a broad stripe of slate color involving also space below eye (narrowly) and rear of loral region; upper portion of nasal tufts, grayish with terminal portion of bristle-like feathers, blackish, this connected with the slate color around eyes by a narrow line of dusky; lower portion of nasal tufts, dull pale yellowish; a sharply defined stripe along lower portion of lores, dull yellow passing gradually into yellowish-white at rear where forming a broad band beneath the slaty ear area, thence extending downward along side of neck to under wing-coverts, which, together with basal half (approximately) of inner webs of wing feathers, are yellowish-white; cheeks, crimson for greater part, the rear portion, dark slate color or blackish slate; chin and throat, white or yellowish-white, sometimes streaked or suffused behind or centrally with grayish; rest of plumage, plain sooty slate-black or blackish-slate, the under parts slightly lighter; feathers of sides and flanks margined terminally with whitish; basal portion of outer webs of wings, white or yellowish-white, that on secondaries usually concealed by greater coverts, that on primaries showing as a small but distinct area beyond tip of primary coverts; bill, slate color; iris, cream-yellow; naked eye skin, grayish olive; legs and feet with scales black, the interspaces pale gray or whitish. Adult Female: Similar to the adult male, *but forehead and front half of crown, grayish-brown or olive and cheek region slate color.*

Nest and Eggs.— Nest: In a dead tree or tall stump, occasionally in the solid trunk of a living tree, usually a coniferous tree, 12 to 80, usually 40 to 50, feet from the ground. Eggs: 3 to 6, white.

Distribution.— Wooded regions of North America, mainly east of the Rocky Mountains.

Next to the rare Ivory-billed, this is the largest of all North American Woodpeckers. Formerly the birds were of wide distribution in the heavily wooded sections of the country, but they have now disappeared from many parts of the eastern United States. When found they are usually in regions of original forest growth, rarely being seen where the woods have been once cut over. The nest of this species is excavated in a dead tree or tall stump, occasionally a living tree is used if a knot-hole or dead spot affords a convenient place in which to begin to dig. Not infrequently the hole is dug to a depth of three feet or more. To perform such a task requires time, and often as much as a month must pass before the two birds working alternately are able to complete their enterprise. I have found their nests at distances varying from eighteen to seventy feet from the ground. These holes, after being abandoned, are a great boon to hole-nesting birds that are not able to excavate hollows of their own. Screech Owls, Sparrow Hawks, and Wood Ducks thus prosper by the industry of their Woodpecker neighbors. From three to six pure white eggs are laid on a bed of fine chipped-off fragments of wood.

Pileated Woodpeckers frequently show an absence of fear of man which one would not expect in a bird that is so distinctly a forest-dweller. Thus, when there are heavy growths of original woods near a village, they will at times come close about houses provided these are surrounded by large old trees. While camping in the hammocks of central Florida, I have now and then walked up to within thirty yards of a Pileated Woodpecker busy at work on some rotting log, without the bird paying the slightest attention to my presence.

As this Woodpecker seems not to possess the faculty of adapting itself to the new conditions created by civilization, it is quite possible that it will not long survive the passing of our primeval forests. T. GILBERT PEARSON.

The food of the Pileated Woodpecker does not interest the farmer or horticulturist for it is obtained entirely from the forest. The bird does not visit the orchard or the grain field, but all of its work in the forest helps to conserve timber. Its animal food consists probably of beetles and ants and its vegetable food of wild fruits.

Drawing by R. Bruce Horsfall

PILEATED WOODPECKER (⅜ nat. size)

As the forests are cut down, this Woodpecker disappears from its old haunts

---

RED-HEADED WOODPECKER

Melanerpes erythrocephalus (*Linnæus*)

A. O. U. Number 406 See Color Plate 62

Other Names.— Redhead; Tricolor; Tri-colored Woodpecker; White-shirt; Jellycoat; Shirt-tail; Patriotic Bird; Flag Bird.

General Description.— Length, 9 inches. Head, red; back, black with white patches; under parts, white.

Color.— ADULTS: *Head, neck, and upper chest, uniform bright crimson,* margined behind by a distinct, (usually more or less concealed) semi-circular band of black across chest; back and shoulders, uniform glossy blue-black, the wing-coverts, black margined with glossy blue-black; primary coverts, primaries, and tail, uniform black, the latter (except two to four middle feathers) tipped with white, the outside pair sometimes edged with white; rump, upper tail-coverts, secondaries, and under wing-coverts (except along margin of wing), uniform pure white, the secondaries with shafts and basal portion (mostly concealed), black; under parts below upper chest, white, the abdomen tinged with dull yellowish or salmon color, sometimes with bright red; bill, bluish-white; iris, deep brown or reddish-brown. YOUNG: Very different from adults; *head, neck, and upper chest, brownish-gray,* streaked or spotted with black, sometimes suffused or intermixed with red on hindneck or on sides of head; back, shoulders, and wing-coverts, black, the feathers margined with pale gray; secondaries, white with one or two broad bands of black (sometimes interrupted) on extremities; under parts, below chest, dull white to very pale brownish-gray, the sides and flanks (especially the latter), sometimes also the breast, streaked with dusky; otherwise much as in adults.

Nest and Eggs.— NEST: Generally in a dead tree but sometimes in a living tree, telegraph pole, or fence post. EGGS: 4 to 6, white.

Distribution.— Eastern United States and British provinces from southeastern British Columbia, Wyoming, Colorado, and Texas, east to the Atlantic coast; north, regularly, to northern New York (breeding in Adirondack region), Ontario, Manitoba, central Alberta, and southwestern Saskatchewan (rare); south to southern Florida and Gulf coast to Texas; rare and local east of the Hudson, where breeding, however, north to Vermont; casual in Nova Scotia, New Brunswick, Utah, New Mexico, and Arizona; irregularly migratory in northern parts of its range.

With the exception of the Flicker the Red-headed Woodpecker is more often seen in the open than any other Woodpecker. His favorite places seem to be the dead tops of forest trees and tracts of forest that have been burned leaving only dead stubs. Lacking these natural sites he will build his home in telegraph poles, fence posts, and similar places.

The Red-headed Woodpecker adds grasshoppers and flies to the regular Woodpecker diet. When he sees a grasshopper he wants he springs upon it and then, unlike the Flicker who remains on the ground hopping about, he returns to his look-out station on the dead stub or fence post. He will pursue a fly for some distance through the air, and having caught it he again returns to his original position to wait for another.

The Red-headed Woodpecker is very fond of beech nuts and other mast. Years in which such food is plentiful he will lay away in the crevices of trees a supply for the winter and it seems to make no difference to him whether later on he eats these same nuts or whether he eats the grubs which have discovered his pantry. Whether or not he spends the winter in the same place where he has passed the summer seems to depend upon the supply of mast.

This member of the Woodpecker family is more noisy than his relatives. Mr. Dawson thus describes this characteristic: "The woods and groves resound with their loud calls, *Quee-o — quee-o—queer.* These *queer* cries are not unpleasant. When one of them flies into a tree where others are gathered, all set up an outcry of *yarrow, yarrow, yarrow,* which does not subside until the newcomer has had time to shake hands all around at least twice. Besides these more familiar sounds the Red-heads boast an unfathomed repertory of chirping, cackling, and raucous noises. The youngsters, especially — awkward, saucy fellows that most of them are — sometimes get together and raise a fearful racket until some of the older ones, out-stentored, interpose."

The red, white, and black of the plumage of this Woodpecker are striking marks. In certain lights the black shows a bluish tint and it is not unusual to hear that a red, white, and blue bird has been seen. This coloration has earned for Red-head the names of "Patriotic Bird" and "Flag Bird." Mrs. Mabel Osgood Wright says

Drawing by R. I. Brasher

RED-HEADED WOODPECKER (½ nat. size)

"He wears the German flag."—Mrs. Wright

that "he is an unmistakable bird, when you are lucky enough to see him, for he boldly wears the German flag in his red, white, and black feathers." Like other highly colored birds he has paid the usual toll to gunners.

No species of Woodpecker in this country, with the possible exception of the Yellow-bellied Sapsucker, has been the subject of so much adverse criticism as the Red-head. It has been accused of eating nearly every variety of cultivated fruit from strawberries to oranges, of pecking corn from the ear, of eating the eggs of poultry and pigeons, of pecking open the skulls and devouring the brains of young poultry, and of destroying the eggs or young of Eave Swallows and other birds. These accusations are well grounded, but the habits are probably only local. These reports have been received from hundreds of localities, but in thousands of other places where the bird abounds no such acts have been observed. Stomach examination confirms to some extent the corn-eating habit, and to a less degree the fruit-eating, but fails entirely to show that the bird habitually eats young birds or eggs. Where this bird has done appreciable harm, it has probably been due to new and unusual conditions likely to be temporary. In its animal food the Red-head does a little harm theoretically by its destruction of predatory beetles, but the harmful species eaten are enough to balance this. On the whole, there seems to be no reason to condemn this Woodpecker except under very unusual conditions. J. Ellis Burdick.

Photo by Alice H. Olds Courtesy of Nat. Asso. Aud. Soc.

RED-HEADED WOODPECKER

Feeding on the railing of veranda

ANT-EATING WOODPECKER

Melanerpes formicivorus formicivorus (*Swainson*)

A. O. U. Number 407

General Description.— Length, 9½ inches. Upper parts, green; under parts, black, green, and white.

Color.— Adult Male: Nasal tufts, front of cheeks, chin, and upper throat, black; forehead and rather narrow band across front of lores to middle or rear of cheeks white, passing into pale sulphur-yellow on lower throat and foreneck; crown, back of head, and nape, bright poppy-red; span around eyes, sides of head, sides of neck, upper chest, lower hindneck, back, and shoulders, plain glossy greenish blue-black; wings, black or brownish-black, the coverts margined with glossy greenish blue-black, the primaries (except three or four outermost) with a basal patch of white, occupying both webs (but interrupted by the black shaft), this white area broader on inner quills; rump and upper tail-coverts, immaculate white; tail, entirely black; lower *chest and sides of upper breast, glossy greenish blue-black streaked with white* (the upper chest also sometimes streaked, at least in center) the remaining under parts, white, the lower breast (except centrally), sides, and flanks streaked with black, the under tail-coverts with narrow shaft-streaks of the same; bill, black; iris, variable in color (pinkish, white, bluish, brownish, or yellow). Adult Female: Similar to the adult male, *but crown glossy greenish blue-black.*

Nest and Eggs.— Nest: Usually in an oak or a pine tree. Eggs: 4 or 5, white.

Distribution.—Western North America from Oregon and western Texas to Panama.

The Ant-eating Woodpecker and its larger brother, the California Woodpecker (*Melanerpes formicivorus bairdi*), conspicuous and gay in their scarlet caps, glossy blue-black coats, and black and white striped waistcoats, are famous for their curious habit of boring holes in trees (often a dead redwood) and filling the holes with acorns. So zealous are these birds, that often when trees in the proper condition for puncturing are not numerous enough, they attack buildings and drill holes in the corners of houses or in the spires of churches. Telegraph and telephone poles and fence-posts are often used as an outlet for their energies.

This habit presents several interesting aspects. In the first place, and from the purely mechanical viewpoint, it is noticeable that the birds evidently have an accurate idea of the necessary relationship between the size of the hole and the size of the acorn. Now, a mouse has been known to struggle long and patiently at the impossible task of pushing or pulling through a hole in a wall, a walnut which was larger than the hole. And with all his general intelligence, a dog will try and keep on trying to fetch through a paling fence a stick much longer than the space between the palings. On the other hand, the House Wren and other birds which build in cavities with comparatively small openings will get long grasses and feathers for their nest through the opening by the, to us, obvious expedient of pushing or pulling them through lengthwise. The significance of all this is not that the Woodpecker and the Wren are naturally wiser or more intelligent than the dog or the mouse, but that the birds are performing an act learned by ages of experience, and now virtually instinctive, whereas the mouse and the dog fail because the problem which confronts them is essentially a new one, and too deep for their natural wit to solve.

Another puzzling aspect of this practice of the Ant-eating Woodpecker is the apparent lack of any sufficient reason for it. It has been suggested that the habit was born of necessity, that necessity arising from the fact that the habitat of the bird is also the habitat of multitudes of ground squirrels, who devour so many acorns that there are not enough left for the Woodpeckers, wherefore they lay away supplies out of reach of the squirrels. But it may fairly be doubted, as a matter of fact, whether the numbers and appetite of the squirrels are together sufficient to threaten any such famine.

Another explanation is that the Woodpeckers store the acorns not because they expect to eat them, but because they know that in time the nuts will rot and in that condition attract insects upon which they may feed. This solution, however, sounds more like the product of a fertile and active imagination than the result of responsible observation and clear-headed reasoning. What can Woodpeckers know about the laws and consequences of decay in the vegetable world? And how does it happen that this particular species, living in a land of unfailing plenty of all kinds of bird food, should have acquired this special knowledge, while their relatives who inhabit regions where food is actually scarce and hard to get show no such wisdom or foresight?

Whatever may be the cause and purpose of this storing habit, it results in much quarreling between the Woodpeckers and the squirrels, Jays, and other thieves in fur or feathers who steal the cached acorns. And even man has been known to put himself in the same category with the pilferers, by replenishing the feed supply for his horses from the Woodpecker's stores. From all this it must not be inferred that these birds subsist entirely on acorns, for insects form a considerable part of their diet, and many of these they take on the wing after the manner of the Red-headed species of the central States.

In flight this Woodpecker may readily be identified by the white patches on its wings and rump. The characteristic call suggests the syllables *ja-cob,* reiterated as the birds fly from tree to tree, and is soft and musical in its quality.

The food of the Ant-eating and California Woodpeckers is not of much economic importance. They cannot be charged with destroying useful insects or many products of husbandry. While they eat considerable fruit, especially almonds, in fact twice as much as the Linnet, they do not habitually infest orchards, and in most localities are not numerous enough to be a serious nuisance. The few insects which they take are nearly all of harmful species, while the acorns which make up the bulk of their diet may be considered of little value. The trees used for storehouses are usually either dead or partly so, and when alive are little harmed by the punctures, which do not usually go through the bark. When, however, holes are made in buildings, telegraph or telephone poles, or fences, they are a real injury, and it is fortunate that such cases are local and exceptional. From the esthetic point of view, however, a strong plea for their protection may be made. It is an interesting and picturesque species, and where they do not make themselves conspicuous by reason of the damage they do they may well be allowed to live.

LEWIS'S WOODPECKER

Asyndesmus lewisi *Riley*

A. O. U. Number 408

Other Names.— Black Woodpecker; Crow Woodpecker.

General Description.— Length, 10½ inches. Upper parts, greenish-black; under parts, gray and red.

Color.— Forehead, lores, around eyes, front half of sides of head, cheeks, chin, and upper throat, dark crimson; rest of head (except lower throat), nape, and upper parts generally, together with rear flanks and under tail-coverts, plain glossy greenish black, the back and shoulders, more bronzy; lower throat, dull black, the feathers (except on upper portion) tipped with pale gray, the foreneck similar, but with much broader pale gray tips; *chest and a broad, sharply defined collar around hindneck, light silvery gray;* breast, abdomen, sides, and greater part of flanks light crimson, intermixed (in fine longitudinal lines or streaks) with pale silvery gray or white, especially on breast, where the reddish color is paler and less strongly contrasted with the pale gray of the chest; under surface of wings and tail, uniform black, faintly glossed with bronzy greenish, at least on under wing-coverts; bill, dull black or dusky; iris, brown.

Nest and Eggs.— NEST: Usually in a natural tree-cavity, or in the deserted hole of some other bird. EGGS: 6 or 7, white.

Distribution.— Western North America, from southern British Columbia and southern Alberta, south to southern Arizona and New Mexico and Western Texas; west to interior valleys and coast ranges of California; east (regularly) to Black Hills of South Dakota, western Nebraska, western Kansas, eastern Colorado, etc.; casually to eastern Kansas and Oklahoma; in winter to southern California, western Texas, and northern Mexico.

Lewis's Woodpecker was one of the birds discovered on the Lewis and Clark expedition and was named in honor of Lewis. In various and interesting respects, he is a decidedly un-woodpecker-like Woodpecker. To begin with, instead of galloping through the air in the undulatory flight of most of his tribe, he is likely to proceed by regular and rather heavy wing-beats, resembling those of the Crow. (On the Pacific coast he is called the Crow Woodpecker.) Again, instead of alighting right-side-up-with-care on the side of a perpendicular tree-trunk or limb, he is likely to land crosswise, on a horizontal limb, like any perching bird. Furthermore, though two or three of his cousins catch flies on the wing, this bird goes on regular aërial cruises after the insects, sailing around, for several minutes at a time, or sometimes darting straight upward high above the tree-tops, and apparently making many captures before returning to his perch.

Perhaps as a result of these habits the bird seems to forget what he is, a good deal of the time, and does comparatively little of the hammering work a real Woodpecker is expected to do. Remembering this we are not surprised to learn that he seldom, if ever, builds, or rather digs, his own house, but occupies the deserted homes of other members of his tribe, or even natural cavities in trees, the last a performance which must make his relatives wag their heads and mutter remarks about degeneracy.

The common Flicker is sometimes seen on the ground where he is most likely to be engaged in probing ant-hills with his long bill, but Lewis's Woodpecker feeds freely on the ground, where he captures crickets, beetles, grasshoppers and various other insects. In this feeding, presumably he finds especially convenient one of his physical peculiarities, which is his ability to raise his upper mandible for about a quarter of an inch without moving his jaws.

Again, this species seems to have developed in some degree the hoarding trait which is so strongly marked in the Ant-eating Woodpecker, for he has been observed stuffing acorns, after having shelled them, into natural cavities in cottonwood trees. Examination of some of these caches showed that they were mere pockets, but that they had been jammed full to their capacity of five or six acorns. Moreover, Mrs. Fanny Hardy Eckstorm, in her book about Woodpeckers, records the interesting and perhaps significant observation that in the San Bernardino Mountains of California this bird has been seen to drive the California Woodpecker away from a tree whose bark he had perforated for storing acorns, and attempt, somewhat clumsily, to do the storing act himself in the holes which the other bird had dug. The possible significance of this hoarding performance is that it may mark the beginning of a trait which hereafter will become a fixed characteristic.

Another un-woodpecker-like habit of this species is that of gathering in large flocks, like Starlings, especially in the mating season. Though at other times the bird is generally very quiet, in this flocking period he is quite noisy, uttering frequently an unmusical and rather rasping call.

While Lewis's Woodpecker eats some useful beetles probably he does no serious harm in this way. His vegetable food amounts to over 60 per cent. of his entire food for the year. He doesn't seem to care much for grain and is not likely to do any harm in that direction. However, he has a pronounced taste for fruit. His shy habits force him to satisfy its craving by wild species; he does not visit the orchard and cultivated areas unless these places are situated in lonely spots. Mr. William L. Finley reports that during cherry season he has often seen this bird carrying cherries to its young in the nest, just as the Robin does; the parent, as a rule, carried the cherry by the stem. (MS.)

An incident of interest is reported from one of the northwestern States. On one side of the river was a large area of wild land and directly opposite was an orchard. Lewis's Woodpeckers persistently visited the orchard when the early apples were ripening. One evening a number of boxes were filled ready for market and were left in the orchard. In the morning it was found that the Woodpeckers had pulled out the papers and pecked the fruit so that it was necessary to open and repack several boxes. The moral in this incident is that the fruit-grower should be careful to leave wild fruit-bearing shrubs and trees around his orchard because when these birds cannot satisfy their desire with the fruit they have been accustomed to, they will without doubt turn to cultivated fruits.

RED-BELLIED WOODPECKER

Centurus carolinus (*Linnæus*)

A. O. U. Number 409 See Color Plate 64

Other Names.— Zebra Bird; Zebra-back; Chad; Shamshack; Ramshack.

General Description.— Length, 9½ inches. Head, red; upper parts, black with narrow white bars; under parts, gray and red.

Color.— Adult Male: Forehead and nasal tufts, light red, the latter usually paler (sometimes dull whitish) in front; crown, back of head, and hindneck, bright poppy-red, more scarlet on hindneck; back and shoulders, regularly and sharply barred with black and white, the white bars usually rather narrower than the black, the wing-coverts similarly barred but white bars relatively narrower, the secondaries also with broad white bars changing to spots on the end quills; primaries and primary coverts, black, the former blotched with white sub-basally, the longer quills (except outermost) narrowly edged with white at ends (except in worn plumage), the others tipped or broadly margined at tip with white; upper rump, barred with black and white, but bars less sharply defined than on back; lower rump, white, usually barred, spotted, or broadly streaked with black (rarely immaculate); upper tail-coverts, white, often immaculate, but (usually) with a narrow shaft-streak of black, at least basally; tail, black, the inner web of middle pair of feathers, white with bars or transverse spots of black (exceedingly variable as to number, size, etc.), the outer web usually with a wedge-shaped longitudinal streak of white on basal half, at least, the lateral feathers tipped with white and with broad (usually interrupted) bars of white on extremities; lores, over and behind eye, side of head, and cheeks, pale buffy-grayish, usually tinged

Drawing by R. I. Brasher

RED-BELLIED WOODPECKER (½ nat. size)

A beneficial tree surgeon

with pale red (sometimes wholly pale red, like frontal region); chin and upper throat, similar but paler (sometimes pale red or tinged with the same), passing behind into pale yellowish smoke-grayish on chest, breast, and sides; middle of abdomen, red, this color sometimes tingeing the breast, etc.; flanks and under tail-coverts, white, barred or streaked with black or with V-shaped markings of the same, the white ground color usually tinged with dull yellowish; bill, blackish or slate-blackish; iris, varying from ferruginous to scarlet. ADULT FEMALE: Similar to the adult male, but *the red of the head restricted to the back of head* and red of abdomen usually much paler as well as more restricted.

Nest and Eggs.— NEST: Usually in a dead limb or tree 15 to 60 feet from ground. EGGS: 3 to 6, usually 4 or 5, white.

Distribution.— Eastern United States; north, regularly, to Delaware, central and western New York, southwestern Ontario, southern Michigan, southern Wisconsin, and southeastern Minnesota, irregularly or casually to northern New York, Connecticut, and Massachusetts; west to southeastern South Dakota, eastern Nebraska, eastern Kansas, Oklahoma, west central Texas, etc., casually to Colorado; south to southern Florida and along Gulf coast to central Texas; accidental in Arizona.

In many parts of the United States all the Woodpeckers that have a plumage mainly black, and more or less spotted with white, are collectively called "Sapsuckers." The Red-bellied Woodpecker is one of several species to which this name is incorrectly applied; Chad is also a common appellation in some of the middle western States. In the South, where apparently it reaches its greatest abundance, the bird is constantly met with, whether one journeys through the pine barrens, or among the heavy growths of deciduous trees that constitute the "hammocks" surrounding many of the ponds and lakes. It is a bird equally at home in the unbroken forests or about the plantations wherever trees are found. In flight it exhibits to some extent the characteristic galloping, undulating movement peculiar to most members of the family, and upon alighting often gives voice to the harsh, brassy cry of *chad, chad,* from which one of its local names has been acquired.

The nest is of the usual Woodpecker type, being made in a hole excavated generally in a dead tree or limb. Sometimes a pair will take possession of a cavity already completed by some other Woodpecker, and while such action may involve a moral question, it at least indicates a disposition to conserve physical effort which by many is to-day rated high among the vital resources of our country.

Only one element in the food of the Red-bellied Woodpecker has much economic significance. The bird evinces a decided taste for fruit, and sometimes injures orchards, as in Florida orange groves. On several occasions, when in that State, I have seen these birds engaged in eating oranges still on the trees. The contents of the stomachs examined by the Biological Survey, however, show that wild fruits are the favorites, and probably only when these have been replaced by cultivated ones is any mischief done. Orange pulp was not positively identified in any stomach, though quite a number were collected in Florida during the orange season. Only a little of the grain eaten is taken when it is a loss to the farmer. In its animal food the bird is almost entirely beneficial, as the insects eaten are largely noxious. T. GILBERT PEARSON.

GOLDEN-FRONTED WOODPECKER

Centurus aurifrons (*Wagler*)

A. O. U. Number 410

Other Name.— Golden-front.

General Description.— Length, 10 inches. Head, yellow; upper parts, black and white, barred; under parts, gray and light yellow.

Color.— ADULT MALE: Front portion of forehead, cadmium yellow, rear of forehead and front portion of the space over the eye, dull buffy grayish-white, passing into mouse-gray on sides and back of head, *this enclosing a crown-patch of bright poppy-red;* hindneck, bright orange (sometimes tinged with orange-red) in front. passing into yellow or yellowish-orange behind; back, shoulders, and upper rump, regularly and sharply barred with black and white, the wing-coverts and secondaries similarly barred, but the white bars relatively narrower; primary coverts and primaries, black the latter with a white sub-basal patch and, except outermost quills, tipped with white; lower rump and upper tail-coverts, immaculate white; tail, black, the lateral feathers tipped with white, the outermost pair with several white spots or indentations along edge of rear portion of outer web, sometimes with one or more similar spots or bars on subterminal portion of inner web; sides of head, sides of neck, chest, breast, and sides, plain pale buffy-grayish, fading into paler (sometimes dull whitish) on chin, front portion of cheeks, and in front of eyes and passing into light yellow on abdomen; flanks and under tail-coverts, white, spotted or barred with black, the markings usually of V-shaped form; bill, dull black or slate-black. Adult Female: Similar to the adult male, *but without any red on head,* the back of the head and the whole crown, gray, the color fading from rather deep gray on the back of the head to pale buffy grayish or dull whitish on forehead, the yellow of hindneck rather paler than in male and, usually at least, without orange tinge, and yellow of abdomen paler, as well as more restricted.

Nest and Eggs.— Nest: Usually in mesquites, pecans, oaks, or telegraph poles. Eggs: 4 to 7, white.

Distribution.— Central northern Texas, south to Valley of Mexico.

Similar in habits to the Red-bellied Woodpecker is the Golden-fronted Woodpecker of Texas and northern Mexico. Along the Rio Grande the birds have been observed to make nesting holes most often in mesquite. Farther up in the State the practice of boring holes in the telegraph poles has become in many cases a serious matter as, not content with one nesting hole a year, each pair will often dig out two or more holes. Yet farther south on the mesquite prairies the birds are known to use one nesting hole year after year. Sometimes these Woodpeckers will make their home in a bird-box near a house.

The Golden-fronts are noisy and conspicuous birds. They do not recognize man as an enemy and their lack of fear has cost many of them their lives to fill pot-pies.

The Golden-fronted Woodpecker shows a decided taste for grasshoppers which make up half of its animal food. Its vegetable diet is composed almost entirely of small fruits or berries.

GILA WOODPECKER

Centurus uropygialis *Baird*

A. O. U. Number 411

Other Name.— Saguaro Woodpecker.

General Description.— Length, 9 inches. Head and under parts, drab; upper parts, black and white.

Color.— Adult Male: Head, neck, and most of under parts plain drab, darkest on hindneck, palest on chin, forehead, and nasal tufts; crown with a broad center patch of bright scarlet vermilion; back, shoulders, and *upper rump, regularly, sharply, and rather broadly barred with black and white,* the white bars, which are usually tinged with pale brownish-buffy, are usually slightly narrower than the black ones; lower rump and upper tail-coverts white, barred (sometimes narrowly) with black, those on upper tail-coverts usually V- or brace-shaped; tail, black, the inner web of middle pair of feathers white (except terminally) broadly barred with black, the outer web with a wedge-shaped streak of white, extending half way down, the outermost pair crossed for most of their length by broad, interrupted, bars of white, the next pair with similar markings on extremities; wings, black, the coverts and secondaries barred with pure white (the bars narrower on coverts, much broader on secondaries), the primaries with a large, broken, patch of white on sub-basal portion of outer webs, the inner quills with a terminal spot or edging of white; abdomen, light saffron-yellow; flanks and under tail-coverts, dull white or yellowish-white, barred with black, the bars usually somewhat V-shaped, at least on coverts; bill, dull black or slate-black. Adult Female: Similar to the adult male *but no red spot on crown,* which is wholly light drab (like general color of head, neck, and under parts), and yellow of abdomen paler and more restricted.

Nest and Eggs.— Nest: Generally in the giant cactus, but sometimes in a cottonwood, a sycamore, or a mesquite. Eggs: 3 to 5, white.

Distribution.— From the Colorado valley in southeastern California and the extreme southeastern corner of Nevada east through southern Arizona and southwestern New Mexico, and south through Lower California and western Mexico.

The peculiarity of the Gila Woodpecker is its apparent preference for the stem of the giant cactus as a home-site. Literal-minded persons may, therefore, contend that to this extent the bird isn't a Woodpecker at all, since the cactus plant does not produce wood. To which it may be replied, with equal seriousness and profundity, that since the bird lives in a country which grows little wood, there is little wood to peck, but from the fact that it pecks the nearest substitute for wood that is available we are justified in concluding that it would peck wood if it could, and therefore, is at heart a Woodpecker. At any rate, the habit has real significance in so far as it bespeaks the persistence of instinct operating through native adaptability, which may be considered a form of intelligence.

It is, of course, comparatively easy for the Gila to make a way through the fiber of the cactus. The pith is cut away to the proper depth, and a chamber of suitable dimensions is hollowed out. In the operation the bird's plumage becomes more or less daubed with sap, but that doesn't seem to bother him. At the entrance and inside the cavity the fluid soon hardens, and the passage-way and chamber become as dry as if they were cut out of solid wood. In the region inhabited by these birds, many, if not most, of the giant cactus stems show one or even several of these nesting holes.

The other habits of the Gila Woodpecker are similar to those of the Ant-eating species, with the important exception that it does not seem to practice hoarding food. It feeds largely on insects, captured in foliage or on the wing, which diet is varied by mistletoe and other berries. It is often seen feeding on the ground in cornfields.

In the report of Mr. F. E. L. Beal, of the United States Biological Survey, on the food of Woodpeckers he says that but one stomach of the Gila Woodpecker had been examined and this was largely filled with beetles of the May-beetle family with a few bones of a lizard. The vegetable part was refuse.

Photo by W. L. Finley and H. T. Bohlman

GILA WOODPECKER

The giant cactus is its favorite home

FLICKER

Colaptes auratus auratus (*Linnæus*)

A. O. U. Number 412 See Color Plate 64

Other Names.—Yellow-shafted Woodpecker; Golden-winged Woodpecker; Clape; Pigeon Woodpecker; Yellow-hammer; High-hole; High-holder; Yarrup; Wake-up; Wood-pigeon; Heigh-ho; Wick-up; Hairy Wicket; Yawker Bird; Walk-up.

General Description.— Length, 11 inches. Upper parts, grayish-brown, barred with black; under parts, lilac-brown, black, and yellowish.

Color.— Adult Male: Crown and hindneck, plain gray interrupted by a crescentic band of bright scarlet, the forehead usually more brownish; back, shoulders, wing-coverts, and secondaries grayish-brown, sharply barred with black, the black bars much narrower than the brown interspaces (except, sometimes, on secondaries) and pointed at the extremities, except on secondaries, where much broader than elsewhere; primaries, dull black and spotted, at least on middle portion, with light grayish-brown or dull pale yellowish (these spots usually rather indistinct), their shafts bright clear yellow; rump, white, mostly immaculate but laterally broken by broad brace-shaped bars of black; upper tail-coverts, white, variously marked (usually transversely) with black; tail, black, the middle pair of feathers duller or more olivaceous basally, usually edged, narrowly, with dull whitish, the inner web often notched or spotted along edge with the same; shafts of tail feathers (except middle pair) bright pure yellow with extremities black; before and above the eye, deep reddish cinnamon, below eye and sides of head together with chin, throat, foreneck, and upper chest, uniform lilac-brown; cheeks, black, forming a conspicuous elongated patch or "mustache"; lower chest, black, forming a conspicuous crescentic patch; rest of under parts pale lilac-brown or dull buff-pinkish fading into white or pale yellowish on sides and on under tail-coverts, conspicuously spotted with black, the spots mostly roundish, larger and subtriangular, sometimes V-shaped, on under tail-coverts; under wing-coverts, pale buff yellow, paler along edge of wing, where spotted with black; inner webs of wings, deep yellow (in certain lights), the basal portion of outer primaries and greater part of other feathers broadly edged with buff-yellow, extremities broadly barred or transversely spotted with the same; under surface of tail, saffron or dull yellow, broadly and abruptly tipped with black, the outside pair of feathers with a terminal spot or edging of whitish, the outer web usually narrowly edged or notched with the same, or with blackish alternating with whitish; bill, black in summer, more brownish or dusky horn color (especially on basal half above) in winter; iris, dark reddish-brown or brownish-red. ADULT FEMALE: Similar to the adult male, *but without the black cheek patch or "mustache,"* this replaced by the color of throat (sometimes tinged with dull grayish).

Photo by H. K. Job Courtesy of Outing Pub. Co.

FEMALE FLICKER FEEDING YOUNG IN THE NEST

Nest and Eggs.— NEST: In tree or stub. EGGS: 5 to 9, white.

Distribution.— Eastern North America from tree limit south to the Gulf coast.

Drawing by R. I. Brasher

FLICKER (⅓ nat. size)

One of the most interesting of the Woodpeckers

The Flicker is the most interesting bird of all the Woodpeckers. The fact that it has been called by so many different names besides that of Flicker shows how very different kinds of people have made very different kinds of observations of the bird. One observer has seen the bird fly into a hole it has chiseled out with its bill near the top of a high dead tree-stub and he has given the bird the name of High-hole or High-holder. Another person has heard the bird calling its *Yarrup-yarrup* while flying about from tree to fence post and to tree again in quest of food; hence the common name of Yarrup. Another person hearing the loud one-syllable call across the fields or the swamp lot has named the bird the Clape. Yet another, hearing the swish of his friendly *weechem* call as he wings along in a wavy up and down flight from ten to a hundred feet above the ground, has named the bird the Flicker.

He is in reality the Yellow-shafted Woodpecker or Golden-winged Woodpecker because of the bright yellow undersides of the wings and shafts of the wing feathers. In the northern part of its range the Flicker averages a trifle larger in size, and he is there known as the Northern Flicker (*Colaptes auratus luteus*). West of the Mississippi the yellow becomes red and we find there the Red-shafted Woodpecker (*Colaptes cafer collaris*).

The Flicker is a friendly neighbor. His interest is so hearty in the life about him. He may be on the limbs of the trees in the characteristic Woodpecker fashion, or he may be on the ground making a desperate noise in the leaves, or he may be up and down, out and in a pasture in the most erratic fashion. His disposition to make friends with the Robins and Bluebirds and even with the English Sparrows has often been noted, and even Swallows and Hawks often meet him on friendly terms. L. NELSON NICHOLS.

Photo by F. C. Pillett Courtesy of Nat. Asso. Aud. Soc.

YOUNG FLICKERS

Four of a family of seven raised in this box

Photo by H. L. Ferguson Courtesy of Nat. Asso. Aud. Soc.

A GROUND-BUILT NEST OF A FLICKER

This resourceful Flicker lived on Fishers Island, New York. No nesting-site, measuring up to Woodpeckers' standards, was available and she therefore hollowed out a place on the ground. The imprint made by her tail as she turned around can be plainly seen

From the point of view of the food analyst the farmer and the horticulturist have very little quarrel with the Flicker. It eats only a few predacious ground beetles. The remainder of the animal food is entirely of harmful species. In its vegetable diet, grain and fruit are the only useful products eaten, and the quantities are insignificant. The bird, like many others, has the bad habit of sowing broadcast the seeds of the poison ivy, but there seems no remedy for this.

ORDER OF GOATSUCKERS, SWIFTS, ETC.

Order *Macrochires*

LIKE the order of Cuckoos, this is a composite order. It includes three sub-orders, each with but one family. These families differ widely from one another in nearly every respect. They are alike on the one point of having small, weak feet, totally unfit for perching. As a result they spend most of their time flying about, and take their food from the air. This in turn has led to a development of the hand or distal-section of the wing — hence the name of the order, *Macrochires*, which literally means "large hand."

GOATSUCKERS

Order *Macrochires;* suborder *Caprimulgi;* family *Caprimulgidæ*

GOATSUCKERS or Nightjars are small to medium-sized (rarely rather large) birds with small, weak bill, deeply cleft mouth, weak feet, long wings, and protective coloration. Their dull colors, in elaborately mottled, freckled, or barred pattern, render them, when at rest, exceedingly difficult to distinguish from their immediate surroundings of stony or sandy ground, dry leaves, or grass, or branches of trees. None of the species are known to build a nest, the eggs (also, as a rule, protectively colored) being deposited on the ground, or other plain surface. The young when hatched are covered with down but need the care of the parents.

The members of this group gather their food either at night or during the twilight hours. Their days are passed in rest. They are chiefly insectivorous, though some of the larger species are known to swallow, entire, small birds. All of their food is caught on the wing. Many of the species are noted for peculiar cries, the Whip-poor-will and Chuck-will's-widow of the United States being well-known examples.

The family is found nearly throughout the warmer portions of the world, and is very numerous in species, about fifty occurring in America. The name "Goatsucker" is derived from an old-time superstition that the common European species subsisted by milking the goats; doubtless this idea was fostered by seeing the birds fly near the goats at night or in the early evening searching for the insects surrounding the animals.

CHUCK-WILL'S-WIDOW

Antrostomus carolinensis (*Gmelin*)

A. O. U. Number 416

Other Name.— The Great Bat.

General Description.— Length, 12 inches. Plumage, a variegation of black, brown, gray, and buff. *Rictal bristles with lateral filaments.*

Color.— Adult Male: General tone of upper parts, brown, more grayish on shoulder, everywhere minutely streaked and sprinkled with black (the marks coarser on shoulder, wing-coverts, and middle tail-feathers); crown, broadly streaked with black, the streaks much broader along center, obsolete on edges; shoulders with irregular large blotches of black, these usually irregularly margined, in part at least, by buff; middle tail-feathers with a center series of very irregular broken spots of black, which often show a tendency toward forming broken bars which become less distinct, or obsolete, toward edge of each web; three outer feathers (on each side) with terminal half or more of inner web white, this encroaching on inner portion of outer web, the remainder of these feathers coarsely and irregularly barred with black and dull tawny; the latter largely predominating on terminal half of outer web, especially on the second and third, and sometimes nearly uniform, the tawny extending across tip of inner web and even tingeing the white along inner edge; wing-coverts with large, irregular spots or blotches of black and with a transverse series of large buff spots across middle portion; primaries and primary coverts dull black, coarsely and irregularly spotted with tawny, the spots much less distinct and more broken on inner webs, which are largely uniform dusky basally; lores, space around eye, sides of head, cheeks, chin, and upper throat, dull ochraceous, narrowly barred with dusky; lower throat, deep buff to buffy-white, forming a conspicuous transverse band, the front rather broadly barred with black; chest and breast brown finely streaked or stippled with dusky (the upper chest more closely barred), the center of the breast with several irregular large spots or blotches of buff or buffy-white; abdomen and flanks, dull buff irregularly barred with dusky and with occasional triangular spots of the general ground color; under tail-coverts, clearer buff, irregularly and very variably barred with dusky; bill, brown; iris, dark brown; feet, brownish. ADULT FEMALE: Similar to the adult male but without the white areas on inner webs of outer tail-feathers, which are irregularly marbled or mottled with black on a light tawny-buff ground, both webs of the three outer feathers (on each side) being tipped with tawny-buff.

Nest and Eggs.— EGGS: 2, creamy or pinkish-white, blotched, marbled, and spotted with pale buff, browns and lilac; laid on the ground in thickets, in swampy, tree-shaded spots, or in pine groves.

Distribution.—Eastern United States; breeding from southern Virginia and southern Ohio (?), southwestern Indiana, southern Illinois, southern Missouri, and southeastern Kansas southward to the Gulf States (Florida to Texas); west to central Texas; in winter south to Bahamas, West Indies, Central America, and Colombia; occasional to Maryland, Massachusetts, Nova Scotia, Ontario, West Virginia, and south-central Kansas.

The largest member in the United States of that interesting family, the Goatsuckers, is the Chuck-will's-widow. In its summer range from Virginia to Illinois southward it is confined chiefly to the coastal plain in the East and the Mississippi basin in the Middle West. It appears not to go into the mountain or Piedmont sections. In winter it retires to our southern borders and in some localities of Florida is very abundant at this season. In general appearance and habits it much resembles the better known Whip-poor-will.

In returning from its winter home the Chuck-will's-widow reaches South Carolina about March 25 and southern Virginia about April 10. We first become aware of its arrival some warm spring evening when the loud cry, from which it gets its name, issues from the thicket or wood lot, for the bird is rarely seen or heard by day. There is a wide-spread belief among the people of the South that this bird is the male Whip-poor-will, although it is twice as bulky as that species. Its cry is variously interpreted as *Chip-fell-out-a-white oak, Twixt-hell-and-white oak,* and various other phrases which usually end in the words "white oak."

The males are supposed to arrive first, the females following four or five days later. Then begins a love-making that for grotesque antics

Drawing by R. I. Brasher

CHUCK-WILL'S-WIDOW (⅜ nat. size)

A mysterious bird of the night, often heard but seldom seen

certainly rivals any other courtship seen beneath the stars. The male struts before the object of his affections, waddling along on his ridiculously short legs with the sublime confidence of masculinity. He makes queer noises, puffing out his throat until he looks as if he had been choked on a lemon. Doubtless these performances appear very fascinating in the big dark eyes of the female.

The birds roost near together during the daytime, sometimes on a fallen tree but more often on the ground. No attempt is made to build a nest of any description, the eggs simply being deposited on the dead forest leaves, which they much resemble. Two is the number laid and the second appears four or five days after the first. Incubation begins immediately and as a result one of the young for a time is larger than its fellow.

When frightened from its eggs the Chuck-will's-widow flies a short distance and with queer cries of *quack, quack,* seeks to distract the intruder's intention. When the nests are molested it is not uncommon for the birds to remove their eggs or helpless young to a distance of several rods. This is accomplished by the simple expedient of picking them up in the mouth one at a time and flying away. In common with many other species they will, if their eggs be taken, lay a second setting. The usual food consists of beetles, moths, and various other night-flying insects. The mouth is very large for the size of the bird and, when open, is two inches across, thus enabling it to take in large objects, which perhaps accounts for the fact that stomachs of these birds have been found to contain both Hummingbirds and Sparrows.

T. Gilbert Pearson.

WHIP-POOR-WILL

Antrostomus vociferus vociferus (*Wilson*)

A. O. U. Number 417 See Color Plate 65

Other Name.— Nightjar.

General Description.— Length, 9½ inches. Plumage, a variegation of gray, brown, black, and buff. *Tail, rounded.*

Color.—Adult Male: General color of upper parts, mixed grayish-brown and brownish-gray, minutely streaked and stippled with dusky; crown, streaked with black, the streaks narrow and linear (sometimes obsolete) on lateral portion, much broader and more drop-shaped along center line, where usually coalesced and forming an irregular stripe; shoulders with large irregular spots or blotches of black, these usually margined, in part, with irregular narrow areas of buff, the back, rump, and upper tail-coverts streaked with black; middle pair of tail-feathers, brownish-gray, freckled with dusky, and crossed by about seven to nine broken irregular bars of blackish, the next pair similar but darker; *three outer pairs, extensively white, at ends,* on both webs, this decreasing in extent from the third to the outermost, on which the white on outer web is much less in extent than on inner web; remaining portion of these three outer feathers, brownish-black broken by incomplete and irregular bars of brownish-buff; general color of wing-coverts, light

Drawing by R. I. Brasher

WHIP-POOR-WILL (3/5 nat. size)

Everybody knows this bird's voice

brown or grayish-brown, finely marked with dusky, and much broken by irregular mottlings or spotting of light brownish-buff, ochraceous-buff, or dull light tawny-ochraceous, the black often in form of irregular shaft-streaks; primaries and primary coverts, brownish-black, conspicuously spotted on outer webs with tawny, their inner webs with bars of the same color, these not extending to shaft, and becoming paler toward edge of the web; terminal portion of primaries (especially on inner webs) confusedly mottled with grayish-brown and dusky; lores and sides of head, narrowly barred with pale tawny and dusky; cheeks, chin, and throat, brownish-black barred (narrowly) with light tawny-brownish, the first usually flecked with white in front; *lower throat crossed by a band of white,* this often suffused with light buff, especially on center portion; chest and breast streaked with pale grayish-brown and dusky and spotted, especially on chest and sides of breast, with pale brownish buff, the abdomen similarly marked but general color paler, the darker markings more in the form of irregular narrow transverse bars; under tail-coverts, light buff, usually with irregular bars (often V-shaped) of dusky; bill, brown; iris, dark brown; feet, brownish. ADULT FEMALE: Similar to the adult male but without white on lateral tail-feathers, the three outer pairs of which are broadly tipped with buffy, and general coloration averaging browner (more suffused with buffy).

Nest and Eggs.— EGGS: 2, white, beautifully marked with spots of brown, yellowish-brown, and purple; laid on old leaves or decayed bits of wood, usually in deep woods, beneath dense underbrush, or in shady ravines.

Distribution.— Eastern United States and southern Canada; north to Nova Scotia, New Brunswick, Maine, Vermont, southern Quebec, Ontario, southern Keewatin, Manitoba, and Saskatchewan; west to eastern edge of the Great Plains, in eastern Nebraska, Kansas, etc., during migration to west-central Texas, casually to eastern Colorado; breeding southward to northern Louisiana, southern Georgia, northwestern Florida, eastern Texas (?), etc.; wintering in Gulf States (Florida to southeastern Texas) and southward through Mexico to Central America.

Few American birds are less frequently seen than the Whip-poor-will, yet few are more widely known. This apparent paradox is due to the bird's call — it can hardly be called a song — which is as familiar as the honest caw of the Crow. Yet comparatively few people can say that they have ever had more than a fleeting glimpse of the bird, while a great many have never seen it at all; and probably never will. It is by far the best known member of its elusive family, of which the other principal American representatives are the Nighthawk, the Poor-will, and the Chuck-will's-widow.

The call of the Whip-poor-will is probably familiar to more people in this country than is the night utterance of any other bird or mammal, because, under the protection of the darkness, the bird does not hesitate to approach human habitations, or even to frequent city parks. The character of the call as it is commonly heard, is so well known that it needs no description. The three whistled notes included in the utterance, are delivered in practically the same rhythm and tempo, and with the same accent, the emphasis being placed upon the first and third syllables, and most emphatically on the third. Comparatively few listeners get close enough to the bird to hear the faint *chuck* which precedes the phrase, and still fewer are aware that it is accompanied by a peculiar bowing motion, the bow coming with the first syllable. Monotony and uniformity may seem to characterize the utterance, but a close listener will discover that the tone and technique of Whip-poor-wills may differ very considerably. This was noted by an auditor who listened carefully for an hour or more one evening to a chorus of fully a dozen of the birds, and who remarked that some of them were distinctly better singers than others.

Photo by H. K. Job Courtesy of Outing Pub. Co.

EGGS OF WHIP-POOR-WILL

They are laid on old leaves beneath deep underbrush

Concerning the remarkable persistence of the Whip-poor-will, Mr. Burroughs records the following amusing illustration: "One April morning between three and four o'clock, hearing one strike up near my window, I began counting its calls. My neighbor had told me he had heard one call over two hundred times without a break, which seemed to me a big story. But I have a much bigger one to tell. This bird actually laid upon the back of poor Will one thousand and eighty-eight blows, with only a barely perceptible pause here and there, as if to catch its breath. Then it stopped about half a minute and began again, uttering this time three hundred and ninety calls, when it paused, flew a little further away, took up the tale once more and continued till I fell asleep."

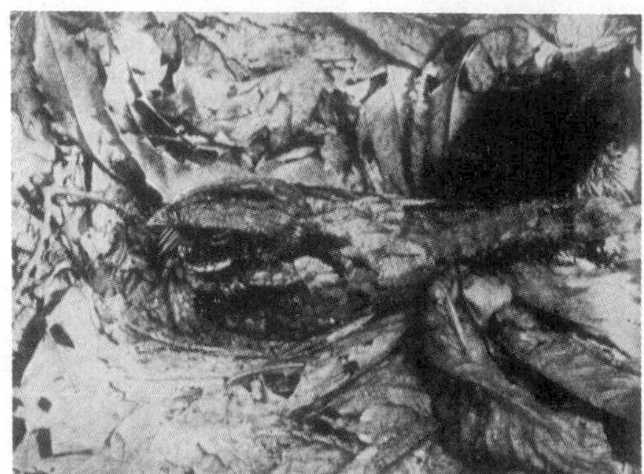

Photo by H. K. Job Courtesy of Outing Pub. Co.

WHIP-POOR-WILL ON NEST

It is interesting to note in connection with Mr. Burroughs's observation, the translation of the scientific name of the Whip-poor-will: the first word, *antrostomus,* means "cave-mouth" and the second, *vociferus,* "strong voice."

Like the other members of its family, the Whip-poor-will when on the ground, where it is apt to be in daytime, is practically invisible, so perfectly does its plumage blend with the fallen leaves and twigs among which it crouches. In fact even when the bird is no more than ten or twelve feet away, and its whereabouts is known positively to within a few feet, a keen and trained eye will sometimes search for fully half an hour before discovering the bird's outline, and meanwhile it will sit perfectly still as if it understood the difficulty under which the observer is laboring. Once flushed, it flies rapidly and absolutely noiselessly for a short distance, only to plunge to the ground and again vanish as if the earth had swallowed it completely. When driven from its eggs the bird flutters along the ground quite rapidly for a few yards, and then begins a series of struggles, accompanied by much flapping of wings and gasping, as if it were hopelessly crippled, all of which performances seem deliberately intended to lure the intruder away from the precious eggs. If followed for a few yards the bird suddenly recovers completely, and vanishes like a ghost.

Stephens's Whip-poor-will (*Antrostomus vociferus macromystax*) does not differ in coloration from the common Whip-poor-will but it averages decidedly larger — about eleven inches in length — and its rictal bristles are much longer and stouter. It is found in southern Arizona, New Mexico, and southwesten Texas, south through the mountains of northern Mexico, wintering south to Guatemala.

POOR-WILL

Phalænoptilus nuttalli nuttalli (*Audubon*)

A. O. U. Number 418

General Description.— Length, 7½ inches. Plumage, a variegation of gray, brown, buff and black. *Tail, square.*

Color.— *General color of upper parts, pale brownish-gray,* palest on sides of crown, shoulders, and upper tail-coverts, the lighter areas in fresh or unworn plumage sometimes pale slivery-gray with a soft downy surface, most of the feathers minutely stippled with darker; crown (which is usually more brownish, sometimes quite dusky, centrally) with very narrow bars (usually more or less brace-shaped) of black, these sometimes widening into spots on center of crown; back and rump also usually with narrow (usually brace-shaped) bars of black or dusky; shoulders with a single narrow, sharply defined black bar enlarged in middle into a usually wedge- or diamond-shaped spot; wing-coverts and inner secondaries, each with one or more narrow bars and a shaft streak of black; other secondaries, irregularly banded with light buff and marbled with pale buffy-gray and blackish, the bands becoming less distinct (more confused) on ends; primary coverts, buff crossed by three bands of black, these connected along inside of shaft; primaries, buff banded with black, their terminal portion finely marbled or streaked with grayish, usually with irregular bars of blackish; upper tail-coverts, sometimes nearly immaculate, but usually with a few narrow bars of black, sometimes banded with darker and lighter shades of grayish; middle pair of tail-feathers, pale silvery-gray to buffy-gray, minutely stippled with darker and with narrow zigzag transverse lines of blackish; second pair, banded with dull black and a mixture of pale brownish-gray and buff, the bands sometimes distinct and fairly regular, oftener indistinct, irregular, or broken, sometimes replaced by a confused combination of mottlings, marblings, and zigzag markings, the grayish areas always broken by blackish or dusky marblings; third pair similar but rather darker (sometimes uniform brownish-black near the tip) and broadly tipped with white; fourth and fifth pairs, similar but with both the uniform brownish-black band near the tips and the white tip, broader; lores, region around eyes, and sides of head, nearly uniform sepia-brown; cheeks and chin, lighter sepia or grayish-brown, minutely freckled with darker, the former usually intermixed with white in front, this sometimes forming a distinct mouth streak; throat, immaculate silky white, this extending farther backward on the sides than on middle portion; extreme lower throat and upper chest, mostly uniform very dark sooty-brown or sooty-black, the lower chest with tips of feathers, pale colored, sometimes pale grayish minutely stippled with darker, sometimes barred with black and pale grayish or white, sometimes a large whitish spot, of variable form; breast and sides, dull white or buffy-white narrowly barred with dusky-brown or black, the barring more close in front, more distant behind; rest of underparts, cream buff to buffy-white, the flanks sometimes with rather distant and rather broad bars of dusky; under wing-coverts, buff usually immaculate but sometimes with a few dusky spots or bars near edge of wing; inner webs of primaries, buff (except tips) with six or seven large curved transverse spots of dusky, of which the end ones do not cross to edge of the web; bill, black; iris, brown; naked eyelids, dull ochraceous; legs and feet, brownish, the former sometimes more lilaceous.

Nest and Eggs.— EGGS: 2, pure white, unspotted; deposited on bare ground in brush at edge of timber or in a bunch of briers or a thicket upon the open prairies.

Distribution.— Western United States, north to southeastern British Columbia, Idaho, Montana, and northwestern North Dakota; east to southeastern South Dakota, eastern Nebraska, western Iowa, eastern Kansas, and western and central Texas; west to California to about latitude of 40°; south to Lower California and central Mexico.

I first heard the song of the Poor-will in a wild cañon in the mountains of New Mexico. In company with Charles F. Lummis, the archeologist, I was camping in the long-silent homes of the cliff dwellers, high up on the white tufa walls of the haunted cliffs of Tyu-on-yi.

Drawing by R. I. Brasher

POOR-WILL (⅜ nat. size)

It was a quiet summer night with the moon shining in great brilliancy. The surroundings were most impressive, and when the sudden cry of *poor-will, poor-will,* was borne on the air from across the cañon, it was as if a voice from the spirit-land had spoken.

In many places through the high semi-desert regions of the southwest this bird may be found. It captures its prey of various insects by short flights much in the manner employed by the Whip-poor-will. It is distinctly nocturnal in its movements. Apparently it never goes abroad in the day-time, and when evening comes it remains in seclusion until the shadows of night have fallen. Sunlight seems to blind it, as may be observed by anyone who chances to come upon the bird by day as it sits drowsing on the fallen leaves beneath some bush or lowhanging tree. If when disturbed it chances to light where the sunlight is bright, one may walk to within a few feet before it appears to notice the approach.

The two white unspotted eggs are usually laid on the bare ground without any attempt at nest building. Two closely related subspecies, viz., the Frosted Poor-will (*Phalænoptilus nuttalli nitidus*) and the Dusky, or California, Poor-will (*Phalænoptilus nuttalli californicus*) are recognized by naturalists. All these birds retire southward when winter appears.

T. GILBERT PEARSON.

NIGHTHAWK

Chordeiles virginianus virginianus (*Gmelin*)

A. O. U. Number 420 See Color Plates 65

Other Names.— Goatsucker of Carolina; Bull-bat; Mosquito Hawk; Will-o'-the-Wisp; Pisk; Piramidig; Long-winged Goatsucker.

General Description.— Length, 10 inches. Plumage, a variegation of black, gray, brown, and buff; *white patch on wing. Tail, emarginate.*

Color.— ADULT MALE: Prevailing color of *upper parts, sooty-black,* very faintly glossed with greenish, much broken by irregular spotting, marbling, and streaks of buff, pale buffy-gray, and whitish, the black greatly predominating on crown, where the sparse markings are irregularly spot-like and buff, and on back where the markings are smaller, in form of irregular narrow bars or streaks; hindneck with buff spots larger, more regularly drop-shaped, forming indication of a broken collar; wing-coverts with rather large and numerous irregular spots of pale buffy-grayish or dull grayish-white, in addition to smaller irregular streaks and marblings, mostly of a more buffy hue; primary coverts, primaries, and outer greater coverts, dull grayish-black, the last margined terminally with pale grayish, the primaries passing into a more grayish hue at tips, the sixth, seventh, and eighth (sometimes ninth also) crossed a little in front of middle, by a broad, sharply defined, space of white, this involving the full width of both webs, as well as the shaft itself; tail, dull grayish-black or dusky, crossed by bands of paler (mostly buffy-grayish and dull grayish-white) marblings and spottings, and crossed by an interrupted broader band of white; region around eyes and sides of head, sooty-black streaked or longitudinally flecked with buffy, cinnamon, or rusty (sometimes nearly plain blackish), the cheeks similar but spotted with buffy; chin, upper and middle part of throat, and span below ears, immaculate white, forming a conspicuous V-shaped patch; lower throat, dark sooty-brown with triangular spots of brownish buff or cinnamon, the chest similar but with the spots dull whitish, the lower chest and upper breast with the markings more transverse or bar-like; rest of under parts, broadly and regularly barred with dark sooty-brown or sooty-blackish and buffy-white, the bars of the two colors of nearly equal width but the whitish ones averaging rather broader than the dusky ones, especially on rear parts, the under tail-coverts with the white interspaces much wider; under wing-coverts, dark sooty-brown or sooty-blackish much more narrowly as well as less regularly barred with buffy or buffy-whitish; the inner webs of *five outer primaries crossed by a broad band of white in front of middle portion;* bill, blackish; iris, blackish-brown; legs and feet, dusky. ADULT FEMALE: Similar to the adult male *but without the white band* on tail, the white on primaries more restricted, the lighter spotting, etc., of upper parts usually more conspicuous (giving a lighter colored cast to the general color of upper parts), under parts more strongly tinged with buffy, and white throat-patch usually suffused with (sometimes entirely replaced by) buff.

Nest and Eggs.— EGGS: 2, grayish-white densely spotted and blotched with gray, black, and pale purple; laid in gravelly spaces of open fields, on large rocks, on gravel roofs in cities, or (more rarely) in open spaces among woods.

Distribution.— North and South America; breeds from southern Yukon, central Mackenzie, central Keewatin, northern Quebec, and Newfoundland south to northern parts of Gulf States and west to edge of Plains from Minnesota to northeastern Texas; migrates through the Greater Antilles and Central America; winters in South America from Brazil south to Argentina.

Drawing by R. I. Brasher

NIGHTHAWK (⅓ nat. size)

Like the Whip-poor-will, the Nighthawk has always been counted a more or less mysterious, not to say uncanny, bird. The term, "Nightjar," as applied to the family, has some justification in the case of the Nighthawk, for the bird's note certainly is not melodious. But the term "hawk" is misleading, since the bird is in no sense a Hawk, but in reality is a flycatcher, and a very industrious and useful one. Indeed, the Nighthawk couldn't be a Hawk if he wanted to be (and he never shows any such disposition), because instead of the powerful talons of the birds of prey, he has feet which are almost rudimentary in their weakness, while in place of the meat-hook-like beak of the true Hawk, he has a short, weak bill and a mouth which is grotesque in its huge proportions.

Still another misnomer applied to this bird, and one almost as absurd as "Goatsucker," is "Bull-bat," the name by which he is commonly known in the South, and the justification for which remains one of the profound mysteries of popular nomenclature. To be sure, the bat has wings and flies, but right there its outward resemblance to a bird, of any kind, ceases abruptly, and it begins to look more like a rat than any other creature. To call the bat a "flying rat" would be much more sensible than it is to call the Nighthawk a "Bull-bat," for the rat and the bat at least belong to the same great class, the mammals, while the birds comprise a totally different one.

On the other hand, it seems strange that the makers of popular names should have entirely overlooked this bird's various and marked eccentricities. Appearing in the skies commonly in the early evening (for his activities are chiefly at the twilight hours), his flight is erratic, as if he were bewildered, and is punctuated by frequent repetitions of a short, nasal, and utterly unmusical call, usually uttered at the termination of fluttering dashes upward. His great flight performance, however, is his astonishing aërial dive, generally from a height of several hundred feet to within a few feet of the tree-tops or the house-tops or *terra firma* itself. It is preceded by no unusual evolutions that are discernible, though it is executed at fairly regular intervals and usually from a considerable altitude. Having reached a proper height by his characteristic fluttering flight, the bird suddenly almost closes his wings and takes his downward, almost perpendicular plunge, the swiftness of which rapidly accelerates until a fairly dizzying speed is attained. The dive continues until the bird seems to be within a few feet of the tree tops or ground, when a sudden spreading of the wings checks the descent and the diver sweeps easily and gracefully upward to renew his apparently aimless wanderings.

Much foolish mystery and needless misunderstanding has prevailed concerning the origin of the booming sound which is heard when the Nighthawk checks his dive and sweeps upward. An apparent misapprehension on the subject is suggested by part of the bird's scientific name, *Chordeiles,* which is derived from the two Greek words, *chorde* meaning "a stringed instrument," and *deile,* meaning "evening." This seems to be in reference to the popular notion that the white spots seen in the wings of the bird when it is overhead are holes, and that the sound referred to, and which might be imagined to resemble the lowest notes obtainable on a bass-viol, is caused by the passage of the air through these holes. Again, the sound by many is believed to be vocal in its origin. As a matter of fact, it is due solely to the rush of the air through the taut feathers of the partly spread wings, in which, of course, any orifice would greatly impede the bird's flight.

The purpose of this thrilling high-dive is not apparent. The suggestion that it is a sexual demonstration is not wholly credible, for the reason that it is often executed by an individual bird with no other member of the species in sight, whereas the characteristic sex demonstration is performed by the male in the presence of the female. Perhaps it is a plunge after a fly or a beetle, though it seems unlikely that the bird could descry an insect at the distance covered by the fall, and it could have no reason for continuing the descent after the prey had been captured. Many another bird would be accused of taking this grand tumble for the fun of it, but a sense of humor seems very foreign to the Nighthawk.

An old delusion — which is still a belief of many ignorant people, especially in the South — is that the Nighthawk and the Whip-poor-will are identical. There is, indeed, some superficial resemblance between the birds, and they have the common habit of perching lengthwise on a limb or fence-rail; but actual comparison of them reveals marked differences, as to both size and coloration. The most conspicuous of the distinguishing marks of the Nighthawk are the plainly marked white wing-bars, which are to be seen clearly from below, and which the Whip-poor-will lacks. The Whip-poor-will furthermore is essentially a bird of the woods, and does not — at least before nightfall — go hawking around in the open after the somewhat crazy manner of the Nighthawk. Close comparison of the birds would reveal the possession by both of a very curious comblike process on the inner edge of the middle claw of each foot. This comb the bird uses in freeing itself of vermin.

The skillful evolutions of a company of Nighthawks as the birds gracefully cleave the air in intersecting circles is a sight to be remembered. So expert are they on the wing that no insect is safe from them. Unfortunately their erratic flight tempts men to use them for targets, and this inexcusable practice is seriously diminishing their numbers, which is deplorable, since the birds are most useful. The Nighthawk is a voracious feeder and is almost exclusively insectivorous. GEORGE GLADDEN.

Photo by H. K. Job Courtesy of Outing Pub. Co.

NIGHTHAWK

Alarmed as she was incubating

The Pacific Nighthawk (*Chordeiles virginianus hesperis*) is similar to the common Nighthawk but its general coloration is lighter, the lighter markings on the back, shoulders, and wing-coverts being more numerous. It breeds from southwestern British Columbia south along the coast to northern California and in the Sierra Nevadas south to southern California. Its winter home is unknown.

Sennett's Nighthawk (*Chordeiles virginianus sennetti*) is even lighter and more grayish in appearance than the Pacific Nighthawk. This member of the family breeds on the treeless plains from Saskatchewan and Manitoba south to central Nebraska. During migration it is seen in Texas, but where it spends the winter is unknown.

The Western Nighthawk (*Chordeiles virginianus henryi*) has a more yellowish appearance, the darker markings being more brownish and the lighter ones more buffy. It breeds from southeastern British Columbia, Alberta, and southwestern Saskatchewan south to southern Texas and the mountains of northern Mexico, and winters in South America.

The Florida or Chapman's Nighthawk (*Chordeiles virginianus chapmani*) is like the common Nighthawk in coloration but is decidedly smaller — only eight and three-quarter inches in length. It breeds in the States of the Gulf coast from Florida to eastern Texas. As is the case with some of the other Nighthawks its winter range is unknown.

SWIFTS

Order *Macrochires;* suborder *Cypseli;* family *Micropodidæ*

SWIFTS never perch on branches of trees. They cling easily to the sides of vertical surfaces — to a rock or to the inside of a hollow tree trunk or a chimney. Like the Woodpeckers they press the tail against the surface for an additional support. Apparently they cannot grasp a branch with their feet in such a way as to maintain a fixed position on it.

Like the Swallows, the Swifts have very small, flat, triangular bills, large mouths, and extremely long wings. They, too, are insect-eating birds and take their prey while flying.

The salivary glands of the Swifts are greatly developed and the mucilage-like secretion is used in making the nests. In the species found in the Orient the nest is composed almost entirely of this substance, and Chinese and Japanese epicures consider them a great delicacy. The common Chimney Swift of the eastern United States makes a nest in shape similar to that of the edible bird's-nest but uses dead twigs and glues them together with the saliva.

Young Swifts are naked when hatched and for about two weeks are fed in the nest. After that they leave the nest and cling to the wall beside it.

Swifts are very beneficial, as their food is entirely made up of insects; and they should be encouraged to take up their residence near human habitations. Because the parasites which use the Swifts for hosts resemble bed-bugs, the birds have been unjustly accused of bringing these pests into houses; but the fact of this matter is that these parasitic insects would quickly die if separated from their hosts.

BLACK SWIFT

Cypseloides niger borealis (*Kennerty*)

A. O. U. Number 422

Other Name.— Northern Black Swift.

General Description.— Length, 7½ inches. Plumage, sooty-blackish, lighter below. Tail, slightly forked, the feathers not tipped with spines.

Color.—Adult Male: Crown and hindneck, deep grayish-brown or sooty, passing into sooty-blackish on back and other upper parts (the wings and tail very faintly glossed with bluish); chin and throat, much lighter grayish-brown passing into much darker sooty on under parts of body and under tail-coverts (the color slightly darker than that of crown); feathers of forehead and crown, narrowly margined at tip with grayish-white, these whitish tips much broader on sides of forehead, blending on edge into a distinct whitish area bordering the upper edge of the velvety-black lores; marginal under wing-coverts, very narrowly margined terminally with pale grayish; bill, black; iris, dark brown. Adult Female: Similar to the adult male but tail less notched (nearly square), under parts, paler.

Nest and Eggs.— Nest: In crevices of sea cliffs of the California coast and on inaccessible mountain walls; a flimsy structure of grass and rootlets snugly tucked away in a niche of the rocks. Egg: One, nearly three times the size of the White-throated Swift's egg, pure white.

Distribution.— Western North America; breeds from southern British Columbia and southern Colorado, south to central Mexico; winters in southern Mexico.

Like the White-throated Swift, this species breeds on inaccessible cliffs, though its nest is sometimes placed on the cornice of a building. Its flight resembles that of the Chimney Swift, but it is much larger than that familiar bird of the eastern States and quieter, too; in fact, Mr. Ridgway, who observed the Black Swifts in Nevada, says they were " perfectly silent " there. An observer of them in Cuba, however, reported that when one of these Swifts pursues another, the pursuer utters a series of soft notes, somewhat like a song. They are often seen hawking for insects above the city of Seattle, but usually at an altitude of from 300 to 500 feet, except when showers are imminent.

To A. G. Vrooman of Santa Cruz, California, belongs the honor of discovering the first authentic eggs of this species.

CHIMNEY SWIFT

Chætura pelagica (*Linnæus*)

A. O. U. Number 423

Other Names.— Chimney Swallow; American Swift.

General Description.— Length, 5½ inches. Plumage, sooty-blackish, lighter below. Tail, less than ½ length of wing, rounded or even, the feathers with spiny tips.

Color.— Adults: Above, plain dark sooty-olive passing into paler grayish-brown on rump, upper tail-coverts, and tail, the plumage slightly glossy, the feathers of crown darker centrally, producing an indistinctly scaly effect, those of the rump and the upper tail-coverts sometimes very narrowly and indistinctly tipped with paler; rigid shafts of tail-feathers, black; wings slightly glossy sooty-blackish, the inner webs of the feathers passing into grayish-brown toward edges; loral region, blackish, the feathers along projecting edges of forehead and crown (especially the portion over the eye), narrowly (sometimes very indistinctly or obsoletely) margined with whitish; remainder of the sides of head, the sides of the neck, and under parts, plain grayish-brown fading into a much paler tint on throat, chin, and cheeks; iris, brown.

Nest and Eggs.— NEST: Inside a chimney; of small twigs glued together with a gelatinous fluid secreted by the salivary glands, forming a semi-circular wall pocket. EGGS: 4 to 6, pure white.

Distribution.— Eastern North America; north to New Brunswick, Nova Scotia, Province of Quebec, southern Labrador, northern Ontario, Manitoba, and Alberta, accidentally to southern Greenland; west to western border of Great Plains and (accidentally?) New Mexico; breeding southward to southern Florida and thence westward along Gulf coast to southeastern Texas; occasional straggler to the Bermudas.

If it is proper to speak of the Chickadee as the "small-boy bird of the woods," it seems appropriate to characterize the Chimney Swift

Drawing by R. I. Brasher

CHIMNEY SWIFT (½ nat. size)

A bird who is never at rest except when he is at home

as the "small-boy bird of the air." All of the Swallows, and especially the Barn Swallow, seem to frolic a good deal on the wing, but their near relative, the Swift, is even more sportive. It is not uncommon to see two of them engaged in what appears to be a contest of speed, and skill in dodging, very like the small-boy's game of tag, keeping up meanwhile their very rapid chipping note, which may be their equivalent of laughter.

The Swift is very rapid and adroit on the wing, but is not so graceful a flyer as the Barn Swallow. However, it apparently has the more endurance of the two, for it is never seen to alight, and undoubtedly is steadily on the wing from the time it leaves its chimney-nest until it returns. Very likely this period of unceasing and rapid flight often lasts for an hour or two, and all of the bird's food is captured and eaten — except such as it takes to its young — while it is on the wing.

Like the Barn and Eave Swallows, the Swift's nesting habits have been changed by its coming into contact with man and his works. Originally the bird's nesting place was in a hollow tree. "I well remember the time," wrote Audubon, "when in lower Kentucky, Indiana, and Illinois many resorted to excavated branches and trunks for the purpose of breeding; nay, so strong is the influence of original habit that not a few still [about 1808] betake themselves to such places, not only to roost, but also to breed. . . . In such instances they appear to be as nice in the choice of a tree as they generally are in our cities in the choice of a chimney wherein to roost. Sycamores of a gigantic growth, and having a mere shell of bark and wood to support them, seem

Photo by H. K. Job Courtesy of Outing Pub. Co.

YOUNG CHIMNEY SWIFTS

Clinging to the wall like bats

to suit them best; and wherever I have met with one of these patriarchs of the forest rendered habitable by decay, there I have found the Swallows [Swifts] of the forest breeding in spring and summer, and afterward roosting until the time of their departure." And to this day, in districts remote from human dwellings, or even near them, it is not uncommon to find the birds obeying this instinct, and nesting as did their forbears who never saw a man-made chimney.

During both the spring and the fall migrations, the Swifts often gather in immense flocks and make use of the same chimney for a sleeping room. Mr. Burroughs describes graphically one of these grand going-to-bed performances, as follows: "One fall they gathered in this way and took refuge for the night in a large chimney-stack near me for more than a month and a half. Several times I went to town to witness the spectacle, and spectacle it was; ten thousand of them, I should think, filling the air above a whole square like a whirling swarm of huge black bees, but saluting the ear with a multitudinous chippering instead of a humming. People gathered on the sidewalk to see them. It was a rare circus performance free to all. After a great many feints and playful approaches, the whirling ring of the birds would suddenly grow denser above the chimney; then a stream of them, as if drawn down by some power of suction, would pour into the opening. For only a few seconds would this downward rush continue; then, as if the spirit of frolic had again got the upper hand of them, the ring would rise, and the chippering and circling go on. In a minute or two the same maneuver would be repeated, the chimney, as it were, taking its Swallows at intervals to prevent choking. It usually took a half-hour or more for the birds all to disappear down its capacious throat."

Photo by S. A. Lottridge

NEST AND YOUNG OF THE CHIMNEY SWIFT

After discovering this nest the photographer paid the owner of the chimney to allow him to tear down enough of it to obtain this picture

A remarkable fact, concerning the Swift is

that no one has yet discovered where it spends the five months between the time it disappears from the northern coast of the Gulf of Mexico in November until it returns in March. This extraordinary mystery was recorded by Wells W. Cooke, assistant biologist of the Bureau of Biological Survey, in his invaluable monograph on *Bird Migration,* as follows: "Much has been learned about bird migration in these latter days, but much yet remains to be learned, and the following is one of the most curious and interesting of the unsolved problems. The Chimney Swift is one of the most abundant and best-known birds of the eastern United States. With troops of fledglings, catching their winged prey as they go and lodging by night in tall chimneys, the flocks drift slowly south joining with other bands, until on the northern coast of the Gulf of Mexico they become an innumerable host. Then they disappear. Did they drop into the water or hibernate in the mud, as was believed of old, their obliteration could not be more complete. In the last week in March a joyful twittering far overhead announces their return to the Gulf coast, but their hiding place during the intervening five months is still the Swift's secret."

GEORGE GLADDEN.

Vaux's Swift (*Chætura vauxi*) is the western representative of the Chimney Swift, ranging through the Pacific coast district from British Columbia to Lower California. Its upper parts are sooty brown and the under parts, gray. In general appearance it is quite Bat-like and it, too, flies abroad at eventide.

WHITE-THROATED SWIFT

Aëronautes melanoleucus (*Baird*)

A. O. U. Number 425

General Description.— Length, 6¾ inches. Upper parts, sooty-blackish with two white patches; under parts, white. Tail, forked with the feathers narrow and stiff but not spiny.

Color.— ADULTS: Crown and hindneck, grayish-brown to very dark sooty-brown, sometimes uniform but usually becoming paler on forehead, and with feathers indistinctly margined with paler, especially on frontal region, the projecting edges of crown, dull whitish, forming a distinct narrow streak over the eye; back, shoulders, wing-coverts, rump, and upper tail-coverts, plain sooty-blackish, the tail similar but rather more sooty (less blackish); *a large patch of white or brownish-white on each side of rump,* pointed in front; wings, dark sooty-brown or sooty-blackish, the secondaries broadly tipped on outer web with dull or brownish-

Drawing by R. I. Brasher

WHITE-THROATED SWIFT (⅔ nat. size)

Its wonderful swiftness of wing and its inaccessible habitat insure this bird's safety—from man, at least

white, the inner webs of primaries passing into pale grayish-brown on edges (except on longer quills); a dusky spot immediately in front of eye, the loral region otherwise whitish; the region around the ear and back of the eye, sooty grayish-brown; the regions below the eye and cheek, chin, *throat, chest, and center portion of breast and abdomen white,* usually tinged with brownish; sides and flanks (broadly) and under tail-coverts, plain very dark sooty-brown or sooty-black; feathers along edge of wing broadly margined with pale grayish-brown or dull brownish-white; iris, dark brown.

Nest and Eggs.— NEST: Glued to cliff or cave sides or in holes in limestone cliffs; constructed of vegetable fiber and feathers, lined with strips of bark and a few feathers. EGGS: 4 or 5, pure white, unmarked.

Distribution.— Western North America; north to Washington, southern Montana, northern British Columbia, and southwestern Alberta, east to western South Dakota, western Nebraska, Wyoming, Colorado, New Mexico, and western Texas (Chisos Mountains), south to Lower California and through Mexico to Guatemala.

There is no very striking physical resemblance between the White-throated Swift and the polar bear, but in one respect they are fortunately alike: neither is, or ever is likely to be, in danger of annihilation by man; the bear because the men who would exterminate him for "sport" or gain (and these do not include his gentle neighbors, the Eskimos) will never invade his habitat in numbers sufficient to threaten his existence; and the Swift because its home on the unscalable peak or precipice is equally inaccessible, except possibly by flying machines, the use of which for this purpose probably would not prove profitable. To be sure, the bird sometimes comes within gunshot and therefore occasionally is "collected," which is to say, shot; but the tremendous speed and the erratic character of its flight make its "collection" an uncertain occupation.

Two of its habitats in which it has been observed, are the lofty cliffs in the Garden of the Gods in Colorado, and the cañon walls of the East Humboldt Mountains, in Nevada. In both places it nests in unapproachable crevices and pockets about half-way up sheer cliffs several hundred feet high, or in towering cañon walls of much greater altitude. On the wing and at other times the bird utters a spirited chatter. It seems also to be rather belligerent, for two birds have been seen to seize each other while in flight, and hold on, as they dropped together in a whirling fall, until near the ground, when they would relinquish their grip and dart away perhaps to resume the combat as soon as they had reached a safe altitude.

Unlike Vaux's Swift, the White-throated seems to have no special preference for the evening hours, but does much of its hunting in broad daylight.

HUMMINGBIRDS

Order *Macrochires;* suborder *Trochili;* family *Trochilidæ*

HUMMINGBIRDS are small to extremely small birds, with the terminal or hand portion of the wing longer than the portion nearer the body. The neck is very long, forming four-sevenths of the vertebral column. The bill is slender, usually awl-shaped, sometimes compressed and often widened and deepened at the base, extremely variable as to relative length (from decidedly shorter than the head to longer than the head, neck, and body together), usually straight, but sometimes excessively curved downward. The tongue is extremely long, slender, capable of extension, split at the tip, each division with the outer edge curled upward and inward for part of its length, forming, in effect, two parallel tubes. The tail is excessively variable in relative length and form — in fact more variable than in any other group of birds.

The nest is open above, is variable as to form and position, but usually cup-shaped and attached to a twig, and is composed of plant-downs or other soft materials, usually stuccoed exteriorly with bits of moss, lichen, or fragments of barks and spiders' webs. The eggs are usually two in number, but sometimes only one, immaculate white in color, and broadly elliptical in shape.

Inhabitants exclusively of America, the Hummingbirds constitute not only the most charming element in the wonderfully varied bird-life of the western hemisphere, but also, without doubt, the most remarkable group of birds in the entire world. No other group of birds is so brilliant in plumage or so different from all others in mode of flight and manner of feeding. The general habits of Hummingbirds are not dissimilar to those of birds in general. They are both aërial and arboreal, but are unable to progress upon the ground or any flat surface by means of their legs and feet alone. They perch readily and frequently upon trees or bushes, or may even cling to rocks or other vertical surfaces; and their nest-building presents nothing that may be deemed peculiar or even specially characteristic. In their flight and manner of procuring their food, however, they differ strikingly from all other birds, in these respects closely resembling certain insects, especially the evening hawk-moths. Their food, consisting mainly of small insects but in part also of the nectar of flowers, is mostly gleaned from blossoms, before which they poise, with wings so rapidly vibrating as to be invisible except as a dim haze or halo partly surrounding the body and producing the humming sound from which these birds derive their vernacular name, the bill thrust inside the flower, and the slender, semi-tubular tongue extended into the depths of the blossom. Some species, instead of feeding from flowers, glean their insect food from the bark of forest trees, following along the branches in suspended flight in the same manner that the others pass from flower to flower. In their feeding from flower to flower, Hummingbirds, like bees, butterflies, and moths, perform the same office in the economy of nature as insects by transferring pollen from one bloom to another and thus assisting in the fertilization of plants. In flying from one point to another, the flight of Hummingbirds, while essentially direct, is usually more or less undulating, and so extremely rapid that the eye can scarcely follow. Often this flight is accompanied (at least in the case of males of some species) by a more or less remarkable screeching or grating sound, produced mechanically by some peculiarity of wing-structure.

Diminutiveness of size and metallic brilliancy of coloring are the chief external characteristics of Hummingbirds, though exceptions to both occur; and in these respects they, as a group, have no rivals. Unfortunately stuffed specimens convey but a faint idea of their splendid coloring, for the perfection of their changeable refulgence can be fully realized only in the living bird, whose every change of position flashes to view a different hue — emerald green replacing ruby red, sapphire blue succeeding fiery orange, or either becoming opaque velvety black — according to the angle at which the sun's rays touch the feathers, an effect which can only partially be imitated with the stuffed specimen by artificially changing its position with reference to the light. Many species have a spot on the forehead at the base of the bill of the most luminous or brilliantly metallic color (usually green) that it is possible to imagine, this spot being surrounded by the most intense velvety black — evidently to enhance the brilliancy of the ornament by contrast, just as a jeweler would, for the same purpose, display a diamond or other gem against a background of black velvet. Often there is a spot of brilliant color and one of a contrasting hue just below it, the result being that first one color, then the other, is flashed forth as the bird changes slightly its position.

RIVOLI'S HUMMINGBIRD

Eugenes fulgens (*Swainson*)

A. O. U. Number 426

Other Names.— Refulgent Hummingbird; Rivoli's Hummer.

General Description.— Length, 5 inches. Upper parts, metallic green; under parts, black, green, and gray.

Color.— Adult Male: Crown, rich metallic violet or royal purple, the forehead blackish, usually glossed with green or bluish-green; hindneck, sides of head, velvety-black or bronze-green, according to light; rest of upper parts, metallic bronze, bronze-green, or golden-green; wings, dark brownish-slate or dusky, faintly glossed with purple or purplish-bronze; chin and throat, brilliant metallic emerald-green, this brilliant green area extending much farther backward laterally than centrally; chest and upper breast, velvety-black or bronze-green, passing into dusky-bronze or bronze-green on lower breast, this into grayish-brown or sooty-grayish on abdomen and flanks; thigh and anal tufts, white; a small white spot or streak back of eye (sometimes a whitish rictal streak also); under tail-coverts, light brownish-gray (sometimes glossed with bronze or bronze-green) margined with whitish; bill, dull black; iris, dark brown. ADULT FEMALE: Above, including four middle tail-feathers, bronze-green, the crown duller (sometimes dull grayish-brown in front); three outer tail-feathers (on each side) with basal half bronze-green, then black, the tip brownish-gray, this broadest on outermost feather, much smaller on third; wings, as in adult male; a white streak back of eye and below this a dusky area; under parts, brownish-gray or buffy-grayish, glossed laterally with metallic bronze or bronze-green, the feathers of chin and throat margined with paler or with dull grayish-white; producing a scaly appearance; thigh and anal tufts, white; under tail-coverts, brownish-gray (sometimes glossed with bronze-green), margined with pale brownish-gray or dull whitish; bill, etc., as in adult male.

Nest and Eggs.— NEST: In sycamores, maples, or firs usually about 40 feet up; constructed of silky plant fibers, grass tips, lined with sycamore down and coated with lichens, fastened on with cobwebs. EGGS: 2, white.

Distribution.— Mountains of southern Arizona, southwestern New Mexico, extreme western Texas, Mexico, and Central America southward to Nicaragua.

The distinctive fact about this Hummer is that it doesn't hum, at least not in the way which makes that term more or less accurate in describing the sound made by the wings of other members of the family. Even when the flight of the bird is exceedingly rapid, which it often is, the whir of its wings is more like the buzz of a big bumblebee or beetle than the almost musical drone made by the flight of other Hummers. Moreover the flight of this species is often so deliberate, comparatively speaking, that the outline of its wings may actually be seen, whereas the little pinions of other Hummers are seen only as faint areas of mist on either side of the body. The tail of the male Rivoli is slightly forked while that of the female is double rounded.

Many years ago it was established beyond a doubt that the diet of Hummingbirds consists largely of insects, rather than solely of nectar; but the latter notion is likely to persist indefinitely because it is a poetic one which appeals to the imagination, and seems in keeping with the fairy-like character of this mite of a bird. The Rivoli Hummer, however, not only depends largely upon insects for its food, but captures many of them in flight. This it often does in the most approved flycatcher manner, by lying in wait, perched on a dead limb in a tree-top, and dashing out after passing insects, few of which have any chance to escape the speed and certainty of this little hunter's movements. The insects found in flowers of honeysuckle and agave are its favorites.

BLUE-THROATED HUMMINGBIRD

Cyanolæmus clemenciæ (*Lesson*)

A. O. U. Number 427

Other Names.— Blue-throated Casique; Blue-throated Hummer.

General Description.— Length, 5¼ inches. Upper parts, green; under parts, brownish-gray.

Color.— ADULT MALE: Above, rather dull metallic bronze-green, passing into olive-bronze on rump, where the feathers have narrow terminal margins of pale brownish-gray; upper tail-coverts, dusky (sometimes faintly glossed with greenish or bluish), narrowly and indistinctly margined with paler; tail, black, faintly glossed with bluish, the outer feathers tipped with white; wings, dark brownish-slate color or dusky, very faintly glossed with purplish; a conspicuous white streak back of eye extending obliquely backward and downward behind upper rear margin of ear region, the latter, together with the lores and space below eye, plain dusky; a chin streak of whitish (this sometimes obsolete); *chin and throat, metallic blue*, the feathers very narrowly and indistinctly margined with brownish-gray; rest of under parts, plain deep brownish-gray or brownish-slate color, the under tail-coverts broadly margined with white; thigh and anal tufts and tuft on each side of rump, white; bill, dull black; iris, dark brown. ADULT FEMALE: Similar to the adult male, but blue of throat replaced by the general dull brownish-gray of under parts.

Nest and Eggs.— NEST: In fork of shrub or sapling, or on a fern; a handsome structure of fine mosses smoothly felted together and lined with down of willow catkins. EGGS: 2, white.

Distribution.— Western Texas, southern Arizona, southwestern New Mexico, and Mexico.

Of its diminutive family the Blue-throated Hummer is the largest member which may be considered an American bird, and this claim is none too firmly established, since it is, after all, essentially a bird of Mexico, and Central America, and favors Uncle Sam's domain only to the extent of appearing in southern Arizona. In other respects, too, this bird is unlike the Hummers who are more nearly American in their range and habits. For, besides being larger (about two inches longer than the common Ruby-throat of the eastern States), it is less active and generally more sedate in its demeanor. It even ventures a little song in the form of a faint twitter, which at least is the most elaborate vocal performance of its species in this country. It has a truly Oriole-like manner of searching for food in the blossoms of the big agave trees.

RUBY-THROATED HUMMINGBIRD

Archilochus colubris (*Linnæus*)

A. O. U. Number 428 See Color Plate 66

Other Names.— Hummingbird; Common Hummingbird; Hummer; Ruby-throat.

General Description.— Length: male, 3¼ inches; female, 3⅘ inches. Upper parts, bronze-green; under parts, red, bronze-green, and white.

Drawing by R. I. Brasher

RUBY-THROATED HUMMINGBIRD
(½ nat. size)

A feathered midget who does not hesitate to tackle a big Hawk

Color.— Adult Male: Above, metallic bronze-green, including middle pair of tail-feathers; wings, dark brownish-slate or dusky, faintly glossed with purplish; tail (except middle pair of feathers), dark bronzy-purplish or purplish bronzy-black; chin, cheeks, region below the eyes, and the sides of head, velvety-black; a small spot back of eye, white; *whole throat, brilliant metallic red* changing to golden or even greenish in different lights; chest, dull brownish-white or very pale buffy brownish-gray, passing gradually into deeper brownish-gray on breast and abdomen, the sides and flanks darker and overlaid by metallic bronze-green; thigh tufts and tuft on each side of rump, white; under tail-coverts, brownish-gray (sometimes glossed with greenish-bronze) centrally, broadly margined with dull white; bill, dull black; iris, dark brown. Adult Female: Above, metallic bronze-green, golden-green, or greenish-bronze, including middle pair of tail-feathers; three outer ones on each side, broadly tipped with white, metallic bronze-green for basal half, the intervening portion black; wings, dark brownish-slate or dusky faintly glossed with purplish; a small spot of dull white back of eye; sides of head, deep dull grayish; lores, dusky; cheeks and under parts, dull grayish-white or very pale brownish-gray (usually more decidedly whitish on chin, throat, and cheeks), the flanks and shorter under tail-coverts usually tinged with pale buffy-brownish; thigh tufts and tuft on each side of rump, white; bill, etc., as in adult male.

Nest and Eggs.— Nest: An exquisite cup, less than two inches across, of felted plant, fern, or dandelion-seed down, covered so perfectly with moss and lichens and fastened with spider webs as to appear a mere protuberance on the limb, and lined with a layer of the finest down. Eggs: 2, pure white.

Distribution.— Eastern North America; north, regularly to southern Labrador, Quebec, Ontario, and Keewatin (to about latitude 52°), and in the interior to northern and central Alberta; west to about middle portion of Great Plains (along streams); breeding southward to middle Florida and along the Gulf coast to west-central Texas; wintering from middle and southern Florida and southern Texas southward through southern Mexico and Central America to Panama; casual in Cuba in migration.

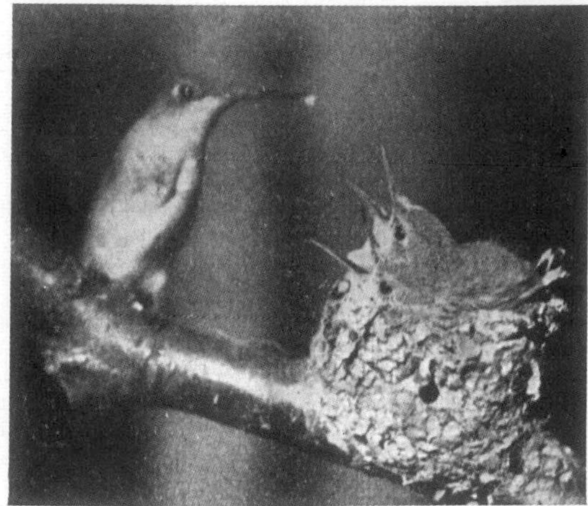

Photo by H. K. Job Courtesy of Outing Pub. Co.

AN INTERRUPTED MEAL

Ruby-throated Hummingbird and young

Hummingbirds are found only in the Americas, but only one, the Ruby-throated, inhabits the eastern United States. It is a dainty little atom of bird-life, and is of exquisite beauty. No other bird can be mistaken for it, its nearest counterpart in nature being the sphinx moth that sometimes comes about flowers of summer evenings. One usually sees this bird when like a great iridescent bee it whizzes across the yard, or pauses before the nectar-bearing flowers of the garden. The wings beat with a rapidity no eye can follow — no camera record.

A great part of the time the Hummingbird perches on the limbs of trees or less frequently on telephone wires. From its perch it makes frequent trips to nearby feeding grounds only to return shortly and resume its usual occupation of alternately preening its feathers and gazing about the landscape.

The nest is a wonderful creation of plant down, covered with lichens and bound together with spider web or fine plant fibers. It is about the size of an English walnut and is saddled on a small limb from twelve to thirty feet from the ground. The young are fed usually on the semi-digested remains of minute insects which the parents regurgitate for the comfort of the nestlings.

These Hummingbirds winter to a limited number in south Florida. The bulk of them, however, go farther south. In the autumn nights these little birds launch out across the Gulf of Mexico straight for Yucatan or Central America. This incredible journey of not less than 500 miles is made without a single stop for food or rest.

T. Gilbert Pearson.

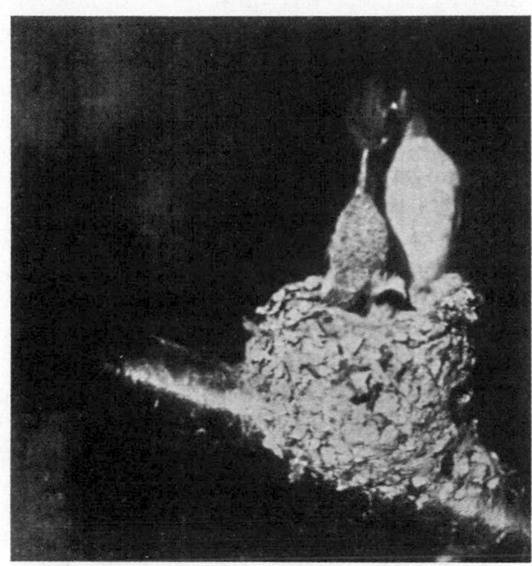

Photo by H. K. Job Courtesy of Outing Pub. Co.

RUBY-THROATED HUMMINGBIRD PUMPING FOOD INTO THE MOUTH OF THE YOUNG BIRD

BLACK-CHINNED HUMMINGBIRD

Archilochus alexandri (*Bourcier* and *Mulsant*)

A. O. U. Number 429

Other Name.— Black-chinned Hummer.

General Description.— Length: male, 3¾ inches; female, 4 inches. Upper parts, bronze-green; under parts, grayish-white.

Color.— Adult Male: Above, rather dull metallic bronze-green, darker and duller on crown; the forehead, sometimes, dull dusky; wings, dark brownish-slate, or dusky, faintly glossed with purple; tail (except middle pair of feathers), bronzy purplish-black; lores, ear region and cheeks, *chin, upper throat, and sides of throat, uniform opaque or velvety-black; lower throat, metallic violet* or violet-purple; chest, dull grayish-white or very pale brownish-gray; the under parts of body, similar, but usually more decidedly grayish centrally; the sides and flanks, darker and glossed or overlaid with metallic bronze or bronze-green; under tail-coverts, brownish-gray; tufts on the thighs and on each side of rump, white; bill, dull black; iris, dark brown. Adult Female: Similar to the male but with under parts, dull white or grayish-white (more purely white on abdomen and under tail-coverts), the throat sometimes streaked or spotted with dusky.

Nest and Eggs.— Nest: On horizontal limb or in the fork of small twigs; constructed of the down found on the lower side of sycamore leaves; resembles a small round yellow sponge. Eggs: 2, pure white.

Distribution.—Western North America; breeds from British Columbia to northern Lower California and northern Mexico and from the Pacific to western Montana and central Texas; winters in western Mexico.

Many observers of that dainty little feathered gem, the Ruby-throated Hummingbird — the sole representative in the eastern States of its wonderful family — have been treated to the remarkable pendulum performance, which it is likely to execute apparently for the purpose of frightening away an intruder who has come too near its nest. A similar act on a much smaller scale seems to be included in the courtship demonstrations of the Black-chinned Hummer of the western States. In this instance, the arc described by the bird in front of the object of his affections — usually perched motionless on a twig — may be no more than a yard in length, and the bird covers it by flying forward and backward, the forward movement being checked apparently by the quick spreading of its tail. Or, the movement may be backward and then forward in a sidewise position; but both show the bird's marvelous skill in the use of its wings and tail.

There is ample proof that this bird feeds freely upon insects, and often such as are caught by gummy sap exuding from the black birch and other trees. Poising in front of these sap-traps — if they may be so termed — these Hummers snap up the helpless insects; as they return frequently to these sources of food supply, they must rely upon them to some extent, though evidently they feed also upon insects imprisoned in flowers.

In an article contributed to *The Auk,* Miss Merriam (Mrs. Bailey) described the clever and interesting method followed by a female Hummer of this species in building her nest. "The peculiar feature of the building," she says, "was the quivering motion of the bird in moulding. When the material was placed, she moulded the nest like a potter, twirling tremulously around against the sides, sometimes pressing so hard she ruffed up the feathers of her breast. She shaped the cup as if it were a piece of clay. To round the outside she would sit on the rim and lean over, smoothing the sides with her bill, often with the same tremulous motion. When she wanted to turn around in the nest she lifted herself by whirring her wings." The male took no part in these building operations, and in fact did not put in an appearance at all. Mrs. Hummer did all of the work, and it took her just six days to complete her beautiful little home, made chiefly of yellow down taken from the under side of sycamore leaves, with green lichen decorations on the outside when the nest was placed among green oak leaves.

ANNA'S HUMMINGBIRD

Calypte anna (*Lesson*)

A. O. U. Number 431

Other Name.—Anna's Hummer.

General Description.— Length: male, 3½ inches; female, 4 inches. Head, rose-red; upper parts, bronze-green; under parts, gray.

Color.—Adult Male: *Whole head except back and ear region, brilliant metallic rose-red,* changing to violet in certain lights, the rear side feathers of throat elongated; a small spot or streak of white behind eye; upper parts, metallic bronze-green, the upper tail-coverts and middle pair of tail-feathers, similar but usually less bronzy, or more bluish-green; tail (except middle pair of feathers), dark grayish, faintly glossed with greenish-bronze; wings, brownish-slate or dusky faintly glossed with purplish; chest, pale brownish-gray or dull grayish-white; rest of under parts, deeper grayish, strongly glossed with metallic bronze-green laterally, the feathers margined with paler grayish; thigh tufts and conspicuous tuft on each side of rump, white; under tail-coverts, brownish-gray glossed with bronze-green or greenish-bronze and broadly margined with pale gray or grayish-white; bill, dull black; iris, dark brown. Adult Female: Similar but crown like back in coloration, and chin and throat usually with an admixture of metallic red or purplish-red feathers, sometimes with a considerable patch of metallic reddish.

Nest and Eggs.— Nest: Similar to that of the Rufous Hummingbird, but covered with green moss and lined with plantdown, fur, or feathers. Eggs: Also similar.

Distribution.— California in general (except parts of northern coast district), and southward (as a resident) to coast district of northern Lower California; during migration southeastward to southern Arizona.

This little Hummer is quite restricted in its range, living through central and southern California mainly west of the Sierra Nevadas. Like the other Hummingbirds, it builds a beautiful little nest, lining the cup on the inside with cotton or plant down and shingling the outsides with green mosses and lichens. Sometimes soft feathers are used as a resting place for the eggs.

In the spring when the eucalyptus trees are in blossom, I have often seen these Hummers chasing each other from tree to tree. One may often find this Hummingbird nesting in the eucalyptus, but it is hard to say that any tree or place is its favorite. I have seen nests saddled on the limb of an orchard tree, or the bird may even select a cholla cactus. I saw one built on the curve of an electric light wire under a porch.

In the early spring, the male often makes quite an effort at singing when he is perched on a wire or dry twig. Some people consider it more a high-pitched squeak than a song, but it is continuous. Mr. Charles A. Allen says, "Its simple little lay sounds like *te-uit, te-uit, te-wieu, wieu, wieu,* repeated over and over again, and when angry it utters a very harsh, rasping screech."

When the eggs of the Hummingbird hatch, the birds look like two tiny black bugs. The first sign of feathers is a light streak of brown along the middle of the back. But the queerest thing in the life of the Hummingbird is to watch the mother feed her young. She collects sweets from the flowers, little spiders and other insects which she swallows, and then she feeds by regurgitation. She braces her tail against the side of the nest, draws her dagger-like bill straight up above and plunges it down the baby's throat to the hilt. Then she starts a jabbing process as if to puncture him to the toes. In this way, she pumps his stomach full of food. It looks like the murder of the infants.

I have never seen a Hummingbird fledgling fall from the nest in advance of his strength, as a young Robin does. When the time comes, he seems to spring into the air fully grown, clad in glittering armor, as Minerva sprang from the head of Jove.

One day as I watched a young Hummingbird in the nest, I learned the reason. He sat on the nest edge, stretched his wings and combed out his tail-feathers with his bill. Then he tried his wings. He began slowly, as if getting up steam. He made them buzz till they almost lifted him off his feet. He had to hang on to keep from going. In this way, he practiced many times during the day, until he mastered the art of balancing and rising in the air.

William L. Finley.

BROAD-TAILED HUMMINGBIRD

Selasphorus platycercus (*Swainson*)

A. O. U. Number 432

Other Name.—Broad-tailed Hummer.

General Description.— Length: male, 4¼ inches; female, $4\frac{7}{10}$ inches. Upper parts, bronze-green; under parts, whitish.

Color.— Adult Male: Above, metallic bronze-green; middle pair of tail-feathers metallic bronze-green (sometimes more bluish-green); rest of tail, dull purplish or bronzy-black, the pair next to middle pair usually glossed with bronzy-green (sometimes mostly of this color), the outer web *edged with cinnamon-rufous,* the next pair sometimes also narrowly edged with the same; wings, dark brownish-slate or dusky faintly glossed with purplish; *chin and throat, bright metallic reddish purple*; chest, grayish-white, passing into very pale gray on breast and abdomen; sides and flanks darker grayish, tinged (especially the flanks) with pale cinnamon, the sides and sides of breast overlaid by metallic bronze-green; thigh tufts, white; under tail-coverts, white with a central area of pale cinnamon or cinnamon-buff (sometimes partly bronze-green); bill, dull black; iris, dark brown. Adult Female: Above, metallic bronze-green, including middle pair of tail-feathers, the latter sometimes blackish or dusky; three outer feathers, on each side, broadly tipped with white, cinnamon-rufous basally, the remaining portion purplish or bronzy-black with bronze-green between the blackish subterminal and cinnamon-rufous basal areas; chin and throat, dull white, the feathers with small center streaks or drop-shaped spots of dusky or dusky bronze; chest, dull brownish-white or buffy grayish-white, the breast and abdomen similar but, usually, more decidedly tinged with buffy; sides and flanks, light cinnamon; under tail-coverts, pale cinnamon (sometimes partly grayish) centrally, broadly margined with white; thigh tufts, white; bill etc., as in adult male.

Nest and Eggs.— Nest: Identical with Rufous Hummingbird; often placed in dwarf willow thickets or on small limbs over running water. Eggs: 2, pure white.

Distribution.— Mountain districts of western United States; north to Idaho, Montana; east to eastern base of Rocky Mountains in Wyoming, western Nebraska, Colorado, New Mexico, and western Texas; west to the Sierra Nevadas (casually to Oakland, California); southward over greater part of Mexico; breeds throughout its general range; winters in Mexico and Central America.

The season for Hummingbirds opened with the locust blossoms next door, which were for days a mass of bloom and buzzings of birds and bees. But when the fragrant flowers began to fall and the ground was white with them, one bird settled herself on our Honeysuckle, and there took her daily meals for a month. Being not six feet from where I sat for hours every day, I had the first good opportunity of my life to learn the ways of one of these queer little creatures in feathers.

After searching and much overhauling of the books, I made her out to be the female Broad-tailed Hummingbird, who is somewhat larger than the familiar Ruby-throat of the East. Her mate, if she had one, never came to the vine; but whether she drove him away and discouraged him, or whether he had an independent source of supply, I never knew. She was the only one whose acquaintance I made, and in a month's watching I came to know her pretty well.

In one way she differed strikingly from any Hummingbird I have seen; she alighted, and rested frequently and for long periods. Droll enough it looked to see such an atom, such a mere pinch of feathers, conduct herself after the fashion of a big bird; to see her wipe that needle-like beak, and dress those infinitesimal feathers, combing out her head plumage with her minute black claws, running the same useful appendages through her long, gauzy-looking wings, and carefully removing the yellow pollen of the honeysuckle blooms which stuck to her face and throat. Her favorite perch was a tiny dead twig on the lowest branch of a poplar tree, near the honeysuckle. There she spent a long time each day, sitting usually, though sometimes she stood on her little wiry legs.

But though my Hummingbird friend might sit down, there was no repose about her; she was continually in motion. Her head turned from side to side, as regularly, and apparently as mechanically, as an elephant waves his great head and trunk. Sometimes she turned her attention to me, and leaned far over with her large, dark eyes fixed upon me with interest and curiosity. But never was there the least fear in her bearing; she evidently considered herself mistress of the place, and reproved me if I made the slightest movement, or spoke too much to a neighbor. If she happened to be engaged among her honey-pots when a movement was made, she instantly jerked herself back a foot or more from the vine, and stood upon nothing, as it were, motionless, except the wings, while she looked into the cause of the disturbance, and often expressed her disapproval of our behavior in squawky cries.

The toilet of this liliputian in feathers, performed on her chosen twig as it often was, interested me greatly. As carefully as though she were a foot or two, instead of an inch or two, long, did she clean and put in order every plume on her little body, and the work of polishing her beak was the great performance of the day. This member was plainly her pride and her joy; every part of it, down to the very tip, was scraped and rubbed by her claws, with the leg thrown over the wing, exactly as big birds do. It was astonishing to see what she could do with her leg. I have even seen her pause in mid-air and thrust one over her vibrating wing to scratch her head.

Then, when the pretty creature was all in beautiful order, her emerald-green back and white breast immaculate, when she had shaken herself out, and darted out and drawn back many times her long bristle-like tongue, she would sometimes hover along before the tips of the fence-stakes, which were like laths, held an inch apart by wires,— collecting, I suppose, the tiny spiders which were to be found there. She always returned to the honeysuckle, however, to finish her repast, opening and closing her tail as one flirts a fan, while the breeze made by her wings agitated the leaves for two feet around her. Should a blossom just ready to fall come off on her beak like a coral case, as it sometimes did, she was indignant indeed; she jerked herself back and flung it off with an air that was comical to see.

When the hot wind blew, the little creature seemed to feel the discomfort that bigger ones did: she sat with open beak as though panting for breath; she flew around with legs hanging, and even alighted on a convenient leaf or cluster of flowers, while she rifled a blossom, standing with sturdy little legs far apart, while stretching up to reach the bloom she desired.

Two statements of the books were not true in the case of this bird: she did not sit on a twig upright like an Owl or a Hawk, but held her body exactly as does a Robin or Sparrow; and she did fly backward and sideways, as well as forward.

Toward the end of June my tiny visitor began to make longer intervals between her calls, and when she did appear she was always in too great haste to stop; she passed rapidly over half a dozen blossoms, and then flitted away. Past were the days of loitering about on poplar twigs or preening herself on the peach tree. It was plain that she had set up a home for herself, and the mussy state of her once nicely kept breast feathers told the tale,— she had a nest somewhere. Vainly, however, did I try to track her home: she either took her way like an arrow across the garden to a row of very tall locusts, where a hundred Hummingbirds' nests might have been hidden, or turned the other way over a neighbor's field to a cluster of thickly grown apple trees, equally impossible to search. If she had always gone one way I might have tried to follow, but to look for her infinitesimal nest at opposite poles of the earth was too discouraging, even if the weather had been cool enough for such exertion. OLIVE THORNE MILLER.

RUFOUS HUMMINGBIRD

Selasphorus rufus (*Gmelin*)

A. O. U. Number 433

Other Name.— Rufous Hummer.

General Description.— Length: male, $3\frac{7}{10}$ inches; female, $3\frac{9}{10}$ inches. Prevailing color of male, red; female is bronze-green above and whitish below.

Color.— ADULT MALE: Crown, dull metallic bronze or bronze-green; rest of upper parts, including lores, eyes and ear regions, and greater part of tail, *plain cinnamon-rufous*, the back sometimes glossed with metallic bronze-green; tail-feathers with an area of purplish or bronzy dusky; wings, dark brown-slate or dusky, faintly glossed with purple; chin, and throat, brilliant metallic scarlet; chest, white passing through cinnamon-buff into cinnamon-rufous on rest of under parts; the under tail-coverts, whitish basally; thigh tufts, white; bill, dull black; iris, dark brown. ADULT FEMALE: Above, metallic green; chin, throat, and chest, dull white, the throat usually with tips of some of the feathers metallic orange-red or scarlet (changing to golden and greenish), sometimes with a large patch of this color; rest of under parts, cinnamon-rufous; fading into dull buffy whitish on breast and abdomen; under tail-coverts pale cinnamon-rufous or cinnamon-buff centrally, broadly margined with white or buffy white.

Nest and Eggs.— NEST: In ferns, bushes, trees, and vines, near creeks; constructed of willow-floss and soft plant-down, covered over with lichens. EGGS: Not distinguishable from those of the Ruby-throat, except that they average slightly smaller.

Distribution.— Western North America; north to coast district of Alaska as far as latitude 61°; east to Alberta, Montana, Wyoming, Colorado, and New Mexico; breeding southward to higher mountains of New Mexico and Arizona, northern California and southward along coast to Santa Clara County and in Sierra Nevada at least to Calaveras County, as well as locally throughout the general range; in winter some migrating southward to Lower California, Santa Barbara Islands, and over highlands of Mexico.

Photo by W. L. Finley and H. T. Bohlman

RUFOUS HUMMINGBIRD

I was standing on the hillside one May morning when I saw a Rufous Hummingbird come down like the rush of a rocket. He turned and whirled up till I could see but the tiniest speck in the sky. Then he dropped headlong like a real meteor, his gorget puffed out and his tail spread wide. He veered just above the bushes with a sound like a whip drawn through the air and as the impetus carried him up, a high-pitched musical trill sounded above the whir of his wings. Again and again he swung back and forth, evidently in an effort to win the heart of some lady. He must have won her, for I think this was one of a pair that had their home in the Virginia creeper at the side of the house.

I have never known just what to think of the male Hummingbird. He is an enthusiastic lover, but he disappears entirely when the nest is finished and incubation begins. I think he was never known to give his wife a hand in caring for the young birds. I found it the same with the Rufous Hummingbird as Bradford Torrey says of his Ruby-throat: he drops out of existence leaving a widow with twins on her hands. Perhaps the male Hummingbird is not an intentional shirk and deserter. I think that somewhere back through the generations of Hummingbird experience it was found that such bright colors about the home were unmistakable clues for enemies. Therefore, it is the law of self-protection for him to keep away from the nest. WILLIAM L. FINLEY.

Photo by Mrs. Granville Pike Courtesy of Nat. Asso. Aud. So

MALE RUFOUS HUMMINGBIRD

Washington

ORDER OF PERCHING BIRDS

Order *Passeres*

THE Perching Birds are the largest group of related birds, and include nearly all of our familiar land birds and more than one-half of the entire number of species. In this order bird life reaches its highest development: the nervous system is acutely sensitive; the special senses, noticeably those of hearing and sight, are keenly developed; the circulation and the respiration are rapid; and the temperature of the body is the highest among animals.

Usually the Perching Birds have four toes, which are so arranged that the bird can grasp a branch or other perch. The hind toe is never raised above the level of the others. The vocal organ is well developed, and according to this development the order is divided into the suborders *Oscines*, or Song Birds, and *Clamatores*, or Songless Perching Birds (Screamers). Twenty-three families of the order occur in the United States and Canada.

The young of this order are born weak, helpless, and nearly naked. They are brooded and cared for by the parents for some time in the nest. After they are a few days old they are covered with down, and later this is replaced with feathers — the juvenal plumage. A more or less complete molt follows in the autumn. The adults also molt in the fall. Some adults have an entire change of plumage in the spring, while others have little or none.

TYRANT FLYCATCHERS

Order *Passeres;* suborder *Clamatores;* family *Tyrannidæ*

FLYCATCHERS belong to the group of songless perching birds. This classification seems a trifle inaccurate, as several of the members have very sweet songs. But the real significance of this appellation is comparative rather than positive; their vocal organs are less highly developed than are those of other perching birds and consequently their singing ability is more limited.

The Tyrant Flycatchers are exclusively American birds. Superficially, both in general appearance and in habits, they resemble the Flycatchers of the eastern hemisphere, but the latter belong to a different family and are more nearly related to our Thrushes. There are about four hundred species and these are most numerously developed in the tropics. In the United States there are thirty species and subspecies. Among this large number of species there are few highly differentiated forms; very much the greater number are birds of dull coloration, with very slightly modified structural characters. The species grade into one another almost imperceptibly.

Some of the general family characteristics are: the shield-like scales that cover the lower section of the short legs; feet small and weak; feathers in the tail numbering twelve; primaries numbering ten, the first well developed and often the longest; wing-coverts more than half the length of the secondaries; shoulders broad; neck short; head large; bill broad and flattened, gradually tapering to a sharp point, abruptly bent downward near the tip, and notched at the beginning of the bend; nostrils near the base of the bill, small and round and not very well concealed by bristly feathers; the gape large and the bristles at the corners usually well developed, sometimes so excessively developed that they extend beyond the tip of the bill when pressed forward. The period of incubation averages about twelve days.

The Flycatchers for the most part inhabit the open country and prefer to live about gardens, orchards, and sparsely timbered hillsides. Several species are not averse to human neighbors and make their nests in the crannies of buildings, while a number of others build in covered sites, such as hollow trees, under bridges, or under the overhanging bank of a stream. Many of the species show a strong liking for the vicinity of water, and are frequently to be found in the neighborhood of streams or pools, and in dry parts of the country every watering trough by the roadside has its attendant Flycatcher. This fondness for the vicinity of water doubtless arises from the fact that insects are abundant in such situations. Most of the species are migratory, though some of them within rather narrow limits.

These birds are extremely agile upon the wing, and turn in the air with extraordinary facility, which enables them to catch the flying insects, of which their food largely consists. Their favorite method of feeding is to perch upon a post, stake, or leafless twig, and from this outlook watch for their prey, and then to sally forth and snap the luckless insect in midair, often with a sharp click of the bill and a sudden turn back toward the perch.

One prominent characteristic, which is more or less marked in the whole family of Flycatchers, is the pugnacity they display toward Crows, Hawks, or other large birds. This is especially shown when the intruders come about the nests of Flycatchers; then they are attacked with the greatest vigor and driven off. This trait is particularly marked in Kingbirds, so that if a pair of them nest in the vicinity of a poultry yard they serve as protectors of the poultry.

Farmers and horticulturists have never accused the Flycatchers of doing any harm to their crops. The most that has been said against them is that certain of the larger species feed to a harmful extent upon honeybees. Stomach examinations, however, do not sustain this accusation. Honeybees do not form an important percentage of the food, and, moreover, a large proportion of those eaten are drones or males, of which, as is well known, there is in every hive a superfluity. The real harm, if any, done by this family of birds is in the destruction of predacious and parasitic hymenoptera, or four-winged flies. Of the former, however, so few are eaten that their loss is of no practical importance. Some parasitic hymenoptera are taken by most Flycatchers, and with certain of the smaller species they amount to a considerable percentage of the food. While theoretically this is harmful to the interests of husbandry, the precise amount of the damage is impossible of calculation. The parasites themselves often destroy useful insects, including other parasites, or are themselves destroyed by other insects, so that the question of the final result involves a problem so delicate and complicated as to preclude exact solution.

SCISSOR-TAILED FLYCATCHER

Muscivora forficata (*Gmelin*)

A. O. U. Number 443

Other Names.— Swallow-tailed Flycatcher; Texan Bird of Paradise.

General Description.— Length, 14 inches. Head, pale gray; body, gray but back with a pinkish tinge; tail and wings, blackish, with white markings. Tail, deeply forked; bill, hooked. Tail of male, 7 to 10 inches; that of female, shorter.

Color.— Crown and hindneck, clear pale gray, the center of crown with a small concealed patch of orange-red, underlaid behind and laterally by white; back and shoulders, light gray, usually suffused with pinkish red or ocher-yellowish (more commonly the former), the shoulders and lower back sometimes almost uniformly the former color; rump, brownish-gray, the feathers darker centrally or with darker shaft-streaks; upper tail-coverts black or dusky, margined with grayish; six middle tail-feathers, black, margined terminally with pale grayish-brown or whitish; three outermost (on each side) white (usually tinged with salmon-pink, sometimes deeply of this color), the terminal portion mostly black, this occupying between terminal third and terminal half of third feather; wings, dusky, the coverts margined with gray or grayish-white, the primaries narrowly edged with light gray; lores, mixed dusky and whitish; upper portion of sides of head, varying from light gray (like crown) to dusky; cheeks, space below eye, chin, and throat, white, shading into very pale gray on chest and breast; sides and flanks, salmon color to almost Saturn red, the under tail-coverts, similar but much paler and more pinkish; under wing patch, bright orange-red, under wing-coverts salmon-color or salmon-pink; inner webs of wing feathers broadly edged with dull pinkish-white; bill, deep horn brown; iris, brown. Young: Similar to adults, but crown-patch missing.

Nest and Eggs.— Nest: Placed in small trees or

bushes, preferably mesquite, 5 to 20 feet up; constructed of plant stems, weeds, thistledown, cotton or wool felted and lined with moss or cotton; sometimes built entirely of cotton. EGGS: 4 to 6, generally 5, white, or creamy, marked with chestnut, brown, and lilac.

Distribution.— Breeds from southern Texas to southern Kansas, less commonly in southwestern Missouri, western Arkansas, and western Louisiana; winters from southern Mexico to Panama; accidental in Illinois, Florida, Virginia, Maryland, New Jersey, Connecticut, Vermont, Manitoba, Keewatin, and even in Mackenzie River valley.

This is one of the most picturesque and graceful of American birds; and he has individuality, too, which would make him conspicuous without these physical peculiarities. His picturesqueness is due chiefly to his long and strikingly marked tail, which he is likely to open and shut when he is excited about anything. This ornament also serves to accentuate the grace or the erratic character of the bird's aërial gyrations, many of which apparently are indulged in simply for the fun of the thing. One of these is a rapidly executed series of ascents and dives, the bizarre effect of which is heightened by the spreading and closing of the streaming tail-feathers, the performance being accompanied by harsh screams emphasized at each crest of the flight wave. Again and for no apparent reason he will interrupt a slow and decorous straight-line flight by suddenly darting upward, uttering at the same time an ear-piercing shriek. Altogether there is something rather uncanny about much of this bird's conduct; and perhaps its unusual ways are responsible for the Mexican peasants' belief that its food is the brains of other birds, which of course, is a hideous slander.

Perhaps, however, this Mexican myth may have been inspired by the bird's fearless attacks upon White-necked Ravens, Caracaras, and other predacious birds, which it will pursue with the utmost fury and persistence, often lighting on their backs, and doing them all the damage it can by savage stabs with its bill. But this is also a performance of our common Kingbird, whom nobody has ever accused of the crime charged against the Scissor-tail. It is an interesting fact that this dare-devil form of attack should be a characteristic of these two members of the same family; also that the Kingbird has a flight trick which suggests the hysterical upward dash of his long-tailed western cousin.

The animal food of the Scissor-tailed Flycatcher amounts to 96 per cent. of the stomach contents, practically all of which is insects and spiders. The vegetable food is composed of small fruits and seeds.

Of the animal food, beetles amount to nearly 14 per cent. and form a rather constant article of diet. Less than one per cent. belong to theoretically useful families. The others are practically all of harmful species. Among these are snout beetles, or weevils, and cotton-boll weevils. Stink-bugs and squash-bugs are among the bugs eaten. Grasshoppers and crickets are evidently the favorite food; they are eaten every month, with a good percentage in all except April. The average for the year is 46 per cent.— the highest for any Flycatcher. In general, grasshoppers and crickets are eaten to the greatest extent by the ground-feeding birds, such as the Meadowlark, while the Flycatchers take the flying bugs. In this case the rule seems to be reversed. It needs but little study of the food of the Scissor-tailed Flycatcher to show that where the bird is abundant it is of much economic value. Its food consists almost entirely of insects, including so few useful species that they may be safely disregarded. Its consumption of grasshoppers is alone sufficient to entitle this bird to complete protection.

SCISSOR-TAILED FLYCATCHER
(⅜ nat. size)

KINGBIRD

Tyrannus tyrannus *(Linnæus)*

A. O. U. Number 444 See Color Plate 67

Other Names.— Field Martin; Bee Martin; Bee-bird; Tyrant Flycatcher.

General Description.— Length, 8 inches. Upper parts, black and gray; under parts, white. Tail, square or slightly rounded.

Color.— Crown and sides of head (except cheeks), black (slightly glossy), the crown with a large concealed patch of orange or orange-red, sometimes inter-

Photo by H. T. Middleton

YOUNG KINGBIRDS

mixed with yellow on margins, underlaid laterally and behind by white; hindneck, slaty-black, passing into plain slate color on sides of neck, back, rump, shoulders and lesser wing-coverts, the feathers of lower rump margined terminally with pale gray or grayish-white; upper tail-coverts, black, margined with white; *tail, black, abruptly tipped with white*, the lateral feathers margined with white for some distance from tip especially the exterior one; wings, dusky, the middle and greater coverts and secondaries edged with white, the primary coverts and primaries more narrowly edged with pale gray; cheeks and under parts, white, the chest shaded with gray, the sides of chest with a distinct gray patch; under wing-coverts, white or yellowish-white terminally, pale brownish-gray basally, those along edge of wing, dusky broadly margined with white; bill, black; iris, brown; legs and feet, brownish-black.

Nest and Eggs.— Nest: Frequently in the orchard, sometimes in tall sycamores near streams, a substantial structure of twigs, weed stalks, grass, roots, particles of wool and down well combined and symmetrically edged, lined with feathers, horsehair, fine rootlets, and wool. Eggs: 3 or 4, white to pale pink with strong bold spots of umber and chestnut.

Distribution.— North and South America; breeds from southern British Columbia, southern Mackenzie, southern Keewatin, northern Ontario, central Quebec, and Newfoundland south to central Oregon, northern New Mexico, central Texas, and central Florida; winters from southern Mexico to Colombia, British Guiana, Peru, and Bolivia; casual in Cuba in migration; accidental in Greenland.

The Kingbird's remarkable courage and persistent aggressiveness in attacking his natural enemies, especially Hawks and Crows, have made his name one to conjure with in the feathered world. Perhaps no American bird, great or small, displays these characteristics in a more marked degree: certainly none makes a more conspicuous display of them; for a Kingbird in hot pursuit of a Hawk or a Crow, dashing down on the bigger bird and striking him repeatedly with his bill, or even actually alighting on his enemy's back and clinging there to do all the damage he can, and screaming incessantly meanwhile, is one of the real spectacles of bird-life. Other birds, to be sure, attack Crows and Hawks, but none are so fearless and persistent as is the Kingbird. In this sense he is a veritable king among birds, though the scientists slander him when they give him a name implying that he is a tyrant, for he attacks consistently only birds he has good reason to hate. Of course, he is likely to declare himself if other birds loiter too near his brooding mate, but any self-respecting bird would do that.

Kingbirds are industrious and skillful flycatchers, a practice which causes them to perch invariably on dead limbs, tree-tops, fence posts,

Courtesy of Am. Mus. Nat. Hist.

KINGBIRD (½ nat. size)

Remarkable for his courage and persistency in attacking his enemies

or similar points of vantage, from which they can get an unobstructed view of at least the immediate surroundings. To such selected perches they are likely to return after dashing flights to capture passing insects. The bird's characteristic note is a sharp and shrill chattering cry, frequently uttered in flight, the phrase (if it may be so termed) being emphasized at its end by a swift upward flutter.

The Kingbird furnishes a conspicuous illustration of the saying, "Give a dog a bad name and everybody will kick him." In this instance, the bad name, "Bee Martin," has been furnished by careless or ignorant observers who insist that the bird destroys honeybees, whereas the careful investigations of experts in the United States Bureau of Biological Survey prove conclusively that no less than 85 per cent. of its food consists of insects, mostly of a harmful nature. It eats the common rose-chafer or rose-bug, and, more remarkable still, it devours blister-beetles freely. As to honeybees, an examination of 634 stomachs showed only 61 bees in 22 stomachs, and of these 51 were useless drones. On the other hand, it devours robber-flies, which catch and destroy honeybees. Grasshoppers and crickets, with a few bugs and some cutworms, and a few other insects make up the rest of the animal food. The vegetable food consists of fruit and a few seeds. The very slight damage that the bird does should count for nothing when compared with the great service it renders not only in destroying noxious insects, but by its persistent warfare upon Hawks and Crows, which often affords efficient protection to nearby poultry yards and young chickens at large.

Photo by H. K. Job — Courtesy of Outing Pub. Co.

A KINGBIRD FAMILY

GRAY KINGBIRD

Tyrannus dominicensis (*Gmelin*)

A. O. U. Number 445

General Description.— Length, 9 inches. Upper parts, gray; under parts, white.

Color.— *Above, plain gray,* the feathers of crown with indistinct shaft-streaks of darker, with a large concealed patch of orange or orange-red underlaid laterally and behind with white; upper tail-coverts, deep grayish-brown margined with gray or rusty brownish; tail, dusky grayish-brown, the feathers margined terminally with pale brownish-gray or dull whitish, their outer webs indistinctly edged with gray, the outermost narrowly edged with whitish; wings, deep grayish-brown, the coverts margined with light gray or grayish-white (the edgings broader and whiter on inner secondaries), the primary coverts and primaries, dusky grayish-brown, very narrowly edged with pale gray; loral region, dusky intermixed with gray; sides of head, dusky or dull blackish, with a few very narrow shaft-streaks of pale grayish; cheeks and under parts, white, the center of chest faintly shaded with pale gray passing into deeper gray on sides of chest, sides, and flanks; the under tail-coverts, usually tinged with pale yellow; under wing-coverts, yellowish-white or pale primrose yellow; inner webs of wing-feathers edged with dull yellowish-white; bill, black; iris, brown.

Nest and Eggs.— Nest: Usually in low mangroves or live oaks but sometimes high in trees, near streams; a frail structure of twigs and grass, lined with small plant stems and moss. Eggs: 3 or 4, creamy or pinkish-white, spotted and splashed with dark brown and lilac-gray.

Distribution.— Breeds from Georgia, southeastern South Carolina, Florida, and Yucatan through the Bahamas and West Indies to northern South America; winters from Jamaica and Haiti southward.

This Tyrant Flycatcher much resembles the more common Kingbird, but may be distinguished from that species by its lighter color and larger size. It is a common inhabitant in many of the West India Islands and is also found in numbers in Florida. Rarely it breeds as far north as South Carolina. The Gray Kingbird prefers the country immediately adjoining the coast, and, although it wanders into the pine woods at times, it is rare to find one more than a mile from salt water. In Old Tampa Bay many of them spend the summer, and one cannot pass along the shore or row a boat for any great distance among the numerous islands without finding one perched on some snag or bush-top. In this territory the nests are built in mangrove bushes and usually over the water. The nest is of rootlets, and occasionally one may be found possessing a meager lining of horsehair. It is so loosely woven that as a rule one may see, through the structure, the form of the eggs within. As an indication of their abundance in a favorite locality one writer speaks of finding twelve occupied nests while paddling a canoe along a four-mile stretch of mangrove-fringed shore-line.

The Gray Kingbirds reach Florida early in April, and after the completion of the breeding season remain but a short time before they again brave the rolling wastes of the Mexican Gulf in their flight to their winter home in the Lesser Antilles and Central America.

T. Gilbert Pearson.

Courtesy of Nat. Asso. Aud. Soc.

NEST AND EGGS OF GRAY KINGBIRD

ARKANSAS KINGBIRD

Tyrannus verticalis *Say*

A. O. U. Number 447

Other Names.— Bee Martin; Bee Bird.

General Description.— Length, 9 inches. Upper parts, gray; under parts, gray and yellow.

Color.— *Crown and hindneck, plain gray,* the crown with a large concealed patch of orange-red underlaid behind and laterally by an admixture of white and yellow; back, shoulders, and upper rump, light yellowish-olive, the lower rump grayer, with feathers darker centrally; upper tail-coverts, black, sometimes with indistinct grayish margins; tail, black, the outer web and shaft of outermost feather wholly white or yellowish-white, except (sometimes) part of terminal portion; wings, deep to dark grayish-brown, all the feathers narrowly margined with paler; *ends of long quills with sharp points;* lores, mixed gray and dusky, sides of head (except lower portion), gray, darker than color of crown; lower front portion of sides of head, region below the eyes, the cheeks, chin, and upper throat, white or grayish white, passing gradually into pale gray on lower throat and chest; rest of under parts, canary yellow, paler on under tail-coverts, shading into light yellowish-olive on sides, flanks, and upper breast; under wing-coverts, pale yellowish-gray margined with pale yellow; inner webs of wing-feathers edged with very pale grayish-yellow or dull yellowish-white; bill, black or brownish-black; iris, brown.

Nest and Eggs.— Nest: In trees, bushes from 5 to 50 feet up, but usually low and in fence posts, corners of houses or nearly any handy spot; built of twigs, leaves, weed bark, wool, cocoons, hair, string, down, rags, and paper. Eggs: Commonly 4, creamy white rather boldy marked with burnt umber and some lavender, chiefly around large end.

Distribution.— Western North America; north to North Dakota, Montana, northern Idaho, and southern British Columbia (Vancouver Island), occasionally to Manitoba, southern Assiniboia, and Alberta (?); east regularly to western Minnesota, eastern South Dakota and Nebraska, middle Kansas, Oklahoma, and western Texas; breeding southward to northern Lower California, southern Arizona, and northern Chihuahua; southward during migration through western Mexico; accidental in Iowa, Wisconsin, Missouri, Maine, New York, New Jersey, and Maryland.

The Arkansas Kingbird is one of the commanding personalities of the western bird-world. Of his presence and his very firm convictions concerning his importance and the deference due to his points of view, you are made well aware immediately you enter his domain, for he always keeps himself very much in evidence. That he is actually quarrelsome is denied by his admirers, who contend that much of his assertiveness is essentially good-natured, and that he doesn't mean really to be ugly except to his natural enemies, Hawks, Crows, Owls, and such like. All and sundry of these he attacks with the most savage fury and persistence, often—like his eastern cousin of the same name and like the picturesque Scissor-tailed Flycatcher — actually lighting on their backs as they fly, and doing them all the injury he can with his beak and claws. He has many tiffs with other birds, though probably some of these are less serious than they appear.

Whatever he undertakes to do he seems to

Drawing by R. I. Brasher

ARKANSAS KINGBIRD (½ nat. size)

Whatever he undertakes to do, he seems to think it important to yell more or less about it

think it important to yell more or less about it. His attacks upon his enemies are accompanied by incessant screaming, and even when he dashes from his perch on telegraph wire or fence post to capture a passing insect, he is likely to announce his success by a shriek of victory as he

Photo by Mrs. Granville Pike Courtesy of Nat. Asso. Aud. Soc.

ARKANSAS KINGBIRD

Through eastern Oregon it commonly nests on a crosspiece of a telephone or telegraph pole

sails back to his station. In these aërial performances he keeps his tail spread to its full width, thereby showing plainly the white outer feathers. It seems natural enough that such a bird should prefer the open country, where he can have plenty of room for his operations, but "through eastern Oregon, where trees are scarce, the Arkansas Kingbird commonly nests on a cross-piece of a telephone or telegraph pole. At Ashland and some of the other towns in northern Oregon they prefer a similar site along the busy street. A farm-building or even a gate-post, wherever two beams come together so the nest can be wedged in, is not an unusual site." (W. L. Finley, MS.)

This bird has been accused in California of eating honeybees to an injurious extent. It was said that the bird lingered near the hive and snapped up the honey-ladened bees as they returned from the field. This statement is not borne out by the facts. Its animal food is open to adverse criticism in only one point — the useful beetles amounting to 5½ per cent. But even if it be admitted that the destruction of these is harmful to man's interests, the amount of damage is so small as to be completely overbalanced by the good done in other directions. The vegetable food, which is less than 10 per cent. of the entire food of the bird, is of so little economic importance that it may be dismissed without further comment. On the whole the Arkansas Kingbird is one of the most useful birds in the region where it is found.

CRESTED FLYCATCHER

Myiarchus crinitus (*Linnæus*)

A. O. U. Number 452 See Color Plate 67

Other Names.— Great Crested Flycatcher; Great Crested Yellow-bellied Flycatcher; Snake-skin Bird.

General Description.— Length, 8½ inches. Upper parts, olive; under parts, gray and yellow. Crown-feathers, erectile.

Color.— Above, plain olive, the crown usually slightly browner, with feathers darker centrally; middle pair of tail-feathers and outer webs of others, deeper brownish-olive with paler olive edgings, the outer web of lateral tail-feathers sometimes narrowly edged with dull whitish; inner web of tail-feathers (except middle pair) *cinnamon-rufous,* the outermost two or three usually with a narrow streak of brown next to shaft; wings, dusky grayish-brown, the middle and greater coverts margined terminally with pale buffy olive, the secondaries edged with the same, the edgings broader and more whitish (sometimes yellowish-white) on inner secondaries; basal half of primaries narrowly edged with cinnamon or cinnamon-rufous; sides of head and neck, gray, tinged with olive; *chin, throat, and chest, plain gray; under parts of body,* light straw *yellow,* the sides of breast and front of sides, pale yellowish-olive; under wing-coverts, pale yellow; inner webs of wing-feathers, broadly edged with pale cinnamon-rufous; bill, horn-brown; iris, brown.

Nest and Eggs.— Nest: In tree or stump cavity or Woodpecker hole, from 6 to 50 feet up; constructed of grass, rootlets, bits of bark, hair, and pine needles; remarkable for the fact that it is almost always encircled with a cast-off snake skin. Eggs: 4 to 8, creamy to deep buff covered with blotches and lengthwise pen lines of brown and purple.

Distribution.— Eastern United States and southern Canada; north to western New Brunswick, New Hampshire, northern New York, southern Quebec, northern Ontario, and Manitoba; breeding southward to central Florida and westward through Gulf States to Texas; south in winter to Cuba and through eastern Mexico and Central America to Colombia; accidental in Wyoming and Cuba.

This bird is famous for its curious habit of almost always including in the material of which it builds its nest part or all of a cast snake skin. Just why the bird does this, no clear-thinking and candid person will attempt to say. To a certain school of nature-writers the reason is, of course, as plain as a pike-staff — the snake skin is employed deliberately by the bird to frighten its enemies away from its nest. But who are the bird's natural enemies? Chiefly certain Hawks

Courtesy of Am. Mus. Nat. Hist.

CRESTED FLYCATCHER (½ nat. size)

Famous for its curious habit of weaving a snake skin into its nest

and Owls, and various other nest-robbing birds like the Crow, Blue Jay, Cuckoo, and Catbird, in addition to red squirrels and snakes. Now, no Hawk or Owl which preys upon birds is afraid of a snake; in fact, snakes are killed and eaten by most of these birds. The other feathered nest-robbers mentioned would be afraid of a live snake, but why should they fear a fragment of dried snake skin? It is exceedingly doubtful if they would even recognize it as the sometime covering of an enemy. And the same applies to the red squirrel; while it seems a bit improbable, to say the least, that a snake would be much terrified by the skin of one of its own kind. Furthermore, what right have we to suppose that this particular bird, and this one alone, knows that other birds are afraid of snakes; that it alone is capable of the intellectual process which would prompt this deliberate deception? For no other bird does the same thing, or anything like it. And finally, how could the snake skin, in part or even in whole, certainly have this effect, since the nest, in which it is often so interwoven as to be almost invisible even in a strong light, is always placed in a cavity where there is little light or none at all?

No, we do not know why this bird follows this peculiar practice. There is no apparent good reason for it; most likely it does not bespeak any design whatsoever, but, as Mr. Burroughs says, reflects simply a whim or fancy.

Yet all who know this Flycatcher well probably will admit that there is a suggestion of the uncanny about him. His characteristic call, a discordant and peremptory *wheep,* is not only unmusical, but has an unearthly ring, as though the bird were trying to conjure gnomes and hobgoblins. And this impression is heightened by the bird's elusive and mysterious manners, and its evident desire to be let alone.

George Gladden.

The food of Crested Flycatchers shows about 94 per cent. of animal matter and 6 per cent. of vegetable. Beetles constitute one-sixth of the food, and of these one-fourth of 1 per cent. are useful species. The remainder are mostly of an injurious character, some of them very harmful. Among them are the notorious cotton-boll weevil, the strawberry weevil, and the plum curculio. While records do not indicate any special preference for the harmful beetles, they do show that these are eaten as often as the average of the different species.

Bugs constitute 14.26 per cent. of the diet;

Photo by S. A. Lottridge

CRESTED FLYCATCHERS

Young in the nest, mother on guard on a limb nearby

they belong to the usual families of stinkbugs, tree-hoppers, leaf-hoppers, and cicadas, with a few assassin bugs. Grasshoppers, crickets, and katydids seem to be among the favorite foods of the Crested Flycatcher. Moths and their larvæ are the largest item of the food — over 21 per cent. Adult moths and butterflies are not a favorite food with birds in general; it is evident that the larvæ, or caterpillars, are generally preferred to the adult insects, but the fact that the adults can fly and so can be taken on the wing apparently recommends them to Flycatchers.

The Crested Flycatcher does little if any harm. It is a very desirable bird to have about the orchard or garden, since it does not attack any cultivated crop. As its natural nesting site is a cavity in a partially decayed tree, it has often been induced to nest in properly constructed boxes, if such are placed in the orchard or other suitable situations. Mr. Burroughs says: "I have seen it nesting in boxes on Henry Ford's farm in Michigan." (MS.) Thus it can be induced to live in orchards and woodlands not now frequented by it because of the lack of nesting sites, and eventually, no doubt, a substantial increase in its numbers can be effected.

PHŒBE

Sayornis phœbe (*Latham*)

A. O. U. Number 456 See Color Plate 67

Other Names.— Phœbe Bird; Pewee; Bridge Pewee; Water Pewee; Barn Pewee; Bean Bird; Pewit Flycatcher; Dusky Flycatcher.

General Description.— Length, 7 inches. Upper parts, grayish-olive; under parts, yellowish-white. Crown-feathers, erectile; tail, emarginate.

Color.— Crown, sides of head, and hindneck dark sooty-brown; back, shoulders, lesser wing-coverts, rump, and upper tail-coverts, plain grayish-olive, paler behind; tail, dusky grayish-brown, the outer webs of feathers passing into light grayish-olive on edges, the outer web of exterior feathers broadly edged with olive-whitish; wings, dusky with pale grayish-olive edgings, these most conspicuous on greater coverts and secondaries, on innermost of the latter broader and more whitish; a slight admixture of dull whitish on lores (especially upper margin) and on lower eyelid; sides of neck, similar in color to back but slightly paler; under parts, dull yellowish-white, the chin (sometimes upper throat also) intermixed with dusky grayish, the sides of chest and breast, light grayish-olive; under wing-coverts, yellowish-white or pale primrose-yellow, tinged with pale grayish, the coverts, near margin of wing dusky-grayish centrally; inner webs of wing-feathers, edged with very pale grayish-buffy; bill, black; iris, brown.

Nest and Eggs.— Nest: Beneath barn eaves, bridges, culverts, ledges, in fact nearly anywhere that affords protection from the weather; constructed of mud, grass, vegetable fibers, lined with some hair, grass, and feathers, and nearly always decorated exteriorly with green moss. Eggs: 3 to 8, normally 5, pure white, rarely speckled at large end with brownish.

Distribution.— Eastern United States and more southern British Provinces; north to Maine, northern New York (Adirondack region), northwestern Ontario; Keewatin and southern Mackenzie; west, at least occasionally, to Athabasca (Little Slave Lake), eastern Wyoming, eastern Colorado, northeastern New Mexico and western Texas; breeding southward to highlands of South Carolina, Louisiana, etc.; winters chiefly within the United States (mostly south of 37°) but migrating to Cuba and eastern and central Mexico; accidental in southern California.

Photograph by C. M. Oswalt Courtesy of Outing Pub. Co.

NEST AND EGGS OF PHŒBE

This is another bird whose nesting habits have been modified by the appearance in its habitat of man and his handiwork. Before his advent Phœbe placed her nest generally in a niche of a shelving cliff, and it was a beautiful little creation of moss and lichens whose color was so nearly that of the immediate surroundings that it was almost invisible. The bird still builds occasionally in such places even when man-made structures are not far away; but most frequently the nest is found on a sheltered projection from a barn or house (often on a ledge under a porch where it may be almost within arm's reach), or on a beam under a bridge. From the last mentioned site the bird is often called the "Bridge Pewee," though the true Pewees are of a different species.

Courtesy of Am. Mus. Nat. Hist.

PHŒBE (⅔ nat. size)

The bird's confiding ways and gentle manners have won real affection from its human neighbors

In this practice we see another instance of what may be termed imperfect adaptability. Evidently Phœbe is intelligent enough to discern some of the advantages of building in or near human habitations. Not the least of these advantages is that she thereby receives protection from her natural enemies, the Hawks and Owls, and predatory animals such as skunks, squirrels, and weasels. Also her natural food (which is composed wholly of insects) is probably more plentiful in the new location than in the old. What she seems to be unable to learn, however, is that a nest of green moss and mud is not exactly inconspicuous when it is tucked away in the angle between a beam and a rafter which are painted red or brown. This is a fair illustration of the occasional blindness, and in this instance, it would seem, the color-blindness, of instinct.

Sometimes Phœbe will take possession of the abandoned nest of a bird of another species, such as a Barn Swallow or a Robin. One observer has reported a nest that was built under a woodshed close to a cord-wood saw, the noisy operation of which did not always frighten the sitting bird from her eggs.

Phœbe is no musician; in fact the bird's invariable two-syllabled call, from which it gets its name, and which sometimes suggests petulance or impatience, becomes a trifle monotonous, when its reiteration is frequent and at brief intervals, which is often the case. Nevertheless the bird's confiding ways and gentle manners have won the real affection of its human neighbors, who should realize as well that it is very useful as a destroyer of noxious insects. In its pursuit of this prey it shows all of the flight-skill and speed which are characteristic of its species. Like its relatives it generally selects a perch on a dead limb or fencepost whence it has an unobstructed view of the immediate surroundings, and it is likely to return to this perch after each darting sally. The sharp snapping of its bill as it seizes an insect is often plainly audible, and it has a trick of switching its tail sideways which is also characteristic.

Photo by A. A. Allen

PHŒBE

At its nest on a cliff

It seems hardly necessary to say anything in favor of a bird already firmly established in the affections of the people, but it may not be amiss to point out that this good will rests on a solid foundation of scientific truth. In the animal food of the Phœbe there is such a small percentage of useful elements (less than 3 per cent.) that they may be safely overlooked, while of the vegetable food it may be said that the products of husbandry are conspicuous by their absence. To its credit are cotton-boll weevils, strawberry weevils, corn-leaf beetles, both spotted and striped cucumber beetles, ants, grasshoppers, locusts, moths and caterpillars, spiders, ticks and thousand-legs. Let the Phœbe remain just where it is. Let it occupy the orchard, the garden, the dooryard, and build its nest in the barn, the carriage house, or the shed. It pays ample rent for its accommodations.

George Gladden.

SAY'S PHŒBE

Sayornis sayus (*Bonaparte*)

A. O. U. Number 457

Other Name.— Say's Pewee.

General Description.— Length, 7½ inches. Upper parts, brownish-gray; under parts, buffy-gray and cinnamon-buff. Tail, emarginate.

Color.—Above, plain brownish-gray, the crown and hindneck decidedly darker; upper tail-coverts, dusky-grayish, usually margined with paler; tail, brownish-black, the outer web of lateral feather edged with whitish; wings, deep brownish-gray with pale brownish-gray edgings, these broader and approaching dull whitish on inner secondaries and terminal portion of greater coverts; sides of head and neck, similar in color to upper portions, changing gradually below into the pale buffy brownish-gray of chin and throat; chest and sides of breast, light buffy brownish-gray, the center portion of chest usually more strongly tinged with buff; *rest of under parts, cinnamon-buff;* under wing-coverts, pale buff or cream-buff; inner webs of wings edged with buffy-whitish; bill, black; iris, brown.

Nest and Eggs.— Nest: Usually beneath bridges in abandoned dwellings, in caves, under ledges, or sometimes in hollow trees; composed of grasses, weeds, bark, moss, wool, cocoons, spiders' webs, lined with feathers and hair. Eggs: 3 to 6, sometimes with a few reddish-brown dots at large end.

Distribution.— Western North America; north to Alaska, Yukon Territory, and southern Mackenzie; east to Manitoba, eastern Wyoming, western Kansas, middle Kansas (more rarely), and (in winter) to coast of Texas — accidentally to Wisconsin and northeastern Illinois; breeding southward to southern New Mexico, southern Arizona, and Lower California — probably breeding in northern and perhaps central Mexico; southward in winter over northern and central Mexico.

In manners, at least, there is some resemblance between Say's Phœbe and its cousin of the eastern States; for both are essentially unassuming and rather timid little birds, and both are apt to nest in protected niches of man-made structures. The western bird doubtless does this less often than the eastern, probably for the very good reason that it has fewer opportunities. Therefore, it is often found in country where there are ledges — which furnish the natural nesting places of the entire tribe — and especially in the great cañons, where its favorite perch is likely to be a big bowlder whence it makes its sallies after passing insects. Nevertheless, Say's Phœbe is common about ranch buildings, mining sheds, and railroad stations. According to Mr. Dawson it is only within the past twenty years that it has taken to nesting in buildings in Yakima County, Washington. Like the eastern Phœbe again, this species shows a strong attachment for the home site it has once used. and will return to build its nest in the same locality or even the same spot.

The western bird is, however, rather more restless than the eastern one, and seems more given to flirting its tail and raising its crest when there is no particular occasion for doing either. Its note is a plaintive two-syllabled utterance, somewhat like that of the eastern Wood Pewee. Its diet is composed almost wholly of insects taken on the wing in true Flycatcher style, and in common with other members of its family (as well as the Hawks and Owls) it ejects from its mouth, in the form of pellets, the hard and indigestible parts of its food.

Its animal food, over 99 per cent. of its entire diet, is the factor that fixes this bird's economic position. The item of this most open to objection is predatory beetles amounting to about 6 per cent. This item is higher with Say's Phœbe than with any other of the Flycatchers, but still is small as compared with the injurious insects eaten. In spite of the fact that the bird eats these useful insects its work on the whole is beneficial, and it should be protected.

BLACK PHŒBE

Sayornis nigricans (*Swainson*)

A. O. U. Number 458

Other Names.— Western Black Pewee; Black-headed Flycatcher.

General Description.— Length, 7¾ inches. Upper parts, sooty-slate; under parts, sooty-slate and white. Tail, emarginate.

Color.— General color, plain dark sooty-slate, the head darker (almost black), the back, shoulders, rump, and upper tail-coverts brownish-slate color; *abdomen, anal region, and under tail-coverts, white,* the last sometimes frequently streaked centrally with dusky; middle wing-coverts, broadly tipped or terminally margined with brownish-gray; greater coverts, edged with brownish-gray and tipped with the same or paler brownish-gray; secondaries, edged with pale brownish-gray or dull white; outer web of lateral tail-feathers edged with white; under wing-coverts dark sooty-gray or brownish-slate, their outer webs mostly white and inner webs extensively white at tip; inner webs of wing feathers edged with pale brownish-gray; bill, black; iris, brown.

Nest and Eggs.— NEST: In sheltered situations, under bridges, eaves, ledges in wells or deserted cabins or houses; a rather large structure of mud pellets, dried grass, bits of wood and vegetable fiber, and hair, lined with feathers. EGGS: 3 to 6, plain white or rarely finely and sparsely dotted with chestnut chiefly around larger end.

Distribution.— Pacific coast district of United States; breeds from southwestern Oregon through California (west of the Sierra Nevada) to Cape San Lucas district, Lower California, eastward through southern California, southern Arizona, and southern New Mexico to central Texas, and over Mexico, except humid Atlantic coast district, to Yucatan.

The Black Phœbe is a little larger than the Phœbe of the East. The black and white of his plumage are sharply contrasted and his friends consider him the handsomest of the Flycatchers. His manners are quiet; he is so demure that he is almost staid. The comforts of civilization are matters of indifference to him. You may meet a Black Phœbe in town to-day and find his nest under the eaves of a kitchen, and to-morrow you may find his brother living just as contentedly in a lonely cañon.

His note is a quiet liquid *hip,* and is usually heard as he darts from perch to perch.

The laboratory investigation of this bird's food showed that about 99½ per cent. of its food consisted of animal matter. Useful beetles amounted to about 3 per cent. of the food. Other beetles of harmful or neutral species reached

Photo by W. L. Finley and H. T. Bohlman

BLACK PHŒBE

Just returning with food for young

10½ per cent. Four-winged flies form the largest item of the food, and for a short time in midsummer ants constitute quite a notable part; but various wild bees and wasps make up the bulk. No honeybees were found.

Bugs in various forms, flies, moths, and caterpillars complete his menu. While the Black Phœbe does not improve every opportunity to destroy harmful insects, it certainly neglects many chances to eat useful ones. The destruction of a few predacious beetles, dragon flies, and parasitic four-winged flies are the sum of its sinning. Throughout its range, it is welcomed and protected.

OLIVE-SIDED FLYCATCHER

Nuttallornis borealis (*Swainson*)

A. O. U. Number 459 See Color Plate 67

Other Name.— Nuttall's Pewee.

General Description.— Length, 7½ inches. Upper parts, dark gray; under parts, white and gray.

Color.—Above, plain slaty-olive or dark smoke-gray, the feathers (especially on crown) darker centrally; tail, dusky, the outer webs of feathers edged with grayish-olive; wings, sooty blackish, the middle coverts margined terminally with grayish-olive, the greater coverts narrowly edged with the same (passing into whitish terminally), the secondaries edged (except basally) with grayish-white, more broadly on inner secondaries; sides of head (including cheeks) and neck plain slaty-olive, like upper parts; chest (*except center line*), sides of breast, sides, and flanks, brownish-gray, tinged with olive, *streaked with darker;* rest of under parts, white (often tinged with pale yellow), the sides of throat and center portion of chest streaked with brownish-gray, the under tail-coverts with broad V-shaped markings of the same; under wing-coverts, brownish-gray narrowly edged with paler; a conspicuous patch of *soft, fluffy white or yellowish-white feathers above flanks* (*on sides of rump*), usually concealed but capable of being spread over secondaries of the closed wing; bill, brownish-black; iris, brown.

Nest and Eggs.— Nest: Saddled on branch or in fork of coniferous tree, generally at great height, 40 to 60 feet, in burned-over tracts; less compactly constructed than the Wood Pewee's, but of similar materials with the addition of some moss. Eggs: Normally 3, identical in color and markings with those of that bird, but larger.

Distribution.— North and South America; breeds from central Alaska, southern Mackenzie, southern Keewatin, central Quebec, and Cape Breton Island and south in the coniferous forests of the western United States to southern California, Arizona, and western Texas, and also northern Michigan, New York, and Massachusetts south along the higher Alleghenies to North Carolina; migrates through Mexico and Central America; winters in northern South America.

The Olive-sided Flycatcher is a bird of very wide distribution. It is included by Dr. Chapman in his book about the birds of the Eastern States, and Mrs. Bailey gives it a paragraph in her work devoted to the ornithology of the West, mentioning especially its occurrence in the fir-tree belt on Mount Shasta, "where its voice is one of the commonest forest sounds, as the evening shadows gathered over the noble trees under which we were camped." It has a habit, not common with the Flycatchers, of perching in the topmost branches of a tree. Without identifying the bird, Thoreau gave this good description of its characteristic flycatching performance: "Looking round for its prey and occasionally changing its perch, it every now and then darts off (Phœbe-like), even five or six rods, toward the earth to catch an insect, and then returns to its favorite perch. If I lose it for a moment, I soon see it settling on the dead twigs again and hear its *till, till, till.*" Apparently Thoreau did not see the bird dart almost if not quite perpendicularly upward, which it often does.

The bird's loud, characteristic and rather commanding call has been variously transliterated. Dr. Chapman thinks he says "Come right here, come right here," in a peremptory manner, and to Mr. Hoffman the syllables resemble *pi-pee'* or *pip, pi-pee'*. Captain Bendire compared the call to that of the Wood Pewee, and says that the syllables are *hip-pui whe,* while a gold miner in the Cascade Mountains, emerging from the bowels of the earth into the sunshine quite naturally thought that the bird shouted to him, "Three cheers!"

In the first analysis the food of the Olive-sided

Flycatcher was found to consist of 99.95 per cent. of animal food and 0.05 per cent. of vegetable.

Bees, wasps, and ants are the staff of life of the Olive-sided Flycatcher and form a large percentage of the food of each month. Beetles amount to about 6 per cent., less than half of 1 per cent. of which are useful. The bird shows a very decided fondness for hive bees, but not the special preference for drones manifested by Kingbirds. The Olive-sided Flycatcher would be a menace to the beekeeping industry, were it abundant in the thickly settled portions of the country.

As it eats no vegetable matter worth mentioning, its record must rest on its insect food, and honeybees constitute entirely too large a quota for the best economic interests. At present it probably does little harm, except when a number of the birds take up their residence in the vicinity of an apiary and make bees a part of their regular diet. The food of this bird is interesting, as it represents the food of a typical Flycatcher; with the exception of the vegetable matter everything it eats could be taken on the wing. Caterpillars, spiders, and millepeds, although found in the stomachs of most Flycatchers, are entirely absent from that of the Olive-sided.

COUES'S FLYCATCHER

Myiochanes pertinax pallidiventris (*Chapman*)

A. O. U. Number 460

General Description.— Length, 8 inches. Upper parts, deep smoke-gray; below, light smoke-gray and yellowish-white.

Color.—*Above, deep smoke-gray,* the crown slightly darker, with feathers darker centrally; wings and tail, grayish-brown, the outer webs of tail-feathers passing into light grayish-olive or olive-grayish on edges, the primaries very narrowly and indistinctly edged with the same; secondaries, edged (except basally) with pale grayish, sometimes approaching dull grayish-white; middle wing-coverts, margined terminally or tipped with grayish-olive or buffy-grayish, the greater coverts edged and tipped, or terminally margined, with same; sides of head and neck similar in color to back, etc., but paler, the loral region somewhat intermixed with whitish; *chest and sides, light smoke-gray,* but usually somewhat tinged with buffy-yellowish, the throat similar but paler, fading into dull whitish on chin; center of breast, abdomen, and under tail-coverts, pale yellowish-white, the latter usually with grayish V-shaped basal or central markings; under wing-coverts, buffy; bill, dusky-brown to nearly black, yellowish below; iris, brown.

Nest and Eggs.— Nest: Saddled on branch of oak or pine, from 15 to 30 feet up, closely resembling the Wood Pewee's but larger; constructed of bits of vegetable fiber catkins, a few dried leaves, fine grass tips, and covered exteriorly with lichens fastened on with cobwebs. Eggs: Generally 3, creamy-buff wreathed with browns and lilac-gray around large end.

Distribution.— Mountains of southern and central Arizona, south into Mexico; accidental in Colorado.

This comparatively little-seen Flycatcher occurs chiefly in uninhabited parts of Arizona, especially in pine and oak timber-growing cañons and gulches. Its manners are essentially Flycatcher-like though its flights are more extended and it is given to sailing about treetops. Its note is like that of the Olive-sided Flycatcher, though the last syllable is prolonged and delivered with a rising inflection. The bird's habitat is chiefly in Mexico.

WOOD PEWEE

Myiochanes virens (*Linnæus*)

A. O. U. Number 461 See Color Plate 68

Other Names.— Pewit; Pewee; Pewee Flycatcher.

General Description.— Length, 6¼ inches. Upper parts, olive; lower parts, grayish-olive and yellowish-white. Tail, emarginate.

Color.—Above, plain olive, slightly paler on rump and upper tail-coverts, slightly darker on crown, where the feathers are darker centrally; tail, deep grayish-brown, the outer webs of feathers passing into lighter grayish-brown or olive along edges; wings, dusky, the middle and greater coverts tipped with pale grayish and with still paler gray terminal margins, the secondaries edged (except basally) with whitish, these edgings broader on inner secondaries; sides of head and neck, similar in color to back, etc., but rather lighter, especially on lower portion; a narrow whitish eye-ring (interrupted on upper eyelid); lores, intermixed with whitish; chin and throat, dull white or yellowish-white; chest (at least laterally) and sides of breast, pale grayish-olive, becoming still paler on sides and flanks; rest of under parts, yellowish-white, the longer under tail-coverts with a central wedge-shaped mark (mostly concealed) of pale olive; under wing-coverts, pale grayish-olive margined into yellowish-white; bill, brownish-black; iris, deep brown.

Nest and Eggs.— NEST: Usually saddled on the horizontal limb of a deciduous tree, in clearings or edge of deep woods, from 10 to 60 feet up; shallow, constructed of fine grasses, strips of bark, bits of vegetable or moss fibers, decorated exteriorly with lichens fastened with cobwebs, with thick felted sides and thin bottom; indistinguishable from a knot on branch. EGGS: 2 to 4, commonly 3, creamy white with a wreath of chestnut, warm brown, and lavender around large end.

Distribution.— North and South America; breeds from Manitoba, Ontario, southern Quebec, and Prince Edward Island to southern Texas and central Florida, west to eastern Nebraska; winters from Nicaragua to Colombia and Peru; casual in Colorado; accidental in migration in Cuba.

"The note of the Pewee is a human sigh," says Mr. Burroughs, and the bird's two-syllabled call frequently conveys very distinctly that idea.

Courtesy of S. A. Lottridge

NEST AND EGGS OF WOOD PEWEE

Drawing by R. I. Brasher

WOOD PEWEE (½ nat. size)

Often the bird seems to be saying, "Dear me!" in a tone which is plaintive and resigned rather than petulant or impatient. Again the syllables are *pee-a-wee,* the first and second slurred and descending; the third of a somewhat higher pitch and more accented, the phrase having distinctly a questioning inflection. About the middle of August the call is likely to be reduced to two syllables, uttered with a falling inflection and strongly slurred. Always the tone is finer and sweeter than is that of the Phœbe, and the bird itself is much more retiring and timid. Its natural habitat is the deep woods (though it is often found in shade trees near houses), where its half-mournful, half-pensive little plaint seems to be part of the silence, and may be heard throughout the daylight hours. Between sunset and darkness the bird often delivers a sort of twittering song of some length and variety of notes, uttered while it is flitting about in apparent excitement the cause of which is not evident.

The Pewee is an industrious flycatcher and follows its craft much after the manner of the Phœbe, that is, by making frequent sallies after passing insects, and usually returning to the same perch. That it is not above taking insects which are not on the wing, is shown by its fluttering pauses above a twig or branch from which it evidently snaps up a bug of some kind, and its not infrequent plunges into the grass, apparently for the same purpose. Like all of the Flycatchers its motions are very swift and certain, as well as graceful; it seems never to miss its prey. It does not flirt its tail as does the Phœbe, from which it may also be distinguished by its smaller size and its plainly marked wing-bars. On the other hand it is considerably larger than the Chebec, or Least Flycatcher.

A curious characteristic of the Pewee is its apparent indifference about betraying the whereabouts of its nest. Many birds consider this a subject of the utmost secrecy, and act accordingly, absolutely refusing to go to their nests as long as an intruder is in sight. Others become tremendously excited and indignant under the same conditions; the wrath and courage of the Brown Thrasher, when his home is threatened, are beautiful to behold. But Pewee is likely to sit quite still and regard you with a somewhat puzzled air as you approach; and if you will remain motionless probably either the male or the female will go directly to the nest, even if it be only a few yards away. Whether this trait reveals confidence or indifference, it might be difficult to say; but anyone who has seen the bravery and rage with which the little bird attacks a prowling red squirrel will not accuse it of lack of solicitude in the presence of a real enemy. GEORGE GLADDEN.

Photograph by A. A. Allen

A WOOD PEWEE AT ITS NEST ON A DEAD BRANCH

The animal food of the Wood Pewee is made up of insects, spiders, and millepeds, and amounts to about 99 per cent. of its total food; the vegetable consists of berries and seeds. The beetles eaten include such harmful species as the clover-leaf weevil, the plum curculio, the corn weevil, and the rice weevil, besides several species of the *Scolytidæ,* a family which includes some of the worst enemies of forest trees.

Bees, wasps, and ants are eaten largely. The Flycatchers, as a group, take a considerable number of useful parasitic species among the bees, wasps, and ants which they eat. The Wood Pewee is probably the worst sinner of the family in this respect. It is safe to say that about one-fourth of the bees, wasps, and ants eaten by the Wood Pewee are of parasitic species. This, however, is probably not so great a fault as may at first appear, and does not necessarily condemn the bird. Flies are the most regular and constant constituent of the food. Among these are horse-flies, robber flies, syrphus flies, tachina flies, and long-legged crane flies. The great bulk of this food, however, belonged to the house-fly family. The syrphus and tachina flies are useful insects, but the great majority of members of the fly families are a nuisance and many of them pests, and it is a benefit to the world to have their numbers reduced; in this respect the Wood Pewee is doing a good work. Moths and caterpillars are eaten by the Wood Pewee every month of its stay in the North, but not quite so regularly nor in such quantities as flies.

Among the bugs which are eaten in small and rather irregular quantities, are tree-hoppers, leaf-hoppers, negro-bugs, stink-bugs, the squash-bug family, assassin bugs, and water striders. All of these are harmful in their habits except the assassin bugs, which destroy caterpillars and other insects, and the water striders, which have no economic significance.

The one unfavorable feature concerning the food of the Wood Pewee is that it eats too many parasitic bees and wasps. There is no doubt that all birds which prey upon bees and wasps destroy some of the useful species, but the proportion in the food of this bird is greater than in other birds whose food has been investigated. As these insects are for the most part smaller than the more common wasps and bees, it would seem natural that they should be preyed upon most by the smaller Flycatchers, which very likely accounts for the fact that the Wood Pewee eats more of them than the Kingbirds. But, even so, the bird does far more good than harm. The loss of the useful bees and wasps can be condoned when it is remembered that with them the bird takes so many harmful or annoying species.

The Western Wood Pewee (*Myiochanes richardsoni richardsoni*) closely resembles its eastern relative in coloration, size, and habits; but its call differs in quality and inflection from that of the eastern bird, the single syllable suggesting the word *deer* or *tweer*. Its nest is deeper and better cupped and is not coated with lichens.

While the Western Wood Pewee inhabits orchards, it does not go there for fruit, but only in search of the insect enemies of the trees. It eats but few useful insects, and does not, as far as investigation shows, attack any product of industry. If, under exceptional circumstances, it destroys honeybees, the occasions are so rare that the bird should not be blacklisted.

YELLOW-BELLIED FLYCATCHER

Empidonax flaviventris (*Baird*)

A. O. U. Number 463 See Color Plate 68

General Description.— Length, 5½ inches. Upper parts, greenish-olive· under parts, yellowish-olive and yellow.

Color.—Above, plain greenish-olive, the feathers of crown slightly darker centrally; tail, deep grayish-brown, with outer webs of feathers passing into greenish-olive on edges; wings, dull black, the middle and greater coverts broadly tipped with pale olive-yellow, the secondaries edged with the same, the primaries dusky grayish-brown very narrowly and indistinctly edged with paler; a pale yellow eye-ring, less distinct but scarcely interrupted on middle of upper eyelid; lores mixed pale yellowish and dusky-grayish; rest of sides of head and sides of neck similar in color to back but slightly paler, *gradually fading below into pale yellow, tinged with olive, on chin and throat; chest and sides of breast, light yellowish-olive,* gradually becoming paler toward flanks; rest of under parts, pale yellow; under wing-coverts, primrose yellow, the outermost coverts with dusky-grayish centers; inner webs of wing-feathers, edged with pale grayish-buffy; bill, brownish-black, wholly pale yellowish below; iris, brown.

Nest and Eggs.— Nest: Usually in upturned roots of trees, or in a fallen tree trunk, in a bed of moss, on deep shady mountain slopes; constructed principally of moss and lichens lined with fine rootlets, pine needles, and fine grass. Eggs: 3 to 5, white, finely spotted with rusty or chestnut.

Distribution.— Eastern North America, north to Newfoundland, southern Labrador, Quebec, Ontario, and Manitoba, accidentally to southwestern Greenland; breeding southward to Maine, northern New York, mountains of Pennsylvania, northern Indiana(?), northeastern Illinois(?), northern Minnesota, and North Dakota; migrating southward through eastern Mexico and Central America to Panama; occasional in migration in western Florida.

The Yellow-bellied Flycatcher is another of the lesser-known members of the species. It frequents both tall tree-tops and thickets, and its habits resemble, in a general way, those of its tribe. Its note, which suggests the syllable *pea,* is uttered by both the male and the female.

So retiring are its habits that the Yellow-bellied Flycatcher is seldom brought into contact with man, and hence its food can have only restricted economic interest. Its bill of fare includes insects of a number of species which are injurious to garden, orchard, or forest, as the striped squash beetle, several species of weevils, tent-caterpillars, and leaf-rollers.

WESTERN FLYCATCHER

Empidonax difficilis difficilis *Baird*

A. O. U. Number 464

General Description.— Length, 5½ inches. Upper parts, brownish-olive; under parts, buffy-olive and yellow.

Color.—Above, plain brownish-olive; tail, grayish-brown, the outer webs of feathers passing into light grayish-olive; wings, dusky, the middle and greater coverts rather broadly tipped with pale grayish-olive (forming two distinct bands), the secondaries edged (except basally) with the same; primaries, grayish-brown, very narrowly and indistinctly edged with paler; a broad eye-ring of pale buffy-yellow, narrower but scarcely interrupted on middle of upper eyelid; lores, pale yellowish intermixed or suffused with dusky; rest of sides of head and sides of neck similar in color to upper parts, gradually fading below into the pale straw-yellow of chin and throat; chest and sides, pale buffy-olive, fading toward flanks; *rest of under parts pale* (*straw*) *yellow;* under wing-coverts pale (primrose) yellow becoming more buffy on edge of wing; inner webs of wing-feathers edged with pale buff; bill, brownish-black, wholly yellowish below; iris, brown.

Nest and Eggs.— Nest: In alders, bushes, stumps, root cavities, under banks, rocky ledges, and even in deserted Woodpecker holes; usually near water; constructed of root stems, vegetable fibers, bark, cobwebs, and grass and often coated with fresh green moss and lined with horse-hair and feathers. Eggs: 3 or 4, creamy white, spotted or ringed with chestnut and brownish-pink.

Distribution.— Western North America, from eastern base of Rocky Mountains and western Manitoba to Pacific coast; north to coast district of Alaska; breeding southward to Santa Barbara Islands, California, northern Lower California, Arizona, southern New Mexico and southwestern Texas; winters in Mexico south to Cape San Lucas, and Tres Marias Islands.

This is one of the group of small olivaceous Flycatchers the accurate identification of which requires sharp eyes and the faculty for noticing comparatively slight differences of color and contour. It is a very common bird in California, especially west of the Sierra Nevadas, and therefore there is no lack of opportunity to study it carefully.

One of the bird's peculiarities will be found to be the wide latitude of choice it displays in selecting a nesting site; for it may make its home high up in a tree, or on a ledge, or in a deserted Flicker's excavation, or a hollow tree, or in an unoccupied shanty, or on the ground in a tangle of the roots of trees, or even on a stranded stump in the middle of a river. Moreover it may build in low country on or near the bank of a stream, or in mountain forests at a considerable altitude. The only kind of country which it seems consistently to shun is the open plain.

The bird's call has the general character of that of most of the wood Flycatchers, the notes resembling the syllables *peet* and *weet,* to which is added a mournful little plaint uttered when the nest is discovered. When that happens, the bird is likely to flutter about the intruder, snapping its bill with considerable energy. The ordinary call note is usually accompanied by a sharp flirt of the tail. The bird's manner of hunting is very similar to that of the other Flycatchers.

In the laboratory investigation of the food of the Western Flycatcher it was proved that he eats less than three-fourths of 1 per cent. of vegetable matter. Only one other Flycatcher, the Western Wood Pewee, eats so little vegetable food. Beetles amount to about 8 per cent. and are nearly all harmful, the exception being a few ground beetles. Bees, wasps, and ants form the largest constituent of the food of this as of most other Flycatchers; they amount to over 38 per cent. Bugs amount to nearly 9 per cent. of the food; flies to a little more than 31 per cent. and include the crane flies, the soldier flies, and the house flies. Moths and caterpillars amount to about 7 per cent. Neither the farmer nor the fruit grower has anything to fear from the Western Flycatcher. Practically it eats no vegetable food, and its animal diet contains less than the normal proportion of useful elements. It should be rigidly protected at all seasons.

ACADIAN FLYCATCHER

Empidonax virescens (*Vieillot*)

A. O. U. Number 465 See Color Plate 68

Other Names.— Green-crested Flycatcher; Small Green-crested Flycatcher; Green Flycatcher; Small Pewee.

General Description.— Length, 6 inches. Color above, grayish olive-green; under parts, yellowish-white.

Color.—Above, plain grayish olive-green, slightly darker and duller on crown; tail, grayish-brown, the outer webs of the feathers passing into grayish olive-green on edges; wings, darker grayish-brown or dusky, the middle and greater coverts broadly tipped with pale buff (*forming two conspicuous bands*), the secondaries edged with the same; a rather broad eye ring of dull yellowish-white, narrower but scarcely interrupted on upper eyelid; lores, dull whitish, suffused with dusky, especially near front of eyes; sides of head otherwise and sides of neck similar in color to back, fading gradually below into the dull yellowish-white of chin and throat; under parts, dull yellowish-white, passing into primrose-yellow behind (whole under parts usually tinged with this color, especially laterally), the chest and sides shaded with pale grayish-olive; under wing-coverts, rose-yellow; inner webs of wing-feathers, edged with pale grayish-buffy; bill, dark horn-brown; iris, brown.

Nest and Eggs.— Nest: Semi-pensile, in forks of

saplings or bushes 5 to 20 feet up, in deep woods; rather carelessly constructed of grass, bark shreds, weed fibers, cocoons and catkins and lined with finer grass. EGGS: 2 or 3, pale yellow-buff, boldly specked and spotted around large end with chestnut-brown.

Distribution.— Eastern United States, north to Long Island, lower Hudson Valley, central New York, southern Ontario, southern Michigan, casually to Massachusetts and Connecticut; west to middle portion of Great Plains, from Nebraska to Texas; breeding southward to northern Florida and thence through Gulf States to Texas; southward in winter to the Bahamas and Cuba and through eastern Mexico, Central America, and Panama to Colombia and Ecuador.

The Acadian Flycatcher is one of the tamest of the wood Flycatchers, but because of its fondness for thickets and solitude, and its comparative inactivity, it is likely to be overlooked. A North Carolina observer noted its apparent liking for rhododendron growths near streams in that State, and another observer found the bird plentiful and calling freely in the great Okefinokee Swamp in Georgia, where its preference for solitude must have been pretty thoroughly satisfied. It perches generally not more than twenty feet from the ground. Its common call-note resembles the syllable *peet* and is uttered at brief intervals and emphasized by a flirting of the tail.

Photo by A. A. Allen

AN ACADIAN FLYCATCHER INCUBATING

Another note, which suggests the syllables *wicky-up,* seems to be articulated with some effort, with the bill elevated and the wings vibrating. One observer refers to the " startling exclamations and mysterious wing whistlings " of the bird; but the latter demonstration may be what Dr. Chapman refers to when he says: "A rarer note may be heard when the bird makes a short, fluttering flight. It resembles the soft murmuring of whistling wings."

Originally the name "Acadian" was given to all the members of the genus *Empidonax* of the Flycatchers. As the ornithologists progressed in their investigations, the other species were separated one by one from the Acadian. This statement explains the curious fact that no Acadian Flycatcher, despite its name, is found in the land of Evangeline.

The habits of the Acadian Flycatcher do not lead it to the garden or orchard, and its food has little direct economic interest. It does not catch many useful insects and, as it does not feed upon any product of cultivation, it may well be considered as one of those species whose function is to help keep the great flood of insect life down to a level compatible with the best interests of other forms of life.

TRAILL'S FLYCATCHER

Empidonax trailli trailli (*Audubon*)

A. O. U. Number 466

General Description.— Length, 5½ inches. Upper parts, olive; under parts, brownish-gray and white.

Color.— Above, plain olive, the crown and hindneck usually very slightly grayer or less brownish than back, etc., the rump and upper tail-coverts paler and more brownish-olive, the outer web of lateral feathers paler, sometimes approaching dull whitish; wings, darker grayish-brown, the middle and greater coverts broadly tipped with pale olive, forming two conspicuous bands, of which the rear one is usually the paler, sometimes approaching dull olive-whitish; secondaries edged with olive-whitish; lores and an indistinct *eye ring, olive-whitish,* the former intermixed with dusky, especially near front angle of eye; rest of sides of head and sides of neck, similar in color to upper parts but slightly paler and grayer, gradually fading below into the white of chin and throat; chest and sides of breast, pale brownish-gray, the sides similar but paler, fading into pale olive on flanks; rest of *under parts, white,* tinged with pale primrose-yellow, at least on flanks, anal region, and under tail-coverts; under wing-coverts, pale primrose-yellow; inner webs of wing-feathers, edged with pale grayish-buff; bill, brown; iris, brown.

Nest and Eggs.— NEST: In forks of shrubs, or bushes near water, one to six feet up; loosely constructed of vegetable fiber, dried grass, and shreds of bark and lined with fine grass, fern down, and horsehair. EGGS: 2 to 4, pinkish or yellowish-buffy, spotted and specked around large end with light chestnut or umber-brown.

Distribution.— Western North America; east, northerly, to western portion of Great Plains, much farther southerly, breeding in Iowa (?), Missouri, southern Illinois, and probably elsewhere in central Mississippi valley; north to coast district of British Columbia and coast district of southern Alaska (?), northern Idaho, and Montana; south in winter over greater part of Mexico to Central America, Panama, and northwestern South America.

Traill's Flycatcher is not only energetic and rather restless, which are common characteristics of its tribe, but shows considerable pugnacity especially in the breeding season; then it is exceedingly likely to attack any other bird who comes near its nest. It is often found in willow or alder thickets along streams, both on high plains and in valleys, and in such surroundings its nest is usually built. One observer reports that, in all of the nests he found, the bird had placed the wool and other soft downy substances on the outside of the walls, and had lined the inside with rough stalks and dried grass. The bird has the characteristic Flycatcher habit of flirting its tail frequently and vigorously.

"In Oregon, Traill's Flycatcher commonly nests in a bush often three or four feet from the ground. The nest resembles that of a Yellow Warbler both in structure and often in location." (Finley.)

A variety of Traill's Flycatcher is found in eastern North America as well as in some of the western districts. The Alder Flycatcher (*Empidonax trailli alnorum*) is the brownest of the Flycatchers. It is rarely found within the depths of the forests; its preference is the swamps which are covered with a low growth of alders, willows, meadowsweet, and other low shrubs. There is a great deal of difference of opinion in regard to the Alder's song; but all the ornithologists agree that it is unlike that of any other Flycatcher. (See Color Plate 68).

The Traill's and Alder Flycatchers, one or the other of the two forms, occupy in the breeding season the whole of the United States except the southeastern part south of northeastern Texas, Arkansas, and the mountains of West Virginia, and extend north into British America. In winter they retire entirely beyond the southern boundary of the United States. No special differences in the food habits of the two have been noticed.

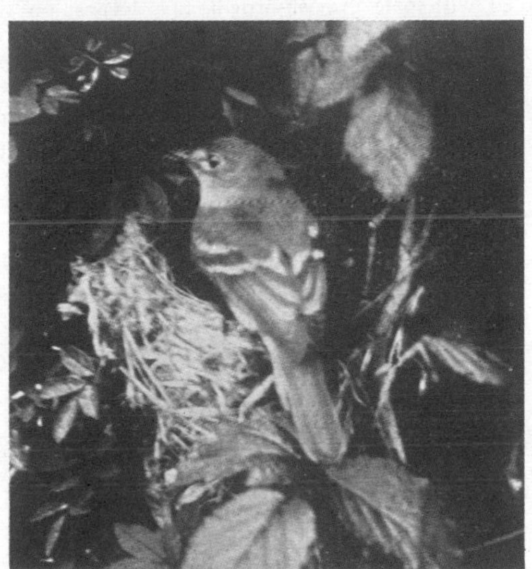

Photo by H. K. Job Courtesy of Outing Pub. Co.

ALDER FLYCATCHER

Female pausing at edge of nest

It is evident from their nesting habits that they are not likely to injure any product of industry, and the contents of the stomachs examined corroborate this observation.

LEAST FLYCATCHER

Empidonax minimus (*W. M.* and *S. F. Baird*)

A. O. U. Number 467 See Color Plate 68

Other Names.— Chebec; Sewick.

General Description.— Length, 5 inches. Upper parts, brownish-olive; under parts, whitish.

Color.— Above, plain brownish olive, the feathers of crown darker centrally; tail, grayish-brown, the feathers passing into light brownish-olive on edges; wings, dusky, the middle and greater coverts broadly tipped with pale grayish-brown, sometimes nearly white on tips of greater coverts, forming two distinct bands; the secondaries edged with the same or with dull yellowish-white; *a broad dull white or yellowish-white eye-ring;* lores, dull whitish suffused with dusky, especially near front angle of eye; rest of side of head and sides of neck similar in color to upper parts, gradually fading below into dull white of chin and throat; rest of under parts, dull white, tinged with pale (primrose) yellow posteriorly, the chest and sides shaded with pale grayish-brown, this deepest on sides of chest and sides of breast; under wing-coverts, pale yellowish-white; inner webs of wing-feathers edged with pale dull buffy; bill, dusky brown; iris, brown. YOUNG: More olive.

Nest and Eggs.— NEST: Placed in fork of sapling, occasionally on horizontal limb; a compact, neat structure of very fine gray bark, fibers, dandelion down, hair, and feathers, lined with fine narrow grasses and a few feathers. EGGS: 2 to 4, *pure white* or with a faint buffy tinge *unmarked.*

Distribution.— Breeds from west-central Mackenzie, southern Keewatin, Quebec, and Cape Breton Island south to central Montana, eastern Wyoming, central Nebraska, Iowa, Indiana, Pennsylvania, New Jersey, and in the Alleghenies to North Carolina; in migration west to eastern Colorado and central Texas; winters from northeastern Mexico and Yucatan to Panama and Peru; accidental in West Indies.

As its name indicates, the Least Flycatcher is the smallest of our common Flycatchers, but it makes up in energy of manner and emphasis of utterance what it lacks in size. As one observer remarked, the little fellow announces his name, *Che-bec,* with such a fervid jerk of both head and tail that he seems to be in real danger of snapping his head off. And this *che-becing* sometimes continues at a rate and with a persistency which almost make one wish that something of the kind might happen.

Courtesy of Am. Mus. Nat. Hist.

LEAST FLYCATCHER (nat. size)

Its energy compensates for its small size

However, the little chap has other characteristics which make one forget this fault. Both sexes, after they alight, have a trick of uttering a series of half-warbled, half-gurgled notes, accompanied by a quivering of the wings and tail, which is characteristic and very pleasing. And the male has a flight song, delivered usually just before dusk as he soars upward from a tree-top, which is interesting, if not highly melodious. Finally the bird makes a decided appeal on account of its obvious friendliness; for it is fully as confiding in its attitude toward its human neighbors as is the Phœbe, and seems especially fond of an apple orchard near a house as a nesting place.

The Chebec's habits are very like those of the other members of its family. It dashes after insects much in the manner of the Phœbe, and these sallies often are directed down into the grass, or against the trunks of trees when insects are seen in either of those places, whether in motion or at rest.

In the food of this Flycatcher there is no evidence of direct injury to the farmer or horticulturist. The bird eats no grain and practically no fruit or other product of husbandry. It must be admitted that the bird destroys more useful insects than could be wished, but the injury it does in this way is comparatively slight. To his credit must be placed cotton-boll weevils, striped squash beetles, cucumber beetles, imbricated clover weevils, plum curculios, moths, and caterpillars.

LARKS

Order *Passeres;* suborder *Oscines;* family *Alaudidæ*

HE Larks are almost exclusively birds of the Old World. They are found in the northern part of Europe and Asia, in Africa, and in India; there is one species in Australia and another in North America. One species, the European Skylark, is a straggler to Greenland and the Bermudas; it has also been introduced into the United States. The Larks belong to the larger group of song birds and many of its members are excellent songsters; the European Skylark is especially renowned in this respect and has been the theme of many a writer both of poetry and of prose.

Among the structural characteristics of this family are: bill, variable in shape, but usually small, conoid, usually moderately thick or rather slender, sometimes very deep and compressed, in some species slender and much elongated; the nostril usually narrow, oblique, sometimes longitudinal, usually at least partly concealed by the feathers of the lores; the bristles at the corner of the mouth indistinct or obsolete; wing rather long, pointed, the longest primaries much longer than the secondaries; tail containing twelve feathers and variable in relative length but always shorter than wing, nearly even, double rounded, or notched; tarsus rather stout, variable as to relative length and covered with scales; middle toe shorter than tarsus but decidedly longer than the side toes which are nearly equal; claws of the forward toes slightly curved, usually short; that of the hind toe much longer, sometimes much elongated and nearly straight, occasionally much longer than the toe; the head usually crested (double crested or "eared" in the Horned Larks).

The Larks are usually streaked brownish above, whitish streaked with brown below, sometimes nearly plain brown, occasionally black or dusky. One species, the Horned Larks, has conspicuous frontal and cheek patches and jugular collar or crescent of black.

The members of this family are terrestrial in their habits. Their nests are built on the ground in open places and they feed on both grain and insects.

SKYLARK

Alauda arvensis *Linnæus*

A. O. U. Number 473 See Color Plate 69

Other Name.— European Skylark.

General Description.— Length, 7½ inches. Upper parts, brown streaked with blackish; under parts, buffy-white tinged and streaked with darker.

Color.— Above, wood-brown everywhere (except on wings and tail) streaked with blackish, the streaks broadest on crown, back, and rump, where margined with deeper brown, some of the back feathers with inner webs paler than the general color; lesser wing-coverts nearly uniform wood-brown; middle coverts, dusky centrally, otherwise brown passing on margins into pale buffy-brown or dull brownish-white; greater coverts with concealed portion dusky, passing toward edges through brown to pale brownish-buff, the secondaries similarly colored but the three innermost with greater part of exposed portion dusky grayish-brown; primaries dusky edged with pale buffy-brown, the outermost with outer web almost entirely pale buffy;

middle pair of tail-feathers dusky centrally, otherwise brown with paler margins; next pair similar in color but darker; others, dusky, the outermost with most of outer web and portion of inner web next to shaft (except basally) dull white, the next with outer web edged with white; a broad but not sharply defined stripe of pale brownish buff over eye; sides of head, brown, indistinctly streaked with darker; lores, dull whitish; cheeks, similar in color to sides of head but paler and more distinctly streaked; under parts, dull buffy white, strongly tinged on chest, sides, and flanks with tawny buff, the last two narrowly and rather indistinctly streaked with darker, the first more broadly and very distinctly and sharply streaked with brownish-black; under wing-coverts, pale wood-brown; bill, pale brownish-buffy; iris, brown; legs and feet, brownish.

Nest and Eggs.— Nest: Always on ground, under a tuft of grass, alongside a rock or clod of earth, in open fields; constructed of plant stems, few leaves, and grasses, and lined with finer blades of the latter. Eggs: 3 to 5, varying from grayish to greenish-white thickly sprinkled with spots of drab and grayish-brown.

Distribution.— Europe in general, except Mediterranean district; accidental in Greenland and the Bermudas, and introduced into the United States.

Several attempts have been made to introduce the Skylark from England into America, but all apparently have failed. In 1887 a few seemed to have taken up their abode in the fields near the old village of Flatbush (now a part of Brooklyn), on Long Island, and one nest with young was found that year in that vicinity. In 1895 another nest and a singing bird were found in the same locality, and according to a responsible observer the species was still represented in that vicinity in 1907, which seems to be the last authentic record of its appearance in this country. It is not improbable that some of the Larks may have lingered in the Flatbush region for a few years after the date named, but in all probability the species is now extinct in America.

HORNED LARK

Otocoris alpestris alpestris (*Linnæus*)

A. O. U. Number 474 See Color Plate 69

Other Names.— Northern Horned Lark; Winter Horned Lark; Shore Lark; Prairie Bird; Road Trotter; Wheat Bird; Spring Bird; Life Bird.

General Description.— Length $7\frac{1}{4}$ inches. Upper parts, pinkish-brown; under parts, white; a black crescent under each eye, and a third one on the breast.

Color.— Adult Male: A broad patch covering front half of crown and rear half of forehead and extending backward laterally to back of head, *where involving an elongated erectile tuft of narrow feathers, black;* front of forehead and broad stripe over eye, pale straw-yellow; lores, space below eye, and lower front part of sides of head, black, this black area bordered behind by light straw-yellow from lower rear margin of eye backward and downward across middle part of ear region, confluent below with the more decidedly yellow area covering chin and throat; upper and rear margin of sides of head, grayish-brown; a broad, somewhat crescentic, patch of black across upper chest invading center lower portion of throat; middle rear portion of crown, back of head, hindneck, lesser wing-coverts, and terminal portion (broadly) of middle wing-coverts, dull red, the upper tail-coverts similar but rather more cinnamon, the longer tapering coverts, grayish-brown edged with paler; back, shoulders, and rump, grayish-brown, the feathers edged with paler, and with a central wedge-shaped area of dusky, these markings larger on lower back and rump; wings (except lesser and middle coverts), deep grayish-brown with paler edgings, the outermost primary broadly edged with white; tail, black, the middle pair of feathers, grayish-brown with basal half (except centrally) more wood-brown margined with dull whitish, the two lateral pairs edged exteriorly with white (except basally), the outermost with terminal portion of inner web light grayish; under parts of body, white, the sides and flanks, dull red streaked with dusky; bill, black; iris, dark brown; legs and feet, black. Adult female: Smaller and much duller in color than the male, the whole crown grayish-brown streaked with dusky, black area on side of head reduced in extent, duller black or merely dusky, the feathers narrowly tipped with dull whitish (except in worn midsummer plumage); throat patch also reduced in size; stripe, space over eye, throat, etc., paler and duller yellow; upper parts, more extensively streaked with little red showing on hindneck or upper tail-coverts; otherwise essentially as in the male. Immature: Similar, but black obscured with yellowish.

Nest and Eggs.— Nest: On ground among moss or tuft of grass; constructed of grass and lined with finer blades and feathers. Eggs: 3 or 4, greenish-gray, thickly spotted with dark olive and pale lavender.

Distribution.— Breeding in northeastern British America, east of Hudson Bay, from Newfoundland, Labrador, and head of James Bay northward; in winter migrating west to Manitoba and the Mississippi valley (eastern portion, chiefly) and southward to Illinois, Ohio, and the Carolinas, casually to Louisiana and the Bermudas; accidental in Greenland.

The Horned Larks are small but hardy birds which frequent the open country and never live in forests. They are found in a great variety of situations, and feed along roads, in weedy or freshly plowed fields, on commons or other waste places, and in closely grazed pastures, meadows, and stubble fields. The beaches and salt marshes of the coasts, the lake shores, muddy flats, and swamps of the interior are thronged with them in fall and winter. In the Far West they live in hot desert valleys, on arid table-lands, on level grassy prairies, in the foothills, and even on bare mountain peaks.

They are readily distinguished from other small ground-loving birds. They are about the size of the Bluebird, their throats are white or yellow, there is a conspicuous black mark across the breast, and just above and behind the eyes are small pointed tufts of dark-colored feathers which are often erected. These black tufts or horns are perhaps the bird's most characteristic feature, and give origin to the common name "Horned Lark," by which it is known over most of the United States. "Shore Lark" is another common name, though a less apt one.

Many of the popular names of the Horned Larks emphasize the fact that they are preëminently terrestrial birds. During the day they run nimbly over the surface in quest of food; at night they roost in small companies on the bare earth. A clod or stone is a favorite perch, and they are rarely seen in a bush or tree. They nest early, the first clutch of eggs often being completed before the snow has disappeared. The nests are of the simplest description, in keeping with the artless character of the bird, being little cups of grass placed in slight depressions in the ground. Two or even three broods are raised in a year, a fact which sufficiently explains the great numbers of the species in some localities.

The flight of the Horned Larks is hesitant. They usually start hurriedly from the ground, uttering short, whistled notes, and it is very characteristic of them that frequently when disturbed they fly straight away for a short distance, only to swing around and alight near the starting point. In the mating season, however, they ascend to great heights and, like the Skylark, sing while on the wing. The song is neither complex nor loud, but it is wild, joyous, and full of the free spirit of the prairie and the open fields.

The birds thus characterized occur at some time of the year in all parts of North America, except the Aleutian Islands, the southern coastal portion of Alaska, extreme southeastern United States, and Central America. This vast range is occupied by only one species, which, however, varies so greatly in different localities that it has been separated into no fewer than twenty-one varieties or subspecies. During the breeding season these geographic forms are restricted to separate areas, but in winter, on account of the tendency of the southern races to wander and of the northern ones to migrate, the subspecies mingle, and as many as seven (Arizona) or eight (California) forms occur in one State. In summer in the United States (including Alaska) there are fifteen subspecies of Horned Larks, and in winter seventeen.

The several members of the family *Alaudidæ,*

Courtesy of Am. Mus. Nat. Hist.

HORNED LARK (½ nat. size)

which includes these forms, are interesting birds. Their habit of walking, instead of hopping, distinguishes them from many small ground birds. They have long hind claws, the prints of which in the snow or along the muddy shores of ponds often indicate where the Larks have been running. They molt but once a year, usually in August, while many birds molt twice and a few three times. The nuptial dress is acquired not by molting, but by the wearing away of the tips of the winter feathers, revealing the brighter colors beneath. The plumage of the Larks is generally neutral in tint, especially when viewed from above, and so harmonizes with their surroundings that it has a protective value, and enables the birds, in a measure, to escape the notice of enemies.

Examination of 1154 stomachs collected in all parts of the United States and southern Canada shows that the food of the Horned Larks consists of insects 20.6 per cent. and vegetable matter, nearly six-sevenths of which are weed seed, 79.4 per cent. The nestlings are highly insectivorous, but soon after leaving the nest they become much more vegetarian than even the adults. The Horned Larks of California differ markedly in food habits from those of other parts of the country, being almost entirely vegetarian. It might appear that the California Horned Larks are decidedly injurious, but a large proportion of the grain is wild and hence of no value to the farmer. Of the grain eaten in the other States, buckwheat is a negligible amount, while practically all of the corn and oats eaten is waste. Although the Great Plains region, the most important wheat-growing area of the country and also the center of abundance of the Horned Larks, is represented by a proportionate number of the stomachs examined, yet the percentage of wheat eaten is only 1.66. In fact, the Larks of this region, considered separately, are even more insectivorous than those from east of the Mississippi, one-fourth of their food being animal matter.

The charges made by farmers that the Horned Larks eat newly sown grain are confirmed, but in attempting to estimate the economic value of the birds it must be borne in mind that the insects they eat compensate many fold for the seed grain taken, even considered bulk for bulk. As a matter of fact, however, the insects eaten constitute almost twice as great a proportion of the food as the grain, including even that which is waste.

It is impossible to estimate in dollars and cents the benefits resulting from the work of the Horned Lark, but it is none the less real on that account. Moreover, the services of the bird cost the farmer practically nothing save a small toll levied here and there upon seed grain. The Horned Lark by its services to agriculture earns a right to live, and deserves protection at the hands of man.

W. L. McAtee, in *The Horned Larks and their Relation to Agriculture.*

Photograph by A. A. Allen

PRAIRIE HORNED LARKS

CROWS AND JAYS

Order *Passeres;* suborder *Oscines;* family *Corvidæ*

CROWS and Jays are large to rather large birds. The bill is variable in shape but always long; the ridge on the top curves at the apex; it is never distinctly notched and usually not at all. The nostril is usually round and completely hidden under a tuft. There are distinct bristles at the corners of the mouth. The wing varies as to relative length: long and pointed in the Ravens and Crows; short and rounded in the Magpies and Jays. The tail varies greatly as to form and relative length, but it is never notched nor forked; usually it is rounded, but often it is graduated, sometimes excessively so.

The Crow-Jay family is so nearly cosmopolitan that only New Zealand and portions of Polynesia are without representatives. The group is most developed, however, in the northern hemisphere. A somewhat singular fact in connection with their distribution in the western hemisphere is that while Jays and Magpies extend from the northern limit of forests almost to the southern extremity of the temperate districts of South America, no part of tropical America being without representatives, the

Crows and Ravens reach their southern limit in the Greater Antilles and on the highlands of Honduras, no peculiar species occurring south of central Mexico or Jamaica, the Greater Antilles lacking any representation of the Jays and Magpies and the Lesser Antilles being without a single member of either group.

MAGPIE

Pica pica hudsonia (*Sabine*)

A. O. U. Number 475

Other Names.— American Magpie; Black-billed Magpie.

General Description.— Length, 19½ inches. Plumage, black with white on shoulders and abdomen. Tail, much longer than wing, graduated for ½ or more of its length; wing, short and rounded; feet, stout.

Color.— Adults: Head, neck, chest, upper breast, back, lesser wing-coverts, lower rump, upper and under tail-coverts, anal region, thighs, lower abdomen, and under wing-coverts, uniform black, the crown glossed with bronze, the back faintly glossed with bluish-green or bluish in certain lights; *shoulders, lower breast, upper abdomen, sides, and flanks, white*; a broad band of grayish-white across upper rump; prevailing color of middle and greater wing-coverts and secondaries metallic steel-blue, varying to bronzy-green; primaries, blackish glossed with greenish-bronze, bluish-green, or steel-bluish; the inner webs of the primaries mostly white; tail, bright metallic bronzy-green, passing into metallic-purple; iris, brown. Young: Similar to adults, but black of head, neck, etc., much duller, without metallic gloss; feathers of throat usually with the basal white spots much larger, often conspicuously exposed and frequently occupying, as large wedge-shaped spots, the central portion of the feathers of chest and upper breast, as well as throat.

Nest and Eggs.— Nest: The nest proper, a bowl of mud and grass, surrounded and arched by an immense number of large and small sticks, is often the size of a barrel! Entrance, a hole on the side. They are located in bushes or trees from 5 to 60 feet up and with the bristling array of sticks pointing in all directions present a formidable appearance. Eggs: 6 to 9, usually 7, pale grayish or greenish regularly and heavily blotched with shades of brown and purple, sometimes hiding the ground color.

Distribution.— Treeless or more sparsely wooded districts of western North America, except coast and interior valleys of California; north to northwestern Alaska; south to southern Arizona, New Mexico (where breeding at 7,000 to 12,000 feet), and western Texas; east to western portion of the Great Plains, and to Lake Winnipeg; rare or casual winter visitant or straggler to southwest side of Hudson Bay, Ontario, Michigan, northeastern Illinois, Wisconsin, Minnesota, Iowa, eastern Nebraska, etc.

Drawing by R. Bruce Horsfall

MAGPIE (½ nat. size)

A mixture of shyness and boldness

In traveling through the arid western country, one often sees a bird of slow but graceful flight, with a long tail and flashing white on wings and breast. These are the unmistakable recognition marks of the Magpie.

The nest of this bird is often conspicuous, for dense trees in which to hide a big nest such as the Magpie builds are sometimes hard to find. The Magpie has learned for his own protection to build in a thorn tree if it is available, and to roof the home over with strong twigs. The entrance is usually on the side. The nest cavity itself is built of mud and lined with fine grasses and roots. As a whole, it is quite a formidable fortress, difficult to penetrate even by a human hand.

Many complaints are lodged against the Magpie. The worst I have heard in the cattle country of the West. Where an animal sometimes has an open sore, the Magpie's taste for flesh and blood leads him to attack the wounded creature by flying down and pecking the sore. This is frequently the case where cattle are being branded.

Trappers often complain of Magpies stealing their bait and eating the smaller animals that have been trapped. Mr. Stanley Jewett, who for several years collected specimens for the Biological Survey of the Department of Agriculture, says that oftentimes when trapping for meadow mice and other small mammals, the Magpie beat him in running the line of traps. A line of traps set out through the sage brush is generally marked by bits of white cotton on the tops of the bushes. A Magpie soon becomes an expert in following these signs, and the trapper is compelled to outwit the Magpie by some other marking. WILLIAM L. FINLEY.

Down in the San Joaquin and Sacramento valleys of California dwells a cousin of the American Magpie. His name is Yellow-billed Magpie (*Pica nuttalli*). He looks very much like his relative, but is smaller, and his bill and the bare skin back of the eye are bright yellow. He is also just as noisy and has just the same mixture of shyness and boldness.

Like the other birds of this family, the Crows, Ravens, and Jays, the Magpie has a cannibalistic appetite and delights in such tidbits as other small birds, their young and eggs. He also eats crawfish and small mammals, especially mice. But his main diet is insects which include destructive black crickets, grasshoppers, grubs, and larvæ. He also likes some fruit, berries, and green leaves.

Photo by W. L. Finley and H. T. Bohlman

YOUNG MAGPIES

Bob-tailed and awkward now

BLUE JAY

Cyanocitta cristata cristata (*Linnæus*)

A. O. U. Number 477 See Color Plate 70

Other Names.— Corn Thief; Nest Robber; Blue Coat; Jay; Common Jay.

General Description.— Length, 11½ inches. Upper parts, grayish violet-blue; under parts, gray and white. Head, conspicuously crested; wings and tail, about equal in length, and rounded.

Color.— ADULTS: Crown (including crest), hind-neck, back, shoulders, rump, upper tail-coverts, and lesser and middle wing-coverts plain dull campanula-blue or grayish violet-blue; sides of the head, chin, and throat, very pale bluish-gray; a black collar beginning on nape (beneath crest) and extending thence downward across end of ear region and alongside of neck and connecting with a broader, somewhat *crescentic, patch across chest, black; greater wing-coverts, secondaries, and tail-feathers, rich cobalt or azure-blue* broadly tipped with white (except middle pair of quills), and barred with black; primaries, plain azure-blue, paler on exterior quills; breast, sides, and flanks, smoke-gray or drab-gray; abdomen, anal region, and under tail-coverts, white; iris, brown. YOUNG: Black bars usually narrower or less distinct; black markings of head and neck less distinct, crown (including short crest) bluish-gray; back, shoulders, rump, upper tail-coverts, and smaller wing-coverts, dull grayish; greater wing-coverts without black bars.

Nest and Eggs.— NEST: Located in conifers or deciduous trees, preferably the former, particularly cedars; a loose, carelessly constructed affair, with ragged rim, though some are fairly well made of sticks, leaves, bark strips, weed stems, lined with strips of bark, grass, pine-needles, rags, paper, string, or any material that seizes the bird's fancy. EGGS: 3 to 6, pale dull olive, greenish-olive, or dull buffy, spotted or blotched with dark olive-brown; one brood only.

Distribution.— Temperate eastern North America, except peninsula of Florida; north on Atlantic coast to Nova Scotia, Prince Edward Island, New Brunswick (resident), etc., in the interior to about latitude 52°, casually 56°; west to eastern Assiniboia, eastern North and South Dakota, eastern half of Nebraska, eastern two-thirds of Kansas, eastern Oklahoma and eastern half (approximately) of Texas; south to the Gulf coast.

The Blue Jay is the clown and scoffer of bird-land. Furthermore, he is one of the handsomest of American birds; also he is one of the wickedest, and therein exemplifies the literal truth of the saying " Fine feathers don't make fine birds." Many have been the attempts to write the Jay down a rascal, and not a few the efforts to rehabilitate and exculpate him. But after all has been said by his defenders, the ugly fact remains, as Mr. Job says, that the bird " has all the mis-

Drawing by R. I. Brasher

BLUE JAY (½ nat. size)

Cannibalistic, noisy, and abusive, but picturesque and popular withal

chievous, destructive, thieving traits of the Crow, and with a lot of audacity or 'cheek' thrown in for good measure."

There can be no doubt that he is a persistent and merciless nest-robber — that he eats the eggs and kills and devours the young of smaller and defenseless birds. Eloquent testimony concerning the commission of these crimes is furnished by the outcry set up by such birds, whenever they catch a Jay lurking near their nests. But we need not take the birds' word alone for it, because he has been caught red-handed by man, more than once, in the very perpetration of these villainies.

Courtesy of S. A. Lottridge

BLUE JAY

An amusing rascal

Yet even those who know and condemn the ways of Jays, are forced to admit that he is an amusing rascal. In the nesting season he is comparatively little in evidence, not only because he has his own family affairs to attend to, but because he devotes a good deal of his time to his cannibalistic practices, concerning which he is anxious to keep the rest of the feathered world in ignorance. But once his family responsibilities are discharged, and there are no more nests to be robbed, his whole demeanor changes, and he becomes the noisiest and most obstreperous creature in the woods.

"Here comes a fool with a gun; look out for him!" he yells, as you enter the woods, said Mr. Torrey; and all the rest of his brethren promptly take up the hue and cry. And let anybody who supposes that Jays can't swear, and employ the most variegated vilification and the most fluent Billingsgate, just stand by and listen to the maledictions of a flock of them as they mob their arch-enemy, the Great Horned Owl.

That the Jay has a sense of humor — which is not common among our birds — also seems very obvious. Often it is humor of the grim kind, but not always, as will be appreciated by those who have read "Baker's Blue Jay Story," in Mark Twain's *Tramp Abroad*. Here we have a most amusing yarn about how a Jay tried to fill up a deserted cabin with acorns; how he worked and swore as the nuts disappeared through the knot-hole in the roof; how one of the flock of Jays who had been attracted by his "devotions," discovered what he had been trying to do, by looking in through the open door, and promptly had a spasm; how the other Jays took a look, one by one, with the same result, and how the whole flock then sat around in the trees and guffawed over the joke — all of this is not merely amusing; it is good ornithology in so far as it reports the way a Jay acts.

James Whitcomb Riley also sketched him accurately when he said (in "Knee Deep in June")

Mr. Blue Jay, full o' sass,
  In them base-ball clothes of his,
Sportin' round the orchard jes'
  Like he owned the premises.

Incidentally it ought to be recorded that the Jay's kleptomaniacal and hiding propensities serve a useful purpose, for they prompt him to carry away and conceal acorns and chestnuts under leaves and in the grass and in hollow trees, with the result that when a forest of conifers is cut away, chestnuts and oaks are likely to appear from the nuts which have been hidden by these birds — and the squirrels. This service, unconscious though it be, ought not to be ignored, even as we reflect, when we remember the boisterous good nature and the clown-like ways of the Jay, that a bird, as well as a man, may "smile and smile and be a villain still."

"That a Blue Jay! Nonsense!" many people exclaim, when told that a very melodious, bell-like note coming from a thicket is one of the calls of a bird whose sole vocal accomplishment, as far as they know, is his harsh cry of *Thief, thief!* But he frequently sounds this note and many others that are really musical, besides which he has considerable skill as a ventriloquist and as a mimic. In the latter capacity witness his frequent and almost perfect imitation of the whistled scream of the Red-shouldered Hawk, which many will insist is a deliberate attempt to terrify the other birds, and is perfectly in keeping with the Jay's love of a practical joke.

GEORGE GLADDEN.

Stomach analysis indicates that about three-fourths (76 per cent.) of the Jay's food consists of vegetable matter and that most of this is acorns, chestnuts, beechnuts, and the like. Such noxious insects as wood-boring beetles, grasshoppers, eggs of various caterpillars, and scale insects constitute about 19½ per cent. of his food. Predacious beetles contribute about 3½ per cent. This leaves but 1 per cent. for the birds and eggs, the mice, fish, salamanders, snails, and crustaceans, that make up the remainder of his diet. According to Mr. F. E. L. Beal, the Jay does not eat the seeds of poison ivy or poison sumac and the distribution of these seeds cannot be charged to him.

In the peninsula of Florida the Blue Jay is smaller and his color is paler and duller. The white tips on the wing- and tail-feathers are smaller. So here he is given the name of the Florida Blue Jay (*Cyanocitta cristata florincola*).

Photograph by Mrs. H. A. Colby

BLUE JAYS

In Maine

STELLER'S JAY

Cyanocitta stelleri stelleri (*Gmelin*)

A. O. U. Number 478

Other Names.— Mountain Jay; Pine Jay; Conifer Jay.

General Description.— Length, 12¼ inches. Fore and upper parts, sooty; rear under parts, blue. Head, conspicuously crested; wings and tail, about equal in length, and rounded.

Color.— *Head (including crest), neck, and upper portion of chest, plain black or sooty-black,* the forehead usually streaked with blue (cerulean or azure) and chin and upper throat usually streaked with pale grayish; back and shoulders, plain dark sooty-brown, rump and under parts posterior to chest, blue; the upper tail-coverts, almost cerulean-blue; wing-coverts and primaries, dull cerulean or Sèvres-blue, the greater coverts usually with narrow bars of black; secondaries, deep cobalt or dull ultramarine-blue; tail, dull cobalt-blue, with terminal portion usually distinctly barred with black; iris, brown.

Nest and Eggs.— NEST: Usually located in firs, sometimes in other trees and bushes from 10 to 50 feet up; constructed of large sticks, moss, grass, cemented with mud and lined with fine dried grasses and hair — a bulky, substantial structure. EGGS: 3 to 5, pale bluish-green, spotted and blotched all over with olive-brown and lavender.

Distribution.—Coniferous forests of northern Pacific Coast district, from shores of Puget Sound northward to eastern shores of Cook Inlet, including Vancouver Island and other coast islands, except Prince of Wales Island and the Queen Charlotte group.

This is another handsome member of a handsome family, but, alas, like his conspicuous and noisy eastern cousin, the Blue Jay, his habits and manners serve to warn us again that "handsome is as handsome does." For his fine clothes cannot conceal from those who know him the fact that he is a nest-robber and a cannibal as well.

Drawing by R. Bruce Horsfall

STELLER'S JAY (⅓ nat. size)

Chack-ah, Mrs. Florence Merriam Bailey says he squalls, as he flirts his tail and dashes about through the woods; and, curiously enough, like the Blue Jay, he has a sort of whistled scream which is singularly like that of the Red-shouldered Hawk. Whether, in either case, this is more than a coincidence, it is impossible to determine, though many who know how Jays act will assert their belief that the imitation is deliberate, and is intended to frighten the other birds.

The fine crest of the Steller's Jay is not always visible when the bird is flying; but, as a keen-eyed youthful friend of Mrs. Bailey remarked, "when they holler they stick that right straight up," a description which Ruskin himself couldn't have improved upon.

As happens with many of the birds, there are several slightly varying local forms of Steller's Jay in the Rocky Mountain section of the United States and Canada. These are known as the Blue-fronted Jay or Sierra Nevada Jay (*Cyanocitta stelleri frontalis*), the Long-crested Jay (*Cyanocitta stelleri diademata*), the Black-headed Jay (*Cyanocitta stelleri annectens*), the Queen Charlotte Jay or Osgood's Jay (*Cyanocitta stelleri carlottæ*) and the Coast Jay or Grinnell's Jay (*Cyanocitta stelleri carbonacea*). Two other geographical forms are found in Mexico — the Aztec Jay and the Blue-crested Jay.

These birds are more shy and retiring than the Blue Jay of the eastern States and seldom visit the orchard or the vicinity of the ranch buildings. The results of stomach examinations show but little variance from those of Blue Jays. A very considerable portion of their food consists of acorns, chestnuts, beechnuts, and the like, together with a little fruit and some insects. The insects are largely wasps and some beetles and grasshoppers. The grain consumed by the Steller's Jay and its kin is probably waste or volunteer. In the 93 stomachs available for the laboratory investigations of the Biological Survey, 13 were found to contain remains of egg-shells. This is the worst item in this Jay's record, since it indicates that the bird is guilty of eating the eggs of smaller birds; but even this is not as bad as it looks. Only 6 of these egg-eating records occurred in June, the nesting month.

FLORIDA JAY

Aphelocoma cyanea (*Vieillot*)

A. O. U. Number 479

Other Name.— Scrub Jay.

General Description.— Length, 11½ inches. Upper parts, blue and gray; under parts, gray. Head, not crested.

Color.— ADULTS: Crown, hindneck, sides of neck, shoulders, wings, upper tail-coverts, and tail, plain dull azure-blue; sides of head, duller blue; back and rump, smoke-gray or drab-gray, the latter tinged with blue; chin and upper throat, grayish-white, gradually shading into light gray on chest; feathers of lower chest, blue, forming a semi-circular collar; breast, abdomen, sides, and flanks, light smoke-gray, fading into white on anal region; under tail-coverts, dull azure-blue; iris, brown. YOUNG: Crown, hindneck, sides of neck and head, deep mouse-gray; back, shoulders, rump, and upper tail-coverts, paler and browner gray; chin, throat, and abdomen, dull whitish; under tail-coverts, light gray; rest of under parts, light grayish, deeper across lower part of chest, where forming a semi-circular collar; wings and tail as in adults, the smaller wing-coverts, however, grayish, and the greater wing-coverts narrowly tipped with pale grayish.

Nest and Eggs.— NEST: In low scrub; a compact, but flat structure of small sticks, plant stems, leaves, lined with moss, wood, or feathers. EGGS: 3 to 5, usually 4, pale bluish or greenish-white, sparsely speckled with chestnut and black, more profusely at large end.

Distribution.— Peninsula of Florida (in oak scrub, irregularly distributed).

The Florida Jay is one of the crestless Jays, and also has the peculiarity of being one of the few American birds whose range is restricted to a comparatively small area — in this instance, the peninsula of Florida. Like his cousin of the New England States, he is a noisy fellow; while his assurance often nearly equals that of the Canada Jay. His preferred habitat is scrub-oak woodland, though favorite perches are the chimney-tops of summer cottages in the sand-dunes near the ocean. From such coigns of vantage in the vicinity of Daytona, he is often found surveying the landscape and haranguing all and sundry who will give him audience.

WOODHOUSE'S JAY

Aphelocoma woodhousei (*Baird*)

A. O. U. Number 480

General Description.— Length, 11 inches. Upper parts, blue and gray; under parts, gray. Head, not crested.

Color.— ADULTS: Head and neck (except chin and throat), wings, upper tail-coverts, and tail, plain, dull azure-blue, brightest on crown where margined laterally by a narrow streak (or series of streaks) of white, the blue dullest on sides of head; *back and shoulders, deep mouse-gray,* sometimes tinged with blue; rump, more bluish-gray; chin, *throat, and chest grayish-white, streaked with bluish-gray,* these streaks broad and very distinct on chest, which is margined laterally by an extension of the blue from sides of neck; breast, sides, and flanks pale mouse-gray or smoke-gray, the abdomen paler, fading into white on anal region; under tail-coverts, light grayish-blue or china-blue; iris, brown. YOUNG: Crown, plain mouse-gray; rest of upper parts (except wings and tail), plain brownish-gray or deep drab-gray; general color of under parts, dull light brownish-gray, paler on chin, throat, chest, and abdomen, deeper and more brownish on upper portion of breast; wings and tail as in adults, but smaller wing-coverts gray and lesser coverts indistinctly tipped with the same.

Nest and Eggs.— NEST: Located in scrub oaks, bushes, thickets, or low trees, usually within 6 feet of ground; a frail structure of small sticks, lined with rootlets and horse-hair. EGGS: 3 to 6, pale bluish-green, lightly spotted all over with brown and lavender, more thickly at large end.

Distribution.— Western United States east of Sierra Nevada; north to southeastern Oregon, southern Idaho, and southern Wyoming; east to Colorado, western Nebraska, New Mexico, and northwestern Texas; south to southern Arizona and New Mexico; west to southeastern California, west to western Nevada.

Woodhouse's Jay is one of the crestless Jays of the Rocky Mountain region and in that respect resembles the perhaps even better known California Jay. It has, however, plenty of individuality, all its own, and also plenty to say, though it is probably less loquacious and withal less assertive than its eastern cousin, the Blue Jay. The common note is a strident scream which has what one observer calls a "wiry" quality that is distinctive. This is the characteristic cry of surprise or anger or alarm, but this Jay has also a variety of other notes including chuckles, gurgles, and chatters, uttered chiefly when a number of the birds are together and undisturbed. Much of this conversation sounds decidedly like that of the Blue Jays, and likely enough is about the same general topics. The language of courtship, addressed by the male to his lady-love when he has enticed her into dense foliage, is as soft and insinuating as any Dove's.

This Jay's preferred habitat is the open hillsides, or scrub-oak and other hardwood timber, which it seems everywhere to prefer to pine woods. Its food is varied, but acorns form a good part of it, and these the bird, true to the thieving propensities of his family, does not hesitate to steal from the store laid away in the bark of trees by the California Woodpeckers. The flight of the bird is steady when considerable distances are being traversed, but shorter movements among trees or in the brush are likely to be covered by combined flapping and sailing. Like most other members of their family, these Jays gather in winter in flocks, and become restless, timid, and decidedly noisy upon little or no provocation.

Pine nuts are an especially favorite item of food of Woodhouse's Jay, but his habits and general diet vary little from those of the California Jay.

Southwestern Texas boasts two species of Jays which are very similar to Woodhouse's Jay. The Blue-eared Jay or Blue-cheeked Jay (*Aphelocoma cyanotis*) has a longer wing than Woodhouse's; it is white on the posterior under parts and its back is more frequently tinged with blue, being sometimes almost a uniform blue. The other species bears the name of the State — Texas (*Aphelocoma texana*). It is similar in the coloration of its upper parts to Woodhouse's Jay (maybe a little paler and less of a blue-gray) but the white line over the eyes is more developed; the under parts are much paler, the chest being devoid of distinct blue streaks and the breast being pale grayish-brown.

CALIFORNIA JAY

Aphelocoma californica californica (*Vigors*)

A. O. U. Number 481

General Description.— Length, 12 inches. Upper parts, blue and brownish-gray; under parts, white. Head, not crested.

Color.— Adults: Entire crown, hindneck and sides of neck, uniform dull cobalt-blue; sides of head similar but darker; back, brownish mouse-gray; shoulders and rump, more bluish-gray, wings, tail, and upper tail-coverts, rather dull azure-blue; chin, throat, and center portion of chest, white, the last streaked with blue; sides of chest, uniform blue; breast, very pale drab-gray fading into dull white on other under parts; the anal region and shorter under tail-coverts pure white; iris, brown. Young: Crown, hindneck, and sides of head, sides of chest, rump, and upper tail-coverts, uniform mouse-gray, the crown slightly more bluish-gray; back, shoulders and lesser wing-coverts, deep drab-gray, a broad space behind ear and eye narrowly streaked with dusky gray; anterior portion of cheek region, chin, throat, center portion of chest, and under parts, white.

Nest and Eggs.— Nest: Placed in low bushes, scrub oaks, dense chaparral, usually low, sometimes in trees 30 feet up; a bulky structure, exteriorly made of interwoven twigs, grass, and moss, containing an inner lining of fine rootlets and horse-hair. Eggs: 3 to 6, usually 4, dark green or buffy of varying shades, thickly spotted and blotched with burnt umber, chestnut, sepia, or lavender.

Distribution.— Pacific coast district of United States (north of San Fernando, San Gabriel, and San Bernardino mountains), north to southwestern Washington, east to, and including, eastern slope of Sierra Nevada and Cascade ranges.

The Jays are one branch of the *Corvidæ* or Crow family, but, in contrast to the Crows, the Jays are of bright and varied colors, generally blue, and often the head is crested. The Jay is a well-known character everywhere, but has a shady reputation.

The California Jay is very different from the deep blue, long-crested Steller Jay, but resembles more the Blue Jay of the East. The general color pattern of the dress is somewhat the same, but it lacks the crest.

A small flock of Jays are a noisy pack in the autumn. They squawk through the woods as if they want everybody to know just where they are, but in the spring after they have paired and are nesting they suddenly go speechless, as if they can't trust themselves to talk out loud. And indeed, they can't when anywhere about the nest. They talk in whispers and flit as silently as shadows through the trees.

While it is so often reported that the Jay goes through the woods stealing eggs and wrecking the homes of other birds, yet I have often questioned whether there are not some good Jays that should not be called thieves. Perhaps there are robber barons among birds, as among men.

In one case where we had a good chance to study the home life of a pair of California Jays, I could find no evidence of their nest robbing. If they robbed other birds, they did it on the quiet some distance from their own home, for in their thicket not many yards away, I found a Robin's nest with eggs and the nest of a Thrush with young birds. The Jays evidently wanted to stand well with their neighbors and live in peace. WILLIAM L. FINLEY.

In southern California two local forms of this Jay are found. Belding's Jay (*Aphelocoma californica obscura*) is smaller and darker than the type species. Its back is a deep brownish mouse-gray with the blue parts a deeper hue; the under parts are decidedly gray in the front, only the lower abdomen and anal region being distinctly white. Xantus's Jay (*Aphelocoma californica hypoleuca*) is smaller, also, but it is much paler; the blue portions of its plumage are a lighter and clearer azure and the under parts are usually whiter or not so much tinged with brownish-gray.

The Island of Santa Cruz, California, has a species all to itself. The Santa Cruz Jay (*Aphelocoma insularis*) is like the Belding's Jay in color but is larger even than the California Jay.

Though Mr. Finley gives the California Jay a good character, others say it excels its eastern cousin the Blue Jay in its bad habits of nest-robbing, and that besides robbing the nests of other wild birds it will even rob hen's nests of their eggs. A woman who lived at the mouth of a small ravine told Mr. F. E. L. Beal of the United States Biological Survey that one of her hens had a nest under a clump of bushes. Every day a Jay came to a tree a few rods away. When it heard the cackle of the hen announcing a new egg, it flew at once to the nest. At the same time the woman hastened to the spot but in most cases the Jay reached there first. This Jay will also attack a young chick and with a few blows of the beak kill it; he then pecks open the skull and eats the brains. Another sin of the California

Photo by W. L. Finley and H. T. Bohlman

YOUNG CALIFORNIA JAY AT NEST

Jay is fruit-stealing. Cherries, apricots, and prunes are the favorites. Analysis showed that while the fruit eaten was only 16 per cent. of the food for the year, it was 44 per cent. of the food in June, 33 in July, 53 in August, and 25 in September. Five per cent. of the food for the year consists of grasshoppers; 4 per cent. wasps and bees; 23 per cent. beetles, bugs, flies, and caterpillars; 6 per cent. grain, of which the major part was oats; and about 42 per cent. acorns, chestnuts, beechnuts, and the like, eaten from September to March, inclusive.

ARIZONA JAY

Aphelocoma sieberi arizonæ (*Ridgway*)

A. O. U. Number 482

General Description.— Length, 12½ inches. Head and tail, blue; body, gray. Wings, longer than tail; head, not crested.

Color.—Above, including sides of head and neck, light dull cerulean-blue; back and shoulders, usually distinctly gray (deep ash-gray to bluish-gray, rarely grayish-blue); chin and upper throat, very pale dull bluish-gray or grayish-white, this grayish-white deepening gradually into smoke-gray on chest, breast, and sides, and this fading into paler gray on flanks and abdomen; the lower portion of the abdomen, the anal region, and under tail-coverts, white.

Nest and Eggs.— Nest: Located in oaks from 12 to 30 feet up; a flat saucer-shaped, flimsy structure, of small sticks and twigs, evenly laid in circles, supporting a woven interior of rootlets, usually unlined otherwise. Eggs: 3 to 7, plain robin-blue.

Distribution.— Southern Arizona, southwestern New Mexico, and northern parts of Sonora and Chihuahua.

"Noisy, fussy, and quarrelsome as all Jays are, I know of no other species which possesses to such an eminent degree the quality of prying into all manner of things which do not concern it, and of making such a nuisance of itself in general, on the slightest provocation or on none at all, as the Arizona Jay does," is the amiable and inviting character given this bird by a western observer, Harry S. Swarth. Like the eastern Jay, this species takes particular delight in badgering a Hawk of any kind. Such a bird, whether it happens to be a Cooper, which is a real and dangerous enemy of all small birds, or a Red-tailed or a Red-shouldered, which are comparatively harmless in the feathered world, a flock of these Jays will follow a long way (if their victim be moving by short flights through the woods), staying at a safe distance, but keeping up an incessant chorus of abuse, threats, and imprecations.

A fox discovered sunning himself on a bowlder or a log, is cordially mobbed as long as the Jays can keep him in sight, and they will follow and curse even a rattlesnake, often lighting near it on the ground and strutting in a ludicrous manner, with the head and body held stiffly upright and about a third of the tail dragging.

This Jay seems to be naturally a very timid bird, but its curiosity is usually greater than its caution, for it may often be attracted to close quarters by a hissing or squeaking noise, if the cause of it remains hidden. Another peculiarity which will often aid in identifying the bird, even when it is not seen, is the singular fluttering sound made by its wings when it is in flight.

The bulk of the food taken by the Arizona Jay is acorns, but wild fruit and seeds, grasshoppers and other insects are also consumed in fair amounts.

GREEN JAY

Xanthoura luxuosa glaucescens (*Ridgway*)

A. O. U. Number 483

Other Name.— Rio Grande Green Jay.

General Description.— Length, 11 inches. Upper parts, blue-green; under parts, pale green. Wing, short and rounded; head, not crested.

Color.— Nasal tufts, broad cheek patch (extending up to and involving posterior half of lower eyelid), crown, back of head, and hindneck, blue; forehead white, or yellowish white; chin, throat, chest, ear region, black; back, shoulders, rump, upper tail-coverts and wings plain yellowish-green or sage-green, usually glossed (often extensively) with blue; the wings rump, and upper tail-coverts, rather lighter or brighter than back; four middle tail-feathers duller or darker green, becoming more bluish-green terminally; four lateral tail-feathers pale yellow; under parts, posterior to chest, including under tail-coverts, pale green often

HAWK OWL *Surnia ulula caparoch* (Müller)
SAW-WHET OWL
Cryptoglaux acadica acadica (Gmelin)
RICHARDSON'S OWL
Cryptoglaux funerea richardsoni (Bonaparte)
All ½ nat. size

Courtesy of the New York State Museum

SCREECH OWL *Otus asio asio* (Linnaeus)
Gray and red phases

SHORT-EARED OWL *Asio flammeus* (Pontoppidan)
All ¼ nat size

GREAT HORNED OWL *Bubo virginianus virginianus* (Gmelin)
⅔ nat. size

BELTED KINGFISHER *Ceryte alcyon* (Linnaeus)

MALE FEMALE

BLACK-BILLED CUCKOO *Coccyzus erythrophthalmus* (Wilson)

YELLOW-BILLED CUCKOO *Coccyzus americanus americanus* (Linnaeus)

All ½ nat. size

HAIRY WOODPECKER
Dryobates villosus villosus (Linnaeus)
MALE FEMALE

DOWNY WOODPECKER
Dryobates pubescens medianus (Swainson)
FEMALE MALE

All ¾ nat. size

ARCTIC THREE-TOED WOODPECKER *Picoides arcticus* (Swainson)
FEMALE
MALE
⅓ nat. size

Courtesy of the New York State Museum

AMERICAN THREE-TOED WOODPECKER *Picoides americanus americanus* Brehm
MALE FEMALE
⅞ nat. size

RED-HEADED WOODPECKER
Melanerpes erythrocephalus (Linnaeus)
ADULT
IMMATURE

All ½ nat. size

YELLOW-BELLIED SAPSUCKER
Sphyrapicus varius varius (Linnaeus)
FEMALE
MALE

NORTHERN PILEATED WOODPECKER *Phloeotomus pileatus abieticola* (Bangs)
MALE FEMALE
About ½ nat. size

NORTHERN FLICKER *Colaptes auratus luteus* Bangs
FEMALE MALE
RED-BELLIED WOODPECKER *Centurus carolinus* (Linnaeus)
FEMALE MALE
½ nat. size

NIGHTHAWK *Chordeiles virginianus virginianus* (Gmelin)
MALE ½ nat. size
WHIP-POOR-WILL *Antrostomus vociferus vociferus* (Wilson)
MALE ½ nat. size

RUBY-THROATED HUMMINGBIRD *Archilochus colubris* (Linnaeus)

MALE FEMALE MALE

All life size

OLIVE-SIDED FLYCATCHER
Nuttallornis borealis (Swainson)

KINGBIRD *Tyrannus tyrannus* (Linnaeus)

All ½ nat. size

CRESTED FLYCATCHER
Myiarchus crinitus (Linnaeus)

PHOEBE *Savornis phoebe* (Latham)

WOOD PEWEE *Myiochanes virens* (Linnaeus)
ADULT IMMATURE

ALDER FLYCATCHER
Empidonax traillii alnorum Brewster

ACADIAN FLYCATCHER
Empidonax virescens (Vieillot)

LEAST FLYCATCHER *Empidonax minimus* (W. M. & S. F. Baird)

YELLOW-BELLIED FLYCATCHER
Empidonax flaviventris (W. M. & S. F. Baird)

All ⅔ nat. size

Courtesy of the New York State Museum

SKYLARK
Alauda arvensis Linnaeus

PIPIT *Anthus rubescens* (Tunstall)
SPRING AUTUMN

All ½ nat. size

HORNED LARK *Otocoris alpestris alpestris* (Linnaeus)
MALE

PRAIRIE HORNED LARK *Otocoris alpestris praticola* Henshaw
MALE FEMALE IMMATURE

All ½ nat. size

BLUE JAY *Cyanocitta cristata cristata* (Linnaeus)
⅔ nat. size

glossed with pale blue; the lower portion of the abdomen and anal region pale yellow.

Nest and Eggs.—NEST: Well hidden in dense thickets; constructed of thorny twigs, and thinly lined with grass, moss, rootlets, and hair. EGGS: 4 to 7, grayish, greenish or buffy white, spotted with brown and lavender thickly around large end.

Distribution.— Lower Rio Grande valley, in southern Texas and northern Tamaulipas and Nuevo Leon, from the coast as far up the valley as Laredo, Texas.

This handsome Jay occurs chiefly in southeastern Texas, and is essentially a bird of Mexico rather than of the United States. It reveals many of the characteristics of its family, including inquisitiveness and pugnacity, and that it has a strong liking for flesh is shown by its practice of lurking near houses and feeding on refuse containing meat. It seems probable, therefore, that it may have the nest-robbing habits which characterize some of its relatives.

CANADA JAY

Perisoreus canadensis canadensis (*Linnæus*)

A. O. U. Number 484 See Color Plate 71

Other Names.— Whiskey Jack; Camp Robber; Whiskey John; Moose-bird; Meat Hawk; Carrion Bird; Grease Bird; Meat Bird; Venison Bird.

General Description.— Length, 11½ inches. Plumage, gray, dark above and light below. Wing, short and rounded; head, not crested.

Color.— ADULT: *Forehead* (including nasal tufts), fore part of *crown,* sides of head, chin, throat, and chest, *white; back, shoulders, lesser wing-coverts, rump, and upper tail-coverts, plain mouse-gray;* wings and tail slate-gray, the primaries slightly more bluish; middle and greater wing-coverts sometimes tipped with white; under parts of body, plain drab-gray, paler (almost, sometimes quite, white) on anal region and under tail-coverts; iris, brown. YOUNG: Above, including crown and hindneck, slate color or brownish-slate; under parts, including chin, throat, and chest, plain brownish slate-gray.

Nest and Eggs.— NEST: Placed in a conifer alongside the trunk; a bulky, high-walled structure of twigs, pine-needles, bark-strips, grasses, and, as the eggs are laid in March or April when the mercury frequently registers 30° below zero, very warmly lined with feathers and down. EGGS: 3 to 5, pearl-gray, heavily speckled with brown and lavender.

Distribution.— From northern limit of coniferous forests south to Nova Scotia, New Brunswick, northern Maine, higher mountains of New Hampshire, Vermont, and northern New York (Adirondacks), northern Ontario, northern Michigan, and northern Minnesota — irregularly, casually, or during winter to Massachusetts, vicinity of New York City, Pennsylvania, southern Ontario, southern Michigan, southeastern Wisconsin, and South Dakota; west to Alberta; north to lower Anderson and Mackenzie rivers, and west side of Hudson Bay.

Drawing by R. I. Brasher

CANADA JAY (⅓ nat. size)

"Whiskey Jack" always looks and acts fuddled, especially when he is planning to steal something

To those who know his habits, "Whiskey Jack" seems about as undesirable a citizen of bird-land as his noisy American cousin, the Blue Jay. Which is to say, he is a nest-robber, and in this rôle is immensely unpopular with his feathered kind, as well as with their human friends. In appearance, however, he bears little resemblance to the American dandy, for there are only black, white, and gray, no bright blue, in his plumage, which furthermore presents an unkempt appearance, so that withal "Jack" looks a good deal like an exaggerated and much disheveled Chicadee. Also "Jack" has a distinctly uncanny air about him as he sits on a branch and regards you vacantly with his beady, black eyes, or flits noiselessly around your camp. But don't make the mistake of supposing that he is really preoccupied or absent-minded, much less timid, for actually he is about the cheekiest thing that wears feathers. All the time, probably, he has his eye on the bacon or the potatoes, which he will not hesitate to steal from under your very nose if he sees the opportunity. Hence his well-deserved name, "Camp Robber." But the man who doesn't enjoy being robbed by such a thief, had better stay at home and sit in the parlor.

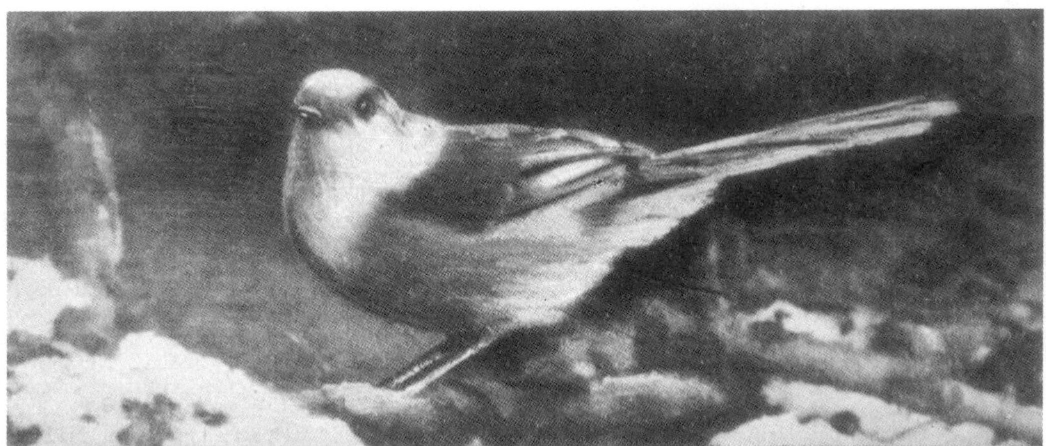

Courtesy of *Field and Stream*

CANADA JAY

He is aoout the cheekiest thing that wears feathers

As a vocalist, "Jack" is considerably more versatile, though no more musical, than the Blue Jay. When he feels so disposed, he can produce an astonishing medley of "chucks," whistles, squalls, squawks, and screams. He doesn't seem to swear as much as the Blue Jay does, but he has been known to provoke profanity from more than one still-hunter, whose presence and purpose he is particularly fond of announcing and then ridiculing for the information and amusement of all the woods-folk within a radius of half a mile.

GEORGE GLADDEN.

There are three variant forms of the Canada Jay. In the West, in the Rocky Mountain region, from central British Columbia, southern Alberta, and southwestern South Dakota south to Arizona and Nebraska, is the White-headed or Rocky Mountain Jay (*Perisoreus canadensis capitalis*). He is larger and lighter colored than the Canada Jay; the whole of his head is white, except the space just around and behind the eyes, which, together with the hindneck, is slate-grayish. In the wooded parts of Alaska and the adjacent part of Canada we find the Alaska Jay (*Perisoreus canadensis fumifrons*). He is a Canada Jay who has put on a dusky hood over his crown leaving only his forehead white. The third variety is found in the eastern part of British America and is named the Labrador Jay (*Perisoreus canadensis nigricapillus*). He is smaller

Photo by H. E. Anthony

OREGON JAY

than the head of his family and decidedly darker in coloration.

The Oregon Jay (*Perisoreus obscurus obscurus* and his variant form, the Gray Jay (*Perisoreus obscurus griseus*), look like Canada Jays, with the wrong color of plumage. The Oregon Jay has brown upper parts and dull white under parts and the Gray Jay has deep mouse-gray upper parts and grayish-white under parts. The Oregon Jay lives in the Pacific coast district from southwestern British Columbia to northern California. The Gray Jay is found in the interior districts of northern California north through central Oregon and Washington to British Columbia. Both are familiarly known as "Camp Robbers."

RAVEN

Corvus corax sinuatus *Wagler*

A. O. U. Number 486 See Color Plate 71

Other Name.— Mexican Raven.

General Description.— Length, 26½ inches. Plumage, black. Wing, long and pointed; tail, much shorter than wing; bill, compressed, and higher than broad; feet, stout.

Color.— Entire plumage, deep glossy black; the wing-coverts, secondaries, innermost primaries and tail, glossed with violet; primary-coverts and longer and outermost primaries, glossed with bluish or greenish; under parts glossed with blue or greenish-blue; iris, deep brown.

Nest and Eggs.— Nest: Located almost invariably on a ledge of inaccessible cliffs; constructed of large sticks well interlaced, the interior well lined with coarse grass, bark strips, wool, and, in maritime sites, with seaweed; the birds are strongly attached to the site, returning year after year. Eggs: 5 to 7, green, olive, drab, profusely spotted and blotched with browns, olive, and lavender.

Distribution.— Oregon, Montana, and South Dakota, south to Honduras and east probably to Missouri, Illinois, and Indiana.

At a distance the Raven looks much like a large Crow, but a closer inspection will reveal certain marked differences. It is decidedly a larger bird and its deep, harsh notes once heard can never be mistaken for the *caw* of the Crow. Ravens breed much in the deep forests of the northwest. On the sagebrush deserts of eastern Oregon their nests are placed among the cliffs of the "rim rocks." Though not distinctly gregarious, in the breeding season certain favorite

Drawing by R. I. Brasher

RAVEN (⅓ nat. size)

A larger brother to the Crow

localities are often used by from two to half a dozen pairs, and the same birds will resort to these places for many years. In the desert regions they eat dead jack rabbits and such other flesh, either fresh or putrid, as may be discovered.

One may see Ravens any summer about the garbage piles back of some of the hotels in the Yellowstone and Glacier national parks. Here they come to share with the bears the refuse from the hotel kitchens. They possess an astonishing variety of coarse cries, grunts, and screams which one may enjoy if in the neighborhood of a pair that are attending to the wants of their offspring. The Raven is found generally throughout Canada and the States of the Northwest.

A closely allied species is the Northern Raven *Corvus corax principalis* which also inhabits Canada but comes down into eastern United States, breeding as far south as the southern Alleghenies. In the North Carolina mountains they are common residents in some sections. Here they come regularly to rural slaughter pens in quest of food. Among the evergreen-covered islands off the coast of Maine I have found several of their nests. These are all built in trees and never more than one pair of Ravens breed on any one island. Farther north in Newfoundland and along the Labrador coast they seem to prefer cliffs overlooking the sea as places in which to establish their eyries.

T. Gilbert Pearson.

Probably the food of the Raven is almost as varied as that of the Crow, yet it is not known to attack cultivated crops of any kind, and the belief that it is destructive to young birds, eggs, and game is rather an inference than the result of observation. Its scarcity precludes the possibility of its doing serious injury of this kind anywhere. There is a strong possibility that it frequents the nesting places of the Gulls and Terns and does some mischief by robbing nests.

WHITE-NECKED RAVEN

Corvus cryptoleucus *Couch*

A. O. U. Number 487

General Description.— Length, 20 inches. Prevailing color, black. Wing, long and pointed; tail, much shorter than wing; bill, compressed, higher than broad; feet, stout.

Color.— Plumage, glossy black, the upper parts (except hindneck) with a violet sheen, the under parts faintly glossed with bluish; *feathers of neck, lower throat, chest, and breast with basal half or more (concealed) pure white;* iris, brown.

Nest and Eggs.—Nest: Located in trees or bushes, usually at no great height from the ground: constructed of sticks, twigs, and grass. Eggs: 4 to 7, pale bluish-green spotted with brown and profusely streaked with zig-zag lines of olive-gray.

Distribution.— Great Plains, from southeastern Wyoming and western Nebraska, southward to central Mexico; westward through New Mexico and Arizona to coast of southern California.

This is a bird of the hot southwestern deserts and valleys where it is commonly called a "Crow," presumably because some of its habits are Crow-like. Certainly it bears little outward resemblance to the almost universally known bird of that name, though it is indeed a member of the same great family.

Where these interesting birds have not been molested, they are usually quite tame and friendly. Under these conditions they pay little heed to the approach of a wagon or a man on horseback; and they often come about the schoolhouses to pick up the remains of the children's luncheons; but after being shot at they become very timid and suspicious. Even in this mood, however, they are often easily attracted within shot by almost any kind of decoy which will appeal to their characteristic Crow curiosity. One collector got all the specimens he needed by tossing into the air a red bandana handkerchief tied around a stone, the result being that he was almost mobbed by the Ravens though he was standing in plain sight.

In winter these Ravens show another family characteristic by gathering into flocks; and they are often seen in groups on the mesas, even during the breeding period. Again, during the cold weather, they often gather about stockyards to feed, and even invade the cities where they do much valuable work as scavengers. Here the bird's natural intelligence is shown by the fact that it soon becomes tame to the point of boldness, which is plain evidence that it is quick to realize that in these surroundings it will not be molested by the very creatures whom it quickly learns to fear in its natural habitat.

The White-necked Raven feeds principally on animal matter, including locusts. Refuse grain also plays an important part in its diet. Its nest resembles that of the common Crow.

CROW

Corvus brachyrhynchos brachyrhynchos *Brehm*

A. O. U. Number 488 See Color Plate 72

Other Names.— American Crow; Common Crow; Carrion Crow.

General Description.— Length, 19¾ inches. Plumage, black. Wing, long and pointed; tail, much shorter than wing; bill, compressed, and higher than broad; feet, stout.

Color.— Adults: Entire plumage, deep black; the back, shoulders, rump, upper tail-coverts, wing-coverts, and secondaries, with a gloss of metallic-violet; the primary coverts, primaries. and outermost tail-feathers glossed with greenish-blue; the middle tail-feathers glossed with duller or more bluish-violet than the back, etc.; under parts slightly glossed with bluish-violet; iris, brown. Immature (in first winter): Similar to adults, but the violet and bluish-green gloss of upper parts less distinct, especially on wings and tail; under parts, duller black. Young: Head, neck, and body, dull sooty or grayish-black, the black slightly glossed with violet; wings and tail as in adults, but less strongly glossed with violet.

Nest and Eggs.— Nest: Usually at good height in conifers or other trees, sometimes 75 feet from ground; a well-made, but coarse, structure of sticks, twigs, grasses, tree bark, very often thickly and evenly lined with the soft inner bark of chestnut, basswood, or other dead trees, giving the interior a warm, yellowish-brown color; fine roots, straw, wool, or hair are also used for linings. Eggs: 4 to 8, from pale bluish-green to olive-green or greenish-buff, irregularly spotted and blotched with brown and olive-gray.

Distribution.— Temperate eastern North America, except peninsula of Florida; north on Atlantic coast to Newfoundland and Magdalen Islands (southern Labrador?), on west side of Hudson Bay to Nelson River, and in the interior nearly to the Arctic coast; west to the beginning of the arid region.

Courtesy of Am. Mus. Nat. Hist.

CROW (½ nat. size)

One of the best known of American birds

Probably a very large percentage of Americans would vote for the Crow, in any contest intended to decide which is the best known bird in America. And probably a large percentage of the persons so voting would mistake a Fish Crow for a Common Crow. For if any such should be observing enough to notice the difference in size between the two birds, he would be likely to account for that disparity by concluding that the Fish Crow was a "small" Crow. However, it is apparent that the Crow is one of the best known of our birds. And to the average farmer, he is likely to be one of the least favorably known.

Photo by Rollin F. Cass Courtesy of Outing Pub. Co.

YOUNG CROWS

The Crow unquestionably is a remarkably clever bird. This is clearly demonstrated in many ways by his conduct in his natural state, and has been borne out in the cases of many hundreds of tamed Crows, who have furnished endless amusement for their owners. Apparently such birds always display a thieving propensity, amounting to what would be considered kleptomania in human beings. They seem to have an especial passion for stealing and hiding any object of a bright color, like a spool of red or blue thread; or any highly polished metal article, like scissors or thimbles. It is an interesting fact that other members of the same family (notably the Magpies and the Jays) evince plainly the same characteristic.

Farmers who try to keep the Crows away from their newly planted corn see plenty of proof of their astuteness. It seems clear that such marauders are sometimes guarded by a sentinel, who gives ample warning of the approach of danger. Other birds, as well as various mammals (for example, the American and certain African antelopes), apparently take similar precautions; but always such an act, if it is intentional, must denote a very high degree of intelligence. Yet we must beware of stultifying ourselves as observers of animal life of any kind, by recording "observations" like the following, which Mr. Burroughs quotes:

"A man sees a flock of Crows in a tree in a state of commotion; now they all caw, then only one master voice is heard; presently two or three Crows fall upon one of their number and fell him to the ground. The spectator examines the victim and finds him dead, with his eyes pecked out. He interprets what he has seen as a court of justice; the Crows were trying a criminal, and having found him guilty, they proceed to execute him. The curious instinct which often prompts animals to fall upon and destroy a member of the flock that is sick or hurt, or blind, is difficult of explanation, but we may be quite sure that, whatever the reason is, the act is not the outcome of a judicial proceeding in which judge, jury, and executioner all play their proper part."

Portia probably wasn't aware, when she said to Nerissa

> The Crow doth sing as sweetly as the lark
> When neither is attended,

that she was stating — with some exaggeration, of course — a fact in American ornithology. Indeed, probably few Americans know that the Crow can sing at all. Yet it is a fact that the bird has a musical little warble which he utters when he thinks he is not "attended."

In a dense forest in Michigan, an observer managed to skulk through the underbrush to within about twenty-five yards of the base of a group of tall spruce trees, in the topmost branches of which a little party of Crows warbled at intervals of a minute or two, for ten or fifteen minutes. That more than one singer was involved seemed certain, but the listener could not determine how many, because the Crows were only dimly discernible through the thick foliage. But it was evident that this was the Crow's "song"; and that the birds did not know they were "attended" was made apparent by the tremendous outcry of protest and abuse which they raised when one of them discovered the audience.

Of the Crow's characteristic note, we have a poetic and eloquent appreciation from James Russell Lowell, when he says: "Yet there are few things more melodious than his caw of a clear winter morning as it drops to you filtered through five hundred fathoms of crisp blue air."

George Gladden.

The Crow is commonly regarded as a blackleg and a thief. Without the dash and brilliancy of the Jay, or the bold savagery of the Hawk, he is accused of doing more mischief than either. That he does pull up sprouting corn, destroy chickens, and rob the nests of small birds has been repeatedly proved. Nor are these all of his sins. He is known to eat frogs, toads, salamanders, and some small snakes, all harmless creatures that do some good by eating insects. With so many charges against him, it may be well to show why he should not be utterly condemned.

The examination of a large number of stomachs shows that the nest-robbing habit, as in the case of the Jay, is not so universal as has been supposed. Neither are many toads and frogs eaten. As frogs are of no practical value, their destruction is not a serious matter; but toads are very useful, and their consumption, so far as it goes, must be counted against the crow. Turtles, crawfishes, and snails, of which he eats quite a large number, may be considered neutral, while mice may be counted to his credit.

In his insect food, however, the Crow makes amends for sins in the rest of his dietary, although even here the first item is against him. Predacious beetles are eaten in some numbers throughout the season, but the number is not great. May beetles, June bugs, and others of the same family constitute the principal food during spring and early summer, and are fed to the young in immense quantities. Other beetles, nearly all of a noxious character, are eaten to a considerable extent. The Crow is no exception to the general rule that most birds subsist, to a large extent, upon grasshoppers in the month of August. Many bugs, some caterpillars, mostly cutworms, and some spiders are also eaten — all of them either harmful or neutral. Probably the most important item in the vegetable food of the Crow is corn. By pulling up the newly sprouted seeds, the bird renders himself extremely obnoxious. Observation and experiments with tame Crows show that hard, dry corn is never eaten if anything else is to be had, and that if fed to nestlings it is soon disgorged. The reason Crows resort to newly planted fields is that the kernels of corn are softened by the moisture of the earth, and probably become more palatable in the process of germination, which changes the starch of the grain to sugar. Crows eat corn extensively only when it has been softened by germination or partial decay, or before it is ripe and still " in the milk." Experience has shown that they may be prevented from pulling up young corn by tarring the seed, which not only saves the corn but forces them to turn their attention to insects. If they persist in eating green corn it is not so easy to prevent the damage.

Crows eat fruit to some extent, but confine themselves for the most part to wild species, such as dogwood, sour gum, and seeds of the different kinds of sumac. They have also a habit of sampling almost everything which appears eatable, especially when food is scarce.

In estimating the usefulness of the Crow, the bird should receive much credit for the insects which it destroys. In the more thickly settled parts of the country it probably does more good than harm, at least when ordinary precautions are taken to protect young poultry and newly planted corn against its depredations.

Photo by H. K. Job Courtesy of Outing Pub. Co.

YOUNG CROWS IN NEST

Five red flannel mouths stretched agape

F. E. L. Beal.

Two smaller forms of the Common Crow are found in North America. The Florida Crow (*Corvus brachyrhynchos pascuus*) is confined to the peninsula of Florida. The Western Crow (*Corvus brachyrhynchos hesperis*) ranges through western North American from east-central British Columbia and Montana south to southern California, Arizona, and western Texas.

The Northwestern Crow (*Crow caurinus*) is found all along the northwest coast of North America from northwestern Washington to the Alaskan peninsula. It is even smaller than the Florida and Western Crows, but it so much like them that Ridgway considered it only another form of the Common Crow.

FISH CROW

Corvus ossifragus *Wilson*

A. O. U. Number 490 See Color Plate 72

General Description.— Length, 13¾ inches. Plumage, black. Wings, long and pointed; tail, much shorter than wing; bill compressed, and higher than broad; feet, stout.

Color.— Entire plumage, glossy black; the upper parts, glossed with bluish-violet (more purplish-violet on lesser wing-coverts and secondaries), the under parts, glossed with bluish-green or greenish-blue; iris, brown.

Nest and Eggs.— Nest: In maritime cedars, about 20 feet up; a platform of sticks with sides of bark, twigs, and grasses, lined with grapevine or other bark, grass, and a few leaves. Eggs: 4 to 6, smaller than, but otherwise exactly similar to, those of the Common Crow.

Distribution.— Atlantic and Gulf coast districts of United States, including peninsula of Florida; north to lower Hudson valley and shores of Long Island Sound (breeding in eastern Connecticut near Rhode Island border), casually to Massachusetts; west along the Gulf coast to Louisiana; not restricted to the immediate coast, but extending back to base of Blue Ridge Mountains (at least in summer), and abundant about lakes and streams in interior of Florida.

The Fish Crow is far more common along the coast and about rivers and lakes than in the fields and wooded uplands. It feeds largely on such forms of animal life as die and float ashore. It is also a great egg-eater. In the south the Heron and Ibis rookeries are constantly robbed by them. As an example of their destructiveness to birds' eggs, there may be mentioned the colony of twenty pairs of Little Blue Herons on Big Lake, North Carolina, from which every egg was taken by Fish Crows while a company of naturalists were photographing in the neighborhood. The Herons left their nests upon the approach of the men but the Fish Crows came boldly upon the scene and inside of an hour had completely plundered every nest.

This bird may be distinguished from the Common Crow by its smaller size and by the richer color of its black plumage. Those who know Crows well can easily tell them apart by their notes. The common variety has a loud clear *caw,* while the Fish Crow possesses a voice with a cracked and high-pitched nasal quality. They are found in eastern United States chiefly along the Atlantic seaboard, or in the Hudson River valley, and in the neighborhood of the Gulf of Mexico. The nest is very compactly built, and in Florida often contains much " Spanish moss." It is placed in tall trees, and in the south pine trees are almost exclusively selected for the purpose.

T. Gilbert Pearson.

The Fish Crow, flying above a school of fish, will suddenly dash down from a considerable height and unerringly seize its prey. Small fish are immediately swallowed, but larger ones are carried to a tree or some other convenient place and torn to pieces. This bird treads for clams just as human beings do, and then dislodges them with its beak, breaks the shell by the same means, and tears out the clams with the aid of its claws. The stomach contents of a number of specimens which were examined showed traces of insects (mostly grasshoppers), carrion, grain, and berries.

Photo by H. K. Job Courtesy of Houghton Mifflin Co.

FISH CROW

Over Florida rookery, bent on nest-robbing

CLARKE'S NUTCRACKER

Nucifraga columbiana (*Wilson*)

A. O. U. Number 491

Other Names.— Clarke's Crow; Meat Bird; Camp Robber.

General Description.— Length, 12½ inches. Body, gray; wings, black. Wings, long and pointed, and, when folded, reaching to the end of tail; tail, a little over one-half length of wing; bill, cylindrical.

Color.— Nasal tufts, front portion of forehead, eyelids, forward portion of cheek region, and chin, white, usually soiled or tinged with dirty yellowish; rest of head, neck, back, shoulders, and under parts (except chin and under tail-coverts), plain smoke-gray or drab-gray, the head somewhat paler than other portions; rump, darker gray than back, deepening into grayish-black on upper tail-coverts; under tail-coverts, pure white; wings and two middle tail-feathers, black, glossed with purplish-blue or violet, especially on wing-coverts and secondaries, the latter very broadly tipped with white; four outermost pairs of tail-feathers white, the fifth pair with outer web mostly white and inner web mostly black; iris, brown.

Nest and Eggs.—Nest: Usually in pines on horizontal branches from 8 to 40 feet up; a large bulky affair; the base of coarse sticks, twigs of white sage, on which is built the true nest of dried grasses, plant-fiber, moss and fine strips of juniper bark, all deftly interwoven into a snug home. Eggs: 3 to 5, finely and minutely specked with brown and pale purple, uniformly marked or wreathed at large end.

Distribution.— Coniferous forests of western North America, from high mountains of New Mexico, Arizona; and northern Lower California to northwestern Alaska; casual in southeastern South Dakota, Nebraska, western Kansas, western Missouri, and Arkansas.

The Clarke Crow or Nutcracker was first discovered by Captain William Clarke near the site of Salmon City in Idaho, August 22, 1805. While this bird is a Crow in actions, yet in dress he is very different. One might think Mother Nature had made him by using an ordinary Crow. She whitened his whole body, but did not finish with his wings and tail; these she left black except with a white patch on the lower part of the wings and the outer feathers of the tail. She made a striking character, typical of the high western mountainous country where the Alpine hemlocks and the jack pines live.

Whenever at Cloud Cap Inn, the log-house hotel which is fastened down with cables on the north slope of Mt. Hood, I like to spend all the

Drawing by R. I. Brasher

CLARKE'S NUTCRACKER (⅓ nat. size)

A conspicuous, noisy, good-natured mountaineer, who keeps you well informed as to his whereabouts and his opinions

time watching the Clarke Crows and Oregon Jays. These birds have learned to come about the hotel for their daily meals all during the summer, and, from the interest that people take in these birds and the squirrels, I sometimes think they are almost as big an attraction as the very mountain itself, for most people do really have a love for outdoor creatures that have changed their normal habits and have become so tame

Photo by W. L. Beatty Courtesy of *Field and Stream*

CLARKE'S NUTCRACKERS

Near Butte, Montana, at an altitude of 7,000 feet

through protection that they will eat from the hand. The scraps from the table are thrown over the cliff down below the Inn on the west side. Here is the best place to study Crows and Jays.

The Clarke Crow is very fond of meat, and for this reason he has often been called "meat bird." His taste for suet or for peanuts often leads the bird to become quite bold and even to take food from the hand. The Oregon Jays are even bolder than the Crows. They are both commonly known as "camp robbers."

In a recent trip through Yellowstone Park, I was surprised to find the Clarke Crow so much wilder than the Rocky Mountain Jay. On account of the protection they receive, many of the wild birds and animals have become so tame that they feed from the hand. While we fed the Jays in many places, I never saw a single Crow come down near the hotel. However, they perhaps do this at different times and places. It may have been that natural food was so abundant in the forests they did not care for the offerings of civilization. All during our trip, we saw them launching out from tree-tops, sometimes with a long swoop, opening their wings and letting themselves curve up before the next drop. Their continuous, harsh, rattling call that sounds like *Char-r! Char-r!* is a familiar and typical sound of the pine timber and rugged mountains. WILLIAM L. FINLEY.

The winter food of the Nutcracker is the seeds of conifers. These he obtains by landing on a branch bearing a cluster of cones; almost before he has gained his balance, he starts off again with an upward flip of his tail and a cone loosened by his foot rattles to the ground. The cone he then picks up in his bill and carries it to some place where he can knock off the scales and get at the seeds. In the spring, summer, and fall he feeds on berries, the seeds of the sundial (lupine), larvæ, butterflies, black crickets, beetles, and grasshoppers. Hulled pine seeds are fed to the nestlings.

PIÑON JAY

Cyanocephalus cyanocephalus (*Maximilian*)

A. O. U. Number 492

Other Names.— Blue Crow; Piñonero.

General Description.— Length, 11½ inches. Plumage, grayish-blue. Tail, almost square; much shorter than wing; head, not crested; bill cylindrical.

Color.— ADULT MALE: General color, uniform dull grayish-blue, paler on posterior under parts, deepening on crown, hindneck, and ear region into a much darker and more purplish-blue, the sides of the head, brighter blue (almost azure-blue); chin, throat, and center portion of chest, broadly streaked with grayish-white; anal region, very pale bluish-gray or grayish-white; iris, brown. ADULT FEMALE: Similar to the adult male, but averaging decidedly smaller and usually much duller in color. YOUNG: No blue on body.

Nest and Eggs.— NEST: Located usually in piñon pines or junipers, from 5 to 12 feet up; a large, bulky, but compact structure, made of sagebrush twigs, weeds, grass, and stems, lined with gray fibrous bark, which is broken by the movements of the bird on the nest into small fibers, forming a felt-like lining. EGGS: 3 to 5, bluish-white, thickly and evenly spotted over whole surface.

Distribution.— Piñon and juniper woods of western United States; north to southern British Columbia, Idaho, etc., south to northern Lower California, Arizona, New Mexico, and western Texas, east to eastern side of Rocky Mountains in winter to Nebraska, casually to eastern Kansas.

The Piñon Jay is a loosely clothed, fluffy bird that combines the form of a Crow with the color and habits of a Jay. It is a very sociable bird. One may often see large flocks of them in the pine timber of southern Oregon and out through the juniper and sagebrush country. They move along very much as Blackbirds do at times, going from tree to tree, or, if feeding along the ground, the rear birds will rise, flying along over the flock and lighting again in front of the main body. The bird perhaps belongs more to the nut-pine country further south. While nuts are a large part of their food, they are very fond of juniper berries and perhaps in search of a change of diet, they flock hither and thither over a large range.

The social nature of the Piñon Jay extends even through the breeding season, for often where one nest is found, others are found near in a sort of a colony. The first naturalist who found the nest and saw the young of the Piñon Jay was Mr. Robert Ridgway. He saw a colony of these birds nesting in the low range of piñon-covered hills in the vicinity of Carson City, Nevada, on April 21, 1868.

In his life history of the Piñon Jay, Captain Charles Bendire says: "Their call note is quite variable; some of them are almost as harsh as the *chaar* of the Clarke Nutcracker, others partake much of the gabble of the Magpie, and still others resemble more those of the Jays. A shrill, querulous *peeh, peeh,* or *whee, whee,* is their common call note. While feeding on the ground they keep up a constant chattering, which can be heard for quite a distance, and in this way often betray their whereabouts."

William L. Finley.

The nuts of the piñon pines are the natural food of these birds. Juniper berries, grain from stubble fields, and insects, the grasshopper in particular, also form part of their general diet.

STARLINGS

Order *Passeres;* suborder *Oscines;* family *Sturnidæ*

STARLINGS are an Old World family containing some one hundred and fifty species divided among forty genera. They are not found in Australia and New Guinea. One species was introduced into America in 1890. They have long, pointed wings and short, square, or slightly notched tails. Although the wing is long, its tip falls short of the tip of the tail. The bill is as long as the head, and blunt at the tip. The feathers of the head, neck, chest, and breast are narrow and long; those of the under parts are pointed also. The plumage of the adult birds is more or less metallic. They have but one molt a year. They are among the most adaptable of birds, and will nest in any convenient place — in the recesses of sea-caves, in the interior of old stone-walls, in the burrow of a Cliff Swallow, or, and this more often, about human habitations. Many pairs raise two broods in a season.

STARLING

Sturnus vulgaris *Linnæus*

A. O. U. Number 493 See Color Plate 74

General Description.— Length, 8 inches. A black bird with a yellow bill.

Color.— General color, *glossy black, the head and neck glossed with purple,* the wing-coverts with blue or violet, other parts with green, becoming bluish, or even sometimes violet, on rear under parts; feathers of back of head, hindneck, back, shoulders, and rump tipped with pale brown, producing *conspicuous triangular specks*; the lesser, middle, and greater wing-coverts, primary-coverts, wings, tail, and upper tail-coverts margined with the same; feathers of under parts of the body, tipped with white, forming narrow wedge-shaped spots, growing gradually larger toward the rear, the under tail-coverts broadly margined with brownish-white; primaries, inner quills, and tail with a central area of brownish-gray, bounded by a submarginal border of dull black; bill, *yellowish, dusky in winter*; iris, brown.

Nest and Eggs.— Nest: Placed in tree cavities, eaves of houses, church steeples, or any location that takes its fancy; made of twigs, grasses, leaves, paper, straw, and lined with fine grass. Eggs: 4 to 6, plain pale greenish or bluish-white.

Distribution.— Western and central Europe; accidental in Greenland; introduced into and partly naturalized in the eastern United States.

The Starling may be recognized at a distance by its general appearance and manner of flight. It is about the size of the Red-winged Blackbird, but has a very short tail. It is dark or dusky in color, and during the breeding season its bill is bright yellow. Those who see it for the first time usually describe it as a Blackbird with a yellow bill. In flight it flutters like a Meadowlark, but seldom sails as much as does the Lark.

In Europe, it is one of the most abundant birds. It is conceded there that the benefits it confers on the farmer far exceed the harm that it does by attacks on fruit or crops; nevertheless, there are many instances on record where the Starling has become a pest to the farmer. The habit of collecting in enormous flocks is the great element of danger. When a great number of any species having grain-eating or fruit-eating propensities is collected in one locality they are capable of doing great harm in a very short time. Such flights, however, are often productive of good.

The forest authorities in Bavaria, during an invasion of the spruce moth or "nun" in 1889-91, noted great flights of Starlings, which were credibly estimated to contain as many as ten thousand in a flock, all busy feeding on the caterpillars and pupæ of this moth. The attraction of Starlings to such centers was so great that market gardeners seriously felt their absence in distant parts of the region.

Miss Gertrude Whiting of New York City writes me that in Switzerland enormous flocks of Starlings come down like black clouds on the vineyards. In ten or fifteen minutes they pluck the fruit absolutely clean, and the cultivator is robbed of his year's crop. In the south of France Starlings are said to be similarly destructive to the olive crop. This indicates what would happen in America were the Starlings to become abnormally numerous.

It is of particular interest to learn what we can of the nature of the Starling in its own country in its relations to other birds. In Europe the Starling is known to eat the eggs and the newly hatched young of Sparrows, but this habit does not seem to have been generally noted. Mr. Clinton G. Abbott, who is very familiar with the bird in Europe, writes me that he considers its pugnacious nature to be by far the most serious objection to the Starling, and that no birds which nest in holes can have any peace at all until all the Starlings are satisfied.

As undesirable qualities are often accentuated when a bird is introduced into a new country, we cannot view the introduction of the Starling without some apprehension. When introduced into New Zealand it became a very destructive pest, and no one can tell what may be the result of its acclimatization here. Since the successful introduction of the Starling in America the Bureau of Biological Survey of the United States Department of Agriculture has been given authority to regulate the importation of foreign mammals and birds into this country, and in the future there is very little likelihood that the zeal of misguided persons who wish to import foreign species will have such results as followed the introduction of the House Sparrow.

Probably we shall never know how many attempts have been made to introduce the Starling into this country. I have learned of several. But the introductions undertaken by Mr. Eugene Scheifflin at Central Park, New York City, are credited as the first to be successful. The first of his importations numbered eighty birds, which were liberated on March 6, 1890, and forty more were released on April 25, 1891. Some of these birds remained in the park or its vicinity and bred there, but in 1891, twenty appeared on Staten Island, and in 1896 they had increased their numbers and had extended to Brooklyn. In 1898, according to Dr. T. S. Palmer of the Biological Survey, the species had obtained a strong foothold in the neighborhood of New York City; it had reached Stamford, Connecticut, and Plainfield, New Jersey. One hundred birds were liberated near Springfield, Massachusetts, in 1897, but Mr. Robert O. Morris of Springfield states his belief that they did not survive the following winter. It may be possible that they went south, but not one was reported from Springfield again until the year 1908. In the meantime the species had spread over the first forty miles of Long Island, up the Hudson River to Ossining and beyond, through much of eastern New Jersey and into Pennsylvania and Delaware.

When the brief period that has elapsed since the introduction of the Starling and the small number introduced are considered, it must be conceded that the increase and the dissemination of the species have been rapid. It has not increased or spread so rapidly as did the House Sparrow, but the Sparrow's numbers sprang not from one importation, but from many, that took place at widely scattered localities during a series of years, something that has been prevented in the case of the Starling. Its increase has been rapid in most of the region now occupied by it, where it is in many places second in numbers only to the Sparrow and the Robin.

Drawing by R. Bruce Horsfall

STARLING (¾ nat. size)

A naturalized American citizen of questionable character

The increase and spread of the Starling is due to its fecundity and its general fitness for the battle of life. It often has two broods in America, as it has in Europe. The Starling's physical fitness for the struggle for supremacy is seen at once on an examination of its anatomy. It is a very hardy, muscular, and powerful bird. It has the physical characteristics of a Crow. It is exceedingly tough and wiry, and the bill, its principal weapon of offense and defense, is superior in shape to that of the Crow. It is nearly straight, long and heavy, tapering, and nearly as keen as a meat ax, while the skull that backs it is almost as strong as that of a Woodpecker. Mentally the Starling is superior to the Sparrow, and, while brave and active in the face of any foe that it can master, it shows the acme of caution and intelligence in its relations with man or any other creature too powerful to master. While it is comparatively fearless where it is unmolested, it is always on guard, and if hunted becomes more wary than a Crow. It is a handsome bird, and though it has little merit as a songster, it has many pleasant whistling and chattering notes and some talent as a mimic. Its alarm note is a harsh, rasping low-pitched call.

Its insect-eating habits, its beauty, and its cheery notes have already made it many strong friends in this country who will protect it stoutly; and this protection, together with the bird's ability to take care of itself and keep out of danger, precludes all possibility of its extermination here if it proves undesirable.

Were rewards or bounties offered with a view to its extinction, Blackbirds, Meadowlarks, and other native species, which consort with the Starling, would be among the chief sufferers. The Starling is here to stay, and we must make the best of it. Whether its presence will result in more good than harm will depend largely on the ratio of its increase. We now know enough of its habits in this country to forecast some of the results that may be expected from an excess of the species.

When any animal is successfully introduced into a new country, and increases rapidly, its advent naturally tends to upset the biologic balance. Its native natural enemies have been left behind in its own country, where it had a settled and established place in a series of natural forces that had been in existence for centuries, and it becomes an interloper in the new land, among conditions and forms of life entirely new. If the species is weak or unfit for its new environment, or if it is introduced into a land differing much in climatic conditions from its own, it may die out; but if it is strong and fit, and if the climate is suitable, it is likely to increase abnormally in numbers, and it cannot so increase without displacing some of the species native to the soil.

The Starling is a hardy, capable, and prolific bird, which, like the Sparrow, has had many centuries of experience in getting its living in populated countries and in cultivated regions in close relationship with man, and it has thriven in such an environment. It thus has an advantage over our native species similar to that enjoyed by the Sparrow, which, subsequent to its introduction here, displaced so many native birds during the latter quarter of the nineteenth century. How can the Bluebird or the House Wren, which have been accustomed to life about human habitations for a comparatively short time, compete with such a bird as the Starling?

The friends of the Sparrow argued that it would fill a void in our city life that no native bird could possibly occupy, inasmuch as it would always have in the streets a plentiful supply of food that would otherwise be mainly wasted, and that it would be able to maintain itself where native birds would starve. No such argument can be advanced in favor of the Starling. If there was an opening for the Sparrow it was filled long ago, and the Starling cannot occupy the place in our urban life now filled by the Sparrow, even if it drives out the latter. No doubt in the city the Starling is preferable to the Sparrow, but it cannot displace the Sparrow without indirectly making trouble for native species also. The Sparrow and the Starling will live together, as in England, but the Starling will drive the Sparrow away from all nesting places that are suitable for its own use, and the Sparrow will in turn eject Tree Swallows, Martins, Blucbirds, Wrens, and other native birds from their present nesting places, that it may secure homes in place of those taken by the Starling. Already this adjustment is going on. First in the city, then in the suburbs, and finally in the country our native birds which normally nest in hollow trees will be driven to the wall if the Starling continues to increase in numbers, and there is now no adequate check to its increase in sight. In America as in Europe the Starling seeks nesting places about buildings. It breeds in dovecotes, such church steeples as furnish safe nesting places, in holes and crevices about houses, in niches under the eaves, in electric light hoods, bird houses, nesting boxes, Woodpecker holes, and hollow trees. Therefore, in seeking nesting places it comes directly in competition with Pigeons, Screech Owls, Sparrow Hawks, Flickers and other Woodpeckers, Nuthatches, Crested Flycatchers, Martins, Bluebirds, Tree Swallows and Wrens, and as it extends its range to the west and south it must compete with other species. In the region already occupied it has proved itself capable of driving out all the above-mentioned species except the Screech Owl, which doubtless will prove its master.

In America the Starling is not regarded as particularly pugnacious except where it has to fight for nesting places or for food. In such cases it is combativeness personified, and its attacks are well directed and long continued. Usually in its competition with the Sparrow there is no fighting; for the Sparrow soon learns that it is no match for the Starling, and the contest degenerates into a straw-pulling match, each bird alternately clearing out the nesting material that the other brings. If the owner of the nest joins battle with the Starling and fights stubbornly it is driven off, or it is sometimes killed in its nest. This daring interloper attacks birds much larger than itself, and the evidence shows that almost invariably it prevails in the end. The Sparrow, the Bluebird, and the Flicker have been credited with repelling it for a time, but eventually the Starling wins, because of its increasing numbers, superior strength, courage, and fitness. As the Starling comes, native birds, whose nesting places it covets, must go, and many of these birds are more desirable than the Starling. The skillful manner in which it evicts the Flicker inspires the observer with a certain admiration for its superior strategy and prowess. The Starlings quietly watch and never interfere while the Flicker digs and shapes its nesting place in some decaying tree; but when the nest is finished to the satisfaction of the Starlings it is occupied by them the moment the Flicker's back is turned. On the return of the Flicker a fight ensues, which usually results in the eviction of the particular Starling then in the hole, which, however, keeps up the fight outside while another enters the hole to defend it against the Flicker, which, having temporarily vanquished the first, returns only to find a second enjoying the advantages of possession. As Mr. Job says, the Flicker is confronted with " an endless chain of Starlings," and finally gives up.

In this or some other way the Starlings, working together, always succeed in driving the Flicker from its home, in which they immediately begin to build. The moment the Flicker gives up vanquished, the Starlings molest it no more, allowing it to hew out another hole, either in the same tree or in one near by, when a similar fight ensues with more Starlings; and so the Flicker is driven literally from pillar to post until it has prepared sufficient homes for the Starlings in its neighborhood and all are satisfied, or until it gives up in disgust and leaves the vicinity of its aggressive neighbors. The principal spring work of the Flicker in the future will be the preparation of nesting places for the Starling. It is probable that the Hairy Woodpecker and the Red-headed Woodpecker also will serve as *carpinteros* for the interloper, but the Downy Woodpecker will be exempt from such service, as the entrance to its domicile is too small to admit the Starling. There is no evidence that the Starling has attempted to dispossess the Screech Owl; but Mr. Clifford M. Case of Hartford, Connecticut, states that he has seen a Starling whip and drive away a male Sparrow Hawk. Many correspondents report that Flickers, Bluebirds, English Sparrows, and Wrens have been driven from their nesting places in old orchards by the Starlings.

The Starling will compete with native birds for their food supply. Mrs. P. R. Bonner of Stamford has observed the intruder frequently attacking Robins and other birds, and driving them away from a lawn where they formerly fed. The Starling is a sphinx-like bird and ordinarily treats other birds with a sort of contemptuous tolerance. In winter it even permits Robins, Blackbirds, and Meadowlarks to join its great flocks; but as these flocks increase they must eventually clean up most of the winter food supply, and leave our native winter birds without sufficient sustenance.

The food of the Starling in America seems to be similar in general character to that which it consumes in Europe. It is particularly useful, there, however, because of its fondness for the destructive land snails, which are very numerous in many regions. It cannot be expected that it will be thus beneficial here, for we are not similarly afflicted in this country. The Starling can give no service here that cannot be equally well performed by our own Blackbirds, Meadowlarks, Bobolinks, Sparrows, and other birds, but it will be useful where these birds are not numerous enough to keep the insect enemies of grass lands in check. Already, however, the Starling has begun to show a capacity for harmfulness which may be expected to become more prominent as its numbers increase. In the breeding season small flocks go to the cherry trees, and as they alight for a few minutes a shower of cherry stones may be heard. Sometimes they strip a tree completely and then go to another. In other cases they feed in a desultory way, taking toll from all the trees in a neighborhood.

Photo by E. H. Forbush

STARLING

At nesting hole with caterpillars for its young

Many observers state that the Starling eats apples, but this habit appears thus far to be confined mainly to apples left on the trees late in the fall, after the crop has been gathered. Flocks sometimes descend on a strawberry bed and considerably reduce the crop.

In the fall, when Starlings gather into large flocks of a thousand or more, they are often very destructive to corn in the ear. In Europe they feed to some extent on small grains, but I have not seen any evidence of that here. In New Jersey in the month of June they seemed to prefer the cherry trees to the wheat fields, and did not appear to molest the wheat at all. A few gardeners claim that they pull sprouting corn and peas.

Mr. Alfred C. Kinsey writes that he noticed the parent birds supplying nestlings with what proved to be the staminate flowers of the hickory. Later on, in different localities, the same peculiarity was noticed. If such feeding becomes extensive, it will bring about a failure of nut crops. He has also noticed these birds on grape vines and in trees wantonly tearing off large pieces of leaves, as well as doing damage to various fruit crops. Some observers assert that the Starling also destroys the buds of trees, but I have been unable to get definite evidence on this point.

EDWARD HOWE FORBUSH, in *The Starling.*

ICTERIDÆ

Order *Passeres;* suborder *Oscines;* family *Icteridæ*

SATISFACTORY vernacular name for this family is wanting. The group has been known by the name of Hangnests, but only certain members build pensile nests. From the superficial resemblance of a small percentage of its members to the Old World Orioles and Starlings, the family has been known as the American Orioles or American Starlings. Other names which have been used, as Grackle, Crow Blackbird, etc., are equally non-distinctive or of limited pertinence. Robert Ridgway says the name Troupial, derived from the French *troupe* and referring to their habit of flocking, has more general applicability than any other term.

In this family the bill varies greatly as to relative length and thickness, but is never conspicuously longer than the head and always more or less conical and sharp; the outlines are usually nearly straight, but sometimes the tip curves downward. The nostrils are never concealed although sometimes the membrane immediately behind them is covered. The bristles at the corners of the mouth are altogether obsolete or but very faintly developed. The wing is extremely variable, but usually the tip is moderately extended and terminates abruptly. The tail is variable as to relative length, form of tip, and shape of the feathers; it is always more than half as long as the wing but never conspicuously longer than the wing, never forked nor notched and is usually rounded, sometimes double-rounded, and occasionally graduated and folded like a fan; usually the tail-feathers, which always number twelve, are of nearly equal width throughout, but sometimes they are wider at the tips and sometimes narrower; in one species, the Bobolink, they abruptly taper to a point and are rigid at the tips.

The *Icteridæ* comprise birds of most various habits. Some live among the trees, and if placed upon the ground they are almost incapable of progression; others are terrestrial (though frequently alighting on trees and sometimes nesting there) and walk upon the ground with the grace and dignity of a Crow; many inhabit reedy marshes, and these usually nest in colonies, building open cup-shaped nests attached to the upright stems of water plants. The Orioles build pensile or hanging nests attached to the branches of trees but do not live in colonies.

Many species are remarkable either for the fullness and richness or other remarkable character of their notes, some of them being songsters of high merit, while others utter only the most harsh and discordant sounds. The Cowbirds are parasitic, like the English Cuckoo, always laying their eggs in the nests of other birds. The plumage varies from uniform black (sometimes with brilliant metallic gloss) or somber brown to the most showy combinations of yellow, orange, or scarlet, and black.

The group is peculiar to America and belongs particularly to the tropical part and to South America and the adjacent islands. Nearly one hundred and fifty species are known, of which by far the greater number are represented only in South America.

BOBOLINK

Dolichonyx oryzivorus (*Linnæus*)

A. O. U. Number 494 See Color Plate 73

Other Names.— Skunk Blackbird; Skunk-head Blackbird; White-winged Blackbird; Meadowwink; Towhee (mistake); Rice-bird; May-bird; Reed-bird; Butter-bird (Jamaica, B.W.I.); Meadow-bird; American Ortolan; Bob-lincoln; Robert.

General Description.— Length, 7 inches. Males in the spring and summer have the upper parts black and white and the lower parts black; males in the fall and winter and females all the year have the upper parts buffy-olive streaked with black, and the lower parts, pale buffy-olive. Wings, long and pointed; tail, shorter than wing with stiff, acute feathers; bill, conical and sharp.

Color.—Adult Male in Spring and Summer: General color, black; *hindneck buff; shoulders, rump, and upper tail-coverts, white* tinged with gray, especially the upper rump, which is sometimes uniform gray; shoulders edged with buff, forming streaks, especially along the center line; inner wing quill and innermost greater wing-coverts margined with pale yellowish passing terminally into grayish-brown; longer primaries narrowly edged with pale yellowish; inner webs of tail-feathers tipped with grayish; feathers of flanks and under tail-coverts margined with buffy or whitish; thighs with feathers on outer side more broadly margined with buff; bill, black; iris, brown. Adult Male in Fall and Winter: Similar in coloration to the adult female, but larger. Adult Female in Spring and Summer: General color above, light buffy-olive; crown with a broad center stripe of pale buffy-olive, and two broad lateral stripes of black, the latter streaked with light buffy-olive; back broadly streaked with black, the edges of some of the feathers light olive-buff, producing two nearly parallel narrow stripes wnen the plumage is properly arranged; rump feathers and upper tail-coverts with central wedge-shaped streaks of dusky (usually mostly concealed); wings and tail, dusky, with conspicuous edgings of pale yellowish and light grayish-olive; sides of head (including a broad stripe over eye), sides of neck, and under parts, light olive-buffy, more decidedly buffy or yellowish across chest and along sides and flanks, paler and straw-yellow on throat and abdomen; sides, flanks, and under tail-coverts, broadly streaked with dusky; a narrow dusky stripe behind eye; iris, brown. Adult Female in Fall and Winter: Similar to spring plumage, but more richly colored, especially the under parts.

Nest and Eggs.— Nest: Wonderfully concealed in a depression of ground in meadows; constructed of dried leaves, weed stems, coarse grass, and lined with finer grasses. Eggs: 4 to 7, pale drab, pearl-gray, or pale rufous, irregularly splashed and spotted with erratic lines and marks of umber, chestnut, lavender, and deep purple.

Distribution.— Eastern and central temperate North America; breeding from Pennsylvania, northwestern West Virginia, central Ohio, central Indiana, northern Illinois, southern Iowa, South Dakota, and Utah, northward to provinces of Quebec, Ontario, Manitoba, Assiniboia, and British Columbia (both sides of Cascade range), to about 40° on the Atlantic coast and 52° in the interior; west to Utah, northeastern Nevada, Idaho, and southeastern British Columbia; during migration southward through the West Indies, and the Atlantic coast of Central America to South America; also to the Galapagos Archipelago and the Bermudas.

Drawing by R. I. Brasher

BOBOLINK (½ nat. size)

The bird with a song like a hysterical music-box

Once upon a time somebody called the Bobolink the "Dr. Jekyll and Mr. Hyde of the bird-world." The Jekyll comparison doubtless originated with the Southern planters, who hated the bird for the damage it did in their rice-fields. Fortunately it has come to have less and less force as rice-growing has diminished in the South, though Robert's reputation in those parts was still bad enough to cause his name to be omitted from the list of birds to whom Uncle

Sam guaranteed protection under the Federal Migratory Bird Law of 1913.

In the Northern States, Robert has always been loved as the handsome and rollicking minstrel of the meadows. In its invariable and infectious spontaneity, and the fine frenzy of its delivery, his song stands alone in the musical utterances of American birds. Thoreau caught the spirit and the technique of the effort when he wrote "This flashing, tinkling meteor bursts through the expectant meadow air, leaving a train of tinkling notes behind." The song baffles description in words, or reproduction by any one musical instrument. William Cullen Bryant's oft-quoted poem contains lines which do some justice to the spirit of the song and of the scene of its delivery, but the refrain, "Bobolink, bobolink; spink, spank, spink," is a feeble effort to reduce its notes to spoken words. Mr. Dawson's transliteration, *Oh, geezeler, geezeler, gilipity, onkeler, oozeler, oo,* really is a clever rendition, in that it suggests clearly the essentially liquid and vowel character of the opening notes. But

Photo by H. T. Middleton

REED BIRD

The Bobolink in fall plumage

Photo by A. A. Allen

FEMALE BOBOLINK

it should be added that, having proceeded thus far, and in a rapid but comparatively restrained manner, Robert is likely to become suddenly a sort of hysterical music-box, and to produce a burst of sound pyrotechnics which make one fear that the next second he is going to explode outright and vanish in a cloud of feathers. This seems all the more probable when the hysteria occurs, as it often does, while he is on the wing.

There seems to be no record that Robert has ever actually blown up, but as far as many people are concerned he literally disappears from the earth very soon after his family responsibilities are discharged; for the fall molt completely transforms his appearance. The sharply outlined black, white, and buff uniform then gives way to a dull mottling of the same colors, which approaches the normal plumage of his striped and demure wife. Then he becomes the Reed-bird, and as such has to run the gauntlet of gunners who lie in wait for him on his southern migration, in order that banqueters may have their "reed-birds on toast." GEORGE GLADDEN.

When Robert on his southward migration reaches Jamaica, B. W. I., he assumes another alias — and a very appropriate one — Butter-bird. Fresh from the rice-fields of the southern

United States both he and his wife are veritable balls of fat and many are killed for food.

Sometimes Robert is not content with one wife and mates with two or more. The young often leave the nest before they are able to fly, but the mother still continues to care for them until they can fend for themselves.

On its northward migration the Bobolink enters the United States from the south at a time when the rice fields are freshly sown, pulls up the young plants, and feeds upon the seeds. Fortunately its stay in this district is not long and it soon hastens onward to its breeding ground in the north. While rearing its young, its chief food and the almost exclusive diet of the nestlings is insects. Among these insects weevils, cutworms, and grasshoppers are conspicuous. After the young are able to fly, the whole family gathers into a small flock and begins to live upon vegetable food. This consists for the most part of weed seeds and grass seeds. Sometimes grain, most commonly oats, in the milk, is eaten; but the damage done in this way is small and is more than offset by the enormous destruction of weed seeds.

As the summer advances the small flocks unite into larger ones and move southward. On their way they frequent the reedy marshes about the mouths of rivers and on the inland waters of the coast region. During this migration they subsist on the wild rice. It is at this time that the Bobolink is commonly known as the Reed-bird and, fattened by its rice-diet, is treated as a game bird.

By the end of August the Bobolink and its family have left their breeding grounds. It reaches the cultivated rice fields in the South as the crop is ripening. A decidedly useful bird in its northern home, the Bobolink becomes a serious pest when it reaches the rice fields. Uniting with various species of Blackbirds, it pillages the fields. The havoc made on the ripening grain by the Rice-bird, as the Bobolink is commonly known in this part of the country, is very great and it not infrequently causes losses of thousands of dollars to individual planters.

COWBIRD

Molothrus ater ater (*Boddaert*)

A. O. U. Number 495 See Color Plate 74

Other Names.— Cow Blackbird; Cow Bunting; Lazy Bird; Brown-headed Blackbird; Cuckold; Cow-pen Bird; Buffalo Bird; Brown-headed Oriole.

General Description.— Length, 8 inches. Males are greenish-black with brown fore parts; females are brownish-gray. Bill, shorter than head, conical, and compressed; wings, moderately long and pointed; tail, about ⅔ length of wing, even or slightly rounded.

Color.— Adult Male: *Head, neck, and upper chest plain brown*; rest of plumage glossy greenish-black, the gloss usually more violet (often distinctly so) on upper back, next to brown of hindneck; iris, brown. Adult Female: Above, brownish-gray, faintly glossed with greenish, the feathers with darker centers and blackish shaft-streaks, especially on back; wings and tail more dusky brownish-gray with paler edgings, these nearly white on longer primaries; under parts, paler brownish-gray usually streaked (narrowly) with darker, the chin and throat much paler (sometimes almost dull whitish), and, together with the chest, unstreaked; iris, brown. Young: Above, varying from dark hair-brown to sooty grayish-brown, the feathers with narrow pale grayish-brown and whitish margins (these usually indistinct and often obsolete on crown and hindneck); the wing-coverts more conspicuously margined with dull buffy whitish; under parts, conspicuously streaked with sooty grayish-brown or hair-brown and dull buffy or whitish, the latter on margins or lateral edges of feathers, the darker color prevailing forward.

Nest and Eggs.—A noted parasite, depositing its eggs, usually singly, in nests of smaller birds, but as many as five have been found in one nest; number of eggs unknown and the circumstances of deposition render a correct conclusion impossible. Eggs are white, spotted and blotched pretty generally over entire surface with chestnut and burnt-umber.

Distribution.— Temperate North America in general, except portions of Pacific coast; north to about 49° in more eastern portions, to 55° 30′ in the interior; west to British Columbia, Washington, Oregon, Nevada, and southeastern California; south in winter to central and southeastern Mexico; breeding south to Georgia, Louisiana, and Texas.

The Cowbird is that interesting phenomenon in nature called a parasite. Like the European cuckoo it leaves all family care to others. It might well serve as the emblem of free love. Many changes have been rung on the fidelity of birds to their mates, on the mating of certain birds for life and the sanctity of such union, but the Cowbird is an exception to all rules of virtue and monogamy among birds. The relations of the sexes are free and untrammeled. Both male and female confer their favors more or less generally and there seems to be practically no jealousy or quarreling. In their wooing, the males swell and bristle something after the manner of a Sage Cock, bowing and spluttering in their attempts to make themselves agreeable. The wings and tail are spread and the birds almost go into convulsions in their efforts to sing but produce nothing more than a rather unmusical *chuck see*. The females receive them all with generous impartiality. The offspring of these brief and happy unions are not nourished and cared for by the community, but are foisted on foster-mothers of other species, while the happy, care-free Cowbirds, with love and song, enjoy the long summer days.

In Massachusetts, the Cowbird deposits eggs from April until late in June and it is probable that within that time at least ten or twelve eggs are laid. Possibly more than half of them, on the average, are destroyed in one way or another, but for every Cowbird that comes to maturity a brood of some other species must perish. When the female Cowbird finds the duties of motherhood imminent she hunts stealthily through woods, bosky dells, shade trees or orchards until she discovers some smaller bird's nest containing one or more fresh eggs. If the owner of the nest is engaged in laying an egg, the Cowbird waits if possible until her victim has left the nest and then, slipping in, deposits her own egg. Sometimes she is unable to find an unoccupied nest in time and has been known to lay an egg in an unfinished domicile or even on the ground. At any rate she leaves it in the most convenient place and apparently continues on her frivolous way with no further thought of it. There is reason for the belief that sometimes eggs deposited on the ground are afterward carried to a nest.

Strange to say, although the foster-parents in some cases seem to discover the intrusion, they do not commonly resent it, although there is some evidence that they occasionally destroy the Cowbird's egg. The Yellow Warbler has been known to build a second nest over it and, when the offense has been repeated, even a third. The victims sometimes desert the nest, but this seems to be a rare occurrence. Usually they incubate and hatch the interloper. The birds chosen as foster-parents frequently are much smaller than the Cowbird, and as the Cowbird's egg is commonly larger than their own, it receives more warmth. For this reason and because it requires a shorter period of incubation it hatches earlier. The young Cowbird, being larger, and getting an earlier start, soon monopolizes nearly all the food, while the

Courtesy of Am. Mus. Nat. Hist.

COWBIRD (⅔ nat. size)

The social parasite of the American bird world

rightful heirs dwindle away and perish. In some cases the young Cowbird claims all the time of the foster-mother during the day, so that her own eggs become chilled and do not hatch; in others the eggs of the foster-parent are punctured, apparently by mother Cowbird. If, after all, any of the rightful occupants of the nest survive, the young Cowbird, taking the middle of the nest, grows so much faster than they that it crowds them out and thus, by hook or by crook, soon has the nest to itself and receives all the food that should have nourished an interesting family. In the meantime it has grown so strong and well-feathered that in about seven days after it leaves the shell it has outgrown the nest and climbed out upon the branches. Later it follows its foster-parents about, begging for food. It is a common sight to see a small Sparrow or Warbler feeding a young Cowbird almost twice its size. The big clown looks as if it might swallow the little bird which ventures to plunge insects and worms into that gaping, capacious, clamoring throat. At last the young Cowbird, being well grown, well feathered, and more than able to take care of itself, searches out the care-free flocks of its kind, joins one of them, and the troubles and cares of its foster-parents are over for the season, unless they attempt to rear a second brood, when the story may be repeated.

Another interesting phenomenon about the Cowbird is its close association with cattle. As it ranges over a large part of North America and well into Mexico, and as it feeds much on insects found in grass land, it uses the cattle as dogs to flush its game. Wherever cattle feed, the Cowbird may be found. It may be seen more commonly in the West than in the East, around and close in front of the cattle, as they graze, chasing and catching insects which flee from the towering kine. The Cowbird passes freely beneath the cow's belly and even alights on her back to seize the insect parasites, flies, etc., that find harborage there. Apparently the Cowbird rarely associates with horses, sheep, or swine but gives its attention chiefly to cattle. In this respect it resembles the introduced Starling, the Rhinoceros Bird, and a few other notable species which seek the company of certain large animals. The Cowbird, however, is not confined to the pasture but visits garden, field, wood, and orchard and often roosts in the marsh, flocking with the Blackbirds.

This species remains quite late in the north and flocks have been seen in winter in southern New England, but the greater number winter in the Southern States where they feed much in the neighborhood of water.

EDWARD HOWE FORBUSH.

The food of the Cowbird has been carefully studied and the tabulated results prove that were its food-habits alone to be considered this bird would have to be placed among the beneficial rather than the harmful species. But it must not be forgotten that in causing the death of multitudes of small birds, all of which are valuable to the agriculturist, the Cowbird is doing an injury for which his beneficial work in other directions can hardly atone. The lives of two to five other young birds is the price of each Cowbird. About 22 per cent. of its food is animal matter and 78 per cent. vegetable. It appears to eat few beneficial insects, avoiding the predacious ground beetles, but eating a few wasps, bees, and ants. Its best work is in destroying grasshoppers. It also eats boll weevils and caterpillars, the latter including cutworms and armyworms. Contrary to expectation it eats few flies or maggots, and there is no proof that it eats intestinal worms from cattle droppings or ticks from the animals themselves.

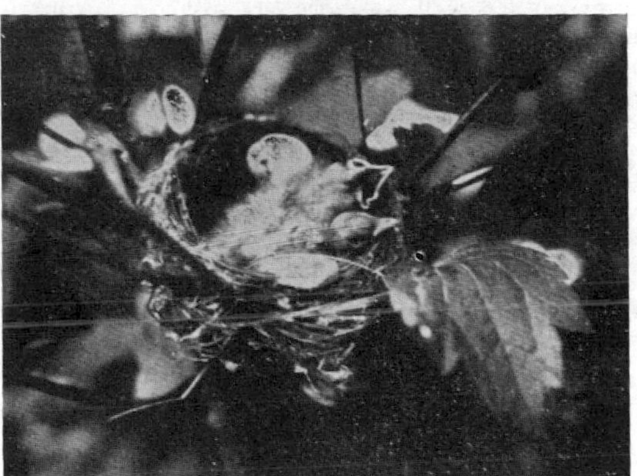
Photo by H. K. Job Courtesy of Outing Pub. Co.

NEST OF CHESTNUT-SIDED WARBLER

Containing a young Warbler, an egg, and a young Cowbird

The Cowbird does no harm to cultivated fruits. Its vegetable food consists mainly of weed seeds and grain, the former predominating and the latter being largely waste.

In Mexico, Lower California, and the adjacent parts of the United States, there is found a small edition of the Cowbird, which is called the Dwarf Cowbird (*Molothrus ater obscurus*).

RED-EYED COWBIRD

Tangavius æneus involucratus *Lesson*

A. O. U. Number 496

General Description.— Length, 8½ inches. Plumage, black, dull in the female and silky in the male. Bill, shorter than head, stout, and conical; wings, moderately long and pointed; tail about two-thirds length of wing, slightly rounded, and the feathers broadest at the tips.

Color.— Adult Male: A conspicuous erectile ruff on sides of neck; head, neck, and body, dark greenish-bronzy, the plumage soft and silky but not smooth, presenting the appearance of having been wet and imperfectly dried; tail-coverts, blue-black, the upper ones glossed with violet; wings, glossy dark greenish-blue, brightest on greater coverts, and inner wing quills less bright, as well as more greenish; on primaries, primary coverts, lesser wing-coverts, dark metallic-violet, the middle coverts violet-bluish; tail, dark metallic bluish-green or greenish-blue; iris, red. Adult Female: Dull black, the under parts, especially throat, sometimes dark sooty-brownish; back and shoulders very faintly, the wings, upper tail-coverts, and tail strongly, glossed with bluish-green; neck ruffs mucl less developed than in the male. Young Male: Dull sooty black or dark sooty, the feathers of the under parts of the body with narrow margins of paler. Young Female: Paler and grayer than the young male; above sepia or grayish-sepia, beneath paler and grayer with indistinct paler narrow margins to the feathers.

Nest and Eggs.— Nest: Builds no nest, laying eggs in other birds' nests. Eggs: Plain bluish-green without spots.

Distribution.— Southern Texas (breeding north to San Antonio), through eastern Mexico, and Central America (to Isthmus of Panama?).

The Red-eyed Cowbird is a handsomer bird than that feathered wretch, the Cowbird. The male, with his red eyes and glistening black coat, and his neck ruff elevated, makes quite an imposing appearance. The coloration of the female is duller than that of the male, but this fine apparel has no effect upon the bird's habits, which apparently are as reprehensible as those of her northern relative.

A close relative, the Bronzed Cowbird (*Tangavius æneus æneus*), lives in Mexico but wanders over the international boundary into Arizona. His reputation is just as shady as that of the rest of his family.

YELLOW-HEADED BLACKBIRD

Xanthocephalus xanthocephalus (*Bonaparte*)

A. O. U. Number 497

Other Name.— Copperhead.

General Description.— Length, 10 inches. Males are black with yellow fore parts; females are grayish-brown. Bill, decidedly shorter than head; wings, long and pointed; tail, over ⅔ length of wing, slightly rounded, the feathers rather hard and stiff.

Color.—Adult Male: *Head, neck, and chest, yellow* or orange; lores, eye region, forward portion of cheeks and chin, black; rest of plumage, uniform black, relieved by a white patch on the wing, involving the primary coverts (except their tips and shafts) and portions of the outermost greater coverts; anal region, yellow or orange; iris, brown. Adult Female: General color, dusky grayish-brown or sooty; no white on wings; a stripe over eye, cheeks, chin, and throat, dull whitish, usually tinged with yellow, passing into light yellow on chest; breast broadly streaked with white; anal tuft yellowish; iris, brown.

Nest and Eggs.— Nest: Fastened to tule stems from one to three feet above water; woven of sedge-grass, rather compact, bulky, thick-edged, and lined with finer blades; breeds in colonies, usually in center of large marshes. Eggs: 3 to 6, usually 4, grayish or greenish-white thickly and evenly spotted and blotched with drab, umber, and purplish-brown.

Distribution.— More open districts of western and central North America; north to southern British Columbia, Assiniboia, Athabasca, Keewatin (to about 58° 30′), and Manitoba; breeding east to the prairie sloughs of the upper Mississippi valley, as far as northeastern Illinois, northwestern Indiana, southwestern Michigan (?), southern Wisconsin, etc.; breeding southward to Arizona, New Mexico, probably to northern Mexico in general; in winter southward over greater part of Mexico; accidental straggler to Ontario, Quebec, Maine, Massachusetts, Connecticut, Pennsylvania, West Virginia, Maryland, District of Columbia, South Carolina, Florida, Cuba, and even to Greenland.

The Yellow-headed Blackbird has been called the Beau Brummel of the *Icteridæ* family. He dresses in a glossy black coat, and over his head, around his neck, and down on his chest he wears a rich yellow mantle. On each shoulder he displays a large, showy epaulette of white. Individuals have straggled as far east as Watertown, Mass., and there is a record of one specimen taken in Florida; but the Yellow-heads are essentially birds of the western prairies and marshes, where they frequently associate with the Red-winged Blackbirds and the Cowbirds, though the flocks may not actually intermingle. Their strongly developed gregarious instinct shows especially in their breeding habits, for large colonies of the birds often nest in close proximity to one another.

The Yellow-head's plumage is so striking and distinctive in its color contrasts that the identification of the bird ought to be easy for anybody. Like other members of its family the bird walks, when on the ground; indeed its gait is a rather pompous strut, and there is a suggestion of insolent superiority in the bird's manner which adds to the appropriateness of its nickname. Its only notes are hoarse chuckles and squeaks, all produced as if the effort caused discomfort, if not actual pain.

The young have lusty appetites, and they present a comical picture when they are able to leave the nest: they grasp a reed with each foot, and the weight of their bodies forces the reeds apart, so that the youngsters assume a sort of spread-eagle pose. But this, however, does not prevent them from keeping their mouths wide open meanwhile, nor does it hush their constant clamor for food.

The Yellow-headed Blackbird must be placed among the birds of doubtful usefulness. Agriculturists justly complain about this bird. It visits grain fields, especially oats and wheat, in large flocks and eats enough of the crop to cause serious loss. In its favor, however, is the eating of insects harmful to vegetation. These constitute about 30 per cent. of its food and are mainly beetles, grasshoppers, and caterpillars. The army-worm not infrequently is on the Yellow-head's menu.

Drawing by R. Bruce Horsfall

YELLOW-HEADED BLACKBIRD (½ nat. size)

The Beau Brummel of his family

RED-WINGED BLACKBIRD

Agelaius phœniceus phœniceus (*Linnæus*)

A. O. U. Number 498 See Color Plate 73

Other Names.— Swamp Blackbird; Red-winged Starling; Red-shouldered Starling; Red-shouldered Blackbird; Marsh Blackbird; Red-winged Oriole; Red-wing.

General Description.— Length, 8½ inches. Males are black with red shoulders; females are dusky above and whitish below with streaks of dusky. Bill, shorter than head; wings, rather long and pointed; tail, ¾ or more as long as wing, and rounded.

Color.— Adult Male: Uniform deep black with a very faint greenish-blue gloss in certain lights; *lesser wing-coverts, bright vermilion (varying to scarlet or even, more rarely, to orange-chrome); middle coverts, wholly buff* (paler at tips, sometimes almost white in midsummer birds); iris, brown. Adult Female: Above, dusky, varied with paler streaks and edgings; crown with center stripe of pale buffy-grayish, the dusky broad lateral stripes streaked with pale buffy or grayish; shoulders, edged on inner webs with pale buffy-grayish, on outer webs with rusty; secondaries, innermost primaries, tail-feathers, and primary coverts narrowly edged with pale grayish or buffy-grayish, the upper tail-coverts margined with the same; greater coverts and outermost primaries edged with dull whitish; lesser coverts broadly margined with brownish-gray or red, or both (often extensively red); middle coverts, black, broadly margined terminally with white or pale buffy; a broad white stripe over eye, finely streaked with dusky, usually becoming buff or salmon color over and in front of eye; a broad stripe of dusky behind the eye; cheeks and under parts, dull white (the chin, throat, and cheeks often buff or salmon-pink), the under parts of the body broadly streaked with dusky (sometimes almost black), these stripes broadest on flanks; under tail-coverts, dusky margined with white or pale buffy; chin and throat sometimes immaculate, but the latter usually marked with small wedge-shaped or triangular streaks of dusky, the sides of the throat margined by a dusky stripe below cheek.

Nest and Eggs.— Nest: In bushes or small trees, but usually in reeds which are interwoven between the outside layer of sedge-grass of which the nest is composed; sometimes in the center of a tussock close to the ground, but usually two or three feet above it, and always in swampy places. Eggs: 3 to 6, usually 5, pale bluish or greenish-white, marked with pen lines of sepia or dark reddish-brown, arranged in a wreath around large end or scattered over entire surface.

Distribution.— Eastern United States and more southern British Provinces to about latitude 62°, except Florida and Gulf coast; west to eastern base of Rocky Mountains.

Drawing by R. I. Brasher

RED-WINGED BLACKBIRD (½ nat. size)

A feathered optimist of bogland

BI-COLORED RED-WING

Agelaius gubernator californicus *Nelson*

A. O. U. Number 499

Other Name.—Bi-colored Blackbird.

General Description.— Length, 8½ inches. Males are black with red shoulders; females are sooty-brown streaked with whitish. Bill, shorter than head; wings, rather long and pointed; tail, three-quarters or more as long as wing, and rounded.

Color.— ADULT MALE: Uniform deep black, with a faint bluish-green gloss in certain lights; *lesser wing-coverts rich poppy-red* or vermilion; middle coverts black, or (if not entirely black) at least broadly tipped with black, the basal portion tawny-buff or ochraceous; iris, brown. ADULT FEMALE: Dark sooty-brown, the back, crown, chin and throat streaked (usually broadly) with whitish, buff, or pinkish, the region over the eye streaked with the same, producing a stripe.

Nest and Eggs.— NEST: In low bushes or flags, along running streams or in swamps; similar in construction to Tri-colored Red-wing's. EGGS: 4 or 5, light bluish-white, marked around large end with dark brown lines and spots.

Distribution.— Northern and central coast district of California and northward to coast of Washington (Cape Disappointment); migrating or straggling eastward and southward in the same States.

TRI-COLORED RED-WING

Agelaius tricolor (*Audubon*)

A. O. U. Number 500

Other Names.— Tri-colored Blackbird; Tri-colored Oriole.

General Description.— Length, 8½ inches. Males are black with red and white on wings; females are brownish-gray streaked with whitish and dusky.

Color.— ADULT MALE: Uniform glossy blue-black, the plumage with a silky luster; *lesser wing-coverts dull crimson; middle coverts white, in abrupt and conspicuous contrast*; iris, brown. ADULT FEMALE: Above, dusky, the plumage with a strong bronzy luster in certain lights; crown, narrowly streaked with brownish-gray, most distinctly along the center, where, however, not forming a stripe; shoulders, with light brownish-gray edgings to inner webs; lesser wing coverts broadly margined with brownish-gray; middle coverts, abruptly margined with white or white and gray; greater coverts, secondaries, innermost primaries, and tail-feathers narrowly edged with light brownish-gray; outermost primaries narrowly edged with white; stripes over eye and on the cheeks of pale brownish-gray narrowly streaked with dusky; space between these lighter-colored stripes nearly uniform dark brownish-gray; chin and throat, pale grayish-buffy, the latter streaked with dusky, especially along sides; chest, streaked with dusky and pale grayish-buffy in about equal amount; rest of under parts, dusky with paler margins to feathers, these most distinct on breast; iris, brown.

Nest and Eggs.— NEST: In alders, willows, and tules; constructed of straw, mud, and coarse sedge-grass, lined with finer similar material. EGGS: 4 or 5, light blue, somewhat deeper than the Eastern Red-wing's, marked with a circle of gray-brown around large end and with black erratic lines and spots.

Distribution.— Valleys of California, northern Lower California, and southwestern Oregon. More common along coast and almost non-migratory.

There are several members of the Red-wing family and some one or more are found throughout North America from Mackenzie south to Costa Rica. The head of the family bears the family name Red-wing. The others are: The Sonora Red-wing (*Agelaius phœniceus sonoriensis*), found in southern California and southern Arizona; the Bahama Red-wing (*Agelaius phœniceus bryanti*), distributed over the southeastern coast of Florida, Florida Keys to Key West, and the Bahamas; the Florida Red-wing (*Agelaius phœniceus floridanus*), found in Florida (except the southeastern coast and keys) and west along the Gulf coast to Texas; the Thick-billed Red-wing (*Agelaius phœniceus fortis*), central North America, from Mackenzie and southern Keewatin south to northeastern Colorado and northern Texas and wandering eastward occasionally; the San Diego Red-wing (*Agelaius phœniceus neutralis*), breeding from eastern British Columbia south to Lower California, New Mexico, and western Texas; the Northwestern Red-wing (*Agelaius phœniceus caurinus*), found along the Pacific coast from British Columbia to Mendocino county, California; and the Vera Cruz Red-wing (*Agelaius phœniceus richmondi*), distributed along the southern coast and through the lower Rio Grande valley of Texas south through eastern Mexico to Central America.

Swamps, morasses and bogs are not considered very cheerful places, but a veritable Slough of Despond would lose its gloom in the presence of one of these feathered optimists with his sleek black jacket and smart red epaulets, and his persistent and jolly *o-ka-lee*. And such are the places the Red-wing loves, and in which it may always be found during the summer months, in the northern reaches of his range. Usually it breeds in large colonies, but single families — a male with several wives — are sometimes found in a small slough. Under this social condition each of the females builds her own nest and rears her own little brood, while her lord and master struts in the sunshine and displays his brilliant plumage.

There is comparatively little variation as between individuals in this bird's characteristic combination of song and call-note, yet it is very differently transliterated by different persons, *O-ka-lee* seems as accurate as any of these attempts, and truer to the note than *conk-a-ree* or *cong-gar-ee,* since the opening tone seems to be very plainly the vowel O, rather than the consonant sound K. Mr. Mathews finds several phrases in the Red-wing's song and makes out of them the following jingle:

O-ka-lee, cong-quer-ree,
You chootea, Olong tea!
Gl-oogl-ee, Conk-a-tree,
Quange-se-tea, Shoo-chong tea!

And then he proceeds to adapt these deliverances to musical notation intended to represent variations of the phrase, with a result which might be entitled, "The Ballad of the Bog."

Other notes of the Red-wing are a dull *chuck,* or a prolonged whistle, sounded frequently in early summer, or a group of sharply accented scolding notes, or a single nasal call, not unlike that of the Nighthawk.

There is marked contrast between the color of the male and that of the female and the latter might easily be mistaken for a bird of a totally different species.

The Bi-colored Red-wing and the Tri-colored Red-wing might well be called California Red-wing and Western Red-wing, for they differ from the Red-wing only in their occurrence and but slightly in their plumage.

"Many complaints have been made against the Red-wing, and several States have placed at times a bounty upon its head. It is said to cause great damage to grain in the West, especially in the upper Mississippi valley; and the rice growers of the South say that it eats rice. No complaints come from the northeastern part of the country, where the bird is much less abundant than in the West and South.

"The examination of 1083 stomachs showed that vegetable matter forms 74 per cent. of the food, while the animal matter, mainly insects, forms but 26 per cent. A little more than 10 per cent. consists of harmful species. Weevils, or snout-beetles, amount to 4 per cent. of the year's food, but in June reach 25 per cent. As weevils are among the most harmful insects known, their destruction should condone for at least some of the sins of which the bird is accused. Grasshoppers constitute nearly 5 per cent of the food, while the rest of the animal matter is made up of various insects, a few snails and crustaceans. The few dragon flies found were probably picked up dead, for they are too active to be taken alive, unless by a Flycatcher. So far as the insect food as a whole is concerned, the Red-wing may be considered entirely beneficial.

"The interest in the vegetable food of this bird centers around the grain. Only three kinds, corn, wheat, and oats, were found in appreciable

NESTS AND EGGS OF RED-WINGED BLACKBIRDS

Placed amid the sweet flags

On a tussock of grass

quantities in the stomachs. They aggregate but little more than 13 per cent. of the whole food, oats forming nearly half of this amount. In view of the many complaints that the Red-wing eats grain, this record is surprisingly small. The most important item of the bird's food, however, is weed seed, which forms practically the whole food in winter and about 57 per cent. of the fare of the whole year. The principal weed seeds eaten are those of ragweed, barn-grass, and smartweed. That these seeds are preferred is shown by the fact that the birds begin to eat them in August, when grain is still readily accessible, and continue feeding on them even after insects become plentiful in April. The Red-wing eats very little fruit and does practically no harm in the garden or orchard. Nearly seven-eighths of its food is made up of weed seed or of insects injurious to agriculture, indicating unmistakably that the bird should be protected, except, perhaps, in a few places where it is overabundant." (F. E. L. Beal.)

Photo by H. T. Middleton

RED-WINGED BLACKBIRD

In some States there is a bounty upon his head

MEADOWLARK

Sturnella magna magna (*Linnæus*)

A. O. U. Number 501 See Color Plate 75

Other Names.— Common Lark; Old Field Lark; Field Lark; Marsh Quail; Medlark; Mudlark; Medlar; Crescent Stare.

General Description.— Length, 10½ inches. Upper parts, brown streaked with black; under parts, black and yellow. Bill, long and slender; wings moderately short; tail, short, with the feathers pointed; legs and toes, long.

Drawing by R. I. Brasher

MEADOWLARK (about ¼ nat. size)

One of the comparatively few birds that walk

Color.— Adult Male: Crown with a narrow center stripe of pale dull buffy, *separating two broad stripes of black,* streaked narrowly with brown, these streaks sometimes obsolete on forehead; a broad stripe, lemon-yellow from nostril to above eye, the remaining portion over the eye dull buffy-white; a narrow stripe behind eye of black; shoulders and the space between them, broadly black centrally edged and tipped with brown, but this passing on extreme edges and tip into buffy-whitish or pale buff, producing *distinct narrow streaks*; rump and upper tail-coverts, buffy, broadly streaked with black; middle pair of tail-feathers black centrally, pale brownish-gray or grayish-brown laterally; three outermost tail-feathers extensively white, the outermost (sometimes the one next to it also) almost entirely white; greater coverts light buffy grayish-brown edged with paler; secondaries similar in coloration to the greater coverts, the tertials usually with the black forming a large central irregular patch, but sometimes broken into regular and widely separated transverse lines or bars; primaries, dusky-grayish, the outermost broadly edged with white, the rest with outer webs broadly edged with light grayish-brown; throat, breast, and abdomen, *bright lemon-yellow; a broad crescent of black on chest,* the extremities of which blend into black spots on the cheeks; sides of breast, white broadly streaked with black, the sides and flanks similar, but tinged with buff and with black streaks rather narrower; iris, brown. Adult Female: Similar to the male, but much smaller; lateral stripes of crown more broadly streaked with brown, the stripe behind eye brown streaked with black, instead of uniform black; sides of head and neck, more buffy; black jugular crescent relatively smaller, the feathers usually tipped with light grayish; yellow of throat, breast, etc., rather duller.

Nest and Eggs.— Nest: Artfully concealed beneath tuft of clover, sedge, or grass; constructed of stems and coarse grass, and lined with fine blades; usually with covered, arched entrance to which a short winding path leads. Eggs: 4 to 6, crystal white thickly or thinly spotted with chestnut and reddish-brown; a second nesting not uncommon and probably usual.

Distribution.— Eastern United States and British provinces north to 54° and as far west as Great Plains. Not strictly migratory, often wintering as far north as lower New England States.

WESTERN MEADOWLARK

Sturnella neglecta *Audubon*

A. O. U. Number 501.1

Other Names.— Common Meadowlark; Field Lark of the West; Lark of the West.

Description.— Length, 9½ inches. Similar to the Meadowlark but different in proportions, the wings averaging longer, the tail shorter; *coloration much grayer and more "broken" above,* the broad lateral crown stripes never uniform black, but always (except in excessively worn plumage) streaked with pale grayish-brown; cheeks always largely yellow; blackish streaks on sides and flanks varied with spots of pale grayish-brown, the ground color of these parts paler buffy (often white); black jugular crescent averaging decidedly narrower; and yellow deeper.

Nest and Eggs.— Nest: On ground beneath a tussock of grass or weeds; constructed of grass, usually roughly arched with same material. Eggs: 3 to 7, white, spotted all over in varying amount with shades of brown and purple.

Distribution.— Western United States, southwestern British Provinces, east to prairie districts of Mississippi Valley, in Minnesota, Iowa, Missouri, Indian Territory, and Texas (occasionally to Illinois, Wisconsin, and southern Michigan, accidentally to Massachusetts?); north to southern British Columbia, southern Alberta, southwestern Saskatchewan, and western Manitoba; south over northern Mexico.

Every once in a while, well-meaning persons arise to remark that the Bald Eagle is not a fit emblem for this country, because he is a robber,

Photo by H. T. Middleton

MEADOWLARK IN SNOWDRIFT

an eater of carrion, and so on. Then they suggest a substitute. One of these substitutes who, a few years ago, had many champions, was the Meadowlark, because, as his friends truthfully averred, he is a beautiful bird and a highly useful one, with no bad habits; besides which he is known, in slightly variant forms, throughout Uncle Sam's domains, and finally because he is distinctly a bird of the Americas. All of this was interesting, and especially the fact that the Meadowlark's kind is not to be found outside of this hemisphere; but for all that, the Bald Eagle apparently was never in serious danger of losing his political job.

The Meadowlark has, however, a just claim on the respect and affections of the people whose country he adorns, and in whose fields he is a characteristic and conspicuous figure. If you see him plainly in the grass, before he takes wing, you can hardly miss his fine yellow breast with its sharply drawn crescent of glossy black; and when he springs into the air and speeds away in his peculiar half-fluttering, half-sailing flight, the white outer tail-feathers are equally conspicuous. Furthermore, you will notice — if you are observant — that on the ground he neither hops nor runs, but always walks, a style of locomotion which is comparatively uncommon among birds; and that immediately upon alighting he flirts his tail vigorously once or twice, thereby showing again the white outer feathers.

Though most of the Meadowlarks obey their migratory instinct, it is not at all uncommon to find the species in meadows covered with snow and swept by the pitiless winds of the coldest winters. From this you may know that he is a hardy bird, and you should guess, also, that he is a great eater of weed-seeds.

The Eastern Meadowlark is no such singer, to be sure, as is his neighbor, the Bobolink, yet there is infinite and invariable cheerfulness in his characteristic whistled phrase, which is always slurred. The Western Lark has a beautiful warbling song, very suggestive of the Baltimore Oriole but more prolonged. It rivals that of the Rose-breasted Grosbeak. By this difference of song you may distinguish between the two forms.

More than half of the Meadowlark's food consists of harmful insects; its vegetable food (27 per cent.) is composed of noxious weeds, grass seeds, and waste grain; and the remainder is made up of useful beetles or neutral insects and spiders. When it is considered that the bird feeds exclusively on the ground, it seems remarkable that so few useful ground beetles are taken. Grasshoppers are the most important item of food of the Meadowlark, amounting to 29 per cent. of the food of the year and 69 per cent. of the food of August. Beetles are next to grasshoppers in importance. Caterpillars, too, form a very constant element of the food. Most of the caterpillars are ground feeders and are overlooked by the birds which habitually frequent trees, but the Meadowlark finds and devours them by the thousands, not even passing by the hairy ones as most birds do.

The Western Meadowlark has been accused in California of eating the seeds of forage plants, especially clover, to an injurious extent. It has also in Southern California been charged with damaging the early crops of peas. Investigation of both of these accusations proved that local or exceptional conditions were the cause of the Meadowlark's fall from grace.

Photo by E. M. Bowland Courtesy of Outing Pub. Co.

NEST AND EGGS OF MEADOWLARK

AUDUBON'S ORIOLE

Icterus melanocephalus auduboni *Giraud*

A. O. U. Number 503

General Description.— Length, 9½ inches. Fore parts, wings, and tail, black; body, yellow. Bill, long and pointed; wings, moderately long; tail, more than ¾ length of wing, rounded.

Color.— Adult Male: Head, upper part of neck, fore portion of upper chest, wings (except lesser and part of middle coverts), and tail, black; inner wing quills and greater wing-coverts broadly edged with whitish; *lower hindneck, back, shoulders, rump, and upper tail-coverts, dull saffron-yellow* or wax-yellow tinged with olive-green, the shoulders partly black; sides of neck, lesser wing-coverts, and under parts (except as described), deep lemon-yellow, sometimes tinged with orange; middle wing-coverts, mostly black. Adult Female: Similar to adult male, but smaller and slightly duller in color, the back, etc., inclining more decidedly to olive-green.

Nest and Eggs.— Nest: Usually in mesquite trees, thickets, or heavy timber, from 6 to 14 feet up; constructed firmly, of dried grass, lined with finer; semi-pensile. Eggs: 3 to 5, pale bluish or grayish-white, with thin hair lines of purple and brown, very rarely with ground color obscured by minute, profuse dust-like specks of brown.

Distribution.— Southern Texas, lower Rio Grande valley; north to San Antonio occasionally.

Audubon's Oriole is essentially a Mexican species, but its northern range brings it into Texas, most commonly in the valley of the lower Rio Grande. It is naturally timid and retiring, and if it notices it is being observed while feeding in the open, is likely to retreat to thick cover.

The whistled note is sweet, with a suggestion of sadness, and the female sings as well as the male, though her voice is weaker. The birds are usually seen in pairs, and show strong affection and solicitude for each other. They have been found in high timber near San Antonio, and are not uncommon in and near Brownsville, Texas.

Drawing by R. I. Brasher

AUDUBON'S ORIOLE (½ nat. size)

A sweet whistler from Mexico who whistles in Texas, too

SCOTT'S ORIOLE

Icterus parisorum *Bonaparte*

A. O. U. Number 504

General Description.— Length, 8 inches. Fore and upper parts, black; under parts, yellow. Bill, long and pointed; wings, moderately long; tail, more than ¾ length of wing.

Color.— Adult Male: Feathers of head, neck, chest, back, and shoulders, uniform black; lesser wing-coverts, edge of wing, under wing-coverts, *under parts of body (except chest), thighs, under tail-coverts deep lemon-yellow*, the rump and upper tail-coverts usually washed with olive; middle wing-coverts, usually paler yellow, often passing into white at tips; rest of wings, black, the greater coverts tipped with white, and some of the wing feathers with narrow white margins; four middle tail-feathers, black with basal portion light lemon-yellow; rest with more than the basal half light lemon-yellow, the terminal portion, black tipped with white. Adult Female: Above, olive-grayish, becoming more yellowish-olive on rump and upper tail-coverts, the feathers of crown, back, and shoulders with darker center streaks, sometimes black with merely the margins grayish-olive; wings, dusky with light grayish-edgings, the middle and greater coverts broadly tipped with white, forming two distinct bands; tail, yellowish-olive with four middle feathers and terminal portion of the remainder darker, more grayish-olive; under parts, plain yellowish-olive, passing into clear yellow on middle of breast and abdomen. Immature Male: Similar in coloration to adult females, but larger.

Nest and Eggs.— Nest: Typical nesting site is in a yucca, about 5 feet up, near water; semi-pensile, rarely pensile; woven of grass, yucca threads, horse-hair, and cotton waste, and lined with fine grass and a felt-like down. Eggs: 2 to 4, marked with blotches and spots of purplish-black, generally without zig-zag lines.

Distribution.— Southwestern United States, Lower California, and Mexican plateau; north to western Texas, New Mexico, Arizona, southern Utah, southern Nevada, and southern California.

Though it ranges as far north as southern Utah and Nevada, Scott's Oriole is mostly a bird of the Mexican border as far as its presence in this country is concerned. In the great desert cañons of Texas, Arizona, and southern California, its clear whistle, much like that of the Meadowlark, is heard to good advantage with the song of the Cactus Wren.

Frequently these Orioles travel through the cañons in groups of from six to a dozen, feeding in the tree-tops. Despite their plumage the birds are often well concealed under these conditions, because their colors harmonize with the foliage. Furthermore, they generally move through the trees by clambering from limb to limb, rather than by flight, so that their movements are not easy to detect. Their presence is betrayed, however, by the loud whistled call of the males.

Drawing by R. I. Brasher

SCOTT'S ORIOLE (½ nat. size)

A brilliant lemon and black inhabitant of the desert cañons

SENNETT'S ORIOLE

Icterus cucullatus sennetti *Ridgway*

A. O. U. Number 505

Other Name.— Sennett's Hooded Oriole.

General Description.— Length, 8 inches. Fore and upper parts, black; under parts, yellow. Bill, long and pointed; wings, moderately long; tail, more than ¾ length of wing.

Color.— Adult Male: Lores, front portion of forehead, eye region, forward half of sides of head, cheeks, chin, throat, and upper chest, uniform black, *with a rounded posterior outline on the chest*; back, shoulders, and lesser wing-coverts, uniform black; middle wing-coverts, white, producing a very broad white band; rest of wings, black, the outer webs of greater coverts tipped with white, the primaries edged with grayish-white; tail, black, the lateral feathers margined at tips with pale grayish; rest of plumage, deep cadmium-yellow, the color most intense on head, neck, and chest. Adult Female: Crown, hindneck, rump, upper tail-coverts, and tail, yellowish-olive, the back of head tinged with dull brownish-gray; back and shoulders, dull brownish-gray; lesser wing-coverts, brownish-gray, more dusky centrally; rest of wings, dusky with pale brownish-gray edgings, the middle coverts broadly tipped with white, and pale edgings to greater coverts becoming white terminally; beneath, gamboge-yellow, paler on abdomen, strongly washed with grayish on sides and flanks.

Nest and Eggs.— Nest: A perfectly wrought cup-shaped, semi-pensile or attached structure, placed in clumps of Spanish moss, sycamores, oaks, figs, palms, or yuccas; constructed mainly of materials similar to tree in which located; typical nests composed almost entirely of Spanish moss; others, fastened to bayonet yucca points, constructed of fiber from edges of their leaves. Eggs: 3 to 5, pale bluish-white, wreathed around large end with brown spots and pencilings.

Distribution.— Lower Rio Grande valley, Texas, and Tamaulipas, Mexico; winters south of the United States to southern Mexico.

Sennett's Oriole seems to occur in the United States chiefly in a narrow strip of land between the Mexican line and the Rio Colorado, in Texas. The vegetation here is composed mainly of almost impenetrable thorny thickets, reinforced by yucca trees and cactus growths. Here, Mrs. Bailey records, she found this Oriole's home, which she describes as "one of the most skillfully wrought nests ever made, a perfect basket hung by the handle to the drooping bayonets in such a way that the sharp points protected it and yet left the bird an easy entrance. The nest was made of yucca fiber, decorative touches being given by bits of gray moss stuck on here and there."

The Arizona Hooded Oriole, or Nelson's Oriole (*Icterus cucullatus nelsoni*) is similar to Sennett's Oriole, but paler and with its forehead entirely yellow. It is found chiefly in Mexico and comes north into southwestern California, southern Arizona, and southwestern New Mexico. Once in a while it ventures into central California. It winters south of the United States.

Drawing by R. I. Brasher

SENNETT'S ORIOLE (½ nat. size)

A Mexican-border bird who builds where you must scratch your hands to get at the nest

ORCHARD ORIOLE

Icterus spurius (*Linnæus*)

A. O. U. Number 506 See Color Plate 75

Other Names.—Brown Oriole; Basket Bird; Orchard Starling; Orchard Hang-nest; Bastard Baltimore.

General Description.— Length, 7 inches. Fore and upper parts, black; under parts, chestnut. Bill, long and pointed; wings, moderately long; tail, more than ¾ length of wing.

Color.— Adult Male: Head, neck, upper chest, back, and shoulders, uniform black; wings (except lesser and middle coverts) black, with narrow whitish edgings; tail, black, the extreme base abruptly yellowish; *rump, upper tail-coverts, lesser and middle wing-coverts, and under parts of body (including under wing-coverts) uniform rich chestnut,* often deepening into bay on breast, the rump and upper tail-coverts inclining to burnt sienna; iris, brown. Adult Female: Above yellowish olive-green, becoming more yellowish on upper tail-coverts and tail, the back duller, with feathers indistinctly darker centrally; under parts, dull canary-yellow, tinged with olive on sides and flanks; wings, dusky, all the feathers margined with light olive-grayish (these edgings approaching white on longer primaries), the middle and greater coverts broadly tipped with dull whitish, forming two bands. Male in Second Year: Similar to adult female, but lores, front portion of cheeks, chin, and throat, black; breeds in this plumage; males more than one year old, but not yet fully adult, are variously intermediate between this black-throated yellow plumage and the fully adult livery; three years are required for full plumage.

Nest and Eggs.— Nest: In groves or orchards from 5 to 20 feet up; a basket-shaped, semi-pensile structure, frequently woven of green grass, lined with feathers. Eggs: From 4 to 6, pale bluish-white, spotted and scrawled chiefly around large end with browns and purple.

Distribution.— Eastern United States and whole of Mexico; breeding from the Gulf coast north to Connecticut, southern New York, southern Ontario, southern Michigan (south of 43°), southern Wisconsin, central Minnesota, and southern North Dakota, but occurring irregularly or casually as far north as southern New Brunswick, Maine, and Vermont; west across the Great Plains; south in winter over whole of Mexico and Central America to northern Colombia; occasional in southern Florida and Cuba in spring migration. Southern limit of breeding range unknown, but probably extending over part of Mexico.

A much rarer bird with generally duller plumage, with a fainter, though more elaborate and really more beautiful, song, a nest which is more like that of other birds, and decidedly retiring manners, the Orchard Oriole naturally has fewer admirers and friends than has the Baltimore. Catesby called it the Bastard Baltimore. Nevertheless he is a handsome and interesting bird, and always adorns the orchards, where, as his name implies, he is likely to be found.

Photo by H. K. Job

YOUNG ORCHARD ORIOLES

There is as much difference between the nests of these two birds as there is in the appearance of the birds themselves. Unlike the Baltimore, the Orchard species makes no use of twine — unless it be by accident — but follows closely the habit of its ancestors and employs almost exclusively green grass blades and stalks, tightly and skillfully woven into a shallower pouch than the Baltimore's nest, but beautiful in color, proportions, and finish. Wilson recorded his careful examination of one of these nests in which he found a grass-strand thirteen inches long, that had been woven through and through the mass thirty-four times. Built of this material, the nest is almost invisible until the grass dries and turns yellow, which, of course, makes it exceedingly conspicuous among the green leaves and usually at just about the time when it contains the helpless young. That the birds have not learned by experience to correct this mistake, must be a poser to those who like to believe in the inerrancy of instinct and the subtlety which the wild creatures are supposed to employ in self-protection. As a matter of fact, this is only one of the many blunders which blind instinct continually makes.

Witmer Stone records the interesting observation that this Oriole often nests in the same tree with the Kingbird, who is also fond of the apple orchards as a nesting site. " For some reason or other," remarks Mr. Stone, " the pugnacious Flycatcher, who usually drives all other birds from the vicinity of his nest-tree, seems able to live on the best of terms with the modest Orchard Oriole."

An unusual nesting site for an Orchard Oriole has been reported from Portland, Conn.; this particular pair had their home forty feet from the ground in an elm.

The Orchard Oriole seldom visits the ground. Among the blossoms at the end of a branch is he most often seen searching for the insects of which his food mainly consists. Plant-lice, small caterpillars, the flies and wasps found about blossoms are his favorite foods. He also feeds on wild fruits, but very sparingly. It has been observed that when the young are able to leave the nest the entire family will adjourn to cornfields where they will feed upon the insect enemies of the corn.

Photo by H. K. Job Courtesy of Outing Pub. Co.

NEST OF ORCHARD ORIOLE

With bill of young projecting

Drawing by R. I. Brasher

ORCHARD ORIOLE (⅞ nat. size)

A beautiful but somewhat elusive bird with a curious nest-building habit

---

BALTIMORE ORIOLE

Icterus galbula (*Linnæus*)

A. O. U. Number 507 See Color Plate 75

Other Names.— Golden Robin; English Robin; Hang-bird; Hang-nest; Fire-bird; Pea-bird; Hammock-bird; Golden Oriole; Baltimore Bird.

General Description.— Length, 8 inches. Fore and upper parts, black; under parts, orange. Bill, long and pointed; wings, moderately long; tail, more than ¾ length of wing.

Color.— Adult Male: Head, neck, back, and shoulders, *uniform black,* that of the throat extending into middle portion of chest; rump, upper tail-coverts, lesser and middle wing-coverts, and under parts of body, *rich orange or orange-yellow;* wings (except lesser and middle coverts), black, *the greater coverts broadly tipped with white,* the wing feathers more or less edged with same; middle pair of tail-feathers, black except the concealed basal portion; remainder of tail, light orange or orange-yellow, crossed near the base by a broad band of black; iris, brown. Adult Female: Crown, hindneck, back, and shoulders, saffron-olive, the feathers with central spots of black or dusky; rump, upper tail-coverts, and tail olive-saffron, brightest (sometimes dull orange) on upper tail-coverts; wings, dusky, the middle coverts broadly, the greater coverts more narrowly, tipped with white, the wing feathers edged with gray (sometimes white on longer primaries); under parts, saffron-yellow or dull orange-yellow, paler and duller on abdomen, tinged with olive on sides and flanks, the throat usually with some black.

Nest and Eggs.— Nest: A remarkable example of bird craftsmanship. Suspension strings are first firmly tied to the branches, these forming the warp through which the plant fibers, milkweed stalks, gray strips of bark, horse-hair, or cord, are deftly woven. The completed structure is gourd-shaped, flaring at bottom and always gray-colored. Extreme ends of large elms are oftenest selected for the site, but nests are found on a large variety of trees, even the conifers. The perfection of their workmanship is proved by the fact that these homes sometimes endure the blasts of four winters. Eggs: From 4 to 6, white with the characteristic pen lines, scrawls, and spots of dark brown and black of the species.

Distribution.— Eastern temperate North America; breeding from more southern United States (Texas to the Carolinas), except along the Gulf coast, northward to Nova Scotia, southern New Brunswick, Ontario, and Manitoba (to latitude 55°); west to eastern Assiniboia, Montana, Wyoming, and Colorado, east of the Rocky Mountains; in winter south through eastern Mexico and Central America to Colombia and Venezuela; accidental in Cuba.

The Baltimore Oriole is a distinct success as a bird. To begin with, he is a superlatively handsome fellow, and comports himself with the ease and confidence of a prince. Again, though he is not a great musician, like the Mockingbird or the Hermit Thrush, there is real individuality, as well as mere cheerfulness, in the quality of his whistled greeting to those who have ears wherewith to hear what is really worth listening to. And finally, his nest is essentially an appropriate and logical domicile for a creature who doesn't care a fig for the law of gravitation, and never even heard of Sir Isaac Newton.

All birds should build their nests after the kind of the Baltimore's — and many do, notably the Warblers and the Vireos. Why should a creature, who is in no more danger of falling than a fish is of drowning, plaster a mass of mud, twigs, and grass on a limb as thick as one's thigh, or in a crotch which would support a five-ton steel safe? Why not sling a stout but dainty hammock from twigs which are plenty strong enough, and swing in the breezes?

Drawing by R. I. Brasher

BALTIMORE ORIOLE (½ nat. size)

A bird whose whistle is as gay as his plumage

It now becomes necessary to explain that it is my Lady Baltimore, and not his lordship, who is the designer and maker of this picturesque and appropriate habitation. Indeed, it appears that while my lady toils, my lord does nothing much but sit around and whistle and look gorgeous. Doubtless if he had both, he would have his hands in his pockets meanwhile. Furthermore, my lady has shown herself a very practical housewife by making use of materials now at hand, instead of sticking to those which her forbears used for ages. For, previous to the appearance of mere man on the scene, the Orioles had employed plant fibers, grass, and other natural materials in their nest-building. Her ladyship still uses these materials, but she reinforces the fabric with almost any kind of string or twine available, not to mention strips of cloth and paper, thus revealing the very interesting and significant fact that her adaptability — which in this instance amounts almost to the human quality called common sense — is stronger than mere instinct, that most powerful factor in shaping the conduct of all animals. In this important respect, the Oriole clearly displays more intelligence than do such birds as the Eave Swallow and the Phœbe, who continue to use nest-building materials which make their homes conspicuous in their new situations.

On the subject of the materials used by Orioles, Mrs. Mabel Osgood Wright records the following interesting observations: "It is asserted that Orioles will weave gayly colored worsteds into their nests. This I very much doubt; or, if they do, I believe it is for lack of something more suitable. I have repeatedly hung vari-colored bunches of soft twine, carpet-thread, flosses, and the like, on the bark of trees

Photo by A. A. Allen

A PAIR OF BALTIMORE ORIOLES

At their nest on the tip of an elm branch

frequented by Orioles and, with one exception, the more somber tints were selected. In the exceptional case a long thread of scarlet linen-floss was taken and woven into the nest for about half its length, the remainder hanging down; but, resuming my watch the next day, I found the weaver had left the half-finished task and crossed the lawn to another tree. Whether it was owing to the presence of red squirrels close by, or that the red thread had been a subject for domestic criticism and dissension, I do not know." On the same subject Mr. John Burroughs writes (in *Riverby*): "One day we saw one weave into her nest unusual material. As we sat upon the lawn in front of the cottage, we had noticed the bird just beginning her structure, suspending it from a long, low branch of the Kentucky coffee-tree that grew but a few feet away. I suggested to my host that if he would take some brilliant yarn and scatter it about upon the shrubbery, the fence, and the walks, the bird would probably avail herself of it, and weave a novel nest. I had heard of it being done, but had never tried it myself. The suggestion was at once acted upon and in a few moments a handful of zephyr yarn, crimson, orange, green, yellow, and blue, was distributed about the grounds. As we sat at dinner a few moments later I saw the eager bird flying up towards her nest with one of these brilliant yarns streaming behind her. They had caught her eye at once, and she fell to work upon them with a will; not a bit daunted by their brilliant color, she soon had a crimson spot there amid the green leaves. She afforded us rare amusement all the afternoon and the next morning. How she seemed to congratulate herself over her rare find! . . . The woolen yarn was ill-suited to the Kentucky climate. This fact the bird seemed to appreciate, for she used it only in the upper part of her nest, attaching it to the branch and in binding and compacting the rim, making the sides and bottom of hemp, leaving it thin and airy, much more so than are the same nests with us. No other bird would, perhaps, have used such brilliant material; their instincts of concealment would have revolted, but the Oriole aims more to make its nest inaccessible than to hide it. Its position and depth insure its safety."

It is interesting to note also that the Oriole's homing instinct is apparently very strongly developed. Probably a pair never use the same nest twice, but there is evidence that the females may build their nests in the same tree for several successive years.

How the Oriole got his popular specific name has often been told, but ought not to be omitted from any sketch of him. It seems that when Cecil Calvert, second Baron of Baltimore, came to live with a company of English colonists in what is now Maryland, the settlement was named Baltimore in his honor. By way of giving the people at home some idea of the natural curiosities of the New World, certain of the colonists sent back to the old country skins of a very beautiful bird which they called an Oriole. As is usual with names invented under such conditions, this one was a misnomer, because the European Oriole is a totally different bird from the one which the colonists so named. It happened, however, that the plumage of this American bird showed the orange and black, which were the family colors of Lord Baltimore, and therefore when Linnæus, the great Swedish naturalist, prepared in 1766 a scientific description of the American bird, he named it in honor of Lord Baltimore.

The Oriole's singularly cheerful call is an even surer sign of the final retreat of winter, than is that of the Robin or the Bluebird. In fact, the bird arrives in New England usually not until early in May, when spring generally is an accomplished fact. Throughout the next two months the males are almost continuously in song, to which the females add a more modest and less sprightly little warble of their own. The "song" usually amounts to little more than two or three call-notes, which can hardly be considered even a musical phrase. An amusing exception to this general rule was furnished by an Oriole who had his home in one of a group of shade trees in East Liberty, a suburb of Pittsburgh, Pa. It was the year when Lottie Collins was astonishing the natives with her famous *Boom, ta ra-ra, boom, de-aye* song, and it happened that the Pittsburgh Oriole repeated exactly, omitting only the first note, the opening phrase of that extraordinary effort, whistling it incessantly as he scouted through the tree-tops.

Thoreau, who had a keen ear for bird-music, and something like a distinct gift for reducing the phrases to words — as nearly as that can be done — thought that an Oriole of his acquaintance said something like, "Eat it, Potter, eat it!" which is ingenious as well as amusing, and about as accurate as such transliterations can be. The scientist, to whom the slightest deviation from literal and firmly established facts is a hideous crime, might be unable to overlook the misrepresentation in Lowell's pretty picture of the Oriole's struggle with the pack-thread, since the male bird is referred to; but, as a matter of fact, his lordship has been known to bring material to his spouse, though, in truth, she does most, if not all, of the actual weaving. However, the person who sees in birds more than a mere opportunity for classification and "orderly" arrangement does not fail to find essential truth and beauty in these lines of a poet who knew birds and loved them well:

> Hush! 'tis he!
> My Oriole, my glance of summer fire
> Is come at last, and, ever on the watch
> Twitches the pack-thread I had lightly wound
> Around the bough to help his house-keeping,—
> Twitches and scouts by turns, blessing his luck,
> Yet fearing me, who laid it in his way.
> Heave ho! Heave ho! he whistles as the twine
> Slackens its hold. Once more now! and a flash
> Lightens across the sunlight to the elm
> Where his mate dangles at her cup of felt.

Even finer, perhaps, are Edgar Fawcett's lines:

> How falls it, Oriole, thou hast come to fly
> In tropic splendor through our northern sky?
>
> At some glad moment was it Nature's choice
> To dower a scrap of sunset with a voice?
>
> Or did an orange tulip, flaked with black,
> In some forgotten garden, ages back,—
>
> Yearning toward Heaven until its wish was heard,
> Desire unspeakably to be a bird?

GEORGE GLADDEN.

One of the cotton-growers' bird friends is the Baltimore Oriole. It generally reaches their district at about the time the boll-weevils are making their annual flight and immediately starts feeding upon them. Specimens which have been examined have contained on the average two weevils each, and one Oriole had eaten nine. Caterpillars form the largest item — 34 per cent.— in the Oriole's bill of fare. Plant and bark lice are so small that they are generally overlooked by most birds. But it is not so with the Baltimore Oriole; he searches for these damaging little pests. The larvæ of the click beetle, which are among the most destructive insects known, form part of the food of this bird, while ants are eaten in the spring, grasshoppers in July and August, and wasps and spiders throughout the season.

During the stay of the Baltimore Oriole in the United States he eats very little vegetable matter — only 16 per cent. of his total food being possible of that classification. He often gives cause for complaint by his bad habit of eating green peas; he sometimes strips the pods to such an extent that crops are severely damaged. Another accusation which he has to answer is that of puncturing ripening grapes; but investigation of this charge seems to prove that the only cultivated grapes he troubles are on vines that run up into trees where he can work unseen. The simple preventive then would be to trim the vine. He is charged with attacking early apples and pears, piercing them with his bill to get at the pulp, and, of course, ruining each apple or pear. But probably more of this damage is done by Red-headed Woodpeckers, Robins, and Blue Jays, and even Catbirds and Grackles, and the Oriole loses his good name because of the company he keeps. However, the amount of damage done by him cannot be very great when there is such a small percentage of vegetable matter in his diet, and the amount of good he does in eating harmful insects should earn for him full protection and encouragement of his presence.

BULLOCK'S ORIOLE

Icterus bullocki (*Swainson*)

A. O. U. Number 508

General Description.— Length, 8½ inches. Plumage, black and orange. Bill, long and pointed; wings, moderately long; tail, more than ¾ length of wing.

Color.— Adult Male: Greater part of crown, hindneck, back, shoulders, lores, streak behind eye, front portion of cheeks, chin, and broad stripe down middle of throat, black; *rest of head and neck (including a broad stripe over eye and sometimes the whole forehead), orange;* the under parts similar, but rather paler toward the rear; rump and upper tail-coverts, orange tinged with olive; lesser wing-coverts, black and orange; exposed portion of middle and greater coverts, white, forming a large patch; rest of wing, including greater portion of inner webs of greater coverts, black, the secondaries (except at base of five or six outermost) broadly, the primaries more narrowly, edged with white; middle pair of tail-feathers black, except at base; next pair mostly black; remaining tail-feathers orange-yellow, with black or dusky at tips; iris, brown. Adult Female: Crown and hindneck, yellowish-olive, becoming grayer toward the back; back, shoulders, and rump olive-grayish, the back sometimes narrowly streaked with dusky; upper tail-coverts and tail, wax-yellow, rather brighter on edges of the tail-feathers; sides of head, stripe over eye, sides of neck, and chest (sometimes most of throat also), saffron-yellowish; chin and center line of throat, more whitish, sometimes blotched with black; rest of under parts, dull buffy-whitish, the sides and flanks tinged with pale olive-grayish, and breast (sometimes abdomen also) tinged with yellow; anal region and under tail-coverts more yellowish, sometimes distinctly yellow; wings, dusky, the middle coverts broadly tipped with white, forming a distinct band, the greater coverts and wing feathers edged with grayish-white.

Nest and Eggs.— Nest: Suspended from branches of poplars, cottonwoods, mesquite, or other trees, sometimes in a cluster of mistletoe, from 5 to 40 feet up; a woven, pensile structure of vegetable fibers, inner bark, and horse-hair, lined with wool, down, horse- or cow-hair. Eggs: 3 to 6, paler and of clearer bluish ground color than the Baltimore Oriole's and marked with erratic hair lines chiefly around larger end.

Distribution.— Western United States and British provinces and plateau of Mexico; north to southern British Columbia, southern Alberta, and southern Assiniboia; east to eastern border of the Great Plains in middle portions of South Dakota, Nebraska, Kansas, Oklahoma, and Texas, more sparingly to eastern portion of the same States; breeding south at least to northern Mexico; in winter south to Mexico; accidental in Maine.

The Bullock Oriole is one of our most striking birds in orange and black. In some parts of the Pacific coast, the bird is especially fond of nesting in an orchard tree near the house. The weeping willow tree is a great favorite. Through the irrigated districts, the bird may always be found among the cottonwoods and poplars.

As a rule, the Oriole builds a strong nest of horse-hair and fibers. It is usually made so strong and elastic that, if pressed together, it springs back into shape. It survives many a hard winter; for often where the Orioles live, one can count the old nests, still hanging, that have been used in years past.

It is difficult at times to try to explain the actions of a bird. I know of a pair of Orioles that lived in a neighbor's orchard. They swung their nest on one of the lower branches of a willow tree. One day, we saw the female Oriole light on a low branch in front of a window. In a few moments, she flew down and lit on the sash. Then she fluttered up against the window, trying her best to hang on. She would turn her head and watch in the glass. The more she looked, the more excited she seemed to get, fluttering against the glass until she was out of breath. The bird kept up these antics every day. It was not merely that she wanted to get inside, for when the window was opened, her curiosity seemed satisfied, but she did not enter the house. When the window was closed again, she kept flying against it, never accomplishing anything except to slide to the bottom.

The Bullock Oriole replaces the Baltimore

from the Rocky Mountains to the Pacific. He has a wholesome, rollicking song which goes well with his dashing color. The orange coloring is extremely beautiful in some individuals. The male is not in his best dress until the third or fourth year. Oftentimes you will see a male that is not really brilliant or that has not attained the orange hue. These are younger birds.

I remember a story told to me several years ago of a pair of Orioles that lived about a eucalyptus grove in California. The male bird was in such fine plumage that an ornithologist shot him for his collection. The next day, the female appeared with a new mate who was as bright and fine looking as the bird she had lost the day before. This bird was shot also, partly because he was in such fine plumage and partly to see if the female would find another as easily. Two days later, she appeared with a third husband who went the way of the two former ones. The female then disappeared for a few days, but returned again with a fourth suitor. The pair built in a eucalyptus tree and soon had a family of young birds. This may be a remarkable case of wooing and winning. It is rather difficult to understand where the supply of male birds came from unless the widow Oriole was breaking up other families.

William L. Finley.

The food habits of Bullock's Oriole differ in no essentials from those of the Baltimore Oriole, the ratio between the animal and vegetable portions being practically the same. It is of interest to note that among the bugs which it eats is to be found the black-olive scale; these amount to nearly 7 per cent. of the bird's food for the year. The major part of its vegetable food is fruit, especially in June and July, when it often eats more cherries and apricots than the owners of the trees think is just. But it is probable that no great harm is done to fruit crops, as the complaints are not many. Injurious caterpillars form a large part of their vegetable food.

Drawing by R. I. Brasher

BULLOCK'S ORIOLE ($\frac{1}{2}$ nat. size)

This is the beautiful Oriole of the West, a good singer and a clever nest builder

RUSTY BLACKBIRD

Euphagus carolinus (*Müller*)

A. O. U. Number 509 See Color Plate 73

Other Names.— Rusty Grackle; Thrush Blackbird; Rusty Oriole; Rusty Crow.

General Description.— Length, 9 inches. Male, black; female, slate-colored. Bill, shorter than head, and narrow; wing, long and pointed; tail, nearly as long as wing, moderately rounded.

Color.— Adult Male in Summer: Uniform black, faintly glossed with bluish green changing to dull violet-bluish on head and neck; under tail-coverts, margined with whitish; bill, black; iris, pale yellow or yellowish-white. Adult Male in Winter: Similar to the summer plumage, but the black obscured by rusty brown on crown, hindneck, back, and shoulders, and by cinnamon-buffy over eye and on cheeks, chin, throat, chest, and sides. Adult Female in Summer: Uniform dull slate color, dark and faintly glossed with bluish-green on upper parts; bill, black; iris, pale yellow. Adult Female in Winter: Similar to the summer plumage but crown, hindneck, back, and shoulders, overlaid by rusty brown, inner wing quills and greater wing-coverts margined with the same, stripe of buff over eye, and feathers of cheeks, chin, throat, chest, and sides tipped with brownish-buff. Young: Above, dark sooty brown, more slate-dusky on wings and tail feathers; inner wing quills and terminal portion of greater and middle wing-coverts margined with rusty; stripe over eye of light rusty; under parts, brownish-gray tinged with light buffy-brown on cheeks, chin, throat, chest.

Nest and Eggs.— Nest: Located in alders or willows within a foot or two of the water; rather bulky, constructed of layers of leaves, grass, and mud, often lined with fine *bright green* grass. Eggs: 4 or 5, light bluish-green thickly blotched and spotted with different shades of chestnut, sepia, and drab; pen lines and scrawls characteristic of other blackbirds, nearly always absent.

Distribution.— Northern and eastern North America; breeding from Nova Scotia, New Brunswick, northern Maine, New Hampshire, Vermont, northern New York and northern Michigan north to Ungava and northwesterly to the Arctic coast and Alaskan shores of Bering Sea; south in winter to the Gulf coast (Florida to Texas); west more or less reguarly, to western border of the Great Plains, casually to Lower California; accidental in Greenland.

When the first sharp frosts come, when the foliage puts on the red and gold tints of autumn and the corn in the fields turns dry and dead, then the Rusty Blackbird begins to appear in the United States, arriving at first in small flocks from the northward. It is well known now over most of eastern North America but it was not always thus. Specimens of the Rusty Blackbird were described nearly a century ago under five different names by a "judicous" British naturalist. Wilson, in referring to this, points out the difficulty of judging correctly from dried skins alone, especially when individuals of a species vary much in size and color. The full-plumaged male Rusty Blackbird is almost pure black with a greenish gloss, while the young bird in autumn is mainly rusty-brown. Nevertheless, no one familiar with the species in life could fail to recognize it in any plumage as its notes are unmistakable. In flight and in the shape of its bill this bird somewhat resembles a Thrush.

Photo by H. K. Job

FEMALE RUSTY GRACKLE SCOLDING NEAR NEST

Bendire and others tell of its song as being "rich, varied, and energetic" and speak of its chuckling, gurgling, wheezing, musical, agreeable notes, "like other Blackbirds," etc. Some of these descriptions may characterize correctly the song in the summer home, but I have heard only a short *chack* or *chuck* and a fine whistle or creak, intermingled more or less with gurgling or choking sounds. This song, if song it can be called, is very characteristic, and when a flock is started from its haunt on some oozy margin and flies to the tree-tops the chorus of *chucks* and weird creaks is inimitable. There is nothing else in the eastern United States that closely resembles it, although the *chuck,* often given separately, is much like that of other Blackbirds.

In spring the bird makes its appearance early in the North, often when snow is on the ground and ice still skims the edges of the streams. It is more of a forest frequenter than most Blackbirds; but it is attracted to water, and may be found in its seasons along the swampy borders of many a woodland lake, swamp, or stream.

As it breeds mainly north of the United States it is seen here principally in migration or in winter. In autumn the flocks are not closely confined to their sloughs and watery retreats, but visit cornfields, stubblefields, and even orchards and gardens. They are fond of corn and other grains and, while many shot on the cornfields have had their crops full of insects, they commonly devour Indian corn in all its stages. At night they roost in marshes or in the button bushes and other vegetation growing about the edges of open water holes in river meadows. There they gather in large numbers, coming in toward dusk in small flocks and roosting, often in company with Red-winged Blackbirds and Cowbirds.

They are among the last of the Blackbirds to go South and sometimes small flocks remain in southern New England well into the winter months. In the South they often frequent rice plantations and cornfields but many retire to the swampy retreats of the Gulf States until the approach of the vernal equinox arouses again the longing which bids them seek the home of their nativity.

EDWARD HOWE FORBUSH.

In the spring the Rusty Blackbird can be found in swampy places wading along the shallow edges of streams and pools. Here he feeds mostly on insects, but eats weed seeds and waste grain. He eats numerous water-beetles and their larvæ, snout-beetles, leaf beetles, May-beetles, and great numbers of other beetles, nearly all of which are harmful. In the autumn he frequents cornfields, stubblefields, and beech woods, eating the same kinds of food as in the spring, but probably the percentage of insects is even higher. He eats but little wheat, oats, or corn except the waste in fields and the allegation that he pulls up sprouting grain has not been proved.

BREWER'S BLACKBIRD

Euphagus cyanocephalus (*Wagler*)

A. O. U. Number 510

General Description.— Length, 10 inches. Male, black; female, brownish-slate. Bill, shorter than head, and narrow; wing, long and pointed; tail, nearly as long as wing, moderately rounded.

Color.—ADULT MALE: Entirely black, the head and neck strongly glossed with violet, the rest of the plumage with bluish-green; more highly glossed in winter plumage; bill, black; *iris, pale yellow.* ADULT FEMALE: Head, neck, and under parts, brownish-slate color, faintly glossed with greenish on under parts of body and with violet on head and neck, especially on crown and hindneck; upper parts darker, especially wings and tail, which are more strongly glossed with bluish-green; bill, black; iris, light yellow.

Nest and Eggs.— NEST: Usually low, sometimes 30 feet up in trees or bushes; often in large colonies; constructed with a rough, coarse foundation of twigs, plant stalks, bark, and rootlets mixed and held together with manure or mud, and lined with finer similar materials with the addition of horse- or cow-hair. EGGS: 5 to 8, usually 5, dull greenish-white or gray profusely marked with erratic streaks and large blotches of sepia.

Distribution.— Western United States and British provinces and greater part of Mexico; north to British Columbia, Alberta, Saskatchewan, and Manitoba (breeding); east to Minnesota, Nebraska, Kansas, Oklahoma and Texas, occasionally, during migration, to Iowa, Wisconsin, Illinois, Missouri, Louisiana, and even South Carolina; breeding south to Lower California, southern Texas; in winter over the whole of Mexico to Guatemala.

Handsomest of all the Blackbird race is Brewer's Blackbird with his glossy black coat shimmering in the sunlight with reflections of purple, blue, and green. And he does not hide his beauty in some woodland solitude, but comes around the barn-yards where he exhibits very domineering manners toward the fowls. His principal nesting places are in the unsettled districts, in the trees or around the edges of marshes. Often, however, he builds in the trees near farmhouses. Like other Blackbirds, he nests in colonies, but these colonies are much smaller, the usual number of families being five to ten.

The love song of this beautiful bird is a rather ludicrous attempt at music making. *Tuck-tuck-qsi! tuck-tuck-qsi!* is one observer's translation of his sputtering plea. But the little lady in dull brownish-slate always seems much pleased with it and soon starts the building of the home. During this operation he shows her a great deal of personal courtesy, but he seems to think it would be beneath his dignity to lend a hand — or rather a beak — to aid her labors.

When fruit is ripe the Brewer's Blackbirds do not hesitate to take a share, and they visit the orchard daily for the early cherries. They claim a share of grain also, but do not appear to eat it at harvest time so much as afterwards. Mr. Walter K. Fisher, writing from Stockton, Calif., reports them as feeding on newly sown wheat that had not been harrowed in, eating nearly all thus left exposed. He describes the birds as in such immense flocks in the grain fields that at a distance they looked like smoke rising from the ground, and says that stomachs of birds taken were full of wheat. On the other hand, Prof. A. J. Cook, of Claremont, Calif., says that he considers it one of the most valuable species in the State. Mr. O. E. Bremner, State Horticultural Inspector, in a letter to the Biological Survey, says: "The cankerworm episode is quite a common one with us here. In one district, Dry Creek Valley, Sonoma County, there has been a threatened invasion of the prune trees by spring cankerworms several times, but each time the Blackbirds came to the rescue and completely cleaned them out. I have often seen bands of Blackbirds working in an infested orchard. They work from tree to tree, clearing them out as they go. If a worm tries to escape by webbing down, they will dive down and catch him in mid-air."

In the cherry season, Mr. F. E. L. Beal of the United States Biological Survey observed these birds in the orchards, and collected a number of them. They were seen to eat freely of cherries, and the stomachs of those taken showed that a goodly proportion of the food consisted of cherry pulp. While these observations were being made, a neighboring fruit raiser began to plow his orchard. Almost immediately every Blackbird in the vicinity was upon the newly opened ground and many followed within a few feet of the plowman's heels in their eagerness to get every grub or other insect turned out by the plow.

On another occasion an orchard was watched closely while the far side was being plowed. A continual flight of Blackbirds was passing in both directions over the observer's head, and practically all of them alighted on the newly plowed ground, fed there for a while, and then returned, probably to their nests. When plowing was finished and harrowing began, the Blackbirds immediately changed their foraging ground, and followed the harrow as closely as they had accompanied the plow.

In so far as its animal food is concerned, but little fault can be found with the Brewer's Blackbird. The insects eaten are fairly well distributed among the various orders, and include

Drawing by R. Bruce Horsfall

BREWER'S BLACKBIRDS (½ nat. size)

They follow the furrow and eat the grubs

only a comparatively small number that are useful. As to fruit, no more is eaten than may be considered a fair return for the destruction of insects. The weed seed eaten must be set down to the bird's credit. All questions, then, in regard to its economic position must rest upon the grain it eats. Most of the grain is taken in the months from August to February, inclusive. The average amount consumed in those seven months is over 75 per cent. of the food, while the average for the other five months is less than 24 per cent., yet this last period covers the time from sowing to the end of harvest. It has a decided partiality for oats, and if abundant would undoubtedly prove a menace to the crop.

J. Ellis Burdick.

PURPLE GRACKLE

Quiscalus quiscula quiscula (*Linnæus*)

A. O. U. Number 511 See Color Plate 74

Other names.— Blackbird; Crow Blackbird; New England Jackdaw; Maize Thief; Keel-tailed Grackle; Purple Jackdaw.

General Description.— Length, 12½ inches. Plumage, black with metallic hues. Bill, about as long as head and decurved at tip; tail, long and graduated. The tail is plicate, or capable of being folded vertically, so that a transverse section is V-shaped, the two edges being brought near together when flying; because of this folding and the graduated form of the tip, the effect, when the bird is flying, is very peculiar, the tail appearing as if much longer on one side than on the other.

Color.— Adult Male: Head, neck, and chest, varying in color from metallic reddish-violet to golden-green; prevailing color of back and shoulders varying from bronzy-purple to metallic olive-green, but this always is broken by bars of metallic green, blue-bronze, or purple (or all of these tints); rump varying in color from purplish-bronze to violet; prevailing color of wings, violet or purple; the lesser and middle coverts usually banded with purple, blue, green, or golden; tail, dark purple, violet, blue or green, or (in worn or faded plumage) black glossed with one of these colors; under parts (posterior to chest), metallic purple, violet, blue, or green, the color varying in different parts, sometimes mixed with golden bronze; bill, black; iris, pale yellow or yellowish-white. Adult Female: Decidedly smaller than the male and much duller in color, the metallic hues more subdued, sometimes very faint.

Nest and Eggs.— Nest: Built preferably in a conifer, placed on a bough but often in fork formed by topmost whorl of branches; sometimes in hollows or cavities of trees near water; a loose, bulky structure of twigs, hay, and grains, frequently cemented with mud. From Kent, Conn., comes the report of the finding of the nest of this bird in the rushes of a marsh, a very unusual site. Eggs: 4 to 6, greatly varying in size and color; ground color greenish, blue to dirty brown, strongly marked with blotches and zigzag streaks or lines of brown and black.

Distribution.— Atlantic coast district of United States, east of Alleghenies; north to lower Hudson valley and northern shore of Long Island Sound; breeding south to uplands of Alabama, Georgia and the Carolinas, to Virginia (?) along the coast; occasional on western side of Alleghenies, in eastern Tennessee; winters mainly south of the Delaware Valley.

Drawing by R. I. Brasher

PURPLE GRACKLE (⅓ nat. size)

Handsome, picturesque, and popular despite his bad habits

In the respects that he is black all over and, when on the ground, walks, and — alas! — is a nest-robber, the Purple Grackle is like a small edition of the Crow. His cannibalistic propensities are well advertised by his neighbors, the Robins, Bluebirds, Thrushes, and Sparrows, who are often seen mobbing him with the utmost fury. And when the birds unite in giving one of their number a bad name, we may be tolerably certain that he deserves it. Furthermore it must be conceded that the Grackle's skulking manners in nesting time and his cold and cruel yellow eyes strongly suggest the birds' arch-enemy, the cat. In fine, that he is a good deal of a villain in bird-land is undoubtedly true, and pity 'tis 'tis true, for there is no denying that the bird's plumage is very handsome; in fact, the iridescent hues on his head, neck, and shoulders are exceedingly beautiful; and he also makes an appeal for popularity on the score that his arrival is one of the surer signs that spring is at hand, and because he presents a fine appearance as he walks, indeed, almost struts, about on the deepening green of the lawns.

Photograph by A. A. Allen

A BRONZED GRACKLE FEEDING ITS YOUNG

A mistake which this Grackle makes is in trying to sing. But perhaps the bird isn't entirely to blame for this, for he may know that the scientists have put him among the *Oscines*, a suborder composed of "song-birds," a term which, however, in this connection, means simply that the bird included possesses well-developed vocal apparatus, and entirely disregards the question as to how he uses that apparatus, or whether he uses it at all. Perhaps the Grackle isn't able to make the scientific distinction between the song-bird who can sing and the song-bird who can't, and therefore supposes himself to be a singer. His demonstration of his proficiency in the "art divine" consists in drawing in his head in turtle fashion, puffing out his body, ruffling up his feathers and then emitting a sort of asthmatic squeak, which suggests the protest of a rusty hinge. When a considerable number of Grackles do this at or about the same time, the result is what somebody has aptly termed a "good wheel-barrow chorus."

The Purple Grackle is found in the Atlantic coast district of North America. In the interior, west to the Rocky Mountains, he becomes the Bronzed Grackle (*Quiscalus quiscula æneus*). In this part of the country his body is a uniform bronze color, except the chest, which varies from

Photograph by H. K. Job — Courtesy of National Association of Audubon Societies

BOAT-TAILED GRACKLES FEEDING WITH WILD DUCKS

This picture was taken from the window of a cabin on a bird-reservation in Louisiana

a greenish-blue to a brassy-green. (See Color Plate 74.) In Florida there is a smaller form of the Purple Grackle, called the Florida Grackle (*Quiscalus quiscula aglæus*).

The Purple Grackle has been proved by the examination of thousands of stomachs to take fully as much vegetable as animal food, the vegetable food being chiefly grain and fruit. This bird needs watching, for the grain he eats amounts to 45 per cent. of his food. About one-third of his food consists of insects most of which are of harmful species. He also eats a few snails, crawfishes, salamanders, small fish, and occasionally a mouse.

During the breeding season the Grackle does much good by eating insects and by feeding the nestlings with them. In the spring he will follow the plow in search of grub-worms, of which he is so fond that he sometimes literally crams his stomach full of them.

BOAT-TAILED GRACKLE

Megaquiscalus major major (*Vieillot*)

A. O. U. Number 513

General Description.— Length, 16 inches. Male, glossy black; female, sooty-brown above and light brown below. Bill, about the length of the head, narrow, and curved downward at the tip; wing, moderately long; tail, as long or longer than wing and graduated for from ½ to ⅓ its length. The tail is plicate, or capable of being folded vertically, so that a transverse section is V-shaped, the two edges being brought near together when flying; because of this folding and the graduated form of the tip, the effect, when the bird is flying, is very peculiar, the tail appearing as if much longer on one side than on the other.

Color.—Adult Male: Head and neck, glossy dark violet, passing gradually into steel-blue on the back and breast, this into dark bluish-green on rump, abdomen, and flanks (duller on rump); lesser wing-coverts, dark steel-blue, the middle coverts green or bluish-green; rest of wings, together with the tail, black, very faintly glossed with bluish-green; thighs, and under tail-coverts, black; bill, black; iris, light yellowish. Adult Female: Crown and hindneck, sepia-brown, rest of upper parts dark sooty-brown, faintly glossed with greenish; a stripe of lighter buffy-brown on the eye; a streak of dusky-brown back of eye; sides of neck, chest, and sides light brownish; chin, throat, and abdomen, similar but paler; flanks, thighs, and under tail-coverts, dusky-brown.

Nest and Eggs.— Nest: In colonies, among reeds, in swamps, in small trees, bushes, removed from water, in saplings or in fully grown trees as high as 40 feet above ground; a large, bulky, rough structure of sticks, grass, bark strips, and roots, generally coated inside with mud. Eggs: 3 to 5, generally 4, brownish-drab tinged with olive or green; irregularly blotched with brownish and black.

Distribution.— South Atlantic and Gulf coasts of United States (including whole of Florida); north to coast of Virginia, west to coast of Texas.

This is the "Jackdaw" of the South and is essentially a bird of the coast districts of that region. It got its popular name from the early settlers of the country on account of its superficial resemblance to the European Jackdaw, which, of course, is a totally different bird. It is very common in the marsh lands of southern Louisiana, Florida, Georgia, and South Carolina, and also on many of the swampy islands along the south Atlantic and Gulf coasts. A rather uncommon characteristic of the species is that in the spring migration the females precede the males. The maneuvers of the females in these spring flocks are also remarkable, their rapid and sustained flight, sharp turns, hoverings, and sudden dives, during which the flock remains closely bunched, suggesting to some observers the employment of signals from a leader. It is much more probable, however, that the evolutions are random and are due to the whims of two or three of the birds, which are instantly accepted by the others.

Like the other members of its family, this Grackle walks when on the ground, and not infrequently the birds catch passing insects by means of flying leaps into the air. Another curious characteristic of the species is the desertion of the females by the males immediately incubation has begun. From that time the males remain in flocks by themselves. Upon the females, therefore, devolves all of the feeding and protecting of the young until they are able, with their mothers, to join the fathers who had deserted them.

In its insect food the Boat-tailed Grackle has no very pronounced tastes, and while it does not cause any great havoc among useful insects, it does not prey extensively upon harmful ones. In common with most other land birds, it eats grasshoppers freely in July and August, and it probably would eat caterpillars if it found them more plentiful than other foods. The animal food it decidedly prefers is small crustaceans — especially the small crabs called "fiddlers"— and these, so far as the interests of agriculture are concerned, are entirely neutral.

In its vegetable diet, the bird certainly does not commend itself to the agriculturist. Its preference for corn is very marked and shows no variance with the change of season. Investigations by the Biological Survey show that in any locality where this Grackle is very abundant it is harmful to the corn crop without rendering any well-defined service in return.

Photo by T. H. Jackson Courtesy of Nat. Asso. Aud. Soc.

NEST AND EGGS OF BOAT-TAILED GRACKLE

Orange Lake, Florida

PART III

ORDER OF PERCHING BIRDS—Concluded

FINCHES

Order *Passeres;* suborder *Oscines;* family *Fringillidæ*

HE Finches are the largest family of birds; there are about twelve hundred species and subspecies scattered over the world except in Australia; about two hundred are represented in the United States. They belong to the larger division of singing birds. All have cone-shaped bills, nine feathers in the hand section of the wing, and a sharp angle at the back of each foot. The line of opening of the bill turns downward near the base, and in some of the Finches the cutting edge of the lower bill is distinctly elevated about the center, this raised portion forming a tooth. At the corners of the mouth are bristles, sometimes indistinct but usually quite easily seen. There are always twelve feathers in the tail, but the shape varies. The nostrils are high up, bare in some species and in others covered with bristles.

The plumage varies from almost plain to highly variegated. The coloring of the Sparrows is adapted to their grassy, dusty habitats and the males and females are similar; while in the subdivision of Finches the males are chiefly bright-colored and the females either duller or with a distinct plumage. Nests are generally placed on the ground or in bushes or in low trees.

These birds are essentially seed-eaters, their strong bills being peculiarly adapted to this kind of food. They do, of course, eat insects also. Because of this indifference to animal food the Finches are less migratory than most birds.

Year by year the usefulness of this family is more and more appreciated by humans. They lay the farmer under a heavy debt of gratitude by their food habits, since their chosen fare consists largely of the seeds of weeds. Some idea of the money value of this group of birds to the country may be gained from the statement that the total value of the farm products in the United States in 1910 reached the sum of $8,926,000,000. If we estimate that the total consumption of weed seed by the combined members of this family resulted in a saving of only one per cent of the crops — not a violent assumption — the sum saved to farmers by these birds in 1910 was $89,260,000.

Their work begins before the seeds are ripe and continues throughout fall and winter and even far into spring. The Sparrows that breed on the farm have to content themselves early in the spring with seeds left from the preceding year. During August the seed-eating of Sparrows is sufficiently noticeable to attract the attention of even a casual observer; for by this time great stores of weed seed have ripened and the young Sparrows, which have been exclusively insectivorous, are ready to take vegetable food. From autumn to spring evidence of the seed-eating habits of Sparrows is so plain that he who runs may read; the lively flocks diving here and there among the brown weeds to feed are familiar adjuncts of every roadside, fence row, and field. A person visiting one of the weed patches in the agricultural region of the upper Mississippi valley on a sunny morning in January, when the thermometer is 20 or more below zero, will be struck by the life and animation of the busy little inhabitants. Instead of sitting forlorn and half frozen, they may be seen flitting from branch to branch, twittering and fluttering, and showing every evidence of enjoyment and perfect comfort. If one of them is shot, it will be found in excellent condition — in fact, a veritable ball of fat.

The most serious charge that can be brought against members of the Finch family is that they distribute noxious plants, the seeds of which pass through their stomachs and germinate when voided from the body. However, it seems likely that this agency of seeding down farms to weeds is infinitesimal when compared with the dispersion of weeds caused by the use of manure containing weed seed and the planting of impure seed, which often contains seeds of foreign weeds of the worst stamp. Birds take seeds for food and it seems probable that such use would preclude the evacuation of any but a most insignificant proportion of uninjured seeds.

Four vernacular names have been applied to this group: Buntings, Grosbeaks, Sparrows, and Finches. "Bunting" means plump, or dumpy, or rounded out, as a sail is filled with the wind, and its application to this family refers to the stocky little bodies of its members. "Grosbeak" has reference to their short, thick bills, but is not altogether appropriate as there are birds in other families with this characteristic. "Sparrow" literally means "flutterer" and has come to us from the Anglo-Saxon *spearwa*, through the mediæval English *sparwe*, *sparewe*, and *sparowe*. "Finch" is also of Anglo-Saxon origin, but its literal meaning has been lost. Robert Ridgway considers it the most appropriate of the popular names for this family in America; he says (manuscript) that in a strict sense the term "Sparrow" pertains to the species *Passer* only, represented in America only by the introduced House Sparrow, or so-called English Sparrow, and in this restricted sense we have no native American true Sparrows; on the other hand there are many true Finches in America.

EVENING GROSBEAK

Hesperiphona vespertina vespertina (*W. Cooper*)

A. O. U. Number 514 See Color Plate 79

Other Names.— Sugar Bird; American Hawfinch.

General Description.— Length, 8¼ inches. Males, yellowish and black; female, gray and black. Bill, heavy; legs, short; tail, short and slightly emarginate; wings, nearly twice the length of tail and pointed.

Color.— Adult Male: *Forehead and stripe over the eye, yellow; crown, black;* rest of head with neck and upper back, plain olive, lighter and more yellowish olive on throat, changing gradually to clear *lemon-yellow on shoulders and rump* and to lighter yellow on posterior under parts, the longer under tail-coverts sometimes partly white; *upper tail-coverts, tail, and wings black; inner wing quills, white* or pale grayish; bill, light olive-yellowish or pale yellowish green; iris, brown. Adult Female: Above, plain deep smoke-gray, the head darker, the rump paler; the hindneck tinged with yellowish olive-green; throat, abdomen, and under tail-coverts white; rest of under parts, light buffy-grayish usually tinged with yellow, especially on sides of chest; wings, dull black with innermost greater coverts largely dull white, inner wing quills largely light gray; the primaries edged with white and pale gray, all except the three outermost quills white at base, forming a distinct patch; upper tail-coverts black with large terminal spots of pale buffy-grayish and white; tail, black with inner webs of feathers broadly white at tips.

Nest and Eggs.— Nest: Usually placed in the top of a conifer from 15 to 50 feet up; sometimes in other trees; a saucer-shaped affair of small twigs, grass, rootlets, bark strips, lined with fine rootlets or horsehair. Eggs: 3 or 4, clear green blotched with pale brown.

Distribution.— Interior districts of North America east of Rocky Mountains; north (in winter) to the Saskatchewan; south, in winter, irregularly, to Kansas, Iowa, Illinois, Kentucky, Ohio, etc.; eastward, irregularly and in winter only, to Ontario, New York, and New England. Breeds in western Canada.

The Hawfinch of England has lived in a populous land and among a people appreciative of the beauty of a beautiful bird. The American relative of the Hawfinch, nesting far out in the less accessible foothills of Alberta and up in the Canadian Rockies, has failed to meet with the poetical disposition and the friendship that belong to the admirers of the Hawfinch. The Evening Grosbeak is in reality a stranger to civilization except in the newer West, and this newer West is a stranger to him. In the winter there may be seen in the northwestern States scattered flocks of these Grosbeaks strikingly marked in their yellow and black. When certain seeds are scarce they will drift on into the eastern States in the middle of winter, reaching New England and the Maritime Provinces. But these years are not often.

During the early months of 1916 the presence of these birds in the East excited an unusual interest. The first record of the Evening Grosbeak in New York city was during the 1911 migration. The ornithological magazines and daily papers had many letters on the observations made of the 1916 migration. Sara Chandler Eastman gave the following interesting and informing record to *Bird-Lore:* "The first record of the Evening Grosbeak at Portland, Maine, was made early in February, when a large flock settled in a mountain-ash on private grounds in the western part of the city. Throughout the months of February and April flocks in varying numbers were observed in different sections of the city, and the birds remained until the eleventh of May, none being seen, so far as known, after that date." The birds were seen both in low pine trees and on the ground. She added that "the males were in beautiful plumage, and it was a rare treat to see them, one's pleasure being greatly enhanced by their fearlessness, as they would permit a close approach without taking flight." Their call is short and cheery, and has been called by Mrs. Bailey, "wild and free."

Down from western Canada through the mountains all the way to Mexico is a variety called the Western Evening Grosbeak (*Hesperiphona vespertina montana*). They breed in the cañons in Arizona and are found not uncommonly near water throughout the southwestern mountain country. In many of the towns of the Pacific northwest they are fairly common winter birds in the street maples and in the parks and woodsides. Mrs. Bailey writes interestingly of their protective coloration. "While watching the birds on Mt. Shasta one day, I was struck by the conspicuousness of one that flew across an open space. As it lit on a dead stub whose silvery branches were touched with yellow lichen, to my amazement it simply vanished."

L. Nelson Nichols.

On his winter visits, the Evening Grosbeak may be found feeding on the buds or seeds of trees. The maple, elder, box-elder, and ash, each give their quota to him. The fruit of the sumac also attracts him. But none of these is valued as highly by him as are the various frozen or dried fruits on vines and trees; of all food his

Drawing by R. I. Brasher

EVENING GROSBEAK (⅓ nat. size)

A beautiful bird of the North who displays misplaced confidence in "civilized" man

preference is for apple seeds taken from frozen apples. A Michigan bird student reports that several of these birds which he kept in captivity for nearly two years refused to eat any kind of grain except a few oats and that only when hard pressed. Insects of any kind that could be secured they absolutely refused to touch.

PINE GROSBEAK

Pinicola enucleator leucura (*Müller*)

A. O. U. Number 515 See Color Plate 76

Other Names.— American Pine Grosbeak; Canadian Pine Grosbeak; Canadian Grosbeak; Pine Bullfinch.

General Description.— Length, 9 inches. Male, pale red and gray; female, gray and yellowish. Bill, short, broad, and thick; wings, long and pointed; tail, long and emarginated; feet, small.

Color.— Adult Male: General color of head, neck, and under parts (except abdomen, flanks, anal region, and under tail-coverts), rather light poppy-red (in summer) or dull pinkish red (in winter), the feathers grayish beneath the surface, this exposed in places, especially on chest; nasal tufts and part of lores and eye region, dusky; abdomen and upper portion of sides and flanks, rather light dull ash-gray or smoke-gray; under tail-coverts, similar but in part darker, broadly margined with white; the space between the shoulders, dusky, broadly margined with red; shoulders, dark grayish, margined with paler gray; rump, superficially, red; upper tail-coverts, broadly margined with red; wings, dull slate-dusky, most of the feathers edged with light grayish and white (the edgings broader and decidedly white on the inner quills), the greater and middle coverts broadly tipped with white, forming two conspicuous bands, which are sometimes, especially the anterior one, tinged with red; tail, slate-dusky edged with grayish (sometimes tinged with red). Adult Female: General color, plain smoke-gray, the crown and rump and part of upper tail-coverts, bright yellowish olive, tawny-olive, or russet, the back and anterior under parts, especially chest, sometimes tinged with the same; otherwise like adult males.

Nest and Eggs.— Nest: Usually in conifers; constructed with foundation and outside walls of twigs and rootlets enclosing a well woven "inner" nest of finer twigs, grasses, and bark strips. Eggs: 4, pale greenish-blue, spotted and blotched with dark umber-brown and lavender.

Distribution.— Northeastern North America, breeding from Cape Breton Island, southern Nova Scotia, New Brunswick, Maine, New Hampshire, Province of Quebec, etc., north to limit of coniferous forests; south in winter to southern New England, New York, northern New Jersey, Pennsylvania, northern parts of Ohio, Indiana, and Illinois, Iowa, etc., casually to District of Columbia, Kentucky, and Kansas; west to eastern Kansas, Minnesota, Manitoba, etc.

Some cold bright winter morning when first we step out into the frost, we hear a pleasing mellow whistle, and see several birds resembling Robins glide up into the apple tree or the clump of spruces in the front yard. Investigation reveals that there are about a dozen of them, moving about in rather a sedate and deliberate manner. Several are on the ground, the rest scattered about in the nearby trees, perhaps biting into frozen apples, or at work on the evergreen cones; in either case trying to get at the seeds encased within. Most of them are dark gray, but one or two look pinkish in the morning sunshine. A rather rare treat is ours, a visit from those nomads of the cold North, the Pine Grosbeaks.

Drawing by R. I. Brasher

PINE GROSBEAK (½ nat. size)

A bird that loves the great pine forests of Canada and the United States

The sight is of some significance. It may imply that the spruces in the northern forests are not bearing the normal crop of cones, and that this is one of the seasons, occurring only about once every half dozen years or so, when there will be a notable influx into the United States of Canadian winter birds. Probably the Crossbills and Redpolls will also be seen, with the accompanying flight of the fierce Goshawks, which prey upon them, also the Northern Shrike, and other northern birds. There is an added incentive now for winter outings, which will pay dividends in health and vigor through getting away from poorly ventilated indoors. Somehow there is a peculiar charm about these birds from the northern wilds which make no account of the fierce cold.

During one such winter some friends of mine

discovered a Pine Grosbeak by a roadside unable to fly, owing to a slight injury to the wing, and took it home. The wing soon healed, and the bird, a young male, became very tame. Frequently it was released from the cage and would fly about the room, alighting on the persons of its benefactors to eat seeds, crumbs, or tender leaves such as lettuce. In spring it had a pretty warbled song. I saw it in late summer when it was molting and had lost most of its tail-feathers.

One year a flock of these interesting birds visited my garden daily from the middle of January to early March. They devoted themselves mostly to the maple seeds on the ground under those trees. I swept off the snow for them, and thus secured their daily return. It was most entertaining to watch them twirl the winged seeds in their bills and bite out the kernels. They are also partial to sumac, mountain ash, or other trees which bear and hold berries, and are not above eating some buds, of which surely there are enough.

In common with the Crossbills this species is said to breed very early, even when there is snow, but like them also it is probably irregular in this respect, as nests have been found in summer. HERBERT K. JOB.

In western North America are several varieties of the Pine Grosbeak. The Rocky Mountain Pine Grosbeak (*Pinicola enucleator montana*) lives in the Rocky Mountains from west central Alberta, Idaho, and Montana to northern New Mexico. The California Pine Grosbeak (*Pinicola enucleator californica*) breeds in the central Sierra Nevadas, in California. The Alaska Pine Grosbeak (*Pinicola enucleator alascensis*) breeds from northwestern Alaska and northwestern Mackenzie to northern Washington and winters south to eastern British Columbia and Montana. The Kodiak Pine Grosbeak (*Pinicola enucleator flammula*) is a bird of southern Alaska coming south in winter along the coast to British Columbia. The differences between these western forms and between them and the common Pine Grosbeak are trifling — a little larger or a little smaller in size, a shade darker or a shade lighter in coloration.

Photo by H. K. Job Courtesy of Outing Pub. Co.

PINE GROSBEAK

In Mr. Job's garden

The economic status of the Pine Grosbeaks is as nearly neutral as that of any bird could be. They do no particular good beyond the possible distribution of seeds of valuable trees and, on the other hand, the few buds they eat from the evergreen and shade trees do not amount to much. Most of their food consists of buds from pine, spruce, and tamarack trees, the berries of the Virginia juniper and the mountain ash, and the seeds of the maples.

PURPLE FINCH

Carpodacus purpureus purpureus (*Gmelin*)

A. O. U. Number 517 See Color Plate 76

Other Names.— Purple Linnet; Purple Grosbeak; Red Linnet; Gray Linnet (immature and female).

General Description.— Length, 6¼ inches. Male, pinkish-purple and brown; female, olive-grayish above, and white below, conspicuously streaked above and below. Bill, shorter than head, conical, and thick; tail, about ¾ length of wing, deeply emarginate.

Color.— ADULT MALE: Crown, deep wine-purple (more crimson in summer); rump, paler, more pinkish wine-purple; back and shoulders, reddish-brown or wine-purplish, streaked with darker; wings and tail, dusky with light brownish-red or light brown edgings, the middle and greater coverts, broadly tipped with dull wine-purple or light brownish-red; eye and ear regions dusky brownish-red; rest of head, together with front and lateral under parts, pinkish wine-purple; abdomen, anal region, and under tail-coverts, white; flanks usually streaked with brown, and longer under tail-coverts rarely marked with narrow streaks of dusky. ADULT FEMALE: Above, olive or olive-grayish (more olivaceous in winter), streaked with dusky and, to a less extent, with whitish; wings and tail, dusky with light olive or olive-grayish edgings; a broad stripe of olive on side of head, and a more broken stripe or patch of the same on sides of throat; ear and cheek regions, mostly whitish, streaked with olive; under parts, white (tinged with buff in winter) broadly streaked with olive, except on abdomen, anal region, and under tail-coverts, the streaks distinctly wedge-shaped or triangular.

Nest and Eggs.— NEST: Usually placed in conifers; a frail open-work structure of grass, rootlets, bark strips, vegetable fibers, thickly lined with hair; resembles a Chipping Sparrow's nest, but larger. EGGS: 4 to 6, dull greenish-blue spotted with shades of brown, black, and lilac.

Distribution.— Eastern North America; breeding from Pennsylvania (especially in mountains), northern New Jersey, Connecticut, southern Ontario, northern Illinois, Minnesota, and North Dakota, north to more eastern British provinces, Hudson Bay, Manitoba; in winter south to Gulf coast.

The haunts of the Purple Finch are the low green forests, not the denser portions, but rather the open woods and swamps where firs and cedars are numerous. He is one of the conspicuous birds of such a neighborhood. From the top of a balsam or a spruce he delivers his song — a rapid, easily flowing, melodious warble, resembling in a measure that of the Warbling Vireo but more variable in character. Sometimes when overcome with emotion he launches into the air with vibrating wings, rising upward and upward, melody pouring from his throat like a torrent down a mountain side, until he has reached an altitude of two or three hundred feet, when with outstretched wings he descends in wide circles to the summit of the very tree from which he started. Occasionally this impassioned outbreak comes with such suddenness as to startle anyone who may be nearby.

Courtesy of Am. Mus. Nat. Hist.

PURPLE FINCH (¾ nat. size)

From the top of a balsam or a spruce he delivers his song

Often he may be seen dancing about a female on the limbs of a tree or on the ground. His wings will be fully extended and quivering, his crest standing as high as possible, his tail spread, and the bright feathers of the rump raised in the air. During this performance he gives voice softly and sweetly to his melodious warble. Presently, apparently overcome by his emotion, he closes his wings and flies to a neighboring tree — but in a short time he repeats his antics.

In addition to his song, he has a sharp call-note, *pip,* uttered while flying, and another, *chip chee,* used when feeding. The immature males, which look like the females, sing almost as well as the full-plumaged males. Several observers have stated that the female sings, but not as sweetly as the male.

In western North America we find in the valleys the California Purple Finch (*Carpodacus purpureus californicus*) and on the mountain slopes Cassin's Purple Finch (*Carpodacus cassini*). The California Purple Finch is about the same size as the eastern bird, but the red is bright rosy instead of wine color. The Cassin's Finch is similar to the California but duller in coloration and he is larger by about an inch.

The scientific name given to this group of birds is very expressive of a bad habit indulged in by them. *Carpodacus* is from the Greek, and translated into English means "fruit-biting." When the trees are budding they do considerable harm in the peach and cherry orchards by eating the buds. Later they have been found feeding on green cherries. In the winter any seed-bearing tree will furnish them with a meal. Though they habitually feed in trees, they often destroy the seeds of noxious weeds. A bird of this species was watched with a glass while feeding in a thicket of giant ragwood. In three minutes he ate fifteen seeds.

HOUSE FINCH

Carpodacus mexicanus frontalis (*Say*)

A. O. U. Number 519

Other Names.— Crimson-fronted Finch; Red-headed Linnet; Linnet; Burion; Red-head.

General Description.— Length, 5½ inches. Upper parts, brownish-gray; under parts, white streaked with brown. Bill, shorter than head, conical, and thick; tail, about ¾ length of wing, nearly even.

Color.—Adult Male: Forehead (broadly), broad stripe above the ear (extending from forehead to back of head), *cheek region, throat* (sometimes upper part of chest also), *and rump, bright red;* rest of upper parts, hair-brown tinged with red; the wings and tail, dusky with pale grayish brown and brownish gray edgings; *under parts* (except throat, etc.) *dull whitish, thickly streaked with hair-brown,* the breast sometimes tinged with pale red; bill, dark horn-brownish; iris, brown. Adult Female: Similar to the adult male, but without any red, that of the upper parts replaced by the general hair-brown, that of throat, etc., by streaks of white and grayish brown, like rest of under parts.

Nest and Eggs.— Nest: Usually about houses, but located anywhere in trees, bushes, sagebrush, hay stacks, old boxes, tin cans, but always near water; carelessly or compactly constructed of any handy material, grass, string, paper, rags, straw, bark strips, or plant fibers. Eggs: 3 to 6, bluish white or pale greenish blue, sparingly marked with spots and lines of sepia or black; rarely unmarked.

Distribution.— Western United States and northern Mexico; north to southern Wyoming, southern Idaho, and Oregon; south to Tamaulipas, Nuevo Leon, northern Chihuahua, northern Sonora, and northern Lower California; east to western border of the Great Plains (middle Texas to western Kansas and southeastern Wyoming).

The House Finch or Red-headed Linnet through many parts of the West is the commonest bird about the dooryard. It is even more abundant and more familiar than the Robin through the northern States. It is especially fond of nesting in vines about the porch, a cypress hedge, or any favorable place not far from the house. The bird is so familiar and abundant through parts of California and it has such a strong taste for the fruits planted by man, that Red-head and his wife are often regarded as a nuisance. However, if a person is willing to trade his cherries, figs, and other fruit for bright bird music and companionship, the Linnet is willing to give full value for all the fruit he takes.

While studying birds at Tucson, Arizona, in the spring of 1910, we found the House Finch one of the commonest residents. We used to watch a pair daily through the Virginia creeper that shaded our porch and window. There were the remains of two old nests, one at the corner of the porch and one in front of the window.

One morning early, we saw the male and female looking at the nest by the window. He of the Red-head turned around and around on the remains of the old nest as if saying, "Come

Photo by W. L. Finley and H. T. Bohlman

HOUSE FINCH

In many places he is regarded as a nuisance

on; we can fix this up. We can add a little to it and have a modern house." But this did not suit the lady, for she turned and flew away in disgust and he followed. Yet in a little while, they were back again discussing the same question. We saw the wife take hold of one of the old strings as if she thought it might be a good idea to use it in the new home. At least, it would save a little hunting. And, indeed, that is just what they did. They built a new nest about six feet away. Occasionally when they got tired of hunting straws and strings for the new house, they pulled a little out of the old nest until the last straw was used.

Out in San Clemente Island off the southern coast of California, we found House Finches were very numerous about the sheep camp. There were no trees in which they could nest, so their homes were found in every odd corner about the sheds. I counted about forty nests, some old, and many new ones containing eggs. The door of the blacksmith shop was tied open and in behind this I found a nest wedged and resting on an inch strip. A House Finch was sitting on five eggs. Had the door been untied, the nest would have fallen to the ground. I found another nest in an old can that was hung against the wall. On nearly every beam and bracket in the sheep sheds, was a Linnet's home. Some of these, I could see, had been used over and over again, the bird, of course, remodeling or building a little on the old home. The birds used the material closest at hand. Many of the nests were made of wool that had been thrown about on the floor. The only fruit about the island was that of the cactus and this seemed to satisfy the Linnets. Whenever a sheep was killed and the Mexicans hung the fresh meat out in the open, the Linnets took their share. I saw where all the meat had been picked from several bones that were hanging up.

William L. Finley.

There are several varieties of the House Finch south of the United States and Mexican border. North of the boundary is one local form, the San Clemente House Finch (*Carpodacus mexicanus clementis*) found in the Santa Barbara Islands, California, and darker in coloration than the House Finch.

Observations in orchards show that in the fruit season, the House Finch is not backward in taking what it considers its share of the crop, and as it spends much of its time there, field observations alone would lead to the conclusion that fruit was its principal article of diet.

Examination of stomach contents proves that such is not the case, and when we find how small is the relative percentage of fruit eaten, it seems strange that its fruit-eating proclivities should have attracted so much attention. But it must be borne in mind that the bird is wonderfully abundant, which is a primary condition under which any species may become injurious. Moreover, it must be noted that not all of the fruit destroyed is eaten. Only one peck from the strong bill is necessary to break the skin of the pear, peach, or cherry, and the fruit is spoiled; the House Finch by no means invariably visits the same individual fruit a second time to finish it, but often attacks a fresh one at each meal. This is proved by the large number of half-eaten fruits, either on the tree or on the ground beneath.

While the strong, conical beak of the House Finch is a very effective instrument in attacking fruit, this is evidently not the use for which nature primarily designed it. Hard-billed birds are supposed to feed on seeds and that this species is no exception has been proved by examinations of contents of over 1200 stomachs. Seeds of plants, mostly those of noxious weeds, constitute about seven-eighths of its food for the year and in some months amount to much more.

CROSSBILL

Loxia curvirostra minor (*Brehm*)

A. O. U. Number 521 See Color Plate 77

Other Names.—American Crossbill; Red Crossbill; Common Crossbill.

General Description.— Length, 6 inches. Male, dull red; female, grayish-olive. Bill, with the tips crossed in adults; wings, long and pointed; tail, short, narrow, and deeply forked.

Color.—Adult Male: General color, dull red (varying from dull brownish scarlet or almost orange-chrome in summer to a hue approaching dragon's blood red in winter), the red brightest on rump, dullest on back and shoulders, where the feathers have dusky brownish centers; middle of abdomen, light grayish;

bill, horn color, more dusky at tips; iris, brown. Adult Female: The red of the adult male replaced by grayish-olive or olive-grayish overlaid with bright yellowish olive or dull saffron-yellow, this brighter color always evident on rump and sometimes prevalent over under parts (except abdomen and under tail-coverts); wings and tail, less dark, more grayish dusky. Young: Wings and tail as in adult female; upper parts, pale grayish mixed or tinged with olive on back and shoulders (sometimes almost white on head, neck, and rump) everywhere broadly streaked with dusky; beneath, whitish, usually tinged with olive, conspicuously streaked with dusky or dusky olive.

Nest and Eggs.— Nest: Placed, like the White-winged Crossbill's, in conifers, usually within 20 feet of the ground; outside "wall" constructed of evergreen twigs, shreds of bark, rootlets with a thick lining of moss, leaves, grass, cottony fibers well felted together, and generally some green bits of hemlock or cedar tips. Eggs: 3 or 4, pale greenish, specked and spotted with shades of brown and purplish gray.

Distribution.— Northern and eastern North America, breeding in coniferous forest districts from southern Alleghenies in northern Georgia (sporadically toward coast in Maryland, Virginia, etc.), Michigan, etc., to Nova Scotia, to Fort Anderson in the interior, and to western Alaska, and southward through Pacific coast district to western Oregon; in winter irregularly southward to South Carolina (vicinity of Charleston), Louisiana, Nevada, etc.; casually to the Bermudas.

The Crossbill is the only American bird with the curious crossing of the bills. No group of water birds or parrots or ducks or tropical birds of any kind have crossed bills. Only this one genus of *Loxia* in the Finch family is so peculiarly fashioned. Because of this singular characteristic, they are among the most interesting birds in the American avifauna.

Drawing by R. I. Brasher

CROSSBILL (½ nat. size)

Don't pity this bird because of his crossed bill; it 's exactly what he needs

All-wise man has been known to point to the Crossbill as one of the "blunders" of Nature, and to sympathize with the poor creature thus "deformed." If such an observer had taken the pains to do a little real observing, he would have discovered that the crossed bills are really a special and very clever adaptation to the bird's feeding habits. For an important part of the Crossbill's diet consists of pine-cone seeds, and these it readily obtains by means of its "deformed" bill. The process consists in inserting the closed bill into the side of the cone, and then opening the mandibles with a movement which tears out the scales and thus leaves exposed the seeds at their bases. These seeds are then seized by the peculiarly shaped, scoop-like tongue. By this operation the bird will cut an apple to pieces in a few seconds to get at the seeds. The mandibles are operated by muscles so powerful that the bird will splinter solid wood with them; and they can be closed tightly enough to hold the smallest seed.

Many of the careful bird observers of the northern States have never seen a Crossbill. This is largely a matter of accident, the bird student not happening to be at the same place as the bird, whose wandering habits are very uncertain. No one can expect to go into any piece of cone-bearing forest and find Crossbills; there may not be a Crossbill within a hundred miles.

Some observations have been made south of Canada in the summer time in most unexpected localities, but it is from November to March that flocks of from a few dozen to a few hundred roam about from forest to forest, and occasionally fly about towns where coniferous trees are scattered or where small frozen apples and hard rose seeds tempt the birds to a side dish. Dr. Merrill reports them as common at Fort Sherman, Idaho, where they can be seen every month of the year and are as tame as English Sparrows. But in the east the eccentric wanderings of the flocks have made their visitations events of importance to bird observers.

Their *kimp-kimp* or *pip-pip,* somewhat like a chicken peeping, is the conversational chatter that can be heard while a few dozen birds are breaking up the cones far up in the trees. The song, given only during the breeding season, is said by Gerald Thayer to be "a series of somewhat goldfinch-like trills and whistles."

Alfred Newton in his *Dictionary of Birds* says of the process of feeding on cone seeds: "Fortunately the birds soon become tame in confinement, and a little patience will enable an attentive observer to satisfy himself as to the process, the result of which at first seems almost as unaccountable as that of a clever conjuring trick."

European Crossbills have been imported into America, but it is not known if the stock has continued. The largest of the Crossbills is the Mexican Crossbill (*Toxia curvirostra stricklandi*) whose northern area extends up into the higher mountains of Arizona and New Mexico. These birds are about an inch longer than the eastern variety. After the breeding season the Mexican variety comes down out of the mountains. Dr. Mearns found them one year among the most commonly seen birds of Arizona, flying about at all times at the watering places and springs.

The White-winged Crossbill (*Loxia leucoptera*) is similar in general appearance to the American Crossbill but somewhat larger, the red of the male rose-red or even crimson, and the wings in both sexes, old and young, with two conspicuous white bars. (See Color Plate 77.) It is less known than the other Crossbills, and ranges a little farther north toward the arctic seas. It seems to be somewhat less common than the Red Crossbill. The flocks seem a little more active and shy, are apt to remain in the tops of trees if food is plenty there, and fly about calling their *cheep, cheep* loudly and less sedately than the Red Crossbill. Many years will sometimes elapse before numerous flocks will be seen in the northern States in winter. Then the conspicuous white wing-bars and the rosy red males will make their appearance for a few winter weeks. Toward spring its song has sometimes been heard in the wandering flocks. Elon H. Eaton says that it is "a beautiful song, perhaps more melodious than that of the Red Crossbill, a low, soft warbling, suggesting somewhat the song of the Redpoll." Its nidification is similar to the Common Crossbill's. The eggs are light blue, spotted around the large end with sepia, black, and lilac; they number three to five and are laid in the winter or early spring when the ground is covered with snow.

L. Nelson Nichols.

The Crossbills are of little importance from an economic standpoint. Very little is known of their summer food; they probably eat some insects. On their winter visits to the United States they show their fondness for the seeds of the arbor vitæ, tamarack, various spruces, firs, and pines. The peculiar structure and strength of their bills enable them to tear open the strongest and toughest cones and extract the seeds. Occasionally they injure an evergreen by cutting the twigs or destroying the terminal buds, but as a rule this damage does not amount to much.

GRAY-CROWNED ROSY FINCH

Leucosticte tephrocotis tephrocotis *Swainson*

A. O. U. Number 524

Other Name.— Gray-crowned Leucosticte.

General Description.— Length, 7¼ inches. Body, brown; crown, gray. Bill, shorter than head; wings, long and pointed; tail, about ⅔ length of wing, and forked; legs short. Generally found on the ground.

Color.—Adult Male in Summer: Forehead and part of crown, black; nasal tufts, grayish white; sides of crown (from above eyes backward) and whole of back of head, plain light ash-gray, very strongly contrasted with the contiguous brown color of the ear regions and hindneck; whole side of head below eyes (whole of ear and cheek regions), neck, back, shoulders, and under parts, chestnut-brown, darker on throat, lighter on back where indistinctly streaked with dusky; feathers of rump and flanks, together with upper and under tail-coverts, broadly and abruptly tipped with pink; the remaining portion of the feathers dusky, especially on the rump and upper tail-coverts; wings and tail, dusky; the lesser and middle coverts, broadly tipped with pink; the greater coverts, primary coverts, and part of wing quills edged with pink or light scarlet, tail-feathers also with lighter edgings but with less of pink; bill, entirely black. ADULT MALE IN WINTER: Similar to summer male but shoulders and space between with distinct edgings of lighter brown, feathers of breast, etc., with narrow, pale margins; the pink markings, especially on wings and flanks, of a softer hue, and the bill yellowish with dusky tip. ADULT FEMALE: Similar to adult male, with the same seasonal differences of color, but averaging paler and duller.

Nest and Eggs.— NEST: In a rocky crevice at high altitudes; constructed of grasses, weed stems, lined with fine grass and a few feathers. EGGS: 3 to 5, pure white, sharp pointed, with a peculiar fine shell texture.

Distribution.— Interior districts of North America; breeding on higher parts (11,000–12,000 feet) of White Mountains and Sierra Nevada, southeastern California, and probably also northward; during migration east to western Nebraska, eastern Colorado, Manitoba, etc.; south to Colorado, Utah, etc.; west to Cascade and Sierra Nevada ranges; north to plains of the Saskatchewan (May).

Amid the snowbanks and glaciers of western North America are found the Rosy Finches. They are optimistic little creatures living the gospel of "come storm or sunshine all is well." When it is cold and stormy they will seek out some sheltered spot and quietly wait for better weather. With the coming of the sun, out they scatter again, just as happy as ever. Where the vegetation is mostly moss and lichens and low-stunted spruce and when the weather is like the typical month of March these birds start their house-keeping.

Hepburn's Rosy Finch (*Leucosticte tephrocotis littoralis*) is similar to the Gray-crowned but the gray of the crown extends down the sides of the head; in typical examples the entire head except a black frontal patch and the throat are light ash-gray. It nests above the timber-line in Alaska and in winter comes south to Nevada, Utah, and Colorado, and along the Pacific coast to Kodiak, Sitka, and Vancouver Island.

The Black Rosy Finch (*Leucosticte atrata*) breeds in the mountains of Idaho and winters in Colorado and Utah. It is a little smaller than the Gray-crowned with the same marking on the head, but the body is brownish black.

The Brown-capped Rosy Finch (*Leucosticte australis*) has no distinct or clear grayish markings on the head. It breeds above the timber-line on the high mountains of Colorado, descending to the valleys and plains and south to New Mexico in the winter.

The food of the Rosy Finches is mainly insects and seeds which have been blown to the mountain heights by the storms. They hunt for the chilled insects and the seeds along the edge of the melting snows and they may be seen with their feathers fluffed, their faces turned toward the wind, busily hopping about and picking up their food, all the time cheerily chattering. Occasionally one will take shelter behind a stone or lump of snow and warm his toes against his warm little body.

REDPOLL

Acanthis linaria linaria (*Linnæus*)

A. O. U. Number 528 See Color Plate 78

Other Names.— Redpoll Linnet; Common Redpoll; Linnet; Lintie; Lesser Redpoll; Little Redpoll; Little Meadowlark.

General Description.— Length, 5½ inches. Upper parts, grayish-brown streaked with dusky; under parts, white and pink or buff; red cap. Bill, small, conical, and acute; wings, long and pointed; tail, long and deeply forked.

Color.—ADULT MALE IN BREEDING DRESS: Forehead (narrowly), dusky; *crown, bright poppy-red;* general color of remaining upper parts, dark grayish-brown or sepia, indistinctly streaked with darker and with grayish-white; rump, mixed pink and grayish-white, broadly streaked with dusky; upper tail-coverts, grayish-brown edged with paler; wings and tail, dusky grayish brown; the middle and greater wing-coverts, narrowly tipped with grayish-white; chin and upper portion of throat, dusky; *cheeks, lower throat, chest, and sides of breast, deep peach-blossom pink;* rest of under parts, white, the sides, flanks, and under tail-coverts broadly streaked with dusky. ADULT MALE IN WINTER PLUMAGE: Much lighter colored than in summer, the prevailing color of back, shoulders, and hind neck, light buffy grayish-brown, distinctly streaked with dusky; the pink of chest, etc., paler (rose pink). ADULT FEMALE: Similar to the male, but without any pink or red on the under parts, the portions so colored on the male being pale buffy or whitish; the seasonal differences exactly as in the adult male. YOUNG: No red on crown, the whole crown being broadly streaked with dusky and pale grayish buffy; sides of throat, chest, and sides of breast, buffy or dull buffy whitish, streaked with dusky.

Nest and Eggs.— NEST: Placed in trees or bushes; bulky, loosely made exteriorly of twigs and grasses, warmly lined with feathers. EGGS: 2 to 5, pale bluish green, speckled around large end with chestnut, burnt-umber, and a few spots of black.

Distribution.— More northern portions of northern hemisphere; breeds southward to islands in Gulf of St. Lawrence; in winter south to more northern United States generally, irregularly and more rarely to Virginia, northern Alabama, southern Ohio, southern Indiana, Kansas, Colorado, southeastern Oregon, coast of Washington, etc.; casual in Bermudas.

The home of the Redpoll is in the northland. There he rears his family in a quiet business-like way. This accomplished he puts on his rosy suit and sallies forth with the snow for a vacation. He joins others of his own kind and is rarely found except in flocks of twenty to fifty, and sometimes there are 200 or 300. While on this winter tour the Redpolls visit and mingle with their cousins the Crossbills and the Goldfinches.

When he is at home the Redpoll has little time for singing — only indulging in a faint warbling or twittering — but with the throwing off of family responsibility he proves that he can sing delightfully. His song is more melodious than that of the Goldfinch; it has the quality of the *tweet* call of the Goldfinch and is delivered in the manner of the Goldfinch's warble. He also has at least four distinct call-notes: a loud twittering call, used when on the wing; a long *buzz,* not unlike one note of the Pine Siskin but thinner and longer; a conversational twitter, used when several birds are feeding together; and a *ker-weet,* very much like the long plaintive call of the Goldfinch but different in tone.

The Redpoll is very unsuspicious and often allows a person to approach very closely without taking alarm. Should one stand still near where they are feeding they will come closer and closer as they feed without a sign of fear.

Drawing by R. I. Brasher

REDPOLL (⅔ nat. size)

A confiding little bird who comes south from the northland, especially when he is hungry

The Greater Redpoll (*Acanthis linaria rostrata*) is a resident of Greenland; in winter he comes south through Canada to northern Illinois, Michigan, northern Indiana, southern New York and Massachusetts. He looks like the Common Redpoll but is of greater size and has a relatively thicker and more obtuse bill. (See Color Plate 78.)

J. ELLIS BURDICK.

Very often when the Crossbill visits us there will be found in his company the Redpoll. After the stronger bird has torn open the cones the other will pick out the seeds. He also attacks cones himself, especially those of the tamarack and arbor vitæ, but not always successfully. To a large extent he feeds on the seeds of the birches and alders. He also eats grass seeds and weed seeds.

EUROPEAN GOLDFINCH

Carduelis carduelis (*Linnæus*)

See Color Plate 79

Other Names.— Thistle Finch; Thistle Bird.

General Description.— Length, 5½ inches. Body, brown; wings and tail, black; red spot on head. Bill, elongate, conical, and acute; wings, long and pointed; tail, rather short and deeply notched.

Color.—ADULTS: Fore part of head, all round, crimson; lores, back part of crown, back of head and neck, and bar from the latter halfway across side of neck, black; rest of head, white tinged with brownish buff; back, shoulders, and rump, plain brown; upper tail-coverts, white; wings and tail, mostly black; greater portion of greater coverts, basal portion of outermost secondaries, and basal half or more of exposed portion of outer webs of primaries, bright lemon-yellow; secondaries, primaries, and middle tail-feathers tipped with white, the inner webs of side tail-feathers, also partly white; sides of breast, sides, and flanks, plain cinnamon-brown or wood-brown; rest of under parts white; bill, whitish tinged with flesh color or lilac; iris, brown. YOUNG: Wings and tail as in adults, but the former with middle and greater coverts tipped with pale brownish, forming two bands; no red on head nor black on head or neck; crown and back of neck light grayish brown, mottled or streaked with darker; the back also streaked with dusky; chin and throat, whitish, the latter flecked with sooty brown; the foreneck, chest, and breast, mottled or spotted with the same.

Nest and Eggs.— NEST: A handsome thick-walled structure of vegetable down, moss, and fine grasses; the few noted in this country indicate a preference for conifer trees as a site. EGGS: 4 to 6, more commonly 5, pale greenish or bluish white, spotted with chestnut around large end.

Distribution.— Europe in general, except extreme northern portions; south, in winter, to Palestine and Egypt. Introduced into the northeastern United States and naturalized in Cuba, in New York city and vicinity, and Cincinnati, Ohio; accidental (?) at New Haven, Connecticut, near Boston, Worcester, etc., Massachusetts, Toronto, Ontario, etc.

The European Goldfinch is well known all over Europe and has been introduced into America. How many times and at what places the attempt has been made to Americanize this favorite of Europeans is uncertain. About 1872 it was introduced at Cincinnati, in 1878 at Hoboken, about 1880 in eastern Massachusetts, and in 1886 in Cuba. There may have been more importations. For a few years these beautiful birds were seen in the vicinity of New York city. In 1900 they were seen at nest building in Central Park. Dr. Chapman saw two in Englewood, N. J., in 1911, but records are very rare. There have been scattered observations in Massachusetts and Connecticut. In 1888 four birds were seen in Toronto and in 1899 one bird in Ithaca, N. Y. A German who knew the bird as the *Distelfink* (Thistle Finch) is confident that he saw one in Chicago in 1911. About New York city they had formerly been seen in flocks of American Goldfinches with which their manners and customs matched perfectly. It would seem that this cheery and attractive little bird is not to become as common as the English Sparrow, and "more's the pity." In Europe the Goldfinch has been a favorite cage bird for centuries. So many thousands were captured in Great Britain alone that Parliament had to take action for the protection of the bird. But it seems never to have been as common again.

GOLDFINCH

Astragalinus tristis tristis (*Linnæus*)

A. O. U. Number 529 See Color Plates 78, 79

Other Names.— Yellow-bird; Thistle Bird; Wild Canary; Catnip Bird; Lettuce-bird; Shiner; Salad-bird; Beet Bird; American Goldfinch.

General Description.— Length, 5 inches. Male in summer has the body lemon-yellow and the wings and tail black; male in winter and female at all seasons have the upper parts olive-brownish and the under parts grayish-white with the wings and tail blackish. Bill, small, conical, and acute; wings, long and pointed; tail, rather short and forked; legs, short.

Color.—ADULT MALE IN SUMMER: General color pure lemon or canary-yellow; the lores, forehead, and crown, together with wings (except small coverts) and tail, black; tail-coverts, middle (sometimes also lesser) wing-coverts, tips of greater coverts, and part of edges of wings, white; bill, orange or orange-yellow tipped with black; iris, brown. Adult Female in Summer: Above, olive-brownish or grayish, sometimes tinged with olive-greenish; the wings and tail, blackish or dusky marked with white or whitish, much as in the male; upper tail-coverts, pale grayish or grayish-white; under parts, dull grayish-white tinged with yellow, especially in the front and on the sides, sometimes entirely soiled yellow, except under tail-coverts. Adult Male in Winter: Similar to the adult female but wings and tail deeper black, with whitish markings more conspicuous. Adult Female in Winter: Similar to the summer female, but more brownish. Young: Somewhat like winter adults, but much browner, all the wing-markings, pale cinnamon, the plumage generally being suffused with this color.

Nest and Eggs.— Nest: Placed in forks of bush or sapling, sometimes on the swaying stalk of a wild blackberry, usually within 5 feet but sometimes 30 feet from the ground; a compact, artistic structure of felted plant down, mosses, grass, leaves, bark strips, usually lined with thistledown; build later than any other birds, from last week in June to second week in September; sometimes reconstruct old Blackbird or other nests, the added material being principally a heavy lining of down. Eggs: 3 to 6, sets of 5 and 6 being common, pale bluish white, unmarked.

Distribution.— United States and more southern British provinces east of Rocky Mountains, north to Manitoba, Ontario, Quebec, southern Labrador, and Newfoundland; breeding southward to the middle districts of the United States; wintering southward to Gulf coast.

The Goldfinch is one of the most interesting birds of American life. It is a bird the most casual observer can enthuse over, and one that the bird student will never tire raving about. The male is such a bright yellow bird with black wings and tail that he readily becomes known as the Wild Canary in any community where he is commonly seen. Then its habit of feeding about where people go to and fro, scarcely heeding the inquisitive humans, has increased the knowledge of the bird. But when the sun begins to warm the earth and air, and summer is here, the Goldfinch is then in his ecstasy. Swinging through the air, its *per-chic-o-ree, per-chic-o-ree* is as sweet in note as any caged Canary's. The abandon and wild delight of the bird at this season while most other birds are feeding their young has brought forth many interesting comments from the nature writers. Dr. Chapman in his *Handbook* says that "their love song is delivered with an ecstasy and abandon which carries them off their feet, and they circle over the field sowing the air with music." After most of the other birds are through with their nesting, and all of the others have already begun, the Goldfinch gathers his thistledown and fine grasses together for the nest in a berry bush or some other low shaded place just out of the sun's rays. The *per-chic-o-ree* changes gradually to notes more directly personal for the mate and young. *Tic-o-ree, o-ree, o-ree* and many variations are heard. There are those who insist that the male calls *ba-by, ba-bee* to the young in the nest. Certainly the notes are as sweet and in-

Drawing by R. I. Brasher

GOLDFINCH (⅔ nat. size)

A beautiful little fellow with jolly manners and a fine canary-like song

sistent as any parent with such a throat could utter.

In the fall the males turn olive, something like the females and immature. They gather into flocks, a few dozen or a few hundreds and haunt the weedy fields and seedy marshlands where the lilt of the Canary-like note is apt to be heard even into the middle of winter. Let the sun but shine a little warmer in the early spring and maybe it will be a Goldfinch instead of a Bluebird that will greet the promise of spring. Its all hail will be *see-see-e* many times repeated.

From ocean to ocean this bird is common. In the Rockies it is larger and lighter with purer tints in winter plumage, and is there distinguished by the varietal name of Pale Goldfinch (*Astragalinus tristis pallidus*). On the Pacific coast the differences are not as great as in the mountains, but great enough to make a separate variety called the Willow Goldfinch (*Astragalinus tristis salicamans*). Down through the luxuriance of southern California they have been known as "gentle-spirited birds" that "seem as light-hearted as butterflies." (Mrs. Florence Merriam Bailey.)

In her *Birds Through an Opera Glass* the same author says of the Goldfinch in the east: "Being a vegetarian, his store-house is always well filled, for if the snow covers the seeds he would gather from the brown weed-tops, he goes to the alders in the swamp; and if they fail him he is sure to find plenty in the seeds of the hemlock, the spruce, and the larch."

L. Nelson Nichols.

In winter this Goldfinch feeds largely on weed seeds, the seeds of birches, and those of the buttonbush. In summer it subsists to a large extent on weed seed, but destroys many noxious insects, such as cankerworms, plant lice, small grasshoppers, and beetles. The habit of feeding on thistles which has given the species the common name of "Thistle Bird" is well exemplified by the following field note: A thistle on which a Goldfinch had been feeding was examined and on its leaves and the ground beneath sixty-seven seeds were counted. They appeared perfect, but close inspection showed a slit through which the meaty kernel had been deftly removed. Dr. S. D. Judd reports having been able to approach within ten feet of four Goldfinches who were feeding on ragweed. Often they would all alight on the same plant at once, then they would

Photo by J. H. Field

NEST AND EGGS OF GOLDFINCH

wrench off the seeds, extract the meat, and drop the shell, their actions resembling those of a Canary at its seed cup. In one instance three alighted on a very small plant, which under their weight bent to the ground. Nothing daunted, they clung to the sprays, heads downward, until they touched the earth, then shifting their position so as to hold the stems under their feet, went on with their meal.

ARKANSAS GOLDFINCH

Astragalinus psaltria psaltria (*Say*)

A. O. U. Number 530

Other Names.— Tarweed Canary; Arkansas Greenback.

General Description.— Length, 4½ inches. Upper parts, olive-greenish; under parts, yellow; wings and tail, black or dusky. Bill, small, conical, and acute; wings, long and pointed; tail, rather short and forked; legs, short.

Color.— Adult Male: *Crown, glossy black;* ear

region, hindneck, back, shoulders, and rump, olive-green; *wings, black with a large white patch at base of primaries;* greater wing-coverts, tipped with white or pale grayish; primaries narrowly and inner wing quills broadly edged with the same; upper tail-coverts, black, margined with olive-green; tail, blackish; *under parts, light yellow.* ADULT FEMALE: Above including crown, olive-greenish, the crown sometimes indistinctly streaked with dusky; wings, as in adult male, but general color grayish dusky instead of black; tail with the white on inner webs of exterior tail-feathers restricted to a squarish spot in middle portion; under parts, light olive-yellow. YOUNG: Similar to adult female, but tinged with buffy-brownish above, the lighter wing-markings buffy, and the under parts a paler and duller, or more buffy, yellow.

Nest and Eggs.— NEST: In small trees or bushes; a counterpart of the American Goldfinch's, but, like the eggs, smaller. EGGS: 4 or 5, pale bluish-green.

Distribution.— Western United States, from coast of California to eastern base of Rocky Mountains; north to northern California, southern Idaho, Utah, and Colorado; south, in winter at least, to southern Lower California and southern New Mexico and Arizona; breeding south to San Pedro Martir Mountains, northern Lower California.

There is a very near relative of the Goldfinch, residing exclusively in the western states; he is the Arkansas Goldfinch. He is a little smaller than the members of the more widely distributed family. A friendly little fellow is he, constantly found in gardens and along the roadsides, sometimes busily feeding among the weeds on the ground and again tossing his song to the winds from the top of some tall eucalyptus tree.

This Goldfinch is a long time acquiring the full adult plumage and first breeds in the immature plumage. This fact led to a great deal of confusion, and the three stages of development were each given a different name until enough specimens had been collected to prove that the variations were due merely to age.

A slightly variant form of the Arkansas Goldfinch is known as the Green-backed Goldfinch (*Astragalinus psaltria hesperophilus*) and is found in the southwestern United States and northwestern Mexico from California and Lower California to Utah, Arizona, and extreme southwestern New Mexico.

The Arkansas Goldfinch feeds almost entirely on weed seeds.

PINE SISKIN

Spinus pinus (*Wilson*)

A. O. U. Number 533 See Color Plate 78

Other Names.— Pine Finch; Pine Linnet; American Siskin; Northern Canary Bird.

General Description.— Length, 4¾ inches. Upper parts, grayish; under parts, white; streaked above and below with dusky. Bill, small, conical, and acute; wings, long and pointed; tail, rather short and forked; legs, short.

Color.—Above, grayish or brownish, conspicuously streaked with dusky, the ground color of the rump paler (whitish or light grayish); wings and tail, dusky or dull blackish; middle and greater wing-coverts, tipped with whitish, and inner wing quills edged with same; basal portion of wing feathers (especially secondaries) and tail feathers, pale yellow, mostly (often entirely) concealed; under parts, dull white, everywhere (except on abdomen and anal region) streaked with dusky.

Nest and Eggs.— NEST: Usually located in a conifer, from 20 to 30 feet up, well concealed; walls roughly constructed of hemlock or other twigs and moss; a saucer-shaped structure one-half foot across; the interior, about two inches in diameter, is carefully and thickly lined with plant down, fur, and hair. EGGS: 4 to 6, pale bluish or greenish white lightly spotted with chestnut and some black.

Distribution.— Northern coniferous forest districts of North America, breeding south to Nova Scotia, New Brunswick, parts of New England, lower Hudson valley, mountains of Pennsylvania, and southward to high mountains of North Carolina, Minnesota, etc., and on the high western ranges quite to the southern boundary of the United States; in winter, south to Gulf coast (including Florida and Texas), valleys of California, etc., and into Mexico; casual or accidental in Cuba.

Someone has said that any bird is frequent enough to be common if you go where it breeds. The Pine Siskin breeds from the Atlantic to the Pacific and yet very few people have ever seen the bird. The reason is that the bird not only confines itself pretty closely to the evergreen mountain forests, but even there it is uncertain in its abode. One year it may be seen in large numbers about one group of mountain peaks and valleys. The next year not a Siskin can be found in the whole district. This uncertainty in its breeding areas is as nothing to the eccentricity of the fall and winter ramblings. Many winters pass without a Siskin being seen about New York city, Boston, Washington, and Chicago. Then again there are winters when they are tolerably common. Its notes are somewhat similar to the Goldfinch's. T. M. Trippe of Colorado wrote to Dr. Coues that "in spring it sings very agreeably, very much like the latter bird [the Goldfinch], but in a lower voice; and like it has the habit of singing in a lively, rambling sort of way for an hour or more at a time."

The birds congregate in large flocks after the breeding season. There is nothing particularly interesting to attract an observer to a flock feeding quietly in the weeds. They look like plain little striped brown Sparrows. Startle them and the flock as one bird will rise and wheel off to a more distant feeding ground. A quick observer will notice the yellow patches on the wings and tail. Then too they may utter weak *tit-i-tit* notes, or on occasions will break out in Goldfinch-like *see-a-wee* notes that betray the close relationship to the Wild Canary. Herbert K. Job calls them Northern Canary Birds, and says that he found them in their nesting grounds in June in northern Nova Scotia; and that they were singing prettily in the shade trees along the streets of Pictou. Wells W. Cooke said that in Colorado the Siskins range from the timber-line in the high mountains down to about 7000 feet above sea level. "Some stay near the timber-line through the winter, but the bulk scatter over the lower valleys and plains."

Herbert K. Job says that it was early in October when he saw the Siskins for the first time. He was hunting Partridge and Woodcock and in an opening in the woods he saw a flock of them alight on a tree. Trembling with excitement he fired into the midst of them and obtained a number of specimens. Never since has he seen so large a flock. The ordinary bird observer may not be so excited as Mr. Job was, but he had better look long and earnestly when he sees his first flock, for it may be many a day before he sees the second.

L. Nelson Nichols.

The Pine Siskin is very similar in his habits to the Goldfinch and the Redpoll and associates very freely with them. Not infrequently he is seen with Crossbills. He feeds principally on the seeds of the white cedar, tamarack, and the various pines and spruces. When the ground is bare he eagerly eats the fallen seeds of maple, elm, and other trees, as well as grass and weed seeds. Frequently he is reported in the spring as feeding on dandelion seeds.

ENGLISH SPARROW

Passer domesticus (*Linnæus*)

Other Names.— European House Sparrow; Gamin; Tramp; Hoodlum; Domestic Sparrow.

General Description.— Length, 5¾ inches. Upper parts, reddish-brown, streaked with black; under parts, grayish-white. Bill, stout, shorter than head; wings, of medium length; tail, about ¾ length of wing; legs, short and rather stout.

Color.—Adult Male: Crown, deep gray or olive-gray bordered laterally by a broad patch of chestnut extending from behind the eye to sides of neck; chin, throat, and chest, black; a small white spot above rear angle of the eye; back and shoulders, rusty brown streaked with black; lesser wing-coverts, chestnut; middle coverts, blackish tipped with white forming a conspicuous bar; rest of wings, dusky with light brown and rusty brown edgings; rump, olive or olive-grayish; tail, dusky edged with light olive or olive-grayish; cheek region and sides of throat, white; under parts of body, dull grayish white, more grayish laterally; bill, black. Adult Female: Crown and hindneck, grayish brown or olive; chin, throat, and chest, dull brownish white or pale brownish gray like rest of under parts; otherwise like the adult male, but back browner.

Nest and Eggs.— Nest: Occasionally built in trees, more often in bird-houses, electric-light hoods, cornices, water-spouts, and similar places; tree-nests large and covered, others open; made of grasses or any easily obtained material, loosely put together, and lined with feathers. Eggs: 4 to 7, generally white, finely and evenly marked with olive, but also varying from plain white to almost uniform olive brown; two broods at least in a season, usually three, and sometimes four and even five.

Distribution.— Europe in general, except Italy; introduced into the United States, where thoroughly and ineradicably naturalized in all settled districts, except southern Florida and a few other extreme outposts; also introduced into Bahamas (island of New Providence), Cuba, Nova Scotia, Bermudas, and southern Greenland.

The English Sparrow or European House Sparrow was introduced into America in 1850. In the fall of that year eight pairs were brought to Brooklyn, N. Y., and liberated in the following spring. Since that time many importations have been made, and small lots of sparrows have been carried from one locality to another until now the bird is naturalized nearly all over the United States. This rapid dissemination is a result of the bird's hardiness, extraordinary fecundity, diversity of food, aggressive disposition, and almost complete immunity from natural enemies.

Drawing by L. A. Fuertes Courtesy of U. S. Dept. of Agriculture

ENGLISH SPARROWS

Male Female

Taking possession of a nesting box provided for a native bird

Although English Sparrows are widely distributed as a species, individuals and flocks have an extremely narrow range, each flock occupying one locality and confining its operations to that particular territory.

The House Sparrow is a persistent enemy of many native birds, especially those which frequent the neighborhood of houses, or which nest in boxes, holes, or other places prepared for them by their human friends. Being a winter resident, he starts his nesting early and when the other birds arrive, all the available nesting sites are occupied and the new-comers must either fight for a place or go elsewhere. Not infrequently he directly attacks Robins, Song Sparrows, Chickadees, Flycatchers, Thrushes, Tanagers, and other birds, while they are feeding and annoys them by repeated calls at their homes.

The filthy habits of these birds are most annoying. They gather in immense flocks to roost, and generally select cornices, ornamental work about the eaves and gables of houses, window-cappings, and the vines which cover the walls of buildings. These they defile with their excrement. Great and serious damage is often caused by their carrying nesting materials into rain-spouts, gutters, and similar places about houses, so that cisterns are defiled, or pipes overflow, causing destruction of or injury to property.

The English Sparrow, when once established increases with wonderful rapidity. At least two broods are raised in a season, but the usual number is three and trustworthy observers have recorded four and five. Very seldom are there less than four birds in a brood and the old birds are generally successful in getting the young on the wing without any accidents. Therefore an immense number of these Sparrows can be raised in a limited area in one season. A dozen pairs in the course of three or four years will have increased, if let alone, to thousands.

The English Sparrow among birds, like the rat among mammals, is cunning, destructive, and filthy. Its natural diet consists of seeds, but it eats a great variety of other foods. While much of its fare consists of waste material from the streets, in autumn and winter it consumes quantities of weed seed and in summer numerous insects. The destruction of weed seed should undeniably count in the Sparrow's favor. Its record as to insects in most localities is not so clear.

In exceptional cases it has been found very useful as a destroyer of insect pests. For example, during an investigation by the United States Biological Bureau of birds that destroy the alfalfa weevil, English Sparrows were feeding their nestlings largely on weevil larvæ and cutworms, both of which are very injurious to alfalfa. In this case the Sparrows, attracted by grain in the fields and poultry runs and by the excellent nest sites afforded by the thatched roofs of many farm buildings, had left the city and taken up their abode in the country where the weevil outbreak subsequently occurred. Unfortunately, however, farmers can rarely expect such aid against their insect foes. Whenever this bird proves useful it is entitled to protection and encouragement in proportion to its net value. Under normal conditions its choice of insects is often unfavorable.

The English Sparrow destroys fruit, as cherries, grapes, pears, and peaches. It also destroys buds and flowers of cultivated trees, shrubs, and vines. In the garden it eats seeds as they ripen, and nips off tender young vegetables, especially peas and lettuce, as they appear above ground. It damages wheat and other grains, whether newly sown, ripening, or in shocks. As a flock of fifty Sparrows requires daily the equivalent of a quart of wheat, the annual loss caused by these birds throughout the country is very great. It reduces the numbers of some our most useful native birds, as Bluebirds, House Wrens, Purple Martins, Tree Swallows, and Barn Swallows, by destroying their eggs and young and by usurping nesting places.

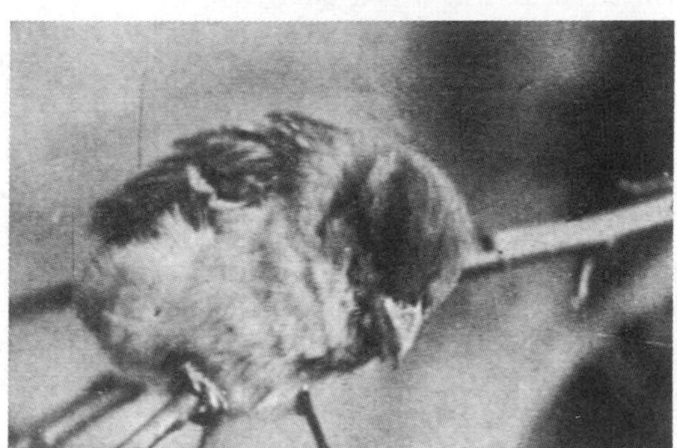

Photo by H. T. Middleton

FEMALE ENGLISH SPARROW

SNOW BUNTING

Plectrophenax nivalis nivalis (*Linnæus*)

A. O. U. Number 534 See Color Plate 80

Other Names.— Snowflake; Snow Lark; Snowbird; Whitebird; White Snowbird.

General Description.— Length, 8 inches. In Summer: Male, white with black markings; female, white, streaked on upper parts with black. In Winter: Both sexes have the upper parts stained with rusty. Bill, with lower section thicker than the upper section; wings, long and pointed; tail, about 3/5 length of wing, forked, and the middle pair of feathers pointed at the tip.

Color.—Adult Male in Summer: General color, pure white; back, shoulders, innermost secondaries, and greater wing-coverts, greater part of primaries, and four to six middle tail-feathers (sometimes rump also), black; bill, black; legs and feet, black, or the former sometimes dark brown. Adult Male in Winter: Similar to the summer plumage, but the white parts (except under parts of body) stained with rusty brown, especially on crown (where sometimes rich dark brown) and hindneck, and the black of the back, shoulders, etc., broken (sometimes almost concealed) by broad margins of rusty and buffy whitish; bill, yellow. Adult Female in Summer: Crown, dusky, the feathers margined with dull whitish or pale grayish buffy; hindneck, dull whitish or pale dull buffy, streaked with dusky; back and shoulders (sometimes rump also), dull black or dusky, the feathers margined with dull whitish (their edgings quite worn off in midsummer plumage); lesser and greater wing-coverts, blackish margined and edged with whitish; greater part of secondaries, three outermost tail-feathers, and under parts (sometimes rump also), white; bill, dusky. Adult Female in Winter: Similar to summer female, but upper parts stained with rusty brown, especially on crown, ear region, and sides of chest, and margins to feathers of back, etc., paler, broader, and more buffy or buffy grayish; bill, yellowish. Young: Head, neck, back, shoulders, and rump, brownish gray tinged with olive, the back streaked with dusky; front under parts paler gray than upper parts, the chest and sides of breast usually very faintly streaked with dusky; under parts of body, mainly white, usually tinged with pale olive-yellowish; wings and tail, much as in winter adults.

Nest and Eggs.— Nest: On the ground in grassy tussocks; a large, well built structure, exteriorly composed of dried grass, moss woven into thick walls, the small, deep center thickly feathered. Eggs: 4 to 6, white or pale greenish white, spotted with raw umber and lavender.

Distribution.— Northern parts of Europe, Asia, and North America; breeding in arctic and subarctic districts; in North America breeding on the barren-ground or tundra region from northern Labrador to Alaska, north and east of the coast ranges, and north to islands of Arctic Ocean (at least to latitude 82°); in winter south to more northern United States, irregularly to District of Columbia, Florida, Georgia, southern Ohio, southern Indiana, Kansas, Colorado, northern California, and eastern Oregon; casually to the Bermudas; south in Asia to northern Japan and China.

When the polar explorers have pushed far beyond the Eskimo villages and out into the wastes where the musk-ox and blue fox live, there they find the Snow Bunting or Snowflake in his nesting home. Across the polar islands along the northern shore of Alaska and only as far south as the bleak and inhospitable shores of Hudson's Bay, these birds may be found in the breeding season. Only in the depth of winter do they drift on down into the northern United States to haunt the snow-swept hillsides of the farms, and the bleak and stormy shores of New England at their bleakest and stormiest season. They are so much whiter than other Sparrows that they seem indeed like animated gusts of arctic weather as they pass along over the ground, the rear birds drifting on over to the front of the advancing ranks. Many a person muffled to the eyes in a cold winter's sleigh ride has seen the Snowflakes feeding cheerily and by choice out in the bitter biting zero weather of wind-swept fields. Sometimes, indeed, they will straggle far south, even to the Gulf coast, but the first sign of advancing spring will send them on their long flights far across Canada to areas little known and to some not yet explored.

Drawing by R. I. Brasher

SNOW BUNTING (½ nat. size)

A hardy and beautiful winter visitor from the northland

While flying, the members of the flock keep up a tinkling whistle, a note that has been likened to the syllable *tee* repeated at intervals by the various members of the flock; when disturbed, they utter a harsh *beez-beez*. What sweet, weird song they sing to the sunrise of the morning of the six-months arctic day, the explorers have yet to tell us. Dr. Elliott Coues gives an interesting account of these birds at Fort Randall on the Missouri River, some distance above Yankton (*Birds of the Northwest.*) The Snowflakes "reached Fort Randall November 15. after a severe cold snap with a light snow-fall, and as I write (January), great numbers are swirling over the ground around and in the fort. They keep pretty closely in flocks numbering from a dozen or so to several hundred, and, though they spread over the ground a good deal in running about after seeds, they fly compactly, and wheel all together. In their evolutions they present a pretty sight, and have not a displeasing stridulent sound, from mingling of the weak chirrups from so many throats."

John Burroughs rises to his best literature as he speaks of this bird (*Far and Near*). "The only one of our winter birds that really seems a part of the winter, that seems to be born of the whirling snow, and to be happiest when storms drive thickest and coldest, is the Snow Bunting, the real snowbird, with plumage copied from the fields where the drifts hide all but the tops of the tallest weeds, large spaces of pure white touched here and there with black and gray and brown. Its twittering call and chirrup coming out of the white obscurity is the sweetest and happiest of all winter bird sounds. It is like the laughter of children. The fox-hunter hears it on the snowy hills, the farmer hears it when he goes to fodder his cattle from the distant stack, the country schoolboy hears it as he breaks his way through the drifts toward the school. It is ever a voice of good cheer and contentment."

In the Far North are found two other members of this branch of the Finch family. They never come as far south as the United States. The Pribilof Snow Bunting, or Aleutian Snowflake (*Plectrophenax nivalis townsendi*) is similar to the better known Snow Bunting but decidedly larger with a relatively longer bill. As his name indicates his home is among the Aleutian Islands; he is also found on other islands of that region and along the Siberian coast of Bering Sea. McKay's Snow Bunting or Snowflake (*Plectrophenax hyperboreus*) is similar to the Pribilof Snow Bunting, but with much more white, the back and shoulders of the adult male being entirely white. This Snow Bunting breeds on Hall Island and St. Matthew's Island, north-central part of Bering Sea; in the winter it migrates to the western portion of the Alaskan mainland.

L. Nelson Nichols.

The Snow Bunting feeds almost exclusively from the ground; the reports of his feeding in trees are rare. Small seeds — pigweed, ragweed, and all kinds of grass — are his chief foods. From Nebraska comes a statement that he always eats locusts' eggs when they are obtainable.

LAPLAND LONGSPUR

Calcarius lapponicus lapponicus (*Linnæus*)

A. O. U. Number 536

Other Name.— Common Longspur.

General Description.— Length 7¼ inches. Upper parts, light brownish, streaked with blackish; under parts, white. Bill, small; wings, long and pointed; tail, more than ⅔ length of wing, and double rounded; hind claw, long and slender.

Color.— Adult Male in Summer: *Head and chest, deep black,* relieved by a broad white or buffy stripe behind eye, continued downward (vertically) behind ear-coverts and then backward along sides of chest; sides, broadly streaked or striped with black; rest of under parts, white; hindneck, deep chestnut-rufous; rest of upper parts, light brownish, broadly streaked with blackish; lesser wing-coverts, grayish, feathers black in center. Adult Male in Winter: Black of head confined to crown, posterior and lower border of ear-coverts, lower part of throat, and patch on chest, all more or less obscured by whitish or pale brownish tips to feathers; sides of head (including lores and greater part of ear-coverts), mostly dull light brownish; rufous on hindneck also similarly obscured. Adult Female in Summer: Much like the winter male, but markings more sharply defined, black areas of chest, etc., more restricted and still more broken, hindneck streaked with blackish and size smaller. Adult Female in Winter: Similar to summer plumage, but browner and less sharply streaked above, hindneck often without trace of rufous, lower parts dull brownish-white, and dusky markings very indistinct.

Nest and Eggs.— Nest: On ground or in tussock of grass; constructed of fine dried grass and moss; lined with feathers or fur shed from the winter coats of the arctic fox. Eggs: 3 to 6, dull white specked and spotted and clouded with umber-brown so thickly as almost to obscure the ground color.

Distribution.— Breeding in arctic and subarctic districts of Europe, northeastern North America, including Greenland, and for an undetermined distance westward to at least the more western portions of Siberia; in North America migrating south in winter (more or less irregularly) to Virginia, South Carolina, Kentucky, eastern Kansas, Oklahoma, and even to Texas; west during migration to eastern portion of Great Plains (Manitoba to Texas).

The general characteristics of the Longspur family are the small acutely conical bill, which is deeper at the base than it is wide; exposed nostrils; long, pointed wing; tail more than half hidden by the pointed upper coverts; and a slender and nearly straight hind claw about the length of the toe. There are three species, differing considerably in details of form. The type species is the Lapland. Smith's Longspur, or the Painted Longspur (*Calcarius pictus*), found on the interior plains of North America east of the Rocky Mountains from the Arctic coast in summer south to Texas in winter, is very similar to the Lapland, but has a slenderer and more pointed bill. The Chestnut-collared Longspur (*Calcarius ornatus*) differs from the other two species in having the tail much shorter than the distance from the carpal or wrist joint of the wing to the end of the wing-quills. The Chestnut-collared is also an inhabitant of the great plains of the United States, but instead of extending his range to the north he prefers Mexico.

A relative of this family — so close a relative that he has adopted the family name for popular use — is McCown's Longspur (*Rhynchophanes mccowni*). He is found on the interior plains of North America, east of the Rocky Mountains. His bill is much larger and relatively thicker and his tail relatively shorter than in his cousins. His nostrils are nearly concealed by well developed soft feathers. The Lapland Longspur and its varieties, the Alaska and Siberian Longspurs (*Calcarius lapponicus alascensis* and *Calcarius lapponicus coloratus*), inhabit a broad subarctic belt around the world during the breeding season. In North America the Alaska occupies the northwestern tundras east to the Mackenzie country. From there east to northern Labrador and Greenland the species is the same as the one that extends across northern Europe and east into western Siberia. It derives its name from that part of the northern Russian tundras called Lapland. The differences noted in America between the Alaska and Lapland are so slight that they may be generally disregarded by the casual student. In the winter they come down to the northern States to stay only as long as the northern barrens are swept by the unbearable storms. While here they are seen in the most numbers in broad prairie lands and along the wide sloping mountain meadows. In the East they are not as commonly seen, but many Snowflake flocks have a few Longspurs. The Shore Larks that feed up and down the wintry seashore of New England and the middle States have also many Longspurs among them.

Toward spring the male becomes a beautiful bird with his black head and breast. He is the most conspicuous creature of the northern barrens when he reaches there in April. Louis A. Fuertes said after an Alaskan trip, that the Longspur sang the most beautiful song north of Bobolink-land. Edward W. Nelson has given much time to the study of the bird. "The Lapland Longspur is one of the few birds, which, like the Skylark and the Bobolink, are so filled with the ecstasy of life in spring that they must rise into the air to pour forth their joy in singing. The males are scattered here and there over the tundra on their chosen projecting points and at frequent intervals mount slowly on tremulous wings ten or fifteen yards into the air. There they pause a moment and then, with wings uppointed, forming V-shaped figures, they float gently back to their perches, uttering, as they sing, their liquid notes, which fall in tinkling succession on the ear. It is an exquisite, slightly jingling melody . . . resembling the song of the Bobolink."

Courtesy of Am. Mus. Nat. Hist.

LAPLAND LONGSPUR (2/3 nat. size)

In April he is the most conspicuous creature of the northern barrens

L. Nelson Nichols.

VESPER SPARROW

Poœcetes gramineus gramineus (*Gmelin*)

A. O. U. Number 540 See Color Plate 82

Other Names.— Bay-winged Bunting; Grass Finch; Gray Bird; Pasture Bird; Grass Sparrow; Ground-bird; Bay-winged Finch.

General Description.— Length, 6¼ inches. Upper parts, grayish-brown, streaked with black; under parts, white. Bill, small; wings, long and pointed; tail, about ¾ length of wing, forked, and with the feathers rather narrow.

Color.— Adults: Above, light grayish-brown (hair-brown) conspicuously streaked with black, the streaks broadest on back, less distinct on rump; lesser wing-coverts, cinnamon or russet with a dusky (mostly concealed) wedge-shaped central space; wings otherwise and tail dusky, the feathers edged with light grayish-brown, especially the larger wing-coverts and secondaries, the former (middle and greater coverts) indistinctly tipped with pale dull buffy, forming indistinct narrow bands; *outermost tail-feathers, largely white;* region over eye, light grayish brown or brownish gray, narrowly and indistinctly streaked with dusky; ear region, browner; a white or buffy white cheek stripe margined below by a series of dusky streaks along each side of throat; under parts dull white tinged with pale buffy on chest, sides, and flanks; iris, brown.

Nest and Eggs.— Nest: Always placed upon the ground, sunk level, in pastures, meadows or along roadsides in the brush; rather bulky, thick rimmed, well cupped but not tightly woven; constructed of dried grass, weed stalks, some bark strips, and lined with fine grass and hair. Eggs: 4 to 6, grayish or bluish-white spotted with burnt umber and chestnut.

Distribution.— Eastern United States and more southern British provinces; breeding from Virginia, Kentucky, Missouri, etc., northward to Nova Scotia(?), Prince Edward Island, New Brunswick(?), Province of Quebec(?), eastern Manitoba(?), etc.; south in winter to Gulf coast (Florida to eastern Texas); casual in Bermudas.

It has been said that what the Veery's song is to the deep woods, the Vesper Sparrow's is to the fields and pastures. There is a certain accuracy in this comparison, and yet the songs are essentially different in spirit; for the Veery's resonant tremolo has an elfin-like ring, which is entirely absent from the Sparrow's simple little expression of quiet thankfulness and very beautiful contentment. Both songs may be heard at any hour of the day, but there seems to be an especial sincerity and spontaneity in the Sparrow's utterance when it blends perfectly, as it always does, with the spirit of the evening and the advancing shadows. Then it is truly vesperian, and in that respect few birds have been more appropriately named.

Some listeners consider the song similar to that of the Song Sparrow, but such similarity certainly is not invariably present; and generally the songs are quite different in mood and musical structure. Mr. Torrey expressed this general difference accurately when he said that the Song Sparrow's utterance is more declamatory and the Vesper's more cantabile. Frequently the Ves-

Photograph by A. A. Allen

FOUR LAPLAND LONGSPURS AND FOUR PRAIRIE HORNED LARKS

per's lay is a simple descending series of notes, very sweet and somewhat violin-like in quality, delivered with increasing rapidity. Not infrequently the song is heard in the dead of night, and occasionally the bird delivers a quite elaborate flight-song as it flutters upward to a height of fifty or seventy-five feet. This effort is very different from the usual leisurely ditty, generally rendered from a conspicuous perch atop a fence-post or bush.

Photo by H. K. Job Courtesy of Outing Pub. Co.

NEST OF VESPER SPARROW

Containing three eggs of the Cowbird

The Vesper Sparrow is shy, after the manner of its kind. Often in the fields or on the roadsides, it will run along for some distance, keeping just ahead of the pedestrian. When it takes to its wings the two white feathers on either side of its tail show very plainly. It has no true crest, but it often elevates the feathers on the crown of its head so that they form a temporary one.

In western North America, except the Pacific coast district, there is a variant form of the Vesper Sparrow, known as the Western Vesper Sparrow (*Poœcetes gramineus confinis*). It averages larger, and has a slenderer bill than the eastern Vesper; it is also slightly paler and grayer and the marks on the chest are not so dark.

Both of these forms are replaced in the Pacific coast district by the Oregon Vesper Sparrow (*Poœcetes gramineus affinis*). The Oregon Vesper is smaller than the Vesper, browner above and distinctly buffy below.

The Vesper Sparrow lives chiefly on different injurious insects, the animal proportion of its food reaching 90 per cent. in the height of summer. Beetles and grasshoppers are most sought after, and next to them come cutworms, army worms, and other smooth caterpillars. It should be accorded the fullest protection because of its value to the farmer.

IPSWICH SPARROW

Passerculus princeps *Maynard*

A. O. U. Number 541 See Color Plate 81

General Description.— Length, 6¼ inches. Upper parts, grayish; under parts, whitish. Bill, small; wings, long and pointed; tail, about ¾ length of wing.

Color.—Adults: Above, pale grayish; the crown and back, streaked with pale brown and blackish; *crown, with a narrow center stripe of pale grayish buff or dull buffy whitish;* broad similar but paler stripe over eye; outer surface of inner wing-quills and greater wing-coverts, pale buffy brown; cheek stripe, pale buff or whitish; under parts, white tinged laterally (sometimes across chest also) with pale brownish buff; the chest and sides, streaked with brown; iris, brown.

Nest and Eggs.— Nest: On the ground in meadow and grassy reaches of Sable Island (so far as known); constructed of similar materials as the nest of the Savannah Sparrow. Eggs: Also similar but larger.

Distribution.— Breeding on Sable Island (and other islands?), off Nova Scotia; migrating southward along Atlantic coast as far as Georgia.

This is a songless Sparrow which occurs, during its migration, on the beaches along the Atlantic and Gulf coasts from Sable Island, Nova Scotia, where it breeds, to Georgia. It is most likely to be found skulking in the beach-grass, generally quite near the ocean. In such surroundings it seems to have been first discovered near Ipswich, Mass., in 1868, and thereafter for several years was confounded with Baird's Sparrow (*Ammodramus bairdi*), a western form, which it only very slightly resembles. It is very timid and when flushed is likely to fly rapidly for a considerable distance, then plunge down into the grass and continue its retreat by running for perhaps fifty yards, so that it is difficult to see the bird a second time. Its associates frequently are Horned Larks, from which it may easily be distinguished, but it somewhat resembles the larger light-colored Savannah Sparrow. Its single note, only occasionally uttered, is a faint *tzip*.

The Ipswich Sparrow is a very rare bird and this fact, added to its exceedingly limited range, prevents it from having any appreciable importance. Grass seed, particularly in winter, forms the staple diet. Lambs-quarters, different polygonums, and dock are also taken. The fruit element consists of bayberries, blueberries, and bunchberries. The animal food is made up of beetles, wasp-like insects, bugs, caterpillars, flies, spiders, and snails. In June the most common article of diet is the little dung-beetle. Tiger beetles are also eaten, a rather unusual element of Sparrow fare, but due, probably, to the abundance of these active insects upon the sand dunes which the bird frequents.

SAVANNAH SPARROW

Passerculus sandwichensis savanna (*Wilson*)

A. O. U. Number 542a See Color Plate 81

Other Names.— Ground Sparrow; Field Sparrow (incorrect); Ground-bird; Savannah Bunting.

General Description.— Length, 6 inches. Upper parts, grayish-brown; under parts, white; streaked above and below with black. Bill, small; wings, long and pointed; tail, about ¾ length of wing, and notched.

Color.— Adults: Above, grayish-brown, conspicuously streaked with black, the broad black streaks on back and shoulders edged with narrower dull whitish or light buffy-grayish; streaks; *crown, with a median narrow stripe of pale grayish or buffy-grayish streaks;* a broad stripe of yellowish over the eye, more decidedly yellow in the front; wings, light brownish with dusky centers to the feathers; tail, dusky grayish-brown, the feathers edged with pale grayish but without any white on inner webs; ear and under eye regions light brownish-gray or dull grayish-buffy, margined above and below by blackish streaks; a broad white or pale buffy stripe on the cheek; under parts, white (sometimes, especially in fall and winter plumage, tinged with buffy on chest and sides) with sides of throat, chest, sides, and flanks conspicuously streaked with blackish, the streaks on chest wedge-shaped, those on throat coalesced into a stripe.

Nest and Eggs.— Nest: Level with ground, generally well concealed in tall grass or tussock; a sparse collection of grass and weed stalks; lined or not. Eggs: 4 or 5, ground color varying from bluish-white to grayish-white, spotted, speckled, and blotched with brown and lavender, sometimes so thickly as to be obscured.

Distribution.— Eastern North America; breeding from Connecticut, Pennsylvania (Bradford, Crawford, Clinton, Elk, and Erie counties), Ontario, northwestern Indiana (Calumet, English, and Wolf Lakes), etc., northward to Ungava (Fort Chimo), western side of Hudson Bay, etc.; migrating south in winter to Gulf coast, Bahamas, and Cuba; casual in Bermudas.

The Aleutian Savannah Sparrow or Sandwich Sparrow (*Passerculus sandwichensis sandwichensis*) is the typical bird of this species. He breeds on Unalaska Island and in the winter comes east and south along the coast to British Columbia and occasionally to northern California. The *sandwichensis* part of his scientific name refers to his being first found on Sandwich Island in the Aleutians by a Russian. The better known member of this family, however, is the Savannah Sparrow.

The peculiarity of this otherwise rather commonplace bird is its habit of singing from the ground. This is very unusual with birds which have any song at all; for though the habit of singing from a more or less conspicuous perch is clearly an inherently dangerous one, since it must have the effect of attracting the notice of the singer's natural enemies, it is persisted in by all but a very few American species, the law of the "survival of the fittest" to the contrary notwithstanding. In point of fact, however, the Savannah's song is a rather insignificant effort. Dr. Jonathan Dwight describes it as "a weak, musical little trill following a grasshopper-like introduction, and is of such small volume that it can be heard but a few rods." As the sun sinks and the quiet of evening deepens the *tsip-tsip-tsip se-e-e-s'r-r-r* (Dwight) is sung more frequently and is audible for a greater distance. The bird's best known note is a sharp *tsip,* frequently heard when it is migrating and still more frequently during the breeding season. This note seems to be used either to express alarm or to scold.

The Savannah is primarily a bird of the fields, especially those near the coast, and is likely to be mistaken for any of several other field Sparrows, for the Vesper, probably, more often than others; but careful study of the bird's coloration, plus its ground-singing habit, will make its identification comparatively easy.

The Savannah is one of the most useful of the Sparrows. Nearly half of its food consists of insects, beetles being most eagerly sought, and in winter it consumes large quantities of grass seeds and weed seeds. Individuals taken in cotton fields in winter were found to have eaten a number of boll weevils.

In western North America, breeding in Alaska but ranging south to Mexico, is the Western Savannah Sparrow (*Passerculus sandwichensis alaudinus*). It is about the same size as the eastern species but the coloration is decidedly paler and grayer.

Other members of this group are: Bryant's Sparrow (*Passerculus sandwichensis bryanti*), somewhat smaller and darker than the Savannah and found in the salt marshes along the coast of California; Belding's Sparrow (*Passerculus beldingi*), still darker in coloration than Bryant's and found in the salt marshes of southern and Lower California; and the Large-billed Sparrow (*Passerculus rostratus rostratus*), differing as its name suggests in the size of the bill and also in not having the upper parts conspicuously streaked; this Sparrow is also found in the salt marshes of southern California and Lower California.

GRASSHOPPER SPARROW

Ammodramus savannarum australis *Maynard*

A. O. U. Number 546 See Color Plate 81

Other Names.— Quail Sparrow; Yellow-winged Sparrow.

General Description.— Length, 4½ inches. Upper parts, gray, buff, brown, and black, mixed; under parts, whitish. Wing, short; tail, short and the feathers narrow and lance-like.

Color.—Adults in Summer: Crown, blackish narrowly streaked with light gray or grayish buffy and divided centrally by a *distinct line of pale grayish buff*; rest of upper parts, mixed grayish, pale buffy, rusty brown, and black, the last prevailing on back and shoulders, *where forming large central or median spots;* hindneck, grayish streaked with chestnut, the chestnut streaks sometimes black centrally; feathers of rump, streaked or spotted with rusty brown, the streaks sometimes black basally; wings, dusky with distinct pale buffy grayish edgings; the lesser coverts, mostly yellowish olive passing into yellow on edge of wing; sides of head, including broad stripe over eye, dull buffy, paler and more grayish on lores, the region above lores yellowish; a dusky streak behind eye; under parts, buffy becoming white or nearly so on lower breast, abdomen, and under tail-coverts; bill, brown, paler on the edge and below; iris, brown. Adults in Winter: Similar to summer plumage, but brighter colored, with less black and more of chestnut on upper parts; the center crown-stripe, deeper buffy; the hindneck broadly streaked with chestnut; the space between the shoulders distinctly edged with buff and gray; buff of under parts deeper, that of chest sometimes indistinctly streaked with chestnut. Young: Crown, dusky with an indistinct center stripe of pale grayish, and indistinctly streaked with the same, or with pale brownish; hindneck streaked with dusky and pale buffy grayish; back and shoulders, dusky or dull blackish; the feathers distinctly margined with dull buffy and pale grayish; middle and greater wing-coverts, margined terminally with dull buffy whitish; under parts, dull buffy whitish; the chest and sides of head streaked with dusky; no yellow over lores nor on edge of wing.

Nest and Eggs.— Nest: On ground or sunk level, in dry fields, clearings, or pastures, and well concealed; bulky; built of dried grass, sometimes semi-arched with deep interior. Eggs: 3 to 5, clear white, spotted and specked rather sparsely, chiefly around large end, with chestnut, black, and lilac gray.

Distribution.— Eastern United States and more southern British Provinces; west to edge of the Great Plains; north, in summer, to Maine, New Hampshire, Ontario, etc.; south, in winter, to Bahamas, Cuba, island of Cozumel, Yucatan, and Gulf coast of Mexico.

It is unfortunate that this bird should ever have received the descriptive designation, "yellow-winged," since the patch of color which appears on its shoulders does not justify that description. Consequently, the absence of yellow wings is likely to mislead an observer who remembers that the bird has been so described. And this likelihood is increased by the extreme shyness of the bird, and its decided disinclination to sit still in plain view if it sees it is being observed. Under such conditions it is almost certain to dive into the nearest cover. So the observer will have to use his eyes quickly and to note accurately the comparatively inconspicuous marking of the plumage.

The insect-like, buzzing song of the bird (whence its name) is, however, quite distinctive, and can hardly be mistaken for that of any other bird of the fields. It faintly suggests the song of the Blue-winged Warbler, which, however, is essentially a bird of the woods. This Sparrow has the skulking habits of most of the members of his family who live in the fields and build their nests on the ground. Also, like other ground birds, the female, when incubating, will sit still until you are within a few feet of her, and then leave her nest very quietly and flutter along the ground, dragging her wings as if she were disabled. This is plainly an instinctive effort to attract attention to herself and away from her precious eggs. If one is determined to discover the nest, it is best to stop short immediately the bird is seen, try to locate that spot exactly, and then mark it with a handkerchief, or a stick thrust into the ground, and long enough to be conspicuous. Then by patiently walking about this spot in circles of slightly increasing diameter, examining minutely every foot of the ground (and please, "watch your step"), the pretty secret may be revealed. But it must be remembered that the nest is built of grasses which blend perfectly with the surroundings, and furthermore, that it is an almost completely enclosed structure, the entrance being at the side, so that it is exceedingly difficult to discover it unless one detects this little door, which is often itself partly concealed.

If the observer has a very sharp and trained eye, he may notice the almost imperceptible path, a few feet long, by which the Sparrow enters and leaves her little home. Knowledge of this trait is also useful if one undertakes to find the nest by watching the bird until she returns to it, which will take a deal of patience, if the little mother sees she is observed. If, however, the bird leaves her perch on a bush, or fence rail, and dives into the grass, wait a few minutes, with your gaze concentrated on that spot and then walk slowly and softly toward it and mark it. From here, by very careful scrutiny of the ground, you may be able to discern the little path, for the bird never flies directly to her nest. These suggestions have been offered, because to find a Grasshopper Sparrow's nest is a real triumph in field ornithology — one, indeed, which many a trained observer has never accomplished.

The vegetable food of the Grasshopper Sparrow is of little importance when compared with that of other species. Grain forms 2 per cent. of the food; weed seed amounts to about one-

Courtesy of Am. Mus. Nat. Hist.

GRASSHOPPER SPARROW (⅔ nat. size)

An extremely shy little bird of the fields

fourth. Insects form its staple diet, and of these, beetles, grasshoppers, and caterpillars are the most important. As a destroyer of insect pests the Grasshopper Sparrow is most efficient, and, both its vegetable and animal food considered, it seems to be individually the most useful species of bird whose food habits have been thus far investigated.

The typical species of the Grasshopper Sparrow family is the Antillean Grasshopper Sparrow (*Ammodramus savannarum savannarum*); it is a resident of Jamaica and Porto Rico and is similar to the Grasshopper Sparrow of eastern North America but decidedly smaller and darker. In the western United States and south over the plains of Mexico, is found the Western Grasshopper Sparrow (*Ammodramus savannarum bimaculatus*). This western species is the same size as the eastern, but of a paler coloration and with more rusty brown and less black on the upper parts.

HENSLOW'S SPARROW

Passerherbulus henslowi henslowi (*Audubon*)

A. O. U. Number 547 See Color Plate 81

Other Name.— Henslow's Bunting.

General Description.— Length, 5½ inches. Upper parts, chestnut, black, and white, mixed; under parts, whitish. Bill, stout; wing, short; tail, not longer than wing, and graduated.

Color.— ADULTS: *Head and neck, buffy olive,* the crown heavily streaked, except along center line, with black, the hindneck, more narrowly streaked; back and shoulders, chestnut, the feathers black centrally and narrowly edged or margined with whitish; wings, mainly chestnut; chin and throat, pale buff or buffy whitish; chest, sides, and flanks, deeper buffy streaked with blackish; abdomen, whitish. YOUNG: Above, dull brownish-buffy, streaked and spotted with black; beneath, light buff, the sides streaked with dusky.

Nest and Eggs.— NEST: In old clearings, pasture lands, or fresh water meadows, on the ground under a clump of grass; built of grass, lined with fine blades and some horse- or cow-hair. EGGS: 4 or 5, pale greenish or grayish white, heavily spotted and blotched with shades of brown and lavender.

Distribution.— Eastern United States, west to edge of Great Plains, north to New Hampshire, New York, Ontario, Minnesota, etc.; breeding south at least to 38°; wintering from about the same latitude to southern Florida and Texas.

Henslow's Sparrow never will be a very popular bird. It is only a plain striped Sparrow, its song is quite insignificant, its breeding home is within inaccessible wet meadows, and it is very retiring. It is really not so very rare in southern New Jersey and Maryland and across the weedy prairies of southern Indiana and Illinois. In many parts of northern Missouri and across Iowa to southern Minnesota, it is actually common. It may not be as rare as has been supposed in the northern part of its range, that is, in the northeastern States and southern Canada; but only a keen ear will notice the explosive *Che-slick* notes far off in the weeds or marsh tussocks. The song as written by P. L. Jouy is *sis-r-r-rit-srit-srit,* and this is as easily unnoticed as in that of the Grasshopper Sparrow that sings its summery lay in the hearing of thousands of people who never hear it at all, because a little distance makes the notes just the simple buzz of spring and summer. The aggressive bird student, however, who sees and hears everything, has made an acquaintance of this little brown Sparrow with its pale olive-green head.

In the winter Henslow's Sparrows are found most commonly throughout the south in the broom sedge of the dry fields. As these fields

HENSLOW'S SPARROW (⅝ nat. size)

But few bird lovers know this plain striped Sparrow

Courtesy of Am. Mus. Nat. Hist.

are neglected in winter and the Sparrows call but rarely, the people of the south know the bird even less than do the people of the north.

Because of its small numbers and irregular local distribution Henslow's Sparrow is of little economic importance. Beetles, cutworms, grasshoppers, soldier bugs, assassin bugs, spiders, blackberries, grass, and plant seeds have been found in the stomachs examined by the members of the United States Biological Survey.

There is a paler race of Henslow's Sparrows in South Dakota that is called the Western Henslow's Sparrow (*Passerherbulus henslowi occidentalis*).

On the prairie marshes of the Mississippi valley and of the central Canadian provinces, southeastward in winter, is another very similar species, known as Leconte's Sparrow (*Passerherbulus lecontei*). (See Color Plate 81.)

L. Nelson Nichols.

SHARP-TAILED SPARROW

Passerherbulus caudacutus (*Gmelin*)

A. O. U. Number 549 See Color Plate 81

General Description.— Length, 5½ inches. Upper parts, olive-brown; under parts, whitish; streaked above and below. Bill, stout; wing, short; tail, rounded, the feathers sharp-pointed.

Color.—Adults: Broad, sharply defined, and conspicuous stripe over eye and broad cheek stripe, deep buff, the latter curving upward behind the ears, but separated from the stripe on the eye by a narrow black or dark brown stripe back of the eye; ear region, grayish; crown, clear bister brown streaked with black, divided by a broad but not sharply defined center stripe of grayish; prevailing color of upper parts, olivaceous, grayer on sides of hindneck and rump, the shoulders and between decidedly darker olive-brown, sharply edged with pale grayish or buffy whitish, producing distinct streaks which are margined internally by a narrower blackish streak; *edge of wing, pale yellow;* under parts, mostly white, but the chest, sides, and flanks tinged with buff, sharply and usually conspicuously streaked with dusky. Young: Crown, blackish *divided by a narrow center stripe,* or series of streaks, of dull buffy; general color of upper parts, light buffy brownish, the shoulders and between broadly edged with buffy, *producing conspicuous streaks;* under parts, buffy, deepest on chest and sides, where streaked, narrowly, with dusky; the abdomen, sometimes nearly white.

Nest and Eggs.— Nest: Always in salt meadow grass, sometimes concealed like the Seaside Sparrow's under a bit of drift sedge; constructed of the same materials as that bird's. Eggs: 4 or 5, pale brownish or greenish white, profusely specked with chestnut.

Distribution.—Atlantic coast of United States; breeding from Massachusetts southward.

The Sharp-tailed Sparrow is a bird of the salt-water marshes along the coast of New England and New York. It has a peculiar habit of perching on a perpendicular reed stalk, where it manages, by spreading its feet wide apart, to assume a partly upright position. On the ground it runs about with its head lowered, among the tussocks, like a mouse, and it is apt to resort to this method of escaping observation, rather than to flight. A distinguishing peculiarity is the form of its tail, which is rather long, and tapers to a point, instead of being square at the end as is that of the Savannah Sparrow; hence, of course, its name. A distinctive plumage marking is the buffy line over the eye and on the sides of the throat. Its song, like that of the Seaside Sparrow, is short and unmusical.

The food habits of the Sharp-tailed Sparrow have many striking peculiarities. The bird shows a greater liking than most species for bugs, and about half of those eaten are leaf-hoppers. These are, it is true, wonderfully abundant in the moist, grassy places where this Sparrow lives, but they are not often eaten by other birds that inhabit the same kinds of places. Of the true bugs — that is, those belonging to the heteropterous division—both the smaller plant-feeding and predacious species are eaten. Perhaps the most curious feature of the bird's food habits is the liking shown for flies. These insects, mainly midges and their larvæ, certain allied insects, and the smaller adult horseflies, constitute 5 per cent. of the food, probably a larger proportion of flies than characterizes the food of any other birds except Flycatchers and those shore-inhabiting species in the Far North which feed so extensively on midges.

There is a difference in the food of the Sharp-tailed Sparrows collected by salt water and those taken near fresh water, owing, no doubt, to differences of environment. The salt-water birds feed on the seeds of salt grasses and occasionally eat wild rice; the fresh-water birds eat other grasses. The salt-water birds eat many sand fleas which are very abundant along the beach, and the birds pick them up either on the clear sand or amid the seaweed or other shore débris. The fresh-water birds do not eat snails, while the others seem to find them very palatable. Birds collected in fresh-water marshes had fed on army worms.

Nelson's Sparrow (*Passerherbulus nelsoni nelsoni*), also known as Nelson's Finch and as Nelson's Sharp-tailed Sparrow, is decidedly smaller than the Sharp-tailed Sparrow. Its coloration is much brighter, the white, pale grayish, or pale buffy streaks of back and shoulders more sharply contrasted with the rich brown or olive ground-color. It breeds in the Mississippi valley northward and winters along the Gulf coast; occasionally it visits the Atlantic coast during migrations. (See Color Plate 81.)

More plainly colored than either the Sharp-tailed or the Nelson's is the Acadian Sharp-tailed Sparrow (*Passerherbulus nelsoni subvirgatus*) which makes its home in the salt-water marshes of the Atlantic coast of the United States and the adjacent Canadian provinces. The conspicuous lighter streaks on the back and shoulders are lacking in this member of the family or else they are not strongly contrasted with the ground color. (See Color Plate 81.)

SEASIDE SPARROW

Passerherbulus maritimus maritimus (*Wilson*)

A. O. U. Number 550 See Color Plate 81

Other Names.— Meadow Chippy; Seaside Finch.

General Description.— Length, 6 inches. Upper parts, olive-grayish, streaked; under parts, white. Bill, stout; wing, short; tail, rounded, the feathers sharp-pointed.

Color.—Adults: Above, olive-grayish tinged with olive especially on back, where feathers are somewhat darker with light grayish edges producing streaks; crown, olive laterally, grayish medially, producing three broad but very indistinct and faintly contrasted stripes; a stripe on the cheek, chin, throat, and abdomen, white; *stripe under the cheek and broad streaks on chest, grayish; edge of wing, yellow.* Young: Above, browner than in adult, the back broadly and crown narrowly streaked with blackish; beneath, whitish; the chest, sides, and flanks buffy and streaked with dusky.

Nest and Eggs.— Nest: Placed in the areas of fine marsh grass, usually beneath dead drift patches of grass, above normal high-water mark (many nests are destroyed every year by extra high tides); constructed almost entirely of dried grass, lined with finer blades. Eggs: 4 or 5, pale greenish or pale brownish white, finely spotted all over and wreathed at large end with rufous and dull purple.

Distribution.—Atlantic coast of United States, in salt-water marshes, breeding from southern Massachusetts (Westport, near Rhode Island line) to Georgia.

As its name indicates, the Seaside Sparrow is a land bird which, nevertheless, evidently loves the sound and the sight of the ocean, for it is most frequently found in the salt marshes along the Atlantic coast from Rhode Island southward. It often has as companions Savannah, Sharp-tailed, Swamp, or Song Sparrows from any of which it may be distinguished by its lack of the reddish cast of color, more or less of which is shown in their plumage, and by its blunt tail. Its song, of four or five notes, can hardly be considered musical; it is delivered from atop a reed, or sometimes as the bird flutters a few feet upward.

There are four varieties of the Seaside Sparrow found in different localities in the southeastern United States. Macgillivray's Seaside Sparrow (*Passerherbulus maritimus macgillivraii*) is found on the Atlantic coast from South Carolina to Florida and, in winter, along the Gulf coast; in coloration it is darker than the Seaside and its back is distinctly and often broadly streaked with black. Scott's Seaside Sparrow (*Passerherbulus maritimus peninsulæ*) is similar to Macgillivray's, but the coloration of the upper parts is more uniform, the markings being less sharply contrasted with the general color; it inhabits the west coast of Florida. The

Louisiana Seaside Sparrow or Fisher's Seaside Sparrow (*Passerherbulus maritimus fisheri*) is much darker than Macgillivray's, often the black on the upper parts exceeding the olive-gray, and the ground color of the underparts being deep buffy; it breeds on the coast of Louisiana and in winter is distributed along the coast of Texas and on the west coast of Florida. The fourth variety is the Texas Seaside Sparrow (*Passerherbulus maritimus sennetti*). As its name would indicate, it is found along the coast of Texas. It is smaller, paler, and much more buffy than the Seaside, with the shoulders and the space between distinctly darker than the rest of the upper parts.

Drawing by R. I. Brasher

SEASIDE SPARROW (½ nat. size)

Closely allied to the Seaside Sparrow but constituting a different species is the Dusky Seaside Sparrow (*Passerherbulus nigrescens*). Its general coloration above is black, indistinctly streaked with olive and grayish; the wing and tail feathers are edged with olive-brown; the under parts are white thickly and broadly streaked with black; the edge of the wing and a spot above the lores are gamboge-yellow. It is found in the marshes at the northern end of the Indian River, east coast of Florida. Of this species, Dr. Chapman says: "In view of the fact that this species is abundant and that the region it inhabits is in no sense isolated, but that both to the north and the south there are marshes apparently similar to those it occupies, the restriction of its range to an area only a few square miles in extent makes its distribution unique among North American birds."

The food habits of the Seaside Sparrow and the Sharp-tailed Sparrow are very similar both in elements and in the proportions of the food. There are, however, some minor differences of details. Thus, the Seaside Sparrow does not take nearly so many sand fleas as its congener, but it feeds on small crabs which so far as known form no part of the food of the Sharp-tailed Sparrow. Because of the limited distribution of these birds they probably do not come in contact to any great extent with cultivated crops. In so far as they destroy insect enemies of salt-marsh hay they are helpful, and in so far as they destroy enemies of insects which prey upon this crop, they are harmful; but otherwise they exercise little influence on agriculture. The birds do not prey on the salt-marsh caterpillars, so destructive to the hay, and they destroy a considerable amount of the seed of the marsh grasses.

LARK SPARROW

Chondestes grammacus grammacus (*Say*)

A. O. U. Number 552

Other Names.— Quail-head; Road-bird; Lark Finch; Little Meadowlark.

General Description.— Length, 6½ inches. Upper parts, brownish-gray streaked with blackish; under parts, white. Bill, stout; wings, long and pointed; tail, long and rounded; feet, small.

Color.—Adults: Crown and ear region, chestnut, the former with a center stripe of pale brownish-gray or grayish-buff; over eye a broad stripe of white, becoming buffy toward the rear; under eye a large white crescent-shaped spot; *under parts,* white becoming buffy grayish-brown on sides and flanks; the chest tinged with the same and marked in center with a blackish spot; back, shoulders, lesser wing-coverts, and upper tail-coverts, brownish-gray or grayish-brown (hair-brown); the back and shoulders broadly *streaked with black*; wings (except lesser coverts), dusky with light grayish-brown edgings, the middle coverts tipped with white (producing a rather distinct band), and the eighth to fifth or fourth primaries with white at the base (producing a patch); middle pair of tail-feathers, dusky grayish-brown, the remaining feathers black, *abruptly tipped with white*, this white occupying nearly if not quite all the exposed terminal half on outermost feather; iris, brown.

Nest and Eggs.— NEST: Located usually on the ground in prairies or dry open meadows, sunk flush with the earth, carefully concealed; constructed of dried grass, weed stalks, lined with finer similar material. EGGS: 3 to 6, pure white or very pale bluish or brownish white, with spots and pen lines of sepia and black, bearing a singular resemblance to Oriole eggs.

Distribution.— Mississippi valley, east of the Great Plains; north to eastern Minnesota, Wisconsin, and southern Michigan, east (regularly) to Ohio, Kentucky, Tennessee, etc., casually or more rarely to Massachusetts, Long Island, New Jersey, Pennsylvania, District of Columbia, Virginia, etc., and (during migration) Florida.

The Lark Sparrow is one of the commonest and most attractive of American birds. It is found in grass country everywhere except in

Drawing by R. I. Brasher

LARK SPARROW (⅓ nat. size)

A familiar bird, common on both city lawns and rocky mesas

the Alleghenies and on the Atlantic coast. In the southwest there is less grass but plenty of sagebrush, and there the Lark Sparrow is also common. No one can travel through America west of the Alleghenies without seeing the Lark Sparrow. And no one who has ever known this Sparrow will ever forget how handsome he is with his chestnut and white head, one black spot on a white breast and a white-edged tail. He runs ahead along the dusty road, he rises out of the June meadows, he walks across the lawns of towns, he perches on rocks and Spanish bayonet and sagebrush and all kinds of wayside bushes. Even out upon the flat and grassless deserts he may be seen flying from cactus to cactus. His absence from the Atlantic coast States is the only fact that prevents his being one of the best known birds of America. Over his great range he is known not only for his beauty, but also for his friendly habit of nesting near the farm buildings and villages.

If nothing else made the bird a favorite, his melodious, long, and varied song, heard almost continuously, would make him beloved. It is a wonder that the poets have not sung his praises. A poetic and intelligent people love the Lark Sparrow already. The writer of poetry will praise him in verse some later year. The song is described by Ridgway as " one continued gush of sprightly music, now gay, now melodious, and then tender beyond description — the very expression of emotion. At intervals the singer falters, as if exhausted by exertion, and his voice becomes scarcely audible; but suddenly reviving in his joy it is resumed in all its vigor

Photo by I. E. Hess Courtesy of Nat. Asso. Aud. Soc.

NEST AND EGGS OF LARK SPARROW

Always carefully concealed

until he appears to be really overcome by the effort."

From the plains to the coast the Lark Sparrow is lighter colored than east of the plains. This makes a subspecies, according to the ornithologist; and the western form is named the Western Lark Sparrow (*Chondestes grammacus strigatus*). There is, however, no practical difference in the habits, song, and beauty of eastern and western birds.

It is very likely that the Lark Sparrow will extend his range eastward in much the same way as has the Prairie Horned Lark. Being a grassland bird the prairie land was the home of the bird before man broke up the eastern forests and made meadows and pastures suitable for homes for grassland birds. Man's progress into the West, creating a continuous area of grassland all the way west to the prairies, has made it possible for the prairie birds to find congenial homes further east. So as man has gone west, some of the western birds have come east.

The food of this Sparrow is made up of seeds of weeds, grasses, and grain, with about 27 per cent. of insects. It is considered to be one of the most valuable of the Sparrows as a destroyer of grasshoppers.

L. Nelson Nichols.

HARRIS'S SPARROW

Zonotrichia querula (*Nuttall*)

A. O. U. Number 553

Other Names.— Hood-crowned Sparrow; Black-hood.

General Description.— Length, 7½ inches. Upper parts, brown, streaked with blackish; under parts, white. Bill, small, compressed-conical; wings, long and pointed; tail, about the length of wing, rounded or slightly double rounded.

Color.—Adults: Crown, cheek region, chin, and throat, *uniform black*, this extended over center portion of chest in the form of a broad streaking or spotting; sides of head, dull brownish buffy becoming more grayish on sides of neck and nearly white next to the black throat-patch, relieved by an irregular blackish or dark brownish spot just back of upper rear portion of ear region; hindneck, brownish varied with blackish; upper parts, light brown or buffy hair-brown; the back and shoulders, broadly streaked with brownish black; middle and greater wing-coverts, tipped with white or buffy white, producing two distinct bands; under parts (except chin, throat, and center portion of chest), white, becoming *dull brownish buffy on sides and flanks*, where streaked with brown or dusky; iris, brown. Immature (young in first winter?): Crown with feathers black centrally, but margined with pale grayish buffy, producing a conspicuously scaly effect; throat, white, or mostly so, with black along each side; middle of chest, blotched or broadly streaked with black or dark brown.

Nest and Eggs.— Probably but one nest has been discovered.

Distribution.— Interior plains of North America, from eastern base of Rocky Mountains to western Missouri, Iowa, Minnesota, Manitoba, etc., occasionally, during migration, to Illinois, and Wisconsin; breeding west of Hudson Bay; south in winter to Texas; accidental in British Columbia and Oregon.

How modern is much of our knowledge of American birds is shown by the fact that the breeding range of the Harris's Sparrow was not known in the nineteenth century. Only the investigation of the country west of Hudson's Bay made since 1900 has established that country as the nesting home of this bird. In the United States it is distinctly a bird of the Missouri River basin, not to breed, to be sure, but to haunt for half the year the shrubbery along the river bottoms and the thickets along the smaller streams. In fact what the White-throat does when it comes down out of the North for three seasons, that also does this Black-hooded Sparrow. Black-hood and White-throat are members of the same genus, but the former has the more restricted area. Black-hood will chirp much in the same tone as the White-throat, will seldom rise much above the bushes, and haunts the damper places in the thickets to rustle about in the dead leaves.

In the spring the Black-hood's song, uttered from the same bushes as the White-throat's, begins something like the hymn-notes of the

White-throat. A change suddenly comes in the middle of the song that makes it very different from the song of any other Sparrow. The close of the song is harsh and drawling, reminding one of the distant rasp of the Nighthawk.

When the winters are severe in the lower Missouri valley, the birds push on in large numbers to central Texas, only to return, as a White-throat would, to more northern wet woods and thickets with the first sign of spring. At this season they are known as Black-hoods, and are a welcome sight in the Dakotas, where they sing their cheery songs from the topmost twigs of the scanty bushes. Their size and their colors make them as conspicuous as Towhees. But civilization loses sight of them during the breeding season and through the heat of summer.

September, though, finds them coming back over the international boundary into the upper Missouri valley. But now the hoods are inconspicuous. Most noticeable now are the heavy markings underneath and the generally reddish appearance. In this garb it is as well to name them after Mr. Harris as to call them by any other name. The birds must search far on down below the Arkansas River to find their black hoods again.

The only nest of this species known was discovered by Ernest T. Seton, August 5, 1907. Writing in *The Auk,* he describes it thus: "It was on the ground under a dwarf birch, was made of grass, and resembled the nest of the White-throated Sparrow. It contained three young, nearly ready to fly."

Figures indicate that it is advisable to afford this species all possible encouragement and protection. The report of the United States Biological Survey was based on the examination of 100 stomachs. As is the case with many of the birds that breed for the most part to the north and merely winter in the United States, the stomach contents were mostly vegetable in character, the animal matter amounting to but 8 per cent. The animal matter was made up of about the same kinds of insects, spiders, and snails that enter into the fare of other Sparrows, but the quantity of leaf hoppers was unusually large (2 per cent. of the food).

Of the vegetable food, 25 per cent. was made up of the seeds of wild fruits and of various plants of uncertain economic position; 10 per cent. of grain, which included more corn than wheat and oats; 9 per cent. of grass seed, mainly pigeon grass, crab grass, June grass, and Johnson grass; 6 per cent. of the seeds of amaranth, lamb's-quarters, wild sunflower, and gromwell, and 42 per cent. of ragweed and polygonum.

Drawing by R. I. Brasher

HARRIS'S SPARROW (½ nat. size)

A comparatively little known bird whose nest was not discovered until 1907

WHITE-CROWNED SPARROW

Zonotrichia leucophrys leucophrys (*J. R. Forster*)

A. O. U. Number 554 See Color Plate 82

Other Name.— White-crown.

General Description.— Length, 6¾ inches. Plumage, gray, light below, and dark with streaks of brown above. Bill, small, compressed-conical; wings, long and pointed; tail, about the length of wing, rounded or slightly double rounded.

Color.—Adults: Crown, with *two broad lateral bands of deep black, inclosing a center one of white* or grayish white of approximately equal width; black of forehead extending backward to the front angle of the eye; a white or grayish-white stripe over eye extending forward above the eye nearly or quite as far as its front angle; hindneck, sides of neck, and ear region, plain gray; back and shoulders, light gray or brownish-gray broadly streaked with chestnut-brown or vandyke-brown; rump and upper tail-coverts plain hair-brown; tail, dark hair-brown with paler edgings; middle and greater wing-coverts, dusky grayish-brown, edged with pale hair-brown and tipped with white, forming two distinct bands; inner wing-quills dusky, margined terminally with whitish, this passing into chestnut-brown toward basal portion of outer webs; primaries, dusky hair-brown narrowly edged with paler; sides of head and neck and chest uniform rather light gray, fading into nearly white on throat, chin, and abdomen; sides and flanks, pale buffy-brown; the under tail-coverts pale buffy or buffy-whitish; iris, brown.

Nest and Eggs.— Nest: Commonly placed on the ground, in dry, high mountain meadows or clearings, sometimes in low bushes; constructed of small twigs, grasses and rootlets, lined with fine grass and hair. Eggs: 3 to 5, pale greenish blue to dull pale brownish white, specked and spotted with chestnut, heaviest at large end.

Distribution.— More eastern British provinces and greater part of United States; breeding from Vermont, Province of Quebec, northeastern Minnesota (?), etc., northward to west side of Hudson Bay and over peninsula of Labrador to southern Greenland, and throughout the high mountain districts of the western United States, from the main Rocky Mountain ranges to the Sierra Nevada, including the intermediate Uinta and Wasatch ranges; breeding southward to New Mexico and Arizona, northward to northern California; migrating southward over greater part of eastern United States, over Mexican plateau and throughout peninsula of Lower California.

Drawing by R. I. Brasher

WHITE-CROWNED SPARROW (⅗ nat. size)

His song has a singular sweetness, all its own

By careless observers this Sparrow is often mistaken for the White-throat, though the difference in the coloration of the two is very marked. In the first place, the White-crown lacks entirely the yellow patch before the eye, the white stripe over the eye, and white patch on the throat, all of which are conspicuous markings of the White-throat's plumage. Then, too, the White-throat's head is much more nearly flat on the crown than is the White-crown's, which is distinctly dome-shaped. On the other hand, White-crowns and White-throats frequently associate, and feed together, and their manners are not unlike.

There is, however, little similarity in the songs of the birds, and the White-throat's will be considered the better of the two probably by most listeners. This is by no means intended to disparage the effort of the White-crowned minstrel, which has a singular sweetness and effectiveness all its own. Indeed, Mr. Burroughs considers the White-crown "a vastly finer songster than the White-throat." As described by Mr. Mathews, "it is composed of six, or at the most, seven notes (unless it is doubled); the first one is twice as long as the others which are of about even value. The intervals are fairly accurate and include anything from a third to a fifth; all the notes are clearly whistled except (generally) the two next to the last, and these are distinctly double-toned or burred; the whole is marked by an even crescendo to the highest note, which is next to or within one of the last, or sometimes actually the last." The song has something, though rather less, of the plaintive quality which characterizes that of the White-throat, and like that bird's is also often heard at night.

In western North America there are two varieties of the White-crowned Sparrow. Gambel's Sparrow (*Zonotrichia leucophrys gambeli*) and Nuttall's Sparrow (*Zonotrichia leucophrys nuttalli*). Gambel's Sparrow averages a trifle smaller than the White-crowned; its coloration is similar, but the lores is entirely white, thus making the light-colored stripe over the eye continuous to the bill. Nuttall's Sparrow also has this uninterrupted stripe, but its general coloration is much darker and its size smaller than Gambel's Sparrow. Gambel's Sparrow is not found in the Pacific coast district of the United States while that is the home-land of Nuttall's Sparrow.

Like most of the family these birds are seed-eaters by preference, and insects comprise very little more than 7 per cent. of their diet. Caterpillars are the largest item, with some beetles, a few ants and wasps, and some bugs, among which are black-olive scales. The great bulk of the food, however, consists of weed seeds, which amount to 74 per cent. of the whole. In California these birds have been accused of eating the buds and blossoms of fruit trees, but buds or blossoms were found in only thirty out of 516 stomachs, and probably it is only under exceptional circumstances that they do any damage in this way. Evidently neither the farmer nor the fruit grower has much to fear from White-crowned Sparrows. The little fruit they eat is mostly wild, and the grain eaten is waste or volunteer.

GOLDEN-CROWNED SPARROW

Zonotrichia coronata (*Pallas*)

A. O. U. Number 557

Other Name.— Golden-crown.

General Description.— Length, 6¾ inches. Plumage, gray, light below, and dark with streaks of brown above. Bill, small, compressed-conical; wings, long and pointed; tail, about the length of wing, rounded or slightly double rounded.

Color.— Adult Male: Crown, deep black, divided medially by a broad *stripe of olive-yellow,* changing rather abruptly to light gray on back of head; upper parts, grayish olive-brown, the back and shoulders broadly streaked with brownish black, these streaks with a marginal suffusion of chestnut-brown; outer webs of innermost greater wing-coverts and inner wing-quills inclining to chestnut-brown; middle and greater coverts, tipped with white, forming two distinct bands; sides of head, dull grayish; under parts, dull brownish gray, somewhat paler on chin and throat, nearly white on abdomen, light buffy brownish color on sides and flanks; under tail-coverts, light grayish-brown or drab, broadly margined with pale buffy; iris, brown. Adult Female: Similar to the male, sometimes hardly distinguishable, but usually with the lateral black stripes of the crown narrower and less intensely black, the yellow of the crown-spot rather paler, and the gray of back of head streaked with dusky. Immature (Young in First Winter?): Similar to adult female, but without any lateral black stripe on crown or well-defined center stripe, the whole forehead and front portion of crown yellowish olive, more or less flecked with dusky, the back portion of the crown, light grayish-olive-brown, streaked with dusky.

Nest and Eggs.— NEST: In alder thickets of Alaska streams; constructed of coarse grass, weed stems, rootlets; lined with fine grass; quite large, and loosely built. EGGS: 4 or 5, pale greenish blue, distinctly speckled with shades of brown and chestnut.

Distribution.— Pacific coast and Bering Sea districts of North America; breeding on the Shumagin Islands, Alaska Peninsula, Kodiak, and more western parts of the Alaskan mainland; migrating southward in winter through southern Alaska, British Columbia, Washington, Oregon, and California, to the San Pedro Martir Mountains, Lower California, the Santa Barbara Islands; occasional straggler eastward.

Alaska is the home of the Golden-crowned Sparrows. They nest during the month of June. After the breeding season, the Golden-crowns are somewhat erratic in their movements. Some stay in the North for a while; others begin straggling off for the South, either alone or in small flocks. As a rule, the Golden-crowns join with the White-crowned Sparrows. Our acquaintanceship with the Golden-crowns begins late in the fall when we see a small flock in the shrubbery and hedgerows through California. It is easy to make friends with these Sparrows by scattering a few crumbs along the paths.

As far as I have observed, the Golden-crowns do not sing much when traveling. I see them each fall on their way through Oregon, but they are silent. I knew the bird best about the campus of the University of California at Berkeley and in Golden Gate Park at San Francisco.

His mood is different from that of other birds. It isn't the sun that makes him joyous; it is the rain. Perhaps the lack of moisture in the California climate makes him homesick. When a rain does come, it reminds him so much of the mist and showers of his northern home that he cannot help breaking into song. The song of the Golden-crown, therefore, is always associated in my mind with a drizzling rain. It is a simple, mournful lay in a high key, quite quavering at times. It is a minor strain, each note lowered a half step.

In his last book, *Field Days in California*, Bradford Torrey speaks of meeting the Golden-crowned Sparrow at Paso Robles. "I was soon close upon a flock of Golden-crowned Sparrows. They were no novelty. I had seen many like them. But these were in song; and that was a novelty; a brief and simple tune, making me think of the opening notes of the eastern White-throat, but stopping short of that bird's rollicking triplets, ending almost before it began, as if it had been broken off in the middle, with a sweetly plaintive cadence. Like the White-throat's, and unlike the White-crown's, the tone is a pure whistle, so that the strain can be imitated, even at first hearing, well enough to excite the birds to its repetition. I proved it on the spot."

WILLIAM L. FINLEY.

For the determination of the food of the Golden-crowned Sparrow, 184 stomachs were available. The animal food amounted to 0.9 per cent., vegetable to 99.1 per cent. The animal food consisted of insects and was pretty well distributed among the various orders. It was evident that the Golden-crowned does not search for insects and takes only those that come in its way. The vegetable food consists of fruits, buds and flowers, grain, and some miscellaneous matter. Fruit amounted to a little more than 1 per cent. of the food and consisted of elderberries, grapes and what was thought to be apple. Buds and flowers averaged 29.5 per cent., grain nearly 26 per cent., and weed seed 33 per cent. This bird does no direct harm to fruit, but by the destruction of buds and blossoms it may do serious harm where it is numerous and visits the orchards.

WHITE-THROATED SPARROW

Zonotrichia albicollis (*Gmelin*)

A. O. U. Number 558 See Color Plate 82

Other Names.— Peabody Bird; Cherrybird (in Adirondacks); Canada Bird; White-throated Crown Sparrow; White-throat; Nightingale (in Manitoba); Canada Sparrow; Peverly Bird.

General Description.— Length, 7¼ inches. Upper parts, rusty-brown, streaked with black; under parts, white and gray. Bill, small, compressed-conical; wings, long and pointed; tail, about length of wing, rounded or slightly double rounded.

Color.—ADULT: Crown, black divided centrally by

a line or narrow stripe of white; a broad stripe over eye, *bright yellow anteriorly (from bill to above eyes)*, white posteriorly; a broad streak of black behind eye; ear and under eye regions, plain gray; *a conspicuous white patch covering chin, upper throat, and greater part of cheek region;* this white patch abruptly defined below against the gray of lower throat and chest, which passes into a more brownish hue on sides and flanks, the latter streaked with grayish-brown; breast, abdomen, and under tail-coverts, white; back and shoulders, rusty-brown streaked with black; rump and upper tail-coverts, light olive or hair-brown; tail, deeper hair-brown edged with paler; middle and greater wing-coverts, tipped with whitish forming two narrow bands; primaries, primary coverts, and outermost greater coverts, edged with lighter and more grayish-brown; the edge of wing, pale yellow; iris, brown.

Nest and Eggs.— Nest: Typical site on ground, in burnt-over clearings of coniferous forests; sometimes in low bushes near streams or borders of fresh-water swamps, in the evergreen woods; a rather bulky structure, of coarse grasses, strips of bark, moss, lined with fine blades of grass. Eggs: 4 or 5, minutely and evenly sprinkled or heavily blotched with dark brown on a pale greenish or pale buffy ground.

Distribution.— Eastern North America; breeding from Massachusetts, northern New York, Ontario, northern Michigan, northeastern Wyoming, eastern Montana, etc., northward to Great Bear Lake, west shores of Hudson Bay, Labrador, etc.; south in winter to Florida and southern Texas

---

This is not only one of the handsomest of the Sparrows; it is perhaps the sweetest singer of them all. The pity of it is that comparatively little is seen or heard of him by humans who would be glad to know him better; for he shows his fetching black, white, and yellow-striped cap, his white ascot tie and his warm brown jacket, and sings his beautiful little song, only on his way to and from his breeding ground in the Canadian forests. This at least is true of the great majority of White-throats, though many breed in northern New York, Maine and in the New England mountains as far south as northern Massachusetts. Both in spring and in fall the birds are likely to travel in little flocks and to spend much of their time on the ground, where they scratch vigorously like Towhees and Juncos. In this operation a White-throat creates a commotion in the dry leaves which suggests the presence of a bird or animal many times its size.

There are few bird utterances at once more characteristic and more appealing than the finished song of this Sparrow. Various efforts have been made to represent the song in words, but all of these attempts are more or less unsatisfactory, for the very good and sufficient reason that they fail utterly to express the spirit of the utterance. " Old Sam Peabody, Peabody, Peabody " is the common New England rendition, from which is derived the popular name of " Peabody Bird," but as W. Leon Dawson, the Ohio orni-

Drawing by R. I. Brasher

WHITE-THROATED SPARROW (½ nat. size)

A shy singer whose wistful, plaintive theme is one of the perfect expressions of the bird world

thologist, says, "the bird does not utter anything remotely resembling Peabody while in Ohio," nor anywhere else, he might have made bold to add.

From a New England farmer, Bradford Torrey had the following story of the origin of another effort to put the song into words:

"A farmer named Peverly was walking about his fields one spring morning, trying to make up his mind whether the time had come to put in his wheat. The question was important, and he was still in a deep quandary, when a bird spoke up out of the wood and said, 'Sow wheat, Peverly, Peverly, Peverly!' That settled the matter. The wheat was sown and in the fall a most abundant harvest was gathered; and ever since then this little feathered oracle has been known as the Peverly bird." (*Birds in the Bush*).

The fault with all of these attempted transliterations, as has been said, is that they quite fail to convey the real genius of the song. Its two commoner forms are reduced to musical notation by Mr. Mathews as follows:

and

The piano conveys only a very faint suggestion of the truly ethereal quality with which the singer invests this simple little phrase. Played with a very skillfully executed tremolo effect well up on the E string of a fine violin, the notes convey a somewhat more definite idea of the song, though the bird's tone is not that of the violin. Essentially the song is a lament—a lament which is wistful and ineffably plaintive, but in which there is no despair, only sweet hopefulness. Stewart Edward White in his book, *The Forest,* has a singularly faithful appreciation of this quality in the song. Ascending from jest to eloquent earnest, he writes:

"The White-throated Sparrow sings nine different variations of the same song. He may sing more, but that is all I have counted. . . . One man I knew he nearly drove crazy. To that man he was always saying, 'And he never heard the man say drink and the ——.' Toward the last my friend used wildly to offer a thousand dollars if he would, if he only would, finish that sentence.

"But occasionally, in just the proper circumstances, he forgets his stump corners, his vines, his jolly sunlight, and his delightful bugs to become an intimate voice of the wilds. It is night, very still, very dark. The subdued murmur of the forest ebbs and flows with the voices of the furtive folk, an undertone fearful to break the night calm. Suddenly across the dusk of silence flashes a single thread of silver, vibrating, trembling with some unguessed ecstasy of emotion. 'Ah! poor Canada, Canada, Canada' it mourns passionately, and falls silent. That is all."

GEORGE GLADDEN.

Like many of the members of its family, this Sparrow is a great destroyer of weed seed and has an especial fondness for the seeds of the ragweed and birdweed. It consumes, also, a great many wild berries and a goodly number of insects. Its food habits in general place it among the useful birds of the farm.

TREE SPARROW

Spizella monticola monticola (*Gmelin*)

A. O. U. Number 559 See Color Plate 80

Other Names.— Snow Chippy; Winter Chip-bird; Winter Chippy; Tree Bunting; Canada Sparrow; Arctic Chipper; Winter Sparrow.

General Description.— Length, 5¾ inches. Upper parts, gray, rusty, and black, streaked; under parts, gray. Bill, small; wings, rather long and rather pointed; tail, shorter than wing, forked or double rounded, the feathers narrow and blunt.

Color.—Adult: Crown, streak behind eye, and patch on sides of chest, brownish; hindneck, sides of head and neck (except as described), and broad stripe over eye, light gray; chin and throat, similar but paler; breast, abdomen, and under tail-coverts, dull white, the first with a dusky center spot or blotch at upper edge, next to the pale grayish of the chest; sides and flanks, pale wood brownish or brownish buffy; back and shoulders, pale grayish buffy broadly streaked with black and, more narrowly, with rusty; rump and upper tail-coverts, plain hair-brown; tail, grayish dusky, the feathers conspicuously edged with pale gray or buffy gray; greater wing-coverts, broadly edged with rufous, dusky centrally; middle and greater *wing-coverts*, dusky, *tipped with white, forming two distinct bands;* iris, brown. Young: Crown, dull brown streaked with blackish; rump, pale buffy grayish indistinctly streaked or mottled with dusky; under parts, whitish tinged with buffy on chest; the sides of throat, chest, breast, and front portion of sides, streaked with dusky; otherwise essentially like adults.

Nest and Eggs.— Nest: Located in low trees, bushes or on ground; constructed principally of dried grass, strips of bark, moss, weed stems, and warmly lined with feathers. Eggs: 3 to 5, pale greenish blue, specked minutely and regularly over entire surface with rufous brown.

Distribution.— Eastern North America, breeding in Newfoundland, Labrador, and region about Hudson Bay (limits of breeding range very imperfectly known); south in winter to South Carolina, Tennessee, Oklahoma, etc.

The word "tree" is misleading as applied to the Tree Sparrow; for the bird is most frequently found on the ground, and does not even nest in trees ordinarily. This is only one of very many instances of strange inaccuracy in popular nomenclature. The vernacular names "Arctic Chipper" and "Winter Chip-bird" are, however, justified by the facts that the bird breeds in the northland, and passes the winter months in the temperate zone. Indeed, the Tree Sparrow and the Slate-colored Junco are the only native members of the Sparrow family which may fairly be counted winter residents within the United States. This, of course, excludes the English Sparrow, "which does not deserve to be considered as a bird, but rather as a feathered rat," as Mr. Job says. The Tree Sparrow has the further distinction of being one of the few American birds who sing real songs in real winter weather, for its pleasing little Canary-like ditty of tinkling notes is often heard in February when there is both snow and blow aplenty.

Photo by H. K. Job Courtesy of Outing Pub. Co.

TREE SPARROW

Feeding on window-sill

The Western Tree Sparrow (*Spizella monticola ochracea*) has decidedly longer wings and tail than the eastern species and its coloration is paler. It breeds from the valley of the Anderson River, near the Arctic coast, westward through Alaska and southward for an undetermined distance. In the winter it comes south through western North America to Arizona, Utah, Colorado, and Texas.

One-fourth ounce of weed seed per day is a conservative estimate of the food of an adult Tree Sparrow. On this basis, in a large agricultural state like Iowa, Tree Sparrows annually eat approximately 875 tons of weed seeds. Only the farmer, upon whose shoulders falls the heavy burden of freeing his land of noxious weeds, can realize what this vast consumption of weed seeds means in the saving and cost of labor. Dr. Judd reports an interesting illustration of the Tree Sparrow's habits which was noticed during a heavy snowstorm in the third week of February. Here and there, where the whiteness of the field was pierced by phalanxes of dry broom-sedge, a flock of a dozen or more Tree Sparrows found good cheer in spite of driving flakes. From one brown patch to another they flew, clinging to the plants while they plucked out the seeds, seldom leaving a stalk unexplored. Frequently two would feed from a single stalk, while a third, made thrifty by the wintry dearth, hopped in the snow below searching for scattered seeds. The snow whirled in clouds across the field, but these little creatures worked on with cheerful, hardy industry.

CHIPPING SPARROW

Spizella passerina passerina (*Bechstein*)

A. O. U. Number 560 See Color Plate 83

Other Names.— Chip-bird; Chippy; Hair-bird; Social Sparrow; Hair Sparrow; Little House Sparrow.

General Description.— Length, 5½ inches. Upper parts, gray, rusty, and black, streaked; under parts, gray. Bill, small; wings, rather long and rather pointed; tail, shorter than wing, deeply forked, the feathers narrow and blunt.

Color.—Adult Male: *Crown, deep cinnamon-rufous to rufous-chestnut*; the forehead, black divided by a center streak of whitish; a broad stripe of white or very pale gray over eye margined below by a *conspicuous streak of black,* the latter extending beyond the ears; ear and under eye regions, sides of neck, and hindneck, gray, the last streaked with blackish; back and shoulders, light brown or drab broadly streaked with black, the black streaks edged with rusty-brown; rump and upper tail coverts, deep olive-gray or mouse-gray, the latter somewhat darker centrally; tail, dusky, the feathers edged with light gray; lesser wing-coverts, mouse-gray with darker centers; middle coverts, dusky broadly margined terminally with white or buffy forming a band; greater coverts, dusky edged with pale wood-brown or buffy-brown, usually passing into whitish or pale buffy at tips of feathers; inner wing-quills, dusky broadly edged with wood-brown or pale buffy brown; primaries, dusky narrowly edged with pale grayish; under parts, white or grayish-white; the chest, sides and flanks shaded with pale gray; iris, brown. Adult Female: Similar to the male and frequently not distinguishable, but usually (?) with the rufous crown slightly less extended and often streaked with dusky. Winter adults have the colors duller, the markings less sharply contrasted, the gray less pure, the chestnut crown obscured by buffy tips to the feathers.

Nest and Eggs.— Nest: Built in bushes, hedges, or almost any kind of tree, especially cedars, usually close to houses, the orchard being a favorite locality; a delicate, open-work structure of fine, curly rootlets, cleverly interwoven and always thickly lined with horse-hair, sometimes constructed almost entirely of this material. Eggs: 3 or 4, rarely 5, bluish-green, thinly spotted with blackish brown, often wreathed at large end.

Distribution.— Eastern United States and British provinces, west to the Great Plains; breeding from near the Gulf coast northward to Nova Scotia, New Brunswick, Prince Edward Island, Province of Quebec, and wooded region on eastern side of the Saskatchewan plains; wintering chiefly in the more southern United States (Florida to Eastern Texas and northward); casual winter visitant to Cuba (and eastern Mexico?).

Drawing by R. I. Brasher

CHIPPING SPARROW (½ nat. size)

This is the familiar and friendly "Chippy" of the dooryard and roadside

This Sparrow is one of the best known and most loved of our door-yard birds. Its confidence in the friendliness of man seems to be no less than that of the Robin and Bluebird, whence one of its names, the Social Sparrow. Another popular name, "Hair-bird," refers to the bird's fondness for horse-hairs as material for its nest. As a matter of fact, this is not good nesting-material, for, the hairs selected are from the mane and tail of the horse, and besides being stiff, and therefore hard to weave into the only

Photo by H. T. Middleton

CHIPPING SPARROW

One of the tamest of our door-yard birds

kind of nest the bird knows how to build, are often so long that two or three ends are likely to be left protruding for several inches. These ends are dangerous snares, in which both old and young birds become entangled, often with tragic results. The persistence of the bird in using this dangerous building material is but another illustration of the blind way in which instinct sometimes works.

The song of this Sparrow is a rapid and rather monotonous reiteration of the same note. It is frequently described as a "trill," but this is inaccurate, as a trill is a rapid repetition of two distinct tones, whereas there is but one tone in Chippy's song. Mr. Burroughs records, as a marked exception, a song of one of these Sparrows in which the tones were in two groups, one at a little lower pitch than the other. The tone is very high,— an octave or so above the highest C of a piano. The bird is often in a conspicuous place — the top of a tree or bush — as he presents this simple little offering; or he may even execute part of it while on the wing, though this seems to be very unusual.

Inexperienced or careless observers frequently confuse this Sparrow with the Field Sparrow; but this is needless if one will remember that the Chipping Sparrow has a *black bill,* and a *grayish line* over the eye and a brown stripe through it, distinguishing marks which the Field Sparrow lacks.

The Chipping Sparrow is one of the most insectivorous of all the Sparrows. Its diet consists of about 42 per cent. of insects and spiders and 58 per cent. of vegetable matter. The animal food consists largely of caterpillars, of which it feeds a great many to its young. Besides these, it eats beetles, including many weevils. It also eats ants, wasps, and bugs. Among the latter are plant lice and black-olive scales. The vegetable food is practically all weed seed. A nest with four young of this species was watched at different hours on four days. In the seven hours of observation 119 feedings were noted, or an average of seventeen feedings per hour, or four and one-quarter feedings per hour to each nestling. This would give for a day of fourteen hours at least 238 insects eaten by the brood. Chipping Sparrows have been noted at the end of May far out in a patch of corn stubble feeding on yellow sorrel that was going to seed. A score of Chipping Sparrows have been seen amid crab grass, which was spreading so rapidly through a market garden in a pear orchard that it was likely to impair the product. They hopped up to the fruiting stalks, which were then in the milk, and beginning at the tip of one of the several spikes that radiated from

Photo by H. K. Job Courtesy of Outing Pub. Co.

CHIPPING SPARROW AT HOME

On Mr. Job's porch, in the woodbine

a common center like the spokes of a wheel and, gradually moving their beaks along to the base, they chewed off the seeds of spike after spike in regular succession. Usually they did not remove their beaks until they reached the base, though some individuals, especially birds of the year, would munch a few seeds in the middle of a spike and then take a fresh one.

Decidedly larger but paler in coloration is the Western Chipping Sparrow (*Spizella passerina arizonæ*). It is found generally over western North America from the Rocky Mountains to the Pacific coast, including Alaska and the more western parts of the interior districts of British America.

The Clay-colored Sparrow (*Spizella pallida*) very much resembles an immature Chippy. It is found on the great plains of North America from the eastern base of the Rocky Mountains to the prairie districts of the upper Mississippi valley. Its nest is usually near the ground like the Field Sparrow's.

Another closely allied species is Brewer's Sparrow (*Spizella breweri*), locally known in its range in the United States west of the Rocky Mountains and south into Mexico as the Sage Chippy. It averages a trifle smaller than the Clay-colored Sparrow, to which it is similar, but it is more narrowly and uniformly streaked above, especially on the crown which lacks the central stripe.

FIELD SPARROW

Spizella pusilla pusilla (*Wilson*)

A. O. U. Number 563 See Color Plate 83

Other Names.— Bush Sparrow; Rush Sparrow; Huckleberry-bird; Wood Sparrow; Field Chippy; Ground-bird; Ground Sparrow; Field Bunting.

General Description.— Length, 5¾ inches. Upper parts, gray, rusty, and black, streaked; under parts, gray. Bill, small; wings, rather long and rather pointed; tail, nearly length of wing, forked or double rounded, the feathers narrow and blunt.

Color.— Adults: Crown, rusty brown; sides of head, light gray (smoke-gray or olive-gray) relieved by a rusty brown streak behind eye; back and shoulders, rusty brown narrowly streaked with black, often streaked also (on edges of feathers) with light dull buffy or clay color; rump and upper tail-coverts, light brown or hair-brown; tail, deep hair-brown, the feathers edged with pale grayish; larger wing-coverts and inner wing-quills, dusky centrally; middle and greater coverts, tipped with whitish, forming two bands; the greater coverts edged with pale brown; outer web of inner wing-quills, broadly edged with pale rusty brown or cinnamon; under parts, pale grayish buffy toward the front and sides, the buffy tinge most pronounced on chest, fading into dull white on each side of chest. Young: Much duller in color than adults, with the chest and sides streaked with dusky; crown, dull brown (not rusty), usually (?) narrowly and indistinctly streaked with dusky; otherwise essentially like adults.

Drawing by R. I. Brasher

FIELD SPARROW (½ nat. size)

A tinkling musician of the open fields

Nest and Eggs.— NEST: Usually placed in low thick bushes, or in tufts of grass on the ground, in clearings, or bushy fields, near woodland; constructed of coarse grass, weed strips, and rootlets, lined with finer grasses and hair. EGGS: 3 to 5, grayish or bluish white spotted with various shades of brown, more heavily around large end.

Distribution.— Eastern North America, west to the edge of the Great Plains; breeding from upper Georgia and South Carolina, northwestern Florida, central Alabama, and Mississippi, and central Texas, northward to Maine, Ontario, Manitoba; wintering in more southern United States, from Florida to Texas, northward to about 39°, occasionally farther.

The Field Sparrow, Chipping Sparrow, and Tree Sparrow resemble one another nearly enough to perplex the inexperienced or hasty observer. Sharp eyes, intelligently used, however, will reveal certain characteristic marks. Look for the *reddish bill* and the *plain breast* of the Field Sparrow; the *white stripe* over each eye, the almost pure *white breast* and the *gray rump* of the Chippy, and the *dark spot* in the middle of the breast of the Tree Sparrow.

The popular specific term "field," is a little misleading as applied to this bird, for its favorite habitat is an old pasture-lot overgrown with weeds and high bushes, or undergrowth along the edges of woodland, rather than cultivated fields, in which it is rarely seen. Nor does it appear, except by accident, in dooryards of human habitations.

Photo by S. A. Lottridge

NEST AND EGGS OF FIELD SPARROW

This Sparrow's habits of running along the ground and skulking through the brush are characteristics which aid in its indentification, and which at the same time reveal its retiring and timid disposition. Its song is a simple but musical little ditty of which Thoreau says: "The Rush Sparrow [a local name for the bird in his time, and one still sometimes used] jingles her small change, pure silver, on the counter of the pastures," a fetching description, though it implies a curious ignorance of the fact that it is the male bird that does the singing. The song is not unlike that of the Chipping Sparrow, in that its notes are all of the same pitch, but it is distinctive in that their delivery is at an accelerated rate which effectually relieves the effect of monotony. The tone is pure and sweet, rather more so than that of the "Chippy." Bradford Torrey recorded that he once heard the song rendered "in reverse order," with an effect which puzzled him until he had identified the singer. This observation conveys a valuable hint as to the variability in the songs of birds. It should always be borne in mind that this variability may be marked even in birds of the same species and the same locality; indeed it is likely that two birds from the same brood may render perceptibly different versions of the same song.

The laboratory investigation of 175 specimens of the Field Sparrow collected during all the months of the year from fifteen States and the District of Columbia showed 41 per cent. animal material and 59 per cent. vegetable. The animal matter consisted of weevils, leaf beetles, ground beetles, tiger beetles, click beetles, May beetles, caterpillars, grasshoppers, leaf-hoppers, true bugs, saw flies, ants, flies, spiders, and parasitic wasps. The last item is the principal point wherein the Field Sparrow differs in its food habits from the Chipping Sparrow — a difference that is not to the credit of this species from the standpoint of usefulness, since these wasps have been proved to be dangerous parasites of many caterpillars. Of the vegetable food 51 per cent. was seeds of grasses of such species as crab-grass, pigeon-grass, broom-sedge, poverty-grass, and sheathed rush-grass; 4 per cent. was seeds of such weeds as chickweed, lamb's-quarters, gromwell, spurge, wood sorrel, and knot-weed; and 4 per cent. was oats. Dr. Judd tells in his *Birds of a Maryland Farm* of watching a flock of Field Sparrows in the middle of November. They spent most of their time swaying on broom-sedge stalks, from which they were busily extracting seeds. Sometimes a bird alighting on a plant would bend it to the ground and hold it down with its feet while picking out the seeds; seldom would one feed from the ground in any other way.

The Western Field Sparrow (*Spizella pusilla*

arenacea) has much longer wings and tail, especially the latter, than his eastern relative, and his general color is grayer. He is found in the more western portions of the Great Plains; he breeds from Nebraska and South Dakota to eastern Montana and winters south to southern Texas and Louisiana.

Worthen's Sparrow or the Mexican Field Sparrow (*Spizella wortheni*) is a straggler from over the Mexican border into New Mexico. He is much like the Western Field Sparrow but his tail is much shorter, the wing-bands less distinct, and the sides of the head gray, relieved only by a white eye-ring.

BLACK-CHINNED SPARROW

Spizella atrogularis (*Cabanis*)

A. O. U. Number 565

General Description.— Length, 5¼ inches. Upper parts, rusty-brown streaked with black; under parts, black, gray, and white. Bill, small; wings, rather long and rather pointed; tail, decidedly longer than wing, double rounded, the feathers narrow and blunt.

Color.— Adult Male: *Front portion of cheek region, chin, and part of throat, black;* rest of head and neck, gray, darker on crown, where sometimes narrowly and indistinctly streaked with dusky, fading into lighter gray or olive-gray on chest and other under parts; the abdomen, white; *back, light rusty-brown* or cinnamon streaked with black; shoulders, similar but with outer webs more decidedly rusty; rump and upper tail-coverts, plain gray or olive-gray; tail, dusky; wing-coverts, dusky centrally, broadly margined, and tipped with pale cinnamon-buffy; greater coverts, dusky centrally broadly edged with pale buffy-brown or wood-brown; primaries, dusky edged with pale grayish. Adult Female: Similar to the adult male and not always distinguishable, but usually with the black of chin, etc., duller and much less extended, often entirely wanting, the entire head being gray, and the gray of crown and hindneck rather browner.

Nest and Eggs.— Nest: In low bushes, in deserts of Lower California, Arizona, and New Mexico; constructed of grass, weed fibers, lined with fine grasses and cow-hair. Eggs: 3 to 5, plain light greenish blue, normally unmarked.

Distribution.— More southern portions of southwestern United States and southward over Mexican plateau, north to southern California, Arizona, and southwestern New Mexico; Lower California, breeding in more northern portions, south in winter to the cape district.

A visitor from the eastern United States to the sagebrush regions of the southwest hears the song of a bird which makes him exclaim: "Why, all those bird-books are wrong! That's a Field Sparrow from home. I know his song." Then he catches sight of a little bird the size of a Chipping Sparrow, except for its longer tail. But instead of the rusty brown crown of the Field Sparrow which he had expected to see, this bird is a stranger with a gray head and a black patch on its throat. To his delight, the bird-lover has added a new acquaintance to his list — the Black-chinned Sparrow. On inquiry he finds that his new friend is fairly numerous within its limited range.

J. Ellis Burdick.

SLATE-COLORED JUNCO

Junco hyemalis hyemalis (*Linnæus*)

A. O. U. Number 567 See Color Plate 82

Other Names.— Snowbird; Black Snowbird; White Bill; Black Chipping Bird; Common Snowbird; Slate-colored Snowbird; Blue Snowbird; Eastern Junco.

General Description.— Length, 6 inches. Fore and upper parts, gray; under parts, white. Bill, small; wings, long and moderately rounded; tail, a little shorter than wing, double-rounded, the feathers narrow at the tips and blunt.

Color.— Adult Male: Head, neck, chest, upper breast, sides, flanks, and upper parts, plain slate-color, darker on head; lower breast, abdomen, anal region, and under tail-coverts, white; six middle tail-feathers, slate-blackish, edged with slate grayish; *two outermost tail-feathers white*; bill, pinkish; iris, dark reddish brown or claret-purple. ADULT FEMALE: Similar to adult male, but the slate-color rather lighter (sometimes decidely so). YOUNG (FIRST PLUMAGE): Above, grayish brown or drab (sometimes slightly rufescent on back), rather broadly streaked with blackish; chin, throat, chest, sides, and flanks, pale dull buffy or buffy grayish, spotted or broadly streaked (except on chin) with dusky; rest of under parts white, the breast usually spotted or flecked with dusky.

Nest and Eggs.— NEST: Usually placed on the ground, under a tuft of grass or weeds, sometimes in rock crevices, or upturned tree roots; constructed mostly of dried grasses, thickly lined with hair, fur, and feathers. EGGS: 4 or 5, white or greenish-white, spotted with rufous-brown.

Distribution.— Breeding from mountains of Pennsylvania, New York, and Massachusetts, Ontario, central Michigan, northern Minnesota, northward to Labrador, western shores of Hudson Bay, and through the interior to the Arctic coast and westward to valleys of the Yukon and Kowak rivers, Alaska; migrating southward in winter to Florida, Alabama, Mississippi, Texas, Arizona, and California, straggling (?) to Point Barrow and coast of Bering Sea (Kotzebue Sound, St. Michaels, etc.), and to eastern Siberia (Tschuctschi Peninsula).

The scientists have taken hold of our old friend the Common Snowbird and done so many things to him that ordinary bird observers and the scientists themselves are quite distracted. First they are disputing over the various races of Snowbirds, not sure just how many different species and varieties to list. They have agreed upon the scientific name "Junco" for the whole group or genus and imposed that Latin name upon the English-speaking world as the common name in place of Snowbird. Maybe the children of the newer generation will look out of the windows on a Christmas morning and say "Oh, see the Juncos!" but the charm of the word "Snowbird" seems to be more worth while in childhood and in poetry at least. Bird students are taking very kindly to the new name but no one seems to know how it started and what it means. Coues says that it is derived from the Latin *juncus* meaning a seed. It was after 1830 that the word "Junco" was first brought into scientific use.

Drawing by R. I. Brasher

SLATE-COLORED JUNCO (½ nat. size)

A sprightly and welcome winter visitor

This is a true winter bird indeed. He remains about his breeding range late into the fall and often goes only a little way to warmer climates when the food supply falls short farther north. The white-edged tail and hood-like coloring of the head makes the bird quite distinctive, and as we see him in the winter his coloring makes him very attractive against the snow or the evergreens. He is a tamer, more genial bird to us than is that other Snowbird, the White Snowbird or Snowflake that stays far afield in all kinds of weather. This Black Snowbird comes near the barns and kitchen doors, dodges in and out of the bushes in the garden, chatters cheerily in the wild cherry and thorn bushes, lisps his characteristic *tsip* from stone piles and stubble rows, and as spring comes, sings from the bushes and shorter trees his low, sweet song which Mrs. Bailey says is "as unpretentious and cheery as the friendly bird itself." And in early spring off he goes for the breeding grounds, often reaching there weeks before the nesting can begin.

The Junco is one of the most common Sparrows of America. In migration he vies in numbers with the other song birds, often being seen by the hundreds wherever there is shelter and food. In the breeding territory he chooses the cool and sheltered, and often damper localities. He breeds commonly in the Adirondacks. But farther south, any mountainous region or valley that is almost cold throughout the summer may shelter its Junco households. Not only in eastern but in western and northern North America up to the limit of trees, and south down through Mexico to Central America the Junco is common.

It is over the Rocky Mountain and Pacific coast Juncos that the scientists have become very much disturbed, and well they might, for nearly twenty varieties of Juncos have been credited to that country. East of the Rockies there is one great variety, the Slate-colored or Eastern Junco that occupies an area greater than any dozen varieties of the West. Far up to the northwest our Eastern Snowbird goes, sometimes pushing on to the limit of trees on the lower Coppermine and Mackenzie rivers. Many cross the Rockies up in that far northwest to the headwaters of the Yukon, and spread out in large numbers down the Yukon and up its tributaries occupying most of central, northern, and western Alaska. Some even fly through the Aleutian Islands to the mainland of Siberia to nest on the inhospitable rocks of a strange corner of the Old World. The other varieties of Juncos do not extend farther north than southern Alaska and northern British Columbia.

A variety of the Eastern Junco is the Carolina Junco (*Junco hyemalis carolinensis*), which exhibits a remarkably short migration route. It inhabits the southern Alleghenies and is slightly larger than the Eastern and not so brownish. Dr. W. W. Cooke said that in the fall migration "no Juncos were seen at Weaverville, N. C. before October 18th, though they nested upon the neighboring mountains, within five minutes' flight."

The other varieties are all Western and they show all sorts of interesting variations of color, but the habits of nesting, feeding, and singing are all very much alike. The White-winged Junco (*Junco aikeni*), larger than the Eastern, has two white wing bars and more white in the tail. The White-wing breeds in the Black Hills and surrounding country, and migrates less than 500 miles to southeastern Colorado for the winter. Within its area it is found in immense numbers.

Maybe the handsomest is the Oregon Junco (*Junco hyemalis oreganus*) with a black head and breast, sharply defined against a mahogany-brown back, white under parts, and pinkish-brown sides. This is a bird of the North Pacific coast. Shufeldt's Junco (*Junco hyemalis connectens*) is like the Oregon but with colors less intense. It is found in the mountains from Alberta to eastern Oregon. Thurber's Junco (*Junco hyemalis thurberi*) has a paler back and is a California mountain bird. The Point Pinos Junco (*Junco hyemalis pinosus*) is like Thurber's but has the throat and breast gray, and haunts the coast of a part of southern California. The Montana Junco (*Junco hyemalis montanus*) is one of the slaty-hooded and brown-backed Juncos. It belongs in the higher Rockies of Idaho, Montana, and north to Alberta. The Pink-sided Junco (*Junco hyemalis mearnsi*) has broadly pinkish sides and ranges in the mountains from northern Montana to Idaho and Wyoming. Ridgway's Junco (*Junco hyemalis annectens*) is discarded by Ridgway himself as only a hybrid. It is found from Wyoming to New Mexico. The Arizona Junco (*Junco phæonotus palliatus*) has no pink sides but has a dark brown back. It ranges from southern Arizona into Mexico, and is said to have less of the manners of a Junco than of a Water Thrush. The Red-backed Junco (*Junco phæonotus dorsalis*) has a bright rufous back and a pink bill. It belongs in the higher mountains of Arizona and New Mexico. The Gray-headed Junco (*Junco phæonotus caniceps*) is of darker gray with belly whiter than the preceding. It finds its home in the higher mountains of Colorado, Utah, and Nevada. South of the United States are found Townsend's, Baird's, Guadalupe, Mexican, Chiapas, Guatemala, and Irazu Juncos. The first three of these are of occasional occurrence in the southwestern United States. All of which means that east of the Rockies we may still love the cheery Black Snowbird that is frequently willing to pick at a dinner laid out near our doors and windows, but that elsewhere we may see all kinds of colors and sizes and variant types, and maybe new kinds of Junco characters and dispositions. L. Nelson Nichols.

The insect food of the Juncos is composed almost entirely of harmful species, of which caterpillars form the the largest item. Juncos do no damage to fruit or grain. They eat large quantities of weed seed (61.8 per cent.), thereby rendering service to agriculture. They should be rigidly protected.

BLACK-THROATED SPARROW

Amphispiza bilineata bilineata (*Cassin*)

A. O. U. Number 573

Other Name.— Black-throat.

General Description.— Length, 5¼ inches. Upper parts, gray; under parts, white. Bill, small; wing, long and slightly rounded; tail, trifle shorter than wing, rounded or double rounded, the feathers broad and rounded at the ends.

Color.— ADULTS: *Conspicuous stripe over eye* and on cheeks, *pure white*; the front portion of the cheek region, together with the chin, throat, and center portion of chest, uniform black, the last with a convex (sometimes angular) posterior outline; rest of under parts, white shading into grayish on sides and flanks; the latter, together with anal region and under tail-coverts, tinged with buffy in winter plumage; upper parts, deep, slightly brownish, gray, becoming more brownish (nearly hair-brown) on back and wings; sides of head (between the two white stripes), plain gray like crown; the tail, *blackish with white on edge and tip of outermost feathers;* iris, deep brown. YOUNG: Similar to adults but without any distinct black markings on head, etc.; the chin and throat, white sometimes flecked with grayish; the chest streaked with the same.

Nest and Eggs.— NEST: Placed in sagebrush, cactus, or other desert shrubs, near ground; constructed of fine shreds of bark, dried grasses, lined with fine blades of the latter. EGGS: 3 or 4, plain greenish or bluish white.

Distribution.— Middle and eastern Texas (except along Gulf coast?), north to Oklahoma, western Kansas, and eastern Colorado (?), south into States of northeastern Mexico.

The Black-throated Sparrow is a very plentiful and beautiful songster of the one area of the United States that certainly does need song. If there is any area in the world that is more dreary than another it is a desert. A song is needed and many of them to cheer the weary humans that travel the long hot routes across the southwestern country. Mrs. Bailey gives the bird the credit due to him when she says: "On all our walks through the thorn brush and climbs over the agave-speared hills we found the lovely little bird everywhere, sitting on top of the bushes singing with head thrown back in fine enjoyment of his bright lay." The bird has a most winsome manner, all out of keeping with the surroundings. Its cheery *tra-ree'-rah, ree'-rah-ree* with many variations can be heard throughout all our southwestern desert country and far down on the Mexican plateau. In most places it is very common, exceeding in frequency all other birds in the area.

Drawing by R. I. Brasher

BLACK-THROATED SPARROW (½ nat. size)

A handsome and sprightly little bird whose sweet song is most welcome in the western deserts

The ornithologists have found slight differences by which they define three species. The eastern race, the common Black-throated Sparrow, extends from western Kansas south through Texas and across the Rio Grande into the nearer Mexican States. The western race is named justly the Desert Sparrow or Desert Black-throat (*Amphispiza bilineata deserticola*), and has much the larger breeding area. It extends from the Pecos country of Texas, west to the Pacific, and from Nevada and Utah south to Lower California, Sonora, and Chihuahua. The third race is the Mexican Black-throated Sparrow (*Amphispiza bilineata grisea*) that ranges over the central Mexico plateau.

Mrs. Bailey gives very clear reasons for enthusiasm for this bird. She says, "When we camped on the arid mesa of the Pecos River, among the sounds that were oftenest in our ears were the songs of the Mockingbird and Nonpareil, the iterant *pe-cos'* of the Scaled Quail, and the calls of the Verdin and Roadrunner, while, mingled with them, always tinkling from the bushes, was the cheery little tune of *Amphispiza.*"

BELL'S SPARROW

Amphispiza belli (*Cassin*)

A. O. U. Number 574

General Description.— Length, 5½ inches. Upper parts, gray; under parts, white. Bill, small; wing, long and slightly rounded; tail, trifle shorter than wing, rounded or double rounded, the feathers broad and rounded at the ends.

Color.— ADULTS: Above (including ear region and sides of neck), deep brownish slate-gray becoming browner on back, where, as well as on crown, sometimes narrowly streaked with blackish or dusky; wings and tail, dull blackish with light brown edgings (pale grayish on primaries), the middle and greater coverts indistinctly tipped with pale brownish buffy or pale wood-brown; eye-ring, cheek stripe, and under parts in general, white; *broad stripe on sides of throat and foreneck, and spot in middle of chest, black or dusky-grayish;* sides and flanks, tinged with buffy and streaked with dusky; edge of wing, pale yellow; iris, brown. YOUNG: Crown and hindneck, dull gray, the former broadly streaked with black; back and shoulders, grayish brown broadly streaked with black; under parts, pale yellowish buff; the chest and sides of throat broadly streaked with blackish, the breast, sides, and flanks with smaller streaks of the same; a buffy whitish eye-ring; wings and tail much as in adults.

Nest and Eggs.— NEST: In bushes, within 3 feet of the ground; composed of grasses, vegetable fibers, weed stems; lined with fine grass and hair. EGGS: 3 or 4, pale greenish-blue finely speckled with dark reddish-brown, chiefly at large end.

Distribution.— Central and southern California (valleys and foothills) west of the Sierra Nevada, and Colorado Desert from about latitude 38°, and south into northern Lower California; also on the Santa Barbara Islands.

On the alkali plains of the Southwest, where only yuccas, sagebrush, and cacti grow, is the home-land of Bell's Sparrow and its variants, the Sage Sparrow (*Amphispiza nevadensis nevadensis*), Gray Sage Sparrow (*Amphispiza nevadensis cinerea*), and the California Sage Sparrow (*Amphispiza nevadensis canescens*). Here, amid the dreary wastes of hot sands, these grayish brown or brownish gray little mites cheerfully go about the duties of their lives, preaching sermons on patience, courage, and the joy of life to all their human friends.

PINE-WOODS SPARROW

Peucæa æstivalis æstivalis (*Lichtenstein*)

A. O. U. Number 575

General Description.— Length, 5½ inches. Upper parts, brown and gray in streaks; under parts, whitish. Wings, rather short and rounded; tail, equal to or longer than wing, graduated, the feathers narrow but with rounded tips.

Color.—ADULTS: Above, gray broadly streaked with chestnut-brown; tail, dusky with broad gray edgings; the middle pair of feathers, gray with a center stripe of dusky; edge of wing, light yellow; sides of head and neck, smoke-gray or dull ash-gray, the latter streaked with chestnut or dark chestnut-brown; a narrow chestnut or chestnut-brown stripe behind eye; chin and throat, very pale dull grayish or buffy grayish white deepening on chest, sides, and flanks into pale grayish-buffy or buffy-grayish; iris, brown.

Nest and Eggs.— NEST: On ground, among palmetto scrubs; constructed of fine dry grasses, in a neat, symmetrical manner. EGGS: 4, pure white.

Distribution.— Breeds in southern Georgia and northern Florida; winters in Florida.

The Pine-woods Sparrow of Florida and its northern variety Bachman's Sparrow, or Southern Pine Finch (*Peucæa æstivalis bachmani*) are striped Sparrows that are distinctly southern birds. In the east they are credited as coming only as far north as southern Virginia, but in the central west they reach southern Ohio, and central Illinois. In the far South they haunt only the pine woods and nest in the palmetto scrub in the pineries. Further north they show greater variations of nesting sites, but always on the ground, with the nest "distinctly roofed-over or domed," according to the description given by Major Bendire. He continues by saying that the nests "are cylindrical in shape, about seven or eight inches long by three in height . . . and the roof a little over half an inch in thickness. . . . The nests are all constructed out of dry grasses exclusively, and are lined with fine grass tops only. Some are much more artistically and compactly built than others."

Yet a greater claim to attention this bird has in its beautiful song. Dr. Chapman in speaking of the Pine-woods Sparrow, goes so far as to say, "In my opinion its song is more beautiful than that of any other of our Sparrows. It is very simple — I write it *chee-e-e-e--de, de, de; che-e--chee-o, chee-o, chee-o, chee-o* — but it possesses all the exquisite tenderness and pathos of the melody of the Hermit Thrush; indeed, in purity of tone and in execution I should consider the Sparrow the superior songster."

The Southern Pine Finch (Bachman's) has a song very similar to the Pine-woods Sparrow's. Its song has been compared to the plaintive song of the Field Sparrow, but louder and far sweeter. As far north as the Ohio River, the Southern Pine Finch may be heard (and seldom seen) in open oak woods. Dr. W. W. Cooke found that it is extending its range north of the Potomac and over the Monongahela.

SONG SPARROW

Melospiza melodia melodia (*Wilson*)

A. O. U. Number 581 See Color Plate 84

Other Names.— Silver Tongue; Everybody's Darling; Ground Sparrow; Hedge Sparrow; Bush Sparrow; Ground-bird; Marsh Sparrow; Red Grass-bird; Swamp Finch.

Drawing by R. I. Brasher

SONG SPARROW (⅓ nat. size)

A sweet singer of the spring and summer and a useful friend the year round

General Description.— Length, 6½ inches. Upper parts, brown and black in streaks; under parts, white streaked with black. Wings, short and rounded; tail, about the length of wing, rounded or double rounded, the feathers narrow and blunt.

Color.— Adults: Crown, brown narrowly streaked with black and divided by a narrow center stripe of gray; hindneck, brownish gray streaked or washed with brown; shoulders and between, black centrally producing streaks, these margined laterally with brown; the edges of the tail-feathers, brownish-gray; rump, olive-grayish streaked with brown; upper tail-coverts, browner than rump and more distinctly streaked; tail, brown; lesser wing-coverts, brown; middle coverts, brown margined terminally with pale brownish gray; greater coverts, brown margined terminally with paler and marked with a broad center tear-shaped (mostly concealed) space of blackish; inner wing-quills, mostly blackish, but outer webs chiefly brown; edge of wing, white; a broad stripe of olive-gray over eye; a broad cheek stripe of dull white or pale buffy, margined below by a conspicuous stripe or triangular spot of black or mixed brown and black; under parts, white; *the chest, marked with wedge-shaped streaks of black* edged with rusty brown, these streaks in lower central portion of chest, or upper breast, *forming an irregular spot*; sides and flanks, streaked with black and rusty-brown; under tail-coverts, white or pale buffy; iris, brown. (In summer the colors grayer, with streaks on chest, etc., narrower, sometimes wholly black; in winter the general coloration browner, the brown parts more rusty.) Young: Much like adults, but without any gray on upper parts; the crown, duller brown with the indistinct center stripe dull grayish buffy and the narrow blackish streaks much less distinct than in adults; ground color of back and shoulders, light buffy brownish or dull buffy; under parts, duller white, often quite buffy, with the streaks narrower and much less distinct.

Nest and Eggs.— Nest: Typical site on ground, in fields, adjoining woods, sheltered under a tussock of grass; sometimes in bushes, cedar or other small trees, or in hollows of apple or other trees; constructed of grass, weed stems, leaves, lined with fine grass and hair. EGGS: 4 or 5, dull pale greenish spotted thickly or sparsely spotted or blotched with shades of reddish or dark brown and lavender.

Distribution.— Breeds in the United States (except the South Atlantic and Gulf States), southern Canada, southern Alaska, and Mexico; winters in Alaska and most of the United States southward.

This is probably the best known of the very large Sparrow family. It lacks the full measure of the Chipping Sparrow's pretty confidence in the friendliness of man, and rather prefers the fields and the roadsides to the immediate vicinity of human habitations; but against these negative qualities are to be placed its more characteristic plumage, and above all its real genius as a songster. Thousands of persons, old and young, who pay little or no heed to the song of the Field Sparrow or the Vesper Sparrow or the Fox Sparrow, recognize instantly the characteristic little *motif* of the Song Sparrow. And the bird lays an additional claim on the friendship and sympathy of all, by the fact that it is a frequent winter resident in the northern States. Though to untrained observation confusingly like some of the other Sparrows, this bird should

Photo of a mounted group in the Am. Mus. Nat. Hist. Courtesy of Nat. Asso. Aud. Soc.

CENTERS OF DISTRIBUTION OF SEVEN OF THE GEOGRAPHICAL RACES OF THE SONG SPARROW

1. Aleutian; 2. Sooty; 3. Heermann's; 4. Mountain; 5. Desert; 6. Mexican; 7. Eastern

readily be identified by its strongly marked breast, its stubby bill, and its slightly forked tail, as shown in flight.

The Song Sparrow takes his singing very seriously. Almost invariably he presents his recital from the top of a bush or a fence post or a comparatively low tree. Always as he begins to sing he throws his head backward, and points his bill at an angle of about 45 degrees, and this position he retains until the song is finished. He seems intent upon sending his little prayer of thankfulness straight up to heaven, by the shortest route. Over and over again the sweet and sincere little petition is offered — and who can doubt that it is heeded? There are very many variations of the song, and sometimes several are presented in succession by the same singer. Mr. Burroughs records one bird who "had five distinct songs, each as markedly different from the others as any human songs, which he repeated one after another. He may have had a sixth or a seventh, but he bethought himself of some business in the next field, and flew away before he had exhausted his repertory." (*Ways of Nature.*) Mr. Mathews devotes several pages, in his *Field Book of Wild Birds and Their Music,* to many variations of the song, reduced to musical notation. The commonest form, however, begins with two notes on the same pitch, followed by a third, four or five tones higher, all of these accented, and followed by a descending run in the same general rhythm. Whatever the form of the song, however, its spirit is always the same, and Mr. Burroughs interprets this very faithfully when he says that it expresses "simple faith and trust."

Photo by S. A. Lottridge

YOUNG SONG SPARROWS

No other bird of the temperate and arctic regions of North America, with the possible exception of the Horned Lark, has proved so sensitive to influences of physical environments, and as a result it has become divided into a large number of geographic forms, some of extensive, others of very circumscribed range. In every case the area of distribution coincides exactly with the uniformity or continuity of physical conditions. Thus the form having the widest distribution is that inhabiting the Atlantic watershed, or the entire region from the Atlantic coast to the wooded valleys of the Great Plains, while those of the most limited range belong to the Pacific slope, where the topographic and resultant climatic features are so varied and complicated. In California nearly every distinct drainage area has its own peculiar form of the Song Sparrow; one form, the Alameda Song Sparrow (*Melospiza melodia pusillula*), is strictly limited to the salt marshes around San Francisco Bay.

The Mountain Song Sparrow (*Melospiza melodia montana*) is found in the Rocky Mountain district of the United States west to and including the Sierra Nevada, in California, north to eastern Oregon, southern Idaho, and southern Montana; south in winter to western Texas and northern Mexico. In coloration it is grayer than the type species, its tail and wings are longer, and its bill is smaller and relatively more slender.

Merrill's Song Sparrow (*Melospiza melodia merrilli*) is very much like the Mountain Song Sparrow; it is slightly darker and more uniform above and the grayish edging to the feathers of the shoulders and the space between them are less strongly contrasted with the darker centers which are usually more brown than black. It breeds from northern California (in the mountains), through Oregon and Washington east of the Cascade Mountains, to northwestern Idaho; in winter it goes south into Nevada, Utah, Arizona, and northern Sonora.

The slender bill of the Desert Song Sparrow (*Melospiza melodia fallax*) is like that of the Mountain Song Sparrow, but its tail and wings average decidedly shorter and its coloration is conspicuously paler and more rusty. It inhabits the Sonoran desert district of southwestern Arizona, southern Nevada, southeastern California, northeastern Lower California, and Sonora.

Heermann's Song Sparrow (*Melospiza melodia heermanni*) is found in the central valleys of California, including the lower levels of the

Sacramento and San Joaquin basin. It is smaller than the type species and darker and browner in coloration.

The San Diego Song Sparrow (*Melospiza melodia cooperi*) is slightly smaller than Heermann's Song Sparrow; the prevailing color of the back is a grayish-olive broadly streaked with black. It lives in the southern coast district of California and the northern Pacific coast district of Lower California.

On the San Clemente, San Miguel, and Santa Rosa islands, California, is found the San Clemente Song Sparrow (*Melospiza melodia clementæ*); it is larger than the San Diego Song Sparrow and grayer in coloration, the back being a light olive-gray with narrower black streaks.

The Santa Barbara Song Sparrow (*Melospiza melodia graminea*) found on the Santa Barbara and Santa Cruz islands, California, is like the San Clemente in color but smaller in size.

Samuels's Song Sparrow (*Melospiza melodia samuelis*) is exactly like Heermann's Song Sparrow in color but in size it is much smaller and its bill is more slender. It is found on the coast slope of central California, except in the salt-water marshes of San Francisco Bay, from Santa Cruz County to Humboldt County.

Similar in size and proportions to Samuels's Song Sparrow but very different in coloration is the Mendocino Song Sparrow (*Melospiza melodia cleonensis*) of the northern coast district of California and southwestern Oregon; its general color is more reddish, the upper parts being a deep rusty olive, conspicuously and broadly streaked with dark rusty-brown, or chestnut, and black; the streaks on the chest are also dark rusty-brown or chestnut.

The Rusty Song Sparrow (*Melospiza melodia morphna*) breeds from the extreme southern portion of Alaska through British Columbia to western Oregon and in winter it travels south to southern California. It is larger than the Mendocino Song Sparrow but its coloration is similar, the rusty brown or chestnut streaks on the back being less strongly contrasted with the rusty olive ground color.

In southern Alaska, on the coast and the islands off the coast is the home of the Sooty Song Sparrow (*Melospiza melodia rufina*). In winter it comes south to the coast of British Columbia, Vancouver Island, and northwestern Washington. It is larger than the Rusty Song Sparrow and darker — sooty rather than rusty.

Four other Alaskan Song Sparrows are the Yakutat (*Melospiza melodia caurina*), the Kenai (*Melospiza melodia kenaiensis*), the Kodiak, or Bischoff's (*Melospiza melodia insignis*), and the Aleutian (*Melospiza melodia sanaka*). The Yakutat is a little larger than the Sooty, the Kenai is larger than the Yakutat, and the Kodiak and Aleutian are still larger. All are grayer in coloration.

The food of this species varies considerably. About three-fourths of its diet consists of the seeds of noxious weeds and one-fourth of insects. Of these, beetles, especially weevils, constitute the major portion. Ants, wasps, bugs (including the black olive scale), and caterpillars are also eaten. Grasshoppers are taken by the eastern bird, but not by the western ones.

LINCOLN'S SPARROW

Melospiza lincolni lincolni (*Audubon*)

A. O. U. Number 583 See Color Plate 84

Other Names.— Lincoln's Song Sparrow; Lincoln's Finch.

General Description.— Length, 5¾ inches. Upper parts, brown and olive, streaked with black; under parts, buff and white, streaked with black. Wings, short and rounded; tail, about the length of wing, rounded or double-rounded, the feathers narrow and blunt.

Color.— Adults: Crown, light mummy-brown, conspicuously streaked with black and divided by a center stripe of olive-grayish; hindneck, back, shoulders, rump, and upper tail-coverts, light olive or buffy olive sharply streaked with black, the streaks broadest on back; outer surface of wings, more rusty brownish especially on innermost greater coverts and secondaries; the greater coverts and inner wing-quills conspicuously blackish centrally; tail, light grayish brown; sides of neck grayish or olive-grayish; ear region similar, but rather darker or browner; cheek region, space behind ear, *broad band across chest*, sides, flanks, and under tail-coverts *buffy*; *the chest*, sides, flanks, and under tail-coverts *streaked with black;* rest of the under parts white, the throat usually flecked or streaked with black.

Nest and Eggs.— Nest: On ground, in marshy land; constructed entirely of grass, lined with finer blades of the same material. EGGS: 3 or 4, white, pale greenish or brownish white rather coarsely blotched with chestnut and lavender-gray chiefly around large end.

Distribution.— North America at large; breeding chiefly north of the United States and in the higher parts of the Rocky Mountains and Sierra Nevada; south in winter to Panama.

"Bird-afraid-of-his-shadow," W. Leon Dawson calls this Sparrow, and then he asks, "Why should a bird of inconspicuous color steal silently through our woods and slink along our streams with bated breath as if in mortal dread of the human eye? Are we such hobgoblins?" Yet this appears to be the characteristic demeanor of the bird throughout its very wide range. And the tendency of this conduct to make the bird little known is strengthened by its habit of arriving in the northern latitudes after most of the other birds are on hand and engaging our attention, and departing in the fall with the general wave of migrating Sparrows, in which it loses its identity.

From the Song Sparrow, which it closely resembles, it may be distinguished by its smaller size, its shorter tail, the buff belt across its narrowly streaked breast, and the olive-gray color of the sides of its head. Its song, which is not often heard, is, according to Dr. Dwight, "not loud, and suggests the bubbling, guttural notes of the House Wren, combined with the sweet rippling music of the Purple Finch, and when you think the song is done there is an unexpected aftermath."

The food of the Lincoln Sparrow resembles that of the Song Sparrow, but more ants and fewer grasshoppers are destroyed than by the Song Sparrow.

In British Columbia and western Washington is a variety of the Lincoln Sparrow called Forbush's Sparrow (*Melospiza lincolni striata*). In migration it is found in California also. The stripe over the eye and the upper parts are more strongly olivaceous and the dark streaks of the back are blacker and more numerous. Its habits are similar to those of its congener.

SWAMP SPARROW

Melospiza georgiana (*Latham*)

A. O. U. Number 584 See Color Plate 84

Courtesy of Am. Mus. Nat. Hist.

SWAMP SPARROW (½ nat. size)

A sprite of swampy country

Other Name.— Swamp Song Sparrow.

General Description.— Length, 5¾ inches. Upper parts, brown streaked with black; under parts, gray. Wings, short and rounded; tail, about the length of wing, rounded or double rounded, the feathers narrow and almost pointed at the tip.

Color.—ADULTS: Forehead, black divided by a center line of grayish or whitish; *crown, chestnut* sometimes streaked with blackish; back of head, blackish laterally, grayish centrally; back and shoulders, light brown broadly streaked with black; rump, olive-brownish streaked with dusky; upper tail-coverts, more rusty brown, distinctly streaked with black; tail, rusty brown; exposed surface of greater wing-coverts and secondaries chestnut; *inner wing-quills black, edged on outer webs with chestnut* and buffy; sides of neck and hindneck, gray; ear region, brownish gray, or light brownish margined above by a distinct streak behind eye of black and chestnut and beneath by a narrower streak of same; chin, throat, and abdomen, white or grayish white; chest, light gray or brownish gray, sometimes narrowly and indistinctly streaked with dusky; sides and flanks (especially the latter), tawny brown; under tail-coverts, buffy with central marks of dusky.

Nest and Eggs.— NEST: Placed on ground in a

bunch of flags or sedge grass, in or on edge of marshes, or wet meadows; constructed entirely of grass and a few leaves, lined with finer similar material. EGGS: 4 or 5, pale greenish or bluish white, clouded with yellowish brown and lilac.

Distribution.— Eastern North America to the Plains, north to the British provinces, including Newfoundland and Labrador; breeds from the northern States northward; and winters from Massachusetts southward to the Gulf States.

Any swamp — within its natural range — whether near the ocean or inland, is good enough for the Swamp Sparrow, and occasionally it spends the winter — if the weather be not too severe — in cat-tail marshes along the coast of Long Island and southern New England. The song resembles that of the Chipping Sparrow, though the quality of the tone is sweeter and fuller.

Walter S. Barrows says, in *Michigan Bird Life:* "In our own experience the song merely suggests that of the Chipping Sparrow, but the notes are less rapid, far sweeter, and have a distinct metallic or bell-like tone which suggests the ring of cut glass."

The bird's plain breast distinguishes it from the Song Sparrow, many of which are found in the swamps in autumn, while in the spring its reddish-brown wings and chestnut-colored crown are not duplicated by any member of its family, save the Chipping Sparrow, which does not frequent swamps and has a more slender figure.

The food habits of this bird are similar to those of the Song Sparrow. It takes more seeds of polygonums than most birds and eats largely of the seeds of the sedges and aquatic panicums that abound in its swampy habitat.

NEST AND EGGS OF SWAMP SPARROW

FOX SPARROW

Passerella iliaca iliaca (*Merrem*)

A. O. U. Number 585 See Color Plate 83

Other Names.— Foxy Finch; Ferruginous Finch; Fox-tail; Fox-colored Sparrow.

General Description.— Length, 6½ inches. Upper parts, gray streaked with brown, or uniform chestnut; under parts, white spotted with chestnut. Bill, large, conical, sharp-pointed, and strong; wings, long and pointed; tail, about ⅚ length of wing, very slightly rounded or double rounded.

Color.— ADULTS: Upper parts, mixed deep rusty and brownish gray in variable proportions. I. GRAY PHASE: Above, olive-gray, the back and shoulders broadly *streaked with rusty brown or chestnut,* the crown tinged with the same; lower rump and upper tail-coverts, cinnamon-rufous; the middle and greater wing-coverts, *narrowly tipped with whitish*; wings and inner webs of tail-feathers, dusky brown; under parts, white heavily spotted on chest, sides of throat, etc., with chestnut-rufous; the sides and flanks, broadly streaked with same. II. RUFOUS PHASE: Above, nearly uniform chestnut or chestnut-rufous, the upper rump, sides of neck, and ear region slightly intermixed with olive or olive-grayish; under parts as in the gray phase, but the chestnut-rufous spots larger, more confluent.

Nest and Eggs.— NEST: On ground, under evergreens; constructed of grass, moss, fine twigs, and a few leaves; lined with fine grass and feathers. EGGS: 4 or 5, pale bluish green, heavily speckled with chestnut or umber-brown.

Distribution.— Northern North America; breeding from Nova Scotia, Magdalen Islands, Anticosti Island, Newfoundland, northern Maine, Province of Quebec, etc., northward and northwestward to valley of Lower Anderson River, Kowak River, and Bering seacoast of Alaska (north of the Alaska peninsula); south in winter to northern Florida and westward to middle Texas, and eastern base of Rocky Mountains; occasional on southern coast of Alaska during migration.

This is not only one of the largest, but is the handsomest and withal perhaps the most characteristic of the American Sparrows. Most of the members of this very large family are modestly garbed, and furthermore there is so much similarity in their plumage, that sometimes it takes a sharp eye and acute observation to distinguish one species from another. But "Foxy" may readily be identified not only by his size, but by his rich tawny coloring (like that of a fox in his summer pelage), as well as by certain of his mannerisms, and by his fine song. It should be remembered, too, that though he is frequently seen in many regions which he traverses in his migrations, he is essentially a migrant as far as the United States are concerned. His real home — that is, the regions in which he breeds — is in the great forests of Canada. In the general latitude of New York and New England, he tarries, in his northward journey, from the middle of March to the end of April, and in his southward passage, from about the middle of October to the end of November. During these visits he is likely to be found both in open woods and in bushes skirting fields.

Drawing by R. I. Brasher

FOX SPARROW (½ nat. size)

A handsome bird whose sweet whistle is all too infrequently heard

When feeding on the ground one of his mannerisms is his habit of scratching with both feet at once, and often with such vigor as to make a considerable commotion in the dry leaves. Another peculiarity of the bird is shown when a flock of them are disturbed while feeding on the ground. Under these conditions, instead of seeking concealment in the brush (as their relatives are likely to do), these Sparrows generally fly to the low branches of the nearest trees where they are apt to remain in plain sight, and whence they return in a few minutes to the ground, if they are not much frightened.

"Foxy's" song — most frequently heard in the United States in spring — is one of the finest of Sparrow ditties. It is a series of whistled notes in descending intervals, and somewhat resembles the lay of the Vesper Sparrow, though the tone is much mellower and sweeter than the Vesper's. Furthermore its technique is distinctive in that the notes are very prettily slurred together like those of the warbling birds. The song is to be heard in the United States when the birds are foraging in little flocks, but even then altogether too infrequently; for many a bird-lover has never heard it at all.

The food of the Fox Sparrow consists of 14 per cent. animal matter and 86 per cent. vegetable.

The animal food is of little interest excepting in the spring when it eats largely of millepedes of the *Julus* group and at the same time developes a taste for ground beetles. The vegetable food differs from that of most other Sparrows, in that it contains less grass seed, less grain, and more fruit, ragweed, and polygonum. Half of the food consists of ragweed and polygonum, and more than a quarter of fruit. It does no direct damage to cultivated fruit, though it occasionally eats the buds of peach trees and pear trees. Bradford Torrey has observed it feeding on the fruit of burning bush.

In western North America, Ridgway recognizes eight forms of the Fox Sparrow. These are all browner than the type species, but vary otherwise and from one another only in small details. They are the Shumagin Fox Sparrow (*Passerella iliaca unalaschcensis*), found in the Shumagin Islands and the Alaska Peninsula; the Kodiak Fox Sparrow (*Passerella iliaca insularis*), found in summer on Kodiak Island, Alaska, and in winter south along the coast slope to southern California; the Yakutat Fox Sparrow (*Passerella iliaca annectens*), living in summer on the coast of Alaska from Cross Sound to Prince William Sound and in winter south to California; Townsend's Fox Sparrow (*Passerella iliaca townsendi*), making its home in the coast district of southern Alaska and in the winter going south to northern California; the Sooty Fox Sparrow (*Passerella iliaca fuliginosa*) summering in the coast district, British Columbia, on Vancouver Island, and in northwestern Washington and wintering south along the coast to San Francisco; the Slate-colored Fox Sparrow (*Passerella iliaca schistacea*), living in the Rocky Mountain district, north to the interior of British Columbia and south to New Mexico and Arizona and east to Kansas; the Thick-billed Fox Sparrow (*Passerella iliaca megarhyncha*), breeding on both slopes of the Sierra Nevadas from Mount Shasta southward; and Stephens's Fox Sparrow (*Passerella iliaca stephensi*), breeding on the mountains of San Bernardino and San Jacinto in southern California.

TEXAS SPARROW

Arremonops rufivirgatus (*Lawrence*)

A. O. U. Number 586

Other Name.— Green Finch.

General Description.— Length, 5¾ inches. Upper parts, olive-green; under parts, white. Wings, short and much rounded; tail, shorter than wing.

Color.— Adults: Above, plain grayish olive-green (wings and tail brighter); the crown, with two broad lateral stripes of chestnut-brown separated by a central stripe of olive or grayish olive-green; sides of head, dull grayish relieved by a streak of chestnut-brown; a narrow ring of dull white around eye; under parts, dull whitish (pure white on abdomen); the chest, sides, and flanks, shaded with buffy grayish; edge of wing, light yellow; iris, brown. Young: Above, dull brownish, including crown; the wing-coverts, edged and tipped with tawny; beneath similar, but rather paler, becoming buffy or tawny on abdomen.

Nest and Eggs.— Nest: In open thickets, or low bushes, within three feet of ground; constructed of weed stalks, grasses, leaves, lined with fine grass and hair; semi-domed, being built obliquely, the upper rim extending over, hiding the eggs from perpendicular view. Eggs: 4, plain, dull white.

Distribution.— Southern Texas and south through northeastern Mexico.

There is nothing very noticeable about the Texas Sparrow and it is a bird that very few Americans will ever see. Its plain olive and brown colors do not attract attention, and its very restricted area within the United States will never make it a well-known bird. The genus to which it belongs is pretty well known all through Mexico and Central America, and has been called the genus of Middle American Sparrows. This species is the only one of the genus that has crossed the Rio Grande. The others are pretty well spread out over Mexico, and down through the Central American States and Panama.

The Texas Sparrow is practically non-migratory and occupies in our area only a small triangle in southern Texas. It does not extend much more than three hundred miles up the Rio Grande and about two hundred miles up along the Texas coast. In Mexico it occupies an area about the same size just across the Rio Grande.

Further south toward Vera Cruz there is a variety that is darker and has been named the Cordova Sparrow.

The Texas and Cordova Sparrows are simple songsters. They frequent thickets and brush fences, and place their nests in thick bushes not far from the ground. Their molts do not make any conspicuous changes in their appearance. As the males, females, and immature all have very much the same appearance, and they live throughout the year in nearly the same places, there is a certain uniformity and dullness in their lives that make this bird different from most American birds, among whom there is something remarkable and interesting happening every year.

TOWHEE

Pipilo erythrophthalmus erythrophthalmus (*Linnæus*)

A. O. U. Number 587 See Color Plate 84

Other Names.— Chewink; Towhee-bird; Swamp Robin; Bullfinch (in Virginia); Red-eyed Towhee; Ground Robin; Towhee Bunting; Jo-ree; Marsh Robin; Bush-bird; Turkey Sparrow.

General Description.— Length, 8 inches. Fore and upper parts, black; under parts, white and brownish. Wings, rather short and much rounded; tail, longer than wing, rounded, the feathers broad with compact webs and rounded tips; feet, stout.

Color.— ADULT MALE: Head, neck, chest, and upper parts, black; sides and flanks, uniform cinnamon-rufous; anal region and under tail-coverts, cinnamon-buffy; breast and abdomen, white; eighth to fourth or third primaries with basal portion of outer webs, white, forming a patch; outer webs of wing feathers, broadly edged with white for part of their length; bill, wholly black in summer; iris, red. ADULT FEMALE: Similar to the adult male, but with the black portions replaced by brown (dull prouts brown above, lighter, more cinnamon-brown or raw umber on throat and chest). YOUNG MALE: Above, dull fulvous-brown, darker and uniform on head, elsewhere indistinctly streaked with dusky; wings, dull black, the coverts edged with buffy brown; wing feathers with a broad lateral stripe of buffy whitish; primaries, marked with white, as in the adult; tail, as in adult male; chin and throat, plain pale buff, with an interrupted blackish stripe on each side; chest, deeper buff, thickly marked with cuneate and arrow-like streaks of dusky; breast and abdomen, dull white.

Nest and Eggs.— NEST: On the ground, under a clump of grass, weeds, or bushes, in deep woods or open, first growth clearings, sunk to level of surface and always exceptionally well concealed; construction rather variable, sometimes carelessly made, at others quite firm and compact; made of leaves, twigs, grass, and vegetable fibers, well lined with grass and rootlets. EGGS: 4, white or pale pinkish white, thickly sprinkled with light chestnut.

Distribution.— Eastern United States and more southern British provinces west to edge of the Great Plains, in Manitoba, North Dakota, Kansas, Oklahoma, etc.; breeding from near the Gulf coast, north to Maine, Ontario, Manitoba, etc.; south in winter to southern Florida, Gulf coast in general, and eastern and central Texas; casual in New Brunswick.

Drawing by R. I. Brasher

TOWHEE (⅓ nat. size)

A skillful ventriloquist "who scratches like a hen"

Both of the names, "Towhee" and "Chewink," by which this bird is commonly known, are intended to represent its characteristic call-note, and the difference between the sound of the two words furnishes an interesting illustration of how differently two persons may hear the same syllables. That many ornithologists, whose hearing should be very keen and discriminating, make the syllables "tow-hee" out of the call is shown by the fact that the American Ornithologists' Union has adopted that name for the bird. Yet to many others the call is much more clearly represented by the syllables, "che-wink," even to the *n* and *k,* though some bird students insist that birds are incapable of uttering any true consonant sound. At any rate, the tone and accent of the call form a singular blend of cheerfulness and inquiry, albeit the quality is a bit nasal.

The bird's song, such as it is, consists of three notes, the first two strongly accented and the second lower by several tones than the first; these followed by several very rapidly uttered notes of the *same pitch* — not a "trill," as they often are described, since a trill is the rapid repetition of two notes of *different* pitch. There have been various efforts to reduce this song to syllables, for example, Seton's transliteration, *chuck-burr, pil-a-will-a-will-a-will,* and Thoreau's rendition, *hip-you, he-he-he-he,* which gives a close approximation to the vowel value of the syllables.

Something strangely like the ventriloquistic faculty seems to be possessed by not a few American birds, and probably many observers have noticed that the Chewink apparently employs it in a very marked degree, their persistence having been taxed to the utmost to locate a Chewink who sang at intervals of every ten or fifteen seconds for several minutes before he was finally discovered, usually in plain sight and not more than twenty-five or thirty yards distant.

This bird has two other peculiarities which distinguish it from most of its kind. One is its way of scratching on the ground, an operation in which it uses its feet alternately, after the manner of the domesticated hen. Indeed, the bird gets much of its food by this ground-foraging, incidentally making a commotion among the dry leaves which suggests the efforts of a much larger bird, or of a squirrel or woodchuck. Again, the Towhee is decidedly unlike other birds in its apparent nonchalance when its nest is approached. It may be dangerous to infer that this seeming indifference is deliberately assumed for the purpose of deceiving the intruder, yet it is difficult to account for it in any other way, for the bird betrays much solicitude once the nest is actually discovered.

The Cowbird seems to have a special preference for the nest of the Towhee and seems to choose the latter to bring up her young more often than she does any other species. Frequently two, three, and even four Cowbird's eggs have been found in a Chewink's nest, and occasionally five or six have been found. In the cases of the larger numbers the nest has generally been deserted as if the Chewinks felt that their good nature had been imposed upon too far. The eggs of the two species resemble each other, but the Cowbird's egg is more likely to be smaller and to lack the pinkish tint which is a usual characteristic of the Towhee's.

Photo by H. K. Job Courtesy of Nat. Asso. Aud. Soc.

MALE TOWHEE FEEDING YOUNG

The two with open mouths are Cowbirds

Wild fruits of all kinds, from strawberries and blackberries to wild cherries and grapes, are eagerly eaten by the Towhee. However, seeds and insects are its principal food. Beetles and their larvæ, ants, moths, caterpillars, grasshoppers, flies, and earthworms are destroyed by the Towhee. Although it cannot be classed as a decidedly useful bird, chiefly because of its haunts, there are no reports of its having damaged cultivated crops or caused loss of any kind to the farmer.

The White-eyed or Florida Towhee (*Pipilo erythrophthalmus alleni*) which is found on the Florida peninsula, is smaller than the common Towhee and has much less white on the wings and tail and its iris is brownish-yellow or yellowish-white instead of carmine-red.

OREGON TOWHEE

Pipilo maculatus oregonus *Bell*

A. O. U. Number 588b

Other Name.— Spotted Towhee.

General Description.— Length, 8 inches. Fore and upper parts, black; under parts, white and brownish. Wings, rather short and much rounded; tail, longer than wing, rounded, the feathers broad with compact webs and rounded tips; feet, stout.

Color.— ADULT MALE: Head, neck, and chest, black, the throat with a white spot, and, very rarely, the back of head streaked with rufous; *upper parts, black*; middle and greater wing-coverts tipped with white, forming two spots; three to four outer tail-feathers with small terminal spaces of white, chiefly on inner webs; the outermost tail-feathers with the outer web edged with white; breast and abdomen, white; sides and flanks, cinnamon-rufous occasionally with dusky spots or bars; anal region and under tail-coverts, paler cinnamon-tawny or ochraceous buff; bill, black. ADULT FEMALE: Similar to adult male, but throat and chest dark sooty brown or sooty black; general color of upper parts, dark sooty brown.

Nest and Eggs.— NEST: In ground, rim sunk flush with the surface, usually near streams; a strong, well built structure of bark strips, grass, or pine needles, lined with grass. EGGS: 4 or 5, very pale greenish white, covered with spots and specks of chestnut and lavender.

Distribution.— Coast district of southern British Columbia, Vancouver Island, Washington, Oregon, and California, south to San Francisco Bay; winters south to southern California.

The group of Towhees, known as Spotted Towhees, and of which the Oregon Towhee is a member, are found in western United States and Mexico among the chaparral. They are very shy and simply refuse to stay where they can be observed; just as you hear one sing and catch sight of him on the top of a bush, he sees you and down he drops to the ground and starts scratching among the leaves under the bushes.

In southern California, in the coast district, and south into Lower California, is found the San Diego Towhee (*Pipilo maculatus megalonyx*). It is a deep glossy black with heavy white markings on the wings. The Arctic Towhee (*Pipilo maculatus arcticus*) has extensive white markings on both wings and tail and its shoulders are heavily streaked with white; it breeds in the plains and among the foothills of the Rockies from southern Alberta to west central Montana and northwestern Nebraska and winters from eastern Colorado and southern Nebraska to southern Texas. The Spurred Towhee (*Pipilo*

Drawing by R. Bruce Horsfall

OREGON TOWHEE (⅗ nat. size)

A scratcher among the fallen leaves

maculatus montanus), distributed from British Columbia south into Mexico and from eastern California to Wyoming, Colorado, New Mexico, and Western Texas, and the San Clemente Towhee (*Pipilo maculatus clementæ*), found on the San Clemente and other islands of southern California, have the white markings much restricted.

These Towhees are not numerous enough to inflict any great damage, no matter what their habits. Should they become very abundant they very likely would injure fruit, but they seem so shy and retiring that the more the country is cleared and put under cultivation the more likely they are to become rare.

About three-quarters of their food consists of vegetable matter. Fruit forms about 18 per cent. and is probably almost entirely wild or waste. Grain averages 4 per cent. for the year with the largest amount eaten after the harvesting season. Weed seed occupies the chief place on their menu and forms nearly 35 per cent. of their food for the year.

Apparently these Towhees do not care for grasshoppers as they form less than 2 per cent. of their food for the year and are eaten very irregularly. Weevils, tree-boring beetles, ants, wasps, bees, and the black olive scale make up most of their animal food.

CANON TOWHEE

Pipilo fuscus mesoleucus *Baird*

A. O. U. Number 591

Other Names.— Fuscous Towhee; Brown Chippy; Cañon Bunting.

General Description.— Length, 9½ inches. Upper parts, brown; under parts, white, brown, and black. Wings, rather short and much rounded; tail, longer than wing, rounded, the feathers broad with compact webs and rounded tips; feet, stout.

Color.—Adults: Above, hair-brown or pale grayish sepia-brown, the crown distinctly ruddy, inclining to cinnamon; middle and greater wing-coverts and upper tail-coverts, usually narrowly and indistinctly tipped with paler; wings and tail-feathers with the general color darker, clearer, and less brown than other portions; side of head, mainly colored like back, etc., but with pale buffy or dull whitish markings; cheek region, chin, and throat, pinkish buff (deeper in winter, paler in summer plumage), the first flecked with dusky, the nearly (sometimes quite) immaculate throat area surrounded by rather large triangular spots or streaks of black; center portion of breast and abdomen, white; sides of breast, sides, and flanks, brown (paler than back); anal regions and under tail-coverts, cinnamon or cinnamon-tawny; iris, brown.

Nest and Eggs.— Nest: Located in thickets or small mesquite trees, near ground, usually within 10 feet, sometimes in dense clumps of cholla or between yucca leaves; deep, large, but loosely constructed of coarse grass, lined with fine roots and horse- or cow-hair. Eggs: 3, speckled, scratched and scrawled with brown, black, or lavender.

Distribution.— Arid districts of Arizona, southern and eastern New Mexico, western Texas, eastern Colorado, and southwestern Colorado, south to northeastern Sonora and northwestern Chihuahua.

The Cañon or Fuscous Towhees form a numerous species that is distinguished by their fluffy brown Sparrow-like appearance. To the Easterner there seems to be less of the Towhee and more of the brown Sparrow about this common dooryard friend of the southwest. It is often called the Brown Chippy from the very persistence of the loud metallic *chip*, whether heard in the streets of towns or out in the dense chaparral and scrub bushes that line the mountain cañons. The flight song is a Robin-like *screep'-eep-eep*, and it has another squeaky but quiet and contented song. In the cañons at dusk a dozen or more of the Cañon Towhees sing this song in concert and the effect is like an evening hymn in a temple to nature's God.

There are many varieties of the Fuscous Towhee. The typical one is the Brown Towhee of the Pacific slope of central Mexico. Throughout California the variety is there known as the California Towhee or Crissal Bunting (*Pipilo crissalis crissalis*), the main distinction appearing to be a deeper colored head than the more eastern bird. Ridgway has seen enough differences in them to make the California Towhee a separate species, but Mrs. Bailey prefers to know them as mere varieties of the Fuscous Towhee. The Anthony Towhee (*Pipilo crissalis senicula*) of southern California is surely but a variety of the California, having darker upper parts and grayer lower parts.

Wherever found, the Fuscous Towhee has no fear of man, and when the breeding season comes the gloomy cañons resound with his songs.

ABERT'S TOWHEE

Pipilo aberti *Baird*

A. O. U. Number 592

Other Name.— Gray Towhee.

General Description.— Length, 9½ inches. Upper parts, brown; under parts, brown and yellowish. Wings, rather short and much rounded; tail, longer than wing, rounded, the feathers broad with compact webs and rounded tips; feet, stout.

Color.— Adults: Above, uniform rather light brown, becoming rather darker and somewhat grayer on wings and tail, the primaries edged with pale brownish gray; beneath, pale wood-brown, paler on breast, deeper and tinged with reddish cinnamon on throat and chest, the lower abdomen yellowish-buffy, the under tail-coverts still deeper, or reddish tawny; chin and throat, streaked with dusky. Young: Above, olive-grayish streaked with dusky; under parts, grayish-white streaked on sides and chest with dusky; wings and tail similar to adults.

Nest and Eggs.— Nest: Usually, in dense chaparral thickets, willow, canebrake or mesquite clumps near streams, within five feet of ground, rarely in trees thirty feet up; rather large, carelessly made of bark strips, weed stalks, grass, twigs, lined with fine inner bark or horse-hair. Eggs: 2 to 4, pale blue, thinly marked or spotted around large end, sometimes over the entire surface, with dark umber-brown and black.

Distribution.—Arid division of Arizona, southern Nevada (bend of Colorado River), southwestern Utah, northwestern New Mexico and southeastern California; south in winter to northern Lower California.

Despite the fact that the Abert's Towhee is the largest of the plain Towhees he is extremely shy. He lives among the mesquites and cottonwoods of the desert region of Arizona, New Mexico, and southeastern California. His note of alarm is *huit huit* according to Bendire.

GREEN-TAILED TOWHEE

Oreospiza chlorura (*Audubon*)

A. O. U. Number 592.1

Other Names.— Chestnut-crowned Towhee; Green-tailed Bunting; Blanding's Finch.

General Description.— Length, 8 inches. Upper parts, greenish; under parts, white and gray. Bill, small; wings, long and pointed; tail, long, equal to or longer than wing, rounded.

Color.— Adults: Crown and back of head, plain rufous or cinnamon-rufous; forehead and sides of head, deep gray or olive-gray; hindneck, back, shoulders, rump, and upper tail-coverts, olive-grayish tinged with yellowish olive-green; wings and tail, mainly yellowish olive-green, the greater wing-coverts and inner wing-quills, duller and grayer; edge of wing, canary-yellow; chin and throat, white forming a sharply defined patch; chest, sides of neck, and sides of breast, gray becoming gradually paler on breast; the abdomen, white; sides and flanks, buffy grayish; under tail-coverts, light buff; iris, cinnamon or reddish. Young: Crown, hindneck, back, and shoulders light olive or grayish brown, streaked with dusky; under parts dull whitish, the chest and sides streaked with dusky; wings and tail as in adults, but middle and greater wing-coverts indistinctly tipped with brownish buffy.

Nest and Eggs.— Nest: Placed in bush, amid shrubbery or on ground, sagebrush, chaparral, mesquite, or cactus preferred; constructed of fine twigs, grass, shreds of bark, lined with fine grass. Eggs: 4, white, pale greenish or grayish white, freckled all over with fine specks of bright chestnut.

Distribution.— Mountain districts of western United States, from more eastern Rocky Mountain ranges to Coast range of California; north to central Montana and Idaho and eastern Washington; south to southern California, southeastern New Mexico, western Texas, and, at least in winter, to middle Mexico, and to southern Lower California; accidental in Virginia.

The Green-tailed Towhee is a beautiful bird with a soft glossy coat touched off with yellowish green and his manners are so gentlemanly that he quickly wins his way to our hearts. "He may generally be found perched on top of a bush and at sight of you will raise his rufous cap inquiringly, turning to look down so that his white chin shows to advantage. When seen hopping over the ground he is as trim as a Song Sparrow, looking about and flashing his green tail till he disappears to scratch in the brush." (Mrs. Bailey.)

This Towhee has the peculiar trait of running along the ground when he is surprised instead of taking wing. His song has many of the characteristics of Finch songs but is phrased like that of the Cañon Towhee. His call note is very similar to that of the Chewink.

CARDINAL

Cardinalis cardinalis cardinalis (*Linnæus*)

A. O. U. Number 593 See Color Plate 85

Other Names.— Cardinal Grosbeak; Redbird; Crested Redbird; Virginia Redbird; Virginia Nightingale; Virginia Cardinal; Kentucky Cardinal; Cardinal Bird.

General Description.— Length, 8¾ inches. Male, red; female, partly red, giving an appearance of being faded. Bill, stout; wings, short and rounded; tail, longer than wing, slightly rounded; head with conspicuous crest.

Color.— ADULT MALE: Front portion of forehead, front part of cheek region, chin, and throat, black, forming a conspicuous cap entirely surrounding the bill; rest of head, vermilion-red, duller on crown (including crest); under parts, pure vermilion-red becoming slightly paler posteriorly, the flanks slightly tinged with grayish; hindneck, back, shoulders, rump, and upper tail-coverts, dull vermilion-red; wings and tail, dull red; bill, red-orange; iris, deep brown. ADULT FEMALE: Wings and tail, much as in the male, but the red duller; red of head and body replaced above by plain grayish olive or buffy grayish, the crest partly dull red, below by pale fulvous or buffy (nearly white on abdomen), the chest often tinged or mixed with red; head, dull grayish, sometimes nearly white on throat.

Nest and Eggs.— NEST: Located in thickets of brambles or grapevines or low saplings; a carelessly constructed, loosely put together affair of small twigs, strips of bark, weed stems, grass, lined with fine rootlets, and horse-hair. EGGS: 2 to 4, white, bluish, or greenish white marked with shades of chestnut, purple, and brown, usually scattered over entire surface.

Distribution.— Eastern United States; north, regularly and breeding to southeastern New York, lower districts of eastern Pennsylvania, western Pennsylvania, northeastern Ohio, northern Indiana, southern Iowa, etc., casually or irregularly to Connecticut, Massachusetts, Maine, Nova Scotia, southern Ontario, southern Michigan, southern Wisconsin, and Minnesota; west to edge of Great Plains, casually to eastern Colorado; south to Georgia, Alabama, and upland region of Gulf States; Bermudas (introduced and naturalized).

The flash of red that comes to view and disappears in other trees is generally the Cardinal. There are other red birds, but none that frequent the stately Southern elms and other large roadside trees as does this most attractive Sparrow.

All through the Southern plantation country this is the bird that typifies everything that is elegant and chivalric not only to the colored cotton pickers and plantation laborers, but to the country gentlemen. Novels have been written in which the Virginia Cardinal and the Kentucky Cardinal and the Carolina Cardinal have given a tone of aristocratic elegance to the plots. The bird is indeed a fine specimen of bird character, whether found on a Southern plantation, or at its northeastern limit in Central Park, New York city, or at its western limit in the dingy chaparral of southern Arizona.

The bird is ever cheerful and active and industrious. The young are cared for eagerly by the male while the female is sitting on a second laying of eggs. Nothing daunts the male in his care of the young that he leads out upon the lawns and berry fields. The search for food, the scent of danger, and the warnings given to the heedless young are common observations made by people who are attracted to them.

The attention the male gives his mate is very noticeable. He is never fearful to fly about

looking after the nest or leading her to some favored food or singing to her from far up in the tallest tree while she is busy at her toilet down by the brook in the valley. And frequently she will answer in a lower note that

Courtesy of Am. Mus. Nat. Hist.

CARDINAL (⅓ nat. size)

A flash of red, coming to view one moment, and disappearing the next

brings from him a quick response. There is a remarkable charm in the Cardinal that brings words of enthusiasm from all who have lived in the country with him and have watched his gracious ways.

His call is a rich and rounded *cue-cue* that penetrates the grove and often brings an answering *cue-cue* from another bird far away. The rapid *hip-ip-ip-ip-ip-ip-ip*, uttered without any loss of power at the end, rings out clear from the tops of the trees and seems to rouse the echoes. Then there is the long drawn out *e-eee*,

Photo by H. T. Middleton

YOUNG CARDINAL

and the *cheer, cheer, cheer* that makes one feel a joy in having such a bird in the neighborhood.

Ridgway has listed about a dozen varieties of the Cardinal but they are mostly in Mexico. Only the Florida (*Cardinalis cardinalis floridanus*) and Arizona (*Cardinalis cardinalis superbus*) and the Gray-tailed (*Cardinalis cardinalis canicaudus*) occupy small areas adjacent to the great areas of the true *Cardinalis* east of Texas and south of the Hudson and the Great Lakes. The Gray-tailed Cardinal is but one of the Mexican varieties that extends up into Texas. But wherever found the Cardinal is a rare sight. Many persons have become much interested in all birds by being first interested in the Cardinal. Some have called him an FFV (member of one of the first families of Virginia). Better yet, he is an FF of America. L. NELSON NICHOLS.

It has been claimed that the Cardinal pulls sprouting grain, but no evidence of damage to either grain or other crops is afforded by the examination of more than 500 stomachs. On the other hand, the evidence is ample that he does much good. The Redbird is known to feed on the Rocky Mountain locust, periodical cicada, and Colorado potato beetle. It is a great enemy also to the rose chafer, cotton worm, plum or cherry scale, and other scale insects, and attacks many other important insect pests, including the zebra caterpillar of the cabbage, the cucumber beetles, billbugs, locust flea-beetle, corn-ear worm, cotton cutworm, southern fig-eater, codling moth, and boll weevil. In addition, it consumes a great many seeds of injurious weeds. Thus its food habits entitle the bird to our esteem, as its brilliant coat and spirited song compel our admiration.

ARIZONA PYRRHULOXIA

Pyrrhuloxia sinuata sinuata (*Bonaparte*)

A. O. U. Number 594

Other Names.— Bullfinch; Bullfinch Cardinal; Gray Grosbeak; Gray Cardinal; Parrot-bill.

General Description.— Length, 9 inches. Plumage, grayish, with red crest and tail. Bill, short, thick, and strongly curved; wings, short and much rounded; tail, decidedly longer than wing, rounded.

Color.—ADULT MALE: Above, brownish gray or grayish hair-brown becoming purer gray (between drab-gray and smoke gray) on head and neck; all the wing-feathers with concealed bases, dusky red; outer webs of primaries and primary coverts, mostly dull red; middle tail-feathers, dusky brownish becoming dark dull reddish in the center and edged with brownish gray; rest of tail-feathers, dull red becoming dusky brownish at the ends, the shafts of all, black on upper surface; longer feathers of crest, dull red; *forehead, chin, throat,* and other center lower parts, thighs, and most of under side of wing, *pure red* (geranium-red to poppy-red), the lores and eye region, duller red; sides of under parts, light brownish gray, paler and tinged with buffy posteriorly; bill, yellowish in summer, horn colored in winter; iris, brown. ADULT FEMALE: Similar to adult male, but lacking the red of face and center under parts (or with it but slightly indicated), the general color of the under parts of a decided buffy hue; bill, yellow in summer, grayish brown in winter.

Nest and Eggs.— NEST: In mesquite, or thorny thickets; resembles that of the Cardinal but more compactly put together and smaller; made of bark strips, twigs, grass, lined with small roots. EGGS: 3, pale bluish white spotted with different shades of brown and lavender, wreathed around large end.

Distribution.— Northwestern Mexico; southern portions of Arizona, southwestern New Mexico, and extreme western part of Texas.

The Pyrrhuloxia belongs to the Cardinal group of Finches. Their habits are those of the Cardinal, but the area in which they are found is but a small part of the country in which the true Cardinals live. The Pyrrhuloxia country is confined to the hot upland areas of the northern plateau of Mexico, and the adjacent parts of Arizona, New Mexico, and Texas.

Some suppose the Pyrrhuloxia to be more "shy and suspicious" than the Cardinal. But the experience of William L. and Irene Finley in photographing a Pyrrhuloxia on the nest, as reported in *Bird-Lore,* is rather the reverse, showing that the bird has about the same confidence in human surroundings as has the Cardinal. The Cardinal traits have been so noticeable that the bird has often been known as the Gray Cardinal. The differences are also conspicuous. Instead of the *cue* note of the Cardinal, the mesquite is musical with his clear, cheerful whistling.

The red crest is the most characteristic feature of the Pyrrhuloxia. Every change of mood in the bird is not only shown but exaggerated by the quick up and down motions of the crest feathers. From listlessness to alertness, and from curiosity to ennui are the changes of a second. These changes are rapid and occur many scores of times every hour.

The eastern variety is called the Texas Pyrrhuloxia (*Pyrrhuloxia sinuata texana*) and has the ring around the bill conspicuously marked with black. From El Paso west into southern Arizona the variety is known as the Arizona Pyrrhuloxia. It is a very fancy name, but it will remain, for it is a very fancy bird.

Like the Blue Grosbeak the Arizona Pyrrhuloxia is more fond of caterpillars and grasshoppers than of other insects. Weevils are next in order of preference. The Parrot-bill ranges over much of the cotton belt of Texas and feeds upon two important cotton pests, one of which — the boll weevil — is one of our most destructive insects. Cotton worms are highly relished, as many as eighteen having been found in a single stomach. In August and September seven-tenths of the Gray Grosbeak's food is weed seed, five-tenths consisting exclusively of the seeds of two of the most important weeds of the South, namely, foxtail and burr grass. So far as known, the Gray Grosbeak eats practically no beneficial insect and damages no crop. This, in addition to the fact that it feeds upon noxious weed and insect pests, entitles it to complete protection.

Drawing by R. I. Brasher

PYRRHULOXIA ($\frac{3}{8}$ nat. size)

A fine whistler, with a red waistcoat and a very dandified air

ROSE-BREASTED GROSBEAK

Zamelodia ludoviciana (*Linnæus*)

A. O. U. Number 595 See Color Plate 85

Other Names.— Potato-bug Bird; Common Grosbeak; Summer Grosbeak; Rose-breast.

General Description.— Length, 8¼ inches. Fore and upper parts, black or blackish-brown; under parts, red and white. Bill, heavy and short; wings, long and pointed; tail, more than ¾ length of wing, even or slightly rounded, the feathers broad and rounded at the ends.

Color.—Adult Male in Summer: Head, neck, back, and shoulders, uniform black; wings, black relieved by a large patch of white on basal portion of primaries, white spots at tips of innermost greater coverts and inner wing-quills, and a broad white band composed of the middle coverts; upper tail-coverts, black with large terminal spots of white; tail, black with inner webs of three outermost tail-feathers white at the ends; *chest, center portion of breast, and under wing-coverts, rose red or light carmine; rest of under parts of body,* *white,* the rump, also white; iris, brown. ADULT MALE IN WINTER: Wings, tail, and upper tail-coverts as in summer; head, neck, back, and shoulders, brown streaked with black, color of head relieved by a center crown-stripe, a stripe over eye, and a cheek stripe of pale buffy or buffy whitish; under parts, brownish white, the chest, sides, and flanks streaked with dusky, the first tinged or suffused with rose-red or rose-pink. YOUNG MALE IN FIRST WINTER: Similar to the adult male in winter, but wings, upper tail-coverts, and tail, grayish brown, instead of black, the last without any white, the first with the white markings much reduced and tinged with brown; back and shoulders, more uniformly brown; chest, sides, and flanks, more deeply fulvous and more heavily streaked, the first with little, if any, red or pink; under wing-coverts and axillaries, rose-pink. ADULTS FEMALE (SUMMER AND WINTER): Much like the young male, but wing-coverts yellow.

Nest and Eggs.— NEST: In low trees and bushes, sometimes on such slender branches that the eggs roll out when the support is bent by a strong breeze; a flat, rather carelessly made saucer-shaped structure of small twigs, wiry rootlets, and grass. EGGS: 3 to 5, greenish blue, spotted and blotched over entire surface with chestnut and shades of brown.

Distribution.— Eastern United States and more southern British provinces, from Atlantic coast to edge of the Great Plains (eastern Kansas to Manitoba); breeding from New Jersey, Pennsylvania, northern Ohio, northern Indiana, northern Illinois, Iowa, and eastern Kansas, north to Manitoba, Ontario, Nova Scotia, etc., and south along the Allegheny Mountains to western North Carolina (3500 to 5000 feet); in winter south to Bahamas, Cuba, Jamaica, and through Mexico and Central America to western Ecuador; casual in Bermudas.

There is no bird in our eastern American avifauna that is better worth an acquaintance than the Rose-breasted Grosbeak. Some birds force themselves upon our attention; we have to go to find the Rose-breast for he is nowhere common. Some birds have commonplace voices, but the Rose-breast has a rich and mellow voice that rings out with abundant vitality in the bush lot at the edge of the forest or across the bushy swamp. Many birds seem to ask for exaggerated

ROSE-BREASTED GROSBEAK (⅜ nat. size)
He is an efficient, resourceful, and virile American
Drawing by R. I. Brasher

description because of their extraordinary beauty. The Rose-breast is a handsome bird in his black and white and rose, much handsomer than most Finches, but not so beautiful as to distract the observer from the life and habits of the bird. And this, the character of the bird, is the finest thing about him.

Almost all observers are impressed with the vital wholesomeness of this Grosbeak. He is seldom nervous and seldom allows trivial things to disturb him. He acts with dignity and yet with a quickness and precision and quiet forcefulness that are almost ideal. As a caged bird he puts up with what he has to and makes the most of what he has. He is a very clean bird. The nest is always clean. Wherever he goes he makes no litter, and whatever he breaks up for food is never scattered, but the remnants remain in small inconspicuous piles. It would almost seem as though the bird had a conscience, and knew what it was to be a gentleman.

Cardinal-like, the male has a great attachment for his mate while she is at the nest. He has been seen standing a few feet away as though glad to be in her company. Sometimes he will sing for her for a long time in a nearby tree. And someone has said that he has carried potato bugs to feed her on the nest. When the young have left the nest his presence with them is very noticeable. Generally silent during these busy weeks, he seems to be the embodiment of good cheer, happier, indeed, it would seem than the scared youngsters that watch his every action as though only in him could they feel any safety in this blood-thirsty world.

Whoever cares to know this really high-class American must go out to his distant haunts. One might happen to see him high up in an elm that shades the highway, or quietly purloining the farmer's crop of potato bugs, or flying sturdily beside a country road "going somewhere," never flying for the sake of flying as do most of the nervous birds. Make a special journey to the wood lot where he lives and spend a morning in his company. You will go home with the feeling of having met one of the best types of efficient, resourceful, and virile Americans.

L. Nelson Nichols.

The Rose-breasted Grosbeak is held in high esteem because of his habit of preying upon the Colorado potato-bug. At least one-tenth of his food is made up of these potato-eating beetles. He is almost the only bird to feed upon these pests; he not only eats the adults but also consumes the larvæ and feeds a great many to the nestlings. Cucumber beetles, canker worms, tent caterpillars, army worms, cutworms, chinch bugs are all greedily sought for.

The vegetable food of this Grosbeak consists of buds and blossoms of forest trees and seeds. He is accused of injuring orchards by eating the blossoms and the fruit and of eating green peas. He does do both of these things, but the little damage he does in this way is more than off-set by his raids on the potato-bug. Mr. Beal examined the stomachs of some Rose-breasted Grosbeaks which had been killed in the very act

Photo by A. A. Allen

ROSE-BREASTED GROSBEAK, HER NEST, AND EGGS

of eating peas. He found a few peas, but there were more than enough potato-bugs to pay for all the peas the birds would have been likely to eat for a whole season. The garden where this took place adjoined a small potato field which earlier in the season had been so badly infested with beetles that the vines were completely riddled. Every day the Grosbeaks had visited the field and after the young left the nests they accompanied their parents. The babes stood in a row on the topmost rail of the fence and were fed with the beetles by the old birds. A careful inspection was made a few days later but not a single potato-bug remained; the birds had saved the potatoes.

BLACK-HEADED GROSBEAK

Zamelodia melanocephala (*Swainson*)

A. O. U. Number 596

Other Names.— Western Grosbeak; Black-head.

General Description.— Length, 8¼ inches. Upper parts, black and tawny; under parts, buffy-cinnamon and lemon-yellow. Bill, heavy and short; wings, long and pointed; tail, more than ¾ length of wing, even or slightly rounded, the feathers broad and rounded at the ends.

Color.— Adult Male: Head, black, the throat light cinnamon-ocher or tawny; wings, upper tail-coverts, and tail, black, the first varied by a broad band of white including the middle coverts, a large white patch on basal portion of primaries, and white spots at tips of greater coverts and inner wing feathers, the last by large white spaces on terminal portion of inner webs of two to three outermost tail-feathers; upper tail-coverts with white terminal spots; collar across hindneck, throat, chest, breast, sides, flanks, and rump, uniform buffy-cinnamon or tawny; *abdomen and under wing-coverts, clear lemon-yellow;* anal region and under tail-coverts, white; shoulders, black centrally, edged or margined with light tawny or cinnamon-buffy; iris, dark brown. Adult Female: Above, dusky grayish brown or olive, streaked, especially on back and along center line of crown, with pale tawny, buffy, or whitish; wings and tail, grayish brown, with white marking much more restricted than in adult males, those on tail nearly if not quite obsolete; chin, sides of throat, cheek region, and a stripe over the eyes, whitish; chest, pale fulvous, cinnamon-buffy, or yellowish buffy; abdomen, usually pale yellow, sometimes white.

Nest and Eggs.— Nest: Located among willows, live oaks or saplings, from five to twenty feet up; a loosely put together, frail structure of fine twigs, weed stems, grass, and rootlets. Eggs: 3 or 4, bluish green, speckled and blotched with chestnut and rufous brown.

Distribution.— Western United States and plateau of Mexico; north in summer, to British Columbia, Idaho, Montana, etc., east to southeastern Dakota, eastern Nebraska and eastern Kansas; breeding south to southern portion of Mexican plateau.

The Black-headed Grosbeak may be used as a striking illustration of the theory of evolution. It resembles the Rose-breasted Grosbeak closely in structure, form, and habits; its notes are almost the same, yet in plumage it differs widely, but still shows relationship. What better evidence is needed to indicate that the two species were once one, and that the only noticeable difference between them that is observable to-day was caused by climatic influences? The pure warbling song of the Black-head as well as its thin alarm note may be recognized, when heard for the first time, by their close resemblance to those of its eastern prototype. The two species seem to show similar tastes in regard to food, as the Black-head attacks the potato beetle and the buds of trees with the same avidity that is shown in the east by its congener. Even the nest and eggs resemble those of the Rose-breast, although in the southern part of its range the Black-head's nest is exceedingly flimsy, so that in some cases the eggs may be seen through it from below.

Apparently the species is more prolific than the Rose-breast, which ordinarily rears but one brood annually. The Grinnells in their *Birds of Song and Story* tell of a pair of Black-heads that raised three broods in their garden, but the glorious climate of California which tends to induce fecundity may be responsible for this.

The male Grosbeak is a handsome bird, startlingly flashy in flight, with its contrast of black, white, and yellow, but is a little coarse or heavy in form. Its big beak, like a huge nose, reminds us of the story of little Red-Riding Hood and the wolf, for it is almost as prominent as the wolf's muzzle, which as a counterfeit grandmother's nose so astonished the child when seen protruding from the depths of the frilled nightcap.

The male like that of the Rose-breast is a good father and relieves his mate on the nest, taking his share of the duties of incubation and chick-rearing. He keeps the nest during a large part of the day and the female takes his place by night: thus the eggs are constantly kept covered and defended.

The Black-headed Grosbeak is a bird of the forest but like its eastern relative it seems to prefer for nesting a place in deciduous woods and shrubbery, especially among the alders along small streams; but when assured of protection it comes as freely about the dwellings of man as does the Rose-breast and even nests in the fig trees. The male pours forth his pure and tender rhapsody from the heights of tall oaks or pines, but does not disdain to sing even while hunting the lowly "potato-bug." Through the long day he sings, even at hot high noon when other less virile songsters are resting and silent.

Edward Howe Forbush.

The Black-headed Grosbeak fills the same place in the West that the Rose-breast does in the East, and economically is fully as important. In parts of its range it is destructive to early fruit and attacks also green peas and beans. However, since by proper precautions such losses may be minimized or altogether prevented, they should not be given too much weight in estimating the value of the bird. Instead of being regarded as an enemy by western orchardists, the Black-head should be esteemed as a friend, since it is a foe to the worst pests of horticulture — the scale insects — which compose a fourth of its food. The black olive scale alone constitutes a fifth of the bird's subsistence, and the frosted scale and apricot scale, or European fruit lecanium, also are destroyed. In May considerable numbers of canker worms and codling moths are eaten, and almost a sixth of the bird's seasonal food consists of flower beetles, which do incalculable damage to cultivated flowers and to ripe fruit. For each quart of fruit consumed by the Black-headed Grosbeak it destroys in actual bulk more than one and one-half quarts of black olive scales, one quart of flower beetles, besides a generous quantity of codling moth pupæ and canker worms. So effectively does it fight these pests that the necessity for its preservation is obvious, while most of its injury to fruit is preventable.

Drawing by R. Bruce Horsfall

BLACK-HEADED GROSBEAKS (½ nat. size)

BLUE GROSBEAK

Guiraca cærulea cærulea (*Linnæus*)

A. O. U. Number 597 See Color Plate 86

Other Name.— Blue Pop.

General Description.— Length, 7¾ inches. Male, blue; female, olive-brownish above and brownish-buffy below. Bill, large, conical, compressed, with nearly straight outlines; wings, long and pointed; tail, about ¾ length of wing, nearly even or very slightly rounded.

Color.—Adult Male: Uniform, slightly glossy, dull ultramarine blue, the feathers of the back dusky centrally; a narrow black spot on crown involving the forehead, the extreme front portion of cheek region, and chin; wings and tail, blackish with dull bluish edgings, the middle wing-coverts with most of the exposed portion, chestnut or cinnamon-rufous (forming a broad band), the greater coverts margined at the ends with the same or a paler color (forming a much narrower band), under tail-coverts margined with white, especially at tips; iris, brown. Adult Female: Above, olive-brownish tinged with tawny, passing into a decidedly more grayish hue (usually tinged with blue) on rump and upper tail-coverts; shoulders darker centrally, forming indistinct streaks; wings and tail, dusky, the latter with dull grayish blue, the former with light brownish edgings; middle wing-coverts, rather broadly tipped with light cinnamon-rufous or tawny and terminal margins of greater coverts usually tinged with the same; under parts, brownish-buffy or clay color, deepest on chest, paler on throat and abdomen.

Nest and Eggs.— Nest: Placed in low brambles, or in deciduous trees as far as thirty feet from the ground; a compact, well built structure of dried grass, plant fibers, leaves, with an intertwined cast-off snake skin; lined with fine brown rootlets and horse-hair. Eggs: 3 or 4, plain light bluish white.

Distribution.— More southern portions of eastern United States, chiefly near Atlantic and Gulf coasts; north regularly, but very locally, to Pennsylvania, New Jersey, Kentucky, and southern Illinois; accidentally to Maine, eastern Massachusetts, Province of Quebec; in winter south to Cuba and Yucatan.

The Blue Grosbeak is an interesting bird of the Southern States. He is not quite so handsome nor has he such interesting notes as the Cardinal and the Rose-breast. And he is not as well known as those distinguished relatives, for nowhere is he common. In short trees and bushes from Maryland to the Gulf coast he may be found probably as often as anywhere. The blue is not so blue as to attract attention. The color is so dark that in certain lights the bird might be mistaken for a Cowbird. He is a very quiet bird. The evidence available would seem to make him more suspicious of man than is the Rose-breast.

Drawing by R. I. Brasher

BLUE GROSBEAK (⅔ nat. size)

You will have to look closely to see the "blue" in this bird's plumage

His song is a weaker effort than the Rose-breast's. It is a rather sweet warble of the Purple Finch nature, and has sometimes been called a beautiful song. No doubt this rare bird far away from the human ear pours forth a very sweet melody to his mate, but no one has yet given a biography of this interesting bird as has been done of his near relatives, the Cardinal and Rose-breast.

The territory of the Blue Grosbeak extends entirely across the southern half of the United States; but west of Louisiana there are so many differences in coloration of the bird that the scientists have made of them a separate variety, the Western Blue Grosbeak (*Guiraca cærulea lazula*). Ridgway is not at all sure that there is but one variety in the Southwest. The Utah and California birds differ from the Arizona birds, and they from the Texas birds. The western is paler colored; and bird observers in those areas seem to know the bird better than do those of the East, showing that his haunts are nearer the homes of men. Even there his haunts are most often along the rushing streams in the brush of the cañons of the foothills.

Blue Grosbeaks do no damage during the nesting period, and, in fact, are of great value to any farm they choose for a home, since they eat large numbers of injurious insects and feed their young exclusively upon them. In certain localities, however, after the breeding season, Blue Grosbeaks collect in flocks, move into grain fields, particularly those of oats and rice, and sometimes do considerable harm. Despite such depredations, the loss of cereals is repaid many fold, since the birds consume almost five times as much insect food as grain. Moreover, some of the insects they devour are especially destructive, such as weevils. More than a fourth of the seasonal food is composed of grasshoppers, including the lesser migratory locust. A tenth of the subsistence is made up of caterpillars and cotton cutworms, enemies of sugar beets and cotton. Because of its effective warfare on these pests, the Blue Grosbeak is an efficient ally of the farmer and deserves to be protected.

INDIGO BUNTING

Passerina cyanea (*Linnæus*)

A. O. U. Number 598 See Color Plate 86

Other Names.— Indigo Bluebird; Indigo Painted Bunting; Indigo Bird; Indigo Finch; Blue Finch; Blue Canary.

General Description.— Length, 5¾ inches. Male, blue; female, olive-brownish above and dull white below. Bill, small; wings, long and pointed; tail, about ¾ length of wing, slightly double rounded.

Color.—Adult Male: General color, plain cerulean blue, changing to bluish green in certain lights, the head more purplish blue, this extending down the foreneck and, usually, strongly tingeing the center under parts of the body; lores and central (mostly concealed) portion of wing-coverts and inner wing-quills, black; secondaries, primaries, primary coverts, dusky edged with greenish-blue; iris, brown. Adult Female: Above, olive-brownish, lighter, and sometimes tinged with greenish-gray on rump and upper tail-coverts; beneath, dull whitish washed or tinged with olive-buffy on chest, sides, and flanks, the chest distinctly streaked with dusky grayish-brown; wings and tail, dusky, the lesser wing-coverts and edges of primaries and tail-feathers, grayish-greenish, the tips of middle coverts brownish. Young: Similar to adult female, but averaging rather browner, especially on under parts, the back sometimes, especially in first plumage, obsoletely streaked.

Nest and Eggs.— Nest: Generally in a low viburnum, witch-hazel, or maple saplings, or other small bushes, or in brambles on brushy hillsides or open clearings near woods; usually in a fork, within five feet of ground; constructed of grasses, leaves, weed stalks, strips of bark, plant fibers, lined with finer grasses and hair. Eggs: 4, plain pale bluish white.

Distribution.— Eastern United States and British provinces; north to Maine, Ontario, Minnesota, etc. (casually to New Brunswick); south in winter to Bahamas, Cuba, and through eastern Mexico and Central America to Panama; west to eastern border of Great Plains, casually to eastern Colorado.

The Indigo Bunting is another bird with a distinct personality. No other bird attracts quite the peculiar attention that this bird does. To get acquainted with him one must be prepared for surprises, and what they all are will not be told here.

The male has such a peculiar color; no bird outside of the tropics has such a peculiar blue as the male Indigo Bird. It isn't an indigo color but rather a deep ultramarine blue. Just as you have made up your mind that that is the right name of the color, you get the bird in a different light and behold he is grayish blue, or azure-blue, or maybe olive-blue. At least there is no confusing him with any other bluish bird. The female, however, is one of the persistently confusing birds to bird students. She has a characteristic *cheep* and twitches her tail from side to side, but in coloring she is a plain little brown-striped Sparrow. There isn't a single distinctive feature that is apt to strike one's eye with a surety that will allow even the most accurate observer to determine on the instant the name of the bird. Most observers see the male in the neighborhood, and by a process of exclusion will decide that the little brown bird is also an Indigo Bunting.

The male is one of the most showy of birds and is not afraid to exhibit himself on a fence rail, or tilting on the reeds, or dodging about in a flock of English Sparrows, or up on a bush or short tree within easy view. The female is suspicious, secretive, silent, and sometimes as hard to see as a mouse in a thicket.

Yet another surprise. The Indigo Bunting seems so busy feeding and going in and out of thickets on some mysterious errands, that he doesn't seem to have much time to sing, while the other birds are doing their best in May and June. Wait till the other birds decrease the volume and intensity of their singing in July, or

Drawing by R. I. Brasher

INDIGO BUNTING (½ nat. size)

"As blue as an Indigo bag" applies to this bird's plumage, but not to his disposition stop entirely; then the Indigo Bunting begins to take an interest in his voice. The summer heat makes the Robin open his bill in the shadow to gasp for breath. The Bobolink is off for the marshes to keep cool. The Song Sparrow hides in the bushes till the extreme heat of the day is over. But the Indigo Bird is never daunted by the heat of July and August days. Many and many a highway can be traversed in the heat of the day without hearing one bird utter even a short note, except the Indigo Bird. He sings from the top of a bush or a short tree or a telephone pole or on the very topmost tiny twig of the very tallest tree in the neighborhood and with the greatest glee "he loudly sings his roundelay of love." The persistence, almost by the hour, of the sweet simple song is one of the surprises of the bird. So far up against the blue he sometimes is that not only color is lost but even his form is often too vague to be identified. The baking hot sun even quiets many of the insects, yet there come the notes of the Indigo Bunting tumbling down from far up in the sky. He certainly has the field all to himself.

Mrs. Bailey gives an interesting account of an Indigo Bird. "I well remember watching one Indigo Bird, who, day after day, used to fly to the lowest limb of a high tree and sing his way up from branch to branch, bursting into jubilant song when he reached the topmost bough. I watched him climb as high into the air as he could, when against a background of blue sky and rolling white clouds, the blessed little songster broke out into the blithest round that ever bubbled up from a glad heart."

Follow the life of the bird as long as he remains in our northern clime, and very many surprising things will be found out about him. Instead of being one of the many species of the large Sparrow family, it would seem that he might be given a scientific family name all to himself.

L. NELSON NICHOLS.

The Indigo Bird is one of our most valuable species and should be given rigid protection. His food consists mainly of seeds and berries with a goodly number of insects. Among the insects are found caterpillars, click-beetles, snout-beetles chafers, bugs of various kinds, and canker worms. In an orchard that was infested with canker worms the Indigo Bird was found eating more than its usual amount of these pests, some stomachs showing as much as 78 per cent. of canker worms.

LAZULI BUNTING

Passerina amœna (*Say*)

A. O. U. Number 599

Other Name.— Lazuli Painted Bunting.

General Description.— Length, 6 inches. Male, blue above and tawny and white below; female, brown and blue above and buffy below. Bill, small; wings, long and pointed; tail, about ¾ length of wing, forked.

Color.— ADULT MALE: Head, neck, rump, and upper tail-coverts, light cerulean or turquoise blue, changing to light greenish-blue (Nile blue); back, shoulders, and lesser wing-coverts, darker and (especially back) duller blue; middle wing-coverts, very

Drawing by R. I. Brasher

LAZULI BUNTING (½ nat. size)

A handsome songster of the western mountains and valleys

broadly tipped with white, the greater coverts more narrowly tipped with the same, forming two bands; wings, otherwise blackish; tail, blackish; chest, tawny-ochraceous; abdomen, under tail-coverts, etc., white; iris brown. Adult Female: Above, grayish-brown passing into dull greenish-blue, or much tinged with this color, on rump and upper tail-coverts, the back sometimes streaked with dusky; wings and tail, dusky, the feathers edged with dull greenish-blue; under parts, dull buffy.

Nest and Eggs.— Nest: Usually located near water, in low willows, weeds, manzanitas, or other brush; constructed of grass, leaves, strips of bark, small twigs, and rootlets, lined with fine grasses and hair. Eggs: 3 or 4, plain pale bluish or greenish white.

Distribution.— Western United States and British provinces; north to British Columbia, Idaho, Montana, etc.; south (in winter) to Mexico; east nearly or quite across the Great Plains to South Dakota, Kansas, etc.

"The Lazuli-painted Finch should be called the Blue-headed Finch; for the exquisite blueness of his whole head, including throat, breast, and shoulders, as if he had been dipped so far into blue dye, is his most distinguishing feature. The Bluebird wears heaven's color; so does the Jay and likewise the Indigo Bird; but not one can boast the lovely and indescribable shade, with its silvery reflections, that adorns the Lazuli. Across the breast, under the blue, is a broad band of chestnut, like the breast color of our Bluebird, and back of that is white, while the wings and tail are dark. Altogether he is charming to look upon." Thus Olive Thorne Miller describes the Lazuli Bunting.

The Lazulis are close relatives of the Painted Bunting; but they are much more shy, except in districts where they are numerous and then they appear to believe that there is safety in numbers.

The Painted Bunting often comes about country homes in the east and sometimes he will venture into a town if there are bushes and trees convenient. The Lazulis love the plains and the foot-hills; they are seldom found very high in the mountains. Their song is almost indistinguishable from that of the Summer Warbler.

Photo by W. L. Finley and H. T. Bohlman

LAZULI BUNTING

Young being fed by their mother

PAINTED BUNTING

Passerina ciris (*Linnæus*)

A. O. U. Number 601

Other Names.— Painted Finch; Pope; Nonpareil; Mexican Canary.

General Description.— Length, 6 inches. Male, blue, green, and reddish above, and red below; female, green above and yellowish below. Bill, small; wings, long and pointed; tail, about 3/4 length of wing, slightly double rounded.

Color.— Adult Male: Head and neck, except chin and throat, purplish-blue; black and shoulders, bright yellowish-green; rump and upper tail-coverts, purplish-red; eye-ring (more or less complete) and under parts, including throat, vermilion red; greater wing-coverts, parrot green; middle coverts, dull reddish-purple, lesser coverts, dull purplish-blue; wings, dusky edged with dull-purplish and green; tail-feathers, dull dusky-reddish or purplish; upper jaw, blackish; iris, brown. Adult Female: Above, plain dull green; beneath, olive-yellowish, clearer yellow on abdomen and under tail-coverts. YOUNG: Above, dull grayish-brown tinged here and there with greenish; middle and greater wing-coverts, narrowly tipped with pale buff or buffy-grayish; under parts, dull grayish-buffy.

Nest and Eggs.— NEST: Located in cat-claw, blackberry, chaparral or other low bushes and saplings or in tall trees; a compact structure, composed of leaves, twigs, grass, bark strips, and lined with fine grasses and horse-hair. EGGS: 4 or 5, creamy or bluish-white, spotted and blotched with reddish-brown and lavender.

Distribution.— Southeastern North America; north to coast of North Carolina, southern Illinois, southern Kansas; south, in winter, to Bahamas, Cuba, the whole of Mexico, and through Central America to Panama; west during migration to Arizona; occasional in winter in southern Louisiana and central Florida.

The Painted Bunting is a southern bird of such a quiet manner that he is not very well known. He spends most of his time in the dense thickets of the river bottoms, or far off in bushy wood lots, or in the almost impenetrable tangles of the steeper hillsides. Far out in the southwest this Nonpareil (as he is better known in the West) is not quite so secretive. There he is found commonly in the mesquite and in the small brush of the river banks.

Drawing by R. I. Brasher

PAINTED BUNTING ($\frac{1}{2}$ nat. size)

A gaudy sprite who seems to know that it may be dangerous to be beautiful

Like the Indigo Bird he sings best in the middle of the summer. But a great deal of the singing is done from the middle of a brush pile or the inside of a thicket of laurel or even in a mass of luxuriant semitropical weeds. Nonpareil seems also to favor the cypress swamps. This shy bird has a very sweet song resembling somewhat the song of the Indigo Bird. There is a conciseness and feebleness about the song that makes it, however, much inferior to the Indigo Bird. Sometimes there is a broken warble that rises to the level of sweetness, but Nonpareil does not lose himself long in his song. Maybe his painted and patched beauty attracts his attention to himself too much.

In Mexico he is quite a favorite cage bird. Americans along the border are therefore apt to speak of the bird as the Mexican Canary. Strange to say, his clear, carrying voice loses none of its quality in the cage, but his varied colors in time are much diminished.

Like most strikingly colored male birds, the Nonpareil struts before his modest colored mate in the mating season. With spread wings and tail he makes a very interesting picture parading up and down on the ground before his mate.

A closely allied species called the Varied Bunting (*Passerina versicolor versicolor*) and its variant, the Beautiful Bunting (*Passerina versicolor pulchra*), wander over the border from Mexico into Texas and Arizona. The Varied Bunting is of accidental occurrence in Michigan.

DICKCISSEL

Spiza americana (*Gmelin*)

A. O. U. Number 604

Other Names.— Black-throated Bunting; Little Meadowlark.

General Description.— Length, 6¾ inches. Upper parts, gray, brown, and black, streaked; under parts, white and yellow. Bill, stout, conical, and compressed; wings, long and pointed; tail, about ¾ length of wing, forked.

Color.—Adult Male: Crown, hindneck, sides of neck, and ear region, plain gray, the forehead and crown usually olive-greenish; over eyes a narrow stripe of pale yellow, sometimes white toward the back; back and shoulders, light brownish-gray or grayish-brown, streaked with black, the rump similar but paler and grayer and without streaks; middle wing-coverts, brownish-gray with dusky shaft-streaks; lesser and middle wing-coverts cinnamon-rufous; greater coverts and wing feathers, dusky centrally broadly edged with pale wood-brownish, the former sometimes tinged with cinnamon-rufous; secondaries, primaries, and tail feathers, grayish-dusky edged with pale buffy-grayish (edging nearly white on outermost primaries and tail feathers); cheek region, yellow toward the front, white toward the back; chin (and usually upper throat), white; breast (sometimes part of abdomen also) yellow, this fading into white on lower abdomen, under tail-coverts, etc.; the sides and flanks, pale brownish-gray; a black patch, of exceedingly variable shape and extent, on lower throat, sometimes continued backward along the middle line of breast to upper part of abdomen or forward (but not including) the chin; iris, brown. Adult Female: Much like the adult male, but coloration much duller; upper parts, more brown, with the crown and rump usually streaked with dusky; stripes over the eye and on the cheeks with less of yellow, sometimes with none; under parts with yellow of breast more restricted; whole throat white, margined on the sides by a streak of dusky; no black spot on lower throat, or else this much smaller than in male; flanks streaked with dusky.

Nest and Eggs.— Nest: Placed on ground sheltered by a tuft of grass, or in trees or bushes sometimes fifteen feet up, but the typical site is on the ground, in meadows or fields; constructed principally of dried grass, with some leaves, weed stems, rootlets and shreds of corn husks, lined with fine grass or horse-hair. Eggs: 4 or 5, plain pale blue.

Distribution.— United States east of Rocky Mountains, and southward in winter through New Mexico, Arizona, Mexico (both coasts), and Central America to Colombia and Trinidad; occasional during migration in Jamaica and on Swan Island (Caribbean Sea); breeding from South Carolina (formerly), Alabama, Mississippi, and Texas north to North Dakota, Minnesota, Wisconsin, Michigan (south of lat. 43°), southern Ontario, etc., formerly to eastern Massachusetts. Now chiefly restricted during the breeding season to the region between the Allegheny Mountains and eastern base of the Rocky Mountains, having, for unknown reasons, become practically extinct since about 1870 throughout the whole of the Atlantic coast plain.

The Dickcissel is so named from the simple song with which he makes cheery the fence-rows and bushy corners of the prairies. It is a simple song, almost too furry and certainly too simple to be counted as good bird music. But the constant repetition comes to influence the listener with pleasure because there is a summery, homely sweetness about the persistency of the notes that matches the season.

The bird has been called the Black-throated Bunting and also the Little Meadowlark. His habits are those of the bush-haunting Sparrows, from whom he is never far away except when in the migratory winter flocks on the Texas plains. There the flocks are ever in motion moving on by flight of the rear ranks over to the front in a continuous forward procession. But up in the more northern areas he is a shy bird. Professor Walter B. Barrows says that it "is one of our most interesting birds, not alone on account of its beauty, but because it varies greatly in numbers in different localities, and in the same locality in different years." This great variation in frequency is most noticeable along the outer edges of its area. In 1871 the bird was common at Colorado city, but it has not been noted as common in the State of Colorado since that time. About Civil War times Dickcissels were not rare in western New York and western Pennsylvania, areas in which they are now counted as only accidental visitors. Along the north side of the Dickcissel area, the birds are common one year, rare the next, absent the next and then back again to common. Different districts over the north side of the Dickcissel range are going through different experiences at the same time. Southern Michigan may be losing Dickcissels over a period of five years while eastern Wisconsin is gaining, the upper Mississippi valley retaining its numbers and southwestern Minnesota losing. How all this is to be accounted for is yet to be worked out by those who are willing to give time to the study of the food and habits of the bird.

Drawing by R. I. Brasher

DICKCISSEL (⅜ nat. size)

Nowhere is the bird classed as one of the leading bird favorites, and yet a person who lives in the central States and the middle west, and does not know this bird is missing an unusually interesting neighbor. This is so because of his song, his unusual beauty, his plump and genial personality, and above all, the uncertainty of his presence. But, do not forget, that more than once experienced ornithologists have proved that it is quite possible and very easy to mistake a male English Sparrow for a Dickcissel.

The Dickcissel is preëminently an eater of grasshoppers. During the months of May, June, July, and August, these insects form over 40 per cent. of his food. Caterpillars — canker worms and other span-worms and cutworms — beetles and snails complete his animal diet. Of course, being a typical seed-eater its staple food during a large part of the year consists of the seeds of weeds and grasses.

LARK BUNTING

Calamospiza melanocorys *Stejneger*

A. O. U. Number 605

Other Names.— White-winged Blackbird; White-winged Prairiebird; Prairie Bobolink.

General Description.— Length, 7¾ inches. Male in summer, black; male in winter and female at all seasons, grayish-brown above and white below, streaked above and below with dusky. Bill, large and conical; wings, long with truncated tips; tail, about ¾ length of wing, even, the feathers rather narrow.

Color.—Adult Male in Summer: Uniform black, with a grayish cast on back, etc.; middle and greater wing-coverts, mostly white, forming a conspicuous patch; inner wing quills, edged with white, and tail-coverts (especially the lower) margined with white; outermost tail feathers, edged with white and sometimes with a large white spot at tip of inner web. Adult Female in Summer: Above, grayish-brown streaked with dusky; wings with a white patch, as in the male, but this smaller, more interrupted and tinged with buffy; under parts, white streaked on breast, sides, etc., with dusky. Adult Male in Winter: Similar to adult female, but feathers of under parts, especially on abdomen, black beneath the surface (this showing where feathers are disarranged); chin, black. Adult Female in Winter: Similar to the summer female, but less grayish-brown and with paler markings more strongly tinged with buff.

Nest and Eggs.— Nest: On ground, sunk to level and usually under shelter of a tussock of grass or weeds; constructed of grass and fine weed stems, lined with fine grasses and vegetable down. Eggs: 4 or 5, plain light-blue.

Distribution.— Great Plains between Missouri River and Rocky Mountains; breeding from middle and western Kansas, eastern Colorado, western Minnesota, etc., to Manitoba and Assiniboia; migrating south and southwest in winter, through Texas (to Gulf coast), New Mexico, and Arizona to plateau of Mexico, Lower California, and coast of southern California; occasional west of Rocky Mountains, and accidental in Massachusetts, New York, and South Carolina in the fall.

The Lark Bunting is a bird of the prairies and might very well have been named from the prairies. Western Kansas and eastern Colorado are the home of most of the Lark Buntings, though they are scattered over a much wider area. Sometimes out on the plains it is called the White-winged Blackbird. That name certainly defines the bird. American bird students, however, associate the name Blackbird with the Troupials instead of the Finches. Just one western schoolgirl has fallen upon the name of White-winged Prairiebird, which name seems to avoid confusion with one of our most popular and widespread American birds, the Lark Sparrow. To show the lack of definiteness about the common name of this bird, it is probably better known as the Bobolink, among the farming families of the prairies, than by any other name. There are many Bobolink traits about the bird, superficial traits to be sure, but enough to make the easterner out on the plain recall his beloved Bobolink of the east.

The Lark Bunting has a rich song during the breeding season. After that the song ceases. The song is poured out frequently on the wing much in the manner of the Bobolink though the song itself has nothing of the Bobolink quality. When many Lark Buntings are singing at once, some from the tops of weeds and others on the wing, the effect is rich and musical.

In habits the birds are rather shy on the breeding grounds, particularly the females. They are found frequently feeding silently among the flowers of the prairie floor. At other times they are silently waiting on top of some bushes or rails. One man says the Lark Buntings are "always sitting around as if they had nothing to do." When the winds blow, this bird does not flee to cover as do many birds. He often stays out in the winds as though he enjoyed them; and he has been seen fighting the gales as though his life depended on going to some destination at that time.

When the migration time comes, the flocks of Lark Buntings are seen on the more southern prairie lands of Texas and the southwestern country. There they are not at all shy, but

Drawing by R. I. Brashe

LARK BUNTING (½ nat. size)

A western schoolgirl has well named him the "White-winged Prairie Bird"

rather friendly and curious of humans and domestic animals. As they fly over in these flocks they utter a cheery, sweet *hoo-ee* with a rising inflection that is distinctive of this bird and very attractive.

TANAGERS

Order *Passeres;* suborder *Oscines;* family *Tangaridæ*

IN the Tanagers, the bill is somewhat conical in shape, decidedly longer than its breadth or depth at the base; the distinct ridge at the top is curved and at the tip is hooked. The nostrils are exposed and rather large and either oval or roundish. There are bristles at the corners of the mouth but these are not conspicuous. The wing is moderate or long and pointed or rounded. The tail is shorter than the wing; it is sometimes notched, sometimes even, and sometimes slightly forked at the end; the feathers are of medium width and rounded at the tips.

In coloration the adult males are more or less red, sometimes entirely so, with or without black wings and tails, the wings sometimes being marked with white, yellow, or reddish bands. The adult females have the red replaced by olive-greenish above and by yellowish beneath, but the wing pattern is the same as in the male. The first plumage of the young differs from the adult coloring in being streaked beneath.

Tanagers are found in temperate North America southward through Mexico and Central America and tropical South America to Argentina, Bolivia, and Peru.

The word "Tanager" is derived from the Latin name *Tanagra* which Linnæus applied to the genus and which is probably of Brazilian origin.

WESTERN TANAGER

Piranga ludoviciana (*Wilson*)

A. O. U. Number 607

Other Name.— Louisiana Tanager.

General Description.— Length, 7½ inches. Male, yellow, black, and red; female, olive-greenish, yellow, and dusky. Bill, stout; wings, moderately long and pointed; tail, shorter than wing, notched.

Color.—Adult Male in Summer: Back, shoulders, wings, and tail, black; back sometimes slightly mixed with yellow; posterior row of lesser wing-coverts, middle coverts, broad tips to outer webs of greater coverts, rump, upper tail-coverts, hindneck, and under parts of body, yellow, the tips to greater wing-coverts, usually paler yellow, sometimes whitish, and the hindneck, sometimes tinged with red; head, crimson, paler on throat; under wing-coverts, light yellow; bill, dull wax-yellowish; iris, brown. Adult Male in Winter: Similar to the summer male but with head yellow (or but slightly tinged with red), obscured on back of head and hindneck with olive-greenish or dusky tips to the feathers; feathers of back, usually margined with yellowish-olive; inner wing quills and the tail feathers margined terminally with white or pale yellow. Adult Female: Above, olive-greenish, the back and shoulders tinged with gray, the rump and upper tail-coverts more yellowish: wings, grayish dusky with light olive-greenish edgings; middle coverts broadly tipped with light yellow and outer webs of greater coverts, broadly tipped with paler yellow or white, forming two distinct bands; tail, grayish-brown with yellowish olive-green edgings; under parts dull yellowish, the under tail-coverts, clear canary-yellow; anterior portion of head, sometimes tinged with red; bill and iris as in adult male.

Nest and Eggs.— Nest: A flat saucer-shaped structure, generally low down on horizontal branch of a conifer or oak, sometimes 30 feet up; constructed of twigs, grass, and bark strips, lined with similar finer material and horse-hair. Eggs: 3 or 4, pale bluish-green, lightly spotted with browns and purple.

Distribution.— Western North American, from eastern base of Rocky Mountains to Pacific coast, northward to British Columbia, Athabasca, Idaho, Montana, and southwestern South Dakota; south in winter over greater part of Mexico to highlands of Guatemala; straggling eastward during migration to more northern Atlantic States.

The easterner, seeing for the first time the wonders of the Pacific slope, hears in the deciduous woods a voice from " back home." It is the song of a Tanager; but when followed to its source the singer is seen to be not the Black-winged Redbird of the east, but a western bird, the most brilliant of them all. It is handsome and striking in plumage and elegant in form. The scarlet, yellow, and black of the male are colors ordinarily associated with tropical birds and not with the songsters of the north, but its lay seems almost exactly that of the scarlet beauty of the eastern woods.

When the territory of Louisiana, then an unknown land, stretched from the Mississippi to the Pacific, this, the most beauteous small bird of that great region, was called the Louisiana Tanager; but the name is inappropriate now; for the bird is only a rare migrant in the Louisiana of to-day. The name Western Tanager is well chosen.

This bird is common on the mountain sides of the Sierra Nevada in California, where it sings from the tops of tall trees, also in the deciduous woods in some of the river valleys of Oregon, Washington, and British Columbia. It is a forest bird and often builds its nest in firs or pines. It is a retiring species, although it can hardly be called shy, and like the Scarlet Tanager it sometimes ventures out of its forest fastnesses into the nearby clearings. This Tanager feeds its young chiefly on insects which it is expert at catching both on trees and on the wing.

Edward Howe Forbush.

The Western Tanager, like the Robin, occasionally becomes a nuisance in the orchard. It breeds in the mountainous regions of California and northward, and as a rule is not common in the fruit-growing sections. There are, however, times during migration when it fairly swarms in some of the fruit-raising regions, and unfortunately this sometimes happens just at the time when the cherry crop is ripening. The bird is a late breeder and does not seem to care to get to its nesting ground before the last of June or early July. It is thus enabled to begin in the southern part of the State when cherries are ripening there, and leisurely follow the ripening fruit northward. The Tanagers are in California every year, and every year they migrate to their nesting grounds in spring and return in fall, but only at long intervals do they swarm in prodigious numbers. Evidently the migration

Courtesy of the New York State Museum

NORTHERN RAVEN
Corvus corax principalis Ridgway

CANADA JAY
Perisoreus canadensis canadensis (Linnaeus)

Both ¼ nat. size

Courtesy of the New York State Museum

FISH CROW
Corvus ossifragus Wilson

CROW
Corvus brachyrhynchos brachyrhynchos Brehm

All ¼ nat. size

RUSTY BLACKBIRD *Euphagus carolinus* (Müller)
ADULT MALE IN SPRING
IMMATURE IN AUTUMN ADULT MALE IN AUTUMN
RED-WINGED BLACKBIRD *Agelaius phoeniceus phoeniceus* (Linnaeus)
MALE IN AUTUMN
MALE IN SPRING FEMALE
BOBOLINK *Dolichonyx oryzivorus* (Linnaeus)
MALE FEMALE
All ½ nat. size

PURPLE GRACKLE
Quiscalus quiscula quiscula (Linnaeus)
MALE

STARLING
Sturnus vulgaris Linnaeus

BRONZED GRACKLE *Quiscalus quiscula aeneus* Ridgway
MALE FEMALE

COWBIRD *Molothrus ater ater* (Boddaert)
MALE FEMALE

All ½ nat. size

Courtesy of the New York State Museum

BALTIMORE ORIOLE *Icterus galbula* (Linnaeus)
MALE FEMALE
ORCHARD ORIOLE *Icterus spurius* (Linnaeus)
FIRST YEAR MALE FEMALE
ADULT MALE
MEADOWLARK *Sturnella magna magna* (Linnaeus)
All ½ nat size

PINE GROSBEAK *Pinicola enucleator leucura* (Müller)
ADULT MALE IMMATURE MALE FEMALE

PURPLE FINCH *Carpodacus purpureus purpureus* (Gmelin)
MALE FEMALE OR IMMATURE MALE

All ⅔ nat. size

CROSSBILL *Loxia curvirostra minor* (Brehm)
IMMATURE MALE ADULT MALE
FEMALE
WHITE-WINGED CROSSBILL *Loxia leucoptera* Gmelin
IMMATURE MALE FEMALE
MALE
All ⅔ nat. size

REDPOLL *Acanthis linaria linaria* (Linnaeus)
FEMALE
MALE

PINE SISKIN *Spinus pinus* (Wilson)
GOLDFINCH *Astragalinus tristis tristis* (Linnaeus)
MALE AND FEMALE IN WINTER
GREATER REDPOLL *Acanthis linaria rostrata* (Coues)
MALE

All ⅔ nat. size

Courtesy of the New York State Museum

EUROPEAN GOLDFINCH
Carduelis carduelis (Linnaeus)

GOLDFINCH
Astragalinus tristis tristis (Linnaeus)
FEMALE AND MALE IN SUMMER

EVENING GROSBEAK *Hesperiphona vespertina vespertina* (W. Cooper)
MALE FEMALE

All ⅔ nat. size

TREE SPARROW *Spizella monticola monticola* (Gmelin)
SNOW BUNTING *Plectrophenax nivalis nivalis* (Linnaeus)
⅔ nat. size

HENSLOW'S SPARROW
Passerherbulus henslowi henslowi (Audubon)
LECONTE'S SPARROW
Passerherbulus lecontei (Audubon)
ADULT
IMMATURE
IPSWICH SPARROW
Passerculus princeps Maynard
SHARP-TAILED SPARROW
Passerherbulus caudacutus (Gmelin)

GRASSHOPPER SPARROW
Ammodramus savannarum australis Maynard
SAVANNAH SPARROW
Passerculus sandwichensis savanna (Wilson)
SEASIDE SPARROW
Passerherbulus maritimus maritimus (Wilson)
ACADIAN SHARP-TAILED SPARROW
Passerherbulus nelsoni subvirgatus (Dwight)
NELSON'S SPARROW
Passerherbulus nelsoni nelsoni (Allen)
All ½ nat. size

WHITE-THROATED SPARROW
Zonotrichia albicollis (Gmelin)

WHITE-CROWNED SPARROW
Zonotrichia leucophrys leucophrys (J. R. Forster)
ADULT IMMATURE

VESPER SPARROW
Pooecetes gramineus gramineus (Gmelin)

SLATE-COLORED JUNCO
Junco hyemalis hyemalis (Linnaeus)
MALE FEMALE

All ⅔ nat. size

Courtesy of the New York State Museum

FIELD SPARROW *Spizella pusilla pusilla* (Wilson)
MALE

IMMATURE
CHIPPING SPARROW *Spizella passerina passerina* (Bechstein)
IMMATURE

MALE
FOX SPARROW *Passereila iliaca iliaca* (Merrem)
All ⅔ nat. size

SONG SPARROW *Melospiza melodia melodia* (Wilson)
SWAMP SPARROW
Melospiza georgiana (Latham)
SPRING
AUTUMN
LINCOLN'S SPARROW
Melospiza lincolni lincolni (Audubon)

TOWHEE
Pipilo erythrophthalmus erythrophthalmus (Linnaeus)
MALE
FEMALE

All ⅔ nat. size

ROSE-BREASTED GROSBEAK *Zamelodia ludoviciana* (Linnaeus)
ADULT MALE
IMMATURE MALE IN AUTUMN FEMALE
CARDINAL *Cardinalis cardinalis cardinalis* (Linnaeus)
FEMALE MALE
All ⅔ nat. size

BLUE GROSBEAK *Guiraca caerulea caerulea* (Linnaeus)
ADULT MALE
CHANGING MALE
FEMALE
INDIGO BUNTING *Passerina cyanea* (Linnaeus)
MALE IN SUMMER
MALE IN AUTUMN
FEMALE
All ⅔ nat. size

ordinarily takes place along the mountains where the birds are not noticed. It is possible that in some years the mountain region lacks the requisite food, and so the migrating birds are obliged to descend into the valleys. This would seem to be the most plausible explanation of the occurrence — that is, that the usual line of migration is along the Sierra Nevada, but some years, owing to scarcity of food, or other cause, the flight is forced farther west into the Coast ranges, where the birds find the ripening cherries. As, under ordinary circumstances, the greater part of the food of this bird consists of insects, many of them harmful, the Tanager has a fair claim to consideration at the hands of the farmer and even of the orchardist.

It is probable that means may be found to prevent, at least in part, the occasional ravages of the Tanager on the cherry crop. The Tanager, like the Robin, prefers to swallow fruit whole, and as the latter takes small wild cherries in preference to the larger, cultivated kinds when both are equally accessible, it is probable that the Tanager would do the same.

Drawing by R. I. Brasher

WESTERN TANAGER (½ nat. size)

A gay mountaineer often found above the clouds

SCARLET TANAGER

Piranga erythromelas *Vieillot*

A. O. U. Number 608 See Color Plate 87

Other Names.— Black-winged Redbird; Firebird; Canada Tanager; Pocket-bird; Scarlet Sparrow.

General Description.—Length, 7 inches. Male: in summer, red with black wings and tail; in winter, red replaced with yellowish-green and yellow. Female: body, yellowish-green above and yellow below; wings and tail, brownish-gray. Bill, stout; wings, moderately long and pointed; tail, shorter than wing, notched.

Color.— Adult Male in Spring and Summer: *Uniform intense (flame) scarlet, the shoulders, wings, and tail uniform deep black*; under wing-coverts white (sometimes tinged with scarlet), with a broad outer margin of black; bill grayish-blue basally, dull yellowish green terminally; iris, brown; legs and feet, pale lavender-gray or lilaceous grayish-blue. Adult Male in Fall and Winter: Wings and tail, black as in summer; rest of upper parts, yellowish olive-green, more yellowish on forehead and crown; under parts yellow, shaded with olive-green on sides. Adult Female in Spring and Summer: Above, yellowish olive-green; wings (except lesser coverts) and tail, dusky brownish gray with olive-greenish edgings; under parts light yellow, shaded laterally with olive-greenish; under tail-coverts, clear canary yellow; under wing-coverts, grayish-white with broad outer margin of grayish olive-green; bill, horn color; iris, brown; legs and feet, bluish-gray in life. Young Male in First Autumn: Similar to adult female but yellow of under parts rather clearer, and middle and greater wing-coverts margined terminally with light yellow; the black first appearing (by middle of September) on lesser and middle wing-coverts and shoulder.

Nest and Eggs.— Nest: On horizontal limb of low saplings, generally low but sometimes 40 feet up, in retired woodlands; a flat, loosely put together structure of stems, roots, and bark strips, lined with rootlets and fine inner bark; some composed almost entirely of brownish rootlets. Eggs: 3 to 5, generally 4, greenish-blue, speckled and blotched with chestnut; occasionally the eggs are very faintly and finely spotted, altogether lacking the usual bold markings.

Distribution.— Eastern United States and more southern British provinces, north to New Brunswick, Nova Scotia, northern Ontario, Manitoba; breeding southward at least to Virginia, Kentucky, Missouri, etc., (in Allegheny Mountains to South Carolina); in winter migrating southward to West Indies and through Mexico, Central America, and northern South America to Bolivia and central Peru; west, casually to eastern Colorado and Wyoming; accidental in Bermudas.

The sudden appearance in deep woods of this remarkable bird, its almost dazzlingly brilliant red and black plumage outlined sharply against the dark green of summer foliage, is nothing less than startling to an observer whose eye is sensitive to color contrasts. And if the observer, instead of being intent upon the length of a bird's bill in relation to that of its hind claw, and the precise number of primary, secondary, and tertiary wing-feathers it possesses, is interested in bird personalities, as expressed in various ways, he is likely to count as a veritable red-letter day the one which brought him a glimpse of this gaudy reminder of what Nature can do when she is in the mood to produce striking effects.

Drawing by R. I. Brasher

SCARLET TANAGER (½ nat. size)

This gaudy fellow might easily be mistaken for a wanderer from the tropics

To speak candidly, this Tanager is usually a rather stupid and lifeless bird in its action. It moves about with an air of being dull-witted or dazed or, perhaps, bored. Also it has a characteristic trick of peering, with its head cocked first to one side and then to the other, as though it were in doubt about something. But perhaps it realizes that it doesn't have to perform or cut capers in order to attract attention, which indeed is the case. On the other hand, it is only fair to add that the bird not only does comparatively little posing in plain sight, but spends much of his time in the tree-tops where he gives the observer only exasperatingly brief glimpses of his radiant apparel. From such places he sounds most frequently his characteristic and emphatic call-note, which has been variously transliterated as *chip-churr, chic-burr,* and *chip-bang,* and also delivers his complete song. This is a carol not unlike that of the Robin, and is described by Mr. Burroughs as a "proud, gorgeous strain," while Mr. Dawson reduces it to the syllables, *terr-que-e-e-ry, ze-erve, pees-croo, be-zoor!* Mr. Mathews remarks the peculiarity that "every note is strongly double-toned or burred," as though the bird were a little hoarse, and supplies this illuminating analysis of the song. "There is a lazy, drowsy, dozy buzz to this beautiful bird's voice which one can only liken to a giant musical bumble bee, or an old-time hurdy-gurdy; the unobtrusive music speaks of summer's peace and rest, soft zephyrs blowing over sighing pine-trees, and tinkling shallows of woodland brooks."

There remains to be noted the extraordinary color difference between the magnificent male Tanager and the neutral, even dull, hues of the female's plumage. When the birds are seen together this contrast is so pronounced that uninformed persons are often incredulous about the relationship, and are disposed to insist that they must represent totally different species.

In the cool early spring as the farmer begins his plowing there may be seen among the Blackbirds following almost at his heels the Black-winged Redbird. He is just as industriously picking up grubs, ants, ground-beetles, and earthworms as his companions. However, as the season advances, he shows his preference for trees, and for the remainder of his stay with us he may be found in the woods and orchards. Here his chief occupation is hunting caterpillars and he has few superiors in this work. Leaf-rolling caterpillars he skillfully extracts from the rolled-up leaves; he is very destructive to the gypsy-moth, taking all stages except the eggs. The larvæ of gall-insects and other injurious larvæ have their places on his menu. When wood-boring and bark-boring beetles and weevils are in season, they form a considerable proportion of his food. He eats very greedily of click-beetles, leaf-eating beetles, and crane-flies whenever and wherever he finds them.

The vegetable food of the Tanager is seeds, berries, and small fruits. He seems to prefer the wild varieties.

SUMMER TANAGER

Piranga rubra rubra (*Linnæus*)

A. O. U. Number 610 See Color Plate 87

Other Names.—Redbird; Summer Redbird; Smooth-headed Redbird; Bee Bird.

General Description.— Length, 7½ inches. Male, red with grayish-brown wings; female, yellowish olive-green above and yellow below with grayish-brown wings. Bill, stout; wings, moderately long and pointed; tail, shorter than wing, notched.

Color.— Adult Male: *Above, plain dull red,* brighter on crown, rump, and upper tail-coverts; wings and primary coverts, grayish-brown edged with dull red; under parts, clear, rich vermilion; the under wing-coverts, paler; bill, light brownish; iris, brown. Adult Female: *Above, plain yellowish olive-green,* more yellowish on crown, lower rump, and upper tail-coverts, the back and shoulders sometimes tinged with grayish; primaries, grayish-brown with light yellowish olive-green edgings; lores, pale yellowish-gray; an indistinct eye-ring of light dull yellow; under parts, dull yellow, the under tail-coverts chrome-yellow; bill as in adult male. Young Male in First Autumn: Similar to the adult female, but more richly colored, the under tail-coverts deep chrome-yellow, the general color of upper parts more ochraceous, with crown, upper tail-coverts, tail, and edges of primaries tinged with dull orange.

The only seasonal difference of color in this species is the greater intensity of the colors in autumn and winter, the opposite extreme being represented in midsummer specimens. Immature males are variously intermediate in plumage between the plumage of the adult female and that of the adult male, the relative proportion of red and yellowish varying according to age, several years being required for attainment of the full plumage. Adult females not infrequently show touches of red, sometimes a considerable amount of this color, but such females may be distinguished from immature males by the duller color of the red.

Nest and Eggs.—Nest: Generally in deciduous trees on a horizontal limb from 5 to 60 feet up; so thinly constructed of bark strips, rootlets, a few leaves, and grass as to show the eggs from beneath; in central and southern States sometimes more compactly built by the addition of down and moss. Eggs: 3 or 4, light green inclining to emerald, spotted and blotched with sepia, lilac, and brownish purple.

Distribution.— Eastern United States in summer, breeding from the Gulf States (Florida to eastern Texas) north to southern New Jersey and southeastern Pennsylvania, southern Ohio, central Indiana, central Illinois, southern Iowa, etc.; casual or occasional visitant north to Nova Scotia, New Brunswick, Maine, Connecticut, Ontario, etc.; in winter south to Bahamas, Cuba, eastern Mexico, Central America and north and northwestern South America.

From New Jersey southward to central Florida the Summer Tanager makes its summer home. It inhabits open woodlands and is partial in some sections to those forests of yellow pine where an undergrowth of small oaks makes conditions attractive for such birds. It is not much given to inhabiting the dense hammocks or the swamps of heavy cypress. It is not a particularly shy bird, and in North Carolina and Virginia it may be seen in many of the towns where shade trees and orchards are plentiful.

To distinguish it from the Cardinal, which is seen in winter quite as often as in summer, and is often called "Winter Redbird," this species is known to many southerners as "Summer Redbird." The nest is built well out on the horizontal limb of some deciduous tree, usually at a height of about fifteen feet. Often the spot chosen is directly over a path or some woodland road.

The bird has a pleasing song. Its usual call-note is loud and clear and somewhat resembles the words *which-a-too*. T. GILBERT PEARSON.

Because of his habit of eating honeybees, the Summer Tanager has been given the name of Bee Bird. Otherwise his food of insects and fruits is of such a character as to be helpful to those who depend in any way upon forest products. In the early summer many large beetles and wasps besides the bees are eaten by him and his family. Later he feeds chiefly on blueberries and other small fruits.

In the southwestern part of the United States we find Cooper's Tanager or Western Summer Tanager (*Piranga rubra cooperi*). It is larger and paler than its eastern congener. It is especially fond of the cotton woods.

SWALLOWS

Order *Passeres;* suborder *Oscines;* family *Hirundinidæ*

WALLOWS constitute perhaps the best defined group among the singing birds, and are characterized by their very short, flat, triangular bills, large mouths, extremely long wings reaching when closed to or beyond the end of the tail, and short legs and weak feet (fitted only for perching). Their tails are never rounded nor graduated but are always notched or forked; there are always twelve feathers in the tail, the outside two sometimes being very much longer than the others.

The plumage of the Swallows is compact, usually lustrous or semi-metallic, at least on the upper parts; sometimes it is dull-colored throughout. They molt but once a year, usually in the fall or winter.

The family is cosmopolitan and there are over one hundred recognized species throughout the world. The warmer countries have the largest number; America is credited with thirty-one species, all but one of which are peculiar to the western hemisphere.

Most migrating birds "fly by night, and feed by day," but the Swallows, as far as known, travel only in the day-time. At night they stop at roosting places used with such regularity as to be known as migration stations. Sometimes these places of rest are in trees but generally they are in marshes. They travel very slowly and whenever they come to a large body of water rather than fly across it they will go around it.

The Swallows are decidedly birds of the air, capturing insects and eating them while on the wing. Most of their time is thus passed in flying, and this probably accounts for the extraordinary development of their wings.

PURPLE MARTIN

Progne subis subis (*Linnæus*)

A. O. U. Number 611 See Color Plate 88

Other Names.— Martin; Black Martin; House Martin.

General Description.— Length, 8 inches. Plumage, steel-blue. Bill, stout; tail, about ½ length of wing, forked for about ⅓ of its length.

Color.— ADULT MALE: *Uniform glossy steel-blue;* lesser and middle wing-coverts glossy dark; rest of wings, and tail, dull black, or sooty-black; iris, brown. ADULT FEMALE: Above, much duller and less uniform steel-blue than in adult male; forehead, sooty-gray;

sides of neck, light-grayish, the hindneck usually crossed by a dull sooty-grayish band or collar, this usually indistinct; *chin, throat, chest, sides, and flanks, sooty-gray;* breast, abdomen, and under tail-coverts, white or pale grayish, usually streaked, narrowly, with dark sooty-gray.

Nest and Eggs.— NEST: In boxes erected for their use, a few pair occasionally returning to primitive conditions and nesting in hollow trees; nesting material consisting of nearly anything handy — leaves, rags, paper, string, straw, or grass. EGGS: 4 to 6, pure glossy-white, unmarked.

Distribution.— Temperate North America, except Pacific coast district; breeding north to Maine, New Brunswick, Nova Scotia, northwestern Ontario, Manitoba, Montana, and Idaho; breeding southward to southern Florida, southern Texas, and plateau of Mexico; in winter, from southern Florida and Mexico to Venezuela and Brazil; accidental in Bermudas and British Isles.

Swallows are everywhere in good repute. Of all the species the Purple Martin is undoubtedly the most popular. Houses are erected for their accommodation in all parts of the country. In some sections of the south there scarcely can be seen a negro's cabin but what has its Martin box, or more often a number of gourds swung from crossed strips erected on the top of a pole. Like other Swallows, these birds nest in colonies when accommodations are adequate; thus a dozen pairs will sometimes occupy as many compartments of a bird-box.

These friends of the Martins in the south do not all provide homes for the birds from an altruistic standpoint, or for sentimental reasons. Martins defend their nests with great tenacity, and drive from the neighborhood any Crow or Hawk that comes within sight; they are, therefore, cherished as important guardians of the poultry yard.

Their nests are made of a miscellaneous collection of sticks, wood-stems, feathers, grasses, and mud. Before the settlement of the United States by Europeans, the Indians of the South encouraged the birds to come about their fields by putting up gourds for their accommodation. This, to be sure, was not practiced extensively enough to provide homes for all the Martins of the country; furthermore we can readily imagine a time of sufficient remoteness when no nesting devices whatever were erected for their use. The original nesting places of the Martin, therefore, were such as nature provided, and these we know were the hollows of trees. So dependent have the birds become on man's bounty, that hollow trees are rarely used by them. In the pine woods on the edge of the Everglades of south Florida, I have found Martins breeding in hollow trees, and not long ago I saw birds similarly engaged in a little grove on the border of Devil's Lake, North Dakota. In some cities they build in the holes of buildings, as for example in Seattle; in other places under the eaves of buildings, as in Bismarck, North Dakota, and in Plant City and Clearwater, Florida.

T. GILBERT PEARSON.

In the Pacific Coast region south into Lower California is found the Western Martin (*Progne subis hesperia*). The male is not distinguishable from the male of the Purple Martin; but the female has the gray of the forehead extending back into the crown, a conspicuous edge of grayish-brown to the feathers of the back and rump, and the under parts grayish-white anteriorly and immaculate white posteriorly.

Drawing by R. I. Brasher

PURPLE MARTIN (⅓ nat. size)

A beautiful and useful bird

The Martins are among the most beneficial of birds. Their food consists almost entirely of insects — wasps, bugs, beetles, and flies. Among the beetles are the boll-weevils, clover-leaf weevils, and nut weevils. Locusts are eaten at all stages.

CLIFF SWALLOW

Petrochelidon lunifrons lunifrons (*Say*)

A. O. U. Number 612 See Color Plate 88

Other Names.— Eave Swallow; Jug Swallow; Barn Swallow; Mud Swallow; Republican Swallow; Crescent Swallow; Rocky Mountain Swallow; Moon-fronted Swallow.

General Description.— Length, 6 inches. Upper parts, steel-blue; under parts, chestnut and whitish. Bill, very short; tail, less than ½ length of wing, slightly notched.

Color.—ADULTS: *Forehead, dull white,* dull pale écru-drab or pale wood brown, forming a conspicuous patch, very sharply defined at rear, its extremities pointed; crown and back of head, glossy blue black; hindneck, hair-brown or brownish-gray; back and shoulders, glossy blue-black, the former streaked with pale gray or whitish; *rump, light cinnamon-rufous;* upper tail-coverts, brownish-gray or hair-brown with paler margins; wings and tail, dusky grayish-brown, the secondaries with paler margins; ear, eye, and cheek regions, chin and throat, rich chestnut; a patch of somewhat glossy-black on lower throat; chest, sides, and flanks, pale grayish-brown, the first usually tinged with pale chestnut; rest of under parts, whitish; iris, brown. YOUNG: Much duller in color than adults; crown, back, and shoulders, dull blackish or sooty; forehead, sometimes dull chestnut or brownish, more often dusky, like crown; sides of head and throat, mixed grayish-brown, dusky, and dull chestnut.

Nest and Eggs.— NEST: A cleverly constructed retort-shaped structure, fastened to cliffs or under eaves of outbuildings at its large end and extending horizontally; made of mud pellets mixed with straw and lined with feathers. EGGS: 3 to 5, speckled and spotted with reddish-brown and lilac.

Distribution.— Nearly the whole of North America; breeding north to Nova Scotia, New Brunswick, Anticosti Island, Province of Quebec, in the interior to Territory of Mackenzie and the Yukon Valley of Alaska, and on the Pacific coast to British Columbia; breeding southward over nearly the whole of the United States (except Rio Grande valley, at least above mouth of the Pecos River) and coast district of northwestern Mexico, as far as Mazatlan and Tepic. In winter, southward through Mexico and Central America, at least to Honduras. Said to occur in winter in Brazil, Paraguay, Argentina, and other parts of South America.

The Cliff Swallow is a bird of large colonies. Though distributed almost all over North America it is entirely absent in the breeding season from large areas. It was formerly supposed that it bred only in the West and that the advent of the Caucasian and his barns tempted the Cliff Swallows eastward to become Eave Swallows. It is likely that many places in the western half of the continent have always been the home of the largest colonies of Cliff Swallows; but the east and southeast have had their scattered colonies of Cliff Swallows both before and after the European settlements were made along the Atlantic shore.

The early explorers of the far West were much impressed by the enormous collections of Cliff Swallow mud bottle nests that were plastered over the great perpendicular rocks in many

CLIFF SWALLOW (⅔ nat. size)

Drawing by R. I. Brasher

places. One very conspicuous place where there was an immense colony was on the face of the high bluffs near the confluence of the Niobrara and Missouri rivers. As the settlements became established in the northwest the Cliff Swallows deserted the rocks in great numbers and became residents under the eaves of the farmers' barns.

They are unusually interesting birds in these large colonies. The air is full of Swallows where there are a few dozen mud bottles along under the eaves of a great barn. Going ever to and fro, in and out of the bottle nests, uttering their single notes continuously, it seems indeed a very busy place. But the individual birds are not in as much of a hurry as the collection seems to be. Many little chestnut-throated birds will be peering out of their nests, others leisurely flying backward and forward in front of the nests as though they were on inspection. Many more are coming in from far distant insect-infected areas with food for the young. Others, having chattered about for a little after feeding the young, are off with the directness of arrows and are soon out of sight. In any area within a few miles and where insects breed to fill the air, these Eave Swallows are up and down, and over and under, now down near the marsh or water, now flying high and round and round in circles; and then suddenly off with arrow-like directness in the direction of the home barn.

When the young are ready to come out of the nest the chattering increases enormously. The young hang on to the outside of the nests apparently fearful to try their wings. But once launched they soon become acquainted with all the methods of wheeling and turning, up-shots and down-dippings, to catch the wary insect on the wing. Then the whole colony deserts the eaves in a few days. Occasionally a pair is delayed behind the others by later hatchings, but it is not many days before they are all gone from the neighborhood.

The flocks of Bank, Barn, and Tree Swallows absorb these Eave Swallows, and together they work to clean the air of the inland lakes of all the flies and mosquitoes. They are up and down over the rivers and swamps and wheeling about over grain fields and pastures. Sometimes they are in hundreds, sometimes in thousands, but always a good proportion of these summer and fall flocks are Cliff Swallows. Then if one goes into the salt marshes of the south, he will find tens of thousands that are on their way for tropical insects for the winter.

The Lesser Cliff Swallow (*Petrochelidon lunifrons tachina*) and the Mexican, or Swainson's, Cliff Swallow (*Petrochelidon lunifrons melanogastra*) are inhabitants of Mexico and countries to the south. The former comes over the boundary into Texas to breed, and the latter visits Arizona for the same purpose. Both are smaller than their more widely distributed relative. The frontal patch of the Lesser Cliff Swallow is fawn color, dull cinnamon, or wood brown; that of the Mexican Cliff Swallow is chestnut or cinnamon-rufous.

Photo by P. B. Philipp Courtesy of Nat. Asso. Aud. Soc.

NESTS OF CLIFF SWALLOWS

Cleverly constructed retort- or bottle-shaped residences

An analysis of the stomach contents of 123 Cliff Swallows showed about one-third of 1 per cent. vegetable matter; this included a few seeds but it was mostly rubbish taken accidentally. In the animal matter, ants, bees, and wasps, amounted to about 39 per cent. No worker bees were found; and as bee-keepers do not regard the destruction of drones as injurious to the swarms this cannot be counted against the Swallows. Bugs — assassin-bugs, leaf-bugs, squash-bugs, stink-bugs, shield-bugs, tree-hoppers, leaf-hoppers, and jumping plant-lice — formed about 27 per cent. Beetles of all kinds aggregated a little less than 19 per cent.; of these, 17 per cent were harmful, some very much so. Gnats, dragon-flies, lace-winged flies, and spiders completed the menu.

The young are fed exactly the same kind of food that their elders eat, but the proportions vary. The soft-bodied insects are more often chosen by the parents for the nestlings as they are more easily digested. Adult Cliff Swallows do not take gravel themselves, but they feed it to the young.

L. Nelson Nichols.

BARN SWALLOW

Hirundo erythrogastra *Boddaert*

A. O. U. Number 613 See Color Plate 88

Other Names.—American Barn Swallow; Barn-loft Swallow; Fork-tailed Swallow.

General Description.— Length, 7 inches. Upper parts, steel-blue; under parts, chestnut and red. Bill, small and depressed; tail, ⅔ length of wing, or longer, and forked for more than ⅓ of its length, the side feathers becoming gradually narrower and more drawn out to the outermost, which are sometimes almost thread-like for the end portion, but always with blunt tips.

Color.—Adult Male: Forehead, chestnut; rest of upper parts, glossy dark steel-blue; wings and tail, dusky faintly glossed with greenish, the middle wing-coverts and inner wing quills broadly margined with glossy steel-blue, the greater coverts glossed with the same; the inner web of the *tail-feathers (except the middle pair), with a conspicuous white spot;* cheek region, chin, throat, and chest, chestnut or deep cinnamon-rufous, the chest margined laterally by an extension of the glossy steel-blue from sides of the neck, these two lateral patches sometimes connected, narrowly, and thus forming a nearly complete collar; rest of under parts, pale cinnamon-rufous; iris, brown. Adult Female: Similar to the adult male and often not distinguishable. Young: Much duller in color than adults; crown and hindneck, sooty-black, much more faintly glossed with blue than back; forehead, dull light-brownish or brownish-buff.

Nest and Eggs.— Nest: A bowl-shaped hemisphere, attached to barn or other buildings, timbers, or on sides of caves; constructed of mud pellets mixed with straw and grass, thickly lined with feathers. Eggs: 3 to 6, white marked with spots of bright Indian red, brown, and lavender.

Distribution.— North America in general, north to Alaska, northern Mackenzie, southern Manitoba, and southern Ungava; breeding southward over whole of United States (except Florida); in winter from southern Florida and southern Mexico, through Central America and South America as far as southern Brazil, Paraguay, Argentina, Bolivia, and Peru, and throughout West Indies; occasional in Bermudas.

Like the Bluebird and the Robin, the Barn Swallow is a bird whose appearance in and departure from the northern reaches of its range have definite seasonal significance, even to those who have no particular interest in ornithology. The poets have had much to say about the bird's comings and goings. "When the Swallows Homeward Fly," the English words of which are translated from the German of Franz Abt's song, "*Wenn die Schwalben heimwärts zieh'n,*" has been known in this country for half a century, and has been sung by many thousands of school children, not to mention yet other thousands of grown-ups. The reference of course

Drawing by R. I. Brasher

BARN SWALLOW (½ nat. size)

Beautiful in flight, appearance, and disposition, and as useful as beautiful

is to the European Swallow, but that bird is very similar in its habits to the American Barn Swallow and has about the same hold on the affections of the people — especially the country people. Like many another poet's, however, good old Franz's ornithology was a bit unscientific, as is shown by the idea he expressed that the Swallows go " home " when they go to southland at the approach of winter. As a matter of fact, this misapprehension is not confined to the poets. Yet, a little reflection should make it clear that the " home " of a bird is obviously its nest, and that the home locality is the locality in which it builds its nest and rears its young. Whatever may be the reason for the southern migration in the autumn (and there are various explanations of that movement), the bird which breeds in the north is no more going " home " when it goes south than a man who lives in New York goes home when he goes to Palm Beach, Florida, for the winter.

The Barn Swallow's habit of building within barns, or on sheltered projections from any structure, has made it perhaps the most domesticated of any of the wild birds. Indeed, under these conditions this Swallow soon comes to occupy a position which seems only a short remove from that of the barnyard fowls; and its twittering as it skims to and fro from its nest, becomes as familiar as is the clucking of the hens, or the challenge of their lord and master, the rooster — and is certainly a great deal more melodious than either. Furthermore, the bird's habit of using barns as building sites has much inherent interest and significance, in that it represents a deliberate departure from its natural instinct to build in caves and under ledges, where it had made its home until man arrived upon the scene and furnished better protection from the elements and from the bird's natural enemies. A similar example of adaptiveness is furnished by the Cliff Swallow and the Chimney Swift, and doubtless all these birds were prompted to adopt the new nesting sites partly by the supply of insects, which of course is greater about barnyards than in the birds' natural habitats.

In a leaflet on the Barn Swallow, prepared for the National Association of Audubon Societies, Mrs. Mabel Osgood Wright discusses the lamentable diminution of the bird's numbers as follows: " We associate the Swallow with comfortable old-fashioned barns, which had open rafters, doors that could not be shut tight, and windows with many panes lacking. Within such buildings, almost as easy to get into and out of as were the caves and broken crags to which they resorted before barns were built, the Barn Swallows used to nest, sometimes in large colonies, while their cousins, the Cliff Swallows, had quarters beneath the outside eaves in a line of gourd-shaped tenements.

" Nowadays, however, in the more thickly settled and prosperous parts of the country, these loosely built old barns have given place to tightly constructed, neatly painted ones; thus, as the new replaces the old in their haunts, many a pair of Swallows drop from their sky-high wooing to find closed doors and tight roofs staring them in the face. So they move on. Whither? Out to the frontiers or into the 'back counties.' This

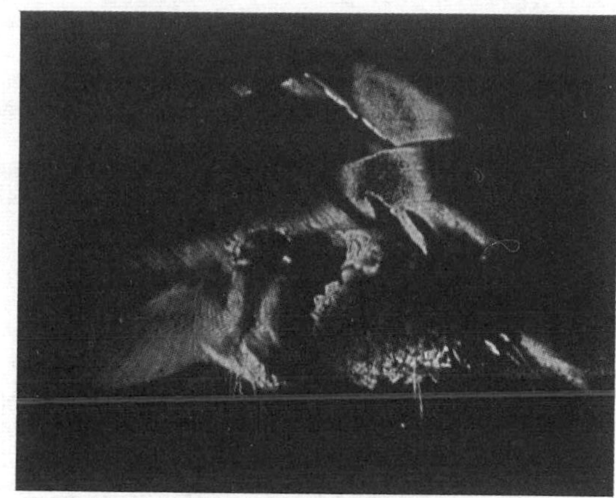

Photo by A. A. Allen

BARN SWALLOW

Poised at its nest under the gable of a barn. Photographed by light reflected from a mirror

accounts, in part, for what seems to be rather than is a decrease; but there is a constant and real loss of Barn Swallows, according to reports from all parts of the country, chargeable to the English Sparrows. These little bandits seem to have a special fondness for despoiling the nests of Swallows of all kinds, tearing them to pieces — perhaps for the sake of the feathers and other good materials for Sparrow-use — and disturbing their owners until the harassed Swallows finally abandon the premises. This is an extensive evil; and it can be prevented only by our taking the trouble to protect our Swallows against their feathered enemies. Cats also catch many Swallows, snatching them out of the air as they skim close to the ground in pursuit of grass-moths and similar low-flying insects. Rats and mice devour their eggs and young to some extent.

"A third and sadder reason why fewer Barn Swallows are now to be seen in a day's drive through the country than used to delight the eyes of bird-lovers, is that for several years they were killed by thousands to make ornaments for women's hats. This is the bird, in fact, which aroused in the mind of George Bird Grinnell, then editor of *Forest and Stream*, such indignation at the waste of bird-life for millinery that he wrote that vigorous editorial in 1886 which immediately led to the founding of the first Audubon Society." GEORGE GLADDEN.

TREE SWALLOW

Iridoprocne bicolor (*Vieillot*)

A. O. U. Number 614 See Color Plate 88

Other Names.— White-breasted Swallow; Blue-backed Swallow; White-bellied Swallow; Stump Swallow; Eave Swallow.

General Description.— Length, 6 inches. Upper parts, greenish steel-blue; under parts, white. Bill, small; tail, not more than ½ length of wing, forked, but depth of notch usually less than ⅕ of its length, the side feathers broad to near tips where they suddenly contract, the tip rounded.

Drawing by R. I. Brasher

TREE SWALLOW (½ nat. size)

A bird which is following the Barn Swallow in accepting man's hospitality

Color.—ADULT MALE: *Above,* including sides of head and neck, and lesser wing-coverts, *uniform glossy greenish steel-blue,* varying to bluish-green; middle wing-coverts dull black, broadly margined with glossy steel-blue or greenish; rest of wings, and tail, dusky, or sooty-blackish, faintly glossed with greenish; lores, velvety-black; cheek region and *entire under parts, pure white;* iris, brown. ADULT FEMALE: Similar to the male, and sometimes not distinguishable, but usually duller in color, the upper parts less brightly steel-blue or green, often dusky grayish-brown with only the tips of the feathers glossy-blue or green; the rump and upper tail-coverts, sometimes uniform grayish-brown; chest, often faintly shaded with brownish-gray. YOUNG; Above, including sides of head and neck, uniform soft dark mouse-gray, the wing feathers margined at the ends with brownish-white; beneath, white, usually shaded across chest with pale grayish-brown.

Nest and Eggs.— NEST: In dead tree trunks, Woodpecker holes, in the vicinity of water, or in boxes erected for its use, made of grasses and feathers. EGGS: 4 to 7, pure white.

Distribution.— North America in general; north to Alaska, Mackenzie, and Ungava; breeding southward to Virginia, Mississippi, Kansas, Colorado, Utah, Nevada, and California; wintering from South Carolina (occasionally northward to New Jersey) and the Gulf States southward to the Bahamas, Cuba (occasional only?) and over greater part of Mexico to highlands of Guatemala; occasional in Bermudas; accidental in British Isles.

The Tree, or White-bellied, Swallow is the first of the Swallows to arrive from the south in the spring and the last of the Swallows to leave in the fall. Hardly has the frost gone out of the ground before the first flight (chiefly adult males) have come on in large numbers. A month or six weeks later the females arrive. Then they choose holes in trees for their nesting sites and make themselves very noticeable with their pure white under parts. They may be commonly seen all spring anywhere within a mile of their nests. In the Far West they are very common in the willow tracts about the ponds and marshes of southern California.

The Tree Swallows do not readily mass together in breeding colonies. In fact they are very jealous of their territory, engaging in fights in the spring to determine which shall leave the neighborhood. Dead tree stubs and rotting upturned tree roots in flooded areas are the usual homes of the Tree Swallows. In some localities Swallow boxes have been erected and are readily occupied. English Sparrows are very apt to try to drive the Swallows out of the boxes. Sometimes they do, but the human proprietor can easily discourage the English Sparrows. The Swallows very readily learn that man is fighting the Sparrows and have been been known to call persistently when annoyed by English Sparrows so that the man may hear them and come to the rescue.

In the summer the Tree Swallows begin collecting into enormous flocks feeding in most all northern marshes. In the salt marshes east and west of New York city they are the most common Swallow in August. In September the large Tree Swallow flocks mix with on-coming flocks of Bank, Barn, and Cliff Swallows, but these other species pass on to the South from the northern States early in October, leaving the Tree Swallow to the last. They in turn go south a few hundred at a time leaving a few scattered birds even to the first of November. Sometimes Tree Swallows will be seen north of the Carolinas all winter, but the great bulk of them are spending the winter in Mexico.

According to Bicknell "the song is hardly more than a chatter. Its ordinary notes are less sharp and rapid than those of the Barn Swallow."

The food of the Tree Swallow, like that of other Swallows, consists almost entirely of winged insects. It would seem that when the first flight arrives in the spring that there would not be any of their particular kind of food for them. To the few stone-flies which they find and take on the wing, they add insects which they pick from the surface of the snow, and from twigs, fences, and sides of buildings. During migrations and in the winter they have a habit of roosting in bayberry and wax myrtle shrubs and at those periods they eat a great many of the berries.

Photo by T. G. Pearson Courtesy of Nat. Asso. Aud. Soc.

NESTING PLACE OF TREE SWALLOW

Heron Island, Maine

NORTHERN VIOLET-GREEN SWALLOW

Tachycineta thalassina lepida *Mearns*

A. O. U. Number 615

Other Name.— Violet-green Swallow.

General Description.— Length, 5½ inches. Upper parts, violet-green; under parts, white. Bill, small, weak, and much depressed; tail, less than ½ length of wing, forked for about 1/5 of its length, the side feathers broad to near ends, where the inner web is abruptly contracted, the tip blunt.

Color.—Adult Male: Crown and hindneck, varying from bronzy-green to purplish-bronze, the lower margin of the hindneck more purplish, often forming a distinct narrow collar; back, shoulders, and lesser wing-coverts, soft bronzy-green, usually tinged with purple or purplish-bronze; center portion of rump, and upper tail-coverts, varying from bluish-green (rarely) to rich violet-purple mixed with blue; wings (except lesser coverts) and tail, blackish, faintly glossed with blue;

ear region, entire under parts, and conspicuous patch on each side of rump pure white; under wing-coverts pale gray, becoming white on edge of wing; iris, brown. Adult Female: Much duller in color than the male; crown and hindneck, varying from grayish-brown, very faintly glossed with bronze or bronzy-green, to decided greenish or purplish-bronze; ear region otherwise, similar to the adult male.

Nest and Eggs.— Nest: In knot holes, deserted Woodpecker holes, hollow trees, or beneath house eaves; constructed of dried grass, lined with feathers. Eggs: 4 or 5, pure white.

Distribution.— Western North America; north to Alaska, east to Montana, Wyoming, Colorado, New Mexico, and western Texas — occasionally to South Dakota; breeding southward to southern California, Arizona, and New Mexico; in winter south to highlands of Guatemala and Costa Rica.

In Oregon, by the first week in March the first Violet-green, or White-breasted, Swallows have returned to their summer homes. For several years, I have watched the Violet-green Swallows return to my bird houses. There is no doubt in my mind that the same birds return to the same places year after year. I have known this on account of peculiarities of birds, their methods of building and the places they have built.

What a sense of location the Swallow has; for his journey from the south leads him through trackless paths of the unmeasured regions of the skies, yet he has some compass and sign posts that seem to guide him. I have often wondered how, from his lofty course, he knows just when he gets back to his old home. I have often wondered where he spends the night. If it rains, he will disappear for a week as suddenly as he came. But the minute another bright day dawns, I know he will be down around my orchard and he will remain till the summer is past. No wonder people used to think the Swallows dived into the mud to spend the winter; they appear so suddenly and are away again so mysteriously.

One thing that is necessary to a Violet-green's nest is a bed of feathers. These are always handier to get about the farm yard. I generally keep a good supply of these on hand when the Swallows are nesting. When I stand on the hillside and blow up the feathers, they ask for nothing better. The Swallows skim past and catch them before they touch the ground. When the feathers begin to appear, it isn't many moments till half a dozen Swallows are in the game. They flit back and forth and soon become tame enough to take the feathers the instant they leave my hand. Then occasionally, I have had a bird that was bold enough to snap a feather from my fingers.

In the western part of Oregon, the Violet-green Swallow formerly nested in old Woodpecker holes and crevices in stumps, or a knot-hole in the corner of a building. It is now one

Photo by W. L. Finley and H. T. Bohlman

NORTHERN VIOLET-GREEN SWALLOW (nat. size)

of the birds that invariably rent a bird house if it is put up about the garden or orchard. Or better still, if a hole is cut in the side of a woodshed and a box put on the inside, it is almost sure to be taken by a Violet-green Swallow.

WILLIAM L. FINLEY.

The food habits of the Violet-green Swallow have no marked peculiarities and are practically identical with those of its eastern relative, the Barn Swallow. Almost all of its food is insects and of these only 3 per cent. can be reckoned as useful.

BANK SWALLOW

Riparia riparia (*Linnæus*)

A. O. U. Number 616 See Color Plate 88

Other Names.— Sand Swallow; Sand Martin; Bank Martin.

General Description.— Length, 5½ inches. Upper parts, grayish-brown; under parts, white and grayish-brown. Bill, small, moderately depressed; tail, about ½ length of wing, forked for about ⅙ of its length, the side feathers moderately contracted near the tips which are blunt.

Color.— ADULTS: Above, plain grayish-brown; chin, throat, cheek region, and under parts of body, with under tail-coverts, white, interrupted by *a broad band of grayish-brown across chest,* continued along sides (where fading out on flanks), the center portion of breast usually with concealed spots of grayish-brown; iris, brown. YOUNG: Similar to adults, but feathers of rump, upper tail-coverts, and inner wing quills broadly margined terminally with pale cinnamon-buff, pale wood-brown, or whitish, the wing-coverts more narrowly margined with the same; feathers of grayish-brown chest-band usually tipped or margined terminally with paler; chin and upper throat often speckled with grayish-brown, and white of under parts sometimes tinged with pale rusty or cinnamon.

Nest and Eggs.— NEST: An excavation, made by the birds, in a sand bank, from a foot and a half to three feet in length, the extremity hollowed out to hold the nesting material of straw, grass, and feathers. EGGS: Normally 5, pure white.

Distribution.— Northern hemisphere; in America breeding from arctic districts southward to Georgia (St. Simon's Island), Louisiana, Texas, Arizona, and northern Mexico; in winter migrating southward through Mexico, Central America, and South America, as far as eastern Peru and Brazil, and to the West Indies.

Drawing by R. I. Brasher

BANK SWALLOW (½ nat. size)

There are but few species of American birds that nest in holes in the ground which they themselves excavate. One is the Kingfishers, whose chief representative is the well-known bird of the eastern United States, and another is the little Bank Swallow. It seems logical that birds which have so queer a common habit, should be in sympathy in other respects, and so it happens quite naturally that the big and brave and self-reliant fisherman in feathers and the timid little insect-hunting Swallow often dig their burrows in the same bank and seem to be on very good terms.

"Honey-combed" is about the only adjective which describes the appearance of a bank in which a colony of these Swallows have made their homes. Thoreau recorded seeing fifty-nine Bank Swallows' holes within a space of twenty by one and a half feet (in the middle), and doubtless this could be exceeded. The bank may be of either clay or sand (in fact there are two or three records of the birds actually having made use of banks of sawdust!), and the bird uses both its bill and its claws in the tunneling operation. As such embankments commonly are the result of the action of water, these Swallows are likely to be seen in the neighborhood of rivers or ponds, though they may utilize the perpendicular surfaces of a brick-yard or of any other excavation left open to the sky, even comparatively narrow railroad cuts. However, they seldom show so decided a liking for human society as is manifested by the Barn and Eave Swallows and their relative, the Chimney Swift. The once quite prevalent theory that the Bank Swallows hibernate in their burrows during the winter months is, of course, preposterous.

The food of the Bank Swallow does not differ appreciably from that of the Tree Swallow with which it often associates.

Photo by H. K. Job Courtesy of Outing Pub. Co.

BANK SWALLOW AT NEST

A hole in a gravel bank

ROUGH-WINGED SWALLOW

Stelgidopteryx serripennis (*Audubon*)

A. O. U. Number 617 See Color Plate 88

Other Names.— Bridge Swallow; Rough-wing.

General Description.— Length, 5¾ inches. Plumage, grayish-brown, paler below. Bill, much depressed and moderately broad; tail, about ½ length of wing, slightly notched. Adult male with barbs of outer web of outermost primary stiffened and abruptly recurved at tip, causing a file-like roughness when the finger is drawn along the quill from base toward tip.

Color.—Adults: Above, including sides of head and neck, plain grayish-brown of very nearly uniform tone throughout, but crown slightly darker than rump; *chin, throat, chest, sides, and flanks, plain pale grayish hair-brown* or brownish-gray, the chin and throat usually somewhat paler than chest and sides; rest of under parts, white; iris, brown. Young: Similar to adults, but upper parts washed or overlaid by pale cinnamon or fawn color; chin, throat, and chest tinged with paler cinnamon or fawn color.

Nest and Eggs.— Nest: Located in a burrow in a sand bank, usually excavated by the birds themselves, wide enough to admit a man's arm, and somewhat broader than high, and from 3 to 5 feet long; large and bulky and usually composed of sticks, weed stalks, grass, and leaves. Eggs: 3 to 7, commonly 4 to 6, white.

Distribution.— Temperate North America, Mexico, and Central America as far as Costa Rica; breeding north to Connecticut, central Massachusetts, southeastern New York, Ontario, northern Indiana, southern Wisconsin, southern Minnesota, North Dakota, Montana, and British Columbia, south to Georgia, Louisiana, Texas, etc., and over greater part of Mexico, as far as State of Vera Cruz; casual northward to northern Michigan and Manitoba; in winter southward through Central America to Costa Rica, occasionally wintering on coast of South Carolina.

Photo by H. K. Job ROUGH-WINGED SWALLOW AND ITS YOUNG Courtesy of Outing Pub. Co.

The Rough-winged Swallow is a much duller looking bird than the Bank Swallow, with which it is apt to be confused. It is a slower flying bird, and those who know it well can tell its flight many rods away; it has fewer twists and zigzags and more gliding and sailing. The bird is not nearly as common as the Barn or Bank or Tree Swallows, though the area over which it breeds extends from southern Canada to central Mexico and from ocean to ocean. They were formerly less common along the northern limit of the range than now, at least it is presumed they have spread further north; even now southern New Jersey has more Rough-wings than has northern New Jersey. Through central and western New York there has been a change in the numbers of this bird from accidental or very rare to fairly common in certain localities.

Their nesting sites are sometimes like those of the Bank Swallow, in sand banks, though it is rare for more than five or six pairs to be found in such a colony. Very often, however, their nests are under bridges or railway trestles or along the under sides of jutting walls; they have also been found in empty pipes and in an old Kingfisher's nest.

One of its associates is the Phœbe. Their nests are sometimes found very close to each other under the same bridge. While Phœbe rushes out upon its prey from a watching station, Rough-wing is up and down the stream deliberately capturing all the insects that get in his way. Occasionally he will rise into the air, going over instead of under the bridge, and sometimes off for a short excursion across a pasture or a meadow; but soon he will be back again doing police duty up and down the stream.

WAXWINGS AND SILKY FLYCATCHERS

Order *Passeres;* suborder *Oscines;* families *Bombycillidæ* and *Ptilogonatidæ*

THE Waxwings are a small family belonging to the larger group of singing birds; they are thus classified because they possess a vocal apparatus but they are not singers in the common acceptation of that term. They are found only in the northern hemisphere and there are but three species known. One of these is peculiar to Japan and the neighboring parts of Asia, another to North America, and a third is circumpolar.

Their wings are rather long and pointed; their tails are less than two-thirds as long as their wings, even or very slightly rounded, with the coverts unusually long, especially the lower which reach nearly to the end of the tail; the feathers of the lores are dense, soft, and velvet-like; there are no bristles at the corners of the mouth, and the head has a long crest of soft blended feathers. The plumage in general is soft and blended.

The prevailing color of the head, neck, and body is a soft fawn hue or wine-color changing to ashy on the rump and upper tail-coverts. The wings and tail are slaty, the tail being sharply tipped with yellow or red preceded by blackish. Two of the species have horny drop-shaped tips to the secondaries which resemble sealing wax. Some of the birds lack these red tips and have other variations from the normal coloration. Concerning this imperfect plumage Dr. Ridgway says: "I am at a loss for a satisfactory name for this plumage or an explanation of its true meaning. It is obviously quite independent of sex; and that it has nothing to do with the age of the specimen, or at least is not evidence of immature age, is almost equally certain. The only very young specimen of the present species that I have seen has the remiges [quill feathers of wing] and rectrices [tail-feathers] colored exactly as in the brightly colored plumage described above, except that the wax-like appendages to the secondaries are smaller. As a rule young birds of *B. cedrorum* [Cedar Waxwing] in the streaked plumage of the first summer lack the red appendages to the secondaries, but sometimes they are present, and the tail-band is usually quite as bright yellow as in adults; therefore it would seem that these two styles of plumage occur both among fully adult and very young birds." The young are much duller than the adults and have the under parts streaked with brownish or dull grayish on a whitish ground.

The nests are bulky and are built in trees. They are constructed of small twigs, rootlets, and the like, mixed and lined with feathers and other soft materials. The eggs, 3 to 5 in number, are pale dull bluish or pale purplish-gray spotted and dotted with dark brown, black, and purplish. The young are cared for in the nest.

The Waxwings live among the trees and feed on berries, fruits, and insects.

Closely allied to the Waxwings are the Silky Flycatchers, a family that is peculiar to Central America and Mexico and which contains but four species. Of these only one extends its range into the United States. This is the Phainopepla. The Silky Flycatchers differ from the Waxwings in their rounded wings, the well-developed bristles at the corners of the mouth, and the wholly exposed nostrils. Their habits, however, are very similar.

CEDAR WAXWING

Bombycilla cedrorum *Vieillot*

A. O. U. Number 619 See Color Plate 89

Other Names.— Cherry Bird; Cedar Bird; Southern Waxwing; Carolina Waxwing; Canada Robin; Récollet.

General Description.— Length, 7¼ inches. Plumage of perfectly blended colors, the effect being a pinkish grayish-brown with yellow on abdomen and tip of tail.

Color.—Adults in Perfect Plumage: Lores and wedge-shaped patch back of eye (connected with loral area above eye), velvety black; chin, dull black; rest of head, together with neck and chest, soft pinkish wood-brown or brownish-fawn color, darker on throat, where shading into the black or dusky of chin, slightly duller or grayer on hindneck; front portion of cheek region and a narrow line (sometimes obsolete) separating the brown of forehead from the black of lores, white; back and shoulders similar in color to hindneck but slightly grayer, the wing-coverts still grayer; secondaries and primary coverts slate-gray, the first with terminal appendages (flattened and expanded prolongations of the shaft) of scarlet, resembling red sealing wax; primaries, darker (slate color), edged with paler gray; rump, upper tail-coverts, and basal portion of tail, paler gray than secondaries, deepening toward end of tail into blackish-slate or slate-black, the tail tipped with a sharply defined band of lemon or chrome yellow; vinaceous-brown color of chest passing into a slightly paler and duller hue on breast and front portion of sides, and this into light yellowish-olive or dull olive-yellowish on flanks and back portion of sides; the abdomen, similar but paler (sometimes nearly white); bill, black; iris, brown; legs and feet, black. Imperfect plumage: Similar to the perfect plumage, as described above, but without red wax-like appendages to secondaries, and yellow band across tip of tail narrower and paler yellow.

Nest and Eggs.— Nest: Generally in an orchard, within 20 feet of the ground; rather bulky, constructed of twigs, leaves, grasses, strips of bark, twine, paper, and rags; lined with fine grass, horse-hair, or wool. Eggs: 3 to 5, bluish-gray to dull olive, marked with spots and blotches of sepia and dark purple.

Distribution.—Temperate North America in general; breeding from Virginia, western North Carolina, Kentucky, Kansas, New Mexico and Arizona (in mountains), and Oregon, northward to Prince Edward Island, southern shores of Hudson Bay, Manitoba, Saskatchewan, and British Columbia; wintering in whole of United States (in wooded districts), and migrating southward to Bahamas, Cuba, Little Cayman, and Jamaica, in West Indies, and through Mexico and Central America to highlands of Costa Rica; accidental in Bermudas and British Isles.

Drawing by R. I. Brasher

CEDAR WAXWING (½ nat. size)

An exquisite of bird land, and as polite as he is handsome

BOHEMIAN WAXWING

Bombycilla garrula (*Linnæus*)

A. O. U. Number 618 See Color Plate 89

Other Names.— Black-throated Waxwing; Lapland Waxwing; Silktail.

General Description.— Length, 7½ inches. Plumage of perfectly blended colors, the general effect being a soft drab.

Color.— Adults in Perfect Plumage: General color, soft drab, becoming more wine-colored forward, more grayish (pale grayish drab or drab-gray) on abdomen, sides and flanks, the rump and upper tail-coverts, nearly pure gray, forehead, region over eye, middle portion of cheeks, and *under tail-coverts, cinnamon-rufous;* lores, streak behind the eyes, chin, and upper throat velvety black; lower abdomen and anal region, pale yellowish or yellowish-white; secondaries, slate-gray, darker on inner webs, their outer webs broadly tipped with white and the shaft of each prolonged into an expanded tear-shaped or linear flattened glossy appendage resembling red sealing wax; primary coverts and primaries, blackish slate or slate-black, narrowly edged with slate-gray, the first broadly tipped on both webs with white; primaries with end portion of outer web sometimes with a narrow terminal margin of yellow or yellow and white; tail, slate-gray becoming darker toward end, broadly tipped with chrome-yellow; bill, black; iris, brown; legs and feet, black. Imperfect plumage: Similar to the perfect plumage, but markings on terminal portion of outer webs of primaries entirely white, red waxlike appendages to secondaries absent, and terminal band of tail, much paler yellow (straw-yellow or pale naples-yellow) and often much narrower.

Nest and Eggs.— Similar to Cedar Waxwing's, but both larger.

Distribution.— Circumpolar. Northern parts of northern hemisphere, breeding in coniferous forests; southward in winter, in North America (irregularly), to Connecticut, Pennsylvania, Ohio, Indiana, Illinois, Kansas, Colorado, northern California, etc., casually to Arizona; breeding from Keewatin and Athabasca to Alaska.

If birds have no conception of manners, how does it happen that half a dozen Cedar Waxwings, sitting close together on a limb — which they often do — will pass a cherry along from one to another, down to the end of the line and back again, none of the birds making the slightest attempt to eat even part of the fruit? This little episode has been witnessed and reported by more than one thoroughly responsible observer of birds. What does it mean? If not politeness and generosity, then what? Mr. Forbush thinks the birds do it only when they are satiated; but how could he be sure of that condition? Obviously not unless he killed all of the birds and examined their stomachs, which, of course, nothing could induce him to do. It would be a sorry way to prove courtesy and kindness, and wouldn't prove anything after all. For if the bird had no room for another cherry, why didn't it simply drop the fruit instead of passing it along? Let the bird psychologists ponder these questions; for the bird-lover the answer is obvious. Besides, he will have observed many other evidences of a gentle and affectionate disposition in these beautiful creatures.

Drawing by R. Bruce Horsfall

BOHEMIAN WAXWING (½ nat. size)

A bird of satiny plumage and elegance

"Who can describe the marvelous beauty and elegance of this bird?" asks Mr. Forbush in an Educational Leaflet written for the National Association of Audubon Societies. "What other is dressed in a robe of such delicate and silky texture? Those shades of blending beauty, velvety black, brightening into fawn, melting browns, shifting saffrons, quaker drabs, pale

Photo by H. K. Job Courtesy of Outing Pub. Co.

YOUNG CEDAR WAXWINGS

blue, and slate with trimmings of white and golden yellow, and the little red appendages on the wing, not found in any other family of birds — all, combined with its graceful form, give the bird an appearance of elegance and distinction peculiarly its own. Its mobile, erectile crest expresses every emotion. When lying loose and low upon the head, it signifies ease and comfort. Excitement or surprise erect it at once, and in fear it is pressed flat.

"In 1908, some fruit-growers in Vermont introduced into the Assembly a bill framed to allow them to shoot Cedar Waxwings. This bill was pushed with such vigor that it passed the House in spite of all the arguments that could be advanced regarding the usefulness of the birds. In the Senate, however, these arguments were dropped, and the senators were shown mounted specimens of the bird. That was enough; its beauty conquered and the bill was defeated."

"Like some other plump and well-fed personages," continues Mr. Forbush, "the Cedar Waxwing is good-natured, happy, tender-hearted, affectionate and blessed with a good disposition. It is fond of good company. When the nesting-season is past, each harmonious little family joins with others until the flock may number from thirty to sixty individuals. They fly in close order, and keep well together through the winter and spring until the nesting-season again arrives. Their manner of flight is rarely surpassed. Often they suddenly wheel as if at command and plunge swiftly downward, alighting in a compact band on the top of some leafless tree. They roam over the country like the Passenger Pigeon, never stopping long except where food is abundant. When hunting for caterpillars in the trees, they sometimes climb about like little Parrots. They often show their affectionate disposition by 'billing,' and by dressing one another's plumage as they sit in a row."

The Waxwings well illustrate the rule (to which, however, there are a few exceptions) that birds with conspicuous or strikingly beautiful plumage are rarely good singers, for their vocal capacities are limited to a faint sibilant note uttered both when the bird is in flight and at rest. Mr. Brewster records hearing the bird utter a series of loud, full notes, resembling those of the Tree Swallow, but these certainly are not common.

The Bohemian Waxwing is another beautiful member of this family, and has habits and a disposition similar to the Cedar Bird. It is comparatively rare, however, as it occurs only in the upper Mississippi valley and some of the mountain States and is infrequently seen at or near the Atlantic coast. GEORGE GLADDEN.

Photo by A. A. Allen

CEDAR WAXWING

At its nest in a thorn bush

The Cedar Waxwing's proverbial fondness for cherries has given it its popular name (Cherry Bird), and much complaint is made on account of the fruit it eats. Observation shows, however, that its depredations are confined to trees on which the fruit ripens earliest, while later varieties are comparatively untouched. This is probably due to the fact that when wild fruits ripen they are preferred to cherries, and really constitute the bulk of the diet of the Cedar Waxwing.

In 152 stomachs examined animal matter formed only 13 per cent. and vegetable matter 87 per cent., showing that the bird is not wholly a fruit eater. With the exception of a few snails, all the animal food consisted of insects, mainly beetles — all but one more or less noxious, the famous elm leaf beetle being among the number. Bark or scale lice were found in several stomachs, while the rest of the animal food was made up of grasshoppers, bugs, and the like. Three nestlings had been fed almost entirely on insects.

PHAINOPEPLA

Phainopepla nitens (*Swainson*)

A. O. U. Number 620

Other Names.— Silky Flycatcher; Shining Crested Flycatcher; Shining Fly-snapper; Black-crested Flycatcher.

General Description.— Length, 7¾ inches. Male, glossy greenish blue-black; female, olive-gray. Crown, crested; bill, short and broad; wings, short and rounded; tail, long and fan-shaped.

Color.— Adult Male: Uniform glossy greenish blue-black; larger wing-coverts, wing, and tail-feathers less glossy black, edged with glossy dark greenish-blue or steel-gray; inner webs of primaries with middle portion extensively white; iris, red. Adult Female: Plain olivaceous mouse-gray, the longer feathers of crest, black edged with gray; wings and tail, dusky (the latter nearly black), faintly glossed with bronzy-greenish; lesser wing-coverts, margined with gray; middle coverts, broadly margined at the ends with white, the greater coverts edged with the same, the primaries, more narrowly edged with white or pale gray; tail-feathers edged with deeper gray, becoming white on outermost feathers; under tail-coverts broadly margined with white; inner webs of primaries, pale brownish-gray basally but without any definite light-colored area; iris, brown.

Nest and Eggs.— Nest: Usually placed in oaks, elders, or mesquite trees from 8 to 25 feet up; flat, saucer-shaped, compactly made of light-colored vegetable substances — plant fibers, blossoms, cottony fibers, small twigs. Eggs: 2 or 3, dull gray or greenish-white thickly spotted with brown, black, or lilac.

Distribution.— Southwestern United States, north, regularly, to southwestern Texas, New Mexico, southern Utah, southern Nevada and southern California, casually or irregularly to west-central Nevada, and to central and northern California; southward throughout peninsula of Lower California and on Mexican plateau.

The Phainopepla, or Shining Crested Flycatcher, is glossy bluish-black in color, with large white spots in the wings, which show only when flying. His mate is brownish gray. They are rather slim birds, nearly as big as a Catbird.

The Phainopepla is a beautiful fellow, with an elegant pointed crest, and plumage shining like satin. He sits up very straight on his perch, but he is a rather shy bird, and so not much is known about his ways. He is a real mountain lover, living on mountains, or in cañons, or on the borders of small streams of California, Arizona, and Texas.

As you see by one of his names, he is a Flycatcher. Sometimes thirty or forty of them may be seen in a flock, all engaged in catching flies. But, like the Cedar Bird, he is also fond of berries. When berries are ripe on the pepper-trees, he comes nearer to houses to feast on the beautiful red clusters. The song of this bird is fine, and, like many other birds, he sometimes utters a sweet whisper song.

The nest is placed on a branch, not very high up in a tree, and is often, perhaps always, made of flower stems with the flowers on, with fine strips of bark, grasses, and plant down.

Drawing by R. I. Brasher

PHAINOPEPLA (½ nat. size)

The handsome and distinguished-looking male does the nest-building while his wife gads about

What is curious, and rare among birds, the male Phainopepla insists on making the nest himself. He generally allows his mate to come and look on, and greets her with joyous song, but he will not let her touch it till all is done. Sometimes he even drives her away. When all is ready for sitting, he lets her take her share of the work, but even then he appears to sit as much as she. Mrs. Bailey found a party of these birds on some pepper-trees, and to her we owe most of what we know of their habits.

OLIVE THORNE MILLER.

SHRIKES

Order *Passeres;* suborder *Oscines;* family *Laniidæ*

THAT the Shrikes should be "song birds," will seem incongruous to many who know how they come by their popular name of "Butcher Birds." But they are so classified by systematic ornithologists, and not without reason; for they not only possess vocal organs, but some of the species actually make use of those organs in producing a sort of warbled song. They are song birds of prey. The Shrike family (*Laniidæ*) have strongly hooked bills; rather short, rounded wings; the tail is nearly as long as the wing, or often longer, and rounded, graduated, or nearly even, but never forked; the plumage is soft, blended, the head never crested, though the feathers of the crown are sometimes rather longer than usual; the plumage is never with brilliant colors (in the typical members of the group) but with plain gray, brown, or rufous predominating, varied with black and white or pale wine-color; the sexes are usually alike in color and the young always have the plumage barred or transversely streaked. The range of the family includes the northern hemisphere in general and portions of the African and Indo-Malayan regions; in the western hemisphere no species are found south of Mexico. The family is rather numerously represented in the Old World, but only one genus and two species occur in America.

The Shrikes are peculiar in several of their habits, especially in their practice of impaling insects, small birds, and small mammals upon thorns. The purpose of this curious habit is not known with certainty; but the most plausible explanation seems to be that suggested by Mr. Seebohm (*History of British Birds and their Eggs*) which is that the Shrike, not having sufficiently powerful feet to hold its prey while it is being torn to pieces, therefore avails itself of the aid of a thorn (or, in some case, a crotch) to hold its food while being eaten. This does not, however, explain why the Shrike's victims are so often found in such positions unmutilated, as if placed there for future use or from mere cruelty.

The food of Shrikes consists of the larger insects (grasshoppers, beetles, etc.), spiders, small frogs, and reptiles, and frequently small birds and mammals, such as mice and shrews. Their favorite position, when resting, is the summit of an isolated small tree or stake, a telegraph wire, or some other prominent perch, from which they can command a wide view in all directions. When flying from one resting place to another the Shrike sweeps downward from its perch and then pursues an undulating flight a few feet above the surface of the ground.

The ordinary notes of the true Shrikes are harsh, often grating, but most of the species are capable of producing a variety of sounds, in some closely approximating a song; some, indeed, are possessed of considerable musical ability, which some persons, doubtless without reason, suppose to be practiced for the purpose of enticing small birds within their reach. Their bulky nests are placed in thickly branched trees, usually among thorny twigs or among intertwining vines, and are usually lined with soft feathers; the eggs, four to seven in number, are spotted or freckled with olive-brown on a whitish, buffy, or pale greenish ground color.

NORTHERN SHRIKE

Lanius borealis *Vieillot*

A. O. U. Number 621 See Color Plate 90

Other Names.— Butcher Bird; Winter Butcher Bird; Northern Butcher Bird; Nine Killer; Winter Shrike; Great Northern Shrike.

General Description.— Length, 10 inches. Upper parts, light grayish-blue; under parts, white; wings and tail, black.

Color.— Above, plain light bluish-gray, changing to *white* on lower rump, upper tail-coverts, shoulders, eyebrow region, and front portion of *forehead;* ear region black, this extending forward beneath lower eyelid *and confluent with a black spot in front of the eye; lores, gray;* wings and tail, black; secondaries and innermost primaries, tipped with white (the latter more narrowly); base of primaries (except three outermost), white across both webs; showing as a patch; outermost tail-feather, white with a black spot near base of inner web; second tail-feather with base and extensive terminal portion, white; remaining tail-feathers, tipped with white; cheek region and under parts, white, the chest and sides of breast marked with wavy bars of dusky-grayish; bill, entirely black in summer, dusky horn color in winter; iris, brown; legs and feet, black.

Nest and Eggs.— Nest: In bushes or thorny trees, principally north of the United States; a large, rude structure of twigs, grasses, leaf and weed stems, lined thickly with moss and feathers. Eggs: 4 to 6, pale bluish green, spotted with brown and dull purple.

Distribution.— Northern North America; breeds from northwestern Alaska, northern Mackenzie, and northern Ungava to the base of the Alaska peninsula, central Saskatchewan, southern Ontario, and southern Quebec; winters south to central California, Arizona, New Mexico, Texas, Kentucky, and Virginia.

Drawing by R. Bruce Horsfall

NORTHERN SHRIKE (½ nat. size)

The Northern Shrike is about an inch longer than the Loggerhead, but the habits of the two birds are quite similar, though in disposition the present species seems to be the more savage of the two. Its appearance always causes consternation among the Sparrows and other small birds upon which it preys. It may be recognized at once by its strong colors—gray, black, and white, — and by its flight, which is peculiarly heavy and with rapid flapping. In the open it flies near the ground, and, like the Loggerhead, gains its perch by a sudden upward glide. The bird's song, heard usually in March or April, is a jumble of notes, some of them musical, the entire effort suggesting that of the Catbird. Its call-notes are harsh and unpleasant.

This Shrike seems to have all of the bad habits of its southern relative, but their odium is relieved by an apparent taste for English Sparrows.

LOGGERHEAD SHRIKE

Lanius ludovicianus ludovicianus *Linnæus*

A. O. U. Number 622

Other Names.— Southern Loggerhead Shrike; Southern Butcher Bird; Butcher Bird; French Mockingbird.

General Description.— Length, 9 inches. Upper parts, gray; under parts, white; wings and tail, black.

Color.— Adults: Above, plain slate-gray, darkest (approaching slate-color) on crown, fading gradually into paler gray on upper tail-coverts and into white on outermost shoulder region; eye region, ear region, and *lores, black,* forming a conspicuous longitudinal patch on sides of head; *wings and tail, black;* secondaries tipped with white; entire under parts, including cheek region, white, the sides and flanks faintly shaded with gray; iris, brown; bill, legs, and feet, black. YOUNG: Above, brownish-gray, the crown and hindneck narrowly barred with narrow lines of darker gray and broader ones of pale buffy or brownish-gray; shoulders, lesser and middle wing-coverts, rump, and upper tail-coverts with more distinct narrow dusky bars and with the paler bars broader, more buffy; chest, sides, and flanks, pale buffy-grayish narrowly barred with dusky; bill and feet, brownish; otherwise similar to adults.

Nest and Eggs.— NEST: Located in thorny trees (hawthorns), hedges, or thickets, usually within 10 feet of ground; a large, carelessly constructed affair of corn stalks, weed stems, coarse grass, roots, paper, and wool and thickly lined with feathers, hair, or wool. EGGS: 5 to 7, grayish or creamy-white, thickly and evenly spotted and blotched with dull browns and lavender.

Distribution.— Coast district of South Carolina and Georgia to southern Florida and westward over the coastal plain of the Gulf States to Louisiana.

The Loggerhead Shrike is the common Shrike of the southeastern States, and over wide regions of its range it is a very abundant species. These "French Mockingbirds," as they are sometimes called, somewhat resemble the famous songster in size and color, but they are very different individuals in habits. When seen the Loggerhead is usually occupying a perch on the top of some small tree, stake, telephone pole, or fence post. From this lookout it will fly down now and then and seize the grasshopper, lizard, or baby snake, which its sharp eyes have detected in the grass often at a distance of 100 feet or more. In common with other Shrikes it possesses the habit of impaling on thorns or barbed wire such objects of food as it has no immediate use for. My observations have led me to believe that it rarely returns to eat what it has thus cached, unless driven to do so by hunger resulting from adverse fortunes of the chase. Undoubtedly the Loggerhead at times pushes its prey on a thorn to help hold it while eating. I once watched one impale a Chipping Sparrow on the sharp splinter of a broken tree and proceed to eat it then and there.

When approaching its nest this bird flies rapidly with quickly beating wings in a straight line, often sinking to within a few feet of the ground until close to the tree, when with a sharp upward turn it will climb the invisible ladder of the air to its nest. This structure is an exceedingly compact affair and often contains a thick lining of chicken feathers. The birds make a great outcry when one disturbs the nest, and will pop their bills in a manner that suggests the grinding of teeth in rage.

In the spring the Loggerhead Shrike often sings, but of all singing birds its musical production is about the poorest. It consists of a series of squeaky whistles, strangling gurgles, and high pitched pipings, all apparently produced with the greatest effort and labor. The notes are not loud and usually can be heard only a short distance. There seems to be no evidence, however, to indicate that the song does not produce the effect for which it is probably designed — that is, discomforting its rival and giving joy to the lady bird of its choice. T. GILBERT PEARSON.

There has been so much discussion of the Shrike's habits and diet that the following observations, concerning a captive Loggerhead, by Dr. Sylvester D. Judd, of the United States Biological Survey, recorded in his *Birds of a Maryland Farm,* are both valuable and interesting:

"The habit the bird has of impaling prey has been the subject of considerable speculation, some writers maintaining that it gibbets its victims alive for the pleasure of watching their death struggles, and others that it slaughters more game at a time than it can eat and hangs up the surplus to provide against a time of want. This theory of prudent foresight may explain why it kills more game than it can eat, but, as the experiments showed, it does not touch the real reason why it impales its prey.

"On the day after the Shrike in question was captured a dead mouse was offered it. The Shrike raised its wings, moved its tail up and down petulantly after the manner of the Phœbe, and then seized the mouse and dragged it about for several minutes, trying to wedge it into first one and then another corner of the cage. Failing in this effort, it tried to impale the mouse on the blunt broken end of branch that had been placed in the cage for a perch, but the body fell to the floor. Then it tried to hold the mouse with its feet and tear it to pieces, but its feet were too weak. A nail was now driven into the cage so as to expose the point. Immediately the Shrike impaled its prey, fixing it firmly, and then fell to tearing and eating ravenously. Several days later the nail was removed and a piece of beef was given to the Shrike. By dint of hard work it managed to hold the beef with its feet, so that it could bite off pieces; but it much preferred to have me do the holding, when it would perch on my wrist and pull off mouthfuls in rapid succession. These experiments indicate that the Shrike is unable to tear to pieces food that is not securely fixed. Hawks can grip their food with their powerful talons and then easily tear it into pieces small enough to be swallowed, but the Shrike's feet have not a sufficiently vigorous clutch to permit this method.

"A series of experiments in feeding insects to this Shrike was also carried out. If the bird was very hungry it did not impale insects. When offered a grasshopper at such times, it would clutch it with one foot, and, resting the bend of its leg on the perch, bite off mouthfuls and swallow them. When not very hungry it impaled grasshoppers and caterpillars. Such prey as the thousand-legs, centipedes, house flies, and blowflies, and in a single instance, a mourning-cloak butterfly, it ate at a single gulp, but very large insects, such as tumblebugs, it always impaled. . . .

"A series of experiments with mice, birds, and other vertebrates was also made. When a live mouse was placed in the cage the Shrike gave chase, half running, half flying. It soon caught the animal by the loose skin of the back, but quickly let go because the little rodent turned on it savagely. In the next attack it seized the mouse by the back of the neck and bit through the skull into the base of the brain, causing instant death. (A Broad-winged Hawk experimented with at the same time always killed its victims with its talons, never touching them with its beak until they were dead.) A honey-locust perch, set with sharp thorns two inches long, had been put into the Shrike's cage, and on this it fixed the mouse, a thorn entering below the shoulder blade and passing out through the breast. Then (10 A. M.) it ate the brains. At 10.30 it picked twenty to thirty mouthfuls of hair from the hind quarters, made incisions and removed the skin, and then ate the large muscles. By 11.30 it had devoured the whole body, including viscera and skin. Several days later the Shrike dispatched a live English Sparrow about as it had the mouse, and impaled the carcass. Then it plucked the breast and ate the pectoral muscles, the lungs, and the heart. Live snakes and lizards were also fed to the Shrike. A toad was put into the cage, and it attacked it, but soon desisted in evident distress, caused probably by the toad's irritating secretions.

"It disgorged indigestible parts of its food in pellets, after the manner of Hawks and Owls. . . . When vertebrates had been eaten their bones were found inside the pellet and the fur, feathers, or scales outside."

The Migrant, or Northern Loggerhead, Shrike (*Lanius ludovicianus migrans*) is practically identical with the Loggerhead in coloration; the gray of the upper parts is paler and the under parts are less purely white. In proportions, however, it is decidedly different: the bill is much smaller and the tail is shorter than the wing instead of the other way round. It breeds from

Photo by Mrs. N. J. Guoser Courtesy of Nat. Asso. Aud. Soc.

LOGGERHEAD SHRIKE

When seen, he is generally perched on the top of some small tree, stake, or the like

northern Minnesota, Wisconsin, Michigan, southern Ontario, southern Quebec, Maine, and New Brunswick south to eastern Kansas, southern Illinois, Kentucky, western North Carolina, and the interior of Virginia. In the winter it is found from southern New England and the Middle States south to Texas, Louisiana, and Mississippi. This Shrike is sometimes known as the Summer Butcher Bird. (See Color Plate 90.)

The White-rumped Shrike, or Mouse-bird (*Lanius ludovicianus excubitorides*) is similar to the Migrant Shrike, but the gray of the upper parts is decidedly paler and changes abruptly to white on the upper tail-coverts; the white of the under parts is purer; and in size it is a trifle larger. It is found in the arid districts of western North America south into Mexico.

The California, or Gambel's, Shrike (*Lanius ludovicianus gambeli*) is so much like the Migrant Shrike that oftentimes it is not distinguishable if only its upper parts are seen, but its under parts are usually either browner or with transverse bars of pale gray or brownish-gray on the chest and the sides of the breast. It breeds in the Pacific coast district from southern British Columbia south to northern Lower California and winters south to Cape San Lucas and western Mexico. It destroys many injurious insects and is a decidedly beneficial specie.

The Island, or Anthony's, Shrike (*Lanius ludovicianus anthonyi*) is the darkest of the members of this species. In coloration it is like the Loggerhead Shrike, but the gray of the upper parts is nearly slate-gray, especially on the crown, and is more uniform, the shoulders almost wholly gray; the under parts are much more strongly tinged with gray; and the outer tail-feathers have much less white. Its range is limited to the Santa Barbara Islands and San Clemente Island, California, and Santa Margarita Island, Lower California.

VIREOS

Order *Passeres;* suborder *Oscines;* family *Vireonidæ*

VIREOS are sometimes called Greenlets; the Latin word *Vireo* means "I am green." They are small, active tree-haunting birds, like the Warblers. They are mainly insectivorous, though they feed also on fruits and berries. As a rule they are fair songsters (they are classed with the *Oscines*, or song birds), although some species are distinguished for the oddity rather than the melody of their notes. The wing (which is typically "nine-primaried") is always longer than the tail, and the plumage is never streaked, barred, or spotted, even in the young. The bill is variable as to relative size, but never longer than the head (usually very much shorter, often less than half as long); and is also very variable as to relative length, depth, and breadth. The wing is variable but always longer than the tail, which is even, slightly rounded, double rounded, or notched, the feathers being rather narrow.

The coloration of the family is decidedly variable, plain olive, whitish, buffy or yellowish hues prevailing, sometimes with bright green and yellow, rarely with blue on the head; usually plain olive, olive-green, or gray above (sometimes relieved by whitish or yellowish wing bars), and plain whitish or yellowish beneath.

As far as known the nest is suspended from a forked branch, and is composed of fine vegetable fibers, mosses, lichens and the like. The eggs are white, usually spotted. The range of the family extends over temperate and tropical America, except the Galapagos Archipelago. The family is peculiar to America, but chiefly tropical, and is represented by about seventy known species, referable to eight genera.

The feeding habits of all the Vireos are similar. Insect food is gleaned from the foliage of shrubs and trees. Probably more span worms and leaf rollers are destroyed by the Vireos than by any other one group of birds. However, they do not confine themselves to these particular species of insects, but, if a plague of any other kind occurs within their range, they will eat the invaders greedily.

RED-EYED VIREO

Vireosylva olivacea (*Linnæus*)

A. O. U. Number 624 See Color Plate 91

Other Names.— The Preacher; Red-eyed Greenlet; Red-eye; Little Hang-nest; Preacher Bird.

General Description.— Length, 6½ inches. Upper parts, grayish-green; under parts, white.

Color.— ADULTS: *Crown, plain mouse-gray, margined on the sides by a narrow line of black or dusky;* rest of upper parts, plain grayish olive-green; *over the eye, a broad stripe of dull white or very pale brownish-*

gray; across the lores, a dusky gray streak, becoming darker at the front corner of eye, and back of the eye a less distinct streak of dusky; ear, under the eye, and cheek regions, pale olive or pale brownish-olive, passing into olive-greenish on sides of neck; under parts, white, the sides and flanks tinged with pale yellowish-olive, the under tail-coverts, tinged with sulphur-yellow; under wing-coverts, pale sulphur-yellow; bill, grayish-dusky or blackish; iris, brownish-red; legs and feet, grayish-blue. YOUNG (FIRST PLUMAGE): Crown, hindneck, back, shoulders, rump, upper tail-coverts, and lesser wing-coverts plain vinaceous brown, varying from pale brown to pale fawn color or deep écru-drab; greater wing-coverts edged and narrowly tipped with pale olive-yellow; under parts white, the under tail-coverts and flanks tinged with sulphur-yellow; sides of head white or brownish-white.

Nest and Eggs.— NEST: In forks of smaller or large trees, usually within 10 feet of ground but often much higher; a beautiful, pensile structure of finely woven vegetable fiber, strips of bark, grasses, and cobwebs and lined with fine grasses, ornamented exteriorly with cocoons, bits of wasps' and spiders' nests. EGGS: 3 to 5, white, sparingly speckled with reddish-brown and umber.

Distribution.— Temperate North America in general, except arid districts; north to Nova Scotia, Prince Edward Island, Keewatin, Saskatchewan, and southern Mackenzie; west to British Columbia (both sides of Cascade range), Washington, Colorado, Utah, etc.; breeding south over whole of wooded region east of Rocky Mountains as far south as Caloosahatchee River, southern Florida, and as far west as Tom Green county, western Texas; wintering from southern Florida to Bahamas, and through Mexico, Central America and South America, as far as Brazil.

If vocal persistence counts for anything, this Vireo should certainly be one of the very best known of our birds, for the male often sings almost incessantly throughout the day, with intervals of rarely more than a few seconds between phrases of his song. Indeed, the pause between the phrases is so brief that to some ears the effect has been that of a continuous song, like the really connected warble of the Robin. To be sure, the Vireo's iteration of its phrases does slightly suggest the Robin's carol, but close attention will reveal that after all they are separate utterances, and not parts of a complete song. Otherwise one would be forced to admit that the song frequently lasted almost literally from early morn to dewy eve. This amazing persistence has earned for the Red-eye from Wilson Flagg the nickname of "Preacher Bird."

The Red-eye's song (if indeed it can properly be called a song at all), usually consists in the ceaseless repetition of two-, three-, or four-note phrases, one of which is delivered with the declarative and the other with the inquiring inflection, as if the bird were saying over and over again, and rather petulantly, "Here I am! Here I am! Don't you see me? Don't you hear me? Here I am! Don't you see me?" and so on *ad infinitum.* Indeed, so anxious is he, apparently, to be both heard and seen, that occasionally he will sit still for several minutes at a time — a most unwarbler-like trick — and give himself entirely to the repetition of his announcement and inquiry, meanwhile facing first one way and then the other, as public speakers do in addressing a big audience out of doors.

The Red-eye is frequently selected by the female Cowbird as the victim upon whom may be imposed the parental responsibilities which she is too lazy to discharge. Mr. Job records a remarkable instance of this kind, in which he photographed several times a female Red-eye solicitously feeding two voracious young Cowbirds, after her own babies had evidently been smothered and thrown out of the nest by the pot-bellied interlopers.

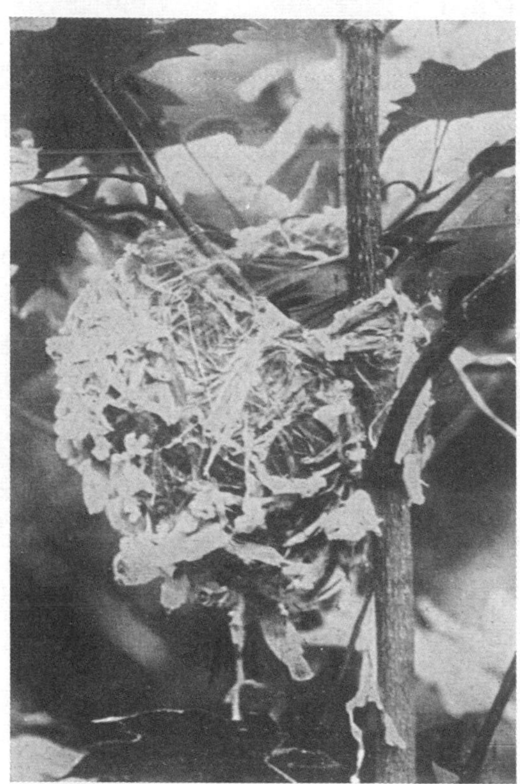

Photo by H. K. Job Courtesy of Outing Pub. Co.

RED-EYED VIREO ON ITS NEST

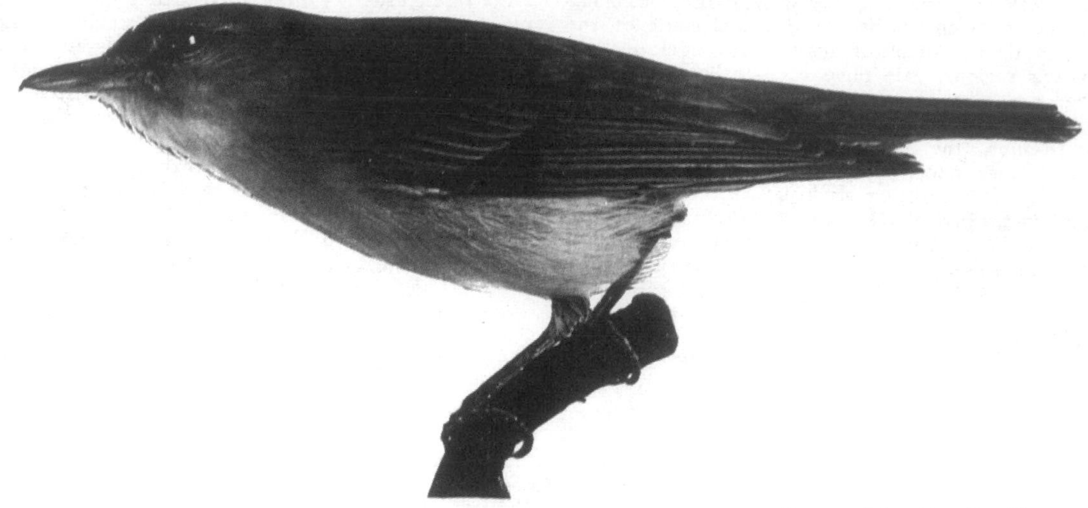

Courtesy of Am. Mus. Nat. Hist.

RED-EYED VIREO (nat. size)

He has the manners of a public speaker

PHILADELPHIA VIREO

Vireosylva philadelphica *Cassin*

A. O. U. Number 626 See Color Plate 91

Other Names.— Philadelphia Greenlet; Brotherly-love Vireo.

General Description.— Length, 5 inches. Upper parts, grayish-green; under parts, yellowish.

Color.— Crown, plain mouse-gray; hindneck, back, shoulders, rump, and upper tail-coverts, *plain grayish olive-green;* wings and tail, dark brownish-gray or hair-brown with light olive-greenish edgings, these broader and more grayish on greater wing-coverts; lesser and middle wing-coverts, olive-gray; a distinct stripe of dull whitish over the eye; a triangular mark of dusky-gray on the lores and a streak of the same color behind the eye; ear and cheek regions, pale olive, becoming paler (sometimes whitish) beneath eye; under parts, mostly dull sulphur or primrose-yellow, the chin and abdomen whitish, the yellow deepest on chest; under wing-coverts, pale primrose-yellow; bill, dark horn color; iris, brown; legs and feet, bluish-gray.

Nest and Eggs.— Nest: In fork of willow or other tree, like rest of the genus. Eggs: 4, similar in size and markings to Red-eyed Vireo.

Distribution.—Eastern North America; breeds from northern and central Alberta, northern Manitoba, northern Ontario, New Brunswick, and Maine to northern Michigan and New Hampshire; winters from Cozumel Island and Guatemala to Veragua.

In its habits, and especially in its characteristic song, the Philadelphia Vireo resembles his much commoner relative, the Red-eye, which, however, is much the more persistent singer of the two. Mr. Brewster notes that "the Philadelphia Vireo has, however, one note which seems to be peculiarly its own, a very abrupt, double-syllabled utterance with a rising inflection, which comes in with the general song at irregular but not infrequent intervals." The popular name "Brotherly-love Vireo" is, of course, in reference to the use of the name Philadelphia, rather than in recognition of any marked degree of brotherly love displayed by the bird. The bird was discovered by Cassin, near Philadelphia, who named it in honor of that city.

WARBLING VIREO

Vireosylva gilva gilva (*Vieillot*)

A. O. U. Number 627 See Color Plate 91

Other Name.— Warbling Greenlet.

General Description.— Length, 5½ inches. Upper parts, greenish-gray; under parts, whitish.

Color.— ADULTS: Crown and hindneck, plain light mouse-gray or smoke-gray, becoming paler on forehead; back, shoulders, and lesser wing-coverts similar in color to crown but tinged (usually very faintly) with olive-green; lower back, rump, and upper tail-coverts, light *grayish olive-green*, or smoke-gray tinged with olive-green; wings (except lesser coverts) and tail, deep brownish-gray with pale brownish-gray edgings; a stripe of dull grayish-white or brownish-white over the eye and extending considerably beyond it; sides of head and sides of neck, pale buffy-gray or pale buffy-brownish; under parts, dull white centrally, *passing into pale buffy-olive or dull pale buffy-yellowish on sides and flanks*; under wing-coverts, very pale primrose-yellow or yellowish-white; bill, horn-brown; iris, brown; legs and feet, pale bluish-gray. YOUNG (FIRST PLUMAGE): Crown and hindneck, plain pale grayish-buff; back, shoulders, lesser and middle wing-coverts, and rump, light buffy-grayish; wings and tail, as in adults, but greater wing-coverts indistinctly tipped with dull brownish-buff or pale buffy-olive; the stripe over the eye, whitish or buffy-whitish but very indistinct, the sides of the head of similar, passing into deeper grayish-buffy on upper part of ear region; under parts, white.

Nest and Eggs.— NEST: On slender, horizontal branches, usually high, sometimes in the extreme top of large elms or other shade trees; a double compact structure, lacking exterior ornamentation of other species, otherwise built of similar material. EGGS: Normally 4, rarely 5, spotted with sepia, umber, and reddish-brown.

Distribution.— Eastern temperate North America; north to Nova Scotia, central Ontario, northern Manitoba, and southeastern Alberta, west to North Dakota, southeastern Montana, South Dakota, Kansas, Oklahoma, and Texas; breeding from the northern limit of its range to the Gulf States (Florida to Texas); winter home unknown, but south of the United States.

The Warbling Vireo seems to be especially fond of tall shade trees growing along village streets, but as it works mainly in the tops of the elms, oaks, and maples, it is much less frequently seen than heard. The sign of its presence, far aloft, is a singularly smooth and running warble, composed of seven or eight notes and suggesting the song of the Purple Finch, than which, however, it is much less hurried and more legato in its execution. Of its general character, Mr. Mathews says: "Although, note for note, the first phrase of Chopin's wild but beautiful *Impromptu Fantasia* does not correspond with this Vireo's song, it cannot be denied that there is a striking similarity in the construction of the two fragments. Both bits of music roll triumphantly toward a high note in a sort of spontaneous ebullition of feeling, and there the matter ends — with the Vireo; but Chopin goes on, and his sprightly embroidery of tones is ultimately succeeded by the substantial form of a slow and dignified melody."

Though this Vireo is a very persistent singer (Ralph Hoffmann estimates that he repeats his song more than four thousand times a day during the breeding season), there is remarkably little variation in the form and accent of the phrase. Almost invariably it is the same rippling run, delivered with the strongly marked crescendo which Mr. Mathews describes.

In western North America there is a smaller and darker form of this bird, known as the Western, or Swainson's, Warbling Vireo (*Vireosylva gilva swainsoni*).

YELLOW-THROATED VIREO

Lanivireo flavifrons (*Vieillot*)

A. O. U. Number 628 See Color Plate 91

Other Name.— Yellow-throated Greenlet.

General Description.— Length, 6 inches. Upper parts, yellowish-olive and gray; under parts, yellow and white.

Color.— ADULTS: Crown, hindneck, and back, plain *yellowish-olive;* sides of neck, ear and cheek regions, and sides of chest, plain yellowish olive-green; a stripe over the eye and a spot under it, front portion of cheek region, chin, throat, chest, and breast, *canary yellow*; abdomen, anal region, and under tail coverts, white; flanks, pale grayish; under wing-coverts, white tinged with yellow; lesser wing-coverts, shoulders, lower back, rump, and upper tail-coverts, plain slate-gray; wings (except lesser coverts) and tail, black; middle and greater wing-coverts (except innermost), broadly tipped with white, forming two conspicuous bands; inner wing quills broadly edged with white (this sometimes tinged with yellow); bill, grayish-black; iris, brown; legs and feet, light grayish-blue. YOUNG: Crown, hindneck, back, shoulders, lesser wing-coverts, rump, and upper tail-coverts, plain soft brownish-gray; line above the lores, eye ring, chin, throat, and chest, very pale yellow, shading into deeper yellow on cheek and under eye regions, and on lower portion of ear region; rest of under parts, white; wing-quills, tail-feathers, and larger wing-coverts as in adults, but edgings of secondaries, pale yellow.

Nest and Eggs.— NEST: Pensile, in fork of deciduous tree from 5 to 30 feet up, in secluded woods; constructed of narrow bark strips and grass compactly woven and artistically decorated with cocoons, spiders' nests, and lichens firmly tied on with spiderwebs. EGGS: 3 to 5, usually 4, pinkish-white, more heavily marked than rest of genus, with umber-brown, sepia, and chestnut.

Distribution.— Eastern United States and southern British Provinces; north to Maine, Vermont, northern New York, southern Ontario, southern Quebec, and southern Manitoba west to edge of Great Plains; breeding south to Gulf coast, from northern Florida to southern Texas; in winter from southern Florida and Cuba southward through eastern Mexico and Central America to Colombia; casual in winter in Cuba and Bahamas.

Like the Warbling Vireo, the Yellow-throated species is essentially a tree-top bird, but probably it is much the more frequently seen of the two, for the reason that its plumage includes quite strong color contrasts, while the Warbling species' colors are comparatively inconspicuous. Also like that species, this bird frequently builds in shade trees, and from their topmost branches sends down its characteristic and frequently repeated song, which somewhat resembles that of the Red-eyed member of the family. A commonly expressed distinction between the two utterances is that the quality of the Red-eye's voice is soprano, while that of the Yellow-throat is contralto; but Mr. Mathews defines the difference more accurately by this analysis: "It is nearer the truth to say, rather, that the Yellow-throat has a violin quality to his voice, or better, a reedlike quality; Bradford Torrey calls it an 'organ tone.' At any rate there is no clear whistle to this Vireo's music, and on the contrary there is to the Red-eye's music. That is the whole matter in a nut-shell! For the rest I may add that the Yellow-throat's tempo is much slower and that he does not indulge in such an interminable amount of singing!"

Photo by A. A. Allen

YELLOW-THROATED VIREO

Incubating twenty-five feet from the ground in a chestnut tree

E. H. Eaton records having found this Warbler nesting in Central Park, New York city, and also in shade trees in Rochester, Medina, Canandaigua, and Buffalo, and adds this further interesting observation: "I have found that in some localities where it was common years ago it has disappeared, and made its appearance in other localities where it was formerly unknown. This shifting of its centers of abundance is difficult to explain, but I have noticed in certain small parks and about many groves and on certain streets where it has been carefully watched, this species has disappeared the next season after it was unsuccessful in rearing its young, due to its having been parasitized by the Cowbird. Probably this cause and other unfavorable circumstances, like the destruction of its brood by Screech Owls or unfavorable weather conditions. left no descendants to repeople the accustomed grove."

BLUE-HEADED VIREO

Lanivireo solitarius solitarius (*Wilson*)

A. O. U. Number 629 See Color Plate 91

Other Names.— Solitary Vireo; Blue-headed Greenlet.

General Description.— Length, 5¼ inches. Fore parts, slate; upper parts, olive-green; under parts, white.

Color.— Adults: *Crown, hindneck, sides of neck, regions around the ears and under the eyes, and cheeks, slate-color or deep slate-gray,* deepening into slate-blackish on back portion of lores; front and upper portions of lores and broad eye-ring (interrupted in the front by blackish loral mark), white; back, shoulders, rump, and upper tail-coverts, plain olive-green, the first usually intermixed with slate-gray; wings and tail, slate-blackish with light olive-green edgings, the outermost tail-feathers with outer web, white; middle and greater wing-coverts, broadly tipped with yellowish-white or pale sulphur-yellow, forming two distinct bands; wing-quills with outer webs broadly edged with yellowish-white or pale sulphur-yellow; chin, throat, and middle under parts of body, white; sides and flanks, mixed sulphur-yellow and olive-greenish, in broad, ill-defined stripes; under tail-coverts, pale sulphur-yellow, yellowish-white, or white faintly tinged with yellow; under wing-coverts pale sulphur-yellow; inner webs of wing- and tail-feathers edged with white; bill, black; iris, deep brown; legs and feet, grayish-blue. Young: Similar to adults but duller in color, with gray of head much tinged with brown, olive-green of back, browner, and white of under parts less pure.

Nest and Eggs.— Nest: Pendant, in terminal forks of horizontal branches within 10 feet of ground; constructed of bark strips, leaves, weed stems, and caterpillar cocoons and firmly fastened with vegetable-strings and hair and lined with fine grasses. Eggs: 3 to 5, white or creamy, spotted with umber and chestnut, chiefly around large end.

Distribution.— Eastern North America; north to Prince Edward Island, Keewatin, Athabasca, and southern Mackenzie; west to border of the Great Plains; breeding southward to Connecticut, Pennsylvania, and North Dakota; wintering in the Gulf States, Cuba, and southward through eastern Mexico to Guatemala.

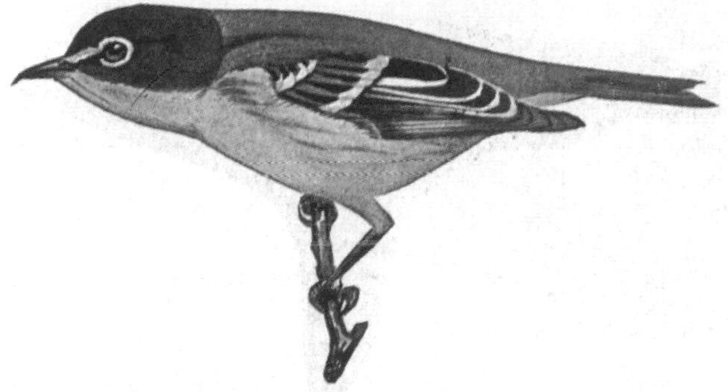

Drawing by R. I. Brasher

BLUE-HEADED VIREO (½ nat. size)

Early to arrive in the spring and often remarkably tame

He whose ears are attuned to the harmonies of nature may find the Blue-headed or Solitary Vireo on warm April days or in early May in the wooded regions of most of the northeastern States. It may be recognized by its bluish head, the white ring around the eye, and the pure white throat. It heralds its presence at this time by its wild sweet song, a charming cadence of the wooded wilderness. Its notes seem more spiritual and less commonplace than those of the familiar Vireos of village and farmstead.

The bird itself is no more solitary in migration than other Vireos, although it is not numerous or gregarious, but in the nesting season it seeks the cool and grateful shade of pine or hemlock trees. It does not avoid mankind but dwells near him only when he lives in its favorite forest retreats. Like some other species it has proved so confiding at times as to allow a person to stroke its back as it sat on its beautiful pensile nest.

This Vireo is one of the conservators of the forest — a caterpillar hunter of renown — one of a number of arboreal birds which guard the trees against the too destructive attacks of quickly multiplying scaly-winged hosts.

EDWARD HOWE FORBUSH.

There are in North America four regional varieties of the Blue-headed Vireo. The Mountain, or Mountain Solitary, Vireo (*Lanivireo solitarius alticola*) is larger and slightly darker in coloration, with the back more often mixed with gray and sometimes with more gray than olive-green; it breeds in the Alleghenies from western Maryland to eastern Tennessee and northern Georgia and winters in the lowlands from South Carolina to Florida. The Plumbeous Vireo (*Lanivireo solitarius plumbeus*) of the southern Rocky Mountain Region is very similar to the Mountain Vireo, but its back and shoulders are entirely gray, the rump and upper tail-coverts gray, tinged with olive-green and its sides and flanks are much more faintly washed with yellow; it breeds from northern Nevada, northern Utah, northeastern Wyoming and southwestern South Dakota south through Arizona and southwestern Texas to the mountains of Mexico. Cassin's Vireo (*Lanivireo solitarius cassini*) is much like the Blue-headed Vireo but averages slightly smaller and much duller in color; it breeds from central British Columbia, southwestern Alberta, and western Montana south through California and western Nevada to the San Pedro Martir Mountains, Lower California; in migration it is found in Utah, Arizona, Colorado, and New Mexico, and in winter in Mexico. The San Lucas, or San Lucas Solitary, Vireo (*Lanivireo solitarius lucasanus*) is like Cassin's Vireo but smaller and with decidedly larger bill and with more yellow and less olive on the sides and flanks; it is a resident of the Cape San Lucas region of Lower California.

Photo by J. Alden Loring

BLUE-HEADED VIREO

This bird is one of the conservators of the forest

BLACK-CAPPED VIREO

Vireo atricapillus *Woodhouse*

A. O. U. Number 630

Other Name.— Black-capped Greenlet.

General Description.— Length, 4¾ inches. Fore parts, black; upper parts, olive-green; under parts, white.

Color.— Lores and a broad eye-ring, white, the latter interrupted on upper eyelid; *rest of head and neck, except chin and throat, uniform black* (oldest birds?) or black and slate-gray (younger birds?); back, shoulders, rump, upper tail-coverts, and lesser wing-coverts, clear olive-green; wings (except lesser coverts) and tail, dull black or dusky with light olive-green edgings; the middle and greater wing-coverts broadly tipped with pale yellow, forming two conspicuous bands across wing; under parts, including chin and throat, white, passing into light olive-yellow or pale yellowish olive-green on sides and flanks; under wing-coverts sulphur or primrose-yellow; bill, black; iris, brownish-red; legs and feet, grayish-blue.

Nest and Eggs.— NEST: Usually suspended from forks of elm, oak, or mesquite saplings, within 6 feet of the ground; a perfectly woven structure of bark strips, grasses, skeleton leaves, spiders' webs, and caterpillar silk. EGGS: 3 to 4, pure white, unmarked.

Distribution.— Southwestern Kansas southward through Oklahoma and west-central Texas; southward in winter to Mexico, as far as State of Sinaloa.

Vireos are likely to be rather deliberate birds in comparison with the Warblers, but the Black-capped Vireo is decidedly energetic in its movements. Furthermore it is the single American member of its family with the head down to the throat black, except for the small white triangular patch running from the eye to the angle of the bill and the forehead.

The bird seems to have been first described in 1851 by Dr. Woodhouse, who took his specimen near the San Pedro River, 208 miles from San Antonio, and later by John J. Clark, naturalist of the Mexican Boundary Commission, who found it in Mexico near the locality in which it was seen by Dr. Woodhouse. Both observers had their attention attracted to the bird by its sharp and unmusical chirp. Its song, Mrs. Bailey says, is unusually varied for a Vireo, though of the general character of those of the White-eyed and Bell's Vireos, rather than that of the Warbling Vireo. "One song contained a run, and its last notes were liquid, loud, and emphatic."

WHITE-EYED VIREO

Vireo griseus griseus (*Boddaert*)

A. O. U. Number 631 See Color Plate 91

Other Names.— White-eyed Greenlet; Politician.

General Description.— Length, 5¼ inches. Upper parts, greenish-olive; under parts, white.

Color.— ADULTS: Above, plain greenish-olive or dull olive-green, usually passing into grayish on hindneck; wings and tail, dusky grayish-brown with light olive-green edgings, the middle and greater wing-coverts rather broadly tipped with pale yellow or yellowish-white, producing two distinct bands across wing; *a stripe above the lores and a narrow eye-ring of canary or sulphur-yellow; a dusky stripe across the lores;* ear and under eye regions and sides of neck, grayish-olive or olive-gray; chin, throat, central portion of chest and breast, abdomen, and under tail-coverts, dull white, passing into *pale yellow washed with olive, on sides and flanks,* the chest and breast tinged with yellow or grayish (or both), the anal region and shorter under tail-coverts also tinged with yellow; under wing-coverts pale yellow or yellowish-white; bill, black; iris, white; legs and feet, grayish-blue. YOUNG: Similar to adults, but upper parts, duller and browner; the stripe above the lores and the eye-ring, grayish-white or brownish-white instead of yellow; chin, throat, and chest, very pale gray or brownish-gray; sides and flanks, pale olive-yellow; iris, brownish (hazel).

Nest and Eggs.— NEST: In low bush, rarely more than 4 feet up, pensile; constructed of grass and bark strips and decorated exteriorly with brown or white spiders' nests, bits of rotten wood, or newspaper and rags and lined with fine grass and some hair. EGGS: 3 to 5, white, lightly spotted with dark purple and chestnut around large end.

Distribution.— Eastern United States; breeds from southeastern Nebraska, southern Wisconsin, New York, and Massachusetts to central Texas and central Florida; winters from Texas, Georgia, Florida, and South Carolina through eastern Mexico to Yucatan and Guatemala; casual north to Vermont, Ontario, and New Brunswick, and in Cuba.

Drawing by R. I. Brasher

WHITE-EYED VIREO (⅔ nat. size)

A voluble little fellow who gives intruders a piece of his mind

---

The White-eyed Vireo is one of the distinct characters of bird-land — pert, abusive, and sarcastic by turns, but always clever and amusing. *Chip-a-wee-o,* Mr. Torrey very accurately transliterated his characteristic and contemptuous salutation as you approach his thicket, and *Whip Tom Kelly* is a word-equivalent which Alexander Wilson found in use in the South —

though this injunction seems a much closer rendition of the Chewink's phrase. "Who are *you*, now?" the bird demanded of Mr. Torrey; and to others he has shouted: "Get out! Beat it!" almost as plainly and peremptorily as a New York policeman says "Gwan" to the corner-loafer.

Photo by H. K. Job Courtesy of Outing Pub. Co.

WHITE-EYED VIREO FEEDING YOUNG

Not even the loquacious Yellow-breasted Chat has so sharp a tongue. Indeed, the Chat is, after all, essentially a clown and a nonsense-vendor, while the White-eye is tart and severe and decidedly inclined to be expostulatory and dictatorial. As Mr. Torrey says: "This Vireo is the very prince of stump-speakers — fluent, loud, and sarcastic — and is well called the politician, though it is a disappointment to learn that the title was given him not for his eloquence, but on account of his habit of putting pieces of newspaper into his nest."

Two regional varieties of the White-eyed Vireo are found within the boundaries of the United States. The Key West, or Maynard's, Vireo (*Vireo griseus maynardi*) is larger, the upper parts average grayer, sometimes with more gray than greenish-olive, and the yellow of sides and flanks averages much paler, sometimes consisting of a mere tinge or wash of pale olive-yellow; it is found in the Florida Keys and the coast district of Florida. The Small White-eyed Vireo (*Vireo griseus micrus*) is similar in color to the Key West Vireo but is even smaller than the White-eyed Vireo; it is found in the Rio Grande valley of Texas and northeastern Mexico.

BELL'S VIREO

Vireo belli belli *Audubon*

A. O. U. Number 633

Other Name.— Bell's Greenlet.

General Description.— Length, 5¼ inches. Upper parts, olive-green; under parts, whitish.

Color.—Adults: Crown and hindneck, dull grayish-brown, sometimes tinged with olive; rest of upper parts, dull olive-green or greenish-olive; wings and tail, deep grayish-brown with paler edgings; middle and greater wing-coverts (except the innermost) tipped with dull whitish, forming two bands; a narrow eye-ring and a streak above the lores of dull white; ear and under eye regions, pale grayish-brown or brownish-gray; a dusky mark at front corner of eyes; central under parts dull white tinged with buffy-yellowish, especially on chest, the sides and flanks light olive-yellow; under tail-coverts, pale sulphur-yellow; under wing-coverts yellowish-white; bill, horn-brown; iris, brown; legs and feet, bluish-gray. Young: Much like adults, but crown and hindneck, soft drab; back and shoulders, dark drab; under parts nearly pure white with sides, flanks, and under tail-coverts tinged with sulphur-yellow, and wing-bands more distinct.

Nest and Eggs.— Nest: A neat, smoothly built structure of bark strips, plant fibers, and leaves and lined with fine grass, down, rootlets, and hair; suspended by brim from forks of small trees or bushes. Eggs: Commonly 4, though rarely sets of 8 are found; white, thinly spotted with brown around large end.

Distribution.— Prairie districts of Mississippi valley, from South Dakota, southern Minnesota, Iowa, northern Illinois, and northwestern Indiana southward to eastern Texas and Tamaulipas; in winter southward over greater part of Mexico and Guatemala; accidental in Massachusetts and New Hampshire.

In its normal range, which is very wide, Bell's Vireo is quite common. It seems to be especially fond of dense patches of brush and briers, and hedge-fences. In its habits, and especially in its song, it resembles the White-eyed Vireo more than any other member of its family. Dr. Coues thought that some of its notes were like those of the Bluebird in the spring, though more hurriedly delivered. Mr. Ridgway likened the song to that of the White-eye, but considered the utterance more sputtering and in that respect similar to that of the House Wren.

The Texas Vireo (*Vireo belli medius*) is found in southwestern Texas and south into central Mexico; it is paler in coloration than its type species, Bell's Vireo, and its tail is relatively longer, its crown and hindneck are brownish-gray instead of grayish-brown, the olive of its upper parts, grayer, and its under parts, whiter.

The Least Vireo (*Vireo belli pusillus*) is a plain grayish little bird of the willows and thickets in central California, southwestern Nevada, and western Texas south to northern Lower California and the valley of Mexico. It is even paler and grayer than the Texas Vireo.

Another species of the Vireo family is the Gray Vireo (*Vireo vicinior*). It is very much like the Least Vireo but the wing-bars are missing. It is also very similar to the Plumbeous Vireo but its coloration is duller and lacks the sharp contrasts of the Plumbeous. The Gray Vireo makes its home in southern California, southern Nevada, the Grand Cañon of the Colorado, and southeastern Colorado south to Lower California, Sonora, and Durango.

WARBLERS

Order *Passeres;* suborder *Oscines;* family *Mniotiltidæ*

WARBLERS are essentially — most of them strictly — insectivorous birds of active habits. Most of them are arboreal, nesting and feeding among the trees and rarely descending to the ground; some are terrestrial, living much upon or near the ground, where they walk in the graceful "mincing" manner of a Wagtail or Pipit, meanwhile tilting the body, as if upon a pivot, and oscillating the tail in the same characteristic manner. Most of them are expert flycatchers. Others creep about the trunks and branches of trees as nimbly as a Nuthatch. The majority of them combine, in various degrees, these several habits.

As a rule the Warblers are birds of beautiful plumage, though their attractiveness in this respect consists in the tasteful arrangement or "pattern" of the colors rather than in their brilliancy. Yellow is the most common and characteristic hue, though this is usually relieved by markings or areas of black, gray, olive-green, or white, usually by two or more of these colors; red is not infrequent, grayish-blue less common; while pure blue, green, and purple are never present, and the plumage is never glossy. There is generally a sexual difference of plumage, and very often the young are different from either adult.

Many of the Warblers have attractive songs; but perhaps the majority, at least among the North American species, are songsters of very ordinary or inferior merit.

The group of Warblers is peculiar to America, where it is the second largest family. It represents the *Sylviidæ* and *Muscicapidæ* of the eastern hemisphere. Over 150 species and subspecies belonging to 21 genera are recognized. It contains a larger proportion of one-type species than most families of song-birds, nearly one-half of the genera being each represented by but a single known species.

There is probably no finer tribute to the beneficial character of these birds than that of Dr. Elliott Coues, who said: "With tireless industry do the Warblers befriend the human race; their unconscious zeal plays due part in the nice adjustment of Nature's forces, helping to bring about the balance of vegetable and insect life, without which agriculture would be in vain. They visit the orchard when the apple and pear, the peach, plum, and cherry are in bloom, seeming to revel carelessly amid the sweet-scented and delicately-tinted blossoms, but never faltering in their good work. They peer into the crevices of the bark, scrutinize each leaf, and explore the very heart of the buds, to detect, drag forth, and destroy these tiny creatures, singly insignificant, collectively a scourge, which prey upon the hopes of the fruit-grower and which, if undisturbed, would bring his care to naught. Some Warblers flit incessantly in the terminal foliage of the tallest trees; others hug close to the scored trunks and gnarled boughs of the forest kings; some peep from the thicket, the coppice, the impenetrable mantle of shrubbery that decks tiny watercourses, playing at hide-and-seek with all comers; others more humble still descend to the ground, where they glide with pretty, mincing steps and affected turning of the head this way and that, their delicate flesh-tinted feet just stirring the layer of withered leaves with which a past season carpeted the ground."

BLACK AND WHITE WARBLER

Mniotilta varia (*Linnæus*)

A. O. U. Number 636 See Color Plate 92

Other Names.— Black and White Creeper; Blue and White Striped or Pied Creeper; Black and White Creeping Warbler; Creeping Warbler; Striped Warbler; Varied Creeping Warbler; Whitepoll Warbler.

General Description.— Length, 5½ inches. Plumage, black and white in stripes. Bill, shorter than head and very slender; wings, long and pointed; tail, even or very slightly forked, the feathers rather narrow.

Color.—Adult Male: Crown with a broad center stripe of white and two still broader lateral stripes of black, slightly glossed with blue; *rest of upper parts* (except wing- and tail-feathers), *slightly glossy blue-black, the back and shoulders streaked with white*, middle and greater wing-coverts, broadly tipped with white (forming two conspicuous bands), and inner wing-quills, broadly edged with white; secondaries and primaries, grayish black narrowly edged with gray; middle tail-feathers, black centrally, gray laterally, the gray broader; other tail-feathers, grayish-black narrowly edged with gray, the two outermost with a large space of white on inner web, and all with inner webs edged with white; eye-ring and a broad stripe above the eyes, white; below this an elongated patch of slightly glossy blue-black covering lores and sides of head; a broad white cheek stripe; under parts, mainly white, but throat usually black; sides, from chest to flanks, inclusive, broadly streaked or striped with blue-black; under tail-coverts, black centrally, broadly margined with white; bill, black; iris, brown; legs and feet, dusky horn color. Adult Female: Smaller and much duller in color, the white everywhere more or less tinged with buffy-brownish; the throat, white; the lores, wholly pale grayish; the sides of head pale buffy-grayish margined above by a narrow streak behind eye of black; streaks of sides much less distinct, becoming grayish on sides of chest; and flanks strongly tinged with brownish-buff; bill, black.

Nest and Eggs.—Nest: On ground at foot of tree, bush, stump, or rock, among upturned roots or alongside a log; rather bulky; constructed of dead leaves, strips of bark, grasses, weed stems, lined with hair; sometimes partly roofed, in half-hearted imitation of the Oven-bird's home. Eggs: Normally 5, white or creamy speckled and spotted all over with brown and chestnut, the markings usually collecting in wreath formation around large end.

Distribution.— Eastern North America, north to upper Mackenzie valley, Hudson Bay, breeding southward to Virginia, Tennessee, Louisiana, Texas, (probably to upper sections of other Gulf States); wintering from the Gulf States southward throughout the West Indies, Mexico, and Central America to Colombia and Venezuela; accidental in California and in the Bermudas.

Bird-names of popular origin often reveal queer misapprehensions as to the birds concerned, but the name "Black and White Creeper," by which this bird has commonly been known, has the advantage of being accurately descriptive. For the bird certainly is black and white; and furthermore it creeps about on the tree trunks and branches with even more celerity and skill

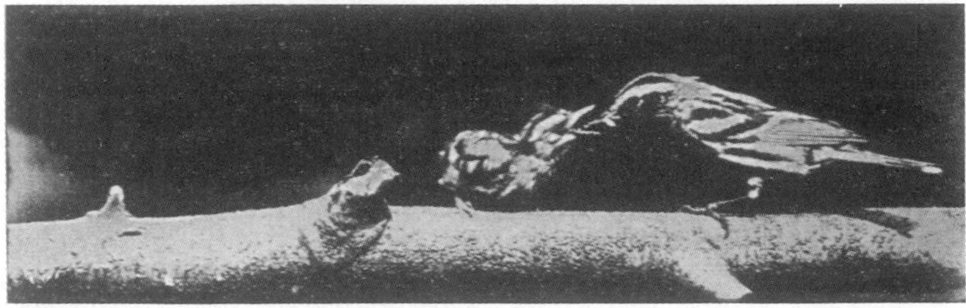

Photo by H. K. Job

MALE BLACK AND WHITE WARBLER FEEDING YOUNG

than is shown by the Brown Creeper, for example. That bird does not attempt to come down a tree trunk head foremost, nor to circle a horizontal limb, feats which are managed with Nuthatch-like ease by the Black and White Warbler. Altogether the Warbler is a much better " creeper " than the Creeper is. However, for reasons which doubtless seem good and sufficient to them, the ornithologists have seen fit to eliminate from the bird's name the term which describes its most characteristic habit, and the inclusion of which certainly would have been of much assistance in identifying the species.

The literal translation of its scientific name, is very appropriate: *Mniotilta* means moss-plucking and refers to its habit of searching in the moss on trees for its insect food; *varia* is variegated and, of course, has reference to the striped effect of its coloration.

The terms " wiry " and " thin " are usually employed in describing this bird's songs, and are perhaps as descriptive as any that could be used. One song consists of eight or ten notes of the same pitch and tone uttered in closely connected couplets, the syllables being like *szee* and *wwee*. The other, which is less frequently heard, though it is longer than the one first mentioned, has about the same beginning, but shows more variation in its development, while the tone, a sort of lisping whistle, is mellower and more musical. About the most that can truthfully be said of these utterances is that the bird seems to have made the best use of a feeble and none too musical instrument.

PROTHONOTARY WARBLER

Protonotaria citrea (*Boddaert*)

A. O. U. Number 637 See Color Plate 92

Other Names.— Golden Warbler; Golden Swamp Warbler; Willow Warbler.

General Description.— Length, 5½ inches. Fore and under parts, yellow; upper parts, yellowish olive-green. Bill, shorter than head, wedge-shaped; wing, rather long and with long pointed tip; tail, slightly rounded.

Color.— Adult Male: *Head, neck, and under parts (except under tail-coverts), rich yellow,* the head sometimes tinged or flecked with cadmium orange; back and shoulders, plain yellowish olive-green, this sometimes extending forward over hindneck and back of head; rump, upper tail-coverts, wing-coverts, and inner wing-feathers, plain gray; secondaries, primaries, and tail-feathers, black, edged with slate-gray, the inner webs of tail-feathers (except middle pair), white tipped with blackish; under tail-coverts, white; under wing-coverts, white, tinged with yellow; inner webs of wing-feathers, edged with white; bill, black in summer, lighter colored in winter; iris, brown; legs and feet, dusky. Adult Female: Similar to the male, but smaller and much duller in color; olive-green of back extended forward over hindneck and crown; yellow of under parts, less intense, tinged with olive, and becoming much paler on abdomen and flanks, the latter strongly tinged with olive; bill, dusky in summer, lighter colored in winter.

Nest and Eggs.—Nest: Usually in deserted hole of a Downy Woodpecker or Chickadee, otherwise in almost any cavity or hole, from 2 to 15 feet up (averaging about 5) and almost always in a stump standing or leaning over water; carefully and thickly lined with moss. Eggs: 5 to 7, commonly 6, varying from creamy-white to buffy-white, glossy, heavily blotched with rich chestnut, lavender, and purple.

Distribution.— More southern portions of eastern United States, breeding from Gulf States (northern Florida to eastern Texas), north to Virginia, southern Ohio, Indiana, southern Michigan, northeastern Illinois, Iowa, southeastern Minnesota, eastern Nebraska, etc., occasionally northward to Massachusetts, southeastern New York, Ontario, and Wisconsin, casually to Maine and New Brunswick; south in winter to Cuba and through eastern Mexico and Central America to Colombia, Venezuela, and Trinidad.

The Prothonotary Warbler is a southern Warbler whose range does not extend as far as Canada. It is common in the Ohio valley and in the Carolinas and on down in the bottom lands of the Mississippi and the rivers that flow into the Gulf of Mexico. But everywhere it must have its home by running water and generally in the willows. It prefers those districts which suffer from spring floods. This has given it the names of the Golden Swamp Warbler and Willow Warbler. There is no use looking for the bird away from a stream or swamp. It does not stray away. With its sweet and penetrating *peet, tweet, tweet, tweet* or *sweet, sweet, sweet, sweet,* it tells the traveler that water is near. When the bird is found he is generally industriously going over and over the area he has chosen, feeding up and down among the bushes and trees and never very far from the nest.

The nesting site is very likely to be an old Woodpecker hole but often a ledge or crotch serves as well. When the hole is deep it is filled to within a few inches of the top, generally with green moss, but with more shallow places the nest building is a much less laborious task.

The bird is rarely seen in the migrating Warbler flocks, for most of these flocks are off for far northern climes. The Prothonotary on the other hand has a special taste for more southern streams and swamp lands.

SWAINSON'S WARBLER

Helinaia swainsoni (*Audubon*)

A. O. U. Number 638

General Description.— Length, 6 inches. Upper parts, olive; under parts, yellowish. Bill, nearly as long as head, narrow, wedge-shaped; wings, moderately long and rather pointed; tail, slightly forked or double rounded, the feathers broad.

Color.—Adults (sexes alike): Crown, plain brown, sometimes with an indistinct center streak of paler, or an indication of one; back, shoulders, rump, upper tail-coverts, and wing-coverts, plain olive; inner wing-quills, warmer brown; secondaries and primaries, dusky edged with light brown or olive; tail, plain olive brown; a narrow stripe over eye of light yellowish-buff; a triangular spot of dusky in front of eye; a streak behind eye of brownish; sides of head otherwise, pale buffy-brownish; under parts, pale dull yellowish, shaded with olive-grayish laterally; bill, light brownish; iris, brown; legs and feet, pale flesh color.

Nest and Eggs.—Nest: Usually built among canes, sometimes in small bushes, from three to ten feet above the ground; generally in swampy locations but sometimes on high land some distance from water, and is a remarkably large affair of water-soaked sweet gum, water oak, pepperidge or holly leaves, lined with fine pine needles and moss. Eggs: 3, rarely 4, plain dull white, creamy or bluish-white, without markings.

Distribution.—Southeastern United States; breeds from southeastern Missouri, southern Illinois, southern Indiana, and southeastern Virginia south to Louisiana and northern Florida; winters in Jamaica; migrates through Cuba and the Bahamas; casual in Nebraska, Texas, and Vera Cruz.

Drawing by R. I. Brasher

SWAINSON'S WARBLER ($\frac{7}{8}$ nat. size)

A strange, rare, southern bird

Swainson's Warbler is a strange, rare, southern bird. He is so strange that one hardly expects to call such a plain brown and white bird gliding so gracefully along under the bushes a Warbler. He is so rare that one may search for days and not find him. Even in the South, one has to confine one's search for him to the coastal swamps from the Dismal Swamp of Virginia down through the "pineland gall" of the Carolinas, west in the vine-tangled semitropical verdure of the Gulf coast and up the Mississippi and some of its tributaries in the thickets of the bottom lands.

In describing the song, Mr. William Brewster says it is "a performance so remarkable that it can scarcely fail to attract the dullest ear, while it is not likely to be soon forgotten. It consists of a series of clear, ringing whistles, the first four uttered rather slowly and in the same key, the remaining five or six given more rapidly, and in an evenly descending scale, like those of the Cañon Wren. . . . In general effect it recalls the song of the Water-thrush. . . . It is very loud, very rich, very beautiful, while it has an indescribably tender quality that thrills the senses after the sound has ceased. . . . Although a rarely fervent and ecstatic songster, our little friend is also a fitful and uncertain one. You may wait for hours near his retreat even in early morning or late afternoon, without hearing a note. But when the inspiration comes he floods the woods with music, one song often following another so quickly that there is scarce a pause for breath between."

WORM-EATING WARBLER

Helmitheros vermivorus (*Gmelin*)

A. O. U. Number 639 See Color Plate 92

Other Names. Worm-eater; Worm-eating Swamp Warbler.

General Description.— Length, 5½ inches. Upper parts, grayish olive-green; under parts, buffy. Bill, decidedly shorter than head, wedge-shaped; wings, rather long and pointed; tail, even or very slightly rounded, the feathers moderately broad.

Color.—Adults (sexes alike): *Crown with two broad lateral stripes of black and a center one of olive-buff;* rest of upper parts, plain grayish olive-green; a broad stripe over eye of pale buff, margined beneath by a rather broad streak of black behind eye; a triangular spot of the same, or dusky grayish, in front of eye; sides of head below this black line, with entire under parts, pale dull buffy, deepest on chest, paler on throat and abdomen (the latter sometimes nearly white), tinged with grayish-olive on flanks; under tail-coverts, pale olive-grayish, edged and broadly tipped with pale yellowish-buff; bill, brown; iris, brown; legs and feet, pale brownish flesh color.

Nest and Eggs.— Nest: On the ground, generally on a woody hillside; constructed of dead leaves and

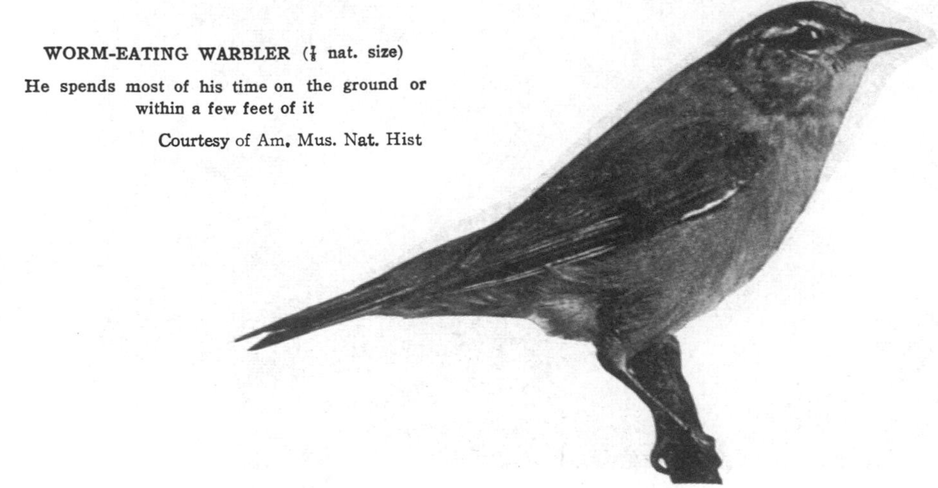

WORM-EATING WARBLER (½ nat. size)

He spends most of his time on the ground or within a few feet of it

Courtesy of Am. Mus. Nat. Hist

nearly always lined with red flower-stalks of hair moss. EGGS: 3 to 6, usually 4, white thinly or thickly marked with spots and blotches of Indian red, lavender, and chestnut sometimes wreathed but more often evenly distributed.

Distribution.— Eastern United States, more common southerly, breeding northward to southern Connecticut, southeastern New York (lower Hudson valley), Pennsylvania, southern Wisconsin (vicinity of Racine), etc., occasional in Massachusetts; in migration casually to Massachusetts, Vermont, western New York, southern Ontario, and southern Wisconsin; winters south to Bahamas, Cuba, Jamaica, and through eastern Mexico and Central America to Panama.

The Worm-eating Warbler is distinctly a ground Warbler, a very differently acting bird from most of the Warbler family. Most of them are rather excitable, nervous birds of the tree-tops. The Worm-eater is a quiet bird that spends most of his time on the ground or within a few feet of it, walking, not running; and sometimes creeping along a tree trunk like the Brown Creeper or the Black and White Warbler. On the ground this bird is rather cocky-acting, stepping along deliberately under the huckleberry bushes or other dense undergrowth, with his tail slightly raised. He has a smart and jaunty air and also a shy disposition that reminds one of a Thrush at his sprightliest.

The Worm-eating Warbler is not so rare as it has been credited. Where bird students have given time to search his haunts, he has been found fairly common as far north as southern New England, southern Michigan, and Nebraska. But the search for him has to be made in ravines and on dry forested hillsides where the undergrowth makes a convenient nesting site. This bird loves his home locality. It has been frequently observed how year after year the birds will come back to the same thicket, building their new nest within sight of the old ones.

Its ordinary song is a weak affair, closely resembling that of the Chipping Sparrow, but Mr. Burroughs says: "The bird has a flight song, uttered near sundown, nearly as brilliant as that of the Oven-bird." (MS.) The call is a sharp *dzt,* and he who watches closely and silently in the tangle when it is heard may be rewarded by a sight of this bird with the buff and black striped head.

BLUE-WINGED WARBLER

Vermivora pinus (*Linnæus*).

A. O. U. Number 641 See Color Plate 93

Other Names.—Blue-Winged Yellow Warbler; Blue-Winged Swamp Warbler.

General Description.— Length, 4¾ inches. Upper parts, olive-green; under parts, lemon-yellow. Bill, shorter than head, narrowly wedge-shaped, the tip very acute; wings, moderately long; tail, about ¾ length of wing, even or nearly even, the feathers narrow.

Color.— ADULT MALE: *Forehead and crown, bright lemon yellow; back of head, hindneck, back, shoulders, rump, and upper tail-coverts, bright olive-green,* more

Photo by H. K. Job Courtesy of Outing Pub. Co.

BLUE-WINGED WARBLER FEEDING YOUNG

yellowish on rump, the upper tail-coverts tinged with gray; wing-coverts and inner wing-feathers, gray, the middle and greater coverts usually tipped with *white, forming two bands*; secondaries and primaries, dusky edged with gray, their inner webs broadly edged with white; tail, gray, the three outermost feathers with inner webs, extensively white, the fourth, sometimes even the fifth, occasionally showing a terminal white spot; lower half of lores and a pointed streak back of eye, black; sides of head below this black streak, with entire lower parts (except under tail-coverts), clear lemon, the sides and flanks slightly tinged with olive-green; under tail-coverts and under wing-coverts, white; bill, black in summer, brownish and paler below in winter; iris, brown; legs and feet, horn-brownish. ADULT FEMALE: Similar to the male but duller in color; olive-green of upper parts covering crown, sometimes the forehead also; lores and mark back of eye, dusky grayish instead of black; gray of wing-coverts and inner wing-feathers tinged with olive-green.

Nest and Eggs.— NEST: On the ground, in a dense tuft of grass or ferns, in clearings or new growth of saplings; constructed of leaves and strips of wild grape bark, lined with very fine grass. EGGS: 4 to 6, usually 5, white or creamy white specked and spotted with sepia brown, lavender, and purple.

Distribution.— Eastern United States; breeding northward to southern Connecticut, southeastern New York, Pennsylvania, northern Ohio, northern Indiana, northern Illinois, southern Iowa, eastern Nebraska, etc.; occasional straggler to Massachusetts, Michigan, and Minnesota; southward in winter through eastern Mexico, Guatemala, Nicaragua, to Colombia.

A prolonged, lisping, drawling " song " of only two notes, *z-zee-e, z-zee-e,*— from the shrubbery along roads or brushy pastures or the open border of woods, proclaims to the initiated the presence of this tiny bird, of rather unique, though not conspicuous, personality. Yellow is its dominating color, but its grayish wings show that it is not the Yellow Warbler. Its note is very characteristic, and not forgotten as easily as are the notes of many other Warblers.

Most of the tribe incline to be northerly in summer distribution, whereas this is one of the small group which are distinctly southerly. Southern Connecticut is as far north along the Atlantic coast as it is at all common, but there it is found in good numbers during the nesting season. Were it not for the characteristic note, it would be considered a much rarer bird than it really is.

In its general manner of conducting itself, it is not different from various other Warblers. It is a busy searcher of foliage and shrubbery, generally not very high up, yet more commonly off the ground, though it readily descends upon occasion. I have often seen it in second-growth woodland, especially where it is a little moist or swampy, but less in deep forests. It is distinctly a bird of the open edge of woodland and of overgrown pastures.

The nest is on the ground, just in from the edge of the woods, in small clearings or openings in low woods, in a bushy pasture, or by a weedy roadside. Usually it is under a small bunch of weeds, often by some little sprout, down which the bird can descend to enter the nest. The structure is deep, rather loose in texture, and is characterized by having its sides formed of dead leaves which curl inward and arch over the top of the nest, helping to conceal it.

Through knowing just the sort of a place to look, I have found more of these nests than of

Photo by H. K. Job

BLUE-WINGED WARBLER

At its nest, on the ground, just in from the edge of the woods

any others of the less-known Warblers. The method is to use a long switch and tap the little thick clumps of weed or small brush in the proper locations, to flush the female, which is a very close sitter.

I shall never forget the first nest which I discovered. Determined to learn the secret, I started one day to beat out a nest. All day long I thrashed the low cover, especially where old fields and second-growth woods adjoined. Toward night I had walked a number of miles and knocked at the door of some tens of thousands of possible hiding places, without results. Standing in a little opening in low woods, just in from a scrub pasture, I decided reluctantly to quit, and mechanically brought down the switch on a handy clump of weeds. The yellow flash which followed gave me a wonderful thrill. In a moment I was gazing with rapture at the five pinkish-white eggs, sparsely ringed about the larger end, and at the deep, well-concealed nest-cup with its typical converging arch of upright dry leaves.

HERBERT K. JOB.

GOLDEN-WINGED WARBLER

Vermivora chrysoptera (*Linnæus*)

A. O. U. Number 642 See Color Plate 93

Other Names.— Golden-winged Flycatcher; Golden-winged Swamp Warbler; Blue Golden-winged Warbler.

General Description.— Length, 4¾ inches. Upper parts, gray; under parts, white. Bill, shorter than head, narrowly wedge-shaped, the tip very acute; wings, moderately long; tail, about ¾ length of wing, even or nearly even, the feathers narrow.

Color.— ADULT MALE: Forehead and crown, lemon-yellow, sides of head, white (sometimes this carried forward over eyes or even to along sides of forehead); rest of upper parts, including middle pair of tail-feathers, plain gray; exposed portion of middle and greater wing-coverts, mostly light lemon-yellow, *forming a large and conspicuous patch on the wing;* wing-feathers and tail-feathers (except middle pair of latter), slate-blackish, edged with gray, the secondaries usually slightly tinged with olive-green; inner webs of three outermost tail-feathers, extensively white terminally; lores, space below eye, sides of head, and throat (sometimes chin also), uniform black; a broad cheek stripe and under parts of body, white, the latter shaded with gray laterally; bill, black; iris, brown; legs and feet, dark brownish. ADULT FEMALE: Similar to adult male but duller in color, with black of throat and sides of head replaced by gray; yellow of forehead and crown, less distinct, sometimes (in younger individuals?) replaced by olive-green; gray of upper parts and of sides usually tinged with olive-green; white of breast and abdomen, duller, often tinged with olive-yellow, especially in winter.

Nest and Eggs.— NEST: On the ground beneath a bunch of weeds or ferns in clearings; neatly made of thin blades of swamp grass, weed bark, rootlets, lined with fine rounded reddish grass. EGGS: 4 or 5, rarely 6, more spherical than average of other Warblers, dull white speckled with chestnut, burnt umber, and lilac-gray.

Distribution.— Eastern United States north regularly to Massachusetts, New York, southwestern Ontario, northern Michigan, southern Minnesota, etc., casually (?) to Manitoba, breeding southward to northern New Jersey, Pennsylvania, northern Indiana, northern and central Illinois, etc., and southward along Allegheny Mountains to South Carolina, and eastern Tennessee; south in winter to Cuba and through eastern Mexico and Central America to Colombia.

The Golden-winged Warbler is an interesting species in that peculiar group of *Vermivora* Warblers distinguished by the peculiar trait of fertile hybridization. Four distinct species are implicated in this mixed breeding, namely, first, the Blue-winged Warbler, which is in reality a blue-winged yellow Warbler; second, the Golden-wing, which is in reality a yellow-winged blue Warbler; third, Lawrence's, which is a blue-winged Yellow with the Golden-wing's throat patch; and fourth, Brewster's, which is a yellow-winged blue, or Golden-winged, Warbler without the throat patch. Birds of this group of Warblers seem to mate indiscriminately and produce fertile descendants. None of them can be said to be very common birds. Indeed Lawrence's and Brewster's are decidedly rare. Some bird students attempt to ignore the crosses. It is immaterial whether the crosses are scientifically recognizable as varieties, or species, or mere hybrids; they do exist as intermediate forms and therefore deserve some kind of name. Lawrence's, Brewster's, and Golden-Wings are all rarer than Blue-wings, and are the most involved in this most unusual condition in the wild-bird world. A hybrid may have either the song of the Golden-wing or the Blue-wing. Most of the hybrids are found in Connecticut and in and near the lower Hudson valley.

Golden-winged Warblers make their homes in open, bushy country, generally near streams or ponds, and not heavily shaded by too many trees. The Golden-wing song is a sweet *zee-i-zee* or *zee-u-zwee* given three or four times and repeated many times when the bird, posing on top of a bush in the spring sunshine, bursts into joyous enthusiasm.

L. NELSON NICHOLS.

LUCY'S WARBLER

Vermivora luciæ (*J. G. Cooper*)

A. O. U. Number 643

General Description.— Length, 4½ inches. Upper parts, gray; under parts, whitish. Bill, shorter than head, narrowly wedge-shaped, the tip very acute; wings, moderately long; tail, about ¾ length of wing, even or nearly even, the feathers narrow.

Color.— Adult Male: *Above, plain mouse-gray;* crown, chestnut, the feathers tipped (except in worn plumage) with gray; *upper tail-coverts, bright chestnut;* lores, eye-ring, and entire under parts, white tinged with pale brownish gray laterally and also tinged with buff, especially on chest; bill, dusky horn color; iris, brown; legs and feet, dusky. Adult Female: Similar to the male and not always distinguishable, but usually with the chestnut crown-patch more restricted (rarely obsolete) and chestnut of both crown-patch and upper tail-coverts lighter or less intense.

Nest and Eggs.— Nest: Usually in deserted Woodpecker holes, behind loose bark of trees, in the giant cactus, or under roots along stream banks, sometimes in knot-holes or any sort of crevice, from 2 to 20 feet above ground; constructed of fine grass, leaves, and rootlets, and lined with horse-hair and feathers. Eggs: 3 to 5, white or creamy, handsomely wreathed around large end with chestnut and umber.

Distribution.— Southwestern United States and Mexico; breeds in Santa Clara valley, Utah, and Arizona; winters in western Mexico south to Jalisco.

Drawing by R. I. Brasher

LUCY'S WARBLER (¾ nat. size)

A little-known Warbler of the southwestern United States and Mexico

The comparatively little known Lucy's Warbler frequents chiefly willow and mesquite thickets in river bottoms and in generally uninhabited regions. According to one observer (Stevens) the specimens he saw " although active and restless were not at all shy," to which he adds that the birds " were continually in motion, flying from tree to tree, and occasionally visiting some low brush in the vicinity." Dr. Gambel, who observed the bird on Santa Catalina Island said its song resembled the syllables *er-r,r,r,r-she-up* in the form of a low, sweet trill.

Mr. Finley found this Warbler quite abundant in the mesquite a few miles south of Tucson. He found several nests one afternoon, each of which was built in behind a chunk of loose bark on the side of a tree about three or four feet from the ground.

NASHVILLE WARBLER

Vermivora rubricapilla rubricapilla (*Wilson*)

A. O. U. Number 645 See Color Plate 93

Other Names.— Nashville Swamp Warbler; Birch Warbler; Red-crowned Warbler.

General Description.— Length, 4¾ inches. Upper parts, gray and olive-green; under parts, yellow. Bill, shorter than head, narrowly wedge-shaped, the tip very acute; wings, moderately long; tail, about ¾ length of wing, even or nearly even, the feathers narrow.

Color.—Adult Male: *Head, hindneck, sides of head and neck, plain gray;* crown, chestnut, the feathers tipped with gray; rest of *upper parts, plain olive-green,* brightest on rump and upper tail-coverts; lores, pale grayish; *a conspicuous white eye-ring;* cheeks and *under parts, bright gamboge yellow* becoming white on lower abdomen and anal region, tinged with olive on sides and flanks, especially the latter; bill, brownish-black; iris, brown; legs and feet, horn-color. Adult Female: Similar to the adult male, but duller in color, and with little, if any, chestnut on crown.

Nest and Eggs.— Nest: On or imbedded in the ground, usually at the foot of a bush in open woods; constructed of leaves, strips of bark, and grass, but sometimes entirely of pine needles, lined with fine grasses and hair. Eggs: 3 or 4, white to creamy speckled with minute dots of reddish-brown, brown, and lilac, more numerous around large end.

Distribution.— Eastern North America, breeding from Massachusetts, Connecticut, northern New Jersey, Pennsylvania, northern Illinois, Nebraska, etc., northward to Grand Menan and the Great Slave Lake district; southward in migration over more southern United States (east of the Rocky Mountains) through eastern Mexico to Guatemala.

The Nashville Warbler was discovered by Alexander Wilson at Nashville, Tennessee, and reported by him in his *American Ornithology.* This bird has ever since borne the name Nashville Warbler. It is not a rare bird in New England if one goes to the birches to look for it. But it is always in birches or poplars that it makes its home; and, if any bird names itself from its preference for a special home-site, this bird certainly names itself the Birch Warbler.

Wintering in Texas and Mexico, this bird follows high ground to its breeding area, keeping well west of the Alleghenies and leaving a few scattered pairs over the central States while the main body goes on to New England. It is therefore a very rare bird in the South Atlantic States, and not at all common at Nashville.

This plain olive-green bird with yellowish under parts seldom comes near enough to show the chestnut crown-patch which gives him his name of *rubricapilla,* and only bird students are familiar with that detail. As he is a nervous bird flitting about in the birches, he does not attract much attention.

The song is a combination of *ke-tsee* with Chipping-Sparrow-like trillings. It has been compared to the song of the Yellow Warbler.

On the Pacific coast there is a variety known as the Calaveras Warbler (*Vermivora rubricapilla gutturalis*) that is brighter and richer colored. They make their homes in manzanita, huckleberry, and short trees, but do not confine themselves to one kind of tree as do the birds of the eastern variety. L. Nelson Nichols.

ORANGE-CROWNED WARBLER

Vermivora celata celata (*Say*)

A. O. U. Number 646 See Color Plate 93

Other Name.— Orange-crown.

General Description.— Length, 5 inches. Upper parts, olive-green; under parts, olive-yellowish. Bill, shorter than head, narrowly wedge-shaped, the tip very acute; wings, moderately long; tail, about ¾ length of wing, even or nearly even, the feathers narrow.

Color.— Adult Male: *Above, plain grayish olive-green,* becoming brighter, more yellowish olive-green, on rump and upper tail-coverts; *crown with a tawny patch,* this color mostly concealed (except in worn midsummer plumage) by grayish olive tips to the feathers; a narrow stripe over eye, eyelids, and general color of *under parts, pale olive-yellowish,* becoming paler (sometimes whitish) on lower portion of abdomen; sides of head, sides of neck, and sides of breast, light grayish olive-green, the chest (sometimes throat also) indistinctly streaked with the same; an indistinct triangular spot or streak of dusky in front of eye and a still less distinct short streak back of eye; under tail-coverts and under wing-coverts, pale yellow; bill, dusky horn color; iris, brown; legs and feet, brownish horn color. Adult Female: Similar to the adult male in coloration, and not always distinguishable (?), but usually the colors are slightly duller, with the tawny-ochraceous crown-patch more restricted, sometimes obsolete.

Nest and Eggs.— Nest: On the ground, among clumps of bushes, in the side of a bank and usually hidden by leaves; large for size of bird and constructed of long, coarse strips of bark loosely interwoven with a few spears of dried grass or plant stems and warmly lined with hair and fur of small animals. Eggs: 4 to 6, white or creamy, finely speckled with chestnut.

Distribution.— Alaska (except coast district from Kodiak eastward and southward) and throughout Rocky Mountain district of British America and United States, breeding southward to Manitoba and high mountains of New Mexico; during migration southward to eastern and central Mexico and eastward over Mississippi valley and Gulf States to South Carolina, Georgia, and Florida; occasionally during migration in New England and Middle Atlantic States (numerous records), and in southern California.

The Orange-crowned Warbler is a bird of the far Northwest. While one plain olive and yellow bird, the Nashville Warbler, is migrating in the spring from southwest to northeast, one of his nearest relatives, another plain olive and yellow bird, this Orange-crowned Warbler, is migrating across the continent in a way to mark a cross (×) on the map of North America. The Orange-crown's route is from the South Atlantic States northwest to Manitoba, the Great Slave Lake, the fur country, and on into Alaska. It is a bird of the upper tree-tops, continually flitting about and uttering a simple song of a few sweet trills of the Chipping Sparrow nature. It seems to be a great wanderer in the fall. It has been seen in many places far from the regular migration route. In January, 1917, an Orange-crowned Warbler was seen on Staten Island, N. Y. Its presence in the central and northeastern States may, therefore, be more common than is supposed. Bird students have found the bird all over the United States.

To this species must of course be added its varieties of the West. The Lutescent Warbler (*Vermivora celata lutescens*) is not a very rare bird in California and is noticeably a much yellower bird than the Orange-crown. It is, therefore, more easily recognized than the Orange-crown. The Dusky Warbler (*Vermivora celata sordida*) of the Santa Barbara Islands is but a dusky variety of the Lutescent.

L. Nelson Nichols.

TENNESSEE WARBLER

Vermivora peregrina (*Wilson*)

A. O. U. Number 647 See Color Plate 93

Other Names.— Swamp Warbler; Tennessee Swamp Warbler.

General Description.— Length, 4¾ inches. Upper parts, olive-green; under parts, white. Bill, shorter than head, narrowly wedge-shaped, the tip very acute; wings, moderately long; tail, less than ¾ length of wing, decidedly forked, the feathers narrow.

Color.— Adult Male: *Crown and hindneck, plain gray;* rest of upper parts, plain olive-green, brightest on rump; wings, dusky, the secondaries edged with olive-green, the primaries with pale gray (edge of outermost primary, white); tail, dull gray, the outer webs of feathers, edged with olive-green, the inner webs, edged with white, that of outermost feather usually with a white terminal spot, lores and short streak over eye, white, the former with a dusky wedge-shaped streak in front of eye; a small streak back of eye, dusky; sides of head, grayish; below eye, cheeks, and under parts, white, the sides and flanks shaded with gray; under wing-coverts, white; bill, brownish black; iris, brown; legs and feet, horn color. Adult Female: Similar to the adult male in coloration, but with gray of crown and hindneck never so pure, being usually tinged with olive-green, and with streak above eye and under parts tinged with yellow.

Nest and Eggs.— Nest: Placed on or close to the ground in heavy growths of spruce, balsam, or kindred trees; constructed of fine vegetable fiber, grass, leaves, and moss, lined with hair. Eggs: 4 or 5, white, spotted with reddish-brown and purplish markings.

Distribution.— Eastern North America; breeds from upper Yukon valley, southern Mackenzie, central Keewatin, southern Ungava, and Anticosti Island south to southern British Columbia, southern Alberta, Manitoba, northern Minnesota, Ontario, New York (Adirondacks), northern Maine, and New Hampshire; winters from Oaxaca to Colombia and Venezuela; in migration occurs mainly in the Mississippi valley; rare on the Atlantic slope; occasional in Florida and Cuba; accidental in California.

The Tennessee Warbler is not a common bird over the eastern part of the United States even in migration. In the Mississippi basin it is fairly common in both spring and fall migrations. But the color and habits of the bird make it discouraging to study. What can one do with a nervous, fidgety lot of dull-colored birds flitting about in the tree-tops with not a wing-bar, nor breast marking, nor change of the tail color? Only when one is so located that he looks down into the tops of trees at the precise moment that a Tennessee Warbler is passing through his part of the country, is it possible to study that bird with any degree of satisfaction.

This Warbler is very rarely found breeding in the United States. Of the great number of Tennessee Warblers that pass on into Canada in the spring, some do not stop to breed in Canada, but, reaching the upper waters of the Yukon, go on down that valley into Alaska, where there are probably more breeding Tennessee Warblers than in any other part of the United States. Although it is in fact a Canadian bird, even in Canada it is not very well known.

"The food of this species is of peculiar interest because it is one of the few Warblers which have proved to be destructive to fruits in a peculiar way. The Tennessee Warbler is known to puncture ripe or ripening grapes and to suck the juice, thereby causing the decay of the berries so punctured and attracting yellow-jackets, bees, and other nectar-loving insects so that whole clusters are sometimes ruined. This work was long attributed to Orioles, Catbirds, and various other species, but has now been definitely fixed on the present species and cannot be denied. Doubtless in some cases the damage so done is considerable, but usually the birds are so scarce that the amount of fruit damaged is absolutely insignificant. Like numerous other Warblers, this species eats the berries of sumac and poison ivy, and, disgorging the seeds afterward, of course spreads these poisonous plants. Except for these two habits the bird is undoubtedly beneficial, since its food consists mainly of insects, among which are immense numbers of leaf-destroying forms, and in particular, plant-lice and the minute leaf-rollers and other forms which few but the Warblers capture." (Barrows.)

PARULA WARBLER

Compsothlypis americana americana *(Linnæus)*

A. O. U. Number 648 See Color Plate 94

Other Names.— Blue Yellow-backed Warbler; Blue Yellowback; Finch Creeper; Southern Parula Warbler.

General Description.— Length, 4½ inches. Upper parts, bluish-gray and yellowish olive-green; under parts, yellow and white. Bill, much shorter than head, narrowly wedge-shaped, and acute; wings, moderately long; tail, forked.

Color.— Adult Male: Head and neck, except chin, throat, lores, and eyelids, dull grayish-blue; lores darker, usually blackish; a small white spot or streak on rear of upper eyelid, and a larger spot of white on lower eyelid; *back between the shoulders, yellowish olive-green, forming a triangular patch;* shoulders, lesser wing-coverts, rump, upper tail-coverts, and middle tail-feathers, plain bluish-gray, rather lighter than color of head; middle and greater wing-coverts, wings, and tail-feathers (except middle pair) blackish or dusky, edged with bluish-gray, the middle and greater wing-coverts broadly tipped with white, *forming two conspicuous bands,* the front one broadest; inner webs of three outermost tail-feathers with a large spot of white near the tip, that on the exterior feather much the largest; chin, throat, and breast, gamboge-yellow; chest, varying from plain yellowish-tawny to deep tawny (the feathers margined with yellow) usually dusky across the upper portion, sometimes forming a rather distinct narrow band, the yellow of the throat also sometimes tinged with tawny; sides of breast, bluish-gray, sometimes tinged with pale chestnut behind; rest of under parts, white, the sides and flanks tinged with grayish; bill, black above, bright yellow below; iris, brown; legs and feet, brownish. Adult Female: Similar to the adult male, but much duller in color, especially the under parts; gray of upper parts, less bluish; yellow of throat, chest, and breast, paler and duller, the chest only faintly, if at all, tinged with tawny, never with a distinct (usually without any) dusky band across upper portion.

Nest and Eggs.— Nest: In a bunch of Usnea moss; constructed by interweaving the strands, adding some soft plant fibers, and lining it with filaments of the same material; entrance on the side. Eggs: Usually 4, sometimes as many as 7, creamy-white somewhat glossy, thickly speckled with brown or reddish-brown.

Distribution.— More southern portions of Atlantic and eastern Gulf Coast districts of United States, breeding from Florida, Georgia, and Alabama, at least to coast of Virginia, probably to Delaware and southern New Jersey; occasional farther northward; also occasional in more southern portions of the interior; apparently wintering mainly in Florida and northern West Indies.

The Parula Warbler has been called the Blue Yellowback, but the name "Parula," meaning a diminutive Parus or Titmouse, was given it because of the Chickadee-like habit of searching for its food; it often hangs to the under side of a limb as though that were as easy a way as right side up. The species has been divided into Northern and Southern Parulas, overlapping in New Jersey and Maryland. The distinction is in the larger size and deeper, richer coloration of the northern variety (*Compsothlypis americana usneæ*). The bird is a fairly common species in the May migration in the northern States.

If one watches long enough he is pretty sure to see the Parula hanging from a limb, and then this little grayish-blue bird will be found to have a very peculiar yellowish-green patch on its back. The peculiar watered-silk effect of the blue and green back is the distinctive marking of this Warbler.

In Florida and the other southern States, where there is a great amount of Spanish moss hanging from the trees, the Parulas are common, and the buzzing song of *chipper, chipper, chipper, chippee-ee-ee-ee* is repeated many times a day. During the breeding season this "sizzling trill," as Dr. Chapman calls it, is one of the most noticeable bird songs in the eastern United States.

Moss is the characteristic nesting site of the bird over its whole area. Usnea moss or beard moss is locally common, but is rare or absent over other large areas. In the moss regions, and there only, will Parula homes be found. The bird is not quite such an artist as he is often given credit for. Frequently the pendants of moss are very attractively formed and often hang by long strong stems so that they swing easily in the breeze. A pair has only to make a hole into a mass of moss, bring in enough material to make a safe bottom for the nest, and the building is done.

L. Nelson Nichols.

OLIVE WARBLER

Peucedramus olivaceus (*Giraud*)

A. O. U. Number 651

General Description.— Length, 5 inches. Fore parts, orange; upper parts, olive-green and gray; under parts, whitish. Bill, shorter than head, tapering to a point; wings, long and pointed, wing-tip very long; tail, deeply notched.

Color.— Adult Male: *Head, neck, and chest, plain orange-ochraceous,* the sides of head with a broad band of black, involving the lores, eye ring, and sides of head; lower hindneck and extreme upper back, yellowish olive-green, this sometimes extending over whole

Drawing by R. I. Brasher

OLIVE WARBLER (¾ nat. size)

A mountain singer of Arizona and New Mexico

hindneck to, and including, the back of head; back, shoulders, rump, and upper tail-coverts, plain mouse-gray; wings and tail, dull blackish; middle and greater wing-coverts, broadly tipped with white, forming two conspicuous bands, of which the one nearer the front is the broader; innermost greater coverts edged with light grayish olive-green; secondaries edged with more yellowish olive-green; primaries narrowly edged with whitish, *the seventh to the third white at base, forming a conspicuous spot;* tail-feathers narrowly edged with pale grayish, usually becoming more olive-greenish basally; inner webs of two outermost tail-feathers largely white, this occupying much the greater part on exterior feathers, the outer web of which is also largely white; middle of breast and abdomen dull white, shading on sides and flanks into light olive-grayish; under tail-coverts, white; bill, blackish; iris, brown; legs and feet, dusky. Adult Female: Crown and hindneck, olive-greenish; sides of neck, head, throat, and chest, dull sulphur-yellow, the chin and throat sometimes nearly white; ear region, dusky, at least in part; lores, dull grayish; below eye, mixed dusky-grayish and dull whitish; rest of plumage, as in adult male, but white wing-bars narrower, and white spot at base of middle primaries smaller, sometimes obsolete.

Nest and Eggs.— Nest: In the fork of a conifer, from 30 to 50 feet up; very neatly constructed of weed stalks, moss, vegetable down, and lichens and tied with spider webs. Eggs: 3 or 4, olive-gray or sage-green, thickly covered with black specks, sometimes almost obscuring the ground color.

Distribution.— Highlands of Mexico, Guatemala, and southwestern United States; north to central Arizona.

The Olive Warbler is confined in the United States practically to the mountainous regions of Arizona and New Mexico. A few may linger in Arizona after the breeding season or even in winter, but mostly the species spends the colder months in the highlands of Mexico and Guatemala. In the pine forests which it frequents, its movements suggest those of the Pine Warbler, according to Dr. Chapman, who found it feeding "leisurely among the terminal branches or hopping along the twigs without displaying the activity of the fluttering Warblers." The same observer thought that the bird's call-note, as he heard it at Las Vegas, Vera Cruz, Mexico, resembled that of the Tufted Titmouse, the syllables being like *peto;* and another ornithologist (Price) has described its song as a "liquid *quirt, quirt, quirt,* in a descending scale."

CAPE MAY WARBLER

Dendroica tigrina (*Gmelin*)

A. O. U. Number 650 See Color Plate 95

General Description.— Length, 5 inches. Upper parts, olive-green with dark streaks; under parts, yellow with black streaks. Bill, shorter than head, tapering gradually to a very acute point; wings, long and pointed; tail, notched.

Color.— Adult Male: Crown, black, sometimes (especially in midsummer) uniformly so, usually with the feathers, at least those of the back of head, margined with olive (sometimes with rusty); sometimes a spot of rusty on center of crown; back, shoulders, lesser wing-coverts, and upper rump, olive-green, the feathers with a central spot of black; lower rump varying from yellowish olive-green to clear canary-yellow; upper tail-coverts, blackish, broadly margined with olive-green; middle wing-coverts, white or pale yellow, only their extreme base dusky; rest of wings, dusky, the greater coverts edged with white, pale yellow, pale gray, or pale olive, the feathers narrowly edged with light olive-green, these edgings broader and paler on inner wing-feathers; tail, dusky with olive-green or grayish edgings, the three outermost feathers with a large patch of white near the tip on inner web, decreasing rapidly in size from the first to the third; stripe over eye, rufous-chestnut, at least in front (the rear part, sometimes yellow); lores and streak behind eye, blackish; *below eye and sides of head, plain cinnamon-rufous;* sides of neck and under parts, yellow, becoming much paler (sometimes white) on flanks, lower abdomen, and under tail-coverts; chest and sides, streaked with black, the throat also sometimes streaked, and often tinged with cinnamon; bill, black; iris, brown; legs and feet, dusky brownish. Adult Female: Above, olive, becoming more yellowish on lower rump, where the feathers are sometimes bright olive-yellow with darker center streaks, the crown streaked or spotted with black; wings, dusky with light olive edgings, the middle coverts, tipped or margined terminally with white, the greater coverts sometimes edged with pale grayish; tail, as in adult male; a rather indistinct streak of dull yellowish over eye; under parts, dull whitish, usually tinged with yellow, especially on breast, chest, and sides of neck, the chest and sides streaked with dusky-grayish or blackish; bill, etc., as in adult male.

Nest and Eggs.— NEST: Usually in low evergreen trees, near ground, in open fields, or cut-over clearings; rather loosely constructed of small twigs, grasses, and leaf stems, fastened with spider webs, and lined with horse-hair; the brim accurately turned into an almost perfect circle. EGGS: Generally 4, dull buffy or grayish-white spotted chiefly around large end with sepia, chestnut, and lilac-gray.

Distribution.— Eastern North America; breeds from southern Mackenzie, northern Ontario, New Brunswick, and Nova Scotia, south to Manitoba, northern Maine, and New Hampshire, and in Jamaica; winters in the Bahamas and the West Indies to Tobago; accidental in Yucatan.

A male Warbler, captured by George Ord in 1809 at Cape May, N. J., was described by Alexander Wilson and named by him the Cape May Warbler. Not till 1825 was a female taken, and this by Charles L. Bonaparte at Bordentown, N. J. This tan-eared Warbler has ever since been eagerly sought, joyously welcomed, and enthusiastically praised. Many of the greatest bird students are not at all familiar with this bird, while some casual observers have had most rare and excellent views of this unusual *dendroica* or tree-dweller. And yet it is said that the nervousness characteristic of most Warblers, though its tree-top habits are those of *dendroica,* The Cape May is also peculiar in its disposition to stop in the spring migration to feed in a small clump of trees and to remain there for three to six days at a time, before going on to its Canadian breeding home. On its arrival there it gives voice to a fine, penetrating, and sweet song, not very different from the *wee-see, wee-see, wee-see* of the Black and White Warbler.

About 1905 Cape May Warblers became more common in western New York, and in

Courtesy of Am. Mus. Nat. Hist.

CAPE MAY WARBLER (nat. size)

Eagerly sought, joyously welcomed, and enthusiastically praised

in the central West as far as the Mississippi it has sometimes been quite common. It may be that the Atlantic coast birds are the scattered individuals far east of the main body of northern migrating Cape May Warblers. Even if this is so, it is also quite certain that there are by no means as many existing individuals of this species as there are of most of the well-known Warblers. A dozen birds together would make them common. Dr. Chapman saw them one spring in Florida on their way north, and in that narrow peninsula through which all of this species migrates, he could very well say that they were common.

The Cape May is a quiet bird, not exhibiting the spring migration of 1916 they were more numerous than ever in the area around the lower Hudson. Either there is a shifting of the birds from western to eastern routes, or else the actual number of individuals is being largely increased. At this rate of increase, the extraordinary excitement over their presence will be reduced in a few years to the normal interest that all Warblers demand from the bird student. On the other hand, of course, they may in succeeding years become as rare as ever.

The Cape May has been found in the company of the Tennessee Warbler indulging in the bad habit of the latter of puncturing grapes and sucking the juice.

YELLOW WARBLER

Dendroica æstiva æstiva (*Gmelin*)

A. O. U. Number 652 See Color Plate 95

Other Names.— Summer Warbler; Yellow Titmouse; Summer Yellowbird; Yellowbird; Yellow Poll; Blue-eyed Yellow Warbler; Golden Warbler; Wild Canary (incorrect).

General Description.— Length, 4¾ inches. Fore and under parts, yellow; upper parts, yellowish olive-green; under parts, streaked with chestnut. Bill, shorter than head, slender, tapering gradually to the tip; wings, moderately long and pointed; tail, slightly rounded.

Color.— ADULT MALE: *General color above, yellowish olive-green,* the crown more yellowish, usually clear yellow on forehead and on the forward portion of crown, often tinged with orange-tawny; upper tail-coverts edged with yellow; back, sometimes streaked with chestnut; wings and tail, dusky, the middle wing-coverts broadly tipped with yellow, the greater wing-coverts and inner wing-feathers broadly edged with the same; primaries, more narrowly edged with yellowish olive-green; inner webs of tail-feathers yellow, tipped with dusky; sides of head and under parts, clear rich yellow, *the chest, sides, and flanks, streaked with chestnut;* bill, blackish; iris, brown; legs and feet, light brownish. ADULT FEMALE: Above, plain yellowish olive-green (usually darker than in adult male), the crown concolor with the back, or at least not distinctly more yellowish; wings and tail, as in adult male, but tips of middle wing-coverts and broad edgings of greater coverts and secondaries less purely yellow, usually yellowish olive-green; under parts, paler and duller yellow than in adult male, usually without streaks, but sometimes with a few, usually indistinct, chestnut streaks on chest and sides.

Nest and Eggs.— NEST: Generally located in hedges and small saplings, within 10 feet of the ground, and strongly fastened in forks; constructed very neatly of grayish colored plant fibers and slender pliable strips of bark and lined with down and feathers; in some cases built entirely of cat-tail down forming an exquisitely soft receptacle for eggs and young. EGGS: 2 to 6, usually 4, with a greenish white ground spotted and splashed around large end with shades of brown, lilac-gray, and some black.

Distribution.— North and South America; breeds in North America east of Alaska and Pacific slope from tree limit south to Nevada, northern New Mexico, southern Missouri, and northern South Carolina; winters from Yucatan to Guiana, Brazil, and Peru.

Photo by H. T. Middleton

MOTHER YELLOW WARBLER

Feeding her one-day-old babes

The Yellow Warbler seems to be one of the few birds, and represents perhaps the only species, which resent and often defeat the Cowbird's parasitic practice of laying its eggs in the nests of other birds and of unloading upon them its parental responsibilities. This the bird docs by building a flooring over its eggs among which a Cowbird has deposited one of her own. That the bird does this deliberately, and with the definite purpose of avoiding the hatching and rearing of the ugly and voracious foundling, is shown by the fact that the intended victim of the Cowbird frequently repeats the floor-building operation twice or even three times, to forestall as many of the parasite's attempts to make it a foster parent. Why the Yellow Warbler should be apparently capable of this discernment, and should resent and defeat the intended imposition, while other Warblers, not to mention various Vireos and Sparrows, evidently not only make no effort to get rid of the egg, but feed the young Cowbird as solicitously as they feed their own young, is one of Nature's riddles of which there appears to be no solution.

For many other reasons besides this eminently practical one, the Yellow Warbler makes a strong appeal to our affections and respect. In its generally rich yellow plumage, set off by a few contrasting colors, it is an exceedingly beautiful little creature, a veritable sunbeam in the masses of dark green foliage where it moves rather slowly for a Warbler, but always with a certain distinctive ease and grace. The syllables of its song, a thin but sweet whistle, repeated at short intervals, suggest the words, *sweet, sweet, sweet, sweeter, sweeter,* or again, *wee-chee, wee-chee, chee, chee,* with sometimes a *chur* or a *wee-i-u* included, and accompany a cheerful and unflagging industry which all may behold, because of the bird's fondness for fruit and shade trees about human habitations. It is also frequently found in willow trees near the water, and in other comparatively open growths, but rarely in dense forests. The bird's conspicuous coloration and its very wide distribution make it one of the best known members of its family so many of which are elusive and difficult to identify. GEORGE GLADDEN.

Regional varieties of the Yellow Warbler are: the Sonora Yellow Warbler (*Dendroica æstiva sonorana*), found in the southwestern part of North America from western Texas westward and south through Mexico to Guatemala and Nicaragua; the Alaska Yellow Warbler (*Dendroica æstiva rubiginosa*), breeding in Alaska and south to Vancouver Island and wintering in Mexico and Central America; and the California, or Brewster's, Yellow Warbler (*Dendroica æstiva brewsteri*), breeding west of the Sierra Nevada from Washington to southern California. The winter home of the California Yellow Warbler is unknown.

BLACK-THROATED BLUE WARBLER

Dendroica cærulescens cærulescens (*Gmelin*)

A. O. U. Number 654 See Color Plate 94

Other Names.— Blue Flycatcher; Black-throat.

General Description.— Length, 5 inches. MALE: Upper parts, black and blue; under parts, black and white. FEMALE: Upper parts, olive; under parts, olive-yellowish. Bill, shorter than head, slender, tapering gradually to the tip; wings, moderately long and pointed; tail, even.

Color.— ADULT MALE: Above, plain dull grayish indigo-blue, the back sometimes spotted or clouded with black; wings, except lesser coverts, black, the middle coverts broadly margined, the greater coverts broadly edged, the wing-feathers narrowly edged, with dull grayish indigo-blue, the inner feathers chiefly of the latter color; *wing bars absent; primaries (except outermost) extensively white basally, forming a conspicuous patch;* all the wing-feathers with inner webs extensively white basally and edged with white; tail-feathers black, narrowly edged with dull indigo-blue, the three outermost with a large patch of white on inner webs near the tips; head (except forehead, crown, and back), chin, throat, sides of chest, sides, and flanks, uniform deep black, that along sides and flanks somewhat broken by white streaking; rest of under parts and under wing-coverts, white; bill, black; iris, brown; legs and feet, dusky brown. ADULT FEMALE: Above, plain olive, relieved by a *white or whitish spot at base of longer primaries;* tail, darker and more grayish-olive, edged with light greenish-gray, the inner web of outermost feather sometimes with an indistinct paler, rarely whitish, spot near the tip; a whitish streak on upper and lower eyelids, the former continued backward for a distance over ears; under parts, including cheeks, pale, dull olive-yellowish, shaded with olive laterally; bill, blackish; iris, brown; legs and feet, dusky horn color. YOUNG MALE IN FIRST FALL AND WINTER: Similar to adult male but white of under parts tinged with yellowish, bluish-gray of upper parts tinged with olive-green, and black feathers of throat, etc., margined with white.

Nest and Eggs.— NEST: In small bushes, seldom higher than 2 feet, close to abandoned wood-roads; very neat, thick-walled structures of weed bark, grasses, twigs, and rootlets, lined with fine brown rootlets and horse-hair and always decorated exteriorly with corky bits of wood and woolly parts of cocoons. EGGS: Usually 4, pale buffy-white or greenish-white, rather thickly blotched with varying shades of pinkish and reddish-brown.

Distribution.— Eastern North America; breeding from northeastern Connecticut, mountains of Pennsylvania, northern Ontario and southern Michigan, northward to Labrador and shores of Hudson Bay; westward, during migration, to base of Rocky Mountains, in Colorado and New Mexico, accidentally to California; winters southward to West Indies and northern South America.

Some of the so-called wood Warblers are "woodsy" only by virtue of relationship, but the Black-throated Blue Warbler is one both by structure and by habit. It is, moreover, a specialized woodland bird, resorting to an especial type of "the woods." Its typical haunts are the densely shaded second-growth on the sides of wooded hills, either well to the north, or else to the corresponding faunal altitude. To suit its fastidious taste there should be rather dense undergrowth, with more or less fallen branches, and more particularly where mountain laurel luxuriates. It might well have been named the "Laurel Warbler." In such places one may note a sweet, simple little song, which in one way reminds one of the Prairie Warbler, in another of the Black-throated Green. Sometimes it comes from up in the trees, but more often from the undergrowth. Here, like most of its tribe, the bird gleans the foliage for insect life, in typical Warbler fashion.

Photo by H. K. Job

NEST OF BLACK-THROATED BLUE WARBLER

In a low fork of the little bush or sapling, a neat little cup will be discovered

The male is a brilliant distinctive fellow, but the female is apt to prove a puzzle. She is hard to discover, and, even when found, is a nondescript demure greenish bird, hard to name, unless one catches a glimpse of the small white patch on the lower middle part of wing. All she has to say, at the most, is an incisive lisping *tsip*.

The region where I became well acquainted with this retiring, modest little sprite was the wooded hills of northwestern Connecticut, perhaps its most southern summer stronghold, except down the ridge of the Alleghenies. Up in the mountain forests of the town of Salisbury, in June and early July, one may almost constantly hear its song. Here, and all through Litchfield County, in similar situations, it nests in low bushy sprouts, usually within a foot or two of the ground, most frequently in mountain laurel. When one knows just where to look, it is not so very hard to locate nests, by persistent beating, tapping the small laurels with a long switch. In the course of time, the little greenish bird is likely to dart forth, with trembling wings, to limp and flutter over the carpet of dead leaves. In a low fork of the little bush or sapling, a neat little cup will be discovered, wonderfully chaste and well-woven, in the deep hollow of which lie the four delicately spotted white eggs. Such a Warbler's nest seems like a locket or a tiny casket of jewels. Its discovery is rich reward for prolonged search. Finding nests of Warblers is a specialized form of "the sport of bird study." It might be called the chess of woodcraft, a test of agility of mind and eye, combined with the very limit of patience. None but a real bird-lover can practice it with any marked success.

HERBERT K. JOB.

Cairns's Warbler (*Dendroica cærulescens cairnsi*) is a variant of the Black-throated Blue Warbler. It breeds in the Alleghenies from Maryland to Georgia and winters in the West Indies. Both the male and female are darker than their cousins.

MYRTLE WARBLER

Dendroica coronata (*Linnæus*)

A. O. U. Number 655 See Color Plate 94

Other Names.— Myrtle Bird; Yellow-rump; Yellow-rumped Warbler; Golden-crowned Flycatcher; Golden-crowned Warbler; Yellow-crowned Warbler.

General Description.— Length, 5½ inches. SUMMER PLUMAGE: Upper parts, bluish-gray, streaked with black; under parts, white, black, and yellow. WINTER PLUMAGE: Upper parts, grayish-brown; under parts, brownish-white with black streaks. Bill, shorter than head, slender, tapering gradually to the tip; wings, long and pointed; tail, nearly even.

Color.— Adult Male in Spring and Summer: Above, bluish slate-gray, streaked with black, the streaks broadest on back and shoulders; *crown with a large, partly concealed, elongated patch of bright lemon-yellow, the lower rump with a triangular patch of paler yellow*; wings, black with gray edgings, the middle and greater coverts rather broadly tipped with white, producing two distinct bands; upper tail-coverts, black, margined with slate-gray; tail, black with gray edgings, the three outermost feathers with a large patch of white on inner web near the tip, decreasing in size from the outermost to the third; a streak over eye and a narrow spot on each eyelid, white, that on upper eyelid sometimes extended backward, sometimes confluent with spot over eye; sides of head, uniform black; cheeks, chin, and throat, white, the lower portion of the last sometimes partly black; chest spotted or clouded with black, this color sometimes nearly uniform; a large patch of light lemon or canary yellow on each side of breast; center line of breast, together with abdomen and under tail-coverts, white; between the yellow lateral patches and the white area of the *breast an elongated patch of black, confluent with throat area, and extending backward to the flanks,* where broken into broad streaks; bill, black; iris, brown; legs and feet, dark brown. Adult Male in Autumn and Winter: Very different from the summer plumage; above, grayish-brown, with black streaks concealed, except on back and shoulders, where much less conspicuous than in summer plumage; yellow crown-patch concealed by brown tips to the feathers; sides of head, brown, like crown, varied by the same white markings as in summer plumage, but these less distinct; chin, throat, and chest, brownish-white, the last streaked with black; lateral yellow breast patches, less distinct than in summer, usually tinged with brownish and flecked with dusky; black side breast areas broken by broad white margins to feathers; wings and tail, as in summer but white bands across former brownish. Adult Female in Spring and Summer: Similar to the summer male, but smaller and duller in color; the upper parts tinged (sometimes strongly) with brown or dusky brownish-gray, instead of black; less of black on chest and sides of breast, and yellow lateral breast patches smaller and paler yellow. Adult Female in Autumn and Winter: Similar to the winter male, but smaller; upper parts more decidedly brown, with streaks obsolete, except on back; yellow crown-patch more restricted (sometimes nearly obsolete); wing-bands, eyelids, etc., pale brown; under parts, pale buffy-brown to the front and on the sides, the median portion of breast, abdomen, and under tail-coverts, dull yellowish-white; yellow patches on sides of breast, indistinct, sometimes obsolete.

Nest and Eggs.— Nest: Placed usually in a coniferous tree but a few feet up; bulky and carelessly built of small spruce and hemlock twigs, vegetable fibers, old leaves and lined with hair, small roots and some feathers. Eggs: 3 to 5, dull white or creamy speckled and blotched with shades of chestnut, brown and lilac-gray, often in wreath around larger end.

Distribution.— North America in general, chiefly east and north of Rocky Mountains; breeding from mountains of western Massachusetts, northeastern New York, northern Michigan, Manitoba, etc., to limit of tree growth, wintering from the United States (except extreme northern portions) southward to West Indies, through Mexico and Central America to Panama; on Pacific coast from central Oregon to southern California; accidental in Greenland and eastern Siberia.

The color contrasts in the plumage of the Myrtle Warbler, its very wide distribution, and the fact that it is often a winter resident in New York and New England, make it one of the best-known members of its species. The patch of bright yellow which is very conspicuous just above the bird's tail serves as a positive identification mark, and gives the bird its common alternative name of Yellow-rumped Warbler. Again, it is the only Warbler with a white throat, excepting the Chestnut-sided, which plainly shows any yellow in its plumage. Furthermore, it moves with more deliberation than is characteristic of many members of this essentially restless and somewhat nervous family; while its habit of feeding much in shrubbery and hedges brings it frequently within easy observation range. Finally its stay in its northern range is much more prolonged than is that of most other Warblers, for it arrives in the latitude of New York city about the last week of April and remains until about the 20th of November. During that month, the Myrtle is of very common occurrence along the southern shore of Long Island, where it feeds in the stunted and then leafless brush, cheerfully unmindful of its bleak surroundings. It takes its name from its manifest fondness for myrtle-berries (or "bayberries," as they are also called), and is very likely to be found wherever that fruit is plentiful.

The Myrtle Warbler has two common call notes: one which suggests the syllable *sweet,* uttered with the inflection of inquiry, and most commonly heard in the autumn; the other, a shorter and less musical note of a sibilant quality. Its most commonly heard summer song has been called a "sleigh-bell trill," and is a tinkling little warble usually involving the reiteration four or five times of the same note, which is followed by two or three a litle higher or lower.

AUDUBON'S WARBLER

Dendroica auduboni auduboni (*J. K. Townsend*)

A. O. U. Number 656

Other Name.— Western Yellow-rumped Warbler.

General Description.— Length, 5½ inches. Upper parts, gray, streaked with black; under parts, black and white; yellow patches above and below. Bill, shorter than head, slender, tapering gradually to the tip; wings, long and pointed; tail, nearly even.

Color.—Adult Male in Spring and Summer: Above, bluish slate-gray, streaked, except sometimes on upper sides and back of head, and hindneck, with black, the streaks broadest on back, shoulders, and upper tail-coverts, where partaking more of the character of wedge-shaped central spots; *crown with a large central elongated patch of rich lemon- or gamboge-yellow; lower rump with a triangular patch of lighter lemon-yellow;* wings, black, the middle and greater coverts very broadly tipped with white, the latter also broadly edged with white, forming a large and conspicuous wing-patch, the wing-feathers narrowly edged with gray (broader on inner feathers); tail, black with bluish-gray edgings (becoming white on outermost feather); inner webs of four or five outermost feathers with a large patch of white near the tip, decreasing in size inwardly; sides of head, bluish slate-gray, like general color of upper parts, darkening (sometimes into nearly black) below and in front of eyes, and relieved by a white spot on upper eyelid and a larger one on lower eyelid; chin and throat, bright lemon-yellow; chest, black, or mixed black and gray; center portion of breast, together with abdomen and under tail-coverts, white; sides of breast, next to white space, black, forming a large patch, confluent forward with the black or partly black throat area, and continued backward over sides and flanks in broad streaks; a large patch of yellow on each side of breast outside the black area; bill, black; iris, brown; legs and feet, dark brown or brownish-black. Adult Male in Autumn or Winter: Much duller and browner than the summer male, and showing much less of black, that of chest and sides mostly overlaid by broad tips or margins to feathers of brownish-white; gray of upper parts much obscured by a wash of brown, and white wing-markings tinged with brown. Adult Female in Spring and Summer: Essentially like the summer male in coloration, but much duller and with less of black on under parts; gray of upper parts, duller, usually tinged with brown; yellow crown-patch smaller and broken by brown or brownish gray tips to feathers; middle and greater wing-coverts, more narrowly tipped with duller white, the latter not edged with white; yellow of throat paler, usually passing into white on chin; chest and sides of breast, white or pale grayish, spotted or clouded with black; lateral breast patches smaller and paler yellow. Adult Female in Autumn and Winter: Similar to the winter male, but smaller and still duller in color, the back without sharply defined streaks of black, yellow of throat and lateral pectoral patches paler and more restricted, and chest and sides of breast without sharply defined partly concealed black spots. Young in First Plumage: Above thickly streaked with dusky on a pale brownish-gray ground color, the latter here and there inclining to grayish-white, the streaks broader and more blackish on back and shoulders; lower rump, grayish-white, narrowly streaked with dusky; under parts, grayish-white, everywhere streaked with dusky.

Nest and Eggs.— Nest: Usually in coniferous trees, on outer limbs from 3 to 30 feet up; constructed of strips of bark, sage brush twigs, or pine needles, lined with rootlets, hair, and feathers. Eggs: Generally 4, rarely 5, olive-whitish or pale greenish-white, thinly spotted with black, brown, and lilac-gray.

Distribution.— Western North America, north to British Columbia, east to western border of the Great Plains; breeding southward (in coniferous woods on high mountains) to southern California, northern Arizona, and New Mexico, eastward to western Nebraska, Wyoming and Colorado; wintering from western United States (in lower valleys) southward over whole of Mexico and Lower California to highlands of Guatemala, eastward to western Texas and western Kansas; accidental in Massachusetts and Pennsylvania.

Because of its resemblance to the Myrtle Warbler, especially as to the arrangement of the yellow patches in its plumage, Audubon's Warbler is often called the Western Yellow-rumped Warbler, but a careful observer is not likely to overlook the broad white wing-patch which is a sure mark of identification of the Audubon and distinguishes it from the Myrtle, or Yellow-rumped, Warbler. Futhermore, the breeding ranges of the two birds are widely separated, and it is only during their fall migration that they are found frequently in the same territory.

Gray plumage is not common among the birds of the Northwest, and for that reason the little Audubon gets a good deal of attention in that region. Moreover he is one of the first of the small birds to arrive at his breeding grounds, where to some extent he is even a winter resident — in Washington, for example.

Mr. Finley questions the statement of some observers as to the nest building being done solely by the female Audubon Warbler. He says: "My experience with this bird is that it is no different than the other Warblers. In some cases, I find the female takes the more important

Drawing by R. Bruce Horsfall

AUDUBON'S WARBLER (nat. size)

A persistent and skillful flycatcher

part in the home building and the care of the young; in other cases, the pair work side by side. The individualities of birds of the same species are often very different. My experience with the Audubon Warbler is that it does not nest in the same tree year after year, although there may be specific instances of this kind. I have noted this fact in some birds, and to me it indicates that the same birds, or at least one of the same pair, have returned. The Audubon Warbler is a frequent resident of our Douglas firs, and through western Oregon and Washington nests much lower than 11,000 feet." (MS.)

They are persistent and skillful flycatchers, and their sallies and aërial zigzagging are very cleverly executed. The call-note is a *tchip* similar to that of the Myrtle Warbler. The song, Bowles says, is "a short though pleasing little warble, surprisingly feeble for so large a bird, and in no way equal to that of its smaller relative, the Yellow Warbler."

In Arizona and northern Mexico is found a variant form of Audubon's Warbler. It is larger and much darker. Its foreneck, chest, and the entire breast except the lower central portion and the yellow patches on the side are uniform black and give to the bird its name of Black-fronted Warbler (*Dendroica auduboni nigrifrons*).

MAGNOLIA WARBLER

Dendroica magnolia (*Wilson*)

A. O. U. Number 657 See Color Plate 97

Other Names.— Black and Yellow Warbler; Spotted Warbler; Blue-headed Yellow-rumped Warbler.

General Description.— Length, 4¾ inches. Upper parts, black with yellow and white patches; under parts, yellow with black streaks. Bill, shorter than head, slender, tapering gradually to the tip; wings, long and pointed; tail, even or nearly so.

Color.—ADULT MALE: *Crown and hindneck, uni-*

form bluish slate-gray, margined laterally by a white streak beginning on upper eyelid and extending over ear region; a white spot on lower eyelid; forehead, lores, space below eyes, *sides of head, sides of neck, back, and shoulders, uniform deep black,* the last sometimes margined with olive-grayish; rump, clear lemon-yellow, the upper portion streaked with black and sometimes partly olive-greenish; upper tail-coverts, black; tail, black, the outer webs of feathers edged with gray, their inner webs (except middle pair) crossed in middle portion by a broad band of white, about one-half inch wide; wings, black, the middle and *greater coverts broadly margined and tipped with white, forming a large and conspicuous patch,* the wing quills and primary coverts, narrowly edged with gray; under parts, except under tail-coverts, rich lemon-yellow, the chest, sides, and flanks, very broadly streaked with black — these black markings sometimes confluent on the chest; under tail-coverts and under wing-coverts, white; bill, black; iris, brown; legs and feet, dusky-brown. ADULT FEMALE: Much duller in color than the male; gray of crown and hindneck duller, passing into dull olive-greenish on back, where usually blotched or spotted with black, rarely mostly black; lower rump crossed by a band of olive-yellow; upper tail-coverts, black centrally margined with slate-gray; tail as in male but black duller; wings, duller black than in male, with less of white on middle and greater coverts; sides of head sometimes as in adult male, usually duller in color, sometimes with olive-grayish replacing black; under parts paler and duller yellow than in male, with chest and sides less heavily marked with black.

Nest and Eggs.— NEST: Generally in a hemlock from 4 to 15 feet up; put together in a slovenly manner and made of twigs, grass, weed stalks, or fine rootlets, but always plentifully lined with horse-hair whenever obtainable (in its absence fine black roots are utilized). EGGS: 4, rarely 5, creamy-white, boldly blotched with shades of chestnut, brown, and a few lilac spots.

Distribution.— Eastern North America, north to Anticosti Island, Magdalen Islands, southern shores of Hudson Bay, and in the interior to the Great Slave Lake district; breeding southward to northern and western Massachusetts, mountains of Pennsylvania northern Michigan, Manitoba, etc.; west to eastern base of Rocky Mountains, casually to California and British Columbia; southward in migration through more southern United States east of Rocky Mountains; in winter, Bahamas, Cuba, Haiti, and Porto Rico, and through eastern Mexico and Central America to Panama.

"Black and Yellow Warbler," the name formerly applied to the Magnolia Warbler, had the advantage of being colorably descriptive, but the disadvantage of being equally accurate in that respect as applied to no less than three other species of the same group, the Prairie, the Canada, and the Cape May Warblers. Hence the change to the popular specific name, Magnolia, was well-considered.

The species is one of the handsomest of a family famous for the beauty of so many of its members. The contrast between its characteristic colors, black, yellow, and white (the white wing-bars being very plainly marked) makes it conspicuous, despite its small size, rapid movements, and fondness for dense spruce foliage in which a neutral-colored bird might easily be overlooked. The bird is also likely to be found in spring in willow thickets near water, while in autumn it shows a liking for scrub-oak and birch timber, especially on hillsides. In its movements, it is quick and fidgety, and it has a trick of partly spreading its tail, thereby showing the characteristic white-banded feathers.

No two writers agree as to the song of this bird. This difference of opinion would indicate that the Magnolia has a greater variety of notes than any other Warbler. Each observer likens its song to that of another bird, and this Warbler seems to have no song peculiar to itself.

CERULEAN WARBLER

Dendroica cerulea (*Wilson*)

A. O. U. Number 658 See Color Plate 94

Other Names.— Blue Warbler; Azure Warbler.

General Description.— Length, 4¼ inches. Upper parts, grayish-blue and black; under parts, white. Bill, shorter than head, slender, tapering gradually to the tip; wings, long and pointed; tail, even or nearly so.

Color.—ADULT MALE: *Above, grayish-blue, brighter on crown, where approaching azure;* sides of back part of crown and back of head streaked with black, sometimes suffused into patches; back and shoulders, streaked with black; upper tail-coverts, black margined with grayish-blue; wings and tail, black margined with grayish-blue edgings, the middle and greater coverts, broadly tipped with white, forming two conspicuous bands; the inner web of tail-feathers with a patch of white near the tip, largest on outermost; sides of head, grayish-blue, relieved by a streak of dusky behind eye, this often margined above by a streak of white; cheeks and under parts, white, *the sides and flanks broadly* *streaked with dusky* (suffused, especially on sides of breast, with grayish-blue), the chest usually crossed by a narrow band of blackish suffused with grayish-blue, this band often interrupted in the middle, sometimes wanting; bill, black, grayish-blue below; iris, brown; legs and feet, brownish-dusky. ADULT FEMALE: Above, varying from light bluish-gray to grayish olive-green, the crown brighter (grayish glaucous-blue to sage-green), entirely unstreaked; wings and tail as in adult male, but edgings, light greenish or olive-grayish instead of bluish; a whitish or pale yellowish stripe over eye; sides of head, grayish or grayish olive-green, darker along upper margin, somewhat streaked with whitish or pale yellowish toward the front; under parts dull white, usually suffused with pale yellow (sometimes strongly so), especially on sides of neck and across chest.

Nest and Eggs.— NEST: Placed in forks of small branches of deciduous trees, at some distance from trunk, and from twenty to fifty feet up; compactly built of fine grasses and plant fibers securely bound together by spiders' webs and decorated with bits of lichen. EGGS: Usually 3 or 4, white, dull bluish or greenish-white speckled with reddish-brown and lilac chiefly around large end.

Distribution.— Eastern United States, chiefly west of the Alleghenies; breeding northward to eastern Nebraska, Minnesota, Wisconsin, Michigan (as far as Mackinac Island), Ontario, western and central New York, eastward to eastern Maryland and western Virginia, southward to Tennessee, Louisiana, etc.; casually or irregularly northward to Connecticut, Rhode Island, Long Island, and New Jersey; west regularly to edge of the Great Plains, occasionally to Rocky Mountains; in winter south to Cuba and Grand Cayman and through eastern Mexico, Central America, and Western South America to central Peru and Bolivia.

Nothing looks more strange in our northern woods than the azure blue of the sky animated in the personality of a Cerulean Warbler. Strange it is because such dainty blues belong rather to the tropics and even there are rare. Blue it is, strong yet dainty, not vivid, seeming even to be too unreal to be enduring. And animated it is, belying the first impression of unreality by an energetic manner that makes the bird noticeable. If the Warbler has a green or brown background he can be seen, but against the heaven's blue he is lost to the eye. Wait for a damp day and he will come down into the lower limbs of the trees and the observations of him will be much improved.

It is mainly in swampy woodland from the Genesee and Monongahela valleys west to the lower Missouri valley that the Cerulean Warbler is common.

This is another bird that, coming up out of the Southwest in migration, has not been content with a Mississippi valley home, but has pushed on into the Northeast. There is some difference of opinion as to the question of its frequency a century ago in the East, but the observations seem to show that there is a decided increase in its numbers in central New York. The accidental records along the Atlantic coast do not seem to be increased by the gradually approaching northeastern boundary.

The Cerulean is not a very attractive singer but he is persistent. His *zee, zee, zee, ze-ee-ee-eep* becomes to the ordinary listener but a part of the buzz of summer.

CHESTNUT-SIDED WARBLER

Dendroica pensylvanica (*Linnæus*)

A. O. U. Number 659 See Color Plate 96

Other Names.— Golden-crowned Flycatcher; Bloody-side Warbler; Yellow-crowned Warbler; Quebec Warbler.

General Description.— Length, 5 inches. Upper parts, white, grayish, and olive-yellow with black streaks; under parts, white with patches of chestnut. Bill, shorter than head, slender, tapering gradually to the tip; wings, long and pointed; tail, notched.

Color.—ADULT MALE: *Forehead and crown, olive-yellow,* the former becoming whitish in front, both sometimes flecked with dusky; lores, space below eye, cheeks, stripe behind eye, and hindneck, black, the last two streaked with white, grayish, or yellowish, back of head usually with a central spot of white or yellowish; sides of head, neck, chin, throat, and under parts, white, *relieved by a broad lateral stripe of rich chestnut,* extending from rear of black cheek stripe along the sides, usually to the flanks, but sometimes not beyond sides of breast; back and shoulders, broadly streaked with black on a white, grayish, and olive-yellow ground, the last-mentioned color usually prevailing; rump, usually yellowish olive-green, sometimes grayish, with or without black streaks; upper tail-coverts, black, broadly margined with light gray (sometimes tinged with yellowish olive-green) tail black with narrow olive-grayish edgings, the three outermost feathers with inner webs extensively white terminally, that on the exterior feather occupying the terminal half, or more; wings, black with yellowish olive-green edgings (becoming grayish on primary coverts), the middle and greater coverts, broadly tipped, the latter also edged, with sulphur-yellow; lesser coverts, margined with gray or olive-gray; bill, blackish; iris, brown; legs and feet, dusky-brown. ADULT FEMALE: Similar to adult male, but duller in color, the forehead and crown, light olive-green rather than olive-yellow, the black areas on sides of head, less deep black often much broken by grayish streaking or mottling, sometimes replaced by grayish, and much more restricted; chestnut of sides averaging less extensive; greater wing-coverts without chestnut-yellow edgings.

Nest and Eggs.— NEST: Usually placed in low bushes or small trees, in or close to clearings or edge of woods; rather loosely woven of coarse grass, strips of bark, and plant down and rather sparsely lined with hair and fine grass. EGGS: Generally 4, rarely 5, varying from white to creamy, speckled with rusty-umber, reddish-brown, and lilac.

Distribution.— Eastern United States and more southern British Provinces; north to Nova Scotia, northern Ontario, and Manitoba; west to edge of the Great Plains, casually to eastern Wyoming; breeding southward to Connecticut, northern New Jersey, Pennsylvania, northern Ohio, central Illinois, Missouri, and eastern Nebraska, and along Allegheny Mountains to western North Carolina (2000 to 4000 feet), northwestern South Carolina, and eastern Tennessee (Roan Mountain, 3500 to 4000 feet); in winter south through eastern Mexico and Central America to Panama; accidental in Greenland.

The Chestnut-sided Warbler is one of the Warblers of intermediate range, neither very northerly nor very southerly. It is a characteristic summer bird of the latitude of southern New England and of the northern Middle States. Scrub pastures and open second-growth woodland are its characteristic haunts. Not only does it wear the color of chestnut, but it is partial to the real article, and wherever, in its range, there is second-growth chestnut, it is likely to be found, flitting through the foliage, ever on the lookout for its insect prey. It is an active bird, yet a gentle one, easy to approach.

Drawing by R. I. Brasher

CHESTNUT-SIDED WARBLER ($\frac{3}{4}$ nat. size)

One of the easiest birds to photograph at the nest

Its song, while rather simple, is quite conspicuous in the scrub which it frequents, and on roadside borders of pasture-land. Sometimes, if one should follow up the song, the male will be found perched in the sunshine at the very top of a young tree, or on a dead branch, singing away at a great rate.

Whereas growing scarcity of birds is usually the prevailing plaint, the Chestnut-sided Warbler is a species which must have had notable increase during the past century, for Audubon only met it once in all his indefatigable searches after birds. Now he could readily find it on thousands of farms.

The nest usually has its quota of four or five eggs about the last of May or first of June in southern New England. It is built with rather looser texture than some other Warblers employ, the Redstart, for example. Yet it is quite a neat little structure, placed in a fork of a bush in its favorite pasture haunts, quite low down, usually about waist high from the ground. Though fairly well concealed by leaves, it is not generally in so dense a mass of foliage as some. I have found a number of these nests by tapping the bushes with a switch and seeing the owner dart out or hearing the slight rustle of her departure.

The delight of finding a nest is greatly enhanced by the tameness of the little owners. They are among the easiest of birds to photograph at the nest, making little objection to incubating or feeding the young in one's immediate presence. In one case I was focusing the camera on the nest, with head under the cloth, when I saw the image of the mother on the ground glass. She let me focus on her, and then take all the pictures I wanted, her feathers fluffed up in a very gentle and pretty protest.

On another occasion when I was bird-sporting with a motion-picture camera and a boy assistant, seeing that the owners of a nest of this species which I had found were remarkably fearless, I had the boy sit quietly by the nest, holding the young in his hand. In a short time the parents, who had found us gentle and harmless, were using him as a convenient roost and were all over him, on legs, arms, hands, and head. It was a wonderful film of these beautiful birds that I thus secured. HERBERT K. JOB.

Photo by H. K. Job Courtesy of Outing Pub. Co.

CHESTNUT-SIDED WARBLER

On its nest, a neat little structure, placed in a fork

BAY-BREASTED WARBLER

Dendroica castanea (*Wilson*)

A. O. U. Number 660 See Color Plate 96

Other Names.— Little Chocolate-breast Titmouse; Bay-breast.

General Description.— Length, 6 inches. Upper parts, buffy-olive, black, and chestnut; under parts, chestnut and buff. Bill, shorter than head, slender, tapering gradually to the tip; wings, long and pointed; tail, notched.

Color.—ADULT MALE: *Forehead, sides of crown, sides of head, lores, and cheeks, black enclosing a patch of rich chestnut;* sides of neck, plain buff; back and shoulders, gray, usually tinged (sometimes strongly) with buffy-olive and broadly streaked with black; rump, similar but with streaks concealed; upper tail-coverts, gray with center streaks of blackish; tail, grayish-black or dusky with light-gray edgings, the inner webs of two or three outermost tail-feathers with a patch of white, that on exterior feather occupying the terminal third or more; wings, grayish-black or dusky with light olive-gray or olive edgings, the middle and greater coverts broadly tipped with white, forming two conspicuous bands across wing; *throat (sometimes chin also), chest, sides, and flanks, plain light chestnut;* rest of under parts, plain pale buff, the under tail-coverts more decidedly buffy; bill, brownish-black; iris, brown; legs and feet, dusky-brownish. ADULT FEMALE: Essentially similar to the male except in extent of the chestnut, which is often almost entirely absent, and never so strongly marked; whole crown usually distinctly streaked with black on a gray, olive, or olive-green ground, the crown and back of the head usually intermixed with chestnut, sometimes with a considerable patch of that color; chestnut of under parts sometimes wholly absent, but usually the area so colored in the male is indicated, especially across chest and along sides; forehead and sides of head never (?) black.

Nest and Eggs.— NEST: Commonly placed in a coniferous tree from five to twenty feet up; a compact, cup-shaped structure made of rootlets, strips of bark, small twigs, and some dried grass. EGGS: Usually 4, bluish-white, finely speckled around larger end with chestnut.

Distribution.— Eastern United States and British Provinces; north to Hudson Bay and Manitoba; west to edge of the Great Plains; breeding southward to northern Maine, New Hampshire, Vermont, New York, and northern Michigan; in winter southward through eastern Mexico and Central America to Panama and Colombia.

The Bay-breasted Warbler is a bird of the Canadian forests noticeable to civilization mainly in its spring and fall migrations. The migration of the bird is one of the most interesting things yet known about it. Between Canada and its winter home in Colombia and Panama, it restricts itself to areas that lead to the upper northern and northeastern waters of the Mississippi basin.

Following the basin down the Gulf coast, the bird makes the great flight across the Gulf of Mexico and the Caribbean Sea to Panama and the adjacent Colombian shores. The bird thus evades Virginia, Florida and the West Indies on the east, and Mexico on the west. Why this little deep buff-colored bird should evolve such a route is a puzzle. In the United States it has been found nesting in the Maine woods and in the White Mountains.

It is a trifle larger than most of the tree-top Warblers, a trifle duskier, and rather quieter in its habits. It has more of the leisurely manner of the Vireo.

There is much variation in the Bay-breast's song and this, together with its resemblances to the songs of the Blackburnian, the Black-poll, the Black and White, and the Cape May Warblers, makes it difficult to identify.

BLACK-POLL WARBLER

Dendroica striata (*J. R. Forster*)

A. O. U. Number 661 See Color Plate 96

Other Names.— Black-poll; Autumnal Warbler.

General Description.— Length, 5½ inches. MALE: Upper parts, gray streaked with black; under parts, white streaked with black. FEMALE: Upper parts, olive streaked with black; under parts, white and yellow streaked with black. Bill, shorter than head, slender, tapering gradually to the tip; wings, long and pointed; tail, notched.

Color.— ADULT MALE IN SPRING AND SUMMER: Entire crown, uniform black; hindneck, streaked with black and white, in varying relative proportion; back and shoulders, broadly streaked with black on a gray or pale olive ground; rump and upper tail-coverts similar but less distinctly streaked, often (especially the rump) without streaks; tail, dusky, with light gray edgings, the inner webs of two or three outermost feathers with a patch of white near the tip (largest on the outside one); wings, dusky with light olive edgings (more yellowish-olive on primaries), the middle and greater coverts broadly tipped with white, forming two conspicuous bands; sides of head, white, including lower eyelid, space below eye, and cheeks; sides of neck, streaked with black and white; under parts, white, broadly streaked laterally with black, the black streaks on sides of throat merging into two stripes converging and usually united on chin, *forming a conspicuous V-shaped mark;* under tail-coverts, pure white; bill, dusky; iris, brown; legs and feet, pale yellowish-brown. ADULT MALE IN AUTUMN AND WINTER: Above, dull olive-green passing gradually into dull gray on upper tail-coverts; back and shoulders (sometimes also the crown, rump, or upper tail-coverts), narrowly streaked with black; wings and tail as in summer plumage, but white wing-bands usually tinged with yellow; over the eye a narrow and indistinct streak of pale olive-yellowish, the upper eyelid whitish; ear region and sides of neck, olive or dull olive-greenish, like color of upper parts; cheeks, chin, throat, chest, breast, and sides, pale olive-yellow or straw-yellow, the sides and flanks indistinctly streaked with dusky; abdomen, anal region, and under tail-coverts, white. ADULT FEMALE: Above, varying from olive-green to gray, streaked with blackish, the streaks usually obsolete or nearly so on rump; wings and tail as in adult male, but white wing-bands tinged with yellow (except in specimens having a gray upper surface); under parts, varying from white to pale olive-yellow (with all intermediate conditions — the under tail-coverts always white), streaked laterally with black or dusky, the streaks usually most distinct on sides of throat and breast.

Nest and Eggs.— NEST: Placed in small spruces from three to eight feet up; constructed of small twigs, rootlets, lichens, and grasses and lined with feathers, fine grasses, and down. EGGS: 4 or 5, creamy or grayish-white, speckled and blotched with varying shades of chestnut, lilac, and gray.

Distribution.— North and South America; breeds from the limit of trees in northwestern Alaska, northern Mackenzie, central Keewatin, northern Ungava, and Newfoundland south to central British Columbia, Manitoba, Michigan, northern Maine, and mountains of Vermont and New Hampshire; winters from Guiana and Venezuela to Brazil; migrates through the Bahamas and West Indies; casual in New Mexico, Mexico, Chile, and Ecuador; accidental in Greenland.

The Black-poll Warbler is frequently associated in its breeding range with its nearest relative, the Bay-breast. Like the Bay-breast, the Black-poll has an extraordinary migration range. The areas over which these two kinds of Warblers travel are, however, quite different. Black-poll, nesting in Alaska and northern Canada as far as the northern limit of trees, passes south in migration pretty well over the whole of the United States east of the Missouri River, concentrating its lines in Florida, and goes on from island to island the whole length of the West Indies, over the Spanish Main, to the interior of Brazil. Not a Black-poll winters north of South America. This means that if a Brazilian bird nests in Alaska, he has five thousand miles to travel twice a year. At the shortest, from the mouth of the Orinoco to the Adirondacks there are twenty-five hundred miles to travel.

Coming north as it does among the latest of the Warblers, Black-poll is very difficult to see. The trees, already far advanced in foliage, easily hide him; and when the Black-poll remains, as he often does, in the tops, he is well out of sight. His song resembles the Black and White Warbler's, but the notes are separated, not in pairs. The hesitating, sibilant notes have crescendo and diminuendo effects that make it possible to distinguish the song from its near relatives. Once learned, the song in the leafy trees is a clue to his presence, and the search may bring him to view.

The Black-poll delays into June before leaving the areas just south of its breeding range, while the more northern breeding birds are on their way to Alaska and the lower Mackenzie. There are a few that nest in the northern tier of States west to Montana, but most often, possibly always, in evergreens, the preference being for short thick clumps of spruces.

Again in the fall the Black-poll seems loath to leave, waiting behind the other Warblers. He does not leave the northern States before October. His Vireo-like movements often make him more noticeable than in the spring. At last he does decide to go, and he is off for the Amazonian forests.

L. Nelson Nichols.

Photograph by R. W. Shufeldt

BLACK-POLL WARBLER

Adult male in spring plumage, from life

BLACKBURNIAN WARBLER

Dendroica fusca (*Müller*)

A. O. U. Number 662 See Color Plate 97

Other Names.— Hemlock Warbler; Torch-bird; Fire-brand; Orange-throated Warbler.

General Description.— Length, 5½ inches. Upper parts, black or blackish with spots of yellow and white; under parts, orange and yellow. Bill, shorter than head, slender, tapering gradually to the tip; wings, long and pointed; tail, notched.

Color.—Adult Male: *Crown and hindneck, black, relieved by an oval patch of orange on middle of crown; a broad stripe of orange over eye confluent behind with a large patch of the same on side of neck;* a spot of rather paler orange-yellow immediately beneath eye, including lower eyelid; loral streak and sides of head, black, the two connected by a narrow streak at the corner of the mouth; cheeks, chin, throat, and chest, rich orange; remaining under parts, pale yellowish (more decidedly yellowish on breast), the under tail-coverts, white; sides and flanks streaked with black, these black streaks commencing at lower rear extremity of ear region; general color of upper parts, black, the back streaked with whitish, especially the exterior row of shoulder-feathers, which have most of the outer web whitish, forming, when feathers are properly arranged, two stripes along each side of back; feathers of rump and upper tail-coverts edged with whitish; two to three outermost tail-feathers white, with black shafts and with a terminal wedge-shaped mark of black; fourth tail-feather also with much white on inner web near the tip, and fifth sometimes with a white edging to the inner web; exposed portion of middle wing-coverts and innermost greater coverts, white, forming a conspicuous patch on wing, the outermost greater coverts, black, broadly tipped with white and narrowly edged with olive-grayish, these edgings broader and paler (sometimes white) on innermost; bill, brownish-black; iris, brown; legs and feet, dusky-brown. Adult Female: Above, grayish-olive; crown, streaked with black with a central spot of pale yellow; back, broadly streaked with black, the outside row of shoulder-feathers with outer webs mostly very pale buffy-grayish or grayish-buffy, forming two broad stripes when feathers are properly arranged; upper tail-coverts, black, margined with brownish-gray; wings and tail, as in adult male but general color much duller blackish, the lateral tail-feathers less extensively white and the white on greater wing-coverts usually not joining that on middle coverts, the white thus usually forming two broad bars instead of a single large patch; broad stripe over eye joining a patch on side of neck, pale yellow; sides of head and lores, grayish-olive; chin, throat, and chest, deep chrome-yellow; rest of under parts, dull yellowish-white, more strongly tinged with yellowish on breast, the under tail-coverts, more nearly white, the longest sometimes with a narrow center streak of dusky; sides and flanks streaked with dusky; bill, iris, etc., as in adult male.

Nest and Eggs.— Nest: An elegant, compact structure of cat-tail down, hemlock twigs, fine grasses, rootlets, and strips of bark and lined with horse-hair and fine lichens; placed almost always in a conifer, spruce or hemlock preferred, usually at great height, in one instance 84 feet. Eggs: Usually 4, grayish or bluish-white, blotched and speckled with cinnamon and olive-brown.

Distribution.— Eastern North America and northern South America; breeds from Manitoba, southern Keewatin, central Ontario, Quebec, and Cape Breton Island to central Minnesota, Wisconsin, northern Michigan, Massachusetts, and Connecticut, and in the Alleghenies from Pennsylvania to Georgia and South Carolina; winters from Colombia to central Peru and less commonly north to Yucatan; in migration to Nebraska, Texas, and Kansas, straggling to Utah, New Mexico, and the Bahamas.

"Torch-bird," Mrs. Mabel Osgood Wright says, would be a good name for this almost dazzlingly brilliant fellow, and Mr. Parkhurst thinks he "might properly be named the conflagration warbler," and continues: "Called, prosily enough, from its discoverer, Blackburn, the name is saved to poetry by the significant play upon words; for while a part of the plumage is black as coal, the crown, sides of face, throat and breast are of a most vivid flame color — a most astonishing combination of orange, black and white, and arranged in such abrupt juxtaposition that, in seeing it for the first time, one will unquestionably pronounce it the most glorious of all the Warblers. Its own color ought to suffice to keep it comfortable in the Arctic Zone." (*The Birds' Calendar*). "The orange-throated warbler would seem to be his right name, his characteristic cognomen," says Mr. Burroughs; "but no, he is doomed to wear the name of some discoverer, perhaps the first who robbed his nest or rifled him of his mate — Blackburn; hence Blackburnian Warbler. The *burn* seems appropriate enough, for in these dark evergreens his throat and breast show like flame."

These are characteristic expressions of the wonder and delight which are inspired by the appearance of this gaudy little sprite of the deep forest. For it is in such growths, and especially in the big conifers, that the bird is most likely to be seen, and frequently in the company of the Northern Parula, Canada, and Black-throated Blue Warblers, all beautiful little creatures, but none so positively gay in apparel as the Blackburnian. Though not really timid, the bird's characteristic movements are quick and nervous, like those of most of its kind. Like theirs, too, its song is thin and essentially sibilant in its quality. *Wee, see, see, see, zi, zi, zi,* Mr. Hoffmann renders one common version of it, while to Mr. Torrey another phrase sounded like *zillup, zillup, zillup.*

YELLOW-THROATED WARBLER

Dendroica dominica dominica (*Linnæus*)

A. O. U. Number 663

Other Names.— Yellow-throated Creeper; Dominican Yellow-throat.

General Description.— Length, 5¼ inches. Upper parts, gray; under parts, yellow and white. Bill, shorter than head, slender, tapering gradually to the tip; wings, long and pointed; tail, even or nearly even.

Color.—Adult Male: Forehead (sometimes crown also, especially side portions), lores, below eyes, and greater part of sides of head, black; back of head, hindneck, back, shoulders, rump, and upper tail-coverts, plain slate-gray, the crown also sometimes gray (except on the sides) streaked with black; wings and tail, black with slate-gray edgings, the middle and greater wing-coverts, broadly tipped with white, forming two conspicuous bands across wing; two to three outermost tail-feathers with inner web extensively white at the end, this on side feather occupying approximately the end half; over the eye a broad white stripe usually becoming yellow (over lores); a crescentic spot below eye, and patch on side of neck (invading center rear portion of sides of head), white; *throat and chest, lemon-yellow,* the chin, usually white; rest of under parts, white, broadly streaked on the sides with black, the broad black streaks on sides of chest joining with a narrow stripe connecting them with the triangular black patch on side of head; bill, black; iris, brown; legs and feet, dusky horn color. ADULT FEMALE: Similar to the adult male and often not distinguishable, but usually with less black on forehead, which is more often gray, streaked with black centrally, and yellow of throat and chest averaging slightly paler.

Nest and Eggs.— NEST: Placed on pine limb, fastened by insect webbing, generally rather high up, or hidden in tufts of Spanish moss; constructed of twiglets, strips of bark, and leaf stems, fastened with moss or cobwebs, and lined with soft vegetable down. EGGS: 3 or 4, dull greenish or grayish-white, spotting of brown and lilac-gray confined to large end, sometimes forming wreaths.

Distribution.—Atlantic coast district of United States; north to lower Maryland and eastern shore of Virginia, casually to New York (Long Island), Connecticut, and Massachusetts; breeding southward to Florida; in winter to southern Florida, Bahamas, Cuba, Grand Cayman, Jamaica, Haiti, and Porto Rico, and occasionally north to South Carolina.

The Yellow-throated and Sycamore Warblers are geographical variations of the same species of Warbler. Both are yellow-throated, both are southern, both haunt the tops of large evergreens, and both have clear ringing songs. From Virginia south to Florida the bird is known as the Yellow-throated Warbler. From Ohio and Missouri south to the Gulf he is called the Sycamore Warbler (*Dendroica dominica albilora*).

He is not a very common bird anywhere, but the clear song of this Dominican Yellow-throat as it rings out from the tops of the tall pines and cypresses of the lowlands of the South Atlantic States is very distinctive. The bird draws attention to itself by this song, which has been written *ching-ching-ching, chicker-cher-wee* and has the ringing character of the Water-Thrush, and the clear distant note of the Indigo Bunting. If one is fortunate enough to be present when the bird comes down into the lower limbs of the forest trees he will see his most attractive yellow throat and see, too, how deliberate is his

YELLOW-THROATED WARBLER (nat. size)

Courtesy of Am. Mus. Nat. Hist.

manner. There is nothing of the excitable disposition that is called "Warbler-like." When he is in a mood to sing, back he goes to the top of a cypress and pours forth his song, often for some minutes, standing quietly on one limb of the tree.

The Sycamore Warbler of the south-central States seems to give his preference to the sycamore trees, and is well named the Sycamore Yellow-throat. Neither is he a very common bird, but his song and beauty are the characteristics that attract people to him.

GRACE'S WARBLER

Dendroica graciæ *Baird*

A. O. U. Number 664

General Description.— Length, 5 inches. Upper parts, gray streaked with black; under parts, yellow and white. Bill, shorter than head, slender, tapering gradually to the tip; wings, long and pointed; tail, even or nearly even.

Drawing by R. I. Brasher

GRACE'S WARBLER (⅚ nat. size)

A pretty bird with graceful manners

Color.— ADULT MALE IN SPRING AND SUMMER: *Above, slate-gray, the crown and back, streaked with black* (sides of crown, sometimes uniformly black); wings and tail, dusky with slate-gray edgings, the middle wing-coverts broadly, the greater coverts more narrowly, tipped with white, forming two distinct wing-bands; two outermost tail-feathers with inner webs extensively white at the end (the white occupying more than the end half on outermost feather, which also has the outer web largely white), the third feather also usually with an elongated white patch at the end or near the end; over the eye a stripe of yellow passing into white beyond eye; a broad dusky loral streak and a narrow dusky streak at corner of mouth; sides of head and sides of neck, plain slate-gray; *spot below eye, cheek, chin, throat, and chest, lemon-yellow;* remaining under parts, white, with sides of chest and breast, sides, and flanks, streaked with black; bill, black; iris, brown; legs and feet, dusky-brown. ADULT FEMALE: Similar to the adult male but duller in color; gray of upper parts, strongly tinged with brown, the black streaks on back, indistinct (sometimes obsolete); white wing-bands, narrower; yellow of stripe over eye, throat, etc., paler; white of under parts, rather duller, and blackish streaks on sides, etc., less distinct.

Nest and Eggs.— NEST: High in pine trees, 50 to 60 feet up; composed of vegetable fiber, straws, string, bud scales, and insect webs. EGGS: 3 or 4, lightly spotted with reddish-brown.

Distribution.— Southwestern United States and adjacent parts of northwestern Mexico; northward through mountains of New Mexico and Arizona to southern Colorado, where abundant in coniferous forests; winters in Mexico.

Grace's Warbler was discovered in 1864 by the great naturalist, Dr. Elliott Coues, who gave the bird his sister's name. It is a pretty name and was a pretty compliment of a kind which ought to have been paid oftener by American ornithologists to their women relatives and friends — in fact, at least as often as there were pretty names available.

Also it is a pity that Americans see so little of this Warbler, because its appearance and its ways are as pretty as its name. But these are facts which are appreciated only by the comparatively few persons who visit or live in the southwestern part of this great country, especially the regions near the Mexican boundary. The bird is, indeed, one of the commonest of its family in Arizona, and is of quite frequent occurrence especially in the neighborhood of that most wonderful wonderland, the Grand Cañon of the Colorado. Here it is found working in the tops of the yellow pine trees, much after the manner of other Warblers. It is also frequently found in similar forests on the Guadalupe Mountains of Texas.

BLACK-THROATED GRAY WARBLER

Dendroica nigrescens (*J. K. Townsend*)

A. O. U. Number 665

General Description.— Length, 5 inches. Fore parts, black; upper parts, gray; under parts, white. Bill, shorter than head, slender, tapering gradually to the tip; wings, long and pointed; tail, even.

Color.—Adult Male: *Head, uniform black, relieved by a broad stripe of white over ear (extending forward to above middle of eye), a small spot of yellow in front of eye,* and a broad cheek stripe of white, extending from lower base of bill to sides of neck, confluent on chin; whole throat and chest, uniform black; rest of under parts, white broadly streaked on the sides with black; hindneck, back, shoulders, rump, and upper tail-coverts, slate-gray or plumbeous, streaked (except on hindneck, and sometimes on rump) with black; wings and tail, black or dusky with gray edgings, the middle and greater wing-coverts, broadly tipped with white, forming two conspicuous wing-bands; inner webs of two outermost tail-feathers mostly (sometimes entirely) white, the third feather with end half or more, white, the fourth also with white on terminal portion; bill, black; iris, brown; legs and feet, dusky-brown, sometimes nearly black. Adult Female: Sometimes scarcely different from the adult male, having the crown and whole throat uniform black, as in that sex, but with gray of upper parts duller; usually, however, with the crown gray (except on the sides), streaked with black; the throat mostly white with a black or dusky patch on each side of lower throat; white of under parts, less pure, with streaks on sides and flanks narrower and grayish dusky; gray of upper parts, duller, with dusky streaks on back and upper tail-coverts much narrower, sometimes nearly obsolete.

Nest and Eggs.— Nest: Low in dense thickets of manzanita, scrub oak, or willows or high among the conifers; compactly constructed, cup-shaped, of plant fibers, grasses, and a few leaf stems and lined with feathers. Eggs: 3 or 4, pinkish-white or cream, spotted around larger end with reddish-browns and purple.

Distribution.—Western North America; breeds from southern British Columbia, Nevada, northern Utah, and northwestern Colorado south to northern Lower California, southern Arizona, and northern New Mexico; winters in southern Lower California and in Mexico.

When the wise men gave names to the different birds, the Black-throated Gray Warbler got its name from the male, for he only has the black throat. His wife wears a white cravat, and, according to my idea, she is a good deal more important in Warbler affairs than he is. This impression was gained by watching at the nest after the eggs were hatched and the young birds were being fed. Mr. Warbler seemed to be away from home practically all the time. He evidently thought his shyness was a good excuse to stay away and let his wife take the burden of hunting food for the young birds.

One day as I was walking along Fulton Creek, I saw one of these Warblers fidgeting on a limb with a straw in her bill. This was interesting, because I had searched this locality trying to find the nest for some time. The site of the nest was twelve feet from the ground in the top of a sapling. It was very advantageously located because just at the side of the sapling was the sawed-off trunk of a fir that was three and a half feet across. Upon this we could climb and aim our camera straight into the nest.

The mother returned home and found two men with a big one-eyed monster, the camera, close to her children. She was scared almost out of her senses. She fell fluttering from the top of the tree. She caught quivering on a limb a foot from my hand. But she couldn't hold on; she slipped through the branches and clutched my shoe. I never saw such an exaggerated case of chills or heard such a pitiful high-pitched note of pain. I stooped to see what ailed her. She acted as if both wings were broken. But a moment later, she limped under a bush and suddenly got well.

The first day I met the male Black-throated Gray face to face, we were trying to get a photograph of the mother as she came to feed. She had got quite used to the camera. We had it leveled at the nest only a yard distant. A gray figure came flitting over the tree-tops and planted himself on a limb right beside his home.

He carried a green cut-worm in his mouth. No sooner had he squatted on his accustomed perch than he caught sight of the camera. With an astonished chirp, he dropped his worm, turned a back somersault and all I saw was a streak of gray curving up over the pointed firs.

The mother foraged the firs for insects of all sizes and colors. She often brought in green cut-worms which she rolled through her bill as dinner they had just swallowed. I don't believe the mother ever saw her children when their mouths were not open. After watching about the home for several days with camera and note book, I discovered that the mother was very impartial to her children. While I could not tell one of the young birds from the other, the mother seemed to be able to do it, for she fed them in turns regardless of position.

Photo by W. L. Finley and H. T. Bohlman

MOTHER BLACK-THROATED GRAY WARBLER FEEDING CUT-WORMS TO YOUNG

a house-wife runs washing through a wringer, either to kill the creature or to be sure it was soft and billsome. This looked like a waste of time to me. The digestive organs of those bob-tailed bantlings seemed equal to almost any insect I had ever seen.

In the days I spent about the nest, I never saw the time when both the young birds were not in a starving mood, regardless of the amount of

The Black-throated Gray Warbler, like the others of its kind, is restless, flitting from tree to tree and singing at times almost constantly. Mrs. Florence Merriam Bailey says, " Its song is a simple Warbler lay, *Zee-ee-zee-ee, ze, ze, ze,* with the quiet woodsy quality of *Virens* [Black-throated Green Warbler] and *Cærulescens* [Black-throated Blue Warbler], so soothing to the ear." WILLIAM L. FINLEY.

BLACK-THROATED GREEN WARBLER

Dendroica virens (*Gmelin*)

A. O. U. Number 667 See Color Plate 97

Other Names.— Green Black-throated Flycatcher; Evergreen Warbler; Green Black-throat.

General Description.— Length, 5 inches. Upper parts, olive; under parts, yellow, black, and white. Bill, shorter than head, slender, tapering gradually to the tip; wings, long and pointed; tail, notched.

Color.— ADULT MALE: Crown, hindneck, back, shoulders, and rump, plain yellowish olive-green, the back sometimes (more rarely the crown and rump also) narrowly streaked with black, and the forehead sometimes with an oval center spot of yellowish; *sides of head and neck, including whole cheek region and a broad stripe over eye, clear lemon-yellow,* relieved by a streak of olive-green behind eye, this sometimes involving greater part of the side of head; *chin, throat, and chest (sometimes sides of breast also), uniform black,* the first, sometimes partly yellow; rest of under parts, white or yellowish white, the breast usually tinged (sometimes strongly) with yellow; sides and flanks, heavily streaked with black, these streaks usually confluent forward with the black throat-patch at its rear margin; wings and tail, dusky with slate-gray edgings, the middle and greater wing-coverts, broadly tipped with white forming two conspicuous bars across wing; inner webs of two side tail-feathers, mostly white, that of the third with a large white end spot, the two outermost with outer webs extensively white; bill, blackish; iris, brown; legs and feet, dark horn-brown. ADULT FEMALE: Similar to the adult male, but chin and throat, usually whitish or pale yellowish, the black of lower throat (if present there) and chest broken (sometimes almost hidden) by whitish tips to the feathers; sides of breast, never uniform black.

Nest and Eggs.— NEST: Nearly always in an evergreen from 15 to 40 feet up, on a limb some distance from the trunk; compactly built of rootlets, bark strips, grasses, wool, and feathers and lined with hair and vegetable down. EGGS: Commonly 4, creamy-white, spotted with chestnut, brown, and lilac-gray mixed with a few darker spots.

Distribution.— North America; north to Nova Scotia, shores and islands of Gulf of St. Lawrence, Newfoundland, southern shores of Hudson Bay, Alberta, etc.; breeding southward to mountains of Connecticut, New York, and Pennsylvania, northeastern Illinois, and along higher Alleghenies to eastern Tennessee, western North Carolina, and northwestern South Carolina; west to edge of the Great Plains; in winter south to West Indies and through eastern Mexico and Central America (Guatemala and Costa Rica) to Panama; occasional in West Indies; accidental in Arizona, Greenland, and Helgoland.

Just as the Black-throated Blue loves the laurel, the Black-throated Green is a devoted habitué of the evergreen groves and forests — of pine, spruce, hemlock. Its drowsy song is one of the typical sounds of the pineries in the warm days of summer, not only in the North, as with the Blackburnian, but well down into the middle States. It is apt to keep well up in the tall trees, and is more readily heard than seen. But patient watching will at length be rewarded by a glimpse of the deliberate little singer flitting through the needle foliage, hanging head downward, to investigate an insect, or hovering before a cluster. Though not confined to evergreens, it is seldom seen, except in migration, at any great distance from its native element.

Since it is quite abundant in many a pinery, it would not appear hard to find its nest. But this

Courtesy of Am. Mus. Nat. Hist.

BLACK-THROATED GREEN WARBLER (¾ nat. size)

A devoted habitue of the evergreen groves and forests

is the secret of the pines and one which is not easy to discover. Usually it is well up in the thickness of the needles, out on some branch, hard indeed to see from the ground. Sometimes however, it is in thick low evergreen growths, but even there it is not much easier to find. As a boy this nest was my despair, and I was long in finding one, in the crotch of a white pine, next to the trunk, some twenty feet up.

Photo by H. K. Job

MALE BLACK-THROATED GREEN WARBLER AT NEST

Though a retired forest dweller, the Black-throated Green is rather a familiar little bird. A nest which I found, in a recent year, gave me wonderful insight into its pretty ways. It was in an unusual situation, in a crotch by the main trunk of one of five chestnut sprouts, growing from the same root, only eleven feet from the ground. As I looked into the then empty new nest, I heard a faint chirp, and there were the little couple right at my elbow.

Many a time through the period of the rearing of that family did I climb an adjacent sprout, and, only two feet from the nest, watch the feeding of the birdlets by the parents, and take photographs of them. When they were nearly grown, I held them in my hand, and the handsome male, perching on my finger tips, tucked grubs into their widely stretched little mouths. One day quite a party came with me to enjoy this sight. A young lady, skeptical of results, was induced to hold one of the little birds. Suddenly the brilliant male alighted on her thumb, to feed the chick, and so startled her that she nearly lost her balance. Then he hopped on her hat as though to see whether he would make becoming trimming for millinery! But no; these feathered gems were made only for nature's foliage, to add the final touch of charm and grace to an already wonderful creation.

Herbert K. Job.

TOWNSEND'S WARBLER

Dendroica townsendi (*J. K. Townsend*)

A. O. U. Number 668

General Description.— Length, 5 inches. Fore parts, black; upper parts, olive; under parts, yellow and white. Bill, shorter than head, slender, tapering gradually to the tip; wings, long and pointed; tail, even or nearly even.

Color.— Adult Male in Spring and Summer: Crown, hindneck, head, chin, throat, and upper chest, uniform black; a broad stripe over eye, broad cheek stripe (curving upward on side of head, and joining rear extremity of the eye stripe), a spot below eye, *lower chest, and breast, clear lemon-yellow;* abdomen, flanks, and under tail-coverts, white; sides and flanks, heavily streaked with black, the forward streaks joining the black throat-patch at rear; under tail-coverts with a center streak of blackish; back, shoulders, rump, and shorter upper tail-coverts, yellowish olive-green, each feather with a central, wedge-shaped spot of black, these markings concealed on rump; longer upper tail-coverts, black centrally, broadly margined with slate-gray; wings and tail, blackish with light gray edgings, and the middle and greater wing-coverts, broadly tipped with white, forming two conspicuous bars across wing; inner webs of three side tail-feathers extensively white at the end, this occupying the end half or more of the outermost feather; bill, blackish; iris, brown; legs and feet, dark horn-brownish. Adult Male in Autumn and Winter: Similar to the spring and summer plumage, but all the black areas much broken or obscured; that of crown and hindneck by broad olive-green margins to the feathers, the black forming central streaks, that of the side of head overlaid by olive-green tips to the feathers, and that of the throat replaced by nearly uniform lemon-yellow, with black appearing as spots or blotches on sides of chest; black streaks of back, etc., concealed. ADULT FEMALE: Very similar in coloration to the autumn and winter adult male, but black streaks on upper parts much narrower (sometimes nearly obsolete, usually mere shaft-lines), the streaks on sides also usually narrower, sometimes indistinct; crown, sometimes blackish, and throat often blotched with black, occasionally extensively so.

Nest and Eggs.— NEST: Usually in willows about 4 feet from ground; constructed of decayed plant fibers, leaves, and roots and lined with rootlets, hair, and plant down. EGGS: 3 or 4, spotted mainly around larger end with brown, lavender, and burnt-umber.

Distribution.— Western North America; breeding from mountains of southern California to Alaska, eastward to eastern Oregon, northwestern Idaho, etc.; during migration eastward to Rocky Mountains, western Texas and southward over western and central Mexico to highlands of Guatemala, Tres Marias Islands, and extremity of Lower California; occasionally eastward to South Carolina.

The Townsend Warbler is perhaps our most beautiful Warbler of the West. To me, its beauty is increased by its shyness. One does not get a good chance to study this restless bird, because, Warbler-like, it is always moving, especially among the firs and hemlocks which, because of their height and density, are not at all favorable for bird study.

I have never found the Townsend Warbler nesting, but I see it occasionally through Oregon and California during the winter season when it is always on the travel. During the season of migration, one may often see this bird traveling with a flock of Audubon Warblers.

Mr. William L. Dawson characterizes the song and the hunting actions of the Townsend Warbler as follows: "The song ran, *dzwee, dzwee, dzwee, dzwee, dzweetsee,* the first four notes drowsy and drawling, the fourth prolonged, and the remainder somewhat furry and squeaky. The bird hunted patiently through the long needles of the pine, under what would seem to an observer great difficulties. Once he espied an especially desirable tidbit on the under side of a needle-beset branch. The bird leaned over and peered beneath, until he quite lost his balance and turned a somersault in the air. But he returned to the charge again and again, now creeping cautiously around to the under side, now clinging to the pine needles themselves, and again fluttering bravely in the midst, until he succeeded in exhausting the little pocket of provender, whatever it was."

WILLIAM L. FINLEY.

Drawing by R. I. Brasher

TOWNSEND'S WARBLER (⅞ nat. size)

The "most beautiful warbler of the West."—Finley

HERMIT WARBLER

Dendroica occidentalis (*J. K. Townsend*)

A. O. U. Number 669

General Description.— Length, 5 inches. Head, yellow and black; upper parts, gray streaked with black; under parts, white. Bill, shorter than head, slender, tapering gradually to the tip; wings, long and pointed; tail, even or nearly even.

Color.— Adult Male: *Forehead, crown, and whole side of head, down to and including cheeks and sides of neck, clear lemon-yellow,* the crown usually spotted or flecked with black; back of head, black; hindneck streaked with black and grayish olive-green, in varying relative proportions (sometimes nearly uniform black); back, shoulders, rump, and upper tail-coverts, gray, usually tinged with olive-green, broadly streaked with black (the black streaks narrower, sometimes obsolete, on rump); wings and tail, black with light gray edgings,. the middle and greater wing-coverts broadly tipped with white, forming two distinct bars across wing; inner webs of two outermost tail-feathers extensively white, this occupying most of the web on the first and about the end half on the second, the third feather usually with a white longitudinal spot or streak near tip, and the first with outer web largely white; chin, throat, and upper chest, uniform black, this black area with a convex outline at the rear; rest of under parts, white, usually faintly shaded toward the sides with gray and sometimes narrowly and indistinctly streaked on sides with dusky; bill, blackish; iris, brown; legs and feet, dark horn-brown, sometimes blackish. Adult Female: Similar to the male, but darker gray above and forehead and crown largely (often mostly) yellow; throat, whitish spotted with dusky; and dusky streaks on back, etc., still narrower, often obsolete; under parts, also similar, but body portions less tinged with brownish, the chest often with a dusky patch (its feathers tipped with whitish) extending more or less over throat, sometimes covering whole throat.

Nest and Eggs.— Nest: In coniferous trees from 25 to 40 feet up, constructed of weed stems, fibrous stalks of plants, pine needles, and small twigs, bound by cobwebs, and lined with soft fine strips of bark and hair. Eggs: 3 or 4, dull white or grayish-white, spotted and blotched chiefly around larger end with browns and lilac-gray.

Distribution.— Pacific coast district of United States; breeding on higher mountains of California, and northward to British Columbia (chiefly west of the Cascade range); in winter south into Lower California and through Arizona, over Mexican plateau to highlands of Guatemala.

The yellow head, black throat, and white breast and belly of the Hermit Warbler are so characteristic that it can hardly be confused with any other bird within its range; and it has a Chickadee-like trick of hanging upside down to the end of twigs which is also distinctive. It is essentially a bird of the great forests of conifers, where it is found much more frequently than in any other surroundings. Its plumage markings make it one of the most conspicuous of the small birds of the great Sierra Nevada forests. Its characteristic song, which a western ornithologist (Barlow) transliterates *tsit, tsit, tsit, tsit, chee, chee, chee,* the last three syllables uttered more rapidly than the first four, though not strong, is penetrating and has considerable carrying power.

Mr. Finley says: "My experience with the Hermit Warbler is that it is shy and retiring and therefore has a good name. It is not very common through western Oregon. The only nest I have found of the bird was in an oak tree. In western Oregon, it lives more in the firs and oaks."

KIRTLAND'S WARBLER

Dendroica kirtlandi (*Baird*)

A. O. U. Number 670

Other Names.— Jack-pine Warbler; Jack-pine Bird.

General Description.— Length, 5½ inches. Upper parts, gray; under parts, yellow. Bill, shorter than head, slender, tapering gradually to the tip; wings, long and pointed; tail, notched.

Color.— Adult Male: Crown, hindneck, sides of neck, and head, bluish slate-gray, the first usually streaked with black; front of forehead, lores, and space between lower eyelid and cheeks, black, gradually blending behind into the gray of the sides of head; *a white crescentic spot or bar on lower eyelid,* and a smaller, narrower mark of white on upper eyelid; back and shoulders, brownish-gray, broadly streaked with black; rump and upper tail-coverts, slate-gray, narrowly (sometimes obsoletely) streaked with black; wings and tail, dusky with pale brownish-gray or grayish-brown edgings, the middle and greater wing-coverts margined near the tips with paler brownish-gray or grayish-brown, sometimes approaching dull white; inner webs of two outermost tail-feathers with a terminal white spot, this about three-fourths of an inch long on the lateral feathers; cheeks, chin, throat, and rest of under parts, pale lemon-yellow, fading into white on under tail-coverts; sides and flanks, grayish streaked with dusky, *the pronounced gray area on each side of breast separated from the yellow of the central portion by a series of broad black streaks;* chest, usually with a few small flecks of dusky, sometimes immaculate yellow; bill, blackish; iris, brown; legs and feet, dark horn-brownish. Adult Female: Similar to the adult male, but duller in color; the bluish slate-gray of crown, hindneck, and rump replaced with brownish-gray; black streaks of back and shoulders rather narrower; yellow of under parts averaging slightly paler, and chest more frequently as well as more extensively speckled or flecked with dusky.

Nest and Eggs.— Nest: To Mr. Norman A. Wood belongs the honor of discovering the nest and eggs of this species, in Michigan. We quote from his article in the *Bulletin* of the Michigan Ornithological Club, March, 1904. "The nest was built in a depression in the ground, at the foot of a jack-pine about five feet tall, and was only five feet from the road. It was partly covered with low blueberries and sweet fern plants. The nest is two inches inside diameter and the same in depth, very neat and compact, and is composed of strips of soft bark and some vegetable fiber, thickly lined with fine dead grass and pine needles. A few hairs from horses' manes or tails complete the lining. Eggs: A delicate pinkish-white thinly sprinkled with several shades of brown spots forming a sort of wreath at the larger end."

Distribution.— Eastern United States and more southern British provinces, chiefly west of the Alleghenies; very irregularly distributed; breeds in Oscoda, Crawford, and Roscommon counties, Michigan; in migration recorded from Minnesota, Wisconsin, Ontario, Ohio, Illinois, Indiana, Missouri, Virginia, South Carolina, Georgia, and Florida; winters in the Bahamas.

Kirtland's Warbler was discovered by Dr. J. P. Kirtland near Cleveland, Ohio, May 13, 1851. He captured a male bird which was scientifically examined, and credited by both Latin and common names to the discoverer. Just as Columbus did not discover America, so it was found, years after Dr. Kirtland's discovery, that as far back as October, 1841, Dr. Samuel Cabot of Boston captured a male on shipboard near the Bahamas. By 1879 there were but nine known specimens of this bird. To this day it is the rarest of North American Warblers. Its winter home has been found in the Bahamas and there only, and its breeding home in Michigan. In 1903 Norman A. Wood located its nesting district in a comparatively small area in the upland between Lakes Michigan and Huron, and between fifty and a hundred and fifty miles south of Mackinaw. No other breeding ground is known. No winter home has been found except the Bahamas. Between these two localities a few stray migrating Kirtland's Warblers have been seen. The records, few as they are, show that the birds are widely scattered during the northward migration.

In the museum the bird looks not unlike a Magnolia Warbler, but with a plainer tail and no spots across the yellow breast. In action it much resembles the Palm Warbler, particularly in a wagging motion of the tail. It has a very stiff and erect attitude in singing.

Norman A. Wood and J. A. Parmelee made thorough studies of the bird in Michigan not far from Mr. Parmelee's home. What they have to say is very nearly all that is known of the breeding habits of the bird. The bird is a frequenter of high, sandy jack-pine plains; makes its home in jack-pine and scrub oak; nests on the ground; walks gracefully over its feeding grounds, and is equally at home in trees or on the ground. It is called by the natives Jack-pine Bird. The song has an Oriole quality and sings very forcibly *chip-chip-che, chee, chee-r-r-r*. From soft and short, the song changes to a clear quick whistle on the *r*. Other songs have been noted with variations.

This bird is so rare that the report of an observation of it would be apt to be doubted by the ornithologists, crediting the observation rather to some more common bird. But no one knows how many times the searchers for Warblers in May have hoped and searched with enthusiasm to see this not impossible find.

L. Nelson Nichols.

PINE WARBLER

Dendroica vigorsi (*Audubon*)

A. O. U. Number 671 See Color Plate 95

Other Names.—Pine-creeping Warbler; Pine Creeper.

General Description.— Length, 5¾ inches. Upper parts, olive-green; under parts, yellow streaked with olive. Bill, shorter than head, slender, tapering gradually to the tip; wings, long and pointed; tail, notched.

Color.— ADULT MALE: *Above, plain bright olive-green,* usually becoming more grayish on shoulders; wings and tail, dusky with dull gray edgings, the middle and greater wing-coverts broadly tipped with dull white or pale gray, producing two distinct bands; inner webs of two outermost *tail-feathers, extensively white at the end, the white on lateral feather occupying nearly the end half,* the outer web also edged with white; sides of head and neck, olive-green, the former relieved by a narrow, usually indistinct, streak over eye and a crescentic spot of yellow below eye, the lores, usually darker olive-green, often becoming dusky in front of eye; cheek, chin, throat, chest, and breast — usually upper portion of abdomen also — yellow, the sides of chest and breast usually streaked with olive-greenish, sometimes distinctly streaked with dusky; rear under parts, dull whitish, the under tail-coverts, gray basally; bill, brownish-black; iris, brown; legs and feet, dusky-brown. ADULT FEMALE: Smaller and much duller in color than the male; above, plain olive or dull olive-greenish, inclining to gray on hindneck and shoulders, sometimes almost wholly dull gray; beneath, pale olive-yellowish in front and dull whitish behind, sometimes wholly dull grayish-white, faintly tinged with yellow on chest, the sides and flanks more strongly tinged with olive or grayish, and sometimes obsoletely streaked with darker, especially on sides of chest; wings and tail, as in the male.

Nest and Eggs.— NEST: Always placed on horizontal limb of pine or cedar, from 6 to 80 feet up, firmly attached and built of strips of grapevine bark, rootlets, leaf stems, and caterpillar silk, lined warmly with deer or other animal hair, this forming a thick ring around the rim. EGGS: Commonly 4, varying from dull white to pale grayish-lilac, marked with specks and spots of brown, umber, and lilac, usually forming a wreath around larger end.

Distribution.— Eastern United States and more southern British Provinces, north to Minnesota, Manitoba (to Lake Winnipeg), Ontario, New York, southern Maine, and New Brunswick; breeding southward to southern Florida and Gulf States, wintering in Southern States (Florida to Texas) and northward to coast district of Virginia, southern Illinois, etc., occasionally to Massachusetts; occasional in Bermudas.

Drawing by R. I. Brasher

PINE WARBLER (⅞ nat. size)

An inconspicuous Warbler, singing its sweet song from the higher parts of the pine trees

The Pine Warbler is a well-named bird, because its nesting sites are always in pine trees. In migration the bird may be found in Warbler flocks in any kind of tree growth, but looking very plain and drab for the bright company in which it finds itself. Wherever there are pines in the States east of the plains and in southern Canada, there the Pine Warblers may be found nesting in the spring. They are common in the pine barrens all the way from Florida to New Jersey and Illinois. North of that they are rare and local. In the winter they retreat to the southern part of the breeding range and enter the straggling winter flocks.

Dr. Elliott Coues says that in the winter in Florida "the bird is of a sociable if not gregarious nature, usually going in straggling companies of its own kind, and often mixing with Titmice, Kinglets, and Nuthatches, the whole throng gaily and amicably flitting through the shady woods, scrambling incessantly on and all around the branches of the trees in eager, restless quest of their minute insect food."

In the winter he begins to sing his monotonous sweet trill and is very persistent at his single tune until the breeding season is over. Then he becomes again the creeper over pitch and red pines that gave him the earlier name of Pine Creeper.

Courtesy of Nat. Asso. Aud. Soc.

YOUNG PINE WARBLER

PALM WARBLER

Dendroica palmarum palmarum (*Gmelin*)

A. O. U. Number 672 See Color Plate 95

Other Names.— Yellow Red-poll; Yellow Red-poll Warbler; Wagtail Warbler; Tip-up Warbler; Yellow Tip-up.

General Description.— Length, 5 inches. Upper parts, grayish-olive; under parts, yellow and whitish; crown and streaks on under parts, chestnut. Bill, shorter than head, slender, tapering gradually to the tip; wings, long and pointed; tail, notched.

Color.— Adults (sexes alike) in Spring and Summer: *Forehead and crown, uniform bright chestnut*, the former sometimes blackish in front where divided by a short and narrow center line of whitish or pale yellowish; rest of upper parts, grayish-olive narrowly and indistinctly streaked with darker, especially on back and shoulders; lower rump and upper tail-coverts, light yellowish-olive or olive-greenish, the larger coverts more brownish, with indistinct streaks of darker; wings and tail, dusky with light grayish-brown edgings, these most distinct on the end portion of middle and greater wing-coverts; inner web of two outermost tail-feathers with a large spot of white, the third sometimes with a small spot of the same; over eye, a narrow stripe of pale yellow; a triangular spot of dusky in front of eye, and a similar but smaller spot behind the eye; sides of head, grayish-brown, sometimes finely streaked in front with dull brownish-white; an indistinct space below eye of dull brownish-white; cheeks, dull whitish, sometimes tinged with yellow; chin, throat, chest, and under tail-coverts, canary-yellow, the intervening under parts (breast and abdomen), dull whitish, usually tinged with yellow; chest (at least on the sides), streaked with brown or chestnut, the sides and flanks less distinctly streaked; sometimes a series of brown or chestnut streaks along each side of throat; bill, brownish-black; iris, brown; legs and feet, dusky-brown. Adults in Winter: Forehead and crown, grayish-brown, streaked with dusky, sometimes with a slight admixture of chestnut, mostly concealed; the strip over the eye, chin, throat, and chest, dull white instead of yellow; otherwise like the spring and summer plumage, but back, etc., browner, and with darker streaks less distinct (sometimes obsolete).

Nest and Eggs.— Nest: On the ground and usually well concealed under a tuft of grass or other vegetation; compactly constructed of fine dry grasses, strips of bark, and moss. Eggs: 4, creamy white, spotted and blotched with reddish-brown, purple, and lavender, more heavily around large end.

Distribution.— Eastern North America, chiefly west of the Alleghenies; breeding in the interior of British America (Keewatin south to northern Minnesota); in winter southern Florida, Bahamas, Greater Antilles, Cozumel Island, Yucatan, and Swan Island, and island of Old Providence, Caribbean Sea; occasional, during migration, in Atlantic States and at eastern base of Rocky Mountains.

The Palm Warbler is the ever-tilting Warbler that comes into the Northern States in April generally a little ahead of the main Warbler flock and greets us from the small bushes near water. This tilting or waving of the tail up and down is the one characteristic that attracts the casual observer to the bird and it has given the names Tip-up Warbler and Yellow Tip-up to the bird.

The Palm Warbler nests in the very northern part of Minnesota and farther north to the Great Slave Lake and west of Hudson Bay. The Yellow Palm (*Dendroica palmarum hypochrysea*) breeds in northern Maine and eastern Canada.

In the fall the Palm comes down into the Mississippi valley, spreading out over a large area; a few even appear along the Atlantic coast from southern New England all the way to Florida, where they focus into the narrow peninsula. The Yellow Palm, on the other hand, comes down through the Atlantic coast States in the fall and meets the Palm in Florida. Then through the winter, both varieties fraternize in the Florida palms and pine fields and fences, gardens and streets, and are among the commonest of the winter birds of the peninsula. The Palm Warbler far outnumbers the Yellow Palm in Florida. Not only this, but the Palms overflow into the West Indies where the Yellow Palm is not found.

The line over the eye is always yellow in the Yellow Palm; in the Palm it is yellow in the spring but white in the fall. The stronger yellowish underparts of the Yellow Palm are a distinctive mark at any season. Even in the spring when they come tilting back north and separate in Georgia for their two routes, it is not safe to guess that all eastern individuals are Yellow Palms and all central individuals Palm Warblers; they have been known to go astray. The *tsee, tsee* trill is common to both. The love of the water courses and the eternal tilting are the same. Only the yellow and lack of yellow are distinctive marks for the casual observer.

L. Nelson Nichols.

PRAIRIE WARBLER

Dendroica discolor (*Vieillot*)

A. O. U. Number 673 See Color Plate 95

General Description.— Length, 4¾ inches. Upper parts, olive-green; under parts, yellow with black streaks. Bill, shorter than head, slender, tapering gradually to the tip; wings, long and pointed; tail, notched.

Color.—Adult Male: Above, yellowish olive-green, brightest on crown and hindneck, slightly intermixed with grayish on upper tail-coverts; *back-feathers, chestnut centrally,* margined or edged with olive-green; wings and tail, dusky with pale grayish-olive edgings, the middle wing-coverts broadly tipped with pale yellow, the outer webs of greater coverts sometimes yellowish at the ends; inner webs of three outermost tail-feathers, extensively white at the ends, this occupying approximately one-half the web on side feathers, successively smaller on the next two; stripe over eye, large crescentic spot below eye, cheeks, and under parts, clear lemon-yellow, paler behind (under tail-coverts, primrose-yellow); a loral streak and a short streak behind eye, a broad curved streak or crescentic patch immediately beneath the yellow spot below eye, and a series of broad streaks beginning on sides of lower throat and continued along sides to flanks, black; bill, dark brown; iris, brown; legs and feet, dusky-brown. Adult Female: Similar to the male and sometimes hardly distinguishable, but usually much duller in color, with the chestnut spots on back indistinct (often obsolete); the black markings on sides of head replaced by dull grayish, and the black streaks along sides less distinct, especially on flanks, where grayish, or obsolete; olive-green of upper parts sometimes partly replaced by grayish, and yellow of lower parts by dull whitish.

Nest and Eggs.— Nest: Usually placed in hickory, dogwood, or maple saplings, barberry, viburnum or low bushes, sometimes in scrub pines or cedars, on dry hillsides and cut-over areas; firmly woven of weed stems, dry grasses, vegetable fibers and stems, and lined with horse-hair. Eggs: Usually 4, white or greenish-white, spotted and blotched with burnt-umber, chestnut, purplish, and lilac-gray.

Distribution.— Eastern United States, breeding north to Massachusetts, southern Ontario, southern Michigan, southern Wisconsin (?), etc., south to Florida, and probably to the Gulf States in general; occurring irregularly north to northern Michigan; west to edge of the Great Plains, in eastern Nebraska, eastern Kansas, etc.; winters from central Florida through the Bahamas and the West Indies.

The Prairie Warbler is not very common on the prairies. It is rather a bird of the southern shrubs and short trees. In most favorable localities from Georgia to Virginia this Warbler nests commonly. Northwest, north and northeast of Virginia it breeds sparingly and locally. Some old fields and bush lots of southern New England, especially if there are barberry and juniper, may attract the Prairie Warblers. In very scattered numbers they may be found from New Jersey and New York to Kansas and Nebraska, but only in the bushes and not on the prairie grasslands. They are distinctly birds of the hillsides. Their chestnut markings on the back are excellent distinguishing characteristics. Better yet is the peculiar song consisting of a thin wiry, lisping trill that can be confused with the song of no other bird. Dr. Elliott Coues in *Birds of the Northwest* gave an interesting account of his bird trips near Washington in his college days. The Prairie Warbler was one of his earliest acquaintances. "Ten to one we would not see the little creatures at first; but presently, from the very nearest juniper would come the well-known sounds. A curious song, if song it can be called — as much like a mouse complaining of the toothache as anything else I can liken it to — it is simply indescribable. Then perhaps the quaint performer would dart out into the air, turn a somersault after a passing midge, get right side up, and into the shrubbery again in an instant; or if we kept still, with wide-open eyes, we would see him perched on a spray, settled firmly on his legs, with his beak straight up in the air, the throat swelling, and hear the curious musician."

OVEN-BIRD

Seiurus aurocapillus (*Linnæus*)

A. O. U. Number 674 See Color Plate 92

Other Names.— Golden-crowned Thrush; Teacher; Nightingale; Wood Wagtail; Golden-crowned Wagtail; Golden-crowned Accentor.

General Description.— Length, 6¼ inches. Upper parts, olive; under parts, white with black spots. Bill, shorter than head, slender, tapering gradually to the tip; wings, long and pointed; tail, even or slightly notched.

Color.— ADULTS (SEXES ALIKE): Crown with *two narrow lateral stripes of black inclosing a much broader center stripe of tawny,* the feathers of the latter tipped with pale olive, especially on back of head which is sometimes uniform light olive; over eye, light grayish-olive fading into a lighter hue of the same on sides of head; rest of upper parts, plain dull olive-green, the inner webs of wing- and tail-feathers, grayish-brown; a whitish eye-ring; lores, grayish-white or dull whitish; cheeks and under parts, white, the chest and sides heavily streaked with black, the flanks more narrowly and less distinctly streaked; a dusky streak below cheeks; under wing-coverts, pale olive-yellow; bill, dark brown, much paler below; iris, brown; legs and feet, pale flesh color in life.

Nest and Eggs.— NEST: Imbedded in ground in dry woods; of dried grass, artfully arched over with dead leaves and so perfectly blending with its surroundings as to be rarely discovered unless the bird is scared from the nest. EGGS: 3 to 6, glossy white marked by specks and spots scattered over entire surface usually more thickly around larger end.

Distribution.— Eastern North America; north to Nova Scotia, Anticosti Island, Labrador (?), southern

Drawing by R. I. Brasher

OVEN-BIRD (⅜ nat. size)

The precision of this bird's gait approaches the unconsciously comical

and western shores of Hudson Bay, and the Yukon Valley in Alaska; west to eastern base of Rocky Mountains in Colorado and Montana, accidentally to British Columbia; breeding southward at least to Virginia, the Ohio Valley, and Kansas, probably much farther, and in the Bahamas; in winter, Gulf coast of United States, Bahamas, Greater Antilles, Swan Island and Old Providence Island, Caribbean Sea, and through Mexico into Central America, and northern South America (Colombia).

Most land birds of terrestrial habits progress on the ground by jumping or running. Comparatively few species walk, and the commoner of these include the Crow, the Larks, the Starling, the Grackles, the Pipits, the Water-Thrushes and the Oven-bird. Of these the Oven-bird is easily the most accomplished walker; indeed there is something which approaches the unconsciously comical in the precision of this bird's gait as it promenades on its pretty pink feet

Photo by H. K. Job Courtesy of Outing Pub. Co.

OVEN-BIRD ON HER NEST

over the leaves and along fallen logs. This impression is heightened by its practice of bobbing its tail during its frequent pauses, an operation which is curiously at variance with its otherwise rather over-dignified demeanor. The Water-Thrushes also walk and bob their tails much after the manner of the Oven-bird, which they also resemble in size and coloration; but there are certain distinctive markings by means of which the birds may readily be distinguished, while the Water-Thrushes' decided preference for the banks of streams is not shared by the Oven-bird. The tail-bobbing habit has given the birds the popular name of "Wagtail" (which is inaccurate in so far as it conveys the idea that the movement is a lateral one); but the Water-Thrushes' natural habitat is recognized by the adjective, "water," which qualifies the remainder of the popular designation, while the Oven-bird is known as the Wood Wagtail. The scientific family name of the Oven-bird and the Water-Thrushes, *Seiurus,* means "to wave the tail."

Besides its walking and its tail-bobbing, the bird has other distinctive peculiarities. The most pronounced of these is the architecture of its nest, from which it takes its name. Like most birds which build on the ground, the female, when forced by the near approach of an intruder to leave her nest, flutters away, dragging one wing as if it were broken, this apparently being a deliberate ruse intended to distract attention from the nest. But the nest usually is so cleverly hidden that it is by no means easy to find, even when the observer thinks he sees the precise point at which the bird appeared.

Again, the common song of the Oven-bird at once challenges the attention. It consists of several repetitions of a two-syllabled note uttered rapidly, and in a quick crescendo. Mr. Burroughs translates this utterance into, "Teacher, *Teacher,* TEACHER, TEACHER," and the note does approximate the sound of the word. The bird puts the accent invariably upon the last syllable — as do some New England schoolchildren — so that what he says is, Tea-cher', *Tea-cher',* and so on, the series often ending with the first syllable alone. This somewhat monotonous chant is metallic and strident rather than musical; but, as Mr. Burroughs says, "Wait till the inspiration of its flight-song is upon it. What a change! Up it goes through the branches of the trees, leaping from limb to limb, faster and faster, till it shoots from the tree-tops fifty or more feet into the air above them, and bursts into an ecstasy of song, rapid, ringing, lyrical; no more like its habitual song than a match is like a rocket; brief but thrilling; emphatic but musical. Having reached its climax of flight and song, the bird closes its wings and drops nearly perpendicularly downward like the Skylark. If its song were more prolonged, it would rival the song of that famous bird. The bird does this many times a day during early June, but oftenest at twilight."

Ornithologists generally agree with Mr. Burroughs that this song is most likely to be heard when the bird is mounting, as he describes, and in the late afternoon or early evening; but at least one careful and accurate observer, Bradford Torrey, recorded (in *Birds in the Bush*) having heard the bird sing it from a perch, or even on the ground, and as early as 6 o'clock in the morning.

It seems clear now that this remarkable flight-song of the Oven-bird is the one which Thoreau heard so often, but failed to identify with the singer, though he knew the "Golden-crowned Thrush," the name by which the Oven-bird was formerly known. No less than fifteen times (between 1851 and 1860) did he note in his journal hearing this mysterious "night-warbler's" song; and, curiously enough, one entry (for May 16, 1858) begins with, "A golden-crowned thrush hops quite near," and ends with, "Hear the night warbler." So anxious did he become to identify this unseen bird that Emerson, with his gentle irony, warned him to desist trying to find out what it was, lest, should he be successful, he should thereafter lose all interest in life.

GEORGE GLADDEN.

LOUISIANA WATER-THRUSH

Seiurus motacilla (*Vieillot*)

A. O. U. Number 676 See Color Plate 92

Other Names.— Large-billed Water-Thrush; Southern Water-Thrush; Wagtail; Water Wagtail.

General Description.— Length, 6¼ inches. Upper parts, grayish-olive; under parts, white with streaks of grayish-olive. Bill, shorter than head, slender, tapering gradually to the tip; wings, long and pointed; tail, even or slightly notched.

Color.— ADULTS (SEXES ALIKE): Above, plain grayish-olive, slightly darker on crown; a conspicuous stripe of white over eye, extending from nostril to beyond end of ear region; a triangular loral spot and broad stripe behind eye of dark grayish-olive, the latter sometimes involving greater part of sides of head, the lower portion of which, however, is always paler and streaked with dull whitish; a crescentic mark of white on lower eyelid; cheeks, white, usually flecked with grayish-olive; *under parts white or buffy-white*, becoming cream-buff on flanks and under tail-coverts; chin and throat, immaculate or with only a few minute flecks; chest, sides, and flanks, broadly streaked with grayish-olive, the streaks on front of chest smaller, more distinctly wedge-shaped; under wing-coverts brownish-gray; bill, horn-brownish; iris, brown; legs and feet, pale flesh color.

Nest and Eggs.— NEST: Placed among roots of fallen timber, old logs, or under mossy banks, always near water and always carefully concealed; exterior of mud-covered leaves which form a solid foundation when dry; inner nest of twigs, grass stems, rootlets and skeletonized leaves, lined usually with dead pine needles. EGGS: 4 or 5, rarely 6, white or creamy, thickly marked with chestnut, rufous, and lilac, more heavily toward larger end.

Distribution.— Eastern United States to South America; breeds from southeastern Nebraska, southeastern Minnesota, and the southern parts of Michigan, Ontario, New York, and New England south to northeastern Texas, northern Georgia, and Central South Carolina; winters from northern Mexico to Colombia, the Greater Antilles, Antigua, and the Bahamas: accidental in California.

Courtesy of Am. Mus. Nat. Hist.

LOUISIANA WATER-THRUSH (½ nat. size)

This Warbler's song is a true voice of the wild

The Louisiana Water-Thrush is one of the comparatively few birds that walk. Like the Oven-bird it also bobs its tail as it proceeds, a peculiarity from which it derives its popular name of Water Wagtail, the "water" being in recognition of its fondness for the banks of running streams. By careless observers the bird is sometimes mistaken for the Spotted Sandpiper (often called the "Tip-up"), because of both birds' habit of bobbing their tails; but their very different appearance should prevent this confusion.

The bird's resemblance to a Thrush begins and ends in its back being of an olive-brown color, while its grayish-white breast is streaked with black. Its manners are totally different from

Photo of habitat group Courtesy of Am. Mus. Nat. Hist.

LOUISIANA WATER-THRUSHES

those of any of the Thrushes, and it is much smaller than the smallest member of this species. Its characteristic movements are very quick and nervous; it is seldom at rest; and its normal timidity is increased during the breeding season, when it is exceedingly wary about approaching its nest (which usually is very cleverly hidden) in the presence of an intruder.

In its striking exuberance and singularly weird and ringing quality, this Warbler's song is a true voice of the wild. The listener whose ear recognizes and whose heart responds to such utterances is thrilled by it. The emotions which it conjures up are perfectly tangible to him, yet it would be difficult to analyze them, and virtually impossible to describe them in words. One appreciative listener speaks of the song as "loud, clear, and exquisitely sweet, beginning with a burst of melody which becomes softer and more delicate until the last notes die away, lost in the ripple of the stream, above which the birds are generally perched." Like the Oven-bird, this Warbler has a flight-song, described by Dr. Chapman as "a thrilling performance which carries the bird above the tree-tops in uncontrollable musical ecstasy."

"This bird frequents wet ground always, but is by no means confined to running streams, since it is a regular inhabitant of more or less stagnant swamps, and is not infrequently found in bushy marshes at some little distance from large woods. It usually nests among the up-turned roots of a prostrate tree, but also hides its nest under the edges of a fallen log or in the sloping bank of a small stream, or even among the tangled roots at the edges of a cut, where a stream has washed away the soil at a bend. In other cases it nests on the ground in an ordinary swamp, placing the nest under the roots of a tree or otherwise hiding it from view." (Barrows.)

A singular feature of its nest-building is the pathway of leaves leading from the nest and forming a doormat sometimes a foot long.

WATER-THRUSH

Seiurus noveboracensis noveboracensis (*Gmelin*)

A. O. U. Number 675 See Color Plate 92

Other Names.— New York Warbler; Small-billed Water-Thrush; Northern Water-Thrush; Wagtail; Water Wagtail; Aquatic Wood Wagtail; Aquatic Thrush; New York Water-Thrush.

General Description.— Length, 5¾ inches. Upper parts, olive; under parts, yellow streaked and spotted with sooty-olive. Bill, shorter than head, slender, tapering gradually to the tip; wings, long and pointed; tail, even or slightly notched.

Color.— Adults (sexes alike): Above, plain olive;

a broad stripe of buff over eye extending from nostril to sides of neck; a triangular spot of dusky-olive in front of eye, and a broad streak of the same behind eye; a crescentic mark of light buffy on lower eyelid; below eye and sides of head, streaked with olive and yellowish or pale buffy; *broad cheek stripe and under parts, sulphur-yellow*; the chest, sides, and flanks, streaked with dark sooty-olive, the lower throat with shorter wedge-shaped marks, the upper throat usually with small triangular spots or flecks of the same; under tail-coverts with concealed portion extensively olive or grayish-olive; bill, dusky-brown; iris, brown; legs and feet, flesh color.

Nest and Eggs.— Nest: Always carefully concealed in a bed of moss at the base of a stump or tree or alongside moss-covered logs, near water and on or near the ground; constructed of particles of moss and lined with moss stems; frequently a few dead leaves and twigs are intermingled to give it stability, and the foundation is often quite substantial. Eggs: 4 or 5, creamy-white spotted with chestnut and lilac, more heavily around larger end; usually smaller than those of the Louisiana Water-Thrush.

Distribution.— Eastern North America; north to Davis Inlet, Newfoundland, and the shores of Hudson Bay; breeding southward to northern New England, mountains of Pennsylvania and West Virginia (spruce belt), southern Michigan (?), northeastern Illinois; in winter southward throughout West Indies and along eastern coast districts of Central America to Colombia, Venezuela, British Guiana, Brazil (?), Trinidad, and Tobago, and to Swan Island and Old Providence Island, Caribbean Sea; occasional in Bermudas; accidental in southern Greenland.

The Northern Water-Thrush is similar to, but somewhat smaller than, the Louisiana Water-Thrush, from which it may be distinguished by its unspotted throat and the white line over the eye. Like its larger relative, it walks and bobs its tail meanwhile, but, unlike the former, during its migrations it is apt to appear in gardens near houses, and is comparatively tame and trustful. By some observers, the song of this species is considered more musical than that of the Louisiana Water-Thrush, though the effort seems to lack the uncanny quality of the larger bird, and its flight-song is a less elaborate, though pleasing, performance.

Grinnell's Water-Thrush (*Seiurus noveboracensis notabilis*) is found in western North America. It is larger than the Northern Water-Thrush, and the coloration of the upper parts is less olive, and the under parts are usually white with little, if any, yellow tinge.

Photo by A. A. Allen

LOUISIANA WATER-THRUSH

With food for young

KENTUCKY WARBLER

Oporornis formosus (*Wilson*)

A. O. U. Number 677 See Color Plate 98

Other Name.— Kentucky Wagtail.

General Description.— Length, 5¾ inches. Upper parts, olive-green; under parts, yellow. Bill, much shorter than head, slender, tapering gradually to the tip; wings, long and pointed; tail, much shorter than wing, slightly rounded, the feathers tapering.

Color.— Adult Male: Crown, black, the feathers of crown and back of head (especially the latter) tipped with slate-gray; rest of upper parts, including sides of neck, plain olive-green; outer web of outermost primary, white; a stripe over eye of lemon-yellow; extending from nostrils to just behind the eye, where curving downward and including the rear half, or more, of lower eyelid; lores, below eye (except the yellow on under eyelid), and greater part of sides of head, uniform black, *this black extended along edge of lower throat and forming a triangular patch;* terminal portion of sides of head, olive-green; under parts, clear lemon-yellow, changing on sides and flanks to olive-green; bill, dark brownish; iris, brown; legs and feet, pale flesh color. Adult Female: Similar to the adult male and not always distinguishable, but usually with the gray tips to feathers of crown broader (even those of the forehead being thus marked) and more brownish-gray, and the black patch on sides of head more restricted and less sharply defined; in some (probably younger) specimens the black of the crown is entirely concealed, and still more rarely there is no black, the whole crown being uniform brownish-gray.

Nest and Eggs.— NEST: Built on ground, in a thicket, in the woods, at the foot of a tree or tussock of weeds; unusually bulky for the size of the bird; constructed of leaves, small twigs, rootlets, and grass and lined with fine rootlets and horse-hair. EGGS: 4 or 5, white speckled with chestnut, umber, and lilac, forming a wreath at large end or evenly distributed.

Distribution.— Eastern United States; breeding from Alabama, Louisiana and Texas, north to southeastern New York, New Jersey, eastern Pennsylvania, Ohio, southern Michigan, southern Wisconsin, Iowa, and eastern Nebraska, west to border of Great Plains (Texas to Nebraska) occurring north (but not breeding?) to southern Connecticut and Long Island; south in winter to Cuba (accidental), Florida Keys (occasional), and through southern Mexico and Central America to northern Colombia.

The Kentucky Warbler is a lover of heavily timbered country, more especially of deciduous forests, where he sings his *turdle, turdle, turdle,* or *peer-ry, peer-ry, peer-ry* much as do the Cardinal and the Carolina Wren. He is a persistent singer giving many hours a day to his musical efforts from the tops of forest trees, and if disturbed while singing will fly to another perch and resume his song.

The nest is built down in the shorter bushes or ranker weeds, or on the ground at the foot of trees. Mr. Dawson says that the easiest way to find it "is to spy upon the female when the nest is a-making." The Kentucky Warbler, like many other ground birds, walks instead of hopping, and bobs his tail in that peculiar manner which has given them the vernacular name of Wagtail — he is the Kentucky Wagtail. Unlike the Oven-bird and the Water-Thrush, his scientific name does not express this characteristic. Instead it means "beautiful autumn bird."

These birds begin to leave early for their winter home. In July many are off by way of Mexico for Colombia, South America.

CONNECTICUT WARBLER

Oporornis agilis (*Wilson*)

A. O. U. Number 678 See Color Plate 99

Other Names.— Bog Black-throat; Tamarack Warbler; Swamp Warbler.

General Description.— Length, 5½ inches. Fore parts, slate; upper parts, olive; under parts, yellow. Bill, much shorter than head, slender, tapering gradually to the tip; wings, long and pointed; tail, much shorter than wing, slightly rounded, the feathers tapering.

Color.—ADULT MALE: Forehead, crown, and sides of head, uniform slate color, *relieved by a conspicuous and uninterrupted eye-ring of white*; chin, throat, and chest, plain slate-gray, paler on chin and upper throat, deeper (sometimes almost slate color) on chest; rest of under parts, pale yellow, the sides and flanks, light olive-green; upper parts (except forehead and crown), plain olive-green, the outer web of outermost primary edged with whitish; bill, dark brownish; iris, brown; legs and feet, pale flesh color. ADULT FEMALE: Similar to the adult male, but slate color of head replaced by grayish-olive, olive or brownish-olive, that of chin and throat by pale brownish-buffy or dull brownish-white, that of chest by a deeper shade of the same color as chin and throat; olive of upper parts browner.

Nest and Eggs.— NEST: On ground in swampy woods; compactly built, entirely of dried grass in some instances, built of shreds of bark, leaf stems, and grass in other cases, and lined with fine rootlets and hair. EGGS: 4, white, or creamy-white, spotted with black, brown, and lilac, forming a wreath around large end.

Distribution.— Eastern United States and British Provinces; north to Maine, New Hampshire, Vermont, Ontario, Michigan, and Manitoba west to Minnesota and (casually) Colorado, breeding in Ontario (?) Minnesota, and Manitoba; in winter south to Bahamas, Colombia, and upper Amazon valley.

The Connecticut Warbler is a strange rare bird; a walker instead of a hopping bird; a bird that is hard to find even when it is in the neighborhood, a bird which comes north by one route and returns by another, and is almost lost to the world in both breeding and winter feeding seasons. In the spring this Warbler, with the white eye-ring and slate-gray bib, comes up out of the West Indies to Florida, then across to the Mississippi and Ohio valleys, and almost disappears in the forests of northern Michigan, Minnesota, and Manitoba. From the extremely few records of this bird during the breeding season, one might suppose there were but a few dozen pairs in existence, allowing even for those that are really never observed by man. Maybe no one but Ernest T. Seton has ever seen a nest of the Connecticut Warbler. He found a nest and eggs on a mossy mound in a tamarack swamp near Carberry, Manitoba, June 21, 1883.

During the breeding season Connecticut has two songs: one, *beecher,* six times repeated, and the other, *free-chapel, free-chapel, free-chapel, whoit.* Free chapel and Beecher and Connecticut do not seem so inappropriately associated in the same bird, so that his Puritan name is quite proper.

In the late summer, the Connecticut Warblers start for the land of the Puritan and show themselves there much more commonly than elsewhere. They do not go south by way of the Mississippi basin, but following east through the St. Lawrence and Great Lakes basin, reach New England in September. These rare Warblers pass on, most of them, unnoticed through the Atlantic coast States and leave Florida in October. The latest known record of this bird was on October 22d in the northern part of Colombia in South America. From then until April the bird is lost to the world. One year on April 9th the bird was seen at Tonantins, a town of the upper Amazon. The earliest Florida date is only a month later.

L. Nelson Nichols.

MOURNING WARBLER

Oporornis philadelphia (*Wilson*)

A. O. U. Number 679 See Color Plate 100

Other Names.— Black-throated Ground Warbler; Crape Warbler; Mourning Ground Warbler; Philadelphia Warbler.

General Description.— Length, 5½ inches. Upper parts, gray and olive-green; under parts, black and yellow. Bill, much shorter than head, slender, tapering gradually to the tip; wings, long and pointed; tail, shorter than wing, slightly rounded, the feathers tapering.

Color.—Adult Male: Head and neck, plain slate-gray deepening into slate color on crown and hindneck, and into almost black on lores; chin, throat, and chest, black, the feathers with distinct terminal margins of slate-gray, these sometimes so broad in front and on the sides that the black is mainly concealed, except on chest; rest of under parts, clear canary-yellow, changing to olive-green on sides and flanks; upper parts, except crown and hindneck, uniform olive-green, the outermost primary edged with whitish; bill, brownish-black; iris, brown; legs and feet, pale flesh color. *No white eye-ring in adult male.* Adult Female: Similar to the adult male, but without any black on chin, throat, or chest, which are smoke gray, much paler (sometimes brownish-white) on chin and part of throat; slate color of crown and hindneck duller, tinged with olive; yellow of under parts slightly paler.

Nest and Eggs.— Nest: In swampy ground among weed bunches or old logs, well concealed and very near the earth, or in the uplands in dry cut-over clearings in small bushes one or two feet above ground; composed of dead weeds, some bark strips, and grass and thickly lined with black horse-hair or black rootlets. Eggs: 4 or 5, white, marked around large end with chestnut and lilac and with small spots of former color scattered over remainder of the shell.

Distribution.— Eastern United States and British Provinces; breeding from mountains of West Virginia (spruce belt) and Pennsylvania, New York, higher districts of New England, Michigan, eastern Nebraska (?), and Minnesota, northward at least to northwestern Ontario, and Manitoba, during migration southward through eastern United States in general (as far west as central Texas), and in winter south to Nicaragua, Costa Rica, Colombia, and Ecuador.

The Mourning Warbler is a quiet Thrush-like bird. If he did not sing in the spring, he might be considered not only scarce but very rare. Even as it is there are many people who have never seen the bird, even in the broad area in which it breeds.

In the cool tangles and thickets of northern hillsides ribbed by cooler gullies, and down in the flat valley swamps where brush and small trees abound, that is where the Mourning Warbler breaks forth into song, because his nest is somewhere not far away from the view of poison ivy, deadly nightshade, or skunk cabbage. A little bush in the rank ferns may be the nesting site. The warmer and more settled parts of the wide breeding area are seldom visited by the

Mourning Warbler. He reserves his song, resembling those of both the Oven-bird and the Water-Thrush, for the distant and wilder regions. He sings *tee, te-o, te-o, te-o, we-se,* loud and clear. Often he will sing a half-hour at a time far up in a tree over a desperately mixed tangle down in which the female sits silently on the nest.

Photo by A. A. Allen

MALE MOURNING WARBLER

At his nest among the nettles

In the late summer they begin their southward journey, appearing frequently along hedgerows, fences full of bushes, and by the highways that skirt the edges of tamarack and cedar swamps. The western birds go south, and the eastern birds go southwesterly until they all meet in one migration route, Louisiana and eastern Texas. Then they are off through Mexico to the winter home in Central America, Colombia, and Ecuador.

There is really nothing about this bird to suggest mourning except the cowl. The cowl is a beautiful bluish-slate set off by a black scarf on the breast. The bird is quiet and retiring in manners, never showy but rather cheerful and self-contained. The *philadelphia* in his scientific name suggests the Quaker garb, and the bird suggests the Quaker manner. Alexander Wilson was not far wrong to call him the Philadelphia Warbler.

L. NELSON NICHOLS.

MACGILLIVRAY'S WARBLER

Oporornis tolmiei (*J. K. Townsend*)

A. O. U. Number 680

Other Name.— Tolmie's Warbler.

General Description.— Length, 5½ inches. Fore parts, slate; upper parts, olive-green; under parts, yellow. Bill, much shorter than head, slender, tapering gradually to the tip; wings, long and pointed; tail, shorter than wing, slightly rounded, the feathers tapering.

Color.— ADULT MALE: Head and neck, slate color, deepening into black on lores, *a conspicuous spot of white on each eyelid,* smaller on the upper; chin sometimes white; throat and chest, darker slate but the feathers margined with pale gray, never forming a "solid" black patch on chest; upper parts (except crown and hindneck), plain olive-green, duller (sometimes slightly tinged with gray) on back and shoulders; outer web of outermost primary, edged with white; under parts of body, clear lemon-yellow, becoming yellowish olive-green on sides and flanks; bill, dusky-brown; iris, brown; legs and feet, light flesh color. ADULT FEMALE: Crown, hindneck, and sides of head and neck, mouse-gray, fading into pale gray on chin, throat, and chest; a distinct white mark on each eyelid, as in the adult male; rest of plumage as in adult male.

Nest and Eggs.— NEST: In some localities, near ground in clump of grass or bushes, in others, in saplings or juniper trees, from 3 to 6 feet up; made of dried grass and lined with fine grass, a few rootlets, or some horse-hair. EGGS: 3 to 5, usually 4, creamy-white, spotted at large end with dark brown, lilac-gray, and a few pen lines.

Distribution.— Western United States and British Columbia; breeding in mountains from Pacific coast ranges to Rocky Mountains, north to British Columbia (including Vancouver Island), south at least to Arizona, New Mexico, and western Texas; during migrations east to western Nebraska, central Texas, etc.; south in winter to Cape St. Lucas and over whole of Mexico and Central America to Colombia.

W. Leon Dawson, the Ohio ornithologist, insists that Macgillivray's Warbler should be called "Tolmie's Warbler," the ornithological powers-that-be to the contrary notwithstanding, and for the following interesting reasons: The bird was discovered (in 1839) by the American ornithologist Townsend, who named it in honor of Dr. W. T. Tolmie, a friend of his and, later, as a factor of the Hudson Bay Company, of all naturalists and such-like wanderers. But when

Townsend died, his collection came into the possession of John James Audubon, who proceeded to give this Warbler the name of Macgillivray, a Scotch naturalist of his acquaintance, who never saw America, much less the bird — alive, at any rate. To this Mr. Dawson objects.

Dr. Coues wrote that he did not remember ever to have seen this Warbler "more than a few feet from the ground, nor elsewhere than in thick brush," and another observer notes its peculiar practice of spending much time actually on the ground, where it scratches industriously among the leaves and searches under dead logs for its insect food. Townsend remarked its sprightly warble, which it delivers with its head and bill raised almost vertically, its little throat swelling with the effort, and Mr. Dawson reduces the syllables of the song to the words, *sheep, sheep, sheep, shear, shear, sheep.* The same observer noted that when the female is flushed from her nest (which is not easy to find), instead of raising an outcry, or attempting to decoy the intruder away, she usually stays near and feeds among the branches with a great show of industry and preoccupation.

Drawing by R. I. Brasher

MACGILLIVRAY'S WARBLER (⅘ nat. size)

Most frequently observed in thickets or on the ground

MARYLAND YELLOW-THROAT

Geothlypis trichas trichas (*Linnæus*)

A. O. U. Number 681 See Color Plate 98

Other Names.— Olive-colored Yellow-throated Wren; Yellow-throat; Western Yellow-throat; Northern Yellow-throat; Northern Maryland Yellow-throat; Black-masked Ground Warbler; Ground Warbler.

General Description.— Length, 4¾ inches. Upper parts, olive-green; under parts, yellow and buffy. Bill, decidedly shorter than head, tapering gradually to the tip; wings, short and much rounded; tail, about the same length as wing and much rounded.

Color.—Adult Male: *Forehead (sometimes including front of crown) and sides of head, uniform black, forming a conspicuous "mask,"* this margined posteriorly by a band of light ash-gray of variable width, sometimes narrow and abruptly defined behind, sometimes covering whole of crown; rest of upper parts, plain dull grayish olive-green, back of head and hinder part of crown tinged with brown; chin, throat, and chest (sometimes breast also), lemon-yellow; under tail-coverts, paler yellow; rest of under parts, pale buffy, becoming light buffy grayish-brown on sides and flanks; edge of wing, yellow; bill, black; iris, brown; legs and feet, flesh color. ADULT FEMALE: Head without any black or gray; crown, grayish-olive, the forehead or front of crown (sometimes both) tinged with cinnamon-brown; sides of head, similar in color to crown, but paler, especially above and around eye; yellow of under parts, paler and duller than in the male, sometimes distinct only on under tail-coverts; otherwise similar in coloration to the adult male.

Nest and Eggs.— NEST: Placed close to ground but raised clear by a platform of dried grass and leaves, and usually in damp locations and carefully hidden beneath a tussock or patch of briers; large and bulky for size of bird; composed of coarse grass, leaves, rootlets, lined with finer grass, and a few hairs. EGGS: 3 to 5, commonly 4, shiny white, specked and blotched with chestnut, purplish-black, brown, and a few spots of lilac.

Distribution.— Eastern North America; breeds from North Dakota, northern Minnesota, northern Ontario, and southern Labrador south to central Texas, northern parts of the Gulf States, and Virginia; winters from North Carolina and Louisiana to Florida, the Bahamas, Cuba, Jamaica, Guatemala, and Costa Rica.

Photo by A. A. Allen

MALE MARYLAND YELLOW-THROAT

Approaching his nest and open-mouthed young

One who has ears to hear what the birds say is in no danger of remaining long unaware of the existence of the beautiful little Warbler, the Maryland Yellow-throat; for his curiously rhythmical cry of "Witchery, *witchery*, WITCHERY, WITCHERY," with uniformly increasing emphasis, is one of the characteristic wood sounds during the bird's sojourn in its northern range. And the male bird is both picturesque and conspicuous, with his bright yellow waistcoat, and the black mask drawn over his eyes, suggesting the villain, which he most certainly is not. On the contrary, besides being both handsome and amiable, he is one of the most industrious and useful of the useful Warbler family.

The Yellow-throat's movements and manners are characteristic of his kind, which is to say, he is a restless and rather timid bird, and much given to darting about hither and thither. But his timidity is less pronounced than that of many other members of his species which pass their time almost wholly in the tree-tops, thereby taxing the patience — not to say the eyesight — of

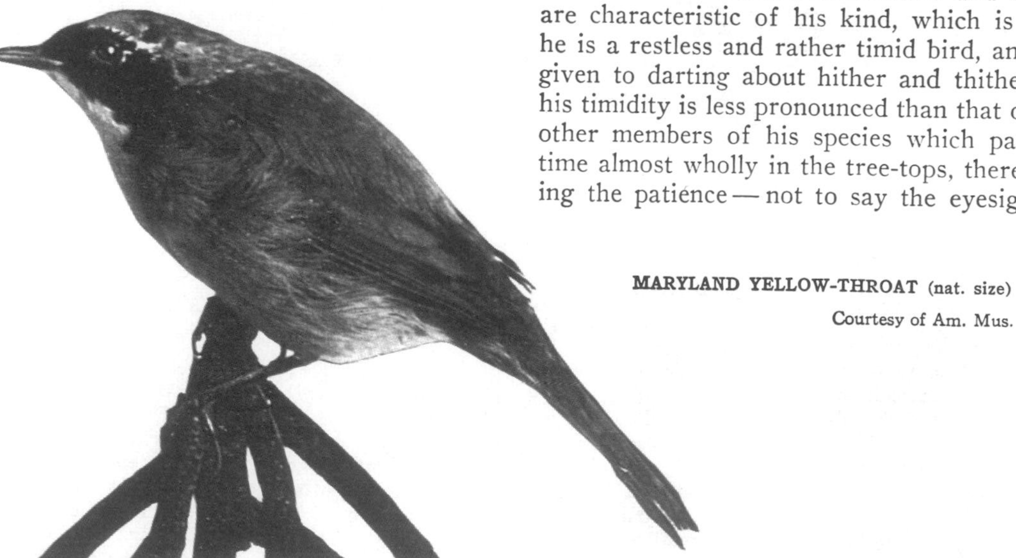

MARYLAND YELLOW-THROAT (nat. size)

Courtesy of Am. Mus. Nat. Hist.

the bird-student; for the Yellow-throat does much of his hunting and frolicking in the brush and thickets near enough the ground to make observation of his movements comparatively easy.

Indeed, the bird manifests something like a distinct friendliness for and interest in human beings, provided they keep at what he considers a safe distance. This, however, does not prevent him from spending much of his time in almost inaccessible marshes, and especially such as have heavy cat-tail growths, in which the bird seems very much at home. In drier surroundings he frequently alights on the ground, where he also places his deep cup-shaped nest, and hence his somewhat misleading popular name of "Ground Warbler," which would be fairly accurate if it were applied to the Oven-bird or the Water-Thrushes. Like these birds, and the Yellow-breasted Chat, the Yellow-throat has a flight song, uttered as he flutters a few feet into the air from a tree-top; but it is little more than a confused and brief inarticulate jumble of notes, and hardly deserves to be called a song at all.

The Yellow-throat is one of the birds which is frequently imposed upon by the Cowbird, and seems entirely to lack the discernment of the Yellow Warbler and the Chat in detecting, and their wit in defeating, the parasite's purpose. Indeed, the female Yellow-throat not only incubates the Cowbird's egg, but solicitously feeds the voracious foundling, sometimes to the neglect of her own young, who may in consequence be almost starved or smothered by the ugly interloper. GEORGE GLADDEN.

There are several regional varieties of the Maryland Yellow-throat, north of the Mexican boundary, differing but little from each other either in size or in coloration. The Florida, or Southern, Yellow-throat (*Geothlypis trichas ignota*) is found in the southeastern United States, breeding from the Dismal Swamp in Virginia south to Florida and along the Gulf coast to Louisiana; in the winter it may be found from the coast of South Carolina to southeastern Texas and Cuba. The Western Yellow-throat (*Geothlypis trichas occidentalis*), is distributed over the arid region of the western United States and the provinces of southwestern Canada; it winters south to Cape San Lucas and Tepic, Mexico. The Pacific Yellow-throat (*Geothlypis trichas arizela*) lives in the Pacific coast district, breeding from southern British Columbia to southern California and wintering south to Cape San Lucas. The Salt Marsh Yellow-throat (*Geothlypis trichas sinuosa*) is limited to the salt marshes about San Francisco Bay.

Photo by W. L. Finley and H. T. Bohlman

MALE PACIFIC YELLOW-THROAT FEEDING YOUNG

YELLOW-BREASTED CHAT

Icteria virens virens *(Linnæus)*

A. O. U. Number 683 See Color Plate 98

Other Names.— Chat; Common Chat; Yellow Chat; Yellow Mockingbird; Polyglot Chat.

General Description.— Length, 7½ inches. Upper parts, olive-green; under parts, yellow and white. Bill, much shorter than head, stout, and arched; wing, moderate in length, rounded; tail, as long or longer than wing, rounded, the feathers narrow with rounded tips.

Color.—Adult Male: Above, plain grayish olive-green, grayer on upper tail-coverts and (usually) lower rump; a stripe (extending from nostrils to a short distance behind eye), a crescentic mark on lower eyelid, and front part of cheeks, white; lores and around eye (immediately beneath the white mark on lower eyelid), black or dark slaty; sides of head, gray (sometimes tinged with olive-green), with narrower and indistinct paler shaft-streaks; chin, throat, cheeks (except in front), chest, breast, upper abdomen, and *front half or more of sides, rich pure lemon-yellow,* sometimes (in highly plumaged specimens) tinged with orange; flanks, pale gray; rest of under parts, white, the under tail-coverts, sometimes tinged with buff; under wing-coverts, yellow; bill and inside of mouth, black; iris, brown; legs and feet, dusky bluish-gray. Adult Female: Similar to the adult male, but slightly smaller, and duller in coloration, the black or dark slate of lores and around eye usually replaced by gray, the yellow of under parts usually less pure or deep (that on sides of breast sometimes tinged with olive), the flanks and under tail-coverts more strongly buffy, and the lower bill usually lighter colored.

Photo by H. K. Job Courtesy of Outing Pub. Co.

NEST OF YELLOW-BREASTED CHAT

Found amid a dense tangle of briers

Nest and Eggs.— Nest: Built in midst of tangled thickets or briers from 3 to 5 feet up; constructed of dead leaves, strips of bark, dried grass, and weed stalks and lined with fine grasses. Eggs: 3 to 5 usually 4, pure white, tinged with pink when fresh, generally fairly evenly spotted with clearly outlined specks of chestnut and lavender, sometimes coalescing into a wreath around larger end.

Distribution.— Eastern North America; breeds from southern Minnesota, Wisconsin, Michigan, Ontario, Central New York, and southern New England south to southeastern Texas, southern parts of Gulf States, and northern Florida; winters from Pueblo, Vera Cruz, and Yucatan to Costa Rica; casual in Maine.

Few birds appear to possess anything like a sense of humor. Most of them seem to be contented enough, and many act and sing — especially in breeding time — as if they were really happy; but these moods evidently are purely subjective; they do not reveal any capacity to make or to take a joke.

A conspicuous exception to this rule is the Blue Jay, who is a natural born mountebank — if there is such a thing in birdland — and another

Courtesy of Am. Mus. Nat. Hist.

YELLOW-BREASTED CHAT (⅔ nat. size)

In Tom-Sawyer-like showing off, he has no equal in the American bird-world

is the Yellow-breasted Chat, the largest and withal the most unwarbler-like of all the American Warblers. Unlike the Jay, the Chat doesn't make other birds the butt of his jokes or the object of his ridicule or wrath. Nor has he ever been accused of the cannibalistic and thieving propensities of the Jay. Indeed, his jests and antics seem often to be directly excited by the presence of man, and intended for his amusement. And in Tom-Sawyer-like showing off before humans he has no equal in the world of American birds.

Speaking of his vocal performances, Mr. Burroughs very aptly says that the Cat-bird "is mild and feminine compared with this rollicking polyglot," and then presents the following capital picture of the bird: "Though very shy, and carefully keeping himself screened when you show any disposition to get a better view, he will presently, if you remain quiet, ascend a twig, or hop out on a branch in plain sight, lop his tail, droop his wings, cock his head and become very melodramatic. In less than half a minute he darts into the bushes again, and again tunes up, no Frenchman rolling his *r's* so fluently. *C-r-r-r-r-r,-whrr,-that's it,-chee, quack, cluck,-yit, yit, yit,-now hit it,-tr-r-r,-when,-caw, caw,-cut, cut,-tea-boy,-who, who,-mew, mew,* and so on till you are tired of listening." (*Wake Robin.*) And as an appropriate exit after one of these deliverances, the bird is likely to take himself off in a curious fluttering flight, with his head down and his legs dangling at full length, as though he were trying to make himself as ludicrous as possible.

Like the Oven-bird and the Water-Thrushes the Chat has a flight song which is a voluble and altogether remarkable effort, containing many notes of real beauty. This he delivers as he rises steadily upward, his legs dangling and his head elevated, the rapidly uttered syllables pouring from his throat with astonishing volubility, until he reaches a height twice or more than that of the surrounding trees. Here he pauses and hovers for a few moments on very rapidly moving wings, the song gradually dying away until it ceases, when he drops almost perpendicularly and regains his old or another perch.

It should be recorded also, to the credit of this peculiar bird, that when the Cowbird attempts to make it the victim of its parasitic practice, the mother Chat often destroys the parasite's egg and her own as well. GEORGE GLADDEN.

Photo by A. A. Allen

ONE OF THE SHYEST OF NORTH AMERICAN BIRDS

The only photograph ever secured of a Yellow-breasted Chat on its nest

The Long-tailed Chat (*Icteria virens longicauda*) of the western United States is similar to the Yellow-breasted Chat; but the wing, tail, and bill are longer, the tail always, or nearly always, longer than the wing; the upper parts are more grayish olive-green, usually more nearly gray than olive-green; white of cheek region much more extended, frequently occupying the entire cheek area; yellow of under parts averages deeper.

HOODED WARBLER

Wilsonia citrina (*Boddaert*)

A. O. U. Number 684 See Color Plate 98

Other Names.— Hooded Titmouse; Hooded Flycatching Warbler; Black-headed Warbler; Mitered Warbler.

General Description.— Length, 5¼ inches. Upper parts, olive-green; face and under parts, yellow. Bill, not over ½ length of head, tapering gradually to the tip; wings, moderately long and pointed; tail, rounded or slightly double rounded.

Color.—Adult Male: Forehead and front of crown, together with lores, sides of head, space around eyes, and cheeks, rich lemon-yellow, the lores sometimes with a little of dusky or black; *rest of head, including throat, together with chest, deep black,* that of the chest with an abruptly defined convex rear outline; hindneck, back, shoulders, lesser wing-coverts, rump, and upper tail-coverts, plain yellowish olive-green, wings and tail, dusky brownish-gray with yellowish olive-green edgings, the middle wing-coverts broadly tipped with that color; inner webs of three outermost tail-feathers extensively white terminally, that on the exterior feathers occupying more than the terminal half; under parts of body, pure rich lemon-yellow, becoming olive-greenish on sides and flanks, the under tail-coverts, paler yellow; under wing coverts, pale yellow; bill, blackish in spring and summer, more brownish in fall and winter; iris, brown; legs and feet, pale flesh color. Adult Female: Similar to the adult male, but with much less of black on head, sometimes with none; if the black occupies approximately the same area as in the male it is much duller and broken with olive-green on crown and back of head and with yellow on throat; usually, the throat is entirely yellow, sometimes with an indication of a dusky collar across the lower portion or on upper chest, and the crown and back of head are blackish only next to the yellow of forehead and sides of head; when there is no black on the head the crown is entirely olive-green, becoming more yellowish on forehead.

Nest and Eggs.— Nest: Generally placed within a foot of ground in bushes; composed of shreds of grapevine and tree bark, dried leaves, and grass, neatly interwoven and fastened with spiders' webs, and lined with fine grass, horse-hair and a few rootlets. Eggs: 3 to 5, but almost always 4, creamy-white sparingly spotted in wreaths around large end with reddish-brown, purple, and dull lavender.

Distribution.— Eastern United States, west to edge of the Great Plains; breeding northward to Connecticut, southeastern New York (lower Hudson valley), central New York, northeastern Illinois, eastern Nebraska, etc.; southward to South Carolina, Alabama, and Louisiana; occasional northward to Massachusetts, northeastern New York, southern Ontario, southern Michigan, and Wisconsin; in winter south to Cuba and Jamaica and through eastern Mexico and Central America to Panama; casual in the Bermudas.

The black domino of the Maryland Yellow-throat is replaced in the male Hooded Warbler by a broad yellow mask, extending over the forehead to the crown of the head and well back of and below the eyes, this yellow patch being sharply set off by a solid black framework, which forms a sort of cap or hood for the bird's head, and a bib for his throat. These markings are very conspicuous, and, being peculiar to this bird, it may readily be identified by means of them.

Like the Yellow-throat, however, this Warbler is found much in brush or the lower branches of trees, within easy observation range. Under these conditions one may not only enjoy to the full the bird's singularly striking and beautiful plumage, but may see as well many evidences of its natural gentleness and friendliness. Even when flushed from her nest, the female bird flutters about, uttering a mildly protesting chirp and showing her outer white tail-feathers, but without the display of fear and rage commonly expressed by other birds under such conditions.

Dr. Chapman, to whose affections this bird evidently makes a very strong appeal, says of its song: "To my ear, the words *you must come to the woods or you won't see me,* uttered quickly, and made to run one into the other, exactly fit the bird's more prolonged vocal efforts, though they are far from agreeing with the attempts at syllabification of others. The call is a high, sharp *cheep,* easily recognized after it has been learned." (*The Warblers of North America.*) Mrs. Wright's interpretation of the song is *Che-we-eo-tsip, tsip, che-we-eo.* There appear to be two song-periods, the first ending early in July and the second occupying about the last week of August.

The genus to which this Warbler belongs, and which includes the Wilson's Warbler and its variants and the Canada Warbler, was named *Wilsonia* by Bonaparte in honor of Alexander Wilson, father of American ornithology.

WILSON'S WARBLER

Wilsonia pusilla pusilla (*Wilson*)

A. O. U. Number 685 See Color Plate 98

Other Names.— Wilson's Flycatcher; Wilson's Flycatching Warbler; Wilson's Black-cap; Wilson's Black-capped Flycatching Warbler; Black-capped Warbler; Black-cap; Black-capped Flycatching Warbler; Green Black-capped Warbler.

General Description.— Length, 4¾ inches. Upper parts, olive-green; under parts, yellow. Bill, not over ½ length of head, tapering gradually to the tip; wings, moderately long and pointed; tail, slightly double rounded.

Color.—Adult Male: Forehead, above and around eye, and entire under parts, lemon-yellow, the sides and flanks slightly tinged with olive-green; *crown, glossy blue-black,* the feathers slightly elongated, distinctly outlined; rest of upper parts, uniform olive-green; the sides of neck and sides of head, similar but rather more yellowish; primaries and secondaries, purplish-brown edged with olive-green; bill, dark brown; iris, brown; legs and feet, light brownish. ADULT FEMALE: Similar to the adult male and often not distinguishable; usually, however, slightly duller in color, with black crown-patch more restricted or obscured by olive-green margins to the feathers; sometimes the black entirely absent, the whole crown, except forehead, being olive-green, the forehead and above eye, yellow.

Nest and Eggs.— NEST: Imbedded in ground in swampy woods; constructed of swamp grass and lined with fine grass and a few hairs. EGGS: 2 to 4, pure white, wreathed around larger end with markings of cinnamon and lavender-gray.

Distribution.— Eastern North America; breeds from the tree limit in northwestern and central Mackenzie, central Ungava, and Newfoundland south to southern Saskatchewan, northern Minnesota, central Ontario, New Hampshire, Maine, and Nova Scotia; winters in eastern Central America from Guatemala to Costa Rica and occasionally north to Michoacán; migrates mainly along the Alleghenies.

The Wilson Warbler is a decidedly busy and restless Warbler full of individuality and energy. He is a jaunty, tail-twitching flycatcher, getting his food any way from leaf-searching and trunk-peering to darting out into the air in the style of the Tyrant Flycatchers. His home is in the bushes that border the woodlands, or in the undergrowth of thin forests, or anywhere along cool streams, but always in the northern parts of America. South of the international boundary he nests only in certain favorable localities. He sings his quick, bubbling warble as a rule far from the haunts of man, though there are places, Ottawa and elsewhere in Canada, where this Blackcap is at home not far out of town.

Drawing by R. I. Brasher

WILSON'S WARBLER (nat. size)

A decidedly busy and restless Warbler, full of individuality

The bluish-black cap is a distinctive mark of the bird. Even if one should wonder to which of the Water-Thrushes or other near relatives the song belonged, the first observation of the yellow under parts and black cap makes the identification certain. In the migrations up and back from Central America by way of Mexico and the country west of the Alleghenies, Wilson's Blackcap is pretty uniform in many places, but very uncertain in other localities. But almost never either in migration or breeding is this bird found in the deep woods.

The Black-caps extend from the Canadian Maritime Provinces across the continent to the Pacific and on down in the higher mountains of the West nearly to the Mexican boundary. But in the Rockies and on the coast there is a varietal difference. In the Rockies and no farther west than eastern Oregon the Blackcaps are larger birds, richer yellow underneath, and with orange rather than yellow foreheads. This variety is named the Pileolated Warbler (*Wilsonia pusilla pileolata*). It occurs much nearer the Arctic Sea than does the Wilson and is one of the common birds in many parts of coastal and interior Alaska. On the Pacific coast from British Columbia to southern California the Blackcaps are about the size of the Wilson, but much brighter colored than the Pileolated. Here the variety is named the Golden Pileolated Warbler (*Wilsonia pusilla chryseola*).

CANADA WARBLER

Wilsonia canadensis (*Linnæus*)

A. O. U. Number 686 See Color Plate 94

Other Names.— Canadian Warbler; Canada Flycatcher; Canadian Flycatching Warbler; Speckled Canada Warbler; Necklaced Warbler; Spotted Canadian Warbler; Canada Necklace.

General Description.— Length, 5¼ inches. Upper parts, slate-gray; under parts, yellow with a necklace of black spots. Bill, not over ½ length of head, tapering gradually to the tip; wings, moderately long and pointed; tail, slightly double rounded.

Color.—ADULT MALE: *Forehead and crown, black, the feathers* (except sometimes those on forehead) *margined with gray, producing a scaled appearance;* forehead sometimes with a center line of yellowish — rest of upper parts, sides of neck and rear part of sides of head, plain slate-gray; upper and front part of lores, cheeks, and under parts (except under tail-coverts), lemon-yellow, the outer portion of sides and flanks slightly tinged with olive; under tail-coverts, white, sometimes tinged with yellow toward anal region; *a conspicuous eye-ring of yellowish-white,* more decidedly yellowish on upper portion; loral spot, space below eye, together with front and lower portion of sides of head, black; this continued (sometimes brokenly) along sides of lower neck (between the gray and the yellow) and continued across the chest in a series of spots or streaks; bill, dusky-horn color; iris, brown; legs and feet, pale buffy-brown. ADULT FEMALE: Above, including sides of neck and sides of head, plain gray, tinged with olive, especially on back and crown, the latter often showing darker centers to feathers of forehead and crown; upper and front portion of lores and conspicuous eye-ring, pale yellow or yellowish-white; loral spot and below eyes, dusky olive-gray, this sometimes continued behind along lower portion of sides of neck; cheeks and under parts, except under tail-coverts, lemon-yellow (slightly paler and duller than in adult male); under tail-coverts, white; chest, streaked with olive, the streaks sometimes partly black; bill, iris, and feet as in male.

Nest and Eggs.— NEST: Commonly on ground, in tussocks of grass, alongside a log, foot of a bush, in upturned roots of trees, or in cavities of banks near streams or pools of water, usually well concealed; composed of dried leaves, grass, and roots and lined with pine needles, rootlets, and horse-hair. EGGS: 4 or 5, white or buffy-white spotted around larger end with reddish-brown and lilac, sometimes mixed with a few black specks or pen lines.

Distribution.— Eastern North America; breeds from central Alberta, southern Keewatin, northern Ontario, northern Quebec, and Newfoundland south to central Minnesota, central Michigan, southern Ontario, central New York, and Massachusetts, and along Alleghenies to North Carolina and Tennessee; winters in Ecuador and Peru and casually in Guatemala; in migration to eastern Mexico; casual in Colorado.

Courtesy of Am. Mus. Nat. Hist.

CANADA WARBLER (nat. size)

Haunts the shrubbery, wild vines, and thick undergrowth

The Canada Warbler is a particularly interesting bird because of his attractive necklace of black pendants on a yellow breast, and because of his sweet warbling liquid song. The song has been spelled *rup-it-che, rup-it-che, rup-it-chitt-it-lit,* and also *t'le we, t'le we, t'le we, t'le we, t'l it wit.* The bird haunts the shrubbery, wild vines, and bushes of thick undergrowth in very much the same localities as the Wilson Blackcap. Damp and dense coverts are where the nests are found. The Wilsons on the way north hardly leave any pairs south of the Canadian zone. Many pairs of the Canada Necklace, however, drop off to breed, all through the northern States, though the main body of the migrants go on to Canada. The Canada is indeed a near relative of the Hooded and Wilson Warblers, and shows it by its habits. Like them it is a flycatcher, taking much of its food on the wing, although like a true Warbler it also gleans among the leaves.

In the spring and fall migrations this bird is not so exceedingly rare as to call for the same enthusiasm, when found by bird observers, that would follow the finding of a Kirtland Warbler. Yet few observations of the bird are made without a thrill of pleasure because of its comparative rarity and beauty.

REDSTART

Setophaga ruticilla (*Linnæus*)

A. O. U. Number 687 See Color Plate 97

Other Names.—American Redstart; Redstart Warbler; Redstart Flycatcher; Fire-tail; Yellow-tailed Warbler.

General Description.— Length, 5¾ inches. MALE: Fore and upper parts, black; under parts, white; patches of reddish-orange and white. FEMALE: Upper parts, gray and olive-green; under parts, white; patches of yellow and white. Bill, about ½ length of head, much depressed, its profile wedge-shaped; wings, rather long and pointed; tail, shorter than wing, decidedly rounded, the feathers broad.

Color.—ADULT MALE: Head, neck, chest. and upper parts, uniform black, with decided bluish gloss, except on wings and tail; *basal portion of wing-quills (except two innermost wing-quills) and more than basal half of tail-feathers except two (sometimes only one) middle pairs, pale orange,* this occupying the full width of both webs; a large patch on each side of chest and breast, and under wing-coverts, orange-red; rest of under parts, white, usually with black between the orange-red lateral patches and the white in middle of breast; longer under tail-coverts, sometimes partly black or dusky; bill, black in spring and summer, more brownish in fall and winter; iris, brown; legs and feet, blackish. ADULT FEMALE: Very different from the adult male. Crown and hindneck, plain mouse-gray; back, shoulders, and rump, grayish olive-green; upper tail-coverts, middle tail-feathers, terminal portion of others, dusky; wings, dusky (not so dark as dusky portion of tail) with light olive edgings; basal portion of wing- and tail-feathers (except one or two middle pairs and two innermost secondaries), light yellow, that on the wings more restricted than the orange-red in the male, often not showing at all on primaries; sides of head, paler gray than crown, especially the lores and region over eye; cheeks, chin, throat, and chest, dull grayish-white; rest of under parts, more decidedly white, *with a conspicuous patch of yellow on each side of chest and breast,* the center portion of breast, together with sides and flanks, sometimes tinged with yellow; bill, dark brown or brownish-black in summer, pale brown in winter; iris, legs, and feet as in adult male.

Nest and Eggs.— NEST: A compact, cup-shaped structure placed in fork of sapling or bush, usually within 15 feet of the ground; composed of plant fibers, strips of bark, and grass, neatly lashed together with spiders' webs, and lined with fine grasses and hair. EGGS: Usually 4, rarely 5, quite variable in coloration; ground color white to greenish or grayish-white, marked with specks and spots of cinnamon-brown or lilac, generally wreathed around larger end.

Distribution.— North America and northern South America; breeds from central British Columbia, west central Mackenzie, southern Keewatin, northern Quebec, and Newfoundland to Washington, northern Utah, Colorado, central Oklahoma, Arkansas, and North Carolina; rarely breeds in the southeastern United States south of latitude 35°; casual in migration in Oregon, California, Lower California, Arizona, and northern Ungava; winters in West Indies and from central Mexico to Ecuador and British Guiana.

The Redstart is not only one of the most conspicuously colored of the Warblers, but is perhaps the most restless and active of this essentially nervous and fidgety family. It is no exaggeration to say that the male bird is almost never still while he is awake, and that the female is motionless only when she is incubating. Not content with incessant hopping, skipping, and fluttering from limb to bough and from bough to twig in its ceaseless search for larvæ and bugs of all kinds, the bird frequently darts off into space, or down to the ground, or against a tree-trunk to snap up an insect which its sharp eyes have detected. These lightning-like sallies may account for its pretty habit of keeping its tail spread and its wings half open and vibrating slightly even as it dances along a limb.

Photo by H. K. Job

FEMALE REDSTART ON HER NEST

"Anyone familiar with the woods in summer," says Mr. Parkhurst, "will recognize in this the fiery little Redstart — a name corrupted from 'redstert,' meaning red tail, this portion of the plumage being doubly noticeable from the amount of reddish-yellow upon it, and from the bird's habit of keeping it partly spread as it moves from limb to limb. The wings and sides of the breast also have a dash of flame color, intensified by the otherwise lustrous black of the male, whereas the female — well, she looks as anyone would be supposed to look, arrayed in goods warranted not to wash. If the male Redstart is a fiery coal, the female is a trail of ashes in his wake." (*The Birds' Calendar.*)

Unlike the Blackburnian Warbler, his rival in color, whose happy hunting ground is the tree-tops where he is hard to find and harder to follow, the Redstart shows a decided partiality for shrubbery and low-hanging foliage near dwellings, wherefore he is much the more frequently and plainly seen of the two. Indeed, either his confidence or his concentration on his work often causes him to dart down and snatch an insect from the ground at the very feet of the astonished and delighted observer.

Like the vocal efforts of most of the Warblers, the song of the Redstart is a lisping and rather unmusical effort, composed generally of the rapid reiteration of syllables like *wee* and *see* or *zee.* In fact, the bird seems to be altogether too busy to sing a real song.

PAINTED REDSTART

Setophaga picta *Swainson*

A. O. U. Number 688

General Description.— Length, 5¼ inches. Fore and upper parts, black; under parts, red; patches of white. Bill, about ½ length of head, much depressed, its profile wedge-shaped; wings, rather long and pointed; tail, shorter than wing, decidedly rounded, the feathers broad and rounded.

Color.— Adults (sexes alike): Head, neck, upper chest, sides, back, shoulders, lesser wing-coverts, rump, and upper tail-coverts, uniform deep black, with a faint bluish gloss; wings and tail, black, the former relieved by a large white patch involving the middle and greater coverts and edges of innermost secondaries, the latter with three outermost feathers extensively white terminally, this white occupying much the greater part of the outermost feather; lower chest, breast, and abdomen, rich vermilion or poppy-red, rarely more orange-red; under tail-coverts, black or blackish broadly tipped with white; under wing-coverts, mostly white; bill, legs, and feet, black; iris, brown. Young, first plumage: Above, plain sooty-black; the wings and tail as in adults, but the white wing-patch tinged with buff; beneath, sooty-grayish passing into dull whitish on center of abdomen; the breast spotted or broadly streaked with sooty-blackish.

Nest and Eggs.— Nest: In cavities under banks or beneath projecting stones; loosely constructed of grasses and vegetable bark and lined with horse-hair. Eggs: 4, pearly-white, thickly dotted with chestnut and lavender.

Distribution.— Higher mountains of central and southern Arizona, and New Mexico, and southward over higher districts of Mexico.

As far as its characteristic movements are concerned, the Painted Redstart might as well be the common Redstart of the Eastern States. For, according to Mr. Henshaw, like that bird his western cousin dances about with his wings and tail half spread, flits nervously from tree to tree, dashing out occasionally to snap up an insect on the wing, seldom stays in the same tree more than a few minutes, and often clings to the side of a tree trunk long enough to dig a grub out of the bark.

The striking red, white, and black plumage of the adult birds makes them very conspicuous in the dense green foliage of the live oaks and conifers which they frequent. They seem to be fond of water and are often found near cascades and spring holes. They may also be seen hopping about on mossy banks and stumps of large trees.

WAGTAILS AND PIPITS

Order *Passeres;* suborder *Oscines;* family *Motacillidæ*

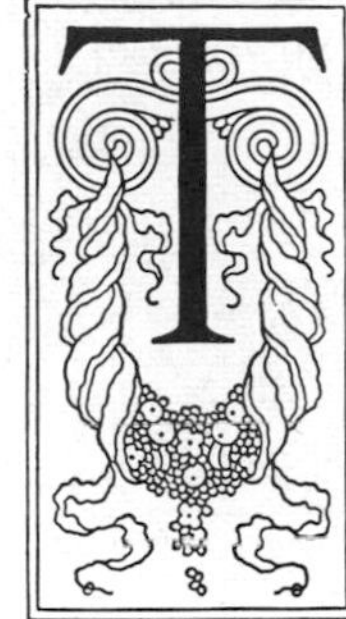

HE Wagtails and the Pipits are *Oscines* or song birds, with the bill slender, notched, and cone-shaped; bristles at the corners of the mouth obvious but only two conspicuously developed; the wing rather long and pointed; the tail variable in relative length but never conspicuously shorter than the wing, usually nearly as long, sometimes longer; the tip even, slightly notched, double notched, rounded, or double-rounded; the tail-feathers rather narrow, usually tapering terminally, but never (except sometimes the middle pair) pointed at the tip; the tarsus slender, always much longer than bill, toes slender, the middle one distinctly longer than the other forward toes; hind toes about equal in length to outer and inner toes or slightly longer, but stouter; claws slender, variable in relative length, that of the hind toe (except in one species) elongated and but slightly equal to or exceeding the toe in length.

The family comprises birds of terrestrial habits, which walk or run gracefully on the ground, instead of hopping, and feed upon insects. The Wagtails are usually of black, gray, and white plumage, but sometimes are partially bright yellow — always unstreaked. The Pipits are of streaked plumage, with brownish or tawny tints prevailing, in which they present a remarkable resemblance to the Larks, as they also do in their habits and the character of their nests and eggs. The family is most developed in the eastern hemisphere, to which the Wagtails are restricted (though one subspecies breeds in the Arctic zone of western Alaska). America possesses only the Pipits represented by about eight species and only two of these eight are found north of the Rio Grande.

PIPIT

Anthus rubescens (*Tunstall*)

A. O. U. Number 697 See Color Plate 69

Other Names.—American Pipit; American Titlark; Prairie Titlark; Hudsonian Wagtail; Brown Lark; Louisiana Lark; Red Lark.

General Description.— Length, 6½ inches. Upper parts, grayish-olive; under parts, pinkish-buff with streaks of dusky.

Color.—Adults in Spring and Summer: *Above, grayish-olive* or hair-brown, the feathers of crown, back, and shoulders, darker centrally, forming indistinct streaks; wings and tail, dusky with pale grayish-olive or olive-grayish edgings, the middle wing-coverts margined terminally with pale grayish-buffy, dull grayish, or dull whitish, the greater coverts also sometimes margined at tips with the same; *outermost tail-feathers with outer web and shaft, except at base, and nearly the terminal half of inner web, white;* second tail-feather with a terminal white space, third sometimes also with a small wedge-shaped mark of white at tip; a stripe over the eyes and the *entire under parts, varying from pinkish-buff to deep cinnamon-buff* or wine-colored buffy cinnamon; the chest, sides, and flanks usually streaked with dusky; bill, dusky-brown; iris, brown; legs and feet, black or brownish black. ADULTS IN WINTER: Similar to the spring and summer plumage, but general color of upper parts much browner or more greenish-gray; the stripe over the eye and the under parts much paler, the streaks heavier.

Nest and Eggs.— NEST: On ground; bulky but compact, made of dried grass and moss. EGGS: 4 to 6, dark chocolate-colored, overlaid with numerous spots and streaks of grayish-brown.

Distribution.— The whole of North America, breeding from Newfoundland, Province of Quebec, high mountains of Colorado and the Sierra Nevada (above timber line, 13,000 feet and upward) northward, including the Shumagin and Aleutian islands, Alaska, and northeastern Siberia; Greenland (breeding); in winter southward over whole of United States and greater part of Mexico to highlands of Guatemala, and to Bermudas.

The American Pipit confines itself to open country entirely, showing a marked preference for wet fields and bogs, especially such as are frequented by Wilson's Snipe. In autumn it is often seen, however, on comparatively dry plowed ground as well as in upland pastures and stubble fields. Usually it occurs in scattered flocks, from a dozen to fifty individuals being distributed over a space of a dozen acres, and when one is started several take flight; but even when fifty are on the wing they never collect into a solid flock, but fly in extended order. When feeding the birds run about rapidly on the ground, very much like Sandpipers, and tilt and flirt the tail much like the Water-Thrushes and some shore birds. When flushed they rise very quickly to a considerable height, mounting by great leaps with their powerful wings, and constantly uttering their sharp double-syllabled call which gives the bird its name of "Pipit." We do not recall ever seeing one alight on a bush or tree and they seldom make use of a wire or fence-post.

Drawing by R. I. Brasher

PIPIT (⅘ nat. size)

A sweet-voiced wanderer from the mountain tops and the subarctic regions

The food appears to consist mainly of worms, insects and such other animal food as can be found in damp places, freely mixed with seeds of various kinds. The bird certainly does no harm and presumably does much good to the agriculturist, but its stay is so short and its numbers in any one locality so small that it probably is not an economic factor of any great importance.

WALTER BRADFORD BARROWS, in *Michigan Bird Life.*

SPRAGUE'S PIPIT

Anthus spraguei (*Audubon*)

A. O. U. Number 700

Other Names.— Missouri Skylark; Prairie Skylark.

General Description.— Length, 6¼ inches. Upper parts, grayish-brown, streaked with dusky; under parts, buffy-white, streaked with black.

Color.—ADULTS IN SPRING: Above, pale buffy grayish-brown broadly streaked with dusky, the streaks broadest on back, narrowest on hindneck; wings and tail, dusky with pale buffy grayish-brown edgings, the middle and greater wing-coverts margined terminally with the same, the outermost primary edged with white; *outermost tail-feathers, white,* with basal half, or more, of inner portion of inner web dusky-grayish; next tail-feather with approximately the outer half white, the inner half grayish-dusky; sides of head, including a stripe over the eyes, and the lores, and the entire under parts, dull buffy-white, becoming brownish-buffy on chest, sides, and flanks, the chest narrowly streaked with blackish, the sides of breast more broadly but less distinctly streaked with grayish-brown; under wing-coverts, white; bill, dusky-brown or brownish-black; iris, brown; legs and feet, pale buffy-brown. ADULTS IN AUTUMN AND WINTER: Similar to the spring plumage, but more pronounced buffy, both above and below; lower throat, chest, breast, sides, and flanks, rather deep dull buff, with dusky streaks on chest rather broader and less sharply defined than in spring.

Nest and Eggs.— NEST: Like that of the American Pipit. EGGS: 4 or 5, pale purplish-buffy or buffy-white, thickly spotted with purplish-brown.

Distribution.— Interior plains of North America; breeding from eastern Montana and northern North Dakota to Assiniboia and the Saskatchewan district of Manitoba; in winter southward to Texas and southern Louisiana, and through eastern Mexico to Vera Cruz and Puebla; occasional in winter on coast of South Carolina.

It does not seem very polite to call a family of birds Wagtails just because they have the habit of jerking their tails as they go about. But that is the name they go by in the books, and we have two of them in the United States. We call them Pipits or Titlarks.

The best known is Sprague's Pipit, called the Missouri Skylark, or sometimes the Prairie Skylark. This bird gets the name of Skylark because he sings while soaring about in the air far over our heads.

The Pipits live on the ground, and walk and run, not hop. As they go, they bob their heads, and jerk their tails. They are a little larger than an English Sparrow, and they go in flocks. They are never seen in the woods, but in open pastures or plains, or beside a road.

Sprague's Pipit is all in streaks of brown and gray, and lighter below. He has a large foot, which shows that he lives on the ground, and a very long claw on the hind toe.

The nest of the Pipit is made by hollowing out a little place in the ground and lining it with fine grasses. Though on the ground it is one of the hardest to find, because it is lightly covered with the dry grasses, and when the bird is sitting, she matches the grasses so well that one can hardly see her, even when looking right at her.

The birds eat insects and weed seeds, and go about in flocks. Even then they are hard to see, because when they are startled they do not flutter or fly, but crouch or squat at once, and stay perfectly still.

This bird is noted, as I said, for his song. It is said to be as fine as that of the English Skylark of which we hear so much. Perhaps his way of singing makes it still more interesting. He starts up on wing, flies a little one way, then the other, all the time going higher and higher. So he climbs on up, up, up, in a zigzag way, till he is fairly out of sight, all the time giving a wonderfully sweet song. It is not very loud, but of such a kind that it is heard when the bird is far out of sight. When he can no longer be seen, one may still follow him with a good field-glass. He will sing without stopping for fifteen or twenty minutes.

Then suddenly he stops, closes his wings, and comes head first toward the ground. It seems as if he would dash his brains out against the earth, but just before he touches he opens his wings and alights like a feather, almost where he started from. He should be as famous as the English bird, and will be no doubt, when he is better known.

OLIVE THORNE MILLER.

DIPPERS

Order *Passeres;* suborder *Oscines;* family *Cinclidæ*

THE distribution of the family of Dippers (*Cinclidæ*) is restricted to Europe and temperate Asia, western North America, and thence southward through the Andes Mountains to the southern part of South America. There are some twelve or fourteen species, six of which are found in America, but only one north of Mexico.

In coloration, plain gray or brown predominates; and this is never relieved by conspicuous markings, such as bars, though parts of the plumage sometimes have darker margins to the feathers which produces an appearance of scales. Some species have the throat and breast, the crown, or part of the back, white. The sexes are alike in color, but the young are paler below than the adults.

The bill is much shorter than the head, slender, much compressed, and the tip rather abruptly curved downward. The wing is short, very concave beneath, with the tip comparatively long and stiff. The tail is decidedly more than half as long as the wing, and even, or slightly rounded, and with the feathers broad and rounded at the tip. The head, neck, and body are covered with down, and the plumage is very dense and soft.

These birds are found only in mountainous or hilly districts, where they frequent the swift, rocky streams in which they find their food of water insects and fish spawn. They are at ease in the water, under which they propel themselves by motion of their wings. Their nest, a structure of moss, is usually placed behind or near a waterfall, and is kept green by the spray which constantly moistens it.

The Dippers are song birds (*Oscines*). Apparently they are allied to both the Thrushes and the Wrens, perhaps more nearly to the latter to whom they bear a closer resemblance in their abbreviated form, though they differ in the more pointed wing as well as in other details. In their aquatic habits and their covering of down they differ from all other perching birds, and for this reason they are often thought of as shore birds.

DIPPER

Cinclus mexicanus unicolor *Bonaparte*

A. O. U. Number 701

Other Names. — Water Ouzel; American Water Ouzel; American Dipper.

General Description.— Length, 8 inches. Slate-color.

Color.— Head and neck, plain gray-brown, darker on the crown, paler on chin and throat; rest of plumage (except larger wing-coverts, wings, and tail-feathers), plain dull slate color, the under parts, slightly paler and more brownish, gradually merging forward into the brown of foreneck; greater wing-coverts, primary coverts, wings, and tail-feathers, dull blackish-slate or dusky margined with slate color; greater under wing-coverts, longer under tail-coverts, and (at least in more early spring specimens) feathers of lower abdomen and flanks, margined terminally with whitish; bill, black; iris, brown; legs and feet, horn-brownish.

Nest and Eggs.— Nest: In a crevice of rocks or among roots of trees, always placed near running water, often where spray keeps the outside damp, and sometimes behind a cascade; a beautiful sphere of soft green moss about seven inches in diameter, sometimes dome-shaped, deeper than wide, with a small round entrance and strongly arched and braced with leaves, grass, and twigs, cemented with mud. Eggs: 3 to 5, plain, pure white.

Distribution.— Mountains of western North America, from Rocky Mountains (including Black Hills of South Dakota) to the Pacific coast, and from the Mexican boundary (western Texas to southern California), and northern Lower California to northern Alaska. (Resident throughout, even in Alaskan localities.)

There is only one member of this family in the United States and that one lives in the Rocky Mountains and the mountains of California.

The body of the Dipper is about as big as a Robin's, but looks much smaller, because his very short tail gives him a "chunky" look. His wings are short and rounded, and his plumage is very soft and so thick that he can go under water without getting wet. He is slate color all over, a little paler on the breast, and his mate is exactly like him, but the young Ouzel has all the under feathers tipped with white, and usually a white throat. Both old and young have shining white eyelids which show very plainly among their dark feathers.

The Dipper is a water lover. The nest is placed close to it, generally near a waterfall, sometimes even behind a waterfall, where he has to go through a curtain of falling water to reach it. It is on a shelf of rock, and shaped like a little hut, with a hole on one side for a door. It is made of soft green moss, which is kept alive and growing by constant sprinkling. Sometimes the waterfall itself keeps it wet, but the birds have been seen to sprinkle it themselves. They do it by diving into the water, then going to the top of the nest and shaking themselves violently.

This bird is a curious fellow. His food is the small insects which live under water, and he is as much at home there as other birds are in the air. He can walk on the bottom with swift running water over his head, and he can really fly under water, using his wings as he does in the air. I have seen him do it.

The Water Ouzel cares nothing for the cold. On cold mornings when all other birds sit humped up with feathers puffed out over their feet to keep warm, he is as jolly and lively as ever. He flies about in the snow, dives under the ice, and comes out at an airhole, and sings as if it were summer weather.

Mr. John Muir, who knows so well the western mountains and the creatures who live there, has told us much of what we know about this bird. He says the Ouzel sings all winter, and never minds the weather; also that he never goes far from the stream. If he flies away, he flies close over the brook, and follows all its windings and never goes "across lots."

When the young Ouzel is out of the nest and wants to be fed, he stands on a rock and "dips," that is, bends his knees and drops, then stands up straight again. He looks very droll.

Drawing by R. Bruce Horsfall

DIPPER (¾ nat. size)

It flies well under water or in the air

Dr. Merriam tells a story which shows how fond the Dipper is of water, especially of a sprinkle, and explains why he always chooses to live by a waterfall. The Doctor was camping out on the bank of a stream where one of these birds lived, and one morning he threw some water out of a cup. Instantly the bird flew into the little shower as if he liked it. To see if he really wanted to get into the water, the Doctor threw out some more. Again the bird flew into it, and as long as he would throw out water, the Ouzel would dash in for his sprinkle.

OLIVE THORNE MILLER.

MIMIC THRUSHES

Order *Passeres;* suborder *Oscines;* family *Mimidæ*

THIS exclusively American group, in habits and general appearance resembling the true Thrushes and Wrens, are all songsters of greater or less merit. Many of them are preëminent as vocalists, while some of the genus *Mimus* are the most brilliant and remarkable vocalists of all birds. This applies especially to the Mockingbirds, though several of the Thrashers are singers of only a little less versatility and charm.

Speaking generally, the members of the family have slender bills, exceedingly variable in shape and relative length, sometimes only half as long, sometimes longer, than the head; usually slightly decurved terminally, sometimes conspicuously so; often straight or very nearly so. The wing is variable as to relative length, but is always more or less rounded, and the tail is also variable, but is never distinctly shorter than the distance from the bend of the wing to the tip of the longest secondaries; usually about as long as the wing or sometimes much longer, always more or less rounded.

This family is now considered scientifically distinct from both the Wrens and the true Thrushes. The Mockingbirds seem to be most nearly related to the Thrushes and evidently occupy an intermediate place between them and the Wrens. Externally the Mockingbirds differ from the Thrushes in their shorter, more rounded wings, and in various anatomical details. The family is most numerously represented, both as to genera and species, in Mexico. Only two of the fourteen genera occur in South America, which has but one genus not found elsewhere. Altogether about fifty species and sub-species and fourteen genera are found.

In coloration the Thrashers have the upper parts plain rufous, brown, or gray, with or without whitish wing bands; under parts buff, whitish, pale brownish, or pale grayish, with or without darker streaks or spots; the lateral tail-feathers with or without white or whitish tips. They build nests open above, composed of twigs and the like, lined with fine rootlets or similar materials, placed in dense (often thorny) shrubs, small trees, or vine-growths, sometimes in brush piles or on ground. The eggs (from 3 to 5) are usually speckled, sometimes plain light greenish-blue.

The Mockingbirds are gray or grayish-brown above, with or without darker streaks, the wings with two whitish or pale grayish bands and whitish or pale grayish edgings, the lateral tail-feathers with more or less white; under parts dull whitish, with or without streaks on flanks. The young have the breast conspicuously speckled or spotted with dusky. As far as is known the nest of the Mockingbird is open above, rather bulky, and is placed in dense shrubs, small trees, or thick vine-growth. The eggs (from 3 to 5) are pale greenish or whitish, speckled or spotted with brown.

SAGE THRASHER

Oreoscoptes montanus (*J. K. Townsend*)

A. O. U. Number 702

Other Name.— Sage Thrush.

General Description.— Length, 8 inches. Upper parts, grayish-brown; under parts, buffy-white, with dark streaks. Bill, much shorter than head and slender; wings, long and pointed; tail, shorter than wing, slightly rounded.

Color.—Above, light grayish-brown, with very indistinct streaks; wings and tail, darker grayish-brown, with pale grayish-brown edgings; middle and greater wing-coverts, narrowly tipped with dull white, producing two narrow bands; outermost primaries, narrowly edged with white; inner webs of three or *four outermost tail-feathers tipped with white,* this about three-fourths of an inch in extent or lateral feathers, greatly decreasing in extent toward middle feathers; an indistinct line of dull whitish over eye; lores, light grayish; speck below the eyes and the sides of head, light grayish-brown, narrowly streaked with dull whitish; cheeks and under parts, dull buffy-white passing into pale cinnamon-buff on flanks, anal region, and under tail-coverts; throat, bordered along each side by a narrow stripe, or series of streaks of dusky or black; lower throat, with sparse wedge-shaped small spots or streaks of dusky; chest, breast, sides, and flanks conspicuously streaked with dark grayish-brown or sooty, the markings on chest in form of wedge-shaped spots rather than streaks; under wing-coverts, pale grayish-buff; bill, dusky; iris, lemon-yellow.

Nest and Eggs.— Nest: In low bushes, especially sage and cactus, from one to three feet above ground; rough, bulky structure of coarse plant stems, dry sage bark, coarse grasses, and twigs, lined with fine stems and rootlets. Eggs: 3 to 5, with a ground color of rich greenish-blue spotted with bright reddish-brown and a few lead-colored spots.

Distribution.—Arid plains, mesas, and foothills of western United States; breeds from the western border of the Great Plains, in western North Dakota, South Dakota, Nebraska, Kansas, and Texas to the eastern base of the Sierra Nevada and Cascade ranges; north to Montana, Idaho, and eastern British Columbia; winters from southern California and mountains of central Texas to northern Mexico and Cape San Lucas, casually to Guadalupe Island.

On the sagebrush plains, or the ragged desert mountains of the West, the Sage Thrasher makes its home. It resembles nothing so much as a young undersized Mockingbird. But for its spotted breast one might easily mistake it for this famous and better known songster. In the early spring, when the snows on the distant mountains are beginning to melt and the long wary ranks of wildfowl are passing northward overhead, the song of this Thrasher rings far and wide over the sandy wastes. One seldom sees it far from the ground. Perched on a sage-bush or a thorny cactus it sings and calls and keeps a lookout for mate or rival. More frequently, perhaps, it is found on the ground, running about among the clumps of bushes. It seems to be equally at home about ranches or far out on the uninhabited deserts. I have met them on the plains when, far as the eye could reach, there was no sign of human habitation, and again have watched them running about the streets of an adobe Indian village, pausing at intervals to raise their wings playfully, glance around, and then resume their travels. The substantial nests of sticks, twigs, and grasses are usually placed in bushes near the ground. The Sage Thrasher appears to be confined very largely to the open countries of the far West.

T. Gilbert Pearson.

Drawing by R. I. Brasher

SAGE THRASHER (½ nat. size)

A fine daylight and moonlight singer of the western deserts

MOCKINGBIRD

Mimus polyglottos polyglottos (*Linnæus*)

A. O. U. Number 703 See Color Plate 101

Other Names.— Mock Bird; Mocking Thrush; Mimic Thrush; Mocker.

General Description.— Length, 10 inches. Upper parts, brownish-gray; under parts, white and gray. Bill, shorter than head; wings, long and rounded; tail, longer than wing, rounded, the feathers moderately broad with rounded tips.

Color.—*Above, plain brownish-gray;* wings and tail, dull blackish-slate with pale slate-gray edgings, these broadest on secondaries (especially the terminal portion, where sometimes inclining to white); middle and greater wing-coverts, narrowly tipped with dull white or grayish-white, forming two narrow bands (these indistinct in worn plumage); primary coverts, white, usually with a subterminal spot or streak of dusky; base of primaries, white, this most extended on the two innermost, where occupying at least basal half of both webs, often much more, that on the longer quills sometimes entirely concealed by overlying primary coverts; outermost tail-feather, white, sometimes with a trace of dusky or grayish on outer web; second, with outer web mostly blackish, the inner web mostly white; third, blackish or dusky, with about half of the terminal and basal portions white; a very indistinct stripe over eye of pale gray; eyelids, grayish-white; lores, dusky; sides of head, grayish, indistinctly streaked with whitish; space below the eyes and cheeks, dull white, usually faintly barred or transversely flecked with grayish or dusky; chin and throat, dull white, margined along each side by a dusky streak; *chest and sides of breast, pale smoke-gray,* passing into a more buffy hue on sides and flanks, the under tail-coverts, pale buff; abdomen and center of breast, white; bill, black.

Nest and Eggs.— NEST: Composed of twigs, grasses and weeds, lined with fine rootlets, moss, and sometimes cotton; placed in many different locations but usually in a deep bramble thicket, or hedge; as a rule they are located within ten feet of the ground, never on it, and have been seen built fifty feet above the earth. EGGS: 4 to 6, bluish-green heavily freckled with several shades of brown.

Distribution.— Eastern United States; northward, regularly (but locally), to Maryland, southern Ohio, southern half of Indiana and Illinois, Missouri, etc., irregularly to Massachusetts, southeastern New York (Long Island, etc.), New Jersey, Pennsylvania, northern Indiana and Illinois, and Iowa, sporadically to Maine, Ontario, southern Wisconsin (breeding), and southern Minnesota; breeding and resident throughout its range, except where occurring accidentally; southward to southern Florida and along the Gulf to eastern Texas, and to the Bahamas; introduced into Bermuda (1893).

The Mockingbird stands unrivaled. He is the king of song. This is a trite saying, but how much it really means can be known only to those who have heard this most gifted singer uncaged and at his best in the lowlands of the Southern States. He equals and even excels the whole feathered choir. He improves upon most of the notes that he reproduces, adding also to his varied repertoire the crowing of chanticleer, the cackling of the hen, the barking of the house dog, the squeaking of the unoiled wheelbarrow, the postman's whistle, the plaints of young chickens and turkeys and those of young wild birds, not neglecting to mimic those of his own offspring. He even imitates man's musical inventions. Elizabeth and Joseph Grinnell assert that a Mockingbird was attracted to a graphophone on the lawn where, apparently, he listened and took mental notes of the performance, giving the next day, a week later, or at midnight an entertainment of his own and then repeating it with the exact graphophone ring. Even the notes of the piano have been reproduced in some cases and the bird's vocalization simulates the lightning changes of the kaleidoscope.

Drawing by R. I. Brasher

MOCKINGBIRD (½ nat. size)

In improvization or mimicry, the most versatile and brilliant of American bird vocalists

The Mocker is more or less a buffoon, but those who look upon him only as an imitator or clown have much to learn of his wonderful originality. His own song is heard at its best at the height of the love season, when the singer flutters into the air from some tall tree-top and improvises his music, pouring out all the power and energy of his being in such an ecstasy of song that, exhausting his strength in the supreme effort, he slowly floats on quivering, beating pinions down through the bloom-covered branches until, his fervor spent, he sinks to the ground below. His expanded wings and tail flashing with white in the sunlight and the buoyancy of his action appeal to the eye as his music captivates the ear. On moonlit nights at this season the inspired singer launches himself far into the air, filling the silvery spaces of the night with the exquisite swells and trills, liquid and sweet, of his unparalleled melody. The song rises and falls as the powers of the singer wax and wane, and so he serenades his mate throughout the live-long night. One such singer wins others to emulation and, as the chorus grows, little birds of the field and orchard wake just enough to join briefly in the swelling tide of avian melody.

The Mockingbird seldom holds himself aloof from mankind, but often makes himself at home in the door-yard, sits on the chimney top and, like the Robin in the North, "knows all the folks." The negroes close the shutters of their cabins at night, but they say that the Mocker "sings down the chimney." Often the nest is placed in shrub or hedge close by the house, and as soon as the young are hatched the parents take pains to proclaim their whereabouts that all may know. Therefore, the young, which are in demand as cage birds, frequently are taken and sold into captivity.

The Mockingbird has many traits that endear it to all. It is brave and devoted, attacking birds twice its size, dogs, cats, and even man himself in defense of its young. Its cries of alarm give warning to all other birds nearby. When kindly treated it may even come in at the door or window. Thus it has won for itself a high place in the regard and affection of the Southern people.

EDWARD HOWE FORBUSH.

Photo by J. H. Field

NEST OF MOCKINGBIRD

Often it is placed in shrub or hedge near the house

The Western Mockingbird (*Mimus polyglottos leucopterus*) is just a paler, larger, and more buffy edition of its eastern congener. Throughout its range through southwestern United States and northern Mexico it exhibits the same traits that have won for the species a scientific name which translated means "many-tongued mimic."

CATBIRD

Dumetella carolinensis (*Linnæus*)

A. O. U. Number 704 See Color Plate 101

Other Names.— Chicken Bird; Cat Flycatcher; Slate-colored Mockingbird; Black-capped Thrush.

General Description.— Length, 8¾ inches. Plumage, slate-gray with black on crown, wings, and tail. Bill, much shorter than head, nearly straight to near tip, where gradually curved downward; wings, moderately long and rounded; tail, slightly longer than wing, decidedly rounded, the feathers narrowly rounded terminally.

Color.— Crown, black, or slate-black, the forehead slate-gray, rear of crown or nape, sometimes more sooty; tail, black, the feathers edged with slate-gray basally; wings, slate-black with broad slate-gray edgings (nearly concealing the darker color); *under tail-coverts, chestnut;* rest of plumage, plain slate-gray, the upper surface darker, or more nearly slate color; bill, black; iris, brown.

Nest and Eggs.— NEST: Rather bulky, made of dry leaves, twigs, roots, and grasses, lined with fine rootlets and grass; placed in bushes, trees or thickets usually within 10 feet of the ground. EGGS: 4 to 6, rarely latter number, plain, deep bluish-green, much darker colored than the Robin's.

Distribution.— Temperate North America in general, but wanting in most of region south of the Columbia River and west of Rocky Mountains; north to Nova Scotia, southern Maine, New Hampshire, Ontario, Manitoba, Saskatchewan, and British Columbia; west to and including Rocky Mountains, in Montana, Idaho, Wyoming, Colorado, New Mexico, and Utah, and in Oregon and Washington to the Pacific coast (accidentally to Farallon Islands, California); breeding southward to northern Florida and along Gulf coast to east-central Texas; wintering from Southern States (occasionally Middle States) southward to Bahamas, West Indies, and through eastern Mexico and Central America to Panama; resident in Bermuda; accidental in Europe.

There is more of the cat about the Catbird than his cat-like call, if birds may be trusted to know their enemies and to treat them accordingly. For, especially during the nesting season, his feathered neighbors are often seen mobbing him with every show of anger and hatred; and, what is more, he acts as if he knew he deserved it. That is, when he is set upon by a pack of Robins, Sparrows, and Bluebirds, and ordered to be gone, he goes, and stands not on the order of his going. Furthermore, besides his most unbird-like snarl, his manners are often distinctly feline, and his habit of slinking through the bushes in which small birds have nests is decidedly suspicious. In short, he is accused of being a nest-robber, and it seems more than likely that the charge can be substantiated. Mr. Burroughs, indeed, says he has "seen him do it."

All this is a great pity, for the Catbird is a distinct personality in bird land, and withal an interesting, if a somewhat pert one. He seems to be very well aware that he is an accomplished and versatile vocalist; in fact, no American bird displays more plainly a desire to "show off." Witness his posing and attitudinizing when he establishes himself atop a bush, where he apparently desires to be the observed of all observers. Then his self-consciousness and his vanity are both apparent and amusing.

As a singer, the Catbird may be ranked third in the remarkably gifted Mimic-Thrush trio, of which the Mockingbird is easily first and the Brown Thrasher a good second. Attentive listeners probably will agree that there is a fundamental resemblance between the songs of these birds, in that each is a prolonged effort, lacking anything like definite construction or consistent rhythm — a mere jumble of notes, varying greatly in volume as well as tonal character, and many of them either actually imitative, or at least reminiscent of the calls or parts of the songs of other birds.

Courtesy of Am. Mus. Nat. Hist.

CATBIRD (½ nat. size)

He is a distinct personality in bird land

The Catbird is given third rank in this trio because his song is likely to include harsh notes of various kinds — some of them imitative — whereas the percentage of such tones is negligible or altogether absent from the characteristic songs of the Thrasher and the Mocker. Somebody has said that the Catbird "sings Chinese," which is rather clever, since there is a certain resemblance between his erratic potpourri and the queer half-musical, half-guttural ups and downs of the Celestial's speech. Despite the foregoing comparisons and comments the Catbird's song is not an unmusical or inferior performance. On the contrary, it is undoubtedly one of the most interesting of bird utterances, and usually contains many melodious phrases as well as piquant musical flourishes. In it one may hear reproduced the characteristic tones of the flute, piccolo, and clarionet, as well as the violin and even the higher tones of the cello. Other birds' notes, or fragments of their songs, which are more or less perfectly reproduced are those of the Wood Thrush, the Robin, the Song Sparrow, the House Wren, the Oriole, and even the Whip-poor-will. With these, as Mr. Mathews says, "the yowl of the cat is thrown in any where, the guttural remarks of the frog are repeated without the slightest deference to good taste or appropriateness, and the harsh squawk of the old hen, or the chirp of the lost chicken, is always added in some malapropos manner. All is grist which comes to the Catbird's musical mill, and all is ground out according to the bird's own way of thinking."

Reports from the Mississippi valley indicate that the Catbird is sometimes a serious annoyance to fruit growers. The reason for such reports may possibly be found in the fact that on the prairies fruit-bearing shrubs, which afford so large a part of this bird's food, are conspicuously absent. With the settlement of this region came an extensive planting of orchards, vineyards, and small fruit gardens, which furnish shelter and nesting sites for the Catbird as well as for other species. There is in consequence a large increase in the numbers of the birds, but no corresponding gain in the supply of native fruits upon which they were accustomed to feed. Under these circumstances what is more natural than for the birds to turn to cultivated fruits for their food? The remedy is obvious: cultivated fruits can be protected by the simple expedient of planting the wild species which are preferred by the birds. Some experiments with Catbirds in captivity show that the Russian mulberry is preferred to any cultivated fruit.

The stomachs of 645 Catbirds were examined and found to contain 44 per cent. of animal (insect) and 56 per cent. of vegetable food. Ants, beetles, caterpillars, and grasshoppers constitute three-fourths of the animal food, the remainder being made up of bugs, miscellaneous insects, and spiders. One-third of the vegetable food consists of cultivated fruits or those which may be cultivated, as strawberries, raspberries, and blackberries; but while we debit the bird with the whole of this, it is probable — and in the eastern and well-wooded part of the country almost certain — that a large part is obtained from wild vines. The rest of the vegetable matter is mostly wild fruit, as cherries, dogwood, sour gum, elderberries, greenbrier, spiceberries, black alder, sumac and poison ivy. Although the Catbird sometimes does considerable harm by destroying small fruit, it cannot on the whole be considered injurious. On the contrary, in most parts of the country it does far more good than harm.

Photo by R. I. Brasher

NEST AND EGGS OF CATBIRD

BROWN THRASHER

Toxostoma rufum (*Linnæus*)

A. O. U. Number 705 See Color Plate 101

Other Names.— Thrasher; Brown Thrush; Red Thrush; Fox-colored Thrush; Sandy Mocker; Sandy Mockingbird; French Mockingbird; Brown Mocker; Brown Mockingbird; Ground Thrush; Mavis; Red Mavis; Song Thrush.

General Description.— Length, 11 inches. Upper parts, brown; under parts, buffy, streaked with dark. Bill, about length of head, curved downward at the end; wings, rather short and rounded; tail, decidedly longer than wing and rounded.

Color.—*Above, plain dull cinnamon-rufous,* becoming paler over eye and on notched terminal portion of outer webs of primaries; middle and greater wing-coverts tipped with white (spring and summer) or pale buff (autumn and winter), producing two distinct bands across wing, each white or buffy band immediately preceded by a narrower and less distinct one of dusky; outermost tail-feathers indistinctly tipped with buff (worn away in summer plumage); sides of head, light rusty-brown, narrowly streaked with dull whitish; cheeks, dull white, usually flecked with brown or dusky, especially on rear portion; under parts, pale buff, approaching buffy-white on chin, throat, and abdomen (entirely buff in fresh autumnal and early winter plumage), the chest, sides, and flanks broadly streaked with brown or dusky, the streaks smaller and narrowly wedge-shaped on upper chest, broader on sides of breast, longer flanks; throat margined along each side by a series of blackish streaks, forming a stripe; bill, dusky; iris, bright lemon or sulphur-yellow.

Nest and Eggs.— Nest: In clusters of thorny vines, within a few feet of the ground, sometimes on it, occasionally in trees, seldom in open situations, out-of-the-way, quiet localities being preferred; a rather flat, loosely constructed structure exteriorly composed of twigs, rootlets, leaves, hair, together with some feathers. Eggs: 3 to 5, varying from pale greenish-white to pale buff, profusely speckled with minute spots of reddish-brown, evenly over entire surface, more rarely forming a wreath around larger end.

Distribution.— Eastern United States and south-eastern Canada; northward to southern Maine, Vermont, New York, northern Ontario, Manitoba and Saskatchewan; breeding southward to northern Florida, Alabama, Mississippi, and eastern Texas, westward to base of Rocky Mountains in Montana, Wyoming, and Colorado; wintering from North Carolina, southeastern Missouri, etc. (more rarely farther northward) to southern Florida and south-central Texas; accidental in Arizona and Europe.

The term "thrush," which is frequently applied to this bird, is another of the many misnomers in popular ornithological terminology, as the bird is not a "thrush" at all, but a member of a totally different family, called *Mimidæ*. In point of fact, about the only resemblance between the Thrashers and other birds commonly called Thrushes is that all show more or less brown in their plumage and have speckled breasts. Right there the outward similarity may be said to end; for certainly in their general form and size (not to mention their habits) there is a wide difference between the smaller Thrushes, with their comparatively short tails and small, plump bodies, and the long-tailed, long-billed and relatively slender Thrashers.

The term "Thrasher" probably is due to the bird's vigorous twitching about of his long tail, a performance which is characteristic especially when he is nervous or angry, and with which he is likely to emphasize certain notes of his song The movement is also suggestive — to a sufficiently fertile imagination — of the flail in the primitive method of thrashing grain. Another explanation — humorous, of course — comes from Mr. Job, who says: "I used to wonder why the bird was called a Thrasher. But after I had actually received a real thrashing from a

Drawing by R. I .Brasher

BROWN THRASHER (⅓ nat. size)

A gifted singer and a brave defender of his home

pair of them, I thought I had some light on the subject." And he then proceeds to describe the courage displayed by this pair in their desperate attacks upon him while he was photographing their nest and young. This is a strongly marked characteristic of the bird, and must excite the admiration of every one who has seen it expressed; for the male bird, especially, is often positively heroic in his persistent efforts to protect his family. Indeed, it behooves the intruder under such conditions to guard his head carefully, for the infuriated bird will often dash directly at one's face, and a single stroke from that long, curved bill, if fairly delivered, undoubtedly would destroy the sight of an eye.

The song of this Thrasher is fairly one of the most musical and delightful of American bird utterances. In its structure — or rather, the lack of any definite structure — it suggests the Catbird's, though it includes almost none of the harsh or nasal notes which often mar that singer's effort. Most of the tones composing the song are like those of the flute or the piccolo, though the violin and the clarionet are also represented. The spirit, also, of the two utterances differs in that the Catbird's is likely to include little phrases which are *sotto voce* in quality, and in the manner of their delivery, as if the singer were addressing them in a personal way to a single listener; whereas the Thrasher's aria, delivered usually from a conspicuous perch at the top of a tree or bush (and most frequently in the morning or the evening), seems to be addressed to all the world within hearing.

Browning, of course, had a different bird in mind, yet he might well have been thinking of our Thrasher's pretty trick of repeating a phrase, when he wrote, in his beautiful poem, "Home Thoughts from Abroad"—

That's the wise Thrush; he sings his song twice over
Lest you should think he never could recapture
That first fine careless rapture.

Of the Thrasher's impassioned manner when the frenzy is upon him, we have this fine picture from Mr. Cheney: "As the fervor increases his long and elegant tail droops; all his feathers separate; his whole plumage lifted, it floats, trembles; his head is raised and his bill is wide open; there is no mistake; it is the power of the god. No pen can report him now; we must wait until the frenzy passes." And now he reminds one of Emma Juch, when she would throw back her head and pour her whole soul into the musical setting of Heinrich Heine's perfect poem, *"Du bist wie eine blume,"*

The lighter and more rollicking significance of the song is cleverly suggested by the following lines in Mrs. Wright's book, *Citizen Bird,* and attributed to "Olive":

My creamy breast is speckled
(Perhaps you'd call it freckled)
Black and brown.

My pliant russet tail
Beats like a frantic flail,
Up and down.

In the top branch of a tree
You may chance to glance at me,
When I sing.

But I'm very, very shy,
When I silently float by,
On the wing.

Whew there! Hi there! Such a clatter.
What's the matter — what's the matter?
Really, really?

Digging, delving, raking, sowing,
Corn is sprouting, corn is growing.
  Plant it, plant it!
  Gather it, gather it!
  Thresh it, thresh it!
  Hide it, hide it, do!
  (I see it — and you.)
Oh! I'm that famous scratcher,
H-a-r-p-o-r-h-y-n-c-h-u-s r-u-f-u-s —
  Thrasher[1]
Cloaked in brown."

GEORGE GLADDEN.

The food of the Brown Thrasher consists of both fruit and insects. An examination of 636 stomachs showed 36 per cent. of vegetable and 64 of animal food, practically all insects, and mostly taken in spring before fruit was ripe. Half the insects were beetles and the remainder chiefly grasshoppers, caterpillars, bugs, and spiders. A few predacious beetles were eaten, but on the whole the work of the species as an insect destroyer may be considered beneficial. Eight per cent. of its food is made up of fruits like raspberries and currants which are or may be cultivated, but the raspberries at least are as likely to belong to wild as to cultivated varieties. Grain, made up mostly of scattered kernels of oats and corn, is merely a trifle, amounting to only 3 per cent. Though some of the corn may be taken from newly planted fields, it is amply paid for by the destruction of May beetles which are eaten at the same time. The rest of the food consists of wild fruit or seeds. Taken all

[1] *Harporhynchus rufus* was the scientific name before the adoption of the present one by the American Ornithologists' Union.

in all, the Brown Thrasher is a useful bird, and probably does as good work in its secluded retreats as it would about the garden, for the swamps and groves are no doubt the breeding grounds of many insects that migrate thence to attack the crops of the farmer.

Photo by H. K. Job Courtesy of Outing Pub. Co.

MALE BROWN THRASHER

Shielding young from the hot sun

Sennett's Thrasher (*Toxostoma longirostre sennetti*) is similar to the Brown Thrasher, but larger, with the brown of the upper parts less red and more golden and the under parts whiter. It is a bird of northeastern Mexico, the Rio Grande valley, and the Gulf coast district of Texas. In the same part of the United States, but distributed over more territory in Mexico, is the Curve-billed Thrasher (*Toxostoma curvirostre curvirostre*). His upper parts are plain brownish gray (clay-color), tail, blackish with four feathers on each side abruptly tipped with white; his under parts are buffy-white, deepening into pale brownish-buff on the flanks and lower regions and with the chest, breast, and upper abdomen spotted with pale brownish-gray.

BENDIRE'S THRASHER

Toxostoma bendirei (*Coues*)

A. O. U. Number 708

General Description.— Length, 9¼ inches. Upper parts, grayish-brown; under parts, buffy-white with streaks of dark. Bill, about length of head, curved downward at the end; wings, rather short and rounded; tail, decidedly longer than wing and rounded.

Color.— *Above, plain light grayish-brown,* the rump and upper tail-coverts, paler, the wings and tail, slightly darker; middle and greater wing-coverts, indistinctly tipped with paler, and wing quills narrowly edged with the same; inner web of exterior tail-feathers rather broadly tipped with dull white, the outer web much more narrowly tipped with the same — the remaining tail-feathers (except middle pair) similarly tipped with whitish, but to a less extent, gradually disappearing toward middle feathers; sides of head, similar in color to upper parts but paler over the eyes and on lores, and around the ears narrowly streaked with dull whitish; cheeks and under parts, dull buffy-white, passing into decided brownish-buff on flanks, anal region, and lower tail-coverts; chest (sometimes sides of lower throat also) with sharply defined small wedge-shaped streaks of grayish-brown, the breast more sparsely marked with more roundish spots of a paler grayish-brown, the flanks sometimes indistinctly streaked with the same; sides of throat, margined with a series of wedge-shaped streaks or small spots of grayish-brown; under wing-coverts, light buffy wood-brown; bill, dusky horn-color; iris, yellow.

Nest and Eggs.— Nest: In the desert trees and bushes, but the customary site is in the cholla cactus about three feet from the ground; small and daintily built in contrast to the nests of others of the genus; composed exteriorly of the regulation sticks, twigs, and grasses and lined with soft materials — wool, feathers, horsehair, fine rootlets, and grasses. Eggs: 3 or 4, generally greenish-white, sometimes grayish or pinkish-white, spotted usually most thickly around larger end with reddish-brown, lavender-gray, and drab.

Distribution.— Desert districts of Arizona, and southeastern California (Colorado Desert) and northern Mexico; winters in Mexico; accidental in Colorado.

While at Tucson, Arizona, one of the first problems of identifying birds of the cactus was to distinguish Bendire's Thrasher from Palmer's Thrasher (*Toxostoma curvirostre palmeri*). From any manual of identification, you will find that the birds look almost exactly alike, except Bendire's Thrasher is a trifle smaller, and its bill is a little shorter than that of Palmer's. But, with these slight differences, it is practically impossible to tell one bird from the other. I soon discovered a difference, however, when I began examining the nests of the two birds. Palmer's Thrasher builds a large bulky nest and, about Tucson, it is found almost entirely in the cholla cactus. The lower part of the nest is made of rough sticks with a lining of fine grasses. The eggs are the size of a Robin's, with blue background uniformly peppered with brown dots. Of some twenty nests examined, all were practically the same.

The nest of the Bendire's Thrasher I found to be a smaller structure and often lined with horsehair, string and fine grasses. The cup of the nest is distinctly smaller than that of Palmer's. The eggs are also smaller. They have a light blue background, but are marked with larger brown blotches, generally more around the larger end. In appearance, the egg is more like that of the Mockingbird or Russet-backed Thrush.

While Bradford Torrey was at Tucson, he experienced considerable difficulty in recognizing Palmer's and Bendire's in the field. He fell back on an old method which he used in distinguishing the Downy from the Hairy Woodpecker, where the dress is alike, but the size is slightly different. It was easier to carry in mind the measurements of the two birds' bills than the comparative measurements of the two birds themselves. So with this point continually in mind and after spending considerable time in the field, he was able by the aid of his glass to tell one bird from the other almost beyond mistake. WILLIAM L. FINLEY.

CALIFORNIA THRASHER

Toxostoma redivivum (*Gambel*)

A. O. U. Number 710

General Description.— Length, 11½ inches. Upper parts, grayish-brown; under parts, buff, grayish-brown, and cinnamon. Bill, about length of head, curved downward at the end; wings, rather short and rounded; tail, decidedly longer than wing and rounded.

Color.— *Above, plain deep grayish-brown,* the upper tail-coverts and tail more decidedly brown (approaching sepia); primaries narrowly edged with paler grayish-brown, and larger wing-coverts usually margined at tip with the same; an indistinct stripe over eye of pale grayish-buff; sides of head and space below the eyes, dusky grayish-brown, narrowly but conspicuously streaked with dull buffy-whitish; cheeks, pale grayish-buff flecked with dusky; *chin and throat, pale buff,* margined along each side by an indistinct (often obsolete) dusky streak; chest, sides of breast, and sides, pale grayish-brown, becoming browner on flanks; center of breast and upper abdomen, pale buff becoming deeper cinnamon-buff on lower abdomen *and passing into cinnamon on under tail-coverts*; bill, blackish; iris, brown.

Nest and Eggs.— NEST: A rough, coarse, shallow platform of sticks, coarse grasses, and moss, with slight depression but always well hidden in the low scrub. EGGS: 2 to 4, usually 3, light greenish-blue with clove-brown, russet, or chestnut spots.

Distribution.— Coast and interior valleys of California and northern Lower California; northward to Shasta County, southward to San Quentin Bay, San Fernando, and San Pedro Martir Mountains.

Drawing by R. I. Brasher

CALIFORNIA THRASHER (⅜ nat. size)

A fine singer, clever mimic, and all 'round good fellow

This Thrasher seems to have more to say than any other member of his notably loquacious and voluble family. " Perched on top of the highest bush in sight," says Mrs. Bailey, " he shouts out *kick-it-now, kick-it-now, shut-up, shut-up, dor-o-thy, dor-o-thy,* and then with a rapid change of mood, drawls out, *whoa-now, whoa-now.*"

Earlier ornithologists did not credit this Thrasher with any imitative faculty, and some went so far as to declare flatly that the bird never reproduced any other bird's note. But John J. Williams is of another mind; for he identifies in the Thrasher's medley the notes of the California Jay, the Valley Quail, the Slender-billed Nuthatch, the Red-shafted Flicker, the Western Robin and the Wren-Tit, who is often tricked into answering the imitation. The entire performance, moreover, suggests the utmost good nature, as if the singer was enjoying intensely his own efforts.

His long, slender and decurved bill this bird puts to good use, for he employs it very dexterously in clearing away leaves and loose grass in order to get at the bare earth, instead of scratching with his feet, as do the Sparrows and Chewinks. Once the earth is cleared, the Thrasher probes into it to the full length of his bill, after the manner of the Woodcock. He is likely to make two or three of these holes in succession, and then watch each one and snap up any insect which comes to the surface through these shafts.

In the defense of their nest a pair of these Thrashers are likely to act very much as do the Brown Thrashers, of the eastern States. That is, they show the same anger and boldness which the eastern bird displays, even to the extent of dashing up to the intruder and striking at him with their bills. In fact, in these attacks the western bird is the more dangerous of the two, because he is more skillful in the use of his long and almost needle-pointed bill, with which he could easily destroy the sight of an eye, or even inflict an ugly flesh wound on the face, either or both of which injuries the birds undoubtedly are entirely willing to inflict.

LECONTE'S THRASHER

Toxostoma lecontei lecontei *Lawrence*

A. O. U. Number 711

General Description.— Length, 11½ inches. Upper parts, grayish-brown; under parts, dull white and buffy-grayish. Bill, about length of head, curved downward at the end; wings, rather short and rounded; tail, decidedly longer than wing and rounded.

Color.— *Above, plain pale grayish-brown,* the primaries edged with still paler; middle tail-feathers, slightly darker grayish-brown; other tail-feathers, deep grayish-brown, the exterior ones broadly tipped with pale grayish-brown; sides of head, pale grayish-brown, narrowly streaked with whitish and dusky; cheeks whitish, transversely mottled or barred with dusky; chin, throat, breast, and upper abdomen, dull white, margined laterally by a streak of dusky below the cheeks; rest of under parts, very pale buffy-grayish, *passing into deep buff on hinder flanks, anal region, and under tail-coverts,* the lower abdomen and front flanks tinged with buff; bill, blackish; iris, reddish-brown.

Nest and Eggs.— Nest: Usually built in the center of a cholla cactus or mesquite bush; a remarkable, bulky, loose, and deep affair, easily detected from a considerable distance; composed of thorny twigs, dried weeds and stems and grasses, lined with finer material and feathers. Eggs: 2 to 4, pale greenish-blue, minutely but sparsely spotted with shades of reddish or yellowish-brown and lavender.

Distribution.— Deserts of southwestern Utah (west of Beaverdam Mountains), southern Nevada (Vegas, Pahrump, and Indian Spring valleys), southern California and Arizona south to San Felipe Bay, Lower California, and Cape Lobos, Sonora.

It is a pity that this fine bird does not select a habitat more habitable for man, who, in order to hear its beautiful song and observe its interesting ways, must go to the Gehenna-like deserts of the Southwest, where the temperature is often 120° in the shade — with no shade. One may easily believe that the rather bleached appearance of this Thrasher's plumage may be due to the savage heat, which, however, seems to have little effect upon the bird's disposition. To be sure, for two or three hours during the middle of the day, when the heat is at its worst, the bird is likely to be silent and to lurk in such cover as there is; but even when the sun is making conditions almost unendurable for human beings the Thrasher may be both seen and heard.

The bird's distinguishing physical characteristics are its remarkable speed and skill in running, and its willingness to trust to its legs, rather than to its wings, to take it out of danger. In this peculiarity it is excelled only by the famous Road-runner. The Thrasher will easily keep ahead of a rapidly trotting horse, and if winged by a shot is pretty likely to escape from a man on foot; for, besides its speed, it can dodge with the quickness of a cat, and it is very clever at taking advantage of any cover. When forced actually to take to its wings, it is likely to fly low through the brush, keeping out of plain sight until it makes a Shrike-like sweep upward to the top of a bush, whence it can see its pursuer.

Though the song includes more metallic and fewer liquid notes than that of the Mockingbird, which it otherwise resembles somewhat, it is a very beautiful effort. The notes are astonishingly loud and resonant, and almost the entire song may sometimes be heard at a distance of nearly a mile. In the dead of night, when the desert lies in tomb-like silence under the wonderfully brilliant stars, the nocturne of this great singer is one of the most beautiful and inspiring of Nature's utterances.

CRISSAL THRASHER

Toxostoma crissale *Henry*

A. O. U. Number 712

General Description.— Length, 12 inches. Upper parts, grayish-brown; under parts, white, grayish-brown, and reddish. Bill, about length of head, curved downward at the end; wings, rather short and rounded; tail, decidedly longer than wing and rounded.

Color.— Above, plain grayish-brown, the tail slightly darker, tipped with paler and more buffy-brown; under parts, similar but paler and slightly more buffy, passing into dull white on throat and chin and into *cinnamon-rufous on rear flanks, anal region, and under tail-coverts*; region below eye and forward part of sides of head, dull whitish, the feathers margined with dusky; rear of same, light grayish-brown streaked with whitish; cheeks, dull whitish, the feathers sometimes narrowly tipped with dusky; chin and throat, margined laterally by a distinct narrow stripe of dusky; bill, dull black, and long and greatly curved; iris, brown.

Nest and Eggs.— Nest: In bushes near ground; large, loosely constructed of coarse twigs, lined with vegetable fibers, coarse grass, small twigs, and a few rootlets. Eggs: Usually 3, plain pale bluish-green.

Distribution.— Deserts of southwestern United States and Mexico; breeds from southern Nevada and southern Utah south to northern Lower California, and Mexico and from southeastern California to western Texas.

The Crissal Thrasher may, as a rule, be distinguished from Bendire's and Palmer's Thrashers by its long, curved bill and the whitish color of the throat bordered by a darker streak. This bird gets its name from the under tail-coverts, which are a rich chestnut color.

Different species of birds sometimes hold to a type locality, so that even if dress or song are somewhat alike, one may get a very fair indication of the bird itself from the place where it hunts and lives. While around Tucson, I found the Crissal Thrasher very shy, yet my experience was that it almost always stayed along the creek or river bottoms in the thick brush. The other Thrashers about Tucson, Bendire's and Palmer's, as a rule were seen out in the open desert living in the cactus.

I got another indication of the shyness of the Crissal Thrasher in trying to get a photograph of the bird at the nest. We succeeded in getting pictures of the nest and eggs and the young birds, but even though we hid the camera in a very careful way nearby, we could never get either of the parents to come close enough for a snap. The eggs are easily distinguished from those of the two other Thrashers mentioned above, because they are pale bluish-green without spots.

William L. Finley.

WRENS

Order *Passeres;* suborder *Oscines;* family *Troglodytidæ*

IN the *Troglodytidæ* or Wren family there are over 250 different forms throughout the world, only some 30 species being represented in the eastern hemisphere. In the tropical part of the Americas this family is most numerously developed. Within the bounds of the United States there are twenty-eight species and subspecies, occupying nearly the whole country from the Atlantic to the Pacific.

With the exception of the Marsh Wrens they all prefer some cozy nook for their homes. The natural sites are in the cavities in trees and rocks but it often happens that farm buildings afford just the place that they desire. Their nests are usually dome-shaped and the eggs are numerous, the clutches varying from 6 to 11. There are usually two broods each year. The eggs are usually white or pinkish speckled with reddish-brown but sometimes they are immaculate white or nearly uniform brown or plain greenish-blue.

In plumage the sexes are alike; and the young do not differ materially, if at all, in coloration from the adults. Red, yellow, green, blue, or other pure colors are never found. On the upper parts brown or reddish hues predominate and these are usually varied with bars, streaks, or speckles of dusky. The under parts are white, gray, buffy, tawny, rufous, or sooty or have two or more of these colors combined; these parts are rarely immaculate and usually are streaked or barred.

The Wrens are small birds. Their bills are long (usually as long as the head although in some cases less) and compressed, usually slender and curved downward at the end. The bristles at the corners of the mouth are usually obsolete but frequently they are quite plain with one or two fairly well developed. The wing is rather short or very short, much concaved underneath and much rounded. The tail varies in its relative length, sometimes shorter than the lower part of the leg; sometimes slightly longer than the wing but usually about half or two-thirds as long as the wing; it is always rounded and sometimes graduated for more than one-third of its length; the tail-feathers are soft and rounded at the tips.

Many members of this family are fine songsters, notably the Cactus, the Carolina, and the Winter Wrens. When alarmed or displeased they give utterance to loud, harsh, and insistent calls. These little birds are never quiet but are always active and seemingly excited about something. The position in which they carry their tails is an indication of their nervous temperament.

Since the Wrens are among our most prolific song birds, it naturally follows that a large amount of insect food must be consumed by the nestlings. The parents are industrious foragers, and, when their home is in a garden, they will search every tree, shrub, and vine for caterpillars and examine every post and fence rail and every cranny or crevice for insects or spiders. No species of this family has been accused of harm, and their presence should be encouraged about farms, ranches, and residences.

CACTUS WREN

Heleodytes brunneicapillus couesi (*Sharpe*)

A. O. U. Number 713

Other Name.— Coues's Cactus Wren.

General Description.— Length, 8½ inches. Upper parts, brown, variegated; under parts, white, spotted with black. Bill, nearly as long as head, stout; wings, much rounded; tail, nearly as long as wing, decidedly rounded, the feathers with broadly rounded tips.

Color.— Crown and hindneck, plain deep brown, the feathers slightly darker centrally; back, shoulders, and rump, paler and more grayish-brown, variegated with white, upper tail-coverts and middle tail-feathers, brownish-gray, rather broadly, but irregularly, barred with dusky, these dusky bars sometimes much broken and confused; tail (except middle feathers), mostly black, the side feathers broadly barred with white, the rest crossed near tip by a broad bar or band of white; the outer webs of all except outermost pair broadly barred or banded basally with brownish-gray; wing-coverts and inner quills, mainly grayish spotted with dusky and also varied with whitish bars or streaks, especially on smaller coverts; primary coverts, primaries, and secondaries (except inner quills), dusky, their outer webs conspicuously spotted with white or brownish-white; a broad, conspicuous, and sharply defined stripe of white over the eye usually margined above by a narrow line of black; a broad brown stripe under the eyes and occupying upper portion of ear region, but extending beyond to side of neck; lores, grayish; rest of sides of head, white, or brownish-white, the lower part of the ear region streaked with black or dusky; chin, throat, and chest, white, spotted (rarely broadly streaked) with black; breast, white or buffy-white, deepening into ochraceous-buff or cinnamon-buff on flanks, abdomen, and anal region, the whole surface marked with streaks or spots of black, these larger and broader on flanks; under tail-coverts, white or buffy with large spots of black; bill, dusky horn color; iris, red.

Nest and Eggs.— Nest: In cactus thicket, yucca, or other thorny bushes, a large flask-shaped structure lying horizontal, with entrance at mouth; constructed of sticks, thorns, straw, and grasses, lined with feathers. Eggs: 4 to 7, white or buffy-white, thickly sprinkled with rich chestnut spots, sometimes hiding the ground color.

Distribution.— Desert regions from southern parts of California, Nevada, Utah, New Mexico, and Texas south to northern Lower California and the northern States of Mexico.

Take it from nearly every standpoint, Mother Nature is strict and harsh with all her children of the desert. Life is spent on the march or on the firing line. Nearly everything is fortified with thorns. The cactus has a panoply of points to protect its soft spongy meat; the mesquite, palo verde, and the delicate white poppy clothe themselves in thorns.

Of all the desert plants, the cholla cactus is the most treacherous. I shall never forget my first experience. It is a favorite nesting place of the Cactus Wren. When I first saw a Cactus Wren's nest, I was anxious to find out what it contained. It was a gourd-shaped bundle of fibers and grasses with a hallway running in from the side. I couldn't look in, so I tried to feel. I ran my hand in as far as I could till the thorns about the entrance pricked into my flesh. I started to pull back. The more I pulled, the tighter the thorns clung and the deeper they pricked. I was in a trap. I reached for my knife to cut some of the thorns off, but had to cringe and let some of the others tear out. I looked at them, but could see no barbs. Yet when they once enter the flesh, one can readily tell they have tiny barbs, for it tears the flesh to get them out.

The Cactus Wren, as a rule, selects the thorniest place in a cholla cactus, although he sometimes nests in a mesquite or palo verde. Like the Tule Wren or Winter Wren, this bird often builds nests that are not used. These are called "cock nests," and are probably built by the male while the female is incubating. It is a question whether they are built from the standpoint of protection, that is having several unused nests about as a ruse, or whether the bird merely builds homes until the pair gets a nest that suits them exactly. At any rate, we examined quite a good many nests before we really found one that contained eggs. We got the impression that some of these birds were doing nothing day after day except building new homes. Some of the Wrens, however, were young, and inexperienced at nest building, for occasionally we noticed where a nest was so poorly built that either the floor dropped out or the roof caved in.

Drawing by R. I. Brasher

CACTUS WREN (⅜ nat. size)

A desert bird that builds in a *chevaux-de-frise* of yucca bayonets and cactus needles

When one thinks of a Wren, he thinks of a tiny fidgety body with an up-turned tail. If he has this in mind when he visits the cactus country, he will likely not know what the Cactus Wren is, for it is a very unwren-like bird. It is larger in size than an English Sparrow or the Bluebird. Its song is unwren-like, but the bird may be recognized by the white throat and breast which are heavily marked with black round spots. Like a Carolina Wren, it sings with head up and tail hanging. WILLIAM L. FINLEY.

Bryant's Cactus Wren (*Heleodytes brunneicapillus bryanti*) is darker and browner above than the common Cactus Wren, and its shoulders, back, and rump are conspicuously streaked with white; three of the lateral tail-feathers are distinctly barred with white; its under parts are more uniformly marked with black. It is distributed over the Pacific coast district of southern California and northern Lower California.

Photo by Mrs. F. T. Bicknell Courtesy of Nat. Asso. Aud. Soc.

NEST OF CACTUS WREN

Though at present the Cactus Wren is found chiefly in the deserts and waste places where its diet is a matter of little or no economic importance, it is not at all unlikely that its feeding habits may some day affect agriculture, and for that reason its natural dietary preferences may well receive some consideration now. Those preferences were pretty clearly shown by examination of forty-one stomachs of the bird taken in southern California; these contained about 83 per cent. of animal matter and about 17 per cent. of vegetable food. Of the insects taken about 27 per cent. were beetles, chiefly weevils and snout-beetles, and all more or less injurious. Among the bugs that had been devoured were black scales, which are very injurious to fruit trees. The vegetable food (17 per cent.) consisted of fruit pulp and weed seeds, all of wild species. It therefore, appears that this Wren's food contains little that is useful to man, while the remainder is made up of elements which are, or would be, harmful on cultivated lands.

ROCK WREN

Salpinctes obsoletus obsoletus (*Say*)

A. O. U. Number 715

General Description.— Length, 6½ inches. Upper parts, grayish-brown, speckled; under parts, whitish streaked with dark. Bill, shorter than head, slender, and straight (except extreme tip); wings, rather long, moderately rounded; tail, about ¾ length of wing, slightly rounded, the feathers very broad.

Color.—Above, grayish-brown or brownish-gray changing on rump to wine-colored cinnamon, most of the surface marked with small wedge-shaped spots or short streaks of dusky; middle tail-feathers, grayish-brown barred with dusky; remaining tail-feathers grayish-brown, broadly tipped with cinnamon-buff and crossed by a broad band of black; a distinct whitish stripe over the eye and a grayish-brown one back of it; eye and cheek regions and lower portion of ear region, dull white or brownish-white; under parts, dull white, passing into pale cinnamon-buff on flanks; throat and chest (sometimes breast also) usually streaked with grayish-brown or dusky; bill, horn color; iris, brown.

Nest and Eggs.— NEST: Usually placed in a cleft of rocks; constructed of a large variety of materials, but principally small twigs, moss, wool, hair, grass, or weeds; a paving in front of nest made of small pebbles, pieces of glass, or rock. EGGS: 5 to 8, usually 5 or 6, glossy white, minutely and thinly speckled with chestnut.

Distribution.— Western North America; breeds from southern British Columbia, west central Alberta, and southwestern Saskatchewan south to Mexico and peninsula of Lower California and adjacent islands, east to western North Dakota, central Nebraska (casually western Iowa), and central Texas; winters in southern part of its United States range and in Mexico.

Wrens seem to have traditions as some people do. I do not remember ever examining the nest of the Parkman, or Western House, Wren and not finding a bit of snake skin woven into the home. Perhaps this answers the purpose of a hearthstone deity or a relic of long ago when the first Wrens must have fought the reptile tribes. The Rock Wren is not unlike its cousin in its household eccentricities. It nests in a rocky crevice. It often makes a path into the nest. "And when it comes to lining the approaches of the chosen cavity, what do you suppose they use?" says Mr. W. L. Dawson. "Why, rocks, of course; not large ones this time, but flakes and pebbles of basalt, which rattle pleasantly every time the bird goes in and out. These rock chips are sometimes an inch or more in diameter, and it is difficult to conceive how a bird with such a delicate beak can compass their removal. Here they are, however, to the quantity of half a pint or more, and they are just as much a necessity to every well-regulated Salpinctean household as marble steps are to Philadelphians."

Drawing by R. I. Brasher

ROCK WREN (⅝ nat. size)

A welcome sign of cheerful life in the torrid western cañons

The Rock Wren is typical of the rimrock regions of the West. He is associated in my mind with the sand and the sage. I have often seen him in the arid desert regions of eastern Oregon. The first time I ever saw him, I recognized him instantly by his general Wren character. He is generally appreciated, for he is often seen where songsters are rather scarce. As Mrs. Bailey says, "Even his song, which at first hearing seems the drollest, most unbird-like of machine-made tinklings, comes to be greeted as the voice of a friend in the desert, and its quality to seem in harmony with the hard, gritty granites in which he lives. Its phrases are varied, but one of its commonest — given perhaps from the top of a cliff while his mate is feeding their brood on a ledge below — is little more than a harsh *kra-wee, kra-wee, kra-wee, kra-wee,* given slowly at first, then after a little bob repeated in faster time."

William L. Finley.

CAROLINA WREN

Thryothorus ludovicianus ludovicianus (*Latham*)

A. O. U. Number 718 See Color Plate 102

Other Names.— Mocking Wren; Great Carolina Wren; Louisiana Wren.

General Description.— Length, 5½ inches. Upper parts, rusty-brown; under parts, buffy-white. Bill, shorter than head, slightly but decidedly curved downward; wings, rather short and rounded; tail, about 4/5 length of wing, rounded, the feathers broadly rounded at the tip.

Color.—Above, plain rusty-brown (nearly prouts-brown to chestnut-brown), duller on crown (especially on forehead), brighter (light chestnut or rufous-chestnut) on rump and upper tail-coverts; rump with concealed roundish spots of white, the feathers dark slate color or blackish-slate basally; wings and tail, duller brown than back, narrowly (sometimes indistinctly) barred with dusky, the exterior tail-feathers and primaries with interspaces between dusky bars much paler (pale buffy or dull whitish, at least in part); middle wing-coverts and some of greater coverts, usually with a small triangular terminal spot of white or pale buffy, margined (except at the ends) with dusky; over the eye a sharply defined and conspicuous stripe of white or buffy-white, bordered above by a narrow black line along the side margin of crown and neck; a broad stripe of rufous-brown back of the eye and occupying upper half (approximately) of ear region, continued (sometimes brokenly) across side of neck; the space under the eye and the lower portion of ear region, dull white, buffy-white, or pale buff, the feathers narrowly edged or margined with dusky, producing streaked or scale-like effect; cheeks, chin, and upper throat, plain dull white; rest of under parts, plain dull buffy-white tinged with buff on chest, sides, flanks, and anal region, or distinctly buff, deepest on flanks; under tail-coverts, buffy-whitish or pale buff broadly barred with black; flanks (occasionally sides also) very rarely barred with dusky-brown; bill, horn color; iris, brown.

Nest and Eggs.—Nest: Placed in brush heaps, holes in logs or rocks, in low bushes, or outbuildings; a large, rough structure of coarse grass, corn leaves, hay, leaves, corn silk, lined with horse-hair, feathers and fine grasses. Eggs: From 4 to 6, varying from white to pinkish-buff, so thickly sprinkled with brownish-pink as to obscure the ground color in some cases.

Distribution.—Eastern United States; breeds from southeastern Nebraska, southern Iowa, Ohio, southern Pennsylvania, and lower Hudson and Connecticut valleys south to central Texas (western Texas in winter), Gulf States, and northern Florida; casual north to Wisconsin, Michigan, Ontario, Massachusetts, New Hampshire, and Maine.

The folk-lore and tradition of the Old World marks the Wren as a tiny bird; American literature follows suit. Darius Green characterizes the family in these immortal words, "the little chatterin' sassy wren, no bigger'n my thumb," but the Carolina Wren certainly is not tiny. In fact it is so large that early American ornithologists referred to it as the Great Carolina Wren, with the accent on the Great.

Courtesy of Am. Mus. Nat. Hist.

CAROLINA WREN (½ nat. size)

It sings nearly the whole year round

Notwithstanding its size it possesses in full the activity, nervousness, excitability, volubility, and curiosity attributed to Wrens from time immemorial. It seems full of song, sings nearly the whole year round, and its voice like that of other Wrens is loud, clear, strong and sweet, but its song does not express the bubbling, outpouring, irrepressible ecstasy that characterizes those of the House Wren and Winter Wren. One of its common phrases is very well expressed by the words *tea-kettle, tea-kettle, tea-kettle.* It has been called the Mocking Wren because some of its notes resemble those of other birds, particularly the whistling call of the Tufted Titmouse and a song of the Cardinal. Its notes are varied but probably it hardly deserves the name of an imitator.

It is not naturally as domestic as the House Wren, being more inclined to the neighborhood of woods and swampy thickets than to that of human habitations. If stared at it is likely to grow nervous and to betake itself quickly to cover, for it usually has a safe harbor under its lee. It is fond of high, thick shrubbery, but can hide readily in old stumps, under logs or in very low-growing vegetation to which it flies when no other cover is near.

Its abundant energy is expressed by both voice and tail and the latter is used freely for gesticulation.

Although this Wren is a cave dweller and nests normally in the hollows of trees or in other natural cavities in the wilderness, it seems more and more to acquire confidence in mankind and quite often builds in some nook in an outbuilding or even in a bird house or nesting box put up for more domestic birds. Rather recently two nests have been found in grape baskets hung up in outbuildings. The only nest with eggs taken in Massachusetts that is now on exhibition in any museum is in the collection of the Boston Society of Natural History. Its history as told by its discoverer is this: He hung for safe keeping high under the ridgepole inside the barn a grape basket containing some sticks of dynamite. A few weeks later when he went to get it the Wren had built her nest in the basket, deposited her eggs and was incubating. The dynamite was removed with great care and replaced with paper, but the bird refused to be comforted and deserted the nest. EDWARD HOWE FORBUSH.

The Carolina Wren has to its credit an apparent disposition to destroy the dreaded boll weevil whose working on cotton-bolls has been a most serious matter in several Southern States. The Wrens live in Texas and Louisiana throughout the year, and frequent thickets and clearings littered with fallen timber. In these surroundings they capture the weevils during their period of hibernation, and it is apparent that they also take them in the Spanish moss during the same period.

The Florida Wren (*Thryothorus ludovicianus miamensis*) is larger than the Carolina Wren and its coloration is darker and richer; the upper parts are rich chestnut to dark chestnut, the stripe over the eye is decidedly buffy, the under parts (except the chin and upper throat) are deep clay color or tawny yellow, the flanks tinged with chestnut and (sometimes the sides also) barred with chestnut or dusky. It is found only in the peninsula of Florida, south of the Suwanee River.

Photo by Jos. Armfield Courtesy of Nat. Asso. Aud. Soc.

NEST OF A CAROLINA WREN

In an old wash-basin

BEWICK'S WREN

Thryomanes bewicki bewicki (*Audubon*)

A. O. U. Number 719

Other Names.— Long-tailed House Wren; Song Wren.

General Description.— Length, 5½ inches. Upper parts, brown; under parts, grayish-white. Bill, shorter than head, slender; wings, short and rounded; tail, about length of wing, rounded, the feathers broadly rounded at the tip.

Color.— *Crown, hindneck, back, shoulders and smaller wing-coverts, plain brown,* the rump, more chestnut-brown; secondaries and greater wing-coverts, brown, the former distinctly, the latter indistinctly, barred with dusky; primaries dusky, their outer webs edged and spotted with pale brownish; upper tail-coverts and middle tail-feathers, brownish-gray, the latter distinctly, the former indistinctly, barred with dusky; a conspicuous and sharply defined stripe of white or buffy-white extending over the eyes to the back of the head, the front portion narrower and usually, more grayish; a broad brown stripe behind the eye occupying upper half (approximately) of ear region; *under parts, dull grayish-white* or very pale gray, becoming more decidedly white on abdomen, the sides and flanks tinged with brown; iris, brown.

Nest and Eggs.— NEST: Located like the House Wren, almost anywhere, in outbuildings, boxes, stumps, watering pots, or any hollow objects, hung in trees or lying on ground, constructed of materials similar to those used by the House Wren. EGGS: 4 to 7, dull white speckled with chestnut, more profusely around large end where often forming a wreath.

Distribution.— Eastern United States; breeds from southeastern Nebraska, northern Illinois, southern Michigan, and south-central Pennsylvania south to central Arkansas, northern Mississippi, central Alabama, and along the Alleghenian highways to northern South Carolina; winters from near the northern limit of its range southward to the Gulf coast and Florida; accidental in Ontario and New Hampshire.

Fussy, nervous, excitable, impatient, restless, and inquisitive, his tail cocked up over his back with true Wren-like pertness, this energetic little bunch of flesh and feathers is much like his well known cousin, the House Wren. But he is a much better singer than Mr. Jenny.

"Not a voluble chatter, like the House Wren's," says W. F. Henninger (in Dawson's *Birds of Ohio*), "but clear, strong and cheery, easily heard for a quarter of a mile — such is the song of Bewick's Wren. Easily distinguished from the former, he has the same teasing ways about him — now peeping into some corner, now examining the wood-pile, now crawling into a knot-hole of a smoke-house, creeping forth like a mouse at the next moment, whisking his erectly carried tail, watching you carefully though fearlessly, he all of a sudden mounts some fence-post, pours forth his proud metallic notes, drops down into the chicken yard, disappears in the pig pen, mockingly scolds at you, sings again, and is willing to keep this game up all day. We do not know which to admire more, his beautiful song or his confidence in man."

This species is also Wren-like in its selection of queer nesting places — an old shoe, the arm of an old coat, a discarded battered tin cup, and so on. Indeed, in this respect these Wrens reveal wonderfully versatile adaptability, which, incidentally, reflects a most gratifying friendliness for and confidence in mere man.

The economic value of this Wren's feeding habits is beyond all question very great. The contents of 146 stomachs examined showed that of its diet for a year a little more than 97 per cent. was composed of insects and less than 3 per cent. of vegetable matter. The only vegetable matter found that could possibly be useful to man was a little fruit pulp. Of the animal food various families of bugs made up the largest percentage. These included several species belonging to the same family as the highly destructive chinch bug, and their destruction by birds undoubtedly is very beneficial. It was also evident that the bird feeds on the black olive scale, a very harmful species. About 21 per cent. of the bird's food consists of beetles, chiefly ladybirds, weevils, and other species. Ladybirds, which constituted about 3 per cent. of the food found in the stomachs examined, are probably the most useful insects of their order, and the bird's destruction of them is regrettable. On the other hand, the bird eats weevils, or snout beetles, to the extent of nearly 10 per cent. of its food, and as all of these are harmful, and some the most injurious of all pests of the orchard or forest, it must be admitted that the Wren pays a fair price for the ladybirds. Beetles belonging to the family of engravers, which live under the bark of trees and greatly damage valuable timber, are also destroyed by these Wrens.

West of the Mississippi are five regional varieties of Bewick's Wren. In the coast region of middle California is Vigors's Wren (*Thryomanes bewicki spilurus*), larger and browner than the type species. In the southern part of the Great Plains is the Texas Wren (*Thryomanes bewicki cryptus*); this member of the family is also larger than his eastern relative but his coloration is grayer. Baird's Wren (*Thryomanes bewicki bairdi*) breeds from California (east of the Sierra Nevada), southern Nevada, southern Utah and southeastern Colorado south into Mexico; he is smaller than Bewick's Wren. Still smaller and with his upper part a duller, or slightly olive, brown is the San Diego Wren (*Thryomanes bewicki charienturus*); he lives in the coast district of southern California and northern Lower California. The Seattle Wren (*Thryomanes bewicki calophonus*) is a deep sepia on his upper parts; his home is the yellow-pine country of the Pacific slope from Southern Vancouver and southern British Columbia south to Oregon.

HOUSE WREN

Troglodytes aëdon aëdon *Vieillot*

A. O. U. Number 721 See Color Plate 102

Other Names.— Brown Wren; Common Wren; Wood Wren; Stump Wren; Short-tailed House Wren; Jenny Wren.

General Description.— Length, 5 inches. Upper parts, brown; under parts, white and grayish-brown. Bill, shorter than head, straight or but very slightly curved downward, tapering gradually; wings, moderate in length, rounded; tail, about length of wing, much rounded, the feathers narrow with rounded tips.

Color.—*Above, brown* (nearest prouts-brown) duller

and grayer on crown, where the feathers have the central portion indistinctly darker; brighter or more rufescent on rump and upper tail-coverts; back and shoulders, sometimes narrowly and indistinctly barred with dusky; upper tail-coverts, narrowly barred with dusky; *tail, greater wing-coverts, and secondaries, brown, narrowly barred with black;* primaries dusky, their outer webs spotted with pale brown, these spots in transverse series forming regular, broad bars; under eye, cheek, and ear regions (except upper portion of the latter), very pale grayish-buffy or dull brownish-white; *chin, throat, and abdomen, dull white,* the last sometimes speckled with dusky; chest and sides of breast, very pale grayish-brown or grayish-buffy, passing into a deeper and more decidedly brown hue on sides and flanks, which are barred (narrowly) with darker brown or dusky; under tail-coverts, dull white tinged or intermixed with rusty-brown and irregularly barred with black; iris, brown.

Nest and Eggs.— NEST: Usually in boxes erected by man for their convenience, under house cornices and eaves, in fact almost anywhere, from the pocket of a scarecrow to an old tin can on the ground; constructed of small twigs, grass, feathers, spiders' webs, and lined with soft strips of bark, down, or feathers. EGGS: From 6 to 8, dull white so profusely spotted with reddish- or pinkish-brown as to obscure the ground color.

Distribution.— Eastern United States and Canada; breeds north to New Brunswick, Maine, Ontario, Michigan, and eastern Wisconsin, and south to Virginia and Kentucky; winters in the South Atlantic and Gulf States, and through eastern Texas to eastern Mexico.

Fussy little "Jenny" Wren has the proud distinction of having forced upon her entire species the popular name which was given her by the early English colonists, in memory of the much milder mannered bird of the old country. As Mrs. Wright says: "We always speak of Jenny Wren; always refer to the Wren as *she,* as we do of a ship. It is Johnny Wren who sings and disports himself generally, but it is Jenny who, by dint of much fussing and scolding, keeps herself well to the front. She chooses the building-site and settles all the little domestic details. If Johnny does not like her choice, he may go away and stay away; she will remain where she has taken up her abode and make a second matrimonial venture." (*Birdcraft.*)

This is an accurate estimate of the character of Jenny who, in truth, is a good deal of a shrew, and a chronic scold on general principles. By the same token, Johnny is likely to present a pretty good imitation of a henpecked husband, for from the moment he promises to love, cherish, and obey Jenny, he hardly dares say his soul is his own. However, he doesn't appear to be in the least depressed by this state of affairs, for his bubbling song is one of the merriest and most spontaneous of bird utterances.

The Latin term *Troglodytidæ,* under which these birds are classified, means literally "cave-dwellers," and is appropriate as applied to the European Wren, which fashions a cave-shaped nest, and also as to the American species (the present one, the Winter Wren and the Long and Short-billed Marsh Wrens) which build in cavities or construct nests after the general pattern of the European species. The House Wren is famous for the odd kinds of cavities which it selects for its nest. It is quick to take advantage of a bird-box of almost any kind, and hollow limbs or trunks of fruit trees are also often

Courtesy of Am. Mus. Nat. Hist.

HOUSE WREN (⅞ nat. size)

A fussy, scolding mite

utilized. In fact the House Wren seems to be especially partial to apple orchards. But lacking a natural or prepared cavity, almost any substitute will do. For example, a discarded straw hat or leather glove is often used, if it is found in the right surroundings, and battered fruit-cans are frequently pressed into service. Nor is the bird in the least concerned as to whether the article with a cavity in it is discarded or not.

This was proved by a photograph, reproduced in one of the magazines a few years ago, which showed a House Wren's nest built neatly in one of the hip pockets of a pair of fishing trousers which some dutiful Mrs. Izaak Walton had hung out on a line to dry. It is a safe conjecture that Izaak had to do his fishing in another pair of trousers until that little domestic affair had been completed.

Photo by H. K. Job Courtesy of Outing Pub. Co.

HOUSE WREN

Emerging from nest in an old can nailed to an apple tree

An experiment of Mr. J. Alden Loring, an experienced field-naturalist of Owego, N. Y., demonstrated in a most interesting and conclusive manner the homing instinct of a particular House Wren. The bird built her nest in a bird-box in Mr. Loring's back yard, and he tamed her so that she would take meal worms out of his hand. Jenny disappeared in the fall and doubtless made the long migratory journey to the southland. The following spring, Mr. Loring saw a pair of the birds examining his bird-box and took his stand as he had the year before, holding out meal worms in his hand. In a few minutes one of the birds alighted on his arm, with very little show of fear, and seized one of the worms. As it had taken much patience and persistence to overcome the bird's fear, Mr. Loring regarded this as conclusive proof that this little Wren was the very one he had tamed the year before. GEORGE GLADDEN.

As regards food habits, the House Wren is entirely beneficial. Practically he may be said to live upon animal food alone, for an examination of fifty-two stomachs showed that 98 per cent. of the contents was made up of insects or their allies, and only 2 per cent. was vegetable food, including bits of grass and similar matter, evidently taken by accident with the insects. Half of this food consisted of grasshoppers and beetles; the remainder, of caterpillars, bugs, and spiders.

Dr. Eaton notices that House Wrens pay frequent visits to the nests of Yellow Warblers, Chipping Sparrows, and other species which live near his home, and peck small holes in the eggs.

In western North America the House Wren is decidedly paler and grayer and his back and shoulders are usually distinctly barred with dusky; he is also larger. The Western House Wren, or Parkman Wren (*Troglodytes aëdon parkmani*), as he is called, breeds from southern British Columbia, northern Alberta, central Saskatchewan, and southern Manitoba south to Lower California, southern Arizona, southwestern Texas, southern Missouri, and southern Illinois. In the winter he is found from California and Texas south into Mexico.

WINTER WREN

Nannus hiemalis hiemalis (*Vieillot*)

A. O. U. Number 722 See Color Plate 102

Other Names.— Wood Wren; Mouse Wren; Spruce Wren; Short-tailed Wren.

General Description.— Length, 4 inches. Upper parts, reddish-brown; under parts, pale wood-brown, speckled with dusky. Bill, shorter than head, very slender, and awl-shaped; wings, short and rounded; tail, ⅔ length of wing, much rounded, the feathers narrow with rounded tips.

Color.—*Above, reddish-brown,* the back, shoulders, and rump barred with dusky; tail, light chestnut-brown or reddish-brown, narrowly (sometimes indistinctly) barred with dusky; wings, similar in color to back, barred with dusky; under eye and ear regions, brownish-buffy, narrowly streaked with brown; a narrow stripe of brownish-buffy over the eye and a narrow stripe of brown back of the eye; cheek region, chin, throat, and chest, light wood-brown or pale cinnamon; the lower throat and chest, sometimes speckled with dusky; rest of ***under parts, speckled or finely marked with dusky*** on a pale wood-brown or cinnamon ground-color; iris, brown.

Nest and Eggs.— Nest: In cavity of stump, or among roots of upturned tree; constructed of small twigs, plant stems, moss, and lichens woven together and warmly lined with moss, fur, hair, and feathers, with a small circular opening. Eggs: 5 to 7 or 8, creamy-white, minutely dotted with reddish-brown and lavender.

Distribution.— Eastern United States and Canada; north to Nova Scotia, Prince Edward Island, New Brunswick, Quebec, Ontario, and Manitoba; breeding southward to Massachusetts, New York, Michigan, and Wisconsin, more rarely to northern Indiana and Illinois and central Iowa, and through mountain districts of Pennsylvania, Maryland, Virginia, and West Virginia to western North Carolina; wintering from near southern breeding limit to northern Florida and thence along Gulf coast to Texas.

"Such a dapper, fidgety, gesticulating, bobbing-up-and-down-and-out-and-in little bird, and yet full of such sweet, wild melody!" is Mr. Burroughs's capital description of the Winter Wren. All too seldom do we hear this "sweet, wild melody," instinct with that indefinable yet eloquent message straight from the soul of Nature. Fortunate indeed is the listener whose heart can receive that message! Yet it is heard by too few who could really heed it, because the singer comes infrequently within the hearing of those whose ears are properly attuned.

The bird's northern migration in April takes it into the depths of the Canadian wilderness and swamps, though it may be found breeding in such surroundings in northern Massachusetts and southern New Hampshire and Vermont, in the Catskills and in northern New York and in the northern part of the lower peninsula of Michigan. Mr Hoffmann describes the song as "long and high, in two equally balanced parts, the first ending in a contralto trill, the second in a very high trill; after a little interval the song is repeated or answered." Thoreau likened the song of a bird he failed to identify, to "a fine corkscrew stream issuing with incessant lisping tinkle from a cork, flowing rapidly, and I said that he had pulled out the spile and left it running." And this probably was the song of the Winter Wren.

The bird somewhat resembles the House Wren, though it is about an inch shorter, this abbreviation being especially noticeable in the Winter Wren's tail, which it holds up, Wren-fashion, over its back but tipped even further forward than are those of his relatives. Another distinguishing mark is the brownish-buffy line over the Winter Wren's eye, which the House Wren lacks. Again, the Winter Wren sings almost invariably from a low perch on a dead limb, or sometimes even when hidden in a brush-heap or in dense undergrowth. Apparently, as Mr. Torrey said, he believes that little birds should be heard and not seen.

Two regional varieties of the Winter Wren are the Western Winter Wren (*Nannus hiemalis pacificus*), found in western North America, breeding from Alaska south to central California and northern Colorado and wintering from southern British Columbia to southern California and southern New Mexico, and the Kodiak Winter Wren (*Nannus hiemalis helleri*), found on the island of that name. Both are larger and darker than the eastern form.

The Alaska Wren (*Nannus alascensis*) and the Aleutian, or Attu, Wren (*Nannus meliger*) are closely allied to the Winter Wrens. They average larger and their coloration is paler and duller. The Alaska Wren is found in the western part of the Alaska peninsula and the islands off the coast while the Aleutian is confined to the western islands of the group of that name.

SHORT-BILLED MARSH WREN

Cistothorus stellaris (*Naumann*)

A. O. U. Number 724 See Color Plate 102

Other Names.— Fresh-water Marsh Wren; Meadow Wren; Grass Wren.

General Description.— Length, 4½ inches. Upper parts, black, pale brown, and whitish in streaks; under parts, white and cinnamon-buff. Bill, much shorter than head, rather stout, nearly straight; wings, short and rounded; tail nearly as long as wing, graduated for 2/5 its length, the feathers narrow, tapering toward the end but with rounded tip.

Color.— *Crown, streaked* with black and light brown, except on forehead, which is sometimes uniform brown; hindneck light brown; *back and shoulders, black, narrowly streaked* with brownish-white; rump, light buffy-brown or cinnamon-brown, streaked or otherwise variegated, chiefly along central line, with black and whitish; upper tail-coverts, light brown, barred with black and tipped with dull whitish; tail, barred with black and light grayish-brown in varying relative proportions; wing-coverts, pale buffy-brown, barred or transversely spotted with blackish; secondaries and primaries, dusky, their outer webs with broad marginal spots of pale buffy-brown producing broad bands on closed wing; sides of head, pale brownish-buff or dull brownish-white, indistinctly streaked with darker; *cheek region, chin, throat, breast, and abdomen white (slightly dull or buffy)*; chest, sides, flanks, and under tail-coverts cinnamon-buff.

Nest and Eggs.— NEST: On or close to the ground, in a tussock of marsh grass, the tops of which are deftly and closely woven together forming roof and sides; construction similar to the Long-billed Marsh Wren's, but shape less clearly defined because of its location; lining made of finer grass, cat-tail down, and some feathers. Eggs: 6 to 8, pure white, unmarked; rarely with a few lavender marks.

Distribution.— Eastern North America; breeds from southeastern Saskatchewan, southern Keewatin, southern Ontario, and southern Maine south to eastern Kansas, central Missouri, central Indiana, and northern Delaware; winters from southern Illinois and southern New Jersey to southern Texas, Louisiana, and Florida; accidental in Colorado.

The curious habit — if it may correctly be termed a habit — of building more than one nest, but using only one, which seems to be a trait of the Wren family — and of other species as well — appears to be quite strongly developed in this little bird. That very common type of observer who is quick to account for the actions of wild creatures, by ascribing them to distinctively human mental operations, explains this particular performance by attributing it to " strategic ability " in the animal concerned. This implies the possession and exercise by the animal of the reasoning power, in fact of actual subtlety, in a degree which none of its other observed acts indicate. Much more sensible explanations of such acts are that they are due to indecision or forgetfulness or sheer stupidity. In some instances the building of a second nest and the desertion of the first may mean that the bird discovered something undesirable about the situation of the first one. But what is to be said of the Phœbe, for example, who was industriously building at the same time three nests within two or three feet of one another on the same beam under a porch, and doubtless would have persisted in this superfluous labor had not her attention been concentrated on one of the nests by the placing of stones over the other two. This may have been an attempt at profound strategy, but common sense prompts the explanation that it reflected downright stupidity.

Photo by H. K. Job Courtesy of Outing Pub. Co.

NEST OF SHORT-BILLED MARSH WREN

Drawing by R. I. Brasher

SHORT-BILLED MARSH WREN (¾ nat. size)

Mouse-like in its ability to scamper through grass and brush and to elude the sharpest eye

As to this particular Wren's needless nest building, we certainly have no good reason to suppose that it bespeaks a strategical faculty, or anything of the kind. If the Phœbe was so forgetful as to build three nests in plain sight, and within a few feet of one another, an equal degree of forgetfulness might easily overtake a Wren, building in a uniform growth of marsh-grass and reeds so dense that nests might be completely concealed from each other though they were placed only a few yards apart.

There are, however, certain facts about the

nest-building and other habits of this Wren which are both significant and interesting. In the first place, it is much more likely to be heard than seen, for it is nothing short of mouse-like in its ability to scamper around through the grass or brush, and elude even the sharpest and most practiced eye. Again, though it usually places its nest in marshy land, the globular structure is seldom built directly over the water, as that of the Long-billed species is likely to be. The entrance to the nest is at the side, but it is usually almost completely concealed.

As its name implies, its bill is shorter than that of its near relative, from whom it may also be distinguished by its striped head and upper back, and by its lack of a white line over the eye. Like the Long-billed bird, it clings to grass and reed stalks in a position as nearly upright as it can assume, and with its tail cocked, Wren-like, over its back. Its song, however, though voluble and delivered with the rapidity characteristic of its family, is composed of notes which are more sibilant and Sparrow-like than are those of other Wrens.

LONG-BILLED MARSH WREN

Telmatodytes palustris palustris (*Wilson*)

A. O. U. Number 725 See Color Plate 102

Other Names.— Marsh Wren; Reed Wren; Cat-tail Wren; Salt-water Marsh Wren.

General Description.— Length, 5 inches. Upper parts, brown and black with white streaks; under parts, white and pale brown. Bill, shorter than head, slender, gently curved for most of its length; wings, moderate in length and much rounded; tail, nearly as long as wing, much rounded, the feathers not tapering and with broadly rounded tips.

Color.— Crown, dull black, brownish centrally, usually with a broad and distinct though never sharply defined center area of olive-brown on forehead and crown, occasionally continued to the hindneck; hindneck, mostly plain brown; *back, black, streaked with white;* shoulders, rump, and upper tail-coverts, plain brown; lesser and middle wing-coverts plain brown; greater coverts, brown, barred with dusky; *over the eye, a narrow stripe of white narrowly streaked with blackish and extending to the edges of the back of the head;* back of the eye, a dusky streak; cheek region and *under parts, dull white, passing on sides and flanks into pale brown,* the chest usually faintly tinged with the same, the sides and flanks sometimes speckled or indistinctly barred with darker brown or dusky; iris, brown.

Nest and Eggs.— Nest: A remarkable coconut-shaped structure of interwoven reeds, strongly fastened to upright sedges or cat-tails, lined with fine grass and cat-tail down, with side entrance and nearly waterproof. Eggs: 5 to 9, chocolate, generally sprinkled with deeper colored specks and spots.

Distribution.— Eastern United States, chiefly east of the Allegheny Mountains; north to Massachusetts and New York; west to western New York and Pennsylvania; breeds southward to the Potomac valley and Atlantic coast of Maryland and Virginia; in winter southward to North and South Carolina, occasionally to western Florida, occasionally wintering in northern portions of its range.

Photo by H. K. Job Courtesy of Outing Pub. Co.

LONG-BILLED MARSH WREN

At its nest with food for its babies

The canoeist who paddles or drifts quietly and slowly along some sluggish river, bordered by broad meadow marshes, may catch sight of a nervous little brown bird hanging to the stems or leaves of rushes, reeds, or cat-tails along the margin and regarding him with alert, apprehensive curiosity. This is the Long-billed Marsh Wren, which may be known by its long, slender bill and a Wren-like habit of flirting and cocking up the tail when excited.

This Wren is fond of the deep and oozy marsh, near slow-running streams or dark, swampy pools

Drawing by R. I. Brasher

LONG-BILLED MARSH WREN (¾ nat. size)

An irrepressible songster and wonderful architect

while the smaller Short-billed Marsh Wren prefers merely moist, grassy, or reedy meadows.

Marsh Wrens, like other Wrens, are irrepressible songsters. They are not satisfied with daylight singing alone but often carol at night. Sometimes when the full moon lights up the marshes the singing of the Wrens becomes almost a continuous performance, ringing over the meadows far and near. This bird breeds abundantly in fresh-water marshes and open swamps and may be found frequently in salt marshes and along the shores of tidal streams. The unique globular nests are hung concealed in the marsh vegetation or even attached to some shrub growing over the water, and with Wren-like industry a pair often constructs several nests. Various theories have been offered to account for this habit. One is that the Wren forsakes its nest the moment it has been disturbed or even touched by human hands. Samuels and others have opined that duplicate nests are built to protect the sitting female, for it is noticeable that the male often lures a visitor to one of the empty nests which, numerous as they often are in the marsh, may puzzle water snakes and other enemies searching for eggs and young birds. Others believe that the male, being full of vigor and vitality, must work off his nervousness in some manner and so occupies himself in nest-building. Excessive nest construction is characteristic of other Wrens also.

Notwithstanding the fact that the Marsh Wren is a common bird in many suitable localities, the inaccessibility of its retreats, its shyness, and the facility with which it keeps under cover have made observation of its habits exceedingly difficult and they are very little known. It has been seen, however, to attack and perforate the eggs of Bitterns, but this may be only a necessary retaliation, as Bitterns and Herons have been known to kill and eat the young of smaller birds.

EDWARD HOWE FORBUSH.

The Long-billed Marsh Wren and its regional varieties are distributed over the United States and southern Canada and south into Mexico in winter. On the Great Plains and prairie districts, where it is slightly larger and redder in coloration, it is known as the Prairie Marsh Wren (*Telmatodytes palustris iliacus*); on the Rocky Mountain plateau its coloration is paler and it is called the Western Marsh Wren (*Telmatodytes palustris plesius*); in the Pacific coast district the markings vary slightly and it is known as the Tulé Wren or California Marsh Wren (*Telmatodytes palustris paludicola*); along the south Atlantic coast are two forms with markings a little different from the others and from each other and these are given the names of Marian's Marsh Wren (*Telmatodytes palustris marianæ*), and Worthington's Marsh Wren (*Telmatodytes palustris griseus*).

NUTHATCHES AND CREEPERS

Order *Passeres;* suborder *Oscines;* families *Sittidæ* and *Certhiidæ*

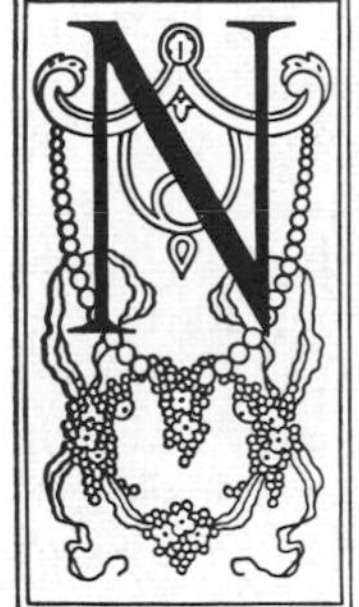

UTHATCHES are small birds which are ranked as *Oscines*, that is " song birds," by the ornithologist, because they have vocal organs, though none are real singers. The characteristic Nuthatch has a straight bill, nearly as long as its head; long and rather pointed wings; and tail from much less than to a little more than half as long as the wing, rounded at the tip. They are generally plain bluish-gray or brownish-gray above, and white, buff, or brownish beneath. In general structure and habits they occupy an intermediate position between the Creepers, and the Titmice, but they differ much from the latter in being perhaps the most expert climbers among birds, as they run nimbly up and down the trunk of a tree or the face of a cliff or stone wall, often head downward, which the Woodpeckers and Creepers are unable to do. The family comprises nearly 40 known species and subspecies. The family is chiefly an Old World one, only four species being represented in America.

The Creepers are found in the northern hemisphere and in Australia. There are five families; but only one, the *Certhiidæ*, is represented in America.

BROWN CREEPER

Certhia familiaris americana *Bonaparte*

A. O. U. Number 726 See Color Plate 102

Other Names.— Common Creeper; American Creeper; American Brown Creeper; Tree Creeper; Little Brown Creeper.

General Description.— Length, 5¾ inches. Upper parts, brown with streaks of grayish-white; under parts, dull white. Bill, slender, sharp, and curved downward; wings, moderate in length, rounded; tail, about length of wing, graduated, the feathers with rigid and sharp tips.

Color.— General color above, sepia or bister-brown (varying in intensity) relieved by conspicuous streaks of dull grayish-white, these broader and less sharply defined on the back, the prevailing color of the lower back being pale brownish-gray or grayish-brown; *rump, russet* or dull tawny-ochraceous; upper tail-coverts, pale raw umber-brown; tail, pale grayish-brown (nearly hair-brown); lesser wing-coverts pale brownish-gray; rest of wings, mainly dark sepia brown or dusky; the outer webs of greater coverts, broadly tipped with whitish and broadly edged toward base with pale buffy grayish; primaries crossed, obliquely, on both webs by a broad band of pale buff or buffy white; a dull whitish or pale brownish-gray strip over the eye; lores and ear region dark sepia brown, streaked with dull whitish; space under the eyes, cheeks, and under parts, plain dull white.

Nest and Eggs.— Nest: A collection of twigs, cottony fibers, bark strips and feathers, placed behind a loosened section of bark, nearly always in a balsam fir tree. Eggs: 5 to 8, white or creamy freckled with cinnamon and lavender specks, often wreathed around large end.

Distribution.— Eastern North America; north to Ontario, Manitoba, etc. (probably to southern Labrador and southwestern shores of Hudson Bay), west to eastern portion of the Great Plains; breeding southward to Massachusetts, New York, northern Indiana, southeastern South Dakota, and southeastern Missouri and along higher Alleghenies to mountains of North Carolina (above 4000 feet); wintering over a large part of its breeding range and south to northern Florida and central Texas.

This is a rather characterless and uninteresting bird, with neutral plumage and somewhat monotonous habits. Alighting near the base of a tree, it hitches its way upward, generally in a spiral course, examining the crevices in the bark with its long, slender, and curved bill, and uttering meanwhile a faint lisping call. Its bill is so weak that it does not attempt actually to dig, as do the Woodpeckers; it simply searches for insects concealed in crevices or underneath the bark which becomes separated from the main growth.

The Tree Creeper somewhat resembles the Nuthatches in its habits, but climbs only upward or at least in an upright position. From one-half or two-thirds of the way up a tree, it is likely to swoop down to the base of another one nearby, only to go through the same operation.

Drawing by R. Bruce Horsfall

BROWN CREEPER (nat. size)

It may readily be identified by these characteristics, plus the peculiarities that it has a noticeably long graduated tail, nearly or quite as long as the wing, with the feathers stiffened and pointed at the end, and that it clings closely to the bark.

William Brewster says that in its breeding ground in the Canadian forests it has a sweet song of four notes, the last of which dies away " in an indescribably plaintive cadence, like the soft sigh of the wind among the pine boughs "; but this utterance is seldom heard during its migration through the United States. Mr. Burroughs has heard it in Ulster county, N. Y., in March.

The food of the Brown Creeper consists of minute insects and insects' eggs, also cocoons of tineid moths, small wasps, ants, and bugs, especially scales and plant lice, with some small caterpillars. As it remains in the United States throughout the year, it naturally secures hibernating insects and insects' eggs, as well as spiders and spiders' eggs, that are missed by the summer birds. On its bill of fare we find no product of husbandry nor any useful insects.

There are four other members of this same Creeper family in North America. They vary but little from the familiar Brown Creeper and from one another. The Mexican, or Sierra Madre, Creeper (*Certhia familiaris albescens*) belongs in the mountains of Mexico as its name implies, but is also found north into southern Arizona. The Rocky Mountain Creeper (*Certhia familiaris montana*) lives in the Rocky Mountains from Alaska, central British Columbia, and central Alberta, south to Arizona and New Mexico; in winters it may be found in southeastern California and probably in Mexico. The Sierra, formerly known as the California, Creeper (*Certhia familiaris zelotes*) is found from the Cascade Mountains of Oregon and the Sierra Nevada of California south to the San Jacinto Mountains and in the winter in the adjacent valleys. The California, formerly known as the Tawny Creeper (*Certhia familiaris occidentalis*), occurs on the Pacific coast from Sitka, Alaska, to the Santa Cruz Mountains, California

WHITE-BREASTED NUTHATCH

Sitta carolinensis carolinensis *Latham*

A. O. U. Number 727 See Color Plate 103

Other Names.— White-bellied Nuthatch; Carolina Nuthatch; Common Nuthatch; Sapsucker (incorrect); Tree-Mouse; Devil Downhead.

General Description.— Length, 6 inches. Upper parts, bluish-gray and black; under parts, white.

Color.— Crown, hindneck, and extreme upper back

uniform black with a bluish or bluish green gloss; back, shoulders, lesser wing-coverts, rump, and upper tail-coverts, uniform bluish-gray; middle, greater, and primary wing-coverts, black margined with bluish-gray (like color of back), the tips of the greater coverts, sometimes whitish forming a narrow indistinct band; inner wing-quills with inner webs black; their outer webs *bluish-gray;* that of third with an elongated patch of black, *rounded at tip,* the tip and edge bluish-gray; secondaries, black, edged with bluish-gray; primaries blackish slate or slate color; two middle tail-feathers, plain bluish-gray, rest of tail-feathers, black crossed by a band of white; a stripe over the eyes, sides of head, sides of neck, and under parts, plain white or grayish-white; anal region and tail-coverts, light chestnut; under wing-coverts, black; under primary coverts and basal portion of inner webs of longer primaries, white forming a conspicuous patch; iris, brown.

Nest and Eggs.— NEST: Usually in a dead stump or tree from 2 to 60 feet up, sometimes in a deserted Woodpecker hole; loosely constructed of soft felted rabbits' fur, leaves, feathers, and hair. EGGS: 5 to 8, white or pinkish-white, spotted with chestnut and a few lavender specks.

Distribution.— Eastern North America; north to New Brunswick and northern Ontario; west to eastern edge of Great Plains; south to Georgia and Gulf States (except coast belt).

The Nuthatches and Chickadees one may reckon among the comparatively few "upside-down birds" he has known, and it is a curious fact that, though they are totally different species, they seem to like one another's society, and frequently are found working and frolicking through the woods together. A bond of sympathy may be detected in their common topsy-turvy habits. It is clear that temperamentally the birds are similar, and that the Nuthatch is as much a small boy of the feathered world as is the Chickadee, though perhaps a somewhat more serious-minded one.

Courtesy of Am. Mus. Nat. Hist

WHITE-BREASTED NUTHATCH

A bird of topsy-turvy habits

The White-breasted species is much the commoner representative of the two which occur in the eastern United States — the other being the Red-breasted. It is a common winter resident in the southern New England States, and in the lower Hudson Valley. It prefers the deciduous trees to the conifers and in that respect differs from the Red-breasted. As has been intimated, it is a decidedly industrious bird and is almost incessantly on the move. It is quite as likely to be upside down as right side up while it explores the trunk and limbs of a tree, and it often clambers entirely around a horizontal limb. The evident ease with which it assumes the inverted position is due chiefly to its lack of dependence upon its tail-feathers, which the true Woodpecker always employs as a prop, and by means of which it holds its body at a perceptible angle from the line of the limb or tree trunk to which it clings. In this position the Woodpecker can strike with its bill a much harder blow than can be delivered by the Nuthatch, which makes little use of its tail either in climbing or in digging. Consequently the Nuthatch's bill is long, pointed, and rather slender, while the Woodpecker's is stout and wedge-shaped at the extremity.

The term "sapsucker," which is often applied to this bird, is an unconscious but unqualified slander, due of course to ignorance. The true Sapsucker is a totally different bird, and does not even faintly resemble the Nuthatches. Probably this confusion arose from the fact that both the Downy Woodpecker, which is about the size of the Nuthatch, though its appearance is very different, and the Hairy, which resembles the Downy but is considerably larger, dig holes in the bark of trees, though not for the purpose of drinking sap. This habit has caused careless observers — of which there is always a bountiful supply — to blame not only the Hairy and the Downy, but even the little Nuthatch, which does not and could not dig holes in bark, for the destructive work of the true Sapsucker. In point of fact, all of the work which the Nuthatch does on the trees is highly useful, since it

Drawing by R. I. Brasher

WHITE-BREASTED NUTHATCH (⅝ nat. size)

From daylight to dark, it busily creeps over trunks and branches of trees in search of insects for food

consists in ridding them of injurious insects and larvæ. For these it searches the crevices of the bark with its sharp bill. The bird also often forces into such crevices soft-shelled nuts, like the acorn or chestnut, sometimes for safe-keeping, or again in order to have them in a position in which it may break the shell with its comparatively weak bill. The notion that the Nuthatch can break the shells of hard nuts like the hickory-nut or the walnut, is, of course, an entirely mistaken one, and to that extent the bird's name is misleading.

The Nuthatch's "song" is a series of short notes resembling the syllables *too-too-too,* uttered most frequently in the mating season; but its more characteristic and common call note is a sharp and often-repeated single syllable, generally transliterated as *yank* or *ank,* and usually described as distinctly nasal. Other observers think, however, that this call sounds much more like the words "part" or "art," — at any rate the consonant "r" is distinctly audible in it. This note often is rapidly reiterated, so that the effect is a sort of chatter, which Dr. Chapman describes as "mirthless laughter."

One of the Nuthatch's most engaging qualities is his friendly curiosity. Stand or sit motionless near the base of a tree in which the bird is working, and he is almost certain to come hitching down the trunk, head foremost, to gaze squarely into your face with his beady little black eyes and inquire politely as to your health and whether all is as it should be with you. If you inform him quietly that you are very well and quite content with your lot (being careful meanwhile to make no movement of any kind), he will express his satisfaction courteously, apologize for being so tremendously busy, and whisk away to the next tree. GEORGE GLADDEN.

The White-breasted Nuthatch gets its living from the trunks and branches of trees, over which it creeps from daylight to dark. Insects and spiders constitute a little more than 50 per cent. of its food. The largest items of these are beetles, moths, and caterpillars, with ants and wasps. The animal food is all in the bird's favor except a few ladybird beetles. More than half of the vegetable food consists of mast — acorns and other nuts or large seeds. One-tenth of the food is grain, mostly waste corn. The Nuthatch does no known injury but much good.

Slightly varying forms of the White-breasted Nuthatch are: the Florida White-breasted Nuthatch (*Sitta carolinensis atkinsi*), found in Florida and along the Gulf coast to Mississippi; the Slender-billed Nuthatch (*Sitta carolinensis aculeata*) of the Pacific coast region from British Columbia to northern Lower California; and the Rocky Mountain, or Nelson's, Nuthatch (*Sitta carolinensis nelsoni*) which lives in the mountain districts of western United States and British Columbia and northern Mexico.

RED-BREASTED NUTHATCH

Sitta canadensis *Linnæus*

A. O. U. Number 728 See Color Plate 103

Other Names.— Red-bellied Nuthatch; Canada Nuthatch; Sapsucker (incorrect).

General Description.— Length, 4¾ inches. Upper parts, bluish-gray and black; under parts, white and reddish.

Color.— Crown, uniform black, with a faint bluish gloss; a *broad white stripe over the eyes* (extending from the sides of forehead to sides of nape, narrower anteriorly); below this *a black stripe* involving the lores and upper portion of ear regions and continued, more broadly, over sides of neck; back, shoulders, rump, middle tail-feathers, upper tail-coverts, wing-coverts, and inner wing-quills, uniform bluish-gray; secondaries and primaries, dull slate color, with gray edgings; tail-feathers (except middle pair), black tipped with gray, the two or three outermost with a band (usually interrupted) or spot of white, both the gray and white most extensive on lateral tail-feather; space under the eye and lower portion of ear regions and lower part of sides of neck, white; chin and upper throat, duller white, gradually deepening downward through pale buff on lower throat to *tawny-buff or reddish-brown* on flanks, anal region, and shorter under tail-coverts, the longer under tail-coverts paler buff or buffy white; iris, brown.

Nest and Eggs.— Nest: In holes of stumps or dead trees, preferably white birch or poplar, from 4 to 20 feet up; constructed of fine grass and pieces of pine bark. Eggs: 4 to 8, grayish-white, thinly or thickly spotted with red-brown around large end.

Distribution.— Forest districts of northern North America and higher mountains of United States; north to Labrador, Keewatin, Yukon district, and southern Alaska; breeding southward to Massachusetts, New York, Pennsylvania, northern Indiana, northern Illinois, central Iowa and along the higher Alleghenies to western North Carolina; in western United States breeding in spruce forests on higher mountains south to Colorado and the Sierra Nevada, in California; breeding also on Guadalupe Island, Lower California. In winter south to or near the Gulf coast and to New Mexico and Arizona, probably to northern Mexico.

The Red-breasted Nuthatch, as may be supposed, is distinguished from the White-breasted species by the different color of its under parts; other plumage peculiarities which may readily be distinguished are the characteristic black-and-white lines which run from the base of the bill to the back of the head, the eye being set in the center of the black streak and just touching the white one. The bird is also noticeably smaller than the White-breasted and prefers the conifers to the hardwood trees for feeding grounds.

The Red-breasted is perhaps even more active and restless than its larger relative, and rather less friendly in its habits, probably because it passes most of its life in the Canadian forests, and therefore sees comparatively little of human beings. Its call note is like that of the White-breasted, but usually is pitched several tones higher; and it has another note which resembles the syllable *hut,* and may be uttered in any of several different pitches.

This Nuthatch has a curious habit of placing a coating of fir balsam or pitch around the entrance to its nest.

BROWN-HEADED NUTHATCH

Sitta pusilla *Latham*

A. O. U. Number 729

General Description.— Length, 4½ inches. Upper parts, grayish-blue; under parts, white; head, brown.

Color.— Entire crown and lateral portions of hindneck, together with upper half of ear regions, plain light grayish-brown; central portion of hindneck white, forming a conspicuous spot; back, shoulders, rump, upper tail-coverts and lesser wing-coverts, uniform bluish-gray, the middle and greater wing-coverts, inner wing-quills, and middle pair of tail-feathers similar but less bluish-gray; secondaries and primaries dull or slate brownish, with pale gray edgings; tail except middle pair of tail-feathers) black, the three outermost feathers broadly *tipped with gray,* the two outermost crossed by a band (incomplete) of white; sides of head, chin, and upper throat white; rest of under parts white, usually tinged with buff, passing into light bluish-gray on sides and flanks; iris, brown.

Nest and Eggs.— Nest: Excavated by the birds in dead stump or tree, from 1 to 40 feet up; made of small bits of grass, cotton, fine parts of pine needles, wool, and feathers. Eggs: 5 or 6, dull white or creamy specked with shades of chestnut and lavender-gray.

Distribution.— Coast pine belt of southeastern United States, from southern Maryland and southern Delaware to Florida and eastern Texas northward; irregularly or casually, to New York, Ohio, southern Michigan, Missouri, Arkansas, and Bahamas.

All through the pine woods of the Southern States the Brown-headed Nuthatch is found. It is a diminutive bird, being much smaller than the common and better-known White-breasted Nuthatch. Rarely is it ever seen out of the open pine woods. It does not have the habit of feeding along the boles of trees like the larger species just referred to, but confines its attention to such insects and their eggs as may be found along the higher branches or among the cones and terminal twigs. The birds usually travel in bands, which may possibly constitute the families of the previous year. In the spring until the young leave the nest rarely more than two are found together. Although very small, these birds possess wonderful power when it comes to excavating their nesting-holes in some rotten stump. Of the hundred or more nests that I have examined, few were more than twelve feet from the ground, although in rare instances they may be as high as forty feet. The entrance to the nest is rarely round like that of the Woodpecker, and sometimes when the wood is hard it looks more like a crack in the tree than like the entrance to a bird's nest. The hole is excavated to a depth of from five to eight inches, and is abundantly lined with soft materials of various kinds, among which one will usually find wings of the pine-tree seeds.

Photo by T. G. Pearson Courtesy of Nat. Asso. Aud. Soc.

NEST OF BROWN-HEADED NUTHATCH

Florida

The bird possesses a characteristic, but not offensive, musk with which the entire nest is scented. By smelling in a hole suspected to be occupied by the Brown-headed Nuthatch, one can readily tell whether the bird has recently occupied it.

In Florida nest-building begins in March. These birds appear to have but few natural enemies, although on one occasion I remember looking into a nest that contained a snake, which I subsequently discovered had swallowed the female bird. T. Gilbert Pearson.

Drawing by R. I. Brasher

BROWN-HEADED NUTHATCH ([illegible] nat. size)

PYGMY NUTHATCH

Sitta pygmæa pygmæa *Vigors*

A. O. U. Number 730

General Description.— Length, 4½ inches. Upper parts, gray; under parts, white and buffy-white.

Color.— Crown and hindneck, plain light grayish-olive or olive-gray, the lower central portion of the latter with concealed portion of feathers, buffy white or pale buff; lores and space back of eyes, blackish or dusky; back, shoulders, wing-coverts (except primary coverts), inner wing-quills, rump, upper tail-coverts, and middle pair of tail-feathers, plain deep bluish-gray, the last with a conspicuous elongated patch of white; rest of tail, black, the three outermost feathers tipped with slate color (very broadly on outer one), the two outer, on each side, crossed, obliquely, by a broad bar or band of white; under the eye, lower half of ear regions, and cheeks, chin, and upper throat white or buffy white; rest of under parts, dull buffy white, passing into pale bluish-gray on sides and flanks; iris, brown.

Nest and Eggs.— Nest: Behind bark crevices or in holes in trees, from 20 feet up, usually in coniferous wood and mountainous sections; constructed of feathers, plant down, bits of wool, and animal fur. Eggs: 6 to 9, crystal white, speckled with Indian red.

Distribution.— Mountains of western North America and Mexico, in coniferous forests; north to British Columbia (Vancouver Island and interior); south to southern Mexico; east to Montana, Wyoming, Colorado and New Mexico; casual in South Dakota and Nebraska.

If the Nuthatch is the small boy of the feathered tree-climbers, the Pygmy is the smallest and most boyish of the "gang." Gregarious and good-natured, he travels in small but noisy flocks through the woods, making a great disturbance over the business of getting something to eat, and enjoying life meanwhile. His companions may be Chickadees, other Nuthatches, Downies, Kinglets, or even Warblers, but he is always very much in evidence and has fully as much to say as any of his comrades. Sometimes he quarrels with the Bluebird when he finds that gentle spirit in possession of a nesting hole which he rather fancies, but generally he is eminently good-natured and not looking for trouble.

Pygmy has the upside-down habits of his immediate relatives, but in an even more pronounced form, and incidentally is more bob-tailed than they are. In fact, his tail is little more than an apology for a tail, and he is not in the least dependent upon it, whether he is going upstairs or down. Lacking this fulcrum he hasn't the carpentering ability of the Woodpeckers; but he isn't in the least averse to hammering, nevertheless, and for such a midget he can strike quite a formidable blow when he is really in earnest about it. Like his Red-breasted cousin he does most of his hunting in coniferous trees, and he conducts his search with much activity and perseverance, though it must be admitted that his operations seem rather hasty and haphazard. A Canadian observer reports that Pygmy has a curious habit of caulking with hair holes and seams around its nest, and sometimes for no apparent reason, since the caulking may serve no necessary or useful purpose.

The White-naped Nuthatch (*Sitta pygmæa leuconucha*) is larger than his congener, the Pygmy; especially is his bill of greater proportions. The white spot on the back of the neck is larger; the gray of the head grayer; gray of the back less bluish; and the under parts less strongly buff. He is found from San Diego county, California, south to San Pedro Martir Mountains. Lower California.

Drawing by R. Bruce Horsfall

PYGMY NUTHATCH (⅝ nat. size)

TITMICE

Order *Passeres;* suborder *Oscines;* family *Paridæ*

THE Titmouse family, which includes the birds of that name, the Chickadees the Bush-Tits, and the Verdins, comprises several species of small birds, classified by systematic ornithologists as "song birds" (*Oscines*), not necessarily because they can sing, but because they have well-developed vocal organs.

The present group have short cone-shaped bills, and obtuse tongues armed at the tip with horny bristles. Wings are well developed and rounded, the tail is usually about as long as the wing and slightly rounded, and the feathers are softer than the stiffened ones of Thrushes and Kinglets. They inhabit the northern hemisphere generally, and chiefly are arboreal, omnivorous, very active, and essentially non-migratory. They are far better represented in the Old World than in the New. North America, including Mexico, possesses less than 30 species and subspecies, and but four genera, while about 70 species and at least five genera belong to Arctic, Indian, and African regions.

The plumage of the members of this family is never spotted, streaked, or barred; plain colors are the rule — grays, browns, and olives for the upper parts and dull white and grays for the under parts. The Titmice may or may not have black on their heads; the Chickadees always have the crown and hindneck uniform black or brown; the adult Verdins have yellow heads; and the Bush-Tits sometimes have the sides of their heads black and, if the general color of their upper parts is gray, their crowns are generally brownish, and if the general color is olive, their crowns are gray. The Titmice are crested, but the other members of the family lack this adornment.

Birds of the Titmouse family, though insignificant in size, are far from being so in the matter of food habits. What they lack in size of body they more than make up in number of individuals. The character of the food of Titmice gives a peculiar value to their services, for it consists largely of the small insects and their eggs that wholly escape the search of larger birds. Throughout the year most of the species of this group remain on their range, so that they are constantly engaged in their beneficial work, continuing it in winter when the majority of their co-workers have sought a milder clime. It is at this season that the Titmice do their greatest good; for, when flying and crawling insects are no more to be found, the birds must feed upon such species as they find hibernating in crevices, or upon the eggs of insects laid in similar places.

TUFTED TITMOUSE

Bæolophus bicolor (*Linnæus*)

A. O. U. Number 731 See Color Plate 103

Other Names.— Tufted Tit; Tufted Chickadee; Crested Titmouse; Peto Bird; Crested Tomtit.

General Description.— Length, 6 inches. Upper parts, slate-gray; under parts, white and reddish. Bill, short and stout; wings, long and rounded; tail, shorter than wing, slightly rounded; head, with crest.

Color.— Forehead, black or sooty black, margined posteriorly with sooty brown; rest of *upper parts, plain slate-gray;* eye region, dull white; ear region, pale gray; cheek region and under parts, dull white, passing on *sides and flanks into light cinnamon-rufous;* iris, brown.

Nest and Eggs.— Nest: Usually in deserted Woodpecker holes or hollow stumps; a collection of moss, leaves, bark strips, and horse- and cattle-hair. Eggs: From 5 to 8, white, thickly spotted with reddish-brown.

Distribution.— Eastern United States; north, regularly, to southern Pennsylvania and New Jersey, central Ohio, northern Indiana, northern Illinois, southern Iowa, and northeastern Nebraska; irregularly or casually to Connecticut, southern New York (Long Island, Staten Island) extreme northern portions of Indiana and Illinois, and southern Minnesota; west to eastern portion of the Great Plains; south to the Gulf coast, including south-central Florida and eastern and central Texas.

Courtesy of the New York State Museum

SCARLET TANAGER *Piranga erythromelas* Vieillot

CHANGING MALE — MALE IN SUMMER — MALE IN WINTER
FEMALE

SUMMER TANAGER *Piranga rubra rubra* (Linnaeus)

FEMALE — MALE
CHANGING MALE

All ½ nat. size

BARN SWALLOW *Hirundo erythrogastra* Boddaert
FEMALE MALE

CLIFF SWALLOW *Petrochelidon lunifrons lunifrons* (Say)
ADULT IMMATURE

ROUGH-WINGED SWALLOW
Stelgidopteryx serripennis (Audubon)

BANK SWALLOW
Riparia riparia (Linnaeus)

PURPLE MARTIN *Progne subis subis* (Linnaeus)
FEMALE MALE

TREE SWALLOW
Iridoprocne bicolor (Vieillot)
ADULT IMMATURE

All ½ nat. size

BOHEMIAN WAXWING *Bombycilla garrula* (Linnaeus)
FEMALE MALE
CEDAR WAXWING *Bombycilla cedrorum* Vieillot
FEMALE IMMATURE MALE
All ½ nat. size

Courtesy of the New York State Museum

NORTHERN SHRIKE *Lanius borealis* Vieillot
ADULT MALE
IMMATURE
MIGRANT SHRIKE *Lanius ludovicianus migrans* W. Palmer
IMMATURE ADULT
All ½ nat. size

WARBLING VIREO *Vireosylva gilva gilva* (Vieillot)
ADULT
YOUNG
RED-EYED VIREO *Vireosylva olivacea* (Linnaeus)
YELLOW-THROATED VIREO *Lanivireo flavifrons* (Vieillot)
WHITE-EYED VIREO *Vireo griseus griseus* (Boddaert)
All ½ nat. size

PHILADELPHIA VIREO
Vireosylva philadelphica Cassin
BLUE-HEADED VIREO
Lanivireo solitarius solitarius (Wilson)

BLACK AND WHITE WARBLER *Mniotilta varia* (Linnaeus)
MALE FEMALE
WATER-THRUSH
Seiurus noveboracensis noveboracensis (Gmelin)
OVEN-BIRD *Seiurus aurocapillus* (Linnaeus)
ADULT JUVENAL
All ½ nat. size

WORM-EATING WARBLER
Helmitheros vermivorus (Gmelin)
PROTHONOTARY WARBLER
Protonotaria citrea (Boddaert)
LOUISIANA WATER-THRUSH
Seiurus motacilla Vieillot

Courtesy of the New York State Museum

BLUE-WINGED WARBLER *Vermivora pinus* (Linnaeus)
BREWSTER'S WARBLER *Vermivora leucobronchialis* (Brewster)
LAWRENCE'S WARBLER *Vermivora lawrencei* (Herrick)
GOLDEN-WINGED WARBLER *Vermivora chrysoptera* (Linnaeus)
MALE FEMALE
ORANGE-CROWNED WARBLER *Vermivora celata celata* (Say)
NASHVILLE WARBLER *Vermivora rubricapilla rubricapilla* (Wilson)
MALE IMMATURE
TENNESSEE WARBLER *Vermivora peregrina* (Wilson)
IMMATURE MALE
All ½ nat. size

PARULA WARBLER
Compsothlypois americana americana (Linnaeus)
MALE
FEMALE

CERULEAN WARBLER
Dendroica cerulea (Wilson)
MALE
FEMALE

MYRTLE WARBLER *Dendroica coronata* (Linnaeus)
MALE
FEMALE

BLACK-THROATED BLUE WARBLER
Dendroica caerulescens caerulescens (Gmelin)
MALE
FEMALE

CANADA WARBLER
Wilsonia canadensis (Linnaeus)
MALE
FEMALE

All ½ nat. size

Courtesy of the New York State Museum

PINE WARBLER *Dendroica vigorsi* (Audubon)
MALE FEMALE
CAPE MAY WARBLER *Dendroica tigrina* (Gmelin)
MALE FEMALE
PRAIRIE WARBLER
Dendroica discolor (Vieillot)
MALE
FEMALE
YELLOW WARBLER
Dendroica aestiva aestiva (Gmelin)
MALE FEMALE
PALM WARBLER *Dendroica palmarum palmarum* (Gmelin)
YELLOW PALM WARBLER *Dendroica palmarum hypochrysea* Ridgway
All ½ nat. size

BAY-BREASTED WARBLER *Dendroica castanea* (Wilson)
IMMATURE MALE
FEMALE
BLACK-POLL WARBLER *Dendroica striata* (J. R. Forster)
IMMATURE MALE
FEMALE
CHESTNUT-SIDED WARBLER *Dendroica pensylvanica* (Linnaeus)
IMMATURE
MALE FEMALE
All ½ nat. size

Courtesy of the New York State Museum

BLACKBURNIAN WARBLER *Dendroica fusca* (Müller)
FEMALE MALE
BLACK-THROATED GREEN WARBLER *Dendroica virens* (Gmelin)
MALE FEMALE
REDSTART *Setophaga ruticilla* (Linnaeus)
MALE FEMALE
MAGNOLIA WARBLER *Dendroica magnolia* (Wilson)
MALE IMMATURE FEMALE
All ½ nat. size

WILSON'S WARBLER *Wilsonia pusilla pusilla* (Wilson)
FEMALE MALE

YELLOW-BREASTED CHAT
Icteria virens virens (Linnaeus)

KENTUCKY WARBLER *Oporonis formosus* (Wilson)
MALE FEMALE

MARYLAND YELLOW-THROAT
Geothlypis trichas trichas (Linnaeus)
FEMALE MALE

HOODED WARBLER *Wilsonia citrina* (Boddaert)
MALE FEMALE

All ½ nat. size

CONNECTICUT WARBLER *Oporonis agilis* (Wilson)
ADULT
IMMATURE
Life size

Courtesy of the New York State Museum

MOURNING WARBLER *Oporornis philadelphia* (Wilson)
FEMALE
MALE
⅔ nat. size

Courtesy of the New York State Museum

MOCKINGBIRD *Mimus polyglottos polyglottos* (Linnaeus)
BROWN THRASHER *Toxostoma rufum* (Linnaeus)
CATBIRD *Dumetella carolinensis* (Linnaeus)
All ½ nat. size

Courtesy of the New York State Museum

HOUSE WREN
Troglodytes aëdon aëdon Vieillot
WINTER WREN
Nannus hiemalis hiemalis (Vieillot)
SHORT-BILLED MARSH WREN
Cistothorus stellaris (Naumann)

CAROLINA WREN
Thryothorus ludovicianus ludovicianus (Latham)
BROWN CREEPER
Certhia familiaris americana Bonaparte
LONG-BILLED MARSH WREN
Telmatodytes palustris palustris (Wilson)

All ⅔ nat. size

The Tufted Titmouse is more common in the South and West than his cousin, the Chickadee, and he is one of the prettiest of the family. He is dressed in soft gray, with a fine, showy, pointed crest. His ways are something like the Chickadee's, but he is, perhaps, even bolder and more pert, and he is easily tamed. All his notes are loud and clear, and he is never for a moment still.

In winter, this bird is found in little flocks of a dozen or more. These are probably all of one family, the parents and their two broods of the year. He is one of the birds who stores up food for a time when food is scarce. In summer, he eats only insects.

The Tufted Titmouse, like others of his race, has a great deal of curiosity. I have heard of one who came into a house through an open window. It was a female Titmouse in search of a good place for a nest. After she had been in all the rooms, and helped herself to whatever she found that was good to eat, she seemed to decide that it was a land of plenty and she would stay.

Drawing by R. Bruce Horsfall

TUFTED TITMOUSE (⅔ nat. size)

A gray-feathered bit of curiosity

The stranger settled upon a hanging basket as nice to build in. The family did not disturb her, and she brought in her materials and made

Photo by S. A. Lottridge

NEST AND EGGS OF TUFTED TITMOUSE

A section of the stub has been removed

her nest. She had even laid two or three eggs, when the people began to take too much interest in her affairs, and the bird thought it best to move to a safer place.

Another of these birds, in Ohio, looking about for something nice and soft to line her nest, pitched upon a gentleman's hair. Unfortunately, he had need of the hair himself; but the saucy little Titmouse didn't mind that. She alighted on his head, seized a beakful, and then bracing herself on her stout little legs, she actually jerked out the lock, and flew away with it. So well did she like it that she came back for more. The gentleman was a bird lover, and was pleased to give some of his hair to such a brave little creature. Olive Thorne Miller.

The characteristic call note of this Titmouse is a two-syllabled, whistled utterance, quite melodious, and sometimes repeated twice, three, or even four, times. To some ears the syllables sound like *peto,* to others more like *tur-ve,* the accent always being on the first syllable. Another single note, less frequently heard, is much like the autumn note of the Bluebird.

BLACK-CRESTED TITMOUSE

Bæolophus atricristatus atricristatus (*Cassin*)

A. O. U. Number 732

General Description.— Length, 6 inches. Upper parts, gray; under parts, grayish-white. Bill, short and stout; wings, long and rounded; tail, shorter than wing, slightly rounded; head, with crest.

Color.— *Forehead, dull white,* sometimes faintly tinged with brown; rest of crown, including crest, black, sharply defined against whitish of forehead; rest of upper parts, including edges of back of head and the region over eye, plain gray, strongly washed with olive, except over the eye where the gray is paler, gradually fading into still paler gray on ear region and sides of neck, and this fading into white or grayish white on cheek region; under parts, grayish-white becoming clearer buffy-white posteriorly, the sides and flanks, pale cinnamon-rufous; iris, brown.

Nest and Eggs.— Nest: In hollows of trees, old Woodpecker holes, or deep cracks of tree trunks; composed of grasses, fine inner bark, feathers, moss, and wool, and usually pieces of snake skin. Eggs: 5 or 6, clear white with small chestnut spots sparingly scattered over entire surface.

Distribution.— Rio Grande valley, and Mexican States of Coahuila, Nuevo Leon, Tamaulipas, San Luis Potosi, and Vera Cruz (highlands).

The Black-crested Titmouse is one of the many birds that lurk chiefly near the southwestern border, and remain unknown to American observers except the comparatively few who see them in that region.

The sharply-defined, black crest gives the bird a clever and rather dandified appearance, and he has the lively manner and cheerful disposition of his well-loved relative, the Chickadee of the Eastern States. The bird occurs very commonly in the Chisos and Davis mountains.

Sennett's Titmouse (*Bæolophus atricristatus sennetti*) is very similar to the Black-crested; he is decidedly larger and his upper parts are much clearer gray with very little, if any, of the olive tinge. He lives in central Texas.

BRIDLED TITMOUSE

Bæolophus wollweberi (*Bonaparte*)

A. O. U. Number 734

Other Name.— Wollweber's Titmouse.

General Description.— Length, 5 inches. Upper parts, deep olive-gray and black; under parts, pale olive-gray and black. Bill, short and stout; wings, long and rounded; tail, shorter than wing, slightly rounded; head, with crest.

Color.— Crown, including crest, black, with a large central patch of deep gray covering whole crown; over the eyes a broad and sharply defined stripe of white extending posteriorly to beneath hind part of crest, where it joins with a broad white band across side of neck; back of the eye a streak of black, broader posteriorly, where it joins with a black band across terminal portion of ear region; rest of ear region, together with the cheek, white; a black spot or short streak at front angle of eye; chin and throat, uniform black, forming a conspicuous patch with sharply defined rear outline; upper parts (except as described), plain deep olive-gray, more strongly tinged with olive posteriorly; under parts of body, pale olive-gray, passing into pale olive-buffy on abdomen and under tail-coverts; iris, brown.

Nest and Eggs.— Nest: In natural tree cavities, three to six feet up; composed of cottonwood down and fern fronds. Eggs: 5 to 7, plain white.

Distribution.— Mountains of southern Arizona and southern New Mexico and south through Mexico to Guerrero, Oaxaca, and Vera Cruz.

The Bridled Titmouse differs radically in appearance from the Black-crest, and notably in the curious markings about the head and throat, which suggest a bridle. In manners and habits however, and especially in gregariousness (excepting during the breeding season), it resembles the other members of its family, though the little companies of twenty or more are less noisy and perhaps less playful than their cousins, the Chickadees.

Drawing by R. I. Brasher

BRIDLED TITMOUSE (nat. size)

The curious markings about its throat suggest its name

CHICKADEE

Penthestes atricapillus atricapillus (*Linnæus*)

A. O. U. Number 735 See Color Plate 103

Other Names.— Common Chickadee; Eastern Chickadee; Black-capped Chickadee; Black-capped Titmouse; Black-capped Tit.

General Description.— Length, 5¾ inches. Upper parts, gray and black; under parts, white and black. No crest; bill, shorter than head; wings, long and rounded; tail, shorter than wing, slightly rounded.

Color.— Entire crown and hindneck (except lateral portion of the latter) uniform deep black; back, shoulders, middle and lesser wing-coverts, plain olive-gray, passing into more buffy gray on rump and upper tail-coverts; wings and tail, dusky slate color; greater wing-coverts and secondaries, broadly edged with pale gray or grayish-white; tail-feathers edged with olive-gray, these edgings becoming white on outermost feathers; chin and whole throat, black; sides of head and neck, white; under parts of body, white, the sides and flanks tinged with buff; iris, brown.

Nest and Eggs.— Nest: In deserted Woodpecker holes, natural cavities, old stumps (preferably white birch), or fence posts; such openings are filled with leaves, moss, grasses, snugly lined with hair, fur from small animals, and feathers. Eggs: 4 to 8, white, spotted with chestnut and lilac-gray.

Distribution.— Eastern North America; north to Newfoundland, Quebec, Ontario, and southern Keewatin; south regularly, to about latitude 40°, in New Jersey, Pennsylvania, Ohio, northern Indiana, northern Illinois, Iowa, etc., in Allegheny Mountains to North Carolina (in spruce belt); irregularly (in winter) to northern Virginia, Kentucky, southern Illinois, Missouri, etc.

In winter especially, the Chickadee is the feathered small boy of the woods. Like the Nuthatches and the Kinglets, frequently his companions, the Chickadee seems actually to enjoy a snowstorm, and announces the fact by language and actions the meaning of which are unmistakable. In the bitterest weather he frolics and frisks from tree to tree, happy and care-free, laughing and joking. Mr. Burroughs says that "the Chickadee has a voice full of unspeakable tenderness and fidelity," which is very faithful to the spirit of the utterance from which the bird is named. This call is often abbreviated by the omission of the first two syllables, but the resulting *dee, dee, dee,* is a very sweet and pleasing little greeting.

Drawing by R. I. Brasher

CHICKADEE (⅓ nat. size)

The feathered small boy of the winter-time — always in fine spirits

Many persons who are familiar with this call are unaware that the Chickadee has two other vocal performances which are widely different from it. One is composed of two notes, and is most frequently heard in the spring; the other involves three notes, and may be heard in the spring or fall. The notes of both are whistled, and their quality is, therefore, very different from that of the characteristic call. By some ornithologists these notes are considered song-like rather than call-like, though it might be difficult to establish this distinction. At any rate, the two-note utterance suggests the characteristic little sigh of the Phœbe, from which, however, it differs in that the tones are purer and sweeter, are more deliberately executed, and are cheerful and hopeful rather than somewhat plaintive.

The three-note group is less frequently heard, but generally is much the more musical and beautiful of the two expressions. Curiously enough these notes reproduce almost exactly the last three notes of the phrase to which are set the words "I'm coming back to you," in the so-called Hawaiian love song "Yakahula." Of course this is a pure coincidence, as is the reproduction by the Wood Thrush of the opening phrase of Faust's "Garden Song to Marguerite." The singularly sweet quality and bell-life resonance of these notes combine to make them almost startlingly beautiful when they are sounded suddenly in the listening silence of a deep forest.

Any one who has a musical ear, and can whistle in a high key, can easily imitate these songs; and, if he will sit still as he does so, he is likely to have the pleasure of bringing the birds to within a few feet of him. Indeed, the Chickadee is one of the most trustful of birds, and by the exercise of a little patience one may often induce the little fellow to take food from the hand or even from between the lips.

While incubating, the Chickadee has an amusing way of trying to frighten away intruders. Mr. Burroughs records the following instance of that performance: "One day a lot of Vassar girls came to visit me and I led them out to the little sassafras to see the Chickadee's nest. The sitting bird kept her place as head after head, with its nodding plumes of millinery, appeared above the opening of her chamber, and a pair of inquisitive eyes peered down upon her. But I saw she was getting ready to play her

Photo by A. A. Allen

CHICKADEE

At its nest hole in a sumach stub

little trick to frighten them away. Presently I heard a faint explosion at the bottom of the cavity, when the peeping girl jerked her head quickly back, with the exclamation, 'Why, it spit at me!' The trick of this bird on such occasions is apparently to draw in its breath till its form perceptibly swells, and then give forth a quick, explosive sound, like an escaping jet of steam. One involuntarily closes his eyes and jerks back his head." (*Far and Near.*)

Like the Nuthatches and a few other birds, the Chickadee doesn't seem in the least to mind being upside down. While searching for insects and larvæ he is frequently seen clinging to a twig in a completely reversed position, in which he seems to be entirely at ease. He also often alights on the side of a perpendicular limb, or trunk of a tree, after the manner of the Woodpeckers, in order to search the crevices of the bark for insects. But he does not attempt to climb up or down as the Woodpeckers and Nuthatches so readily do; and it is noticeable that his position is usually at an angle with the perpendicular, this in consequence of his not having either feet or a tail adapted for climbing.

GEORGE GLADDEN.

Examination of 289 stomachs of this Chickadee shows that its food consists of 68 per cent. animal matter (insects) and 32 per cent. vegetable matter. The former is made up of small caterpillars and moths and their eggs. Prominent among the latter are the eggs of the tent-caterpillar moths, both the orchard and forest species. As these are two of our most destructive insects, the good done by the Chickadee in devouring their eggs needs no comment. During the winter the Chickadee's food is made up of larvæ, chrysalids, and eggs of moths, varied by a few seeds; but as spring brings out hordes of flying, crawling, and jumping insects, the bird varies its diet by taking also some of these. Among the bugs may be mentioned the plant lice and their eggs, which are eaten in winter. The beetles taken nearly all belong to the group of snout beetles, more commonly known as weevils, and nearly all are known to the farmer or fruit raiser as pests; the plum curculio and the cotton-boll weevil may be taken as fair examples. Spiders constitute an important element of the food and are eaten at all times of the year, the birds locating them when they are hibernating in winter as well as when they are active in summer. The vegetable food of the Chickadee consists largely of small seeds, except in summer, when they are replaced by pulp of wild fruit.

In western North America are three variant forms of the Common Chickadee. The Long-tailed Chickadee (*Penthestes atricapillus septentrionalis*) breeds from Alaska, central Mackenzie, and southwestern Keewatin south to New Mexico and eastern Kansas and from eastern Oregon east to western Minnesota and western Iowa. In winter it is found south as far as central Texas. It is larger than the Eastern Chickadee and its plumage is paler, with the white edgings on the wing and tail-feathers broader and more conspicuous.

Photo by Harriet S. Rider Courtesy of Nat. Asso. Aud. Soc.

THE BIRDS' CHRISTMAS TREE

Receives a visit from a Chickadee

The Oregon Chickadee (*Penthestes atricapillus occidentalis*) is smaller and darker than the eastern Chickadee, its back varying in color from deep mouse-gray to deep hair-brown or light olive, and the white edgings of tail and wing feathers more restricted. It is found in the Pacific coast district from the Columbia River to British Columbia.

The Yukon Chickadee (*Penthestes atricapillus turneri*) is found in Alaska, north and west of Cook Inlet. It most resembles the Long-tailed Chickadee. It is slightly smaller, with coloration grayer above and the under parts and white edgings of feathers more purely white.

The Carolina or Southern Chickadee (*Penthestes carolinensis carolinensis*) and its variants, the Plumbeous, or Texan, Chickadee (*Penthestes carolinensis agilis*) and the Florida Chickadee (*Penthestes carolinensis impiger*), are smaller than the Black-capped Chickadee, with relatively shorter tails and larger bills, with little, if any, white on wings and tails, and with the black throat-patch abruptly defined posteriorly. They are found in the southeastern United States east to eastern Texas, and north to Indiana, Ohio, Pennsylvania, and New Jersey.

MOUNTAIN CHICKADEE

Penthestes gambeli gambeli (*Ridgway*)

A. O. U. Number 738

General Description.— Length, 5¾ inches. Upper parts, olive-gray; under parts, black and white. No crest; bill, shorter than head; wings, long and rounded; tail, shorter than wing, slightly rounded.

Drawing by R. Bruce Horsfall

MOUNTAIN CHICKADEE (½ nat. size)

Its call has an accent of good cheer and tenderness

Color.— Crown and hindneck, uniform black, with a faint bluish gloss; *over the eyes a white stripe;* cheeks, chin, throat, and upper chest, uniform deep black, very sharply defined posteriorly; sides of head and neck between the two black areas, white; back, shoulders, lesser wing-coverts, rump, and upper tail-coverts, plain olive-gray or mouse gray, the rump more strongly tinged with olive; wings and tail, dull slate color with gray edgings; sides and flanks (broadly) and under tail-coverts, olive-gray (paler and more tinged with olive than back); center of lower chest, breast, and abdomen, white; iris, brown.

Nest and Eggs.— Nest: In natural cavity or a deserted Woodpecker hole, from 2 to 20 feet up; made of grasses, rootlets, sheep's wool, cattle hair and, very frequently, rabbits' fur. Eggs: 5 to 9, plain white unmarked or spotted with reddish-brown.

Distribution.— Mountains of western United States, from the Rocky Mountains to the coast ranges; north to British Columbia, northern Idaho, Montana, etc., south to western Texas, New Mexico, Arizona, and northern Lower California.

The Mountain Chickadee of the West is a shade larger, and of slightly different coloration than its well beloved eastern relative, but in habits and disposition the birds are very similar. The western bird moves in short, fluttering flights from tree to tree, is much given to clinging to twigs upside down, and shows the same friendly curiosity about human loiterers in his neighborhood that is characteristic of his eastern cousin; and his call, though somewhat different in the arrangement and quality of its syllables, has the same accent of combined good cheer and tenderness. It is in the coniferous regions of the mountains that he is found.

ACADIAN CHICKADEE

Penthestes hudsonicus littoralis (*H. Bryant*)

A. O. U. Number 740a See Color Plate 103

General Description.— Length, 5½ inches. Upper parts, brown; under parts, black, white, and reddish. No crest; bill, shorter than head; wings, long and rounded; tail, shorter than wing, slightly rounded.

Color.— Crown and hindneck, plain, soft *grayish-brown;* back, shoulders, lesser wing-coverts, rump, and upper tail-coverts, *brown;* wings and tail, dull slate color with slate-gray edgings; mouth and eye regions, white, gradually shading into pale gray on ear region and this into clear gray or olive-gray on sides of neck; cheek region, chin, and throat, uniform sooty black; under parts of body, white medially, the sides of chest shaded with gray, the *sides and flanks, cinnamon-brown;* iris, brown.

Nest and Eggs.— Nest: In natural cavities in trees or stumps; constructed of moss and fur. Eggs: 6 or 7, indistinguishable from those of common Chickadee.

Distribution.— Southeastern British provinces and extreme northeastern United States, Maine, mountains of New Hampshire, Vermont, and northeastern New York; casually or irregularly southward to Massachusetts, Rhode Island and Connecticut.

The gray-brown cap, brownish back, and reddish sides of this little denizen of the northland, distinguish him sharply from his essentially black-and-white, livelier, and more ubiquitous cousin, the Common Chickadee, but in general the manners of the two birds are not markedly dissimilar. Naturally enough, different observers give different renderings of the bird's call notes. One (Wright) speaks of its "sweet warbling song," while another (Brewster) has heard only "low, chattering conversational sounds, a low chip much like that of the Common Chickadee," and "an abrupt, explosive, *tch-tchip,* and a nasal drawling *tchick, chee-day-day,*" which he thinks is easily distinguishable from the familiar call of the Common Chickadee.

The records show a remarkable flight of this bird into the southern New England States in the winter of 1914–15. Why the flight, no one seems to have explained clearly, but it has been conjectured that it may have been due to the injury done by insects in northern Maine and New Brunswick to the spruce forests which furnish a large part of the bird's normal food supply. At any rate, the Acadian Chickadees became comparatively common that year in eastern Massachusetts where they do not usually appear in such numbers. They were seen in the company of Golden-crowned Kinglets, Fox Sparrows, and other Chickadees, and it was noticed that they fed freely upon the seeds of the goldenrod and upon the berries of the red cedar; also that they did not expose themselves much.

Evidently there was a flight somewhat similar to this in the winter of 1913–14, and of this we have an account in the *Auk* from a correspondent in Watch Hill, R. I., which seems worth quoting in part. "As this was the second record of this species in the State," he writes, "and there was what might almost be called a flight for a so rare a bird, I tried to collect one with a cap and golf sticks, but was unsuccessful, succeeding merely in getting very close."

Courtesy of Am. Mus. Nrt. Hist.

ACADIAN CHICKADEE (⅜ nat. size)

The Hudsonian Chickadee (*Penthestes hudsonicus hudsonicus*) is larger than the Acadian and its upper parts are slightly grayer. It is found in nôrthern North America, breeding from Alaska and the tree-limit in central Mackenzie and central Keewatin south to southern British Columbia, central Alberta (usually Montana), northern Manitoba, central Ontario, and Ungava; sometimes in the winter it wanders as far south as northern Illinois.

Another subspecies is the so-called Labrador Brown-capped Chickadee (*Penthestes hudsonicus nigricans*) of which there was an interesting southward flight in the winter of 1916–17, as far as Staten Island, N. Y.

CHESTNUT-BACKED CHICKADEE

Penthestes rufescens rufescens (*J. K. Townsend*)

A. O. U. Number 741

General Description.— Length, 5 inches. Upper parts, brown; under parts, brown and white. No crest; bill, shorter than head; wings, long and rounded; tail, shorter than wing, slightly rounded.

Color.—Crown and hindneck, plain sepia brown, becoming darker along lateral margin; *back, shoulders, and rump, plain chestnut;* upper tail-coverts and lesser wing-coverts, brownish-gray or hair brown; wings and tail, deep brownish-gray with paler gray edgings, these broader and paler (sometimes nearly white) on inner wing-quills and terminal portion of greater wing-coverts; cheek region, chin, throat, and upper part of chest, uniform dark sooty-brown, abruptly defined posteriorly; sides and flanks, chestnut; under parts of body otherwise, white; under tail-coverts tinged with brown; iris, brown.

Nest and Eggs.— Nest: In a dead stump from 12 to 40 feet up; lined with hair, fur, feathers, and moss. Eggs: 5 to 7, white, usually unmarked, but sometimes minutely specked or spotted with chestnut or reddish.

Distribution.— Pacific coast district, from northern California to Prince William Sound and head of Lynn Canal, Alaska; east to Montana.

Titmice personify inquisitiveness. They are feathered interrogation points; prying into each hole, crack, and cranny; interviewing and questioning every passer-by. In this respect the Chestnut-backed Chickadee is typical of the Titmouse family, but why is it colored so differently from other Chickadees which inhabit the same region? Here is a question for future ornithologists to answer.

This sprightly, cheerful little acrobat of the trees is common in some of the timberlands of the Northwest; but is not by any means confined to them, as, like other Titmice, it visits the homes of man and is as fearless as the common Chickadee. Nevertheless, the great coniferous forests of the humid Pacific coast region seem to be its favorite hunting grounds; and there, far up amid the foliage of tall pines, firs, and cedars that tower toward the sky, it flutters, turns, pries, creeps, and clings, searching out destructive insect enemies of its sheltering friends, the trees.

Often invisible by reason of the dense greenery, its cheery notes are the only indications of its presence that are perceptible to the foot passengers in the shades below. As a matter of course, it is seen more commonly in open deciduous woods. It is by no means averse to settled regions, and may be found along roadways and even in orchards and shade trees.

The old nursery rime, "Little Tommy Tittlemouse, lives in a little house," applies perfectly to this species; for its snug domicile in the hollow of a tree has doorway, floor, and roof and is carpeted or lined with a felting of hair, fur, wool, or feathers. It is a safe, comfortable little house quite sufficient for the owner's simple needs. Moreover this Chickadee nests in bird houses put up for other birds and the habit grows.

While the young are in the nest the parents work with tireless industry; searching bark, leaf, and twig for insects with which to fill the many little gaping, hungry mouths protruding upward from the well-filled nest. In the search for food the parents are constantly on the move; swinging, twisting, hanging, fluttering, climbing, and even turning an occasional half-somersault in air when pursuing some winged insect that seeks safety in precipitate erratic flight. The Chickadee views the world from all angles, and is quite as much at home wrong side up as right side up. It plays a continual game of hide and seek or "tag, you're it," which it seems to delight in, but it is played mostly in the line of business — the serious business of getting a living.

When the young are fledged and able to fly they are near replicas of the parents, but somewhat abbreviated and even more fluffy. Away they all go, fluttering and scampering through the labyrinth of coniferous branches, often in company with Golden-crowned Kinglets, Oregon Chickadees, Mountain Chickadees, Creepers, or Warblers. When winter winds rage over the forests, when rain and snow storm into their fastnesses, the Chickadees pack their little stomachs well with insects' eggs, pupæ, or seeds and hie themselves to some snug sheltered refuge in the trees where, warm and dry, they sleep away the long winter nights.

Edward Howe Forbush.

The California, or Nicasio, Chickadee (*Penthestes rufescens neglectus*) and Barlow's Chickadee (*Penthestes rufescens barlowi*) are geographical varieties of the Chestnut-backed. They are found in central California in the coast district. The California has less chestnut on its sides and flanks, which exteriorly are pale gray. The Barlow's has the sides and flanks entirely pale gray.

BUSH-TIT

Psaltriparus minimus minimus (*J. K. Townsend*)

A. O. U. Number 743

General Description.— Length, 4¼ inches. Upper parts, gray; under parts, brownish-white. Bill, very small, deeper than broad; wings, long and pointed; tail, longer than wing, much rounded, the feathers narrow but with the tips broad and rounded.

Color.— Crown and hindneck, plain, warm brown or drab; back, shoulders, lesser wing-coverts, rump, and upper tail-coverts, plain deep smoke gray; wings (except lesser coverts) and tail, darker gray (dull slate color) with pale gray edgings; sides of head similar in color to crown but much paler and duller; under parts, dull brownish-white, deepening on sides and flanks into pale, dull écru-drab; iris, light yellow.

Nest and Eggs.— Nest: Placed in low oaks, in bunch of mistletoe or mesquite from 5 to 20 feet up, a long gourd-shaped structure, flaring at bottom, entrance near top on side; not strictly pensile, being fastened to a number of twigs along sides; from eight to ten inches long and four or five in diameter, the walls three times as thick at bottom as at top, where about one-half inch through; constructed exteriorly of dry sage leaves, plant down, moss, lichens, and cobwebs, thickly lined with smaller feathers. Eggs: 4 to 6, pure white.

Distribution.— West slope of coast mountains in Oregon, California, and northern Lower California, north to the Columbia River, south to Nachoguero valley, Lower California (also to San Pedro Martir Mountains, and San Fernando?).

One can hardly help falling in love with the Bush-Tit. He is such a tiny bird, not larger than your thumb. He goes along in such a bustling, business-like way. He is quite fearless. One can make friends with the Bush-Tit as easily as with his cousin, the Chickadee. Any one who has studied bird character would know that the two are related even if he did not know that both are members of the Titmouse family.

The Bush-Tit builds a real bird mansion, a long, gourd-shaped home from eight to ten inches or even longer, with a round entrance at the upper end. I once watched a pair of these birds lay the foundation for a typical long pocket-nest. I say " lay the foundation," but really the Bush-Tit does not follow our ideas of architecture, for he builds from the top down. This pair began making a roof to the home, then a round doorway, and next they began weaving the walls of moss, fibers, and lichens. From the

Drawing by R. I. Brasher

BUSH-TIT (nat. size)

A fearless little mite, no bigger than your thumb

doorway, there was a sort of a hall down to the main living-room. This was warmly lined with feathers. To make a soft feather lining required a good deal of hunting. The feather lining was not really completed till after the eggs were laid. Whenever one of the Bush-Tits would come upon a feather, he would pick it up and bring it home. The Bush-Tits reminded me of some people who build a house, but are not able to furnish it throughout, so they pick up the furnishings later on from time to time.

In some parts of Oregon where moss hangs in long bunches from the limbs, the Bush-Tit uses this natural beginning for a nest. I saw one of these birds build its home by getting inside of a long piece of moss and weave this into the wall of the nest. At another time, I saw a Bush-Tit's nest twenty inches long. The little weavers had started their home on a limb and it was evidently not low enough to suit them, for they made a fiber strap ten inches long and then swung their gourd-shaped nest to that, letting the nest hang in a bunch of willow leaves.

I never had had a good idea of the amount of insect food a Bush-Tit consumed until I watched a pair of these birds a few days after the eggs were hatched. Both birds fed in turn and the turns averaged from five to ten minutes apart. The parents were busy from dawn till dark. They searched the leaves and twigs, branches, and trunks of every tree. They hunted through the bushes, grasses, and ferns. They brought caterpillars, moths, daddy-long-legs, spiders, plant lice, and many other kinds of insects. One pair of Bush-Tits about a locality means the destruction of a great many harmful insects. If we could but estimate the amount of insects destroyed by all the birds about any one locality, we should find it enormous. Without the help of these assistant gardeners, the bushes and trees would soon be leafless.

WILLIAM L. FINLEY.

VERDIN

Auriparus flaviceps flaviceps (*Sundevall*)

A. O. U. Number 746

Other Names.— Gold-Tit; Yellow-headed Bush-Tit.

General Description.— Length, 4½ inches. Head, yellow; upper parts, brownish-gray; under parts, pale brownish-gray and white. Bill, much shorter than head, conical, and tip acute; wings, long and rounded; tail, nearly as long as wing, rounded.

Color.— ADULTS: Head, dull gamboge or wax-yellow, clearer yellow on cheeks, chin, and throat (where the yellow sometimes extends over upper chest), more olivaceous on crown and back of head, the back portion of forehead sometimes tinged with orange-rufous (rarely with a distinct though partially concealed

Drawing by R. I. Brasher

VERDIN (nat. size)

A tiny fellow who has learned to use his own roof for protection during the winter season spot of this color); hindneck, back, shoulders, rump, and upper tail-coverts, plain brownish-gray (between smoke-gray and hair-brown), the rump usually tinged with yellowish olive; wings and tail, decidedly darker with pale brownish-gray or grayish-brown edgings, the lesser wing-coverts, uniform bright reddish-chestnut or bay; under parts of body, pale brownish-gray, becoming nearly white on lower abdomen and under tail-coverts. YOUNG: Essentially similar to adults, but without yellow on head or chestnut on lesser wing-coverts, which are of the same color with the back.

Nest and Eggs.— NEST: At end of branch of thorny trees or bushes, in brushy valleys of high dry country away from timber and among the desert thickets; a remarkable large retort-shaped structure with small round entrance on one side, composed exteriorly of thorny twigs and leaf and flower stems, closely interwoven, and lined with feathers. EGGS: 3 to 6, bluish or greenish white, speckled with reddish-brown, heaviest at large end.

Distribution.— Southern Texas, New Mexico, Arizona, southwestern Utah, southern Nevada, and southern California, northern Lower California, and Mexico.

One day, while we were passing a little gully west of Tucson, Arizona, I saw what looked to be a small bunch of grass or roots caught on the bare limb of a cat's-claw. It looked like a piece of drift caught by the high water. Out of curiosity, I went closer and found a small round hole in the side. In a few minutes, here came a tiny olive-gray bird, yellow on the neck and head and a chestnut patch on the shoulder. He was about the size of a Chickadee and I could tell he was a cousin of the Chickadee by his actions. This was our introduction to the Verdin.

Photo by W. L. Finley and H. T. Bohlman

VERDIN, NEST, AND YOUNG

The nest was hung out on a plain bare branch with not a leaf to hide it

I was not accustomed to seeing a nest hung out on a plain bare branch with not a leaf to hide it. When I looked about, I saw that the Verdin didn't have much choice for a nest-site, for there was nothing for a mile around except cactus, creosote, and cat's-claw. The best a Verdin can do for self-protection is to make her home look like a little bundle of drift, roof the house with thorns and make the doorway on the under side. I had to look all around before I discovered this doorway.

This bird, which I took to be the female, had a morsel in her bill. She hopped into the house and was out again and off on the hunt, paying no attention to us. We sat down about fifteen feet away. In a few moments, the male Verdin came headlong with a mouthful of green measuring-worms. He brought up with a surprised jerk and fidgeted as if he didn't know just what to do. He was evidently saying to himself, "Who are they? What do they want?" He came to the conclusion he would fool us, so he

Drawing by R. I. Brasher

WREN-TIT (½ nat. size)

Prudent to the point of secretiveness

swallowed the bite and went hunting through an adjoining bush to show us that he was merely skirmishing to appease his own appetite and that he had neither nest nor children.

When we first found the Verdin's nest, the doorway was a round hole in the side. By getting the light just right, we could look inside. A week later when we visited the same home, we were surprised not to see the door at all. The birds evidently thought we had been too curious, so they built a little roof and porch, sloping it out and straight down, so that I had to get down on my hands and knees to look up to find the doorway, for the entrance was now in the bottom.

The Verdin makes use of his home not only during the summer to raise a family, but he often uses it in winter as a sleeping place. Many birds abandon the nest as soon as the children leave home and it then falls to ruin. Not so with the Verdin; he keeps his in repair. He is such a tiny fellow, he needs a protected place for sleep. So he has learned to use his own roof during the winter season. WILLIAM L. FINLEY.

WREN-TITS

Order *Passeres;* suborder *Oscines;* family *Chamæidæ*

LTHOUGH the characters of the single genus which constitutes the family of Wren-Tits are in the main intermediate between those of the Titmice family and those of the Wren family, they are not all so, and there can be no question, says Robert Ridgway, that it is an isolated type and should be regarded as a distinct family.

The chief anatomical characteristics of the Wren-Tits are: bill much shorter than the head, compressed, and strongly curved above; well-developed bristles at the corners of the mouth; the feathers of the neck and chin terminated by distinct though fine bristles; wings rather short and much rounded; tail, much longer than wing, graduated for nearly one half its length, the feathers rather narrow, but gradually widening to the tip, which is rounded. They are found in the Pacific coast district from Oregon south to northern Lower California and east to the interior of California.

WREN-TIT

Chamæa fasciata fasciata (*Gambel*)

A. O. U. Number 742

General Description.— Length, 7 inches. Upper parts, brownish-olive; under parts, pale buffy-cinnamon.

Color.—Above, plain brownish-olive, the crown, hindneck, wing and tail feathers slightly grayer, sides of head and neck, paler grayish-olive than crown and hindneck; under parts, pale buffy-cinnamon deepening into drab or buffy-drab on sides, flanks, and under tail-coverts; iris, white.

Nest and Eggs.— NEST: In low bushes, seldom more than 4 feet up, compactly put together with thick walls; constructed of fine strips of bark, roots, grasses, and lined with horse hair or cattle hair. EGGS: 3 to 5, usually 4, pale bluish-green.

Distribution.— The eastern and southern shores of San Francisco Bay and in the adjacent Santa Clara Valley.

The Wren-Tits have long had the distinction of being the only family of perching birds peculiar to the continent of North America. The one species is found exclusively in the Pacific coast district of the United States.

The Wren-Tits are divided locally, because of slight variations, into four groups — the type species (*Chamæa fasciata fasciata*), the Pallid Wren-Tits (*Chamæa fasciata henshawi*), Coast Wren-Tits (*Chamæa fasciata phæa*), and Ruddy Wren-Tits (*Chamæa fasciata rufula*). They are small terrestrial birds, living in the dense chaparral of the hillsides and the lower mountain slopes. Prudent to the point of secretiveness they will remain securely hidden from sight while their merry *Keep-keep-keep-keep-keep-it, keep-it, keep-it* (Mrs. Bailey) rings in your ears.

KINGLETS AND GNATCATCHERS

Order *Passeres;* suborder *Oscines;* family *Sylviidæ*

THE *Sylviidæ* family is part of the larger group of singing birds. It is found in the northern hemisphere in general and in the greater part of the tropical countries of the western hemisphere; it is most numerously represented in the northern part of the eastern hemisphere. It contains a wide variety of forms. The relatively few American forms belong to two groups, one of which, the Gnatcatchers, consisting of a single genus, is peculiar to America, while the other includes two genera, one of which, the Kinglets, is circumpolar and the other, the Willow Warblers, is of northern Europe and Asia, but is sometimes included among the birds of North America because of the occurrence of a single Siberian species (*Acanthopneuste borealis*), in western Alaska.

The American forms of the family are distinguished by the following characteristics: bill, much shorter than the head, slender, and rather broad and depressed at the base; nostril at least partly exposed, sometimes partly covered by bristly feathers turned upward; distinct bristles at the corners of the mouth; wings, rather long but with rounded tip; tail, variable as to relative length but usually decidedly shorter than the wings (longer only among the Gnatcatchers), even, notched, slightly double-rounded, or (in the Gnatcatcher group) much rounded, the feathers usually broad and rounded at the tips but sometimes (in the Kinglet genus) somewhat pointed.

Drawing by R. B. Horsfall Courtesy of Nat. Asso. Aud. Soc.

GOLDEN-CROWNED KINGLETS

In coloration, the *Sylviidæ* are plain olive, olive-green, brown, or bluish-gray above; wings and tail, sometimes crown also, black, and side tail-feathers partly white in the Gnatcatchers, the crown of the Kinglets with a yellow, orange, or red patch, and under parts whitish, yellowish, or pale grayish. The sexes are usually alike or nearly so, and the young as a rule do not differ materially from the adults — the young of the Kinglets lack the patch of color on the crown, and the female and young of the Gnatcatchers never have black on the crown.

The Kinglets and Gnatcatchers are closely related to the Thrushes, but their diminutive size and the unspotted young are unfailing differences. The *Sylviidæ*, however, probably render more service to man than the Thrushes. Their diet is more nearly exclusively insectivorous and they destroy numbers of leaf-eating larvæ and plant lice.

GOLDEN-CROWNED KINGLET

Regulus satrapa satrapa *Lichtenstein*

A. O. U. Number 748 See Color Plate 104

Other Names.— Golden-crested Kinglet; Golden-crowned Wren; Flame-crest; Fiery-crowned Wren; Gold-crest.

General Description.— Length, 4¼ inches. Upper parts, gray; under parts, olive-whitish.

Color.— Adult Male: Front portion of forehead and a broad stripe over the eyes, dull white or pale gray; within this *a broad V-shaped mark of black, inclosing a narrower one of yellow, within which is a large patch of bright orange or cadmium orange,* occupying center of crown and projecting over back of head; back of head (beneath rear portion of orange-colored crest), hindneck, and upper back, mouse-gray; rest of back, grayish-olive, changing gradually into brighter or more greenish-olive on rump and upper tail-coverts; wings and tail, dusky with light yellowish-olive edgings; the middle and greater wing-coverts, broadly tipped with pale olive-yellow or yellowish-white; secondaries crossed by a basal (concealed) band of pale yellow, immediately succeeded by an exposed one of dusky; an indistinct, or at least not sharply defined, dusky streak across the lores and back of the eyes, and, usually, a similar streak at the corner of the mouth; rest of sides of head, together with under parts, plain dull olive-whitish, the sides and flanks faintly tinged with more yellowish-olive; iris, brown. Adult Female: Similar to the adult male, but orange crown-patch entirely replaced by canary-yellow.

Nest and Eggs.— Nest: Spherical, about four and a half inches in diameter, composed exteriorly chiefly of green moss, lined with fine strips of bark and fine rootlets, surmounted by numerous feathers of various wild birds, arranged with points of quills downward and forming a screen that effectually conceals the eggs; semi-pensile or not, being sometimes supported beneath and sometimes fastened by top and sides to the needles of the coniferous tree in which it is usually placed, generally at a height 50 or 60 feet from the ground. Eggs: 5 to 10, varying from creamy-white to buff, sprinkled with numerous spots or blotches of pale brown, chiefly around larger end, and placed in the nest cavity in a double layer as the space is too small to hold them in one.

Distribution.— North America east of Rocky Mountains; north to Labrador, Keewatin, etc.; breeding southward to Massachusetts, central New York, northern Michigan, northern Minnesota (?), etc., and along Allegheny Mountains to western North Carolina (in spruce belt); wintering southward to northern Florida, and westward along Gulf coast to south-central Texas.

Drawing by R. Bruce Horsfall

GOLDEN-CROWNED KINGLET (nat. size)

A dainty, feathered mite

RUBY-CROWNED KINGLET

Regulus calendula calendula (*Linnæus*)

A. O. U. Number 749 See Color Plate 104

Other Names.— Ruby-crowned Wren; Ruby-crown; Ruby-crowned Warbler.

General Description.— Length, 4½ inches. Upper parts, olive; under parts, grayish-buffy.

Color.— Adult Male: Above, plain grayish-olive on the head, gradually assuming a more decided olive hue on back, the rump and upper tail-coverts, more greenish-olive; a large, concealed fan or *wedge-shaped patch of clear vermilion-red beginning at center of crown* and overlapping back of head; wings and tail, dusky with light yellowish-olive or olive-yellow edgings, middle coverts narrowly tipped with pale grayish-olive, the greater coverts more broadly tipped with dull white (forming two bands across wing), the inner wing quills broadly edged with dull whitish; a broad whitish eye-ring, interrupted on upper eyelid, the eyelids themselves, black; rest of head, gray fading into pale grayish-buffy on chin, throat, and chest, the remaining under parts similar but more yellowish, especially on flanks, the abdomen and under tail-coverts olive-whitish; iris, dark brown. Adult Female: Similar to adult male, but without the red crown-patch.

Nest and Eggs.— Nest: Semipensile, placed almost invariably near or at end of a coniferous tree usually within 25 feet of ground; neatly and compactly built, with soft thick walls made of moss, fine strips of bark, grasses, and cocoons and lined warmly with feathers and hair. Eggs: 5 to 9, dull white or pale buffy, speckled chiefly around larger end with light brown.

Distribution.— North America in general, in wooded districts, north to the limit of tree growth, in Labrador, northern Keewatin, Mackenzie, Yukon, and Alaska (to valley of Kowak River); breeding southward to Quebec, northern Michigan, and high mountains of New Mexico, Arizona, and northern California; in winter southward entirely across United States, and over whole of Mexico to highlands of Guatemala.

The genus to which the little Kinglets belong is called *Regulus*, the translation of which is "petty king," in recognition of the patch of yellow, orange, or scarlet, shown on the top of the birds' head and which suggests a crown. These dainty little feathered "Hop-o-My-Thumbs," as Mr. Burroughs aptly called them, are the smallest of our birds, the Hummingbirds alone excepted. There is but a slight difference in their size, and little in their general coloring, excepting the distinctive marks indicated by their names; and their habits also are similar.

In the Ruby-crowned species this mark is likely to be altogether overlooked, unless the bird is excited or angry. "How does the Ruby-crowned Kinglet know he has a bit of color on his crown which he can uncover at will, and that this has great charms for the female?" asks Mr. Burroughs. "During the rivalries of the males in the mating season, and in autumn also, they

Drawing by R. I. Brasher

RUBY-CROWNED KINGLET (⅔ nat. size)

A delicate, active mote of a bird whose cheerful song is louder than its size would indicate

flash this brilliant ruby at each other. I witnessed what seemed to be a competitive display of this kind one evening in November. I was walking along the road, when my ear was attracted by the fine, shrill lisping and piping of a small band of these birds in an apple-tree. I paused to see what was the occasion of so much noise and bluster among these tiny bodies. There were four or five of them, all more or less excited, and two of them especially so. I think the excitement of the others was only a reflection of that of these two. These were hopping around each other, apparently peering down upon something beneath them. I suspected a cat concealed behind the wall, and so looked over, but there was nothing there. Observing them more closely, I saw that the two birds were entirely occupied with each other.

"They behaved exactly as if they were comparing crowns, and each extolling his own. Their heads were bent forward, the red crown patch uncovered and showing as a large, brilliant cap, their tails were spread, and the side feathers below the wings were fluffed out. They did not come to blows, but followed each other about amid the branches, uttering their thin, shrill notes and displaying their ruby crowns to the utmost. Evidently it was some sort of strife or dispute or rivalry that centered about this brilliant patch." (*Far and Near.*)

It is not to be inferred from this graphically described episode that these feathered mites are pugnacious or quarrelsome creatures. Certainly Mr. Burroughs could not have meant to convey any such idea. Rather it was simply a little difference of opinion such as may arise between any two birds. Even human beings have been known to hold different opinions concerning the same subject, each defending his view and condemning the other's by language and conduct sometimes no less violent than that of Mr. Burroughs's Kinglets. As a matter of fact, not only are both species of Kinglets essentially peaceable, but they seem normally to be happy-hearted and care-free, like their larger cousins, the Chickadees, in whose company they are often found, and with whom they seem always to be on most friendly terms.

Like the Chickadees, too, the Kinglets, averaging about an inch shorter and much more fragile in their appearance, seem to enjoy the bitterest and stormiest winter weather. How such delicate creatures manage not only to survive a characteristic New England winter storm, but to be cheerful and industrious through it all, is a nine-days' wonder. Yet it is undeniably true that strong, hardened and warmly-clad men have perished in storms and cold which do not affect even the apparent happiness of these weak little folk with only a thin coat of feathers to protect their bodies from the killing blasts. What constitutions they must have!

Unlike the partly concealed marking which gives the Ruby-crowned Kinglet his name, the corresponding ornamentation of the Golden-crowned species is always plainly observable if the bird's head be in full view. In the thick foliage of coniferous trees, the bird is not easy to observe closely, but it is very conspicuous in deciduous trees from which the foliage has fallen.

The songs of the two birds differ greatly. That of the Golden-crowned bird, Mr. Brewster says, "begins with a succession of five or six fine, shrill, high-pitched, somewhat faltering notes, and ends with a short, rapid rather explosive warble. The opening notes are given in a rising key, but the song falls rapidly at the end. The whole may be expressed as follows: *tzee, tzee, tzee, tzee, ti, ti, ter, ti-ti-ti-ti.*" The song of the Ruby-crowned species is much more elaborate and musical. In describing it as he first heard it, Dr. Chapman writes: "The longer and more eagerly I followed the unseen singer, the greater the mystery became. It seemed impossible that a bird which I supposed was at least as large as a Bluebird could escape observation in the partly leaved trees. The song was mellow and flute-like, and loud enough to be heard several hundred yards; an intricate warble past imitation or description, and rendered so admirably that I never hear it now without feeling an impulse to applaud. The bird is so small, the song so rich and full, that one is reminded of a chorister with the voice of an adult soprano."

Both the Ruby-crown and the Golden-crown are represented in western North America by variant forms. The Western Golden-crowned Kinglet (*Regulus satrapa olivaceus*) has shorter wings and tail and a more slender bill than his eastern brother and the olive of his upper parts is brighter and more greenish. He breeds from Kodiak Island and Kenai Peninsula, Alaska, south through eastern Oregon to San Jacinto Mountains, California. The winters he spends from British Columbia to the highlands of Mexico and Guatemala. The Sitka, or Grinnell's Ruby-crowned, Kinglet (*Regulus calendula grinnelli*) is similar to the more widely distributed Ruby-crown, but he has a shorter wing and a larger bill, and his coloration is decidedly darker. He breeds in the Pacific coast district from Alaska to British Columbia and winters south to middle California.

BLUE-GRAY GNATCATCHER

Polioptila cærulea cærulea (*Linnæus*)

A. O. U. Number 751 See Color Plate 104

Other Names.— Common Gnatcatcher; Little Bluish-gray Wren; Small Blue-gray Flycatcher; Sylvan Flycatcher.

General Description.— Length, 4½ inches. Upper parts, bluish-gray; under parts, whitish.

Color.— Adult Male: Crown and hindneck, plain bluish-gray, the back, shoulders, rump, and lesser wing-coverts slightly paler and less bluish; *front portion of forehead and sides of forehead and crown, black, forming a conspicuous U-shaped mark;* wings, dull slate color with pale gray edgings, these much broader and much paler gray (sometimes whitish) on inner wing quills; upper tail-coverts and tail, black, *the outermost tail-feathers extensively white,* with blackish shafts, the white occupying the whole of the exposed portion of both webs on the outermost feather, extending more nearly to base on outer web than on inner, the second feather with terminal half (approximately) white, the third broadly tipped with white; sides of head, pale bluish-gray; a white eye-ring; under parts, white, the throat, chest, and sides, especially the chest, faintly shaded with pale bluish-gray; bill, black; iris, brown. Adult Female: Similar to the adult male, but gray of upper parts less bluish, and without the U-shaped mark on forehead and sides of crown.

Nest and Eggs. Nest: Interior about 1½ inches deep and about the same in diameter, perfectly cup-shaped, gracefully contracted at brim; composed of soft, silky milkweed or cat-tail down, withered blossoms, or other dainty material, pinned together with fine grasses, old leaf stems, and horse-hair; exterior decorated with lichens, held on by spider-webs; usually saddled on a horizontal limb, sometimes in a sapling fork, about 15 feet from the ground; in the former situation it resembles a knot on the limb. Eggs: 4 or 5, greenish or bluish-white speckled with chestnut, umber-brown, or lilac.

Distribution.— Eastern United States; north (breeding) to New Jersey, southeastern and southwestern Pennsylvania, southern Ontario, southern Michigan, northern Illinois, southern Iowa, and eastern Nebraska, occasionally or accidentally to Long Island, Connecticut, Rhode Island, Massachusetts, Maine, northern Michigan, and Minnesota; breeding southward to Florida, Louisiana, and southern Texas; wintering in Florida and other Gulf States and southward to Bahamas, Cuba, and Mexico to Yucatan and Guatemala.

Drawing by R. I. Brasher

BLUE-GRAY GNATCATCHER (¾ nat. size)

A fussy and fearless little fellow who doesn't hesitate to attack a bird five times his size

The Blue-gray Gnatcatcher is one of the sweetest singing birds of the southland, but owing to the weakness of its voice it can be heard only a short distance. In spring one may pass through a woodland resonant with the songs and cries of mating birds and never suspect that one of the most abundant of all the feathered inhabitants of the region is the little gray Gnatcatcher. In form it strikingly resembles a Mockingbird, but its diminutive size precludes the possibility of confusion with that bird.

The lichen-covered nest is usually placed on the horizontal limb of an oak or other deciduous tree. The nest is begun in the early spring and may easily be seen from the ground below. It is usually placed in such a position, however, that when the leaves on the surrounding twigs are fully grown, it is completely hidden from view. Both birds labor at the task of nest building, and also share alike the duties of incubation and caring for the young. Many kinds of birds maintain a discreet silence when near the nests, but not so with the Blue-gray Gnatcatcher. Sometimes he may be found exercising his vocal power to his little utmost when the female is brooding only a few feet away. On more than one occasion I have watched a male Gnatcatcher singing with might and main as he sat on the eggs taking his turn at housekeeping.

As the name of this bird implies, it is insectivorous in its feeding habits. Hence it is migratory. Until of late it has been supposed that none of the species passed the winter north of Florida. Recently, however, Arthur T. Wayne has proved that some of them spend the colder months in swamps as far north as South Carolina.

In the western United States and Mexico is found the Western Gnatcatcher (*Polioptila cærulea obscura*), a variant form of the Blue-gray. The gray of its upper parts is slightly duller and the black at the base of inner web of the outer tail-feathers is more extended than in the Blue-gray.

T. Gilbert Pearson.

THRUSHES

Order *Passeres;* suborder *Oscines;* family *Turdidæ*

THE Thrushes belong to the singing birds. Their bills are slender and small and the upper mandible grows slightly thicker toward the apex. The space in front of the eyes is wide.

The various members of the Thrushes present wide differences in general appearance, form, coloration, and habits. Some live among the trees, others on the ground, and others among rocks. Some eat fruits, others insects — though many kinds feed upon both fruits and berries and insects. They may be plainly colored or of brilliant hues, though the latter is exceptional, the former being the rule.

The young of the Thrush family differ from the adults in having the upper and under parts spotted, whether that is or is not the case in the adult. This family trait is particularly noticeable in the Robin. The autumn molt is the only complete change of feathers during the year. In the spring the points of the feathers are cast off and any extremely worn feathers are replaced by new ones. The young birds have a complete molt before they migrate in their first autumn.

The family is remarkable for the number of excellent songsters it contains, the European Nightingale and the American Hermit Thrush, Veery, and Wood Thrush being renowned in this respect.

The Thrushes, as a group, are nearly cosmopolitan, only parts of Polynesia having none. They are most numerously represented in Europe and northern and central Asia. The family is well developed in the Americas, especially in the mountainous district extending from Mexico to the central Andes, the total number of species and subspecies now known to occur in the two continents being about one hundred and fifty.

TOWNSEND'S SOLITAIRE

Myadestes townsendi (*Audubon*)

A. O. U. Number 754

General Description.— Length, 8 inches. Plumage, brownish-gray, paler below. Bill, short and broad; wings, moderately long, rounded; tail, about the same length as wing, double rounded; legs, short and slender.

Color.— Above, plain brownish-gray, the under parts similar but slightly paler, especially on chin, throat, and abdomen; the under tail-coverts broadly but rather indistinctly tipped with dull white; an eye-ring of dull white; lores, dusky; wings, dark grayish-brown, with lighter brownish-gray edgings, the secondaries and inner primaries buff basally (mostly hidden by greater and primary coverts), and with a broad dusky space intervening between this buffy portion and the grayish-edged terminal portion; inner quills margined terminally with dull white (except in worn plumage); middle pair of tail-feathers concolor with back, or the outermost with terminal half of outer web dull white, the inner web broadly tipped with white, this white extending along shaft for a considerable distance, the second feather with a similar but much smaller white tip; under wing-coverts mixed pale brownish-gray and dull white; under surface of wing feathers, showing an oblique basal and subbasal band of buff; bill, black; iris, brown.

Nest and Eggs.— NEST: On the ground, or on a log or stump, or in rubbish; often in a bank-niche by a stream or sometimes in a rocky crevice; rather large and loosely made of sticks, grasses, or pine-needles and weed stalks; on this large foundation is placed the real nest, made of finer bits of similar material, but the whole carelessly and loosely constructed; the mass of material hanging below frequently betrays the nest, especially when it is placed among rocks. EGGS: 3 to 6, bluish-white, freckled with reddish-brown.

Distribution.— Mountain districts of western North America; breeding (in pine forests) from Alaska (heights above Bennett; 1500 feet above Caribou Crossing; Lake Lebarge; Yukon River, 20 miles above Circle) and Northwest Territory (Miles Canon; Semenow Hills) and from the coast ranges to the Black Hills of North Dakota and western Texas south to Mexico; wintering from Oregon, Montana, etc., southward; straggling, in autumn or winter, to Kansas, Nebraska and northwestern Illinois.

Along the wooded heights of the western mountains, the Townsend's Solitaire has its abode. Of all the North American Thrushes it is the loftiest dweller. Along the steep mountain slopes, where streams from melting snows dash downward to join the river below, this bird may be found. At times one may come upon it running along the ground over bowlders and logs in a manner very similar to that of the Robin. It is in such places that the nest of twigs

Drawing by R. I. Brasher

TOWNSEND'S SOLITAIRE (¾ nat. size)

A sweet and elusive singer in the mountain solitudes

and pine-needles is hidden, and so well is it concealed that a most laborious search is often necessary to find it. The pretty spotted eggs number from three to six.

The male Solitaire has a most pleasing song. From the top of some tree far on the heights it rings out bold and clear with a vividness of expression that harmonizes perfectly with the wild surroundings. At other times, when near the nest or late in the evening, its notes are usually subdued, and these minor strains are wonderfully appealing as one sits alone in these mountain solitudes where few birds are to be heard.

Visitors to the Yellowstone National Park or the Glacier National Park often see these birds along the mountain roads or trails. The Solitaire is about the size of the Wood Thrush, but is of more slender build. Its form, color, and movements suggest a lazy Mockingbird, and the resemblance is heightened by the white wing-bars that traverse the gray wings. The approach of winter early drives it to lower levels in quest of food.

T. GILBERT PEARSON.

Since this little fellow avoids civilization and makes his main habitation in the inaccessible mountain gorges of the West, his food consists largely of wild berries.

WOOD THRUSH

Hylocichla mustelina (*Gmelin*)

A. O. U. Number 755 See Color Plate 105

Other Names.— Song Thrush; Wood Robin; Bell Bird; Swamp Robin.

General Description.— Length, 7¾ inches. Upper parts, brown; under parts, white, spotted. Bill, about ½ length of head, slender, curved downward at the tip; wings, long and pointed; tail, not more than ¾ length of wing, even, the feathers slightly sharpened at the extreme tip; legs, long and slender.

Color.— *Crown, tawny-brown passing into cinnamon-brown on back and shoulders,* this into grayish-olive on rump, upper tail-coverts, and tail; wings, similar in color to back but slightly less cinnamon; a distinct eye-ring of white; lores whitish, suffused with dusky grayish in front of eye; sides of head, dusky grayish-brown, narrowly streaked with white; cheeks, white flecked with dusky; under parts, white tinged with buff on chest; a broad streak below cheeks of black or dusky along each side of throat; *chest, sides, and flanks, marked with large roundish or broadly drop-shaped spots of brownish-black; bill, dusky horn color,* the basal half below pale flesh color; iris, dark brown.

Nest and Eggs.— NEST: Usually in thickets, placed in the crotch or on horizontal limbs of saplings, six to twelve feet from ground; composed externally of leaves, grasses, small twigs, and stems placed when damp and cemented with mud, the whole quite firm and solid when dry; bits of paper or rag are frequently added as a sort of decoration; the lining formed

Courtesy of Am. Mus. Nat. Hist.

WOOD THRUSH (⅔ nat. size)

He frequently makes his home near human habitations

of fine rootlets and grasses. EGGS: 3 or 4, plain greenish-blue, like the Veery's and intermediate in size between that bird's and the Robin's.

Distribution.— Eastern temperate North America; north to New Hampshire (White Mountains), New York (breeding at Lake George), northern Ontario, northern Michigan, etc., accidentally to Maine and northeastern New York; west to middle portion of Great Plains (along wooded valleys); breeding southward to northern Florida and thence westward through Gulf States to eastern Texas; in winter southward through eastern Mexico and Central America to Nicaragua and Costa Rica, also to Bahamas, Cuba, Jamaica, and Porto Rico; straggler to the Bermudas.

The Wood Thrush is unlike any other woods-dwelling member of his famous family in the respect that, though deep woods are his natural and generally preferred abiding place, he frequently makes his home near human habitations. He seems never to become domesticated in the degree that the Robins and the Bluebirds do and his demeanor is always more shy and retiring than theirs. Nevertheless he is often found conducting his family affairs in the shade trees or shrubbery very near the homes of men, and so he becomes much better known to them than do the Hermit, the Olive-backed, the Veery, and the other Thrushes who remain essentially birds of the woods. He is, besides, the handsomest member of his tribe, and has withal the most elegant manners.

It is generally too fanciful to find resemblances between bird notes and spoken words, but no one with an ear for time and tune can deny that bird songs may — by coincidence, of course — repeat known musical phrases. So sane and accurate an observer as Herbert K. Job finds in the phrase of the Wood Thrush a distinct suggestion of "the opening appeal in Weber's 'Invitation to the Dance,' and again the 'sweetly solemn thought' of Handel's 'Largo' from 'Xerxes.'" Another bird lover says that to his ear, two successive renditions of the Wood Thrush's phrase, if the second is pitched at the usual interval above the first, reproduce very closely the first two phrases of Faust's beautiful appeal to Marguerite (in the garden), when he sings:

These two phrases are all that are claimed for the Thrush, and the pause between them is, of course, much longer than is the time value of the quarter-rest, according to the usual tempo of Gounod's music; but otherwise the phrases, in their intervals, strongly suggest Faust's impassioned address. We need not strain the probabilities by fancying that Gounod may have borrowed the song of our Thrush, but we may, at least, take a little pride in the fact that our woods had heard and learned to love this song centuries before the great French composer put much the same music into one of his sweetest melodies.

Photo by H. K. Job Courtesy of Outing Pub. Co.

WOOD THRUSH INCUBATING

The food of this bird consists largely of insects, with a small percentage of fruit. The insects eaten include grasshoppers, crickets, cutworms, ants, caterpillars, and beetles, including the potato beetle. The fruit consumed is chiefly of wild varieties, such as frost grapes, wild blackberries, wild cherries, and the seeds of the spice bush and southern magnolia. Since the Wood Thrush is a decidedly useful species and adapts itself readily to civilized surroundings, its presence about the farm and garden should always be encouraged.

GEORGE GLADDEN.

VEERY

Hylocichla fuscescens fuscescens (*Stephens*)

A. O. U. Number 756 See Color Plate 105

Other Names.— Wilson's Thrush; Tawny Thrush; Nightingale.

General Description.— Length, 7¼ inches. Upper parts, tawny-brown; under parts, buff and white, streaked and spotted with dark. Bill, about ½ length of head, slender, gradually and increasingly curved downward toward the tip; wings, rather long and pointed; tail, not more than ¾ length of wing, even, the feathers slightly sharpened at the extreme tip; legs, long and slender.

Color.— Above, plain tawny-brown, the wings and tail slightly duller brown, especially the former; lores, dull grayish-white; eyelids, similar, *the color not forming a distinct eye-ring*; sides of head, rather light dull tawny-brown, narrowly streaked with dull brownish-white; cheeks dull buffy-white, becoming decidedly buffy behind, where streaked with tawny-brown; *chin and throat buffy-white, gradually passing into pale buff on chest,* the latter tinged with brown laterally; the upper chest and sides of lower throat, streaked with tawny-brown; the lower chest, spotted with a paler and slightly grayer tint of the same; sides and flanks light buffy-grayish; the sides of breast sometimes faintly spotted with a darker shade of the same; rest of under parts, white; bill, dark horn color, the basal half below pale grayish-flesh color; iris, dark brown.

Nest and Eggs.— Nest: At base of bush or small tree; made of leaves, strips of grapevine or other bark, weed stems, and roots, and lined with fine rootlets or grass; nests have been found in tree hollows fifteen feet from the ground, but the usual location is on or near the ground. Eggs: 3 to 5, plain greenish-blue, like a small Robin's egg.

Distribution.— Eastern North America; breeding from northern New Jersey, Pennsylvania, northern Ohio, northern Indiana, northern Illinois, central Iowa, and southeastern South Dakota, northward to Newfoundland, Magdalen Islands, and Ontario, and southward along the Allegheny Mountains to western North Carolina (3500–5000 feet); wintering in South Carolina (?), Florida (?), Cuba, coast of Yucatan, Costa Rica, Panama, and northern South America.

The Veery is essentially a bird of the deep woods and the "silent places." He is fully as shy as the Hermit, while his song heightens the impression of mystery produced by his evident desire to avoid notice. Indeed, comparatively few persons certainly identify the song with the singer. A reprint of the *American Ornithology,* by Wilson and Bonaparte (a real Bonaparte, and writing about birds!), with poorly executed wood-cuts after Wilson's fine drawings, was a standard work as late as 1885, but not a word is there in it about the Veery! For, as we know now, the very man, Alexander Wilson, in whose honor the bird is often called "Wilson's Thrush," seems himself never to have heard the unique and beautiful song of this bird.

Courtesy of Am. Mus. Nat. Hist.

VEERY (⅖ nat. size)

A bird of the deep woods and silent places

The distinctive characteristic of the Veery's tone is a peculiar resonant quality, very like that produced by whistling into a long, metal tube of, say, a foot in diameter. Resonance in some degree is not an uncommon quality in the tones of several of the Thrushes, notably the Hermit; but it is the prevailing characteristic in the Veery's song. Nor is there any common bird whose vocalization involves such a perfectly adjusted tremolo effect, as dainty and innocent of apparent effort as the ripples which greet the lightest zephyr from the surface of a motionless pool.

The song has been likened to a " spiral, tremulous, silver thread of music," and has been represented by means of *connected* spirals in a uniformly descending line. The " spiral " idea is accurate, though it should be elaborated by the explanation that each curve is in the form of a finely shaded and evenly divided crescendo and diminuendo. The singer frequently begins by repeating this curve once, followed by three more renditions, and those by two more, each group being distinct (though the rest interval is very brief), and at a pitch slightly lower than the preceding one. Furthermore the entire song is in diminuendo, the last notes being noticeably softer than the first. In this respect the song is exactly the reverse of the Oven-bird's, which begins with the lowest note and increases consistently in volume and pitch to the final and highest one. The Warbler's tone, however, lacks the tremolo and resonant qualities of the Thrush's.

Ernest Thompson Seton has said that while it seems almost profane to represent this faint, soft, silvery tinkling of the Veery's song by uncouth syllables, yet he thought the best idea of the mere articulation would be suggested by the syllables *veero, veery, veery, veery,* from which no doubt the singer got its name.

During the nesting season the Veery frequents the woodlands almost exclusively and consequently its work is not of any great value to farmer or fruit-grower. It gets most of its food from the ground and like all Thrushes it feeds largely upon beetles, snails, and a great variety of insects and small fruits whenever obtainable. The Veery confines its fruit-food almost exclusively to wild fruit and cannot be considered in any way injurious.

The Willow Thrush (*Hylocichla fuscescens salicicola*) is a form of the Veery which is a little duller in coloration, the brown of the upper parts less tawny and the brown streaks on the upper chest and the sides of the lower throat averaging slightly darker. It breeds from southern British Columbia, central Alberta, central Saskatchewan, and southern Manitoba south to central Oregon, Nevada, Utah, northern New Mexico, and central Iowa; it winters in South America, south to Brazil.

Courtesy of S. A. Lottridge

NEST AND EGGS OF VEERY

Usually placed on or near the ground

GRAY-CHEEKED THRUSH

Hylocichla aliciæ aliciæ (*Baird*)

A. O. U. Number 757 See Color Plate 105

Other Name.— Alice's Thrush.

General Description.— Length, 7¾ inches. Upper parts, grayish-olive; under parts, whitish with grayish-dusky spots. Bill, about ½ length of head, slender, gradually and increasingly curved downward toward the tip; wings, rather long and pointed; tail, not more than ¾ length of wing, even, the feathers slightly sharpened at the extreme tip; legs, long and slender.

Color.— *Above uniform grayish-olive,* the tail slightly browner; sides of head, mostly grayish-olive, paling slightly around eyes, but *not showing a distinct eye-ring,* sides of head narrowly streaked with whitish; the upper portion of lores, dull whitish; *cheeks* buffy-whitish, tinged with *grayish-olive* and streaked with a darker shade of the same; under parts, white, passing on sides and flanks into pale olive-gray; chest, varying from buffy-white to pale cream-buff; a broad streak below cheeks of dusky along each side of throat; chest (sometimes lower throat also) marked with triangular spots of grayish-dusky, those on lower part of chest more transverse; breast, especially laterally, with transverse spots of light grayish-olive; bill, dusky, the basal half below pale brownish flesh-colored; iris, dark brown.

Nest and Eggs.— Nest: In low trees, from 2 to 7 feet up, occasionally on the ground; compact and large, composed of interwoven dry grasses, leaves, strips of fine bark; lined with fine dried grass; often dried moss enters largely into its composition. Eggs: 3 or 4 (usually the latter number), greenish-blue, speckled with spots of rusty and yellowish-brown.

Distribution.—Eastern and northern North America; breeding from Newfoundland (Canada Bay), Magdalen Islands (?), Labrador, Ungava, and Keewatin, to Mackenzie, Alaska (except portion south and east of Cross Sound), and northeastern Siberia; migrating southward through eastern United States (west to eastern Montana) to Cuba, Santo Domingo, Panama, and northern South America.

The annual northward concert tour of this sweet singer may extend from Peru to Alaska. This you may learn by consulting his itinerary set forth in the above paragraph devoted to his distribution. In the long journey he makes frequent stops to fill short engagements which are much appreciated by those who know of his coming, and are familiar with his program. Then he hurries on to attend to his (to him) much more important family matters.

Courtesy of Am. Mus. Nat. Hist.

GRAY-CHEEKED THRUSH (½ nat. size)

In Alaska he may be heard singing twenty hours out of the twenty-four

In Alaska, within a hundred miles or so of that strange "Land of the Midnight Sun," his song is heard throughout all of the twenty-odd hours of daylight during his stay, and very often during the short, make-believe night. Near Port Clarence, north of Bering Strait, Mr. Burroughs heard him singing continuously in July, when there was daylight from about 2 A. M. to about 10 P. M. Incidentally he observed one member of the species doing a thing which, he says, he had never seen any Thrush do before. This bird "hovered in the air fifty feet or more above the moor and repeated its song three times very rapidly." The English Skylark is famous for its flight song, which inspired one of Shelley's most beautiful poems; and there are certain American singers which have the same pretty habit, notably the Bobolink, the Yellow-breasted Chat and the Oven-bird. The Thrushes, however, are essentially singers from perches, and the Robin especially is likely to select the topmost twig of the tallest tree available, from which to carol his evening lay. But, as Mr. Burroughs says, the gray-cheeked singer he heard had "no lofty trees to perch upon," so he "perched upon the air."

It would seem that, with so much time to practice, this Thrush ought to be a pretty good singer, and though he is not the equal of his cousins, the Wood Thrush, the Hermit, and the Veery, his is by no means a poor or indifferent effort. The quality of the tone is not unlike that of the Veery, though it is somewhat thinner. Mr. Hoffman expresses it in the following syllables: *te-deé, de-eà, te-dee-ee,* adding that there is a slurring effect on all of the long syllables. The call-note is a sharp, impatient *feé-a,* often repeated in an ascending pitch.

During its spring sojourn this bird feeds chiefly on insects, but in the fall it prefers wild fruits and berries, such as sour gum, dogwood, poke berries, and frost grapes. Three stomachs of the Gray-cheeked Thrush taken in May contained sawfly larvæ, ants, caterpillars, May flies, ground beetles, weevils, and scarabæid beetles.

A smaller form of this bird, called Bicknell's Thrush (*Hylocichla aliciæ bicknelli*), is often seen in the higher Catskills and in the dwarfed coniferous timber high on the mountains of northern New England. This Thrush was discovered on Slide Mountain and it is often called the Slide Mountain Thrush.

RUSSET-BACKED THRUSH

Hylocichla ustulata ustulata (*Nuttall*)

A. O. U. Number 758

Other Name.— Russet-back.

General Description.— Length, 7¼ inches. Upper parts, olive-brown; under parts, white and buff with spots of olive-brown. Bill, about ½ length of head, slender, gradually and increasingly curved downward toward the tip; wings, rather long and pointed; tail, not more than ¾ length of wing, slightly notched, the feathers slightly sharpened at the extreme tip; legs, long and slender.

Color.—Above, plain olive-brown, *a conspicuous eye-ring; lores, pale buff,* the latter obscured with olive-brownish, especially near central portion; sides of head, olive-brown, with narrow shaft-streaks of pale buff or buffy-whitish; cheeks, buffy, streaked with olive-brownish; chin, throat, and chest, buff, the chin and throat sometimes buffy-white, the sides of lower throat and whole chest with triangular marks of deep olive-brown, these markings narrower and more wedge-shaped in front, broader behind, those on central portion of chest darker, sometimes approaching a sooty hue; a streak below cheek of olive-brown along each side of throat; breast, abdomen, and under tail-coverts, white, the upper portion of the first (especially on lateral portions) transversely spotted with light olive-brown; sides and flanks, pale olive-brown; under wing-coverts, pale buffy, suffused with pale brownish; bill dusky brown or blackish, the basal half pale dull fleshy below; iris, deep brown.

Nest and Eggs.— Nest: In bushes, saplings, or thickets, usually within a few feet of the ground and near water; a large compact structure of twigs, bark strips, mosses, grass, and leaves. Eggs: 4 or 5, light greenish-blue, spotted with light brown, chiefly around large end.

Distribution.— Breeding in Pacific coast district of United States, British Columbia, and southern Alaska, from southern California, probably also northern Lower California, to Juneau, Alaska; during migration, southward, western Mexico, Guatemala, Costa Rica, to eastern Ecuador and British Guiana.

"If we take the quality of melody as a test," says John Burroughs, "the Wood Thrush, the Hermit Thrush and the Veery Thrush stand at the head of our list of songsters." Yet it is often difficult to say whether the song of one bird surpasses that of another, because bird songs are largely matters of association and suggestion. The song of the Russet-back is best late in the day after all other birds have ceased singing. It comes just before dusk from the shaded cañons or from the firs on my hillside just above the river. It is a vesper hymn I love better than all others.

Every year I find two or three pairs of Russet-backed Thrushes nesting on our ten acres. One can always tell the nest of this bird by its position and by the material used. As a rule, it is in among the dark foliage or a dark clump of bushes not far from the ground. The nest is made almost entirely of moss and leaves. After the foundation of the home is built, the Thrush seeks some leaves from the damp ground. These she flattens out and molds into the bottom of the home with her breast. She collects moss for the walls and when the home is completed, it often looks like a ball of moss fastened in the briers or branches.

The Thrush is so different from the Robin. When I go out to the Robin's nest in the orchard, the owners are so angry they dash around yell-ing, "Help! Murder! Get out of here or we'll knock your head off!" Whenever I visited the Thrush's home, the mother stayed on the nest until I almost touched her, then she slipped through the branches with a low whistle for her mate. He was near at hand. They were anxious, but they did not relieve their feelings with a great noise and fuss, as the Robins did. The Robins are noisy; the Thrushes shy and quiet.

As I watched each time the Thrush mother came to feed her young, she lingered at the nest edge. I often saw her sit for several moments at a time looking at her babies and caressing them with a real mother's love.

WILLIAM L. FINLEY.

While this Thrush is very fond of fruit, its partiality for banks of streams keeps it from frequenting orchards when they are far from water. It is most troublesome during the cherry season, at the time when the young are in the nest. It might be inferred from this that the nestlings are fed on fruit, but such is not the case to any noticeable extent. The parent birds eat the fruit themselves, while the young, as is usual with nestlings, are fed mostly upon insects. The old birds eat some fruit throughout the season, but do not seem to attract much attention by their depredations on prunes and the later fruits. As the Thrush is one of the "soft-billed" birds, its attacks on fruits are limited to the thin-skinned varieties. It is as often seen on the ground pecking at fallen fruit as attacking the cherries on the trees. It probably confines its depredations upon the later fruits to such as have already been broken into by stout-billed birds.

This Thrush is an efficient destroyer of insects, and during its sojourn in the fruit region a little more than half of its food consists of harmful insects. In the investigation of this bird's diet 157 stomachs were examined and 52 per cent. of animal matter to 48 per cent. of vegetable was found. The animal portion was insects, spiders, earthworms, sowbugs, beetles, caterpillars, ants, wasps, and grasshoppers. The vegetable portion in addition to the skins and pulp of cherries contained seeds of blackberries, raspberries, elderberry, pepper tree, and weeds.

In its insect diet the Russet-backed Thrush is almost wholly beneficial, as it eats but few predacious beetles or other useful insects. As young Thrushes are fed almost exclusively upon insects and as they eat almost continuously from morning till night, they must destroy an enormous number of these harmful creatures. The Russet-backed Thrush must be considered as one of the positively beneficial birds.

OLIVE-BACKED THRUSH

Hylocichla ustulata swainsoni (*Tschudi*)

A. O. U. Number 758a See Color Plate 105

Other Names.— Alma's Thrush; Swainson's Thrush; Swamp Robin.

General Description.— Length, 7¼ inches. Upper parts, olive-brown; under parts, white and buff with spots of olive-brown. Bill, about ½ length of head, slender, gradually and increasingly curved downward toward the tip; wings, rather long and pointed; tail, not more than ¾ length of wing, slightly notched, the feathers slightly sharpened at the extreme tip; legs, long and slender.

Color.— Above, *uniform grayish olive-brown; conspicuous eye-ring* and lores pale buff; sides of head, olive-brown, with narrow streaks of pale buff; cheeks, buffy streaked with olive-brownish; chin, throat, and chest, buff; the chin and throat sometimes buffy-white; the sides of lower throat and whole chest with wedge-shaped marks dark olive-brown; these marks narrower and darker in front, broader and lighter behind, those on central part of chest sometimes sooty-blackish and usually on a cream-buff ground color; a streak below cheek of olive-brown along each side of throat; breast, abdomen, and under tail-coverts white; the upper portion of the first transversely spotted with olive-brown; sides and flank, grayish-olive; bill, dusky brown; the basal half below pale dull flesh color; iris, deep brown.

Nest and Eggs.— NEST: In a bush or small tree, usually from five to eight feet from ground, in secluded situations; composed of grasses, leaves and shreds of bark; in the more northern parts of the bird's range, moss enters frequently into the nest construction. EGGS: 3 or 4, with a ground color of greenish-blue, speckled with varying shades of reddish-brown, rufous, or light umber-brown.

Distribution.— North America in general except Pacific coast district south of Cross Sound and Lynn Canal; breeding from Massachusetts (Berkshire County, 2000 to 3500 feet), mountains of eastern New York (Catskills), Pennsylvania, and West Virginia (spruce belt), northern Michigan, Colorado (Rocky Mountains), Utah (Uinta and Wasatch mountains), Nevada (East Humboldt Mountains), and California (Sierra Nevada) northward to Alaska (Kenai Peninsula; Iliamna District; Yukon valley; Kowak valley, etc.), Yukon Territory (Dawson, Lake Marsh; Lake Lebarge; Caribou Crossing), Mackenzie and shores of Hudson Bay; in migration southward over whole of Mexico and Central America to Peru, Brazil, and Argentina; occasional in Bermudas and Cuba.

This Thrush deserves to be much better known. To be sure he breeds chiefly in the Canadian forests and when seen in the central and eastern States (about the middle of May) is likely to be on his way to the northern wilderness; but his breeding range extends as far southward as the Catskills, in New York, and he is not an uncommon spring and summer resident on Greylock Mountain in northwestern Massachusetts, in the White Mountains, and in the lower peninsula of Michigan. In these regions he may be seen and heard frequently — by those who know what to look and to listen for.

Ocular identification of the bird may be a puzzling operation for the unpracticed or careless observer, since there really is considerable resemblance between the Olive-backed, the Gray-cheeked, the Veery, the Wood, and the Hermit Thrushes; yet the plumage of each bird shows one or more individual peculiarities by which each may be certainly and quickly identified. Besides, each species has a distinctive song, or peculiar call notes which the careful listener soon detects.

Stewart Edward White, who, besides being a mighty hunter of both the timid and the dangerous game animals of America and Africa, is an accurate and sympathetic observer of bird-life, has recorded a careful analysis of this Thrush's song, as he heard it on Mackinac Island; together with some ingenious and amusing statistics concerning the industry and persistence of the singer. Analyzing the song Mr. White says that it "begins low and ascends by two regular steps of two notes each, and ends with several sharp notes. The first note of each step is higher than the second, and the second of the next is about the same as the first note of the first step." To Mr. White the song said *gurgle, gurgle ting, chee chee chee*. Then come his statistics, which are astonishing as well as amusing.

Holding his watch on one Thrush, he noted that the bird sang, with extreme regularity, on an average nine and a half times a minute. The recital began commonly at about 3:15 A. M. and the song was repeated at the usual intervals until about 9 A. M. when an intermission began which lasted until about noon. Then the recital was resumed and the song delivered as before, but at longer intervals than during the morning performance. At about 4:30 the singer got into his pace again, and kept it up steadily until about 7:30. Therefore, Mr. White estimates, if this Thrush sang but eight times a minute for eight hours and forty-five minutes, plus occasional songs for about twenty minutes, he must have sung 4360 songs a day, or in, say six weeks, his normal singing period, no less than 168,000 songs!

The food of the Olive-back is similar to that of other small Thrushes, and, the larger part of the animal food at least, comes from the ground, where the birds search busily for it, turning over the leaves, probing the moss and decayed vegetation and picking up worms, snails, and insects of various kinds, particularly beetles and ants. Dr. Sylvester D. Judd in his report to the Department of Agriculture, *Birds of a Maryland Farm,* said that he had examined the stomachs of two Olive-backed Thrushes collected in May and found that they had eaten ants, wasps, ground-beetles, darkling-beetles, and ground-spiders. This bird is fond of wild fruits of all kinds and eats large quantities. Being an inhabitant of woodlands rather than orchards or gardens, it does no damage to the horticulturist, but on the other hand renders him little service.

Courtesy of Am. Mus. Nat. Hist.

OLIVE-BACKED THRUSH (½ nat. size)

According to one count he sang 4360 songs a day

HERMIT THRUSH

Hylocichla guttata pallasi (*Cabanis*)

A. O. U. Number 759b See Color Plate 105

Other Names.— American Nightingale; Swamp Angel; Swamp Robin; Rufous-tailed Thrush; Solitary Thrush.

General Description.— Length, 7 inches. Upper parts, russet-brown; under parts, white with spots of dark. Bill, about ½ length of head, slender, gradually and increasingly curved downward toward the tip; wings, rather long and pointed; tail, not more than ¾ length of wing, even, the feathers slightly sharpened at the extreme tip; legs, long and slender.

Color.— Above, plain russet-brown, *the upper tail-coverts and tail reddish-brown*; a conspicuous eye-ring of dull white; lores, dull whitish mixed with dusky grayish; sides of head, grayish-brown with very narrow shaft-streaks of dull whitish; cheeks and under parts dull white, the chest and hinder part of cheeks tinged with pale cream-buff; a dusky or sooty streak below cheeks along each side of throat; sides of lower throat with narrow wedge-shaped streaks of dusky; chest with large triangular spots of dusky grayish-brown or sooty; these more wedge-shaped on upper chest, broader and more rounded on lower chest; upper breast, especially on lateral portions, spotted with grayish-brown or brownish-gray; sides and flanks, light brownish-gray; bill, dusky brown or blackish, the basal half below pale grayish flesh color; iris, dark brown.

Nest and Eggs.— Nest: Placed on or close to the ground; rather bulky and made of grass, a few small rootlets, leaves, sometimes bits of dried moss, and rather carefully lined with finer pieces of the same material. Eggs: 3 or 4, plain greenish-blue.

Distribution.— Eastern North America; breeding from Massachusetts (Marthas Vineyard; Taconic Mountains, Berkshire County, 1000 to 2900 feet); Connecticut (Bear Mountains, Norfolk); New York (Catskills, 2300 to 2600 feet; Peterboro; Lake Ronkonkoma, Long Island?), mountains of Pennsylvania, Ontario, northern Michigan, etc., northward to Labrador, and through Manitoba and Athabasca, to Mackenzie; during migration southward to Gulf States (Florida to Texas) wintering northward (regularly) to about 39°, occasionally to lower Hudson valley, New York.

If, while you are walking through deep and slightly swampy woods, a bird somewhat smaller than a Robin, with an olive-brownish back and a dully speckled breast starts suddenly from the ground, flies quickly to a low branch, looks about, nervously tilting its *short, reddish-brown* tail and uttering a soft *whew* or *chuck* meanwhile, and then vanishes like a wraith, mark him well, for you have seen a Hermit Thrush, singer of the purest natural melody to be heard in this or, perhaps, any land. The "American Nightingale," he is sometimes called; but there are candid and competent critics who contend that in purity and sweetness of tone, as well as in technique, the Hermit's phrase is really finer than that of the celebrated English bird.

Courtesy of Am. Mus. Nat. Hist.

HERMIT THRUSH (⅔ nat. size)

It is often remarked that the gaudy bird is rarely a good singer, and the color scheme of the Hermit's plumage is subdued and inconspicuous to a degree. Furthermore, the bird's manners are modest and retiring to the point of actual timidity. Always the Hermit seems to be trying to elude notice, and hence his appropriate name.

Of the Hermit's song, at its best, it is difficult to speak with moderation, and it is quite impossible to describe it adequately in words. The quality of the tone is not reproduced faithfully by any musical instrument. There is in it perhaps more of the flute than of any other instrument, though the tone is much mellower, more velvety, and there is a distinct suggestion of the reed quality especially in the lower registers.

Elementally the song is very simple. Often it is reminiscent of the characteristic phrase of the Wood Thrush. It differs, however, from all the Thrush songs in that it is usually begun with a long, liquid, mellow note. This introductory tone glides into the first phrase, composed of several perfectly slurred tones in an ascending and descending scale. Within a few seconds the phrase is repeated at a pitch about a minor third higher; then it is delivered again and again in a steadily ascending scale, until fairly dizzying vocal heights are attained. Here the singer pauses for a few minutes, only to go back to the lower pitch and proceed as before.

Following are records of the songs of two Hermits as reduced to musical notation by F. Schuyler Mathews:

Rendered on a piano these phrases convey only a very faint suggestion of the matchless beauty of this song. A very fine flute or a piccolo, if perfectly handled, or a violin with skillful use of harmonics, would more nearly suggest the singer's tone, which, after all, as has been said, really cannot be accurately reproduced by any musical instrument.

To Mr. Burroughs it suggests "a serene religious beatitude as no other sound in nature does," and in his book, *Wake Robin,* he records this fine appreciation.

"A few nights ago I ascended a mountain to see the world by moonlight; and when near the summit the Hermit commenced his evening hymn a few rods away from me. Listening to this strain on the lone mountain, with the full moon just rounded from the horizon, the pomp of your cities and the pride of your civilization seemed trivial and cheap." No wonder the bird is called the "Swamp Angel"!

Another of this great artist's temperamental peculiarities is that he rarely sings responsively with others of his kind, which the Wood Thrush often seems to be deliberately trying to do. And again, unlike the Wood Thrush, and more particularly such birds as the Robin, the Catbird, and the Brown Thrasher, who seem to enjoy singing to a human audience, the Hermit is likely to become altogether silent if he sees or suspects the presence of a listener. Undoubtedly it is for these reasons, and because of the bird's solitary habits, that this really wonderful song is comparatively little known. Even the great ornithologists, Wilson and Audubon, apparently never clearly identified it. Both give the Wood Thrush full credit for his musical genius, but Audubon evidently had never heard the song of the Hermit! GEORGE GLADDEN.

In spring and summer the Hermit Thrush feeds mainly on insects, but in fall and winter it partakes largely of various wild fruits and berries. Examination of sixty-eight stomachs showed animal matter to the extent of 56 per cent. and vegetable 44 per cent. The proportion varies little in the different months. On the whole, the food of the Hermit Thrush is remarkably free from useful products, destruction of which is a loss to mankind. The worst that can be said of the bird is that it eats and scatters the seed of poison oak, but it does not do this to a marked degree.

In the western part of North America there are five variants of the Hermit Thrush. The Alaska Hermit, or Kodiak Dwarf, Thrush (*Hylocichla guttata guttata*) is ranked as the type species; it breeds in the coast district of Alaska and winters south to Lower California, Mexico, and Texas. In size it is a little smaller than the Eastern Hermit and the brown of the upper parts is grayish instead of russet.

The Dwarf Hermit Thrush (*Hylocichla guttata nanus*) breeds in the coast district of Alaska and British Columbia and in the winter goes south to California, Arizona, and New Mexico. It is darker than the Alaska Hermit, the back being a sepia-brown.

The Monterey Hermit Thrush (*Hylocichla guttata slevini*) is smaller, paler, and grayer than the Alaskan. California is its home and the winter is spent in Mexico and Lower California.

The Sierra Hermit Thrush (*Hylocichla guttata sequoiensis*) is slightly darker and decidedly larger than the Monterey and larger but paler and grayer than the Alaskan. It is found in the high mountains of southern California north to southern British Columbia. In the winter it goes to western Texas and over the border into Mexico and Lower California.

Similar in coloration to the Sierra Hermit but decidedly larger is Audubon's, or the Rocky Mountain, Hermit Thrush (*Hylocichla guttata auduboni*). It breeds from British Columbia and Montana south to Nevada, Arizona, and New Mexico and winters in western and central Texas and south over Mexico to Guatemala.

ROBIN

Planesticus migratorius migratorius (*Linnæus*)

A. O. U. Number 761 See Color Plate 106

Other Names.— Fieldfare; Common Robin; Robin Redbreast; Redbreast; Migratory Thrush; Canada Robin; Northern Robin; American Robin.

General Description.— Length, 10 inches. Head, black; upper parts, gray; under parts, reddish and white. Bill, decidedly shorter than head, compressed, terminal ⅔ gradually and increasingly curved downward; wings, rather long and pointed; tail, shorter than wing, even or slightly rounded, the feathers broad.

Color.—ADULT MALE IN SPRING AND SUMMER: Head *black;* chin white; throat streaked with white and black; back, lesser wing-coverts, rump, and upper tail-coverts plain, deep mouse-gray or brownish slate-gray; larger wing-coverts and tertials darker, becoming pale mouse-gray on edges; primary coverts dark brownish slate, or dusky, edged with pale gray; tail dull slate-black or sooty black, with narrow grayish edgings; chest, breast, upper abdomen, sides, flanks, and under wing-coverts *plain, deep cinnamon-rufous;* lower abdomen, anal region, and under tail-coverts, white, the latter with concealed portion mainly gray; *white spots at the extremities of the outer tail-feathers, showing plainly when the bird is in flight;* bill, yellow; iris, deep brown; legs and feet, dark horn color or blackish brown. ADULT MALE IN AUTUMN AND WINTER: Similar to the spring and summer plumage, but gray of upper parts tinged with olive; cinnamon-rufous feathers of under parts edged with white and other slight variations of the normal plumage. ADULT FEMALE: Similar to the male, but usually much duller in color, with gray of upper parts lighter and browner and encroaching more on head, the blackish feathers of under parts paler. YOUNG: Head as in adults, but the black duller; back and shoulders, grayish-brown or olive; rump and upper tail-coverts, brownish-gray; wings and tail as in adults, but wing-coverts with terminal wedge-shaped spots or streaks of pale rusty, buff, or whitish; chin and throat, white or pale buffy, margined laterally with a stripe of blackish or a line of blackish streaks; under parts cinnamon-rufous, conspicuously spotted in very young birds with black, the lower abdomen white or pale buffy.

Nest and Eggs.— NEST: A thick but symmetrical bowl, made of mud reinforced with leaves and twigs, in which are frequently woven leaves, twine, paper and rags. It is lined with soft grass, and may be placed (frequently quite near the ground) in any kind of tree, or upon any suitable projection from a house, or within or without barns, sheds, and other outbuildings. EGGS: 4 or 5 (occasionally 6), greenish-blue, unmarked; usually two broods a season and sometimes three.

Distribution.— Eastern and northern North America; breeding from the southern Alleghenies (in western North Carolina, etc.), Pennsylvania, New Jersey, the New England States, Ohio, central and northern Indiana and Illinois, Iowa, northward to the limit of tree growth in Ungava (Fort Chimo), and northwestward to the valley of Kowak River in northwestern Alaska; westward nearly to the Rocky Mountains (to the Pacific at Cook Inlet, Alaska); in winter southward to southern Florida and along the Gulf coast to Texas; accidental or occasional in the Bermudas and Cuba; accidental in Europe (as escapes from captivity?).

The Robin's remarkably wide distribution, its conspicuous plumage (notably the fine red breast and black head of the male), its reputation as a harbinger of spring, and above all its evident fondness for human society, have combined to make it probably the best known bird in America. Its chief rival seems to be the Bluebird, whose range is virtually as great as that of the Robin, and whose plumage is also very beautiful, while its peculiarly sweet and joyous warble is a surer sign of approaching spring than is the appearance of its larger relative. For, although practically all of the Robins who breed in the temperate zone migrate to warmer latitudes in the autumn, their places are taken by birds who have bred further north, so that the species is usually well represented in its northern range even in the dead of winter and where the snow lies deep. At these times, and especially when the weather is very severe, the Robins are most likely to be found in wooded swamps, where there is plenty of cover.

The Bluebird also displays charming confidence in the friendliness of man, and occasionally stays in the north during the winter months; but the Robin is, after all, the more characteristic of the two birds, and the more in evidence, too, because of its fondness for the lawns, and the trustfulness which it displays by building its nest and rearing its lusty family (who also take

Drawing by R. I. Brasher

ROBIN ($\frac{2}{3}$ nat. size)

Everybody knows the Robin and ought to welcome and protect him

to the lawns as soon as they are able to get there) often on the woodwork or in the vines of a porch within a few feet of a window or door. As an instance of the curious and stupid things a bird may do in the way of nest-building, Mr. Burroughs tells the following story:

"I was amused at the case of a Robin that recently came to my knowledge. The bird built its nest in the south end of a rude shed that covered a table at a railroad terminus upon which a locomotive was frequently turned. When her end of the shed was turned to the north she built another nest in the temporary south end, and as the reversal of the shed ends continued from day to day, she soon had two nests and two sets of eggs. When I last heard from her, she was constantly sitting on that particular nest which happened to be for the time being in the end of the shed facing the south. The bewildered bird evidently had had no experience with the tricks of turntables."

Photo by H. T. Middleton

YOUNG ROBIN

The Robin's song has, perhaps, been a little overpraised, doubtless because of its significance in the spring. It is, in fact, a cheerful rather than a melodious warble, composed of ascending and descending phrases, the final one, it must be admitted, likely to end in imperfect vocalization which suggests a lack of control of the vocal cords, and produces an effect not unlike that of the ludicrous break in the tones of a lad whose voice is changing. The call note also is bright and incisive rather than musical.

Another characteristic note of the Robin is sounded when danger is at hand, especially in the form of a cat. This is a peculiar, wailing cry, in a sort of undertone, and expresses both fear and sorrow. Very likely it may be evoked by other enemies, but it more often means a cat and a very young Robin nearby. The bird's foreboding under these conditions is really pitiful; for usually it displays great courage when its young are threatened in the nest, and frequently will swoop down on a prowling cat and actually strike it with its beak, meanwhile shrieking and screaming incessantly. This to-do often attracts other birds, who make common cause with the Robin against their common enemy, with the result that puss may be literally driven away.

Incredible though it may seem, until within a few years ago, the Robin was classified, in several of the southern States, as a "game bird," and as such was killed in countless thousands for food or for "sport." This slaughter of a beautiful and highly useful song bird is now forbidden by the Federal Migratory Bird Law, which became a statute on March 4, 1913, and under which all migratory game and insect-eating birds are made wards of Uncle Sam.

Spencer Trotter says that "Our American Robin was known to the early southern colonists as the 'fieldfare' and is so termed by Catesby. The bird has many of the qualities of its British congener."

The economic status of the Robin probably has received more attention than that of any other bird. There is no denying the fact that the bird eats or injures a great amount of small fruit, especially cherries and berries in their season. On the other hand, it is equally certain that the Robin destroys enormous quantities of noxious insects. Nor should it be forgotten that the bird's raids upon cultivated fruits and berries are due largely to the destruction by man of the wild fruits and berries (especially wild cherries) which form part of its natural and preferred diet.

An examination of 350 stomachs of Robins shows that over 42 per cent. of its food is animal matter, principally insects, while the remainder is made up of small fruits and berries. Over 19 per cent. consists of beetles, about one-third of which are useful ground beetles, taken mostly in spring and fall, when other insects are scarce. Grasshoppers make up about one-tenth of the whole food, but late in August comprise over 30 per cent. Caterpillars form about 6 per cent., while the rest of the animal food is made up of various insects, with a few spiders, snails, and angleworms. All the grasshoppers, caterpillars, and bugs, with a large portion of the beetles, are injurious, and it is safe to say that noxious insects comprise more than one-third of the Robin's food.

ARCADIAN CHICKADEE
Penthestes hudsonicus littoralis (H. Bryant)

CHICKADEE
Penthestes atricapillus atricapillus (Linnaeus)

RED-BREASTED NUTHATCH
Sitta canadensis Linnaeus

FEMALE
WHITE-BREASTED NUTHATCH
Sitta carolinensis carolinensis Latham
MALE FEMALE

MALE
TUFTED TITMOUSE
Baeolophus bicolor (Linnaeus)

All ⅔ nat. size

GOLDEN-CROWNED KINGLET
Regulus satrapa satrapa Licht.
MALE
FEMALE
RUBY-CROWNED KINGLET
Regulus calendula calendula (Linnaeus)
MALE
FEMALE
BLUE-GRAY GNATCATCHER
Polioptila caerulea caerulea (Linnaeus)
FEMALE
All ⅔ nat. size.

WOOD THRUSH
Hylocichla mustelina (Gmelin)
HERMIT THRUSH
Hylocichla guttata pallasi (Cabanis)
GRAY-CHEEKED THRUSH
Hylocichla aliciae aliciae (Baird)
VEERY
Hylocichla fuscescens fuscescens (Stephens)
OLIVE-BACKED THRUSH
Hylocichla ustulata swainsoni (Tschudi)
All ½ nat. size

Courtesy of the New York State Museum

ROBIN *Planesticus migratorius migratorius* (Linnaeus)
ADULT IN SPRING IMMATURE FALL
BLUEBIRD *Sialia sialis sialis* (Linnaeus)
MALE IMMATURE FEMALE
All ½ nat. size

Vegetable food forms nearly 58 per cent. of the stomach contents, over 47 being wild fruits, and only a little more than 4 per cent. being possibly cultivated varieties. Cultivated fruit, amounting to about 25 per cent., was found in the stomachs in June and July, but only a trifle in August. Wild fruit, on the contrary, is eaten in every month, and constitutes a staple food during half the year. The depredations of the Robin seem to be confined to the smaller and earlier fruits.

In view of the fact that the Robin takes ten times as much wild as cultivated fruit, it seems unwise to destroy the birds to save so little. Nor is this necessary, for by a little care both may be preserved. Where much fruit is grown it is no great loss to give up one tree to the birds; and in some cases the crop can be protected by scarecrows. Where wild fruit is not abundant, a few fruit-bearing shrubs and vines judiciously planted will serve for ornament and provide food for the birds. The Russian mulberry is a vigorous grower and a profuse bearer, ripening at the same time as the cherry, and, so far as observation has gone, most birds seem to prefer its fruit to any other. It is believed that a number of these trees planted around the garden or orchard would fully protect the more valuable fruits.

Two variant forms of the American Robin occur within the bounds of the United States. The Southern, or Carolinian, Robin (*Planesticus migratorius achrusterus*) is smaller in size and its color is paler and duller. It is found in the southeastern States. The other is called the Western Robin (*Planesticus migratorius propinquus*). It averages slightly larger than its eastern congener, and the gray of its upper parts is a little more olive and the red of the under parts paler. It is found from Alaska to Mexico and from the Pacific coast to the Great Plains.

Photo by H. T. Middleton

ROBIN ENTERING NEST

VARIED THRUSH

Ixoreus nævius nævius (*Gmelin*)

A. O. U. Number 763

Other Names.— Oregon Robin; Alaska Robin.

General Description.— Length, 10 inches. Upper parts, slate color; under parts, tawny and white, crossed by a band of slate-black. Bill, much shorter than head, slender, and nearly straight; wings, rather long and pointed; tail, shorter than wing, even.

Color.— Adult Male: Above, plain slate color, the feathers, especially those of crown and back, sometimes (in certain lights) slightly darker centrally; wings (except lesser coverts) dusky, with slate-gray edgings, the middle coverts with a large terminal spot (usually triangular in form) of tawny, the greater coverts also broadly tipped with the same (mostly on outer web), the secondaries edged subterminally with a paler and duller tint of the same, the primaries (except two or three outermost) cinnamon-buff on basal portion of outer web and edged with the same half way to tip, the outer web of secondaries also buff basally (concealed by greater coverts), the inner feathers often tipped with pale buffy; two or three outermost tail-feathers with a whitish spot at tip of inner web (largest on the outside feathers); a conspicuous stripe above ears of tawny, extending from middle of upper eyelid (sometimes from above lores) to nape; lores below eyes and sides of head uniform slate-black; *cheeks, chin, throat, and breast uniform tawny,* the chest crossed by rarely interrupted band of slate-black, the feathers sometimes margined with a more slaty hue; sides and flanks similar in color to breast but paler, the feathers broadly margined with olivaceous slate-gray; abdomen, white; under tail-coverts brownish-slate-gray basally, extensively white terminally, the white usually suffused with tawny; under wing-coverts white basally, broadly slate-gray terminally; inner webs of wing feathers crossed by a broad basal band of pale buffy; bill, brownish-black; iris, brown. ADULT FEMALE: Much duller in coloration than the adult male; upper parts varying from olivaceous slate-gray to brownish-olive (still browner on crown); the markings on wings and tail as in the male; tawny color of under parts paler; the band across chest indistinct and never (?) uniform blackish or slate color — usually with feathers dusky centrally (more or less concealed), margined with dull buffy-grayish; white of rear under parts usually (?) relatively more extended than in male.

Nest and Eggs.—NEST: Placed in low bushes always on or near the banks of a stream; it is rather large for the bird; the foundation is a carefully constructed arrangement of interlaced slender twigs; upon this base is erected the main structure of closely interwoven fine grasses, moss and long gray lichens. EGGS: Usually 4, pale greenish-blue, sparsely spotted with dark umber-brown.

Distribution.— Western North America; breeding from northern California, northward to the limit of spruce forests in northern Alaska; the eastern breeding limit is unascertained, but probably includes the spruce forests of the interior mountain districts, at least in British Columbia, possibly to northern Idaho and Montana; wintering from Kodiak Island southward to southern California (as far as Colorado River), and occurring during migration in Montana (Cœur d'Alene Mountains) and straggling eastward to Kansas, New Jersey, New York, and Massachusetts.

Drawing by R. Bruce Horsfall

VARIED THRUSH (½ nat. size)

Act like Robins, but dressed differently

Frequently we have inquiries from people as to a strange bird that comes in the midst of winter down into our western Oregon valleys. It looks and acts like an ordinary Robin, but its dress is so changed from this well-known bird.

The Varied Thrush, Alaska Robin, or Oregon Robin, as it is sometimes called, lives back in the mountains in the wilder sections where the timber is most dense. The bird has a weird and mysterious note, a sort of a monotone song that can be imitated by using a combination whistle and voice note. I have never heard any different song or note from this bird except one summer when we were traveling through the coast mountains of Oregon when a young bird flew along the bank by a wood road. We gave chase and caught it. But the moment I closed my hand on the bird, it cried out in alarm and down swooped a mother Varied Thrush. She was frantic. She let out a variety of exclamatory notes and phrases such as I had never heard in the vocabulary of any bird. It was a surprise to me to know that this solitary, single-note singer was like a Shakespeare in the bird world, for she used such a large vocabulary.

When John Burroughs was a member of the Harriman Expedition to Alaska in 1899, he met this bird for the first time. His thoughts are recorded in some verses which were written at the time:

O Varied Thrush! O Robin strange!
Behold my mute surprise.
Thy form and flight I long have known,
But not this new disguise.

The Varied Thrush is driven down from the high mountains by the snows of winter. When he first comes into the valleys, the later fruits are still hanging on vine and tree. He seems to be ravenously hungry for the sweet-tasting fruit that has been planted by man. His taste sometimes turns to grapes and apples to such an extent that some farmers think him a nuisance.

If one wishes to have Varied Thrushes about his home during the winter, all he has to do is to leave some apples hanging on one of the old trees of the orchard. After the leaves have fallen, the Thrushes will stay as long as the apples last. They seem to live almost entirely on this fruit, especially when the snow is on the ground.

WILLIAM L. FINLEY.

BLUEBIRD

Sialia sialis sialis (*Linnæus*)

A. O. U. Number 766 See Color Plate 106

Other Names.— Eastern Bluebird; Wilson's Bluebird; Blue Robin; Common Bluebird; Blue Redbreast; American Bluebird.

General Description.— Length, 7 inches. Upper parts, bright blue; under parts, cinnamon-chestnut and white. Bill, small and slender; wings, long and pointed; tail, shorter than wing, distinctly notched; legs, short.

Color.— ADULT MALE: Upper parts, uniform bright blue, the shafts of wing- and tail-feathers black; and tips of wing-feathers (especially primaries) dusky; sides of head including cheeks (sometimes including

Drawing by R. I. Brasher

BLUEBIRD (⅓ nat. size)

His soft warble, beautiful blue coat, warm waistcoat, and gentle manners make him the most welcome herald of spring

also chin and sides of upper throat), lighter and grayer blue; throat, chest, breast, sides, and flanks, uniform dull cinnamon-chestnut; abdomen, anal region, and under tail-coverts, white, the last with longer feathers tinged with pale grayish-blue, the shorter ones with pale cinnamon-rufous; under wing-coverts, pale grayish-blue; bill, black; iris, dark brown. ADULT FEMALE: Above, bluish-gray tinged with light grayish-brown (especially in autumn and winter), passing into bright blue on rump, upper tail-coverts, and tail; wings, blue, the inner quills and innermost greater coverts edged with pale brownish-gray or whitish, the outermost primary edged with white; front and lateral under parts, dull rufous-cinnamon (paler in summer, deeper in fresh autumn plumage), the chin and upper throat paler; abdomen, anal region, and under tail-coverts, white.

Photo by S. A. Lottridge

NEST OF BLUEBIRD

Section of tree cut away to show nest. The birds entered through hole above

Nest and Eggs.— NEST: The natural nesting-sites are in deserted Woodpecker holes, hollows of decayed trees, or crevices of rocks; it was one of the first birds to take advantage of "modern conveniences" and quickly appropriated boxes placed around the farm houses for its occupancy; hollows in old rail-fences are often used and in some parts of New England a large percentage of nests are so located; more rarely the pair usurp a Swallow's nest; the nest is composed of grass, weed stalks, a few bits of bark, and lined with finer grass-blades. EGGS: 4 to 6, rarely 7 and usually 5, plain light bluish-white in color.

Distribution.— United States and southern Canada east of Rocky Mountains; north to Nova Scotia, southern New Brunswick, southern Maine, Vermont, northern New York (Adirondacks), northern Ontario and Manitoba, occasionally to northern New Brunswick, northern Maine and southern Quebec; west to eastern base of Rocky Mountains, in Montana, Wyoming and Colorado; breeding southward to southern Florida and along the Gulf Coast to southern and west-central Texas; Bermudas (resident); accidental in Cuba.

This beautiful and singularly lovable bird divides with the Robin the grateful mission of bringing to its northern human friends the welcome news that spring is at hand. In the article on the Robin, it is explained that many individuals of that species remain during the winter months in northern latitudes of the United States. Few Bluebirds do this; and their appearance in the spring is, therefore, much more significant than is the Robin's. To be sure, the Bluebird's migratory instinct occasionally gets the better of his meteorological discretion, so that his greeting to his northern breeding grounds is sometimes a howling "north-easter," bringing snow and freezing temperatures which drive him back to the southland, or not infrequently cost him his life.

A real tragedy of this kind occurred in the spring of 1895, when many species of migratory birds, but especially the Bluebirds, were caught in the wave of severely cold weather which swept through the Middle and Gulf States. Thousands of Bluebirds perished in the storms and bitter cold which lasted for a week or more; their frozen bodies were found everywhere — in barns and other outhouses where the poor things had vainly sought shelter; in the fields and woods and even along the roadsides. In the localities affected, they were almost exterminated. To many people it was a sad spring in those regions.

Much dubious ornithology has been produced by poets from whose minds facts are crowded out by fancies, but James Russell Lowell revealed a trained eye, as well as an appreciation of the beautiful, when he wrote (in "Under the Willows") of

> The Bluebird, shifting his light load of song,
> From post to post along the cheerless fence,

a pretty spring habit of the bird which has delighted many a wayfarer.

Like the Robin, the Bluebird shows a decided fondness for human society. Orchards are favorite natural resorts of the bird, and furnish plenty of home-sites in the shape of hollow trunks or limbs of trees, for the bird always prefers a cavity of some kind wherein to place its nest. The wise owner of such trees will do his utmost to encourage this tenancy. Indeed, if he will scatter through his orchard a goodly supply of Bluebird homes, in the form of short sections of hollow limbs, covered at the top and bottom, and with an auger-hole doorway, he will soon have plenty of Bluebird tenants, who will pay their rent many times over by destroying injurious insects and worms. For, with the possible exceptions of the House Wren and the Purple Martin, the Bluebird is as willing as any bird to set up housekeeping in a dwelling for him made and provided.

The sentimental aspects of the society of Bluebirds will not be overlooked by people who appreciate manifestations of very genuine domestic peace and happiness. None of our common birds are so demonstrative in their expressions of devotion to each other, and in their affectionate solicitude for their young. The note of lament which is so plainly expressed in the Bluebird's abbreviated warble as it prepares to follow the retreating summer, brings a sympathetic echo from many a human heart.

George Gladden.

The Bluebird has not been accused, so far as known, of stealing fruit or of preying upon crops. An examination by the United States Biological Survey of 855 stomachs showed that 68 per cent. of the food consisted of insects and their allies, while the other 32 per cent. was made up of various vegetable substances and was found mostly in stomachs taken in winter. Beetles constituted 21 per cent. of the whole food, grasshoppers 22, caterpillars 10, and various other insects 9, while a number of spiders and myriapods, about 6 per cent., comprised the remainder of the animal diet. All these are more or less harmful, except a few predacious beetles, which amounted to 9 per cent. The destruction of grasshoppers by Bluebirds is very noticeable in August and September, when these insects make up about 53 per cent. of the diet. So far as its vegetable food is concerned the Bluebird is positively harmless. The only trace of any useful product in the stomachs consisted of a few blackberry seeds, and even these probably belonged to wild rather than cultivated varieties.

The Azure Bluebird (*Sialia sialis fulva*) wanders over the Mexican border into Arizona. It is much like the type species, though the browns of its plumage are paler, the grayish-blue nearer a gray-white, and the blue of the upper parts greener.

WESTERN BLUEBIRD

Sialia mexicana occidentalis *J. K. Townsend*

A. O. U. Number 767

Other Name.— California Bluebird.

General Description.— Length, 7 inches. Male: Upper parts, cobalt-blue; under parts, blue and red. Female: Upper parts, grayish-brown and blue; under parts, grayish-brown, brownish-gray, and cinnamon-rufous. Bill, small and slender; wings, long and pointed; tail, shorter than wing, distinctly notched; legs, short.

Color.— Adult Male: Above, plain rich cobalt-blue, brighter blue on rump, upper tail-coverts, tail, and outer webs of primaries; shafts of feathers of wing and tail, sometimes also of shoulder, the upper tail-coverts sometimes with streaks of black; a patch of chestnut on back between shoulders; sides of head, chin, throat, upper central (usually also whole center of) chest, and breast, uniform blue, slightly paler and duller than color of upper parts, the blue gradually fading on abdomen and flanks into pale gray; sides of chest and breast and front part of sides, chestnut, this extended across chest, connecting the two lateral areas, extending along sides to flanks; under tail-coverts, blue edged basally with pale gray; under wing-coverts, darker blue; bill, black; iris, dark brown. Adult Female: Crown, hindneck, dark brownish-gray; back and shoulders, light grayish-brown forming a distinct patch; rump and lesser wing-coverts, dull blue, the former rather brighter, passing into bright blue on upper tail-coverts and tail; middle and greater wing-coverts and inner quills, dusky grayish-brown edged with paler brownish-gray or bluish; secondaries, dull bluish; the primaries, lighter and brighter blue narrowly edged with whitish, the outermost broadly edged with white; sides of head, throat, center portion of upper chest, and breast, light brownish-gray passing into dull grayish on chin; sides of chest and breast and more or less of sides, dull cinnamon-rufous; abdomen and flanks, pale grayish-brown; under tail-coverts pale dull grayish-blue, edged with pale brownish-gray, usually with a dusky shaft-streak; under wing-coverts, dull grayish-blue or bluish-gray; bill and iris as in male.

Nest and Eggs.— Nest: In holes of dead trees, between the trunk and loose bark, and, in the more settled parts of its range, in boxes supplied for the purpose; comprised of sticks, straw, hay, or any similar material. Eggs: 4 or 5, uniform pale blue, somewhat deeper in shade than those of the Eastern Bluebird.

Distribution.— Pacific coast district from Los Angeles county, California, to British Columbia, chiefly from the coast to the western slope of the Sierra Nevada and Cascade ranges, but extending eastward through eastern Oregon and Washington to northern Idaho and western Montana (breeding); northward to British Columbia (Vancouver Island); southward in winter as far as San Pedro Martir Mountains, Lower California.

This form so strongly resembles the Common Bluebird of the Eastern States that only a trained eye would detect the color difference between the two birds. Its habits and disposition, too, are virtually those of the eastern bird, nor is there any material difference between the economic status of the two, both undoubtedly doing very valuable work in the destruction of insect-pests.

In an examination of 217 stomachs of the Western Bluebird, animal matter (insects and spiders) was found to the extent of 82 per cent. and vegetable matter to the extent of 18 per cent. The bulk of the former consisted of bugs, grasshoppers, and caterpillars. Grasshoppers, when they can be obtained, are eaten freely during the whole season. Caterpillars also are a favorite food and are eaten during every month of the year; March is the month of greatest consumption, with 50 per cent., and the average for the year is 20 per cent. Two stomachs taken in January contained 64 and 50 per cent., respectively, of caterpillars. Beetles also are eaten and comprise mostly harmful species. The vegetable matter consists of weed seeds and small fruits. In December a few grapes are eaten, but elderberries are the favorites whenever they can be found.

The southern Rocky Mountain region has two slightly differing forms of Western Bluebird. The Chestnut-backed Bluebird (*Sialia mexicana bairdi*) ranges through Utah, Colorado, and western Texas south into Mexico; the San Pedro Bluebird (*Sialia mexicana anabelæ*) breeds in San Pedro Martir Mountains.

MOUNTAIN BLUEBIRD

Sialia currucoides (*Bechstein*)

A. O. U. Number 768

Other Name.—Arctic Bluebird.

General Description.— Length, 7¼ inches. Male: Upper parts, cerulean-blue; under parts, turquoise-blue and white. Female: Upper parts, gray and turquoise-blue; under parts, brownish-gray and white. Bill, small and slender; wings, long and pointed; tail, shorter than wing, distinctly notched; legs, short.

Color.— Adult Male: Above, plain rich cerulean-blue, the wings and tail slightly more cobalt-blue; shafts of wing- and tail-feathers, black, and terminal portion of primaries, dusky; *sides of head, chin, throat, chest, breast, and sides plain turquoise-blue,* decidedly paler and less bright than color of upper parts; abdomen, hinder flanks, anal region, and shorter under tail-coverts white; longer under tail-coverts pale turquoise tipped or margined with white; bill, black; iris, dark brown. Adult Female: Crown, hindneck, back, and shoulders plain mouse-gray, sometimes faintly tinged with greenish-blue; rump, upper tail-coverts, tail, and wing (except inner feathers), turquoise-blue; inner quills and greater wing-coverts, similar in color to back, but darker, edged with paler, and sometimes tinged with blue; lesser and middle wing-coverts dull greenish-blue, or else dusky brownish-gray margined with bluish; an eye-ring of dull white; sides of head similar in color to crown but rather browner; chin, throat, chest, breast, and sides, pale brownish-gray passing into dull white on abdomen, hinder flanks, anal region, and under tail-coverts, the longer of the latter with dusky shaft-streaks and sometimes tinged with blue; bill and iris as in the male.

Nest and Eggs.— Nest: Placed in a hollow limb,

abandoned Woodpecker hole, corners of barns and outbuildings, and even under the eaves of porches or houses; in parts of the West, old abandoned mine shafts are utilized; the nest is built almost entirely of dried grass, and is lined occasionally with a few feathers and fine strips of cedar or other tree bark. EGGS: From 4 to 7, usually 5, plain greenish-blue.

Distribution.— Mountain districts of western North America; north to Mackenzie and Yukon Territory; breeding southward to higher mountains of New Mexico and Arizona (San Francisco and Mogollon Mountains), and Chihuahua, eastward to eastern Wyoming (Black Hills) and northwestern Texas, westward to the Sierra Nevada and Cascade ranges; wintering southward from southern California and Colorado to Guadalupe Island, Lower California, northern Sonora, and northwestern Chihuahua and eastward to Kansas, Oklahoma, and Texas.

Though it is somewhat larger, and has a proportionately shorter tail, the Mountain Bluebird presents a general appearance very similar to that of its eastern relative. As its name indicates, however, it has a distinct liking for the mountains. Wells W. Cooke found the birds in Colorado above timber-line to at least 13,000 feet. Another observer records being greeted by a little family of them near the summit of San Antonio Peak ("Old Baldy,") in southern California, at an altitude of nearly 10,000 feet, at that time far above the clouds, through whose dense billows the highest of the surrounding peaks protruded like islands in a motionless sea. The indescribable weirdness of the scene, and the unearthly quiet, which had deeply impressed the lone wanderer, had no apparent effect upon the Bluebirds, whose warbling was as sweet and gentle up there above the clouds as that of their eastern brethern in a Connecticut Valley orchard.

Their insect food is obtainable at all times of the year, and the general diet varies only in the fall, when some fruit, principally elderberries, is eaten, though an occasional blackberry or grape is also relished.

Drawing by R. I. Brasher

MOUNTAIN BLUEBIRD (½ nat. size)

A gentle mountaineer often found far above timber-line

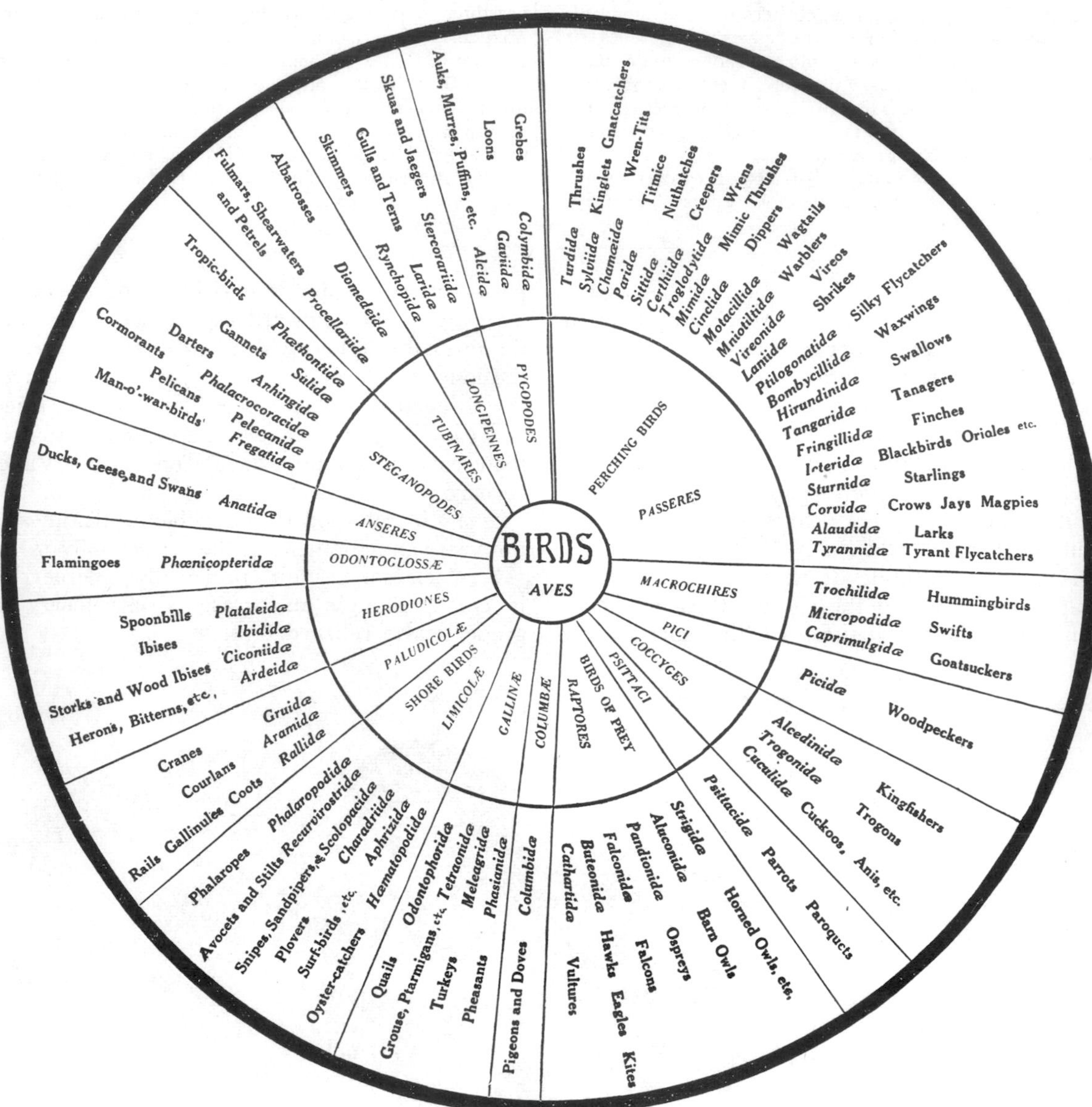

The above Chart is limited to a consideration of the birds of America, and follows the terminology of the official Check List of the American Ornithologists' Union, and of the preceding pages of the present work. It will be noted that the Class, Birds, comprises seventeen Orders in North America, the names of which are listed in the second circle. These Orders are subdivided into Families. Beginning with the lowest form, the Grebes, the gradual development of bird life can be traced around the circle to the highest form, the Thrushes.

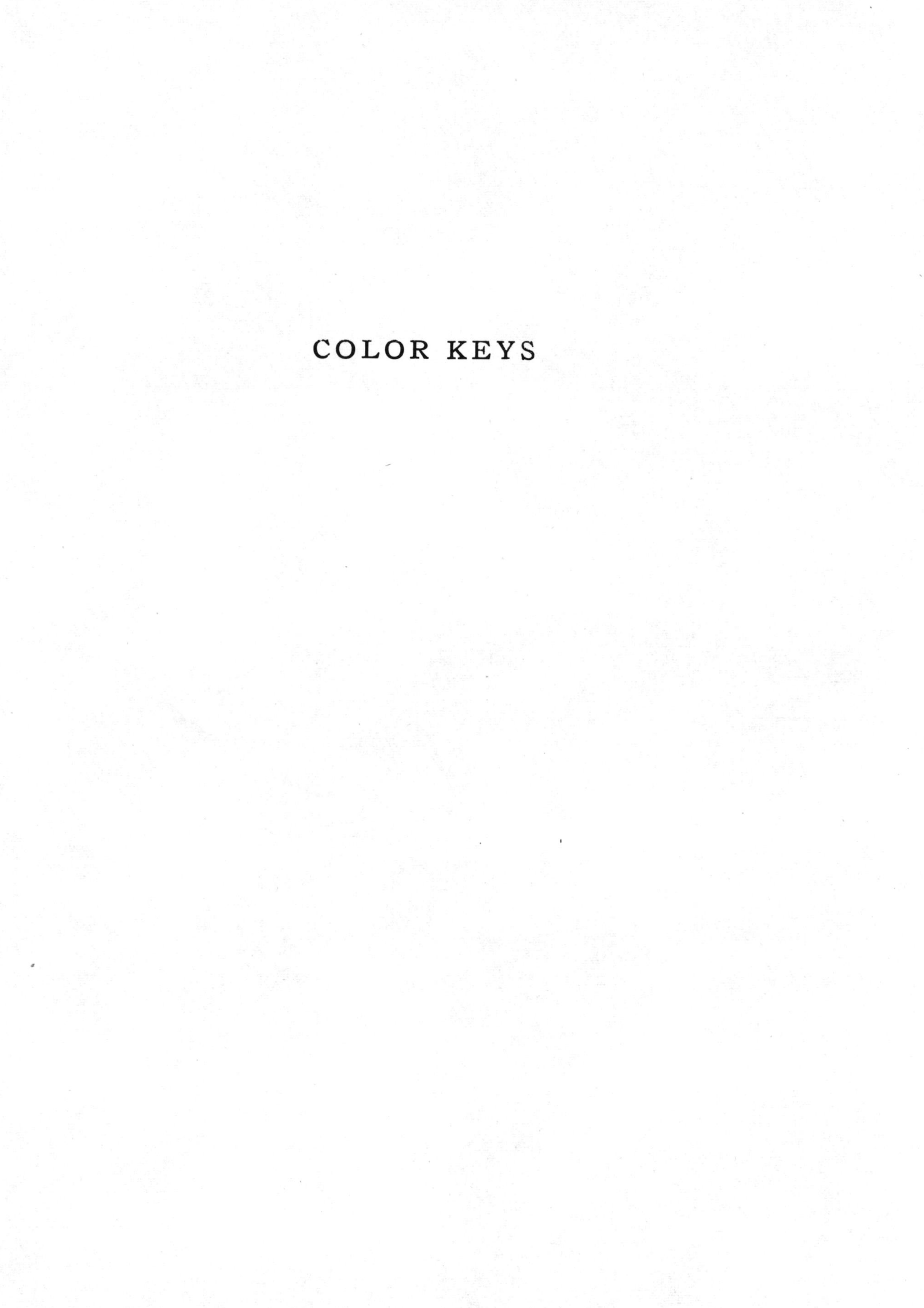

COLOR KEYS

COLOR KEY TO WATER BIRDS

BLACK

Size of Duck or Larger

Sooty Shearwater
Water Turkey
Cormorant
Double-crested Cormorant
Brandt's Cormorant
Man-o'-war-bird
Black Duck
Florida Duck
Scoter
White-winged Scoter
Surf Scoter
Black-footed Albatross

Smaller than Duck

Fork-tailed Petrel
Least Petrel
Kaeding's Petrel
Storm Petrel
Wilson's Petrel
Black Tern
Black Rail
Coot
Black Oyster-catcher

BLACK AND WHITE

Size of Duck or Larger

Western Grebe
Loon
Black-throated Loon
Murre
California Murre
Brünnich's Murre
Razor-billed Auk
Great Auk
Great Black-backed Gull
Black Skimmer
Laysan Albatross
Scaup Duck
Lesser Scaup Duck
Ring-necked Duck
Golden-eye (head purple)
Barrow's Golden-eye (head greenish)
Buffle-head
Harlequin Duck
Labrador Duck
Steller's Eider
Spectacled Eider
Northern Eider
Eider
King Eider
Canada Goose (back brown)
Hutchins's Goose (back brown)
White-cheeked Goose (back brown)
Cackling Goose (back brown)
Brant (back brown)
Black Brant (back brown)
Merganser
Hooded Merganser (head green)
Mallard (head green)
Shoveller (head green)
Old-squaw
Yellow-crowned Night Heron

Smaller than Duck

Horned Grebe
Eared Grebe
Tufted Puffin
Puffin
Cassin's Auklet
Crested Auklet
Least Auklet
Ancient Murrelet
Black Guillemot
Pigeon Guillemot
Dovekie
Pomarine Jaeger
Parasitic Jaeger
Long-tailed Jaeger
Sooty Tern
Greater Shearwater
Leach's Petrel
Black-crowned Night Heron
Black-necked Stilt
Black-bellied Plover
Golden Plover
Oyster-catcher
Black Turnstone
Purple Sandpiper
Aleutian Sandpiper
Pribilof Sandpiper
Greater Yellow-legs
Yellow-legs
Solitary Sandpiper
Western Solitary Sandpiper

BLACK, RED, AND WHITE

Size of Duck or Smaller

Holbœll's Grebe
Red-throated Loon
Red-breasted Merganser
Wood Duck
Redhead
Canvas-back
Red Phalarope
Red-backed Sandpiper

WHITE

Size of Duck or Larger

Ivory Gull
Glaucous Gull
Glaucous-winged Gull
Yellow-billed Tropic-bird
Red-billed Tropic-bird
Gannet

Snow Goose
Greater Snow Goose
Whistling Swan
Trumpeter Swan
Roseate Spoonbill
White Ibis

Wood Ibis
Great White Heron
Egret
Whooping Crane
White Pelican

Smaller than Duck

Ross's Gull
Snowy Egret

Little Blue Heron (white phase)
Avocet (primaries black)

BROWNISH

Size of Duck or Larger

Skua
Booby (whitish below)

Brown Pelican
White-fronted Goose

Limpkin

Smaller than Duck

Bittern

Noddy

BROWNISH, MIXED OR STREAKED WITH YELLOWISH OR WHITE

(Usually lighter below)

Size of Duck or Larger

Gadwall
European Widgeon

Baldpate
Pintail

Smaller than Duck

Cory's Shearwater
Least Bittern
King Rail
California Clapper Rail
Clapper Rail
Louisiana Clapper Rail
Caribbean Clapper Rail
Virginia Rail
Sora
Yellow Rail
Woodcock
Wilson's Snipe

Dowitcher
Long-billed Dowitcher
Stilt Sandpiper
Pectoral Sandpiper
White-rumped Sandpiper
Baird's Sandpiper
Least Sandpiper
Semipalmated Sandpiper
Western Sandpiper
Marbled Godwit
Pacific Godwit

Hudsonian Godwit
Willet
Western Willet
Upland Plover
Buff-breasted Sandpiper
Spotted Sandpiper
Hudsonian Curlew
Long-billed Curlew
Eskimo Curlew
Turnstone
Ruddy Turnstone

RED

Larger than Duck

Flamingo

BLUISH-GRAY ABOVE, WHITE BELOW

Size of Duck or Larger

Herring Gull
California Gull
Ring-billed Gull
Fulmar
Pacific Fulmar
Blue Goose
Emperor Goose
Great Blue Heron

Smaller than Duck

Kittiwake
Pacific Kittiwake
Laughing Gull (head black)
Franklin's Gull (head black)
Bonaparte's Gull
Sabine's Gull (head black)
Heermann's Gull (head white)
Gull-billed Tern
Caspian Tern
Royal Tern
Cabot's Tern
Forster's Tern
Common Tern
Arctic Tern
Roseate Tern
Least Tern
Northern Phalarope
Sanderling
Knot (breast chestnut)
Surf-bird

All the Terns in this group have the crown black

SLATE-GRAY

Larger than Duck

Little Brown Crane
Sandhill Crane

Smaller than Duck

Florida Gallinule
Louisiana Heron (white below)
Little Blue Heron (dark phase)

CHESTNUT

Size of Duck or Larger

Green-winged Teal (back mottled gray and white, breast spotted with black)
Blue-winged Teal (head gray, white crescent in front of eye)
Cinnamon Teal (back mottled with dusky and brown)
Ruddy Duck (crown black, cheeks and chin white)
Glossy Ibis (back irridescent blackish)
White-faced Glossy Ibis (back irridescent blackish, face white)

GREENISH

Smaller than Duck

Green Heron (throat streaked with dark chestnut)

GRAYISH-BROWN ABOVE, WHITE BELOW

Smaller than Duck

Semipalmated Plover
Ringed Plover
Piping Plover
Snowy Plover
Wilson's Plover
Mountain Plover
Killdeer (two black bands on breast)
Wilson's Phalarope (neck rufous)

PURPLE

Smaller than Duck

Purple Gallinule

COLOR KEY TO LAND BIRDS

BLACK

Size of Crow or Larger

California Vulture
Wild Turkey
Black Vulture
Raven
White-necked Raven
Rough-legged Hawk
Zone-tailed Hawk
Crow
Dusky Grouse
Franklin's Grouse
Bald Eagle (young)
Black Gyrfalcon
Everglade Kite
Audubon's Caracara
Fish Crow
Hudsonian Spruce Partridge

Size between Crow and Robin

Ivory-billed Woodpecker
Lewis's Woodpecker
Groove-billed Ani
Purple Grackle
Brewer's Blackbird
Rusty Blackbird
Pileated Woodpecker
Boat-tailed Grackle
Starling

Smaller than Robin

Purple Martin
Cowbird
Red-eyed Cowbird
Phainopepla
Catbird
Black Swift
Dipper

BLACK AND WHITE

Size of Crow or Larger

Bald Eagle
Swallow-tailed Kite
Duck Hawk
Osprey

Size between Crow and Robin

Magpie
Nighthawk
Pigeon Hawk

Smaller than Robin

Hairy Woodpecker
Black-headed Grosbeak
Downy Woodpecker
Texas Woodpecker
White-headed Woodpecker
Williamson's Sapsucker
Towhee
Arctic Towhee
Snow Bunting
Slate-colored Junco
Seaside Sparrow
Barn Swallow
Arctic Three-toed Woodpecker
Three-toed Woodpecker
Ant-eating Woodpecker
Nuttall's Woodpecker
Red-cockaded Woodpecker
Kingbird
Bobolink (male, summer)
Black Phœbe
Cliff Swallow
Lark Bunting
White-throated Swift

BLACK AND RED

Smaller than Robin

Red-winged Blackbird
Bicolored Red-wing
Scarlet Tanager
Western Tanager
Painted Redstart

BLACK, RED, AND WHITE

Size of Robin

Rose-breasted Grosbeak
Red-headed Woodpecker
Red-bellied Woodpecker
Golden-fronted Woodpecker
Gila Woodpecker
Tricolored Red-wing
Red-breasted Sapsucker

BLACK AND ORANGE

Smaller than Robin

Baltimore Oriole

BLACK AND YELLOW

Size of Robin

Audubon's Oriole
Bullock's Oriole
Scott's Oriole
Sennett's Oriole
Yellow-bellied Sapsucker
Yellow-headed Blackbird
Evening Grosbeak
Meadowlark (brown above)
Western Meadowlark (gray above)

Smaller than Robin

Goldfinch
Arkansas Goldfinch

BLACK AND BROWN

Smaller than Robin

Orchard Oriole

WHITE

Size of Crow or Larger

White Gyrfalcon
Snowy Owl
White-tailed Kite (upper parts pale-gray, shoulders black)

Size between Crow and Robin

Willow Ptarmigan (winter)
Rock Ptarmigan (winter)
White-tailed Ptarmigan (winter)

Smaller than Robin

Snow Bunting (some brownish)

BROWNISH

Size of Crow or Larger

Golden Eagle
Turkey Vulture
Great Horned Owl
Ruffed Grouse
Spotted Owl
Marsh Hawk (young, rump white)

Size between Crow and Robin

Chuck-will's-widow
Sparrow Hawk
Boat-tailed Grackle (female)
Whip-poor-will
Mourning Dove
California Thrasher

Smaller than Robin

Cañon Towhee
Abert's Towhee
European Goldfinch (face red, wing-patch yellow)
Olive-sided Flycatcher (streaked above and below)
Crested Flycatcher
Chimney Swift
Vaux's Swift
Cedar Waxwing
Bohemian Waxwing
Gray-crowned Rosy Finch
Carolina Wren
House Wren
Winter Wren
Brown Creeper (streaked lengthwise with lighter)
Say's Phœbe
Bank Swallow
Rough-winged Swallow

BROWNISH, MIXED OR STREAKED WITH YELLOWISH OR WHITE

(Usually lighter below)

Size of Crow or Larger

Goshawk (young)
Red-tailed Hawk
Harris's Hawk
Red-shouldered Hawk
Swainson's Hawk
Rough-legged Hawk (light phase)
Gryfalcon
Prairie Falcon
Broad-winged Hawk
Road-runner
Prairie Chicken
Heath Hen
Sage Hen
Sharp-tailed Grouse
Barred Owl
Long-eared Owl
Short-eared Owl
Barn Owl

Size between Crow and Robin

Cooper's Hawk (young)
Pigeon Hawk (young)
Sharp-shinned Hawk (young)
Hawk Owl
Saw-whet Owl
Richardson's Owl
Burrowing Owl
Screech Owl
Willow Ptarmigan (summer)
Rock Ptarmigan (summer)
White-tailed Ptarmigan (summer)
Bob-white
Masked Bob-white
Mearns's Quail
Poor-will
Brown Thrasher
Flicker (transversely barred with black on back)

Smaller than Robin

Red-winged Blackbird (female)
Bobolink (male in autumn, female, and young)
Williamson's Sapsucker (female)
Pygmy Owl
Elf Owl
Coues's Flycatcher
Purple Finch (female)
House Finch
Redpoll
Pine Siskin
Lapland Longspur
Ipswich Sparrow
Savannah Sparrow
Grasshopper Sparrow
Henslow's Sparrow
Sharp-tailed Sparrow
Lark Sparrow
Harris's Sparrow
White-crowned Sparrow
White-throated Sparrow
Golden-crowned Sparrow
Tree Sparrow
Chipping Sparrow
Field Sparrow
Pine-woods Sparrow
Song Sparrow
Lincoln's Sparrow
Vesper Sparrow
Swamp Sparrow
Fox Sparrow
Skylark
Pipit
Sage Thrasher
Cactus Wren
Rock Wren
Bewick's Wren
Short-billed Marsh Wren
Long-billed Marsh Wren
Wren-Tit
Wood Thrush
Veery
Gray-cheeked Thrush
Olive-backed Thrush
Russett-backed Thrush
Hermit Thrush
Ground Dove
Inca Dove

RED

Size of Robin or Smaller

Cardinal
Summer Tanager
Crossbill
White-winged Crossbill
Pine Grosbeak (upper parts gray)
Purple Finch (male)
Varied Bunting (forehead and rump blue)
Painted Bunting

BLUE

Size between Crow and Robin

Arizona Jay
Florida Jay
California Jay (below white)
Woodhouse's Jay (below gray)
Steller's Jay (head black)
Blue Jay

Smaller than Robin

Bluebird (breast rufous)
Mountain Bluebird (white below)
Western Bluebird (breast and back rufous)
Blue Grosbeak
Indigo Bunting (male)
Lazuli Bunting (male)

GREEN

Size between Crow and Robin

Carolina Paroquet
Thick-billed Parrot
Coppery-tailed Trogon
Green Jay

Smaller than Robin

Rivoli's Hummingbird
Ruby-throated Hummingbird
Blue-throated Hummingbird
Black-chinned Hummingbird
Anna's Hummingbird
Broad-tailed Hummingbird
Rufous Hummingbird

GREEN AND WHITE

Smaller than Robin

Texas Kingfisher
Violet-green Swallow
Tree Swallow

GRAYISH

(Usually lighter below)

Size of Crow or Larger

Mississippi Kite (ashy below)
Great Gray Owl
Marsh Hawk (rump white)
Goshawk (finely barred below)
Sennett's White-tailed Hawk (shoulders rufous)

Size Between Crow and Robin

Clarke's Nutcracker
Sharp-shinned Hawk (rufous, barred, below)
Cooper's Hawk (rufous, barred, below)
Screech Owl (gray phase)
Yellow-billed Cuckoo
Black-billed Cuckoo
Canada Jay

Size of Robin or Smaller

Robin (rufous below)
Bendire's Thrasher
Leconte's Thrasher
Crissal Thrasher
Mockingbird
Northern Shrike
Loggerhead Shrike
Townsend's Solitaire
Scissor-tailed Flycatcher
Gray Kingbird
Phœbe
Wood Pewee
Western Wood Pewee
Least Flycatcher
Yellow-bellied Flycatcher
Horned Lark
Black-chinned Sparrow
Black-throated Sparrow
Arizona Pyrrhuloxia (crimson in center below)
Bell's Sparrow
Dickcissel
Warbling Vireo
Philadelphia Vireo
Black-capped Vireo
Bell's Vireo
Tufted Titmouse
Bridled Titmouse
Black-crested Titmouse
Chickadee
Mountain Chickadee
Hudsonian Chickadee
Acadian Chickadee
Chestnut-backed Chickadee
Bush-Tit
Verdin

BLUISH-GRAY

(lighter below)

Size between Crow and Robin

Band-tailed Pigeon
Passenger Pigeon (rufous below)
White-winged Dove
Mountain Quail
California Quail
Scaled Quail
Gambel's Quail
Belted Kingfisher
Piñon Jay
Varied Thrush (below rusty, black chest-band)

Smaller Than Robin

Red-breasted Nuthatch (rufous below)
Brown-headed Nuthatch
Pygmy Nuthatch
White-breasted Nuthatch
Blue-gray Gnatcatcher

GREENISH-GRAY

(usually white or yellowish below)

Size of Robin or Smaller

Arkansas Kingbird
Green-tailed Towhee (crown rufous)
Texas Sparrow (crown brown, white center stripe)
Yellow-throated Vireo
Red-eyed Vireo
Blue-headed Vireo
White-eyed Vireo
Ruby-crowned Kinglet
Golden-crowned Kinglet
Alder Flycatcher
Traill's Flycatcher
Acadian Flycatcher
Western Flycatcher
Yellow-bellied Flycatcher

COLOR KEY TO WARBLERS

BLACK AND WHITE STRIPED

Black and White Warbler
Myrtle Warbler
Black-poll Warbler
Audubon's Warbler

BLACK AND RED

Redstart

BLACK AND YELLOW

Townsend's Warbler
Golden-cheeked Warbler
Blackburnian Warbler
Hermit Warbler
Magnolia Warbler

BLACK AND GRAY

Golden-winged Warbler
Black-throated Gray Warbler

BLACK, GRAY, AND YELLOW

Yellow-throated Warbler
Grace's Warbler

YELLOW

Prothonotary Warbler
Cape May Warbler
Wilson's Warbler
Blue-winged Warbler
Yellow Warbler

OLIVE ABOVE; YELLOW BELOW

Yellow-breasted Chat
Maryland Yellow-throat
Mourning Warbler
Ovenbird
Black-throated Green Warbler
Olive Warbler
Hooded Warbler
Belding's Yellow-throat
Macgillivray's Warbler
Kentucky Warbler
Yellow Palm Warbler
Kirtland's Warbler
Prairie Warbler
Lawrence's Warbler
Black-throated Blue Warbler (female)

OLIVE ABOVE; WHITE BELOW

Chestnut-sided Warbler

DUSKY OLIVE ABOVE; WHITISH OR YELLOWISH BELOW

Swainson's Warbler
Tennessee Warbler
Pine Warbler
Louisiana Water-Thrush
Bay-breasted Warbler
Worm-eating Warbler
Nashville Warbler
Water-Thrush
Connecticut Warbler

GRAY ABOVE; WHITE BELOW

Brewster's Warbler
Virginia's Warbler
Lucy's Warbler
Parula Warbler

GRAY ABOVE; YELLOW BELOW

Canada Warbler

BLUE ABOVE; WHITE BELOW

Cerulean Warbler

BLUE AND BLACK; WHITE BELOW

Black-throated Blue Warbler (male)

GLOSSARY

GLOSSARY

(*For the scientific names of the orders, suborders, and families of birds, consult the Index.*)

Abdominal. Relating to the abdomen or belly.

Abnormal. Irregular; not conforming to the type.

Acuminate. Terminating in a long tapering point.

Acute. Sharp-pointed.

Adult. Of breeding age, usually with fully mature plumage.

Aërial. Inhabiting the air; performed in the air.

Air-sac. Any one of the spaces, in different parts of the bodies of birds, which are filled with air and connected with the air passages of the lungs.

Albinism. An abnormal condition of plumage, in which white replaces the ordinary colors.

Albino. Affected with albinism.

Algæ. Seaweed.

Alpine. Pertaining to high altitudes, chiefly near timber line.

Altricial. Young are helpless.

Amphipod. Of or belonging to the Amphipoda, a suborder of crustaceans including the sand fleas and allied forms.

Anal region. The feathered region immediately surrounding the anus or vent.

Annulated. Surrounded by rings of color.

Anterior. Forward; in front of.

Anus. The vent.

Apex. Tip or point.

Apical. Relating to the tip or point.

Aquatic. Pertaining to or living in the water.

Arboreal. Pertaining to or living in trees.

Attenuate, attenuated. Growing gradually narrower toward the tip, but not sharply pointed.

Auriculars. Ear-coverts; ear region.

Avi-fauna. The bird-life of a given region.

Axillaries, axillars. The elongated feathers growing from the axilla or armpit.

Bar. A transverse mark.

Basal. Relating to or situated at the base. The basal part of a feather is that part where it enters the skin; the basal part of the bill is that part nearest the head, and not the lower mandible.

Belt. A broad band of color across the breast or belly.

Bevy. A flock, as of Quails.

Bicolor. Of two colors.

Boreal. Northern; used by scientists to designate a division of the earth comprised of its northern and mountainous parts.

Bristle. A small hairlike feather near the angle of the mouth, or rictus.

Bronchi. One of the subdivisions of the windpipe.

Calcareous. Chalky; limy.

Cambium. In certain shrubs and trees the ring of tissue which separates the wood from the bark.

Carnivorous. Flesh-eating; feeding or preying on other animals.

Carpal. Pertaining to the carpus or wrist.

Carpal joint. The bend of the wing.

Caudal. Relating to the tail.

Cere. A soft swollen area at the base of the upper part of the bill.

Cervical. Pertaining to the cervix or hind neck.

Cinereous. Ash-colored; of a clear bluish-gray.

Clavicle. The collar bone.

Clutch. A complement of eggs; a brood of chicks.

Coalesce. To unite; to grow together.

Collar. A ring of colored feathers encircling the neck.

Commissure. The line formed by the closed mandibles of a bird's bill.

Complement. The full number, as of the eggs of a bird; clutch.

Compressed. Flattened from side to side; the opposite of depressed.

Concentric. Having a common center, as rings or circles one within another.

Concolor. Of the same color as (some other object); of uniform color.

Confluent. Running into or blending in a complete whole; — said of colors in plumage.

Coniferous. Bearing cones, as the cypress and pine.

Conoid, conoidal. Resembling or approaching a cone in shape.

Contour feathers. The common feathers that form the general covering of a bird, determining its shape.

Corrugate, corrugated. Furrowed; wrinkled.

Cosmopolitan. Not restricted to any locality; found in all countries; world-wide.

Covert. Any one of the special feathers covering the bases of the quills of the wings and tail of a bird. They are called upper tail-coverts, lower tail-coverts, greater coverts, lesser wing-coverts, etc., according to location.

Covey. An old bird with her brood; a small flock; — used chiefly of Grouse and Partridges.

Crepuscular. Active at twilight.

Crescentic. Crescent-shaped.

Crest. A tuft of feathers on the top of the head.

Crested. Furnished with a crest.

Crown. The top part of the head.

Crustacea. A large class of water-breathing animals, including the water fleas, barnacles, shrimps, etc.

Crustacean. One of the Crustacea.

Cuneate. Wedge-shaped.

Curculio. Any snout beetle.

Cygnet. A young Swan.

Cylindrical. Shaped somewhat like a cylinder, as the bills of the Mergansers.

Deciduous. Shed at certain periods or seasons.

Decurved. Bent downward, as the bill in certain birds. Compare recurved.

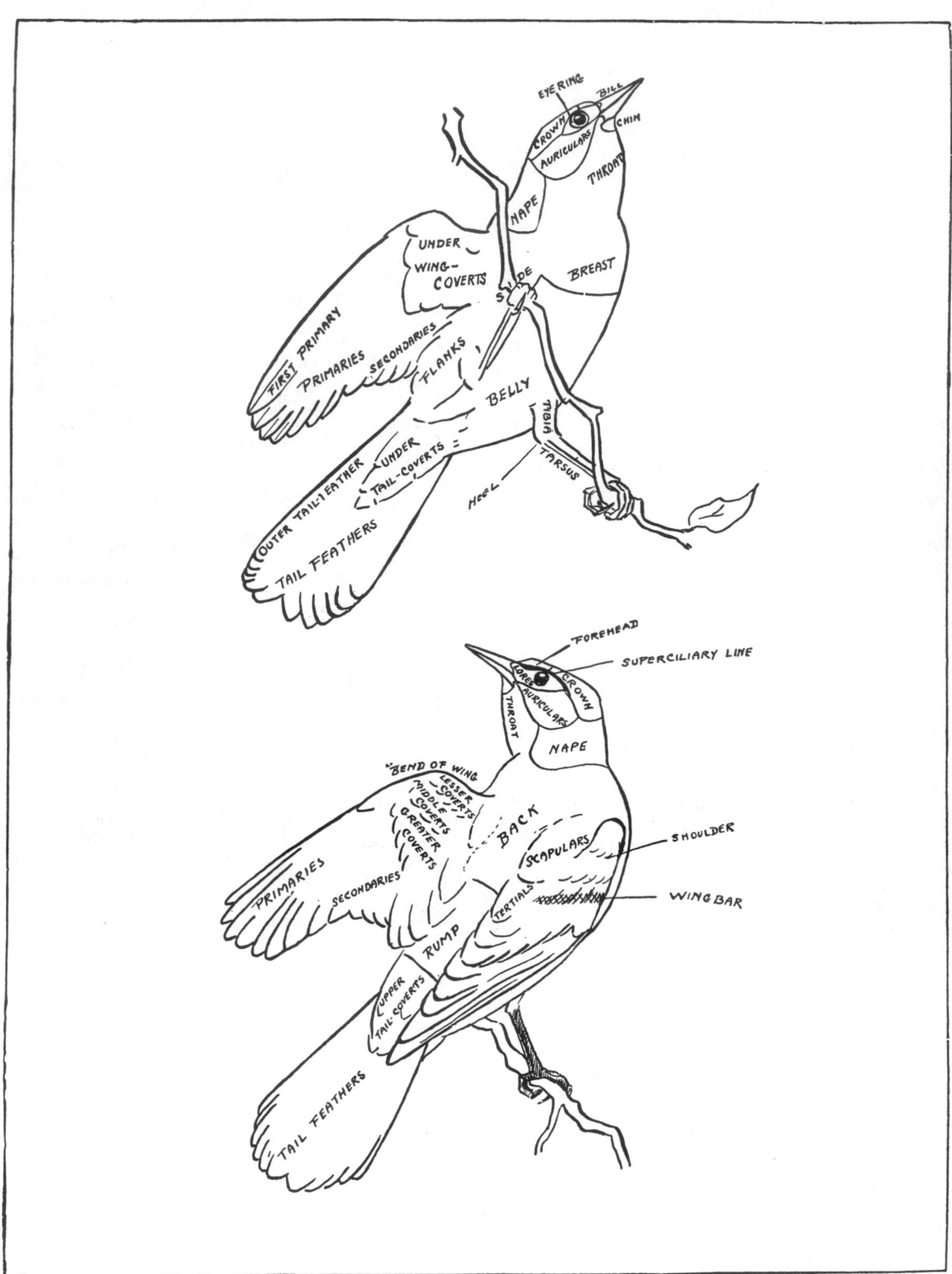

Drawing by Henry Thurston

THE TOPOGRAPHY OF A BIRD

Baltimore Oriole

Deflated. Emptied of air; — the opposite of inflated.

Depressed. Broader than high; the opposite of compressed.

Dichromatic. Having two phases of color, independently of age, sex, or season.

Distal. Toward or at the extremity; the opposite of proximal.

Distribution. Natural geographical range of a species or group.

Diurnal. Active in the daytime.

Dorsal. Situated on or near the back; pertaining to the back.

Down. A covering of fluffy, soft feathers; young birds are covered with down before they acquire ordinary feathers. Down feathers have very short stems, with soft barbs.

Ear-coverts. The feathers overlying the ears of most birds; auriculars.

Eared. Having tufts of feathers resembling ears.

Ear-tufts. Tufts of elongated feathers on each side of the crown or forehead, that can be erected.

Eclipse plumage. A term applied to the incomplete molt of the males of certain birds.

Economic value. The usefulness, or otherwise, of a bird judged by its food, its relation to agriculture, etc.

Elongate. Used in the sense of lengthened or extended; elongated.

Emarginate. Having the margin cut away; notched.

Environment. The external conditions and influences affecting the life and development of an animal.

Epignathous. Upper mandible longer than, and decurved over, lower.

Erectile. Capable of being erected or dilated.

Exotic. Foreign; not native; introduced from a foreign country.

Facial disks. The area about the eyes of owls.

Falciform. Sickle-shaped; scythe-shaped.

Family. A group of genera agreeing in certain characters, and differing in one or more characters from other families of the order to which they belong.

Fauna. The animal life of a region.

Felt. Matted fibers of hair, wool, fur, etc.; to cause to mat or to adhere together.

Ferruginous. Like iron rust in color; yellowish-red; brownish-red.

Filament. A barb of a down feather.

Filamentous. Threadlike.

Filiform. Threadlike.

Flag. Any one of the secondaries of a bird's wing; also, the long feathers on the lower part of the legs of certain birds, as the Owls and the Hawks.

Flush. To cause a bird to start up and fly.

Fore-neck. The throat; sometimes includes chin, throat, and chest.

Frontal. Pertaining to the forehead.

Frugivorous. Feeding on fruit.

Fulvous. Tawny; dull yellowish with a mixture of brown and gray.

Fuscous. Dark brown; smoky brown.

Gallinaceous. Like the pheasants and the domestic fowls; hen-like.

Gape. The opening of the mouth.

Genus [plural, **genera**]. A group of species agreeing in certain characters, and differing from other genera of the family to which they belong; also a single species showing unusual differences.

Glaucous. Of a whitish-blue or whitish-green color.

Gonys. The outline of the lower mandible, from the tip to the point where the branches fork.

Gorget. A patch on the throat, distinguable from the surrounding parts because of its color or for some other special cause.

Granular, Granulated. Having numerous small elevations on the surface; lumpy.

Greater coverts. The hindmost series of wing-coverts, which immediately overlap the basis of the secondaries.

Gregarious. Living in flocks.

Ground color. The main color of the general surface.

Gular. Pertaining to the throat.

Habitat. Natural abode; the kind of environment in which the bird occurs.

Hibernate. To pass the winter in a lethargic or torpid state.

Hybrid. Offspring of parents of different species.

Hymenopterous. Relating to the Hymenoptera, an order of insects which includes the ants, bees, wasps, sawflies, etc.

Immaculate. Unspotted; unmarked.

Immature. Not adult, although full-grown.

Incubation. The act of sitting on eggs; brooding.

Indigenous. Growing or living naturally in a country or region; native; not imported.

Inflated. Filled with air; the opposite of deflated.

Insectivorous. Feeding on insects; of or pertaining to insects.

Interscapulars. The feathers in the middle line of the back, between the scapulars or shoulders.

Iridescent. With changeable colors or tints in different lights.

Iris. The colored circle of the eye surrounding the pupil.

Isochronal. Recurring at regular intervals; uniform in time.

Isotherm. In physical geography a line marking points on the earth's surface having the same temperature.

Jugular. On, or relating to the jugulum, as a jugular collar.

Jugulum. The lower throat or foreneck; immediately above the breast; sometimes called the upper breast.

Juvenal plumage. The plumage immediately succeeding the natal down.

Lamella [plural, **lamellæ**]. A thin plate or scale.

Lamellate. Having lamellæ, as the sides of a Duck's bill.

Lamellirostral. Having a lamellate bill, as the Ducks, Geese, and Swans.

Larva [plural, **larvæ**]. A grub, caterpillar, maggot, etc.

Lateral. At or toward the side.

Lesser wing-coverts. The smaller wing-coverts, those covering most of the shoulder, or area in front of the middle coverts.

Linear. Line-like.

Littoral. Pertaining to or inhabiting the shore; coastal region.

Lobate, lobated. Having lobes or flaps along the sides of the toes.

Loral. Relating to the lores.

Lore. The space between the eye and the bill;— generally used in the plural, lores.

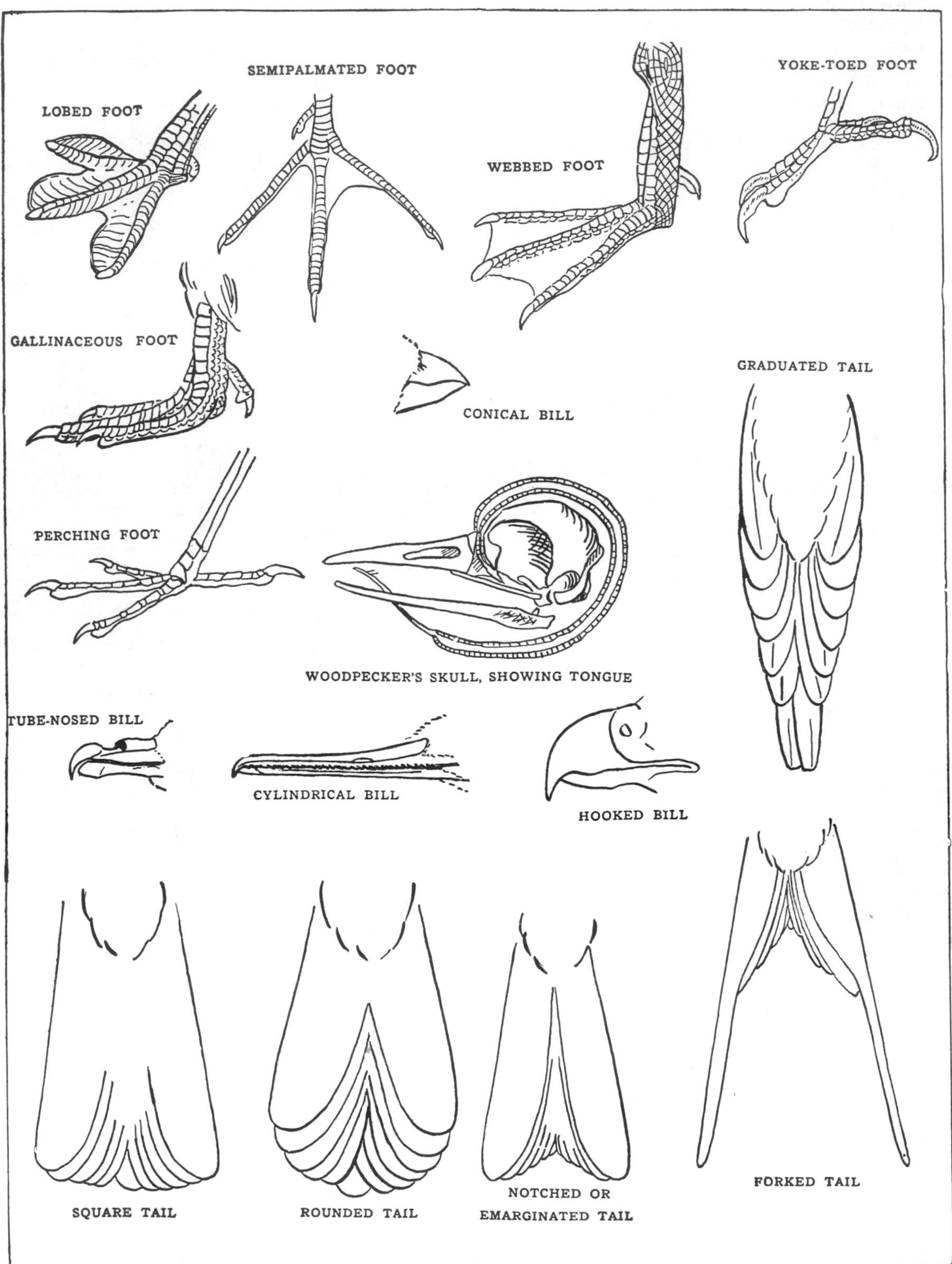

Drawing by Henry Thurston

Lower tail-coverts. The feathers overlapping the base of the tail-feathers beneath.

Maculate. Spotted; blotched.

Malar region. The side of the lower jaw behind the horny covering of the mandible; cheek region.

Mammal. An animal the female of which suckles her young.

Mandible. Either of the jaws of a bird's bill.

Mantle. A term used to include the back, the scapulars, and the upper surface of the wings.

Marine. Pertaining to, existing in, or formed by the sea.

Maritime. Living or found near the sea; bordering on the sea.

Mat. The lining of down in the nest of a Duck.

Maturity. State of being mature; having attained its complete adult plumage.

Maxilla [plural, **maxillæ**]. The upper jaw;— used loosely for either jaw.

Median, Medial. Along the middle line.

Melanism. An unusual development of black or nearly black color in the plumage.

Melanistic. Affected with or showing melanism.

Middle wing-coverts. The coverts between the greater and the lesser coverts.

Migrant. Any bird found in certain districts during migration only.

Migratory. Moving, either occasionally or regularly, from one climate or region to another.

Milliped, millipede, milleped, millepede. Any one of the insects commonly known as thousand legs.

Mollusks. Shellfish such as clams, oysters, whelks, etc.

Molt. The periodical shedding or casting of the feathers.

Monogamous. Mating with only one of the opposite sex. Compare polygamous.

Mustache. A conspicuous stripe of color beneath the eye; maxillary line.

Nail. The horny plate or tip on the beak of Ducks and certain other birds.

Nape. The part of the hindneck back of the occiput; the nucha.

Nidicolous. Reared for a time in the nest.

Nidification. Nest building.

Nocturnal. Moving about at night; done or occurring in the night.

Nucha. Nape.

Nuchal. Relating to the nucha or nape.

Nuptial plumes. Ornamental feathers acquired at the approach of the breeding season, and molted at its close.

Obscure. Indistinct; ill-defined.

Obsolete. Indistinct.

Occipital. Relating to the occiput.

Occiput. The back part of the head.

Ocellated. Like, an eye or ocellus; having ocelli, as parts of the plumage in certain birds.

Ocellus [plural, **ocelli**]. An eye-like spot of color.

Ochraceous. Of the color of ocher; resembling ocher.

Olivaceous. Olive-colored; of an olive-green color; resembling the olive.

Omnivorous. Eating both vegetable and animal food.

Oölogical. Pertaining to oölogy, or the study of eggs.

Opaque. Without gloss; dull; not transparent.

Order. A group of families agreeing in certain characters.

Ornithological. Pertaining to ornithology.

Ornithologist. A student of ornithology.

Ornithology. The branch of zoölogy which treats of birds; a treatise on the study of birds.

Pectoral. Relating to the breast.

Pelagic. Oceanic; living on or at the surface of the sea far from the coast.

Pellet. A small ball, ejected from the mouth by certain birds, and containing the non-digestible portions of their prey.

Pendulous. Hanging downward; suspended loosely; swinging.

Pensile. Suspended; hanging, as the nests of certain birds.

Perforate. Pierced through.

Piscivorous. Feeding on fish.

Plicate. Folded like a fan.

Plumage. The entire covering of feathers. See, also, eclipse plumage, juvenal plumage.

Plumbeous. Of a deep bluish-gray color; lead-colored.

Plumelets. Small plumes.

Plumicorns. Ear-tufts; popularly called horns or ears.

Polygamous. Having more than one mate at one time. Compare monogamous.

Polygamy. The habit of having more than one mate at the same time.

Post-nuptial. Occurring after the breeding season.

Postorbital. Back of or behind the eye.

Precocial, præcocial. Covered with down and able to run about when newly hatched.

Predacious. Preying on other animals.

Primary. Any one of the quill feathers of the pinion.

Primary coverts. The stiff coverts which overlie the bases of the primaries.

Produced. Extended.

Proximal. That end of a feather or limb which is nearest to the point of attachment;— the opposite of distal.

Psilopædic. Young are naked when hatched, and are fed by parents.

Ptilopædic. Young are feathered.

Pupa [plural, **pupæ**]. In insects the stage between the larva and the adult stage.

Pupil. The central spot or disk of the eye, enclosed within the iris.

Quill feathers. The primaries.

Rectrix [plural, **rectrices**]. A tail-feather.

Recurved. Bent upward;— used of a bird's bill. Compare decurved.

Regurgitation. The casting out (of food) from the stomach and mouth.

Remex [plural **remiges**]. Any one of the longer flight feathers.

Resident. Any bird that stays in a certain district permanently.

Reticulate. Netted; resembling network.

Rictal. Pertaining to the rictus.

Rictus. The edges and corner of the mouth; the gape.

Rufescent. Tinged with red; reddish.

Rufous. Brownish-red; rust-colored.

Scapular region. The longitudinal area of feathers overlying the shoulder blade.

Scapulars. The feathers of the scapular region; shoulders.

Scutellum [plural, **scutella**]. Ascute or plate or shield.

Seasonal. Pertaining to or occurring with the change of the seasons.

Secondary. Any of the flight feathers of the forearm.

Secondary coverts. The greater wing-coverts.

Secretive. Inclined to keep out of sight; retiring to a degree.

Semi-. A prefix meaning half, partly, or imperfectly.

Semi-lunar. Like a half-moon in shape.

Semipalmate, semipalmated. Having the front toes webbed only half, or part, way to their ends.

Semi-pensile. Partly hanging or suspended.

Serrate, serrated. Saw-toothed; notched like a saw on the edge.

Setaceous. Bristled; bristly.

Shaft. The horny axis or stem of a feather.

Sibilant. Hissing; making a hissing sound.

Sinuate, sinuated. With the edge cut away less abruptly than when emarginate.

Skin. In zoölogy, the skin of a bird or animal with its covering of feathers or fur and other external parts, as the bill and feet.

Soporific. Tending to cause sleep.

Species. A group of animals possessing in common certain characters which distinguish them from other similar groups; a distinct sort or kind of animal.

Speculum. A mirrorlike or brightly colored area on the wing of certain Ducks.

Stock species. Same as type species.

Sub-basal. Almost or nearly at the base.

Sub-caudal. Under the tail.

Sub-marginal. Nearly at the margin or edge.

Sub-orbital. Below the eye.

Subspecies. A variety or race; a form connected with other forms of a species by individuals possessing intermediate characters.

Subterminal. Almost at the end.

Subtropical. Of or pertaining to the regions bordering on the tropics; nearly tropical.

Subtruncate. Terminating abruptly.

Superciliary. Above the eye.

Superior. Upper; topmost; uppermost.

Supraloral. Above the lores.

Supra-orbital. Above the eye.

Tail-coverts. The feathers which cover the base of the tail, above and below.

Tarsus [plural, **tarsi**]. The shank of a bird's leg.

Taxidermist. One who prepares, stuffs, and mounts in lifelike form the skins of animals.

Terminal. At the end or tip.

Terminology. The special terms used in any science.

Terrestrial. Inhabiting or belonging to the ground or land in distinction from water, trees, etc.

Tertiaries. The inner secondaries.

Tibia. The part of the leg next above the shank; the "drumstick."

Transverse. Crosswise.

Traversed. Crossed.

Truncate, truncated. Cut squarely off.

Tuberculated. Having tubercles, that is, small knob-like prominences on some part of an animal.

Tumid. Enlarged; distended; swollen.

Type. Typical form. A type species is that form used as the basis for the original description of a species. A type genus is that genus from which the name of the family or subfamily to which it belongs is formed.

Under tail-coverts. The feathers covering the base of the tail below.

Under wing-coverts. The coverts of the under surface of the wing.

Uniform. Entirely of the same color or shade, as "uniform sooty-black."

Upper tail-coverts. The feathers overlying the base of the tail above.

Vent. The anus.

Vermiculate, vermiculated. Marked with fine wavy lines like worm-tracks.

Vernacular. Term used in the sense of common, as opposed to scientific.

Vernal. Pertaining to spring.

Vertex. The crown; the central part of the top of the head.

Vinaceous. Wine-colored.

Visitor. Any bird found, regularly or irregularly, in a certain district at certain seasons only, as spring, summer, autumn, or winter; not a permanent resident.

Volunteer. Self-sown.

Web. The series of barbs on each side of a feather.

Zone. A broad band of color completely encircling the body of a bird.

BIBLIOGRAPHY

BIBLIOGRAPHY

BOOKS

American Ornithologists' Union
Check-list of North American Birds.

Apgar, Austin Craig
Birds of the United States East of the Rockies.
American Book Co.

Audubon, John James
Birds of America.
J. J. Audubon (first edition).
R. Lockwood & Son (later edition).

Bailey, Florence Merriam (Florence A. Merriam)
A-Birding on a Bronco.
Birds of Village and Field.
Birds through an Opera Glass.
Handbook of Birds of the Western United States.
Houghton Mifflin Co.

Baird, Spencer Fullerton
Review of American Birds.
Smithsonian Institution.

Baird, Spencer Fullerton, and others
A History of North American Birds.
Little, Brown & Co.

Barrows, Walter B.
General Habits of the Crow.
U. S. Department of Agriculture.
Michigan Bird Life.
Michigan Agricultural College.

Baskett, James Newton
Story of the Birds.
D. Appleton & Co.

Baynes, Ernest Harold
Wild Bird Guests.
E. P. Dutton & Co.

Beal, F. E. L.
Birds of California in relation to the Fruit Industry, Parts I and II.
Food of our more Important Flycatchers.
Food of the Bobolink, Blackbirds, and Grackles.
Food of the Woodpeckers of the United States.
Some Common Birds Useful to the Farmer.
U. S. Department of Agriculture.

Beal, F. E. L. and McAtee, W. L.
Food of Some Well-known Birds of Forest, Farm, and Garden.
U. S. Department of Agriculture.

Beebe, C. William
Geographic Variation in Birds with especial reference to Humidity.
Sci. Contribs. N. Y. Zoölogical Society.
The Bird.
Henry Holt & Co.
Two Bird-Lovers in Mexico.
Houghton Mifflin Co.

Beetham, Bentley
Photography for Bird-Lovers.
Charles Scribner's Sons.

Bendire, Charles E.
Life Histories of North American Birds.
Smithsonian Institution.

Biological Survey, U. S. Department of Agriculture
Bulletins and reports on birds.

Boraston, John M.
Birds by Land and Sea.
John Lane Co.

Brewer, Thomas M., and others
A History of North American Birds.
Little, Brown & Co.

Brewster, William
Minot's The Land Birds and Game Birds of New England.
Houghton Mifflin Co.

Brooks, Earle A.
The Food of West Virginia Birds.
West Virginia Department of Agriculture.

Burroughs, John
Complete Works.
Houghton Mifflin Co.

Chapman, Frank M.
Bird-life.
Bird Studies with a Camera.
Camps and Cruises of an Ornithologist.
Color Key to North American Birds.
Handbook of Birds of Eastern North America.
The Warblers of America.
D. Appleton & Co.

Cheney, S. P.
Wood Notes Wild.
Lee & Shepard.

Cooke, Wells Woodbridge
Bird Migration.
Distribution and Migration of North American Ducks, Geese, and Swans.
Distribution and Migration of North American Gulls and their Allies.
Distribution and Migration of North American Herons and their Allies.
Distribution and Migration of North American Rails and their Allies.
Distribution and Migration of North American Shorebirds.
Distribution of the American Egrets.
U. S. Department of Agriculture.

Cory, Charles Barney
Birds of Eastern North America.
Field Museum of Natural History.
How to Know the Ducks, Geese, and Swans.
How to Know the Shore-birds.
Little, Brown & Co.

Coues, Elliott
Key to North American Birds.
Dana Estes & Co.

Davie, Oliver
Nests and Eggs of North American Birds.
David McKay.
Dawson, William Leon
Birds of Ohio.
Mrs. Elizabeth C. T. Miller.
Birds of California.
Birds of Washington.
The Occidental Publishing Co.
Dearborn, Ned
The English Sparrow as a Pest.
U. S. Department of Agriculture.
Eaton, Howard Elon
Birds of New York.
New York State Museum.
Eckstorm, Fannie Hardy
The Bird Book.
D. C. Heath & Co.
The Woodpeckers.
Houghton Mifflin Co.
Elliott, Daniel Giraud
North American Shore-Birds.
The Gallinaceous Game Birds of North America.
The Wild Fowl of the United States and British Possessions.
Lathrop C. Harper.
Finley, William L.
American Birds.
Charles Scribner's Sons.
Finley, William L., and Irene
Little Bird Blue.
Houghton Mifflin Co.
Fisher, A. K.
The Hawks and Owls of the United States in their relation to Agriculture.
U. S. Department of Agriculture.
Flagg, Wilson
Year with the Birds.
Educational Publishing Co.
Forbush, Edward H.
Game Birds, Wild-fowl, and Shore Birds.
The Starling.
Useful Birds and their Protection.
Massachusetts Board of Agriculture.
Grinnell, George Bird
American Duck Shooting.
American Game Bird Shooting.
Forest and Stream Publishing Co.
Grinnell, Elizabeth and Joseph
Birds of Song and Story.
A. W. Mumford.
Hamilton, D. W.
Our Common Birds.
Dominion Book Co.
Headley, Frederick Webb
The Flight of Birds.
Witherby & Co.
Henshaw, Henry W.
American Game Birds.
National Geographical Magazine, Vol. 28, No. 2.
Herrick, Francis H.
Home Life of Wild Birds.
G. P. Putnam's Sons.
Hoffmann, Ralph
Guide to the Birds of New England and Eastern New York.
Houghton Mifflin Co.
Hornaday, William T.
The American Natural History.
Charles Scribner's Sons.
Wild Life Conservation in Theory and Practice.
Yale University Press.
Howell, Arthur H.
The Relation of Birds to the Cotton Boll Weevil.
U. S. Department of Agriculture.
Huntington, Dwight Williams
Our Feathered Game.
Charles Scribner's Sons.
Our Wild Fowl and Waders.
Amateur Sportsman Co.
Ingersoll, Ernest
Wild Life of Orchard and Field.
Harper Brothers.
Job, Herbert K.
Among the Water-fowl.
Doubleday, Page & Co.
Blue Goose Chase.
Baker & Taylor Co.
How to Study Birds.
A. L. Burt Co.
Propagation of Wild Birds.
Doubleday, Page & Co.
The Sport of Bird Study.
A. L. Burt Co.
Wild Wings.
Houghton Mifflin Co.
Jones, Lynds
The Birds of Ohio.
Ohio State Academy of Science.
Judd, Sylvester D.
Birds of a Maryland Farm.
The Bobwhite and other Quails of the United States in their Economic Relations.
The Grouse and Wild Turkeys of the United States and their Economic Value.
The Relation of Sparrows to Agriculture.
U. S. Department of Agriculture.
Keeler, Charles A.
Bird Notes Afield.
Elder & Shepard.
Keyser, Leander S.
Birds of the Rockies.
A. C. McClurg & Co.
Lange, Dietrich
Our Native Birds: How to Protect them and Attract them to our Homes.
Macmillan Co.
Lord, William Rogers
Birds of Oregon and Washington.
J. K. Gill Company.
Lottridge, Silas A.
Animal Snapshots and How Made.
Familiar Wild Animals.
Henry Holt & Co.
Lowe, Percy R.
Our Common Sea-Birds.
Country Life, Ltd.
McAtee, Waldo Lee
Our Grosbeaks and their Value to Agriculture.
Our Vanishing Shorebirds.
The Horned Larks and their Relation to Agriculture.
U. S. Department of Agriculture.
McAtee, W. L., and Beal, F. E. L.
Some Common Game, Aquatic, and Rapacious Birds in Relation to Man.
U. S. Department of Agriculture.

MacClement, William Thomas
New Canadian Bird Book.
Dominion Book Co.
Mathews, Schuyler
Field Book of Wild Birds and their Music.
G. P. Putnam's Sons.
Maynard, Charles Johnson
Eggs of North American Birds.
DeWolfe & Fiske Co.
The Birds of Eastern North America.
Charles J. Maynard.
Merriam, Florence. See **Bailey, Florence Merriam**
Miller, Olive Thorne (Harriet Mann Miller)
Bird-Lover in the West.
In Nesting Time.
Little Brothers of the Air.
The Children's Book of Birds (includes the First Book of Birds, and the Second Book of Birds).
True Bird Stories.
Upon the Tree-Tops.
Houghton Mifflin Co.
Minot, Henry Davis
The Land Birds and Game Birds of New England.
Houghton Mifflin Co.
Nehrling, Henry
Our Native Birds of Song and Beauty.
G. Brumder.
Newton, Alfred
Dictionary of Birds.
Macmillan Co.
Oldys, Henry
Pheasant Raising in the United States.
U. S. Department of Agriculture.
Parkhurst, Howard Elmore
How to Name the Birds.
Song Birds and Waterfowl.
The Birds' Calendar.
Charles Scribner's Sons.
Pearson, T. Gilbert
Bird Study Book.
Doubleday, Page & Co.
Stories of Bird Life.
B. F. Johnson.
Pike, Oliver G.
Bird Biographies and other Bird Sketches.
Farther Afield in Birdland.
Scout's Book of Birds.
Frederick A. Stokes Co.
Reed, Charles K.
American Ornithology.
Western Bird Guide.
Charles K. Reed.
Reed, Chester Albert
American Game Birds.
Charles K. Reed.
Birds of Eastern North America.
Camera Studies of Wild Birds in their Homes.
North American Birds' Eggs.
Doubleday, Page & Co.
Rich, Walter H.
Feathered Game of the Northeast.
T. Y. Crowell Co.
Ridgway, Robert
A Manual of North American Birds.
J. B. Lippincott Co.
A Nomenclature of Colors for Naturalists and Compendium of Useful Information for Ornithologists.
Little, Brown & Co.
The Birds of Middle and North America.
U. S. National Museum.
Ridgway, Robert, and others
A History of North American Birds.
Little, Brown & Co.
Sage, John Hall, and Bishop, Louis Bennett
The Birds of Connecticut.
Connecticut Geological and Natural History Survey.
Sanderson, Lyle Ward
Chickadee-dee and his Friends.
Frederick A. Stokes Co.
Sandys, Edwyn William, and Van Dyke, Theodore Strong
Upland Game Birds.
Macmillan Co.
Sharp, Dallas Lore
Roof and Meadow.
Century Co.
Stejneger, L., and others
Riverside Natural History.
Houghton Mifflin Co.
Thoreau, Henry David
Notes on New England Birds.
Houghton Mifflin Co.
Torrey, Bradford
A Rambler's Lease.
Birds in the Bush.
Everyday Birds.
Field-Days in California.
The Foot-Path Way.
Houghton Mifflin Co.
Trafton, Gilbert Haven
Bird Friends.
Methods of Attracting Birds.
Houghton Mifflin Co.
Van Dyke, Theodore Strong
Game Birds at Home.
Fords, Howard, & Hulbert.
Weed, Clarence Moores, and Dearborn, Ned
Birds in their Relations to Man.
J. B. Lippincott Co.
Wilson, Alexander, and Bonaparte, Charles Lucien J. L.
American Ornithology.
Bradford & Inskeep.
Wright, Mabel Osgood
Birdcraft.
Citizen Bird.
Gray Lady and the Birds.
Macmillan Co.

In the above list each firm mentioned is the publisher of the one, two, or more books immediately above its name, and not credited to another firm; in other words, Houghton Mifflin Co. publish all the books by Bradford Torrey included in this bibliography, but only one of those of Herbert K. Job's.

PERIODICALS

The Auk. Organ of the American Ornithologists' Union. Quarterly. Address, care of the Academy of Natural Sciences, Philadelphia.

Bird-Lore. Organ of the National Association of Audubon Societies. Bi-monthly. Address, D. Appleton & Co., New York City.

The Condor. Organ of the Cooper Ornithological Club. Bi-monthly. Address, Pasadena, Calif.

The Bluebird. Organ of the Cleveland Bird Lovers Association. Monthly. Address, 1010 Euclid Avenue, Cleveland, Ohio.

Journal of the Maine Ornithological Society. Quarterly. Address, Portland, Maine. (Suspended.)

The Oölogist. Monthly. Address, Lacon, Ill.

Wilson Bulletin. Organ of the Wilson Ornithological Club. Quarterly. Address, Oberlin, Ohio.

INDEX

INDEX

B

C

D

E

F

G

H

I

J

M

N

O

P

Q

R

T

U, V

W

X, Y, Z